Excavations at
Kilise Tepe 1994–98

Kilise Tepe from the southeast before excavation in 1994.

The mound is silhouetted against the dark green of the river flats bordering the Göksu and the Gelembiç Çay, behind which the barren sides of the valley recede upwards into the summer haze.

McDONALD INSTITUTE MONOGRAPHS

Excavations at Kilise Tepe 1994–98

From Bronze Age to Byzantine in western Cilicia

Volume 1: Text

Edited by Nicholas Postgate & David Thomas

BRITISH INSTITUTE AT ANKARA
BIAA Monograph No. 30

Published jointly by:

McDonald Institute for Archaeological Research
University of Cambridge
Downing Street
Cambridge, UK
CB2 3ER
(0)(1223) 339336
(0)(1223) 333538 (General Office)
(0)(1223) 333536 (FAX)
dak12@cam.ac.uk
www.mcdonald.cam.ac.uk

British Institute at Ankara
10 Carlton House Terrace
London, UK
SW1Y 5AH
(0)(20) 7969 5204
(0)(20) 7969 5401 (FAX)
biaa@britac.ac.uk
www.biaa.ac.uk

Distributed by Oxbow Books
  United Kingdom: Oxbow Books, 10 Hythe Bridge Street, Oxford, OX1 2EW, UK.
    Tel: (0)(1865) 241249; Fax: (0)(1865) 794449; www.oxbowbooks.com
  USA: The David Brown Book Company, P.O. Box 511, Oakville, CT 06779, USA.
    Tel: 860-945-9329; Fax: 860-945-9468

Undertaken with the assistance of the Institute for Aegean Prehistory.

ISBN: 978-1-902937-40-3 (2-vol. set)
ISBN: 978-1-902937-41-0 (vol. 1)
ISBN: 978-1-902937-42-7 (vol. 2)
ISSN: 1363-1349
(Volumes to be sold as a set)

© 2007 McDonald Institute for Archaeological Research

All rights reserved. No parts of this publication may be reproduced, stored in a retrieval system, or transmitted, in any form or by any means, electronic, mechanical, photocopying, recording or otherwise, without the prior permission of the McDonald Institute for Archaeological Research.

Edited for the Institute by Chris Scarre, Graeme Barker (*Series Editors*) and Dora A. Kemp (*Production Editor*).

Cover illustration: *Early Bronze Age domestic vessels from Level Vj (see Fig. 222) (photograph: Bronwyn Douglas).*

Printed and bound by Short Run Press, Bittern Rd, Sowton Industrial Estate, Exeter, EX2 7LW, UK.

Contents

Contributors	vii
Figures	ix
Tables	xvii
Preface	xix
Abbreviations and conventions	xxii
Note on numbers	xxiii

Part A Introduction

Chapter 1	Introduction to the Project and the Publication *by* Nicholas Postgate	3
Chapter 2	The Site of Kilise Tepe *by* Nicholas Postgate	9
Chapter 3	The Kilise Tepe Area in Pre-Classical and Hellenistic Times *by* Nicholas Postgate	15
Chapter 4	The Kilise Tepe Area in the Byzantine Era *by* Mark Jackson	19
Chapter 5	The Excavations and their Results *by* Nicholas Postgate	31

Part B The Surface Collection

Chapter 6	The Surface Collection *by* David Thomas	45

Part C The Excavations

Chapter 7	Introduction to the Excavations *by* Nicholas Postgate	67
Chapter 8	Fire Installations *by* Nicholas Postgate	71
Chapter 9	Pits *by* Nicholas Postgate	79
Chapter 10	Level V: the Early Bronze Age *by* Lucy Seffen	87
Chapter 11	Level IV: the Middle Bronze Age *by* Nicholas Postgate	103
Chapter 12	Level III: the Late Bronze Age *by* Sarah Blakeney	111
Chapter 13	Level II: the End of the Bronze Age and the Iron Age *by* Nicholas Postgate & David Thomas	121
Chapter 14	The East Slope *by* Nicholas Postgate	165
Chapter 15	Trenches South of the Church *by* Nicholas Postgate & Mark Jackson	171
Chapter 16	The Church *by* Mark Jackson	185
Chapter 17	The Northwest Corner *by* Mark Jackson	199
Chapter 18	The Northeast Corner Sub-surface Clearance *by* Mark Jackson	211
Chapter 19	Architectural Fragments *by* Mark Jackson & Dominique Collon	215

Part D The Pottery

Chapter 20	Introduction to the Pottery *by* Nicholas Postgate	237
Chapter 21	Pottery Fabrics and Technology *by* Carl Knappett & Vassilis Kilikoglou	241
Chapter 22	Detailed Fabric Descriptions *by* Carl Knappett	273
Chapter 23	The Early Bronze Age Pottery *by* Dorit Symington	295
Chapter 24	The Middle Bronze Age Pottery *by* Dorit Symington	319
Chapter 25	Pottery from Level III *by* Connie Hansen & Nicholas Postgate	329
Chapter 26	Pottery from Level II *by* Connie Hansen & Nicholas Postgate	343
Chapter 27	Geometric Pottery *by* Nicholas Postgate	371
Chapter 28	The Mycenaean Pottery *by* Elizabeth B. French	373

Chapter 29	Comparison of the NAA Data for Six Mycenaean-style Samples from Kilise Tepe with Chemical Reference Groups from Mainland Greece, Crete, Cyprus and the Levant *by* JONATHAN E. TOMLINSON	377
Chapter 30	Hellenistic Ceramics and Lamps *by* LISA NEVETT & MARK JACKSON	379
Chapter 31	Pottery from Level One *by* MARK JACKSON	387

Part E   *The Small Finds*

Chapter 32	The Small Finds: Introduction *by* NICHOLAS POSTGATE	437
Chapter 33	Seals with Hieroglyphic Inscriptions *by* DORIT SYMINGTON	441
Chapter 34	Other Glyptic *by* DOMINIQUE COLLON	445
Chapter 35	Miscellaneous Clay Artefacts *by* DOMINIQUE COLLON & DORIT SYMINGTON	449
Chapter 36	Loomweights *by* DOMINIQUE COLLON & DORIT SYMINGTON	469
Chapter 37	Spindle Whorls *by* DORIT SYMINGTON & DOMINIQUE COLLON	481
Chapter 38	Beads *by* DOMINIQUE COLLON & DORIT SYMINGTON	499
Chapter 39	Glass *by* DOMINIQUE COLLON	505
Chapter 40	Mosaic Tesserae *by* DOMINIQUE COLLON	511
Chapter 41	Metalwork *by* DOMINIQUE COLLON & DORIT SYMINGTON	515
Chapter 42	Bone, Horn and Ivory *by* POLYDORA BAKER & DOMINIQUE COLLON	531
Chapter 43	Fossils *by* DOMINIQUE COLLON	541
Chapter 44	Lithics *by* TIM REYNOLDS	545
Chapter 45	Smaller Stone Artefacts *by* DOMINIQUE COLLON & DORIT SYMINGTON	559
Chapter 46	Larger Stone Artefacts *by* DOMINIQUE COLLON	567
Chapter 47	Coins *by* KORAY KONUK	577

Part F   *Environmental Studies*

Chapter 48	Environmental Studies: Introduction *by* NICHOLAS POSTGATE	581
Chapter 49	The Archaeobotanical Assemblages *by* JOANNA BENDING & SUE COLLEDGE	583
Chapter 50	Processing, Storing, Eating and Disposing: the Phytolith Evidence from Iron Age Kilise Tepe *by* MARCO MADELLA	597
Chapter 51	Fish Remains from Bronze Age to Byzantine Levels *by* WIM VAN NEER & MARC WAELKENS	607
Chapter 52	Human Remains *by* JESSICA PEARSON	613
Chapter 53	Dating *by* PETER IAN KUNIHOLM, MARYANNE W. NEWTON, ROY SWITSUR & NICHOLAS POSTGATE	619

Vol. 2 contents (printed as a separate volume)
Figure list   v

Appendices
Appendix 1   Archaeobotanical Data   627
Appendix 2   List of Excavation Units   641

References   685

Figures
Artefact Drawings   705
Maps, Plans and Sections   817
Colour Figures   861

Contributors

POLYDORA BAKER
English Heritage, Research Department, Fort Cumberland, Fort Cumberland Rd, Eastney, Portsmouth, P04 9LD, UK.
Email: Polydora.Baker@english-heritage.org.uk

S.M. BARNETT
Luminescence Laboratory, Department of Archaeology, University of Durham, South Road, Durham, DH1 3LE, UK.

JOANNA BENDING
Department of Archaeology, University of Sheffield, Northgate House, West Street, Sheffield, S1 4ET.
Email: j.bending@sheffield.ac.uk

SARAH BLAKENEY
35 Harding Way, Cambridge, CB4 3RW, UK.

DOMINIQUE COLLON
c/o Department of the Middle East, The British Museum, London, WC1B 3DG, UK.

ELIZABETH B. FRENCH
26 Millington Road, Cambridge, CB3 9HP, UK.
Email: LISACAMB@aol.com

CONNIE HANSEN
Ingerslevsgade 188 st. TH, 1705 Copenhagen V, Denmark.

MARK JACKSON
Historical Studies, Armstrong Building, Newcastle University, NE1 7RU, UK.
Email: m.p.c.jackson@ncl.ac.uk

CARL KNAPPETT
Department of Archaeology, Laver Building, North Park Road, Exeter, EX4 4QE, UK.
Email: C.J.Knappett@exeter.ac.uk

KORAY KONUK
Chargé de Recherche CNRS, Institut Ausonius CNRS – Université Bordeaux 3, Pessac, France.
Email: koraykonuk@gmail.com

PETER IAN KUNIHOLM
Aegean Dendrochronology Project, Cornell Tree-Ring Laboratory, B-48 Goldwin Smith Hall, Ithaca, NY 14853-3201, USA.

MARCO MADELLA
Director, Laboratory for Palaeoecology and Plant Palaeoeconomy, Department of Archaeology and Anthropology, Institució Milá i Fontanals, Spanish Council for Scientific Research (CSIC), C/Egipcíaques, 15, 08001 Barcelona, Spain.
Email: marco.madella@icrea.es

LISA NEVETT
Associate Professor, Department of the History of Art and Department of Classical Studies, University of Michigan, Ann Arbor, 110 Tappan Hall, 519 S. State Street, Ann Arbor, MI 48109-1357, USA.
Email: lcnevett@umich.edu

MARYANNE W. NEWTON
Aegean Dendrochronology Project, Cornell Tree-Ring Laboratory, B-48 Goldwin Smith Hall, Ithaca, New York, NY 14853-3201, USA.

JESSICA PEARSON
School of Archaeology, Classics and Egyptology, University of Liverpool, Brownlow Street, Liverpool L69 3GS, UK.
Email: jessica.pearson@liverpool.ac.uk

NICHOLAS POSTGATE
Trinity College, Cambridge, CB2 1TQ, UK.
Email: jnp10@cam.ac.uk

TIM REYNOLDS
Lecturer in Archaeology, School of Continuing Education, Birkbeck, University of London, 26 Russell Square, London, WC1B 5DQ, UK.
Email: te.reynolds@bbk.ac.uk

LUCY SEFFEN
13 The Linnets, Cottenham, Cambridge, CB24 8XZ, UK.
Email: lucy.seffen@hotmail.co.uk

ROY SWITSUR
Department of Forensic Science and Chemistry, Anglia Ruskin University, East Road, Cambridge, CB1 1PT, UK.

DORIT SYMINGTON
109, Old Woking Road, West Byfleet, Surrey, KT14 6HY, UK.
Email: dorit.zone@virgin.net

DAVID THOMAS
Archaeology Program, La Trobe University,
Bundoora, Victoria 3086, Australia.
Email: dcthomas@students.latrobe.edu.au

JONATHAN TOMLINSON
Canadian Institute in Greece, Dionysiou Aiginitou 7,
GR-115 28 Athens, Greece.
Email: jtomlinson@cig-icg.gr

WIM VAN NEER
Koninklijk Belgisch Instituut voor
Natuurwetenschappen, Afdeling Antropologie
en Prehistorie, Vautierstraat 29, B-1000 Brussel,
Belgium.
Email: Wim.VanNeer@natuurwetenschappen.be

MARC WAELKENS
Faculteit Letteren, Blijde Inkomststraat 21, B-3000
Leuven, Belgium.
Email: marc.waelkens@arts.kuleuven.be

Figures (vol. 1)

Chapter 1

1.	Sn. İlhame Öztürk with Kilise Tepe exhibit in Silifke Museum.	4
2.	Bar chart of grants awarded to the Kilise Tepe project.	4
3.	Bar chart of Kilise Tepe project expenditure 1994–2004.	5
4.	Pie diagram of Kilise Tepe project expenditure 1994–2004.	5

Chapter 2

5.	Kite photograph of Kilise Tepe.	10
6.	Promontory to north of the tepe, showing decayed conglomerate surface.	11
7.	Göksu river and the remnants of the bridge, looking upstream from Kışla.	11
8.	Kilise Tepe and the Göksu valley from the east.	12
9.	North end of Kilise Tepe before excavation, with tree and spring to the left.	12
10.	Plane tree and spring at north end of tepe, conglomerate outcropping on the left.	13

Chapter 5

11.	Robber trench in H19, from north before excavation.	31
12.	Rock-cut steps above the spring, from east.	32
13.	Rectangular basin north of tepe, from south.	32
14.	Rectangular basin north of tepe, outflow channel from above.	33
15.	Rock-cut feature on ridge south of tepe.	33

Chapter 6

16.	Surface of L14, before surface collection.	48
17.	Kilise Tepe: areas worked 1994–98.	49
18.	Centre of tepe after surface collection.	49
19.	Byzantine foundations in L20 to O20 after sub-surface clearance.	50
20.	Surface marks.	54
21.	Surface distribution: architectural fragments.	55
22.	Surface distribution: decorated sherds.	55
23.	Surface distribution: Early Bronze Age sherds.	55
24.	Surface distribution: feature (non-body) sherds.	56
25.	Surface distribution: Hellenistic sherds.	56
26.	Surface distribution: Iron Age sherds.	56
27.	Surface distribution: informative sherds.	57
28.	Surface distribution: large stones.	57
29.	Surface distribution: total number of sherds (to the nearest 50).	57
30.	Surface distribution: percentage of informative sherds.	58
31.	Surface distribution: red Hittite wares.	58
32.	Surface distribution: Roman/Byzantine sherds.	58
33.	Surface distribution: small stones.	59
34.	Surface distribution: stone artefacts.	59
35.	Surface distribution: Terra sigillata sherds.	59
36.	Surface distribution: tile fragments.	60
37.	Surface distribution: percentage of datable sherds.	60
38.	Surface distribution: trefoil rim sherds.	60

Chapter 7

39.	Example of a unit sheet.	68
40.	Example of a pit sheet.	68
41.	Example of a fire installation sheet.	69
42.	Example of a wall sheet.	69

Figures

Chapter 8
43.	FI95/5 in Rm d4, looking south.	71
44.	FI95/3 (K20, Rm e9; see Fig. 498 for location).	72
45.	FI95/3 in Rm e9, as first exposed, looking south.	72
46.	FI96/1 in I19d; Level I/IIh, looking west.	72
47.	FI96/11 (I19 Level IIe/f; see Fig. 499 for location).	72
48.	FI96/7–8 (I19 Level IIg/h).	73
49.	FI96/7–8 in I19; Level IIg/h, looking south (see Fig. 48).	73
50.	FI96/25 in Rm e3; Level IId/e, looking north.	74
51.	FI96/5 (I19 Level IIg/h).	74
52.	FI96/5 in I19d; Level IIg/h, looking south (see Fig. 151 for location).	75
53.	FI96/16 (K14 Level 2).	75
54.	FI96/16 in K14a; Level 2, looking east (see Fig. 53).	75
55.	FI94/9 in Rm e10, looking east (see Fig. 498 for location).	75
56.	FI95/9 (J20, Level IIIe Eastern Courtyard; see Fig. 491 for location).	76
57.	FI95/9 in J20 in Level IIIe Eastern Courtyard, looking south (see Fig. 56).	76
58.	FI97/7 (H20 Level Ve; see Fig. 484 for location).	76
59.	FI95/4 (I14 Level 1/2k).	77
60.	FI94/2–3 (H20 Level IVb; see Fig. 488 for location).	77
61.	FI94/2–3 in H20d; Level IVb, looking south (see Figs. 60 & 488).	78
62.	FI94/7 in Level IIc Rm 15, looking east (see Fig. 492).	78

Chapter 9
63.	P94/29 (J19 Level I).	79
64.	Lined Byzantine pit P94/10 in J20b, before excavation (see Fig. 508).	80
65.	P94/10 after excavation.	80
66.	P98/72 (K18 Level IIc Rm 6; see Fig. 492 for location).	81
67.	P96/29 (I14 Level 2, Rm 97; see Fig. 505 for location).	81
68.	P97/88 (H20 Level Vf4, Rm 53; see Fig. 483 for location).	82
69.	P95/13 in Level IIc Rm 1, looking south (see Fig. 492 for location).	82
70.	Stone-lined pit P94/57; Phase E4a in R19, looking NW (see Fig. 501 for location).	83
71.	Robber trench P94/2 in J19d, cutting surface 1602; looking north (see Fig. 499 for location).	83

Chapter 10
72.	Phase Vl bedrock, looking west.	88
73.	Jar **193** (H20/676) in situ, looking NE (see Fig. 474).	89
74.	Phase Vj Rm 82 destruction; objects **199**, **201**, **211** (H20/736-8), looking north (see Fig. 476).	90
75.	Phase Vj juvenile skeleton **2842** (H20/785), looking east (see Fig. 476).	90
76.	Phase Vg Rm 64 cut by pits P97/82, 88, P98/17, 58; wall W246 to the right; looking south (see Fig. 481).	94
77.	FI98/5 constructed against Phase Vg W246, looking SW (see Fig. 481).	94
78.	South section of H20d, showing burnt deposit on sequence of clean Level Vg floors in Rm 62.	95
79.	H20c: east section through levels Vg–i.	95
80.	Phase Vf4 Rms 50–53 looking west, cut by P97/82 and P97/88 (see Fig. 483).	97
81.	Phase Ve FI97/7, looking north (see Fig. 484).	100
82.	East section H20d, showing Phase Ve FI97/1 (see Fig. 512).	100

Chapter 11
83.	Rm 41 looking NW, showing burnt floor surface with central hearth and unbaked vessels at NW end of room.	103
84.	Rm 41 FI96/22, looking west (see Fig. 487).	104
85.	Rm 41, plastered installation in west corner, looking SW (see Fig. 487).	104
86.	Rm 41 pots **517** and **523** (H19/358-9) plastered against installation, looking NW.	104
87.	Combed ware jar **525** (H19/366) with clay bung **1492** in place.	104
88.	Doorway in W105, leading from Rm 42 into Rm 41, looking south (see Fig. 487).	105
89.	Detail of doorway in W105, showing plastered steps and door socket.	105

Figures

90.	*Rm 41, bricks of collapsed wall lying across destruction debris, looking SE.*	106
91.	*Rm 43, loomweights **1706–9** (H20/205–8) in situ.*	106
92.	*Storage vessel H19/223, coated with grey lining (see Fig. 488).*	108

Chapter 12

93.	*Repositioned 'plaster' lining I20/83 from around pot I20/81.*	115
94.	*Eastern Courtyard: FI97/10, looking north (see Fig. 491).*	116
95.	*Carbonized figs (J20/108) with modern strung figs above for comparison.*	118

Chapter 13

96.	*View of Level IIc Stele Building, looking west with Rms 4 and 5 at centre (see Fig. 492).*	122
97.	*View of Level IIc Stele Building, looking SW, with Rm 4 at centre.*	122
98.	*Painted design on bench, east side of Rm 1 (see Fig. 99).*	123
99.	*Painted design in red paint (see Fig. 98).*	123
100.	*Stele Building Rm 3, looking east, with FI96/18 at centre and 'altar' in corner.*	124
101.	*Rm 3, west side looking north, with FI96/18 and plastered sill on left (before excavation of K19a).*	124
102.	*Staircase in SW corner of Rm 3, looking SW.*	124
103.	*Altar in east corner of Rm 3, from NW, after exposure of IIb phase.*	125
104.	*Altar viewed from the back, also showing holes for timbers in east end of W796.*	125
105.	*Miscellaneous items from around the altar.*	125
106.	*Plastered socket in north wall of Rm 3 (W796), looking SE with plastered sill to right.*	126
107.	*Rm 3: plastered socket behind plaster of south wall (W624), looking SW.*	126
108.	*Rm 3 stele **2829** (K19/104) and dish **781** (K19/97) in situ, looking east.*	127
109.	*Rm 3, Level IIb phase of hearth FI96/18, looking SW (centre of hearth previously removed).*	127
110.	*Rm 3: cross-section through IIb foor lines west of FI96/18.*	127
111.	*Storage jar **909** (K19/294) in SW corner of Rm 4.*	128
112.	*Rm 4: carbonized beam in west wall (W797).*	129
113.	*Rm 4: basket impression against east wall, looking NE.*	129
114.	*Rm 5 with storage jar emplacements; collapsed west wall of Rm 20 (W626) in foreground, looking NW.*	130
115.	*Rm 5: stacks of bricks forming wall W619, looking SW.*	130
116.	*Rm 5: detail of door jamb in W619, looking south.*	130
117.	*Rm 5: storage jar emplacements in north corner.*	131
118.	*Rms 5 and 6, looking NE with Rm 7 and W436 in the left foreground.*	131
119.	*Rm 6: upright mudbrick features against W436, looking east.*	132
120.	*Rm 7, with Rm 6 in foreground, showing stone and mudbrick features against east face of W436.*	132
121.	*Rm 7, west corner, showing wall plaster and carbonized wood on foundation stones of W437.*	133
122.	*Rm 7, south corner: carbonized timbers in W437 and W436.*	133
123.	*Rm 7, south corner: goat horn **2494** (J18/393) in situ in W437.*	133
124.	*Rm 7: cache of astragali **2421** (J18/345) under floor by SW wall.*	134
125.	*Rm 7: 'slates' lying on floor, below destruction debris, looking east.*	134
126.	*Rm 7: bone implements **2469** in P97/49.*	135
127.	*Rm 7: early walls in sounding through W437.*	135
128.	*Rm 8: barley seeds in J19/340.*	136
129.	*Rm 8: Level IIc destruction debris, looking NE.*	136
130.	*Rm 20, looking north, with stone paving.*	138
131.	*Rm 20, north corner with stone footings of W626 and W627.*	138
132.	*Rm 20, SW corner; jars in destruction debris.*	139
133.	*Rm 21: burnt timbers of threshold, with square socket, looking NE.*	140
134.	*Rm 21, looking west, showing extent of bluish-grey ash on floor.*	140
135.	*Rm 22, NW corner: collapsed mud brick from W958, looking north.*	141
136.	*Rm 22, looking east, showing pottery from unit 5979, P98/85 and unexcavated P98/49 in foreground.*	141
137.	*Burnt mud brick and burnt wooden threshold overlying stone foundations of wall W444.*	142
138.	*Foundation of W631 in doorway, between Rms 20 and 24, looking west.*	142
139.	*K20d, looking NW with W121 at left and Rms 11 and 15.*	143

Figures

140.	*Level IId postholes in K19c (see Fig. 496), looking NW with storage jar **909** in Level IIc Rm 4 behind.*	148
141.	*H18b/d, Rm e1 foundations (W779, W782), looking SW (see Fig. 497).*	153
142.	*Rm e5: roof(?) beams on floor (J18/315, 321; see J18b in Fig. 497).*	154
143.	*Rm e6, looking west: stone-faced benches against W426 and W441, FI97/9 on the left.*	155
144.	*Rm e6: FI97/9, showing black and white pebbles, looking SW.*	155
145.	*Rm e9: loomweights in situ against W712 (see Fig. 498 nos. 1–3), looking SW.*	157
146.	*Rm e9: group of loomweights in situ (see Fig. 498 nos. 4–11), looking east.*	157
147.	*FI96/14 (I19 Level IIf).*	159
148.	*Level IIf kiln FI96/14, after clearance of fuel-chamber, looking north (see Figs. 147 & 499).*	160
149.	*Kiln FI96/14, looking south.*	160
150.	*Interior of kiln FI96/14, detail of SW end.*	160
151.	*SE corner of I19d to show FI96/15 and possibly associated features.*	161
152.	*Level IIf kiln FI96/15 looking east, across top of plaster of western side to plastered internal face of eastern side.*	162
153.	*FI96/15 interior, detail of NE corner.*	162
154.	*FI96/15, after removal of west half of structure.*	162
155.	*Rm f3 looking SE with W424 and emplacements for jars (see Fig. 499).*	163

Chapter 14
156.	*Q19d: phase E3b stone-lined drain 2120, looking NW (see Fig. 501).*	168
157.	*Byzantine walls W933–5 in S18, looking NW (see Fig. 500).*	169

Chapter 15
158.	*Q10a: storage jar Q10/41, in situ, looking SW (see Fig. 502).*	171
159.	*N12a: W500–502, looking north (see Fig. 503).*	172
160.	*I14a/b: Level 3 Rms 91–4, looking west (see Fig. 504); west edge of ditch right foreground.*	174
161.	*Rm 91: **637a** (I14/160), one of two storage jars found in situ in NW corner (Scale 1:10).*	174
162.	*Level 1 in J14b and K14a looking NW.*	178
163.	*J14b and K14a, looking east; walls W406/403 and W400/407 running parallel, and associated cross-walls.*	180
164.	*K14b and L14a in foreground, looking west.*	180
165.	*M14a–b, looking east, showing room formed by W923, W922 and W924.*	181

Chapter 16
166.	*Aerial view of church (kite photograph courtesy of Jan Driessen).*	186
167.	*K17d/L17c, looking east.*	188
168.	*I17c/d, looking east: W507 and, top left, plaster and associated W519, overlapping W506.*	191
169.	*Nave and north aisle, looking east, with pavement and associated plaster floor.*	192
170.	*Nave: west side of pavement looking south in J16.*	192
171.	*West end of pavement, looking NW, with fallen voussoirs and column base E (**191a**) in foreground.*	192
172.	*Single-chambered church, looking east.*	193
173.	*Single-chambered structure, looking SW.*	194
174.	*Floor of the chapel/chancel together with the remains of the south wall of the chapel (from SE).*	194
175.	*Later apse (W516) built onto the internal floor of the much larger earlier apse (W512), looking west.*	194
176.	*Church, looking west: in foreground late W515, with six columns (**191–2**) in alignment.*	195
177.	*L16a, looking south: skeleton **2840** in grave outside east end of church; note stones of W522 beneath skull.*	196

Chapter 17
178.	*J19d, looking south: tumble from W717, lying on surface 1605; cut by modern robber pit P95/33.*	202
179.	*J19a, looking north: column base 190 in situ in P96/17.*	203
180.	*Level Id Rm B in K19, looking NW.*	206
181.	*K20d, looking NE: stone-lined P95/6 in foreground.*	206
182.	*P95/6 before excavation, looking south.*	207
183.	*P95/6 after excavation, looking north.*	207

Figures

Chapter 18
184.	Byzantine wall foundations in L20 and M20, after surface clearance, looking west.	211
185.	N20a: walls W215–16 after surface clearance, looking south.	212

Chapter 19
186.	Different chisel marks on stone fragments.	217
187.	Architectural fragment **44**, with acanthus leaf.	218
188.	Stone basin **57**.	219
189.	Trough fragment **59**.	220
190.	Column fragments **60**.	220
191.	Architectural fragment **61**, with floral decoration.	220
192.	Architectural fragment **68**, with floral pattern.	221
193.	Architectural fragment **70**.	221
194.	Architectural fragment **71**.	221
195.	Miniature column **112**.	223
196.	Incised marble slab **127**.	225
197.	Decorated marble fragments **129**.	225
198.	Fragment of capital **130**.	225
199.	Fragment of capital **131a**.	225
200.	Fragment of capital **131b**.	226
201.	Capital **132**, underside.	226
202.	Capital **132**, side view.	226
203.	Dressed stone **136**.	226
204.	Decorated capital **189** at Kışla school.	228
205.	Detail of column base A **192a**, showing alpha mark.	229
206.	Column base B **192b**, showing vertical slots for screens.	229
207.	Detail of column base C **192c**, showing lambda mark.	229
208.	Column base D **192d**, showing slots for screen, looking NW.	230

Chapter 21
209.	Dendrogram 1: EB II.	250
210.	Dendrogram 2: EB III.	252
211.	Dendrogram 3: MBA (with the exception of 99120, which belongs in Level III).	254
212.	Dendrogram 4: LBA.	255
213.	Dendrogram 5: Level IIa–d.	258
214.	Dendrogram 6: Level IIf.	265
215.	Principal components scatterplot.	266
216.	Sc vs Cr scatterplot.	266
217.	Sc vs Ce scatterplot.	267
218.	Cs vs La scatterplot.	267

Chapter 23
219.	Sample 'scored ware' and other sherds with striations.	297
220.	Sample metallic ware sherds.	298
221.	Sample sherds of metallic ware with painted bands.	298
222.	Early Bronze Age ceramic assemblage from Level Vj destruction.	300
223.	Selected vessels from Level Vj destruction.	300
224.	White painted sherds, including **224** (top left) and **220** (bottom centre).	301
225.	Red cross bowl **352**.	310
226.	Cup **400**, with incised pot mark just visible on left.	312
227.	Incised lid **404**.	314
228.	Cypriot Red polished III juglet **410–11**.	314
229.	Sherds with incised and white-filled decoration, from miniature vessels.	314

Figures

Chapter 24

230.	Unbaked storage vessel **508** in situ *against north wall of Rm 41*.	320
231.	Storage jar **523** *from Rm 41 (see Fig. 86)*.	320
232.	Combed ware jug **529** *(on right) and other typical combed ware sherds*.	321
233.	Lids: *on left* **453** *with painted decoration; on right* **531** *with combed decoration*.	321
234.	Cup with high-rise handle **490**.	321
235.	Lower part of storage jar **558a** with disc base.	325
236.	Beak-spouted jug **549**.	326

Chapter 25

237.	Storage jars *in situ against north wall of Rm 91, looking west*.	336
238.	Neck and handle of Red Lustrous Wheel-made ware lentoid flask (**672**).	339
239.	Interiors of libation arm fragments from unit 4211, to show manufacturing technique.	340

Chapter 26

240.	Lentoid flasks and other storage vessels from Rm 20 Level IIc destruction debris.	347
241.	Pottery from fill of Level IIf kiln FI96/14.	349
242.	a) Jug **707** (I19/83); b) side view.	350
243.	Cylindrical pot stands **715–17**.	351
244.	Shallow bowl with grooved rim **718**.	352
245.	a) Side view of shallow bowl with grooved rim **719**; b) top view.	352
246.	Ring-based bowl with bevelled rim **720**.	352
247.	Bowls with painted strips on internal rim (**736–8**).	353
248.	Bowls with plain rim and cross-hatching on exterior, including **751** *(bottom left)* and **754** *(right)*.	354
249.	Bowls with plain rim and diagonal lines on exterior, including **763** *(top centre)* and **758** *(bottom right)*.	355
250.	Jars with squared rim and cross-hatching, including **794** *(top left)*.	358
251.	Upper part of jar **800** built into base of FI96/11.	359
252.	Miscellaneous jars with cross-hatching: **802** *(left)*, 2 sherds of **801** *(top)*, **805** *(bottom right)*.	359
253.	Jar sherds with pendent semi-circles, including **855** *(on left)* and **856** *(top centre)*.	363
254.	A variety of decorated feet from pilgrim flasks, including **925**, **932**, **936** and **938**.	369

Chapter 27

255.	'Geometric' sherds from the ditch in I14: **940–44**.	371

Chapter 28

256.	Mycenaean deep bowl **957**.	376

Chapter 30

257.	Hellenistic sherds from pit P94/41 in Q19, including **980–81** and **989**.	381
258.	Selected Hellenistic sherds from units 2100 and 2107.	382
259.	Hellenistic cooking pot **1007**.	386

Chapter 31

260.	Fragments of Byzantine tiles: **1468b**, **1468a**; **1467**, **1467**, **1464**.	401
261.	Fragments of Byzantine tiles with moulded curve in corners: **1469b**, **1466**, **1469a**; **1469c**.	402

Chapter 33

262.	Hieroglyphic seals (**1470**, **1471**, **1472**, **1473**).	443

Chapter 35

263.	Bovid figurine **1505**.	450
264.	Base of statuette **1510**.	451
265.	Hellenistic plaque **1511**, showing comic actor.	451

266.	*Human figurine* **1512**.	451
267.	*Head of horse head figurine* **1515**: *a) side view; b) front view.*	452
268.	*Head of animal figurine* **1516**, *side view.*	452
269.	*Head of Hellenistic female figurine* **1519**.	453
270.	*Head of horse figurine* **1523**.	453
271.	*Perforated clay disc* **1529**: *a) front view; b) side view.*	454
272.	*Perforated clay disc* **1532**.	454
273.	*Assorted clay discs, drawn examples:* **1540**, **1546**, **1570**, **1575**, **1582** *and* **1595**.	456
274.	*Decorated clay ball* **1596**.	459
275.	*Re-used sherd with incised design* **1623**.	461
276.	*Ottoman pipe bowl* **1624**.	461
277.	*Horned clay support* **1625**.	462
278.	*Clay spit support* **1627**.	463
279.	*Clay crescents: top)* **1635**, **1734**; *centre)* **1634**; *bottom)* **1636**, **1638**.	464
280.	*Stamped clay crescent* **1634**.	465
281.	*Stamped clay crescent* **1638**.	465
282.	*Dimensions of clay ovoids (***1639–78***).*	467

Chapter 36

283.	*Weights of clay loomweights weighing up to 1250 g; see also* **1760** *(3800 g).*	470
284.	*Group of 14 loomweights from Middle Bronze unit 1258.*	472
285.	*Selected loomweights from floor of Rm e9 (***1735–59***).*	475

Chapter 37

286.	*Weights of spindle whorls, grouped by period or type.*	482
287.	*Spindle whorls from Level V.*	483
288.	*Spindle whorls from Level Vf, views from above and side.*	485
289.	*Spindle whorls from Level Vf: a) view from above; b) view from side.*	485
290.	*Spindle whorls from Level Ve (except* **1851** *from Vf): a) view from above; b) view from side.*	487
291.	*Spindle whorls from Level IVa (except* **1975** *from IIIc): a) view from above; b) view from side.*	489
292.	*Spindle whorls from Level IV: a) view from above; b) view from side.*	490
293.	*Spindle whorls from Level IV: a) view from above; b) view from side.*	490
294.	*Spindle whorls from various levels: a) view from above; b) view from below.*	491

Chapter 38

295.	*Assorted beads from Level II (except* **2002** *from Vf).*	500

Chapter 39

296.	*Glass handles.*	507
297.	*Glass bangles.*	508

Chapter 41

298.	*Copper adze* **2213**.	515
299.	*Copper bracelet terminal* **2215**.	516
300.	*Detail of needle* **2233** *head to show folded eye.*	517
301.	*Copper pins and needles from Levels II, III and V.*	518
302.	*Projectile points from Level II.*	518
303.	*Detail of blade* **2248** *to show X mark.*	519
304.	*Copper ring* **2259**, *side view to show herring-bone design.*	519
305.	*Copper chain links* **2268**.	520
306.	*Copper ring* **2271**: *a) one face; b) other face; c) side view.*	520
307.	*Section from copper rim of hoplite shield* **2272**.	520
308.	*Copper fragments from rim of hoplite shield(s)* **2273–4**.	521
309.	*Tweezers* **2276** *from Level Vf.*	521

310.	*Copper studs **2290**, found with astragali **2421**.*	522
311.	*Metal column **2293**.*	523
312.	*Copper cross **2294**.*	523
313.	*Silver figurine of divine triad **2306**.*	524
314.	*Iron nails etc. **2343**, **2370**, **2331**, **2370**, **2331**, **2372**, **2339**, **2341**, **2412**, **2336**.*	527

Chapter 42

315.	*Selected astragali from hoard **2421** in Level IIc, Rm 7.*	532
316.	*Two deer astragali from **2421**.*	533
317.	*Three worked astragali **2423** from 5362 (Level Vf).*	534
318.	*Notched bone implements **2469** (nos. 1, 4, 10 and 11).*	537
319.	*Perforated tube of antler **2483**.*	538
320.	*Bone bar **2486** with dowels each end.*	539
321.	*Carved bone artefact **2491**.*	539
322.	*Antler **2493** (K18/96).*	539

Chapter 43

323.	*Fossil bi-valve shells from different levels.*	541
324.	*Fossilized uni-valve shells.*	542
325.	*Fossils: **2517**, **2521**.*	542
326.	*Fossilized coral **2518**.*	542

Chapter 45

327.	*Fragment of decorated disc **2603**.*	560
328.	*Segment of carved disc **2605**.*	560
329.	*Carved stone **2610**.*	560
330.	*Fragment of stone incense burner(?) **2611**.*	561
331.	*Stone maceheads from Level IVa, **2614** & **2615**.*	561
332.	*Sandstone mould for metalwork **2616**.*	562
333.	*Stone jewellery mould **2617**.*	562
334.	*Stone palette **2619a**.*	563
335.	*Fragment of black stone vase **2641**, with lion in relief.*	564

Chapter 46

336.	*Stele **2829** obverse with red-painted design, after cleaning and re-assembling (see Fig. 469).*	576

Chapter 47

337.	*Coin of Gordian III, obverse (**2832**).*	577
338.	*Coin of Arcadius (2nd period — AD 402–408) (**2936**): a) obverse; b) reverse.*	577
339.	*Coin of Leo I (**2837**): a) obverse; b) reverse.*	577
340.	*Anonymous follis, c. AD 980–1025 (**2838**).*	578
341.	*Follis of Michael VII Ducas (**2839**): a) obverse; b) reverse.*	578

Chapter 49

342.	*Discriminant analysis comparing ungrouped Kilise Tepe wild type assemblages to ethnographic data.*	588
343.	*Ddiscriminant analysis comparing grouped Kilise Tepe wild type assemblages to ethnographic data.*	588
344.	*Multivariant correspondence analysis.*	589
345.	*Multivariant correspondence analysis focusing on the cluster present around the origin.*	589
346.	*Cereal grain composition for samples containing 50 grains or more and from definite phases (18 samples).*	593

Chapter 50

347.	*Relative and absolute frequencies of silica skeletons from the coprolite and the residues from pots.*	600
348.	*Relative and absolute frequencies of silica skeletons from the floor, the courtyards and the structural fill.*	600

349.	*Relative and absolute frequencies of silica skeletons from the pit samples.*	600
350.	*Correspondence analysis plot of the pit samples and two controls.*	601

Chapter 51
351.	*Size distribution of all the cyprinids.*	609
352.	*Percentage contribution of Anatolian freshwater fish, marine species and exotic freshwater fish through time.*	610

Chapter 52
353.	*Cranium 2840, from grave at east end of Church: a) left side; b) back.*	614
354.	*Metatarsal 2845 to show kneeling facets: a) top; b) side.*	615

Chapter 53
355.	*Dendrochronology chart.*	619
356a.	*Plot of the wiggle-match for sample J20/172 against the INTCAL04 calibration data set.*	620
356b.	*Composite probability plot of the radiocarbon dated decades calculated for the Kilise Tepe sample J20/172.*	620
357a.	*Plot of the wiggle-match for sample J18/398 against the INTCAL04 calibration data set.*	620
357b.	*Composite probability plot of the radiocarbon dated decades calculated for the Kilise Tepe sample J18/398.*	620

Tables

Chapter 1
1.	*Grants awarded to the Kilise Tepe project (Total = £282,744).*	4
2.	*Kilise Tepe project expenditure (Total = £283,815).*	5

Chapter 6
3.	*Summary of a selection of previous surface surveys and collections in the Near East.*	46
4.	*Summary statistics.*	53
5.	*Correlation analysis.*	53
6.	*Summary of distribution maps.*	54

Chapter 10
7.	*Overview of Levels III–V in H19–20 and I–J20.*	87

Chapter 21
8.	*Kilise Tepe ceramics samples list.*	244
9.	*Chemical data for ceramic samples.*	262

Chapter 25
10.	*Sherd counts for Level III by phase.*	330

Chapter 26
11.	*Sherd counts for Level II by phase.*	344

Chapter 29
12.	*Comparative data.*	377
13.	*Similarities found.*	378

Chapter 31
14.	*Level One pottery provenance, fabric nos.*	424

Part D Appendix
15.	*Summary of luminescence results.*	429

Chapter 35
16.	Clay ovoid data.	466

Chapter 42
17.	Deposit 5870: distribution of astragali by species, sex and body side.	531
18.	2421: deposit under floor of Rm 7 (unit 5870).	532
19.	2422: astragali from altar area in Rm 3 (unit 6209).	533
20.	2469: dimensions of notched bone implements.	536

Chapter 44
21.	Total numbers of tools.	546
22.	Blank form distribution.	550
23.	Raw materials in the collection.	552
24.	Raw material usage.	552
25.	Chert blank composition.	553
26.	Obsidian blank composition.	553
27.	Quartz blank composition.	554
28.	Limestone blank composition.	554
29.	Data for units yielding ten or more pieces.	555
30.	List of units yielding between five and nine pieces.	557

Chapter 49
31.	Context details of archaeobotanical samples analysed in this report.	584
32.	Summary of codes used in statistical analyses and the identification categories they represent.	586
33.	Categorization of wild seed characteristics expected to influence behaviour in crop processing.	587
34.	Presence of potential crop types by phase.	588
35.	Categorization of samples based on their overall composition and the results of crop-processing analysis.	590
36.	Summary of content of sub-samples taken from the same archaeological units.	591
37.	Summary of samples from Level IIc.	592

Chapter 50
38.	Contexts sampled for the analysis of phytoliths with level and unit of provenance and the field description.	598
39.	Absolute and relative frequencies of the phytolith types encountered in Kilise Tepe samples.	599
40.	Correspondence analysis of Kilise Tepe samples with the identified clusters and the phytolith types.	601

Chapter 51
41.	The fish remains in the various levels of Kilise Tepe.	608
42.	Skeletal element representation of the unidentified cyprinids.	608

Chapter 53
43.	Radiocarbon data.	621

Preface

The threat of submersion under a hydro-electric reservoir offered the opportunity to excavate 13 metres of archaeological deposits on a hill overlooking the valley of the Göksu in the province of Mersin, or in classical terms, of the Calycadnus in Rough Cilicia. These 13 metres proved to represent nearly 4000 years of human occupation, from the Early Bronze Age until late in the Byzantine era. As we had expected, the site became an outpost of the Hittite Empire in the late second millennium BC, but it soon emerged that it was also used in the Early Iron Age and then again in the Hellenistic period. Then a substantial basilica was built towards the centre of the mound in early Byzantine times, from which the site takes its modern name of Kilise Tepe.

The defining characteristic of the site is its position athwart one of the two major routes between the Anatolian interior and the southern seaboard. At times the material record we recovered looks towards the Mediterranean, participating in the cultural and political world of Kizzuwatna, Que and Hilakku, Cilicia, or the Çukurova, but in the late second millennium BC or the first millennium AD the imperial sway of Hattusa or Byzantium is plain to see.

The continued occupation of the site and the enigmatic Stele Building in the obscure centuries after the fall of the Hittite capital provides one of the principal points of interest, with radical changes in both the architecture and the ceramic repertoire calling for explanation in terms of the social and political transformations of the age. Yet at all times — in the Early Bronze levels of the third millennium BC, in the Middle Bronze, and through the Hellenistic centuries into the world of Byzantium — Kilise Tepe fills a void in the archaeological record, with the nearest excavated settlements several days of pre-motorized travel distant.

The Byzantine church and the contemporary occupation was an added bonus, providing an opportunity to observe a record of occupation from an era when the great majority of our evidence takes the form of ecclesiastical architecture.

The present volume is inevitably a compromise, born of the tension between the pressures from different sides to produce a report promptly, and the desire to present as definitive a record as possible. Although this is what is commonly described as a final report, in fact it is intended more as the beginning of a process than the end. Like most research, the work at Kilise Tepe has raised at least as many questions as it has resolved, and the value of the work is likely to rest at least as much in the formulation of these questions as in some of the answers it affords. As this volume goes to press, plans are under way for a resumption of work at the site which will address some of these questions and recover some more precise answers: how does the material evidence of Hittite presence relate to its system of political control? How and when exactly did local traditions or innovations overtake the Hittite order? When and from where did external influences on the local ceramics make their appearance? Such questions combine to explore the nature of the transition from the palace cultures of the Late Bronze Age to the new world of the classical era, one of the crucial axes in the history of the Old World.

*   *   *   *

Over and above the core funding provided by the British Institute at Ankara, the project received significant and recurrent support during its fieldwork phase from the British Academy, the (Arts and) Humanities Research Board, the McDonald Institute for Archaeological Research, and Trinity College, Cambridge (Cary Robertson Fund). The generosity of these institutions, tabulated on p. 4 below, is acknowledged here with much gratitude. Likewise the grants which we received towards the costs of post-excavation study and the preparation of this publication from the same bodies, and also from the Institute for Aegean Prehistory (INSTAP), the Mediterranean Archaeological Trust, and the C.H.W. Johns Fund of the University of Cambridge are tabulated there and very warmly acknowledged here.

A special word of thanks must go to the McDonald Institute, which has throughout provided the 'base camp' for the project in addition to recurrent financial support. Without the facilities of the Institute mounting the field seasons and writing up the results would have been enormously more difficult, and we are deeply grateful to Chris Scarre, the Deputy Director throughout the duration of the project, and to Colin

Renfrew and Graeme Barker as successive Directors for their moral and practical support.

*   *   *   *

The excavations at Kilise Tepe were initiated by Nicholas Postgate in 1994 on behalf of the British Institute at Ankara. Under the provisions for rescue excavations, the direction of the project in the field was shared jointly with the Director of the Museum at Silifke, initially Şinasi Başal (in 1994–97), and then İlhame Öztürk (in 1998). As representatives of the General Directorate in the field we were fortunate to benefit from the support and company of Erhan Özcan in 1994, Fatih Ferli in 1995 and 1996, Musa Tombul in 1997, and Mustafa Ergün in 1998. We are privileged to be able to thank the General Directorate for their backing throughout, and recall especially the advice and assistance of Prof. Dr Engin Özgen and the late Osman Özbek at the beginning.

*   *   *   *

The digging, movement of earth and stones, collection of surface materials, sieving and floating, trowelling, brushing and shovelling was done by our local workmen. Some came from Zeyne (Sütlüce) or nearby Şarlak, some from Kışla, a few from neighbouring places. They all worked willingly, most of them hard, and some very skilfully. To them all we are grateful.

From 1995 to its conclusion in 1998 Dr Caroline Steele acted as Assistant Director to the project. Although busy on site as an area supervisor, she shouldered more than her fair share of the day-to-day management of the project seven days a week and almost 24 hours a day. On site at different times David Thomas, Nicholas Jackson and Mark Jackson also assumed overall responsibility for the supervision and recording in different areas. Their contributions and those of all the colleagues and students from Britain, Turkey and several other countries, were of course critical to the conduct of the excavation. They cannot be separately attributed unit by unit, but we have indicated here the years and location of their principal work: Sanna Aro-Valjus: J14 (1995); Nurettin Aslan: (1996); Francesca Balossi: R18 (1995), H18–19, I18 (1996); Sarah Blakeney: I19, I20, J20 (1994–97), L19 (1998); Graham Chandler: Q10 (1994); Iain Cheyne: H20 (1996), J19 (1998); Ilknur Demir: H20 (1997); Martin Densham: H20 (1994); Berrin Ergin: K14 (1994); Jon Gower: I14, J14 (1995–96), H20 (1997); Emily Hayes: K19 (1997); Lisa Hopkins: H19, H20 (1996); Vedia Izzet: J19 (1998); Mark Jackson: the Church and adjacent areas (1997–98); Nicholas Jackson: J20, K19, K20, L14 (1994–96); Carl Knappett: J19 (1996); Ergün Laflı: Church (1996); Jennifer MacCormack: H19, H20 (1995); Gaille Mackinnon: J19, J20, K20 (1994–96); Aidan O'Lynn: surface (1994); Sara Owen: Q18, R18 (1994); Tom Pollard: survey (1994), surface (1994–95); Lucy Seffen (née Mutter): J18, K18 (1997), H20 (1998); Töre Sivrioğlu: Church (1997); Caroline Steele: K14, M14 (1994, 1996), J19 (1997), K19 (1998); David Thomas: Q19, Q20, surface (1994), J18, K18 (1997-8); Leylâ Umur: N12 (1994); Andrew Wilson: H20 (1994); Marysia Zapasnik: H20 (1998).

For most of our field seasons the work of the Leverhulme project was in progress (see p. 581). This was under the direction of Sue Colledge, who was at site for the 1995–97 seasons and set up and supervised the flotation system and sieving systems for the recovery of wet and dry samples. Jo Bending joined her to assist with the recovery and sorting of botanical samples in 1996–97. Polydora Baker was also present working on the zooarchaeological materials in 1995–97, and returned to the site in 1998 and to the museum in 1999 to complete study of the material recovered from the excavation outside the framework of the Leverhulme programme. In 1997 she was assisted by Rebecca Sheldon. Finally the micromorphological samples were collected by Wendy Matthews during visits to the site over the three years of the Leverhulme project.

The pottery was initially sorted in the orchard near the spring below the tepe. This was entrusted to Sara Da Gama Howells in the first season, 1994, under the guidance of Dorit Symington, and in subsequent seasons (1995–98) was undertaken by Connie Hansen. 'Back at the house' the more detailed cataloguing and recording of the excavated pottery in 1994 was in the hands of Dorit Symington, while Dominique Collon took charge of the voluminous surface material. Subsequently Dorit Symington concentrated on the description of the Early and Middle Bronze Age ceramics, while Connie Hansen analysed the Late Bronze and Iron Age pottery, both assisted at times by Carl Knappett, especially in 1997–98 when he was studying the full range of ceramics with a view to selecting samples for analysis. The Byzantine ceramics were taken in hand in the latter seasons by Mark Jackson. As their contributions to this volume indicate, in the course of short visits the Hellenistic pottery was studied by Lisa Nevett (in 1995) and the Mycenaean by Elizabeth French (in 1999).

Most work on the finds took place 'back at the house', in the school building at Zeyne. There the objects register was primarily entrusted to Heather Baker (1994–95), Rebecca Sheldon (1996–97) and Kathy Hadley (1998), although there was usually assistance

Preface

from 'members of the cast', including Bronwyn Douglas. Others who gave assistance with the finds were Çiğdem Koçyiğit and Meltem Karanfil (1996), Kadriye Şahin (1997), while Tim Reynolds carried out his exhaustive study of the lithic material in 1998.

Conservation in the first season was entrusted to the capable hands of Andrew Wilson, followed in 1996–98 by the equally capable and dedicated Franca Cole. Martin Densham took the photographs in the first season, followed in 1996–98 by Bronwyn Douglas. From her hand are virtually all photographs in this volume, with the exception of the first season and the ceramic thin-sections, and the project owes much to her professional input. The pottery drawing was principally done by Dominique Collon, in 1994 and occasionally in later seasons, Tessa Rickards, in 1995–98, and Elizabeth Postgate, in 1995–96. The Byzantine pottery was mostly drawn by Mark Jackson. The great majority of finds illustrations are also from the hand of Tessa Rickards.

Post-excavation work in the Museum at Silifke continued in 1999 and 2000, and again in 2003. Collaborators in 1999 were: Mark Jackson, Sarah Blakeney (also 2000, 2003), Franca Cole, Bronwyn Douglas, Elizabeth French, Jessica Pearson, Polydora Baker, Connie Hansen, Dorit Symington, Dominique Collon, and Caroline Steele (also 2000 and 2003).

*   *   *   *

The preparation of the publication naturally extended long after the conclusion of fieldwork. The full manuscript was first assembled in May 2004. It was then revised and expanded in the light of suggestions from the publishers' reader, and resubmitted in its present form in August 2005. After this time the editors and the individual authors have not normally been able to take account of other publications.

Of the two editors of the volume, Nicholas Postgate is responsible for its overall composition and contents, while David Thomas, in addition to his own identified contributions, gave the typescript its final shape and format, carried out most of the laborious cross-referencing between sections, assembled and organized the photographs and other illustrative material. Only the contributors will be conscious of how many drafts their contributions were put through, and how long they have had to wait for them to see the light of day: for their patience and good will we are deeply grateful, and the errors which will inevitably have escaped us will not be theirs.

Not named as authors are others whose post-excavation work on the documentation was an essential preliminary to the drafting of the manuscript, notably Tom Pollard, Caroline Steele, Nicholas Jackson, David Thomas, and for the Byzantine materials Mark Jackson. Equally essential are those who have helped on the technical side in producing the drawings and other images. Substantial work on inking and mounting the drawings was done in the years after 1998 by Tessa Rickards, Elizabeth Postgate, Sarah Blakeney, Adam Scott, and Lucy Seffen. Most of the inked drawings were scanned by Gary Reynolds Ltd. Some of the photographs were printed by Gwil Owen of the Faculty of Archaeology and Anthropology in Cambridge, the remainder, the majority, were then scanned digitally by Ian Bolton of the Anatomy Visual Media Group in Cambridge. To Dora Kemp we are deeply grateful for the care and expertise with which she has converted our 'manuscript' into these two volumes.

*   *   *   *

We are grateful to many colleagues for their help with specific points, both during the excavations and in the preparation of the publication: Stuart and Shirley Blaylock, Rainer-Maria Boehmer, Lucilla Burn, Nicholas Coldstream, Alain Davesne, Jan Driessen, David French, Elizabeth French, Marie-Henriette Gates, Eric Handley, Vronwy Hankey, David Hawkins, Ellen Herscher, Stephen Hill, Maria Iacovou, John Meadows, Stephen Mitchell, Roger Moorey, Gwil Owen, Tahsin Özgüç, Jürgen Seeher, Emre Şerifoğlu, St John Simpson, Joanna Smith, Anthony Snodgrass, Kate Spence, Geoffrey Summers, Dorothy Thompson, Leylâ Umur (née Çehreli), John P. Wilde, and Levent Zoroğlu. In addition, Jo Bending received much help from Glynis Jones, Amy Bogaard and Michael Charles, Jessica Pearson from Theya Molleson, Mark Jackson from Jim Crow, Kevin Greene, and Richard Bayliss, and from the Newcastle University Robinson Bequest and Runciman Studentship.

Both during and before and after each season we were consistently supported by the British Institute of Archaeology at Ankara, not only successive directors, David Shankland, Roger Matthews and Hugh Elton, but other staff of the Institute, including Keith Jordan, Yaprak Eran, Gina Coulthard back in London, and most especially Gülgün Girdivan. In Zeyne we benefited from the support of Arif Ali Çelik, and for more than ten years, from the first season to the final throes of the publication, from the help and advice of Yakup Kahveci and the staff of the Yaka Hotel in Kızkalesi.

J.N. Postgate
Cambridge 2007

Abbreviations and Conventions

approx.	approximately
archit.	architectural
assoc.	associated
bot.	botanical
carbon.	carbonized
ceram.	ceramic
ctyd	courtyard
cyl.	cylinder, cylindrical
dec.	decorated, decoration
destr.	destruction
Di.	diameter
E	east
EB(A)	Early Bronze (Age)
ext.	(on) exterior
FI	Fire Installation
frag.	fragment
H.	height
incl.	including
int.	(on) interior
KLT	Silifke Museum Kilise Tepe catalogue number
L.	length
LB(A)	Late Bronze (Age)
LR(A)	Late Roman (Amphora)
max.	maximum
MB(A)	Middle Bronze (Age)
min.	minimum
mini.	miniature

Myc.	Mycenaean
N	north
NAA	Neutron Activation Analysis
NE	northeast
NW	northwest
obj.	object
occ.	occupation
P	Pit number
perf.	perforated, perforation
pers. comm.	personal communication
pt.	point
pub.	published
Rm	Room number
S	south
SE	southeast
sp. whorl	spindle whorl
SW	southwest
Th.	thickness
unexc.	unexcavated
unpub.	unpublished
W	West; Wall number
W.	width
Wt	weight
+	Height above datum (see p. xxiii)
~	Approx. height above datum (see p. xxiii)
( )	incomplete dimension

Note on numbers

1. Grid squares

See Figure 17 p. 49 for the site grid and co-ordinates. Each 10-m square is identified by a capital letter and two-figure number (e.g. K20). Within each square the quadrants are a = NW, b = NE, c = SW and d = SE (see p. 67).

2. Site datum

A datum arbitrarily fixed at 100.00 was established in 1994 (at a point near the centre of the mound, at 1150, 1150, the NW corner of P14). This is approximately 142 m above sea level (see Pollard, in Baker *et al.* 1995, 148). Precise readings related to the arbitrary 100-m datum are given in the form +99.75; approximate or average heights in the form ~99.75.

3. Artefact numbering

The numbers in **bold** for catalogued objects have been assigned for the purpose of this volume. Both the descriptive catalogue entries and the plates of illustrations are arranged in this sequence, and the simple number will thus direct the reader to both the entry and an illustration if it exists. In a few instances it has been necessary to omit a number or to insert extra entries in the sequence, identified by the addition of a, b etc. (e.g. 637a and 637b). When an item has no drawing its number in the catalogue is enclosed in square brackets, e.g. [2291].

On site, or later in the house, most artefacts, other than potsherds, were assigned an 'object number' of the type K20/345, under which they are recorded in the electronic data base and listed in the museum storage records (see p. 440). For an earlier numbering system used in 1994 and 1995, which was superseded and is not used in this volume, see p. 67. Each season a relatively small number of the most significant finds were also assigned a Museum Number of the type KLT 67; this is also given in the catalogues. In 1997–98 some finds were placed in the museum category of Etütlük: these are not given KLT numbers but are also stored in the central museum storeroom, unlike the remaining finds which are in the annex.

While whole vessels, especially those found *in situ*, were assigned object numbers, most sherds were not, but were solely identified by their unit number (see below) and a drawing number (e.g. D1234) which only features in this volume when the item is not catalogued.

4. Unit numbers

Each separately recorded archaeological operation was assigned a 'unit number'. The surface clearance units were identified by 3-figure, excavation units by 4-figure numbers. A list of these is given in Appendix 2 (pp. 629–70). The unit number is the essential link between each object or assemblage of sherds, bones, etc. and its provenance. The main bulk of the retained potsherds and bones are identified, bagged and stored in the museum annex solely by their unit number.

5. Dimensions

These should be self-evident for the most part. In object descriptions linear dimensions are in centimetres, weights in grammes. Incomplete dimensions (where the object is broken) may be indicated by enclosing them in round brackets — e.g. L. (19.7).

In the excavation sections lengths are normally given in metres, except where features measuring less than a metre are being described in which case centimetres are normally used.

Part A
Introduction

Chapter 1 **Introduction to the Project and the Publication**   3
   The background   3
   The project   3
   Objectives and results   4
   The publication   7

Chapter 2 **The Site of Kilise Tepe**   9
   The mound and its surroundings   9
   The natural setting   10
   The geographical context   11

Chapter 3 **The Kilise Tepe Area in Pre-Classical and Hellenistic Times**   15
   The Bronze Age   15
   The Iron Age   16
   The Hellenistic era   17

Chapter 4 **The Kilise Tepe Area in the Byzantine Era**   19
   The Isaurians   19
   Sites in the Göksu region   20
   Architecture in the landscape   22
   The major Göksu sites   23
   Seventh century and after   25
   Conclusion   28

Chapter 5 **The Excavations and their Results**   31
   Summary of the work on site   31
   Fortification, access and the environs   31
   Periods represented at the site   33
      Early and Middle Bronze Age   33
      Late Bronze Age   33
      The end of the Bronze Age   34
      The Iron Age   34
      The later first millennium BC   34
   The Level III to Level II transition   35
   The Level II destructions   36
   The Vg destruction   37
   Two aspects of the stratigraphic sequence   37
   Food production and consumption   38
   Textile production   38
   Ceramic production   39
   External relations   39

Chapter 1

Introduction to the Project and the Publication

Nicholas Postgate

The background

Prehistoric sites in the Göksu valley were surveyed in the 1950s by J. Mellaart, and again by D.H. French in 1965, and as far as we are aware it is here that the site of Kilise Tepe first features in scholarly literature. It is reported in Mellaart's survey under the name of Maltepe (Mellaart 1958a, 315); this appears to result from a confusion with a site near Zeyne, on the other side of the Göksu, whose name is given on official maps, and known to the locals, as Maltepe (Fig. 471; also described under this name by Heberdey at the end of the nineteenth century: Heberdey & Wilhelm 1896). When we began work in 1994 it rapidly became apparent that the mound we were investigating was known locally as Kilise Tepe, and this has been accepted officially as the site's name by the General Directorate.

In his survey report Mellaart writes of abundant pottery of the third, second and first millennia BC, and from his 1965 visit to the site (still under the name of Maltepe) French publishes more material which made it clear that the site was occupied in the Late Bronze Age (French 1965, 184–5; particularly diagnostic is a fragment of red-burnished libation arm). Neither survey was concerned with the Classical or later periods, and neither mentions collecting material of this date from the site.[1]

The project

During the 1980s plans were drafted for the construction of a hydro-electric dam on the lower Göksu, at a locality known as Kayraktepe, just below the road bridge SE of Değirmendere. As planned, this would have led to the flooding of Kilise Tepe. D.H. French was alert to the potential interest of a Late Bronze Age site in this region, and it was thanks to his prompting that in 1993, when the British Institute of Archaeology at Ankara was considering its future field activities, application was made to the authorities in Ankara to start a rescue excavation at Kilise Tepe in advance of the barrage construction. Agreement was reached in principle with the authorities to open excavations at the site, and in accordance with the current procedures for rescue projects, the work was set up under the joint direction of Şinasi Başal, representing the Silifke Museum, of which he was Director, and J.N. Postgate on behalf of the British Institute. Subsequently in 1998 İlhame Öztürk succeeded Ş. Başal as the Director of the Museum and hence as Joint Director of the Kilise Tepe project.

Work started on site in July 1994, the advance party initially commuting daily from its base at the Yaka Hotel in Kızkalesi. Subsequently we moved into a large temporarily unused school building on the outskirts of Zeyne, convenient for its size and copious water, but across the Göksu and about 10 km from the site up a steep and in places winding road. The finds (except discarded potsherds) were all brought back to the house and processed there. At the site itself a splendid oriental plane tree (çınar) creates a welcome shaded space round the spring at the foot of the north end of the tepe, and after an initial unsuccessful experiment with a tent on the top of the mound we did not find it necessary to erect any other structure (except small sanitary facilities). Approximately half our work force (averaging around 30) came from the village of Kışla, 1 km away, next to the road bridge over the Göksu, the other half from Zeyne. Work on site was between 6 am and 1.30 pm, once we had realized that in the heat of July and August very little could be expected of workmen or staff in the half hour between 1.30 and 2.00. Wednesdays were a day off for all concerned, and Sundays also for the workmen, while the staff continued recording work both on site and in the house.

We excavated at the site for five consecutive summers, in 1994–98 inclusive, although in the fifth and final season we were concentrating on preparing materials for publication. At the end of that season we had to vacate the school premises unexpectedly early, for the happy reason that it was being prepared for re-use as a school, and thanks to the collaboration of the Museum Director we moved our entire body of excavated materials (some 370 plastic crates) down to

Figure 1. *Sn. İlhame Öztürk with Kilise Tepe exhibit in Silifke Museum.*

safe and convenient storage in the annex to the Silifke Museum, where we were able to complete the season's work. Subsequently some members of the team spent time working in the museum in the summer of 1999, and in summer 2000 we were able to check further details and install a Kilise Tepe exhibit in the museum display (Fig. 1). Finally two weeks were spent ordering the finds and checking final details for this volume in April 2003. Our debt to our colleagues in Turkey and to the staff of the excavation team is obvious, and is detailed in the Preface. There too we gladly record the debt we owe to the various institutions which have supported the work, both at the time of the excavation and after it during the protracted publication process. It may be of interest to our contemporaries, and perhaps even more to succeeding generations to tabulate here the amounts and purposes of the financial support the project has received over the 10-year period (Tables 1 & 2; Figs. 2–4).

All the expenditure figures are approximate, and it should be observed that there is one aspect of the project not reflected in these tables, and that is the time contributed without remuneration by several of the crucial members of the team, both to the work in the field and subsequently during the preparation of the publication. These include Dominique Collon, Connie Hansen, Mark Jackson, Carl Knappett, and Dorit Symington, each of whom has, over a number of years, given substantial amounts of time to the preparation of their section of the volume; and of course the first editor's own time. If this work were realistically costed it would add very substantially to the sum total, but happily there are still some areas of academic enterprise which do not have to be measured in money and these contributions to the work are mentioned only to remind us that the listing of monies received does not tell the whole story.

Objectives and results

The decision to start excavation at Kilise Tepe related to the known presence of Late Bronze Age settlement at the site. Given its location on a major route linking the interior with the sea coast, the fact that it was

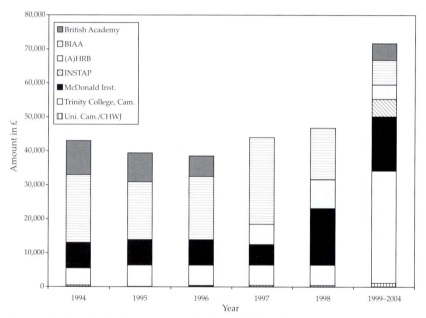

Figure 2. *Bar chart of grants awarded to the Kilise Tepe project.*

Table 1. *Grants awarded to the Kilise Tepe project (Total = £282,744).*

	1994	1995	1996	1997	1998	1999–2004	Total
British Academy	10,000	8500	6000			4900	29,400
(A)HRB				6000	8500	4271	18,771
BIAA	20,000	17,000	18,600	25,500	15,189	7240	103,529
Trinity College, Cambridge	5000	6310	6000	6000	6000	33,037	62,347
McDonald Institute	7500	7500	7500	6000	16,650	15,981	61,131
INSTAP						5100	5100
University of Cambridge/CHWJ	400		302	370	360	1034	2466
Total	42,900	39,310	38,402	43,870	46,699	71,563	282,744

threatened by the proposed barrage at Kayraktepe, and its relatively small size, the site seemed to offer an opportunity to address a number of related issues within a limited time. While there could be no expectation of documentary sources from the site, given its size and location, it was occupied when adjacent areas of Anatolia and the eastern Mediterranean were to some degree in historical times, and as a small, though potentially defensible, site, it promised to provide an insight into conditions in the margins of the major contemporary polities, and at the same time to supply a chronological sequence which could also be related to events elsewhere.

By contrast with some other parts of the Near East and Mediterranean, the low density of known pre-Classical archaeological sites in this region of Rough Cilicia is remarkable, and excavated sites are even more widely separated. Before we began work at Kilise Tepe, the nearest excavated Late Bronze Age sites to Mersin to the north and west must have been Kamankale Höyük and Beycesultan, about 300 and 400 km away respectively. Any excavation in so large a vacuum is bound to contribute to bridging the gaps in our knowledge of the material cultural record, and thus to the gradual mapping of culturally defined regions, which have a validity of their own whether or not they can be associated with ethnic or even political criteria. 'On the evidence of the pottery, the Göksu valley belonged to Cilicia rather than the Konya plain' (French 1965, 186), and excavation confirms that the material culture of Kilise Tepe belongs at most periods

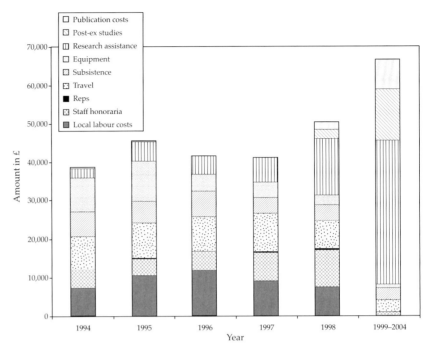

Figure 3. *Bar chart of Kilise Tepe project expenditure 1994–2004.*

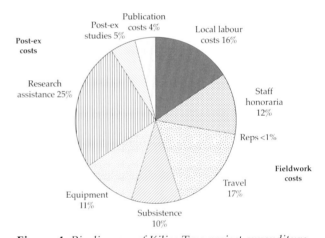

Figure 4. *Pie diagram of Kilise Tepe project expenditure 1994–2004.*

Table 2. *Kilise Tepe project expenditure (Total = £283,815).*

Season	Fieldwork						FW Subtot	Post-excavation			PE Subtot	Total
	Local labour costs	Staff honoraria	Reps	Travel	Subsistence	Equipment		Research assistance	Post-ex studies	Publication costs		
1994	7335	4906	0	8511	6441	8856	36,049	2400	0	240	2640	**38,689**
1995	10,594	4550	0	9087	5712	10,399	40,342	5222	0	116	5338	**45,680**
1996	11,695	5180	0	9017	6595	4415	36,902	4653	0	0	4653	**41,555**
1997	9122	7470	118	10,006	4053	4057	34,826	6288	0	0	6288	**41,114**
1998	7366	9673	410	7312	4033	2484	31,278	14,843	2300	1871	19,014	**50,292**
1999–2004	0	900	0	3369	2925	985	8179	37,267	13,262	7777	58,306	**66,485**
Total	46,112	32,679	528	47,302	29,759	31,196	18,7576	70,673	15,562	10,004	96,239	**283,815**

with Cilicia, and thence indirectly to the eastern Mediterranean *koine*, especially during the first millennium BC. The principal exceptions to this are in Early Bronze Age III, when like Tarsus on the coast, Kilise Tepe displays a ceramic repertoire with connections reaching across inland Anatolia to the west (see Symington, pp. 297ff. below), and then again in the Late Bronze Age when it shares with Mersin, Tarsus and Kinet Höyük the standardized ceramics associated with the Hittite Empire.

This is all pertinent to the defining quality of Kilise Tepe, which is its position astride a major channel of communication, at various times connecting very different worlds. Throughout pre-Classical times, the material culture of the inland plateau was palpably different from those of the contemporary western seaboard, of the Cilician plain and East Mediterranean, and of Syria beyond the Amanus. In the Middle Bronze Age the world of central Anatolia was a discrete but thriving block, delimited by the Taurus from the literate and urban Near Eastern world, and recognizably distinct, even though at this date there is no collective designation known to us in the shape of a toponym like the later 'Land of Hatti'. Later in the Bronze Age one of the abiding enigmas of Anatolian and Greek archaeology has been the extent to which the kingdom centred at Hattusa, and the rulers — whether one or several — of the Mycenaean world, interacted with each other. Recent advances in our understanding of the historical geography of western Asia Minor have placed the interpretation of events recorded there in the Late Bronze Age on a better-focused basis, and suggest that there must have been some contact on a diplomatic and occasionally military plane; yet the extreme scarcity of Mycenaean artefacts in central Anatolian sites, and of recognizably central Anatolian products on the Aegean littoral or overseas, suggest that the two worlds remained at a distance from each other in commercial and cultural affairs. Sites like Kilise Tepe should be helpful in monitoring the nature of interaction between zones.

At the start of work there was an expectation that in the Late Bronze Age the site had been a relatively small provincial settlement within the confines of the Hittite empire. This seems to have been met in the shape of our Level III, but the immediately succeeding level raises a series of more complex questions which now constitute one of the chief interests of the site. In the closing decades of the Hittite Empire a large swathe of Anatolia to the southwest of the heartland round Hattusa was defined as the kingdom of Tarhuntassa and entrusted to a cadet branch of the royal family (see p. 16). Even though the precise borders between this new kingdom, 'Hatti proper' to the north, and former Kizzuwatna to the east remain undecided at present, the Göksu valley must either have been in or have bordered on it, and must have been affected by the political shifts. The most intriguing aspect of our work at the site has been the transition from classic 'Hittite' ceramics in Level III to something different in the early phases of Level II, accompanied by a break in the architectural tradition. At other small settlements which fell under direct Hittite administration (such as Gordion in the west and Tille and Norşun Tepe in the east), it is generally accepted that the disappearance of typical Hittite ceramics coincides more or less with the fall of Hattusa, conventionally dated to 1190 BC. At Kilise Tepe the picture is less clear: at present our best guess is that the shift from Level III to II took place some decades before the fall of Hattusa, and might thus have some connection with the establishment of the Tarhuntassa kingdom. On the other hand it is also possible that some form of Hittite rule survived here in the south later than at Hattusa (see p. 16). The position at Tarsus on the Cilician coast is far from clear in this respect, and it is to be hoped that renewed work at both Tarsus and Mersin will help to address these questions.

The end of the palace regimes around 1200 BC ushers in one of the most crucial transformations of the Old World. Explanations will continue to be sought for the roughly simultaneous collapse of palace regimes as far apart as Hattusa and Ugarit, and for the gradual establishment of a new order, which in Anatolia saw the emergence of new polities, with the petty kingdoms of Tabal in the centre flanked by Phrygia in the west and Urartu in the east. Interpreting the archaeological correlates of such political developments is hard, but crucially important, given that our written sources fall silent as the literate bureaucracies vanish. The association of an archaeologically attested destruction with a precise historical event is notoriously dangerous (as the examples of Tarsus and Gordion in the Iron Age have shown). Nevertheless, the Stele Building and the adjacent East Building were burnt down, and in general our settlement cannot have been immune from the regional collapse around the end of the thirteenth century. The evidence of our IId level indicates some continuity into the mid twelfth century, but thereafter the stratigraphic record becomes very scanty and hard to disentangle. This is not of course a coincidence. It is large solid buildings which provide easily recognizable archaeological strata, not successions of flimsy mudbrick structures, but in unstable conditions large-scale economic enterprises are not possible. There would be no accumulations of capital or large-scale labour force available to carry out major building projects. Hence not only in Anatolia, but also in (for instance) Mesopotamia it is very hard to identify stratigraphic layers which correspond to the eleventh, tenth and ninth centuries BC. Nevertheless, at Kilise Tepe these post-Hittite levels have yielded new ceramics and as at Boğazköy or Gordion in recent years, we begin to see indications of what life was like after the Late Bronze Age collapse.

These geographical and chronological interfaces of the second millennium BC were issues which we certainly hoped the excavation would be able to address, as well as recovering a cultural sequence for most of the third millennium from sounding the lower levels. We were less prepared for later material. The presence of occupation in the earlier first millennium (our Levels IIe–h) was not evident from the reported surface collections. If we had known the site by its correct name meaning 'Church Mound' (rather than Maltepe) before starting work we might not have been surprised to encounter a Byzantine basilica, but since the earlier surveys had concentrated on pre-Classical ceramics, we did not expect Hellenistic and later occupation levels across the entire mound.

The occupation of the site down into the eighth or seventh centuries BC brings us back once again into the margins of recorded history. Presumably the occupants belonged to the Luwian population groups which are still in the area in Classical and Roman times, but in the absence of any ceramics we can assign to the sixth or fifth centuries it appears that the site may later have been abandoned for a time. The Greek colonization so evident along the coastal fringe at (e.g.) Kelenderis and Soli may not have penetrated the valley. The remnants of more than one hoplite shield, the enigmatic ditch along the west side, and the first-millennium fortification wall along the east side all hint at the political unrest of these times when the coastal powers and the Taurus states were squeezed between the imperial advance of the Assyrians, Neo-Babylonians, and finally Achaemenids on one side and the inland kingdoms of Phrygia and Lydia on the other. One cannot help feeling that the local population may have viewed the advent of the Hellenistic age with some relief, and that a more stable political scene may have permitted the resumption of occupation at the site.

The consequence of the extensive later occupation has been to reduce the amount of horizontal exposure achieved, while increasing the chronological depth. We are now able to monitor the nature (and indeed the presence or absence) of the settlement over some three millennia. At each period it helps to shed light on the geographical relations between plain and sea, but at the same time there are strong elements of continuity in the material record. Not only the botanical and zoological data but also the evidence for the ceramic clay sources and the constant recurrence of weights from vertical looms, point to a local continuity of the subsistence economy independent of the wider political scene.

The publication

In the ten years and more since the start of this project archaeological recording and publication have been in constant flux, and many things would be done differently if we started now. Nevertheless, we heartily endorse the wish of the General Directorate that excavation projects should be published within five years of the completion of the fieldwork (even if we have not exactly succeeded in meeting that deadline), and we believe that publication in book form remains the best option at present. Our intention in this report is to fulfil a number of simple objectives:

- to provide a description of the process and results of excavation in sufficient detail for readers to assess the nature of the evidence and to form their own opinions as to the correctness of our conclusions;
- to describe and illustrate the ceramic repertoires of the different periods represented at the site, indicating relations to other sites;
- to describe and illustrate all significant artefacts, especially those found in context;
- to present studies of environmental materials, over and above the detailed statistical work already placed in the public domain as part of the Leverhulme project (Matthews & Postgate 2001).
- to offer our own general conclusions about the nature of the occupation at the site at different periods and to position it in its historical and cultural context.

In this way, the volume is intended to meet our obligation to publish. While there is still work in progress on the animal bones, and more detailed study on some of the ceramics would certainly be profitable, this is designed as a comprehensive report on all five seasons' work. In that sense it is 'final', but like all excavation, our work has raised at least as many questions as it has resolved, and the accounts offered here are no more than starting points for further research, whether in the field or in the museum. Tension between the pressure to put our results promptly into the public domain, and providing exhaustive studies of artefact types has usually been resolved in favour of swift publication. We have tried to provide geographically and chronologically relevant comparanda for individual finds, but in terms of both quantity and quality the artefacts recovered often fail to give a coherent body of evidence which would justify a fresh general study of the different categories. With the publication of this report we consider the materials from the site now to be released for study by any interested colleagues without reference to ourselves. To this end, we have prepared the finds data base for deposit with the Archaeology Data Service hosted by the University of York (http://ads.ahds.ac.uk), along with other files from the excavation archive, including the storage lists for the material in the Silifke Museum. We have also deposited low-resolution versions of the scanned photographs, plans and plates of illustrations, and the data bases with a Cambridge University digital archive called DSpace (https://www.dspace.cam.ac.uk). This should enable others to establish the existence, and identify the storage location, of all items we recorded (whether or not included in this volume), and to know where in the museum to find the pottery or bone assemblages from a given unit. We hope that the combination of the published report and the archived electronic files will in future make it possible for colleagues to see our entire finds repertoire and at the same time to know the details of each item's provenance. Of course nothing can entirely replace the original field notebooks when establishing the provenance of an object, but in the List of Excavation Units (Appendix 2) we have tried to give a helpful codified summary of the nature of each context.

We have dithered long and hard over the organization of the material within the publication. Our initial intention was to put the Hellenistic and Byzantine periods in a separate volume of their own, but as time proceeded it became clear that this would not work for more than one reason: in many cases we cannot be certain of the date of less well-stratified finds from Level I; much of what we needed to say about the site in general was applicable to both the early and the later periods; the description of the excavated features of Level I cannot be separated from the Level II remains immediately below; and some material would have had to be duplicated to make the 'later' volume usable independently. Consequently this report covers all periods at the site, and we have used the two volume format to allow the user to have the illustrative matter open at the same time as the text.

Our desire to present a complete view of the site and its contents has probably led us to include some bodies of data which may be thought excessively detailed. The process of excavation not only destroys the physical remains, but also divorces items found from their resting place, and this separation is often reflected in the separate publication of both site and finds. Our aim has been to correct this as far as possible. After each section of the excavation narrative (Part C) the units used are listed, together with any artefacts from them which are included in the publication. A complete list of excavation units is given in the appendix. Many of these receive no other mention in the volume, but even they are relevant because of their relationship to other units which do feature, and the single unit list removes the need for repeated explanation. For a full record of what was recovered from each unit the reader would need to consult the electronic archive.

For the user of the volume there is a note on the numbers used in the volume (p. xxiii), for which some explanation is needed here. A block of 100 unit numbers for identifying each differentiated archaeological context was allocated to each 10-m grid square (see p. 67). Any potsherds from a context were assigned this number, as were all other finds, whether artefacts or samples, in addition to a number of their own. For the details of the numbering see p. 237 (for potsherds) and p. 440 (for the finds). This 'object number' is the unique identification for all our objects, and is mentioned in every catalogue entry, and used for objects marked on plans, although for ease of reference a separate series of consecutive numbers (in bold font) has been assigned to all objects in this volume.

Chapter 2

The Site of Kilise Tepe[2]

Nicholas Postgate

The mound and its surroundings

The Göksu valley, which furnishes one of the two main routes from Turkey's southern shore through the Taurus to the Konya plain and the rest of the central plateau, must be deemed one of the country's national treasures (Frontispiece; Figs. 8 & 472). The clear turquoise ribbon of the Göksu threads its way southeastwards from high in the mountains west of Ermenek to reach the Mediterranean at Silifke, or rather at the mouth of the delta the river has created to the south of the Classical and modern town. The valley itself, however, is by no means uniform, nor is the road which follows it. Coming from the interior, the traveller leaves the Konya plain not far south of Karaman, and after a gentle climb to the pass at Sertavul, begins to descend thickly pine-grown slopes high on the eastern shoulders of the valley, with the Göksu itself glimpsed occasionally flowing far below. Dropping steeply down, leaving the monastery of Alahan high above to the left, one passes into a very different landscape around the regional centre of Mut, Roman Claudiopolis (earlier Ninica: see Mitchell 1979). Here the Göksu is joined from the west by the Ermenek Su, and the narrow valleys of their upper courses give way to a wide low-lying basin, where the stream has cut through one terrace after another, to yield a curiously barren landscape. Remaining patches of the geological terraces, harbouring olive groves and cereal crops in early summer, stand isolated from one another by high eroded scarps, whose steep bare yellow and white limestone slopes are studded only sparsely with pines and low evergreen bushes like prickly oak. The river has trenched so deep that most of the terrain lies below the 1000-ft (= 325-m) contour, and the Göksu itself near Kilise Tepe is at less than 100 m above sea level. Consequently it is not surprising that on the climatic map of Turkey the Mut basin shares with Adana and Mersin in the Çukurova the privilege of being in the country's highest temperature zone in July and August (*Yeni Türkiye Atlası*, Ankara 1977). Similarly, the annual rainfall here is low, less than 500 mm, and in July, August and September it receives on average less than 5 mm of rain per month.

The modern road from Konya to the sea follows the course of the river past Kilise Tepe and then skirts along the left bank of the steep gorge, as far as Değirmendere, where it flattens out to cross to the other bank on the bridge just above the proposed site of the Kayraktepe dam. Then it climbs the pine-clad slopes past the monument to Frederik Barbarossa, who drowned in the river, before dropping down past the castle to the modern town of Silifke, the Hellenistic port of Seleucia. Like other modern commentators we have tended to assume that this has always been a major route linking the Konya plain to the sea, and there is evidence of pre-Classical presence in the rock relief at Keben at the SE end of the gorge, which seems Hittite although its precise date remains undetermined.

A milestone reported from further up the gorge, about 3 km NE of the modern road near Yenisu (Sayar 1992, 57), indicates that the route was used in the first century AD, but in Roman times the major roads to the interior from the sea seem to have passed either side of the Göksu. One branched left off the valley above Mut to lead across the plateau and down to the sea at Corycus (Kızkalesi), via the regional capital of Olba/Diocaesareia (see map in Mitford 1980, 1260). The other went southwestwards from Mut, perhaps following the modern road which crosses the Göksu near Kilise Tepe and then climbing the side of the valley to reach the plateau at Gülnar (Ottoman Aine Pazar) before dropping steeply down past the fortress of Meydancıkkale to the coast at Aydıncık (ancient Kelenderis). This route would pass through Zeyne, near which stands the Byzantine church of Ala Kilise, and from there an alternative would have been to drop down to Silifke through pine woods via Gökbelen, a route followed in reverse by Heberdey and partly at least identical with the Roman road marked by Mitford (1980, 1260) after Calder & Bean 1958 as passing through Pracana. It seems fair to suggest that the choice of route to the coast will have depended in part on the traveller's precise destination, and in part on the political conditions at the time.

Chapter 2

Figure 5. *Kite photograph of Kilise Tepe (plane tree and spring, top right: courtesy of Dr Jan Driessen.)*

The natural setting

Kilise Tepe (36°30' N; 33°33' E) occupies the largest of a row of flat-topped conglomerate-capped bluffs which look westwards over the Kurtsuyu and Göksu valleys, approximately 50 m above the present river level (Fig. 8). Unfortunately the 50-m-contour interval on our map is not sufficiently sensitive to reproduce the outline of these bluffs, but they run along a roughly north–south line for about 1.5 km from the modern village of Kışla, which overlooks a bend in the river,

to the modern asphalt road in the north. The bluffs vary somewhat in character. The promontory on which our site sits measures nearly 200 m north–south at the level of the conglomerate surface, and on its western side is some 16 m higher than the gently sloping land below it (cf. Fig. 5). To the north of the site is a 20-m-high promontory which has a distinct conglomerate layer on top (see Fig. 6), and frequent fallen boulders littering its sides; yet its eastern part has an accumulation of 1 m of soil on its top and is therefore cultivable. Before it was occupied Kilise Tepe itself must have been very similar to this. To the south, between Kilise Tepe itself and the village, are several much less imposing outcrops on which the conglomerate cap is very indistinct, but which are nonetheless uncultivated because the conglomerate is too close to the surface.

The land around the site is given over entirely to agriculture (wheat, olives, vines, fruit trees and poplars). Ploughing continues right up to the foot of the bluffs (see Fig. 9) and begins again at a higher level from their top edge. In places between the bluffs and the rivers are patches of land which can be irrigated, either via channels along the left bank of the Kurtsuyu or using mechanical pumps from the Göksu, sometimes supplemented by flow from springs which surface at the base of the bluffs. On the upper level, vines, olives, and cereal crops are grown where there is the necessary soil cover on the gently sloping ground forming the sides of the basin to the east.

There must have been a combination of reasons favouring the choice of the Kilise Tepe bluff for a settlement. Its position in a cultivable zone taken with the steeply sloping sides provided subsistence and security, but the decisive factor may well have been the perennial spring at the northern foot of the mound. On a wider plane the choice of the site must have been influenced by its position at the intersection of routes. Before the construction of the bridge the old road to Zeyne crossed the Göksu by a ferry at the bend of the river just west of the modern village of Kışla. This will have served traffic for Zeyne, Gülnar and beyond, coming both from downstream (via the old road through Gedik) and from Mut along the left bank of the Göksu. That the road through Zeyne was important earlier too is shown by the remains of a major stone bridge across the river some 1 km upstream from the old ferry, just above the confluence of the Gelembiç Çay (Fig. 7). It seems likely that this was a Byzantine construction and its location so close to Kilise Tepe cannot be coincidental.

If the river crossing is partially responsible for the siting of Kilise Tepe, the same must apply to the smaller mound of Çingentepe which stands close to the modern road as it begins to climb towards Şarlak and Zeyne through the cultivated slopes on the opposite bank of the river. This is a small mound by any standards, though not much smaller than Kilise Tepe itself, and surface sherds indicate that it was occupied from the Bronze Age into the Iron Age (French 1965, 180). Today there are no permanent houses in the immediate area and the surrounding fields, which are irrigated from Pınarbaşı, are mostly cultivated by residents of Şarlak and Zeyne, who may decamp to sleep near their fields for part of the summer. Çingentepe does not give the impression of a fortified settlement, and it presumably owes its continued occupation to the combination of the river crossing and the favourable agricultural environment. A small investigation of the site would certainly be of significance for our understanding of Kilise Tepe. It is possible to imagine that at times this was a local village, by contrast with the administrative and military centre across the river at Kilise Tepe, and it would be interesting to see if the architecture and artefactual repertoire reflected this.

Figure 6. *Promontory to north of the tepe, showing decayed conglomerate surface.*

Figure 7. *Göksu river and the remnants of the bridge, looking upstream from Kışla.*

The geographical context

One of the most striking impressions to an archaeologist moving to Cilicia from southern Mesopotamia is the different density of excavated sites, although of course there is an even greater contrast with Cyprus, just across the water. The only two pre-Classical sites within 150 km of Kilise Tepe are Mersin and Tarsus, and since relatively little material of Iron or Late Bronze Age date was excavated at Mersin, the majority of our comparative material inevitably comes from Tarsus, supplemented by survey information on other Cilician sites.

In the following survey of how Kilise Tepe slots into the existing picture for different periods this paucity of evidence will recur time and again to prevent us from reaching any solid conclusions, and many

Figure 8. *Kilise Tepe and the Göksu valley from the east.*

Figure 9. *North end of Kilise Tepe before excavation, with tree and spring to the left.*

questions will require more work in the field for their resolution, but there is another aspect which perhaps deserves comment, and that is the question of scale. Succinctly, the natural landscape of some parts of Anatolia does not now, and probably never has, supported a density of occupation comparable to that of Cyprus or Sumer. Down on the Çukurova, where Gjerstad and Seton-Williams surveyed, the alluvial fan of the Ceyhan shows a fair number of sites reported from different periods. The striking feature of the Mellaart and French surveys of the Göksu valley is how few pre-Classical sites were found. No one has attempted a similar survey for the huge tracts of territory to east and west of the river between the coastal strip and the central plateau. Nevertheless, it seems likely that, if it were attempted, there too very few significant höyüks would be identified, since Classical and Byzantine remains have been reported quite widely in these areas. The question which arises is whether we are looking at a genuine sparsity of early settlement, or a failure of the evidence. Settlement is certainly relatively sparse today — only 15–22 persons per km^2 in the rural areas of the Taşeli plateau between the Göksu and the sea according to figures cited by Bazin (1991, 247) — but before opting for this comparison, the nature of the evidence needs to be considered.

There are two parallel sources of bias. One concerns the formation of the sites themselves, the other the process of detection. In a flat terrain, whether the Çukurova or the Konya plain, even quite small ancient sites betray their presence by breaking the natural surface and we can expect modern observers to be relatively efficient in locating them, whether from the ground or with remote sensing. Conversely, in a naturally hilly landscape man-made hills are much more difficult to spot. Before this, though, there may be underlying differences which need to be taken into account. In the first place, builders far from sources of stone in the middle of an alluvial plain will prefer mud brick, and one effect of this will be the relatively rapid formation of mounds. In areas where stones are regularly used (even if only for foundations) the temptation to re-use them when re-building will tend to reduce the rate of accumulation (but this can only be taken as a very general prediction, and as we shall see in the case of Kilise Tepe there may well be other factors at work). Moreover, one of the reasons why mounds grow is that even when abandoned they provide obvious advantages as the location for settlements, both in terms of security and also because they are unsuitable for agriculture. Off the alluvium there are often no such factors favouring one site over another, since there may be plentiful slopes and defensible locations, and even on flat ground there may well be insufficient depth of soil for agriculture. Hence the pressure to re-use an earlier inhabited space is less and we could expect much less continuity in the localization of settlements. Moreover, where the terrain slopes, the effects of erosion from rain wash are greatly increased and we might expect any abandoned settlement rapidly to lose the soil matrix which forms the substance of höyüks, and be left with the bare bones of stone buildings, often no more than the foundations.

Finally, the presence of modern settlements introduces an unknown quantity into the evidence of archaeological surveys. Occupied villages are difficult to study, given both the practical obstacles of the standing architecture and the social constraints on ferreting around in other people's houses and yards.

Figure 10. *Plane tree and spring at north end of tepe, conglomerate outcropping on the left.*

For all these reasons it is extremely difficult to be sure whether in pre-Classical times we are really looking at very sparse settlement, or only at very poor visibility. Some of the uncertainties might be resolved by intensive survey, but the historical and contemporary evidence for widespread transhumance in the region indicates that much of the population may indeed be archaeologically invisible — see the excellent survey of Yakar 2000, 350–58; Cribb 1991, 111–32; and further below, p. 18. Because the Kilise Tepe project was established as a rescue excavation we did not undertake survey in the region, but this needs doing in future. The use of remote-sensing images might enable identification of other settlement sites, and in some areas, such as the immediate surrounds of Kilise Tepe, intensive field walking is indicated to see if we should expect scatters of sherds away from visible sites. Modern villages also need to be visited to investigate whether any of them show signs of earlier occupation.

Chapter 3

The Kilise Tepe Area in Pre-Classical and Hellenistic Times

Nicholas Postgate

The Bronze Age

While the detailed pattern of settlement round Kilise Tepe is very imperfect, it may be helpful to review briefly the archaeological activity in the wider region to provide what context there is for the Kilise Tepe assemblages and link it to the historical scene in the Konya plain and Cilicia. During the Early Bronze Age, broadly the third millennium BC, to the north the major city at Karahöyük (Konya) has been excavated by Professor Sedat Alp since the 1960s. One of the principal members of the Anatolian city-state network revealed to us by the Middle Bronze Age archives from Kültepe (Kanesh), it is clear that like Kanesh itself the city was already important in the third millennium. At the other corner of the central plain stands Acemhöyük, another major city with a similar history. In the Middle Bronze Age these two vast sites must have been cities with a *karum* and mentioned in the Assyrian texts. Here is not the place to give opinions as to their identification.[3] The point we need to note is that alongside the major cities the business archives mention smaller towns at which the Assyrians maintained an agency (*wabartum*), and of these we have no excavated examples in the south part of the plain. They seem likely to have existed, but the survey of the Konya region being carried out by D. Baird supports Mellaart's perception of a 'collapse and radical transformation of settlement following the mid-third millennium BC, and the persistence of this situation throughout the second millennium' (Baird 2003). In particular, one would expect a centre of some kind in the Karaman area, south of Karadağ, which is not included in the Baird survey (e.g. perhaps the large Late Bronze Age site near Karaman observed by D.H. French: Hawkins 1995, 56 n. 201), and if we are thinking about the role of Kilise Tepe it is obvious that until we know the configuration of settlement at this point, where the Göksu traffic would arrive on the plateau, we are lacking an important piece of the jigsaw.

In the Late Bronze Age the lack of evidence from the plateau is even more striking, since neither Karahöyük nor Acemhöyük seems to have remained an important centre in the later part of the second millennium. As far as archaeological excavation is concerned the Konya plain is a virtual vacuum during the time of the Hittite empire. When we look inland for contemporary material at this date we usually have to go as far as Boğazköy itself. The historical sources indicate that this cannot entirely correspond to reality. Konya itself may have taken over as the regional centre from Karahöyük, being mentioned in the Bronze Tablet as Ikkuwaniya (III.48); while Wašhaniya, a *karum* in the Middle Bronze Age (I.83), and Parsuhanda (Muwatalli Prayer) still exist.[4]

It is not unduly surprising therefore that for ceramics and other materials to compare with our Kilise Tepe finds we usually have to look in the opposite direction, to Tarsus. No doubt Mersin, some 30 km closer to us, would have been culturally closer as well, but here excavated remains of the Late Bronze Age were largely confined to the fortifications and did not yield stratified sequences or a rich variety of artefacts, and recent work at the site has principally been concerned with earlier or later levels (see most recently Jean 2003, 83–4). Kazanlı, tested by Garstang while working at Mersin, would also have been very relevant but little was found or published from there.

In political terms these sites on the coastal plain probably all belonged in the later second millennium to the territory of Kizzuwatna, a kingdom in its own right in the sixteenth/fifteenth century under Išputahšu (whose sealing was found at Tarsus), but now thought by some to have been annexed to Hatti before the reign of Suppiluliuma I.[5] In the treaty between Sunassura of Kizzuwatna and a Hittite king, the frontier at the seaboard falls east of Lamiya. This name has long been identified with the Classical river Lamos, some 40 km to the west of modern Mersin,[6] which is stated by Strabo to mark the boundary between Cilicia Pedias and Tracheia. No reason has yet been found to disprove the connection, which would imply that at this time the Calycadnus fell within directly administered Hittite territory.[7]

A change came in the reign of Muwatalli II, who moved south from Hattusa to a new capital called Tarhuntassa. Subsequently the capital was moved back by Urhi-Tešub, but then soon after his accession Hattusili III created a separate kingdom of Tarhuntassa and entrusted it to his nephew Kurunta, a son of Muwatalli. The relationship between the Great King and the Tarhuntassa royal house was regulated, like that with Carchemish, by a formal treaty which specified the mutual boundaries, and the original treaty of Hattusili with Kurunta (under the name Ulmi-Tešub) was revised by his son Tudhaliya IV. The text of this treaty (Otten 1988) was inscribed on a bronze tablet, and gives valuable, though not always easy, information on the geography.[8]

The details of the borders of the Land of Tarhuntassa show that it stretched as far west as Perge (Parha) on the south coast, and it is clear that the mutual frontier with the lands of the Great King fell in the Konya plain. Here the relief of Kurunta discovered in 1994 above a spring at Hatıp, 17 km to the SW of Konya, brings Tarhuntassa territory at least this far north,[9] while further east Emirgazi with its Tudhaliya IV inscriptions[10] presumably fell on the Hattusa side of the frontier.

There remain areas of uncertainty. The Bronze Tablet refers to both the 'Hulaya River land' and the 'Land of Tarhuntassa' and it is far from clear how they relate to each other. All the same, section 8 of the treaty indicates that Tarhuntassa territory (here described as Hulaya River land) reached as far as the sea, and without rehearsing all the arguments, it is hard to suppose that it did not include the Göksu valley. Along with others, I tend to assume that the Hittite port of Ura was at or near Silifke, and must therefore have fallen within Tarhuntassa's boundaries.[11] If so, not far to its east the old distinction between Hittite territory and Kizzuwatna was carried forward to provide the eastern frontier of Tarhuntassa. Although there remain areas of uncertainty about the geography, it still seems likely, and significant for our understanding of the role of Kilise Tepe, that the Calycadnus valley was under a different political administration from the Cilician plain.[12]

The Iron Age

After the fall of Hattusa, conventionally dated to 1190 BC, post-imperial successor dynasties retained some power on the southern and eastern flanks of former Hittite territory. This is clearly the case at Malatya and Carchemish. It is possible that the inscriptions of Hartapu on Karadağ, on the plain below at Kızıldağ, and further east at Burunkaya near Aksaray, represent the continuation of the Tarhuntassa dynasty and were erected in the twelfth century, but their use of the title Great King could have been contemporary with the last Hattusa rulers.[13] Unfortunately, with the cessation of the Hattusa archives and the fragmentation of the political scene, that is virtually the only snippet of historical information relating to our part of Anatolia for more than three centuries. True, the evidence of the seventh-century Karatepe inscriptions may justify considering Greek legends about a ruler of Cilicia called Mopsus to have a historical kernel,[14] but even if we take his reported activities at face value we would not know which century to assign them to.

Wherever it was, the city of Tarhuntassa itself must eventually have fallen victim to the general disruption of the twelfth century, and plays no role in the historical geography of our region in the Iron Age. Both the archaeological and the historical evidence for Cilicia at this time remain very scrappy.[15] Most of the historical detail comes from Assyrian and Babylonian royal inscriptions and is therefore superficial and one-sided, while the texts left us by indigenous rulers do not help much with the geographical scene. Plain Cilicia has a new name, Quwe,[16] and in the ninth century it belonged to the Aramaean/Neo-Hittite amalgam which succeeded to the Hittite empire in NW Syria. To the north it bordered on the petty states of Tabal, and like them found itself squeezed between Assyria, Urartu in the east, and the rising power of Phrygia to the NW. It fell under Assyrian control, or at least influence, already in the ninth century. In the later eighth century under Tiglath-pileser and Sargon Quwe was incorporated into the Assyrian provincial system, and it was still within Assyrian territory at the very end of the seventh century.[17]

However, Assyria's hold on Cilicia was by no means secure. While cities on the plain were still occupied, as attested archaeologically at Tarsus, Kinet Höyük, and Sirkeli near to Adana (Hrouda 1998), the Assyrians found that power tended to be in the hands of local rulers with their capitals at previously unknown places in the mountains ringing the alluvial plain. This pattern repeats itself from Shalmaneser on (see for instance the table in Desideri & Jasink 1990, 132). Around 710 BC the governor in Quwe (which city was adopted as the provincial capital is not known) was in correspondence with Midas of Phrygia, but Assyrian control of the area was no doubt badly shaken by Sargon's death in battle in the Taurus region five years later. In attempting to restore control Sennacherib was opposed by a former vassal called Kirua described as the 'city ruler' of Illubru, who had made the populace of Hilakku rebel, and was able to involve cities of the plain, Tarsus and Ingira, in the revolt.[18] The location of Illubru itself is unknown,[19] but since it belonged in Hilakku, and his defeat is described as taking place in mountainous terrain, it seems probable that this was another hill-top dynast. Similarly Esarhaddon was obliged to campaign in mountains against Sanduarri, the local ruler of Kundi and Sissu (Borger 1956, 49–50; Grayson 1975, 83). It is possible that he is identical with Azatiwatas, the author of the Karatepe inscriptions (see Hawkins 2000, I/1, 44–5), who was based in the mountains to the NE of the plain but claimed domination of Adana and its region.

This was the situation in Quwe, Plain Cilicia (Pedias). Kilise Tepe must have fallen within Hilakku, broadly equivalent to Rough Cilicia (Tracheia), which was briefly under Assyrian control in the reign of Sargon, around 710 BC (Hawkins 1972–75). What applied to Quwe did not necessarily hold good for Hilakku, but the terrain ensured that here too most rulers were back in the hills, although examples are few. Kirua of Illubru (see above) may have come from west of Tarsus, and in the sixth century the Babylonian king Neriglissar marched on mountainous paths to attack Appuašu of Pirindu in his strongholds. One of these was named Kirši, and has been identified as Meydancıkkale near Gülnar, 32 km from the coast at Aydıncık, on the evidence of an Aramaic inscription found at the site.[20] Once again the instability of the politics of the region is reflected in a new set of names: the land of Pirindu must coincide at least partially with Assyrian Hilakku, and the two cities of Appuašu mentioned by the chronicle, Ura' and Kirši are also new.[21] In any case the fortress of Meydancık seems to have been a new foundation in the Iron Age, as the excavations at the site have not yielded any evidence for occupation as early as the seventh century, or any ceramics comparable to our Level II material (Davesne & Laroche-Traunecker 1998, 64).

Turning from the strictly political to more general considerations, the pattern of coastal settlements oriented to the sea, some possibly colonies from other parts of the Mediterranean, co-existing with inland polities prudently centred on hill-top fastnesses, foreshadows conditions in Classical times (see Jackson, p. 19), when Cilicia was famous as the home of pirates. Just to the east of the Göksu valley was a tenacious local dynasty and priesthood centred on the temple at Olba — Diocaesaria, modern Uzuncaburç, which must have been important already before the time of Alexander (see e.g. Houwink ten Cate 1961, 32ff.). Further west in Hellenistic times the cities of Hamaxia and Laertes were 'both set back from the coast on ridges of the Taurus' (Hopwood 1991, 305). According to this pattern Meydancıkkale, 32 km back from the coast at Kelenderis, could perhaps be seen as the hilltop redoubt for the rulers controlling the port, but Kilise Tepe, although only 40 km from Silifke as the crow flies, nestles behind the most precipitous section of the Göksu gorge and its *raison d'être* must have had more to do with the Mut basin and its rich agricultural potential.

Nevertheless, the evidence of our ceramics suggests close links with the south, rather than the inland plateau: at Kilise Tepe we have seen no Phrygian or central Anatolian material or even influence (cf. Yakar 2000, 374). Culturally both the ports and cities of the Cilician plain and the hilltop towns belonged in an East Mediterranean environment. No doubt much of the population was of Luwian descent,[22] but alongside the hieroglyphs of Karatepe and Çineköy we find inscriptions in Phoenician (cf. Desideri & Jasink 1990, 142–4), and later the rulers of Meydancıkkale, like much of the rest of the Near East under the Achaemenids, used Aramaic. Not only at Tarsus but in the hills at Karatepe the Iron Age ceramics show strong links with Cyprus in the eighth–seventh centuries. While this was not necessarily a case of Cypriot artefacts being imported (see Knappett, p. 261 for evidence for local production), there can be no doubt that our region was an active partner in the cultural amalgam.

The Cyprus connection is not the only Greek dimension. The legend of Mopsus in Classical sources is reflected in the Karatepe and Çineköy inscriptions,[23] and Greek historians recorded that Greeks were involved in the revolt against Sennacherib in 696 BC. A Greek presence at Kilise Tepe is suggested by the fragments of hoplite shield (**2272–4**) recovered from two different parts of the site, but this may of course have been a temporary situation or even a single day. With the exception of a handful of sherds from the ditch in I14, we recovered no pre-Hellenistic Greek pottery at Kilise Tepe (see Chapter 27). On present evidence, we have no reason to think that the site was occupied at all between the seventh century and the Hellenistic period, in other words during the Neo-Babylonian and Achaemenid empires. This contrasts sharply with coastal cities of Tarsus, Mersin (Yumuktepe) and Kelenderis (Aydıncık), for instance, and it seems likely that the Greek population was less concerned with the interior than the interior was with the coast.[24]

The Hellenistic era

In Hellenistic times Cilicia was initially ruled by the Seleucids, but later was governed from Egypt by the Ptolemaic dynasty (see Elton 2004, 233–4; Van Neer & Waelkens, Chapter 51). There seems to be nothing among our Hellenistic ceramics which need be earlier than the foundation of Seleucia at the mouth of the Göksu in the early third century. Under the Ptolemies we know that as usual the South Anatolian coastal towns were actively engaged in Mediterranean trade. In the third century BC Alexandrian merchants imported wine and honey from Coracesium (modern Alanya) just along the coast in Pamphylia,[25] and grew 'Cilician' vines (Orrieux 1985 citing Pap. Cairo Zenon 59033: Edgar 1925, 54–5). Cilicia was no doubt already a source of timber for the Egyptian economy (and the Ptolemaic navy), as it was later (cf. Hopwood 1991, 307). For more on connections with Egypt see Van Neer & Waelkens (Chapter 51); our evidence for import of Nilotic fish may suggest one of the commodities for which these Anatolian products were exchanged.

Elton has commented that in our region 'the extent of Hellenization ... was not as developed as in Lycia, Pisidia or Pamphylia' (2004, 236). The modern village next to the site is called Kışla, which means winter-quarters, and across the river we have Çingentepe ('gypsy mound'); these may serve as a reminder that transhumance is a normal and long-standing lifestyle in this region (see for instance Yakar 2000, 355; Bazin 1991). To this day there are transhumant groups in this part of the country, such as the Sarıkeçili, who move between the coast near Aydıncık and the region of Ermenek, passing Meydancıkkale en route, and others who move between the coastal strip east of Silifke to yaylas high up in the Göksu catchment area.[26] Some of the elaborate cemeteries near the coast in Roman times may have belonged to tribal transhumants whose actual residences are never likely to surface in the archaeological record, but who were just as indigenous to Rough Cilicia as the more settled population (Hopwood 1991).

Chapter 4

The Kilise Tepe Area in the Byzantine Era[27]

Mark Jackson

The ancient settlement at Kilise Tepe was located roughly halfway between Seleuceia and Claudiopolis, the two most important cities in the Late Roman province of Isauria (Ammianus Marcellinus 14.8.1–2; see Fig. 472). Isauria occupied the central Taurus mountain region of southern Asia Minor to the east of Pamphylia, and the west of Cilicia and was bounded to the north by Lycaonia on the central Anatolian plateau. It is no coincidence that Seleuceia and Claudiopolis lay in the Calycadnus (Göksu) river valley which runs through the heart of this mountainous province. The region is fertile, well-watered, and its population would have had access to a variety of natural resources available across the landscape. In addition, the Göksu valley represents a major route through the Taurus Mountains facilitating communication between central Anatolia and the Mediterranean (Fig. 472).

The location of a number of mounds such as Kilise Tepe on the terraces and lower slopes of the valley, testifies to the intensive settlement and exploitation of the valley's hydrology, natural resources and communication routes by communities in the past (Mellaart 1958a,b; French 1965; Postgate 1995, 139–42). Yet the ruins of some of the finest monuments known from the region lie high on the upper slopes of the Göksu valley at Alahan, Mahras Dağ, Alakilise, and Meryemlik. These buildings belong to Isauria's important ecclesiastical heritage and form a significant part of the published Byzantine archaeological record from the province.

In an attempt to summarize some of the remains of the valley and to give a broader context for the site at Kilise Tepe, this chapter aims to provide a summary interpretation of the Byzantine research into the region.[28] It will be argued that the spatial relationship between the rural settlements such as Kilise Tepe located near the valley floor and the remains of the monumental ecclesiastical sites on the mountains above, offers great potential for understanding the past dynamics of Early Byzantine everyday life in the valley.

The Isaurians

Certain historical sources have been used to suggest that the people of Isauria, located in the fourth century near the geographical heart of the Late Roman world, represented a serious internal threat to the security of the Empire (Edwards 1999, 515; Elton 1996, 63; Shaw 1999, 155). Indeed the Isaurians were responsible for numerous uprisings in the third, fourth and fifth centuries (J. Matthews 1989; Lenski 1999). Isauria was also involved in the civil wars in the late fifth century at the time of the Emperor Zeno (Elton 2000a). The nature of Isaurian ethnicity is also discussed by Elton (2000b). These sources however represent the perspective of the government and the inhabitants of the urban centres. Matthews has argued that many of the uprisings suggest a reaction against harsh treatment by government authorities and a response to periodic economic hardship:

> ... they were not random, meaningless events or gratuitous outbursts of aggression against the Greco-Roman cities and their territories, but expressions of some more profound economic adversity, producing a response of a more general character (J. Matthews 1989, 367).

It would appear, however, that attacks were made from the highlands and that the lowland Isaurians were periodically in need of protection from their neighbours (J. Matthews 1989, 357; Lenski 1999). Other documentary sources support the interpretation that the traditional label of the Isaurians as 'bandits' did not hold true for all inhabitants of the province. Of note is the significant role played by the Isaurian bishops in the theological disputes of the early Christian church (Frend 1972; Hild & Hellenkemper 1990, 86–91), the celebration of the skill of Isaurians as architects and builders (Mango 1966) and the general fertility of the Isaurian valleys (Ammianus Marcellinus 14.8.1). Perhaps the best evidence for further understanding of the nature of life in Isauria will come ultimately from the archaeological remains.

Chapter 4

Sites in the Göksu region

The archaeological record of Isauria has attracted attention from academics for over a century in a rather sporadic and *ad hoc* manner. Yet their work, especially in the Göksu valley, does provide a very important foundation for future research on the Byzantine archaeology of the region.

Early publications from the Göksu tend to represent traditional architectural studies of individual buildings, sculptures and epigraphy encountered on tours through the area. They also provide important information on the topography, settlements and antiquities now often very different or destroyed (Davis 1879; Heberdey & Wilhelm 1896; Headlam 1892; Guyer 1909/10; Sterrett 1884–85; Wilson 1895, 180–82; Sykes 1915, 534–6).

In particular, Leake provided an important description of the remains of a colonnaded street at Mut in the early nineteenth century (1824, 108, cited in Mitchell 1979, 428), and Headlam finally provided convincing evidence for Mut as the site of Claudiopolis (1892, 22–3, no. 1).

The ancient settlement at Sinobuç, 6 km north of Mut, is located on a pointed hill, flanked by vertical cliffs except on the east side, where a defensive wall separated the hill from lower ground whose plough soil is littered with pottery sherds (Ramsay 1890, 495; Headlam 1892, 26–33; Heberdey & Wilhelm 1896, 120; French 1984; Bean & Mitford 1970, 224–9). The ornately decorated tombs on the slope below the wall were dated by Gough from first–fourth centuries (Gough 1958, 6). There are also unpublished rock-cut tombs in the cliff to the north.

The ancient city of Adrassus may be located 29 km west of Mut at the site known as Balabolu (Alföldi Rosenbaum 1980, 13; Heberdey & Wilhelm 1896, no. 212). Balabolu is best known for its large necropolis that consists of over 100 sarcophagi, on a spur of a plateau above the Değirmendere gorge. In contrast to Sinobuç from where there is arguably no evidence for Christian settlement (Mitford 1980, 1246, but note Headlam 1892, 27–9), the site at Balabolu has a church and many of the sarcophagi can be identified to date from Hellenistic through to the sixth century (Alföldi Rosenbaum 1980, 27).

The settlement of Sibyla was identified incorrectly at Dağ Pazarı by Wilson (1895, 181) and has now been located 11 km NNE of Mut near Mavga Kalesi (Hild & Hellenkemper 1990, 410).

Pottery littered on the site at Aşağıköselerli near Zeyne on the lower terraces of the Göksu can be dated to the Hellenistic and Roman periods. Brief visits to the nearby sites of Maltepe and Çingentepe suggested mostly sherds earlier than Hellenistic in date.

A number of sites have been located at strategic communication points in the mountains and on the hilltops to the south of the lower Göksu valley. Remains of Byzantine hilltop settlement have been excavated at Meydancıkkale (Davesne & Laroche-Traunecker 1998); the well-preserved remains of a Hellenistic heroon, and rock-cut tombs survive at Kise; Çığ Tepe is a hilltop site littered with much Hellenistic pottery and undressed stones from walls and buildings. At Nuruköy, on the top of a plateau overlooking the Göksu valley, Byzantine activity is confirmed by remains that include sarcophagi bearing carved crosses and alpha and omega designs and the remains of a large building, that may have been a church (Hild & Hellenkemper 1990, 368; Heberdey & Wilhelm 1896, 118).

The first attempt at a systematic approach to the Göksu region was the identification of a number of prehistoric sites by French (1965), but no detailed multi-period archaeological survey of the valley had been attempted subsequently until Elton's fieldwork (2002b).

The source of much of the modern research on the Byzantine archaeology of the Göksu was the late Michael Gough who carried out important excavations and surveys during the 1950s and 1960s. Unfortunately the results of much of this work, complemented by years of local knowledge were never published in final form because of his premature death. The relative lack of fieldwork inland since Gough means there is much to be said about specific Byzantine sites where he carried out research, notably at Alahan, but also at Aloda (Gough 1955; 1957), Dağ Pazarı (Gough 1958; 1959a,b; 1960; Hill 1979; 1998) and Mahras Dağ (Gough 1974; Harrison 1980). Elsewhere in Isauria, excavation at the Late Roman town of Anemurium, on the southernmost tip of Asia Minor, was carried out by James Russell during the 1970s and has resulted in the publication of a ceramic sequence by Caroline Williams which has been invaluable for subsequent research in the region including surveys along the coast (Russell 1980; Williams 1989; Blanton 2000). A literature review and gazetteer of much of the published material has been compiled (Hild & Hellenkemper 1990), and analyses of ecclesiastical sites studied by scholars earlier this century have been reinterpreted in the light of new fieldwork (Hill 1996; Mietke 1999). Yet few publications have attempted a proper study of the province during the first millennium AD, and part of the reason for this is the rather limited nature of fieldwork.

Distribution maps for settlements in Isauria are relatively blank, symptomatic of research rather than the actual situation (Mitford 1980, 1260). The early sixth-century text of the Synekdemos of Hierokles provides evidence for 22 cities in Isauria (Hier. 708, 2). Jones has argued that, since Hierokles omits 11 cities known from other sources, this represents evidence for the number of cities in the empire being reduced at this time (Jones 1973, 716–17). However the picture has not been helped substantially by methods of archaeological research. Significantly, no evidence of the Byzantine remains at Kilise Tepe was reported until excavation began there in 1994 (Baker *et al.* 1995, 142–3); earlier publications had not included references to the Hellenistic, Roman or Byzantine occupation at the site (Mellaart 1958a, 315; French 1965, 180).

A large number of abandoned rural settlements, many of which include standing buildings, survive along the coastal hills of Isauria and Cilicia. These rural settlements are the size of moderate villages. Öküzlü for example contains 50–70 houses, and yet research projects investigating them have generally been small-scale. Surveys have focused mostly on the Early Byzantine churches, which in general represent a distinct group and remain the best-preserved structures (Hill 1996). The settlements that have been the focus of brief architectural study are thought to date between the Hellenistic and Early Byzantine periods, but their dynamics remain obscure (Eyice 1981; 1988, 21, 26–9; Hild & Hellenkemper 1990). In reality, detailed surveys of these buildings have only recently begun (Eichner 2000; Mietke 1996) and even fewer whole settlements have been surveyed. No excavation has been published from any of the houses.

Much of the ancient success of the settlements on the foothills near the coast may have been due to their exploitation of the local resources, especially olive oil and timber, and their role as producers for the coastal cities. Elaiussa Sebaste located nearby on the coast has undergone recent archaeological excavation (Equini Schneider 1999). Neither Seleuceia[29] nor Claudiopolis has received more than survey and very limited excavation (Keil & Wilhelm 1931; Bean & Mitford 1970, 196–8; Topçu 1984).

Evidence from the coastal cities complements that from elsewhere in the eastern Mediterranean and suggests that they underwent a major transition during the Late Roman and Early Byzantine periods. The dynamics of the urban environment through this period have been attributed variously to events and processes in both society and the ancient environment. Ideological shifts resulting from the conversion of the Empire to Christianity manifested themselves in changes to the built fabric of the city, thus for example at Seleuceia the temple of Apollo Sarpdonos was converted to a church in the fifth century (Topçu 1984; Bayliss 2001). There were also environmental shifts in this period, such as the silting of the harbour at Elaiussa Sebaste. Much has been made of the impact of the Justinianic Plague of AD 542 on Anemurium (Russell 1958) but its influence should not be seen as a single determining factor on population (Stathakopoulos 2000). The subtleties of these changes have often been attributed to single agents but as Kazhdan & Cutler (1982) have observed the reasons for the transition in Early Byzantine settlement are far from simple.

A broad overview of these settlements suggests a period of prosperity in the Early Byzantine countryside. The whole question is open to interpretation, however, and further archaeological research is needed to investigate this topic in Isauria. Analysis of urban change at Anemurium and the lack of datable churches after the fifth century in general have been used as evidence to support the view that the region was in a state of decline after the fifth century (Hill 1996, 9–10). Future interpretations will benefit from examination of a range of buildings from the settlements within their topographical setting rather than focusing merely on the monumental structures. This is crucial since without survey and excavation of a cross-section of buildings, interpretations will rarely be able to address evidence for the changes undergone by these rural settlements through time.

The seventh century was a period of political and military change in Byzantium as a result of wars first with the Persians and subsequently with the Muslim Arabs. The following two centuries were a time when the population of Isauria found itself lying just inside the new frontier with the Islamic world.

Detailed familiarity with the local ceramic type-sequences is vital for the interpretation of settlement dynamics in both archaeological excavation and survey. The local ceramics of the eighth and ninth centuries especially are unknown in many parts of Asia Minor. Research by the author seeks to provide a clearer understanding of the Roman–Byzantine sequence in the Göksu region.

Kilise Tepe provides us with an archaeological site ideally located to consider the nature of Byzantine settlement in Isauria precisely because of its unprotected location on the valley floor in an area of potential agricultural prosperity on a major supply route Seleuceia, which was one of the major military fortresses of the Byzantine world. It is through the archaeological excavation of sites like this that we can begin to build up a picture of the dynamics of Byzantine settlement before, during, and after this turbulent time. And it is with the help of excavated ceramic sequences generated from these excavations that we can begin to consider material collected by field surveys.

Between the tenth and eleventh centuries the Armenians began to colonize Cilicia and there followed a further period of political and social change. In the eleventh century following the battle of Manzikert in 1071, the Selcuk Turks began raiding into central Anatolia. 'Immediately following Manzikert, Byzantine administrative authority collapsed in Asia Minor, and in the vacuum Turks, Armenians and Normans attempted to found states' (Vryonis 1971, 104).

Claudiopolis is recorded as being besieged, Seleuceia, Corycus and Pracana sacked or destroyed (Vryonis 1971, 166–7). Cilicia was divided between the Franks and the Armenians in the twelfth century during which time the coastal cities experienced substantial amounts of construction (Lilie 1993, 107; Edwards 1982; 1987). The crusader army marched inland to Pracana in Isauria to fight the Selcuk Turks in 1146–47 (Cinnamus, 38) and in 1190 Frederick Barbarossa whilst on the Third Crusade, died attempting to cross the Calycadnus (Göksu river) (Brundage 1962, 164–6).

Architecture in the landscape

Analysis of the published archaeological sources might suggest that the domestic architecture of the Göksu valley has survived poorly relative to the upland areas nearer the coast. Indeed many of the ancient settlements of the Göksu may be concealed beneath modern villages. The conspicuous mound at Kilise Tepe, unknown to have Byzantine remains until the excavations began in 1994, demonstrates the need for Byzantinists to focus not only on the standing remains of stone buildings but to adopt a more strategic field methodology which encompasses the breadth of occupation in the landscape. Recent survey of the Konya plain in southern Lycaonia using innovative new research methods together with fieldwalking techniques not yet applied to Isauria, has clearly demonstrated evidence for dense settlement of the plain, with a village every 2–3 km in the Hellenistic continued into the Early Byzantine period (Baird 2003; 2004).

This evidence for settlement in central and southern Anatolia may be compared broadly with results from the limestone hills of northern Syria (Tchalenko 1953–58; Sodini *et al.* 1980; Tate 1992; Magness 2003) to suggest that much of the eastern Mediterranean region was a dense network of rural settlements in the early Byzantine period. Unlike the frontier provinces of Asia Minor where relatively little fieldwork has been carried out on the period between the sixth and tenth centuries, the changes undergone by Syria at this time have been a focus of research for some time.

The interpretations of the fluctuations in Syrian settlement are still heavily influenced and to some extent generated by the methodologies and approaches which have been applied to them. They have led to a variety of contrasting histories (Foss 1995; Kennedy 1985; 1992; Tchalenko 1953–58; Tate 1992; Magness 2003).

Of importance for us here is the question of settlement in the period immediately before the growth of the Islamic empire. Magness has recently provided a critique and reassessment of the evidence for settlement in Syria and Palestine from an archaeological perspective and has questioned, in particular, Kennedy and Tate's interpretations of the chronology of settlement in the limestone hills of Syria. Tate provided an interpretation for Déhès, based largely on inscriptions and wall typologies, of a gradual increase in settlement density up to AD 550 and a continuity of investment in churches up to AD 610 (Tate 1992, 173–81, 337). Kennedy has suggested that the picture of uninterrupted rural prosperity until the seventh century is too simple and that settlement began to 'decline' in Syria from AD 550 but was followed by growth and investment which took place again later under the Umayyads (Kennedy 1992, 291; Magness 2003, 198).

Magness argues against Kennedy's suggestion of decline at the end of the Byzantine period, and proposes that there was very significant growth and prosperity between the mid sixth and mid seventh centuries and that in fact although there were changes in settlement in the eighth and ninth centuries, there was significant evidence for continuity at Déhès and other settlements into ninth and tenth centuries (Magness 2003, 198–9).

Sodini indeed noted an increase in ceramic material during the seventh and eighth centuries (Sodini *et al.* 1980, 300); the dating of these types is affirmed by Magness who suggests that analysis of the stratigraphy from which the pottery came may be interpreted as evidence for domestic refuse and inhabitation associated with the eighth and ninth century and continued occupation at Déhès until the tenth century. Thus she argues (2003, 199), from the archaeological evidence, that the 'decline' put forward by Kennedy for the mid sixth century, and by others attributed later to the Persian and Arab invasions of Syria, had a much less significant impact than has been argued in the past.

The nature of settlement in Byzantium at this time is still disputed. Regions are not likely to be *identical* in patterns of prosperity; however, it appears from the work on the same areas in Syria that interpretations for the period after AD 550 disagree markedly. Researchers considering Isauria need to be aware of these debates.

Magness's work provides a reminder of the importance of the correct dating of local ceramic type sequences (Magness 2003, 2; Sodini & Villeneuve 1992, 195–6) and their relationship to archaeological contexts (Magness 2003, 199) as well as the inherent dangers of relying on coins and texts for interpreting archaeological evidence. Magness provides us with a picture, based largely on archaeological evidence for inhabitation rather than textual references, of some change but of relative continuity in settlement from many parts of northern Syria up to and following the seventh century. Similar questions should be asked about the nature of the archaeological evidence of the Byzantine–Arab frontier zone in Anatolia in this period.

A distinction should be made between the villages in Syria and religious sites, though they were often closely related. Many monasteries and pilgrimage sites grew up during the Late Roman period when there was a general prosperity of settlements in the countryside. The pilgrimage sites can be connected to the development of the practice of asceticism (Brown 1971, 83–4). Ascetics played a significant part in the spread of Christianity into the countryside (Kennedy & Liebeschuetz 1988, 74–5). They moved into remote locations where they performed a number of roles including local arbitration for rural communities (Brown 1971, 86–7): 'Eventually the power was institutionalized and the hermit was replaced or supplemented by the abbot of a monastery' (Kennedy & Liebeschuetz 1988, 74).

The huge late fifth-century pilgrimage centre of Qal'at Seman in Syria which was built around the pillar of St Simeon the Stylite is one of the most famous examples of the institutionalization of a saint's power (Kennedy & Liebeschuetz 1988, 68). Hermits and monasteries were found throughout the diocese of Oriens and especially flourished in Monophysite areas. Thus monasteries and pilgrimage sites became a familiar part of the Late Antique countryside in Syria and Egypt (Brown 1971, 82–3). Isauria too was part of the Monophysite archiepiscopal diocese of Antioch and was renowned for its monastic traditions (Frend 1972, 150). The growth in ecclesiastical sites in the countryside of Oriens should be viewed within this context.

The theological debates of the fourth and fifth centuries frequently split the bishops within Isauria whose decisions first over the Arian dispute and later over Monophysitism and Orthodoxy demonstrate that Isauria was not merely a provincial backwater but that its bishops entered into the theological debates of the time. Interestingly it is precisely from this period that the majority of the surviving church buildings survive.[30]

The major Göksu sites

The majority of the research concerning the Göksu valley over the past 120 years has concentrated on a relatively small number of very significant ecclesiastical sites. The two most famous are located at Meryemlik, which lies on a hill, about a kilometre outside ancient Seleuceia, and at Alahan (Gough 1985; Hill 1996, 68–83), high on the side of the Göksu valley c. 15 km north of Mut. Both of these two places are well attested as centres of pilgrimage (Mango 1991; Hill 1996, 68–72).

The focal point of the pilgrimage centre at Meryemlik was the underground cave of Saint Thecla. Although the site has never been excavated, investigations earlier this century produced evidence for at least four churches including the cave church, two large cisterns and baths (Herzfeld & Guyer 1930; Hill 1996, 208–34). Documentary sources record that the site contained rest houses for pilgrims and was famous for its garden full of birds (Miracles of S. Thecla 24, 36: 17–21 in Dagron 1978). The two churches from the site which have dominated attention are the Basilica of St Thecla, which lies over the cave and the Cupola Church.

Alahan has two churches linked by a 200-m-long terrace. The space between the churches is furnished with a baptistery, tombs, a shrine, and a colonnade as well as buildings interpreted from epigraphic evidence as guest-houses (Hill 1996, 69). Alahan exhibits a quality and style of stone carving comparable to that of other local sites. In particular, carved niches in the west wall of the East Church at Alahan have been compared to similar examples inside the apses of the church and 'pastophory' at Mahras Dağ and examples from the Domed Ambulatory Church at Dağ Pazarı (Hill 1996, 200). The architectural decoration at Alahan lies within a broader tradition of stonemasonry for which the Isaurians were famous (Mango 1966).

The Cupola Church at Meryemlik and the East Church at Alahan have been compared in plan and interior space to other churches from Isauria which belong to a similar architectural scheme (Forsyth 1957). They include two other buildings from the Göksu region, the church at Alakilise (Guyer 1909/10) and the Domed Ambulatory Church at Dağ Pazarı, and also the Tomb Church at Corycos on the coast (Hill 1996, 45).

The church at Alakilise is built high on the mountain above Zeyne (Sütlüce) on the west side of the Göksu. The site lay on the ancient road to Kilise Tepe which crossed a now ruined bridge close to the modern village of Kışla.[31] Alakilise was investigated by Guyer, who published a brief summary of his field notes (Guyer 1909/10). This very substantial building which has been interpreted as a 'Domed Basilica' (Hill 1996, 83–4), had collapsed and remained *in situ* but has unfortunately been used recently as a source of building supplies by locals.

The architectural importance of these buildings derives from their employment of centrally planned elements within the design of a traditional basilica (Mango 1966, 364; Gough 1972, 199; Hill 1996, 45–50). Hill has argued however that the 'domed basilicas' of Isauria[32] represent a precedent for the great domed churches in Constantinople, such as Hagia Sophia following the 'throwing together' of provincial architectural traditions in Constantinople under the Isaurian Emperor Zeno (Hill 1996, 46). The dating of this innovation in Isauria is in fact still debated. Most have linked buildings from the group with varying degrees of certainty to Zeno (late fifth century: Mango 1966, 364; Gough 1972; Hill 1996, 51, 70). Others dispute his involvement (Mietke 1999, 121; Elton 2002a).

Both sites would have facilitated the movement of pilgrims or formal processions around the various opportunities for stationary liturgy during the Late Roman/Early Byzantine period in much the same way as they did in cities (Hill 1996, figs. 1, 45; Bayliss 1999, 60–63). Other sites also had monumentalized approaches: there are huge numbers of sarcophagi on the path to the Tomb Church at Corycos and the remains of another *via sacra* at Dağ Pazarı were recorded by Wilson (1895, 181–2). The veneration of saints' relics became an important part of both public and private life in the Late Antique world. Prior to relics being brought inside the city walls, pilgrimage sites associated with the veneration of saints' relics and holy men developed outside the cities (Bayliss 1999, 63). People journeyed to venerate *loca sancta* or relics, or holy men and women often at local rural shrines. Thus these shrines played a significant part in the lives of people in the countryside.

Monumental sites featuring colonnades, tombs, baths, baptisteries and churches developed in the countryside as the shrines of holy men were embellished with architecture. Such sites were an important feature of the Calycadnus valley. Evidence from Meryemlik and Alahan suggests earlier phases of both sites were centred around caves, but that with time the sites became highly developed architecturally involving buildings and monuments more typical of the cities than in the countryside. These places, together with smaller ecclesiastical sites within settlements such as at Yanıkhan, formed a network of foci for the local population in the province. The Calycadnus valley also lay on an overland route to the East and thus these sites may have played a significant role in the journeys of those travelling to the Holy Land.[33]

A close examination of the churches from Cilicia and Isauria has shown that at least 37 churches from Cilicia and Isauria had eastern passages (Hill 1996, 29). Hill has argued a strong case from the evidence at the South Church at Yanıkhan that these passages enabled the building to function both as a parish church and as a martyrium (Hill 1996, 29). The passages facilitated movement of people around the apses for the purpose of the veneration of relics as took place in Sinai where pilgrims processed around the relic of the burning bush at The Monastery of St Catherine (Hill 1996, 31; Forsyth 1968, 17–18; Mietke 1999, 120).

There appears however to be a difference not only in design, but also in layout and location between the domed basilicas and the typical Isaurian village basilicas. The former occur at significant locations in the wider landscape, are associated often with other monumental buildings, and are constructed to a very high standard whereas the typical Isaurian basilicas seem to occur in locations which are significant to their own context but usually represent little more than agricultural settlements. In this sense the architectural complexity of the buildings clearly reflects the context of the building and very probably its role in society. Even in rural contexts, there does, however, appear to have been the facility in the design to afford procession, which may have been associated at times with veneration of relics as at Yanıkhan, or perhaps more generally as part of eucharistic liturgy.

The large sites at Alahan, Alakilise, and Meryemlik must have been a constant visual presence, even at night, for those living in the Calycadnus valley. The gradual construction of monuments along the paths to these sites suggests growth through time which may be due to a number of factors. These monuments which have dominated discussions were not the first phases at the sites — they embellished what came before. It is tempting to assume that those with authority at these sites may have exercised more than ideological control over the local inhabitants. The ecclesiastical authorities might have had access to resources that would have given them significant political and economic powers, perhaps to rival or even partner those in the cities. Control of local painted-pottery production at the pilgrimage site Abu Mina in Egypt demonstrates the potential of ecclesiastical institutions of the time to exploit economic potential. Ceramics were made specifically for pilgrims to take away and for use locally (Dark 2001, 81, 120). There are clear similarities in broad tradition between the painted wares of North Africa, as well as elsewhere in the eastern Mediterranean, and the painted wares of the Göksu valley. The production sites in the Göksu are yet to be established (Williams 1985, 41–7; Collon 1995, 157–9; Jackson, this volume, pp. 394–5).

Whatever the true role of these foundations for the local inhabitants, many of these buildings are still standing long after their construction date; the East Church at Alahan for example is virtually complete today except for its roof. One of the important questions to address is the duration and nature of use of these sites. The changing uses of these monuments through time and the aspects of everyday life of the inhabitants are more likely to be provided by excavation of material culture associated with subsidiary structures. At the same time, the buildings at these ecclesiastical sites form part of a broader archaeological landscape which itself will benefit from field survey in conjunction with excavation of the archaeological strata at a range of settlements. The lower slopes of the Göksu valley can be exploited for crop production and modern villages make the most of water and other resources (Postgate 1995, 139). High on the mountains above the valley, former hermitages of ascetics were monumentalized. These institutions may well have become a significant part of the local economic and political system in addition to wielding ideological authority over the people working on the land below.

Seventh century and after

After the mid seventh century, the remains of buildings in the Near East have often seemed less archaeologically visible since the traditional dating tools apparently cease to be useful at this time. Few texts survive from that period, Late Roman fine wares apparently cease to be traded and after the late seventh-century bronze coins tend to go out of circulation (Hendy 1985, 643). As a consequence, the period between the eighth and the tenth centuries has been considered as the Byzantine 'dark age'. This picture is compounded by our methodologies, since local pottery sequences, which promise to contribute much to our understanding of the period in particular, are generally poorly understood. As a consequence we have a relatively scanty picture of the nature of rural settlement in Isauria during the first millennium AD.

Major changes however took place in the Middle East and Asia Minor in the seventh century AD. In the early seventh century the Sassanian Persians invaded Asia Minor. Clive Foss has argued that the Persian armies inflicted serious damage on the cities of Byzantine Anatolia in AD 616 in the invasion which resulted in the siege of Chalcedon and the threat of attack on Constantinople. He noted that Byzantine coins were struck at Seleuceia in AD 616 and 617 and argued that this represented evidence for the establishment of the Byzantine military headquarters there. However, he also noted that coins in AD 618 cease to be minted at Seleuceia and were minted instead on the other side of the Taurus inland at the site of the earlier Hellenistic fortress at Zengibar Kalesi (Isaura Nova). This evidence has been used by Foss to suggest that the region was taken by the Persians in c. AD 618, and that as a result, the Byzantine army fell back to Isaura which became the Byzantine forward fortress in the face of Persian invasions (Foss 1975, 729–30, 734). Russell argues that there was no evidence of destruction or abandonment at this time at Anemurium. The withdrawal to Isaura and the end of minting there after only one year may be a sign that much of Isauria was protected by this tactic (Russell 2001, 60–61). Only careful excavation at a range of sites will enable this question to be addressed further.

Following the expulsion of the Persians from Byzantine territory in the East, and after less than 20 years of peace, the Byzantine provinces of Syria and Palestine were again overrun, this time by a new enemy in the form of the Muslim Arabs. The Taurus mountain region was transformed into a new frontier zone between the late Roman Empire and the Arab territories. The frontier was not strictly linear but represented a buffer zone between the two powers (Haldon & Kennedy 1980, 97). The armies of both empires raided into each other's lands through the passes in the Taurus range. Once a route for pilgrims and traders travelling to the Holy Land and the East, in the seventh century the pass through the Göksu valley became a strategic military supply-route to the Byzantine fortress at Seleuceia.

Isauria thus fell within, and at the SW end of, the eastern frontier of the newly created Anatolikon Theme which represented the Byzantine military unit designed to combat the new security problem (Whittow 1996, maps VI & VIII, 92–3, 114).

Smooth Cilicia is known to have been a no-man's land between the Arab and Byzantine Empires until AD 717 when it was settled by the Arabs (Haldon & Kennedy 1980, 79; Whittow 1996, 167). Much has been made of the reference in Al-Yakūbi which provides evidence for the Byzantine inhabitation of the Taurus. He describes Tarsus, one of the Arabs' newly occupied cities of Cilicia, lying on level ground surrounded by mountains inhabited by the Byzantines (Rūm) (Haldon & Kennedy 1980, 109).

For two centuries therefore, the Isaurian Taurus fell just on the Byzantine side of the frontier zone and was one of the areas targeted by Arab raids (Haldon & Kennedy 1980, 83). However the nature of the situation for people living in the region at this period derives largely from textual references rather than archaeological evidence, since, in reality, little is known about the nature of settlement in the region. Archaeological work at Tarsus by Professor Zoroğlu may yield further important contributions to our understanding of the area under Umayyad control (Zoroğlu *et al.* 1999) and current work at Ayaş by Professor Equini-Schneider will provide further information on the nature of settlement on the coast at this period (Equini-Schneider 1999; 2003). This will be an important addition to the evidence from Anemurium where inhabitation seems to have come to an end by the early eighth century (Williams 1977, 175; Russell 1980), but the mountain region further to the west at this time remains relatively poorly understood.

At the start of the Arab wars Seleuceia was a city in the large Anatolikon Theme. Later, reorganization of national security, certainly from the ninth century, resulted in the city's appointment as capital of the *Kleissoura* or 'frontier province' of Seleukeia demonstrating the continued strategic value of the region (Haldon & Kennedy 1980, 86). Textual information illuminates the kinds of military tactics employed in defence of Anatolia (Dennis 1985). The responsibility of defence in these geographical areas was placed on the local populace who controlled the passes in particular (Dennis 1985, 116, 138; Trombley 1998, 99).

There are limited passes through the mountains into Anatolia. The actual invasion routes based on historical sources remain unclear (Ahrweiler 1962, 7). Lilie provides a list of Arab raids into Asia Minor (1976, 112–22).

The natural route of entry into Anatolia from Tarsus is the Cilician Gates. Many other raids entered Anatolia through passes further to the east (Arvites 1983, 219–20). The location of the fortress at Seleuceia which would have protected the Göksu pass and the coastal route behind should not be underestimated. The very fact that there was a military fortress there emphasizes its strategic location.

> Such fortifications closely reflected the strategic networks of the regions in which they were established, both in respect of communications and routes of ingress and egress, as well as — depending upon the region — of economic activity and the movement of resources (Haldon 1999, 251).

That Isauria was invaded seems to be attested in the texts. We have references to battles at least two of which may concern Isauria. Ibn Al-Athir records that the Arabs took Dalisa — which Brooks suggests may have been the Isaurian city of Dalisandus (1898, 197). And an Arab force was soundly defeated in AD 960 at Adrassos, located in a pass through Isauria possibly at Balabolu (Ramsay 1890, 367–8; Alföldi Rosenbaum 1980, 13). The traditional frontier for the exchange of prisoners in AD 945 was the Lamos gorge probably further east of the Göksu (Ramsay 1890, 380; Haldon & Kennedy 1980, 86).

Archaeological research will be critical for the understanding of both sides of the frontier zone (Haldon & Kennedy 1980, 116; Whittow 1996, 94). The nature of settlement in the Taurus Mountains in general and its changes during this period remain relatively unknown. Certainly, relatively little investigation has taken place to examine the archaeological evidence for life in Isauria at this time.

Scholars have postulated that the frontier region probably became less populated because of the military threats (Haldon & Kennedy 1980, 99). Haldon & Kennedy argue that crops within the frontier zone would have been subject to raiding and assume that there would have been a consequent drift away from crop farming towards cattle and especially sheep raising (1980, 100–101); this view is echoed by Whittow (1996, 180). They also argue for the gradual transfer of power to a new military elite able gradually to acquire cheap land in the depopulated zone, which was later repopulated from the tenth century by Armenian mercenaries (1980, 98). Many of these arguments are based on textual sources but might be tested with excavated faunal remains. Unfortunately, good sources of palynological data are less available in this area than in Lycia where broad trends in vegetation can be reconstructed (Neil Roberts pers. comm. 1999; Bottema 1999, 15).

The extent to which Isauria, and more specifically the settlement in the Göksu valley, was affected by the new Arab–Byzantine frontier is an important question for archaeologists to consider. The period raises all sorts of questions about the nature of frontiers, agriculture, and possible changes in land use, land ownership and settlement patterns from the previous period.

Excavations of rural sites in the region offer us the opportunity to consider closely the changes at specific locations. Kilise Tepe in particular offers an ideal opportunity to address these questions because of its status as a relatively small rural settlement located on the floor of one of the biggest passes through the Taurus just inside what is traditionally seen as Byzantine territory.

In the Göksu valley, the rock-cut church known as Aloda is one of the few sites which has been proposed as evidence for occupation during this 'dark age' period (Gough 1955; 1957). This structure was one of many rooms carved into the cliff above the modern town of Diştaş in the upper Göksu valley. Its walls are covered with two layers of painted plaster, the earlier decorated with geometric designs and the later with figural. Gough argued that the figural motifs belonged to the tenth century based on comparisons with those from Karabaş Kilise in Cappadocia (Jerphanion 1928, pl. 199). He suggested that the earlier geometric designs painted on the layer of plaster beneath, which contain no images, may have derived from the Iconoclast period c. AD 726–843 (Gough 1957, 156ff.). Yet Ousterhout has argued that many churches without figural decoration have been called iconoclast without solid basis (1998, 26).

The church's paintings, if dated correctly by Gough, represent the only identifiable evidence for occupation in the valley during this period. No other structures have been positively dated to after the seventh century and before the twelfth century in the region. In view of the durability of a cave and the unsystematic methods used to examine settlements of the region, the lack of other published evidence for structures from the period is hardly demonstrative of a lack of occupation at the time.

The nature of settlement in the Göksu during the period of Arab wars has yet to be determined from excavated remains. In broader terms, it is unknown what happened to the settlements of the Early Byzantine period during the following centuries. This is partly due to the reliance in previous years on building phases for the determination of chronology rather than occupation sequences in archaeological stratigraphy.

The length of use of the East Church at Alahan and the date when it became derelict are both unknown. The Early Byzantine phase of the West Church at Alahan was built at a similar time to the East Church. The secondary construction phase at the site is represented by a substantial rebuild of the baptistery and by a single chambered church built on the site of the West Church (Gough 1963, 105–9; 1964, 185–8). This phase of activity remains one of the keys to the chronology at the site. The buildings of the later phase were built out of *spolia* from the primary phases and may therefore have represented an episode of reconstruction following a destruction event or a period of decline at the site. A number of human skeletons[34] were found in the cemetery which lay around this later chapel. These were transported to Ankara for analysis by a human osteologist but have never been published (Gough 1963, 106). This phase is an indication of significant later use of the site and represents very important evidence for our understanding of the chronology of Alahan and settlement in the Göksu valley in general after the Early Byzantine period. Hill has therefore suggested that all these phases are likely to have lasted until the seventh century based on the dating of the local painted pottery which Gough called 'Monastic Ware' (Hill 1996, 74). No other pottery or datable material culture has been linked to this phase apart from a late pavement to the west of the church, associated with green glazed pottery dated to twelfth–fourteenth (Gough 1962, 177) or c. thirteenth century (Williams 1985, 52). These could have been left after the abandonment of the building.

The West Church at Alahan (Gough 1962, 175–7; 1964, 187–8) and the Necropolis Church at Anemurium (Russell 1980, 34) provide very important evidence for our understanding of the construction of medieval 'chapels' in Isauria since until the excavation at Kilise Tepe, they were the only two other excavated buildings of this type from the province. In reality their features and proportions are not really very comparable (Hill 1996, fig. 8; Gough 1962, 175). The later structure at Anemurium was rectangular in shape and reused the outline of the earlier chancel. It was built against the surviving Early Byzantine apse and represented the fourth phase of architecture in the building. It was attributed to the twelfth century by its excavator (Russell 1979, 184–5). The later chapel on the West Church at Alahan was dated to the twelfth century by Gough but has been attributed to the seventh by Hill (Gough 1964, 187; Hill 1996, 74).

Unfortunately, there is no consensus on the date of this later building at Alahan, nor on the length of time between the destruction of the former phase and the construction of the later. Neither is it known whether the East Church was still functioning at the time, although this would seem likely in view of its state of preservation today.

Gough excavated at both Alahan and Dağ Pazarı. Subsidiary buildings, living quarters and associated material culture often provide more useful information on the duration of occupation than monumental structures. The excavation at Alahan demonstrated that a number of the areas of the site had a series of building phases, but unfortunately, when the site was published after Gough's death the strata of the excavation were only linked to the material culture in summary form, making the re-interpretation of phasing and dating problematic (Gough 1985).

The substantial quantity of coins from the site mostly date between the fourth and the sixth centuries, however there was one coin of the mid seventh and another of the eleventh century (Harrison 1985, 27). There was also 'a fair amount' of seventh-century pottery from the site (Harrison 1985). The distribution of coins and fine ware at Alahan reflects the typical pattern of availability which ceases in the mid seventh century. Little evidence from the site can be positively dated between the mid seventh century and the eleventh century. The lack of coins or fine ware need not mean an end to the occupation. Gough attributed his

'Monastic Ware' to the primary phase of architecture at the site 'provisionally', i.e. fifth–seventh century (Gough 1964, 190). Although this seems likely, the discovery of similar motifs on later material from elsewhere in the Mediterranean, as well as on Late Roman wares, does raise the question whether this local material might have continued in use later (Sauer & Magness 1997, 476–7; Dark 2001, 43 & fig. 17). Establishing close dates for these local ceramics is of crucial importance for the production of a more detailed picture of settlement dynamics in the region.

Gough's excavations at the Late Roman walled city at Dağ Pazarı 65 km north of Seleuceia, in 1957–59, identified secondary building phases following the destruction of both the Domed Ambulatory Church and the baptistery of the Basilica Church (Hill 1996, 158; 1998, 327, 334). The dates of their destruction and the construction of the second phases remain elusive as the excavations were never fully published. Coins[35] from Gough's excavations at Dağ Pazarı represent six dating to the fourth century, two to the early fifth century, three to the late sixth century, one to the early seventh and one to the mid eleventh century. Full publication of Gough's work together with further fieldwork at the site promises important results on the nature of the Late Roman site and its continuity into the medieval period.

In Isauria, excavation of Early Byzantine churches at Alahan and Anemurium has revealed the presence of smaller buildings located in the naves of the earlier structures. These structures, although of a similar small scale, are not known to conform to a standard architectural type. Their dates of construction are largely unproven and the dates of the destruction of the buildings over the remains of which they are built are also unknown. Analysis of buildings of this class needs to establish, at each site, when the Early Byzantine basilicas were destroyed and how long it was until they were replaced by the smaller structures, to see if there are regional trends.

The reduced scale of buildings has been used as evidence for the reduction of population from the seventh century onwards due to the Islamic raids (Hill 1996, 10). The reduction in scale of church buildings in Isauria needs to be considered alongside similar evidence all over the Byzantine Empire, even in cities and castles where populations would have been sizable. The new forms might be better linked to a change in the perceived needs of a church from those offered by a large congregational basilica to the more intimate and personal space afforded by the smaller secondary buildings. Such considerations would not have determined liturgy *per se*, but the variation in design does suggest a shift in the perceived requirements of the building. Architectural alterations of this kind would have contributed to a very different experience of both the interior space and the exterior of church buildings. People may have come to use the space outside the building rather than to congregate within it as in Early Byzantine times.

Associated buildings represent the context of churches. In order to understand the nature of Byzantine sites, churches need to be excavated as part of this broader context (Mango 1986, 8). A greater understanding of the local ceramic assemblages will not only help to date the structures with which they are associated but will enable an interpretation together with other finds within their archaeological context to facilitate interpretation of the dynamics of everyday life of these people.

The Göksu valley would have been a major agricultural region for the upland province of Isauria. Cities and country were both undergoing changes in the Late Roman and Early Byzantine periods. At this time the Near Eastern countryside seems to have experienced prosperity in many rural areas. This conflicts with the argument for *agri deserti* which it has been argued occurred all over the Mediterranean between the late third and sixth centuries (Jones 1973, 812–23). In spite of this the low status of many of the small cities and bishoprics in the province can be demonstrated by the fact that Bishop Musonius of Meloe earned less than a private in the army (Jones 1973, 906). In particular, there is evidence for the construction of significant ecclesiastical sites which may have rivalled established authority in the cities for the control of the countryside. These new centres exercised not only ideological, but also economic and political authority over their local areas. Such authority was enforced by their role as *loca sancta* and by their very locations high on the sides of the Göksu valley, where pilgrimages would have been made as part of a festival calendar.

Conclusion

The excavation at Kilise Tepe provides evidence for a significant agricultural community which would have lived in the valley below Alakilise, one of these monumental churches. Kilise Tepe was surrounded by fertile irrigated land and had its own water supply. The excavation of the Late Roman and Byzantine levels at the site provides new evidence for the way the local ceramic sequence changed through time, which will be of importance for the necessary future survey of the valley. The pottery together with associated finds provides us the opportunity to examine the nature of everyday life at this rural settlement, for example: the nature of food preparation, animal husbandry and crop production in the region, together with details of methods of storage for subsistence. Of crucial importance are the changing dynamics of the settlement through time, identifiable partly as construction and destruction events reflected in the changes in architecture; but also through longer changes recognizable only through the relationship between these buildings and successive archaeological strata and the associated artefacts.

Chapter 5

The Excavations and their Results

Nicholas Postgate

Summary of the work on site

Once the mapping of the site was completed, and a 10-m grid established, work began on the complete surface clearance of the mound. This served the purpose, among others, of affording a preview of the artefactual debris present below the surface — principally of course the ceramics — and hence of the stratigraphic sequence (see Part B, pp. 45–62). It became clear that we should expect 'late' material right across the top of the site, and that if we wanted to probe earlier layers we should look at the steeply sloping sides of the mound for a promising place to start. At the NW corner a large, relatively recent, robber trench had been sunk through some of these earlier layers (see Fig. 11), and seeing in the resulting cross-section plastered mudbrick walls and floors associated with a thick layer of burnt debris (subsequently labelled Level IVa), we elected to start excavation at the northern end. It emerged that the highest, Byzantine, level here more or less directly overlay the late second-millennium Stele Building of Level II, and this area, from L19 in the east to H18 at the north end of the western side of the tepe, remained the main focus of our excavation throughout the five seasons. Our report on Levels V through to II at the NW corner, which provided a stratified sequence from the Early Bronze Age down to about the seventh century BC, is given on pp. 87–164, and on the Byzantine remains in Level I on pp. 199–210.

An area was also opened on the east slope, where the prevalence of Late Bronze Age sherds led us to hope (falsely) that the Bronze Age architecture might be closer to the surface. The work here, which defined an Iron Age fortification wall along the rim of the site and exposed disjointed remains of Byzantine, Hellenistic and Iron Age date, is described on pp. 165–70.

In the first season a 5-m-wide trench was sited from west to east across the centre of the mound. In the event we opened only the western 50 m of this (I14–M14) as it proved relatively unrewarding. Its Byzantine and Hellenistic levels are described on pp. 178–83. At two points along its length we continued downwards: a 5 × 5 m sounding was taken down through some 3 m of Iron Age deposits in K14a (see pp. 177–8), and in I14, where the trench met the west edge of the tepe, well-preserved Iron Age and Late Bronze architecture was encountered, cut by a massive but enigmatic ditch (pp. 173–7). Two other 5 × 5 m trenches placed diagonally at regular intervals in N12 and Q10 were opened, but not taken down below the Iron Age (see pp. 171–3).

To the north of the I14–M14 trench an area about 20 m N–S by 30 m E–W was opened to recover the plan of the church (see pp. 185–97), but excavation here did not go below the church itself.

Fortification, access and the environs

The approximate limits of the site must always have been determined by the natural outline of the con-

Figure 11. *Robber trench in H19, from north before excavation.*

Figure 12. *Rock-cut steps above the spring, from east.*

Figure 13. *Rectangular basin north of tepe, from south.*

glomerate outcrop, which provides steep drops at the northern end and along the western side in particular. Today the eastern slope is less steep, and as our excavations showed, there was building here in Byzantine times and, closer to the top, in the Iron Age and earlier. Probably the underlying conglomerate was less steep here, permitting buildings to spread down the slope, but in the later Iron Age (after about 750 BC) or in the Hellenistic period a moderately substantial fortification wall was constructed along the NE rim of the mound (Wall 300, see p. 167). There was no sign of this at the NW corner; either it was not thought necessary because of the steep drop there, or it once existed and has fallen away entirely. Neither did we see any trace of a fortification wall along the western side or at the south end. However, in the later Iron Age or early Classical period a very large ditch was dug parallel with the western edge of the mound in I/J14 (see pp. 176–7). It is possible, but by no means certain, that this had a defensive purpose.

We have no evidence for access to the site at different times. It seems plausible that at most times the easiest route to the summit would have been from the terrace to the south, from which the tepe itself projects, and there are no discontinuities in the profile of the sides which might indicate an alternative approach. We noted in 1994 that:

> … at the south-east corner of the mound, where the wash apron meets the edge of the promontory, there are several extremely large slabs of conglomerate, some up to 10 m. in length, which appear to be arranged in a series of ramps (Pollard, in Baker *et al.* 1995, 149).

We have not investigated these slabs further, and are therefore still unable to say whether they may have had any association with an access route.

As already mentioned, the spring at the foot of the north end must have been one of the site's principal attractions, but it was a long way down from the top and when the site was fortified separate defensive measures must have been taken to protect the water supply, though we have observed no trace of structures round it, other than a terrace bordering a flat space round the plane tree. Just above the modern spring head two or three steep narrow steps can be seen cut into the conglomerate at the base of the slope (Fig. 12). We cleared the earth from these in 1998. Nothing further of interest was revealed, but it remains probable that these were the end of a steep route for pedestrians down to the water from the NW end. Although a few pre-Classical potsherds were found in this operation, they cannot be taken to date the steps.

Our permit related to the excavation of the mound and did not include survey. While preparing the contour plan of the tepe in 1994, and during the work on site each summer we saw very little evidence of occupation in the fields immediately surrounding the mound. In two places rectangular basins have been cut into natural conglomerate rock. One was carved into the top of a large conglomerate boulder on a low spur on the flanks of the promontory north of the mound (Figs. 13–14).[36] Another was cut out of a large conglomerate slab on the western edge of the ridge to the south of the mound (Fig. 15).[37] Both may have been connected with grape or olive pressing and we are unable to suggest a date for them. Our workmen told us of the illicit opening of tombs in earlier years. We could find no clear sign of this on the side of the next-door bluff facing the east slope of Kilise Tepe, but on the far side of the modern Mut–Silifke road there was an area of partially ploughed land in which a number of stone-lined tombs had been emptied of their contents. Given that intramural burial does not seem to have been a regular practice during any of the occupation periods at the site, it seems probable that these are part of a cemetery belonging to the Kilise Tepe population, but we saw nothing to indicate their date, except they did not have an east–west orientation and are presumably pre-Christian.

Figure 14. *Rectangular basin north of tepe, outflow channel from above.*

Figure 15. *Rock-cut feature on ridge south of tepe.*

Periods represented at the site (Fig. 473)

The excavation of the NW corner provides most of our evidence for the nature of the settlement and its history, but the picture can be supplemented by evidence from other areas investigated. Here we summarize the representation of the successive periods in the different parts of the site as a preface to the detailed account of each excavated area in Part C.

Early and Middle Bronze Age
Although the surface collection recovered plentiful EBA material from the southern end of the site, our excavation only reached these periods in the sounding in H19–20. While they include individual architectural features of some character, the area uncovered was not sufficient to offer any clues to the wider context, nor indeed to yield any complete building plans. As far as we can tell, these were regular domestic rooms, with plastered floors and mudbrick walls often on stone foundations. Without a larger sample of contemporary architectural practice it is impossible to say if Rm 41 in Level IVa with its impressive central hearth (Middle Bronze Age, see pp. 103ff.), or the very carefully re-plastered surface of Rm 62 in Level Vg (EB III, p. 95), were in any way exceptional. Nor can we interpret with any confidence the rather unusual features in Level Vj (EB II, pp. 89ff.) without parallel instances.

Late Bronze Age
Directly overlying the Middle Bronze Age Level IVb in H19 are the walls of Level III. It is clear that these constitute a definite break with the past architectur-

ally, and this is reflected by the ceramics, which belong to the widely distributed Late Bronze Age tradition associated with the Hittite empire. The petrographic and chemical analysis of this material indicates that some of it was imported from beyond the immediate vicinity of the site (see p. 270), and there are clearly implications for the settlement's relations with the outside world at this time. One of the most characteristic ceramic types in Level III is the libation arm (see pp. 340–41, **684–92**). Although one example of this form was found in the Late Bronze Age building in I14 (see below), it was much more frequent in the I19–20 and H19 deposits. There is a natural assumption that such vessels had a cultic function, and given the likelihood that in the earlier phases of Level II there was a shrine in this part of the site, we hold it possible that our Level III rooms were also associated with some kind of cultic activity (see below, p. 111). Given the partial plan, though, it would be premature to say more.

In view of the distribution of Late Bronze Age sherds on the surface it is likely that most of the site was occupied at this time, but the only other LBA remains we excavated were on the west side of the tepe in Level 3 of I14 (see pp. 173–5). The architecture here has all the appearance of one or more regular dwelling houses, including the provision for domestic storage represented by the two *in situ* jars in Room 91. The ceramic repertoire indicated that this was broadly contemporary with Level III at the NW Corner.

The end of the Bronze Age
Nothing later than Level III survived in H19 and H20, and the investigation of Levels I and II at the NW end of the mound occupies the area to the east of this (i.e. I-K20, I-L19, and I-K18). The transition from Level III to the Stele Building, and the Stele Building itself, raise knotty problems which are discussed at some length below (pp. 35–6). As described there, the 'Stele Building' of Level IIa–c seems likely to have had a public role and this would be understandable: it occupied the most protected point on the site, in a prime position for surveying the Göksu and the routes which followed it downstream or crossed it below the site (see above, pp. 9–11). Built on the destroyed IIc Stele Building was its IId successor, which belongs to the middle of the twelfth century to judge from the Mycenaean ceramics. In terms of the sequence at Tarsus, some or all of the IIa–d sequence belongs to LBA IIb, but since this spans the downfall of the Hittite Empire and there appears to be some continuity in the ceramics from IId to IIe it is not clear how helpful it is to assume some major cultural break at this point; in terms of the ceramics and architecture the larger break at Kilise Tepe is between Level III and Level II.

The Iron Age
The principal unresolved question about the later phases of Level II is where, if at all, there was a break in the sequence of occupation (and, if we retain the terms, at what point the Iron Age takes over from the end of the Bronze Age).[38] While some of the painted pottery from phase IIe does seem to inherit features from earlier phases (see pp. 343ff.), any IIe version of the Stele Building that may have existed is entirely lost, except perhaps in the south where a couple of rooms (mainly in J18) seem to respect the earlier phases.

The stratigraphic transition from IIe to IIf is not easy to identify precisely, either in the Western Courtyard or in J18, but more sophisticated and imported painted wares first make a convincing appearance in Level IIf, and if there was a break in occupation it seems likeliest to be at this point in the sequence. A larger body of well-stratified material would be very desirable to resolve this point (see below, p. 343). Unfortunately in neither of the other parts of the site where contemporary levels were dug is the stratigraphy informative. In I/J14 the earlier Level 2 architecture was founded on a thick layer of packing which constituted a clear break from the LBA house(s) of Level 3, and the sherd material suggested it was contemporary with IIe/f.

In I14, K14 and on the East slope it is clear that during the Iron Age (Level 2) there were domestic houses and associated open spaces which served to accommodate storage pits, but the areas exposed were not enough to reveal entire building plans or evidence for streets. In the NW corner, on the other hand, there are no domestic structures that we can assign to IIf or the rather arbitrary succeeding phases IIg and IIh. What seems almost certain is that in IIf the NW end of the mound was partly used for the manufacture of painted and unpainted pottery in a style common to large parts of the East Mediterranean (**707–35**). This style is generally attributed to the end of the eighth and beginning of the seventh centuries BC, and these pots are therefore quite close in time to the handful of sherds, mostly from the I14 ditch, in Greek Geometric styles (**940–46**), underlining the Mediterranean connections of the settlement at this time.

The later first millennium BC
At present we have no artefacts we can assign to the sixth–fifth century BC — unless we count the hoplite shields (**2272–4**) — but, if it was abandoned, occupation of the site resumed fairly early in the Hellenistic age, and the evidence of the surface collections suggests that most of the tepe was occupied at this date. Excavations at the north end of the mound revealed no evidence for occupation during the Roman period,

and the surface collection tends to confirm a reduced settlement size, though the southern part of the site did include small numbers of Roman period fine wares. There was increased activity during the Late Roman period and occupation at the site probably continued unbroken until the church and site were abandoned, perhaps some time in the eleventh century AD. It is only in the Byzantine period, discussed below by Mark Jackson (Chapters 16–18), that we have any idea of the layout of buildings on the site.

The Level III to Level II transition

We referred above to a definite break at the end of Level IV, and there is an equally distinct change at the end of Level III. Since this discontinuity is accompanied by an equally striking change in the ceramic tradition (see pp. 344–5), an explanation is called for in terms of the cultural and political history of the settlement. This obliges us to consider the evidence for the date of the building, which is unfortunately still difficult to fix. There are four potential dating methods:
1. the general position of the ceramics (and other artefacts) within the known sequence for this part of Anatolia;
2. the Mycenaean vessels from Level IId (pp. 373ff., **955–65**);
3. dendrochronological data for beams in the IIc walls (Chapter 53);
4. C14 dates (Chapter 53).

All of these agree on a broad date for the Stele Building within the fourteenth–twelfth centuries BC, but only the Mycenaean pottery offers more precision.[39] It indicates that Level IId of the Stele Building, on the floor of which the IIIC Mycenaean pottery was lying when it was destroyed, must date after the destruction of Hattusa, and thus according to conventional views after the termination of the main Hittite dynasty. If, as has often been done, the end of the Hittite Empire is treated as the end of the Bronze Age, it would mean that the transition from Bronze to Iron Age falls at some point during the life of the Stele Building, which would not have been an obvious moment at which to place a major cultural hiatus if we were looking solely at the evidence from Kilise Tepe.

When we started work at Kilise Tepe the very obvious cultural break between Levels III and II led us to think broadly of Level III as our 'Late Bronze Age', and of Level II as the beginning of the Iron Age. This was not based on any precise chronological considerations. It was in part the assumption that a change of such magnitude should signal some kind of transition, and the fall of the Hittite empire seemed to offer an obvious candidate. This was tied to the fact that the ceramic repertoire in Level III was familiar from imperial Hittite levels across Anatolia, whereas some at least of the Level II wares seemed to be distinctly local in inspiration and distribution. This observation seemed to fit very well with the dissolution of central political authority characteristically associated with the collapse of empire.[40]

However, the picture is not as simple as that. If the end of Level III had coincided with the burning of Boğazköy,[41] the entire Stele Building sequence would have to be contemporary with the post-imperial successor dynasties. In southern Anatolia these may be represented by the inscriptions of Hartapu. If he was in fact ruling after the fall of the Hattusa dynasty, these show that, as at Carchemish and Malatya, an attempt was made to preserve the Hittite imperial tradition in the south and east. Kilise Tepe might therefore have been isolated from the full effects of the disruption which affected Boğazköy, and since we would expect the Hartapu dynasty to draw some of its legitimacy from its traditional connections with the royal family, whether that of Hattusa or the cadet branch ruling Tarhuntassa, perhaps we should not be looking for major changes in the material culture at this point in time.

However, it now seems improbable that the life of the Stele Building prior to the IId destruction could be compressed into the years between 1190 and the manufacture of the Mycenaean pottery (~1175–1150). This would imply that the major architectural and cultural shift at the beginning of Level II took place well before the fall of Hattusa, and must be attributed to some other cause. Given that our LHIIIC pottery from Level IId is comparable to the Mycenaean material from the post-destruction LB IIb at Tarsus, and pointing to the typical LB II storage vessels caught up in the burning of Level IIc Room 20, Dorit Symington (2001, 170f., and pers. comm.) would equate our earlier Level II material with Tarsus LB IIa. She would stress the continuities in the ceramic material between our Levels III and IIa–c, and see them both as corresponding to Tarsus LB IIa and Kinet Höyük periods 15–13. This would still allow us to equate the destruction of the IIc Stele Building with the events leading to or following from the fall of Hattusa. In this case we could assign a time span of a few decades to the IId phase before its destruction in turn, and this would agree well with the expected date for the Mycenaean pottery.

On the other hand, the significant cultural changes at the beginning of Level II still need to be accounted for.[42] We are not aware of any comparable break within the Tarsus LB IIa horizon, or the corresponding levels at Kinet Höyük. One is obliged to enquire whether any political event known to have affected the Kilise Tepe region could account for the changes. The continuous stratigraphic accumulation in the Stele Building before the IIc destruction suggests, though it does not prove, the passage of some decades, and this is not contradicted by the dendrochronological data (which indicate a date of 1350 BC for the timbers used in the walls of IIc Rm 7). If we look back in Hittite political history some decades, there are several occasions which could perhaps have had an impact: Muwatalli's initial creation of Tarhuntassa as a substitute capital, the move back to Hattusa by Urhi-Tešub, the hand-over of Tarhuntassa to Kurunta and his dynasty by Hattusili, and Suppiluliuma II's campaign against Tarhuntassa and Lycia. Whether any of these was the sort of event which would lead to the changes seen at Kilise Tepe is open to question.

If asked to interpret the archaeological break, in ignorance of the events documented at Hattusa, one would be inclined to suggest that it marks the end of centralized political control of the Göksu valley, and the advent of an era of local polities. If, for chronological reasons, it cannot be attributed to the wholesale collapse of the major powers around 1190, and the transition to the small states which emerge in the ninth–eighth centuries, we have to find a way in which decentralization could have taken place within the lifetime of the empire. The ceramic standardization observed in Level III is paralleled at other sites ruled from Hattusa, as recently described by Gates (2001). If, as she suggests, it was a conscious and deliberate process associated with the political style of the Hattusa monarchy, for Kinet Höyük and Tarsus it perhaps followed the Hittite annexation of Kizzuwatna, and it would not be surprising to see Kilise Tepe included in the same process. Then the lapse of this standardization and the adoption of very different locally made wares could signal the withdrawal of the controlling hand of Hattusa and the establishment of the Tarhuntassa monarchy. This would shed unexpected light on the nature of the decentralization and imply that the establishment of the separate dynasty was not merely a cosmetic act. It may seem to give too much weight to a change in pottery production, but there is also the architectural change to account for. In any case, without more detailed work on the ceramic assemblages, this cannot be more than a hypothesis for the present.

The Level II destructions

Near Eastern archaeology is littered with attempts to equate destructions with historically attested events. From Ebla to Tarsus the temptation to match two different records has led us astray.[43] The assumption that the sack of a city is bound to leave a recognizable destruction level, or that an impressive enough destruction must find a mention in the (usually one-sided) historical narratives we happen to know, is obviously risky (cf. also the comments of Fischer *et al.* 2003, 5–7). Seeking a precise historical event to explain our own destructions at Kilise Tepe is equally dangerous, but it would be perverse to ignore the fact that several Anatolian sites share destruction levels at about the end of the Bronze Age, which have sometimes been attributed to the political disruption accompanying the fall of Hattusa. Egyptian texts describe these disruptions and attribute them to the 'Sea Peoples'. Modern commentators tend to be either sceptical or convinced, and Drews, who writes without reticence of 'The Catastrophe', is typical of the convinced position (Drews 1993; see pp. 8–11 for a summary of Anatolian sites affected). However, even he would not maintain that all such destructions took place simultaneously.[44]

Despite our difficulties with the precise chronology, there is no doubt that the IIc and IId phases of the Stele Building were destroyed by fire at about this juncture in history. In IIc the East Building suffered from the same conflagration, and although no humans were caught up in the destruction, and only a single handful of valuable items (the silver triad and associated jewellery, **2306**–7), it seems unlikely that the grain-filled jars in the Stele Building and the pilgrim flasks in Rm 20 would have been willingly left to burn. Moreover, this destruction layer was not just a few pieces of charcoal lying in black ash on a floor: it included lumps of brickwork some of which were fused and distorted by the heat of the fire. In one case a copper/bronze arrowhead (**2247**) was embedded in the fallen brickwork, though this is the only specific evidence which might point to a hostile agency. On the other hand, there are some indications (though no decisive proof) that those who used the building were not entirely unprepared for the fire (see p. 147).

Less of the destroyed remnants of the IId building survived the attentions of later builders, but the similarity of that material to the IIc destruction was enough for us to confuse the two at an early stage. There is no doubt that the building was thoroughly destroyed; but the general layout of the area persisted despite these two destructions, and there was enough continuity — as shown by the continued use of the Western Courtyard, and the way IIe walls respect the IId and IIc alignment — for us to reject the idea of any abandonment of the site at this stage

So to sum up, the Stele Building and the East Building, which were probably government establishments of some kind, were destroyed by a fierce fire at the end of Level IIc, which might be roughly contemporary with the destruction of Boğazköy. Subsequently a version of the Stele Building was built over the ruins, but the East Building was not replaced. This IId phase was by no means identical to its predecessor, but a set of Mycenaean bowls was kept there and duly caught up in a second destruction around the middle of the twelfth century. Thereafter the site of the Stele Building did continue in use for a while, in phase IIe, but as explained above, neither stratigraphic evidence nor external synchronisms allow us to be certain if occupation continued uninterrupted into the later Iron Age.

The Vg destruction

Uncertainty as to the significance of the destruction of buildings dogs us in other levels too. A major conflagration overcame the house in H20 at the end of phase Vg. As observed by Dorit Symington (see below) this could be interpreted in the wider context of events during which a large number of sites in western and southern Anatolia were destroyed at the end of EB II, an event attributed by Mellaart to the influx of Luwian population groups into Anatolia (Mellaart 1971, 406ff.). In the Konya plain, according to Mellaart, every EB II mound showed signs of destruction, mostly followed by desertion. Cilicia also seems to have been affected, and at Tarsus there are signs of hastily built fortifications before the final destruction of the EB II settlement (Goldman 1956, 20f., 31f.).

With a process which affected both the Konya plain and the Çukurova it is unlikely that the Göksu valley would have escaped unscathed. Although at Kilise Tepe occupation seems to have resumed without a hiatus in the architectural tradition (see p. 97), the ceramic break between Vg and the succeeding phase Vf is absolute, not to say dramatic, bringing in a pottery tradition of West Anatolian character that typifies EB III. This is essentially that known from Troy II, including the *depas amphikypellon*, tankards, wheel-made plates and red cross bowls, with a wide distribution in Anatolia which extended to sites beyond the Amanus. However, as with all our conflagrations (except IIc) there is nothing, in the small area of Vg we excavated, to tell us if the burning was accidental or deliberate, and whether it was confined to a single building or spread further across the settlement.

Two aspects of the stratigraphic sequence

While each level at the site requires its own interpretation independent of the others, there are two general observations which emerge from a consideration of the sequence as a whole. The first concerns the nature of domestic floor surfaces. Since participating in Diana Kirkbride-Helbaek's excavation of the Neolithic site of Umm Dabaghiyah in northern Iraq I have always been struck by the care lavished in earlier prehistory on domestic living surfaces. Lime plaster is standard in the Levantine Pre-Pottery Neolithic, and one has only to look at Çayönü to see how much value was attached to some floors. At Kilise Tepe the best floors we have are in the Early Bronze Age levels. The quality varies with the type of space, but for interior spaces thick layers of carefully prepared clay, often yellowish when not burnt, are used, and regularly renewed, as coating for floors and walls into our Level III, the Late Bronze Age. Clay plaster was used in the Stele Building but less generously, especially on the floors, and in phase IIe (e.g. in J18) the whitish floor plaster was extremely thin and fugitive.[45]

In Level I the concept of floor plaster seems to be almost wholly absent. Hardly any of the Hellenistic or Byzantine walls in I-M14 showed any traces of wall plaster or any recognizable associated floor surface.[46] One reason could be that we usually only recovered stone foundations, and packing from beneath the floors, whereas plaster would normally be applied only to a mudbrick superstructure with its base at about the same level as the floors. On the other hand, it could be that they really did not use carefully laid clay floors, because there were other floor coverings, such as mats, carpets, or a combination of both, which made this unnecessary.

Our second general observation concerns the transition from one level or phase to the next, which generally involved a new construction, whether or not along the same lines as the previous phase. The rebuilding of a house was not a light matter. One of the reasons for the deep deposits of some Neolithic and Chalcolithic Anatolian sites is the practice of infilling the earlier version to a considerable depth (cf. Çatalhöyük, Aşıklı, Can Hasan: see Özdoğan & Özdoğan 1998). Ritual acts for the inauguration of a new dwelling survive in the Middle East to this day, and rituals and incantations for those building houses are attested in ancient Mesopotamia. In our Bronze and Iron Age levels the normal processes of rebuilding did not entail leaving the earlier phase standing to any height; on the contrary we find walls shaved down close to their foundations, even removing the associated floor levels. It is all the more remarkable that by contrast buildings which had burnt down were left more or less as they stood.

There are several episodes in the sequence in the NW corner in which the buildings were destroyed by a serious fire. These are from earliest to latest: Vj and Vg (EB II), IVa and IVb (MBA), IIId (LBA IIa), IIc and IId (LBA IIb). In all other cases no burnt horizon marks the transition from one phase or level to another, and this applies not only to minor changes, from floor to floor, and changes within a level which involved architectural reconstruction, but also to the interface between clearly different levels, e.g. the end of IIIe to IIa. The vertical space occupied in our 12-m sequence by these six single events is disproportionate, and poses a question. Why were the burnt remnants of a destroyed building not cleared away before rebuilding on the site? Pragmatically, one would imagine that a competent builder would wish to clear his site down to a solid flat surface before starting on his new building.

Obviously various explanations could be considered. It is not beyond the bounds of possibility that a destruction was so considerable that the site was effectively abandoned for a long time, so that when it was reoccupied there was no memory of what lay beneath, and it appeared to be a homogeneous mound. However, we have no reason to suppose any long breaks in occupation until the Classical period, and even if this were true for the transition from Vj to Vi, or IVb to IIIa, it certainly cannot apply to IIc to IId. The builders of IId adopted the outline of the IIc Stele Building, and they built across the irregular debris of the burnt rooms. One imagines that any modern builder would be unhappy to lay floors across a surface which varied between hard-fired mudbrick walls and lumps of brick, loose burnt ashy soil, and even (in Rm 8) large empty jars still standing in position.

Moving back in time, it seems equally strange that when in the LBA the IIId building burnt down, tipping the NW wall into the courtyard and depositing a large uneven mass of brick and potsherds in the centre of it, this debris was simply left in place and the surrounding space packed with fill to give an even ground level for the IIIe reconstruction. Likewise in the MBA the walls and contents of Level IVa were left in place after the fire. Although the stubs of the walls of Rm 41 were shaved off at about 50–60 cm from the floor, 18 courses of loose toppled brickwork from its east wall were left above the burnt fill of the room as they had fallen — hardly an ideal substratum for a new building. With Vj in EB II the position is slightly different: here the burnt remains of the building were left in place, and heavily burned bricky material used to pack the space between the walls which stand up to 1 m. Above this, layers of packing were laid before the construction of the next phase (Vi), but not before at least one juvenile burial had been inserted over the destroyed walls.

That the treatment of buildings when no longer used might be charged with significance has been convincingly argued for Neolithic Anatolia by M. and A. Özdoğan (1998, 589–92). Here too it is hard to avoid the conclusion that the similarity of these examples is not entirely coincidental. Is it possible that in some cases destruction by fire was a deliberate valedictory act by the users of the building? Or do the surviving burnt strata attest to a long-standing tradition on how to treat the remnants of a building which had been destroyed by fire? It might be supposed that there was a taboo against recreating a building which had suffered a disaster, but this is not the place to pursue such speculation or to assemble comparable cases.[47]

Food production and consumption

The programme of quantitative analysis described below (p. 581) and published as an electronic archive (Matthews & Postgate 2001) involved the study of animal and plant remains and therefore of subsistence practices at the site. (For an overview of the botanical remains see Colledge (2001).) Individual finds of plant remains are studied below by Bending and Colledge in Chapter 49. Individual bone artefacts and animal bones are catalogued by Baker in Chapter 42; in addition to the animal bone studied as part of the quantitative analysis (Baker 2001), work is continuing on the much larger volume of material recovered during the routine processes of excavation.

Textile production

It is hard to avoid the impression that the production of textiles was always a major activity at Kilise Tepe. Spindle whorls are among the commonest artefacts in all levels (with the exception of Level III), and at the NW corner the groups of loomweights found in EB II, EB III, MB and Iron Age (IIe) contexts indicate that weaving was carried out here for a good 2000 years. Not enough of the architecture was recovered in any of these levels to allow us to say for sure whether the rooms or courtyards where the weights were found belonged to an ordinary domestic house or to something more approaching a workshop; only with IIe is there perhaps a hint of something more specialized.[48] The easy assumption is that there was normally a supply of wool from local flocks and that the population, and perhaps each individual household, were self-sufficient in basic textiles. An alternative would be to surmise that production was to some extent for export, and that the prevalence of weaving in the NW corner, which we guess was the elite end of the settlement, suggests that it was controlled by, and contributed to the status of, the local leaders. Our evidence is simply inadequate to choose between these broad alternatives, or to be sure of the significance of the absence of textile artefacts from Levels III and IIa–d, but the evidence of Classical writers shows that at times there was indeed an export industry for goat-hair products from Cilicia.

Roman authors (Columella, Pliny the Elder and Varro) tell us that 'the major exported commodities from Rough Cilicia were products derived from sheep and goats, in particular goats' hair cloth' (Hopwood 1991, 307). 'Cilician' was still the name of coarse goat-hair fabric in the third century AD and as late as Procopius. Flocks of goats are a familiar sight in the Göksu valley today, and the Sarıkeçili transhumants on the Taşeli plateau to the west mainly keep goats.[49] I am not aware of a surviving textile industry, although one occasionally sees a loom in domestic houses. The evidence of the animal bones at Kilise Tepe indicates that they outnumbered sheep (Baker 2001, goat:sheep at a proportion of 1.3:1). If this strengthens the conclusion that the residents of Kilise Tepe were regularly engaged in textile production, it must remain uncertain whether the flocks which produced the majority of their raw hair and wool came from flocks pastured permanently round the town, or moved with shepherds from transhumant tribes, and whether or not they owned the animals themselves as urban landlords (a practice attested in Roman times: Hopwood 1991, 307).

Ceramic production

Even when the ceramics at the site belong unequivocally to traditions well known from elsewhere — as with the LH IIIC Mycenaean vessels from Level IId, or the IIf kiln pottery with its parallels in Tarsus and Cyprus — it is only by technical analysis that we can determine whether or not they were locally produced. Thus the thin-section petrographic analysis is an essential part of our results, and there is no need to repeat Knappett's conclusions here (see Chapters 21–2). It was perhaps to be expected that most of our pottery at most periods was locally produced, and this underlines the abnormality of the Late Bronze Age situation. Even then, it appears that much of the pottery of Level III was locally produced, and although new painted wares make their appearance in Level III the clay sources do not seem to be new. It is very striking that hand-made painted wares make an appearance at Boğazköy in the levels immediately after the destruction, and these have been attributed to a re-assertion of earlier, perhaps local, traditions ('die auf die Früh- und Mittelbronzezeit zurückgehenden Keramiktraditionen': Genz 2000, 40). A similar phenomenon has also been observed in Greece at the end of the Bronze Age (Snodgrass 2002).

We have already referred to the historical and anthropological evidence for close links between settlements in the hills and the cities and ports of the plain, whether in the pre-Classical Iron Age, or in Hellenistic and Roman times, and these seem to be borne out by the evidence of the pottery. It is unsurprising that connections seem to be to the south, and only exceptionally in LBA through the Konya plain to the centre of Anatolia. In EB III Symington identifies a western Anatolian influence, but the Mycenaean finds from the thirteenth and twelfth centuries and the Cypriot style material with a handful of Geometric style sherds from the eighth–seventh century betray the expected Mediterranean links, as do the imported Hellenistic wares.

External relations

Imported pottery is also valuable as a possible by-product of Kilise Tepe's role as a way station on a trade route from the Mediterranean littoral to the centre of Anatolia. This must surely be valid at those times when there was an active trading enterprise supplying the centre, but we must acknowledge that at times, such as the eighth century when central Anatolia was dominated by Phrygia, there is precious little evidence for links between the central plateau and the East Mediterranean. It seems possible that the Göksu valley participated in the seaward culture of Cilicia to the exclusion of an inland connection. Of course it is true that absence of ceramic evidence is not evidence of absence of traders, as the example of Kültepe proves, and it seems unlikely that there was no traffic from the Konya plain to the Mediterranean in the Middle Bronze Age.[50]

The most characteristic evidence of trade, other than texts, would be sealings, found in quantities at major sites like Karahöyük (Konya). A few small fragments of sealing (**1480–83**) were recovered at Kilise Tepe, enough to confirm that the practice was present at the site but not to allow us to suggest what had been sealed or by whom.

Notes

1. Mellaart published one sherd he characterizes as Chalcolithic (1954, 184 no. 79), but no other sherds identifiable as Chalcolithic turned up in the course of our total clearance of the surface (see Chapter 6), and to judge from the drawing it could well belong to our Level II painted tradition, which includes hand-made pieces (and was of course unknown before we began excavating).
2. Parts of this section are adapted from our first report on Kilise Tepe in *Anatolian Studies* (Baker *et al.* 1995).
3. For a recent vote in favour of Karahöyük (Konya) = Purušhattum see Hawkins 1995, 51 n. 176.
4. For connections with the Konya plain see e.g. Symington, below Chapter 23.
5. My thanks to Dorit Symington for pointing this out to me, see e.g. Freu 2001, 25–36; Jasink 2001, 52–3.
6. See for instance Desideri & Jasink 1990, 82–3. Boundaries can be very tenacious despite political change. This line seems to correspond closely to the western limit of Cilicia Pedias in Roman times (see e.g. Mitford 1980, 1241; later perhaps further west, see p. 1248). For the possibility that the Neriglissar chronicle refers to the River Lamos as the limit of Babylonian-held Cilicia see Houwink ten Cate 1961, 17; but note that the river's name is not mentioned in the Chronicle.
7. A similar argument applies to the toponym Saliya which occurs in the Sunassura treaty and in the Bronze Tablet: see Symington 2001, 174.
8. For a detailed discussion of the geography as illuminated by the Bronze Tablet see Hawkins 1995, 49–53.
9. Reported in Bahar *et al.* 1996, 42–5 with Levha I–II and X–XV; for the text see Dinçol 1998.
10. The Emirgazi altars were found at a site some 115 km due east of Konya. For the text see Hawkins 1995, 86ff.
11. The thorny question of Ura's location has not been helped by the Bronze Treaty Tablet. Beal 1992b proposes Kelenderis (= Gilindere = Aydıncık). This is a prime natural harbour (see Zoroğlu 1994) and the identification has its attractions, but like Hawkins in Baker *et al.* 1995, 148, I am not sure they outweigh its drawbacks. It seems certain that Meydancık was not Tarhuntassa, no pre-Classical levels are yet reported from Aydıncık, for which in any case the town of Saranduwa listed in the Bronze Treaty provides at least as plausible a candidate (Gurney 1997, 138). Ura in the second millennium need not be the same as the place mentioned by Neriglissar which seems to be located in mountains. Note the comment of Laroche that Ura' 'signifie "grand(e)"...' (in Lemaire & Lozachmeur 1987, 382).
12. But see Jasink 2001, and Dinçol *et al.* 2000; 2001, who bring the SE border of Tarhuntassa much further to the west than earlier scholars, running almost straight through Kilise Tepe (map in Dinçol *et al.* 2001). One advantage of this would be to permit Ura, if at the western end of the Cilician plain, to fall under direct Hittite administration in the thirteenth century when it was acting as a major port for grain imports.
13. Hawkins 2002, 148.
14. Discussed in Houwink ten Cate 1961, 44–50, though note that since then the Madduwattas texts have been re-dated to the fourteenth century and are hardly pertinent.
15. The evidence has often been presented, e.g. in Houwink ten Cate 1961, 17–44; Desideri & Jasink 1990; Zoroğlu 1994; and most recently Hawkins 2000, I/1, 41ff. Since then we also have the colossal bilingual statue of Urikki from Çineköy near Adana (Tekoğlu & Lemaire 2000).
16. The toponym Kizzuwatna does survive into the ninth century, being mentioned by Shalmaneser III as a stronghold within the territory of Quwe (Grayson 1996, 55 iv.27).
17. As indicated by Kataja & Whiting 1995, no. 51:5 where lands in Quwe are included in a grant similar to those of Assur-etelli-ilani, the last Assyrian king.
18. The title LÚ.EN.URU is not to be read *hazannu* as in some earlier transcriptions, and was used by the Assyrians to refer to local rulers who did not qualify as 'kings', e.g. of the Median chieftains.
19. Though often identified with Namrun (Byz. Lampron), see Desideri & Jasink 1990, 126; the idea of Forlanini cited there that it might be Soli/Pompeiopolis on the coast seems unlikely to me, as in my view the text of Sennacherib implies that Kirua was himself of Hilakku.
20. Lemaire & Lozachmeur 1987, 368ff., also in Davesne & Laroche-Traunecker 1998, 307–27.
21. Unless of course Ura' is identical with second-millennium Ura, as assumed in Beal 1992b but by no means, to my mind, certain (see note 11 above).
22. For Neo-Assyrian evidence at Tarsus cf. Desideri & Jasink 1990, 145. For Hellenistic times, Houwink ten Cate 1961. In the Roman period in coastal settlements belonging to Cilicia Tracheia, including Corycus (Kızkalesi) the onomasticon is still 'overwhelmingly Luwian' (Mitford 1980, 1255).
23. See most recently Tekoğlu & Lemaire 2000, 1005–6.
24. See Zoroğlu 1994, esp. 21–4 for the Greek connections of Kelenderis.
25. See French 1992, 172–3, citing the archive of the Alexandrian Zenon, who lived in Alexandria (but was a native of Caria).
26. Cribb 1991, chap. 7; Cribb shows that such groups need only be families with a long-term village base who have adopted a transhumant mode elsewhere in the response to the economics of animal husbandry.
27. The end of the Late Roman and the start of the Early Byzantine period cannot be fixed by a date *per se*. 'It is quite correct to argue that the last emperor of the Romans died in 1453 when the Turks stormed Constantinople. However this has the danger of implying a degree of continuity between the empire of 600 and that of 1000 (let alone that of 1400) which did not exist. Hence I think it more helpful to term the empire after the mid-seventh century the "Byzantine empire"' (Whittow 1996, 97). Others argue for the start of the Early Byzantine period in the fifth century (Dark 2001, 7). This chapter will broadly follow this terminology but will

examine the Göksu from the fourth century through to the eleventh.

28. Topics in this chapter are discussed in more detail in the author's PhD thesis (Jackson 2001).

29. In the fourth century, Seleuceia (Silifke), the capital city of Byzantine Isauria located near the mouth of the Calycadnus, became the seat of the Metropolitan archbishop of the province. It was also the base for the military governor a *dux et praeses* or *comes* from the early fourth century until the sixth century, and continued to be a major military fortress in later centuries (J. Matthews 1989, 357), as well as the base of the Byzantine naval fleet *Kibyrrhaiotai* against the Arabs (Brooks 1901, 71). As a port, on the Mediterranean coast of Asia Minor, also located close to Cyprus, Seleuceia benefited from trade across the eastern Mediterranean and therefore belonged to the series of cities and towns that grew prosperous during the late Roman period along the southern coast of Asia Minor.

    80 km inland to the NNW of Seleuceia, Isauria's second city Claudiopolis (Mut) was also located at another strategic position, guarding the juncture of at least five major routes in the central Taurus. Neither of these ancient cities has been excavated extensively but limited archaeological evidence available from both suggests that, in the Roman period, they had been furnished with many of the trappings of a provincial Roman city including colonnaded streets and monumental buildings (Mitchell 1979, 428; Keil & Wilhelm 1931, Taf. 3; Topçu 1984).

30. Following the condemnation of Arianism at the Council of Nicaea in AD 325, 24 Isaurian bishops gathered at Seleuceia for the synod in AD 359 which met to resolve the continuing Arian dispute (Hild & Hellenkemper 1990, 86). At least 11 attended the Council of Constantinople in AD 381, following which Seleuceia became the metropolis (Ramsay 1890, facing 362). The Isaurians were also clearly affected by the Monophysite disputes of the fifth and sixth centuries. Basil of Seleuceia backed by 16 Isaurian bishops was outspoken against the Monophysites in the mid fifth century (Hild & Hellenkemper 1990, 87). The Isaurian Emperor Zeno (AD 474–81) himself was a Monophysite and by the early sixth century, the fact that Johannes of Klaudiopolis is recorded as the only bishop in Isauria to have stood against Severos of Antioch on the side of Orthodoxy demonstrates the strength of Monophysite influence in the diocese by that time. The Orthodox emperor Justin I finally banished 9 out of 12 Monophysite bishops from Isauria following the death of his Monophysite predecessor Anastasius (Severos of Antioch, 6 Ep. 1.52). These disputes flared again in AD 533 when Eugenios was ordained Bishop of Seleuceia by the instigator of the Jacobite Monophysite doctrine Baradais (Hild & Hellenkemper 1990, 89–90).

31. The footings of this stone bridge and the remains in the river, possibly noted by Wilson (1895, 180) were surveyed at the end of the 1998 excavation season by the author. Another ruined bridge was also observed on the river near Evkafçiftliği.

32. It should be noted also that similar arguments have been proposed for other structures from elsewhere in Asia Minor, for example the Church of St John the theologian at Alaşehir, Philadelphia, in Phrygia (Buchwald 1981).

33. It is interesting to note however that Egeria did not take the Calycadnus pass but retraced her journey back along the coast to travel inland via Tarsus and the Cilician gates (Wilkinson 1971, 123).

34. Which might provide a valuable source of information, for dating the cemetery, and for the pathologies of the local population.

35. These were kindly conserved, photographed and catalogued for the author by Franca Cole, Bronwyn Douglas and John Tanner respectively (Jackson 1999b, 26).

36. This measures 1.20×0.90 m, and was a maximum of 0.80 m deep, with a small channel cut through the south lip, and a small niche ($25 \times 15 \times 15$ cm carved into the middle of the back side (see Fig. 14).

37. This measures $c. 4 \times 2$ m, was 0.40 m deep at the back, and showed no sign of a channel.

38. This is not the place to engage in discussion of the terminology of Bronze and Iron Age, a topic which was addressed in detail at a conference on Iron Age chronologies organized by Prof. A. Çilingiroğlu at Izmir in May 2005. We have retained here these broad 'Ages', even though in current usage the Iron Age seems to take over from the Bronze Age about a century earlier at Boğazköy than at Tarsus, but as far as possible I have refrained from using the terms 'Early Iron Age' or 'Middle Iron Age', since here again the transition from one to the next is placed at different times at different sites, and at Tarsus, which it would be logical for us to follow in view of its relative proximity, the criteria for differentiating the two phases seem vague and their absolute chronology uncertain.

39. This is partly because the commonly accepted chronology of Mycenaean ceramics is, like the dating of the end of the Bronze Age in Anatolia, ultimately dependent on Egyptian chronology. The date of 1190 BC conventionally accepted as the approximate date of the destruction of Hattusa can safely be used in conjunction with the prevalent dating of Mycenaean pottery because if one needs to be shifted, the other will shift with it.

40. This short statement should be read in conjunction with the discussion in Part D on pp. 343ff.

41. For a description of the evidence for this event, see Bittel 1983, 26–8. The revised interpretation of the archaeological evidence for the destruction offered by Seeher 2001 does not significantly affect its general association with the fall of the empire.

42. Principally the entirely new architectural layout, and the introduction of the new red-painted pottery, a phenomenon which is not well attested at Tarsus or Kinet, and appears to post-date the Hittite Empire elsewhere. Note also that pieces of libation arm, whether in Red Lustrous Wheel-Made ware or another fabric, do not persist as a regular component of the ceramic assemblage after Level III.

43. For Tarsus, see at length Forsberg 1995, 51–81. The most telling point is that there is no evidence that Sennacherib's army 'destroyed' the city (the most that is said is

that they 'conquered' the cities of Ingira and Tarsus and 'carried off their plunder'). See now also the redating of the Destruction Level at Gordion, formerly linked to historical references to a Cimmerian invasion around 700 BC, by about a century to *c.* 800 BC (De Vries *et al.* 2003).
44. Note for instance Tille Höyük where the principal destruction layer is presently assigned to the late twelfth century (Blaylock 1999; Summers 1993); or Fraktin (cf. Drews 1993; Bittel 1983, 31 & 34).
45. For floor surfaces at Kilise Tepe, both plastered and not, as observed in micro-morphological thin section see W. Matthews 2001, §9.
46. One exception is in I14 and J14 (see pp. 179–80 on units 3421–2 and 3314). The Level Ic cobbled surface in K18b is no exception, since it belonged to an exterior space.
47. Compare, nearer to Kilise Tepe in time and space, similar situations at Tarsus (Goldman 1956, 347) and at Porsuk in the LBA.
48. Unless the 40+ 'notched pins' (**2469**) from a pit in the IIc Stele Building were also used in textile production.
49. According to Bazin 1991, 249; see also Cribb 1991, 117: a 'commercial herd' of mixed sheep and goats, but a 'subsistence herd' of goats only.
50. It seems unlikely that the Göksu valley was a route used by the merchants from Assur. If it was, it would have been to reach Karahöyük (Konya), but in fact we know from the archives that incoming trade was channelled through Kanesh even when it was aimed at the other major cities of the interior such as Purušhanda, Wahšušana or Wašhania.

Part B

The Surface Collection

Chapter 6 **The Surface Collection**   **45**
   Theory behind surface collection   45
   Surface surveys in the Near East   45
   Distorting factors   47
   Methodology employed at Kilise Tepe   48
   Data analysis methodology   49
   Presentation of the data   50
   Statistical analysis   51
   Summary statistics   52
   Correlation analysis   52
   Artefact distributions   52
   Initial results of the surface collection   61
   Conclusions   61

Chapter 6

The Surface Collection

D.C. Thomas[1]

Theory behind surface collection

The repeated, but not necessarily continuous, occupation of sites in regions where mud bricks have been the primary building material for millennia results in artificial mounds acquiring distinctive morphologies. Thus, although fieldwalking, geophysical surveys and aerial and satellite photography are increasingly being used to enable a more comprehensive analysis of archaeological landscapes (Banning 2002; Philip *et al.* 2002; Summers & Summers 1998; Ur 2002; 2003), mounded urban settlements (known as höyük/hüyük, tell or tepe in the Near East), are the most readily recognizable archaeological sites.

Through time, two general types of mound are formed — sealed tells and shelved tells (Rosen 1986, 47). Sealed tells develop when the top of the mound is occupied to its full extent. As the mound becomes higher and its edges steeper, buildings tend to be constructed slightly in from the edge. The occupied surface area thus decreases through time, sealing the earlier deposits.

As Baird (1996, 42) notes, however, the extent of the area occupied during different periods often varies, so that one or more parts of the mound may become higher than others. Köseli, a site surveyed by the Konya Plains Survey, is a good example of such 'shelved' tells — it covered 1.5 ha in the EB I–II periods, but decreased in size to 0.8 ha in the Iron Age.

Datable and diagnostic surface material often indicate the periods of occupation, varying spatial extent of occupation and differential use of space at a site, although a simple relationship rarely exists between surface artefacts and sub-surface features (Binford 1972, 179). Archaeologists now readily accept that the haphazard collection of artefacts on the surface is unlikely to yield a representative sample from a site, particularly from a palimpsest. Consequently, increased emphasis has been placed upon methodical surface collection, sample size and site-formation processes, in an attempt to maximize the amount of information that could be gleaned from surface survey data. Optimum areas for excavation may then be highlighted (Green 1993, 2–3), although Binford has argued that without a programme of stratified sampling and/or a prior knowledge of the culture history of a site, '... densities of items cannot be used as a guide to excavation' (Binford 1972, 164).

Surface surveys in the Near East

Numerous unsystematic archaeological surveys have been conducted in the Near East, those of particular relevance to Kilise Tepe being by Mellaart, French and Hall in the Konya plain (Mellaart 1961; 1963; French 1970) and by Mellaart and French in the Göksu valley (D. French 1965). A new survey in the Göksu valley is currently being directed by Hugh Elton of BIAA (Elton 2002b).

French visited Kilise Tepe (under the mistaken name of Maltepe) three times in the course of 1963/64 and noted tunnelling activity by treasure-seekers (D. French 1965, 179–80). He was primarily interested in prehistoric material and collected and classified a varied assemblage of EB and second-millennium wares and types. No Neolithic or Chalcolithic sherds were found (D. French 1965, 186) and no mention was made of Classical sherds although, given the depth of Byzantine deposits found during our excavations, they must have been visible on the surface.

Other more innovative surface surveys were conducted in the late 1960s in Turkey: at the site of Ayngerm in southeast Anatolia (Whallon 1980) and at Çayönü and Girik-i-Haciyan (Redman & Watson 1970) — see Table 3. Both surveys collected a *c.* 10 per cent sample of the surface artefacts and displayed the data as contour maps in an attempt to convey the changing distribution of sherds through time.

Contrary to Binford, Redman & Watson found a strong relationship between surface and sub-surface artefact distributions for the first 50 cm of deposits in their test excavations. They also noted that areas of high concentrations of surface material usually reflect

Table 3. *Summary of a selection of previous surface surveys and collections in the Near East.*

Site	Period	Approx. site size	No. of squares	Size of squares	Area collected	No. of artefacts	Comments/Conclusions
Çayönü, Turkey	Pre-ceramic	250 m max.	83	5 × 5 m	2100 m² 10%	c. 15,000	Simple random sample
Ayngerm, Turkey	Prehistoric	200 × 125 m	99	5 × 5 m	2475 m² 10%	n.a.	Revealed sealed aceramic deposits
Tepe Yahya, Iran	fifth mill. BC–first AD mill.	180 m diam.	2	variable	13.5 m²	268	Also 'off-site' collection; disproportionate 'late' material
Girik-i-Haciyan, Turkey	Halafian	250 m max.	109	5 × 5 m	2725 m² 10%	c. 15,000	Stratified unaligned systematic sample
Çatalhöyük East, Turkey	Neolithic–Byzantine	13.5 ha	298	2 × 2 m	1192 m² 1%	23,585	Wall lines revealed; sampled squares' deposits sieved
Çatalhöyük West, Turkey	Chalcolithic	8.5 ha	213	2 × 2 m	852 m² 1%	20,953	Wall lines revealed; sampled squares' deposits sieved
Kilise Tepe, Turkey	EBA–Byzantine	170 × 140 m	219	10 × 10 m	21,900 m² 90%	c. 48,000	Total collection from much of tepe surface
Uruk, Iraq	Ubaid–Parthian?	480 ha	n.a.?	20 × 20 m (min.)	430 ha 90%	n.a.	Used distribution maps to investigate the layout of the city
Abu Salabikh Main, Iraq	Early Dynastic	16.8 ha	210	10 × 10 m	21,000 m² 20%	not stated	Much of city plan traced
Abu Salabikh West, Iraq	third–fourth mill.	250 × 190 m	106	10 × 10 m	10,600 m² 20%	not stated	Much of city plan traced

disturbed sub-surface deposits (Redman & Watson 1970, 285). Thus, if archaeologists want to excavate well-preserved, *in situ* features close to the surface, they should avoid dense concentrations of surface artefacts, rather than necessarily be drawn to them.

Whallon concluded from his fieldwork that surface collection tells the archaeologist little on its own, although at Ayngerm it did yield an interesting insight into the nature of the tepe. The contour maps showed that flint and obsidian were concentrated along the periphery of the mound. Whallon argued that differential displacement by run-off or gravity could not explain the lack of sherds in these areas. He suggested that these lithics were eroding from an aceramic layer which was buried beneath later, ceramic period deposits on the top of the mound (Whallon 1980, 216).

The importance of mound structure was also demonstrated by the surface collection at Tepe Yahya, in Iran (Vidali *et al.* 1976). Artefacts were collected from two squares on the tepe and from 3 × 3 m squares at 50-m intervals on twelve radials running from the site. Of the sherds collected from the top of the tepe, 78 per cent (209 sherds) belonged to what they classified as later periods (750 BC–AD 700), whereas only 34 per cent (430 sherds) of the sherds from the radial collections were assigned to these later periods. This over-representation of the later periods among the site sherds is even starker given their estimate that 90 per cent of Tepe Yahya's mound accumulated between mid fifth–early second millennium BC (Vidali *et al.* 1976, 241, 245).

In the mid-1980s large-scale surface surveys were carried out at several sites in Iraq. At Uruk, the whole of the undisturbed surface of the site was surveyed (Finkbeiner 1991). The 480-ha size of the site, however, meant that detailed recovery and spatial coverage had to be balanced. Artefacts were collected from 20-m squares across much of the site, but where sediments overlay the ancient surface and artefacts were scarce, 100-m squares were used.

Finkbeiner and his colleagues hoped to investigate the nature and layout of the city through time, by plotting the distribution of artefacts and pottery. Particular attention was paid to industrial waste. Much of the recording occurred in the field, with only artefacts deemed to be of particular interest receiving more attention. While recognizing the constraints and their achievement, Postgate has argued that their methodology would have been stronger, had they kept a proportion of the collected artefacts as control samples (Postgate 1994, 292).

Stone's research into the anatomy of a Mesopotamian city (Mashkan-shapir/Tell Abu Duwari) also suffers from the fact that sherds were only recorded in the field (Stone 1994; Stone & Zimansky 2004). Tell Abu Duwari is a 72-ha, single period site, dating to the early second millennium BC and has an estimated 3 million sherds on its surface. Stone decided that the massive task of collecting and storing even a proportion of the surface sherds would be relatively uninformative, although their distribution might be informative. The distribution was investigated using 50-m squares. Linear concentrations of sherds were interpreted as resulting from the dumping of garbage in streets and thus helped to define the layout of the city.

Surface survey techniques were advanced by work at the sites of Abu Salabikh (Postgate 1983, 3–18; Matthews & Postgate 1987) and Jemdat Nasr in Iraq (Matthews 1989). Teams of workmen collected all objects lying on the surface from 10-m squares, removed loose soil and then scraped the surface clean. Wall lines often became apparent after *c*. 10 cm of deposits had been scraped away, allowing the archaeologists to draw tentative, but detailed plans of the layout of buildings close to the surface of these sites, without significantly disturbing the archaeological deposits. The surface and sub-surface finds could then be interpreted in relation to defined spatial units.

In the mid-1990s, these techniques were refined and applied to the site of Çatalhöyük, in Turkey (Matthews 1996a, 73–5; 1996b, 79–81). In addition to large-scale scraping, the absolute densities of artefacts and their relative frequencies were investigated. Dense vegetation was cleared from 2 × 2 m squares at 20-m intervals across the site; 36 litres of surface earth was then collected and put through a 5-mm sieve. Differences emerged between the East and West mounds at Çatalhöyük. On the East Mound, which dates to the Neolithic period but has a high concentration of post-Neolithic occupation in the southeast, 54 per cent of the artefacts were sherds, whereas on the predominantly Chalcolithic West Mound, 82 per cent of the artefacts were sherds. Bone fragments were twice as common per square metre on the East Mound than on the West. Matthews suggests that these differences may be explained by increased use of pottery in the Chalcolithic period and the differential treatment of refuse through time (Matthews 1996a, 75–6).

Distorting factors

The morphology of a mound can affect the remnants of material culture found on the site's surface, as much as the nature and history of its occupation. 'As the topographic form is gradually flattened, potsherds move downslope and initially concentrate around the lower periphery of a mound...' (Rosen 1986, xiii).

Mound slopes consist of a variety of aspects, lengths and gradients, and thus experience different erosional processes; these largely consist of natural weathering, and attrition by gravity and water run-off. Rosen noted, however, that many mounds in Mesopotamia have steep northwest faces and gentle southeast slopes. She concluded that this was a result of the prevailing winds and associated rainfall patterns. Soil creep occurs more on the exposed face, whereas run-off affects the gentler slopes, which also tend to be better vegetated and therefore more stable. Artefacts collecting at the base of a mound may then be re-buried by silts, some derived from the run-off from the mound — a mound should, therefore, be thought of as part of a dynamic system of erosion and deposition.

The structure of the mound and its stage of evolution are other significant factors. Settlements with perimeter walls tend to form mounds with steeper sides. They will erode less quickly than other mounds, although marked changes in slope and increased erosion may occur at breaches in the walls and at former gateways.

Human agency can also affect a mound and its surface artefacts, in a variety of ways through time. On palimpsests, repeated occupation of the site may protect earlier archaeological deposits. More often, however, buried deposits are disturbed by later occupants of the site digging storage and refuse pits, graves and pits to extract stone and earth for mud bricks. The speculative digging for precious artefacts at archaeological sites is another common, age-old practice.

Long after the abandonment of a site, the land may be cultivated. Ploughing can bring artefacts to the surface, as well as bury them, resulting in a mixed ploughsoil deposit and the disturbance of sub-surface features to a depth of up to 30–50 cm. Many fields in the Near East are still ploughed perpendicular to the slope, thus creating downslope channels, concentrating run-off and increasing erosion. Different ploughing strategies and frequencies may result in significant and variable displacement of artefacts.

The surface artefacts and their distribution are also directly affected by other well-documented natural and cultural agencies (Redman & Watson 1970, 280; Schiffer 1987; Wood & Johnson 1978; Postgate 1983, 8–10). Faunal turbation — animal burrowing — may bring artefacts to the surface and contaminate deposits (Hardy-Smith & Edwards 2004, 267–71), while carnivores may gnaw, displace and add to faunal remains exposed on the surface. Human visitors often pick up, keep, move and/or drop artefacts, as well as disturbing them unwittingly merely by wandering across the site. Finally, the physical characteristics of the artefact — its size, shape, weight, durability and visibility — will also affect its distribution, survival and subsequent chances of collection.

Chapter 6

Figure 16. *Surface of L14, before surface collection.*

The work of numerous archaeological projects, particularly since the 1960s, has highlighted the variety of approaches it is possible to take when looking at surface materials. Perhaps their greatest achievement has been to turn surface material into a resource in itself, adding a less destructive element to the analysis of archaeological data, particularly in a regional context. Such studies have also demonstrated that although surface material can yield a useful insight into the unexposed deposits at a site, no simple relationship exists between the two. A wide variety of natural and cultural influences have to be considered when attempting to interpret the distributions of surface artefacts.

Methodology employed at Kilise Tepe

In the light of the various approaches to surface material outlined above, the surface of Kilise Tepe was systematically cleared of artefacts during the 1994 and 1995 seasons. Our aims were to analyse the distribution of ceramics, stones and other artefacts lying on the surface, to record any surface marks and to gain a preview of the buried cultural assemblage. We hoped to discover whether any correlations exist between the exposed remains of human activity, surface marks and sub-surface features and to provide comparative material, should surface surveys be conducted at other sites in the Göksu valley or further afield.

The relatively small size of the tepe (measuring c. 120 × 100 m, N–S × E–W, across the top) allowed us to dispense with designing a sampling strategy and to collect all the exposed material culture on the accessible parts of the tepe. The first season's surface collection concentrated upon the top of the tepe (Thomas, in Baker *et al.* 1995, 149–51), while in 1995, the surface collection area was extended to the tepe's southern and eastern flanks (Fig. 16), the northern and western slopes being too precipitous to be practical to survey.

A contour survey of the tepe was made by Tom Pollard and an arbitrary grid of 10 × 10 m squares was set up (Fig. 17; Pollard, in Baker *et al.* 1995, 148–9). Before beginning the collection in each square, the supervisor sketched any surface marks, depressions, slopes, etc. onto a 'scrape sheet' at the scale of 1:100, and added any general comments about the square. These often included a subjective appraisal of the density of the stone coverage in the square (light, medium or dense) and a comment on the vegetation cover.

A process of trial and error revealed that the most efficient way of conducting the surface collection was to use a team of five or six workmen and one supervisor in each square. The surface material was scraped into small piles and then sorted by hand onto sacks, to ease its subsequent transfer into wheelbarrows (Fig. 18). All ceramic sherds were collected in labelled baskets and washed. Stones were regarded as potential indicators of sub-surface structures. They were divided into piles of large stones (>15 cm) and small stones (<15 cm); any worked or decorated stones were kept. The number of large stones was then counted and a rough estimate of the volume of large and small stones was recorded, using level wheelbarrow loads as the unit of measurement.

Initially, all unusual stones and objects were collected. Many of these were later discarded as amorphous lumps of rock, but the procedure encouraged the workmen and supervisors to be vigilant. Before each pile of stones was emptied into the wheelbarrow, the supervisor checked through it for any missed sherds and artefacts. The workmen were generally quick to recognize sherds, but occasionally missed larger pieces of pottery and fragments of tiles. On a good day, a team of workmen could clear the surface of 10 squares (1000 m^2).

Several unavoidable factors affected the consistency of the surface collection. Supervisors and workmen inevitably differed in their practices and thoroughness, but the general procedure and recording technique applied across the mound were designed to compensate for this. The greater the stone density, the harder it was to clean the surface and to maintain concentration, although fears of disturbing scorpions among the stones were largely unfounded. Dense thistle coverage hampered the recovery of ceramics and small artefacts, while the time of day and position of the sun affected the visibility of surface marks. The effects of these variables, however, appear to be minimal and the fact that some of the surface marks join up strengthens their potential significance, given that they were noted independently, square by square and not in a general sweep across the mound.

The methodology changed slightly between 1994 and 1995. In 1995, only the number of large stones, and not the number of wheelbarrow loads of large stones, was counted. Surface marks on slopes were deemed to be less informative than those on the top of the tepe because they would probably relate to short stretches of walls from different periods, rather than to coherent buildings. They were thus ignored in 1995. Excavations in 1994 also showed that a largely featureless 20–30 cm of topsoil/ploughsoil lay immediately below the surface over much of the site. This disturbed layer prevented the tracing of mudbrick and plaster lines which was achieved with such success at Abu Salabikh, Jemdat Nasr and Çatalhöyük. The plans of several stone structures were, however, revealed by sub-surface scrapes — see Fig. 508 and Figs. 19, 184 & 185).

In total, 129 squares on the top of Kilise Tepe and a further 90 squares on the slopes were cleared in 1994 and 1995. The total area cleared was 21,900 m², and about 57,500 surface sherds were processed by Dominique Collon.

Data analysis methodology

The imperfect and challenging nature of a lot of archaeological data is well documented and discussed (see Clarke 1973; Schiffer 1987; Shanks & Tilley 1992; among others). As we have seen, surface collection data are not exempt from these issues; in fact, they are potentially more difficult to interpret than excavated material.

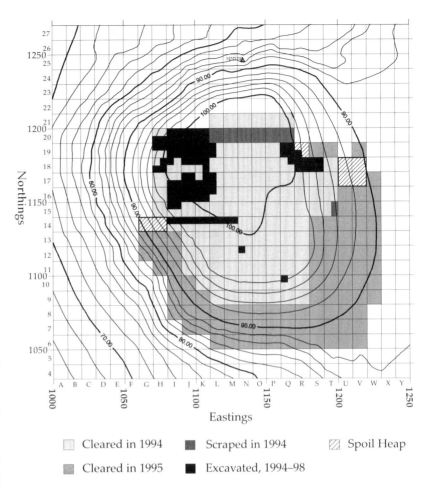

Figure 17. *Kilise Tepe: areas worked 1994–98. 10-m squares.*

Figure 18. *Centre of tepe after surface collection.*

Figure 19. *Byzantine foundations in L20 to O20 after sub-surface clearance.*

Not only do the biases inherent in surface data, therefore, have to be considered, but also biases imposed upon the data by archaeologists' choices of collection strategy, classification criteria and analytical techniques. When 'total' collection is attempted, the most fundamental of these biases is that of classification criteria.

'The adequacy of a survey, then, depends in part on the surveyor's perception of the importance of certain classes of archaeological data' (Plog *et al.* 1978, 386). Each person will approach the classification of an assemblage of artefacts differently, depending upon their experience, knowledge, personal preferences and idiosyncrasies. This is particularly so with a ceramic assemblage.

At Tepe Yahya, attempts were made to test the consistency of Lamberg-Karlovsky's pottery classifications by submitting random batches for re-classification, with acceptable results (Vidali *et al.* 1976, 238). This approach, while satisfying the reader of Lamberg-Karlovsky's level of consistency, does nothing to address the problem of consistent inaccuracies in classification. Although diagnostic sherds may be illustrated, projects often discard the majority of surface artefacts after classification, due to storage constraints, thus making any future re-assessment of their assemblages impossible — Adams, for example, adopted this strategy during his influential, extensive surveys in Iraq (Adams 1981); similarly, the surveys at Uruk and Mashkan-shapir classified sherds in the field rather than collect and store them (Finkbeiner 1991; Stone 1994).

Since subjective classifications and artefact discard are likely to remain archaeological realities, a project should state its methodology clearly, openly admit any apparent limitations and weaknesses and make available as much of the data as possible, in an attempt to allow other researchers to assess the validity of the conclusions.

All the surface pottery from Kilise Tepe was kept and washed. Diagnostic sherds were then selected and recorded. The classification of the Kilise Tepe surface collection sherds was initially conducted by Dorit Symington. Dominique Collon later took over sole responsibility for the classification of the surface collection material (from unit 183 on). She went through Symington's records to standardize terminology and re-examined the sherds extracted from the units, to check for consistency.

Presentation of the data

Counts and distributions have been collated for the following temporal and typological categories (followed by their abbreviations), which were used in Tables 4–5 and Figs. 21–38:

    Early Bronze Age Wares - EBA
    Red Hittite Wares - RH
    Iron Age Wares - IA
    Hellenistic Wares - Hellen
    Terra Sigillata Wares (real and imitation) - TS
    Late Roman/Byzantine Plain Wares - Rom./Byz.
    Painted Sherds - Paint
    Trefoil Rim Sherds - Trefoil

The ceramic assemblage is considered in more detail in Part D. The following brief notes (after Collon, in Baker *et al.* 1995) are merely intended to expand slightly on the categories chosen:

- Little material attributable to the Middle Bronze Age was found among the surface sherds. This period is well represented among the excavated sherds, thus discounting the impression of a hiatus in occupation that the surface collection gives.
- The most distinctive ware of the Late Bronze Age is a dense red fabric, self-slipped and polished or burnished — Red Hittite Wares.
- An apparent gap in the sequence occurs between the Middle Iron Age and the Hellenistic period, but this may be because wares between *c.* 600–300 BC have not been recognized. Iron Age parallels were taken from Tarsus (Goldman 1963).
- The Hellenistic wares were relatively distinctive and seemed to belong predominantly to the third–second centuries BC. Types included Bowls,

Kraters, Skyphoi, Fish Plates, Unguentaria, Flasks and Jars.
- Roman fine wares were largely absent from the surface collection assemblage, with the exception of a few, fragmented Terra Sigillata/imitation sherds.
- Late Roman/Byzantine plain and cooking wares are often difficult to differentiate from other cooking wares. There were no close parallels with either cooking wares from Alahan (Williams 1985) or with the mid-seventh-century Byzantine pottery from Anemurium (Williams 1977). Numerous sherds of locally painted pottery, similar in style to some of those found at Alahan and Dağ Pazarı, were found.
- The surface sherd assemblage included very little material recognizable as post-Byzantine. One possible exception is the presence of heavy jar, or even pithos, sherds with incised and impressed decoration. Some of these are published by Collon (Baker *et al.* 1995, 170–72); items 13:4–9 in particular seem to represent a ware which we did not encounter in the excavations, although without parallels it would be premature to conclude that it must be late.
- The number of sherds which could be assigned to temporal periods in 1994/5 was low. If the surface collection assemblage was re-classified in the light of five seasons of excavations, however, it would probably be possible to assign a larger proportion of sherds to a general period of occupation. Limited time and resources have prevented us from doing this.

Data were also collected for the following, more general categories in each square:
- Small Stones (number of wheelbarrow loads) - SSWB;
- Large Stones (counts) - LS;
- Total Sherds (recorded to the nearest 50) - TotSh;
- Total Diagnostic Sherds (totals of the above temporal and typological categories) - TotDiag;
- Decorated Sherds (including painted ones) - DecoSh;
- Feature Sherds (rims, handles, bases, etc.) - FeatSh;
- Tile Fragments - Tile;
- Drain Fragments (presence/absence) - Drain[2];
- Knapped lithics - Lithic;
- Stone Processing Tools (grindstones, pounders, querns, etc.) - Grind;
- Bone and Shell (presence/absence) - Bone;
- Metal Fragments - Metal;
- Architectural Fragments (dressed stone, bricks, pieces of marble, etc.) - Arch;
- Miscellaneous Artefacts (glass, figurines, clinker, spindle whorls, stamped sherds, etc.) - Misc.

These categories were refined after classification, in the light of the resultant data. Several small categories were discarded since they included too few finds to be significant — Metal and Misc, for example. The stone artefact categories Lithic and Grind were amalgamated into a single stone artefact category — StTool. A bag of bones was collected from virtually every square. Bones exposed on the surface are often fragmentary, relatively modern, badly weathered and affected by animal activity — it was therefore decided to ignore them in our analysis.

Refinements to our methodology between 1994 and 1995 meant that we counted the Total numbers of Sherds (TotSh) in 1995, rather than estimating numbers (by the number of *sepet* loads), as in 1994. Numbers of Tiles were quantified by bucket-load (*c.* 40 buckets in total) in 1994, whereas the actual number of tiles (over 350) was counted in 1995: Tile data were therefore omitted from the statistical analysis, as were the presence/absence Drain data.

Statistical analysis

The surface collection data were collated onto Microsoft *Excel* spreadsheets. This allowed basic statistical analysis to be performed upon the data and eased its transferral into Golden Software's *Surfer32* programme, which was used to produce the surface distributions. The use of a GIS package such as *IDRISI* was considered, but we decided that this type of analysis was unlikely to produce significant results at Kilise Tepe and therefore did not justify the extra investment of time and effort.

Tables 4 and 5 show the Summary Statistics and Correlation Analysis results. They are shown in their entirety, with results considered to be significant highlighted in bold. The number and percentage of squares recording 0 data are also included in Table 4 since they will obviously affect the statistics and should be acknowledged when attempting to interpret the results. Most of the summary statistics should be familiar to archaeologists; some of the more obscure measures are summarised below (following Shennan 1997).
- The Standard Error is calculated by dividing the estimate of the population Standard Deviation by the square root of the number of observations in the sample — the larger the sample, the more representative it will be of the true population variability.
- Sample Variance is the average of the squared differences between the mean and data values — i.e.

the Standard Deviation is the square root of the Sample Variance.
- Kurtosis is the length of the tails of a distribution — long-tailed distributions are leptokurtic; short-tailed distributions are platykurtic.

Differences in the types of data analysed should be noted. Most of the categories are counts. Small Stones (SSWB) is the number of wheelbarrow loads, rather than actual counts, while the Total Number of Sherds (TotSh) consists of classes to the nearest 50 sherds. Given the imperfect nature of the data, some readers may question the point of analysing and presenting the data in this way — by doing so, we hope to provide as much potentially meaningful data, as clearly and objectively as possible.

Summary statistics

In general, Table 4 shows that counts per square have low mean values, with small amounts of variation. The mode and median are often 0. The largest variation occurs among the Painted, Early Bronze Age and Total Diagnostics categories and this is reflected in their larger than average Range scores. Four categories (Rom/Byz, TS, IA, Trefoil) have Sum scores around or below 100 — with 219 squares, this means that these sherd types were only found in less than every second square. The Summary Statistics do not augur well for further analysis, although it is possible that categories with low square counts may show clear clustering in their distributions, which may be of interest.

Correlation analysis

Table 5 results from the comparison of two sets of variables. Regression describes the form of the relationship between the variables (often in the form of a scattergram and a line of 'best fit'), while correlation analysis measures how well the data fit the relationship. Its values (r) range from –1.0 for a perfect negative relationship, through 0 (no relationship) to +1.0, a perfect positive relationship.

Normally distributed data is desirable when carrying out correlation analysis, as for most statistical analysis. The nature of the Kilise Tepe data, with its generally small counts and abundance of 0s should be remembered. In Table 5, I have highlighted values of ±0.5 or more. These correlations should not be emphasized too strongly, since the coefficient of determination (r^2) is a more realistic assessment of the strength of a relationship — an apparently moderate correlation $r = 0.4$ yields a small coefficient of determination $r^2 = 0.16$.

The strongest correlations in Table 5 reflect the most complete and largest data categories — the Total Number of Sherds and the Number of Diagnostics. Early Bronze Age, Painted and Red Hittite Wares figure among the moderate/strong correlations, again probably reflecting their higher sherd counts and therefore contribution to the Number of Diagnostics. It should, however, be noted that Early Bronze Age and Painted correlate moderately. It may also be significant that a moderate negative correlation exists between Large Stones (LSWB) and the Total Number of Sherds (TotSh).

Covariance Analysis, which also measures the relationship between two sets of data, was applied to the surface collection data, but since the results were broadly similar to those of Correlation Analysis, they are not shown here.

Artefact distributions

Surfer32 was used to create artefact distributions from the surface collection data. It is designed to interpolate irregularly spaced XYZ data onto a regularly spaced grid, from which distribution maps can be produced (Keckler 1994, 1-1). The software offers a variety of interpolation techniques and the facility to use regularly spaced data if it exists. To a certain extent, the interpolation technique chosen is less important than consistently applying it to all the data, but the less the data is manipulated the better. The regularly spaced data option was used to produce shaded contour distributions for the Kilise Tepe data, with medium smoothing.

Data from each square were assigned to the mid-point co-ordinates of the square. The distribution maps were then combined with a surface model derived from the 1994 contour survey of Kilise Tepe to produce Figures 20–38. Only artefact distributions which were deemed to be informative are shown. On the basis of subjective, visual interpretation, the distribution maps are summarized in Table 6.

Kilise Tepe is similar in morphology to other mounds in the Near East, analysed by Rosen (1986, 31). It has a steep north/west face and more gentle slopes to the south and east. Excavations in Q19 in 1994 revealed a major stone wall running parallel to the edge of the top of the mound. If this wall continues around the mound, it is possible that the slight indentation in the contours on the eastern side of Kilise Tepe (Northings 1175–1180) indicates the location of a gateway.

The most striking point revealed by the distributions is the huge difference in the total sherd densities

The Surface Collection

Table 4. *Summary statistics.*

	SSWB	LS (count)	Nosh. (n50)	Deco.	Feat.	Deco. + Feat.	Tref.	Rom/ Bzy.	Terra Sig.	Hellen.	EBA	RH	IA	TotPer Sh.	Info. Sh.	Lithics	Grinders, etc.	Metal	Arch.	Misc
Mean	3.49	77.28	283.33	28.99	45.40	74.39	0.46	0.49	0.20	1.79	3.22	2.66	0.11	8.47	82.86	0.60	1.00	0.26	0.75	0.34
Standard error	0.19	4.55	20.27	2.68	3.00	5.22	0.06	0.07	0.04	0.19	0.41	0.24	0.02	0.55	5.62	0.06	0.10	0.05	0.13	0.06
Median	2.50	67	150	19	32	50	0	0	0	1	0	1	0	6	55	0	0	0	0	0
Mode	2	0	100	10	14	29	0	0	0	0	0	0	0	2	38	0	0	0	0	0
Standard deviation	2.82	67.35	299.97	39.63	44.38	77.32	0.94	0.99	0.54	2.79	6.09	3.53	0.35	8.12	83.23	0.90	1.49	0.73	1.87	0.93
Sample variance	7.95	4536.60	89,984.71	1570.77	1969.45	5978.33	0.89	0.98	0.30	7.78	37.03	12.48	0.12	65.93	6926.94	0.82	2.23	0.54	3.50	0.87
Kurtosis	9.98	17.30	2.09	18.24	2.89	7.55	7.20	6.47	9.17	13.00	7.26	5.27	9.50	3.05	7.07	1.70	2.87	12.82	20.91	79.65
Skewness	2.59	2.94	1.70	3.92	1.79	2.48	2.49	2.52	3.03	3.02	2.54	1.94	3.09	1.58	2.38	1.51	1.83	3.48	4.06	7.50
Range	20	600	1300	289	221	475	6	5	3	21	36	23	2	46	521	4	6	4	15	11
Minimum	0	0	0	0	0	0	0	0	0	0	0	0	0	0	0	0	0	0	0	0
Maximum	20	600	1300	289	221	475	6	5	3	21	36	23	2	46	521	4	6	4	15	11
Sum	763.50	16,925	62,050	6349	9943	16,292	101	107	43	392	706	582	25	1855	18,147	132	218	56	164	74
Count	219	219	219	219	219	219	219	219	219	219	219	219	219	219	219	219	219	219	219	219
Confidence level (95.0%)	0.38	8.97	39.95	5.28	5.91	10.30	0.13	0.13	0.07	0.37	0.81	0.47	0.05	1.08	11.08	0.12	0.20	0.10	0.25	0.12
No. of 0 counts	7	16	4	8	4	4	163	157	189	93	133	83	196	14	2	73	73	146	159	146
% of 0 counts	3.20	7.31	1.83	3.65	1.83	1.83	74.43	71.69	86.30	42.47	60.73	37.90	89.50	6.39	0.91	33.33	33.33	66.67	72.60	66.67

Table 5. *Correlation analysis.*

	SSWB	LS (count)	Nosh. (n50)	Deco.	Feat.	Tref.	Rom/ Bzy.	Terra Sig.	Hellen.	EBA	RH	IA	TotPer. Sh.	Lithics	Grinders, etc.	Metal	Arch.	Misc.
SSWB	1.00																	
LS (count)	0.40	1.00																
Nosh. (n50)	-0.31	-0.01	1.00															
Deco.	-0.15	-0.04	0.65	1.00														
Feat.	-0.24	0.02	0.93	0.69	1.00													
Tref.	-0.14	0.01	0.45	0.35	0.52	1.00												
Rom/Bzy.	0.13	0.06	-0.17	-0.02	-0.08	-0.05	1.00											
Terra Sig.	0.06	0.08	-0.24	-0.13	-0.18	-0.08	0.32	1.00										
Hellen.	0.03	-0.03	-0.13	0.02	-0.06	-0.07	0.11	0.14	1.00									
EBA	-0.26	0.00	0.76	0.59	0.73	0.34	-0.14	-0.19	-0.13	1.00								
RH	-0.20	-0.08	0.45	0.35	0.44	0.41	-0.17	-0.17	-0.11	0.40	1.00							
IA	-0.11	-0.12	0.01	0.11	0.02	0.02	0.08	0.00	0.02	-0.02	0.01	1.00						
TotPer. Sh.	-0.25	-0.04	0.68	0.59	0.69	0.40	0.00	-0.06	0.22	0.85	0.67	0.05	1.00					
Lithics	-0.02	-0.01	0.08	0.17	0.11	0.09	0.12	0.08	-0.02	0.08	-0.01	-0.07	0.07	1.00				
Grinders, etc.	-0.07	0.08	0.38	0.07	0.37	0.19	-0.09	-0.14	-0.11	0.21	0.30	-0.07	0.23	0.00	1.00			
Metal	0.06	0.02	-0.12	0.01	-0.05	0.05	0.26	0.17	0.12	-0.07	-0.07	0.03	0.00	0.20	-0.02	1.00		
Arch.	0.16	0.13	-0.15	-0.10	-0.18	-0.18	-0.05	-0.06	-0.08	-0.14	-0.20	0.02	-0.23	0.07	-0.02	0.00	1.00	
Misc.	0.04	0.02	0.08	0.06	0.11	0.07	-0.10	-0.06	0.11	0.01	-0.04	-0.01	0.01	0.17	0.01	0.02	0.10	1.00

Table 6. *Summary of distribution maps.*

Slopes of Tepe	Top of Tepe	Clustered
Percentage Diagnostics	Small Stones - esp. NW & E	Late Roman/Byz. Sherds
Trefoil Rims	Terra Sigillata - esp. S & SW	Stone Artefacts
Red Hittite Wares	Hellenistic Sherds	Architectural Fragments
Total Sherds		Large Stones
Early Bronze Age		
Decorated Sherds		
Feature Sherds		

found on the southern and eastern slopes, compared to the top of the tepe. This probably reflects a capping of fairly sterile, Byzantine and perhaps also Hellenistic fill deposits across the tepe which was encountered in most of our excavation trenches.

A similar 'skirt' of artefacts was found around the East Mound at Çatalhöyük, where densities of artefacts were greater to the south of the mound. Çatalhöyük obviously does not have such a depth of overlying Classical deposits. From his analysis of the pottery, Last concluded that the end result of taphonomic processes is lateral movement of material downslope from the top of the mound, although sherd size and shape are also significant factors (Last 1996, 145). Similar taphonomic processes may have contributed to the distribution patterns found at Kilise Tepe.

The similar concentration of Diagnostic, Painted and the temporally indistinct Trefoil Rim sherds on the slopes suggests that most sherds at Kilise Tepe were not differentially affected by taphonomic processes. The general distributions may be partly explained by differential erosion — the flat top of the tepe is presumably a relatively inactive erosional area compared to the slopes. The additional effects and extent of ploughing can only be surmised, although ploughing is likely to bury, as well as to expose, sherds.

Other important factors are the profile of the underlying conglomerate bedrock and the gradient and length of the slopes. An initially steep slope, on the edge of the conglomerate shelf, is likely to remain steep through time, as the tepe becomes higher. The north/west slopes are short, steep, high energy slopes — once a sherd starts to move, it is likely to move a considerable distance, as was shown by the subsequent dumping of excavation spoil down these slopes (visible in Fig. 5). The gradients on the south/east slopes are more moderate and the slopes longer.

If the tepe's shape is related to the prevailing wind direction, surface run-off from the top of the tepe is likely to be in a southeasterly direction, which may also partially account for the overall sherd distribution. The general distribution of small stones should also be considered at this point. Small stones are more likely to be affected by surface run-off than large stones, so their prevalence on the 'low energy' top of the tepe, compared to on the slopes adds weight to the case for differential erosion contributing to the sherd distributions.

The different patterning among the distributions becomes more informative, however, when the various sherd categories are investigated. The dearth of Islamic sherds and the tepe's flat top suggest that the site was not significantly occupied after the Byzantine period. Consequently, Late Roman/Byzantine Plain wares

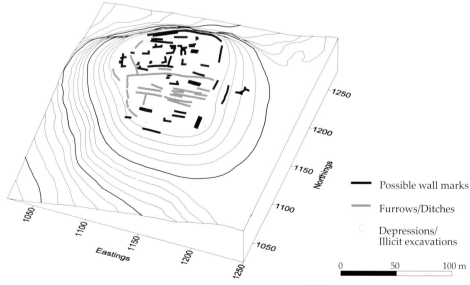

Figure 20. *Surface marks.*

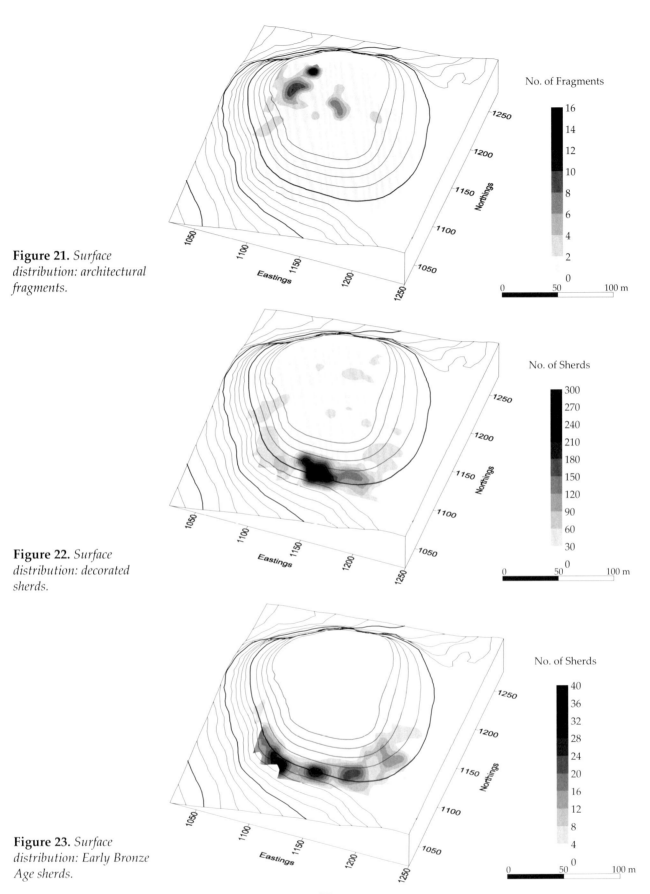

Figure 21. *Surface distribution: architectural fragments.*

Figure 22. *Surface distribution: decorated sherds.*

Figure 23. *Surface distribution: Early Bronze Age sherds.*

Chapter 6

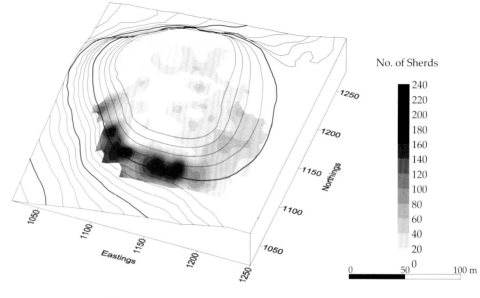

Figure 24. *Surface distribution: feature (non-body) sherds.*

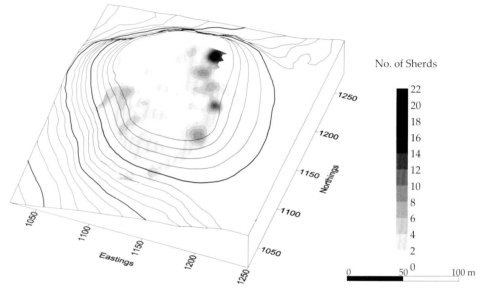

Figure 25. *Surface distribution: Hellenistic sherds.*

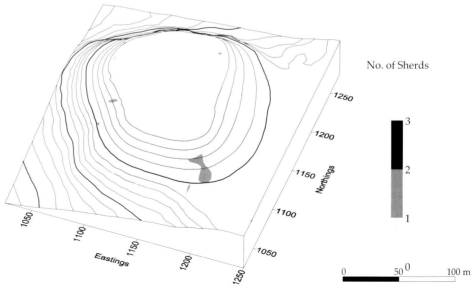

Figure 26. *Surface distribution: Iron Age sherds.*

The Surface Collection

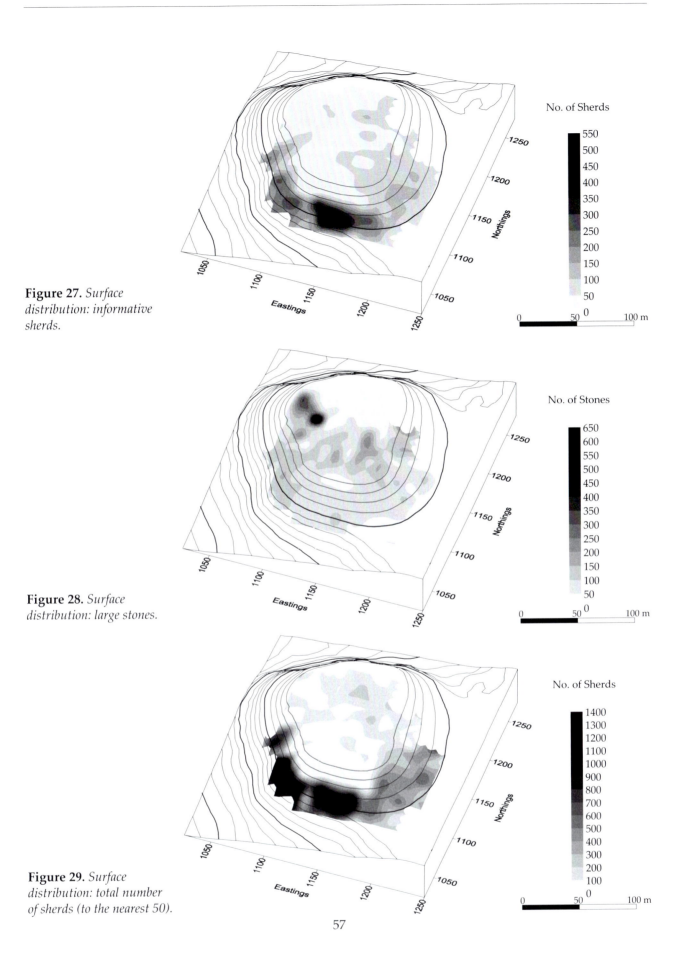

Figure 27. *Surface distribution: informative sherds.*

Figure 28. *Surface distribution: large stones.*

Figure 29. *Surface distribution: total number of sherds (to the nearest 50).*

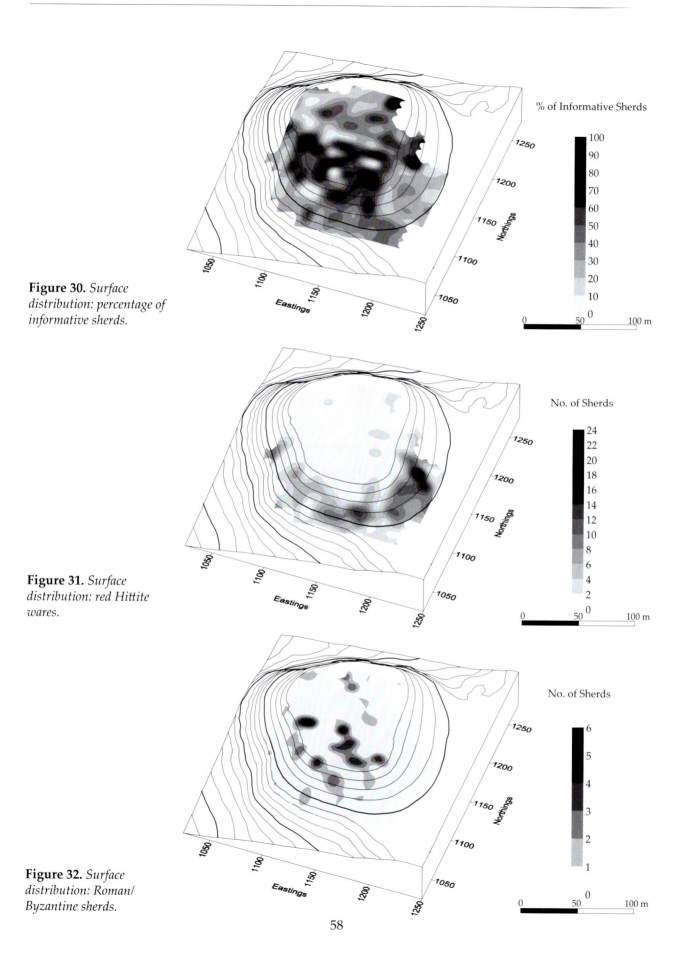

Figure 30. *Surface distribution: percentage of informative sherds.*

Figure 31. *Surface distribution: red Hittite wares.*

Figure 32. *Surface distribution: Roman/Byzantine sherds.*

The Surface Collection

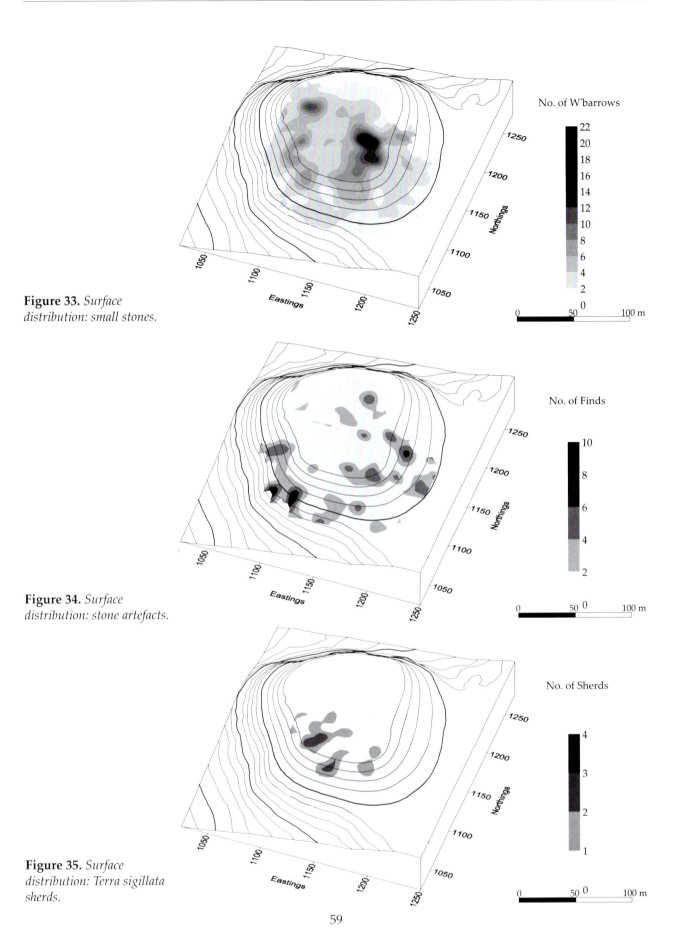

Figure 33. *Surface distribution: small stones.*

Figure 34. *Surface distribution: stone artefacts.*

Figure 35. *Surface distribution: Terra sigillata sherds.*

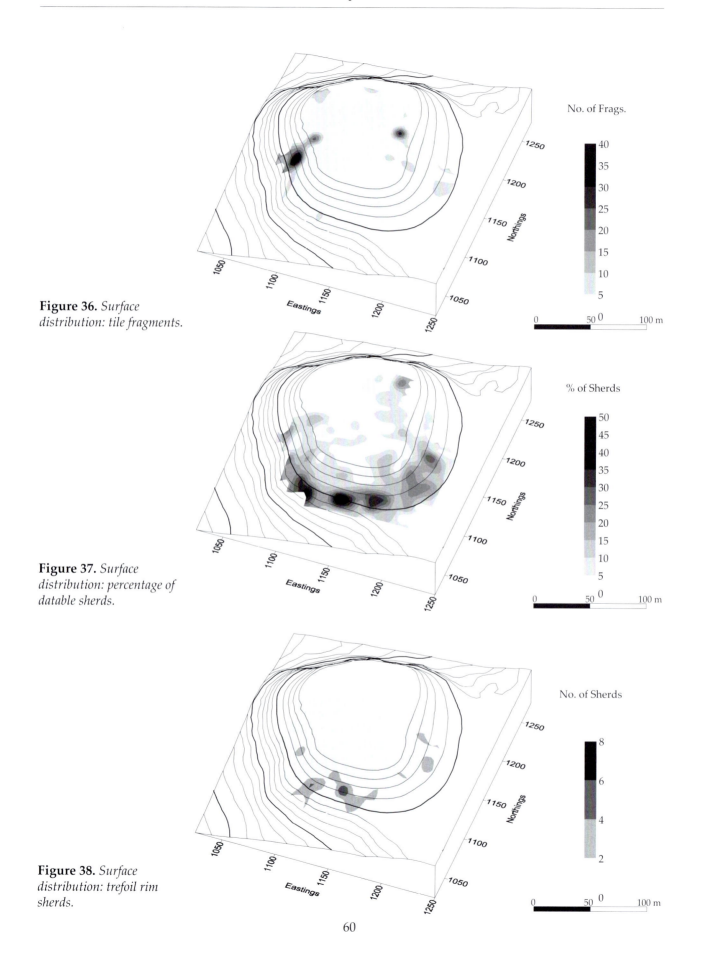

Figure 36. *Surface distribution: tile fragments.*

Figure 37. *Surface distribution: percentage of datable sherds.*

Figure 38. *Surface distribution: trefoil rim sherds.*

and Terra Sigillata would be expected to be prominent among sherds collected from the top of the tepe, since these periods' deposits should be close to the surface. Conversely, since Kilise Tepe appears to be a sealed tell, rather than a shelved tell, earlier periods' sherds would not be expected on the top of the tepe, other than where illicit excavations have taken place or where later periods' pits have been dug deep into earlier levels.

Terra Sigillata sherds appear to be quite localized in their distribution on the top of the tepe. Late Roman/Byzantine Plain wares have a more diffuse distribution, but are concentrated in broadly the same area as Terra Sigillata sherds. Terra Sigillata sherds are relatively distinctive, so their distribution is probably real rather than the result of any inconsistencies in classification. If these imported/imitation wares are regarded as prestige items, their localized distribution may point to the presence of a building or an area of different status to that of the rest of the tepe.

Curiously, Hellenistic sherds are distributed more evenly across the top of the tepe than the later sherds. This may suggest that Hellenistic occupation of the site was spatially more extensive than Late Roman/Byzantine occupation, although factors such as the ease of recognizing sherds from these periods and the type of buildings and volume of sherds they may have contained should be considered. Subsequent work demonstrated that Kilise Tepe was the site of a Byzantine church, so we would expect fewer sherds to accrue on the site of the church than in domestic areas. As noted above, Large Stones (LS) and Architectural Fragments are concentrated in the northwest of the top of the tepe, where few Classical sherds were collected.

Given a presumed thick deposit of Roman/Byzantine archaeology on the top of the tepe, the pre-Classical periods should be represented in greater frequency among sherds eroding from the sides of the tepe. This is the case — Red Hittite wares and Early Bronze Age wares occur in great numbers on the cleared slopes. A difference is evident, however, in that Early Bronze Age sherds are more concentrated in the south and Red Hittite wares in the east. There is no obvious reason for this, other than possible differences in the underlying deposits. It should be remembered, however, that sherds on slopes are likely to have moved, so excavation trenches particularly targeting these periods should be located upslope from the densest concentrations.

The other distributions appear less informative. Stone Tools are generally found on the slopes, rather than the top of the tepe. Some clustering is evident, but the numbers of artefacts involved is low.

Initial results of the surface collection

The principal result of the surface collections was to confirm the presence of several different archaeological periods at Kilise Tepe, although undiagnostic Byzantine sherds dominated the collected assemblage. This strengthened the general impression that Kilise Tepe was capped by a significant amount of Byzantine, and in some areas Hellenistic, occupation, sitting on top of a more or less continuous build-up of prehistoric deposits. Surface collection on the southern and eastern slopes of the mound yielded a higher proportion of Bronze Age sherds than on the summit of the tepe. It was also noted that the northern half of the tepe may not have been ploughed as intensively or recently as the southern half.

Some of the surface indications suggested that stone walls were closer to the surface in the northern half of the tepe (Fig. 19) and this appeared to be borne out by excavations in the east (squares Q19 and R18) in 1994. It seemed probable that these walls would date to the Byzantine period, although excavations proved the perimeter wall in the east to be earlier. The likelihood that one of the possible buildings indicated by the surface marks was a church, as suggested by the modern name of the site, was increased by higher densities of large stones and architectural fragments in the northwest and by the discovery of at least three fragments of carved stone ornaments, of the type found on capitals (see Chapter 19). The surface collection thus helped focus subsequent seasons' excavations aimed at locating the church.

Conclusions

The data from the surface collection at Kilise Tepe are far from perfect, but when considered in the light of other surface surveys, it is possible to postulate explanations for some of the distinct patterns that have emerged in the distribution plots. The characteristics of the tepe are crucial to the surface distributions, in both its morphology and composition. Kilise Tepe fits Rosen's model relating mound shape to the prevailing wind. Slope type appears to have a significant effect on the distribution of artefacts, while the predominance of Roman/Byzantine sherds on top of the mound and earlier sherds around the edges is similar to that found at Tepe Yahya.

The results of the correlation analysis, linking Number of Sherds, Number of Diagnostics, Early Bronze Age, Painted and Red Hittite wares, confirm the visually comparable distributions of these artefacts. The locations of the main excavation trenches were selected before the surface collection was completed, so we have not as yet tested the correlation of surface and sub-surface material. That said, future work at the site could use the results of the surface collection and focus on the marked concentrations of Decorated and Early Bronze Age sherds in the south, Red Hittite wares in the west and the cluster of Terra Sigillata sherds in the centre of the tepe.

The slight differences in methodology between the 1994 and 1995 seasons are regrettable and limit the analysis possible on several of the less important categories of finds. Equally, some of the patterning found in the data may be related to inconsistencies in our methodology, and the varying ease or difficulty of classifying some types of ceramics.

The sherds from the surface collection obviously often become more readily identifiable when compared with a large assemblage of well-stratified material from a local excavation. In general, the surface material would have served as a fairly accurate predictor of the occupation periods uncovered by excavation at the site (exceptions being principally the Samian ware and the decorated pithos sherds — see above p. 51). The diagnostic material from the surface has been retained and is available for further study, but inevitably, the re-assessment of surface ceramics receives an increasingly low priority as the ceramics from the excavations mount up. This paradox should be considered by those championing, and indeed requiring, surveys prior to excavations. We did not have the luxury of well-stratified, local comparanda in 1994–95, but we hope that the on-going archaeological survey of the Göksu valley and future excavations will benefit from the Kilise Tepe assemblage and surface collection analysis.

Notes

1. Thanks are due to Dr Dominique Collon, Professor David Mattingly and Professor Nicholas Postgate for their helpful and pertinent comments relating to this chapter. The author, naturally, remains solely responsible for any remaining misinterpretations and errors.
2. These were later interpreted as imbrices by Mark Jackson, our Byzantine specialist, and thus should have been considered along with tiles.

Part C

The Excavations

Chapter 7 **Introduction to the Excavations**	**67**
Excavation and recording procedures	67
Numbering of squares and finds	67
The excavation record	67
Arrangement of the descriptions	67
The stratification	68
Chapter 8 **Fire Installations**	**71**
Hearths	71
Tannours	74
Pebble-based installations	74
Large ovens	76
Continuity	77
Groupings	77
Contents	78
Chapter 9 **Pits**	**79**
Storage pits	79
Level 1	79
Earlier levels	80
Fills	82
Location	83
Other types of pit	83
Contents	84
Chapter 10 **Level V: the Early Bronze Age**	**87**
Introduction	87
Note on phasing	88
Level Vl	88
Level Vk	89
Level Vj	89
Level Vi (early)	91
Level Vi (late)	92
Level Vh	92
Level Vg	94
Level Vf	97
Level Ve	99
Chapter 11 **Level IV: the Middle Bronze Age**	**103**
Level IVa	103
Level IVb	108

Chapter 12   Level III: the Late Bronze Age   **111**
  Level IIIa–c   111
  Level IIId   112
    The Western rooms (Rms 33–6)   112
    Room 33   112
    Room 34   113
    Room 35   113
    Room 36   113
  The Central sector (Rms 30–32)   114
    Room 32   114
    Room 30   114
    Room 31   115
  Eastern Courtyard   116
    FI97/10   116
  Area NW of Wall 109   117
  Level IIIe   117

Chapter 13   Level II: the End of the Bronze Age and the Iron Age   **121**
  13.1. Level IIa–c   **121**
  Stele Building   121
    Room 1   121
    Room 2   123
    Room 3   123
    Room 4   128
    Room 5   130
    Room 6   131
    Room 7   132
    Room 8   136
    Rooms 9 and 10   136
    The nature of the Stele Building   137
  The East Building   137
    Room 20   138
    Room 21   139
    Room 22   140
    Room 23   141
    Room 24   142
  The Northeast Annex   142
    Level IIc   143
    Phase IIb   143
  The Western Courtyard   144
    Levels IIa–b   145
    Level IIc   146
  The IIc destruction   147
  13.2. Level IId   **148**
    The site   148
    The IId building   149
  13.3. Level IIe   **152**
    H18   152
    The Western Courtyard   153
    Other IIe material   153
    Room e5   154
    Room e6   154
    Room e7   156
    Rooms e9 and e10   156
  13.4. Level IIf and later deposits   **158**
  Level IIf (west half)   158
    Kiln FI96/14   160

    Level IIf (east half)   161
        Kiln FI96/15   161
        Room f3   162
    Later deposits (IIg–h)   163

Chapter 14   The East Slope   165
    Phasing for East Slope   165
    Excavation in R18 (phase E5)   165
    The sequence in Q19b/d (E4a–c)   166
    Wall 300 (phase E3a)   167
    Drain in Q19d (phase E3b)   167
    Walls 301 and 303 (phase E2b–c)   168
    Phase E2a   168
    S18 Byzantine walls (phase E1)   169

Chapter 15   Trenches South of the Church   171
    15.1. Square Q10   **171**
    15.2. Square N12   **172**
    15.3. Levels 2–3 in I14   **173**
        Level 3   173
        Level 2 early   175
        Level 2 late   175
        The ditch   176
    15.4. Level 2 in K14   **177**
        Upper Level 2   177
        Middle Level 2   177
        Lower Level 2   177
    15.5. Level 1 in I-M14   **178**
        Introduction   178
        Earlier Hellenistic phase   178
        Later Hellenistic phase (I14/J14a)   179
        Later Hellenistic phase (J/L14)   180
        Later Hellenistic phase (M14)   181
        Late Roman deposits (L14a/b)   182
        I14a–M14b conclusion   182

Chapter 16   The Church   185
    Introduction   185
    Early Byzantine basilica   185
    Single chambered church   185
    Chronology   186
    Details of the excavation of the Early Byzantine basilica   188
        The north side-chamber   188
        East wall and passage behind apse   189
        The apse   189
        The north aisle   190
        The south aisle   190
        The narthex   190
        Evidence for activity to the NW of the church   191
        Nave   191
        Single chambered structure built over the Early Byzantine basilica   193
        Second phase of later structure   194
        Interpretation   194
    Burials east of the single chambered structure   195
        Burial 5626 (P98/38)   195
    Later robbing of the church site   196
    Summary   196

Chapter 17   **The Northwest Corner** — **199**
   Level Ia, Hellenistic phase — 199
   Level Ia (later) — 200
   Level Ib — 200
      Introduction — 200
      Detailed discussion of Level Ib — 201
      Phase Ib in I19c/d and H18b/d — 202
      Deposits associated with the Level Ib walls — 202
      The external courtyard surface — 203
      Pits post-dating the courtyard surface — 203
   Level Ic — 204
   Level Id — 204
      Introduction — 204
      The east side of the courtyard — 205
      Level Id Room A — 206
      Level Id Room B — 206
      Level Id Room C — 206
      The west side of the courtyard (I18/19) — 207
   I18a Level Id — 207
   The later deposits in the courtyard area — 208
   Level Ie — 208
   Conclusion — 208
      Phasing summary — 210

Chapter 18   **The NE Corner Sub-surface Clearance** — **211**

Chapter 19   **Architectural Fragments** — **215**
   Dressed limestone fragments — 216
      a) Fragments of flat slabs — 216
      b) Limestone fragments with claw-chisel marks — 217
      c) Curved dressed fragments — 219
      d) Fragments with mouldings — 219
      e) 'Trough-like' fragments — 219
      f) Column fragments — 219
      g) Decorated fragments — 220
   Dressed marble fragments — 222
      a) Slab fragments — 222
      b) Fragments of mouldings — 224
      c) Screen(?) fragments — 224
      d) Column fragments — 224
      e) Decorated fragments — 224
      f) Capital fragments — 225
   Column bases — 229

Chapter 7

Introduction to the Excavations

Nicholas Postgate

Excavation and recording procedures

Numbering of squares and finds
Throughout most of the excavated areas our normal practice was to divide each 10-m square into four 5 × 5 m squares, referred to as 'quadrants' and identified by a (= NW), b (= NE), c (= SW) or d (= SE). Thus the NE quadrant of K20 is referred to as K20b. Each separately distinguished operation to remove soil was assigned a four-figure 'unit number'. Any item, whether an artefact or a sample, recovered from each context was assigned this unit number, but was also identified by a unique 'object number' of its own. In some categories several artefacts, e.g. miscellaneous stones or sherds of glass, might be grouped in a bag which received a single number. The general assemblage of potsherds from each unit did not receive an object number, but any ceramic items which for whatever reason needed to be identified individually were also assigned an object number of their own.

In the first two seasons the object number assigned to a find consisted of the unit number followed by a slash and a further running number, e.g. 2378/3. This had the virtue of simplicity, but in the course of the two seasons it became apparent that it had significant disadvantages leading to confusion: the principal being that as each sequence of numbers from a context was open-ended, it was difficult to establish an integrated list and to notice omissions. Consequently in the third and following seasons a single sequence of object numbers was used for each square, e.g. K20/237, though of course objects were also still given their unit number. This system was also imposed retrospectively on the finds from 1994 and 1995, and these are the numbers used throughout this publication.

The excavation record
The trench supervisors recorded the process of excavation in the following ways:
1. A bound A4 notebook with alternating graph and text pages was used as a daily record, with sketches and sometimes measured plans.
2. A pre-printed form was used for each unit (see Fig. 39 for a completed example). In principle this was a retrospective account of the unit, once the operation had been concluded.
3. Measured plans and sections were drawn on separate sheets of drafting film. These are in most cases at 1:20, although a scale of 1:50 was used for larger areas and 1:10 for detailed features. An effort was made to draw all sections along the main 10-m grid lines, but internal sections between quadrants (a/b etc.) were only recorded when it seemed valuable. Based on this record a few composite sections are presented in this volume (Figs. 512–27). These are not designed to provide a comprehensive account in the same way as the horizontal plans, but should give the reader a sense of the vertical composition of different parts of the site, and illustrate a few specific features, such as the ditch in I14 (Figs. 514–15).
4. In theory each pit, fire installation, and wall was described on a pre-printed form designed for the purpose (see Figs. 40–42 for completed examples). In practice this did not always happen, and details of those features which were not entered on the pre-printed sheets are sometimes to be found in the A4 notebooks.

Once excavated, the earth and stones from an operation would normally be dumped over the side of the mound. Exceptions to this procedure involved the occasional retention of 'whole earth' samples, described below (p. 581), and dry sieving at the site for the controlled recovery of faunal material.

Arrangement of the descriptions

The account of the excavations which follows in this chapter starts from the earliest levels and ends with Level I. It therefore reverses the sequence in which the information was observed, and it is not an attempt to abbreviate the narrative accounts of the trench supervisors. It aims to describe the principal architectural features, not the process of excavation. In some areas this does not leave much to describe, because the

Chapter 7

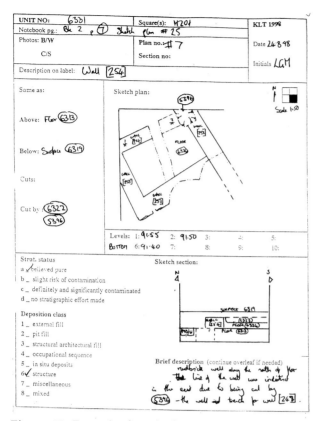

Figure 39. *Example of a unit sheet.*

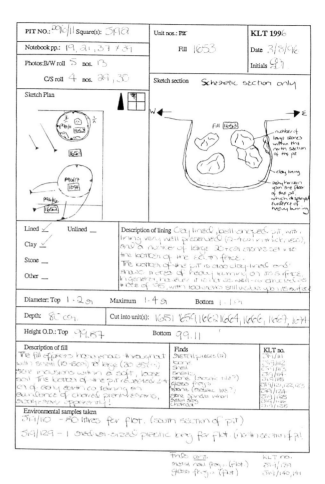

Figure 40. *Example of a pit sheet.*

majority of the deposits, and of the time and trouble devoted to them by the excavators, were taken up by the fill of many pits (e.g. in I19 or R18). Punctuating our account of the architecture with a description of every intrusion would serve no useful purpose and make it unreadable. Instead we have provided first a general description of the pits and their contents (pp. 79–85). For similar reasons, we have also placed our survey of the range of fire installations in this introductory section (pp. 71–8).

After each section of the text we list the excavation units which contribute to the preceding description. They are grouped broadly according to their stratigraphic nature ('fill', 'destr. debris' etc.). These groupings are a rough guide only, and not intended to replace the details given in the main Unit List (Appendix 2). Pits are not usually listed individually but grouped with other intrusive events under 'cuts', and the distinction between 'packing' (beneath a floor or wall) and 'fill' (overlying a feature) cannot be consistently applied. It is also not a comprehensive list, since many units will not be listed under any section of the text for a variety of reasons — they may not be stratified, they may belong to pits not described in the text, or they may have been assigned to features such as walls which are not included in this context. After each group are listed any artefacts reported in this volume from the units included. While the detailed relationship between the process of excavation and the architecture and stratigraphy of the site can only be conveyed by the entire record of excavation, this part of the text will not only guide the user of this report to the ceramic and other finds from each area, but also give an indication of the nature of each provenance and its relationship to the architecture.

The stratification

Six major periods were encountered in the course of the excavations, in conventional terms the Early, Middle and Late Bronze Ages, the Iron Age, and the Hellenistic and Byzantine eras. Figure 473 indicates how these correlate with our level-by-level stratigraphic nomenclature. Inevitably our interpretation of the stratification changed during the excavation, and the system used in this volume is a compromise between terminology used during the excavation and the ideal which we might have applied with hindsight.

Introduction to the Excavations

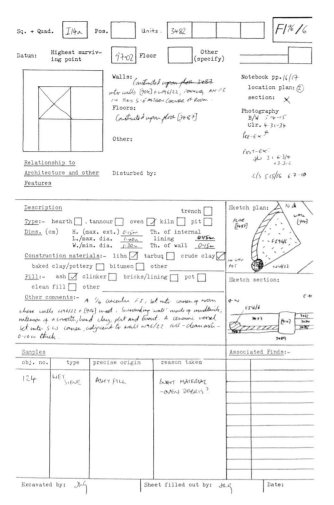

Figure 41. *Example of a fire installation sheet.*

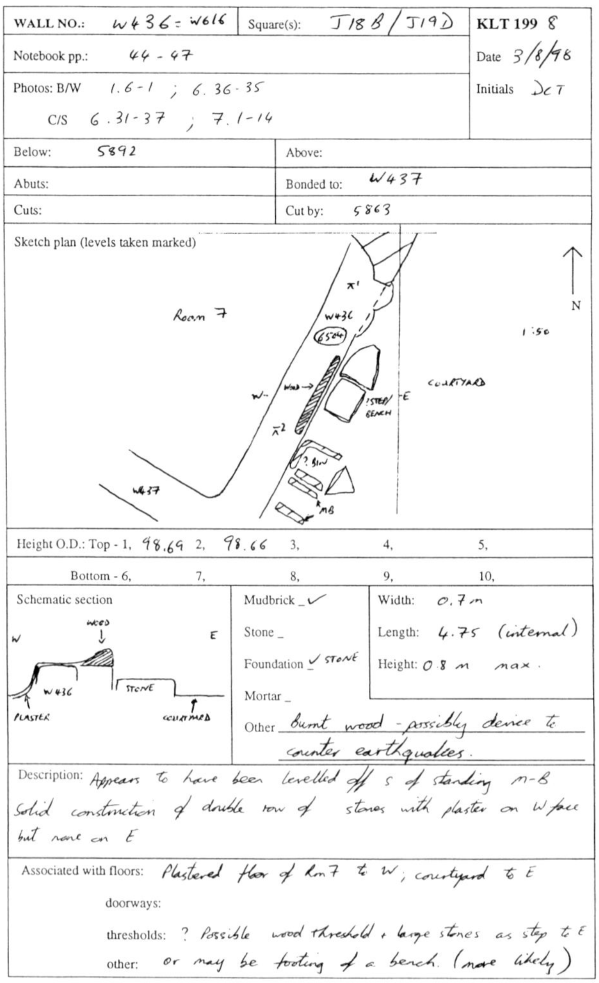

Figure 42. *Example of a wall sheet.*

Two major points of inconsistency should be singled out for explanation. In the first place, stratigraphic conditions varied from one part of the mound to another. At the NW corner, from which our numbering of levels was taken, substantial Byzantine activity had removed virtually everything belonging to the Hellenistic period, and our Level I therefore includes within it all material after the pre-Classical Iron Age (for the subdivision of Level I see Jackson, pp. 199 ff.). In the central trench (I-M14) and on the east slope we were able to distinguish a Byzantine and a Hellenistic architectural level much more clearly. The Iron Age levels below these are undoubtedly in part contemporary with Level II in the NW corner, and in I14 we have a Late Bronze Age level which corresponds in time with Level III; but we are not able to demonstrate any stratigraphic connection between the two areas, nor to claim any precise equivalences, and we have emphasized this by using Roman numerals (Levels I, II, III) for the NW corner sequence but Arabic (Levels 1, 2, 3) for other parts of the mound.

The other major inconsistency concerns the lettering of the phases in the NW corner. The details of this are explained in the introduction to Level V (p. 88).

Chapter 8

Fire Installations

Nicholas Postgate

About seventy features were designated as fire installations (and allocated an FI number) over the five seasons of excavation. The most important fire installations are described in their architectural contexts. Here it may be helpful to survey the different kinds and note their chronological and spatial distribution.

In general our use of the term 'fire installation' is intended to avoid the difficulty of deciding between e.g. 'hearth' and 'oven', both because English usage is imprecise and because in some cases it is impossible to establish the exact nature of the feature from the surviving fragmentary remains. Where appropriate we use the word 'hearth' to refer to any open feature used to accommodate a fire, whether flat or with constructed sides. There are also fireplaces let into the ground, which should perhaps be considered 'firepits'. The term 'oven' is used for installations with a superstructure, with 'kiln' reserved for industrial furnaces. A special type of oven is the 'tannour'.

Hearths

An elaborate central hearth was an important feature of at least two of our buildings. In Level IVa the rather irregular Rm 41 had the big lime-plastered circular hearth FI96/22 as its central feature (di. 1.20 m, with a rim some 8 cm high, see p. 103).

The burnt IIc Stele Building had a hearth at the centre of Rm 3 (FI96/18; Figs. 100–101, 109–110 & 492). The hearth itself was a simple, slightly oval (76 × 90 cm), clay feature, over a pebble base, but placed on a low rectangular platform and protected to the west by a partition wall. A similar hearth was already present in the earlier IIa/b phases of the room. Neither here, nor in Rm 41, can we be certain if the room was roofed or not. The size of these hearths might seem too big for an interior room, but their careful construction, and other features of the rooms tend to suggest they were under cover. In either case, from their position at the centre of a large space it seems likely that these hearths had a primarily social, not culinary, function.

Later FI95/5, a very fragmentary but also unusually carefully constructed installation in Rm d4 may have been the Level IId equivalent of FI96/18. It was not centrally placed but constructed against the SW face of W721, and beneath the layer of plastered pebbles was a low semi-circular mudbrick emplacement, plastered round its edge (Fig. 43). The only other plastered brick base we noted was FI97/6 in Rm 17, the annex to the IIc Stele Building (Fig. 494), which had an angular outline but the remnants of a circular pebble layer above it.

In a few other cases we find hearths built into the furniture of an internal room and backed against a wall face. In Rm 83 of Level Vj a feature which could have served as a hearth was probably built against the east wall (Fig. 476), but it showed no sign of having been used for a fire and has not been classed as a fire installation. FI97/5 in H20c Level Vi may have been against a wall, but its south end was beneath the baulk and not excavated. The earliest clear example is therefore FI98/5 in the phase Vg reception room Rm 63 (Fig. 481), which was constructed of thin stone slabs each side and filled with soft grey ash. It was 30 cm in width but projected as much as 60 cm into the room. Further fragments of stone may indicate that it was also covered by a slab and could thus more properly considered an oven (Fig. 77).

Figure 43. *FI95/5 in Rm d4, looking south.*

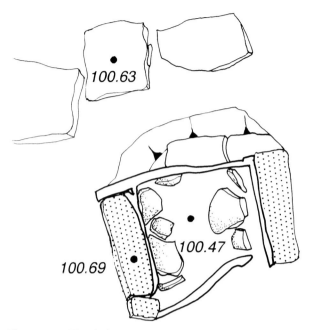

Figure 44. *FI95/3 (K20, Rm e9; see Fig. 498 for location).*

Figure 46. *FI96/1 in I19d; Level I/IIh, looking west.*

Figure 45. *FI95/3 in Rm e9, as first exposed, looking south.*

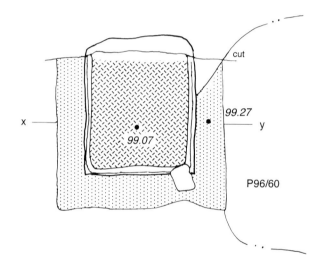

Figure 47. *FI96/11 (I19 Level IIe/f; see Fig. 499 for location).*

FI95/8 in Rm 11 (Level IIc; see Fig. 492) was built against the eastern end of W121, and like FI95/5 seems to have had a mudbrick base beneath the layer of pebbles. One example was installed against the south wall of Rm e6 in Level IIe (FI97/9; Fig. 144). Its back was provided by two upright stones, no doubt to protect the wall face, and another stone was used to retain the pebbles on which the clay floor surface was laid. Of about the same date was FI95/3 against the north wall of Rm e9 in K20 (Figs. 44, 45 & 498). It was about 50 cm wide, with the two sides supplied by mud bricks (30 × 20 × 10 cm) placed on edge and resting on potsherds, and the front open to the room. On the base were the remnants of a crushed unbaked clay vessel, and in the clean grey ashy fill of the interior were sherds from one or more coarse pots.

Occasional other installations had a rectangular brick surround. In Rm e3 in H18 bricks on edge had been used to mark off the south end of the room and to contain a segment of floor used as a hearth at each side (FI96/17 to the west, and FI96/19 to the east, see Fig. 497).

While Rm e6 seems likely to have been roofed, this is less certain for Rm e9 which was a work space housing a loom, and for Rm e2. In the late phases of the Western Courtyard a number of square fireplaces seem to have stood on their own in the open, isolated from any architecture, and are likely to have served for domestic activities including cooking. These include FI96/1 from Level I or IIh in I19d, a square feature 62 × 62 cm cut into the ground (Fig. 46), and FI96/11 in a IIf phase of the Western Courtyard (Figs. 47 & 499). This was a square (42 × 42 cm) formed by mud bricks, with a plastered base incorporating several sherds from a large jar (**800**), sunk at least 20 cm into the courtyard surface (and thus probably not open to the north, although it was cut at this point). To its east an oval cut (P96/60, *c.* 22 cm deep, 2.20 m E–W, 0.90 m N–S) seems to have respected its east wall and may therefore have been associated.

Most hearths were circular. A few were mere burnt patches of ground, like FI96/3 in K20c (1.25 m long; IIb/c) or FI96/23 near the doorway in Level IVa Rm 42 (Fig. 487), which was no more than a shallow depression in the floor, some 40 cm in diameter. In the IIb Western Courtyard FI97/12 (Fig. 494) was a simple circular hearth of this sort, and similarly FI95/6 in the annex to the IIc Stele Building, Rm 18, was a flat circular feature with a diameter of 80 cm (Fig. 495; with three flat stones probably laid deliberately at its centre). In the subsequent phase (IId) a rectangular hearth (FI95/1; 1719) was laid directly above this, suggesting that the shape was relatively unimportant. In the Western Courtyard there were often circular hearths, sometimes more than one in use together. These include FI97/13, a IIb circular hearth at +98.19, and just to its north two burnt patches at +98.08 (not assigned an FI number: Fig. 494); *c.* 2.5 m to the SW there was an-

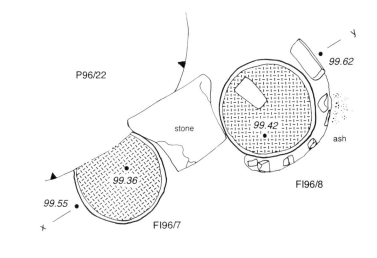

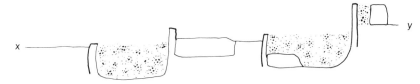

Figure 48. *FI96/7–8 (I19 Level IIg/h).*

Figure 49. *FI96/7–8 in I19; Level IIg/h, looking south (see Fig. 48).*

other hearth FI97/12, at +97.87 but probably contemporary too. Two circular fire installations, FI97/7–8, in the IIg phase of the Western Courtyard with bases at +99.36–99.42 (Figs. 48 & 49) were certainly contemporary. That on the west (FI96/7) was a simple circular clay-lined pit, di. 34 cm, and sunk some 10 cm below the associated ground surface (1773); 30 cm to its east, and separated by a large stone, was FI96/8 which was slightly larger (di. 37 cm), was also clay-lined, and was protected by an edging of stones round its south and east sides where the associated

Figure 50. *FI96/25 in Rm e3; Level IId/e, looking north.*

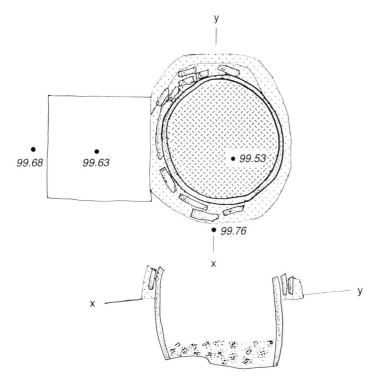

Figure 51. *FI96/5 (I19 Level IIg/h).*

surface was higher. Some 50 cm to the north there also was a flat circular pebble-based hearth of about the same size (FI96/9).

Tannours

Some fragmentary tannours (by which is meant ceramic or unbaked clay cylinders serving as bread ovens) were present in the Level I layers closest to the surface, e.g. in L19a FI98/1, 55 cm in diameter with a clay wall 3 cm thick resting on small stones, and in L19a/c FI98/2 (5933), a cylinder of fired clay 6 cm thick, 80 cm in diameter and standing 45 cm high, both clearly of Byzantine date. FI94/17 at the north side of N12 was also in a Byzantine level; it was circular with a brick lining from 10 to 15 cm thick and had a diameter of 90 cm.

In Level II cylindrical ovens were exceptional. One was a ring of clay in H18b (FI96/25; Fig. 50; di. 42 cm, standing 25 cm high, baked but now very crumbly). Another was FI96/5, assigned to IIg/h, but perhaps associated with the IIf kiln in the SE corner of I19d (Figs. 51–2, 151; di. 46 cm; depth 23 cm): this had a baked clay lining 2 cm thick, protected round the outside with white plaster 4.5 cm thick, and it seemed to have been countersunk some 20 cm into the associated courtyard surface, with a plaster surround above this point. Against its west side was a square box measuring 40 × 40 cm with the same white plaster.

Pebble-based installations

Like FI96/18 in the centre of Rm 3, more formal hearths mostly had a smoothed clay base laid on a bed of river pebbles, sometimes as much as 15 cm deep. The earliest instance of this practice is FI97/1 in an open area in Level Ve (on plan Fig. 486). It was exceptionally large (di. 1.85 m), with four consecutive layers of pebble-based clay, to a total depth of 30 cm (see Fig. 512). Pebble bases recur frequently in the earlier phases of Level II, but are not represented among the installations in I19 in phases IIf–h. The roughly square IIb hearth FI96/4 in Rm 15 had two layers of pebbles separated by a layer of flat stones. In the carefully made rectangular example FI96/16 in K14a the pebbles lay on a lower clay lining, which is continuous with a clay rim enclosing the hearth (Figs. 53 & 54; see p. 177). FI94/13 in R18a also had a clay lining beneath the pebbles, but this was not the regular practice. Exceptional is FI96/12 (on plan Fig. 497), a large circular hearth with a mudbrick rim, where there seems to have been a pit packed with clay ovoids underlying the pebble base (see p. 153).

In some cases where we only have a fragmentary patch we cannot tell whether it belonged to a simple open hearth or to an enclosed oven. Where more was

Fire Installations

Figure 52. *FI96/5 in I19d; Level IIg/h, looking south (see Fig. 151 for location).*

Figure 54. *FI96/16 in K14a; Level 2, looking east (see Fig. 53).*

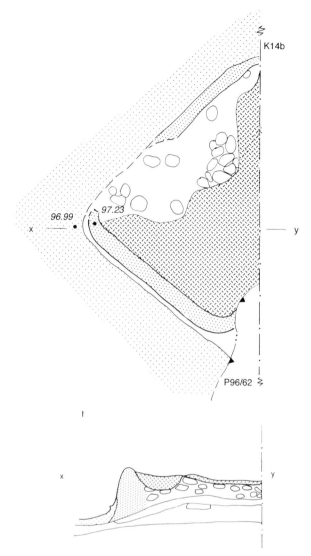

Figure 53. *FI96/16 (K14 Level 2).*

Figure 55. *FI94/9 in Rm e10, looking east (see Fig. 498 for location).*

preserved the longer dimension is usually around 1 m. There was sometimes evidence for a shallow kerb, as in FI96/16 in K14a (see above), but in at least one instance it appears certain that it was a low oven roofed with a shallow clay dome. This was FI94/9 in Level IIe in K20: it had a diameter of 60 cm and at least 20 cm of the top survived curving over (Fig. 55; on plan Fig. 498). Unfortunately it was observed in cross-section at the end of one season and did not survive for detailed recording the following year. An earlier instance is FI95/9 (Figs. 56 & 57; on plan Fig. 491) on the east side of the Eastern Courtyard in Level IIIe, where not only were there the beginnings of an inward slope on the wall, but pieces of the upper structure were still scattered across the base.

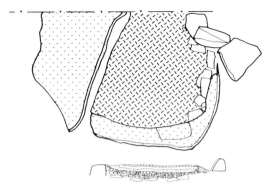

Figure 56. *FI95/9 (J20, Level IIIe Eastern Courtyard; see Fig. 491 for location).*

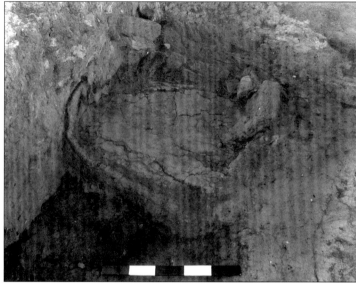

Figure 57. *FI95/9 in J20 in Level IIIe Eastern Courtyard, looking south (see Fig. 56).*

Large ovens

The two largest free-standing ovens encountered were FI97/2 in the Level IIb Western Courtyard, and earlier than this FI97/10 in the Eastern Courtyard of the IIId building. Neither of these was built over a layer of pebbles; the fuel chamber of FI97/2 was probably sunk at least 20 cm into the courtyard floor, while FI97/10 seems simply to have been established on the flat ground. Another fire installation which might fall into this category is FI96/13 in Rm e2 (H18; on plan Fig. 497), also larger than usual and clearly located in a domestic working area, although circular and based on pebbles.

Two other self-standing oblong ovens or hearths were probably in open spaces. Each was edged with vertical bricks or stones, and it remains uncertain whether either of them was roofed over. FI97/7 (Fig. 58) in H20d Level Ve (Fig. 484) had two successive clay bases, with upright brick edging down the two long sides with a surviving height of 0.40 m, and a total length of 1.80 m. Its floor sloped gently down to the SE. This was a substantial installation, and should perhaps be seen as an early version of the courtyard ovens in IIIe and IIb just mentioned. On a smaller scale was

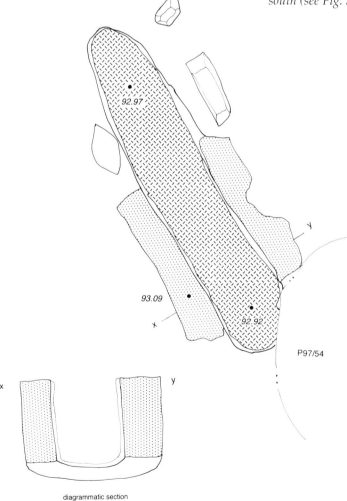

Figure 58. *FI97/7 (H20 Level Ve; see Fig. 484 for location).*

FI95/4 belonging to the later Level 2 phase in I14a (Fig. 59). It was a stone-lined oval pit (0.5 × 1 m) sunk into an open space and surrounded by ashy deposits which presumably derive from its use. Some modest 'industrial' purpose cannot be ruled out for this one. Whether the oblong installation FI98/4 (I19c in Level II; on plan Fig. 494) was similar to either of these is impossible to say, since it was so badly eroded.

There are just two definite kilns, FI96/14 (Figs. 147–50) and FI96/15 (Figs. 151–4), from the same time and place (Fig. 499). Each had a narrow rectangular fuel chamber sunk into the ground, lined with small stones and clay or lime plaster, and was probably spanned by an internal floor on which the items to be fired (presumably pottery) would have been placed. What remained of the superstructure of FI96/15 seems to have been clay-lined, with traces of internal arches. FI96/15 may also have been associated with a pair of open hearths to its north, and/or a tannour-like oven against the wall to its west (see above, FI96/5). Both kilns were probably in an open courtyard, with one end built into one of the courtyard walls. There is unfortunately very little to indicate the nature of the building to which these kilns were attached.

A group of roughly contemporary pottery kilns was found at Tarsus. They were larger but in other respects similar, with long narrow fuel-chambers usually lined with brick or stone, and in some instances with remnants of the firing platform surviving (see Goldman 1963, 14–17).

Continuity

Continuity in the position of the hearth suggests continuity in the use of space. This is best attested by the central hearth of Rm 3 of the IIc Stele Building, but another example is offered by FI96/20, seen in the side of P96/64 in J19a, where the pebbles of a second clay surface were laid directly 9 cm above the first.

Groupings

Kitchen areas often had more than one installation together. A small 'kitchen range' in Level IVb comprised two adjacent pits of differing size and depth (FI94/2–3; Figs. 60 & 61). They

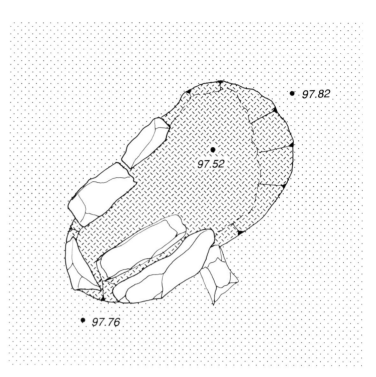

Figure 59. *FI95/4 (I14 Level 1/2k).*

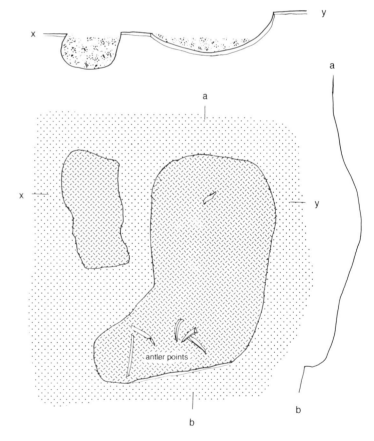

Figure 60. *FI94/2–3 (H20 Level IVb; see Fig. 488 for location).*

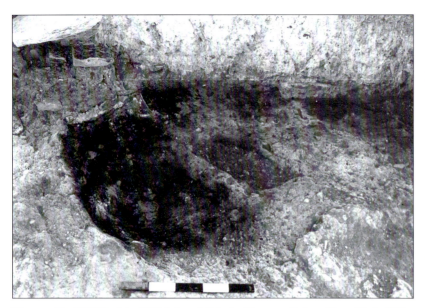

Figure 61. *FI94/2–3 in H20d; Level IVb, looking south (see Figs. 60 & 488).*

Figure 62. *FI94/7 in Level IIc Rm 15, looking east (see Fig. 492).*

had no clay plaster or other lining, but plenty of evidence of use including antler tines in among the black ash. They were probably set against a wall to the SE, although it had been cut away.

In Level IIc Rm 15 a row of three ovens was positioned along the NW wall of the room (FI94/7; see Figs. 62 & 492). This was a very busy scene, as close to them near the NE wall of the room were also FI94/11 and FI94/10 (see below and Fig. 492). Perhaps not coincidentally, a very similar row of three adjacent hearths was found just beneath the surface resting on the masonry of W714 where it formed the NW wall of Rm 12 (FI94/8); these must date to phase IId.

Contents

Apart from fragments of the installation itself, traces of its use often survived. As just mentioned, in FI94/2–3 (Level IVb) frequent tips from antler tines suggest that an antler may have been used for poking the fire, a purpose to which it would be well suited. In H18 a long iron fork (**2322**) found lying on the floor of the hearth may well have been a fire tool and thus not coincidentally left there (FI96/19). Ash was of course regularly deposited both inside and outside the installations. Wet-sieved and flotated samples from such contexts occasionally yield botanical remains, though not as frequently as one might hope or expect. Micro-morphological samples were also taken through ash deposits, e.g. Level Vi ash deposits with 'remarkably well preserved calcitic pseudomorphs of plants and other organic remains' which W. Matthews (in Matthews & Postgate 2001, 5.5.2 on 1853) interprets as rake out from a fire installation. It seems likely that other forms of laboratory analysis might cast light on the types of fuel used and on the temperatures reached in individual cases, but even in the case of the suspected kilns there were no signs of really high temperature.

Chapter 9

Pits

J.N. Postgate

Over the five seasons of excavation 457 'pit numbers' were assigned in our sequential list (P94/1–57; P95/1–87; P96/1–128; P97/1–91; P98/1–94). Not all of these could in fact be described as pits: some were too small, and are more like post-holes, others may be no more than emplacements for jars or shallow cuts resulting from building or other activities, and some are the holes of animals, either foxes or badgers to judge from their size.

Undoubtedly some features which could or should have been given pit numbers are not included in the list, either because they were simply not seen during excavation, or because the excavators did not think they merited the status. Occasionally one pit may have been given two different numbers (in two different squares or seasons). In many cases the excavator assigned one or more unit numbers to distinguish different components of the fill. A separate number was also often given to the outline or cut of the pit (such units corresponding to no volume of earth and yielding no contents), but this was not a general rule. Details of dimensions, construction and contents were recorded on a standard 'pit sheet' (see Fig. 40 for an example), as well as in the site notebooks.

In the following excavation narrative (Chapters 10–18) units relating to pits are listed after each section. If the pit number is not specified it can be discovered from the Unit List (Appendix 2), which also gives information about its stratigraphic level and purity. Individual pits are not usually described in the text, except for those which can be clearly identified as in use at the same time as a building and so contribute to our understanding of its nature.

Storage pits

These form the largest class of features which can reasonably be called pits (as opposed to 'cuts' or 'holes') and it seems simplest to describe them first, before other examples which do not fall into any neat category.

Level I
Bell-shaped pits with a distinct clay lining were of Byzantine date and were grouped at the NW corner of the site (P98/82 was a lone example in the SW angle of the nave of the church). As with the great majority of all pits only the lower part survived, so that one can only guess at the original depth. P94/29 is the nearest we have to a complete profile (Fig. 63); this pit in J19d survived to a depth of 1.10 m and the diameter narrows from 1.40 m at the base to no more than 0.40 m at top, which must be near the original rim. It was a relatively small example, since P94/13 was 1.50 m deep and had a diameter of 1.63 m at the highest surviving point, P97/37 in J18b was 0.85 m deep, with a diameter of 1.30 m at the base and only 0.90 m at the top, while the largest, P94/7 in J20c measured 2.2 × 2.3 m with a surviving depth of 1.60 m. While clay linings do occasionally occur in earlier levels, those of Byzantine pits are especially thick. 5 cm was normal, and in P94/10, which was a large pit (di. about 2 m) with atypically

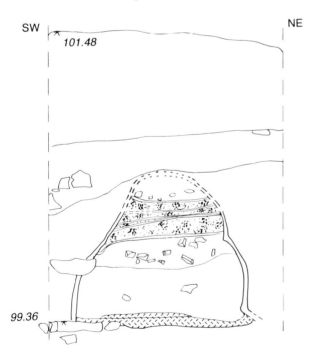

Figure 63. *P94/29 (J19 Level I).*

Figure 64. *Lined Byzantine pit P94/10 in J20b, before excavation (see Fig. 508).*

Figure 65. *P94/10 after excavation.*

vertical sides, the lining was as much as 10 cm thick in places (Figs. 64–5). P98/82 in the church area (Fig. 507) was clay-lined and close to cylindrical with sides only tapering slightly towards the top (50 cm deep, di. at base 60 cm, at top 50 cm).

Carefully made clay-lined pits of this kind seem likely to have served for food storage, and this obvious assumption is confirmed by carbonized grains recovered from the base of P96/19 (spelt) and P96/11 (barley, see Bending p. 591). We noted that there was often a black ashy deposit across the base of the pit (as in P96/11, but also in P95/15), but are not able to determine whether this was accidental or deliberate. It is conceivable that fire was used to cleanse the interior, but it seems unlikely that if the pit was to be reused much of the resultant ash and soot would have been left inside. P94/7 (see above) also had a distinct black deposit (1309) at its base, beneath a clay lining. On a layer of black ash at the base of P94/29 (see above) there was the skeleton of a young animal; we cannot imagine that this relates to the original purpose of the pit and it may be simply a case of secondary use as a rubbish pit. The same must presumably apply to P95/33 from which came a number of whole jars (see Jackson, p. 200).

Earlier levels

There were no examples of such bell-shaped pits in the Iron Age levels. In some later Iron Age contexts investigated by us (Levels IIf–h in I19 and E5 in R18 in particular, but also the contemporary phases of H18, K14a and L19) there was a remarkable concentration of successive pits, their outlines intersecting one another to the extent that in places nothing remained but segments of pit fill. They were usually accurately circular in plan, with a diameter at the base of between 0.90 and 2.00 m, although a few even larger examples were over 2 m in diameter: P98/86 di. 2.5 m (K18b); P98/71 di. 2.30 m (L19a/c); P98/85 di. 2.04 m (L19c, phase IIc); P95/13 = 23 (Figs. 69 & 492); P95/81 (I14a), di. 2.15 m sloping down to 1.8 m. The base was flat, and the sides were usually more or less vertical, though they did sometimes slope slightly in towards the top (this seems to have been usual in I14, which may reflect a chronological difference). In these phases the original top of a pit virtually never survived, because the later ones had cut away the upper part of the earlier ones, and their own upper parts had been sliced away by later building work or by the erosion of the mound surface.

A few earlier pits had a clay lining: in Level II P94/2 in I20b/d and P95/77 in I14a (8 cm thick); earlier

P96/87 in H19 from Level IVb, with a clay-lined base, and P96/103 in H20 Level Vh/i. The majority were however unlined, except that their base was often distinguished by a bright white layer of decayed vegetation, normally about 1 cm but occasionally as much as 5 cm thick. This layer might also extend some way up the vertical sides (in the case of P97/7 as far as the surviving top, 60 cm above the base). The study of this substance by Marco Madella (Chapter 50) confirms our suspicion that this represents the decay of a deliberate straw lining, and that the primary purpose of the majority of these pits must have been grain storage.

In earlier phases storage pits with phytolith linings were not quite so frequent and rather less standardized. Three examples in the Level IIc Stele Building are of particular interest. The burnt debris inside each of them shows that they were in use at the time of the destruction. We therefore know their full depth, and it is clear that there were no elaborate arrangements (such as brick or stone surrounds) for their closure. P97/6 alongside the foundations of the outer wall of the building in the Western Courtyard was large and irregularly shaped (at the top 1.94 × 2.10 m, and 1.26 m deep, giving a capacity of about 8 m³). On the other side of the building in Rm 6, P98/72 (see Fig. 66) was also quite large, measuring 2 m E–W and 1.5–1.6 m in depth, but more nearly circular, and P98/94 in the next door space Rm 24 was a smaller circular pit (di. 1.00 m, depth more than 0.75 m). P97/6 was found with a layer of black ashy material on the sides and base, which is presumably the result of burning the straw lining preserved as phytoliths in other cases. In the case of P98/72 in Rm 6 successive layering gave evidence of re-use, but none of these three pits seemed to have contained a store of grain at the time of the destruction (though plenty of food plant remains were recovered from inside the building).

A similarly burnt and abandoned building in I14 Level 2 provided another example of a pit in its

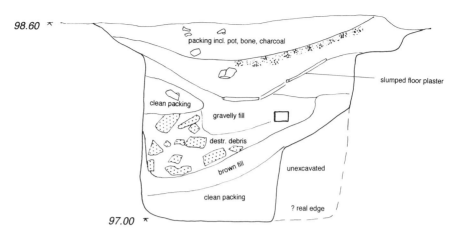

Figure 66. *P98/72 (K18 Level IIc Rm 6; see Fig. 492 for location).*

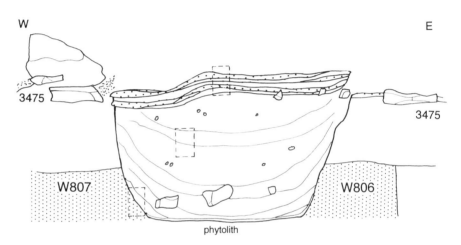

Figure 67. *P96/29 (I14 Level 2, Rm 97; see Fig. 505 for location).*

context (P96/29; Fig. 67, on plan Fig. 505, in section Fig. 514). Here some evidence remained of a stone rim around the top of the pit, and at least one stone slab projected over the edge. One must assume that storage pits might be opened and resealed more than once during their lifetime. Similar too was probably P95/49 in Rm e9, Level IIe in K20 (plan Fig. 498). The sherds of several large storage jars were scattered on the floor surface of the room, and also filled this pit which must have been contemporary (di. 1.60 m, depth 0.94 m). It is uncertain if this space was roofed or not, but the collection of loomweights (**1735–60**) from the same surface indicates that it was a working area.

Although typical storage pits were not identified in Level III and only rarely in Level IV (see P96/87 above), phytolith-lined examples are attested at least as early as Level Vf (P97/63; P98/17) and from Ve (P97/7; P97/27; P97/34; P97/54), helping of course to identify the excavated area in H20 as an open domestic space in Ve/f. Several of these were large, and two

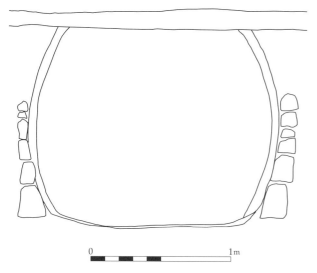

Figure 68. *P97/88 (H20 Level Vf4, Rm 53; see Fig. 483 for location).*

in phase Vf were stone-lined: P97/88 (Vf) di. 1.60–1.70 m, depth 1.50 m, with a well-made stone lining all round, and phytolith-lined base (Fig. 68); and P98/17 which was stone-lined only on its north and west sides, but had phytolith lining as well. In other periods stone linings do occur, but infrequently: there are two well-constructed cylindrical pits lined with medium-sized stones on the eastern slope. One in R18 (P94/44, di. ~2.5 m) is later Iron Age (phase E4a) and another very similar one nearby (P94/57, di. ~1.8 m; Fig. 70) is presumably of the same date. At least two smaller pits dug into the site of the Stele Building had rather irregular stone linings: P97/20 in K19b, and P98/35 in K19d which had a phytolith lining as well (both shown on Fig. 523). In these two instances the use of stones might just be a response to unstable soil conditions in the vicinity, but this would not apply to the larger well-constructed examples on the east slope and in Level Vf. A stone-lined Byzantine (or possibly earlier) pit in J14a survived to a depth of 1.10 m (P95/56).

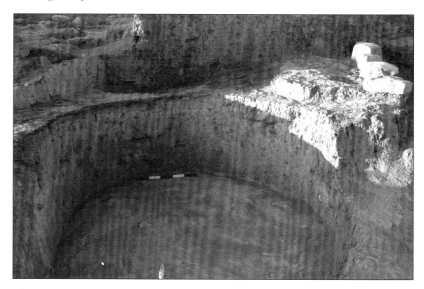

Figure 69. *P95/13 in Level IIc Rm 1, looking south (see Fig. 492 for location).*

Fills

In some cases the fill of the lower part of the pit was composed of layers of soil alternating with white phytoliths (making it difficult to decide when the base of the pit had finally been reached), and sometimes also of black ashy or burnt orange striations. This would seem to be evidence of serial reusage for the same purpose, and is attested in most phases. Good examples include the courtyard pit in Rm 6 (P98/72), P97/69 in the Western Courtyard of the Stele Building (see Fig. 491), and P94/53 from phase E5a on the east slope. Although the plant structure of the lining material does survive in these white layers, the grains themselves, not being stored in a carbonized state, were not normally recovered.

Other examples of accumulated layers of phytoliths are in H18b: P96/78 (2624); H18b+d: P96/86 (2631, 2636); H20d: P97/7 (1288); I19b: P95/1 (1708), P95/3 (1714), P95/34 (2886), P97/69 (5501); J19d: P97/73 (3943 etc.); K14: P95/22 (3031, 3047), P96/33 (3078); K18a: P98/72 (6122 etc.); K19d: P98/35 (4569–70, 5956); L19c: P98/66 (5970); R18a: P95/5 (2402), P94/53 (3012 etc.). See also W. Matthews in Matthews & Postgate 2001, 5.3 and 9.3.6.

Location

While it is only in the Stele Building and in I14 that we can be sure of the precise context of storage pits — in unroofed spaces associated with individual buildings — these presumably reflect the normal practice. In Levels IIf–h in I19/20 it was clear that the storage pits had been positioned over a period of time in an open space. Without knowing precisely from which surface each pit was sunk we are not able to reconstruct how the later pits were positioned in relation to earlier ones. It would seem unlikely that when a new pit was dug, it would actually intersect the outline of an old one just abandoned. Where we meet such an intersection, we must presumably conclude that the old one had been back-filled some time previously, so that its position was no longer evident. Perhaps the back-filling of a pit would have coincided with a general renovation of the courtyard which could have involved clearing away a surface layer and then raising the overall ground level, obscuring its outline. Certainly the fill of the majority of pits in the IIf–h horizon was relatively clean and homogeneous, suggesting a deliberate operation.

Figure 70. *Stone-lined pit P94/57; Phase E4a in R19, looking NW (see Fig. 501 for location).*

Figure 71. *Robber trench P94/2 in J19d, cutting surface 1602; looking north (see Fig. 499 for location).*

Other types of pit

Not all storage pits were identifiable by their phytolith lining, and the purpose must in some cases remain uncertain. The size of the pit, the regularity of its construction, and its architectural context are all criteria which contribute to interpretation. Whereas food storage pits were rarely placed within a room while it was in use, a hoard of astragali (**2421**) was buried under the floor of Rm 7 of the IIc Stele Building, in a small depression evidently intended for the purpose. Also within the IIc building, but very much larger, was P97/73 occupying the east half of Rm 10 (see plan Fig. 492), which we think must have been in use during the building's lifetime, and had a mudbrick surround on its east side. This could have been a grain storage pit, and it had a capacity of over 11 m³, but we have no certain explanation for its unusual location.

In the pre-Byzantine phases of L19 there were several unusual pits. P98/44 was oval and very large, 3.20 × 2.80 m, though only 0.75 m deep. The bottom was filled with very loose brown soil and above this was a layer of bricky fill mixed with many small stones. Since the base and sides had a white phytolith lining it was presumably a storage pit despite its unusual size and shape. Probably similar was P98/51 which measured *c*. 2.70 × 1.60 m and survived to a depth of 0.62 m; it too had a phytolith lining on base and sides, and was filled with loose brown earth, beneath a layer with charcoal lumps at the top.

Completely enigmatic, and only partially excavated, was P98/49, a vertical-sided, unlined shaft dug into the Level IIc East Building. Within K19d this measured 3.30 × 2.00 m, but the unexcavated part extended into L19c, K18b and L18a. Since it was not emptied to its base the depth is unknown, but it was not less than 1.30 m. Its fill was solid clean earth with occasional whole mud bricks, and no doubt deliberate. Since a well shaft is an improbability on top of this conglomerate promontory it is hard to see what purpose it could have served.

P97/77 in K19 was a large circular pit sunk into the concreted destruction debris of Rm 20, and at the base contained a large piece of hoplite shield (**2272**), which leads us to attribute it to the Hellenistic residents of the site or their immediate predecessors. P94/41 in Q19c (see Fig. 500) was probably of similar date, since its fill contained a fair amount of imported Hellenistic pottery; it measured 2.70 m E–W and being relatively wide and shallow did not look like a storage pit.

Of Byzantine date is P96/17 (on Fig. 509) from which we recovered an entire column base (**190**) displaced from the church, packed round with large unshaped building stones (Fig. 179). It seems possible the intention was to use the base as a support, and that the pit was dug simply to let it into the ground. Similarly P95/6 in K20d (on Fig. 509) looked as though it had been intended to take the base of a large post wedged in place by the stones found packed into it (Figs. 181–3). In the NW part of I18 there was a large space which had been filled with loose building stone, but looks more like a construction feature and was not assigned a pit number.

Contents

It does not need to be stressed that the contents of the pits as we found them are not usually a guide to their original use. An unwanted pit may have been refilled deliberately in one operation, whether the fill was clean soil (cf. above) or miscellaneous debris, or if left open it may have filled up gradually by natural processes or have been used for occasional rubbish disposal. It seems unlikely that many of these pits were designed in the first instance for rubbish disposal, since the steep edge of the tepe offered an easy route for instant disposal of unwanted matter. However, once dug and no longer required for their original purpose they sometimes had obviously been used for waste material.

Usually mixed deposits within a pit look like nothing more than a load of earth with a normal admixture of sherds, bones etc., but in a few instances the assemblage appears to have had a less secondary origin. In the large (>2 m di.) IIf pit P98/70 in K18b at least 7 loomweights (**1783–9**) and fragments of two grindstones (**2762** and **2816**) had been dumped. The fill of P95/81 in I14 Level 2 was predominantly black ashy, but included various items of bone, ivory and metal (see p. 175). A small pit of Level III date (P95/63 in H19b, 4212) contained a quantity of animal bone, including a pig skull, but also shell, obsidian and a piece of copper wire. The jars found in the Byzantine pit P95/33 (see above) seem likely to have fallen in or been put there to dispose of them.

Similar conditions probably account for the occasional recovery from pits of larger animal bones or even skeletons, which were too substantial to have lain around for long under foot without getting in the way. Examples include a pig's skull from P95/63 from Level III (see above); a *Bos* skull J20/63 from P95/13 (Level IId–f); and fragments of a dog skeleton (**2498**) from the IId/e pit P97/86 in K19. From Level I pits, either Hellenistic or Byzantine, came another dog skeleton **2497** (P97/40 in K19d) and the kid's skeleton **2496** (P94/29).

As noted above, in the courtyards and also Rm 10 of the IIc Stele Building we found a few pits which must have been standing open (and possibly empty) when it was destroyed. These contained the primary debris from the destruction of the building which also lay in depth across the floors of the rooms. More puzzling are a few pits dug through the destruction debris of the Stele Building, apparently before its reconstruction in phase IId: P96/101 (in NE corner of Rm d5); P96/119 (against east wall of Rm 4); P96/121 (di. 2.50 m, at north end of Rm 4, respecting its wall faces). These seem to have been backfilled with more or less the same material as they had dug through. One might suppose that they were attempts to recover items from the destroyed building, but if so it is curious that they are regularly circular in outline, rather than haphazard shafts. In retrospect the easiest explanation might be that they were indeed storage pits, but belonging to an open area in the IId phase, so that the burnt debris derives from the destruction of the IId, and not the IIc phase. Nevertheless, at the time of excavation the excavator was clear that P96/119 and P96/121 at least had been sunk from below the IId floor surfaces, and that the debris must have been from the IIc destruction.

A different case is P97/49: this was dug into the NW corner of IIc Rm 7, and inside it were found a jar (**915**) and over 40 small bone tools, fragile when found because of the burning they had suffered, but not otherwise apparently unserviceable (**2469**, Figs. 126 & 318). If the pit was in use at the time of the destruction, conceivably it had served for the storage of these bone artefacts, perhaps along with a now perished organic container, since otherwise it is hard to see how they would have ended up so tidily inside it.

A similar situation in the following phase seems to be implied by P96/102 which was dug into the destruction of IIc Rm 3; the matrix of the fill consisted of black burnt matter within which was an unusually rich assemblage of material including worked and unworked animal bone (**2437**, **2459**) and broken and burnt pottery. This plainly derived from destruction debris, but it must have been from the IId destruction since it included several pieces of Mycenaean pottery, one of which joined one of the fragments found still resting on the IId floor of Rm 7 to the south (**959**). The pit can therefore hardly have been dug for storage from a subsequent phase, especially since it is sealed by a (probably) Level IIe wall. The best assumption seems to be that it was standing open at the time of the IId destruction.

Chapter 10

Level V: the Early Bronze Age

L. Seffen

Introduction

The surveys of the 1950s and 1960s established the presence of Early Bronze Age sherds at Kilise Tepe, but given the depth of later deposits and the limited time that was at our disposal, our only prospect of access to the earliest stratified levels at the site was by taking advantage of the eroded edges of the mound, in an operation we often referred to as our 'Deep Sounding'. Step trenches down the side of a mound are notoriously deceptive, but a very large shaft, which turned into a tunnel leading south under the centre of the tepe, had been dug into the north end of the mound by local villagers in former years. Inspection of the cross-section it had left revealed clear plastered wall faces and a floor associated with a thick layer of burnt material (Fig. 11). This looked enticing (and later turned out to be Level IVa). Excavation therefore began in H20d, and was subsequently extended into H20c and H19a+b. In the course of time this evolved into two different operations: in H20d and H19 the emphasis was on the later phases, i.e. the Middle and Late Bronze Age remnants of Level III and Level IV(a and b). In H20c, thanks to the steep slope of the mound, the highest surviving level was IVa, giving us easy access to the Early Bronze Age here. The robber shaft was almost entirely within H20c, and initially we were doing little more than square up and straighten its sides, but below the base of the shaft phases Vh down to Vl were intact. These earlier phases were fully cleared within H20c, although at first it was only the eastern half of the quadrant that was carried down to bedrock, meaning that phases Vi to Vl were each dug in two strips. Later, to increase the volume of earth investigated, the higher EBA phases (Ve down to Vg) were also dug in H20d, under the MBA deposits already excavated as Level IV. The location and area exposed in each phase is summarized in Table 7.

Although the Deep Sounding successfully delivered a stratigraphic sequence covering most of the third millennium, with no obvious reason to suppose a gap in occupation, the small area exposed means that there is little that can safely be said about the nature and purpose of the buildings. General statements based on an area never more than 5 × 10 m, and often less,

Table 7. *Overview of Levels III–V in H19-20 and I-J20.*

Level	Period	C14 samples (see p. 621 for details)	Date range (cal. BC)	Squares	Area exposed (m², approx.)	Fig.
IIIe	LBA	J20/125	1440–1210	I19, I-J20	73	491
IIId	LBA			H-I19, H-J20	230	491
IIIc	LBA			H19	26	490
IIIb	LBA	H19/157	1920–1610	H19-20	60	489
IIIa	LBA			H19-20	60	489
IVb	MB	H19/197	2120–1770	H19-20	50	488
IVa	MB	H19/357	2140–1770	H19-20	80	487
Ve late	EB III			H20	25	486
Ve middle	EB III			H20	25	485
Ve early	EB III			H20	25	484
Vf4	EB III			H20	32	483
Vf1–3	EB III			H20	25	482
Vg	EB II	H20/456	3100–2600	H20	45	481
Vh late	EB II			H20	39	480
Vh early	EB II			H20	42	479
Vi late	EB II			H20	17	478
Vi early	EB II			H20	17	477
Vj	EB II			H20	17	476
Vk	EB			H20	17	475
Vl	EB			H20	8	474

are bound to be dangerous. It is regrettable that we could not achieve a wider exposure for any of the better-preserved phases, but this proved impracticable. Extending to the south and east would have meant clearing several metres of tightly stratified overlying material, while to the north the slope of the mound left little if any deposits, and further west, where phases Vh to Vj were probably close to the surface, there is more disturbance in the shape of recent robber pits.

Below Vh the remains of all phases except Vj are too scrappy to make even the vaguest of generalizations, and Vj itself looks rather different in nature from anything above it. Above this the consistent orientation of the walls in phases Vh, Vg and Vf, and in particular the constant presence of a NW–SE wall (surmised in Vh, W246+249 in Vg, W244 in Vf1–3), suggest a degree of continuity, compatible with the tight sequence of rebuilding which makes the different phases so tricky to disentangle. This continuity is reinforced by the consistent use of fine yellow plasters on walls and floors in Vh and Vg (and perhaps Vf too, although only some patches of floor are available for comparison). It is unfortunate that we have not recovered anything approaching a complete plan for the buildings of these levels, because the indications are that they were well planned and constructed, and well cared for. The quality of the floor plaster in Vg in particular, as attested by the micromorphological evidence, but also more generally the yellow clay plastering of both floors and walls in Vh, Vg and Vf, raise the possibility that as in later levels some of the rooms were not exclusively utilitarian.

In our introductory chapter (p. 37) we have noted that there is a definite change in the pottery between Vg and Vf, and by comparison with the ceramic sequence at other sites this would mark the transition from EB II to EB III. As described by Symington (pp. 295, 306), the destruction of Vg would therefore coincide with similar destructions at other Anatolian sites. Nevertheless, here at Kilise Tepe it appears that if the burning of the Vg building was a result of hostile action, it did not lead to the complete abandonment of the site but was followed by a rebuild on similar lines. On the other hand, above Vf the pits, fire installations, and other scrappy features attributed to Ve indicate an open area and thus a change of use for the area of H20d. In architectural terms, the significant breaks are between Vf and Ve, and between Ve and Level IV.

Note on phasing

In Levels I to IV at the NW corner of the mound, the major levels are sub-divided into phases, identified by letters, with 'a' the lowest in each case (see Table 7). Thus the latest phase of Level III, phase IIIe, is followed by the first (and lowest) Level II phase, IIa (see Fig. 473).

The phasing of Level V reverses this system. The phases in H19 and H20 were initially given letters in alphabetical sequence, starting with 'a' at the surface and continuing to phases 'k' and 'l' above bedrock. Subsequently, phases 'a' and 'b' were redesignated Levels IIIb and IIIa, respectively, while phase 'c' was renamed IVb and phase 'd' IVa. Everything below this is deemed to be Level V, but here we have retained the original letters for the phases, so that uniquely in Level V the lettering for the phases runs from top to bottom, from Ve to Vl.

We are aware that this is very inconsistent, but inverting the order would have required a major overhaul of our records during the preparation of the report, and doubtless have resulted in errors and greater confusion.

Level Vl (Fig. 474)

The earliest cultural material recovered by us was a jar lying in a shallow pit in bedrock at the base of the H20c sounding. Bedrock was reached here at ~88.60–88.70 (Fig. 72), and was the natural conglomerate of the terrace on which the tepe is formed. The stratum immediately above it was rich in pebbles deriving from the disintegrated surface, which can be observed today on the neighbouring hill to the east (Fig. 6). No traces of architecture were observed, but in the NE corner of the

Figure 72. *Phase Vl bedrock, looking west.*

excavated area this layer sealed a shallow scoop about 20 cm deep in the natural rock (P97/30; base at +88.49), in which lay a jar (**193** H20/676: Fig. 73).

Level Vl units and finds[1]
Natural conglomerate: 1893, 5431
Cut: 1894
| Jar | 1894 | *H20/676 | **193** |

Level Vk (Fig. 475)

The earliest architecture in the deep sounding consisted of three wall foundations of stone construction, which may have enclosed a space — roofed or unroofed — of about 3.90 m by more than 2.20 m. W241, in the NW corner of the excavated area, was built directly over the natural conglomerate, and a single course of medium-sized stones some 10 cm high and 50 cm wide survived. In the east of the sounding were W230 and W231. Under both these walls at +88.67 was a compact surface (1892), which seems likely to represent levelling material prior to their construction, and they seem to have rested directly on a further surface (1891) at ~88.90. A small posthole (6 cm di., 11 cm deep) was let into this surface at some 50 cm from the SW face of W230 (1889–90). W230 running NW–SE had one course of stones ranging in size from 13 × 8 × 25 to 40 × 23 × 13 cm. At its NW end it was cut by a later grave P97/5. At the SE end it was bonded to W231 which ran at right angles to it; it was not possible to determine if either wall foundation continued eastwards under the baulk. W231 also had one surviving course of stones and was of the same construction as W230; it was parallel to W241, and stopped approximately 50 cm from the edge of the sounding. This could represent the location of an entrance through the wall.

Above 1891 and the equivalent layer in the west half (5429), was a layer of packing between the walls (1885); to the SE of W231 (1886) and NE of W230 the equivalent layer was mixed with pebbles which may indicate that these areas were external.

Since the stones of W241 lay directly on the natural conglomerate, it may have been structurally earlier than W230 and W231 which stand on two layers of packing. This would not necessarily mean that it belongs to a different building phase, and it seems best to leave it in Phase Vk.

The Vk walls and room fill were sealed by two or three layers of homogeneous earthen fill to a depth of 10–20 cm. Their upper surface sloped down to the west, but provided the material for the base of the Vj walls.

Level Vk units and finds
Construction surface: 1891, 5429
Posthole: 1889–90
Packing: 1884–6, 1892
| Pub. ceramics | 1892 | | **194–5** |

Packing below Vj walls: 1879, 1882–3, 5427–8
| Hearth guard | 5427 | H20/836 | **1630** |
| Loomweight | 5427 | H20/794 | **1679** |

Level Vj (Fig. 476)

This was a better-preserved occupation phase with three or four rooms of a building excavated, and a number of pots and other domestic furnishing preserved *in situ* when it was burnt down. It is also of special interest in providing virtually the only intact human interment in the prehistoric levels of the site, which seems to have been placed intentionally within the destruction debris of the building.

The main architectural feature was W225, a substantial mudbrick wall running NNE–SSW across the quadrant. It was 50 cm wide, had stone foundations and survived to a height of 25–34 cm. At three points postholes were sunk in the centre of its brickwork. There were no traces of timber in these holes, and if there were posts here we are not able to say if they belonged to a wooden frame above the brickwork or were incorporated within it. Abutting the north face of W225, approximately halfway along its length, was W227. This was a narrower mudbrick wall with one course of stone foundations, 30 cm in width. It separates Rm 83 on the east from Rm 82 to the west. These two rooms, together with their walls and the neighbouring areas, had suffered a violent fire, which had changed the colour and consistency of the walls and floors, and also of most of the finds caught up in the conflagration.

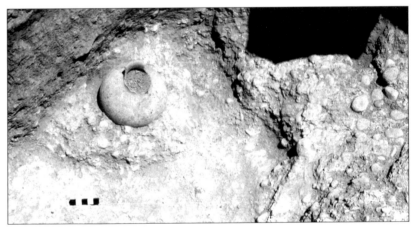

Figure 73. *Jar* **193** *(H20/676) in situ, looking NE (see Fig. 474).*

Rm 83 had a well-preserved plaster floor, only cut by an intrusive grave in the NW corner (P97/5). At the

Figure 74. *Phase Vj Rm 82 destruction; objects **199**, **201**, **211** (H20/736–8), looking north (see Fig. 476).*

Figure 75. *Phase Vj juvenile skeleton **2842** (H20/785), looking east (see Fig. 476).*

east side of the room a low (8 cm) plastered platform was built onto this floor. It had a rounded west end, and may have backed up against the eastern wall of the room (if this was continuous with the incurving plastered face in the SE corner of the room). However, since it showed no evidence of use as a hearth, it may rather have been associated with a threshold giving access to the room from the east. On the west side of the room a secondary mudbrick feature had been constructed on the floor along the plastered wall-face. It stood some 50–60 cm high, and the top was rounded and plastered continuously with its east face. It is impossible to be sure if this was a subsidiary wall, perhaps topped by a wooden superstructure, or some other feature, such as a high step or shelf. (W226 is shown extending north to the limit of the sounding, but the presence of P97/5, and the fact that W227 was cut by the SW edge of P97/5 (not shown on plan) makes it unlikely that the brickwork of the wall survived here, although the restoration may be correct.) At the centre of the room a large block of fallen brick masonry stood nearly 1 m high from the floor, and south of the platform, in the corner of the room, a jar was lying under the destruction debris (**202** H20/614).

The same destruction material was present in Rm 82 on the other side of W227. It is noticeable that there is no plaster on the wall-faces enclosing this space, and this is probably because the walls have been removed down to floor level. The floor here is 40 cm higher than on the east side of the wall, suggesting that we should see Rm 82 as a raised platform area; although it is true that to the south of W225 the contemporary floor is only some 20 cm lower, so that Rm 83 may also have been sunken. On the plaster of the floor in Rm 82 (which was exceptionally finely prepared, see W. Matthews 2001, §9.3.1 on unit 5412) rested the base of a large vessel (H20/743; base di. 41 cm), with **196** H20/725 inside it and two other pots nearby (**197** H20/735 and **204** H20/734). Other household goods, including loom-weights and a baked clay stand (**1625**), were not directly on the floor but scattered through the destruction debris, which extended over the line of W237 and into Rm 81. They may therefore have been on a flat roof. W237 was entirely mud brick, without a stone base, and was perhaps more of a partition than a wall. The gap between it and W236 may represent a doorway between here and Rm 82. Here the destruction fill was deeper, although no plastered floor was seen. Three more jars (**199** H20/737, **201** H20/736, **211** H20/738: Fig. 74) lay against the destroyed face of W236 which delimits Rm 81 to the west.

The western limits of Rm 82 are not clear, since both the floor and the overlying destruction peter out here. Rm 80 may have been an interior room in view of the plaster along the west face of W236. South of W225 Rm 84 also had a plastered floor, and wall-face, suggesting it was an interior space. There was a circular plastered feature within it, not preserved to its full height, and two postholes cut the floor, close to the south face of W225.

The destruction debris extended across the line of W225 and overlay Rm 84. It also sealed a number of large stones which were scattered over the western part of W225 and the south side of Rm 82. In between and beneath these lay the complete skeleton of a juvenile (**2842** H20/785: Fig. 75), in a gently flexed position on its right side. The skull lay under one of the large stones, and other stones gave the appearance of having been deliberately placed each side. It looked as though the skull had been deliberately crushed, but as David Thomas points out, it could well be that it was intended as the roofing slab of a small cist which collapsed onto the skull after the inhumation. No artefacts were found with the skeleton, and it did not seem to have been placed in a cut.

Level Vj units and finds
Walls 225–6: 1874–5

Pub. ceramic	1874+1859		270
Loomweight	1875	H20/623	1682

Destr. debris above Rms 81–2: 5406

Jugs	5406	H20/744, 816	198, 200
Cup	5406	H20/980	206
Pub. ceramics	5406		207, 210, 212, 214, 280
Basin	5406	H20/829	216
Jar	5406	H20/720	217
Stopper	5406	H20/770	1491
Loom support	5406	H20/742, 755	1625–6
Loomweights	5406	H20/740–41	1683–4
Red pigment	5406	H20/817	

Rm 81
Occ. surface: 5424

Pub. ceramic	5424		213

Destr. debris (N area): 5406, 5412, 5417

Jugs	5406	*H20/736–7	199, 201
Bowl	5406	*H20/738	211

Rm 82
Occ. surface: 5411, 5424

Pub. ceramic	5424		213

Destr. debris (S area): 5406, 5412, 5417

Jug	5406	*H20/725	196
Juglet	5406	*H20/735	197
Large vessel	5406	*H20/743	
Cup	5406+1858	*H20/734	204
Cup frag.	5406	H20/980	206

Rm 83
Occ. surface: 1861
Feature: 1873
Destr. debris: 1858–9, 1871

Pub. ceramics	1858		203, 271
Loomweights	1858	H20/545, 551	1680–81
Cup	1859	H20/567	205
Spit support	1859	H20/561	1628
Sp. whorls	1859	H20/563, 566	1836–7
Point	1859	H20/569	2453
Polished bone	1859	H20/570	2482
Polisher	1859	H20/562	2627
Human bone	1859	H20/879	2843
Jug	1871	*H20/614	202
Pub. ceramics	1871		208, 281

Rm 84
Occ. surface: 1870
Feature: 1869
Destr. debris: 1864, 5416

Pub. ceramic	1864		209

Packing: 5427, 1879

Hearth guard	5427	H20/836	1630
Loomweight	5427	H20/794	1679

Cuts into Rm 84: 1866–8, 1880–81, 5422–3

Grave overlying W225: 5407

Human bone	5407	*H20/785	2842

Level Vi (early) (Fig. 477)

In the west half of H20c, immediately overlying the phase Vj destruction material, at ~90.30 a yellow clay floor was laid (5403). A hearth was let into it in the south (FI97/5). This is partly under the south baulk, but measured 70 cm E–W, and more than 70 cm N–S; along its west side is a raised rim 8 cm in height and about 12 cm wide. About 1 m to the NW a large pottery vessel (H20/709) was sunk into the floor, with its mouth at floor level (+90.32). In the east half of the quadrant (which was excavated the previous season in 1996) some stone wall foundations survived to a height of 20–30 cm (W791–2). W792 ran for 2 m N–S, with W791 abutting it at right angles on its eastern side and running for about 50 cm before disappearing under the baulk.

These early Vi features are difficult to place within a stratigraphic framework without recourse to the section. Here it is possible to see that much of Vi has been robbed out or levelled to make way for later construction. A layer of hard yellow clay at the base of 1852 (~90.37), described as being 'associated with small remaining patches of thin white plaster surface', is probably the floor belonging with this phase, and would have been laid against mud brick resting on the stone foundations. At the north side of the quadrant the base of a pottery jar (**273** H20/544) had been sunk through the packing (1853) beneath this floor and into the underlying Vj destruction material; the sides of the cut had been lined with white plaster suggesting that it may have belonged with the floor at the base of 1852. It was at this level, beneath the plastered floor of the later phase of Vi, that a cut appeared against the north baulk; this may represent the top of P97/5, but the contents were very loose, and it may be that at this level it is no more than an animal burrow. West of W792 the deposits were cut by Pit P96/96. This was 68 cm in diameter, and was emptied to a depth of 60 cm where the top of W226 was exposed.

Level Vi (early) units and finds
Packing over Vj: 1863, 1898–9, 5402

Sp. whorl	1863	H20/607	**1849**
Hammerstone	1863	H20/617	**2628**
Human bone	1863	H20/863	**2844**
Pub. ceramics	1898		**230, 240**
Human bone	1898	H20/875	**2849**
Pub. ceramic	1899		**272**
Human bone	1899	H20/872	**2846**
Pub. ceramics	5402		**222–3**
Hammerstone	5402	H20/707	**2629**

Packing below white floor: 1853

Pub. ceramics	1853		**218, 231–2, 234, 242, 282–4**
Mortar	1853	H20/534	**2671**

Occ. layer: 5403

Pounder	5403	H20/715	**2781**
Human bone	5403	H20/798	**2848**
In situ jar	5403	*H20/709	

F197/5: 5404

Sunk into Vj: 1858

Pithos	1858	*H20/544	**273**

Level Vi (late) (Fig. 478)

The remnants of the later phase of Vi consisted of stone wall foundations standing one course high but yielding no coherent plan, and a small area of plastered floor in the NW. W235 and W234 were aligned NNE–SSW and ran next to each other along the west side of the quadrant. W233 extends eastwards some 1.5 m from the south end of W234, at a sharp angle. The stones numbered W790 in the eastern half of H20c may represent foundations for a continuation of W233, but if so they appear to have been displaced, and they are more likely to be the result of later disturbance which removed the eastern part of the wall. It is not possible to be certain which, if any, of these walls were in use simultaneously, though they must have been roughly contemporary.

The principal value of the patch of floor at +90.49 in the north of the quadrant is that it seals the area of P97/5, a pit filled with loose earth which cut into the plastered floor of Rm 83 in Level Vj. This pit contained the disarticulated bones from the lower half of an adult human (**2845**).

Level Vi (late) units and finds
Packing above white floor: 1852

Pub. ceramic	1852		**220**
Bone point	1852	H20/799	**2454**
Grinder	1852	H20/506	**2700**
Human bone	1852	H20/554	**2847**

Cut into Level Vj Rm 83: 1872

Human bone	1872	H20/615	**2845**

Cuts into Level Vi: 1855, 1865–6, 5400–401

Level Vh (Figs. 479–80)

Phase Vh was reached in both H20d and H20c, and is therefore exposed for 10 m from west to east. It had three clearly definable sub-phases, which belong to part of a substantial building, with a similar layout and alignment to Vg above, and well-constructed walls with thick plaster on the floors. For a C14 determination between 3150 and 2600 from the packing layer above the floor of Rm 70 (1838) see p. 621.

The earliest sub-phase is designated Vh1 (Fig. 479). Parts of four rooms of this building were excavated, three of them separated by W252 running from the SE corner of H20d to the centre of the north baulk. This was a substantial, 53 cm wide, plastered mud-brick wall with four courses of stone foundations. It survived to a height of 65 cm in the north, and was not fully exposed in the south. Halfway along its east side Pit 97/82 has cut away its junction with W251: this was also a plastered mudbrick wall, but only 38 cm wide and survived to a height of no more than 20 cm. It separated Rm 73 in the north from Rm 74 to the south. Both of these rooms had well-preserved plastered floors. Rm 73 had a small vessel (**221** H20/1058) sunk into its floor at +91.55. Rm 74 is mostly unexcavated. On the other side of W252 to the west was Rm 72, a large room with a minimum width of 2.85 m, and a length of 5 m or more. It had a thick yellow plaster floor at a lower level than the rooms to the east, and much cut in the SE by later pits. In the north a plaster line was traced marking the south face of the northern wall of Rm 72, a continuation of W786. This line breaks at 1 m from the east wall, and both the plastered face of W252 and the plaster of the floor continue to the north of the line, indicating a doorway at this point. There is a shallow depression in the floor here (some 13 cm in depth), which would make sense if this was an entrance leading into the room from an area lower than the floor of Rm 72 itself.

The western wall of Rm 72 is presumably concealed beneath the Vg floor, which remains unexcavated, but the Vh floor continued beneath the associated Vg wall (W246). In H20c, to the west of the presumed wall, is Rm 70. At its northern end it was bounded by the southern version of W786. Only the stone base of this wall survived, standing up to 50 cm high, with a plaster line 1.5 cm thick along the south face. Assuming that there was a western wall to Rm 72, the eastward continuation of the floor plaster along the south face of W786 must indicate that there was an opening here connecting Rm 70 with Rm 72. In this part of the room, some 50 cm south of the wall face, lying at the base of unit 1836 which was a layer of earthen fill, were a juglet (**268** H20/434), a spit-stand (**1627** H20/435), and also a round stone. Below this an earlier layer of fill lay directly on a well-made yellow clay floor at +90.75, continuous with the wall plaster. Further west, the W786 plaster turns towards the south, marking the east face of a mudbrick wall we did not spot; the floor plaster probably stopped along the same line (although this was not recorded), since both wall and floor plaster were subsequently identified in the south section, and the plaster lines shown on the plan no doubt belong to this wall's western face in Rm 79. The zig-zag plan of this plaster perhaps results from a doorway or an internal bench. The floor in this space looked identical to the Rm 70 yellow clay surface, but stood some 10 cm higher, at +90.87.

In the later phase Vh2 the north wall of Rm 72 was taken down and Rm 71 was constructed (Fig. 480). W252 remained in use (as did Rms 73 and 74 on the other side of the wall), but the three other walls of the room, W253–5, were newly built. These are of mud brick surviving to a maximum height of 30 cm, mostly resting on stone foundations. For a stretch of 1.05 m at its western end W253 rested on large stone slabs, which overlay the plaster floor of Rm 72, and W255 had one course of stones underneath its entire length. The lowest part of W254 was not excavated, but further to the west in H20c the northern side of W786 seems likely to have been the foundation for a continuation of this repositioned northern wall. Any floor which might have belonged with this phase of the wall, and have run across the top of the southern part of W786, would have been removed by the modern robber trench, the base of which cut through the top of phase Vh in H20c.

The final sub-phase Vh3 survives only in the NW of H20d as a patchy surface which ran up to the west face of W252 at +91.62. This suggests that the building remained in use for another phase, but these later deposits are mostly cut away by the Vg architecture.

Level Vh units and finds
Walls 786, 251: 1849, 6330
Pub. ceramics	1849		275, 285
Grinder	6330	H20/1049	2703

Rm 70
Occ. surface: 1846, 1850
Packing: 1851, 5405
Pub. ceramics	1851		233, 239, 241
Querns	1851	H20/509, 512	2701–2
Pounder	1851	H20/498	2782
Pub. ceramics	5405		219, 274

Cut into Rm 70: 1857
Antler	1857	H20/550	2481

Packing above floor 1850: 1838
Pub. ceramics	1838	224, 235–6, 244, 247–50, 252, 269, 276–8	
Scraper	1838	H20/461	2554
Door socket	1838	*H20/450	2672
Pounder	1838	H20/460a	2783
Hammerstone	1838	H20/460b	2784
C14 sample	1838	H20/456	see p. 621

Fill below Vg occ. surface: 1836
Pub. ceramics	1836		251, 253–6, 261–2, 279
Juglet	1836	*H20/434	268
Spit stand	1836	*H20/435	1627
Mortar	1836	H20/427	2673

Rm 71
Occ. surface: 6319, 6326
Packing above surfaces: 6310, 6317, 6323
Lithic chips	6323	H20/1063	2586

Cuts into Rm 71: 6322

Rm 72
Rm fill: 6308–9, 6312, 6329
Pounder	6308	H20/1040	2786

Occ. surface: 6313

Rm 73
Destr. debris and deposits above floor: 5399, 6318
Occ. surface: 6307
Bowl	6307	*H20/1058	221

Packing below floor: 6320
Flint sickle	6320	H20/1062	2543

Fill below packing: 6321, 6333
Cut into Rm 73: 6324

Rm 74
Packing above floor: 6325

N of W786
Packing below 1838: 1847
Pub. ceramics	1847		225, 245, 267
Jar	1847	H20/477	265
Core	1847	H20/479	2575

Figure 76. *Phase Vg Rm 64 cut by pits P97/82, 88, P98/17, 58; wall W246 to the right; looking south (see Fig. 481).*

Figure 77. *FI98/5 constructed against Phase Vg W246, looking SW (see Fig. 481).*

Level Vg (Fig. 481)

The remains of Vg resemble Vh in the quality, layout and alignment of the construction, suggesting a degree of continuity between the two phases. The architecture of Vg is among the best preserved on the site, thanks to a fierce conflagration, with mud brick and the plaster on floor and walls baked hard, and some rooms filled with concreted rubble (Figs. 76 & 77). On the other hand we have regrettably little in the way of artefacts from this phase. The scarcity of objects on the floors suggests that the building had been cleared out before the fire, and since most of the stratified Vg material consists of walls or building rubble, there is a shortage even of sherd material.

Our area of excavation is divided in two by the NW–SE line of W246 and W249, parts of which were standing to a height of 0.70 m. Unfortunately much of the western sector in H20c had been dug away by the modern robber pit, while in the east later wall-trenches and a series of large storage pits from phases Vf and Ve (P98/17, P98/58, P97/82, P97/88 and P96/13) have removed much of the floors and walls.

East of W246 there was much less evidence of high temperatures, and less burnt debris (although this is due in part to the higher floor levels). Parts of three rooms survived here. In the NE corner Rm 65 was delimited by W250 to the SE, but the stones of the Vf foundation of W248 have removed its western side. Its clay-lined floor is at virtually the same level as the floor of Rm 64 to the east, but with only a little ashy deposit on it. Rm 64 had a hard, lightly burnt, plaster floor running up to W250 in the north. This wall was cut away by later building as can be seen on the section (Fig. 512). It survived as two courses of stone within a foundation trench cut down onto the Vh floor below. The SW wall of the room had also been cut away, and only a plaster line and the edge of the floor indicated its approximate line. If there was access between Rms 64 and 63 it was probably where P97/82 has cut away floor and wall in the NW corner of the room.

Like its Vh counterpart Rm 72, Rm 63 looks like a principal reception room. Unfortunately a good deal of its floor-surface was taken out by at least four large pits, but a small patch of floor with associated wall-plaster in the SE corner gives it a width of about 2.5 m, and it must have been more than 4.5 m in length. On the west side of the room a stone-lined fire installation FI98/5 projects about 60 cm from the east face of W246, with an internal width of 30 cm (Fig. 77). It was constructed from two slabs of slate (or a similar stone) which were set upright into the floor, giving a height of about 30 cm. They were plastered inside and out, and the plaster extended onto both the floor and the wall-face. Further stones lined the back of the oven against the wall. The feature was filled with fine ash, and broken slabs of stone on the base of the oven suggest it originally had a stone capping. The south section of H20d shows that the earliest floor of this room was some 20 cm lower down at ~91.65, meeting the eastern face of W246 just below the point where the stone foundation gives way to the mudbrick superstructure; the fire installation may have been used in both phases.

Wall 246 itself was a substantial mudbrick wall 50 cm wide with stone foundations 6 courses deep (Fig. 77). It stood to a height of 53 cm above the final, burnt, floor in Rm 63, and 92 cm above the floor of Rm 62 in the west, which was thus 40 cm lower but had plainly been burnt in the same event. The plastered mud-brick face of W246 projected some distance over the floor in Rm 62, and this fact, as well as the profile of the wall in the southern section indicates that a segment of the mudbrick masonry had shifted and slumped to the west (perhaps as a result of the weakness caused by the burning of internal timbers?). This slumped wall face is shown on the plan by a dashed line. In the north W249 was originally a continuation of W246. However the foundation trench for a large phase Vf1 wall (marked on the plan as W785 and W247) cut a 70 cm wide section through it. The bottom of the plaster line along the west face remained however, and it is obviously possible that W247, although itself later, was replacing a robbed out Vg predecessor in the same position.

To the west of W246/249 little survived the robber pit, but the walls that did were baked hard by the fire, which must have been more intense this side of the wall, and the intervening spaces were filled with hard-fired building rubble to a depth of 70 cm. In the south was Rm 62. Both the wall and floor of this room

Figure 78. *South section of H20d, showing burnt deposit on sequence of clean Level Vg floors in Rm 62.*

Figure 79. *H20c: east section through levels Vg–i. At top destruction debris resting on Vg floor, and plastered door jamb. Base of sounding with Vi foundations at ~90.60, with pedestalled Vh foundations centre left, and large stones belonging to threshold 6327 directly beneath Vg floor, centre right. Micromorphological samples at right.*

had been liberally plastered. It was clear from the cross-section in the south baulk that the burnt floor was only the last in a succession of very carefully plastered yellow clay floor surfaces making a 15 cm thick band (Fig. 78), and therefore that the room had been refurbished on several occasions before it was burnt down (in contrast to Rm 63 to the east which seems to have undergone only a single reflooring over the same period). Micromorphological study of this sequence of floors confirms the extreme cleanness of the floors and the regularity of their replastering, and suggests that Rm 62 was singled out for special treatment (see W. Matthews 2001). It is unfortunate that most of this room is probably under H19a, and its northern and western limits are difficult to define. To the north a feature (6327, visible in Fig. 79) runs SW from W246 to which it is bonded. It has stone foundations four courses deep, the lowest of which was a single large stone measuring 90 × 50 × 15 cm. Over the top course of stones a layer of wood was laid, and over this wood the feature was plastered. The stones continue into H20c, giving a total length of about 1 m, and their solidity suggests that they belong to a load-bearing wall rather than an internal fitting. However, to the west the floor plaster extends northwards as far as the line of W785, and since the feature had a small slope down to the south this suggests that it may have been a shallow step inside the threshold, which is readily understandable since at the NE corner of Rm 61 the floor was 11 cm higher than in Rm 62.

Whether these were in fact two separate rooms is difficult to decide. The plastered floor of Rm 62 stretches north until it is cut by the stone foundations numbered W785, which are a continuation of W247 belonging to phase Vf1. In the NW W784 was a small surviving part of the mudbrick walls. It stood to a height of seven courses of mud brick over only one course of stone foundations (compare the six courses of stone for W246). Its east face was plastered and corresponds to the plastered west face of the return from W249, in which there was the impression of a vertical post (Fig. 79, on left). These are undoubtedly the two jambs of a doorway. The debris in this area included very large blocks of mud brick, severely burnt. No sign of a threshold was noted, but a large stone door socket (**2672** H20/450) was found at a lower level (+91.03). This seems likely to be associated, though if so it has probably been displaced. The plaster on the jamb of W784 curves round as though another wall ran to the south, no more than 25 cm further to the west, which would have made Rm 61 a small room about 1.70 × 1.80 m.

In the SW corner of H20c the robber trench had left a fragment of the plastered face of W787, with a small piece of the associated floor. This wall would have been parallel to W246, and certainly belonged to this phase to judge from the absolute height of the floor surface, the hard-fired wall plaster, and the identical burnt rubble which filled the room to the surviving height of the walls (some 40 cm). This area is designated Rm 60, but depending on the position of the north wall of Rm 62, it could have belonged to the east end of either Rm 62 itself, or another room to its north.

Level Vg units and finds
Walls 246, 249–50: 6305, 6315–16

Pounder	6305	H20/1037	**2630**
Grindstone	6315	H20/1052	**2706**
Quern	6316	H20/1061	**2707**

Cuts into walls: 5379, 6335

Lithic sickle	5379	H20/966	**2541**

Rm 60
Destr. debris: 1839, 1841
Packing below floor: 1845

Pub. ceramic	1845		**243**
Sp. whorl	1845	H20/474	**1838**

Rm 61
Destr. debris: 1831, 1844

Pub. ceramic	1831		**263**

Cuts into Rm 61: 1832, 1834

Rm 62
Destr. debris: 1833, 5374, 5387

Grindstone	5374	H20/888	**2704**

Room fill: 1835

Pub. ceramic	1835		**259**

Occ. surface: 5391

Loom support	5391	H20/1082	**1629**

Feature: 6335

Rm 63
Packing: 5383

Bowl	5383		**260**
Platter	5383		**286**

Destr. debris: 5380, 5382, 5388

Pounder	5380	H20/964	**2785**
Loomweight	5388	H20/987	**1685**
Sp. whorls	5388	H20/1004–5, 1011	**1839–41**

Occ. surface: 5393
Fl98/5: 6303

Rm 64
Destr. debris: 5384, 6304

Pub. ceramics	5384		**237, 257–8, 266**
Bead	5384	H20/969	**2008**
Human bone	5384	H20/1033	**2850**

Occ. surface: 5389
Packing below floor: 6314
Mixed packing in Rm 64: 5397

Sp. whorls	5397	H20/1009, 1020	**1844, 1852**
Palette	5397	H20/1008	**2618**
Lithic blade	5397	H20/1007	**2596**

Rm 66
Destr. debris: 5398

Grindstone	5398	H20/1020	**2705**

Fill: 5385, 6306

Level V: the Early Bronze Age

Level Vf (Figs. 482–3)

After the destruction of Vg, this phase seems to represent a period of uninterrupted occupation, with new buildings regularly constructed on top of older buildings that had been cut down to their floor level, or even to the foundations of their walls. Therefore the remains from this level are often not associated with any floors or walls. This was clearly seen in the sections. Also two large later pits P97/82 and P97/88 cut through much of the Vf deposits, further destroying the architecture. Four sub-phases were identified, the latest of these (Vf4) being the best preserved, as shown on Figure 483. The other Vf plan (Fig. 482) shows the preceding three fragmentary sub-phases together, which between them occupy no more than half a metre in depth. In all sub-phases, the walls that do survive seem to be aligned in the same direction, and there is evidence to suggest that throughout this phase the central part of H20d could have been an external area. There was no *in situ* inventory of artefacts on the floors, but the fill of the rooms was relatively rich in ceramic and lithic debris.

Figure 80. *Phase Vf4 Rms 50–53 looking west, cut by P97/82 and P97/88 (see Fig. 483).*

The earliest sub-phase (Vf1) is only represented here by the wide stone foundations of W248 and of W247, which abuts it to the south. Wall 247 was 70 cm wide with four courses of large stones (40 × 35 × 30 cm) remaining. Wall 248 was constructed using large stones for the bottom course with smaller (15 × 15 × 10 cm), often rounded, stones for the remaining four courses. In the north section of H20d the trench containing the foundations of W248 can be seen, cutting through the phase Vg floor of Rm 65 and into the late Vh wall W252. A clay floor is also visible in this section, to the east of W248, at the same level as the top of its surviving stone foundations, but this was not identified within the trench. Most of the stone foundations of W247 were robbed out, with only a stretch of 1.70 m left where it joined W248; the trench that originally held them survived, and was seen cutting through the brickwork of W249 in Level Vg. This allows us to associate it with the remnant of stone foundation shown in H20c on Figure 481 labelled W785. Other early Vf1 architecture may have existed in the SE of H20d. In section it can be seen that the Vg mudbrick walls and room fill have been cut into, with the replacement material containing much mud brick. However this was poorly preserved and there was no sign of the usual stone foundations, so it may have been no more than bricky fill.

Level Vf2 consisted of a small, poorly preserved wall stub W245. It was 80 cm long and 48 cm wide and constructed from one course of stones and blocks of mud brick. This seemed to be contemporary with a mudbrick feature seen in section, made of three mud bricks, each of a different colour ranging from grey to yellow, stacked one above the other (5373). A patchy green clay floor, which we had difficulty tracing, ran underneath 5373 and directly overlay a thick band of Vg debris. It is assigned to Vf2 because in the north baulk it is plainly later than W248 of Vf1, a sub-phase which must have been cut away completely further east.

Level Vf3 was also very shallow. However, perhaps because it was sealed by Vf4 packing material and not cut into by later architecture (at least in the south of H20d) there are two well-preserved stone wall foundations W243 and W244. W243 survived two courses high running NE–SW for a distance of 1.12 m. It was cut by P97/82 and P97/88, but had probably continued to make a right-angled junction with W244, which was of a very similar construction and also two courses high. No other walls are definitely contemporary with these, and although there was a surface to the north and west of W244, it is not known whether this was associated with the wall or cut by it. The rest of this structure has been cut by pits P97/82 and P97/88, and has been levelled by the builders of sub-phase Vf4. We have no criteria to help us decide if we are looking at part of the internal rooms of a house or an external space. However, south of W243 is a cylindrical pit (P98/17; di. 1.65 m) with a stone lining 8 courses (1.16 m) deep on its north and west sides (W242). This was dug during Vf3, and means that the area south of W243 is likely to have been an open space.

Phase Vf4 (Figs. 80 & 483) was the best-preserved Vf sub-phase. In the NE and east of H20d there were parts of Rm 51 and Rm 52. Rm 51 was bounded by W239 to the west and W232 to the south. Both of these walls stood 70–80 cm high, and had stone foundations with a shallow layer of their original mud bricks on top of them. W239 was only 30 cm wide. It was plastered on its eastern face where it met the plastered floor of Rm 51. W232, which ran NE–SW separating Rms 51 and 52, was noticeably larger than W239, being 54 cm wide, with large foundation stones. Parts of its original plastered northern face survived, but most of its mud bricks were not preserved and therefore much of the plaster was lost with them. Rm 52 had a plastered floor which ran up to W240 in the south. This wall was very similar to W232 and W239, was 44 cm wide and survived to a height of 45 cm.

Wall 232 continued to the west, and what may be an entrance way of some kind can be seen 1.30 m west of the point where W239 and W232 join, between Rm 50 in the north and Rm 53 in the south. These rooms have no clay floors and may be external areas.

The walls further to the west may or may not have belonged to another building. This part consisted of a mudbrick wall (numbered W238 in H20d with a continuation W735 in H20c) aligned NW–SE, only roughly parallel with W240 and W239. Abutting this was W736, running NE–SW on the same line as W232. These walls were about 60 cm in width, and had large foundation stones with some courses of mud brick surviving above them. In the case of W735 and W736 this mud brick stood up to eight courses and 90 cm in height. Both of these walls had traces of pinkish plaster on their western faces suggesting that Rm 54 and Rm 55 were interior rooms. Only a small area of these rooms could be excavated, the remainder of Rm 55 having been removed by the modern robber trench, and of Rm 54 being buried beneath the south baulk. The fill of Rm 55 was very mixed, with mud bricks and stones in brown soil, as well as a number of loomweights. No internal floor was identified in either room. W735 seems to end in a door jamb where there are some fallen stones, in what may have been a doorway between Rm 55 and Rm 50.

Level Vf units and finds

General units from Vf1–Vf3
Packing: 1823–6, 5363, 5365, 5367–9, 5372, 5390

Pub. ceramics	1823		228, 291, 303, 317–18, 323, 325, 422
Pub. ceramic	1823+1825		395
Sp. whorls	1823	H20/392, 394	1864–5
Human bone	1824	H20/877	2851
Pub. ceramics	1825		321–2, 326, 361, 423
Pub. ceramics	1826		229, 295–6, 320, 324, 329–30, 433, 436
Bone tube	1826	H20/404	2471
Jar	5363+5351	H20/1015	379
Pottery discs	5363	H20/1013–14	1537–8
Sp. whorl	5363	H20/924	1847
Astragali	5363	H20/916a	2425
Antler frag.	5363	H20/916b	2493
Grindstone	5363	H20/957	2708
Pub. ceramic	5367		368
Tweezers	5367	H20/921	2276
Pub. ceramics	5368		300, 313, 332
Flint sickle	5368	H20/937	2540
Worked stone	5368	H20/929	2667
Pub. ceramic	5369		428
Bead	5369	H20/931	2001
Astragalus	5372	H20/1076	2426
Lithic flakes	5372	H20/933	2588
Pub. ceramic	5390		305

Fill: 1829

Pub. ceramics	1829		290, 298–9, 311, 327–8, 331, 333, 374, 384
Clay scraper	1829	H20/424	1586
Fossil	1829	H20/423	2525
Human bone	1829	H20/878	2852

Mixed: 1843, 5371, 5381

Unstratified cuts into Vf: 1832, 5364, 5375, 5377, 5394

Lithic sickle	5364	H20/913	2553
Lithic flake	5364	H20/915	2596
Bead	5394	H20/1000	2004
Lithic blade	5394	H20/999	2596

Level Vf1
Wall trench: 5376, 5378

Bowl	5376	H20/1065	312
Pub. ceramic	5376		362
Pub. ceramic	5378		429

Level Vf2
Packing: 5370

Pub. ceramics	5370		287, 307, 440
Pottery disc	5370	H20/983	1550
Mortar	5370	H20/973	2674
Quern	5370	H20/930	2710

Cut: 5392

Pub. ceramic	5392		441
Pottery disc	5392	H20/1075	1549
Lithic sickle	5392	H20/992	2542

Mudbrick feature: 5373
Posthole: 5386

Level Vf3
Mixed: 5361

Sp. whorl	5361	H20/900	1843

Level V: the Early Bronze Age

Wall 244: 5356
Pub. ceramic	5356		**288**

Packing: 5350 (Rm 52), 5354 (Rm 50), 5359–60, 5366
Pub. ceramics	5350		**316, 444**
Sp. whorl	5350	H20/855	**1848**
Pub. ceramics	5354		**294, 308, 310, 427, 431**
Pot	5359		**404, 443**
Sp. whorl	5359	H20/893	**1845**
Lithic knife	5359	H20/892	**2569**
Pub. ceramic	5360		**314**
Grindstone	5360	H20/897	**2709**
Pub. ceramics	5366		**289, 306, 364**

Fill: 5357 (Rm 50)
Cut: 5337, 5349, 5362, 6300
Shell	5349	H20/852	**2508**
Mortar	5349	H20/988	**2675**
Pub. ceramics	5362		**292, 363, 438–9**
Juglet	5362	H20/920	**397**
Sp. whorl	5362	H20/904	**1850**
Needle	5362	H20/902	**2226**
Astragali	5362	H20/1032	**2423**
Lithic blade	5362	H20/914	**2596**

Level Vf4
Packing in foundation trench for W735 and 736: 1819
Pub. ceramic	1819		**375**
Denticulate	1819	H20/375	**2572**

Walls 238–40, 735–6: 1817–18, 5320, 5326, 5347
Grinder	1817	H20/367a–c	**2775**
Pub. ceramics	1818		**293, 354**
Sp. whorl	5320	H20/855	**1848**
Perf. stone	5326	H20/830	**2665**
Pub. ceramic	5347		**335**
Astragali	5347	H20/843, 1031	**2424–5**
Bone needle	5347	H20/886	**2465**
Hammerstones	5347	H20/848–9	**2788–9**

Rm 50
Packing: 1814
Stone tumble: 1816
Fill: 1813, 1820, 5342
Pub. ceramics	1813		**336–8, 340, 372, 399, 434**
Cup	1813	H20/359	**398**
Pub. ceramics	1820		**309, 380–81, 412–13, 424**
Sp. whorl	1820	H20/380	**1851**
Lithic sickle	1820	H20/379	**2534**
Pub. ceramic	5342		**442**

Rm 51
Occ. surface: 5336
Fill: 5335
Incised disc	5335	H20/837	**2603**

Rm 52
Occ. surface: 5314
Fill: 5310
Sp. whorl	5310	H20/689	**1883**
Bead	5310	H20/807	**2044**

Rm 53
Packing: 5352
Pub. ceramic	5352		**432**

Fill: 5323, 5327, 5331–2, 5334, 5338
Lithic sickle	5323	H20/754	**2535**
Grinder	5323	H20/732	**2779**
Sp. whorls	5327	H20/750, 752–3, 756	**1856, 1863, 1867–8**
Lithic core	5327	H20/751	**2580**
Lithic blade	5331	H20/765	**2592**
Pub. ceramic	5332		**387**
Sp. whorl	5334	H20/813	**1854**
Sp. whorl	5332	H20/774	**1855**
Lithic blade	5334	H20/812	**2566**
Lithic core	5334	H20/797	**2583**
Flaked lithics	5334	H20/797	**2590**

Cuts into Rm 53: 5324, 5328, 5330, 5340–41, 5351
Pub. ceramics	5328		**348, 365–6, 388, 405–8**
Sp. whorls	5328	H20/757, 805, 826	**1857–8, 1862**
Bead	5328	H20/825	**2002**
Metal hook	5328	H20/808	**2221**
Lithic core	5328	H20/759	**2581**
Clay cube	5340	H20/823	**1598**
Flaked lithics	5340	H20/827	**2590**
Grinder	5341	H20/824	**2775**
Pub. ceramic	5351		**386**

Rm 54
Packing: 5353
Pub. ceramics	5353		**315, 430**

Destr. debris: 5339
Cuts into Rm 54: 1299
Pub. ceramics	1299		**449, 466**

Rm 55
Fill: 1812
Pub. ceramics	1812		**297, 350, 358, 371, 377, 394, 409**
Juglet	1812	H20/344	**410–11**
Loomweights	1812	H20/345, 347–52, 354–5	**1686–94**
Sp. whorl	1812	H20/346	**1846**
Endscraper	1812	H20/343	**2556**

Cleaning Vf4 rooms: 5344
Pub. ceramics	5344		**227, 349, 396, 474**
Lithic blade	5344	H20/887	**2567**
Grinder	5344	H20/846	**2731**
Human bone	5344	H20/839	**2853**

Cut into Vf and lower phases: 5333
Pub. ceramics	5333		**392, 463**
Sp. whorls	5333	H20/784, 792	**1870–71**
Metal needle	5333	H20/775	**2227**
Bone needle	5333	H20/786	**2464**
Shell	5333	H20/789	**2500**
Flint core	5333	H20/780a	**2584**
Lithic chips	5333	H20/780	**2586**
Flaked lithics	5333	H20/780	**2590**
Grinder	5333	H20/779	**2770**

Level Ve (Figs. 484–6)

The remains of this latest Early Bronze Age level were very scanty, cut by numerous pits and by later architecture. The features assigned to this level have been represented on three plans, but these do not correspond to precise chronological sub-phases, as these were impossible to disentangle.

Chapter 10

Figure 81. *Phase Ve FI97/7, looking north (see Fig. 484).*

Figure 82. *East section H20d, showing Phase Ve FI97/1 (see Fig. 512).*

The earliest feature found from Ve was a fire installation FI97/7 (Fig. 81). This consisted of two layers of clay making up a long tongue-shaped base. On top of this along each side were placed two rows of mud bricks, baked orange. The whole feature measured 1.80 m long, 0.70 m wide and 0.40 m deep.

The middle phase of Ve (Fig. 485) consists entirely of a large number of pits, not all of which are shown on the plans. We noted a total of 13 pits cut into H20d at this level, 11 of them with phytolith linings. The number of pits and absence of walls indicates that in this sub-phase this whole area was an open space, as it probably was also at the time of FI97/7.

In the final sub-phase of Ve there was some building. The two walls shown in Figure 486 (W224 and W229) are probably partially contemporary. The foundation of W224 was 50 cm wide and consisted of one course of angular and rounded stones (on average 30 × 25 × 10 cm), running SW–NE. These were laid within a foundation trench with its base at +93.85 at the SW end. At its NE end the stones either abutted or partly overlay those of W229. (The foundation of W229 was not drawn with sufficient accuracy to resolve this issue and it is represented on Figure 486 by a broken line.) In any case W229 was the earlier construction: it was also 50 cm wide and consisted of one course of angular stones (35 × 18 × 12 cm max.), running NW–SE. The stones were laid within a trench, with its base at +93.75.

Both walls are cut by Level IVa building work, W224 in the west by the foundation trench for W106, and W229 in the north by the trench for W228. W224 was let into a layer at +94.14–94.21 (numbered 1283 to its north and 1281 to its south), which was associated with a few features, presumably pre-dating the structure. One feature is FI97/1 (Fig. 82). This was a roughly circular hearth (half under the east section), 1.85 m in diameter and made up of four layers of clay alternating with four layers of small round pebbles to a depth of 30 cm. The hearth appeared to be laid into deposit 1281. Towards the centre of the area was a square patch of well-packed orange material (1284). Cut into layer 1281 to the SE of this patch was a large posthole 35 cm in diameter at the top, 30 cm deep, and with sides tapering to a 17 cm diameter base. Some 2 m to the north, just west of FI97/1, was a similar posthole (1277), 28 cm in diameter, 26 cm deep and lined at the bottom with flat stones. Both these features, and the wall foundations which are presumably marginally later, were sealed by packing in at least three layers (1275 under 1272 under 1269). These layers represent the transition to Level IVa.

Level Ve units and finds
FI97/1: 1274
FI97/7: 5311, 5312
Clay feature: 1284
Fill: 1281, 1283, 1287, 1289, 1811, 5300–302, 5304, 5306–7, 5313, 5318–19
Pub. ceramic   1281

Level V: the Early Bronze Age

Loomweight	1283	H20/619		**1700**
Lid	1287	H20/622		**453**
Pub. ceramics	1287			**457, 462**
Human bone	1287	H20/873		**2861**
Pub. ceramics	1289			**450, 456, 469**
Loomweight	1289	H20/637		**1701**
Sp. whorls	1289	H20/636, 643		**1878, 1880**
Copper pin	1289	H20/642		**2236**
Arrowhead	1289	H20/629		**2533**
Pub. ceramics	5300			**446, 468**
Ceramic disc	5300	H20/665		**1573**
Perf. clay obj.	5300	H20/655		**1597**
Loomweight	5300	H20/654		**1695**
Lithic knife	5300	H20/652		**2568**
Human bone	5300	H20/870		**2859**
Jar	5301	H20/730		**448**
Loomweight	5301	H20/660		**1697**
Sp. whorl	5301	H20/656		**1875**
Metal pin	5301	H20/834		**2237**
Sickle blades	5301	H20/657a–b		**2536–7**
Lithic blade	5301	H20/657c		**2594**
Rubber	5301	H20/659b		**2631**
Grindstone	5301	H20/659a		**2712**
Pub. ceramics	5302			**472–3**
Clay sphere	5302	H20/666		**1596**
Sp. whorl	5302	H20/670		**1877**
Lithic sickles	5302	H20/673, 684		**2538–9**
Sp. whorls	5304	H20/672, 674		**1872, 1874**
Human bone	5304	H20/862		**2856**
Pub. ceramics	5306			**451, 454, 460, 467**
Pub. ceramic	5313			**415**
Sp. whorl	5313	H20/695		**1876**
Bone awl	5313	H20/692		**2455**
Bone point	5313	H20/698		**2456**
Bone tube	5313	H20/769		**2472**
Human bones	5313	H20/871, 876		**2860, 2862**
Pub. ceramics	5318			**464, 471**
Loomweights	5318	H20/712-13		**1696, 1698**
Human bones	5318	H20/861, 864		**2855, 2857**
Pub. ceramic	5319			**339**
Sp. whorl	5319	H20/719		**1869**
Human bone	5319	H20/869		**2854**

Packing: 1267, 1809–10, 1815

Shell	1267	H20/286		**2509**
Pub. ceramics	1810			**347, 382–3, 455**
Bowl	1810	H20/335		**352**
Sp. whorl	1810	H20/336		**1873**
Bead	1810	H20/337		**2005**
Flaked lithics	1810	H20/333		**2590**

Cuts into Level Ve: 1252, 1259, 1276–7, 1279–80, 1282, 1285–6, 1288, 1290, 1293–4, 1821–2, 5303, 5305, 5309, 5315–17, 5321, 5325, 5329, 5346

Pub. ceramic	1288			**452**
Loomweight	1288	H20/678		**1699**
Lithic blade	1288	H20/634		**2591**
Sp. whorl	1290	H20/639		**1879**
Sp. whorl	5315	H20/699		**1881**
Pub. ceramic	5317			**465**
Sp. whorl	5317	H20/703		**1892**
Lithic chips	5317	H20/704		**2586**
Human bone	5317	H20/865		**2863**
Sp. whorl	5321	H20/722		**1882**
Stone axe	5321	H20/721		**2597**
Human bone	5321	H20/866		**2858**
Pounder	5322	H20/729		**2632**
Jug	5346	H20/838		**447**

Note

1. Each of the phases in the excavation chapters is followed by a list of the principal units and the published finds. The units are arranged in their broad stratigraphic sequence: i.e. wall, packing, floor, features on floor, deposits on floor, fill, cut. The finds are listed in unit order, and then volume number (in bold). Items asterisked (*) are shown on plan. Note that this is not the complete list of finds for each unit, merely of the published finds. Complete lists can be retrieved from the project data base, when it becomes available on-line.

   To save space, published ceramic sherds from the same unit are listed as 'Pub. ceramics', unless the object has an object number, which usually indicates that it was relatively complete and/or significant. Where it exists, the object number is included, partly because this is the number identifying objects on the plans; it is also the object's number in the project archive and store.

Chapter 11

Level IV: the Middle Bronze Age

J.N. Postgate

The Middle Bronze Age at Kilise Tepe is represented by just two architectural levels, with a combined depth of about one metre, and occupying an area of some 50–80 m² in H19a+b and H20c+d at the NW corner of the tepe. The layout of the buildings is different in the two phases, and quite different from Ve below and IIIa above. Each of the two phases had a single occupation layer, which had been terminated by a fire. The buildings appear to have been largely functional, with evidence for domestic storage and textile production. A good number of clay vessels, both fired and unbaked, were found *in situ* on the floors, along with a variety of other utilitarian items, in particular a coherent group of loomweights on a IVa surface. Symington's study of the pottery and other artefacts from these two phases places them in the MBA period by comparison with other sites, especially Mersin and Tarsus, and this is supported by the C14 determination from Level IVa, see p. 621. There was no sharp break in the ceramic repertoire between Level Ve and IVa, or from IVa to IVb, suggesting continuous occupation. By contrast, the new architectural layout in Level III is accompanied by clear changes in the ceramics, and a gap in occupation before the Late Bronze Age cannot be ruled out.

Level IVa (Fig. 487)

Level IVa, excavated in 1996, comprised parts of two well-preserved rooms on the west (Rms 41 and 42), and a less well-defined, probably open, area to the east (Rm 43). Rms 41 and 42 were aligned in the same NW–SE direction as the buildings of the previous occupation levels in this area of Kilise Tepe. Rm 41 was a large space, measuring *c.* 4.5 m from SW to NE, and 6 m along its NE side; the SE wall (W749) was not fully exposed, and joined W107 at an obtuse angle, so that the length of the SW side must have been about 7 m (Fig. 83). The SW wall itself, a continuation of W748, had fallen or been removed, but its position was betrayed by the floor of the room, since it gave way along the expected line to a deposit of 'grey-brown gritty soil' which presumably filled the space the wall had occupied. The other walls survived to heights of between 49 and 61 cm, and all were close to 50 cm in width, and of mud brick, plastered on both faces. We did not penetrate below floor level, and it is not known if the walls had stone foundations.

The room itself had a yellow plaster floor, of rather uneven height at around ~94.40. It had been laid over flat paving stones, and was badly damaged by the fire. In the centre of the room was a fine, circular lime-plastered hearth (FI96/22), 1.20 m in diameter, with its surface a few centimetres above the surrounding floor level at +94.44 (Fig. 84). The raised kerb is about 10 cm wide, with a single shallow groove in the top round the west side and a double groove on the east side. To the NW this hearth and the adjacent floor were broken

Figure 83. *Rm 41 looking NW, showing burnt floor surface with central hearth and unbaked vessels at NW end of room (see Fig. 487).*

Chapter 11

Figure 84. *Rm 41 FI96/22, looking west (see Fig. 487).*

Figure 85. *Rm 41, plastered installation in west corner, looking SW (see Fig. 487).*

Figure 87. *Combed ware jar **525** (H19/366) with clay bung **1492** in place.*

by a wide shallow cut (P96/128) filled with crumbly grey soil and some small stones (<15 cm); it is hard to account for this intrusion, since it can scarcely have been contemporary with the use of the hearth, but it was sealed beneath the destruction debris.

In the western corner, against the line of W748 was a mudbrick installation (Fig. 85) of irregular shape, set into the floor, and cut off at about the same height as the walls. Plastered into concave depressions against its southern face were two large pottery jars (**517** and **523**, H19/358–9: Fig. 86). The floor in the nook between this feature and the NW wall was some 25 cm higher than in the main part of the room. Between it and the doorway were found a couple of loomweights (**1732–3**, H19/283 and 301), and several fragments of flat unbaked clay lining with vegetable temper, grey on one side and pale orange (presumably from heat) on the other (H19/251; erroneously marked as being in Room 42 on plan). In the north corner of the room the floor dipped down to a bench along the face of W105 on which stood a huddle of eight unbaked clay vessels (some of which were already exposed in 1994: Fig. 230; Baker *et al.* 1995, pl. XXIVb). These were plainly storage

Figure 86. *Rm 41 pots **517** and **523** (H19/358–9) plastered against installation, looking NW.*

containers, although botanical remains were not recovered from them.

Against the foot of W107 stood a small jar still with its clay bung (**525** H19/366: Fig. 87), and between this and the hearth was a circular plastered feature, which the excavator thought could have been a support for a timber post. On the west side of the room at a roughly comparable location was a posthole. In the destruction material on the floor, as well as a few lengths of burnt timber there were numerous pieces of 'slate'. These seem likely to have fulfilled the same function as in Rm 7 of the Level IIc Stele Building (see p. 134), which like Rm 41 is a wider space than one would normally expect to have a single roof-span. Whether Rm 41 itself was roofed remains uncertain; on the one hand the handsome hearth and the storage vessels seem more likely to have been indoors, but the size of the room and the underfloor paving rather point to an open area. Possibly it was not formally roofed but sheltered along one or more of its sides.

Figure 88. *Doorway in W105, leading from Rm 42 into Rm 41, looking south (see Fig. 487).*

To the west of the bench a doorway led through W105 into Rm 42. It was 80 cm wide and had three shallow plastered steps leading down some 40 cm on to the floor of Rm 42 (Fig. 88). A stone door socket on the east side of this doorway, against the NW face of W105, indicates that the door itself was on the NW side of the wall, inside Rm 42 (Fig. 89). Against the wall-face to the west of the doorway was the remnant of an unbaked plastered container, and fragments of similar vessels were common in the fill above the floor.

Figure 89. *Detail of doorway in W105, showing plastered steps and door socket.*

The NW part of Rm 42 was lost to the erosion of the face of the mound, and most of the rest of the floor had been removed by the robber trench in H20c. Where the floor survived it was of yellow plaster. In the west of the room, against W748, there was a hearth (FI96/23) 40 cm in diameter, consisting of a shallow (4 cm deep) scoop into the floor. In the eastern corner of the room there was a mudbrick bench built along W105. This had a plastered northern face, though the shape of the west end was unclear. The circular outline of an unbaked clay vessel remained in place on the bench towards its west end (**518** H20/139). The surface of the bench continues along W105 as far as its outer corner with W107. Where W107 would have continued, there is instead another plastered bench (likewise without a stone foundation), with a circular unbaked clay vessel (H20/159) set into it, just north of a 20-cm-wide gap in which was found a cylindrical clay object, possibly a pot stand (**1632** H20/155). At least three ceramic vessels were lying on the floor in front of these two benches (**516** H20/156, **519** H20/157, and H20/158, a globular cooking pot with horizontal handle); a loomweight and a pierced stone were also recovered (**1726** and **1825**).

During the excavation of H20d we were mystified by the NE wall of Rm 42. The bench remained standing some 10 cm high, but there was no sign of the wall against which it must have backed. We concluded that the wall proper must have fallen out to the NE and subsequently have been cleared away (like the SW wall of Rm 41). Later, during the excavation of the earlier phase Ve, a vertical edge running parallel with the bench was noted, cutting through

Figure 90. *Rm 41, bricks of collapsed wall lying across destruction debris, looking SE.*

Figure 91. *Rm 43, loomweights **1706–9** (H20/205–8) in situ.*

W224 and associated Ve deposits. This can be identified as a foundation trench for the Level IVa wall, and an alignment of stones towards its NW end must be a remnant of the foundation. The absence of stones further SE suggests that when the debris of the wall was cleared away, the opportunity was taken to reuse some of its foundation stones. A similar cut-line was also observed at the H19/H20 grid line, suggesting that the missing wall may at some stage have continued beyond the east end of W105 overlapping the northern part of W107. A line of eight postholes (1271; 20 cm deep and 8 cm di.) was observed at intervals of 30 cm along the NE side of the trench at a height of +94.10, and may have been associated with whatever structure the trench was made for.

In any case, it is likely enough that this wall fell, since there is clear evidence of the destruction of the rest of the building by a major fire. For a C14 determination between 2300–1650 BC for material off this floor see p. 621. Black ashy deposits covered the floors, and surrounded the storage vessels in the north corner of Rm 41 to a depth of 80 cm. In places on the floor of Rm 41 were remnants of wooden beams (H19/361–2) and above the ashy debris the bricks of W107 lay tilted on their edge in sequence as they had fallen (see Fig. 90). At least eighteen courses were counted here, and since the bricks are uniformly 9 cm thick, and W107 itself remained standing 20 cm above the floor, we can see that the minimum height of this wall was 1.8 m. Given that it is no more than 50 cm in width, and seems to be unsupported throughout its length by any cross-wall, it is not surprising that it collapsed in this way. On the other hand, the NE wall of Rm 42 was buttressed along its SW side by the bench, and hence could well have collapsed outwards instead.

The slope of the mound meant that little remained of Level IV to the west of Rm 41, and the little that did was not informative. There is a rubbly stone foundation (W799) running more or less parallel to the line of W748, making a passage some 50 cm in width. W799 was mostly tumbled, but was constructed of stones and approximately 60 cm wide. There was no sign here of the deep destruction debris so evident further east, and this must imply either that any such destruction material was cleared away along with the south part of W748, or that for some reason the fire and its effects did not extend in this direction.

On the other hand, in Rms 43 and 45, to the east and south of Rm 41, the burnt destruction debris was also present. In Rm 43 there were no signs of architecture, and we assume that this was an open space. Next to the baulk with I20 the excavator noted a 'large number of large sherds, … in association with some signs of intense burning in the soil and a severely burnt pile of bone/antler fragments'. No other features were noted here, and it is probable we did not reach the contemporary surface. Further north in H20d the transition from fill beneath the Level IVb floor to the phase Ve deposits proved hard to identify, but at a horizon at about +94.65 a cluster of about 20 loomweights (**1702–22**: Figs. 91 & 284), associated with a good deal of broken pottery, suggests that there was a rough courtyard surface here.

To the north of this area was a wall foundation W228, well defined in the SW, where it is 80 cm wide, but degenerating into an area of tumbled stone further to the NE. Since this is thoroughly sealed by the IVb surface above it, it must belong broadly to phase IVa, but the absence of the NE wall of Rm 42 makes it difficult to decide whether W228 was precisely contemporary with the main building. It may itself have been more a terrace or boundary wall to the open area to the south than part of a building, and this impression is strengthened by the presence of a large unshaped conglomerate boulder (more than 1 m across) partially extending into I20, the top of which stands at +95.10: this can hardly have been inside a room.

Level IVa units and finds
Packing above Ve but below IVa packing: 1272, 1275

Pub. ceramics	1272		458, 470, 491
Ceramic lid	1272	H20/593	531
Loomweight	1272	H20/591	1727
Sp. whorls	1272	H20/586, 588–9	1885, 1888, 1893
Macehead	1272	H20/592	2614
Whetstone	1272	H20/580	2649
Grinder	1272	H20/587	2713
Human tooth	1272	H20/874	2864
Pub. ceramic	1275		478

Rm 40
Packing: 4267

Pub. ceramic	4267		489
Clay disc	4267	H19/320	1527

Rm 41
Wall 105: 1298

Sp. whorl	1298	H20/647	1889

Occ. surface: 4278

Cup	4278	H19/373	490
Unbaked vessels	4278	H19/349, 365	509–10
Unbaked vessel	4278	*H19/367	508
Storage vessel	4278	*H19/358	517
Storage jar	4278	*H19/359	523
Handled cup	4278	*H19/366	525
Cup	4278	H19/389	526
Pub. ceramic	4278		528
Metal object	4278	H19/355	2239
Clay bung	4278	H19/371	1492
C14 sample	4278	H19/357	see p. 621

Benches: 1296–7
Destr. debris: 1239, 4273–4

Pub. ceramics	1239	*H20/122, 124	506–7
Storage vessel	1239	*H20/123	521

Packing: 4257, 4261, 4263–4

Pub. ceramics	4257		532, 536
Sp. whorl	4257	*H19/247	1901
Bead	4257	H19/254	2009
Shell	4257	H19/246	2501
Fossil	4257	H19/250	2527
Pierced stone	4257	*H19/249	2668
Human bone	4257	H19/382	2867
Clay lining(?)	4257	*H19/251	
Copper bead	4261	H19/293	2007
Microlith	4261	H19/266	2551
Human bone	4261	H19/384	2868
Coarse vessel	4264	H19/285	511
Loomweights	4264	*H19/283, 301	1732–3
Sp. whorl	4264	*H19/282	1886
Flint sickle	4264	H19/277	2545

Rm 42
Packing below floor: 1246, 1807–8

Pub. ceramic	1807		522
Flint core	1807	H20/321	2577
Stone mould	1807	H20/323	2616

Wall 107: 1241

Pub. ceramic	1241		484
Loomweight	1241	H20/147	1728
Sp. whorls	1241	*H20/145–6	1890–91

Occ. debris: 1240, 1242

Pub. ceramics	1240		499, 512, 518, 530
Pub. ceramics	1242		477, 488
Jar	1242	H20/152	520
Sp. whorl	1242	H20/151	1894

Occ. surface: 1243, 1245, 1247, 1806

Pub. ceramic	1243		498
Cooking pot	1243	*H20/156	516
Storage vessel	1243	*H20/157	519
Clay support	1243	*H20/155	1632
Pierced stone	1243	H20/154	1825
Vessel	1243	*H20/158	
Circ. feature	1243	*H20/159	
Grinder	1245	H20/166	2714
Loomweight	1806	H20/316	1726
Lithic sickle	1806	H20/315	2563

Posthole in floor: 1248
Destr. debris: 1236, 4258

Unbaked vessel	1236	H20/118	513
Unbaked vessel	4258	H19/253	514
Human bones	4258	H19/383, 385	2865–6

Rm 43
Packing below walls: 1263–4

Jar	1263	*H20/272	476
Loomweights	1263	H20/274–6	1723–5
Sp. whorl	1263	H20/280	1895

Wall 734: 1270

Bone tube	1270	H20/581	2483
Macehead	1270	H20/583	2615

Occ. surface: 1251
Packing: 1253, 1265, 1269

Pub. ceramics	1253		485–6, 501
Sp. whorl	1253	H20/178	1899
Glass handle	1253	H20/180	2094
Rubber	1253	H20/179	2810

Loomweights	1269	H20/576–7	**1729–30**
Lithic blade	1269	H20/578	**2560**
Destr. debris: 1258, 4276			
Pub. ceramics	1258		**479–83, 487, 492–6, 500, 503–4, 515, 524, 527**
Bulla	1258	H20/252	**1483**
Loomweights	1258	H20/190–98, 210, 220–22, 224, 226, 237, 250	**1702–5, 1710–14, 1716–22**
Loomweights	1258	*H20/205–8	**1706–9**
Sp. whorl	1258	H20/234	**1896**
Bead	1258	H20/241	**2006**
Fossil	1258	H20/236	**2526**
Lithic sickle	1258	H20/242	**2544**
Lithic blade	1258	H20/230	**2562**
Unpub. ceram.	1258	*H20/188, 201, 204	
Jar	4276	H19/388	**475**

Posthole: 1271
Cut: 1273

Rm 44
Dest. debris: 4269

Copper pin	4269	*H19/304	**2237a**

Rm 45
Destr. debris: 4277

Level IVb (Fig. 488)

This later MBA phase was present over much the same area as IVa, though the mound slope means that it did not extend so far to the north. No clearly defined structures were discovered in this level, and most of it must have been an open space or courtyard, but plastered features survived, overlain by building debris.

In the centre of the excavated area plaster lines delineating a low vertical edge were traced and formed three sides of a rectangular shape, measuring *c.* 2.50 × 3 m. It seems likely that this was a low platform whose upper surface had been plastered but later cut down. Along the inside of the westernmost plaster line were four unevenly shaped postholes of different sizes. On a burned surface to its SW were two grindstones (**2718–19**, H19/226–7) lying next to wooden timbers, presumably a fragment of collapsed architecture, and up against the plastered face was the base of a large storage vessel coated with a grey lining (H19/223: Fig. 92; two storage jars in Rm 30, Level IIId, had a similar coating, see p. 115). For a C14 determination on charcoal from this context see p. 621 (H19/197: 2140–1740 BC).

Within the plaster lines (and so presumably incorporated into the platform during its use) was a fill of occupational debris in which were found two spindle whorls (**1897–8** H19/235, 239) and a pierced stone (**2669** H19/236). To the north and west of these lines a roughly plastered floor was traced across the whole area at a level of between +95.12 and +95.38. The fill above the floor contained large amounts of charcoal. This, along with the building debris mentioned above, may represent the displaced remains of a burnt out room.

In the north the plaster floor extends to the edge of the tepe, though damaged in the east by a large animal tunnel. In this area a variety of objects were found lying on the very uneven floor, mostly vessels and potsherds but also clay crescents. Some of the pots seemed to have been resting on unbaked clay to keep them stable. The whole area lay under a layer of burning, although in some places the floor clay had been protected from it by a fallen brick, stone or pot. There were few architectural features. In the SE of H20d a small circular post-hole was cut into the floor. To the SW of this were found side by side two contemporary clay-lined hearths let into the floor, which here had a thin white plaster (see pp. 77–8, Fig. 61). The larger (FI94/3) was more heavily burnt and shallower (18 cm) and measured 90 × 50 cm. In among the charcoal which filled it were 5 or 6 deer antler fragments burnt completely black, as well as other bone. The smaller hearth (FI94/2) measured 50 × 20 cm, was deeper (some 24 cm) and filled with ash. Two large slabs of stone were set on the floor south of the hearths.

In the SE part of the excavation area (the east side of H19b) was a

Figure 92. *Storage vessel H19/223, coated with grey lining (see Fig. 488).*

Level IV: the Middle Bronze Age

burnt horizon, representing a continuation of the H20d surface. It stretched across the IVa destruction debris without an intervening layer of fill. Various stray finds were recovered at this level, but since it was directly superimposed by Level III foundation materials it proved difficult to be certain whether they belonged on the IVb surface or were contained in the base of the later packing episode. Hence unit 4248, which yielded a mixture of MBA ceramics with 'examples of the characteristic shallow bowl with internal thickened rim' (see p. 325) almost certainly includes material from Level III.

Level IVb units and finds

Packing above IVa walls: 1232–3

Palette	1232	H20/109	**2619**
Loomweight	1233	H20/113	**1731**

Packing material: 1226, 4255, 4260, 4262, 4268, 4272, 4275
NB. the findspot of several of these items, beneath the IVb floor, is shown on Fig. 487.

Jar base	1226	*H20/72	
Tripod jar	1226		**557**
Clay disc	1226	H20/76	**1599**
Sp. whorl	4255	*H19/239	**1898**
Pub. ceramics	4268		542–3, 560–61, 567
Stone axe	4268	*H19/314	**2598**
Mortar	4268	*H19/315	**2676**
Mortar	4268	*H19/324	**2677**
Astragali	4268	H19/318	**2428**
Copper pin	4272	*H19/338	**2238**
Lead wire	4272	*H19/331	**2302**
Lithic blade	4272	H19/337	**2561**
Stone axe	4272	*H19/330	**2599**
Astragali	4272	H19/327	**2427**

F194/2: 1229
F194/3: 1230

Burnt antler	1230	*H20/97–8	**2493**

Destr. debris: 1218–20, 1228, 1231, 1249, 1842, 4249

Jug	1219	*H20/35	**546**
Unpub. ceram.	1219	*H20/36	
Jar	1219	*H20/37	**558**
Clay crescents	1220	*H20/47, 53a+b, 54	**1635–8**
Loomweight	1220	H20/58	**1826**
Worked stone	1220	H20/57	**2666**
Seed sample	1220	*H20/49	
Unpub. ceram.	1220	*H20/45, 50, 52	
Pub. ceramics	1231		538, 555
Unpub. ceram.	1231	*H20/101	
Bowl	4249	H19/202	**535**
Jug	4249	H19/205	**548**
Jugs	4249	*H19/191, 193	**550–51**
Pub. ceramic	4249		552
Clay ball	4249	*H19/208	**1528**
Sp. whorl	4249	*H19/211	**1902**
Sp. whorl	4249	H19/194	**1904**
Hammerstone	4249	H19/210	**2633**
Stone object	4249	*H19/212	
Grinder	4249	H19/186	**2715**
Grinders	4249	*H19/200, 207	**2716–17**
Unpub. ceram.	4249	*H19/190, 192, 201	
Charcoal	4249	*H19/197	see p. 621

Occ. debris: 4251

Handle	4251		**544**
Quern	4251	*H19/226	**2718**
Grinder	4251	*H19/227	**2719**
Bones	4251	*H19/216–17	
Unpub. ceram.	4251	*H19/223, 230	
Charcoal	4251	*H19/225	

Occ. surface: 4254

Pub. ceramics	4254		537, 540
Sp. whorl	4254	*H19/235	**1897**
Pierced stone	4254	*H19/236	**2669**

Cut: 1254–7, 1261–2, 4253, 4259, 4270–71

Flaked lithics	1261	H20/266	**2590**
Sp. whorl	1262	H20/268	**1900**
Ceramic disc	4270	H19/329	**1551**
Bowl	4271		**533**
Sp. whorl	4271	*H19/316	**1887**
Sp. whorl	4271	H19/309	**1905**

Packing directly below base of Level IIIa: 1227, 4248

Jug	1227	H20/79	**547**
Jar	1227	*H20/84	**554**
Pub. ceramic	1227		556
Lid	1227	H20/78	**559**
Loomweight	1227	*H20/89	**1734**
Sp. whorl	1227	H20/90	**1906**
Unpub. ceram.	1227	*H20/82	
Clay crescent	1227	*H20/91	
Pub. ceramics	4248		541, 562–5
Loomweight	4248	*H19/182	**1827**
Copper blade	4248	*H19/181	**2214**
Bone tube	4248	H19/376	**2473**
Worked bone	4248	*H19/175	**2484**
Whetstone	4248	H19/169	**2650**
Grinders	4248	*H19/173–4, 176, *179	**2723–6**
Quern	4248	*H19/172	**2722**

Chapter 12

Level III: the Late Bronze Age

S.H. Blakeney

Since Late Bronze Age sherds were collected from various parts of the surface, and houses of this date were excavated in I14, there is every reason to suppose that the entire top of the site was occupied at this time. However, the overburden of 3 to 4 metres meant that the only substantial exposure was at the NW corner, where five architectural phases of Level III were identified (in squares I20, H19, and I19 with small areas also excavated in H20 and J20). These phases are referred to as Level IIIa–e: IIIe is the latest, limited to a reuse of the phase d Eastern Courtyard, and immediately underlying the construction of the Level II Stele Building; IIId is the best represented phase, from H19 to J20; while phases IIIa–c, although doubtless present in I19 and 20, were only uncovered further down the slope to the west in H19a+b and H20d.

The builders of phase IIIa must have cut down into the destruction material of Level IVb when laying their stone foundations, but the architectural layout is entirely new. There is thus a clear stratigraphic break at both start and end of Level III, which is also reflected in changes in the ceramic repertoire. Units such as 4248 in which material from Level IV is mixed with typical LBA sherds (see p. 109) are either the result of the Level III building work or of our failure to pick up the precise transition. Hence it is not possible for us to say whether there was a significant break in time between the end of Level IVb and the foundation of Level IIIa.

On the whole, wall foundations in Level III tend to be constructed with two lines of largish stones (roughly 25 × 20 × 10 cm), deliberately laid with the smoother more squared-off face placed at the outside edge of the wall, and the inner core of the wall filled with much smaller rough stones. Where preserved the superstructure was mud brick, usually a single row of large bricks covering the full width of the wall.

The interpretation of the Level III architecture is hampered by its division into an earlier, western, half in H19–20, where phases IIId and IIIe were mostly absent, and the later plan in I19–20, where the IIIa–c phases remain unexcavated. However, if we allow ourselves to assume that the later or earlier phases respectively would have been similar, and describe the resulting reconstituted layout as a coherent whole, it becomes clear that Rm 32 was probably a central component of the plan, flanked to the NE by a storage room (Rm 30) and on the SW by other smaller rooms of which we have very little more than the foundations in different phases. At all times there seems to have been a major wall running SW–NE along the line of the back of Rms 30 and 32, but the presence of Rms 35 and 36 in Level IIId and their predecessors in IIIa–c raises the possibility that the building also extended further to the NW and that Rm 32 was enclosed by rooms on at least three sides. Whether the scale of the architecture, and the quality of some of the wall plaster should be taken together with the frequency of libation arms as evidence that it had a cultic function is a matter of personal inclination.

Our description starts from the earliest phases in the west, where essentially only the foundations of some small rooms survived, and then continues eastwards to the rather better-preserved remains of IIId and IIIe.

Level IIIa–c (Figs. 489–90)

These three early phases of our Late Bronze Age levels were reached only in H19a+b. As usual, the walls probably all had foundations of undressed stone (occasionally incorporating discarded grindstones), topped with mud brick. Those of the two earlier phases, IIIa–b, had been cut down to foundation level when rebuilding the succeeding phases, and no associated occupation surfaces were firmly identified. Instead these levels are composed of uniform fill with horizontal stratification, most clearly observed in the east section of H19 (Fig. 512). It is therefore difficult to be sure which strata were associated with each wall phase. In the absence of clearly identified trenches cut to take the stone foundations the fill surrounding the IIIb and IIIc walls may well consist largely of soil from the demolished structures, and the sherds may belong to the immediately preceding phase. (This applies equally to the C14 sample H19/157 which was in fill associated with the IIIb wall W745; it suggests a date between 1920 and 1610 BC, which seems too early for the building, see p. 621.) Level IIIa however was laid directly upon the shaved down walls and destruction material of Level IVb, and the associated fill, which was not destruction debris, must have been introduced from elsewhere.

The only clear dimension for the rooms of these phases is the distance of 1.60 m between W102 and W103, making a narrow room. Otherwise all we can say about these phases is that although the exact position of the walls varied with time, their alignment was constant. Thus in IIIc (Fig. 490) W741 was partly constructed over an earlier foundation belonging to IIIb (also numbered 741). With only fragments of rooms and no *in situ* furnishings we cannot guess at the function of these structures, although we might surmise that they were forerunners to Rms 33–36 in Level IIId, which are similar in scale and alignment. The steady accumulation of levels and occasional rebuilding argues a period of continuity, without major changes in the use of space, and this is supported by the ceramic repertoire, which appears remarkably constant from the earliest to the latest Level III phases.

Level IIIa–c units and finds
Walls 102, 703, 740–41, 744–6: 1210, 4241, 4244, 4245, 4247

Grinder	1210	H20/20	2730
Mortars	4241	H19/*108–9	2679–80
Grinder	4241	*H19/106	2728
Quern	4241	*H19/107	2729
Sp. whorl	4244	H19/155	1975
Quern	4245	H19/160	2727
C14 sample	4245	H19/157	see p. 621
Clay wheel	4247	*H19/167	1600
Mortar	4247	H19/164	2678
Grinders	4247	H19/*161, 165	2720–21

Packing: 4240
Worked bone	4240	H19/146	2485

Occ. surface: 4239, 4242
Unpub ceram.	4239	*H19/144	

Fill: 4227–8
Copper shaft	4227	H19/375	2235
Shell	4228	*H19/105	

IIIa/IVb packing: 1221, 1223 (for 1226–7 see p. 109)
Sp. whorl	1221	H20/59	1908
Hearthguard	1223	H20/68	1631

IIIa/b packing: 4236–7, 4243, 4246 (for 4248 see p. 109)
Jug	4236	H19/130	549
Human bone	4236	H19/379	2872
Pub. ceramic	4237		683
Sp. whorl	4237	H19/134	1907
Human bone	4237	H19/380	2871
Sp. whorl	4243	*H19/152	1986
Lithic blade	4243	H19/222	2596

IIIc packing: 4217–18, 4223–4, 4230–32, 4234–5, 4238
Pub. ceramics	4217		600, 627, 656
Fossil	4217	H19/78	2518
Mortar	4217	H19/76	2681
Pub. ceramics	4223		578–9, 648
Pub. ceramics	4224		629, 639, 670
Pub. ceramic	4231		642
Sp. whorl	4231	H19/111	1993
Fossil	4232	H19/117	2503
Human bone	4234	H19/378	2873
Pub. ceramics	4235		539, 545
Human bone	4235	H19/125, 386	2869–70
Lithic sickle	4238	H19/138	2546
Human bone	4238	H19/381	2874

Level IIId (Fig. 491)

This phase is represented across a 20-m stretch from the east side of H19/20 to the west half of J20. It will be described in three sections, from the remnants of rooms on the west to the open space on the east side.

The Western rooms (Rms 33–6)
Little of phase IIId survived in H19/20, though what there is suggests continuity with the preceding phase. The stone foundation of W833 stands directly on the foundations of phase IIIc, while in H20d the IIId stones of W100 rest on those of W104. The alignment of the architecture is constant, although walls shift their position slightly, so that the west wall of Rm 36, W101, is slightly NW of its IIIb predecessor W103. Further south, it looks as though Rms 34 and 33 have been shifted eastwards. Here again we have little other than foundations and their packing, with no occupation surfaces surviving. Only in the extreme SE corner of H19b did we identify a short stretch of the mudbrick superstructure of W833. This was plastered on each face, suggesting that both Rm 33 and Rm 32 were internal rooms belonging to a single structure, and thereby that these western rooms belong to the same building as Rms 30 and 32.

Room 33
Only a corner of Rm 33 was excavated against the south baulk of the quadrant. Its NW wall (W737) was a parallel line of foundation stones some 60 cm wide, similar in construction to and founded at the same level as W738. No clear mud brick was seen overlying this foundation, although the return to the SE, W833, was standing to a height of 50 cm, a stone foundation with four well-laid courses of mud brick on top. As seen in section between H19 and I19 it measured 56 cm in width and appeared to be constructed of a single row of mud bricks 10 cm in height and separated by

grey mortar. Plaster lines on the inside faces of both walls suggest that Rm 33 was an interior space.

Within the room a thin layer of hard yellow clay at +96.83 just below the surviving stones probably represents a plastered floor. There were no finds associated with this surface. Below it the packing of the room was described as a hard yellow clay deposit c. 10 cm deep, with a high concentration of animal bone and pottery.

Level IIId units and finds — Rm 33
Packing: 4208

Room 34
No floor survived in this squareish space (2.85 × 2.0 m) NW of Rm 33, but its approximate level may be deduced from a roughly semicircular patch of burnt orange clay against W737 in the SE corner at +96.60, close to the surface of the mound. This was about 1 m wide and mixed with pebbles, and very likely was the base of a hearth sunk below the floor. The walls were all reduced to their foundation level (or in the case of the SW wall completely eroded), and this means that no doorways could be identified.

The surviving stones of W737 and W638 were not bonded with W739 nor founded as deep, and the excavator was therefore unsure if they were contemporary. It seems likely that W739, which stood to a height of five courses of stone and was 75 cm in width, represents a major external wall, continuing the line of W100 in I20, and although it may have been founded earlier than W737–8, it may have remained in use with them.

The space between the foundations was occupied by a compact brown fill roughly 30 cm in depth. The excavation unit used for the upper level of this material was 4205, which together with 4211 below it supplied many of the potsherds selected for publication as typical of Level III. Immediately above this was the eroding mound surface (4201) formed of a fractured yellow bricky material regularly encountered cladding the slope from H19 into K20. Cut into it was a small pit (P95/47; di. 25 cm) filled with rubbly material including small chunks of yellow clay.

Level IIId units and finds — Rm 34
W739: 4206
Lithic core	4206	H19/31	2587

Foundation trench for W738: 4210
Occ. layer below 4227–8: 4229
Bead	4229	H19/100	2057

Fill in Rms 32, 34: 4211, 4225, 4227–8
Pub. ceramics	4211	570, 572, 576–7, 580–83, 586, 588, 590–93, 598–9, 604, 616–19, 621–2, 630–32, 634, 637–8, 641, 645–7, 654, 660–61, 664–6, 679, 682, 686	
Astragalus	4211	H19/49	2429
Fossil	4211	H19/50	2502

Packing between W737 and W738: 4205
Pub. ceramics	4205	569, 571, 584–5, 587, 589, 594, 597, 601–3, 620, 624, 635–6, 640, 653, 655, 658–9, 667–8, 671, 689	
Re-used potsherd	4205	H19/21	1587
Sp. whorl	4205	H19/18	1963
Lead wire	4205	H19/23	2303

Cut: 4204, 4212–13
Pub. ceramic	4212		573
Rhyton	4212	H19/390	678
Copper needle	4212	H19/63	2228
Mortar	4212	H19/66	2682

Packing: 4201
Pub. ceramic	4201		948

Room 35
Although W739 may have been a major architectural divide, it was not the edge of the settlement at this date because at least two further rooms were present to its north, separated by the short remaining stub of W101. Rm 35 was to its west, and the slope of the mound had removed most, if not all, of its floor surface. What remained had been cut by a pit (P95/83), and above this was no more than loose topsoil.

Level IIId units and finds — Rm 35
Packing: 1216, 4207
Sp. whorl	1216	H20/30	1903

Occ. surface: 1212
Fill: 1213
Cut: 4222

Room 36
East of W101 was Rm 36, the remaining part of which measured 2.70 m NE–SW and 1.50 m NW–SE. W100 to its SE was exposed for 1.5 m before it entered the unexcavated part of I20c. It survived as a single course of undressed stones (including the mortar fragment **2683**) and measured some 56 cm in width. The jumble of stones within the room did not amount to a recognizable feature. Close to the edge of the mound in the NE corner of the room a small area of surface marked by a thin grey/yellow layer (1208) was noted at +95.58; if this surface was present further south we did not notice it. A small posthole (1206) was discovered at the junction of W100 and W101 and would have cut through any floor.

Most of the fill of this room was yellow bricky 'hill wash', due to the nature of the slope of the mound at this point and little of significance was found within it (max. depth of 60 cm).

Level IIId units and finds — Rm 36
Walls 100–101: 1209
Mortar	1209	H20/14	**2683**

Packing: 1217
Ceramic disc	1217	H20/34	**1552**

Surface: 1208, 1211, 1215
Ceramic disc	1215	H20/29	**1539**
Clay crescent	1215	H20/27	**1634**

Posthole: 1206
Fill: 1205, 1207

The Central sector (Rms 30–32)

Along with the fire installations in the Eastern Courtyard and the material in the destruction debris there, these rooms provide a tantalizing glimpse of a significant building, partly because of the large size of the rooms, and partly because only here did an occupation floor survive in association with plastered wall faces. Rm 30 plainly served at least partly for storage; Rm 32 was probably a more important space, but was not excavated to floor level. The plan suggests that the two rooms must have been connected through a doorway, not preserved. It is hard to say whether this pair of rooms had any direct connection with the open space to the east, as there is no evidence for access to them from the NW or NE.

Room 32
This space measures 4.75 m across, but its full length is unknown as a SE wall has not been located. It might have been a continuation of W830, but if so it would have been removed by two pits, P97/70, a large (di. 2.18 m) pit with 1 m of fill containing much bone and sherd material, and, cutting into it, P98/18 which had a fill of light brown loose packing, with charcoal inclusions (5537). Had its SE wall been here, the room's length would have been about 6 m. Towards the southern corner of the room the SW wall is indicated by the plastered NE face of W833, giving a width of 5 m, but the line of the stone foundation of W738 seems to show that the northern half of the room was half a metre narrower. On the opposite side of the room the interior face of its NE wall (W112) was also plastered, with at least three consecutive coatings of pinkish-white plaster, suggesting that despite its width this was a carefully maintained interior space. The floor was reached only in a 1-m-wide strip along the south side of I19a where an occupation level described as a grey charcoaly deposit (5541) extended from the face of W833 eastwards until cut by P97/70. In the side of P97/70 an orange deposit was observed in cross-section some 0.35 m below the surviving top of W112 (hence ~96.80). Below this there was a sequence of horizontal yellow bricky layers, probably from successive replasterings of the floor, and in the east baulk of H19b a floor sequence shows at ~96.50. Above the latest occupation layer the fill throughout the room was clean clayey material some 25–30 cm deep (5539/5540). Within this at the centre there was a section of collapsed mudbrick masonry measuring 1.67 m in length, and 0.38 m in width, showing three grey bands of mortar 13 cm apart, although actual brick sizes were not visible. The courses ran transversely across the room, so perhaps they fell from the upper part of the SE end wall.

Overlying deposit 5539 up to the top of W112 was deposit 5536, described as a similarly clean yellow bricky fill, with a depth of 25 cm. The packing of the room thus reached a total depth of 50–55 cm.

Level IIId units and finds — Rm 32
Fill: 1202–3, 1431, 1433, 4027, 4214–15, 5536, 5539–41
Metal/slag	4214	H19/411	**2420**
Ceramic discs	5536	I19/192, 199	**1554, 1589**

Occ. surface: 4030

Cut: 5516, 5537–8
Worked bone	5537	I19/208	**2458**

Room 30
Rm 30 is the best-defined room in the building, measuring some 3.15 × 1.80 m, with parts of all four walls surviving, and two successive occupation floors. Towards the south the mudbrick superstructure of the walls survives with at least three clear coatings of pinkish-white plaster on the inner faces, but the north ends of both east and west side walls (W112 and W113) had been eroded down to the stone foundations. These meet the foundation stones of W100, which therefore must count as the NW end of the room, but built across the room against the SE face of W100 is a mudbrick structure (W742). This was a double row of bricks with an average size of 35 × 38 cm, giving a width of 70 cm like W112. Its function is unclear: it may be a secondary wall, but as it survived no more than 15 cm above the upper floor it could equally well have been a bench or even the base of stair.

Both the SW side wall, W112, and the SE end wall, W830, were of plastered mud brick with stone footings and although W830 was narrower they were similarly constructed. The foundations of W112 appeared to be stepped down to the north. At the southern end the mud brick above the stone foundation was preserved to a height of +97.16, 40 cm above the upper floor. The wall was some 70 cm in width, built of two rows of bricks measuring about 33 × 33 cm; the plaster on the wall faces was not removed so the height of the brick courses was not determined. W830 was only some 55 cm in width. The plaster was well preserved on its internal face and had been continuous with the upper floor surface. Even below this the wall-plaster continued down across the face of the stone footing, running down to the earlier floor surface, and turned the corners on to W113 and W112.

The earlier floor of the room (5528) was only reached in I19, and was plastered continuously with the stone footings of the walls. The only features surviving were two jar bases at the south end near W830, one measuring 17 cm and the other 19 cm in diameter, at ~96.40. There were no surrounding sherds and the bases were presumably left in place when the second floor was laid some 30 cm higher up. Within the yellow bricky packing between the two floors (5527) were found a copper pin (**2240** I19/179), a copper ring (**2255** I19/178; see Fig. 491 for the position of each), and a copper needle (**2229** I19/172).

On the upper surface associated with W742 (5521/4028) the only occupation deposits were collected in a shallow circular depression (not marked on plan) halfway along the room towards the SW wall: it was no more than 5 cm deep, and about 1.10 m in diameter, and the fill (4029) was dark soil mixed with charcoal, so that it could have acted as an informal hearth. Along the NE side of the room there were two large jar bases. I20/81 was a flat base of reddish-brown clay some 45 cm in diameter and sunk 18 cm into the floor. Sherds from it, including parts of the rim and a handle, and fragments of a 'plaster' lining (I20/83) were lying on the floor around it (see Fig. 93, showing parts of this lining repositioned). The lining, some 4.5 cm in thickness, had been reinforced by reed or coarse cord, the impressions of which remained within the thickness of the clay. The reconstructed internal diameter of the lining (i.e. the external diameter of the vessel I20/81) was 96 cm at the highest surviving point. Close to the jar base and these plaster fragments were an intact antler (**2493** I20/76) and the upper jaw of a cow (I20/77), which also seemed to be *in situ*.

The jar I19/177 was about 2 m further south, also alongside W113. It was of a gritty brown fabric and had two handles; the rim did not survive. Around it on the upper floor surface, some 20 cm above the flat base, were many sherds from its upper body together with fragments of 'plaster'. These come from a light grey unbaked clay coating 4 cm thick which formed a protective surround to the vessel (I19/176; see Fig. 491); within the thickness of the clay there were the impressions of string and reed stems, suggesting that the covering functioned to seal the jar as well. This is of course very similar to I20/81 to the north, and a vessel similarly coated with a layer of clay was also found in Level IVb (see p. 108).

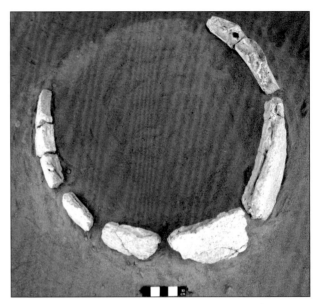

Figure 93. *Repositioned 'plaster' lining I20/83 from around pot I20/81.*

These remnants of the use of the room were buried beneath a succession of roughly horizontal clay packing layers which reached a depth of 55–65 cm at the southern end of the room, but were largely removed further north by the slope of the mound.

Level IIId units and finds — Rm 30
Primary floor: 5528
Packing between two floors: 5527 (some)

Pilgrim flask	5527	I19/173	677
Copper needle	5527	I19/172	2229
Copper pin	5527	*I19/179	2240
Copper ring	5527	*I19/178	2255

Later floor: 1437, 4028, 5521, 5527 (some)

Plaster coating	4028	I20/83	
Pestle	4028	I20/82	2634
Large jar	4028	*I20/81	
Plaster coating	5527	I19/176	
Large jar	5527	*I19/177	

Fill above later floor: 1432, 4024, 4026, 4029, 5505, 5509, 5519–20

Antler	4024	I20/76	2493
Jawbone	4024	I20/77	
Pub. ceramic	4027		623
Bead	5519	I19/174	2029

Room 31
The space numbered Rm 31 to the south of Rm 30 was bordered on the east by the flimsy mudbrick wall W831 (average width 36 cm). A packing deposit was excavated to a depth of 25 cm below the surviving top of W831, at which point excavation ceased, and no floor level was reached in this space.

Level IIId units — Rm 31
Fill: 5507, 5510

Eastern Courtyard

In I20 and J20, to the east of the building comprising Rms 30–34, was an area we believe to have been open to the elements and have called the Eastern Courtyard. It was bounded to the NW by W109, and to the SW by W113. Limits to the east and south were not identified, which gave the courtyard minimal dimensions of 6.80 × 6.00 m. Of W113 only the lowest course of stones survived where it met W109, but at its SE end the stones of W113 stood several courses and 72 cm high with remnants of the mudbrick superstructure above them.

On the NW side W109 survived only as a single course, two stones and about 50 cm wide. These were very close to the mound surface, and it was not possible to decide if the uneven line of stones north of the wall belonged to it, to another contemporary wall, or to a wall foundation of later date (e.g. IIIe). In I20b the courtyard surface was traced through a break in the wall (1.10 m wide), which must have been a point of access into the Eastern Courtyard, and to the east of this the continuation of W109 is narrower (40 cm) and differently constructed (just a single line of large stones with a few smaller stones wedged in).

In the northern part of the courtyard the floor was of yellow clay baked hard, presumably by the fire that affected the building later. The southern and eastern part of the floor was light green in colour and more difficult to trace, but overlay a layer of yellow clay packing. The floor was at a height just below the stones of W109; in Rm 30 too the first occupation floor was level with the base of the stone footings. On the west side the courtyard floor ran under the stones of W111 (phase IIIe) which were not removed, and presumably up to the foot of W113.

Directly overlying this surface in I20d was an ashy deposit up to 5 cm thick. This did not carry across to the eastern and southern areas of the courtyard, and it is unclear whether it derives from occupation activities or is the first phase of the destruction debris which elsewhere lay directly on the courtyard surface. This debris must have resulted from an intense fire, which had almost melted some of the mud bricks involved in it. On the north side of the courtyard at least five courses of mud bricks could be seen lying tilted on their edges as they had fallen from their stone footing (see Fig. 518). These gave brick dimensions of 37 × 23 × 10 cm. The destruction debris was deepest in the NW part of the courtyard where it was up to 90 cm thick, dropping to 5 cm at the SW corner and in the area of the courtyard excavated in J20a. The debris was composed of a mixture of lumps of mudbrick masonry, fragments of bricks, and loose ash. Much pottery was also mixed in, but only sherds from parts of vessels, none whole, and none *in situ* (mostly unit 1428).

Later the debris had been levelled off to some extent with packing laid above and around it. Directly above this across the area of the courtyard in I20 (but not picked up in J20a) there was a sequence of thin horizontal layers, some ashy, some rubbly, and some perhaps a rough surface, underlying the main clean packing layer which formed the solid foundation for the IIIe courtyard.

Level IIId units and finds — Eastern Courtyard
Packing below floor: 4022–3
Floors: 1382, 1435
Destr. debris: 1376, 1408, 1410, 1428–9

Pub. ceramics	1376		643, 687
Glyptic	1376	J20/126	1484
Re-used potsherd	1376	J20/117	1588
Pub. ceramics	1428		568, 574–5, 595–6, 605–15, 625–6, 628, 633, 644, 649–52, 657, 662–3, 669, 673, 680, 688, 690–91
Libation arm	1428	I20/94	688

Levelling fill and intermediate layers: 1425, 1427, 4018, 4021

Worked bone	4018	I20/70	2486

Cuts in courtyard: 1409, 1421

FI97/10

Little of this feature remained standing (Fig. 94). The best-preserved part was in the north, where there survived a line of loose stones some 1.5 m long and at least 0.75 m or two courses high. From their west end there was a return represented by two stones *in situ* (and others, loose, higher up), and the inside edge of these stones was prolonged southwards by the gently

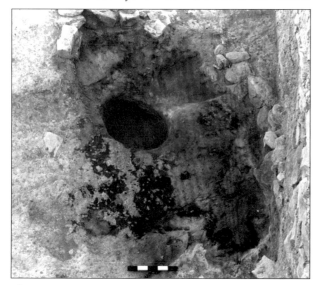

Figure 94. *Eastern Courtyard: FI97/10, looking north (see Fig. 491).*

curving line shown in plan (Fig. 491) dividing clean bricky material on the west from black ashy soil to the east. At about 4.5 m from the NW corner this line turns to form the south side of the feature, and disappears under W130; there it probably joined the eastern edge, which is marked by a line of loose stones, the east side of which is also concealed from us by the deposits underlying W130. The resulting space measures some 4.5 m N–S and 2.5 m E–W.

Within this space was a sequence of ashy layers, of which the lowest is a black sooty deposit overlying a clay base burnt red-brown in places. In the south half of the area this basal clean clay layer is more or less flat, but from the middle of the west side to the inner face of the northern wall of the feature it slopes gently up about 25 cm. Above the ashy sequence was a deposit of very distinctive powdery blue-grey wood ash, and above this again at the centre a reddish-brown earth layer on which were lying three distinct carbonized logs and a number of thinner laths. The longest surviving log was no more than 50 cm, but their south or west parts had all been truncated by pits (P97/91 or P97/55), so they may once have been considerably longer. Dendrochronological samples were taken from them, as detailed below. Above the carbonized wood at the centre, but elsewhere lying directly above the powdery blue-grey ash, was a deposit of rubbly, yellow/white clinkery material admixed with dirty blue powdery ash (5703; north of P97/55 1389, 1390). This material lay over the stones of the north wall of the feature, and sloped down to the east, where some of it seems to have extended beneath the loose line of stones, suggesting that they are in a secondary context. It also sealed the pit which cut through two of the carbonized logs (P97/91; J20/171–2), but not the larger pit further south (P97/55, the base of which more or less coincided with the floor of the feature). Above 5703 was cleaner packing (5701, 5702), which underlay the IIIe surface strewn with carbonized figs.

What all this seems to represent is a large area devoted to burning on successive occasions. There are no very revealing structural details (such as firechambers, access, or flues), but the deposits within its confines clearly indicate that this was a fire installation. The lines of stones along the north and east sides are too loose to have been the walls of a kiln, and do not show signs of intense burning, but they could have served to wall off an area within which fires were lit. The rather flimsy timbers could have come from a roof, if it were high enough to avoid the flames, in which case the associated earth layer may have come down with it, but it is perhaps more likely they derive from a vertical screen. The sequence of ashy lines, culminating in the blue-grey ash, derives from the usage of the fire installation. The clinkery layers obviously belong after its disuse, and must represent material brought in from elsewhere, since nothing within the feature suggests such high temperatures.

Level IIId units and finds — FI97/10
Ashy fill of FI97/10: 5705
Occ. deposits: 5700
Fill associated with north side of FI97/10: 5704
Fill deposits overlying FI97/10: 1389–90, 5701–3
Carbonized logs   5703   *J20/171–2, 180   see pp. 619–23
Copper frag.   1390   J20/162   **2235**

Area NW of Wall 109

W109 is probably only a later version of an earlier (IIIa–c) continuation of the alignment represented in H19 and H20 as W739 and W100. This no doubt delimited one building complex, but although virtually nothing survives to its NW, there is just enough to be sure that it was not the limit of all building in Level III. A short length of scrappy stone wall-foundation (W110) appears to be tacked on to the NW side of W109. It ran NW–SE, was 62 cm in width, and was not constructed like the other walls of the building (stones of different sizes were randomly laid).

A hard yellow surface (1411) was found to the east of W110 and north of W109 extending up to the east, and about 1 m northwards (to the break of slope). It overlay a similar surface (1416), which was only 20 cm lower than the surviving top of W110. Above 1411 was a loose packing deposit 1407. This in turn was covered by the hard clay deposit which follows the contour of the mound (here 1405/1404; probably later than Level III). Overlying and to the west of the western part of W110 was a loose rubbly deposit, which was only excavated for about 10 cm before being left (1412).

Units and finds — NW of wall 109
Surface: 1411, 1416
Packing: 1404–5, 1407, 1412
Bone bobbin   1404   J20/9   **2491**
Pub. ceramic   1405   **949**

Cut: 1414–15

Level IIIe

The phase labelled IIIe was only identified in the Eastern Courtyard. Over the IIId destruction debris left here were packing levels, the last of which was clean bricky fill c. 20–25 cm in depth. This was presumably put down at the same time as, or shortly after, the construction of W111, which had a well-constructed stone foundation clearly sitting on top of the destruction debris of the IIId phase. Three courses of stone

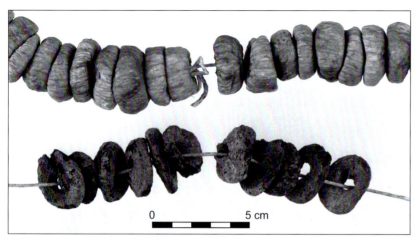

Figure 95. *Carbonized figs (J20/108) with modern strung figs above for comparison.*

remained at its greatest height, with the stones in the wall arranged so that the flat, straight-edged stones were used to provide the two faces of the wall, and rougher, coarser stones formed the core. The stones were bonded with a dark brown mortar and there were the remains of a mudbrick wall overlying the stone foundation at its southern end, although no separate bricks were discernible.

W111 was built up against the east face of W113, the western wall of the courtyard in the IIId phase. Either the two walls were in use simultaneously, with W113 remaining in use during IIIe as the east wall of Rm 32, or W111 formed the east wall of the IIIe successor to Rm 32. It is impossible to be certain, because any IIIe floors to Rm 32 must have stood appreciably higher than the IIIe courtyard surface and have been removed by Level II construction work.

The other limits of the courtyard remain unknown. As in IIId, no southern or eastern edge to it was reached in Level IIIe; and the stones of W109 in Level IIId were so close to the surface that any IIIe successor to this wall, which may well have existed, would have been removed by erosion. Given the size of the space it is unlikely to have been an internal room, but the area could easily have been shaded by a wooden shelter (although no postholes were noted).

Phase IIIe was probably a fairly perfunctory reconstruction, as the courtyard surface was very uneven. This was particularly so in J20, where it rose and fell sharply as it lay over the collapsed remnants of the big IIId fire installation (FI97/10). The surface dropped to about +97.09 on the eastern edge, where there was a hearth or oven belonging to this phase (FI95/9). This was set into a piece of hardened clay flooring; the cross-section (Fig. 56) shows its circular clay rim with a base of small circular pebbles and burnt clay. Remnants of the clay wall that would have arched over the whole oven were found on its clay floor, and the fill above this included collapsed material from the superstructure. On the same floor a little to the north was a small circular depression which had two stones placed in it, and probably served some purpose ancillary to the oven.

Elsewhere to the west there was no well-plastered floor above the packing layer, but the occupation surface was very distinctive, as especially in I20 a large area of it was covered in a deposit some 20 cm thick in places and rich in ash and charcoal. It was readily recognized by the carbonized figs that had been pierced and hung on string (charred strands were found in some of the holes: see p. 592; Fig. 95). Perhaps these had been hanging from the roof and fell to the floor in the fire that engulfed the building in this phase. (Note though the observation of W. Matthews 2001 in §9.3.4, that 'the figs appear to have been charred prior to deposition as there is no shrinkage of charred remains from surrounding burnt and unburnt debris'. The occurrence of at least one burnt fig in 1376, assigned to IIId, may be because the burnt IIIe surface lay directly above the IIId burnt material where it was at its highest above and around the fallen mud-bricks on the west side of J20a, and the two layers were not correctly differentiated.) A C14 determination from this ashy layer suggests a date between 1440–1210 BC (see p. 621).

A succession of packing deposits, mostly of clean or charcoal-flecked clay, accumulated over the IIIe floor of the courtyard to a depth of *c.* 60 cm. They were all sealed by a distinctive pinkish-white deposit a few centimetres thick (4011, described as 'orange layer' in the unit list) that appeared to seal all the Level III building in I20 and I19 prior to the Level IIa foundations.

Especially in the southern part of the courtyard much of the IIIe (and indeed IIId) deposits had been removed by a cluster of successive storage pits from Level II (see Chapter 13). In the SE corner of J20a, south of FI95/9, both IIIe and IIId courtyard levels had been cut through during the erection of the Level II Stele Building, and large untrimmed rocks (some shown on Fig. 492) had been inserted in the trench to shore up its NW corner.

Level IIIe units and finds
Packing below floor: 1375, 1426, 4017
Pub. ceramic	1426		**681**
Sealing	4017	I20/67	**1481**

Occ. surface: 1379, 1418, 4016
Carbon. figs	4016	I20/64	

F195/9: 1377–8, 1380

Destr. debris: 1327, 1372, 1381, 1388, 4015
Carbon. figs	1372	J20/108	
C14 sample	1372	J20/125	see p. 621
Whetstone	1372	J20/110	**2651**
Painted tile	1388	J20/143	**1600a**
Copper shaft	1388	J20/164	**2235**
Carbon figs.	1388	J20/147	

Packing: 1371, 1375, 1383–4, 1387, 1399, 1417, 1420, 1436, 4012–14, 5506
Carbon. fig	1371	J20/105	
Pub. ceramic	1417		**675**
Sp. whorl	1417	I20/19	**1965**
Grinder	1417	I20/23	**2772**
Sp. whorls	1436	I20/38	**1987**
Pub. ceramic	4012		**739**
Grinder	5506	I19/165	**2734**

Chapter 13

Level II: the End of the Bronze Age and the Iron Age

J.N. Postgate & D.C. Thomas

Of the strata grouped as phases of Level II at the NW end of the tepe, phases IIa–d, and probably also IIe, form a sequence, punctuated by destructions and rebuildings, which follows on from the Late Bronze Age phase IIIe with no sign of a major gap in time. We have addressed elsewhere (see pp. 35–6) the date of these levels, the best evidence for which is provided by the Mycenaean LHIIIC pottery on the floor of phase IId, assigned to the middle of the twelfth century. Equally, on the evidence of the ceramics, the IIf architecture, and the occupation responsible for the deposits and pits assigned by us to IIg–h, must belong to a later sequence of the eighth–seventh centuries BC. In between, the status of phase IIe remains uncertain: there is some reason to see it as continuous with IId, and since this single phase does not seem likely to have lasted four centuries, it seems possible there was a break in the use of the site between IIe and IIf. This, however, remains very uncertain.

13.1. Level IIa–c

The major architectural remains of the earlier sequence consist of the 'Stele Building' (named after the painted stele discovered in its central room), and the western end of another substantial structure to its east, called the 'East Building'. Both this and the Stele Building itself were built of mud brick on stone foundations and they were destroyed together at the end of phase IIc by an intense fire, which seems to have affected the East Building most severely, resulting in the collapse and 'meltdown' of the mudbrick walls. While the two buildings are broadly contemporary, it seems that the main part of the Stele Building was built first, with southern and eastern rooms being added later, and the East Building was subsequently constructed against it, with Rm 5 of the Stele Building perhaps being created in the same operation. The impression that the Stele Building was the more substantial, and possibly more significant, structure may partially be a reflection of its more complete plan and better preservation.

Be that as it may, for us the outstanding feature, both horizontally and vertically, is the Stele Building in its IIc phase, and it is inevitable that our account of other phases and adjacent parts of the site is tied in to it. Within the Stele Building proper deposits belonging to the earlier phases, IIa (which is the initial foundation), and IIb (subsequent occupation before the main IIc phase), were only excavated in limited soundings beneath the IIc floors. They did provide us with evidence for the continuous occupation of the building before the IIc destruction, architectural details of the earlier phases, and flotation samples and micro-stratigraphic sections. In all, seven soundings were excavated beneath the phase IIc Stele Building, in Rms 2, 3, 4 and 7. Since their placing was, and their interpretation is, determined by the layout of the IIc phase, they are described and discussed under these rooms. Similarly, the sounding beneath Rms 11 and 15 is discussed, together with the walls in J20b, after phase IIc under the North-East Annex (pp. 143–4).

Stele Building (Fig. 492)

The Stele Building in Level IIc was a more or less freestanding square structure with external dimensions of approximately 18 m NE–SW by 14 m NW–SE. To the NW of it was an open space we have called the 'Western Courtyard', and there was probably open space also along its SW side. Beyond its NE wall was a domestic area known as the 'North-East Annex', and only on the SE side was the East Building constructed up against it. By the end of our work in 1998 all rooms in the building had been cleared down to the IIc floor level (see Figs. 96 & 97). The resulting plan consists of ten rooms, although 'Room' 6 is probably an external area and to judge from their size Rms 3 and 7 may not have been entirely roofed.

Room 1

The NW angle of the Stele Building is occupied by Rm 1, a rectangular room running NE–SW, with internal dimensions of *c.* 6.75 m by 3.0 m. Against the southern end-wall of the room and the southern half of the two side-walls is a plastered bench some 60 cm deep and 30–50 cm high. On the plastered vertical face of the eastern bench, there was an indistinct design in red paint (Figs. 98 & 99), and an emplacement for a pottery jar was set into the bench-top above this. The SE corner of the bench has been cut by pits P96/79 and P97/67.

In the north half of the room the floor slopes very markedly down to the north, perhaps reflecting subsidence of the NW corner of the building or compression of an underlying pit. What remains of its clay plaster between pits P95/13 and P94/12 had been burnt to a hard, smooth, black surface (1325), to the extent that when we first encountered it we thought it part of a large fire installation. A small posthole was found in the SE, cut into the floor beside the bench.

The highest surviving parts of the walls of the room are stones bedded onto mud brick. The explanation for this is that here and elsewhere in the original Stele Building the IIc builders left the lower part of the IIa/b mudbrick walls standing and laid the new IIc walls on top of them, with a new stone foundation (possibly of only a single course). As a result, the IIc floors are lower than the IIc foundations, and plastered continuously with the re-used internal faces of the IIb walls.

The bench in the south does not seem to permit reconstruction of a doorway or steps into Rm 9, and it is therefore probable that a doorway led through the north end of W122 into Rm 2. The wall at this point was badly damaged by later pits and the proximity of the mound surface, so the

Figure 96. *View of Level IIc Stele Building, looking west with Rms 4 and 5 at centre (see Fig. 492).*

Figure 97. *View of Level IIc Stele Building, looking SW, with Rm 4 at centre.*

Level II: the End of the Bronze Age and the Iron Age

Figure 98. *Painted design on bench, east side of Rm 1 (see Fig. 99).*

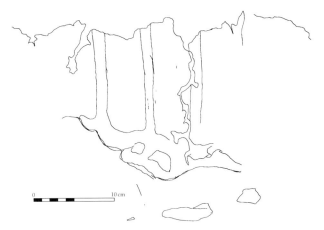

Figure 99. *Painted design in red paint (see Fig. 98).*

absence of clear evidence for a doorway is not decisive. The slope of the mound also made it impossible to establish whether or not there was access to Rm 1 from outside the building, through the NE or the NW wall, since they were both destroyed down to floor level or below.

Level IIa–b units and finds — Rm 1
Packing: 1391, 1393
Ceramic disc   1393   J20/188   1558

Level IIc units and finds — Rm 1
Packing: 1336
Benches: 1356–7, 1396
Copper needle   1396   J20/158   2232

Occ. surface: 1325
Pub. ceramic   1325   951
Sp. whorl   1325   J20/50   1941

Destr. debris: 1333, 1685
Fill: 1397
Iron nail   1397   J20/176   2388

Cuts: 1398

Room 2

This central northern room of the Stele Building measures 5.6 × 2.8 m. The SW corner of the room leads through into Rm 3, across a shallow step, or sill, which may have incorporated timber and/or bricks. The opening is 2 m wide and therefore unlikely to have had a door; it is delimited in the east by a square, plaster-lined feature abutting W796 (see under Rm 3 below). The room itself has no distinguishing features, and its floor has been cut by several small pits (P96/107, P96/119 and P96/120), by pit P96/82, which also cuts W797, and by

a small posthole, in the west, against W122. A jug (**912** K20/198) lay on the floor towards the middle of the room, with part of another vessel (K20/197) nearby.

A sounding measuring 1.40 m by 1.60 m was made beneath the IIc floor against the south wall of the room (W796). It revealed layers of packing, below a single phase IIc surface. The packing was uniform, clean and clayey. The sounding went down 80 cm without identifying any earlier floor surfaces.

Level IIa–b sounding unit — Rm 2
Packing: 4540

Level IIc units and finds — Rm 2
Plastered feature: 2900
Occ. surface: 1148, 1355, 1984, 2902
Pub. ceramics   1984   K20/198   912
Unpub. ceram.   1984   *K20/197

Destr. debris: 1134, 1147, 1321, 1323, 1348, 1350–51, 1353–4, 1361, 1939, 1943, 1989
Copper shaft   1353   J20/90   2235
Sp. whorl   1943   K20/135   1989
Bone point   1943   K20/134   2463
Pub. ceramic   1989   2488
Pounders   1989   K20/195–6   2795–6
Rubber   1989   K20/194   2812

Fill: 1936, 1991
Cuts: 1996

Room 3

The apparent heart of the Stele Building is the central space called Rm 3 (Fig. 100). It is roughly square, measuring 5.3 × 5.0 m, and at the centre is a low rectangular platform, raised only some 10 cm or so above the floor, forming the emplacement for a hearth (FI96/18: Fig. 101). The hearth itself is approximately circular and some 80 cm in diameter. Its baked clay surface was 5 cm below the surface of the platform, and like other hearths of this date rested on a base of small pebbles.

Chapter 13

Figure 100. *Stele Building Rm 3, looking east, with FI96/18 at centre and 'altar' in corner.*

Figure 101. *Rm 3, west side looking north, with FI96/18 and plastered sill on left (before excavation of K19a).*

Figure 102. *Staircase in SW corner of Rm 3, looking SW.*

The whole raised feature measures 2.3 × 1.7 m. Its west end is a short stretch of plastered mudbrick wall, found standing some 40 cm high; its original height is unknown. From its north and south ends two small 'wings' 18–19 cm wide extended eastwards and formed a shallow kerb to the north and south sides of the platform, while at its SE corner the edge of the platform curves gently down to the floor of the room. This floor surface slopes noticeably downwards into the SE corner of the room (+98.76 against the north wall, +98.46 by the south wall next to the stele). It is not clear to us if this is deliberate or accidental, but it may have been a feature inherited from phase IIb (see below), and it does suggest that this part of the room served a rather different purpose from the north and west sides.

At the SW corner of the room three broad steps in plastered stone (c. 1.4 m wide and 0.4 m deep) led up into Rm 10 to the south (Fig. 102). The east side of this stair was extended to form a shallow plastered sill abutting the south side of the hearth platform, and the stairs led up from a passageway some 85–95 cm wide between the western wall of FI96/18 and W122, leading through towards Rm 2. Along the east face of W122 at least two postholes (diameters of 35 cm and 20 cm) seem to have been plastered into the mud brick, and others could have existed.

Apart from the hearth, the most significant feature of Rm 3 is the diagonal mudbrick structure in its NE corner (Figs. 103 & 104). The more we examined this, the more difficult it became to interpret it as anything other than an altar. The following description is based primarily on the detailed observations of Caroline Steele. The feature is formed by a row of 'half' bricks (c. 34 × 14 × 14 cm), which were laid across the corner of the room, leaving a triangular space behind them. The front and sides (but not the back) of the brickwork were plastered and replastered more than 10 times, both before and during the IIc phase. Although there was no surviving upper surface, close observation of the highest piece of plaster showed it beginning to curve inwards, indicating that in phase IIc there was a flat top standing about 80 cm above the floor at +99.57.

The original altar dated to phase IIa/b since its plaster extended down to the IIa foundation stones, and behind the IIc replasterings the top of the brickwork of the earlier phase was identified at +99.30 with a further 6 cm of plaster above it. At first the IIa/b altar measured 35 × 91 cm. It was free-standing, and the plastered faces of W796 and W797 continued behind it to meet in the corner. In time the numerous replasterings added 8 cm to each side and at least 5 cm to the front of the altar. The plaster sometimes curled round the rear corners but the back of the feature was not itself plastered. The plaster is mostly applied in thin layers of whitish clay, although occasionally it was thicker and included vegetable matter. Two astragali were found within the plaster as it was removed. When the thickness of the plaster reached 5 cm the space between the NW side and W796 was largely filled in by a wedge of hard white plaster material, and from then on the junction with the wall was plastered round continuously.

Figure 103. *Altar in east corner of Rm 3, from NW, after exposure of IIb phase.*

It is clear that the Phase IIa/b altar was left standing when the upper parts of the IIb building were levelled off to take the IIc walls. The top of the altar was then raised and the triangular space behind it filled in, although it is impossible to say if this was a single operation or a gradual accumulation. At the level of phases IIa/b the fill consisted of largely sterile, white, clay material, but the mixed Phase IIc fill (6209) included numerous astragali, natural shells and clay, stone and shell beads (Fig. 105).

The enigmas of this corner do not end here. A vertical rectangular shaft with plastered sides was found in the thickness of the north wall of Rm 3 (W796), where it abuts the east wall (W797). Within this 'box' had been a large wooden beam, standing upright. The carbonized base of this beam rested on the Phase IIa/b foundation stones. The plastering on the exterior (south) face of the shaft was covered by the in-filling episodes behind the altar. This feature appears to be related to another large, burnt beam (dendrochronological sample K19/467, see p. 621) which ran horizontally to the east, through the brickwork of W797, and almost meets the vertical beam. They do not, how-

Figure 104. *Altar viewed from the back, also showing holes for timbers in east end of W796.*

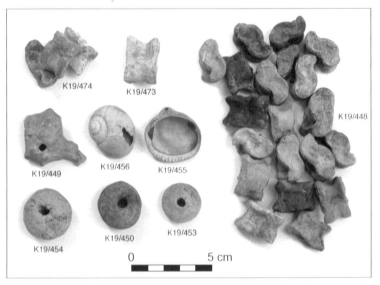

Figure 105. *Miscellaneous items from around the altar: astragali* **2422**: *K19/474 (3), 473, 448 (20); shells K19/449, 456, 455; spindle whorls, left to right:* **1938, 1936, 1937**.

Chapter 13

Figure 106. *Plastered socket in north wall of Rm 3 (W796), looking SE with plastered sill to right.*

Figure 107. *Rm 3: plastered socket behind plaster of south wall (W624), looking SW.*

ever, appear to have been constructed together and it is impossible to be sure if one or both belong to the IIa or the IIc construction phase.

To the west, W796 ends in another enigmatic rectangular feature (2900), internally plaster-lined (Fig. 106). It measured about 80 cm along its NE–SW axis, occupying the width of the wall, and 60 cm from NW to SE along the line of the wall. The base at +98.42 was about 80 cm below the IIc floor level in Rm 2. There was no plaster lining against the mud brick of W796 at its east side, but the north side, where it gave on to the floor of Rm 2, was clearly plaster-lined. On its base, formed by stones probably belonging to the IIa foundation, this 'box' contained burnt bricks and stone mixed with soot, and above this pieces of carbonized beams and other destruction material like that elsewhere on the floors of the IIc building. The burning led us at first to assume it was a fire installation, but this now seems unlikely.

Any interpretation has to take into account the very similar plastered feature on the opposite side of Rm 3, in a corresponding position midway along its south wall, W624 (Fig. 107). It was slightly smaller, measuring some 75 cm, the thickness of the wall, by 60 cm NW–SE along the line of the wall; its depth below the floor is about 45 cm, but on its north side there was a distinct vertical plaster edge projecting about 10 cm above the level of the floor. Although we have considered explanations such as ventilation shafts or 'cupboards' this detail strongly suggests that when in use these two 'boxes' were not open shafts but may have housed substantial square timber posts, against the face of which plaster was applied. That each shaft was filled with destruction debris would then indicate that the posts were removed shortly before or after the destruction.

With a thickness of 90 cm the east wall of the room (W769) was more substantial than the others, which could be taken as an indication that it was intended to stand higher. Its brickwork was bonded with the SW wall of Rm 4; neither of these walls showed any sign of the rather haphazard IIc stone foundations laid across the earlier mud brick in other parts of the building, and this suggests that the IIa/b mudbrick walls were left standing to a higher level here.

When we came to clear Rm 3 we found it was filled with a deep deposit of heavily burned material, including lumps of mudbrick masonry (these especially round the west wall of the hearth), single bricks, and fragments of timber. In the SE of the room, where the walls still stood as much as 1 m above the floor and the destruction debris was correspondingly deeper, a large slab of sandstone (2829 K19/104: Figs. 108 & 469) was found, which had been cracked into over 70 fragments by the heat of the fire as it lay. It seems likely to have stood upright as a stele, although there was no obvious emplacement for it. A design in thin red-painted lines was painted on each face, but even on the better-preserved and flatter face (on which it was lying) the lines are hard to discern, and the significance of the design remains obscure. Between the stele and the SW wall, within the destruction material, was a two-handled dish (**781** K19/97), and between it and the SE wall some carbonized seeds including barley (see Table 37, p. 592), and the bones of a snake.

Level IIc units and finds — Rm 3
Packing: 3960, 6405–6, 6411
Jar	3960	J19/363	784
Sp. whorl	3960	J19/351	1976
Needle	6411	J19/424	2231
Rubber	6411	J19/422	2635

Door socket: 1558, 4572
F196/18: 1695, 6400, 6402, 6404
Clay disc	6400	J19/410	1530

Shaft in W624: 3909
Staircase: 1694
Altar: 1559, 4567, 6209
Clay object	6209	K19/451	1604
Sp. whorls	6209	K19/450, 453	1936–7
Sp. whorl	6209	K19/454	1938
Astragali	6209	K19/448, 460–61, 472–4	2422

Occ. surface: 1557, 1689, 6401, 6403, 6412
Fossil	6403	J19/417	2529

Occ. deposit: 1688
Destr. debris: 1554, 1560, 1618, 1640, 1642, 1686, 1699, 3906
Clay ball	1554	K19/90	1531
Sp. whorl	1554	K19/93	1968
Grinder	1554	K19/92	2775
Stone stele	1554	*K19/104	2829
Ceramic tray	1560	*K19/97	781
Copper shaft	1642	J19/116	2235
Grinder	1686	J19/224	2772
Copper adze	3906	J19/270	2213
Carbon. seeds	1560	K19/96	
Snake vertebrae	1560	K19/96	

Cuts: 1556, 6407–8

In Rm 3 a sounding 2.55 × 1.48 m was excavated in the NE corner, in front of the 'altar' and sectioning the doorway into Rm 4. About 75 cm of deposits were removed (4535). Beneath solid, clean packing, a series of floors was reached at +98.42, *c.* 30 cm below the phase IIc floor, lying on what appeared to be an earlier wall. The sounding was extended to the south (4551) and a hieroglyphic bi-facial lentoid seal (**1473**) and three beads (**2033** and **2051**) were recovered from the resultant flotation sample.

In the centre of the room the history of the hearth was also investigated (Figs. 109 & 110). An earlier IIc clean clay floor was identified some 7 cm below the final surface. The platform, its associated floors, and bricky packing beneath were removed. On the north and west sides of the room this exposed ashy

Figure 108. *Rm 3 stele* **2829** *(K19/104) and dish* **781** *(K19/97) in situ, looking east.*

Figure 109. *Rm 3, Level IIb phase of hearth F196/18, looking SW (centre of hearth previously removed).*

Figure 110. *Rm 3: cross-section through IIb foor lines west of F196/18.*

Seal	4551	K19/342	**1473**
Beads	4551	K19/345a–b	**2033, 2051**

Cuts: 6416–17, 6421

Room 4

This long room, measuring 6.75 × 2.20 m, housed a number of storage vessels. It was only accessible from the doorway leading into it through the east wall of Rm 3. This is only 58 cm wide, and would have been easily secured. In Rm 3 on the south side of the doorway against W769 there was a plastered rectangular socket measuring 30 × 40 cm and sunk 50 cm below the floor. This would have taken a solid door-post, and is unique in the building, thus confirming the importance of securing Rm 4.

In the SW corner of the room, a large jar (**909** K19/294) remained *in situ*, sunk some 30 cm below the floor (Fig. 111), and contained a quantity of burnt coarse-sieved einkorn (K19/99; see Bending, p. 592; Madella, p. 602). Other jars were found just inside the threshold (**785** K19/117), and near the south wall (**913** K19/115). Parts of another pithos were found on the floor in the NW corner (K20/233), and next to it, against the end wall of the room, a smaller flat-based jar was let into the floor (K20/235; base di. 7 cm). Near the east wall were sherds from another jar (**897** K19/105), and to its south the clear impression of the base of a basket was visible (see below). North of the large jar K19/294, by the entrance, there had been a small round clay installation.

Figure 111. *Storage jar* **909** *(K19/294) in SW corner of Rm 4.*

deposits up to 10 cm thick overlying a thick yellow clay floor (at +98.46 in the NW corner, evidently the same floor as in the sounding by the 'altar'). The associated hearth was formed like its successor on a pebble base. This extended 90 cm E–W, and was enclosed, on the west side at least, within a mudbrick surround and capped with a clay surface standing some 15 cm proud of the floor, and about 15 cm below the IIc version (Fig. 110). There seemed to be a border to the floor deposits on the west side which coincided with the line of the IIc partition wall, but at this level we saw no sign of 'wings' protecting the north and south sides. Excavation did not reach to the base of the walls, and there may well have been earlier phases of this hearth.

While investigating the hearth the SE corner of Rm 3 was also examined. Thinner IIb ashy deposits continued here, but the situation was obscure because even during the use of the IIb hearth it seems that this corner of the room was occupied by a cut which sloped down to the SW and SE wall faces, where it was nearly half a metre deeper than the IIb floor (+97.99). Later this cut was filled with rubble, overlying a thick layer of white plant material similar to that often found in the storage pits. The later compaction of the filling of this cut probably explains why the IIc floor sloped perceptibly down to the SE corner.

Level IIb units and finds — Rm 3
Occ. surface: 6415, 6419
F196/18: 1696, 6413
Loomweight	1696	J19/255	**1794**

Fill: 6409, 6414, 6423–4
Clay disc	6414	J19/427	**1529**

Packing: 4535, 4551, 6418, 6420, 6422
Bead	4535	K19/322	**2060**

The floor surface in Rm 4 was not always easy to trace, partly because it was cut by several pits (P96/121, P96/127, P97/3, P97/21), and partly because it was not all at one level. In the south half of the room it was broadly at the same height as that of Rm 3, but the north end stood some 20 cm higher, and it is possible that this was not a gradual slope but caused by a step or similar feature associated with a horizontal beam which had run across the room in line with the NE wall of Rm 3 (W796). Only the western end of this beam was found, completely carbonized (Fig. 112); it was built or inserted into the mud brick of the western wall of Rm 4 (W797) and met the enigmatic vertical beam set into the eastern end of W796 (described above under Rm 3). One possible explanation could be that in an earlier phase the horizontal beam had belonged to an eastward extension of W796, which was later taken down.

The circular basket was *c*. 58 cm in diameter and made of withies *c*. 0.5–0.8 cm thick. Its base had been impressed into the room's clay floor (Fig. 113), and was found below charcoal (possibly burnt, slender roof

Figure 112. *Rm 4: carbonized beam in west wall (W797).*

Figure 113. *Rm 4: basket impression against east wall, looking NE.*

beams), sherds from a large pot and much carbonized wheat. It is possible that the pot had contained the wheat and was originally on a shelf or on the roof of Rm 4.

The destruction debris in Rm 4 was similar to that in Rm 3, and 50–70 cm in depth.

Level IIc units and finds — Rm 4
Wall 613: 4546

Sp. whorl	4546	K19/317	**1916**

Occ. surface: 1549, 1561, 1995, 2908, 4521, 4563(?)

Clay stopper	1561	K19/102	**1495**
Grain sample	1561	K19/99	see p. 592
Pot	2908	*K20/235	
Pithos sherds	2908	K20/233	
Storage jar	4521	*K19/294	**909**
Bone disc	4521	K19/303	**2487**
Sp. whorl	4563	K19/343	**1915**

Basket impression: 1590
Destr. debris: 1555, 1566, 1568, 1570, 1572, 1589, 1594

Pilgrim flask	1555	*K19/100	**918**
Jar	1555	*K19/105	**897**
Jug	1566	*K19/115	**913**
Fossil	1566	K19/113	**2510**
Jar	1568	*K19/117	**785**
Carb. wheat	1570	K19/124, 126	
Jar stopper	1572	K19/130	**1496**
Bead	1572	K19/146	**2012**
Projectile point	1572	K19/150	**2247**

Packing: 1551–2, 4542

Pub. ceramic	1551		**924**

In the SW corner of Rm 4, a sounding was placed so as to bisect the threshold and expose a section through the material below the IIc floor for micromorphological sampling. It measured 1.35 m SW–NE and 1.43 m NW–SE. The sounding was 0.75 m deep, and revealed uninformative packing layers.

At the north end of the room another sounding exposed the IIa foundations. The bases of the north (W121) and east (W613) walls, which are of course the outer walls of the building were of relatively flat rectangular stones, some as much as 60 cm in length, at about +98.60, and surmounted by several courses of less regular stones to a height of as much as 1 m in places. (Above this the stones of the IIc re-foundation were laid at ~99.50, and of the IId re-foundation at ~100.25.) By contrast, the IIa foundation of the party wall between Rms 2 and 4 was a single course of rectangular stones laid at ~98.35.

In the fill close to the east face of W797 this operation came on a flat ceramic plate with a large collection of animal bones lying on it. The assemblage of some 90 bones included at least one partial sheep(?) skeleton, as well as a few miscellaneous bones of juvenile/immature animals. Many bones show cut marks. In addition to the predominant sheep/goat bones the context included two red deer phalanges, one pig femur, and one fragment of cattle tibia (information courtesy of Polydora Baker). At +98.26 this was just below the base of the IIa foundation stones, but in the constricted context it is impossible to say for sure if it was connected with the building.

Level IIa–b units and finds — Rm 4
Sounding SW corner, packing: 4534

Sounding north end, packing: 2904–5, 2907

Copper bangle	2904	K20/229	**2256**
Plate	2907	not numbered	
Animal bones	2907	K20/232	

Figure 114. *Rm 5 with storage jar emplacements; collapsed west wall of Rm 20 (W626) in foreground, looking NW.*

Figure 116. *Rm 5: detail of door jamb in W619, looking south.*

Figure 115. *Rm 5: stacks of bricks forming wall W619, looking SW.*

Room 5

South of Rm 4 is another smaller storage space, Rm 5 (Fig. 114). It appears to be a later addition to the main Stele Building, tacked on in makeshift fashion after the East Building was erected, using the west wall of the East Building (W626), along with the plastered exteriors of W622 and W769. W619 which closes the fourth side on the SW, is hardly a wall, being formed of a row of three stacks of single large, mud bricks 50 cm square (Figs. 115 & 116). Towards its west end was a plastered wood and stone sill in the space 1.2 m wide between two stacks. Plaster mouldings on their faces may indicate fittings for a screen-like door. The flimsy nature of W619 suggests that security was not a concern here (unlike Rm 4) and that it was not designed to take any weight, perhaps no more than an awning for shade rather than a mud roof.

The interior of Rm 5 measures 3.28 × 2.80 m. Its floor is very soft, and, like that of Rm 6, unplastered; in fact it was at very much the same level, and seems to be the same surface running under wall W619, which has no stone foundations, providing further evidence that Rm 5 was a later closing-off of the northern part of a large, external area. Five depressions in the floor, along the west and north walls, mark the locations of jar emplacements (Fig. 117).

Like the rest of the buildings, Rm 5 suffered a fierce fire. Directly on the floor was a thick deposit of fine, black material, and above this the burnt architectural debris, filling the room to a depth of more than 80 cm. Many fragments of large storage jars and considerable quantities of charred lentils and barley were found within the destruction debris. Although the jars themselves were no longer in position, the south face of W622 betrayed their presence: for some 20–30 cm above the floor its plaster was light brown and unaffected by fire, suggesting that it been somehow protected from the fire. Above this for some 50 cm the wall face was burnt black, except for one unburnt patch at the west end, which had evidently been sheltered from the fire by the jar standing there, while above this again the entire wall-face had been exposed to the full effects of the fire and was baked to a hard brown consistency.

The eastern wall, belonging in fact to the East Building, consists of a jumble of highly vitrified mud brick, which bears witness to the intensity of the fire and suggests that the room may have housed combustible commodities, such as oil.

Level IIc units and finds — Rm 5
Occ. surface: 4513
Pub. ceramic 4513 890

Destr. debris: 4507, 4510
Copper nail 4507 K19/196 2224
Copper shaft 4507 K19/203 2235
Astragali 4507 K19/475 2435

Packing above destr. debris: 4506
Iron nail 4506 K19/194 2388
Fossil 4506 K19/191 2530
Stone palette 4506 K19/190 2620

Room 6

This 'room' was probably an open space between the two buildings (Fig. 118). W444 on the east, which belongs to the East Building, is on a different orientation to both buildings and gives Rm 6 an irregular plan which measures over 6.4 × 6.0 m and was thus probably too wide to roof. Its southern limit lies outside the excavated area, but it is certain that W437 did not continue across it.

This space led into Rm 5 to the north (which as we have seen may have been separated only subsequently from Rm 6), and into Rm 24 to the east. It is more difficult to decide whether it also gave access to Rm 10 in the west. Although pit P97/57 has removed most of the critical evidence, there was enough to show that there was a doorway leading out of the NW corner: beneath the north edge of the pit at the SW end of the line of mud bricks which extends from W769 to form the east wall of Rm 10, was a rectangular slot some 20 cm deep measuring 35 × 25 cm. This resembles the post emplacement by the door from Rm 3 into Rm 4, although here it would have had to belong to a door erected within the thickness of the wall. Any threshold had been removed by the pit, whose south side cut down to the stone foundations of the NE corner of Rm 7. For this possible doorway see further under Rm 10.

The surface of Rm 6 is burnt orange and dips to the SW. It is cut by several pits, the most significant of which is P98/72, located in the centre of the courtyard. This is over 3 m in diameter and was in use at the same time as the building, since the base was filled with destruction debris including carbonized grain, later covered with cleaner fill. From the rim of the pit it appeared that there had been successive re-plasterings during its usage, and these had periodically reduced its size, as the pit was not completely emptied each time (see cross-section Fig. 66 on p. 81).

Several enigmatic features were found along W436 in the SW of the area (Figs. 119 & 120). The two large, flat stones may be the remains of a courtyard bench. The pit to the east, P98/52, seemed to have a mudbrick 'collar' around its northern edge. Further south along the wall, a shallow possible storage bin was found, with three free-standing large mud bricks beside it. These bricks must have been deliberately placed on their sides, although what function they performed, if any, remains unclear.

Level IIc units and finds — Rm 6
Occ. surface: 5899
Posthole: 6163

Figure 117. *Rm 5: storage jar emplacements in north corner.*

Figure 118. *Rms 5 and 6, looking NE with Rm 7 and W436 in the left foreground.*

Destr. debris: 4384, 4387, 4507 (see Rm 5), 4509, 4515–16, 4558, 5892
| Bead | 4509 | K19/208 | 2068 |
| Copper frag. | 4515 | K19/277 | 2291 |

Occ. deposits: 4511, 4518, 4537, 5886
| Copper shaft | 4518 | K19/282 | 2235 |
| Hammerstone | 4537 | K19/314 | 2794 |

Packing: 4506 (see Rm 5), 5811, 5819
Iron blade	5811	J18/249	2320
Quartz core	5811	J18/250	2582
Stone vessel	5811	J18/251	2640

Cuts: 5814, 5893, 6122, 6125–6, 6139, 6141, 6145, 6164
Loomweight	5814	J18/258	1777
Copper shaft	5893	J18/389	2235
Astragalus	5893	J18/412	2434
Worked bone	6126	K18/263	2462
Grinder	6139	K18/277	2739

Room 7

Rm 7 is a large, almost square room measuring 5.45 m NW–SE by 5.00 m NE–SW (Fig. 120). All four walls were plastered on their internal faces, although they had been cut down nearly to the floor by the IId building operations and/or later pits. The stones exposed in the northern half of wall W620 probably represent a threshold, leading into Rm 8 to the west. On the internal face of the SE wall (W436) the stone foundation stood *c.* 20 cm above the plastered floor surface, with the floor plaster running up the stone faces. The external face of this wall, however, was not plastered all the way down to the courtyard surface in Rm 6, as the foundation stones and lower mud bricks there exhibited signs of burning.

Much of W436 appears to have been levelled off at its solid stone foundations, while mud brick from W437 seems to have been selectively removed, detaching it from the wall plaster which was left free-standing (and buckling from lack of support; see Fig. 121). Both walls had lengths of burnt wooden beams resting on their foundation stones (samples of which were taken for dendrochronological dating, Chapter 53 p. 621; Fig. 122). The same practice was observed elsewhere in the IIc building, and is conventionally explained as a measure to resist earthquake tremors. W437 also had a 20-cm-long, burnt goat horn (**2494** J18/393) set into it, towards its eastern end (Fig. 123). No functional purpose for this is evident, but it did not look accidental.

Figure 119. *Rm 6: upright mudbrick features against W436, looking east.*

The floor of the room had a well-laid cream-coloured plaster surface, 1–2 cm thick. The function of the room seems to have included storage, since against the SE wall there was a shallow depression, probably the emplacement for a pot, and deposits of carbonized olive stones and barley were observed in the floor close by, to the north. The only find on the floor was half an up-turned grindstone (**2684** J18/379). More unusual was

Figure 120. *Rm 7, with Rm 6 in foreground, showing stone and mudbrick features against east face of W436.*

Level II: the End of the Bronze Age and the Iron Age

Figure 121. *Rm 7, west corner, showing wall plaster and carbonized wood on foundation stones of W437.*

Figure 122. *Rm 7, south corner: carbonized timbers in W437 and W436.*

Figure 123. *Rm 7, south corner: goat horn 2494 (J18/393) in situ in W437.*

the hoard of 99 astragali (**2421** J18/345) found against the SW wall (Fig. 124). They had been pushed into a small hole (15 cm in diameter, 10 cm deep) in the ground and the floor re-plastered over them. In among them we recovered 12 small copper studs or rivets (**2290** J18/346), perhaps from a perished container. Whether this cache was deposited here as some kind of dedication, or secreted for eventual recovery, is hard to say. Caches of astragali are not infrequent in the second millennium BC across the Near East, in some cases associated with temples (see on **2421**, p. 531).

Against the walls and across the floor of the room was a layer of highly vitrified destruction debris, in places 60 cm deep, and including large pithos sherds and numerous (over 30 in the east half alone) medium-sized, flat slate-like stones (the largest examples measuring 31 × 23 × 5 cm and 46 × 37 × 5 cm). These stones lay in a jumble, several 'slates' high, directly on top of Rm 7's plastered floor, or with a very thin, black deposit between the two in places (Fig. 125). The burnt mudbrick tumble was above these deposits. It is clear that the slates, which were also found among the destruction debris of Rm 8, must have formed part of the building at the time it was destroyed, but their precise function remains enigmatic. That they acted as roof-tiles in the normal sense seems improbable: not only are they too thick and mostly too small to be effective, but the thin, black deposit over which they lay

Figure 124. *Rm 7: cache of astragali **2421** (J18/345) under floor by SW wall.*

Figure 125. *Rm 7: 'slates' lying on floor, below destruction debris, looking east.*

no means certain that the space was roofed in this fashion (cf. similar stone slabs in Level IVa Rm 41, p. 105). The quality of the floor-plaster in Rm 7 certainly suggests it was a covered space, but the 5-m span in each direction would have required exceptional timbers. A piece of carbonized timber was found on the floor near the SE corner, but the well-plastered floor shows no signs of posts or pillars to support even a partial shelter, unless the grindstone near the centre of the room could have served this purpose.

Another problem is the question of access from the northern part of the building. At +98.33 and +98.40 the floors of both Rm 7 and Rm 8 are a metre or more lower than Rms 9 and 10, where the floor had in all likelihood been removed by the IId builders. There is no sign of a doorway in their NE walls (W615 and W618, although part of W618 was removed by a modern robber pit). Nor is there a trace of a staircase such as led down from Rm 10 into Rm 3. It seems necessary to assume that either the SW wing was not connected directly to the rest of the building, or, more likely, access was by ladder or by wooden staircase. Conceivably relevant to this were some curious discontinuities in the bonding of the bricks along the south face of W615, in the NW corner of the room.

In the same corner a circular storage pit (P97/49) had been dug. This was sealed by a phase IId wall and contained characteristic phase IIc destruction debris. At first sight it seems improbable that it could have been in use during phase IIc since it is just inside the doorway leading into Rm 8. However, the exact position of this presumed doorway is uncertain, and the fact that the pit seems to respect both walls forming the NW corner means that it could have been contemporary; indeed, it is conceivable that it was under a wooden stair or sloping ladder leading down from Rm 10. Whatever its date, the contents of P97/49 were of interest. They included a pottery jar (**915**) in the fill, and lying at the bottom there was a group of more than 40 broken, burnt bone needle-like implements of unknown purpose (**2469**; Fig. 126).

does not seem sufficient to represent the remains of an organic roofing structure on which the slates would have been laid.

In the nearby village of Kışla a layer of flat stones is often laid along the top of mudbrick walls to act as a water-proof emplacement for roof beams, and this suggests one possible explanation. However, it is by

Level IIc units and finds — Rm 7
Walls: 6500, 6504
Dendro. sample   6500   J18/397
Dendro. sample   6504   J18/398

Level II: the End of the Bronze Age and the Iron Age

Figure 126. *Rm 7: bone implements* **2469** *in P97/49.*

Occ. surface: 3929, 3938, 5895–6
Destr. debris: 3932, 3934, 5815–16, 5887, 5891
Pub. ceramic	3934		795
Pub. ceramic	5816		904
'Roof tile'	5887	J18/373	3
Mortar	5887	*J18/379	2684

Packing above dest. debris: 3928, 3931, 3937, 5809, 5889, 5894
Copper shaft	3928	J19/296	2235
Sp. whorl	5889	J18/380	1942
Pub. ceramics	5894		783, 914
Copper wire	5894	J18/387	2283
Goat horn	5894	*J18/393	2494
Quern	5894	J18/391	2742

Cuts: 3935, 3964, 5870
Jug	3935	J19/320	915
Bone tools	3935	J19/322	2469
Copper frag.	3935	J19/321	2235
Copper studs	5870	*J18/346	2290
Astragali	5870	*J18/345	2421

Two soundings below Level IIc were dug in Rm 7. In the NW corner, along the SW face of W615, east of and partially overlapping pit P97/49, a 1.5 × 0.80 m sounding (3963, 3965) was sunk beneath the IIc floor (here at +98.42), through about 70 cm of clean packing. Under this (at +97.58–97.67) was a 1- to 2-cm-thick band of well-stratified floors, composed of two successive pale green clay coatings each overlying a thin brown layer. Below these a further 25 cm of fill was removed (the base of the sounding being at +97.44).

In the south of Rm 7, at the junction of W436 and W437, a 3.80 × 1 m trench was excavated parallel to W436, cutting through the phase IIc plastered surfaces and clean sub-surface packing in Rm 7, through W437 itself, and through the courtyard deposits south of the wall (Fig. 127). A white plaster surface was noted within the packing, but it was not until the removal of another spit of clean, yellow, silty packing (5898), that clear differences in the colour of the packing emerged. These differences probably represented fill on either side of a mudbrick wall belonging to phase IIb.

Figure 127. *Rm 7: early walls in sounding through W437.*

South of the plaster line a 1-m stretch of deposits was then removed, in an attempt to discover the depth of the phase IIb wall. Below some 20 cm of light grey/yellow packing, and a further 35 cm of light brown/grey, fairly homogeneous, clean packing fill (6503), a spread of foundation stones was exposed, probably belonging to a 70-cm-wide phase IIb wall with a later, poorly constructed, secondary N–S wall laid across it (Fig. 127). Excavation stopped at this point.

Level IIa-b units and finds — Rm 7
Sounding in NW, packing: 3963, 3965
Sp. whorl	3963	J19/374	1914
Bead	3963	J19/372	2032
Pounder	3963	J19/373	2791

Sounding in south, packing: 5897–8, 6501–3

Chapter 13

Room 8

This small room in the SW corner of the Stele Building measured 4.2 × 3.3 m. Like Rm 7 its plastered internal wall-faces had been cut down almost to floor level, although the upper destruction debris included lumps of concreted brickwork which derived from at least the eastern wall (W620). A presumed doorway in the north end of W620 would have led east, into Rm 7; if there was a doorway through the SW wall (W621), evidence for it was removed by a series of later pits.

The clay floor of the room had mostly been burnt to a hard orange consistency. Against the north wall two large thick-walled storage jars (J19/339 and J19/340) remained *in situ*, associated with a quantity of burnt seeds (J19/341, cleaned barley, see p. 592; Fig. 128), and to judge from fragments of handle and other sherds found in the vicinity, there were probably more than these two jars along this wall. At two other places the floor of the room had circular impressions from pot bases, in one case with large sherds associated in the destruction debris. J19/383 was a flat base *in situ* with smoothed slipped surface inside and out, therefore probably a bowl; its precise location was not recorded.

Towards the centre of the room, in *c.* 40 cm of destruction debris (Fig. 129), was a concentration of burnt, flat, dark grey stone slabs, lying, like some of the pithos sherds, on and among loose, ashy fill. The stone slabs were similar to those found in Rm 7 and doubtless served the same purpose.

Figure 128. *Rm 8: barley seeds in J19/340.*

Level IIc units and finds — Rm 8
Destr. debris: 3927, 3932, 5817

Clay disc	3927	J19/317	**1540**
Beads	3927	J19/298, 326	**2076–7**
Pounder	3927	J19/319	**2793**
Unpub. ceram.	3927	J19/*339–40, 383	
Carbon. barley	3927	J19/341	Sample H

Rooms 9 and 10

Throughout most of the Stele Building the phase IIc floors were readily identifiable, if only because of the burnt destruction debris lying on them. In Rms 9 and 10, however, neither floors nor debris were convincingly present. Since there was a staircase leading up into Rm 10 from Rm 3 we expect its floor to have been higher, but there was no surface associated with the highest surviving part of the stairs, and the floor of Rm 10 must have been above +99.41, which is as much as 80 cm above Rm 3. In the absence of identifiable IIc floors elsewhere in Rms 9 and 10, one is forced to conclude that in both rooms the floor levels stood higher than elsewhere and were removed by later building activity (presumably during the construction of phase IId).

Rm 9 measures *c.* 3.88 × 3.00 m, while the longer, narrower Rm 10 measures *c.* 5.60 × 2.84 m. In the absence of their occupation surfaces, the function of these rooms can only be deduced from their position in the building, and the features in the east end of Rm 10 only complicate the picture. Here a curving arrangement of mud bricks respects both the north and east walls of the room and the NE rim of a large pit (P97/73). This has a diameter of more than 2.20 m, and its base at +97.53 is 1.65 m below the brick rim at +99.18. It would therefore have had a capacity of at least 11 m³. The fill of most of the pit was typical IIc

Figure 129. *Rm 8: Level IIc destruction debris, looking NE.*

destruction debris, with lumps of burnt and unburnt brick, ash, and pieces of storage vessel. However, at about 1.20 m above the base this was sealed by a succession of fine orange strata, which ran up and over the edges of the pit. They were initially interpreted as belonging to a fire installation, but it soon became clear that this was wrong, and on reflection the likeliest explanation is that they were deposited naturally as a form of silt in the depression caused by the pit during the time between the abandonment of the destroyed IIc building and its IId reconstruction.

The consequence is that at the moment of the IIc destruction we have to imagine the east end of Rm 10 as largely given over to a deep pit, the rim of which was noticeably higher than the floors of the rooms to north and south, but lower than the ground surface further west in Rms 9 and 10. Behind the brick edge to the north and east the interior faces of W624 and W769 were plastered, and they are also likely to have been exposed at the time. This would not have been the only pit associated with the IIc building which was in current use at the time of the destruction and filled with debris from it (cf. P98/72 in Rm 6, and P97/6 in the Western Courtyard).

To explain why one half of Rm 10 was much lower than the other the only obvious solution is to assume another staircase, contrived over the top of the pit itself. We have already seen that there seemed to be access from the NW corner of Rm 6, and the difference in levels would require some kind of stair: the Rm 10 floor was higher than +99.41 and the Rm 6 ground surface around +98.60. That this is the correct interpretation may also follow from a consideration of access to the Stele Building as a whole. We have found no evidence of an entrance to it from the north (although a doorway at the north end of Rm 1 cannot be ruled out). If there was not one, then the staircase in Rm 3 must have provided access to all of Rms 1–4, and the western end of Rm 10 must in turn have given access to the main entrance of the building. At first we thought Rm 9 represented a very plausible candidate for an entrance lobby, but painstaking examination of the mudbrick west wall of this room and associated strata running up to it in the Western Courtyard failed to provide any sign of a doorway or possible associated features. It is therefore tempting to conclude that one entrance at least was through Rm 10, and as we have seen, there may have been a door-socket in the NW corner of Rm 6. Since P97/73 was unquestionably standing open when the building was destroyed, the entrance from Rm 6 must have led up and over the east end of Rm 10 before reaching *terra firma* at the west end, from which one could turn right, down the stairs into the main part of the building (or go straight on into Rm 9, or possibly take another descent over a pit into the NW corner of Rm 7). It may seem strange to have had a principal entrance over a storage facility, but the use of space under stairs for storage is not unknown in antiquity and today.

Level IIc units and finds — Rm 9
Packing: 3952, 3962
Destr. debris: 3947, 3950
Cuts: 3951, 3955
Grinder   3951   J19/349   2740

Level IIc units and finds — Rm 10
P97/73: 3917, 3943, 3957, 3967–9
Grinder   3968   J19/375   2743
Copper tool   3969   J19/370   2217

The nature of the Stele Building

The excavation of the Stele Building has yielded intriguing glimpses as to its purpose. With eight to ten rooms, the building appears to be too large to be a typical house. It also lacks the kitchen and drainage facilities we might expect in a domestic residence. The paucity of loose *in situ* finds means that we have to rely largely on fixtures in the various rooms to suggest their function.

Rms 4, 5 and 8, with their pot emplacements and carbonized plant-foods, were presumably used for storing considerable quantities of foodstuffs and perhaps liquids. The pits in Rms 6 (outside) and 10 may also have been for grain storage. Even the benches in Rm 1 might have served for some kind of storage, seeing that at least one vessel stood on them.

Rm 3, with its central raised hearth, 'altar' and stele was at the core of both the building's plan and presumably its *raison d'être*. In the absence of any contemporary houses to compare with it, we cannot know if the elaborate central hearth is special, but both the stele and the altar are most easily explained by assuming a cultic function, which is supported by the well-documented association of hoards of astragali with religious buildings in the eastern Mediterranean region (see Gilmour 1997 and p. 531). This need not mean that the entire building is a 'temple', since it could have been only Rm 3 which functioned as a shrine, but the scale of the storage arrangements in the building does at least suggest a public facility. Dorit Symington has suggested that we may have here one of the 'seal houses' referred to in Hittite texts and the association of all four official seals with the building also favours an administrative function.

The East Building

In contrast to the Stele Building, what we have of the East Building is a single period plan (Fig. 492). It is

Figure 130. *Rm 20, looking north, with stone paving.*

Figure 131. *Rm 20, north corner with stone footings of W626 and W627.*

not a normal domestic house, and this is perhaps also hinted at by the silver figurine and jewellery caught up in the destruction. However, the rooms which survive seem utilitarian. With higher ground floors to the north and west, it seems possible that these were at least semi-basement rooms, leading off the open area labelled Rm 24, and that if there was a more formal part of this building it was either on a higher storey, or perhaps more likely, in view of the shakiness of some of the walls, to the east, beyond W959.

Room 20

This space is L-shaped, measuring 6.7 × 3.4 m at its maximum (Fig. 130). At its south end the west wall, W626, supplies the east wall of Rm 5, and its northward continuation was built alongside the east wall of Rm 4. To the north the floor surface of both Rm 20 and Rm 21 runs up to a stone footing, but the mud brick which as usual forms the upper part of the wall (W627) was on a different alignment, standing back from this line some 80 cm in the west to 30 cm in the east, thus apparently leaving the stones to act as a rough bench along the north side of these two rooms. At the NW corner, where the north and west walls should join, although the stones of W626 and W627 did meet, there was a gap at the level of the mud brick, as though stones or perhaps a heavy timber post had been extracted (Fig. 131). As explained above, W627 was effectively a terrace wall backed against the higher ground to the north. W628, which separates Rms 20 and 21, looks secondary. It is only one brick (38 cm) wide and the gap above the stone footing between the brick of walls W627 and W628 was filled with chunks of mud brick and stones, rather than laid materials. There is no sign of a doorway through it. In the SE corner of the room the timbers in W631 probably mark an entrance from Rm 24, and there was possibly also a threshold leading through W629 into Rm 22.

Parts of the floor of Rm 20 were paved with unshaped stone slabs, irregularly laid in unplastered soil. Across this surface lay a dense layer of black ashy deposit and then *c.* 1 m of destruction debris — mainly calcined and distorted mud bricks tumbled

clear that it suffered from the same conflagration as the Stele Building, but was a separate structure. The rooms we see on the plan were probably built at the same time as, or during, the IIc phase, and they were included in the IIc destruction, after which, in phase IId, this part of the site was flattened and left as an open area. The space north of W627, marked on the plan as Rm 23, showed no sign of the IIc destruction, and it is virtually certain that as in Rms 9 and 10 the ground level here was much higher, so that after the destruction the levelling of the site sliced into earlier deposits. South of W627 the IIc floors in Rms 20–22 were significantly lower than those within the Stele Building (except for Rms 7 and 8 in the southern wing).

Its scale, and the number of storage vessels found within it, tend to suggest that the East Building too is from the superstructure. It was deepest in the south, and caught up in the destruction here were several pottery vessels, including pilgrim flasks, a trefoil-mouthed jug with clay stopper and at least two heavy storage jars (**694–700, 702–3** K19/364, 379–84, 386–7, 405, 412: Fig. 132). The position of these vessels within the destruction debris (rather than in the lowest black ash on the floor) suggests that when the building collapsed some of them may have been hanging on walls, or resting on shelves, or even in a higher storey. Also baked into this debris was the silver figurine of a triad of deities (**2306** K19/327), in close association with a group of silver, copper and frit jewellery (**2018, 2035, 2043, 2241, 2307**, K19/346, 348–51), concreted together by the heat.

Figure 132. *Rm 20, SW corner; jars in destruction debris.*

With its roughly paved floor and irregular shape Rm 20 has many of the characteristics of an open space (cf. Rm 41 in Level IVa). Without the plan of the eastern and southern parts of the building, it is impossible to say whether it was a forecourt giving access to Rm 22 and connecting rooms, or was merely a dead end formed by the space remaining between the backs of the two main structures. If Rm 22 was in fact a courtyard (see below), then it is possible Rm 20 was roofed; in this case the paving, unusual in a domestic room, might point to its use for animals, which is not necessarily incompatible with storage.

Level IIc units and finds — Rm 20

Walls: 4589–90, 6210

Fossil — coral	4589	*K19/466	2519
Sp. whorl	6210	K19/458	1972
Copper bangle	6210	K19/457	2257

Occ. deposit: 4557, 4598

Copper wire	4557	K19/337	2258

Destr. debris: 4525, 4528, 4531, 4548, 4552–3, 4555, 4562, 4564, 4578, 4597

Grinder	4552	K19/325	2772
Storage jar	4553	K19/400	704
Beads	4553	K19/349–51	2018, 2035, 2043
Copper pin	4553	K19/348	2241
Silver figurine	4553	K19/327	2306
Silver pin	4553	K19/346	2307
Stone axe	4555	K19/336	2600
Pub. ceramic	4562		988
Astragalus	4562	K19/341	2436
Pilgrim flask	4564	K19/361	693
Bowl	4564	K19/391	701
Storage jar	4564	K19/356	706
Pilgrim flasks	4578	*K19/382, 387	694–5
Jug	4578	*K19/386	696
Trefoil jug	4578	*K19/383	697
+ Jar stopper	4578	K19/385	697
Trefoil jug	4578	*K19/380	698
Jar	4578	K19/381	700
Pithos	4578	*K19/384	702
Storage pot	4578	*K19/379	703
Pub. ceramic	4578		705
Trefoil jug	4597	*K19/405	699
Jar stoppers	4597	K19/406, 409	1498–9
Copper wire	4597	K19/410	2281
Metal/slag	4597	K19/407	2420

Packing: 4522
Cut: 4561

Chain link	4561	K19/338	2399

Room 21

This room measures 4.5 × 2.1 m. The doorway halfway along W958, linking it with Rm 22 to the south, is 1.18 m wide and 0.68 m deep. The threshold is represented by two stretches of burnt wood and stones, with a square socket at the west end of the inner piece of wood (Fig. 133). The socket is 16 cm square, sunk 6 cm into the ground, and lined with baked clay; from its shape and position it seems more suited to a fixed door jamb than to the turning door post usually associated with such sockets.

The most notable feature of Rm 21 is its surface (Fig. 134). The whole floor, except around the edges of the room (where an underlying brown floor similar to that in Rm 22 was visible), was covered by a deposit of bluish-grey ash forming a rectangle of about 3.7 × 1.8 m. The origin of this striking effect is not known; the ash may derive from an organic floor covering such as a rug, but we have no technical confirmation of this. At the western end of the blue ash was a circular area of burnt, white deposits, 70 cm in diameter, indicating the location of something organic which was inciner-

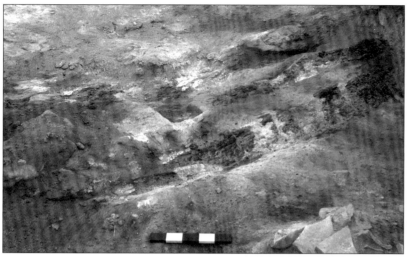

Figure 133. *Rm 21: burnt timbers of threshold, with square socket, looking NE.*

ated in the fire. Along the north side of the room this same surface sloped up to several stones from the footing of W627, and their continuation here in line with stones at the north edge of Rm 20 may point to a time before the rooms were partitioned by W628. Lying on the floor near the centre of the room were a couple of large potsherds, one of them a painted jar rim (**803** L19/74), the other a heavy jar base. Above the floor was the usual layer of destruction debris. This was up to 70 cm deep with burnt brick on the south side of the room against W958, but sloping down towards the north side where it was mainly black ashy and no more than 10 cm in depth.

Level IIb unit — Rm 21
IIb packing: 5977

Level IIc units and finds — Rm 21
Occ. surface: 5980
| Jar rim | 5980 | L19/74 | **803** |

Destr. debris: 5976
| Loomweight | 5976 | L19/64 | **1829** |
| Sp. whorl | 5976 | L19/61 | **1940** |

Packing: 5973
Pub. ceramic	5973		**894**
Animal figurine	5973	L19/53	**1505**
Human bone	5973		**2878**

Room 22

Rm 22 was probably a rectangular room, although in the absence of its south wall this must remain uncertain. It measures 5.7 m E–W and more than 3.2 m N–S. The west end of the room was severely affected by the fire, and bricks from W959 were caught up in the calcined destruction debris (Fig. 135). At the east end of the room W959 is cut back to make room for a wood-fronted bench. This is more than 2.10 m long, and 0.40 m deep, and the upper surface, which was marked by the same dark brown deposit as the room floor, stood about 35 cm above it. The bench occupies the full width of this end of the room, and indeed it seems to have been prolonged northwards through the thickness of W958, leaving a square space where the two walls should meet, similar to that at the NW corner of Rm 20. To the north, technically in Rm 21, the plaster on wall W958 curves round to meet wall W959, while in the south, the east end of W958 is plastered, where the niche starts.

The floor in Rm 22 is at the same level as the south end of Rm 20, but some 10–15 cm below that of Rm 21,

Figure 134. *Rm 21, looking west, showing extent of bluish-grey ash on floor.*

and covered in soft dark-brown burnt soil. In the NE corner of the room was a badly broken storage jar with flat base (di. 25.5 cm) and one handle preserved (L19/77), and lying on the floor some 30 cm in front of the doorway was a patch of broken pottery (5979), which may once have been more extensive, as it lay just next to the NE corner of P98/49. This huge pit (2.8 m E–W and more than 3.2 m N–S) was filled with very clean solid clay, with some mud bricks, and had been dug with vertical sides from Level I, from a height of at least 2 m above the Rm 22 floor; we did not empty it below the floor level or identify its southern limit. Immediately to its east was another large pit, P98/85 (Fig. 136). This was roughly cylindrical, 2.04 m in diameter, with vertical sides and a well-defined base some 1.1 m below the floor. It belongs with phase IIc, and seems to have been in use prior to the destruction of the building because apart from a small quantity of loose grey soil mixed with pieces of charcoal, it was filled with the debris of destruction — large blocks of mud-brick mixed with loose burnt soil and charcoal lumps.

Figure 135. *Rm 22, NW corner: collapsed mud brick from W958, looking north.*

The size of Rm 22, its position in relation to Rms 20 and 21, and the presence of a contemporary pit, all suggest that it may have been an open central courtyard. The soft brown floor deposit might tend to belie this but Rm 6, which was surely open to the sky, had a similar surface.

Figure 136. *Rm 22, looking east, showing pottery from unit 5979, P98/85 and unexcavated P98/49 in foreground.*

Level IIc units and finds — Rm 22
Occ. surface: 5979, 5981
| Storage jar | 5981 | *L19/77 | |

Destr. debris: 4596, 5975, 5982
Jar stopper	4596	K19/403	1497
Copper rod	4596	*K19/411	2282
Pub. ceramics	5975		804, 932
Jar stopper	5975	L19/65	1500
Unpub. ceram.	4596	*K19/412	

Cut: 5978

Room 23

This is not so much a room, as undefined space north of Rm 20, where the final IIc level was probably higher than the standing remains of W627. This wall would have been sliced off during IId building work, to which the stone wall base shown in K20d, abutting the east end of W121, probably belongs. Some of the deposits removed by us were accordingly contemporary with the earlier use of the Stele Building in Phase IIb.

Level IIb units and finds — Rm 23
Feature: 6206
Packing: 6203, 6205, 6207
| Pub. ceramic | 6203 | | 745 |
| Astragalus | 6203 | K19/464 | 2432 |

Level IIc units and finds — Rm 23
Occ. surface: 6201
Packing: 6200
Astragalus   6200   K19/465   **2438**

Cut: 6202
Jar stopper   6202   K19/436   **1501**
Astragalus   6202   K19/435   **2439**

Room 24

Like Rm 6, Rm 24 was probably an open area, linking the Stele Building and the East Building. The excavated NW part measures 4.2 × 2.8 m. In the west, W444 which separates Rm 24 from Rm 6 was irregular and appeared to have slumped to the east, off its stone foundations (Fig. 137). A wood-lined, stone threshold, or perhaps step, (width *c.* 1.6 m) in W444 leads down from the higher courtyard surface of Rm 6, while at the north end of Rm 24 another wood-lined threshold (width *c.* 1.7 m, over a double row of stones), gives access to Rm 20 (Fig. 138).

The surface in Rm 24 was well preserved, with evidence of burning, and dipped to the SE. The material lying across it took several forms, but included unmistakable highly vitrified destruction debris in the north and a jumble of individual, tumbled mud bricks in the SW of the room — possibly a collapsed arch or vault. In the SW it was cut by pit P98/94. This pit was full of mixed destruction debris, indicating that it was open when the building was destroyed.

Level IIc units and finds — Rm 24
Destr. debris: 6143, 6159–61
Fossil   6161   K18/303   **2520**

Fill: 6146, 6153, 6156
Cuts: 6158, 6162

The Northeast Annex

NE of the Stele Building in phase IIc was an irregular triangular space given over to a variety of fire installations. Although there appears to be no direct

Figure 137. *Burnt mud brick and burnt wooden threshold overlying stone foundations of wall W444; Rm 6 to left, Rm 24 with P98/94 to right; looking north.*

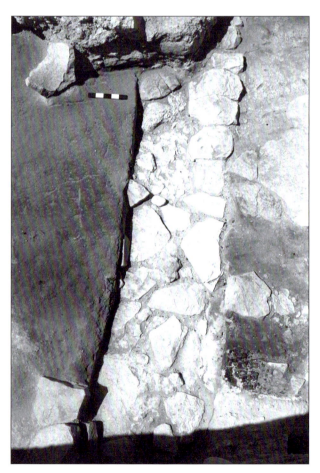

Figure 138. *Foundation of W631 in doorway, between Rms 20 and 24, looking west.*

access between here and the main building, we guess it must have served as its domestic annex, if only because the Stele Building proper is noticeably lacking in a kitchen area with ovens.

The 'annex' is bounded on the NW by the solid stone foundations of W714, and on the NE by a less substantial mudbrick wall (W716). In the IIc phase this space was divided by W715, leaving a larger domestic area to the NW (Rm 15) and a smaller one to its SE (Rm 11) — see Figs. 139 & 492. Earlier, in IIa–b the space was divided differently (see below). W714 continues to the NE, but no detail survived of the space beyond W716 numbered Rm 12.

Figure 139. *K20d, looking NW with W121 at left and Rms 11 and 15.*

Level IIc

Rm 15 measures *c.* 6.5 × 5.0 m (max.). Since the SW stretch of W714 was badly denuded, it is impossible to say if there was access to the room from the west, although it seems more likely that the wall continued without a break to meet W121, and that access was from the east, via Rm 11. There was a gap in the upper brickwork at the centre of W715 which suggested a doorway here, in which case it had a raised threshold, as the plaster on the SE face was continuous.

There was a variety of fire installations. Built against the face of W714 (and directly below the surface of the site) was a range of three small hearths with clay kerbs (FI94/7; Fig. 62), while FI94/10 against W716 was a much larger oven (di. 1.2 m) with a brick surround and plaster floor over a pebble base. Between them was a free-standing circular oven (FI94/11), 50 cm in diameter, with its walls surviving to 12 cm, likewise with a burnt clay base over pebbles. Three late pits had left only a fragment of FI95/7 in the southern part of the room *in situ*; it also had a pebble base and clay surface, but at +99.98 it may have belonged to an earlier floor. In Rm 11 against the NE face of the Stele Building was a larger hearth with a pebble layer over a mudbrick base (FI95/8). In the NW corner of K20b, was another range of three small hearths (FI94/8), but these were placed directly on the foundation stones of W714 where it forms the NW wall of Rm 12, and are therefore probably of IId date.

The density of fire installations suggests that this was a domestic quarter, and that the area was probably un-roofed. The ground surface in Rms 11 and 15 stood a good 70–100 cm higher than in Rms 2 and 4 of the Stele Building, yet after the removal of later packing both spaces were covered with the same heavily burnt destruction material as overlay the stones of the IIc rebuild of W121 between them. This suggests that while the floors of the Stele Building itself had probably been kept clean, this informal domestic area to the NE had been less assiduously cleared of debris so that the ground level had gradually risen.

Level IIc units and finds — Rm 11
Occ. surface: 1949
FI95/8: 1953
Destr. debris: 1945

Pub. ceramic	1945		883
Sp. whorl	1945	K20/145	1939
Bead	1945	K20/147	2072

Level IIc units — Rm 12
FI94/8: 1108, 1112

Level IIc units and finds — Rm 15
Occ. surface: 1131, 1135, 1141–2, 1146, 1931, 1948

Clay stand	1131	K20/227	1633
Mortar	1131	K20/40	2685
Beads	1135	K20/44	2053

FI: 1106, 1144–5, 1952
Destr. debris: 1942, 1944

Sp. whorls	1942	K20/125, 219	1943, 1956
Beads	1942	K20/130–31	2013, 2019
Tessera	1942	K20/228	2203
Pub. ceramic	1944		758
Bead	1944	K20/140	2078

Cuts: 1138–40

Phase IIb (Fig. 493)

Within Rm 15 a small sounding was sunk beneath the phase IIc floor to recover a sequence of stratified earlier material. The floors were regular with cleanish deposits on them, although there always seems to have been an oven. On the first occupation surface below IIc was a pebble-based fire installation (FI96/4) against the NE face of W121. This was about 1 m square, with a kerb 13 cm high; beneath its clay floor at +99.65 were two layers of pebbles with a layer of flat stones between. It stood directly above the stones of W794, which ran NE from W121, and parallel to W793. W793 was the forerunner of W714 and its foundation stones had been exposed by the diggers of P94/13. The floor of this earlier phase was at ~99.30, and at this date there was an oven (FI96/10) in the west corner of the room. This had also been sectioned by the pit P94/13; it was 75–80 cm in diameter, with a kerb 10–15 cm thick and a clay floor laid over a bed of pebbles 8 cm deep.

We did not excavate to the SE of W794 and are unable to say whether W715 was already present at this time, since it is an obvious possibility that it was built later, after the removal of W794.

Although the deposits each side of W793 were not fully excavated, its foundation courses, as revealed in the north side of P94/13, were of large roughly rectangular slabs, and they clearly constitute the continuation of W118, which was exposed in the SE corner of J20b, and was also founded on large slabs at the same level. W118 is bonded with W119, which survives for a stretch of 1 m before it is cut by the slope of the tepe. Rm 14, in the angle formed by the two walls, had an occupation surface (1316) at ~98.94, which must be roughly contemporary with the IIb deposits in K20c. This is the only remnant of a solid structure, which has now been eroded but was at least partially contemporary with the Stele Building although built to a different alignment. Further east the space NW of W793 showed no further occupation levels, although at +99.13 there was part of a large jar buried in bricky fill and eroding out of the mound surface (**911** K20/218). To the west of W119 there were further scrappy traces of walls which cannot be convincingly related to either building, and the only item of interest here was the discovery of a hieroglyphic seal (**1472** J20/33).

Level IIb units and finds — sounding under Rm 15
Packing: 1977, 1986
Bead	1986	K20/189	2047

Fill: 1981
Occ. surfaces (earlier): 1971–2, 1975–6, 1978
Clay stopper	1971	K20/167	1494
Beads	1971	K20/168, 173	2011, 2034
Human bone	1971	K20/238	2876
Astragalus	1971	K20/240	2431
Grinder	1976	K20/178	2737

FI96/10: 1973
Occ. surfaces (later): 1149–50, 1935, 1958, 1965, 1967
Bead	1935	K20/116	2052
Bead	1965	K20/163	2025
Antler frag.	1965	K20/162	2493
Quern	1967	K20/157	2736

FI96/4: 1966

Level IIb units and finds — Rm 13
Packing: 1962, 1968–9, 1982
Sp. whorl	1962	K20/153	1935
Astragalus	1962	K20/239	2433
Grinder	1962	K20/156	2738
Antler frags.	1968	K20/158-9	2493
Pub. ceramic	1982		911

FI96/3: 1961

Level IIb units and finds — Rm 14
Packing below IIb floor: 1326, 1332
Pub. ceramics	1332		684, 826

Occ. surface: 1316
Fill: 1313
Cut: 1307

Level IIb units and finds - west of W119
Stratified deposits: 1317, 1328
Seal	1317	J20/33	1472
Sp. whorl	1328	J20/55	1918

The Western Courtyard (Figs. 494–5)

The area to the NW of the Stele Building, which in Level III had been occupied by a substantial building, was in Level II an open space we have called the Western Courtyard. Since it is here that the sequence from IIa to IIe is most clearly visible, and from here that the bulk of our stratified IIa–b ceramics came, the area merits description.

When the stone foundations of the IIa Stele Building were laid, the space to its west was flattened, cutting down the brickwork of the Level IIId/e walls, and it remained a largely open area throughout the life of the Stele Building, into phase IIe or later. During this time the area accommodated small impermanent structures tacked on to the NW wall of the main building, occasional fire installations, and any number of pits. In the earlier phases the pits seem to have been fewer and larger (notably P97/6); later on, in IIe and also during IIf and even later, the ground was honeycombed with intersecting pits so that very little of the horizontal accumulation of occupation deposits remained in place.

The area of pits probably extended northward into I20d and J20c, where much of southern part of the Level IIId–e courtyard had been removed by a number of intersecting pits (notably P94/1: Fig. 491; P94/5, P95/12, P95/28, P95/34, P97/55 and P97/71 (both Fig. 492)). The precise attribution of all such pits to one phase or another is impossible: their upper rims had almost all been removed by erosion (thanks to the slope of the mound), and/or by later building activity, but to judge from the ceramics they do not seem to post-date phase IIf and some can be assigned to an earlier phase of Level II on the basis of stratigraphy.

Despite the disturbance, three successive occupation surfaces could be traced across most of the area; the first and second of these could be tied stratigraphically to phases IIc and IId of the Stele Building respectively. The IIc surface in the Western Courtyard was at ~98.30–98.60, about the same level as the floors of Rms 7–8 inside the building. When the Stele Building was reconstructed after the burning of phase IIc, the IId room floors were laid as much as 1 m higher (+99.29 in Rm d7), but the courtyard surface by the SW corner of the building was raised only some 30 cm. Hence the Stele Building was effectively placed on a platform, or, viewed another way, the Western Courtyard was left as a sunken area. Much the same happened after the IId destruction, and this means that whereas any IIe material in the Stele Building proper was completely removed by later (Iron Age or Byzantine) activities, the contemporary IIe level in the Western Courtyard lay much lower and forms our third and highest occupation surface (at ~99.00). The accumulation in the Western Courtyard is therefore important in that it gives us a sequence from the earliest until the latest attested phase of the Stele Building.

Levels IIa–b (Fig. 494)
Before the Level IIc reconstruction of the Stele Building the principal feature of the courtyard was a square room tacked on to the NW wall of the building (Rm 17). Further to the west there were wall foundations on a quite different alignment which no doubt belonged to a separate structure or structures, virtually nothing of which survives.

Directly above the cut-down mud brick of Level III in I19 was a distinctive layer of whitish material with a pink tinge (5518, 5533), continuous except where it had been cut by later pits. Above this was a layer of fill (5531, 5535) into which were sunk the stone foundations of W832. This wall is probably the west end of W829 (= 825), and W828 [+98.02] is a return from its east end, going NW to connect in some way with W108.

East of W828 is a surface notable for the reddish deposit lying on it (2884; +97.76). This deposit and the surface on which it lies belong with the patch of pebbles shown against the east face of W823 (FI97/11). This was presumably a hearth base, though its clay surface has not survived. It looks semicircular on the plan but was probably originally roughly circular since its western half would have been removed by the laying of the foundation of W823. Only some 20 cm to its south was another pebble-based hearth (FI97/6). This has also lost its clay capping, but it rested on a low platform (8 cm high) built of two courses of small stones (typically 10 × 10 × 4 cm) and plastered on its surviving north and east sides. To the south it abutted W826, but its west side had been removed by a combination of P97/19 and the foundation of W823.

The stratigraphy makes it quite clear that Rm 17, a space *c.* 2.20 m (SW–NE) by 2 m (NW–SE) enclosed by the three walls W827, W823 and W824, was constructed later than W828 and W829 further west. Inside the room at the north end the floor level (2890) lies at +97.91, and it ran across the top of W826 to reach W824. Outside to the west a surface at ~97.70–97.80 (2881) was cut by the stones of W823, but these are probably a foundation course and it is possible that the main courtyard floor belonging with Rm 17 was removed by later construction work. For not very long after its construction Rm 17 was demolished and for a while the space became part of the open courtyard again, with a succession of occupation surfaces separated by layers of packing. From this time two patches of burning were noted in the north of I19b on a surface (2879) at +98.02. At the same place in a later phase a shaved-down hearth at +98.19 was associated with surface 2872, which was also pierced by three postholes in an east–west row. A second hearth was also observed in the SW corner of I19b, where the courtyard surface had sloped down noticeably to +97.90 (FI97/12).

The latest occupation surface (2867) was a clear reddish clay layer up to 5 cm thick, best observed on the north side of I19b, where it sloped down towards the south from +98.51 to +98.31. Directly above this was a thick layer of packing probably associated with the IIc reconstruction of the main building.

Further to the south, but with no direct stratigraphic link, a relatively large pebble-based hearth (FI97/3) was located at +98.07 and is probably roughly contemporary. It partly overlay the mud brick of W836, which with W835 and W834 appears to form a dog-leg enclosure wall along the SW side of the courtyard. Only the tops of these walls were uncovered, but they seem likely to belong to the initial Level IIa construction phase, along with the stone foundations on the same alignment further north in I19a. The large fire installation FI98/4 at the west side of I19c appears to respect the face of W834 and it may therefore belong to this phase; but it was too close to the surface and badly damaged for any certainty on this score.

Level IIa/b units and finds — Western Courtyard
Occ. surface: 1329, 2867, 2872, 2879, 2881, 2884, 2897, 5500, 5511, 5530

Pub. ceramic	2880+2884		789

FI: 1334–5, 1367, 2895, 2898–9
Packing: 1359, 1362, 1365, 1369–70, 1385–7, 1392, 1395, 1399, 1417, 2864, 2866, 2869, 2871, 2873, 2875, 2877–8, 2880, 2889, 2891, 2894, 3973, 3976–7, 3979, 3980-82, 4010, 4012, 4019–20, 4201, 5502, 5508, 5517–18, 5531–3, 5535, 5702

Bead	1365	J20/135	2049
Beads	1370	J20/103a–b	2048, 2071
Pub. ceramic	1386		676
Bead	1395	J20/160	2059
Glyptic	1395	J20/169	1485
Loomweight	1395	J20/168	1828
Beads	1395	J20/160–61	2059, 2070
Pub. ceramic	1417		675
Pub. ceramic	2864		805
Pub. ceramic	2871		810
Pub. ceramics	2873		809, 917
Pub. ceramic	2875		808
Pub. ceramic	2877		916
Worked bone	2880	I19/157	2457
Jar stopper	3977	J19/385	1493
Ceramic disc	3981	J19/394	1557
Bead	3981	J19/393	2050
Ceramic disc	4010	I20/60	1575
Pub. ceramic	4012		739
Pub. ceramic	4201		948
Pub. ceramics	5502		736–8, 750, 790, 806
Sp. whorl	5517	I19/153	1933
Sp. whorl	5518	I19/151	1930

Fill: 1331, 1420, 2885, 2888, 2892, 4009, 4011, 4013, 5504, 5514–15, 5529

Sp. whorl	1331	J20/56	1934
Pub. ceramic	5514		898
Needle	5514	I19/150	2230

Cuts: 1363–4, 1366, 1368, 1373–4, 1394, 1403, 1409, 1421, 2865, 2883, 2886, 3974–5, 3978, 3983, 4001–8, 5501, 5516, 5523, 5537–8

Bead	1363	J20/127	2067
Worked bone	1363	J20/186	2461
Bone point	1364	J20/131	2460
Bead	2883	I19/145	2031
Copper shaft	2883	I19/144	2235
Seal	4001	I20/43	1471
Sp. whorl	4001	I20/44	1966
Bead	4001	I20/46	2017
Pub. ceramic	4003		771
Pub. ceramic	4004		740
Bead	4004	I20/54	2075
Arrowhead	4004	I20/52	2246
Nail	4004	I20/53	2330
Astragali	4004	I20/51a	2430
Bone pin	4004	I20/51b	2466
Pub. ceramic	5501		752
Bead	5501	I19/158	2030
Grinder	5523	I19/163	2735
Pub. ceramic	5523		744
Worked bone	5537	I19/208	2458

Level IIa/b units and finds — Rm 17
Occ. surface: 2890
Packing: 2882, 2893

Pub. ceramic	2882		791
Stamp seal	2882	*I19/126	1470
Wire coil	2882	I19/156	2263
Pub. ceramic	2893		792

Level IIc (Fig. 495)

In phase IIc a small square room was once again built against the NW wall of the Stele Building, but further west the earlier buildings have vanished and the only structure seems to be a roughly rectangular enclosure housing a large oven (FI97/12). At the east side of the courtyard, in a corner formed by the west wall of the Stele Building (W820) and a less substantial stone foundation which abuts it (W819), was P97/6, which was unusual for a number of reasons. It was large, with a diameter of about 2 m, although not especially deep (1.26 m). The sides and base of the pit were coated with a distinctive black ashy deposit, and on the east side this was continuous with ashy debris which lapped over the sides and into the interstices of the stones of the IIc foundation of the Stele Building (and was spread across other parts of courtyard as indicated in Fig. 495). This detail shows that the pit was standing open when the IIc phase was burnt down, and in fact the lower part of the fill of the pit was a loose mixture of mud brick, ash and plaster which obviously derived from the destruction of this phase. In the western half of the pit this was overlaid by large blocks of clean brick material, which presumably also came from the walls of the building. Three relatively large pieces of pottery were incorporated in the fill and can be safely attributed to this phase (**741** I19/124, **788** I19/112, and I19/117, the upper part of a pilgrim flask).

Just as the east side of the pit obviously respects the outer wall of the Stele Building, so its north side respects W819. This formed the south side of Rm 18, a small room (2.80 m NE–SW × 2.60 m NW–SE) tacked on to the west side of the main building, very like Rm 17 in phase IIa/b. It too had a hearth at its north end (FI95/6, followed in a second phase of use by the smaller rectangular FI95/1, which lay directly above it but some 25 cm higher). The two large stones at the south end of the room seemed to be *in situ*, and it is probable that the break in the mud brick of W733 represents the doorway.

The base of W732 was noticeably higher than the IIc surface elsewhere in the courtyard. This reflects a steep slope up towards the NW corner of the Stele Building, such that the IIc floor in the NW corner of J19 stood at +99.09, more than half a metre higher than in the rest of the courtyard. A similar rise was also present in phase IId, and the correct identification of these two surfaces was checked with care. W730, shown to the west of W733 on Figure 495, although standing at almost the same level, is probably an isolated fragment from phase IId.

In IIc at less than 1 m from W733 was the east angle of W822, which (despite the interference of P96/111) seems to have belonged to Rm 19, a freestanding structure within the courtyard, presumably at least in part intended to house the large fire installation FI97/2. The other walls were W821 to the NE and W818 to the SW; any NW wall to the room had disappeared with the erosion of the mound, but there are two possible entrances to it, in the SW and in the NE where the surface 2850 runs through the line of W821. Between these walls the surface was some 15 to 25 cm lower than in the south and east, while the fire installation itself lay still lower, and was probably countersunk. The details of this feature were hard to reconstruct, probably because the superstructure had fallen into the fuel chamber leaving a confusing picture, but the plastered side stood some 20 cm high, and it was certainly a closed oven rather than an open hearth.

Level IIc units and finds — Western Courtyard

W733: 1726

Quern	1726	I19/206	2744

Occ. surface: 2845, 2850, 2852, 2862, 1728 (Rm 18)
FI95/6: 1727
FI97/2: 2834, 2854
Destr. debris: 2840, 2843, 2849, 2851

Stone bowl	2840	I19/123	2639
Copper shaft	2843	I19/115	2235
Whetstone	2851	I19/109	2661
Hammerstone	2851	I19/110	2792

Fill: 2846, 2861

Pub. ceramic	2846		802
Ceramic disc	2846	I19/111	1572
Quern	2861	I19/118	2741

Packing: 2841, 3970

Pub. ceramic	2841		801
Bone tube	3970	J19/378	2474

Cuts: 2848, 2856, 2858, 2863

Bowl	2848	*I19/124	741
Jar	2848	*I19/112	788
Bead	2848	I19/114	2061
Stone object	2848	I19/107	2619a
Human bone	2848	I19/187	2877
Pilgrim flask	2858	*I19/117	

The IIc destruction

That the entire Stele Building, the adjoining rooms of the East Building, and the North-East Annex were destroyed in a single episode seems certain, as already stated, p. 36) but there remain questions about what happened before and after that event. It seems possible that the users of the building had warning: few artefacts were found *in situ* on the floors, but perhaps more tellingly several of the pot emplacements in Rms 4, 5, 7 and 8 no longer held vessels (and **909** K19/294 in the corner of Rm 4 was too large to remove easily). Commenting on the material on the floor of Rm 6 (unit 4511), W. Matthews has also noted that 'the presence of a thick layer of loose aggregates across the floor of this and other rooms, suggests this building may have been abandoned for a period of time, prior to final destruction by fire' (2001, §9.3.4). It also seems possible that if we have interpreted the large sockets in the north and south walls of Rm 3 correctly, large timbers may have been removed from them before the destruction. Moreover, there were few signs of substantial burnt roof timbers among the debris in other rooms which were presumably roofed (e.g. Rms 1, 2 and 4), and if they had been taken off in advance it might also explain the dispersal of 'slates' across the floors of Rms 7 and 8.

There can be no doubt about the destructive effects of the fire itself, which seems to have been hottest in the region of Rm 20 where the mud bricks had been fused *in situ* into a vitrified mass. The source of artefacts found within the destruction deposits has to remain in doubt. Plainly the stele in Rm 3, which had been shattered by the heat into more than 70 pieces, must be approximately *in situ*, but did the complete plate found next to it belong with it, or fall from above? How did the silver figurine and associated jewellery find their way into the vitrified mass of brickwork fallen into Rm 20? These are unanswerable questions, especially since we cannot be sure whether we should reconstruct an upper storey, and if so over which of the rooms. Nevertheless, the presence of such valuable items makes it unlikely that the inhabitants were fully prepared for the destructive effects of the fire.

A number of pits seem to have been dug through the destruction debris before the construction of the IId building, and possible implications of this are discussed in the next section. Evidently some time must have elapsed between the fire and the construction of a new building in IId, but probably not long.

13.2. Level IId (Fig. 496)

Although very poorly preserved, the structure which occupied the site of the Stele Building in phase IId seems to have been similar enough to be judged its successor. It is aligned identically, and occupies a very similar footprint, though it extends further to the SW and its SE wall was pushed out slightly into the space formerly occupied by the west end of the East Building. Along the NE side the IId walls are constructed directly on the brickwork of IIc. Not enough survives of the rooms to demonstrate a continuity of function: the only clues are the domestic installations in Rm d3 and the elaborate hearth against the NE wall of Rm d4. The presence of imported Mycenaean pottery on the floor of Rm d10 is important for dating the building, but does not help much in determining its function.

The site
After the destruction of the IIc Stele Building, both the walls and the tumbled, burnt masonry filling the rooms were levelled off at about 1 m above the IIc floors. In some areas a burnt, 'trample horizon' was found, directly above this destruction debris, with the IId occupation surface proper laid over an intervening layer of packing.

From this intermediate level a number of pits were dug through the burnt debris of the IIc destruction. They were of different shapes and sizes, but recognizable by the loose ash and chunks of brick with which they had been back-filled. These pits (unlike others which had phytolith linings, and were probably IId storage pits) were unlined and were all placed within the rooms of the IIc building, avoiding the walls. Clear instances shown on Figure 492 are: P96/119 in Rm 2, P97/21, P96/121, P96/127 (cut by P96/121), and P97/3 in Rm 4. From their contents these intermediate IIc/d pits risk confusion with a few pits which were actually in use during the IIc phase, and which were also filled with destruction material, but in most if not all cases the upper rim of these intermediate pits is well above the IIc floors, and they are clearly cut through the destruction. Their purpose remains obscure. One obvious possibility is that attempts were made to recover objects known to have been buried in the ruins, but mostly the pits do not look like the burrowings of robbers. Equally this can hardly have been a good context for grain storage pits nor is there any sign that they were so used.

Whatever their function, these pits do suggest that some time elapsed before the erection of a new building on the site of the IIc destruction. The same impression is given by the rough IId surface identified in much of K19c and adjacent quadrants. A number of postholes were sunk through this surface in a roughly rectangular arrangement (Figs. 140 & 496). 24 postholes were excavated, although they are not all necessarily related. They are, on average, 15 cm in diameter, the largest being 64 cm deep. They were cut into a compact mudbrick-like material. They enclose an area *c.* 2.4 × 2.0 m and suggest some form of shelter or other ephemeral structure. There are no coherent signs of room walls or floors in this space.

To the NE and SE of the destroyed IIc Stele Building, no attempt appears to have been made to rebuild in the triangular space occupied by Rms 15 and 11, or over the East Building, during phase IId. (A possible exception to this would be the row of three hearths FI94/8 built on top of the stone foundation of W714. These were so close to the surface that we cannot judge whether they are really IId or merely of late IIc date; see p. 143.) In both areas the IId phase was marked by a heavy layer of ash but no structures. In the east section of K19, extending into L19, there was a clear initial IId surface tilting down to the south in conformity with the shape of the destroyed IIc buildings (represented by unit 1545 at +99.72). Above this was a layer of packing designed to create a roughly levelled open space, capped by a level clay floor which also respects the east face of W770 (1535 at +100.22, not shown on plan), and corresponds to the IId occupation phase inside

Figure 140. *Level IId post-holes in K19c (see Fig. 496), looking NW with storage jar **909** in Level IIc Rm 4 behind.*

the building. A few postholes were found cutting IId surfaces to the east of W770, similar to those in K19c but at a higher level and in a less coherent pattern.

On the other side, the IIc Western Courtyard was re-plastered over a thin layer of IIc destruction debris and remained open as before, with the possible exception of W730 shown on Figure 495. In turn this IId courtyard surface has a layer of grey ashy debris — and in places two such layers — lying on it, beneath a further layer of packing (2823) which underlies the IIe surface.

The IId building

Between these open spaces only fragments of the phase IId structures have survived the attentions of the builders and pit-diggers of the Iron Age, and especially of the Byzantine period. These remains are best preserved in the NE, and in the south of the former Stele Building, where both the IIc and the IId rooms were at a lower level; indeed, the IId architecture in the south range was so much lower that at first we assumed it belonged to the IIc phase. Even here, the IId walls and floors had been severely truncated by later activities. While the very partial IId plan we have recovered respects the broad lines of the underlying IIc structure, there are major differences in its internal layout which show that no attempt was made to replicate the earlier building. There is no doubt that the IId building was destroyed by fire like its predecessor. Burnt destruction debris similar to that in the open spaces to east and west was identified on IId floors in Rms d7–10.

The most coherent IId architecture is Rm d3 in the NE of the excavated area. This room is about 4 m long from west to east, and because the SW wall (W771) diverges, its N–S width varies from 2.4 m in the east to 3 m at the west end. The stone foundation of the IId wall (W795) was laid alongside the SW face of the IIc wall (W713) which here remained standing higher than elsewhere because of the higher ground level in Rms 11 and 15. By contrast, W770, the SE wall of the IId building, was positioned almost 1 m further to the east than W613 in IIc, more in line with the west wall of the East Building.

W771 forms the southern limit of Rm d3 and continues to the west, where it also forms the southern wall of a second small, rectangular room, Rm d2, before returning to the north as W725. W772 between the two rooms presumably included a doorway, either at the centre, where pit P96/82 has cut away much of the wall, or at the south end, where no stones were noted.

The yellow clay floor of Rm d3 was laid directly on top of IIc destruction debris at ~99.70 (and about 65 cm above the underlying floor of IIc Rm 4). Against the north wall was a circular hearth (FI96/28). A later unplastered surface (1542/1987), was about 20 cm higher than the original floor (at ~99.89). Belonging to this phase in the SE corner was a small, plastered mudbrick bin, with the impression of a jar base inside it, and some 90 cm to its north a storage vessel in unbaked clay stood against the wall. Close to the NE wall was a small pit, perhaps the emplacement for another pot (P96/97). An unbaked clay vessel stood *in situ* against the NW wall. These features combine to indicate a domestic function for the room, but not a large volume of storage capacity.

Rm d2 to the west measures *c.* 4 × 3.20 m. Its original floor (1988) was a weathered, compact surface, sealing IIc destruction debris at the same height as Rm d3, and capped by a second layer of clay flooring (1980). These probably correspond to the floor surface against the south face of W713, excavated in 1994 (1133). Although the floors had stones and bricky debris on them no informative detail survived. The whole space has been severely disrupted by pits, with P94/24, P96/53 and P96/82 in particular removing potentially crucial information about access to the room from the vicinity of walls W725 and W772. The south wall of the room is restored on the assumption that W721 connected with W771. The IIc wall W713 served as the north wall of the room, possibly with an extra course of stones and mud brick laid on top of it.

Further west, erosion has removed any IId deposits that might have existed, and to the south of this the patches of flooring and stretches of wall are too fragmentary to be certain even that we are looking at a single building, let alone permit a confident restoration of its plan. The surface shown in J19b had ashy debris lying on it and itself lay directly on top of the bricky IIc destruction debris. It seems therefore to be 'trample horizon', and the single course of stones labelled W721 rested on it. At the same level as this foundation, and apparently laid against its south face, was FI95/5, a pebble-based hearth with clay surface and the remains of a kerb, resting on a curved brick platform of about 1 m diameter, with plastered edges. This arrangement is unusually elaborate, and if one were looking for continuity with the IIc Stele Building, one would have to see FI95/5 as the IId equivalent of the central hearth in Rm 3, and Rm d4 therefore as the counterpart of Rm 3.

Unfortunately we have no clues to the layout of the IId building in this central area; at one stage we believed that W763, in the NE corner of J19d, was of IId date, but its stones lie directly above a large pit (P96/102) which has itself to be of IId date, so that W763 must belong to IIe at the earliest, and the same may apply to W722 and W723 further west. In the fill of P96/102 were found, along with a large block of mud brick and other fresh destruction material, a large piece of deep bowl and other Mycenaean sherds, one of which has a physical join with a piece from the IId destruction level in Rm d10 (5802; **960**). This makes it probable that P96/102 was either standing open at the time of the IId destruction (and therefore intended for storage), or dug immediately after the destruction, suggesting an intermediate phase of activity between IId and IIe, similar to the IIc/d transition.

As with W713 to the NE, so the line of the main IIc SW wall (W618–W615) was inherited by IId, with the stone foundations of W724 laid over the IIc brickwork. It served as the NE wall of Rm d7, which measured roughly 4 m NW–SE by 3.30 m NE–SW. Its unplastered floor, at +99.15–99.29 was appreciably lower than the basal IId surfaces further north, and this must reflect the lower level of these southern rooms in phase IIc. Along its NE side, against the face of the short surviving stretch of W724, was a mudbrick bench with a plastered face, which turns to run along the SE wall of the same room (now lost except for a few stones). On the west side of the room an unbaked clay storage vessel (J19/282) was probably resting on a similar bench against a short surviving stretch of wall (W767). The floor was covered in destruction material, which included large beam fragments, two flat stones, and a baked mud brick.

The SW limit of Rm d7 is indicated by W768, a short stretch of mudbrick wall, only some 40 cm wide and plastered on both faces. We have no indication of how much further Rm d8 extended to the SW, but it seems certain that the IId building(s) here reached further than the IIc Stele Building's SW wall. The SE corner of Rm d7 was removed by a large cut or pit, the base of which is shown as P97/85 on Figure 492. This unfortunately has removed any connection between the SE and SW walls of the room and Rm d10 to the SE.

The IId floor of Rm d10 is at about the same level as in Rms d7 and d8, and the fragment of brickwork numbered W429 seems to have been the northern jamb of a doorway which would have led through from Rm d8 into d10. A fragment of the threshold still survived beneath the burnt destruction material, which also covered most of the relatively well-preserved Rm d10 floor (5873/5877), delimited on the NE by W433. Any eastern wall was removed by the construction of Rm e6 in phase IIe. The space must have been at least 5 m NW–SE and 4 m NE–SW, and is reminiscent of Rm 7 in phase IIc, which occupied a similar space further to the north. The IId floor was cut by two small postholes and dipped slightly to the south and west.

In the destruction material, in J18b south of W433 (5864), just to the east of W429 (5802), and in the extreme NW corner of this room in J19c (3921), were parts of several Mycenaean bowls, with joins between units. Other pieces evidently from the same original deposit were found in the IId destruction layer in K18a (4382; Rm d9), and also in later pits and other disturbed contexts in the vicinity (in K18a: 4334 and 4338; J19c: 3918), and more surprisingly, in the fill of P96/102, 5 m to the north (see above).

Immediately north of W433 is a space designated Rm d9, which with the plastered face of W614 to the NE looks like a corridor some 2 m wide, although both shape and function must remain uncertain. Only two patches of IId floor remained here, one against the north face of W433, and the other in the NW corner of K18a where it had been preserved by having the IIe W426 built above it. In each place the plastered IId floor surface was covered in burnt destruction debris, similar to that in Rms d7 and d10.

The sunken IIe Rm e6 in K18a also cut through IId deposits down to just above the IIc surface. Where IId floors survive here, it is thanks to IIe walls and benches being built directly on top of them. To the east of Rm e6 only half of K18b was excavated to IId levels; again much of the deposits had been removed by pits. What remained were short stretches of a low IId mudbrick wall, W442/W443, either side of a probable doorway, and a IId surface (6150). This surface was compact and grey and was cut by two small, oval pits and a posthole (6151). It was stratified above a burnt 'trample surface' (6156) lying directly on top of the IIc destruction debris, which was cut by a posthole (6154) and had a large mud brick lying in a shallow depression. Once again, the features cut into the 'trample surface' suggest that some time elapsed between the IIc destruction and the construction of phase IId proper.

Intermediate IIc/d pits units and finds
Level IIc Rm 2: 1996
Level IIc Rm 3: 1588, 1690

Cooking pot	1690	J19/256	905
Myc. vessel	1690		955
Myc. deep bowls	1690		959, 961, 963–5
Bowl	1690		762
Glyptic	1690	J19/280	1482
Ceramic disc	1690	J19/257	1560
Copper shafts	1690	J19/234, 278	2235
Copper frags.	1690	J19/274	2296
Astragali	1690	J19/225	2437
Bone points	1690	J19/228	2459
Antler frags.	1690	J19/225, 229, 232, 236	2493
Whetstone	1690	J19/226	2652

Level IIc Rm 4: 1550, 1562, 1565, 1569, 1588, 1592, 1994, 1999, 2906

Ceramic disc	1550	K19/82	1559
Sp. whorls	1592	K19/163, 165	1919, 1957
Copper pin	1592	K19/168	2242
Door socket	1565	K19/109	2821
Jug	1994	K20/211	786
Sp. whorl	1994	K20/203, 205, 207	1920–21, 1945
Wire coils	1994	K20/202	2261

Level II: the End of the Bronze Age and the Iron Age

Obsidian chips 1994 K20/208 2588

Level IId units and finds — Rm d1
Occ. surface: 3946
Packing: 1320, 1324, 1344, 3911
Copper ring 1324 J20/45 2259
Wire ring 1324 J20/46 2260

Phase IId–f cuts in area of d1: 1337–42
Bead 1342 J20/69 2073
Copper shaft 1342 J20/68 2235

Level IId units — Rm d2
Occ. surface: 1133, 1980, 1988
Clay wheel 1988 K20/209 1524

Cut: 2901, 2903
F194/9: 1137
Destr. debris: 1132
Pub. ceramic 1132 760

Level IId units and finds — Rm d3
Wall 795: 1992
Ceramic disc 1992 K20/200 1541

Occ. surface: 1542
Antler frag. 1542 K19/68 2493

Occ. deposit: 1987
Destr. debris: 1541, 1983
Pub. ceramics 1541 751, 761, 895, 923
Cyl. clay obj. 1541 K19/66 1605

Cut: 1546, 1997

Level IId units — Rm d4
Occ. surface: 1635
F195/5: 1628, 1633–4
Packing: 1637
Cut: 1613–14, 1616–17

Level IId units and finds — area south of Rm d4
Cut: 1657
Pub. ceramic 1657 896

Level IId units — Rm d5
Occ. surface: 1543
Copper frags. 1543 K19/78 2296

P96/92: 1544

Level IId units and finds — area south of Rm d5
Occ. surface: 4504–5, 4527, 4532
Fill or packing: 4503, 4526, 4529–30, 4554
Cuts: 4512, 4514
Pub. ceramic 4502+4514 754
Antler frag. 4514 K19/275 2493

Level IId units and finds — Rm d6
Occ. surface: 3942
Cooking pot 3942 J19/332+333 907
Copper pin 3942 J19/328 2235

Packing: 1681, 3940–41, 3945

Level IId units and finds — Rm d7
Bench: 3905

Occ. surface: 3904, 3926
Pounder 3926 J19/294 2797

Fill above IId surface: 3903
'Weetabix' frags. 3903 J19/282

Destr. debris: 1693
Pub. ceramic 1693 794

Packing: 1691, 3901
Pub. ceramic 1691 936
Loomweight 1691 J19/243–4 1790–91
Grinder 1691 J19/262 2770

Level IId units — Rm d8
Occ. surface: 3933
Destr. debris: 5807

Level IId units and finds — Rm d9
Fill and IId floor deposit: 4367, 4383, 5880
Sp. whorl 4367 K18/143 1944
Iron blade 4367 K18/146 2320
Astragalus 5880 J18/410 2440

Destr. debris: 3916, 4382
Packing above IId destr.: 1692, 5866
Cuts into IId: 1697–8, 3925, 3930
Loomweight 1698 J19/260 1795
Needle 3930 J19/310 2233

Level IId units and finds — Rm d10
Packing below IId floor: 5879, 5881
Sp. whorl 5881 J18/362 1994

Wall 433: 5882
Grinder 5882 J18/364 2745
Rubber 5882 J18/365 2813

Occ. surface: 5805, 5864, 5873
Copper frag. 5873 J18/354 2284
Myc. bowl 5802+5864 962

Postholes: 5871, 5876
Occ. deposit: 3920–21, 5877
Pub. ceramic 3918+3921 960
Myc. bowl 3921 J19/324 957

Destr. debris: 3922, 5802, 5862
Pub. ceramic 1690+5802 959
Myc. bowl 5802+5864 962

Fill: 5868
Cuts into IId: 2399, 5808, 5810, 5812–13, 5818, 5820, 5874, 5888
Pub. ceramic 2399 764
Loomweight 2399 J18/232–3 1775–6
Arrowhead 2399 J18/237 2249
Iron blade 2399 J18/231 2320
Astragalus 5808 J18/429 2441
Pub. ceramics 5812 753, 759, 925
Grinder 5813 J18/254 2770
Loomweight 5874 J18/353 1782
Nail 5874 J18/350 2225
Quern 5888 J18/371 2746

Level IId units and finds — Rm d11
Packing below IId floor: 6135
Occ. surface: 4386, 6150

151

Postholes: 6151, 6154
Fill above IId surface: 6131–3, 6147

Stele(?) frag.	6131	K18/283	2830
Lithic sickle	6147	K18/294	2548

Cuts: 6142, 6148

Mortar	6142	K18/282	2687

Level IId units — area south of W614
Fill above IIc Rm 6: 5890
Occ. surface: 4560

Iron nail	4560	K19/194	2388

Cut into Level IIc Rm 6: 6155

Level IId units and finds — area east of W770
Trample sealing IIc destr.: 1545
Packing below occ. surface: 1540, 4523, 5958, 5969

Pub. ceramics	1540		856, 921

Occ. surface: 1535

Pub. ceramic	1535		899
Clay leg	1535	K19/62	1507
Iron frags.	1535	K19/61	2419

Fill or packing: 4517, 4520, 4524, 4550, 4584–7, 4595, 5959, 5966, 5968,

Grinder	4517	K19/279	2745
Fossil shell	4586	K19/395	2504
Pub. ceramic	4587		772
Pub. ceramic	5966		797
Pub. ceramics	5968		793, 938
Human bone	5968	L19/71	2879

Cuts: 1547–8, 1587, 4519, 4533, 4549, 4588, 5971

Fossil	1587	K19/152	2524
Metal/slag	4533	K19/300	2420

Level IId units — area north of W713
FI94/8: 1108, 1112

Level IId units and finds — Western Courtyard
Occ. surface: 2829
Fill: 2825
Packing: 1712, 1724, 2831, 2842

Bead	1712	I19/18	2074
Copper shaft	2842	I19/105	2235

Cut: 2853

13.3. Level IIe (Fig. 497)

The safest description of our label IIe is 'any layers between IId and IIf'. The remains attributed to this level have suffered more than most from the attentions of subsequent builders and pit-diggers, and the lack of connection between different areas means that they may well represent more than one phase.

In two areas an occupation phase later than IId but similar to it was noted: in the Western Courtyard, where the conformity of the IIe surface to its IId (and indeed IIc) predecessors indicates a continuity, and in K18a, where the alignment of Rm e6 follows that of the IId architecture, suggesting an awareness of the earlier phase. The IIe material has survived in these two areas because it stood deeper. Any actual IIe building which may have stood on the site of the higher parts of the IIc/d Stele Building, north of Rms e5–7, consists at most of a few scraps of stone foundation.

Further to the NE, in K20, Rms e9 and e10 are isolated from the rest of Level IIe. Their walls are on a different alignment, and this suggests that they may post-date Rms e5–7 and the IIe surface identified in the Western Courtyard. Equally uncertain is the precise stratigraphic relationship between this surface and the rooms in H18 to the SW of the courtyard.

H18
Here, excavations in H18b/d revealed some fragmentary domestic structures which must at least approximately belong to this phase, although a precise stratigraphic link is lacking. Along the NW edge of the mound both W781 and W783 are stretches of wall conforming to the contour of the surface. They resemble, and could have joined, W817 in I19c, assigned to phase IIf, but it is equally possible they were independent structures whose alignment and position were dictated by the shape of the mound at the time. Inside them, to their east, several fire installations were found in Rm e3.

FI96/25 in the NE corner of H18b, was originally thought to be a large pot, but was then recognized to be a cylindrical tannour (H18/122: Fig. 50, p. 74), sunk into the floor and truncated by the cut for W780. Further south, two different fire installations were found at either side of the room, connected by a line of bricks. On the west, FI96/17 consisted of a surround of up-ended mud bricks and a rough stone foundation. It contained a discrete deposit, including occasional sherds and plaster fragments. FI96/19 was more ephemeral. Its fill consisted of burnt chunks of mud brick and carbonized kindling; within the fill was a long iron fork (**2322** H18/146), which could well have been a fire-tool. The fire installations were associated with a plastered floor (2645), into which several pits had been cut from above. This floor, which extended south of pit P96/86 into the space numbered Rm e2, had been burnt and was buried under a layer of burnt destruction debris which may have been the same as that on the IIe surface in Rm e4 (see below). Much of the surviving area of Rm e2 was taken up by another large fire installation (FI96/13); this was a hearth with a diameter of about 1 m and a mudbrick surround surviving to a height of 24 cm. The clay floor was 3–4 cm thick, resting on a layer of small pebbles, under which were larger pebbles, and under them small flattish stones. The concentration of ovens and the irregular shape of the area occupied by Rms e2 and e3 suggest that this was an open space devoted to cooking; whether it served a structure unexcavated to the east under I18, or belonged with Rm e1, must remain undecided.

Only the north end of Rm e1 was exposed by our excavations, while the western part of the room has been affected by erosion, and the southern part by an animal burrow. It measured *c*. 1.50 m by over 2.60 m, and had a plastered floor. Features include a small posthole, an *in situ* basin of low-fired or unfired clay (H18/162) and a small central pit, P96/126, containing destruction debris and thus probably contemporary with the floor. The north and east walls of the room, W779 and W782, were of mud brick resting on a single course of foundation stones (Fig. 141). W782 had plaster on both faces at its base.

Figure 141. *H18b/d, Rm e1 foundations (W779, W782), looking SW (see Fig. 497).*

Level IIe units and finds — Rm e1
Occ. surface: 2667
Destr. debris: 2656, 2658–9
Clay basin   2658   H18/162
Ceramic disc   2659   H18/161   1543

Fill or packing: 2650
Clay object   2650   H18/155   1606

Cut: 2660

Level IIe units — Rm e2
Occ. surface: 2645
Destr. debris: 2653, 2655
Fill or packing: 2630, 2652

Level IIe units and finds — Rm e3
Occ. surface: 2645
F196/17: 2634
F196/19: 2643
Iron fork   2643   H18/146   2322

Destr. debris: 2635, 2640–41, 2646
Ceramic disc   2640   H18/142   1542
Jar   2646   H18/146   843

Fill or packing: 2632–3, 2637–9, 2644, 2647
Loomweight   2632   H18/102   1801
Loomweight   2633   H18/107   1802

Cut: 2648–9, 2651, 2657
Ceramic disc   2649   H18/156   1561

The Western Courtyard
The IIe open area in I19 has been called Rm e4. Where not removed by pits and animal burrows, there survived an occupation surface (2820) overlain by *c*. 10 cm of destruction debris consisting of collapsed mud brick, some plaster, ash and charcoal (2818). The surface 2820 was a bright yellow, hard deposit with 2–3 cm of brown ash directly above it. Sherds from a broken pot, vetch seeds (*Lathyrus sativa*; see p. 593) and four short lengths of burnt wood were found lying on this surface. Unlike earlier and later phases in this area, we found no trace of contemporary walls or fire installations, although the intersecting pits in the east part of the area could easily have removed all trace of a hearth or oven. For the same reason, we cannot establish an exact correspondence of the levels in I19b with the two IIe floors further to the south and west.

Other IIe material
Pits, the robber trench and animal burrows (blamed by us on badgers) have accounted for much of phase IIe in J19. One feature of interest in J19a is the hearth FI96/12, which must have had a diameter of about 1.20 m, with a mudbrick surround. Like other hearths, the clay floor was laid over a bed of river pebbles, some 15 cm deep, but beneath these there was a further 15 cm layer of oval clay lumps laid within a shallow pit, which presumably served a similar function. Forty of these were recovered and catalogued (**1639–78**).

The attribution of this hearth to phase IIe is uncertain as there is no architectural context surviving here, but further to the south a jumbled intersection of walls remaining in J19b/d suggests that there was a building here as in earlier phases. It is possible to hypothesize, by projecting wall W723 southwards, that it might have joined with similarly projected walls W766 in the west and W719 in the east. The method of construction of these stone wall-foundations is comparable and the absolute levels are virtually the same.

Chapter 13

Figure 142. *Rm e5: roof(?) beams on floor (J18/315, 321; see J18b in Fig. 497).*

Another tentative suggestion could be for a doorway in the narrow, stone-free gap between the western part of W722 and W723. It is not clear how W719 relates to Rm e6, which survives at a lower level. It might originally have been part of the same wall as W439, to the east of Rm e6.

Level IIe units and finds — Rm e4
Occ. surface: 2820
Destr. debris: 2818
Bot. sample   2818   *I19/72

Fill or packing: 1704, 2823, 2827, 2832, 2837
Pub. ceramics	1704		787, 900, 946
Pilgrim flask	1704	I19/11	919
Loomweight	1704	I19/8-9	1796–7
Sp. whorl	1704	I19/7	1923
Stone bobbin	1704	I19/10	2602
Ceramic disc	2832	I19/106	1553

Cuts: 1795, 2801, 2804–7, 2812, 2824, 2833, 2859
Bead	2806	I19/211	2063
Projectile point	2806	I19/60	2250
Iron blade	2806	I19/57	2311
Clay object	2812	I19/61	1608

Room e5

As was the case in phases IIc and IId, the IIe ground surface seems to have been appreciably lower SW of the line represented by W766 and W719, and as a result, the remains of IIe are better preserved here. For ease of reference an open area in J18a/b has been designated Rm e5. This wide, open expanse is delimited by the intrusive phase IIf walls W424 and W720/W764, although its original northern extent may have extended up to wall W766, which is cut by W764. The area is characterized by packing or ephemeral surfaces in J18b, but better defined surfaces in J18a. The floor in J18b was cut by numerous pits, but burnt wooden beams (samples J18/315 and 322 and one non-sampled piece, 1.40 m long) lying among grey, compact packing on one surface, with olive pips in the fill above it, suggest a roof collapse (Fig. 142). The sizeable stones in the NW of J18b might belong to the remnants of walls, or might be the remains of surrounds for the pits. In the south of J18b, two (probably originally three) distinct mudbrick 'steps' seem to indicate an access route down to this open area from a building to the south.

Two different surfaces were found in J18a. In the south half of the quadrant was a white plastered surface (2394), cut by pit P97/29 and a small animal burrow. To the north, the surface is more irregular, but is of interest for two reasons. Firstly, a horseshoe-shaped bin feature, of single mud bricks laid end to end, was constructed on it. The bin was *c.* 1.10 m wide and the bricks averaged 40 × 12 × 19 cm. It contained unremarkable light brown to grey fill, but had a quite distinct base. It was not clear whether the bricks respected an earlier phase of wall W424, or were cut by it. No wall trench was noted, either during excavation or in the section, so perhaps the former is more likely.

The second point to note in this area is the irregular but deliberate stone cobbling that was found to the north (2393), with a circular ashy spread on it, presumably marking an unguarded fire-place. The deposits beneath the phase IIe cobbling were heavily pitted (notably by P97/85), and perhaps the phase IIe builders were aware of this and laid the cobbling here, rather than anywhere else, to provide a more stable surface.

Room e6

The stratigraphic relationships of this room in K18a clearly assign it to our phase IIe. It was sealed beneath the mudbrick packing of phase IIf, and cut through the heavily burnt phase IId fill and floors into destruction debris belonging to phase IIc. The room has thus a 'sunken' appearance, relative even to the phase IIe surfaces to the west.

The room itself is well constructed and preserved, measuring internally *c.* 4.80 (E–W) by 3.40 m. Its mudbrick walls have stone foundations. Mudbrick benches faced with stone line all but the southern wall, which disappears into the baulk (Fig. 143). Two distinct surfaces associated with the walls were defined. The lower (4376), described as 'cream plaster' some 5 cm thick, lay at +98.77, as much as 80 cm below the highest surviving stretch of wall. It presumably belonged with the initial construction and the only associated features were a couple of postholes some 40 cm apart near the centre of the room.

A layer of packing some 10 cm deep (4372/4374) separates this from the upper surface at +98.87, on which was a well-preserved fire installation, FI97/9 (Fig. 144), built against the south wall of the room (W435). This consisted of a back wall of two upright stones some 30 cm high, with a horseshoe-shaped raised base composed of an outer ring of white pebbles (*c.* 6 × 4.5 × 3 cm) set in mud brick or clay, and an inner circle made up of smaller pebbles, burnt black to brown and set in red to brown clay (though in places a lower layer of pebbles was still white). Below the surface of the hearth the front edge of the pebble base was retained by a vertical stone.

Rm e6's benches averaged 70 cm wide and 35-40 cm high. The line of facing stones suggests that the western bench was built first, followed by the northern bench and the eastern one, although construction was presumably broadly contemporary. The eastern 'bench' was composed of two parts: a stone-lined storage feature (4378) and a short stretch of bench (4375). No clear base was found relating to the bin, while the bench was laid on top of the upper plastered floor and seems to have been added after the bin was constructed. The northern and eastern benches were topped with coarse yellow plaster, while W426 had white plaster on its northern face too, indicating that there must have been some free space between it and the IId wall base W614 and associated surfaces to the north.

Two small postholes (max. di. 8 cm, 13 cm deep) were dug through the sub-floor packing, or possibly an intermediate floor, into the lower floor (4376). An ephemeral, possible fire installation was noted in the NE corner of the room, east of two large flat stones, which had yellow bench plaster running over them

Figure 143. *Rm e6, looking west: stone-faced benches against W426 and W441, FI97/9 on the left.*

Figure 144. *Rm e6: FI97/9, showing black and white pebbles, looking SW.*

and were set into the upper floor. The function of the stones remains unclear — they may have acted as steps, or if Rm e6 was a domestic room, as seems likely, as flat processing areas.

Access to Rm e6 seems to have been from the west. A narrow gap in W434, 60 cm wide, probably indicates the doorway. It possibly re-uses a phase IId foundation stone (from W433) as a threshold — alternatively, the stone could merely be part of W434. Although not all of W435 was exposed on the SW, it seems unlikely to have included a door in its east end, given the location of the fire installation.

Towards the centre of the room a near complete cooking pot (**906** K18/134), was found lying broken directly on the upper surface (+98.91). Long, narrow strips of burnt wood were found in the destruction material fill (4363) above this floor in various places. These pieces of wood were presumably roof beams and the packing probably represents roof collapse.

Room e7
To the east of Rm e6, W439, a scrappy mudbrick wall with stone foundation and a possible bench on its south side, ran up to, but did not bond with, W441. The area to the south of the bench was heavily disturbed by pits, and to the north there was a band of packing with no convincing occupation surface of this phase.

Level IIe units and finds — Rm e5
Occ. surface: 2393–4

Loomweight	2393	J18/218	**1772**
Sp. whorl	2393	J18/219	**1977**
Bead	2394	J18/224	**2054**

Fill or packing: 5849, 5853–5, 5857–9, 5861, 5867, 5869, 5883

Clay object	5849	J18/309	**1611**
Spearheads	5849	J18/308	**2393**
Stone weight	5849	J18/312	**2647**
Bead	5854	*J18/321	**2062**
Burnt beam	5855	*J18/315	
Carb. wood	5855	J18/322	
Bear's claw	5855	J18/323	**2495**
Clay ball	5867	J18/343	**1613**

Cuts: 5827–8, 5831, 5843, 5847, 5850–52, 5860, 5863, 5865, 5872

Clay figurine	5827	J18/288	**1508**
Clay object	5843	J18/299	**1609**
Loomweight	5847	J18/306	**1779**
Clay object	5850	J18/327	**1607**

Level IIe units and finds — Rm e6
Packing below W446: 4385
Wall 434: 5878

Obsidian core	5878	J18/366	**2585**

Bench: 4366, 4375, 4377–9, 5875

Rubber	4379	K18/161	**2814**

Occ. surface: 4342, 4352, 4356, 4359–60, 4363, 4371–2, 4374, 4376

Lithic scraper	4352	K18/106	**2557**
Human bone	4352	K18/264	**2880**
Loomweight	4356	K18/117	**1830**
Sp. whorl	4356	K18/120	**1922**
Iron blade	4356	K18/116	**2308**
Arrowhead	4359	K18/121	**2248**
Cooking pot	4363	*K18/134	**906**
Grinder	4377	K18/159	**2772**

FI97/9: 4373
Post-holes: 4388
Destr. debris: 4338, 4344–5, 4365, 4369–70
Fill or packing: 4335–7, 4339, 4341, 4343, 4346, 4348, 4355, 4361, 4364

Re-used potsherd	4337	K18/92	**1591**
Grinder	4338	K18/87	**2772**
Grinder	4338	K18/88	**2772**
Pounder	4346	K18/104	**2799**
Antler	4348	K18/96	**2493**
Pounder	4348	K18/97	**2798**
Copper frags.	4364	K18/138	**2296**
Iron blade	4364	K18/144	**2320**
Slingshot	4364	K18/136	**2624**

Cuts: 4340, 4353–4, 4357–8, 5884

Pub. ceramic	4353		**774**
Jar stopper	4353	K18/111	**1502**
Clay object	4353	K18/113	**1610**
Pub. ceramics	4358		**884, 887**

Level IIe units and finds — area north of Rm e6
Packing: 4350–51

Grinder	4350	K18/101	**2749**
Grinder	4350	K18/102	**2770**
Pub. ceramic	4351		**767**

Level IIe units and finds — area north of Rm e7
Packing: 6127–9

Copper ring	6127	K18/255	**2262**
Rubber	6129	K18/260	**2815**

Rooms e9 and e10 (Fig. 498)
In K19, where deposits were not so deep as in squares to the south, phase IIe (and IIf) material seems to have been shaved off by Byzantine builders, but remains of IIe occupation did survive in the SE of K20. Here walls we encountered just below Byzantine foundations were isolated from the IIe and IIf levels further south, and cannot therefore be directly linked with them stratigraphically. Indeed, at first we took this for an earlier Byzantine phase, but subsequent study of the potsherds (cf. especially **811**) revealed our mistake.

The northern limit of Rm e9 is marked by a wall-foundation of a single row of large stones (W710). The NW corner of the room is lost to a combination of the mound slope and the foundations of W116, and only a 3 m stretch of the west wall of the room survives to a height of no more than 15 cm further south, mainly mud brick with rough mud plaster on the east face. We did not excavate in L20, and further to the south and east, this level only survived as a patch of floor in K19b. The resulting space measures a minimum of 6 m (E–W) by 7.40 m (N–S), and is therefore likely to have been unroofed.

FI95/3 was a small but neatly constructed fire installation built on the floor surface (1924) up against the southern edge of W710 (Fig. 45, p. 72). Its western and eastern sides were made of single mud bricks (average size 30 × 20 × 10 cm), and the north and south ends of heavily vegetable-tempered plaster. The interior was also quite thickly lined, though with a higher grade of plaster, resulting in a slightly more rounded shape. Its width overall was 50 cm and its excavated depth 23 cm. The fill produced one large handle sherd; the remains of a crushed unbaked vessel were also recovered at the bottom. There were no pebbles beneath the floor of the hearth, but the bricks each side rested on a layer of potsherds. P95/42 nearby may have served to gather ashy rake-out from the hearth.

The floor of the room, at ~100.50, was not well preserved, but was sealed by a clayey layer in which there were parts of whole vessels, scattered large sherds, and some 19 loomweights in a group (see Fig. 498). Two other loomweights were found at about 1 m from the main group, to the west and SE, and a group of three close to the face of W712 in the SW corner (Fig. 145). (Two loomweight fragments, **1799–800,** found nearby in a pit and a disturbed context in K19b are of different types and probably do not belong with the main group). The weights in the main group seem to have been lying in some order, forming at least two curved alignments of four weights, and another of three (Figs. 146 & 498). Immediately north of the main group was P95/42, described as a well-defined shallow scoop with ash lenses on the bottom, and just to the east of this were two large mud bricks: one stood vertically on its edge, the other lay flat, but they were not built into the floor surface. Further south there were fewer artefacts lying on the floor, but a tumble of stones, no doubt subsequent to its use. Towards the west side of the room there was a circular pit (P95/49) inside which were many large sherds from 6 or 7 large pottery jars (**910**). Some potsherds found scattered on the surrounding floor also belonged to these jars, and we must conclude that the pit was dug and used at the same time as the floor. Fragments of other vessels collected from this floor surface plainly belong typologically with our Level IIe material rather than anything later. However, W710 and W712 observe a different alignment from all the earlier Level II phases, and also from the IIe walls on the south side of the area, indicating either that it is not strictly contemporary with IIe elsewhere (which is easily conceivable, given the three centuries or so between

Figure 145. *Rm e9: loomweights* in situ *against W712 (see Fig. 498 nos. 1–3), looking SW.*

Figure 146. *Rm e9: group of loomweights* in situ *(see Fig. 498 nos. 4–11), looking east.*

IId and IIf), or that a significant change to the layout of the architecture took place at this time.

The only feature we observed in Rm e10 to the west of Rm e9 is the pebble-based hearth F194/9, which retained part of its domed superstructure (Fig. 55, p. 75). This was seen clearly in 1994 in the cross-section of a temporary baulk in K20c, but its east half could not be recognized when excavation resumed in 1995, and no floor which was definitely associated with the west face of W712 was identified.

Level IIe units and finds — Rm e9
Packing below floor: 1938
Clay disc	1938	K20/121	**1532**
Ceramic disc	1938	K20/122	**1590**

Occ. surface: 1533, 1911, 1916, 1924–5
Pub. ceramic	1911		**811**
Loomweights	1911	K20/64–74, 76–88	**1735–58**
Pub. ceramic	1924		**763**
Loomweight	1924	K20/104	**1760**
Sp. whorl	1924	K20/102	**1958**
Iron tang	1924	K20/100	**2323**
Mortar	1924	K20/101	**2686**
Storage jars	1924+1930	K20/237	**910**

Depression in surface: 1923
Loomweight	1923	K20/98	**1759**

P95/49: 1929–30
Metal/slag	1929	K20/221	**2420**
Storage jars	1924+1930	K20/237	**910**

FI95/3: 1910
Destr. debris: 1913, 1918
Bead	1918	K20/94	**2026**

Cuts: 1922, 1950–51, 1954–7, 1959–60

Level IIe units — area north of Rm e9
FI (unnumbered): 1926

Level IIe units and finds — Rm e10
Occ. surface: 1125
Packing: 1128, 1136, 1921, 1934
Cut: 1121, 1127, 1129
Pub. ceramic	1121	**863**

Level IIe units — area north of W700
Occ. surface: 1533
Packing: 1534

Level IIe units — area north of W722
Occ. surface: 1632
Cuts: 1536, 1612

Level IIe units and finds — K19b/d east of W770
Misc. deposits: 4544, 4547, 4568, 4579, 4582, 4592
Cuts: 4569–70, 4573–6, 4580–81, 4583, 4593–4, 4599
Whetstone	4569	K19/365	**2662**
Quern	4570	K19/366	**2750**
Pub. ceramic	4573		**769**
Pounder	4574	K19/373	**2800**
Quern	4593	K19/404	**2751**
Pub. ceramic	4594		**885**
Bird figurine	4594	K19/402	**1506**

Level IIe units and finds — L19 (this square not included on plan)
Fill: 5952, 5972
Cuts: 5953–4, 5965, 5970, 5974
Grinder	5954	L19/36	**2752**
Quern	5954	L19/37	**2753**

13.4. Level IIf and later deposits (Fig. 499)

The latest significant architectural remains discovered beneath the Byzantine levels at Kilise Tepe belong to phase IIf. The two main points of interest are the storage facility Rm f3 in J18, and the two kilns at the south side of I19, one of which supplies an approximate chronological fixed point in the shape of the quantities of Cypriot-style White Painted ware dumped in it. Elsewhere in our main excavation trenches, the slope of the tepe dips steeply off to the north and west, and the subsequent Byzantine buildings and pits have removed any coherent phase IIf deposits that existed.

Level IIf (west half)

Across I19c/d there are several surfaces assigned to IIf, but the phase is best represented by a hard, yellow floor (1798), cut by a line of three postholes, c. 20 cm in diameter and c. 30 cm deep. A thin layer of burnt occupation debris (1799) lay on this floor, but neither floor nor burning could be convincingly followed to the north or east, where there were areas of packing, severely disturbed by intersecting pits and a large animal burrow. An earlier phase consists of a thin ashy occupation deposit (2815) resting on a hard yellowish layer of clean packing (2814). To judge from its level above datum, the square fireplace FI96/11 seems to belong to a surface slightly later than this, but must have pre-dated the 1798 floor and the associated kilns.

To the SW the upper surface (1798) was delimited by, and contemporary with, W759 running NW–SE. The highest surviving stone in this wall was at +99.17, only some 15 cm above the floor, but the stones of the foundation had been set in a shallow foundation trench which clearly cut through the phase IIe floor, as shown in the IIe plan (Fig. 497). At the NW end of this wall shallow alignments of stones returned to the NE and SW (W816 and W817, respectively). Both the upper floor and 2814 below it ran across the stones of W816, which must therefore belong to an earlier sub-phase of IIf with no associated occupation surface surviving. To the NE, W760 parallel to W759 was stratigraphically isolated thanks to animal activity; although founded lower it may have been at least partly contemporary, in which case Rm f2 would have been 3.40 m wide.

On the other side of W759 is Rm f1. Here, towards the SE end of W759 a stone-lined rectangular kiln had been constructed against its SW face. This kiln, FI96/14 described below, makes it likely that Rm f1 was an open area, but most of the IIf deposits here had probably been removed and replaced by later packing, cut by animal burrows. Since quadrants I18a and b were

Level II: the End of the Bronze Age and the Iron Age

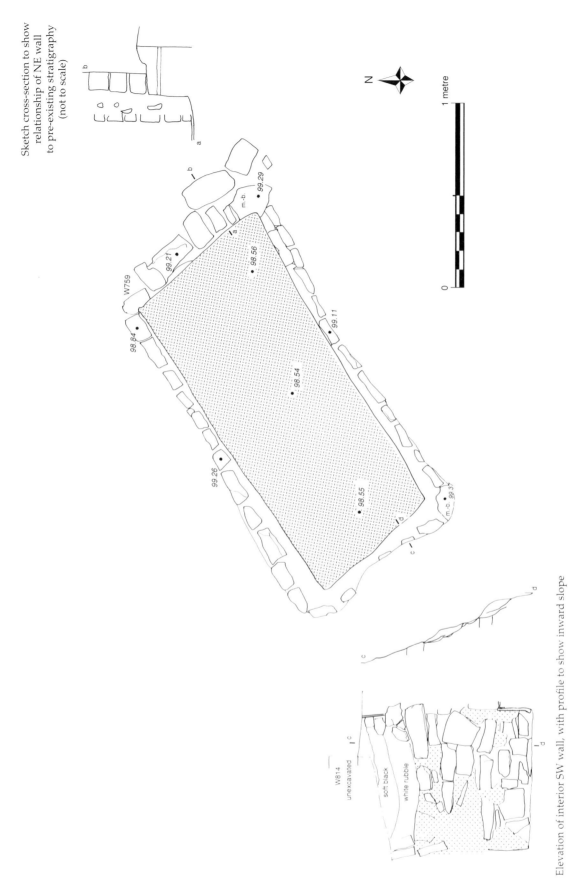

Figure 147. *F196/14 (I19 Level IIf).*

Figure 148. *Level IIf kiln FI96/14, after clearance of fuel-chamber, looking north (see Figs. 147 & 499).*

Figure 149. *Kiln FI96/14, looking south.*

Figure 150. *Interior of kiln FI96/14, detail of SW end.*

not excavated in this phase, nothing is known about the southward extension of the plan.

To the SW, scrappy remnants of occupation survived in H18b. If the N–S wall, W780, is indeed contemporary, its different alignment merely confirms that Rm f1 is outside the building. This wall was cut by a large pit, P96/78, with another large pit, P96/86, further to the south, but neither wall nor pits can be confidently attributed to the same phase as the kiln FI96/14. The tepe slopes steeply to the west at this point, with scatters of stones and the tops of phase IIe walls and fire installations sticking up through the phase IIf packing.

Kiln FI96/14 (Figs. 147–50)

This structure measured 2.10 by 1.04 m (Fig. 147). The fuel chamber, which was sunk into earlier deposits, measured internally *c.* 1.85 by 0.83 m, and was lined with 5 to 6 courses of small (4–6 cm high, 8–10 cm long) and medium-sized (12–20 cm high, 20–30 cm long) rough stones; one stone at the north end is noticeably larger (21 cm high, 30 cm long and 18 cm deep). Three really large stones (one *c.* 45 cm long, another *c.* 55 cm long and another 33 cm square) formed the NW corner foundation of the kiln wall. The stones forming the NE end of the kiln were integrated into the masonry of W759, although they extended a further two courses down to the base of the excavation for the fuel chamber (see sketch on Fig. 147). Behind the stones, except at the NE end, the space against the sides of the cut is filled with scrappy packing (2844), including loose, small stones (*c.* 5 cm), dusty soil and some moderate-sized potsherds.

On all four sides, the deep cracks between the stones were plugged by a coarse, heavily vegetable-tempered plaster, up to 2.5 cm thick, burnt on its face to a buff colour, grading to a blackish grey inside, against the stones. It looks as if this plaster was not carried across the flat faces of the stones, although it could just have rubbed away. For the most part the stones look whitish buff on their surfaces, but at the base of the lining, when there is no plaster, they are black and sooty, up to 10 cm from the floor (and as much as 30 cm above the floor at the south end). Some of the plaster stretches down almost to the floor and it too is blackened for *c.* 2 cm above the base. In the NW corner, the plaster stands as much as 65 cm above the hard clay base, burnt chocolate brown to black, and for the top 15 cm of this, it has a comparatively reddish tinge. At the SW end, in I18a, the lining stood more than 80 cm above the floor, and at this point fragments of a burnt clay superstructure still survived.

The chamber was packed with loose light grey ash, and a very high concentration of potsherds. These proved to come from a homogeneous group of painted and unpainted jars, plates and other forms (**707–35**), which belong to the wares known from Cyprus as White Painted IV and Plain White IV, and are generally dated to the end of the eighth and beginning of the seventh century BC (see pp. 350 & 370).

Level IIf (east half)

There is no straightforward stratigraphic link between Rms f1–2 and the IIf architecture further to the east (Fig. 499). That they are approximately contemporary is an assumption based on the fact that they both overlie IIe material, and are both associated with our later Iron Age pottery. In more detail, the south section of I19 (see Fig. 516) demonstrates that the eastern kiln (FI96/15) is at a similar level to FI96/14, and the similarity of the two kilns suggests they are at least roughly contemporary.

Kiln FI96/15 (Figs. 151–4)
This was located in the SE corner of Rm f2, in the angle of walls W755 and W765. The western side of the structure was of mud brick and the eastern was similar, though backed up against the west face of W765. The lower part, which was sunk below ground, was lined with small rectangular stones (typically 5–10 cm). The interior length of this fuel chamber is 1.20 m, and its width 45 cm, widening to about 55 cm further up. At about 90 cm above the base of the fuel chamber the plastered internal face stands some 20 cm further back from the lower stone lining. A trace of the superstructure was still visible against the east face: two patches of blackened vertical plaster were framed by unburnt areas suggesting an arrangement of low arched partitions some 30 cm high and 30–40 cm wide (see Fig. 152). At the base of the fuel chamber was a 30 cm deposit of extremely fine grey

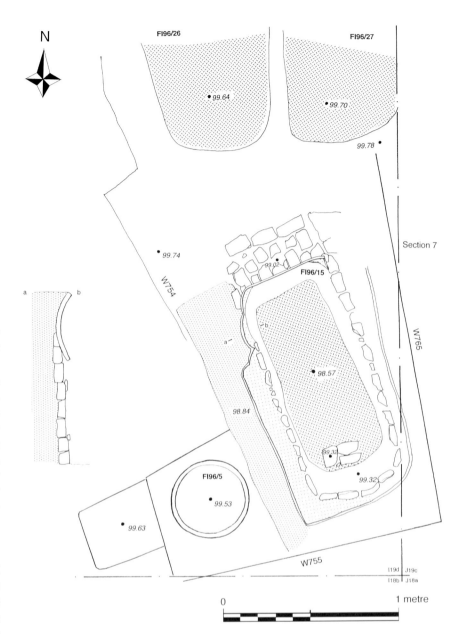

Figure 151. *SE corner of I19d to show FI96/15 and possibly associated features.*

material resembling the white phytolith pit linings, and above this was about 70 cm of very loose soil containing lumps of fallen mud brick and plaster, no doubt deriving from the superstructure. Access to the kiln was presumably from the north, across the stone-built end wall, which stood to at least 50 cm above the base of the chamber. There was an area of bricky packing against its NE edge, and further to the north two similar hearths (FI96/26–7) with burnt, cracked plaster bases were let into the bricky area. Although they were originally assigned to phase IIg they are probably associated with the kiln. Also in the angle where the kiln abuts W755 there were a tannour

Figure 152. *Level IIf kiln FI96/15 looking east, across top of plaster of western side to plastered internal face of eastern side (note the lighter outline of the arched superstructure; see Figs. 151 & 499).*

Figure 153. *FI96/15 interior, detail of NE corner.*

Figure 154. *FI96/15, after removal of west half of structure, showing cross-section through north and south walls and intact internal face of east wall.*

(FI96/5), and an adjoining square plastered box, both of which may have belonged to the same phase.

Room f3
FI96/15 must have been contemporary with W755 and W765, in the angle of which it was built, at least for some of their existence. These two fragments of wall were also at least partly contemporary with the stone foundations of W764, running E–W across the south side of J19c, and W424, which runs southwards from the same point. In the space framed by these walls, called Rm f3, excavation in J18 and K18 provided us with the only well-stratified IIf deposits.

Here an area of mudbrick benches, floors and packing was uncovered, associated with W424 and W764 (with its east end numbered W720).

In the surviving western part of Rm f3 two principal consecutive phases were distinguished. In the later (IIf2), plaster-lines and individual mud bricks were clearly visible. The plaster-lines relate to a series of mudbrick benches which were built against the stone walls. One wide bench occupies the west end of the room against W424: on this were the emplacements for and the bases of, two large pottery storage jars (Fig. 155). Two or three similar benches seem to have been constructed, one against and the others parallel to W764, and these may have been 'stepped' down to the south leaving only a narrow 'corridor' of floor running E–W through the middle of the room. On the south side of this corridor, the benches stepped up again, and no doubt backed up against an unexcavated south wall.

The eastern limit of this space is unknown. W764 is cut by the large, modern robber pit in J19d (Fig. 71), and then by a Byzantine wall-cut further to the east, and the floors and other features within the room could not be followed as far as the east side of J18b. W438, a fragment of stone wall in K18b, does not align with the other phase IIf walls. A thick deposit of grey mudbrick packing continues to the east, where the plaster-lines peter out. No southern limit was found, either, since J18c/d to the south were unexcavated, but it should be noted that the north edge of a wall of comparable absolute level (W425) was encountered when cutting access steps to the trench in the southern baulk of J18b (see Fig. 519).

At least one earlier phase of IIf was found below these benches and floor. This phase, IIf1, had western and southern benches (2383 and 2385, surviving to +99.78 and +99.67, respectively) associated with *c*. 20 cm of red/grey packing/fill (2370 and 2378) overlying a compact, whitish-grey surface at (2390), with sherds trampled into it, at +99.42. The more easterly fill (2378) included a dense concentration of sea shells (J18/181) and a cluster of loomweights (**1762–5**). A thin mudbrick wall, W427, lay on top of the western bench, perpendicular to wall W424 and a shallow, possible posthole (2388) was cut into the floor. The southern bench was one course thick, with a tilted, possible socket stone at its base. Into the fill beneath the bench a strange posthole-type feature (5821) had been cut.

The nature of this building is hard to determine. Its use in its two main phases seems to have been similar. The benches and the storage jars (possibly for water) suggest some kind of domestic use, but on a large scale, so possibly communal. The masonry of W424 is solid, whereas that of W764 and 765 is sloppy with loose and ill-fitting stones. W755 seems also to have been solidly constructed, and this suggests that the core of the building may lie under I18b, and that our Rm f3 was an external addition to the plan. With its mudbrick benches it is not likely to have been completely unroofed, but its width of more than 5 m would have been difficult to span, and it is possible that some of the postholes cut in the floor or benches supported flimsy structures designed to provide shade and shelter.

Much of the rest of the space to the north and east of Rm f3 is covered with uninformative packing or fill during phase IIf, with isolated patches of floor (6116, with up-turned pot K18/227 (**747**) on it and 6136 in K18b, for example) and occasional enigmatic truncated features, as well as the tops of phase IId and IIe fire installations. Pits, which were singularly empty of any artefacts, a large animal burrow, and Byzantine wall cuts further blur the picture, and attribution to IIf rather than IIe or IIg–h is usually uncertain.

Figure 155. *Rm f3 looking SE with W424 and emplacements for jars (see Fig. 499).*

Later deposits (IIg–h)

Architectural remains between phase IIf and the Byzantine levels were scant. The sequence here was rather arbitrarily divided into two further phases called IIg and IIh, since the sherds from both fill and pits in this area still appeared to be pre-Greek. In J18a, W424 was overlain by two overlapping single course walls, W422 and W423. We have no clear indications of their date, but if they were a late (and careless) rebuild of W424 they may have been contemporary with some of the frequent pits, some probably for storage, which occupied the Western Courtyard area in I19 after the abandonment of the two IIf kilns there. These were virtually the only features in the area except for a few smaller fire installations, six of which are described above in Chapter 8 (FI96/1, 5, 7–9 and 11).

Level IIf units and finds — H18
Wall 777: 2619
Ceramic disc	2619	H18/61	1544

Packing: 2626
Bone spatula	2626	H18/86	2479

Fill: 2624–5, 2627–8
Cuts: 2629, 2631, 2636
Pub. ceramic	2631		849
Iron blade	2631	H18/112	2320
Iron frags.	2631	H18/97	2419
Iron frags.	2636	H18/120, 168	2419
Bone tube	2636	H18/128	2475

Level IIf units and finds — I19
Packing: 1786, 1790, 2808, 2816
Pub. ceramic	1786		934
Pub. ceramic	1790		833

Chapter 13

Occ. surface: 2814
Bead	2814	I19/100	**2036**

Occ. deposit: 2815
FI96/11: 2821
Pub. ceramic	2821		**800**

Wall 760: 2828
Pub. ceramic	2828		**937**

FI98/4: 5542
Occ. surface: 1798
FI96/14: 1783, 2817, 2826, 2844, 2847
Jugs	1783	I19/64–5, 82–5, 96–7	**707, 712–13, 735**
Jars	1783	I19/88a–b, 89, 94–5, 218–19, 223–4, 228–31	**708–11, 723–4, 728–34**
Bowls	1783	I19/86–7, 93, 221–2, 225–7	**714, 718, 720–22, 725–7**
Pot stands	1783	I19/90–92	**715–17**
Other ceramics	1783		**881–2**
Loomweight	1783	I19/73	**1798**
Bead	2817	I19/100	**2036**

FI96/15: 1777, 2802-3, 3914–15, 3936, 3966
Iron frags.	2802	I19/77	**2419**
Pub. ceramic	3915		**776**

Destr. debris: 1799
Pub. ceramics	1799		**765, 812, 836, 848, 879**
Iron tang	1799	I19/51	**2324**

Cuts: 1708, 1713–18, 2800, 2809–10, 2813, 2819, 2822, 2835, 2857

Southern squares — J18/K18
Walls W424, 427, 438: 2335, 2355, 2389, 6110, 6123
Grinder	2335	J18/101	**2772**
Pub. ceramic	2355		**1177**
Socket stone	6123	K18/261	**2822**

Packing: 2323, 2325, 2340, 2349, 2351, 2356, 2358, 2360–61, 2370, 2374, 2378, 2380, 2386, 2391–2, 2396, 5823, 5825–6, 5829, 5833, 5838, 5840–42, 6111–12, 6116–17, 6136–8
Grinder	2351	J18/138	**2754**
Glass	2356	J18/132	**2108**
Pub. ceramics	2370		**766, 773, 778–9, 799, 820, 834, 853, 859, 866, 869, 876**
Bead	2370	J18/236	**2038**
Pub. ceramics	2378		**749, 872, 889**
Loomweights	2378	J18/183–5, 188	**1762–5**
Sp. whorl	2378	J18/187	**1967**
Shells	2378	J18/181	
Pounders	2380	J18/186a–c	**2801–3**
Clay ball	2391	J18/210	**1612**
Loomweights	2391	J18/203–4, 208–9	**1766–9**
Loomweights	2392	J18/212–13	**1770–71**
Bead	2392	J18/214	**2037**
Clay figurine	2396	J18/230	**1509**
Loomweights	2396	J18/227, 229	**1773–4**
Pub. ceramic	5829		**864**
Sp. whorl	5829	J18/282	**1995**
Iron nail	5829	J18/291	**2388**
Metal/slag	5829	J18/281	**2420**
Projectile point	5840	J18/296	**2392**
Astragali	6111	K18/226, 304	**2443–4**
Grinder	6138	K18/276	**2770**

Occ. surface: 2368, 2390, 5824
Pub. ceramics	2390		**743, 858**
Iron nail	5824	J18/274	**2335**

Features: 2322, 2332–3, 2359, 2362–4, 2366, 2369, 2371–2, 2382–3, 2385, 2387–8, 2395, 2397, 5800, 5821
Pub. ceramics	2362		**755, 825, 878**
Metal/slag	2366	J18/164	**2420**
Ivory object	5800	J18/411	**2489**

Fill: 2327, 2341–2, 2365, 2377, 2379, 2381, 2384, 5848, 6113, 6115, 6120
Iron nail	2365	J18/427	**2388**
Iron object	2365	J18/19	**2417**
Bead	2377	J18/178	**2020**
Pub. ceramic	2381		**835**
Bone tube	2381	J18/192	**2476**
Pub. ceramics	2384		**831, 850**
Pub. ceramic	6113	*K18/227	**747**
Pub. ceramic	6120	K18/238	**908**
Iron chopper	6120	K18/247	**2309**
Iron nail	6120	K18/273	**2388**

Cuts: 2324, 2326, 2328, 2331, 2347, 2367, 2375–6, 5801, 5803, 5834–6, 5844–6, 6108–9, 6114, 6118–19, 6121, 6124
Iron frags.	2331	J18/95	**2419**
Bone pin	2347	J18/133	**2468**
Loomweight	2376	J18/177	**1761**
Pub. ceramic	5801		**756**
Sp. whorl	5846	J18/317	**1990**
Pub. ceramics	6109		**798, 845, 871**
Loomweight	6118	K18/234	**1788**
Pub. ceramic	6119		**746**
Pub. ceramics	6121		**775, 857**
Loomweights	6121	K18/241–3, 245a–e, 249	**1783–7, 1831**
Grinder	6121	K18/244	**2762**
Rubber	6121	K18/246	**2816**

Level IIf units and finds — J19
Wall 764: 3918
Pub. ceramics	3918		**950, 954**

Fill: 3919

Level IIf units and finds — L19
Packing: 5951
Fill: 5955
Cuts: 5946–7, 5949–50, 5960–64
Cylinder seal	5949	L19/33	**1474**
Counter	5950	L19/34	**1533**
Pub. ceramic	5964		**797**

Chapter 14

The East Slope

J.N. Postgate

The results of our work on the eastern edge of the mound fall into four parts. A 25-m stretch of wall was investigated along the edge of the mound (W300); within this wall a complex sequence of stratified architecture was revealed in Q19d; outside the line of the wall in R18 was a bewildering succession of earlier pits; and finally further down the slope in S18 we came upon some relatively well-preserved stone walls of the Byzantine period. Our motives, like our results, were mixed. The choice of Q19 as a starting point was dictated by the exposed breach in the outer face of W300 which revealed that it was substantial enough to be a fortification wall. We did not continue with the work in Q19c after the first season because the sequence was too complex to be profitable, and instead moved outside the wall into R18, where Late Bronze Age sherds at the surface offered the hope of reaching Bronze Age levels without any later overburden. In the event this aspiration was also thwarted by the number of pits which had destroyed any buildings and stratigraphic relationships in the west half of R18, and by the Byzantine builders who had cut deep into the earlier deposits in S18.

Phasing for East Slope

There were at least three main periods of construction in Q19, which have been combined with the Byzantine structure in S18 to provide a period coding as follows.

1 Byzantine architecture in S18;

2a Hellenistic (cuts into) surface;
2b W301 and W302 to west of W303;
2c W303;

3a W300 (over top of P94/44);
3b Drain and associated fill;

4a P94/44 (and by analogy, P94/57);
4b Q19c/d, mudbrick walls W304–308;
4c Layers below mudbrick wall W304;

5a Pits in R18a/c earlier than W300;
5b Stratified deposits in R18a/c earlier than W300, and pits sealed by such deposits;
5c W931–2 and W947 and associated deposits;
5d Stratified deposits beneath 5c.

To distinguish these phases from the levels in the main excavation area these periods are preceded by an E (for East slope) in the unit lists (and in the chronological chart Fig. 473), which has not always been repeated here in the text.

Excavation in R18 (phase E5) (Fig. 500)

The surviving east edge of the foundation of W300 happens to coincide almost exactly with the west side of square R18, and consequently all the deposits in this square were lower, and probably also earlier, than the wall. This is clearest in the case of features which were stratified beneath the stones of the wall itself: these included the stone-rimmed pit P94/44 (discussed below under phase 4a), and a small hearth with a plastered base resting on a layer of pebbles (FI94/13), both almost directly beneath the lowest course of masonry. The deposits below the wall went down for a further 2 m, and the majority were composed of the fill of numerous intersecting pits, some as big as 2 m in diameter. Excavation of this area was unusually difficult, because the size and fine horizontal stratification of the fill of some of the pits meant that in their dissected state they were easily mistaken for occupation layers. (This explains the thirteen separate units used in the excavation of P94/53, for instance.) The ceramics indicate that all the pits were of Iron Age date, and this is confirmed by the resemblances between these pits and those of Level IIf–h in I19–20. Even more than above the Western Courtyard of the Stele Building, the pits in R18 had left extremely little in the way of stratified occupation deposits between them. As there, the pits were earth-cut and often lined with distinctive and sometimes thick layers of white phytolith-rich material. All this strongly suggests that the western side of R18a/b was an unroofed space, perhaps a courtyard, used as a food storage area.

Further to the east, and hence lower down the slope, there were scrappy remnants of mudbrick architecture (W931–2, W946–7). Although here too there were some intrusive pits, and some which were definitely sealed by stratified material, the blocks of brickwork which could be plotted clearly show that this area was built up, and would have enclosed the area of storage pits on its east side. Although no great volume of soil was moved in phases 5c and 5d, a reasonable quantity of sherd material was recovered from here, comparable to the IIa–d material in the NW area, and with nothing demonstrably later. It is clear that in phase 5 (i.e. in late second or earlier first millennium) the settlement extended east of the modern rim of the mound summit. This follows the line of the fortification wall (W300), which was fixed at least 5 m back from the eastward extent of occupation in phase 5.

R18 units and finds

Topsoil, section straightening and other mixed matter: 2000, 2008, 2010–11, 2015, 2021, 2023, 2028, 2041, 2045, 2051–2, 2400–401, 2403, 2405, 2407, 2432, 2439, 2456–7, 2465

Fossil	2010	R18/17	2522
Grinder	2010	R18/16	2772
Stone weight	2023	R18/38	2648
Pub. ceramics	2401		814, 860
Fossil	2403	R18/104	2512
Pub. ceramic	2405		868
Pub. ceramic	2407		861
Grinder	2407	R18/119	2407
Pub. ceramic	2456		898

Cuts from surface: 2001, 2009, 2012–13, 2410, 2419, 2421, 2425, 2447–8, 2472, 2474

Phase E5a
Cuts stratified below W300 or cut by other such cuts: 2022, 2024–7, 2030–31, 2033–4, 2036–7, 2038–40, 2042–3, 2046–50, 2402, 2404, 2406, 2411–13, 2415–18, 2422–3, 2426–7, 2430, 2434, 2438, 2440–41, 2443, 2449, 2461, 2466

Sp. whorl	2030	R18/51	1951
Lithic bladelet	2040	R18/62	2596
Sp. whorl	2047	R18/80	1927
Grinders	2048	R18/81, 83	2770
Grinder	2048	R18/82	2777
Antler frags.	2402	R18/99, 101	2493
Stamp seal	2406	R18/112	1478
Pub. ceramic	2411		851
Grinder	2412	R18/130	2775
Pub. ceramics	2418		837–8
Grinder	2434	R18/165	2774
Mortar	2461	R18/208	2693

Mixed cuts and stratified deposit (5a/b): 2004–5
Cuts sealed by stratified 5b deposits: 2016–17, 2020, 2414, 2420, 2428, 2444–5, 2451–2, 2454–5, 2458–9, 2471, 2473

Sp. whorl	2016	R18/29	1950
Human bone	2414	R18/263	2881
Astragalus	2428	R18/147	2451
Human bone	2453	R18/264	2882

Phase E5b
Stratified layers between cuts: 2002–3, 2006-7, 2014, 2018–19, 2029,
2032, 2035, 2044, 2053, 2408, 2424, 2429, 2431, 2433, 2435–7, 2442, 2446, 2450, 2453, 2464, 2470

Clay wheel	2018	R18/32	1525
Grinder	2424	R18/144	2772
Pub. ceramic	2433		927
Pierced disc	2435	R18/171	1563
Grinder	2435	R18/169	2777
Bead	2436	R18/175	2041
Bone tube	2436	R18/173	2478
Ceramic disc	2446	R18/188	1564
Worked bone	2453	R18/195	2470
Bead	2464	R18/215	2014

Phase E5c
Stratified layers associated with walls: 2460, 2462–3

Pub. ceramic	2462		952
Bead	2462	R18/210	2069
Bead	2463	R18/258	2015
Grinder	2463	R18/212	2758

Phase E5d
Occ. deposits beneath W931–2: 2475–6

Copper shaft	2476	R18/227	2235

The sequence in Q19b/d (E4a–c) (Fig. 501)

The earliest excavated features in Q19 are assigned to phase 4, which primarily refers to three mudbrick walls enclosing a small room (phase 4b). Outside this, to the east, was an area of mud bricks designated W304, which must be roughly contemporary; beneath these bricks two layers were excavated and are assigned to 4c.

The stone-lined pit P94/44 has been designated 4a: it is overlaid by the foundations of the fortification wall (W300), and it may have respected the stone foundations of W305. Its relationship to W304 is not certain: it might have cut through the brickwork but it is equally possible that both features were in use at the same time. What is plain is that it cannot be earlier than W304, and therefore that W304 must, like the pit, predate the fortification wall W300. It seems possible that P94/44 was sunk from an external ground-surface just outside W305, and belongs with it, but since the surviving top of the pit-lining is directly overlaid by the stones of W300 it is equally possible that the pit had been dug from a higher level. The part of the pit west of W300 was emptied to a depth of about 50 cm (i.e. base at ~99.20). The upper fill, 2118, was a uniform sandy brown deposit containing fragments of saddle-quern and grindstone; the lower fill, 2123, some 10–15 cm only, was more orange in colour with many stones in it. The walls of the pit were lined with several courses of similarly sized coarsely dressed stones, narrowing towards the base. This lining emerges into the NW corner of R18, and from this it is clear the diameter of the pit was in the order of 2.5 m. A similar pit lined with at least 5 courses of small stones was noted at the surface further down the slope some 3 m to the north in R19 (internal diameter 1.70–1.80 m) and no doubt belongs to the same time (P94/57).

Phase E4a–c units and finds — Q19b/d
Layers below W304: 2135, 2139–40
Fill east of W304: 2134
P94/44 in Q19: 2118, 2123

Copper tang	2118	Q19/62	2219
Grinder	2118	Q19/63	2758
Grinder	2118	Q19/60	2775

P94/57 in R18: 2133, 2138

Antler frag.	2138	Q19/98	2493

Immediately to the west of P94/44 is a small room (3.20 m E–W by 2.30 m or more N–S) enclosed by narrow (40 cm thick) mudbrick walls on a rough foundation of smallish stones (W305-7), which has been designated phase 4b. As noted above, P94/44 may respect the eastern wall, but it could be later or even earlier. The mud brick was mostly eroded down close to the foundations, and entirely missing in places. The fill between the walls was unremarkable, but there was a 10-cm layer of burnt debris lying on an unplastered surface, which probably represents an occupation phase. The inside face of W307 seemed to include a number of stones, some of which lay over mud brick; in places a vertical plaster line runs beneath these stones, indicating either that their position here post-dates the use of the room, or that they represent a later scrappy reconstruction. If the latter, a posthole (2128) sunk through the burnt occupation layer at about the centre of the room might belong to this secondary phase: it was 52 cm deep and about 10 cm in diameter, about 1.80 m from the face of W306 to the north and 1.50 m from the east and west wall-faces. A short stretch of narrow mudbrick wall also projected northwards (W308), but our excavation did not extend into the north and west parts of Q19c. In the angle of this wall and W306 was a relatively small pit, P94/43, which seems to respect the wall-faces and contained much cooking ware.

Phase E4b units and finds
Room in Q19c/d, occ.: 2110, 2130
Room in Q19c/d, fill: 2115, 2117, 2119, 2127–8

Ceramic disc	2127	Q19/80	1582

P94/43: 2125, 2129

Wall 300 (phase E3a) (Figs. 500–501)

The length and width of this wall, and its position along the edge of the tepe, indicate that it was a fortification wall, although it naturally also served as a terrace wall. Its stones in Q19 lay close beneath the surface, and the cross-section of the wall provided by the robber cut stands at least 1.2 m high. South of this cut the wall had been robbed further, or had tumbled down hill, so that only the inner west face and half its width survived. To the north, however, the base of the outer wall-face remained partially intact, showing two to three courses of neatly laid dressed stone. Some 4 m to the north the line of this face turns to the east, creating a projection which continues north for some 2.20 m, where it returns to the main line; beyond this point the original face is lost to erosion. This feature projects only some 45 cm, hardly enough to suggest a tower or to have served a significant structural purpose. North of Q19 the stones of the wall were cleared along the eastern face, but these seemed to give way at the north end of Q20 to mudbrick masonry, which we did not pursue further (although there were traces on the untouched surface of the site which suggested that a narrow brick wall curved round in conformity with the edge of the mound, perhaps inside or above the stone foundations if they also continued).

The bottom course of W300 was laid on top of clear stratified deposits, which were investigated further in R18, and the wall was also laid across the surviving top of a large stone-lined pit (P94/44, see above). Some of the earth overlying the masonry in Q19d seemed to respect the east face of W303, and that this wall was later is confirmed by the evidence of Q18 (see below). Here the surface soil was merely cleared enough to show that the interior face of the wall survives for a further 5 m to the north.

We did also briefly investigate in T15, where some lumps of conglomerate broke the slope of the mound and appeared to be *in situ*. The tops of these rocks were between +93.70 and +94.05, but they were not part of a natural outcrop. If they did belong to the same defensive wall, its length would have been at least 55 m, and it would here have been constructed significantly below the rim of the tepe as it is today.

Phase E3a units
Clearance of wall tops in Q18: 2201–3
Stones in T15: 2501

Drain in Q19d (phase E3b) (Fig. 501)

In Q19d a substantial drainage channel ran parallel to the inside face of W300, at about 2.5 m from it (Fig. 156). It was formed of two parallel lines of vertically set stone slabs about 50 cm apart, and about 4 m of its original length has been recovered. To the north it has been destroyed by the activities of P94/42, to the south it continues into Q18. The base was formed of similar slabs (and smaller stones) laid horizontally, and over side the main wall. On the other hand, it could equally be contemporary with W303, though not with W301 which overlies it, in which case the same conclusion would apply for the later phase.

Phase E3b units
Cut for drain: 2126
Stone-lined drain: 2120
Fill of drain: 2116
Possibly associated fill: 2112–13

Walls 301 and 303 (phase E2b–c) (Fig. 500)

In Q18b the well-defined western edge of W300 is overlaid by the stone foundations of W303, implying that at least the stone masonry of the main wall had been cleared down to this level (while the outer eastern face might of course have remained functional as a low revetment below this point). W303 runs for a total of 5 m in Q18 and a further 6 m in Q19, and must presumably have acted as a flimsy substitute for W300 along the edge of the mound, since it lacks cross-walls and can hardly have belonged to a building. As we have seen, it might have been contemporary with the drain. In Q19, about 1 m to its west, the foundation of W301 ran parallel to it. This still survived to a height of about 40 cm, three courses high, and even more noticeably than W303 its western face was neater. It stood higher, and stratigraphically was later, than W303, and it may be that these are two successive facing walls for the inside of the main wall, which could of course have had an earthen or mudbrick superstructure. To the north W301 turns, or meets a cross-wall (W302), but too little survived here to give a clear picture, and we cannot be sure if it continued northwards from this point.

Figure 156. *Q19d: phase E3b stone-lined drain 2120, looking NW (see Fig. 501).*

these lay about 10 cm of ashy fill. Otherwise the fill of the drain was unremarkable. There was no evidence for capping stones, so we may assume it was open, and therefore unlikely to have run beneath a building. The trench into which it was laid is plainly visible in the south section of Q19, about 40 cm deep and nearly 1.5 m across. This section makes it certain that the drain is later in date than the mud bricks of W305, and by extension than the rest of the room. Levels taken on the base slabs at three points (as shown in Fig. 501) indicate a very gentle downward slope from north to south (+100.23 down to +100.20 near the south end, over a stretch of 3.5 m).

Whether this feature should be considered contemporary with W300 must remain uncertain. If it was, there is hardly enough space between the two to accommodate a building, and we would have to conclude that there was an open space immediately in-

Phase E2b–c units and finds
Cut for W301: 2122
Grinder	2122	Q19/71	2775

Fill against W301: 2100–102, 2105, 2121
Pub. ceramics	2100		980–81, 989
Clay pipe	2100	Q19/17	1624
Iron nail	2102	Q19/25	2379

Fill under W301: 2108
Stone vessel	2108	Q19/43	2643

Cut for W303: 2124

Phase E2a (Fig. 500)

Dug into the south side of Q19c was a large pit (P94/41) which was remarkable less for its shape or size than for its contents, which included a fair quantity of large Hellenistic sherds including **966, 971, 984, 1001** (as well as two iron projectile blades and a loomweight). While there is no watertight stratigraphic connection, the pit is dug from no lower than the subsoil layer in which the base of W301 stands, and it seems probable that it is either contemporary with or later than the wall.

There is little else of Hellenistic or later date to report. A small hearth (FI94/2) on the west wide of Q19c was exposed directly beneath the surface but no related architecture was seen. Further north, in Q20, no clear architectural features were visible after surface clearance, but evidence of Hellenistic activity was present: in the NW corner of Q20c a group of loomweights was turned up in, or directly below, the plough soil (**1809–18**, Q20/3–12). Immediately to their north the pit P94/46 contained parts of at least two large jars, one with two handles and one with one handle (**1006–7**, Q20/25–6). Another metre or two to the north there was a loose ashy deposit containing a collection of heavy sherds, which included a large part of a Hellenistic krater (**985**, Q20/23). In the SW corner of the sounding we laid out to recover these heavy sherds there was a clay-lined feature filled with very soft soil (P94/45), but it was not further investigated.

Figure 157. *Byzantine walls W933–5 in S18, looking NW (see Fig. 500).*

Phase E2a units and finds
Sub-surface clearance, Q19: 173, 178
Glass bangle	173	Q19/2	2154
Glass bangle	178	Q19/8	2155
Iron nail	178	Q19/11	2385
Fossil	178	Q19/5	2507
Lithic sickle	178	Q19/6	2549
Stone vessel	178	Q19/13	2645

Sub-surface clearance, Q20: 184, 2151
Loomweights	184	*Q20/3–12	1809–18
Loomweight	184	Q20/19	1819
Glass bangle	184	Q20/16	2156
Sp. whorl	184	Q20/17	2000
Sp. whorl	2151	Q20/21	1820
Lead rectangle	2151	Q20/22	2300

In situ pottery: 2103–4, 2142
Krater	2103	Q20/23	985
Pub. ceramic	2104		979
Jar	2104	Q20/25	1006
Cooking pot	2104	*Q20/26	1007

Cuts: 2106–7 (P94/41), 2109, 2141
Pub. ceramics	2106	984, 1001, 1446, 1461
Pub. ceramics	2107	966, 971, 1388
Loomweight	2107	*Q19/38	1808
Projectile blades	2107	Q19/37	2396a

S18 Byzantine walls (phase E1) (Fig. 500)

In the second season we were tempted by the frequency of Late Bronze Age sherds on the surface to extend our work down the eastern slope in R18 and S18, in the hope that this would give us direct access to second-millennium deposits. In R18 as we have seen, this was partially justified, but the regular stone walls revealed further down the slope in S18 proved to belong to the Byzantine era, when the builders cut back into earlier deposits. W935, which bulged outwards slightly, had a well finished eastern face of dressed stones, while its west 'face' consisted merely of a packing of small stones, making it evident that this was a terrace wall. Since there was no sign of further building beyond the east face of W934, it seems likely that this row of rooms was a semi-basement belonging to a house whose upper floor extended back up the slope into R18b/d but has been entirely eroded.

In the fill above the cross-wall (W933) were many large undressed stones, and similar fill was cleared out of the rooms to its north and south. In the southern room the fill also included some Byzantine tiles. As in other parts of the mound, we were unable to identify any definite occupation surfaces associated with these walls, although the walls were standing to a height of up to 1 m (Fig. 157). Below the fill containing large stones (which no doubt derived from the upper parts of the walls), was a soft fill without stones. We saw no sign of a doorway, and nothing betrayed the function of the rooms with the possible exception of large fragments of a storage jar just north of W953.

Phase E1 units and finds — S18
Lower fill without stones: 2507–8
Loose fill above and between walls 2504–6
Grinders   2506   S18/19–20   **2767–8**

Topsoil over whole square: 2500
Glass bangle   2500   *S18/4   **2157**
Stone disc   2500   S18/1   **2613**

Chapter 15

Trenches South of the Church

J.N. Postgate & M.P.C. Jackson

Although most of our excavation work was concentrated on the NW corner and the east slope, we also put some trenches into the southern half of the site. In the first season three 5 × 5 m trenches were placed diagonally across the southern half of the tepe from NW to SE, in squares K14, N12 and Q10. In each case the upper levels consisted of stone architecture without identifiable floor surfaces. Subsequently a 50-m strip trench was dug across the middle of the site from I14 to M14 (see p. 31), and this then incorporated K14a. In most of this strip we did not go down below Level 1, and the results at this level are described by Mark Jackson below (pp. 178–83). He also gives the description of N12 (pp. 172–3), since it was virtually entirely Byzantine. Earlier levels were investigated at the centre of the strip in K14a, where a sequence back into Early Iron Age levels was recovered (pp. 177–8), and at the western end (I/J14) where in addition to the enigmatic ditch we exposed two main building levels, of Iron Age and Late Bronze Age date (pp. 173–7).

15.1. SQUARE Q10 (Fig. 502) by J.N. Postgate

In Q10 only the NW quadrant, Q10a, was excavated. At least four building phases are represented here, of which the two highest are certainly Byzantine. Phase 1 is principally represented by walls W600–602 in the west half of the quadrant which appear to be contemporary, giving the SE corner of a space delimited by W601 and W602, with W600 some 70 cm to the south making a corridor-like space. There was no sign of a doorway at the east end of W600, and although the masonry rested on a surface between about +98.80 and +98.90, there was no recognizable floor. In the NW corner of the quadrant at about the same level as the base of these walls was an area roughly paved with stones, suggesting that this was an exterior space. A gap of some 60 cm between the paving and the inside face of the two walls could perhaps be interpreted as having been beneath benches built along the walls but no longer present.

Phase 2 is attested as a clear thick clay band, laid in two superimposed layers to judge from the north section, about 5 cm below the base of the phase 1 walls. The band stretched under all three walls (W600–602), and on it stood sherds from a cylindrical pot (Q10/46). This was 45 cm in diameter and must have been truncated in the construction of the upper walls. Although this floor is not associated with any identified walls, its eastern limit coincides pretty much with the east side of the upper building, and the evidence of the north section suggests that it rose steeply at the east edge, presumably to meet the face of a wall now lost. The clay flooring suggests a roofed space, but if so it must have been a large room.

Phase 3 is represented by W603. This was a wall foundation of small loose stones running more or less E–W; its north face was within the north baulk. It was first observed to the east of the phase 2 floor surface where it had been cut down to the level of the

Figure 158. *Q10a: storage jar Q10/41, in situ, looking SW (see Fig. 502).*

171

floor, and in fact it continued beneath it to the west side of the quadrant. It therefore belongs to an earlier architectural phase, but there was nothing else we excavated which can be definitely associated with it. However, there were at least three pits to the south of W603 in the east half of the quadrant, and it is possible that some or all of them were contemporary with it. In the south side of P94/36, and possibly not belonging to its fill but left in place when the pit was dug, was a large storage jar (Q10/41; see Fig. 158).

Both P94/36 to the south and P94/39 further north cut into W604, a wall mainly of mud bricks but some stones, running more or less due north and beneath the base of W603. Without any associated walls or floors, it is hard to offer any interpretation of this wall, or to assign it to a period. Some of the sherds recovered from the excavation units about the level of its base were of Iron Age types with painted decoration, including a target design and a handle with herring-bone decoration, but this more likely reflects the date of the fills underlying the wall than that of the wall itself.

Units and finds – Q10
Surface soil: 230
Stamped sherd	230	Q10/45	1489

Sub-surface soil: 3100–102
Pub. ceramic	3100		1059
Glass ring	3100	Q10/7	2158
Copper coin	3100	Q10/6	2832
Pub. ceramics	3101		1093, 1134, 1197–8, 1360, 1365, 1374, 1448, 1450
Pub. ceramics	3102		1003, 1005, 1412, 1447

Fill of phase 1 building: 3103, 3105, 3107
Obsid. bladelet	3103	Q10/19	2596
Unpub. jar	3105	*Q10/46	

Fill to east of phase 1 building: 3104, 3106, 3108
Pub. ceramic	3106		1410

Fill east of W604: 3111, 3113–14
P94/36: 3109–10
Sounding SW of P94/36: 3117–18
Unpub. jar	3117	*Q10/41	
Iron nail	3118	Q10/43	2388

15.2. SQUARE N12 (FIG. 503) *by M.P.C. Jackson*

N12a is situated along the N–S central axis of the mound about 15 m from the top of the slope on the south side of the tepe. The excavation of this quadrant produced evidence for foundations and lower courses of Level 1 buildings in association with floors and fire installations; the operation in this area also made a significant contribution to the Level 1 ceramic assemblage.

The walls themselves were similar in construction technique to those associated with other Level 1 architecture from the site; they consisted of roughly worked facing stones on each side, and a rubble core bonded with clay, not lime mortar. The foundation courses were offset by 5 cm from the standing walls (Fig. 159).

Three interconnected stone walls were excavated in this quadrant: W500 ran roughly SW–NE across the trench. Parallel with W500, but lying 1 m to the south of it was a second wall W502, 0.60 m wide. W500 and W502 were both bonded at their west ends into a third wall W501, which ran perpendicular to them.

Thus W500 and W501 formed the SW corner of a room in the north part of the trench and W502 and W501 formed the NW corner of a separate room in the south part of the trench, leaving a space 1 m wide between W500 and W502. Differences were noted between the construction of the walls in the two rooms. W500 survived to three courses of foundations and W502 only to two. The less well-constructed south room may have been a subsidiary building to the north room. A large number of pithos sherds were found in the southern room (3204–5) but not in the northern part of the square (3202).

Hard white floors were found beneath topsoil and general fill, and were excavated as 3214 north of W500, 3210 to the south of W502, and 3209 in the area between the two walls. Associated with these floors were two fire installations: FI94/17 was framed by tiles and was found in the north room partly in N12a but continued north into unexcavated

Figure 159. *N12a: W500–502, looking north (see Fig. 503).*

N13c; and FI94/18 was found to the south of W502 in the southern room (not shown on plan).

The units above these floors were to some extent delimited by the walls, but the excavator observed that there was little structure to the stratigraphy in these units. The units sealed below the floors were excavated to the bases of the foundation walls. Fabric 1a Byzantine painted sherds were found in lower topsoil in this square especially unit 3204, and other Byzantine sherds were recovered both from above and below the floors. They were also found in fill (3208).

The upper units were found to contain a significant number of Hellenistic black-slipped vessels as well as a Late Roman C Ware red-slipped sherd which was found in lower topsoil (**1008** 3201); a large number of Hellenistic sherds were found below the floor of the building too. These ceramics suggest earlier Hellenistic occupation below the Byzantine building at this point on the mound. The finds, including a ring, spindle whorl, iron nails and animal bones, are not unusual and provide little evidence for the interpretation of such a small area; however the presence of two clay figurines (**1511–12**) should be noted.

Level 1 units and finds — N12
Fill below surfaces: 3211–13, 3215
Pub. ceramic   3212   1375

Pub. ceramic   3213   1372

Surfaces excavated with fill below: 3209–10, 3214
Pub. ceramics   3209   1047, 1384

FI94/17: 3203
Pub. ceramic   3203   1406

FI94/18: 3206
Fill above surfaces: 3207–8
Pub. ceramic   3207   1079
Projectile pt.   3207   N12/25   2396
Pub. ceramics   3208   1143–4
Figurine   3208   N12/39   1512

Cut: P94/40 (3216)
Topsoil and lower topsoil: 3200–202, 3204–5
Marble slab   3200   N12/4   98
Pub. ceramics   3200   1026, 1110, 1141, 1226, 1245,
                                  1267, 1362, 1423, 1449
Sp. whorl   3200   N12/8   1999
Iron nail   3200   N12/11   2376
Fossil   3200   N12/2   2513
Pub. ceramics   3201   1008, 1414
Pub. ceramics   3202   1075, 1287
Pub. ceramics   3204   1024, 1106, 1142, 1196,
                                           1234–5, 1444
Iron nails   3204   N12/16–17   2353–4
Pub. ceramics   3205   1045, 1074, 1199, 1272, 1288, 1426
Figurine   3205   N12/22   1511
Iron nail   3205   N12/20   2355
Iron chain   3205   N12/18   2404

15.3. LEVELS 2–3 IN I14 *by J.N. Postgate*

The Byzantine and Hellenistic levels of the 50-m strip across the mound from I14 at the west edge to M14 in the centre are described below (pp. 178–83). It was only at the west end of this trench and in K14 that we investigated earlier levels. In I14 the most notable feature was a massive ditch running parallel with the west side of the tepe and largely back-filled with big stones. This was probably of Late Iron Age date (see discussion below), and it had been cut through an occupation sequence which comprised only two Iron Age occupation phases, the earlier a building level, the later a surface without associated structures, and a single Bronze Age building level. These correspond broadly with Levels II and III at the NW end of the mound respectively, but it should be borne in mind that there is no stratigraphic link between the two areas, and the correlation is based solely on the ceramic evidence. To emphasize the lack of connection Arabic numerals have been used for the levels in I14 (and also other areas outside the NW corner), and in our lists the I14 units have mostly been assigned either to Level 2 or 3 without further precision, although the notation 2k has been used for the ditch, which represents a striking departure from the two earlier Iron Age occupation strata here.

Level 3 (Fig. 504)
The earliest material excavated in I14 is a small area at the base of the ditch (3717). This was a deposit of fill with small stones, whose architectural context could not be established in the small area accessible.

A plan comprising parts of four rooms was recovered in I14a/b (Fig. 160). Two or three buildings are probably present. In I14a Rm 92 must be the eastern part of one, while Rm 91, enclosed by W803 and W804, is the western end of another. W809 seems likely to constitute the southern side of a third unit represented by Rm 93, which shares a wall with Rm 92, while Rm 94 is doubtless an open space. There was a well-defined floor surface in Rms 91–3, but not in Rm 94. In Rm 92 there was a patch of burning on the floor, and the surface was overlain by an occupation deposit rich in sherds (3494). The best floor surface at the south side, in Rm 94, was some 20 cm or more higher than the floor of Rm 92, and the stones in the area between the east end of W805 and the south end of W806 evidently served as a rough step down into Rm 92.

Below the floor, Rm 94 was cleared to a rough surface at about +96.20, the level of the base of the stone foundation course for W803 and W805. It seems un-

Chapter 15

Figure 160. *I14a/b: Level 3 Rms 91–4, looking west (see Fig. 504); west edge of ditch right foreground.*

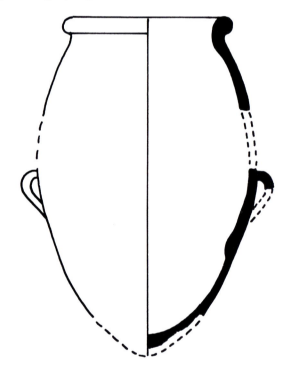

Figure 161. *Rm 91:* **637a** *(I14/160), one of two storage jars found* in situ *in NW corner (Scale 1:10).*

likely that there was a proper door in the SE corner of Rm 92, and hence likely that it was an open courtyard giving access to the interior of the house through the doorway at the SW corner. The sherds from the side of a large vessel, shown in plan, may have been protection for the threshold, which was slightly raised, but none of the presumed room to which it gave access fell within our excavation, and indeed it has probably all fallen victim to a combination of the construction of W901 and the slope of the mound: this suggests that here, as on the eastern side of the tepe, the Bronze Age settlement extended beyond the modern and Hellenistic rim of the mound.

In the NW corner of Rm 91, which is virtually all that had survived the digging of the ditch, two large storage vessels remained *in situ* (**637a–b** I14/159–60: Fig. 161). They had both been sliced away by the upper slope of the ditch, but the interior of the base of **637b** was at +95.38, meaning it was sunk about 75 cm into the floor, and that of **637a** at +95.69, sunk 45 cm below the floor. The walls were as usual of mud brick with stone foundations, and had been shaved down fairly regularly to a height of about half a metre above the floors, though they stood higher in the NE, and W808 had been cut down almost to floor level. Above this the rooms were filled with packing to the surviving height of the walls.

After a period of disuse represented by a couple of pits cutting through the room fill, the walls and fill of these four rooms were sealed across the full extent of the space west of the ditch by a deposit described as a broad band of clean yellow charcoal-flecked clay some 40 cm deep (3489), representing the interface between Levels 2 and 3. This deposit was not a construction phase of the overlying Iron Age building because it had been cut by a number of pits before it was built.

Level 3 units and finds — I14
Rm 91, floor surface: 3708
Clay 'wheel'	3708	I14/161	1601
Bead	3708	I14/186	2066
Storage jars	3708	*I14/159–60	637a–b

Rm 91, packing: 3702, 3705
Metal/slag	3702	I14/157	2420
Bead	3705	I14/168	2058

Rm 92, floor surface: 3709
Rm 92, occ. deposit: 3494

Rm 93, floor surface: 3713
Rm 93, packing: 3711

Rm 94, floor surfaces: 3714, 3716
Sp. whorl	3714	I14/182	1929
Quern	3714	I14/183	2733

Rm 94, packing: 3712

Pub. ceramic	3712		930

Pits sealed by 3489: 3703–4

Clay object	3703	I14/164	1603
Human bone	3703	I14/190	2875
Sp. whorls	3704	I14/153, 156	1955, 1988

Packing sealing Level III: 3489

Pub. ceramic	3489		757
Ceramic disc	3489	I14/175	1556
Pierced clay	3489	I14/151	1602
Sp. whorl	3489	I14/150	1932
Lead strip	3489	I14/152	2297
Grinder	3489	I14/174	2772

Level 2 early (Fig. 505)

The building erected above 3489 seems also to have been an unremarkable dwelling house, on a similar alignment to Level 3 but with a quite different layout. In the east half of I14a and into I14b was a burnt occupation level cut by a number of pits. Its western limit was provided by W904. The north section of this was built of a single row of large rectangular mud bricks, tilted down to the east in the destruction of the building. W800 was a short stretch of stone foundation with mudbrick superstructure making a return, and in the SE corner of Rm 95 was a fire installation (FI96/6). The hearth was built against the two walls, with a curving front wall of mudbrick material 15 cm thick and standing no more than 15 cm high. The overall dimensions are 1.30 m NW–SE and 1.40 m NE–SW. The interior was a smooth flat burnt clay surface. In the SW corner, where the front rim would have met the face of W800, the base of a pot was set into the floor.

South of W800 was Rm 96, delimited to the east by the southern part of W904. Rm 97 was probably an external space, and the occupation surface (3460/3475) was marked by ashy spreads occupying the spaces between the many pits, some at least contemporary with the surface. The largest of these, P96/29 partly under the north baulk, had a stone edging round the rim (see above, p. 81). The ashy spread was delimited in the SE by W802. Its stones as planned are more or less flush with the floor surface, and rested in a shallow foundation trench (base at +96.80). Above these three further courses of the same wall were present, reaching a height of about one metre (at +97.85), and the excavator suggested that the entire wall may have been a stone structure delimiting the courtyard area, since the stone foundations under contemporary mudbrick walls were not usually more than one or at most two courses.

Level 2 early units and finds — I14

Rm 95 floor surface: 3487
FI96/6: 3482
Rm 95 packing: 3473

Sp. whorl	3473	I14/120	1925

Rm 96 floor surface: 3486

Rm 97 floor surfaces: 3460, 3475
Two postholes into 3489: 3498 and 3701
Posthole into 3475: 3700
Rm 97, burnt debris overlying floors: 3458–9, 3474

Quern	3458	I14/99	2756

Rm 97 packing: 3457, 3472

Packing: 3448, 3451
Pits into 3489 cut or sealed by 3473–5: 3462–3, 3491, 3495, 3498–9, 3710

Copper shaft	3491	I14/166	2235
Sp. whorl	3495	I14/147	1931

P96/29: 3478

Clay object	3478	I14/127	1617
Metal/slag	3478	I14/128	2420

Other cuts into 3460/3475: 3476–7, 3479–80, 3488, 3493, 3496–7

Clay object	3477	I14/125	1616
Grinder	3493	I14/141	2770

Fill below 3432 and above walls: 3445, 3448, 3451
Pits etc. sealed by 3432/3466: 3461, 3468–71

Iron object	3471	I14/131	2326

Pits below 3432: 3443–4, 3446–7, 3449–50, 3452–3, 3455–6

Bead	3446	I14/191	2039
Bead	3446	I14/195	2056
Copper celt	3446	I14/78	2216
Copper haft	3446	I14/79	2218
Iron nail	3446	I14/193	2388
Metal/slag	3446	I14/190	2420
Sp. whorl	3455	I14/85	1947
Tesserae	3455	I14/92	2161
Copper pin	3455	I14/88	2243
Astragalus	3455	I14/86	2446
Worked ivory	3455	I14/87	2490

Level 2 late

The burnt occupation debris in Rooms 91–4 was sealed by layers of fill, the highest of which (3432 = 3466) was flattened and served as at least a temporary surface. The sherd material from 3432 puts it broadly contemporary with phases IIf–h at the NW corner. No structures were associated with this phase, with the exception of FI95/4, which was an oval hearth measuring some 50 × 30 cm, and sunk some 30 cm below the surrounding surface. The SW end was lined with stones set upright in the cut, and partly blackened and cracked by fire. In the fill were sizeable fragments of charcoal (average size some 3 cm) and fine black ash. Four patches of fine white ash, roughly 30 cm across, were noted to the south and east of the hearth (3407), and these partly overlay a larger spread (1.30 × 1.40 m and up to 10 cm deep) of fine black ash in the same area (3409). The hearth appears to cut the fill of P95/25 (3411). Several other contemporary features including a number of postholes were noted in the surface, but did not yield any significant pattern.

Level 2 late units and finds — I14
Late surface: 3432, 3466
Clay object	3466	I14/107	**1615**

F195/4: 3410
Loomweight	3410	I14/31	**1822**

Ashy deposits on late surface: 3407, 3409
Iron nail	3409	I14/29	**2377**

Postholes etc. into late surface: 3413, 3416, 3417/3428, 3418/3429, 3440–41)
Fill overlying late surface: 3406, 3431
Grinder	3406	I14/24	**2757**
Incised stone	3431	I14/67	**2605**

Pits cutting late surface: 3411/3425, 3412/3426, 3414/427, 3425, 3434-5, 3436–7, 3438–9
Pub. ceramics	3412		**813, 847, 1442–3**
Iron frags.	3412	I14/34a, b	**2320, 2388**

The ditch (Figs. 504–5)

The late Iron Age surface just described was mostly overlain by Byzantine or Hellenistic walls and fill (see pp. 178ff.), but at the east side of I14 extending into the west side of J14 it had been cut through by a massive ditch. This was first observed as a roughly horizontal area of small stones resembling a cobbled surface. Subsequently it became clear that this was only the top of a deep deposit filling the ditch to its brim (see sections, Figs. 514–15). Against the west side of the cut the smaller stones gave way to much larger rocks, angular untrimmed stones (up to 50 × 50 × 40 cm in size), presumably deriving from destroyed buildings. It was clear from their disposition that these had been thrown into the ditch from the west side, no doubt as deliberate fill. Beneath them was a mixture of loose ashy lenses, black, white and reddish, in among a more compact brown matrix, containing quantities of charcoal fragments (on average 2 cm), potsherds, and numerous animal bones in better condition than usual on the site. On the base of the ditch, and for about 20 cm up the sides was a 'crusty, hard white … lining' about 0.5 cm thick. It seems probable that the filling episode took place in two phases, during the first of which the ditch was used as a refuse tip, while in the later phase it was deliberately back-filled with rejected building stone to the level of the surrounding ground surface, with the layer of small stones representing an intentional final levelling.

The base of the ditch, at the south side of I14b, was at +95.26, giving it a depth of just over 3 m, a substantial municipal hazard. The sides sloped quite steeply, though not completely regularly, with its width at the base at least 1.5 m, and at the rim more like 4.5 m.

The west side of the ditch ran approximately NNW–SSE in the 5-m stretch exposed by us in I14b, and the 2.5 m stretch of the east side exposed in the north half of J14a ran parallel to it. Here the cut for the east side was definitely identified at ~97.60 (although it may have been present higher up). Parallel to this, and some 60 cm to its east there was a stretch of stone-built wall (W810) standing some two to three courses and 40 cm high (max. +98.13). The similar alignment suggests that the ditch was dug at a time when the superstructure of the wall was in use, but in view of the relative heights, it was probably a below-surface wall foundation, and there was no other context with which it could be associated eastwards.

As to the purpose of this ditch we remain in the dark. It must presumably continue to the north and south; there were no indications of the ditch's presence on the surface of the mound outside our 5 m trench, but this is to be expected since the highest identified ditch filling (i.e. the top of 3424) was at +98.33, i.e. nearly 70 cm below the mound's surface, and it lay beneath a Level 1 structure. So deep a trench would seem only to have had a defensive purpose, but if so it is a curious device, apparently running parallel to the edge of the tepe, some 8 m back from the top of a steep slope.

To date the back-filling of the ditch, the most telling evidence comes from the handful of Greek Geometric type sherds recovered from the fill. As noted on p. 371, these seem likely to belong to around the seventh century BC. This is convenient, for the ditch pre-dates a Hellenistic building, but is cut through the highest Iron Age surface in I14 (3432, see above). It is strange that except for a surface find we noted no other Geometric-style pottery on the site, though one cannot rule out the possibility of a few unrecognized pieces. The occurrence of a very distinctive plate rim (**719**) in the same fill suggests that these sherds could be contemporary with the pottery from the IIf kiln in the NW corner. However, even if this is correct, it does little to date the digging and usage of the ditch, since earth taken for backfill could easily derive from either considerably later or considerably earlier deposits. All we can say for sure is that it belongs at some time between the Level IIe phase as found in the NW corner and the Hellenistic architecture in I-M14.

Units and finds – ditch
Cut for ditch: 3370, 3433, 3467
Fill of ditch: 3368, 3424, 3465
Antler frag.	3368	J14/105	**2493**
Metal/slag	3368	J14/106	**2420**
Pub. ceramics	3424		**854, 901**
Clay sphere	3424	I14/60	**1614**
Loomweight	3424	I14/56	**1832**
Glass bangle	3424	I14/54	**2117**
Pub. ceramics	3465		**719, 933, 940–44**
Mortar	3465	I14/136	**2689**

Grinder	3465	I14/105	**2775**
Metal/slag	3465	I14/104	**2420**

Packing west of ditch: 3430

Ceramic disc	3430	I14/65	**1580**
Iron nail	3430	I14/63	**2388**

15.4. LEVEL 2 IN K14 *by J.N. Postgate*

In an attempt to reach well-stratified Iron Age and Bronze Age levels at the centre of the mound, a sounding was made below the Level 1 layers in K14. It was not very revealing: while we did excavate a fair quantity of Iron Age deposits, we seem to have been in an open area without substantial architecture, and most of our time and effort was devoted to disentangling a complex succession of pits. Figures 520–21, the south and west sections, give an idea of the nature of this area.

Upper Level 2
Below the Hellenistic architecture the upper Iron Age levels, where they were not removed by pits, seemed to be no more than layers of fill. One of these layers (3046) was spread across the full width of the quadrant with its base at ~98.50 and this has been taken as a dividing line between the upper and middle phases here.

Upper Level 2 units and finds — K14a
Fill east and west of W915, Level 1 or 2: 3033–4, 3043–4

Stamped bowl	3011+3043	K14/36	975
Pub. ceramic	3043		839

Fill along south side: 3026–7, 3035, 3037–8

Copper pin	3037	K14/78	2244
Fossil	3037	K14/79	2521

Fill (other): 3036, 3046

Metal/slag	3036	K14/76	2420

Cuts into middle or lower Level 2 deposits: 3048–9, 3064, 3066–7

Copper frags.	3067	K14/129	2296

Middle Level 2
Below 3046 the nature of the deposits did not change significantly. At ~97.80 the area on the south and west sides at least was sealed by a yellow packing layer (3069+3070) and this is taken as the base of the middle Level 2 deposits; the corresponding level in the NW corner was the transition from 3056 to 3058. Nowhere was there any sign of architecture or an occupation surface. At least two large pits were dug and abandoned within this sequence: P96/38, with a diameter of 1.96 m at the base, narrowing to 1.85 m towards its top, was cut on its west side by P96/45, which was larger, with a diameter of about 2.80 m and a surviving depth of 0.65 m.

Middle Level 2 units and finds — K14a
Fill/packing: 3050–56, 3063, 3065, 3068–70

Pub. ceramic	3063		928

Cuts into lower Level 2 deposits: 3074, 3076–8, 3080–81, 3083, 3086, 3089, 3096

Bead	3078	K14/132	2064
Metal/slag	3078	K14/133	2420
Mortar	3080	K14/124	2688
Bead	3083	K14/152	2040
Counter	3096	K14/151	2612

Lower Level 2
Below this were clear signs of architecture. Unfortunately the pits make it impossible to reconstruct an intelligible plan, but in this lower phase, sealed by later deposits about 1.5 m below the Level I walls, we have the first recognizable building level, at a height similar to that of Level 2 early in I14 (see p. 175).

In the NW corner at ~97.40 a well-prepared floor surface was reached, at the base of 3059, associated with FI95/10. This was a fragment of hearth at +97.34, merely a small patch of hard-fired and burnt clay, associated with soft layers of brown and orange fill. The basal floor was at +97.23, nearby was a small ash-filled pit some 20 cm deep (3082); mud brick in the west section (Fig. 521) must have belonged to the same phase. At this level some 2 m to the east were a relatively well-preserved hearth (FI96/16) and ashy deposits probably associated with it. The hearth (Figs. 53 & 54, p. 75) was roughly rectangular, oriented so that a triangular segment was exposed at the east side of K14a, at least half remaining unexcavated in K14b. The surface of the hearth, at +97.23, was clay plastered, over a bed of river pebbles (from 3 × 4 to 8 × 9 cm) about 8 cm deep, laid over a thin clay plaster surface. The approximate dimensions of the interior were 80 cm NW–SE and 1 m NE–SW; this was contained by a clay rim about 10 cm thick and 25 cm high, fired hard on the exterior, and the floor (3097) ran up to this.

On the south side, below the 3069+3070 horizon, where not cut once again by a pit, there were fragmentary walls and associated surfaces, belonging to the same phase as FI96/16 and FI95/10. The principal evidence was supplied by two mudbrick walls (W811 and W812) forming an angle projecting from the south baulk, but they were succeeded by a fragmentary stub of mud brick (numbered W813) above the south end of W812, and above this again by a one-course stone foundation along the same line as W812 but immediately below the layer of packing which seals the entire phase (3069 = 3070).

Lower Level 2 units and finds — K14a
Packing, etc.: 3058, 3071, 3073, 3075, 3085, 3095
Copper frags.	3095	K14/141	2296

Posthole into 3058: 3057
Occ. deposits: 3079, 3087, 3090, 3092–3
Bead	3087	K14/153	2021
Bead	3087	K14/135	2079
Pub. ceramic	3090		953

Ceramic disc	3090	K14/155	1562

Occ. surface: 3059, 3072, 3084, 3091, 3097–8, 3803
Astragalus	3091	K14/157	2448
Ceramic disc	3097	K14/156	1577
Human bone	3097	K14/158	2884
Astragalus	3097	K14/159	2449

FI95/10: 3082
FI96/16: 3099
Fill below Lower Level II occ. surface: 3094, 3800
Pub. ceramic	3094		902
Metal/slag	3800	K14/150	2420

15.5. LEVEL 1 IN I-M14 by M.P.C. Jackson

Introduction
A 50 × 5 m trench was laid out across the central east side of the mound between I14a and M14b, i.e. running parallel with the church, but 10 m to the south. This trench was dug during the first two seasons and except for soundings to deeper levels in I14 and K14 consisted mostly of the excavation of Level 1 deposits. These can be summarized as: buildings and associated features in two main phases dated by finds to the Hellenistic period, and evidence for later occupation in L14, in the form of late Roman/early Byzantine pottery and finds.

The proportion of well-stratified contexts was limited by the fact that well-preserved floor deposits were found only in I14. Isolated patches of floor surface were located in other areas but they were not found in clear association with walls. Topsoil was deeper in L14b, which seemed to represent an area between buildings, and the major concentration of late Roman pottery was found here.

Figure 162. *Level 1 in J14b and K14a looking NW, showing W406/403 along the south side of trench and W400/407 along north side (over W921) (see Fig. 506).*

Earlier Hellenistic phase (Fig. 506)
The earlier of the two phases of Level 1 architecture was uncovered principally in the centre of the trench in J14a/b and K14a/b. It was represented by a narrow rectangular structure aligned almost exactly E–W and with a length of 14.30 m, from its end wall W915 in K14b in the east to W414 in J14a in the west. Its north wall is numbered W404 + W921 + W917, and the south wall W406 + W403 + W402 (Fig. 162). The whole structure enclosed a space measuring 12.80 m long by 2.60 m wide. These walls were all bonded together and constructed in a single phase and each was built from two lines of facing stones with small amounts of rubble core. No floors were associated with these walls, and the visible remains, with no obvious doorways, presumably represent no more than the foundations.

At the west end of the structure in J14b, above the fill which respected the south face of W404, were a layer of occupation debris (3321), and a concentration of potsherds (3327). This fill (3348) was also cut by three pits: P95/20 (3322), P95/30 (3339) P95/29 (3337), and all were sealed beneath the packing layer 3317 below the later wall W409.

At the east end of the building in K14b, a pit P95/22 (fill 3031), containing ash, some mud brick, and Iron Age ceramics, was sealed beneath the later wall W401. It was half-sectioned along the K14a/b quadrant line. This pit was similar to FI94/14 (3002) from K14a which contained substantial quantities of Hellenistic material; both had surfaces interbedded with ash. The fill at the east end of the room — to the west of W915 — was 3034 and contained Iron Age material.

Built onto the east end of this structure, were two walls which appear to represent extensions of the north and south walls east of W915 from K14b into L14a. These were W916 and W918 respectively. The construction and alignment of these walls was quite different to those of the rectangular structure to which they were bonded: both were constructed from single lines of considerably larger stones than used in the rest of the structure; the north wall W916 continued straight, but the south wall W918 tapered northwards.

Both these walls disappeared into the east section of K14b and were not excavated in L14a. Fills 3033 and 3036, which contained Iron Age material, were removed from the space between walls W916 and W918 to the east of W915. No floors were identified in this space.

Outside the building in the west side of J14a two consecutive surfaces were discovered running up to the west face of W414: 3316 and beneath it 3318. 3316 had a group of potsherds lying on it which included pieces of Hellenistic fine ware. These surfaces lay below 3314 which represented the later phase surface in J14a.

Earlier Hellenistic units and finds
Fills sealed by this phase: 3026, 3027
Internal fills: 3303–7, 3348

Pub. ceramic	3305		1455
Metal/slag	3305	J14/12	2420
Iron nail	3306	J14/16	2388
Ceramic disc	3348	J14/74	1581

External fills: 3308
Occ. debris: 3321, 3327
Surfaces W of W414: 3316, 3318

Shield frag.	3316		2274
Iron spearhead	3316		2394
Pub. ceramic	3316		1108

Cuts: 3322, 3337, 3339

Pub. ceramic	3322		1002

Cuts sealed by later architecture: 3030–31

Iron blade	3031	K14/67	2320
Palette	3031	K14/70	2621

Later Hellenistic phase (I14/J14a) (Fig. 506)
The removal of topsoil in I14 revealed the side walls and plastered floor of an interior room, with associated burnt fill. The structure would appear to have been destroyed by fire, preserving some of its remains *in situ*. Both walls continued into the sections to the north and south.

The western wall of the room survived only as a below floor foundation wall W902, which was visible in the north section I14b, where it was clearly associated with the west edge of the floor (3421) (see Fig. 514). A spread of stones (3403) found in I14a/b partly lying on floor 3421 may well have represented the fallen remains of this wall. W902 on the east side was a dry stone wall, standing 0.50 m and three courses high. A doorway 1.35 m wide led through it to another plastered space on its east (3422; 3314 in J14a). This floor stretched for at least 2.20 m from the wall face, but its eastern limit and any associated wall were lost.

The plaster floors of these two rooms were well preserved and were laid on compact clay and cobbles. The plaster had been applied in a continuous layer through the doorway and from the floor up onto both sides of W902, and was particularly thick on the west face of W902. The height of the plaster floor on the west side of the doorway was +98.86. The plastered floor to the east of the doorway was some 10 cm higher, and the floor sloped upwards to the north. This rise in the floor levels may have been due in part to the proximity of this structure to the edge of the mound.

Contents of the rooms: Topsoil spits cleared from above the floor area in I14b, contained a relatively large proportion of Hellenistic ceramic material. Directly above the floor (3421) in I14b there was a layer of about 10 cm of burnt room fill from which came a miniature metal column, **2293**. A corresponding burnt layer 5–10 cm deep (3423) was found to the east of W902 on floor 3422 below topsoil.

In J14a, to the south of the doorway on the east side of W902, the base of a large unbaked clay vessel (J14/52) was set into the floor (3314). It contained a Hellenistic black-slipped sherd. Other finds were sealed within the floor and in the fill on top of the floor. A fragment of lamp (J14/111), of a type dated late third to late second century BC (similar to **991**), was found within the matrix of the plaster floor itself in J14.

Above the floor in J14a was a layer of fill (3310), which extended into the east side of the quadrant. Here it sealed the stones of W411, which represented the west wall of the later phase building in J14 (see below). Two irregularly shaped pits (P95/18 and P95/19) had been cut through fill material 3310 into surface 3314 below; the pit fills were loose and ashy. P95/18 (3312) was on the west side of the quadrant, and P95/19 (3313) in the NW corner. These pits would appear to be the latest features in this part of the trench.

The similar orientation of the building in I14b to the later phase walls in J/K14 may be taken to suggest that it belongs to the same phase, and this is confirmed by the stratigraphic evidence of 3314 which sealed surfaces respecting the west face of W414 (3316 and 3318), and was laid on packing which extended over the earlier phase walls W414 and W406 as 3331. In J14b, the later walls were constructed onto a similar packing layer (3317), which divided the secondary phase from the earlier phase below. The corresponding deposits further east in K14 were 3006, which sealed the top of W403, 3016 and 3029.

Later Hellenistic units and finds — I14/J14a
Floors: 3314, 3421–2
Ceramic disc	3314	J14/27	**1583**
Bead	3314	J14/29	**2024**
Shield frag.	3314	J14/24	**2273**
Grinder	3314	J14/26	**2775**
Lamp	3314	J14/111	
Pub. ceramic	3421		**1418**
Iron nail	3422	I14/53	**2388**

Occ. debris: 3419, 3423
Pub. ceramic	3419		**1373**
Metal column	3419	I14/45	**2293**
Pub. ceramics	3423		**1070, 1225, 1227, 1254**

Fills: 3310, 3403
Marble slab	3403	I14/16	**76**
Pub. ceramic	3403		**1133**
Iron nails	3403	I14/18, 197–8	**2350–52**
Spatula	3403	I14/196	**2416**
Grinder	3403	I14/20	**2766**

P95/18–19: 3312–13
Topsoil: 3400–402
Clay object	3400	I14/5	**1621**
Glass bangle	3400	I14/4	**2116**
Glass base	3401	I14/9	**2104**
Bead	3401	I14/11	**2042**
Iron frag.	3401	I14/8	**2391**
Stamp seal	3402	I14/13	**1475**

Later Hellenistic phase (J/L14) (Fig. 506)
A single phase of walls, with a zigzag shape incorporating four opposing corners, was found to extend from J14a as far as L14a.

The most substantial wall belonging to this later phase was W400/407 (Figs. 162–3). This was a single wall running WSW–ENE, four courses high, along the north side of J14b and K14a for a distance of more than 10 m. It was built from two lines of facing stones with little or no rubble core and measured 55-60 cm wide. W411, the west return of W407, ran almost perpendicular to it into the north section of J14a, and was aligned parallel with W902 in I14b.

A second wall, W408 also ran north from W407 into the north section of J14b, 1.28 m east of W411 (Fig. 163). A small room was thus formed north of W407, bounded by walls W411 and W408 to the west and east respectively. The surviving tops of these walls were found together with patchy greyish 'plaster' surface and patches of ashy material on a hard mudbrick layer directly below the topsoil, which was excavated as 3301. Fill was removed from south of W400/407 as 3302 in J14b, and lower fills (3303, 3311 and 3315) were removed from the room north of W407 between W411 and W408.

In K14a, two fire installations were found below the topsoil, within the room space created by walls W400 and W401. FI94/14 (di. 60 cm) rested on surface (3006), and there were spreads of ash and clinker on the same surface in the area around the fire installation (3003–4). The surface

Figure 163. *J14b and K14a, looking east; walls W406/403 and W400/407 running parallel, and associated cross-walls.*

Figure 164. *K14b and L14a in foreground, looking west: W943 in foreground returning westwards as W942 to meet south end of W401.*

was cut by a second fire installation FI94/15. The fill from this oven was excavated in two stages, above (3007) and below (3008, 3011) a large stone within the fill. 3008 contained a deep echinus bowl (**967**). Part of bowl **975** was found in FI94/15 (3011). Discovery of these vessels was complemented by the fact that all these units contained Hellenistic black-slipped fine ware sherds.

In K14b topsoil (3012) was removed to reveal the top of W401 and W942 (Fig. 164). W401 was the perpendicular return of W400/407 at its east end. It ran to the south for 3.05 m. It was 60 cm wide and was constructed in a similar way to W400/407 but survived only three courses high.

Figure 165. *M14a–b, looking east, showing room formed by W923, W922 and W924.*

W942, the main return of W401, ran in an ENE direction for 4.76 m and then returned as W943 in a SSE direction to disappear into the south section of L14a after 2.80 m. W942 was found immediately below the topsoil (3012), flanked on both sides by grey fills (3014, 3013).

It was postulated that the area to the east and north of walls W401 and W942 in K14b might represent an internal space of a building. The fill here was 3013. Lying on this was a small area of surface, which was cut by ovoid pit P95/7 (in the NE corner of K14b). This elongated pit may have been dug to remove stone from the earlier phase wall W916 lying at its base — like a similar pit to the south P95/8. A layer of ash was found below 3016; this was thought to represent the top level of the earlier phase. To the south of W942, fill (3014) was excavated to reveal an area of stones and a blue grey surface (3035) which ran under W942, sealing the earlier phase walls W915 and W918 beneath. No finds were located on this floor.

Later Hellenistic units and finds — J/L14
Packing below floors: 3006, 3016, 3029, 3035, 3317, 3331
Ceramic disc	3016	K14/53	1547
Loomweight	3016	K14/58	1806
Glass rims	3016	K14/56a–b	2082, 2086

FI94/14 3002, 3004
| Pub. ceramic | 3002 | | 1262 |

FI94/15 3007, 3008, 3011
Echinus bowl	3008	K14/28	967
Pub. ceramic	3008		1381
Stamped bowl	3011+3043	K14/36	975
Pub. ceramic	3011		983
Loomweight	3011	K14/38	1805

Fills below topsoil: 3003–5, 3013–14, 3301–2, 3311, 3315

Lead sheet	3003	K14/7	2299
Loomweight	3005	K14/19	1804
Iron strip	3005	K14/21	2411
Glass base	3013	K14/46	2110
Pub. ceramics	3301		1019, 1132
Copper object	3301	J14/3	2292
Iron nail	3301	J14/7	2388
Copper ring	3302	J14/8	2265

Cuts: 3015, 3020, 3022–4, 3312–13
Topsoil: 3012, 3300
Pub. ceramics	3012		990, 1077
Iron arrowhead	3012	K14/41	2398
Human bone	3012	K14/40	2841
Pub. ceramic	3300		1370

Later Hellenistic phase (M14)
In M14a/b, the tops of walls representing three sides of a room were uncovered only 0.20 m below the surface beneath the topsoil (Fig. 165). The walls all measured *c.* 0.65–0.72 m wide and were built from two lines of facing stones with a narrow rubble core, and had a similar alignment to the later Hellenistic phase in J/K14. The west wall W923 and the east wall W924 ran from the south section in a NNW direction to join the north wall W922, which was orientated WSW–ENE. A short interior partition wall W926 abutted the east side of W923. The internal measurements of the room were 4.00 m E–W and more than 3.25 m N–S, since the building continues south into M14c/d. Unit 3501 was excavated from the first appearance of W922 and W923. The fill below this was then removed as 3505 inside the structure and 3506 outside it.

The SW corner of a second structure (W928 and W929) was found in the NW corner of M14b, aligned similarly to the better exposed structure in the south. This lay 2.40 m east of the junction of W922 and W924.

The similar orientation of both these buildings to the second phase of architecture further to the west is noteworthy.

The base of a large Hellenistic kantharos (**982**) was found in the NW corner of M14b. The other pottery from M14 was all of Hellenistic date, but since no floors were identified in direct relationship with the walls it cannot be argued conclusively that these were occupation deposits from the structures.

Later Hellenistic units and finds — M14
Fill, internal 3505
Fill, external 3506

Silver wire	3506	M14/14	2304

Fill below topsoil: 3501

Pub. ceramics	3501		1223, 1457
Iron nail	3501	M14/9	2388
Grinder	3501	M14/10	2775

Topsoil: 3500, 3504, 3507

Kantharos	3507	M14/20	982
Pub. ceramic	3507		987
Lamp	3507	M14/18	993

Late Roman deposits (L14a/b)
Up to 0.58 m of topsoil from squares L14a and L14b, was excavated from the original ground surface at +100.55–78. Topsoil in this part of the trench was relatively deep compared to that from the quadrants on either side. This may have been due partly to the comparative lack of structural remains belonging to the later Hellenistic phase in this section of the trench. The sum of the excavation in these quadrants however consisted of the removal of only the top few contexts to a depth of *c.* 0.70–1.00 m.

Features identified in L14a were few: below the topsoil, a patch of grey plaster surface was revealed which was only 0.40 × 0.75 m in area (3602). Lying on this surface was a substantial amount of stone tumble, within the fill of which the base of a ceramic statuette was found (**1510**). The removal of this surface and the fill below it revealed scatters of large stones and the later phase wall W943 in the SW corner of L14a (mentioned above). Light grey fill (3606) was excavated over the whole quadrant to a final depth of +99.55, but was not excavated right to the base of W943. No surface was found in association with this wall.

The topsoil in L14b lay above a fragmentary area of cobbled surface (3604). This was found towards the south of the quadrant, but was not discovered in direct association with any other features. The pottery from the unit contained late Roman material including the distinctive imported gritty fabric LR1 amphorae.

The top of another wall, W944 was located within the light grey fill immediately below the topsoil along the south edge of L14b. This wall was four courses high and was aligned exactly E–W. It had no relationship with the walls of the later phases in L14 or M14 and was consequently attributed to the earlier architectural phase with which it lay parallel.

Units from L14a/b included some Hellenistic pottery, but mostly consisted of later material including closed forms with knobbed handles, body sherds with painted spiral and bird motifs (3601, 3603), imported gritty late Roman amphorae (from 3600, 3601, 3603, 3604) and at least one late Roman 'rolled rim' Cypriot type cooking vessel (**1395** from 3602). This is interesting, since little architecture was found in this area and pottery found in association with the neighbouring buildings suggests a Hellenistic date for the structures. At this date the cobbled surface in L14, similar to that found in K18b (p. 204), suggests an open area between these structures.

Subsequently the concentration of Late Roman ceramics here provides evidence for disposal of domestic material, which attests to occupation of this area following the Hellenistic period. No occupation deposits from the Late Roman period were discovered *in situ* within structures at this part of the site. The differentiation of the Late Roman and Hellenistic ceramics was distinct between units and is clearly linked to the different deposits associated with the open area in L14, and the structures located on either side.

Late Roman units and finds – L14a/b
Fill matrix for walls: 3603–4, 3606, 3608

Pub. ceramic	3603		1139
Pub. ceramics	3604		973, 1260
Stone bowl	3604	L14/22	2644
Pub. ceramic	3606		1018
Pub. ceramic	3608		1236
Ceramic disc	3608	L14/27	1584
Glass vessel	3608	L14/28	2093

Fill below topsoil: 3602

Statuette	3602	L14/10	1510
Pub. ceramics	3602		1031, 1044, 1069, 1073, 1256–7, 1327, 1395
Wick-holder	3602	L14/13	2280
Iron blade	3602	L14/8	2316
Archit. frag.	3602	L14/14	184

Topsoil: 3600–601

Pub. ceramics	3600		1258, 1424
Glass handle	3600	L14/1	2102
Lamp	3601	L14/9	991
Pub. ceramics	3601		1046, 1049, 1058, 1087–8, 1136–8, 1145, 1182, 1204, 1242, 1255, 1280, 1348
Fossil	3601	L14/16	2511

I14a–M14b conclusion
It would appear that the walls excavated in the trench from I14a–M14b were all associated with units that contained Hellenistic material i.e. two main architectural phases of Hellenistic date were recovered. The excep-

tion is L14, which appears to have been largely devoid of buildings and which contained substantial amounts of late Roman and Byzantine ceramic material.

It is possible that the buildings in the other squares may have had occupation dating later than the Hellenistic. The apparently intrusive spiral painted sherds **1132** (3301) and **1133** (3403) (from the fill below topsoil and the wall collapse respectively) may be significant, but appear to post-date the other material from the destruction deposits associated with the buildings. This is a difficult problem since so few floors survive from the area; certainly some of the floor deposits were directly associated with Hellenistic dated cultural material but the high concentration of Late Roman/Byzantine ceramic material in what may be an open area between buildings in L14 suggests that refuse may have been thrown from buildings into this area.

Chapter 16

The Church

M.P.C. Jackson

Introduction (Fig. 507)

The church was uncovered on the highest point of the mound in Squares I17, J17, K17, L17; I16, J16, K16, L16; I15, J15; an operation resulting in the excavation of an area c. 35 × 20 m totalling c. 700 m² (see Fig. 17, p. 49).

Two discrete concentrations of stones were noted during the pre-excavation surface survey (see Thomas, Fig. 28). The more westerly of these two areas, located in square K16, included a dense concentration of tile fragments and was proved on excavation to be the location of a single chambered church built over the levelled foundations of a larger Early Byzantine basilica. Work on the church was begun in 1995 by Caroline Steele and Ergün Laflı, and continued in 1996 by Carl Knappett and Ergün Laflı, followed in 1997 and 1998 by Mark Jackson.

The surface of the mound had been ploughed, so much of the 'excavation' represented the clearance of largely unstratified overburden from above the preserved archaeological features below. The best deposits were excavated at the east end, where the overburden was up to 0.50 m deep. The topsoil became steadily shallower until it was as little as 0.15 m deep towards the west end of the area.

The excavation area was expanded over the course of the project to uncover the majority of a basilical building which survived mostly as below-floor foundation walls. This was the earlier of the two churches (see Figs. 166 & 176). The later structure, a single-chambered church, was located in K16, stratigraphically above the east end of the nave of the basilica.

Early Byzantine basilica

The overall dimensions of the basilica were determined in 1998, the final season of excavation. It measured 29 m long by 16 m wide and consisted of a nave and two aisles, a narthex, and an apse (the external diameter at its chord was 6.30 m). The apse was flanked by two side-chambers, joined by a narrow passage which ran between the apse and the east wall. This building survived mostly as foundation walls, except in the north side-chamber where the floor was found intact and associated with a small section of standing wall two courses high. This room provided the best information on the construction of the building: the foundation walls were built with two lines of undressed, mortared, facing stones with a rubble and mortar core. This foundation was capped by large slabs which stretched the full width of the foundation; it was onto these slabs that the upper courses were laid. The upper courses also consisted of two lines of undressed facing stones with a mortar core.

No brick was noted in the construction of the building but the large amount of *imbrices* and *tegulae* recovered during the excavation would suggest that the building had once had a tiled roof. Fragments of dressed stone were recovered in relatively small quantities from the area of the church itself, but found reused in other areas of the site providing some evidence for both limestone and marble architectural features in the building (see Chapter 19).

A cobble and stone deposit interpreted as the exterior surface outside the church was found to the north of the northern side-chamber in K17b. Lying on these cobbles and stones a thin plaster surface was found, which ran most of the length of the 1 × 10 m trench dug to connect the stratigraphy of the church to that in the NW corner. This surface was associated with the west side of the phase Ic structure W430 in K18b and may be interpreted as the former surface between the two buildings in that period. The cobble surface was also reused as part of the phase Id courtyard. The surface in this long narrow trench was post-dated by two unexcavated burials, aligned E–W and capped by stones, discovered in K18d and K17b.

Single chambered church

The secondary church was built on top of the surviving foundation walls of the early Byzantine basilica following the removal of its standing walls. It was an

Figure 166. *Aerial view of church (kite photograph courtesy of Jan Driessen).*

almost square structure which measured externally *c.* 7 m (N–S, reconstructed) × 6.8 m (E–W), with an apse extending 1.6 m east from the building (length of chord of apse *c.* 3.25 m). Thus the chamber formed inside was *c.* 5.70 m (reconstructed) × 5.5 m.

The north and south walls were built over the stylobates of the earlier church; and the apse was constructed within the line of the earlier apse. The walls of this building were also constructed of two lines of facing stones filled with a mortar and rubble core.

Four column bases arranged in a square inside the later structure may relate to two others found to the west of the building beneath a paved floor set on mortar (Fig. 176).

No direct evidence was recovered to provide a date for this later structure. The apse of the building would appear to have been blocked at some time after its initial construction.

Three burials were located to the east of the later church, situated stratigraphically above the walls of the destroyed earlier building. In an effort to provide a *terminus ante quem* for the destruction of the basilica, and to suggest a date for the use of the later building, a skeleton, which subsequently proved to have been female, was excavated (5626, see pp. 195–6). With a view to obtaining a scientific date for the burial, a femur from the skeleton was exported at the end of the 1998 season. Following analysis by the AMS Radiocarbon Lab. in Oxford the sample was dated to 857±35 BP (calibrated date most likely to be AD 1110–1270: Bronk Ramsey *et al.* 2000, 473–4).

Chronology

Based on plan alone, the basilica at Kilise Tepe is typical of churches in the early Byzantine World dating any time in the fourth to sixth centuries (Mango 1986, 38). However, the basilica in Cilicia and Isauria is seldom dated to as late as the sixth century (Hill 1996). Some buildings may have been repaired as late as the sixth century and a few constructed later but most are dated to the fourth and fifth centuries. Hill has argued, based on an inscription, that the 'Cathedral' at Corycus — if assigned correctly by Forsyth to the seventh century — represents the latest known basilica in the region, since it has been attributed to AD 629/30. Others however, have dated it to the fifth century (Forsyth 1961, 137, n. 32; Herzfeld & Guyer 1930, 107–8; Hill 1996, 9–10, 120; Hild *et al.* 1984). No inscriptions were found during the excavations at Kilise Tepe.

The Church

In spite of efforts made, the basilica unfortunately could not be closely dated by pottery or finds associated stratigraphically with it, or by direct association with neighbouring buildings. The excavation of the church did provide stratified ceramic material below floors, but these were of relatively early date. The material under the nave floor consisted of Hellenistic fine wares; the material from beneath the floor at the east end of the church was local fabric painted with broad lines of red/brown paint of uncertain date, probably either Hellenistic or Roman.

In fact the discovery of Hellenistic material beneath the church reflects the pattern of Hellenistic finds discovered below Early Byzantine levels in the areas both to the north and to the south of the church.

Significant occupation of the mound during the late Roman period/early Byzantine period is attested by pottery and coins from other parts of the site, and typologically it is consistent to argue that the building would have been built to serve the purposes of this apparently thriving community.

Clearly at some point the basilica at Kilise Tepe was destroyed, but no conclusive evidence was recovered from the excavation of the church, which might be used to support an interpretation of how or when this event took place. It is clear, however, that there was a substantial episode of clearance and reconstruction after the event on the site of the church itself. Elsewhere on the site, for example in the NW corner, architectural elements, apparently from the fabric of the original church, were incorporated into secondary features. Most notably these items of *spolia* include the column base from P96/17 (**190**; Fig. 179, p. 203) in J19a and a capital fragment **132** from P95/6 (1902). These features in the NW corner post-date the courtyard phase. Two interpretations can be made based on this observation: firstly that the church and the Level Ib phase were both levelled by the time of these reconstruction events; secondly that the features which incorporate the architectural elements from the church appear to be associated with buildings and features which date to the fifth century AD or later, to judge from coins and pottery.

It is unclear how long after the initial destruction of the church the later activity took place. But clearly the original church was substantially razed by the time the secondary structure was built. Similarly, the Level Ib walls were post-dated by the courtyard and pits containing *spolia*. Although this relative relationship appears to suggest that the Level Ib walls and the first phase of the church are contemporary, their stratigraphic relationship was not conclusively confirmed.

There seems to have been major clearance work after the destruction of the church, as also after the destruction of the Level Ib phase, which might be taken to suggest that the site was abandoned for a period before the reconstruction. Clearly the significance of the location of the earlier building was perceived by the re-builders since the reconstruction took place on the same site. However the architects responsible for the later structure created a building of much smaller scale and of completely different form to its predecessor. This may be taken to suggest a distinct change in the perceived needs of the second community from those of the first. It would be simplistic to attribute this change in scale to a reduction in population or resources at the site.

Construction of single chambered chapels over the remains of early Byzantine basilicas is a common phenomenon in Cilicia and Isauria as well as elsewhere in Anatolia (see above, p. 28; Jackson & Postgate 1999, 543). Since there is a general reduction in church size in many Mediterranean settlements including cities, the change in scale may be more likely linked to changes in liturgy.

Hill has argued that single chambered structures were first built in Cilicia prior to the seventh century (Hill 1996, 10). There has been however no synthesis of the information relating to these buildings, many of which remain undated. Many of them certainly date to the Armenian period. A useful study by Edwards has concentrated on the typological differences between certain Byzantine and Armenian single chambered chapels found within Cilician castles (Edwards 1982, 173).

At Kilise Tepe, no direct evidence was found to support or dismiss a seventh-century date for the construction of the single chambered church at Kilise Tepe, although it is tempting to link the Level Ic and Id phases of the NW corner to this structure. The blocking of the apse appears to represent a secondary phase of the structure, but its period of use is unknown. The only independent date which aids our understanding of the chronology of the later structure is the radiocarbon date obtained from the skeleton in burial (5626). This suggests that the cemetery immediately to the east of the later structure was in use as late as the twelfth century.

Isolated finds from Kilise Tepe, including very few sherds of glazed ceramics and certain later coins, corroborate this date as evidence for relatively late settlement at the site. Some of these finds are related to a very late pit (P97/1) and surface in J18a, but few other finds have been identified to structures from that period.

Chapter 16

Details of the excavation of the Early Byzantine basilica

The north side-chamber
The best-preserved part of the early Byzantine basilica at Kilise Tepe was the north side-chamber which was excavated in K17d and L17c. This was the only place where the walls survived above the foundation levels.

After topsoil removal in L17c, two clearly different deposits were revealed: on the west, the fill overlying the walls and floor of the north side-chamber of the church, a dusty grey rubble deposit (5104 and 5106), containing undressed stones up to 25 × 15 × 10 cm; on the east, the material outside the church to the east of the north side chamber, a soil deposit (5103 and 5105) containing almost no stones.

Below 5104 in L17c and 9636–7 and 9643 in K17d lay two courses of W521 built on the church foundation. This represented the only section of standing wall belonging to the basilica church found during the excavation. W521 survived for 1.10 m along the north edge of K17d, from where it ran into L17c, where it was less well preserved. The wall was constructed of two lines of facing stones with a mortar and rubble core measuring 52–54 cm wide and 40 cm high. W521 was built onto large slabs which formed an offset foundation course beneath it. These slabs thus 'capped' the lower foundation courses. The foundation capping slabs measured *c.* 85 cm and protruded beyond the width of the standing wall both on its interior and exterior.

The hard deposit 9657 existed level with the exterior offset foundation of the church. This and the two units below are thought to have represented an external surface to the north of the church. 9657 lay above two units: the first (9658) contained a substantially high proportion of stone, this in turn lay above a similar but softer deposit containing cobbles and pottery (9659). The large amount of cobbles and stone in these units and the relationship with the church and the surfaces to the north in K18b, would support the interpretation that these units represented the exterior surface on the north side of the early Byzantine church. The elevation of the upper surface of 9657 was +100.26–8.

A deposit of this description and elevation was discovered running north in the trench dug to connect the church with the excavation in the NW corner of the tepe. It was cut by a burial in K17b and a second in K18d, but is most likely to represent a continuous surface running all the way to K18b where it was found, like the later courtyard, to lie on the layer of cobbles to the west of wall W430 (units 9677 in K17b and 6011 in K18d; cf. 4398 in K18b; see p. 208).

Within the room, ploughed topsoil was removed followed by a layer of rubble. Sealed below this rubble was a layer of fine ashy deposit 10 cm thick lying on top of the original floor of the north side-chamber. This floor was a mortar surface, which extended to the base of the interior face of the side-chamber walls, thus running over and concealing the interior offset of the large foundation capping stones. The floor surface was unlike that found in the nave area both in composition and appearance: there were no signs of broken marble within it. Its matrix contained angular stones of *c.* 15 cm and distinctive rounded pebbles *c.* 2–3 cm diameter. The floor surface was very smooth and did not preserve the impressions of paving slabs on it. Its elevation varied from +100.44 to +100.56. No finds were discovered on the floor of this room (see Fig. 167).

On the east side of the room the standing wall had been robbed, but the capping slabs of foundation W522 still lay *in situ* preserving the impression of the standing walls in the mortar surviving on them. On the NW side of the north side chamber, all but two of the foundation capping slabs of W511, and all those at the west end of W520 had been ripped out. Their positions were found occupied by the rubble filled robber trench for W511 and for W520. When this fill was cleared, the tops of the

Figure 167. *K17d/L17c, looking east; north side chamber of church following excavation, showing plastered surface and W506, W511, W521.*

next course of foundations of W511 and W520 were revealed 0.13 m below the height of the broken floor which had previously run over the slabs. The foundation wall below these capping stones consisted of two rows of undressed facing stones bonded with a rubble and mortar core measuring c. 85 cm wide.

A sondage was dug in K17d which demonstrated that walls W511 and W520 were of a single phase. Both were built at the same time as W506, the north wall of the church.

North side-chamber units and finds
Topsoil: 5101–2, 5111, 9606, 9608, 9621–3, 9635, 9639, 9684–5

Iron nail	5101	L17/1	2387
Tessera	9623	K17/40	2193
Tesserae	9642	K17/57	2196

Robber trenches: 5109, 9624, 9626, 9628, 9630, 9632, 9645

Glass bangle	9624	K17/44	2148
Marble tile	9626	K17/46	84
Tesserae	9628	K17/48	2195

Rubble fill of north side chamber: 5104, 5106–7, 9609, 9636–7, 9643

Tessera	5104	L17/2	2209
Mortar	9607	K17/26	2694
Archit. frags.	9607	K17/25, 27	83, 182
Iron nail	9636	K17/52	2348
Pub. ceramic	9643		1286
Glass bangle	9643	K17/58	2149
Tesserae	9643	K17/60, 62, 64	2197–8, 2212

Ashy deposit beneath rubble on floor: 5107, 9627, 9629, 9631, 9638, 9641
Mortar floor: 5110, 9610
Soil fill outside church: 5103, 5105, 5108, 5112–13, 9614–15, 9617–18, 9620, 9625, 9633–4, 9654, 9656–7, 9686

Iron nail	5103	L17/7	2349
Iron nail	5112	L17/5	2384
Tesserae	9614	K17/30	2190
Pub. ceramics	9615		1201, 1290
Tesserae	9615	K17/31–2	2191–2
Worked bone	9618	K17/36	2492
Pub. ceramic	9625		1033
Tessera	9625	K17/43	2194
Pub. ceramic	9633		1306
Pub. ceramic	9657		1237
Glass base	9657	K17/72	2111
Pub. ceramic	9686		1184

Possible surface outside church: 5114, 9658, 9659, 9662

Pub. ceramic	9658		1228
Metal/slag	9659	K17/78	2420

East wall and passage behind apse
During the excavation of the north side chamber, the foundation of the east wall of the building W522 was located in L17c. It was also found in L16a where it ran 35 cm east of the apse wall foundation W512. The same mortar surface discovered in the north side chamber (9610 and 5110) stretched south to L16a (= 5633), between these two walls. Here too the capping stones of the foundation walls had been robbed, but this surface would have run c. 20–25 cm over each of the offset foundations up to the base of their standing walls, thus forming the floor of a passage that narrowed to c. 75–85 cm behind the apse. This passage would have allowed access between the north and south side-chambers.[1] A section of this mortar floor was removed from between the walls. Pottery was recovered from 5634 below the floor (**1215, 1217, 1219**).

The apse
The apse of the early Byzantine basilica, measuring 6.30 m across its chord, was a substantial, almost semi-circular, wall which measured 0.95–1 m wide.[2] It survived only as a foundation except for two foundation capping stones on its north side (elevation +100.53). The north edge of these stones was covered by the same lime-mortar surface as 9610 uncovered in K17d; this was found on both the interior as well as the exterior of the apse.

A 2 × 4 m trench excavated along the east side of K16d exposed a 75 cm deep robber trench dug on the south side of the apse to a depth of +99.73. This activity had not removed the entire foundation, which continued down below the limit of our excavation. The western extent of the mixed fill of this robber context was not fully excavated. It was seen from the section to continue into the NW side of K16d. On the SE side of K16d a small area of lime-mortar surface 1.25 × 1.10 m was found, which may have represented the remains of the floor of the south side chamber (elevation of this possible floor was +100.51; this may be compared to the elevation of the north side chamber floor which was from +100.44 to +100.56).

The robbing of the apse may have taken place relatively recently since the SE corner of the later chapel was also damaged in K16d.

Apse units and finds
Topsoil: 4805, 4810–11, 5600, 5603, 5620–21, 5627

Glass bangle	4805	K16/24	2147

Robber trench: 4812, 5623, 5625

Glass rim	4812	K16/35	2084
Tessera	4812	K16/34	2184
Human bones	4812	K16/31, 38	2887–8
Tesserae	5623	L16/13–14	2206–7
Pub. ceramic	5625		1129

Grave fill: 4813

Human bones	4813	K16/36	2889

Fill inside area of apse W512 (see later structure below)
Rubble fill over W512: 5601–2, 5604

Tesserae	5601	L16/1	2204

Mortar floor between W512 and W522: 5633

Pub. ceramic	5633		1214

Fill below mortar floor: 5634, 5638–9
Pub. ceramics	5634		**1215, 1217, 1219**
Metal/slag	5638	L16/32	**2420**
Pub. ceramic	5639		**1333**

Soil fill outside church: 5622, 5624, 5629–31, 5635–7
Pub. ceramic	5630		**1130**
Pub. ceramic	5631		**1100**
Pub. ceramic	5636		**1389**

Possible surface outside church: 5632
Metal/slag	5632	L16/25	**2420**

The north aisle

The north aisle was excavated to the elevation of the surviving foundation walls in order to complete the plan. It measured 16.35 m long and was 3.80 m wide at the west end, tapering to 3.25 m wide at the east end.

The foundation of the north stylobate W517 ran parallel with what survived of the south stylobate W509 and perpendicular to the west wall of the structure W510. W517 survived relatively intact but only at its extreme east end were the large foundation capping slabs found — the rest of these, and any column bases, had been robbed. No floor was located in the north aisle. As in the north side chamber, it had presumably existed at a level above these capping slabs, impressions of which were also noted on the surface of the north wall foundation W506.

The excavation of a sealed deposit 9682 at the far east end of the north aisle immediately north of W514 and to the west of W511 revealed mixed soil with hundreds of loose mosaic tesserae **2199** and a discrete area of small chipped fragments of marble K17/96 clearly caused by the breaking up of marble blocks. Unit 9682 lay at an elevation of 100.50 m similar to that of the surface 9610/5110 in the north side-chamber (100.48 m) and seems to represent evidence for a destruction phase.

W506 tapered considerably towards the east end where it appeared to be bonded to walls W520 and W511. It was not bonded at the west end with either the west wall W510, or with any part of the narthex.

The tapering alignment of W506 and its position relative to W520 led to the decision to excavate its construction trench (P98/37) located on its north side in K17d. This revealed its foundation to be 1.30 m deep and the trench to be filled with a single fill (excavated as three units).

The removal of these units revealed that W520 was clearly bonded with W511 and W506 in a single episode of construction. Clinging to the west side of the foundation W511 was a very hard deposit of soil which was different to the rest of the construction trench fill.

W511 may have been constructed against the west side of its own construction trench before the trench for W506 was dug. W506 was built on the south side of its construction trench and continued parallel with the north stylobate for 4.25 m, before kinking to the north to run past the north end of the west wall W510.

North aisle units and finds

Topsoil: 5000, 9601–2, 9646
Archit. frags.	5000	J17/1, 2	**20, 145**
Iron nail	5000	J17/12	**2367**
Iron ring	5000	J17/11	**2407**
Iron strip	5000	J17/9	**2414**
Incense burner	5000	J17/8	**2611**
Pounder	5000	J17/7	**2807**
Pounder	9601	K17/7	**2808**
Socket	9601	K17/6	**2824**
Iron nail	9602	K17/8	**2370**

Fill outside church: 9647–8, 9650–53
Pub. ceramics	9650		**1041, 1131, 1153**

Possible surface outside church: 9649
Pub. ceramic	9649		**1307**

Fill below topsoil: 9603
Archit. frags.	9603	K17/16, K17/28	**82, 117**
Sp. whorl	9603	K17/10	**1981**
Tesserae	9603	K17/12–13, 19–21	**2185–8, 2211**
Iron nail	9603	K17/22	**2372**

Construction trench fill north side of W506: 9664, 9666–7
Pub. ceramics	9666		**1293, 1363**

The south aisle

The south aisle was 3.48 m wide at its west end. The south wall W505 and south stylobate W509 were both truncated near the west end of the aisle during a later phase of activity at the site. W505 survived only 0.45 m long and W509 was truncated 6 m from the west end of the aisle and post-dated by a dry stone wall W518 running from J15b.

The truncation of the south stylobate and its association with W518 thus clearly represents a phase of activity later than the destruction of the basilica in this area — possibly contemporary with the later chapel.

South aisle units
Topsoil: 4700 (see below for 4700 finds)

The narthex

At the west end, the removal of ploughsoil in squares I15a, I15b, I16 and I17c and I17d revealed evidence for a narthex with an unusual layout. The west end lay very close to the western edge of the mound overlooking the Göksu valley. Stray finds in this unstratified material included an early fifth-century coin (**2836** - Arcadius AD 383–408).

The south wall of the narthex W505 projected 5.50 m west of the south aisle into I15 where it turned to form the west wall of the narthex W503. W503 ran 10.30 m to the north, but it stopped 4.80 m short of the north wall W506 with a short return to the east.

Narthex units and finds
Topsoil: 4400, 4402, 4600–601, 4900–603

Iron arrowhead	4400	I15/8	2397
Archit. frag.	4600	I16/25	103
Marble panel	4600	I16/37	111
Mini. column	4600	J16/7	112
Dressed stone	4600	I16/30	136
Archit. frag.	4600	I16/38	137
Columns	4600	J16/6	141
Dressed stone	4600	I16/24	157
Marble	4600	I16/35	158
Pub. ceramics	4600		1265–6
Glass stem	4600	J16/8	2106
Glass bangle	4600	J16/3	2119
Tesserae	4600	I16/28, 36	2165–6
Spatula	4600	J16/4	2275
Metal strip	4600	I16/21	2301
Iron nails	4600	I16/20, 22, 29, 31–2	**2358–61, 2381**
Chain ring	4600	J16/5	2405
Ceramic disc	4601	I16/16	1548
Loomweight	4601	I16/3	1835
Glass handle	4601	I16/17	2095
Tesserae	4601	I16/4, 9, 14	2162–4
Cyl. stone	4601	I16/19	2670
Worked stone	4603	I16/18	1
Coin	4900	I17/12	2836
Marble	4901	I17/6	104
Iron blade	4901	I17/4	2317
Iron nail	4903	I17/8	2362
Iron rod	4903	I17/9	2412

Evidence for activity to the NW of the church
A section of the north side of the north wall W506 immediately to the west of W510 was missing as if a wall running north from the building had been robbed — no robber trench was recognized during the removal of topsoil. Further west, W506 reduced in width from 0.85 m to 0.75 m. The relationship of the west end of this wall with the rest of the narthex was enigmatic and may be due partly to subsequent activity on the church and the area to its NW.

A single line of stones W519 ran into I17d from I17b over the truncated west end of W506, 4.25 m from the west end of the north aisle (see Fig. 168). A spread of uneven plaster surface found directly below W519 in the NE corner of I17c and the NW corner of I17d could be taken to suggest possible further evidence for related structures to the NW of the building in I17a and I17b. Unfortunately further interpretation of the events relating to these fragmentary remains was not clear.

Nave
The nave was 16.35 m long by 5.5 m wide (Figs. 168–9). Much of the area between the stylobates of the early structure, to the east of the west wall W510, and extending west beneath the west wall of the later structure W513 was covered in a mortar surface. This surface survived 1–2 cm higher than the elevation of the surviving stylobate foundations in J16.

This mortar layer (4721) was distinct in composition from the mortar surface in the NE side chamber (9610, 5110, 5633). The surface in the nave area contained no rounded pebbles but instead was characterized by a large proportion of broken marble fragments. It is not certain that this surface was associated with the primary phase of the early Byzantine basilica (see below).

In the surface of the mortar layer impressions of large slabs were visible which must have been laid onto it when it was still slightly wet. The slabs had been aligned parallel with the stylobates. Five stone slabs, including one of marble with a smooth undecorated surface, were also found lying on this mortar in the NW corner of the nave in J16a. These stones just encroached over the edge of the stylobate, though they may have been subject to slight disturbance either when the other stones were robbed or as a result of ploughing activity (see Fig. 507).

A sondage was made through the mortar layer in the SW corner of the nave in J16c in order to determine the depth of the south stylobate wall W509 and

Figure 168. *I17c/d, looking east: W507 and, top left, plaster and associated W519, overlapping W506.*

Chapter 16

Figure 169. *Nave and north aisle, looking east, with pavement and associated plaster floor.*

Figure 170. *Nave: west side of pavement looking south in J16; column base F (191b) in foreground and, to the right, fallen voussoirs.*

Figure 171. *West end of pavement, looking NW, with fallen voussoirs and column base E (191a) in foreground*

to examine deposits below the floor. No construction trench was found on the north side of W509 and no earlier church surface was found beneath the mortar layer. A pre-church floor surface, associated with a clay-lined pit P98/82 (fill 4724) below 4720, 4723 and 4725 which contained Hellenistic pottery, was cut by the foundation trench for the south stylobate, against the north side of which W509 was built. Removal of further deposits revealed that the foundations of W509 and W510 were about 1.28 m deep.

It is assumed that there would have been a colonnade on each of the stylobates but no evidence was found for them on either of these walls. Six column bases were found — not sitting on the stylobates as might be expected — but within the body of the nave (Fig. 176). They were labelled A–F (**191–2**; Figs. 205–8). A further column base (**190**; Fig. 179) was also found north of the church in pit P96/17 fill (1654) in J19. These together with the capital fragment **132** from pit P95/6 would all appear to demonstrate secondary reuse of these architectural elements.

Two of the column bases were found concealed beneath the mortar surface with just their circular tops protruding. The northern of the two was **191b** (J16/161), the southern was **191a** (J16/162). They were aligned N–S 2.70 m from each other, and lay 1 m closer to the north stylobate than to the south one. They were located 6.30 m from the west end of the nave, and 9.70 m from the east end in J16b. Both column bases set below the mortar layer were constructed into the stone pavement, which survived in the body of the nave on the mortar. This surviving section of stone pavement included a slab of marble **172** (J16/164) which had clearly been reused from a previous location. These two column bases lay almost in line with four more column bases found to the east in K16.

A small sondage beneath the mortar around column base **191a** (J16/162) revealed that it was not laid on an earlier floor surface. Clearly the column bases must have been put down prior to the laying of the mortar and the stone floor, but presumably as part of the same operation. Very few fragments of pottery were recovered from the sondage; those found included a sherd of Hellenistic black-slipped fine ware.

Running between these column bases along the west side of the surviving section of pavement was a line of stones raised 2-3 cm above the stone pavement (Figs. 170–71); the raised stones also ran along the north side of the stone pavement. Immediately to the west of this paved area the mortar was damaged by a number of large ashlar voussoirs which seemed to be lying *in situ* where they had fallen (Figs. 170–71). The alignment of the unmortared wall W518 running from unexcavated J15b into J16c towards **191a** (J16/162) should be noted (see Fig. 507).

Nave units and finds
Topsoil in J16 (over nave): 4700, 4705
Dressed stone	4700	J16/14, 21	2, 17
Column	4700	J16/37	60
Marble tiles	4700	J16/35–6	105–6
Marble panel	4700	J16/39	120
Columns	4700	J16/26–7, 43, 49	121–3, 163
Marble cyl.	4700	J16/24	126
Capital	4700	J16/15	130
Dressed stone	4700	J16/20, 22, 45	142, 161–2
Glass bangle	4700	J16/33	2120
Tesserae	4700	J16/16, 34	2168–9
Iron blade	4700	J16/113	2320
Iron nails	4700	J16/11, 25, 28–30	2363–6, 2382
Chain link	4700	J16/31	2406
Iron strip	4700	J16/12	2413
Mortar	4700	J16/13	2695
Grinder	4700	J16/17	2775

Soil rubble below topsoil: 4706
Archit. frag.	4706	J16/153–6	165–8
Column bases	4706	J16/161–2	**191a–b**
Marble slabs	4706	J16/163–4	171–2
Copper sheet	4706	J16/166	2287
Iron nails	4706	J16/152, 165	2346–7
Metal/slag	4706	J16/160	2420

Mortar Floor in J16d: 4721
Deposits below floor in SW corner of Nave in J16d: 4726
Mortar Floor in J16c: 4721–2
| Iron nail | 4722 | J16/167 | 2388 |
| Metal/slag | 4722 | J16/167 | 2420 |

Deposits below floor in nave and around column base in J16c: 4720, 4723–5, 4727

Single chambered structure built over the Early Byzantine basilica

The excavation in K16 provided evidence for a single-chambered church located over the surviving foundation walls of the Early Byzantine church (Fig. 172). The north wall of this building W514 was three courses high, preserved 0.10 m below the ground surface and measured 6.80 m long. It was constructed over the north stylobate wall W517 of the earlier building. A small curved wall W516 which may be interpreted as the apse of this small church projected 1.60 m east of the structure (Fig. 175). The west wall of the building W513 was the southern return of W514 but stopped after 3 m to form a doorway c. 1 m wide. A line of white marble stones marked the entrance (Fig. 173). The south wall was not excavated but given that the distance from the exterior of the north wall to the centre of the door was c. 3.5 m, it may be suggested that the entire structure including the apse measured 8.4 × 7 m.

The west wall of the later structure W513 was built directly on top of the same mortar layer as the paving in J16. W513 did not survive on the south side of the doorway; but there, the mortar layer was clearly associated with a line of stones which formed part of a fragmented paved floor surface in K16 (Fig. 174). The association of the mortar layer and paving with the fragmented paving further to the east is clear and would suggest they are all contemporary.

The fill of this structure in K16 consisted of rubble and blackened soil (4802). Beneath this fill four column bases arranged in a square and a blackened fragmentary paved floor were uncovered.

The apse W516, found on the east side of the structure, was built onto the internal floor of the much larger apse W512 of the earlier phase (floor = 9610 in K17 and 5633 in L16: Fig. 175). This wall was faced with undressed stones on the east side and had a mortar and rubble core but no surviving facing stones on the west side. It stood to the same elevation height as the north wall W514 and was aligned with the later structure, not the earlier apse.[3]

The elevation of the fragmentary stone floor in K16 (+100.15) was less than that of the top of the surviving stylobate (+100.22–6) onto which the north wall of the later structure was constructed. It also lay below the elevation of the mortar floor to the west of the structure in J16 (+100.32–5) and the mortar floor inside the small apse to the east (+100.43).

Figure 172. *Single-chambered church, looking east.*

Figure 173. *Single-chambered structure, looking SW: fragmented paving with white marble edging and associated mortar beyond.*

Figure 174. *Floor of the chapel/chancel together with the remains of the south wall of the chapel (from SE).*

Figure 175. *Later apse (W516) built onto the internal floor of the much larger earlier apse (W512), looking west.*

The four column bases did not lie on the fragmentary stone floor nor did they fit neatly into it. The best associated of them suggests that they were incorporated into this floor. It was not possible to determine conclusively whether the column bases were brought in at the same time of the construction of this floor or at a later date.

Second phase of later structure

The small apse W516 was blocked in a subsequent phase of the later structure by a crudely built wall W515 (Fig. 175). The base of this wall lay at an elevation lower than the broken paved floor of the structure which had been robbed away on the east side of the structure — suggesting that the blocking had taken place after the destruction of this floor. The masonry of W515 differed substantially from the rest of the building and included *spolia* from an earlier structure: a large broken marble column 0.80 m long, which tapered from 1.59 m circumference to 1.51 m circumference over its length, and a large limestone block with moulding 0.44 × 0.60 × 0.44 m (Fig. 172).

Interpretation

The paved floor on the mortar layer could have occupied the nave of the Early Byzantine church and the broken paved floor could have been part of a bema at the east end of the building — with the four columns serving as the base for a ciborium. If this were the case, the four column bases and paved floor would have been reused following the destruction of the Early Byzantine basilica and incorporated into the construction of the single-chambered building. The line of the chancel screen would have been replaced by the west wall W513, the solea would have become the entrance to the later building which would have adopted the earlier bema floor in the new construction.

One could argue however, that the floors of the Early Byzantine basilica were not found because they had all existed at a level similar to the floor in the north side-chamber — i.e. above the foundation capping stones. These stones no longer survived over the rest of the church foundations. Thus the original floors would have been destroyed following the destruction of the rest of the upper levels of the church, in which case the mortar surface and associated paved floor which survives in the nave must relate to the later phase.

This second proposition is strengthened by the fact that, if the mortar surface in the nave belonged to the primary phase one would not expect the column bases to be sealed beneath it, but instead resting on the stylobates. The positions and elevations of all six column bases would suggest strongly that they also were all placed in a single contemporary building phase secondary to their original use.

Figure 176. *Church, looking west: in foreground late W515, with six columns (191–2) in alignment.*

Thus it may be postulated that in preparation for the construction of the later structure, the six column bases were set down together.

The mortar layer within the earlier nave was laid in order to provide a foundation for the stone pavement which also includes at least one fragment of marble *spolia*. The crushed marble contained within the mortar may well have derived from the burning of the furniture of the early structure.

The stone floor could then have been laid inside the later building together with the column bases. In this position they could thus be argued as contemporary with the later structure.

Single chambered structure units and finds

Topsoil: 4800, 4802
Archit. frag.	4800	K16/3	127
Capital	4802	K16/15	67
Marble panel	4802	K16/14	128

Fill of later structure: 4803–4
Column bases	4804	K16/18–21	192a–d
Glass bangle	4804	K16/17	2146

Deposits inside small apse W516: 4807
Deposits outside small apse inside W512: 4808–9
Dressed stone	4808	K16/28	27
Dec. stone	4808	K16/27	68

Burials east of the single-chambered structure

The area to the east of the later structure was used for burials. During the course of the excavation three burials were found directly east of the later church, and two to the north of the church area. The two to the north and one to the east lay in a stone built cist. The cist to the east was situated directly over the destroyed apse of the early Byzantine church in the SE corner of K16b. This was partly uncovered and planned, but not excavated.[4] A second burial, that of a child, was buried in a hole cut into the north side of the apse — following the discovery of human teeth during cleaning of the pit, this was not formally excavated. The other burial to the east of the church was placed directly in a grave in the ground over the top of the extreme east wall of the early Byzantine basilica. This was completely excavated, primarily with a view to ascertaining a scientific date which might provide a *terminus ante quem* for the destruction of the basilica and might be used to infer a date for the construction and use of the later structure.

Burial 5626 (P98/38)

Beneath some 20–50 cm of topsoil a grave (5626: Fig. 177) was located running E–W in L16a. The cut for the burial was clearly visible at its east end where it cut soil deposits 5622, 5623 and 5624, but was much harder to detect at its west end where it cut the loose rubble fill of the robber trench of W522, excavated later as 5623, 5625 and 5628.

The full length of the grave cut may be estimated to have been *c.* 1.70 m long by 0.50 m at its widest. The burial contained the well-articulated skeleton of a woman buried on her back with her head to the west and feet to the east (**2840**). Her left leg was straight, the right leg slightly bent in order to fit into the grave. Two rectangular stones had been placed lengthwise 41 cm apart on either side of the grave cut. The shoulders seemed to have been hunched to fit the body between these two stones. No other stones or tiles were found

Chapter 16

Figure 177. *L16a, looking south: skeleton **2840** in grave outside east end of church; note stones of W522 beneath skull.*

event seemed to have destroyed the SE part of the single-chambered building and may therefore be seen as comparatively recent.

Summary

The Early Byzantine church at Kilise Tepe was once an imposing structure situated at the highest point on the western side of the mound. It was constructed as a basilica with nave, two aisles, side chambers, apse, eastern passage and irregular-shaped narthex; measuring in total 29 × 16 m. No useful *terminus post quem* was found in deposits beneath the floors or in the construction trenches of the building, which contained latest finds dateable to the Hellenistic period. The church may be attributed to the fourth–fifth centuries AD based on typological comparison of its plan with dated examples from elsewhere. At some point during the latter half of the first millennium AD, the church was almost completely destroyed — so that little more than its foundation walls survived. The site of the church was subsequently reused. There is no evidence to suggest how great the time gap was between the destruction of the first building and the construction of its successor. The later structure was a single-chambered structure lying over the east end of the earlier church. The siting of a smaller chapel over its basilical predecessor is typical at a number of sites in the region. Later structures of this broad type were built over a period of many centuries (Jackson & Postgate 1999, 543), so it is therefore not possible to date the structure simply by typological association with others from elsewhere.

Finding a means to date the later structure during the excavation at Kilise Tepe proved difficult. The discovery of *spolia* from the church in deposits in the NW corner may be interpreted as evidence for reconstruction activity following the destruction of the church. These buildings and features appear to be related to a complex succession of events broadly datable after the fifth century but still within the early Byzantine period.

However, evidence from the excavation shows that the cemetery east of the later church was in use as late as the twelfth century. This may be taken to suggest that the building itself *may* also have been used at that time. There is nevertheless no direct evidence for the construction date of the chapel — which may have been built much earlier. The later structure has at least two architectural phases and the site could have been

in association with the grave. Fill (5626) from the burial contained some mosaic tesserae, a few sherds of pottery and a relatively large number of fine white plaster-like stones less than *c.* 5 cm diameter. The head was tilted slightly to the right and the jaw was open. Beneath the skull was found the handle of a pithos (L16/16). This had been used to prop up the dead woman's head. The woman's left arm had been bent at right angles and laid across her stomach. The fingers of her left hand were clenched in a fist as if holding something no longer surviving e.g. a posy. The right arm was bent at the elbow and the right hand tucked awkwardly almost under the wrist. L16/15 (**2391**) and L16/8 (**2420**) were both metal fragments which came from fill 5626; L16/8 was found very close to, or in, the fragmentary left knee of the skeleton.

Burial 5626 — units and finds
Adult grave: 5626

Human bones	5626	L16/7, 9, 11, 12, 31	2840
Tesserae	5626	L16/5, 17	2205, 2208
Iron frag.	5626	L16/15	2391
Metal/slag	5626	L16/8	2420
Jar handle	5626	L16/16	
Fossil	5626	L16/6	2532

Later robbing of the church site

The southern part of the building suffered extensively from destruction and stone-robbing both during and after the medieval period. Excavations in K16d revealed a single context of rubble (4812) running right down onto the robbed apse wall to a depth of 0.70 m, which was interpreted as fill of a robber trench. The west section of this trench suggested a continuation of the context and was not excavated in view of time pressures during the excavation. The same robbing used as a cemetery even after the building itself fell out of use. Coins from Kilise Tepe dated to the tenth and eleventh centuries (see Konuk, Chapter 47) and a few glazed ceramics, however, were discovered in other parts of the site, which suggest a relatively long period of continued occupation at Kilise Tepe.

A twelfth-century date for the later structure would admittedly complement the dating of certain other single chambered chapels in Cilicia. The evidence from Kilise Tepe as it stands seems to suggest an earlier construction date, but the typologies and dating of these buildings warrant further investigation in the future. If possible the use of further scientific dating techniques would help to resolve the problem of chronology.

The general reduction in scale of churches should not necessarily be considered a result of reduced resources and population but at least in part a response to changes in liturgy. Such a small building would clearly afford very different liturgy from its predecessor but liturgy may have involved the congregation of large numbers, or procession, in the paved area outside the building itself.

The early Byzantine basilica would not only have dominated the settlement on the mound, but would also have been visible from a great distance. The later structure would have been a much less imposing feature of the settlement and would have been a far less conspicuous symbol in the valley.

Notes

1. Eastern corridors and passageways are well attested in Isaurian and Cilician churches (Hill 1996, 28–37).
2. An apse of similar size still stands at the Necropolis Church at Anemurium (Russell 1980, 31–40).
3. It could not, therefore, have been e.g. the remains of a *synthronon* of the earlier building and may be interpreted as an apse.
4. There was some concern, in particular voiced by the local villagers, about whether we should excavate human burials. Time constraints also played a part in the decision not to excavate all those found. It is unfortunate that more skeletons were not recovered, as information on both the dating and osteology of a number of individuals would have been more significant than that from just one.

Acknowledgements

In particular thanks to Prof. J.N. Postgate, and also Dr C. S. Steele, Dr D. Collon, John Gower, and Bronwyn Douglas for advice during the excavation; to Bekir Can, Salih Asgun, Serdar Kılınç and Mehmet Kale, workmen from Kışla, Şarlak and Zeyne. It was very helpful to receive interest in the building from a number of people who provided invaluable discussion at various times in particular Mr J.G. Crow, Dr R. A. Bayliss, Prof. J. Russell, Dr M. Ballance and Dr S. Hill. Any remaining errors are naturally the author's sole responsibility. We would also like to acknowledge the support of the NERC who provided a contribution to the cost of the AMS dating of the femur and offer thanks to Dr P. Pettitt at Oxford AMS Laboratory who conducted the analysis.

Chapter 17

The Northwest Corner

M.P.C. Jackson

Excavations in the NW corner of Kilise Tepe began in 1994; this area of the site was gradually expanded throughout the five-year project with the result that by the end of 1998 a significant amount of Level I material from four main phases had been excavated. Level I features in the NW Corner were found in squares H18b, d; I18a; J18a, b; K18a, b; I19; J19; K19; L19a, c; and K20.

Many of the Level I finds were recovered from unstratified ploughed topsoil. This overburden, c. 0.40 m deep, lay principally over the remaining Level I deposits, except towards the edges of the mound where erosion had caused earlier phases to be exposed nearer the surface.

The interpretation of the four sub-phases within Level I was based on the observation of a Hellenistic pit phase, succeeded by at least three phases of walls. An exterior courtyard surface, which was found to seal the first phase of architecture, was punctured by numerous pits prior to its covering by a succession of later surfaces and fills. The courtyard area therefore records a more complex sequence of sub-phases than the associated buildings.

Unfortunately, no complete interior floor surfaces were found in association with these walls. Excavation suggested that the Level I floor surfaces were more difficult for the excavators to recognize by comparison with earlier period floors. This may be because floors were destroyed when standing walls were levelled to their foundations for the construction of new buildings, or may be due to the greater use of reed matting or carpets in this period (cf. above, p. 37).

The excavation of the NW corner at Kilise Tepe provides evidence for substantial changes in both the scale and the design of buildings and their associated spaces during the first millennium AD. It has yielded substantial quantities of finds including locally produced painted pottery as well as imported ceramics and coins, which were found in comparatively small numbers at this inland site. The excavation of this rural settlement may be contrasted to the urban and ecclesiastical sites which often form the foci of much research into the Early Byzantine period. The results of the NW corner have therefore provided new evidence, for example, on the processing of crops from the surrounding area, as well as for our understanding of changes to this part of the site through time.

Level Ia, Hellenistic phase

The Hellenistic phase in the NW corner of the site consisted almost entirely of pits. These were identified by the diagnostic Hellenistic ceramics which they contained. Only a few additional deposits in the NW corner were excavated which may be considered to have been Hellenistic. These were found in K19 and were associated with the remains of two walls: W610 and W611.

Unit 1578, which was found within the space created by these walls contained Hellenistic ceramics. 1591 was the unit beneath walls W610 and W611, and apparently sealed a further unit 4502. 4502 however contained a coin **2838**, dated c. AD 980–1025. The coin is probably therefore intrusive.

Also in K19, units 1527, 1528, 1567, 1577 and 1583, contained some Hellenistic material; 1577 and 1583 were cut by Level Ib wall W612.

Hellenistic material was found within packing fill 1117 pre-dating the surface 1116, which may have been associated with the Level Ib wall W116 and the occupation deposit 1104.

The whole of the NW area was heavily truncated by pits preceding the Level Ib phase. These pits contained Iron Age as well as Hellenistic finds, which were used to facilitate their dating. The area was substantially levelled prior to the construction of the Level Ib walls. Many of the pits survived only as decapitated bases following these levelling operations. Their relative dating was thus less easily established stratigraphically since the tops of the features were divorced from their former surfaces. Some were characteristic bell-shaped, clay-lined pits (see above, pp. 79–80) that contained a variety of finds. Often they contained burnt material and traces of grain at their bases. This evidence supports the interpretation for their initial purpose as grain storage pits prior to later use as refuse pits.

The dating of certain pits was attributed with some confidence to the Hellenistic period based on the diagnostic ceramics they contained: P94/11 (1311); P96/32 (1517); P96/24 (1521); P97/08 (1573); P97/09 (1575); P97/39 (4500); P97/40 (4501). P97/77, in K19d, was cut down, during Hellenistic times, to the level of the phase IIc floor in Rm 20. This pit's fill (4539) included a piece of Hellenistic crater (**988** but recorded as from unit 4562, IIc destruction) and part of the bronze facing from a Greek hoplite shield (**2272**) with guilloche decoration.

Other pits have been attributed to the Hellenistic period, but their attribution is more tentative due to the nature of the finds within them: P97/16 (1582); P94/17 (1118); P94/22 (1123); P94/7 (1304).

Level Ia (later)

Certain other pits appear to have been dug later than the Hellenistic period, but to pre-date the Level Ib phase. For example, Pit P95/33 (1625/6) is thought to have pre-dated the Level Ib wall W717. Others were sealed by the same courtyard surface which also sealed the Level Ib walls (see below).

Level Ia units and finds
Level Ia Hellenistic Fill: 1117, 1520, 1527–8, 1577, 4502

Pub. ceramic	1117		841
Grinder	1520	K19/84	2764
Quern	1520	K19/469	2765
Pub. ceramics	1527		920, 935
Ceramic disc	1527	K19/53	1535
Tripod leg	1527	K19/52	1618
Arrowhead	1577	K19/180	2253
Iron strip	1577	K19/181	2409
Dog skeleton	1577	K19/135	2499
Coin	4502	K19/185	2838
Antler frag.	4502	K19/182	2493

Hellenistic pits in K19: P94/11 (1311); P96/32 (1517); P96/24 (1521); P97/08 (1573); P97/9 (1575); P97/39 (4500); P97/40 (4501), P97/77 (4539)

Pub. ceramic	1517		968
Ceramic disc	1575	K19/140	1565
Pub. ceramics	4500		840, 870, 1409, 1460
Copper nail	4500	K19/178	2223
Metal/slag	4500	K19/177	2420
Dog skeleton	4500+4501	K19/179	2497
Shield	4539	K19/313	2272

Probable Hellenistic pits: P94/17 (1118), P94/22 (1123), P94/7 (1304), P97/16 (1582)

Later Ia pits which pre-date the post Level Ib courtyard surface: P95/21 (1619–20), P95/32 (1623–4), P95/33 (1625/6), P96/19 (1656), P96/35 (1660), P96/36 (1661), P96/90 (1683)

Pub. ceramics	1626		**1021, 1159–60, 1279, 1368, 1377, 1382, 1402, 1422, 1427, 1433, 1437–41, 1462**
Sp. whorls	1626	J19/79, 83	**1996–7**
Glass bangles	1626	J19/71a–b, 85a–e	**2135–9**
Tesserae	1626	J19/71	**2179**
Copper tang	1626	J19/82	**2220**
Copper chains	1626	J19/409	**2268**
Copper sheet	1626	J19/76	**2288**
Copper shaft	1626	J19/76c	**2235**
Iron frags.	1626	J19/40, 86	**2391**
Metal/slag	1626	J19/439	**2420**
Pub. ceramic	1660		**1367**
Dec. marble	1661	J19/137	**131**
Pub. ceramics	1661		**1386, 1401**
Glass bangle	1661		**2144**
Metal/slag	1661	J19/138	**2420**

Level Ib (Fig. 509)

Introduction

Level Ib was the primary Level I phase of architecture in the NW corner of the mound. The phase was represented by a substantial complex of large interconnecting walls, constructed on a grid pattern.

Excavation revealed the western end of a single building complex larger than the area of excavation. The sub-surface clearance complemented this area and demonstrated that walls of the Level Ib complex continued east into square M20, and appeared to run into M19, which remained unexcavated. The resulting plan illustrates a considerable area of this substantial Level Ib phase building. It was a rectilinear structure, and was aligned roughly E–W (in fact 15° WSW/ENE).

Its relatively large walls measured *c.* 1.00 m wide, although they varied in width by up to about 0.10 m, and were well built from roughly fashioned facing stones *c.* 0.30 × 0.20 × 0.15 m, and a rubble core, which was bonded with clay and mud.

Usually these Level Ib walls were set in shallow wide construction trenches cut into deposits of earlier phases. The fills of these cuts contained a high concentration of residual Iron Age pottery and were characterized by a mixture of rubble debris and loose patches of yellow clay.

No surfaces were found to be clearly associated with the Level Ib walls. Many of the patchy surfaces found lying close to the walls were in fact cut by the foundation trenches and thus belonged to earlier levels. In L19a and L19c, these foundation trenches were clearly identified on the inside of the walls, where they left *in situ* a 'rectangle' of earlier deposits in the area between them.

A clue to the lack of floors associated with the Level Ib walls was found during the excavation of W952 in L19c, where it was demonstrated that these stone walls represented the foundations for a building whose standing walls were made of mud brick. Associated floors may have existed therefore at a level near to the tops of the stone foundations and the bottoms of the mud brick. If this was the case, then surfaces associated with the Level Ib phase in the area to the north and west would have been removed in the past, probably by subsequent levelling activity.

The Level Ib phase plan suggests that the building complex measured c. 15.20 m N–S, and at least 21.5 m E–W. The lack of walls in the NW of the trench may be due partly to its proximity to the edge of the mound where erosion is greatest.

The excavation exposed 16.80 m of the south façade of the complex, which continued unexcavated further into L19d. The wall was broken at its west end by a well-constructed 'opening' 6.25 m wide. On the east side of the area, in squares L19 and L20, were three similar-sized rectangular rooms, lying parallel to each other. The wide opening in the south wall provided access to a large rectangular space immediately to the west of Rm 3. The north wall of the complex (W116) was poorly preserved.

Detailed discussion of Level Ib
The excavated part of the south wall of the complex measured 21.5 m long. It ran from J18 to L19c and was represented by wall numbers W421 in J18, W612 in K19d, and W952 in L19c. This was not the full length of the wall, which continued further into L19d where it remains unexcavated. Wall W421 (3.92 m long), represented the west side of a 6.25-m-wide opening in the south wall, the east side of which was formed by W612 in K19d. The ends of both walls forming the 'opening' were well preserved. W612 ran east into L19c as W952.

The sub-surface clearance in L20 revealed a return of the north wall W202, i.e. W203; this may have run south to meet W952 in L19d. Further evidence for the tops of features from the sub-surface clearance in M20 however, appears to represent a possible continuation and return of the north wall W202 in M20b to meet W214 and form a building at least 33 m E–W (see Fig. 510). This suggests that the complex may have been considerably larger than that excavated. The SE part of the building where the deposits are deepest remains unexcavated.

The SW corner of the complex was located in J18b where the west wall W717 and the south wall W421 joined. W717 ran north for 5.40 m into J19d where it was damaged by a large modern robber hole (Fig. 178). Just beyond the robber hole, W717 ended abruptly c. 1.20 m from the north side of J19d.

W717 ran parallel with, and 1.60 m to the east of, a similar wall: W425. At its south end, W425 ran into the south section of J18b heading in the direction of the church; at its north end, W425 was truncated by the same modern pit as W717. No trace of W425 was found any further to the north. The robber hole removed stone from both walls and the material between them, removing any possibility of establishing a direct relationship between the two. Their similar scale and alignment however suggest that there was a link between these walls and perhaps also W700 to the east, but no direct evidence was provided by the excavation to support this.

Three rooms, aligned E–W, were created by the walls at the east end of the excavated part of the complex. They were constructed from a grid of internal and external walls all of similar scale and all built as part of the same operation.

The relatively good preservation of the structures in L19a and L19c enables the majority of the dimensions of the rooms to be measured and others given with some confidence. The most southerly: Rm 1 measured 4.16 × 6 m (reconstructed), Rm 2 measured 3.20 × 6 m, and the northern Rm 3 measured 3.60 × 6 m.

Stone wall W952, representing the south wall of Rm 1, was the best preserved of all the Level Ib walls. The top of this wall was +101.22 and base +100.13. At the east end, where it survived best, it stood to 1.10 m high, i.e. six courses. Here, it was found to be topped by a mudbrick upper wall. This evidence may be used to propose that all the standing walls of this building were made of mud brick and that the stone walls found merely represented the foundations for the mudbrick courses. Unfortunately, no internal floor surfaces associated with this wall were located. However, in the NW corner of Rm 1, a fire installation FI98/1 (fill 5915) was found. This was uncovered at the base of topsoil (5906) in L19a on a patchy surface (5911) that was not found to run up to W953. A second tannour FI98/2 was found crossing the centre of L19. The western half was excavated, but the eastern half was not. Further excavation might resolve whether this feature and the associated floor belonged to this phase or an earlier feature preserved beneath the building.

The north parts of Level Ib, Rms 2 and 3, were uncovered by the sub-surface clearance. The south part of Rm 2 was excavated in L19a where there was little evidence for contemporary surfaces and features. However, damage was noted on the north side of W954, which had been the result of later activity.

Another wall, W700 in K19, continued the line of W954 for about 5 m into the centre of K19. K19 was to become the location for a large concentration of Level Id activity that removed any further evidence for W700. Some of the later walls appeared to respect or reuse the west end of W700 (see Level Id description and combined Level Ib/d phase Fig. 509).

Figure 178. *J19d, looking south: tumble from W717, lying on surface 1605; cut by modern robber pit P95/33.*

W116, the north wall of the complex near the edge of the mound, appears to have been less well preserved, or possibly less well constructed, than the walls to the south. W116 ran for 12 m WSW–ENE across the north side of J20d, K20c and K20d, until it joined W202 and the north end of W708 in the SE corner of K20b. It was set in a visible foundation trench. A short return of this wall was found in J20.

Phase Ib in I19c/d and H18b/d

In I19c/d a large stone wall W750 was found running E–W below the packing layer (1733, 1740–42, 1744) for Level Id walls W727 and W729. This wall was 7 m long and returned to the south at its west end. The return was rediscovered in I18a as W814, which then returned east as W815. These walls were interpreted as Level Ib walls since they predated the Level Id phase and were of similar construction to the other Level Ib walls. The packing layers below W727 and the ash layers contained Hellenistic pottery. Fill from east of W814 and north of W815 was recovered as 2711 but it contained no diagnostic ceramics later than Iron Age.

Deposits associated with the Level Ib walls

In J18 the division between the Level II deposits and the Level I deposits was a 2–5 cm spit of packing deposits (2353–4). This was removed to reveal Level IIf mudbrick benches beneath. The Level Ib walls W425 (base +100.13) and W421 in J18a and K18a (base +100.21) were built directly onto the packing layers (2353–4).

On the west side of W425 was deposit 2344 which contained no diagnostic ceramics. Two units of fill lay on the packing layers to the east of W425: 2343 and 2350. 2343 was excavated from between W421 and W425 and 2350 from the area to the south of the walls. Both of these units contained a high concentration of painted sherds.

In J18b, W425 and 2344 were subsequently sealed by units 2337 and 2339, which represented the original surface of a later courtyard. The equivalent surface in J18a was 2311.

All the deposits in this area associated with the large walls W421 and W425 therefore lay above the Level IIf Iron Age phase and beneath the courtyard surface. Thus 2311, 2337 and 2339 post-dated the destruction of walls W421 and W425 and the deposits (2343 and 2350) found associated with them. Surface 2311 contained a very worn mid–late fourth-century AD coin (**2835**). Units 2337 and 2339 contained significant quantities of Fabric 1 painted ceramics.

The Level Ib walls in L19 were found in construction trench 5929 which cut the earlier Iron Age deposits (5921).

Pit P95/33 (1625/6) in J19d, which was apparently sealed by W717, was the latest dated feature to be cut by a Level Ib wall. It contained five partially preserved cooking vessels and a very high proportion of cooking pot sherds. The pit also contained a few small fragments of fine, black-slipped pottery and three sherds of painted pottery. The excavator worried about contamination by a modern robber pit which cuts the west side of P95/33 (Fig. 178). A flotation sample revealed the presence of pistachios, almonds, olives, lentils, and free-threshing wheat (see Bending, Appendix 1.7 samples 22–3).

To the north and south of W116 in K20 external surface 1103, and possible occupation fill 1104 were considered by the excavator to be associated with the wall. Three pits to the north of the wall were located, but only P94/13 was excavated. It contained a Cypriot Red Slip ware rim dated to the late Roman period fifth–sixth century AD. There was however no direct evidence to suggest a link between the dates of the pit and the dating of W116 in this area.

Level Ib units and finds

Level II pits cut by Level Ib walls: P96/40 (1530); P96/53 (1537)

Pot stand	1537	K19/56	1619
Iron haft	1537	K19/57	2325

Packing above Level II deposits: 2311, 2344, 2353–4

Pub. ceramics	2311		1294, 1431
Glass bangle	2311	J18/53	2124
Tesserae	2311	J18/56–7, 62	2171–3
Iron nail	2311	J18/52	2383
Iron nail	2311	J18/54	2388
Iron frags.	2311	J18/55	2419
Metal/slag	2311	J18/50, 59	2420
Coin	2311	J18/58	2835
Glass bangles	2344	J18/121a–b	2125–6
Fossil	2344	J18/113	2531
Pub. ceramic	2354		1109

Possible refuse dump lying on packing above Level II, between Level Ib walls: 2343, 2350, 2711

Lamp	2343	J18/120+147	996
Pub. ceramics	2343		1017, 1029, 1062, 1096, 1150, 1175–6, 1190, 1193–5, 1216, 1218, 1299, 1334, 1405
Glass rim	2343	J18/114a	2085
Glass rim	2343	J18/114b	2107
Iron nails	2343	J18/119	2343
Fossil	2343	J18/123	2505
Slingshot	2343	J18/117	2625
Pub. ceramics	2350		1151–2, 1305, 1364
Iron nail	2350	J18/134	2334

Fill of Ib wall foundation trenches: 1114 (W116)
Fill around Ib walls: 1571
Possible Ib occupation surfaces: 1103–4, 1915, 5911

Iron nail	1104	K20/13	2333
Iron blade	1915	K20/92	2320
Lamp	5911	L19/14	992

Features on possible Ib surfaces: F195/2 (1909), F198/1 (5915) on surface 5911, F198/2 (5933)

Tessera	1909	K20/63	2202

Level I features cutting same earlier deposits as Level Ib walls: P94/13 (1105) late Roman or later, P94/14 (1107), P94/10 (1307), P97/8 (1573)

Incised pebble	1105	K20/17	2607

The external courtyard surface

The levelled Level Ib walls in the centre of the NW corner were sealed by an external courtyard surface which was uncovered in J19, J18a–b, the east side of I19d and K18a.

The patchy nature of the surface, and the excavation of each quadrant at different times meant that the original courtyard surface was not clearly traced across the entire area. It is tentatively suggested, however, that the following units probably represent the primary phase of the courtyard: in J18a, 2308; in J18b, 2337; in I19, 1733 and 1729; in J19d, 1605; in J19b, 1627; and 1651 in J19a/c.

Lying on surface 2308 an important collection of finds were discovered: iron nails (**2340–42**), a broken cross (**2294**), a sickle blade and other iron blades (**2312–13**), a finger ring (**2266**), fragments of glass (**2122**), shells, and mosaic tesserae (**2170, 2178**). 1627 was noted to have contained a large amount of Byzantine roof tiles.

In J18b, 2337 seals the Level Ib walls (W421 and W425); therefore, this courtyard surface clearly post-dates the destruction of the Level Ib phase in that quadrant. However in J19d, the remnant of foundation wall W717 (1606) protrudes through the courtyard surface (1605) and stone tumble from the wall W717 lay on its east side on surface 1605 (Fig. 178).

External courtyard units and finds
Initial courtyard: 1605, 1627, 1651, 1729, 1733, 1740, 2308, 2337, 2339

Pub. ceramics	1605		1036, 1271, 1322, 1376, 1458
Ribbed sherd	1605	J19/462	1158
Glass bangle	1605	J19/33	2130
Tessera	1605	J19/33b	2210
Wick holder	1605	J19/34	2278
Pub. ceramics	2308		1295, 1394, 1429
Glass bangle	2308	J18/36	2122
Tesserae	2308	J18/42, J19/43a	2170, 2178
Copper ring	2308	J18/40	2266
Copper cross	2308	J18/34	2294
Iron sickle	2308	J18/35	2312
Iron blades	2308	J18/39	2313
Iron nails	2308	J18/32, 37–8	2340–42
Human bone	2308	J18/414	2886
Pub. ceramics	2337		1174, 1300
Tessera	2337	J18/111	2174
Pub. ceramics	2339		1098, 1149, 1191, 1247, 1291, 1347, 1349, 1398
Cooking pot	2339		1436

Pits post-dating the courtyard surface

The surface of the courtyard was subsequently cut by numerous pits, many of which were clay-lined. The contents of the clay-lined pits suggests that they

Figure 179. *J19a, looking north: column base 190 in situ in P96/17.*

were used initially for the storage of grain at various stages of processing, but that they were later used as refuse pits.

Six pits were cut through 1651 which spread over quadrants J19a and J19c. They were cut either directly through 1651 or from a later deposit.

One of the pits P96/17 (fill 1653) contained a column base similar to those reused in the church (Fig. 179; see also Fig. 176). The reuse of architecture from the church is also paralleled in P95/6 in K20, which re-used a capital fragment in its lining (Figs. 182 & 183).

The clay-lined pits contained fairly homogeneous fills, with occasional stone, ceramic, metal and bone inclusions. Some display evidence of burning on pit bases.

Pits cutting courtyard units and finds
Pits cutting courtyard 1651 in J19a/c: P96/11 (1653; J19a); P96/16 (1652; J19a/c); P96/17 (1654; J19a); P96/21 (1658; J19c)

Pub. ceramic	1653		1358
Sp. whorl	1653	J19/125	1998
Glass bangle	1653	J19/140a	2143
Tesserae	1653	J19/115, 124, 140b	2180–82
Iron nail	1653	J19/111	2388
Iron pin	1653	J19/139	2389
Metal/slag	1653	J19/126	2420
Pub. ceramic	1652		1421
Column base	1654	J19/106	190

Pits cutting courtyard 1627 in J19b: P95/14 (1603–4); P95/15 (1608–10); P95/16 (1611–12); P95/17 (1613–14); P95/31 (1621–2)

Dressed stone	1604	J19/29	24
Marble slab	1604	J19/28	79
Pub. ceramics	1604		685, 1303, 1308
Tesserae	1604	J19/25, 31	2176–7
Copper ring	1604	J19/445	2269
Copper shaft	1604	J19/26	2235
Metal/slag	1604	J19/30	2420
Coin	1604	J19/27	2837
Dressed stone	1609	J19/42	25
Pub. ceramic	1609		922
Glass bangles	1609	J19/38, 43	2131–2
Pub. ceramic	1610		1399
Glass bangle	1610	J19/48	2133
Grinder	1611	H18/170	2775
Pub. ceramic	1621		1313
Bead frag.	1621	J19/62	2023
Marble column	1622	J20/66	125
Column base	1622	J19/66	190
Glass bangle	1622	J19/68	2134

Pit cutting courtyard 1605 in J19d:
Modern robber pit

Pits cutting courtyard 2337 in J18b: P97/37 (2338); P97/44 (2352)

Pub. ceramic	2338		1211
Ceramic disc	2338	J18/159	1576
Iron link	2338	J18/142	2400
Pub. ceramic	2352		1456

Pits cutting courtyard 2308 in J18a:
P97/1 (2305)

Level Ic (Fig. 509)

In K18b, W430 blocks part of the large opening in the Level Ib phase wall represented by W421 and W612. A distinctive external surface was connected to the west side of W430. It consisted of bluish-black, rounded river cobbles *c*. 15 cm in size which had been laid both on their sides and flat.

The external surface ran from W430 across K18b west into the extreme SE corner of K18a, at a height of +100.33 where part of the Level Id courtyard surface not laid on cobbles (4320) ran over it. This surface was uncovered running southwards as far as the north side-chamber of the church. The surface between these buildings was cut by two later unexcavated burials in K18d and K17b.

W430 ran diagonally across K18b in a NW–SE direction 35 cm below the topsoil. It was 6.95 m long, 0.60 m wide and 4 courses high and was differentiated from the later Level Id walls by its more substantial construction, lower elevation, and orientation. Its top lay at an elevation of +100.76 and its base at +100.19. The most distinctive aspect of this Level Ic wall was the way the stones used in its construction were laid on their sides rather than flat.

W430 represented the west wall of a building and was bonded at its south end to W432. W432 ran east, perpendicular to W430 from K18b into L18a, where it remains unexcavated. A less substantial and slightly curved wall W431 (top +100.74, base +100.48) lay inside the room creating an internal partition wall.

The fill of the room between the walls W430 and W432 and the internal partition wall W431 was excavated as unit 4395, and lay on top of a packing deposit (6101), at +100.50. A large concentration of Byzantine pottery including one almost complete painted vessel in fragments and a second half-preserved (**1094, 1112**) were recovered from the fill (4395) within this space created by W430 and W431.

The ceramics from the fill of this Level Ic room included painted pottery with spiral decorations similar to those found in 2343 between Level Ib walls W421 and W425.

Level Ic units and finds
Floors: 6101
Room fill: 4393, 4395

Metal/slag	4393	K18/202	2420
Pub. ceramics	4395		1094, 1112, 1127, 1239, 1246, 1283

Level Id (Figs. 509–10)

Introduction
Excavation in the NW corner clearly revealed a phase of architecture just beneath the plough soil. These

walls were found to lie at a higher elevation than the Level Ib walls; some ran over the remains of Level Ib structures, demonstrating that they represented a phase post-dating the Level Ib architecture and deposits. This was the latest phase of architecture in this part of the site and was named Level Id.

Level Id walls were recognized principally in K19, K20, and L19 (Fig. 509). A second set of walls, also interpreted as Level Id, was found on the west side of the area in I19. The Level Id walls were much less substantial than the Level Ib walls. They measured c. 60 cm wide and mostly survived one or two courses high.

No Level Id architecture was found in J18 and J19 in what is presumed to have been an open courtyard area between buildings. There, the Level Id phase was represented by a dense concentration of ashy layers interspersed with surfaces, totalling up to 50 cm in depth. Like the Level Id walls, these ashy deposits clearly post-dated remains of Level Ib walls but also post-dated the pits cut into the base of the courtyard. On the NW side of the area, where the mound begins to slope downhill, there were no Level Id deposits.

The excavation demonstrated that unlike the Level Ib walls, which were built as a single operation, the subsequent activity provides evidence for a succession of construction events grouped for interpretation as Levels Ic and Id. These walls are complemented by the large number of surfaces and fills excavated in the courtyard area. The Level Id walls however, although broadly contemporary with each other, were not constructed simultaneously as a single complex, but appear to have built up gradually over a period of time. The general picture portrayed by the evidence for the Level Id phase is of a set of structures representing a much less ordered and more haphazard approach to construction than those of the Level Ib phase.

The way in which a number of Level Id walls seem to respect the Level Ib phase walls, in particular in K19, suggests that the earlier walls were to some extent reused and incorporated within the later phase. The Level Ib walls appear to have survived in parts, at least as visible foundations, into the period represented by the Level Id phase. The tops of the Level Ib walls, for example, were covered by the bottom layer of ash deposits in the courtyard area in J18b, and were reused for the foundations of two later walls W951 and W950 in L19. Although the Level Id walls may at times have reused sections of surviving wall from earlier periods, in general they do not replicate or follow the regular grid-like pattern of the Level Ib walls. They form a variety of different shaped internal and external spaces. The major limitation in our understanding of this phase was caused by robbing and re-use of stone in the past as well as by ploughing and erosion on the surface of the mound in more recent times. This destroyed parts of some walls and surfaces making the interpretation of their relationships problematic.

The description of the Level Id deposits will begin with those associated with structures on the east side of the courtyard. It will then describe deposits excavated on the west side of the courtyard, followed by those comprising the courtyard area itself.

The east side of the courtyard

In K19, the Level Id walls form a variety of irregular-shaped internal spaces. To some extent the walls of this phase, in particular those running E–W, respect the lines of the earlier Level Ib walls. This demonstrates some continued influence of the previous phases on the form of the later structures. The walls formed what appears to have been a complex arrangement of small rooms. Although there may have been sub-phases within the Level Id phase which have not survived, it would appear that some of the earlier structures continued to stand contemporarily with the later ones.

The surface below the plough soil in K19d, 1567 was very ashy. The corresponding surface in K19c was 1502 and 1564; these units contained some Hellenistic material, which was presumably residual from earlier phases.

The plough soil in K19d (1500 and 1501) appeared in fact to have been the disturbed fill of the buildings in this part of the site. Both units contained substantial quantities of painted Fabric 1 sherds including painted local pottery and imported Late Roman wares. Similar sherds were found in the fills of the structure in K18b whose SW wall was represented by the Phase Ic wall W430. Few finds other than pottery were discovered associated with the units in K19. The stratigraphic integrity of most of these fills was not without question, because of the ploughing and lack of clearly identifiable internal floors.

The west and north sides of the Level Id building were formed by walls W704, W701 and W702. Butting onto the north end of Level Ic wall W430, W704 ran for c. 10 m in a NW direction continuing the line of W430 at an orientation slightly more to the north. Wall W704 ran roughly parallel to the east walls of the excavated part of the building W951 and W703. The south wall was W950.

The partial uncovering of W950 in L19c demonstrated that the building was larger than the excavated area. It ran from the unexcavated quadrant L19d, across L19c to the SW corner of K19d in a WSW direction. The excavated length of W950 was c. 10 m. It consisted of two lines of large facing stones with a rubble core, and measured 18 cm high and 68 cm

Chapter 17

Figure 180. *Level Id Rm B in K19, looking NW: W704 to the west with W705 running up to and over W612 in foreground.*

Figure 181. *K20d, looking NE: stone-lined P95/6 in foreground.*

wide. Some courses contained stones that were laid diagonally on their edges. W950 was abutted by W591.

Level Id Rm A

W950 ran over Level Ib wall W952; similarly, W591 ran north almost perpendicular to W950 crossing over the top of Level Ib wall W593. Together W950 and W951 formed the SE corner of a space, which has been called Rm A. The north end of W951 was poorly preserved.

Level Id Rm B

A space called Rm B, *c*. 5 × 3 m was aligned NW–SE along the east side of W704. Rm B was bounded by W706 to the south and a short length of wall running over W700 to the north, and by W705 to the east (Fig. 180). W705 measured only 1.90 m and was very poorly preserved; but its short length may in fact demonstrate that the room had a large entrance on the east side. Fill excavated from Rm B in K19d was 1510, the continuation of topsoil 1501; both were considered by the excavator to represent occupation deposits. This interpretation was supported by the large number of finds in this area compared to other quadrants. A coin **2839** dated to the late eleventh century was found in 1514. This was the coin with the latest date found at Kilise Tepe. Another slightly earlier coin **2838** (4502; mentioned above, p. 199) was found in the same square apparently below its original depositional context.

Level Id Rm C

Immediately north of Rm B, was a small space, labelled Rm C, which was bounded by W701 to the north and W704 to the west. A doorway was located in the gap between walls W701 and W702. A door socket (di. 13 cm), was found at the east end of W701.

One of the most interesting features in this phase was discovered in K20d. A row of three postholes was uncovered below the topsoil bounded to the north by the contemporary wall W707 (Fig. 181). One of these postholes, pit P95/6 (1902), incorporated in its lining part of a carved stone capital (**132**).[1] This reused architectural fragment presumably had come originally from part of a monumental building. It is tempting to suggest that the capital came from the church and to attribute the Level Id pit to a construction event at some point after the destruction of the church (Figs. 182 & 183).

W707 (1903), ran due ENE across K20d. There was no clear association between W707 and wall W701/W702. It represented a relatively poorly preserved Level Id wall 3 m long, 0.80 m wide. No trace of it was found during the sub-surface clearance in L20c.

East side of courtyard units and finds
Plough soil interpreted as disturbed occupation deposit: 1500–501

Dressed stone	1500	K19/5	29
Pub. ceramics	1500	1053, 1057, 1063, 1072, 1076, 1080	
Ring	1500	K19/4	2408
Pub. ceramics	1501	974, 1011, 1013, 1015–16, 1032, 1035, 1038, 1064, 1081, 1090, 1092, 1097, 1161–70, 1173, 1183, 1200, 1205–6, 1210, 1232, 1248–52, 1273, 1282, 1314, 1316, 1318–19, 1324, 1326, 1330, 1335, 1343, 1359, 1385, 1391, 1396, 1428	
Clay seal?	1501	K19/17	1477
Clay wheel	1501	K19/13	1526
Glass sherd	1501	K19/434a	2091

Figure 182. *P95/6 before excavation, looking south.*

Figure 183. *P95/6 after excavation, looking north.*

Glass handle	1501	K19/430, 434b	**2100–101**
Glass bases	1501	K19/8c, 431	**2112, 2115**
Glass bangle	1501	K19/8d	**2151**
Iron nail	1501	K19/14	**2388**
Lithic scraper	1501	K19/15	**2555**
Quern	1501	K19/10	**2763**
Grinders	1501	K19/9, 476	**2777, 2779**
Juglet	1501+1512	K19/479	**1027**

Fill between walls: 1514

Pub. ceramics	1514		**862, 1207, 1209, 1451**
Sp. whorls	1514	K19/26, 27, 31	**1928, 1960, 1978**
Coin	1514	K19/28	**2839**

Occupation surfaces below plough soil: 1502, 1510, 1564, 1567

Clay disc	1564	K19/111	**1593**
Glass bangles	1564	K19/107a–b	**2152–3**
Pub. ceramics	1567		**1071, 2264**
Copper wire	1567	K19/123	**2264**
Iron nails	1567	K19/119	**2331**
Astragalus	1567	K19/116	**2450**
Fossil	1567	K19/127	**2528**

Cut associated directly with Level Id walls: P95/6: 1902, 1906

Capital	1902	K20/52	**132**
Sp. whorl	1906	K20/59	**1985**

The west side of the courtyard (I18/19)

The courtyard to the west of wall W704 was c. 12 m wide and was flanked on the west side by W727 in I19d. W727, which measured 3.6 m, and ran roughly N–S, lay on the east side of an area of paved surface in I19d; the second wall, W729, of the same construction as W727, ran along the south side of the paving. Evidence for a mortar and chipped stone feature running along the north side of the pavement suggested that there had once been a wall here but that it had been subject to erosion.

The area of paving stones (1701) was constructed onto a compact yellow clay surface (1702), which represented the surface of the courtyard to the east. Therefore this building immediately post-dated the earliest phase of the courtyard.

This surface and the surviving two walls by which it was bounded were atypical of other excavated Level I buildings. The walls were both bonded with lime mortar and pebble aggregate. These walls were unusual since most Level I walls were made from stone bonded with clay. Lime mortar was discovered to the south of this area in I17c to the NW of the church. The only other place lime mortared walls were located outside the church area was in N20 and O20 (see the sub-surface clearance, p. 212).

To the east of W727, a series of surfaces with ash deposits interspersed filled the courtyard as far as W704 in K19. The latest surface in the courtyard area in I19d was 1729, the equivalent of 1649 in J19. The precise stratigraphic relationship between this surface and wall W727 was removed by an animal burrow.

I18a Level Id

P96/88, probably cut from topsoil, its fill consisting of stones, removed the north limit of W775 in I18a. The north edge of the cut was located in I19d where its fill was 1732.

West side of courtyard units and finds
Packing below Level Id walls and courtyard layers post-dating Level Ib walls: 1702–3, 1733, 1740–42, 1744

Bone tube	1744	I19/210	**2477**

Paved floor: 1701
P96/88: 1732, 2701–3

Pub. ceramic	1732		**1411**
Glass bangles	1732	I19/23	**2118**
Fossil	1732	I19/22	**2510a**
Archit. frag.	2701	I18/5, 10	**63, 139**

Glass base	2701	I18/6	2105
Mortar	2701	I18/9	2691
Metal/slag	2702	I18/7	2420
Stone basin	2703	I18/11	57
Tessera	2703	I18/16	2167

The later deposits in the courtyard area

The initial courtyard surface which was cut by numerous pits (discussed above, p. 199) was subsequently covered in a series of ashy fills and surfaces. In total, these were about 50 cm deep and were best preserved and most meticulously excavated in J19c and I19d, but continued into I19, J18a and J18b. Painstaking excavation in J19c and I19d revealed four layers of ash fill lying between a series of five surfaces. The latest ash fill in J19c and I19d was (1648=1730) which was sealed by the latest surface (1649=1729) at +100.45–50.

This operation demonstrated that these were almost sterile layers with few finds or ceramics; for this reason the same deposits were dug as a single unit in J18a as 2306, and in J19b and J19d as 1602. It was noted that the ash in J18a contained numerous medium-sized stones. The ash deposits in J18b (2329 and 2330) were less deep than those to the NW.

The sequence of ash layers and surfaces respected the Level Id walls in K19, and respected W727 in I19. Some of the surfaces were extensive, others very patchy. The courtyard sloped towards the NW and the ash layers were found to be deepest in J19 near the bottom of the downward slope.

The ash layers were not found in K18, where a later surface of the courtyard ran over the cobbled surface associated with Level Ic wall W430 in K18b.

Units in K18a excavated to the west and east of wall W420 included 4304, 4307 and 4308. W420 curved northwards from the south intersection of J18b and K18a where it remained unexcavated.

Later deposits in the courtyard area units and finds
Ash layers: 1644, 1646, 1648, 1650, 1730, 1737, 1739
Marble tile	1650	J19/102	80
Glass bangles	1650	J19/104–5	2141–2
Antler frag.	1650	J19/100	2493

Surfaces: 1643, 1645, 1647, 1649, 1651, 1729, 1731, 1733, 1738, 1740
Mixed ash and surfaces: 1602, 2306, 2329–30
Pub. ceramics	1602		1107, 1154–7, 1312, 1387, 1432
Glass bangle	1602	J19/19	2129
Tesserae	1602	J19/20	2175
Iron nails	1602	J19/18, 448	2344, 2378
Metal/slag	1602	J19/16, 403	2420
Iron nail	2306	J18/23	2339
Flaked lithic	2306	J18/20	2590

Units in K18a below topsoil associated with W420: 4303–4, 4306–9
Pub. ceramics	4303		1238, 1244, 1351, 1361, 1453
Pub. ceramic	4304		1331
Pub. ceramics	4307		1095, 1180, 1224, 1325, 1338, 1342, 1352, 1397
Copper bracelet	4307	K18/24	2215
Metal/slag	4307	K18/26	2420
Pub. ceramics	4308		1066, 1117, 1188, 1212, 1336, 1341, 1416
Glass bangle	4308	K18/31	2150
Iron handle	4308	K18/39	2418
Lithic chips	4308	K18/32	2586
Pub. ceramics	4309		1030, 1118–19, 1222, 1241, 1259, 1269, 1284
Glass	4309	K18/29	2088
Grinder	4309	K18/28	2779

Units in K18a/b, below W420, above exterior courtyard surfaces: 4310, 4312–14, 4316–17, 4320, 4397–8
Iron nail	4310	K18/38	2388
Stone vessel	4310	K18/35	2642
Grinder	4310	K18/36	2775
Grinder	4312	K18/41	2770
Human bone	4312	K18/265	2885
Lamp	4314	K18/67	995
Pub. ceramics	4314		1042, 1048, 1120, 1221, 1275, 1285
Iron nails	4314	K18/44, 63	2388, 2336
Antler frag.	4314	K18/61	2493
Pub. ceramic	4316		1378
Glass	4316	K18/48	2089
Pub. ceramics	4317		1050, 1355
Pub. ceramics	4320		1067, 1181
Glass	4320	K18/59	2090
Glass handle	4320	K18/60	2098
Pub. ceramics	4397		1128, 1274

Level Ie

To the west of W430, i.e. outside the building, patches of a possible surface were found at +100.68, below lower topsoil (4392), which contained glass, and a stone and cobble scatter.

In J18 an isolated patch of trampled surface (2302) was found beneath topsoil deposits at +100.75. A number of finds were discovered on this surface including dressed stone. This surface sealed a pit P97/1 (2305) which was cut into ash deposits (2306) (see below) and contained: a green glazed sherd, a knobbed amphora handle and painted Fabric 1a pottery.

Level Ie units and finds
Surface: 2302, 4392
| Pub. ceramics | 4392 | | 1051, 1086, 1099, 1125, 1277, 1337, 1340, 1357 |

P97/1 (2305)
| Pub. ceramics | 2305 | | 1054, 1148, 1420 |
| Iron strip | 2305 | J18/24 | 2410 |

Conclusion

The earliest phase of Level I in this area was represented by a series of Hellenistic pits, Level Ia. No other features excavated in this part of the site could be assigned securely to the Hellenistic period except for two fragmentary walls W611 and W610. Hellenistic pottery was found associated with very few other features.

Level Ib walls were the most substantial of the Level I architecture from the NW corner. They survived only as stone foundations for a large rectilinear complex that was well planned and built in a single operation.

Evidence from L19 suggests that these foundations would have been topped by mudbrick standing walls. The best-preserved features of the building phase were three rooms lying next to each other in L20 and L19, and a large opening 6.25 m wide on the south side of the complex.

The Level Ib foundation walls had been cut into earlier Iron Age deposits. They also appear to post-date W611 and W610, the walls associated with the Level Ia Hellenistic pit phase. This stratigraphic relationship suggests that the Level Ib phase was later than the Hellenistic pit phase, but is proposed with some hesitation because of the scanty survival of Hellenistic deposits. The most reliable dating evidence associated with the Level Ib walls comes from a significant dump of pottery (2343) including locally painted sherds and an LRA3 amphora toe. This material was found, apparently dumped, between two phase Ib walls sealed under a later external courtyard surface.

The external courtyard was located in J19, J18a/b, K18a/b and I19d. This surface apparently sealed earlier phases which had been levelled beneath it, including the Level Ib wall complex. In J18a the Iron Age deposits below the courtyard were sealed by 2311, a packing deposit which contained a very worn mid–late fourth-century AD coin (**2835**). This lowest level of the courtyard must, therefore, date from after the fourth-century date of the coin. In J19b, the surface of the courtyard was cut by a number of pits including P95/14 (1604), which contained a mid fifth-century coin (**2837** - dated Leo I AD 457–74); P95/14 must therefore date later than the mid fifth century.

The exact dating of these deposits will depend on the period of circulation of these two coins i.e. the time between their minting and their burial. The date of the courtyard surface is potentially significant since it seals the Level Ib wall phase, together with a significant amount of painted pottery from 2343. A mid fifth-century date for the surface, for example, would suggest both that the Level Ib phase had been destroyed, and that the locally painted pottery had been in use at Kilise Tepe prior to that date.

The initial surface of the open 'courtyard' area in J18 and J19 also contained a number of interesting finds including a metal cross and iron objects. Following the puncturing of the courtyard by the pits, it was covered by a sequence of ash fills interspersed with external floor deposits.

Phase Ic is represented by a small set of secondary walls that were built onto the SE side of the earlier Level Ib complex blocking part of the large opening in the south wall. Clearly they respect the earlier phase but represent a substantial alteration to its original design. The Level Id phase appears to have been an extension to the initial construction of the Level Ic walls.

Pottery from within the space created by the Level Ic walls was found in units 4393 and 4395. These ceramics consisted of many late Roman amphorae fragments and Fabric 1 painted sherds including two almost complete closed vessel profiles. This therefore represented a very similar assemblage to that excavated as 2343, found between the two Level Ib walls in J18. It was also very similar to 1501 excavated below the topsoil in K19.

The latest architectural phase identified in the NW corner was named Level Id. This was represented principally by a network of stone foundation walls, which may be divided into two groups: one in the east and one in the west of the excavated area, separated by the courtyard area in between. The walls on the east side were best preserved in K19 where they were found to have been built on top of the earlier levelled Phase Ib walls, using them as foundations. They were however much less ordered than those of the earlier Level Ib phase, and would have formed a variety of irregular-shaped rooms and spaces. In general, the walls of the Level Id phase had been subject to considerable damage by ploughing, and represented the lower foundations of walls built across the tops of the earlier Level Ib phase walls. Fill found in association with these walls contained significant quantities of pottery. This material, although not well sealed appeared not to have been substantially contaminated and must therefore have been relatively well protected from ploughing and post-depositional movement by the surrounding walls. Unfortunately, floor surfaces were not identified so the potential of linking the ceramics securely to either of the wall phases was limited. The major levelling of the Level Ib walls suggests a possible period of abandonment prior to the subsequent construction phases.

Very scanty evidence for later occupation (Level Ie) was found in J19 where a late surface was cut by a bell-shaped pit P97/1 (2305). The pit contained, among other things one of the only sherds of glazed pottery recovered from the site.

Phasing summary

Level Ia (second century BC) - Hellenistic pit and wall phase;

Level Ib - Area levelled and large walls constructed;

Early fifth century AD - destruction and levelling of large wall phase; destruction sealed by laying of the initial courtyard surface;

Mid fifth century AD - pits dug into initial courtyard;

Level Ic - secondary wall phase; Level Ic courtyard predates the later phase of courtyard in K18b;

Level Id - tertiary wall phase constructed; subsequently respected by ash and floor sequence;

Level Ie - later pit P97/1 cutting late surface that seals ash layer.

Note

1. 12 m to the SW of pit P95/6 a column base (**190**), similar to those reused in the church, was found in pit P96/17 (1654).

Chapter 18

The Northeast Corner Sub-surface Clearance

M.P.C. Jackson

The removal of topsoil layers in order to expose the tops of underlying archaeological features was conducted during the 1994 season over an area 50 × 10 m. This strip was cleared along the north side of the tepe running E–W in squares L20, M20, N20, O20, P20 and was called the 'sub-surface clearance'. The operation succeeded in revealing a number of features at the west end which corresponded very well with Level I features excavated in later seasons in the NW corner and provided further information on the NE side of the tepe (Fig. 184). Pottery and small finds from the clearance were collected and plans produced of the visible features.

The most clearly identifiable features in L20 and M20 were the tops of two different phases of walls (Fig. 184, also Fig. 19). The earlier phase consisted principally of three walls which measured c. 1.05 m wide and consisted of facing stones with a dense rubble core, topped by mud brick. Walls W202 and W204 run parallel with each other roughly E–W, to join the west side of a third wall W203 running N–S which disappeared into the south section of L20. These walls in L20 clearly belong to the northern of three rooms which formed part of the Level Ib structure excavated in the adjacent NW corner (see Fig. 510).

Less prominent features uncovered in the sub-surface clearance in M20 also hinted that the massive Level Ib complex of walls may have continued even further to the east. In particular, a horizon of stones W213 running parallel to W202 in M20 and a second horizon of stones W214 running N–S roughly perpendicular to W213 seem to be aligned with the walls of the Level Ib structure. W214 may have been the fill of a robber trench since it was associated with small sections of surviving wall but elsewhere it appeared as a ditch-like feature. The south end of W214 was associated with a ridge of harder clay running perpendicularly in a SSW direction. This clay feature aligns with the mud brick topped Level Ib wall W954 in L19a, and may represent the continuation of that wall.

The later phase in L20 and M20 consisted of a complex network of walls which post-date the Level Ib phase. These survived in a rather fragmentary state. A short length of wall W206 in the centre of L20c returned ENE as W207. W207 was joined to a further wall W201 running north. W207 and W201 both ran up and over the earlier walls W202 and W203 respectively.

On the east side of L20, the sub-surface clearance revealed the tops of further walls belonging to the same later phase which joined to form a roughly square-shaped room orientated NNW–SSE (Fig. 184).

The west wall of this structure W209 was 4.75 m long and ran roughly SSE–NNW tapering towards, and finally overlapping, the earlier Level Ib wall W203 at the north end where it joined W207. The southern wall of the room was formed by W210 which ran west past W209 over earlier wall W203 into L20c, where it survived

Figure 184. *Byzantine wall foundations in L20 and M20, after surface clearance, looking west (see Fig. 508).*

Figure 185. *N20a: walls W215–16 after surface clearance, looking south.*

only as an isolated line of stones near the SE section of L20c. The east side of the room was formed by wall W211 which ran both to the north and to the south of W210. The north end of W211 returns to the west, but stopped after 2.5 m. It would appear that this short stretch of wall is built on top of an earlier wall W208, visible at the east end of this return as W213, and possibly a continuation of W202.

W211 was cut 2.5 m south of the join with W210, probably by a pit 1.40 m in diameter, but appears to continue on the south side of the pit to disappear into the south section. A second pit was found on the east side of W211 near the middle of M20.

No discrete features crossed from M20 into N20. In the centre of N20, two walls were located (Fig. 185). W215 running 5 m N–S was joined halfway along by W216. W216 ran east for 4 m and possibly may have continued further. These walls were 0.65–68 m wide consisting of well-faced stone foundations with a rubble core. Remains of a hard pink clay floor surface were found both north and south of W216. An area of burnt deposit measuring $c.$ 2 × 1.5 m, which may represent the top of a pit, was located to the north of the east end of W216. This T-shaped wall had no other associations except a possible feature represented by a stone scatter to the south of W215.

One of the most intriguing discoveries of the sub-surface clearance was a wall W217 running along the south edge of N20 which joined to W218 in O20. This was a well-faced wall bonded with mortar and measuring in total at least 12.80 m long and 1 m wide. Immediately north of this wall in O20 an area of mortar surface 3 × 1.8 m was located. The discovery of a mortared wall here was particularly interesting since the early church and walls W727 and W728 in I19 were the only other mortared walls discovered on the site. The east end of W218 stopped abruptly in the SE corner of O20 providing little evidence for a return or associated deposits.

O20 and P20 revealed a number of features which were mostly associated with extensive signs of burning. Two walls in P20, W221 and W222, which ran N–S parallel with each other, 5.20 m apart, together with W220 which extends west from W221, all appear to belong to the same phase. W220 ran into O20 and survived only 1.10 m long as W219 in the centre of O20. W221 ran N–S along the west side of P20 and disappeared south into P19. The north end of W221 seemed to stop level with the south side of an expanse of mudbrick located running E–W along the north side of O20. This mudbrick expanse delimited the north side of an oval area of what appeared to be collapsed and burnt mud brick. The east side of W221 was respected by a large area of clay, which may have represented a surface. A similar patch of surface was found 2.5–4.0 m on the east side of W222. To the south of P20 a stone pavement was uncovered lying on a similar clay surface but at an elevation 0.10 m lower than elsewhere in the square.

Conclusion

The evidence from the west end of the sub-surface clearance clearly revealed the northernmost of the three Level Ib rooms excavated in L19a/c. Feature 214 and the ridge of clay found in the SE corner of M20 also suggested the possibility that this large structure may have continued up to 12 m further to the east. A second phase of walls, post-dating the Level Ib walls found in L20 and M20, may be interpreted as further evidence for Level Ic/d walls.

The discovery of the 12.8-m-long mortared wall represented by W217 and W218 in N20 and O20 provides opportunity for comparison with walls from the church area, and raises the possibility of more monumental structures being uncovered at the site. The parallel walls and the substantial proportion of burnt deposits in O20 and P20 were notable.

It is clear from the plan of the sub-surface clearance that more than one phase of buildings was exposed. Little in the way of interlocking features, which might have offered a clue to their phasing, were identified except at the west end where the features complement the excavated area well.

Units and finds — sub-surface clearance
L20 surface: 137, 241

M20 surface: 138; sub-surface: 231
| Dressed stone | 138 | M20/1 | **39** |
| Dressed stone | 231 | M20/2 | **40** |

N20 surface: 139; sub-surface: 232
| Dressed stone | 139 | N20/1 | **43** |

O20 surface: 140; sub-surface: 185
Figurine head	185	O20/6	**1519**
Glass sherd	185	O20/7	**2080**
Stone palette	185	O20/5	**2623**

P20 surface: 176; sub-surface: 210
Bowl	210	P20/4	**978**
Loomweight	210	P20/6	**1824**
Fossil	210	P20/2	**2523**

Chapter 19

Architectural Fragments

M.P.C. Jackson & D. Collon[1]

Surface collection (Chapter 6) and excavations at Kilise Tepe (Chapters 15–18) recovered blocks and fragments of both carved local limestone and imported marble. Other architectural fragments that may have been removed from the site were located at the spring on the north side of the mound and at the nearby village of Kışla. The surround of the spring (Fig. 10) was built in 1961 from ashlar blocks that bear similar tool marks to worked stones found on the site of the church. At Kışla, a small column capital is stored at the school (**189**). Other blocks are likely to have been taken to Kışla while the village was under construction earlier in the twentieth century AD, but no other recognizably ancient examples were identified.

The surface survey revealed that the major concentration of masonry lay on the site of what turned out to be the church (p. 55, Fig. 21). Certain of the limestone blocks found could be identified as *voussoirs*, others had 'moulded' decoration on at least one edge and may be considered to represent door or window 'mouldings' and other architectural features which are visible today in many of the standing churches of the region. The excavation also revealed a number of carved architectural features, most notably: columns, column bases and column capitals, mostly located in good archaeological contexts. However, none of these were found in what may be considered their original position — i.e. they had been re-used almost without exception for a secondary purpose. This re-use took place both on the site of the church, and in features excavated to the south in the I14a–M14b strip, and to the north at the NW corner. These contexts represent important evidence for occupation at the site after the demise of the early Byzantine church.

In total relatively few fragments of dressed stone survive from Kilise Tepe. The distribution map of the find-spots of individual fragments shows that the major concentration of dressed stone comes from the area of the church (see p. 61). No evidence for another monumental structure or potential origin for architectural pieces was found on the site. However, an area of mortared wall and mortar surface that may represent evidence for another substantial building was exposed by the sub-surface clearance in squares N20 and O20 on the NE side of the mound (see Fig. 19).

Evidence from the small secondary church suggests that architectural features from the earlier structure were re-employed in its construction. These included four column bases in the centre of the chamber, and a broken marble column and a carved block, both used as part of the wall that blocked up the apse (see p. 194; Figs. 169–72). Small fragments of marble had been placed across the doorway of this church to mark the entrance.

In contrast to the secondary building, the early church was a structure of considerable size. None of the carved architectural features of the building survived *in situ*, only the lower walls remained. Originally, however, each of the stylobate foundations flanking the nave would have carried a line of columns resting on bases and topped with capitals.

The discovery of certain large carved blocks would suggest the employment of more ornate stones around doorways and windows and for architecturally significant points — notably arches — even though the walls may have been made of small stones with a mortar core as suggested by remains in K17. Flat marble slabs may have been used on floors but also as screens and panels in the interior.

At least one re-used marble paving slab was laid within the mortar floor surface located in the central area of the church. The mortar floor itself may well be a clue to the fate of at least some of the early church decoration since it contains many fragments of marble — burnt to create the surface for the paving slabs. The dating of the floor is uncertain, but the sealing of column bases underneath it would suggest that it belongs later than the construction of the early church, which would have employed the column bases on the stylobate. Marble used for its construction may well have come from the original building. It may be assumed that the column bases were used in the early church, but whether they were made specifically for that building or whether they may have come from an even earlier structure in the vicinity remains open to question. Note that four of the column bases had secondary slots cut into them, which would have served no purpose in the locations at which we found them, thus implying at least three phases of use.

The paucity and fragmentation of the pieces are evidence for the extensive use of the site as a source of building materials both in antiquity and in more recent times and indicate that stones were broken up on site. Most of the claw-chisel dressed limestone fragments seem to have come from quite small blocks; this is due partly to the natural cleavage of the limestone.

Excavations revealed evidence for a total of seven column bases: six on the site of the church (**191–2**: Figs. 205–8) and a lone example buried in a pit to the north of the church in J19 (**190**: Fig. 179). Only one significant part of a marble column was found — situated in the blocked apse of the later structure (Fig. 172); fragments were, however, located in at least six other contexts. In addition to fragments of large columns which were made of grey/white marble, a small porphyry (red/brown) marble column was found (**112**: Fig. 195). This may have been employed in a window — but could also represent part of an altar table.

The dating of the architectural fragments is interesting because it is clear they were used in more than a single period. Original dating of most of the pieces may be inferred from their presumed employment within the early Byzantine church, typologically dated to the fourth–fifth centuries. Stylistic comparison of the features themselves is problematic, except for the sharp pointed acanthus carving on certain of the fragments from capitals (**130–31**: Figs. 198–200), which would suggest that they at least were made during the Byzantine period. Capital **132** was a variation of an Ionic capital which was found in secondary context, in a pit in K20 (P95/6) (Fig. 181).

Large quantities of fragments of terracotta roofing tiles were found across the surface, especially in squares I–Q, 15–19 (Thomas, in Baker *et al.* 1995, 150), and are discussed briefly on pp. 51, 60, Fig. 36, and illustrated as **1463–9** (see also Figs. 260–61).

Catalogue

Note: for these architectural pieces the measurements, as preserved, are given below in the following order: L. × W. × Th.; where + is added to a measurement, this means it is incomplete due to breakage. In the catalogue, and throughout the volume, items with their number enclosed in square brackets are not illustrated on the pages of drawings (though they may be shown in photograph).

Dressed limestone fragments

Unless otherwise stated, the limestone is beige or honey-coloured, sometimes slightly pink. It seems to be quite soft and the natural cleavage seems to have produced relatively small blocks (see below).

a) Fragments of flat slabs

There are a few fragments of slabs that are roughly finished on both sides. They could have been used as paving slabs. Most of the surviving slab fragments, however, are made of marble (see below). One piece (**1**) is broken in two but is complete and approximately circular.

[1]   I16/18   4603
Two pieces of stone which form a flat, circular object made out of light-coloured stone. One surface is darker grey.
Di. 23.0; Th. 2.0

[2]   J16/14   4700
Dressed stone. Fragment of pale buff-coloured stone. Roughly triangular in shape, with a smooth, upper face. There are small traces of mortar on the upper surface and on one edge, which is very straight. The other two edges and the back are more irregular and may be broken.
L. 10.6; W. 5.9; Th. 2.0

[3]   J18/373   5887
Level IIc, Rm 7
Architectural feature/roof tile? A piece of sedimentary rock. Flat surfaces but not worked, irregular rectangular-shaped.
L. 20.0 max.; W. 15.7 max.; Th. 3.0 max.

[4]   K16/25   4806
Tile fragment. Flat and smooth on both surfaces, with possibly the remains of some type of 'adhesive' along one edge.
Th. 2.0

[5]   L7/5   321
Architectural fragment. Part of a rectangular slab of grey stone with a curvilinear groove incised on one face. The groove is *c.* 1.0 cm wide with an external diameter of 11.0 cm, which looks as though it has been worn by a bolt or part of a hinge rubbing against the stone as a door was opened and shut.
L. 15.0+; W. 13.0; Th. 5.0 max.

[6]   L15/7   102
Dressed fragment. A roughly rectangular slab of grey, laminated stone. Presumably cut into this shape, although no sign of chisel marks, etc. — the shape is too regular to be natural. Chipped at one end.
L. 31.5; W. 14.0; Th. 2.0

7   O15/7   105
Dressed stone fragments
(a) fragment of buff-coloured stone with one dressed surface: 9.6+ × 8.0+ × 4.4+
(b) fragment of buff-coloured, dressed stone with a border and groove: 7.3+ × 5.5+ × 5.4+
(c) fragment of buff-coloured stone with one dressed surface. The opposite face has some dressed marks but is otherwise irregular: 9.5+ × 8.3+ × 6.0+

(d) part of a slab of buff-coloured stone with a dressed edge (no chisel marks visible): 12.0 × 9.1 × 3.9
(e) part of a slab of grey stone with a straight edge (no chisel marks visible): 24.0 × 14.0 × 3.0.

b) Limestone fragments with claw-chisel marks

These are the most numerous of the architectural remains but even so they are meagre and fragmentary, with no complete block surviving. There are many fragments of mouldings but these are also fragmentary and are rarely similar. With the exception of the column and trough-shaped fragments — (f)–(g) below — there is one broken block measuring 20.2 × 14.3 cm (**51**), but otherwise the largest dimensions recorded are 14 or 15 cm. Three of the blocks had an original thickness of 6.5 cm, which appears to correspond to the lines of cleavage of the limestone.

The blocks were broken along the natural cleavage of the limestone but shaped on the two opposing sides with a broad, flat chisel with about six teeth. This was generally used diagonally in short, oblique chisel strokes, sometimes creating a chevron pattern; for narrow areas it was used at right-angles. There is evidence for rougher chiselling and even deep gouging of the stone and some fragments show the use of a chisel which left fine, flat-topped ridges (see especially **188**).

Three different types of chisel marks are shown on Figure 186. The claw-chisel may have been used to create a rough surface onto which a plaster coating would adhere, as is the case at Alahan. This may explain why it is rare to have more than one face with claw-chisel markings.

Figure 186. *Different chisel marks on stone fragments.*

Plain fragments with single surviving face dressed

[8] G12/2 305
Fragment of buff-coloured stone with traces of one dressed face.
L. 9.4+; W. 9.8+

[9] H13/1 303
Fragment of buff-coloured stone with traces of one dressed surface.
L. 10.6+; W. 8.2+; Th. 3.1+

[10] H17/3 160
Two pieces of buff-coloured stone, each with one dressed surface.

[11] H18/1 2600
Two pieces of grey dressed stone. Diagonal incised lines on one surface.

[12] H19/403 162
Two fragments of buff-coloured dressed stone:
(a) small, dressed on one side.
(b) dressed on one side, with border and groove: 6.6 × 6.2 × 2.1.

[13] I13/2 302
Piece of buff-coloured stone with one dressed face.
L. 9.8+; W. 8.3+; Th. 3.3+

[14] I14/7 3401
Fragment of buff-coloured stone, roughly dressed on one (extant) surface.
L. 13.7+; W. 4.1+; Th. 7.9+

[15] I16/41 156
Two fragments of buff-coloured stone, only one of which has a dressed surface.

[16] I17/13 157
Fragment of buff-coloured stone, with one dressed surface.

[17] J16/21 4700
Fragment of buff-coloured stone, dressed on one face; some mortar adhering to part of the same face.
L. 8.2+; W. 7.1+; Th. 6.9+

[18] J16/108 144
Fragment of buff-coloured stone, dressed on one face.
L. 14.3+; W. 9.3+; Th. 3.3+

[19] J16/110 144
Piece of buff-coloured stone with one dressed surface.

[20] J17/1 5000
Small piece of buff-coloured stone, with one dressed surface.
L. 6.2+; W. 5.5+; Th. 2.4+

[21] J17/19 145
Dressed fragment. A fragment of buff-coloured stone with a flat, dressed surface and roughly circular edge — possibly shaped this way.
L. 19.7+; W. 9.2+; Th. 4.8+

[22] J17/20 145
Dressed fragments. Two pieces of buff-coloured stone, each with one dressed surface.

Figure 187. *Architectural fragment 44, with acanthus leaf.*

[23] J18/404 146
Dressed fragment. A fragment of buff-coloured stone, with one dressed surface.

[24] J19/29 1604
Dressed stone fragment. An edge of a dressed stone block. One face has chisel marks, the adjacent face has been chipped smooth.
L. 5.2+; W. 3.7+

[25] J19/42 1609
Dressed stone. A piece of buff and grey stone with two parallel faces, one of which has chisel marks; the other is flat.
L. 3.45+; W. 2.7

[26] J19/407 147
Dressed stone, crystalline.

[27] K16/28 4808
Dressed stone with pattern. A pale beige stone with parallel lines running along one surface.

[28] K18/308 121
Two fragments of buff-coloured stone, each with one dressed surface.
(a) L. 10.8; W. 6.5; Th. 4.0
(b) L. 9.1; W. 7.6; Th. 5.3

[29] K19/5 1500
Flake of buff-coloured stone, dressed on one surface.
L. 6.7+; W. 5.5+; Th. 1.8+

[30] K19/417 149
Fragment of stone, dressed on one surface.

[31] K19/418 149
Fragment of buff-coloured stone with one dressed surface.

[32] K19/421 149
Fragment of buff-coloured stone with one dressed surface.

[33] K19/424 149
Two pieces of buff-coloured stone, one with a single, dressed surface; the other is a corner with two adjacent dressed surfaces.

[34] K19/425 149
Fragment of buff-coloured stone with one roughly dressed surface.

[35] L15/5 102
Small piece of stone, dressed on one surface only.

[36] L18/1 122
Fragment of pale buff stone with one dressed surface.
L. 4.5; W. 4.2; Th. 2.5

[37] M15/4 103
Fragment of buff-coloured stone, dressed on one surface.
L. 11.1+; W. 9.1+; Th. 6.0+

[38] M18/3 123
Fragment of buff-coloured stone with one dressed surface.

[39] M20/1 138
Small fragment of buff-coloured stone, dressed on one surface.
L. 4.2; W. 2.8; Th. 1.9

[40] M20/2 231
Flake of buff-coloured stone, dressed on one surface.

[41] N16/9 109
Fragment of a roughly shaped, buff-coloured dressed stone.
L. 12.2+; W. 10.8+; Th. 4.6+

[42] N17/5 117
Two fragments of buff-coloured stone, each dressed on one surface.

[43] N20/1 139
Two fragments of buff-coloured stone, each with one dressed surface.

44 O15/5 105
Decorated, architectural fragment of buff-coloured stone. One acanthus leaf type design with the base of another, separated by a groove.
L. 9.5+; W. 10.2+; Th. 5.1+
Fig. 187

[45] O16/3 110
Four fragments of stone, each with one dressed surface; three are of buff-coloured stone, the fourth is of pale grey stone.

[46] P18/4 126
Small fragment of grey/buff stone with one dressed surface.
L. 4.9; W. 4.1; Th. 2.4

[47] Q18/5 128
Flake from the dressed surface of a stone block.

Plain fragments with two adjacent faces dressed

[48] H15/5 159
Fragment of buff-coloured stone with two adjacent dressed surfaces.
L. 6.7+; W. 4.1+; Th. 2.7+

Architectural Fragments

49   I12/3   306
Dressed stone fragments:
(a) fragment of buff-coloured stone with one dressed face: L. 8.3+; W. 6.2+; Th. 2.7+
(b) as (a), with a groove along one side of the dressed face: L. 8.4+; W. 9.2+; Th. 5.5+

[50]   I15/12   155
Two fragments of dressed stone:
(a) one dressed surface
(b) a corner, with two adjacent dressed surfaces.

[51]   I17/16   157
Fragment of a stone block, dressed on two adjacent faces.
L. 20.2+; W. 14.3+; Th. 8.7+

[52]   J17/21   145
Two fragments of buff-coloured stone, one with a single dressed surface, the other with two adjacent dressed surfaces.

[53]   J18/1   2300
Fragment of dressed stone with patterning; incised, parallel lines on two sides.

[54]   K19/426   149
Piece of buff-coloured stone with one dressed surface.

c) Curved dressed fragments

These are curved on both faces but the outer one is somewhat rough, whereas the inner one was finished with a claw-chisel; it is therefore the interior diameters which are given below:

[55]   M14/5   191
Piece of buff-coloured stone. Curved in top view, with straight parallel sides. Top edges are rounded.
W. 8.3; Th. 4.5; Int. di. ? × 4.0 × 8.0 × 3.5

[56]   P10/3   229
Curving piece of buff-coloured, shelly stone, dressed on both its exterior and interior surfaces, which are parallel.
L. 13.9+; W. 6.2+ Th. 3.5; Int. di. 19.0 × 2.6 × 11.5 × 4.0

A further curved fragment, included in K17/104 (**149**), could alternatively be part of a moulding (as on **192a–d**) but too little remains to be sure.

d) Fragments with mouldings

Apart from the simplest, stepped mouldings or scooped angles, only two other mouldings are represented by more than one example, which is remarkable if we consider that such mouldings would have edged doorways and windows and there would therefore have been numerous blocks with the same mouldings. The mouldings are on small, broken pieces and are plain without the elaborate decoration of Alahan (with two possible exceptions — see under (g) below). For the small stepped mouldings, the claw-chisel was generally used at right-angles instead of diagonally. See also **150** and **150a**.

Figure 188. *Stone basin 57.*

e) 'Trough-like' fragments

Three large but fragmentary blocks have been roughly shaped on the exterior (only one has a preserved end and base with claw-chisel markings). They have been hollowed out equally roughly with one end open and may have been beam supports (Figs. 188 & 189).

[57]   I18/11   2703
White, corner section of a stone basin with grooves carved into the sides and base. The max. thickness is measured at the side edge rim; the basin's thickness at the deepest part of the depression is 3.6 cm. Claw-chisel marks on the base and end which has a stepped overhang some 5.5 cm above the base.
L. 24.0; W. 18.0; Th. 9.1 max.; Int. w. 17.0+
Fig. 188

[58]   K19/420   149
Fragment of buff-coloured stone with one dressed surface. Similar to **57**, but without the chisel marks and overhang.

[59]   P11/6   219
The end of a trough(?) of buff-coloured stone. Only one surface (an end?) is completely preserved. Attached to it are small parts of the base and two sides. Since the interior face is only partly extant, it is not clear whether it ran all the way up to the top edge, or whether a fourth side is missing, thereby forming a box.
Ext.: 17.0+ × 20.0 × 9.0; Int. w. 12.5; Th. 3.2 (at base)
Fig. 189

f) Column fragments

60   J16/37   4700
Three fragments of a column on a round base (Di. 19.0; H. 3.4) above which there is a moulding with a sharp ridge (Di. 19.0; H. 1.5) and a shaft (Di. 18.0), preserved on one fragment to a height of 12.0+ cm. The shaft has claw-chisel markings which may indicate that it was plastered whereas the base was not. On one of the three fragments is a dowel-hole which is roughly square at the bottom (3.2 × 3.4 cm), 4.5 cm deep and widening at the top.
Fig. 190

Figure 189. *Trough fragment 59.*

Figure 191. *Architectural fragment 61, with floral decoration.*

they too have decoration based on the acanthus but with an almost Gothic ornamentation of florets, and the background has been drilled out to form deep, dark holes.

61, **67–8** are probably fragments from larger capitals; **67** (27.0+ × 36.0+ × 19.0+) gives an indication of the original size of one piece. These pieces have the simplicity and sharp cutting of the marble capitals, associated, on **67** where the upper parts of some of the leaves are better preserved, with the deeply drilled-out areas characteristic of the other limestone capitals (in none of these cases are florets preserved but they may have existed). Note that in the case of **69**, red paint has been preserved.

Figure 190. *Column fragments 60.*

The seven column bases found in the excavations are discussed on pp. 191–2 and catalogued below as numbers **190–192**.

g) Decorated fragments

Most, if not all, of these small fragments seem to have belonged to capitals. The possible exceptions are **65**, where the decoration is bordered by a plain band, and **72** which has a very fragmentary Greek key motif; both could have adorned jambs or lintels.

It is generally impossible to tell whether the capital was round, rectangular or trapezoidal in plan but most of the limestone fragments seem to have come from small capitals. Like the larger marble capitals,

61   H19/402   162
Carved, architectural fragment representing the base of stems curving outwards. Fine-grained, buff-coloured, shelly stone.
W. 16.5+; Th. 8.6+
Fig. 191

62   I17/15   99
Fragment of decorated capital(?). Dimensions not recorded.

[63]   I18/10   2710
White limestone fragment, with curved grooves carved into one surface.
L. 5.5 max.; W. 3.3 max.

[64]   J19/9   1601
Carved architectural fragment made out of off-white, calcareous stone. On the only preserved side is carved a design of stems(?)

Figure 192. *Architectural fragment **68**, with floral pattern.*

with an oval hollow between two of them. Part of the lower face may also be preserved.
L. 22.2; W. 14.5

65   K16/7   4801
Piece of masonry with part of a carved design on one side.
L. 12.8; W. 5.8

66   K16/8   4801
White masonry fragment with carved patterns on one surface. There is black staining on the decorated side.
W. c. 13.5

[67]   K16/15   4802
Limestone capital. Carved decoration on one side. A hollow some 15.0 cm in diameter was later cut through the capital.
L. c. 36.0; W. c. 26.0

[68]   K16/27   Etütlük 96   4808
Decorated stone fragment with a flower-type pattern on one surface. Dimensions are of the pattern, which is not complete.
L. 7.8; W. 8.2
Fig. 192

[69]   K19/415   149
Two fragments of buff-coloured stone, each with one dressed surface. A third fragment, of grey stone, has a carved design, probably floral, on one side, which appears to have been coloured red:
11.0 × 7.6 × 7.7.

70   K19/416   149
Carved, architectural fragment made out of off-white stone. On one side is the base of a leaf design; an oval-shaped hollow between two stems is partly filled with mortar. No other surface is preserved, but at the back of the top side, as seen from the carved surface, there are the broken stumps of another carved face.
L. 15.0+; W. 8.0+; Th. 6.9+
Fig. 193

Figure 193. *Architectural fragment **70**.*

Figure 194. *Architectural fragment **71**.*

71   K19/422   149
Carved architectural fragment made out of off-white stone, carved on one side with base of stems of a floral or leaf design.
W. 9.0+; Th. 6.2+
Fig. 194

72   K19/423   149
Decorated architectural fragment of buff-coloured stone. Three sides are preserved, with a carved design on one. The other two sides are somewhat uneven.
L. 11.2+; W. 6.3+; Th. 2.5+

Dressed marble fragments

Marble was used for slabs, screens, columns and capitals. There are two main types: a white marble which can be brilliantly white but weathers to cream or grey, and a white to grey marble with darker grey streaks. The former was used predominantly for thin slabs, screens and capitals and the latter was used for thicker slabs, columns and some capitals. The distinction is not always clear, however, with small, weathered fragments. The largest columns may have stood on the bases, dressed with the claw-chisel, which were found in the church, and a similar base of the same size was observed in a municipal car-park in the old town of Silifke. The possibility exists that the bases (and the columns?) came from elsewhere and they could have been looted from a Hellenistic or Roman building. However, the fact that the same streaky grey marble was used for the columns and some capitals should be noted.

a) Slab fragments
These slabs were probably used for paving; none is complete. The following slabs have one face smoothed and the other left rough:

[73] I13/3 302
Architectural fragment of off-white marble; part of one flat face and edge.
L. 7.0+; W. 7.5+; Th. 3.0

[74] I16/39 156
Marble slabs:
(a) fragment of a thick tile(?), made out of white quartz, with one smooth polished surface: 18.0 × 15.5 × 4.0
(b) fragment of an edge of a tile, made out of grey quartz with two adjacent polished surfaces: 8.0 × 2.2 × 4.0

[75] N16/3 109
Marble slab. Fragment of tile(?), with one flat, well-polished surface, of grey-streaked, crystalline quartz.
L. 9.0+; W. 6.8+; Th. 2.7+

The following slabs have both faces smoothed but one is better finished than the other; all are made out of grey-streaked marble.

[76] I14/16 3403
Marble slab. Fragment of a tile made out of off-white/light grey, banded, quartz-like stone. Two parallel flat surfaces.
L. 13.0; W. 8.0; Th. 2.4

[77] I20/6 1401
Marble slab. Fragment of grey and white, banded, quartz tile. Two smoothed polished surfaces.
L. 7.0+; W. 4.0+; Th. 1.9+

[78] J18/99 2334
One marble piece — flat with rounded edge. Broken on the sides. An architectural fragment?
L. 9.4; W. 5.3; Th. *c.* 2.0

[79] J19/28 1604
Marble slab. Fragment of a tile made out of grey, quartz-like stone. Two flat, parallel surfaces; part of a rounded edge is preserved.
L. 14.7+; W. 12.1+; Th. 2.0

[80] J19/102 1650
Marble fragments (tile?). A light grey stone with flat, smooth surfaces.
L. 13.0; W. 10.5; Th. 3.3

[81] K15/5 100
Fragment of tile(?) made out of very pale grey, marble-like stone. Two parallel, very smooth surfaces; no edges extant.
L. 5.5+; W. 3.5+; Th. 2.0

[82] K17/16 9603
Marble architectural fragment.
L. 8.0; Th. 2.7

[83] K17/25 9607
Marble architectural fragment which has flat surfaces and an edge.
Th. 3.5

[84] K17/46 9626
Marble tile. An irregularly shaped piece of white marble, flattened on both surfaces.
L. 9.5+; W. 9.0+; Th. 1.5

[85] K17/96 9682
Seven chunks of marble of various shapes and sizes, none of which appear to join. Max. thickness is 2.6 cm. All are less than 6.0 cm in length.

[86] P16/1 111
Fragment of a tile made out of marble-like stone. Two well-polished surfaces.
L. 13.7+; W. 6.7+; Th. 2.75

Other small fragments of fairly thick tiles (white, whitish or grey) with one smoothed face preserved have been found.

[87] H15/3 159
Marble slab. Fragment of tile made out of white quartz, with one flat, polished surface.
L. 4.2+; W. 3.4+; Th. 2.3+

[88] H16/1 158
Marble slab. A small fragment of tile made out of white quartz with one flat, polished surface.
L. 3.7+; W. 1.2+; Th. 2.2+

[89] H17/2 160
Marble slab. Fragment of tile(?) made out of white quartz, with one flat, well-polished surface.
L. 6.6+; W. 4.1+; Th. 2.0+

[90] H19/406 162
Marble slab fragments:
(a) two fragments of grey, quartz tile: 5.2 × 3.6 × 4.1 and 3.8 × 1.8 × 2.2
(b) one fragment of tile(?) of white, granular stone: 3.2 × 2.6 × 1.0
(c) a piece of off-white, crystalline stone with two parallel, roughly

flat surfaces and a rounded edge: 2.7 × 2.4 × 0.8

[91]   J15/2   143
Two dressed fragments:
(a) a fragment of a grey, quartz tile with one smooth, polished surface: 11.2+ × 6.2+ × 4.8+
(b) a fragment of an off-white, quartz stone with one flat, smoothed surface, too deep to be a tile: W. 14.3; H. 13.2; Th. 6.8

[92]   J15/4   143
Fragment of dressed stone and sixteen un-worked fragments.

[93]   J16/109   144
Marble slab. Four fragments of white and grey quartz(?), all with one flat, polished surface. Fifteen un-worked fragments.

[94]   J17/15   145
Dressed fragment. Fragment of grey quartz with one smooth, polished surface. Probably an architectural fragment other than a tile, since part of an edge is projecting upwards from the flat surface along one break.
L. 7.6+; W. 2.1+; Th. 4.4+

[95]   J18/408   146
Marble slab. Fragment of tile made out of white/grey quartz with a single flat, polished surface.
L. 5.3+; W. 3.2+; Th. 1.5+

[96]   L17/4   119
Marble slab. Two fragments of white and grey quartz, one with a well-polished surface, probably a tile.

[97]   N11/6   217
Marble slab. Fragment of tile made out of off-white quartz with one flat, polished surface.
L. 10.3+; W. 8.3+; Th. 5.0+

[98]   N12/4   3200
Marble slab. Fragment of pale grey, granular quartz with one flat, polished surface; somewhat damaged.
L. 7.2+; W. 5.4+; Th. 2.4+

[99]   Q20/1   183
Marble slab. A small piece of tile made out of white quartz, with one smooth, polished surface.
L. 4.0+; W. 2.8+; Th. 1.9+

[100]   T17/2   171
Marble slab. Fragment of white, quartz tile with one flat, polished surface.
L. 10.5+; W. 5.6+; Th. 2.9+

The following are fine marble slabs, white unless otherwise stated, worked on both faces, and possibly part of screens rather than floor tiles; they are generally very fragmentary.

[101]   H17/1   160
Inscribed marble slab. Fragment of white quartz tile, inscribed 'AS' on one side (possibly 'AS', if the mark below the S is deliberate), with random scratches on the other side.
L. 4.0+; W. 3.2+; Th. 1.1+

[102]   H18/175   161
Marble slab. Fragment of tile(?), with two well-polished, flat surfaces and a rounded edge.

Figure 195. *Miniature column* **112.**

L. 5.4+; W. 4.0+; Th. 2

[103]   I16/25a–b   4600
(a) flat, thin piece of white marble in two joining fragments: 9.8 × 5.5 × 1.0
(b) flat, thin piece of white marble: 9.0 × 5.5 × 1.1

[104]   I17/6   4901
Fragment of marble; flat surfaces.
L. 3.7+; W. 4.0+; Th. 1.3

[105]   J16/35   4700
Fragment of a thin, off-white marble tile.
L. 10.9+; W. 7.6; Th. 1.3

[106]   J16/36   4700
Fragment of plain, white, marble tile; no edges.
L. 6.8+; W. 4.5+; Th. 1.2

[107]   K20/4   1101
Fragment of a tile made out of white and grey quartz.
L. 3.6+; W. 2.9+; Th. 1.2

[108]   N17/3   117
Fragment of a tile(?), made out of grey-streaked marble, with two flat, very well-polished surfaces.
L. 6.2+; W. 4.6+; Th. 1.7

[109]   O14/1   188
Marble slab. A small fragment of tile made out of white quartz, with two smooth, well-polished surfaces.
L. 4.5+; W. 2.8+; Th. 2.2

[110]   P19/2   142
Marble slab. Fragment of a tile made out of off-white quartz.
L. 3.2+; W. 2.9+; Th. 1.0

b) Fragments of mouldings

111   I16/37   4600
Marble panel block. A rectangular block with two smooth sides at a sharp right-angle. Other sides are rough and the ends are broken. White, weathered to grey; see **117** for a larger version of the same profile.
L. 18.0; W. 4.0

112   J16/7   KLT 62   4600
Miniature column fragment of dark pink marble. Squared base surmounted by five ridges, the lowest wider than the others. On top of those is a plain column, broken at the top.
L. 11.0+; W. 5.8 (base); Th. 5.2 (base)
Fig. 195

113   J18/83   2320
Section of white marble with a smooth, curved convex surface. Perhaps an architectural fragment broken on the right along a straight line.
L. 7.4+

[114]   J19/11   1601
Fragment of a tile(?) made out of mid-grey quartz. Two flat, parallel surfaces, one of which has a curved, upturned edge, along which it is broken.
L. 16.0+; W. 6.8+; Th. 3.4

[115]   J20/6   1301
Tile fragments(?):
(a) fragment of white, quartz tile, with one smooth, polished surface: 2.6 x 2.4 x 1.2
(b) fragment of tile(?), with one flat, polished surface, the other carved with a raised rounded border: 6.4 x 5.5 x 2.8

[116]   K16/22   4800
Carved section of white marble moulding, particularly finely cut and smoothed.
L. 20.0+; W. 9.0; Th. 4.3

[117]   K17/28   9603
Piece of heavy, white, weathered to grey, marble-like stone with two corners at roughly right angles. Appears to widen towards the opposite (broken) surface. See **111** for a smaller version of the same profile.
L. 14.0+

c) Screen(?) fragments

These fragments are carefully worked on both faces in a mottled white marble and have been carefully smoothed. Since they were clearly meant to be seen from both sides and are sturdily made, they were probably fragments of screens, perhaps slotted between columns (cf. Alahan and note the grooves in the Kilise Tepe column bases). Whether they were set vertically or horizontally is not clear and although the fairly clean break at one end of **118** might indicate the point up to which it was slotted, there are no marks of slotting on the largest piece.

118   99/14   99
Surface find
White stone, with two parallel grooves at one end and the corner of an excised panel at the other. Design is mirrored on the other side.
L. 21.0; W. 11.0; Th. 3.7

[119]   I19/4   1700
Small, flat piece of marble with two parallel grooves on either side, broken along the second groove; thinner but with similar mouldings to those of the middle section of **120**.
L. 6.9+; W. 7.5+; Th. 4.6 max.

[120]   J16/39   4700
Carved marble panel. Squared, deep edge, with the same carving on both sides, namely, a groove and ridge, and then a recessed part further down on either side.
W. 14.5+; Th. 6.5 max.

d) Column fragments

Most of the fragments are from columns of grey-streaked marble with a diameter of *c.* 36.0–40.0 cm although this was not easy to measure due to the fragmentary nature of the pieces. The columns probably tapered towards the top, so fragments with different diameters could have come from the same column or a range of columns:

[121]   J16/26   4700
Piece of the surface of a column made out of off-white marble.
L. 27.0+; Th. 5.6+

[122]   J16/27   4700
Fragment of the surface of a marble column. Re-used, since there are patches of mortar adhering to both front and back.
W. 21.0+

[123]   J16/43   4700
Column fragment(?).

[124]   J18/3   2300
Marble column fragments — two small pieces.

[125]   J19/66   1622
Fragment of pale grey, marble column. Smooth texture.
W. 29.0 max.

Smaller columns are represented by the limestone fragments referred to above and to the following marble example.

[126]   J16/24   4700
Fragment of a cylindrical piece of grey-streaked marble.
Th. 4.6+

e) Decorated fragments

Several flat pieces bear decoration on one smoothed face; they look as though they could come from screens but the reverse is very rough — either broken, unfinished or not meant to be seen. Note that on one of the pieces, the design has been incised, on two the design has been left in reserve and the background

Architectural Fragments

Figure 196. *Incised marble slab* **127**.

Figure 197. *Decorated marble fragments* **129**.

has been chiselled away in roughly straight lines or grooves and on the fourth piece the techniques have been combined.

127 K16/3 4800
Fragment of a slab of mottled, creamy white marble, decorated with an incised, swirling acanthus leaf design; the background is chiselled away in roughly horizontal lines, leaving the design in flat relief. Part of one squared edge is extant. Straight finished edge (L. 12.0+), plain border (W. 2.5).
L. 17.0+; W. 11.0+; Th. 4.0
Fig. 196

128 K16/14 4802
Marble panel. Mottled, creamy white; part of the smooth surface has been chiselled away in roughly horizontal lines to form the background for two buds(?) and part of a leaf or lily-like flower, leaving the design in flat relief.
L. 14.0; W. 12.0; Th. 3.5

[129] N16/4 109
Two decorated marble tile fragments:
(a) mottled white, weathered; plain band on right(?) side (W. 3.5+); part of the smooth surface of the remainder has been chiselled away

Figure 198. *Fragment of capital* **130**.

Figure 199. *Fragment of capital* **131a**.

in diagonal lines to form the rough background for a lily-like flower in flat relief: 8.0 × 7.5 × 2.0–2.5
(b) mottled, white, partly weathered to grey; incised lines — perhaps, by comparison with **127**, part of an acanthus leaf; finished edge: 7.0+ × 9.0–10.0 × 2.5
Fig. 197

f) Capital fragments

The fragments of marble capitals are generally larger than those of limestone. They are exceedingly well cut with designs based on acanthus leaves with sharply-defined planes and clear, bold execution.

[130] J16/15 4700
White, weathered to creamy grey marble; a piece of a straight-fronted capital and part of the right side at an angle to it, decorated with acanthus leaves, with deeply excised triangular areas between the leaves. Decorated front: 9.0 × 20.0; side: 7.0 × 9.0
L. 6.0+ max.; W. 25.5+ max.; Th. 15.0+ max.
Fig. 198

Chapter 19

Figure 200. *Fragment of capital **131b**.*

Figure 201. *Capital **132**, underside.*

Figure 202. *Capital **132**, side view.*

131   J19/137a–c   1661
Three marble fragments:
[131a] white; top, bottom and right side missing; flaring, trapezoidal in plan with flat back and front and a preserved left side set at about 120 degrees to the front and separated from the back by

Figure 203. *Dressed stone **136**.*

an undecorated band 5.0–6.0 cm wide at right angles to the back where it could have been set into a wall. A plain corner separates the decoration of acanthus leaves on the side and front. On the front, above the acanthus leaves, there is a horizontal band resembling the arm of a cross, which narrows towards the centre of the capital and extends as far as a double circular motif which, if it was centrally placed, would make the capital roughly 34.0 cm wide at the highest preserved point.
18.0+ × 22.0+ × 16.0
Fig. 199

[131b] white weathered to cream marble; large piece of stone with all faces broken except for a fragment of acanthus leaf (11.0 × 8.0).
20.0+ × 20.0+ × 27.0+
Fig. 200

131c white weathered to cream marble; curved fragment of bottom of capital surmounted by two leaves pointing downwards. Decorated portion: 11.0 × 18.0; Max. preserved dimensions: 20.0+ × 18.0+ × 10.0+

132   K20/52   KLT 61   1902
Capital fragment. White marble, banded with grey. The underside has a circular, dressed face, and there is a carved, curvilinear design at both ends. The upper side and the long edges are broken.
L. 51.0+; W. 41.0+; Th. 21.0+
Figs. 201 & 202

[133]   H15/4   159
Marble slab. Fragment of tile made out of white quartz with one flat, polished surface.
L. 7.3+; W. 4.2+; Th. 2.0+

[134   number not used]

135   I14/204   209
Fragment of buff-coloured stone, dressed on one surface, with a border.
L. 7.2+; W. 6.7+; Th. 5.8+

[136]   I16/30   4600
Three joining pieces of a length of dressed stone. Buff-coloured soft stone. The back is smooth, the two sides have been quite roughly chipped, and the front has chisel marks. One end is also roughly chipped, but the other is broken. Along one edge the front face is recessed by fairly rough working.
W. *c.* 6.3; Th. *c.* 6.3
Fig. 203

137   I16/38   4600
Limestone block with slightly incised patterning and a ridge on one side. Lines continue on the base.
L. 13.5; W. 7.7

[138] I17/14 157
Two fragments of buff-coloured stone, one dressed on one surface only, the other a corner piece dressed on two adjacent surfaces with a third surface flat but with no tool marks.

139 I18/5 2701
Several fragments of white stone, carved with small grooves on some surfaces. The largest fragment has a flat surface adjacent to the curving surface (on which the patterns are found). Dimensions are for the largest fragment.
L. 28.5 max.; W. 14.0 max.

140 I19/5 1700
Dressed stone:
(a) fragment of dressed stone with one chiselled surface. Re-used, since the broken surfaces have traces of mortar on them. Buff-coloured stone.
L. 9.0+; W. 7.7+; Th. 3.0+

(b) curved piece of buff-coloured, dressed stone. One long, straight edge, and a straight back.
L. 24.0+; W. 14.6+; Th. 6.6

[141] J16/6 4600
Three fragments of a column of off-white marble. Only one piece, the largest, has part of curved face preserved.
W. 11.0+; Th. 8.5+

142 J16/22 4700
Fragment of a dressed stone block, cut from buff-coloured stone. There are two dressed faces at right-angles to one another, with a recessed edge between them.
L. 13.2+; W. 9.2+; Th. 5.1+

[143 number not used]

[144] J16/101 144
Corner of a carved architectural fragment made out of buff-coloured stone. It has one curved surface, separated by an angular groove from a right-angled corner.
L. 24.5+; W. 11.0+; Th. 9.5+

145 J17/2 5000
Fragment of buff-coloured stone, dressed on two adjacent faces, with a recessed edge.
L. 14.2+; W. 6.8+; Th. 8.2+

146 J17/13 145
Piece of buff-coloured stone, dressed on one side; carved with two parallel ribs and grooves.
L. 20.2+; W. 13.3+; Th. 7.0+

147 J18/9 2301
Light-coloured, dressed stone fragment with a dot patterning.
L. 13.0; W. 11.0

[148 number not used]

[149] K17/104 120
Seven fragments of dressed buff-coloured stone. Five are dressed on one surface only; of these, the dressed surface of one is curved. The remaining two pieces have two adjacent dressed surfaces.

150 K17/98 99
Carved stone. Convex moulding.

[150a] K17/68 9649
Carved stone with a ridge and two grooves.

[151] L17/11 119
Dressed fragments:
(a) small fragment of buff-coloured stone with one dressed surface
(b) piece of buff-coloured stone with an obtuse-angle corner along which a vertical groove runs.
H. 14.0; W. 13.2; Th. 6.8

152 N16/6 109
Dressed fragments:
(a) two fragments with one dressed surface each
(b) corner fragment with two adjacent dressed surfaces
(c) fragment with the corner of a carved panel: H. 10.3+; W. 9.4+; Th. 7.4
(d) fragment of an obtuse-angled corner with a vertical groove along its edge: H. 7.9+; W. 13.3+; Th. 7.0+

[153 number not used]

[154] X14/3 1000
Decorative architectural piece in the form of two stems(?) curving upwards and outwards in opposite directions. At the back, ridges from manufacture remain. The fabric, where visible, is red or yellow with quite frequent red inclusions of medium size (up to 0.2 cm). The surface, although much encrusted, is yellow-buff, where visible.
W. 7.4; Th. 4.2

[155 number not used]

[156] I14/1 3400
Dressed fragments:
(a) buff-coloured stone, dressed on one face only. 11.5+ × 6.5+ × 3.2+
(b) architectural fragment of buff-coloured stone. Top/bottom(?) is roughly dressed. Two adjacent sides at an obtuse angle are separated by a vertical V-sectioned groove. One side is smooth, the other has diagonal chisel marks.
L. 16.2+; W. 15.9+; H. 9.4+

[157] I16/24 4600
Fragment of dressed stone.
L. 11.3+; W. 8.2+; Th. 4.6+

158 I16/35 4600
Piece of carved, off-white marble. The back is flat, the top edge is concave, the front has a groove parallel with the top edge, and beneath that, curves down sharply to a broken edge. Traces of mortar are visible in the groove along the top edge.
W. 11.5; Th. 4.2 (1.05 min.)

[159 number not used]

[160] J12/3 212
Roughly dressed stone; no visible chisel marks. Buff and grey-coloured.
L. 43.0; W. 8.1; Th. 4.6

[161] J16/20 4700
Tall, thin piece of dressed, buff-coloured stone. One surface has a recessed edge. Both front and back are smooth; one side has marks of working, the other side, next to the recessed edge, is very rough. Cf. **136**, although unlike that piece, the front of this has no marks from a toothed chisel.
L. 15.4; W. 7.4; Th. 6.3

Figure 204. *Decorated capital* **189** *at Kışla school.*

[162] J16/45 4700
Dressed stone.

[163] J16/49 4700
Fragment of the curved face of a column made out of light grey, banded, crystalline stone (marble?).
L. 20.0+; Th. 4.8+

[164] J16/103 144
Dressed fragment. A roughly shaped stone block with one curved edge. No chisel marks visible. Cut from buff-coloured stone.
L. 20.4; W. 17.1; Th. 9.0

[165] J16/153 4706
Regular shape; perhaps a block from fallen architecture.
L. 49.0; W. 21.0

[166] J16/154 4706
Concave at narrower, top end; sloping sides. Perhaps a block from fallen architecture.
L. 48.0; W. 36.5–37.0 (top), 40.0–43.0 (bottom)

[167] J16/155 4706
Concave on one face; perhaps from fallen architecture.
L. 49.0; W. 28.0

[168] J16/156 4706
Regular shape; perhaps from fallen architecture.
L. 49.0; W. 31.0

[169–170 numbers not used]

[171] J16/163 4706
Marble slab.
L. 70.0 × 62.0; 54.0 × 62.0

[172] J16/164 4706
Marble slab.
L. 101.0; W. 63.0

[173] J17/14 145
Carved stone.

[174] J18/407 146
Dressed(?) fragment. No trace of chiselled surfaces, but one surface has a V-shaped groove carved in it.

[175] J19/95 1641
Dressed stone. A white stone with lined markings on one surface. There is a slight orangey patch on the 'base' side.

[176] J19/406 147
Two fragments of buff-coloured stone, each with one dressed surface.

[177] J20/3 1301
Faced marble(?) fragment.

[178] K14/5 3001
Fragment of buff-coloured stone, dressed on three adjacent surfaces.

[179] K14/161 193
A piece of buff-coloured stone with one flat surface, carved with a matting effect of ridges and grooves, quite worn in places. Could merely be chisel marks, but seems more regularly executed than the usual way of dressing stone at Kilise Tepe.
L. 8.1+; W. 6.6+; Th. 3.4

[180 number not used]

181 K17/107 120
Piece of buff-coloured stone, dressed on one side, with two parallel ridges.
L. 14.0+; W. 9.9+; Th. 6.8+

[182] K17/27 9607
Large, rectangular, brown, stone slab. Flat on opposite surfaces.

[183] K19/427 149
Small piece of buff-coloured stone with deep, diagonal chisel marks on the only extant dressed surface.

[184] L14/14 3602
Piece of a corner of a dressed stone block, cut out of buff-coloured stone. Dressed on two adjacent faces.
L. 10.0; W. 7.1

[185] N18/1 124
Three fragments of buff-coloured stone, each with one dressed surface.

[186] O15/6 105
Fragment of a buff-coloured, stone block with traces of dressing on one edge and grooves on the adjacent side.
L. 10.3+; W. 9.2+; Th. 3.6+

[187] O16/2 110
Carved, architectural fragment of buff-coloured stone, with three extant registers. The lower consists of deeply hollowed ovals with a hollowed circle at the top of each, separated by grooves. The middle consists of a row of roughly triangular-shaped excisions, rounded at the top, while the upper part, largely broken away, has three circles cut out of it.
W. 9.5+; Th. 4.6+

[188] K14/173 193
Carved fragment.

[189]   Kışla village
Capital.
34 × 31; Di. 33.8
Fig. 204

Column bases

The seven more or less complete marble column bases found are discussed above, p. 216. Six of them were *in situ*, although in secondary locations, within the church, the seventh (**190**) in a pit stratified below later courtyard debris in J19 at the NW corner. They all bore claw-chisel markings and had similar mouldings. Three of them had a mason's mark (**191b**, **192a** and **192c**). In three others (**190**, **192b** and **192d**) two secondary slots had been cut through the mouldings at the centre of two adjacent sides. This was presumably to accommodate vertical architectural screens or similar features, although in their present positions the slots could no longer have served this purpose, thus indicating at least three phases of use for these bases.

[**190**]   J19/106   1654
Found in pit P96/17.
Column base. Marble. One corner broken away. Mouldings as on **192a–d**. On upper surface a shallow V-shaped groove (W. 2.5 cm) radiating from central hole (di. 6.5; depth 5) towards one corner, and two faint incised lines 0.5 cm apart, parallel with base (cf. **192b**). One wedge-shaped slot approx. at centre of one side (and another probably at 90 degrees to it but now broken away). In all respects a pair to **192b** in the Church.
Base 72 × 74; Di. of top 59; H. 30 (H. of base 8, H. of mouldings 22).
Fig. 179

[**191a**]   J16/162   4706
Column base E (south). Marble. No mason's mark, no slots. Not fully excavated (Fig. 171).
Di. of top 51

[**191b**]   J16/161   4706
Column base F (north). Marble. Centre point marked by shallow depression (c. 0.5). Not fully excavated, but at least upper mouldings similar to other column bases. Mason's mark 'N' (Fig. 170).
Di. of top c. 52

[**192a**]   K16/19   4804
Column base A. Marble. Mouldings as on **192b**. Base broken at two corners. Mason's mark in form of alpha (Fig. 205). (Without secondary slots but with a mason's mark, like **192c**.)
Base 65 × 65; Di. of top 58.

[**192b**]   K16/18   4804
Column base B. Marble. For mouldings see Figure 206. On upper surface a shallow V-shaped groove (W. 2 cm) radiating from central hole (Di. 6.5; depth 4.5) towards NW corner, presumably for injecting molten lead, and two faint incised lines 0.5 cm apart, along E–W axis (cf. **190**). Slightly wedge-shaped secondary slots 6–8 and 7–9 cm wide cut at centre of north and east sides.
Base 74 × 72; Di. of top 57; H. 29 (H. of base 8; H. of mouldings 21).

[**192c**]   K16/21   4804
Column base C. Marble. NW and SE corners broken away. Mouldings as on **192b**. Centre point marked by shallow depression (c. 0.5). Mason's mark in form of lambda (Fig. 207). Cf. **192a**.
Base 70 × 69; Di. of top 53; H. of base 7, H. of mouldings c. 20.

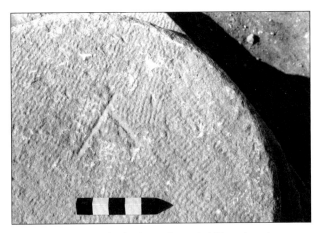

Figure 205. *Detail of column base A **192a**, showing alpha mark.*

Figure 206. *Column base B **192b**, showing vertical slots for screens.*

Figure 207. *Detail of column base C **192c**, showing lambda mark.*

Chapter 19

Figure 208. *Column base D **192d**, showing slots for screen, looking NW.*

[**192d**] K16/20 4804
Column base D. Marble. Mouldings as on **192b**. Slightly wedge shaped secondary slots 6–8 cm wide cut at centre of east and south sides. Not fully excavated.
Base 74 × 74; Di. of top 55; H. of mouldings 22.
Fig. 208

Notes

1. The basic catalogue of pieces was prepared by Dominique Collon, with an introductory text and additional detail supplied later by Mark Jackson.

Part D

The Pottery

Chapter 20 **Introduction to the Pottery**	**237**
Recovery and recording	237
Presentation of the ceramics	238
Chapter 21 **Pottery Fabrics and Technology**	**241**
Aims of the study	241
Methodology	241
Local geology and clay resources	242
Techniques of preparation	242
Equipment used	242
Descriptive system	242
Technique of chemical analysis	243
Clay, sand and rock samples	243
Special focus on resources from Tarsus	248
Clay briquettes in thin section	248
Level Vj–g (EB II)	249
Chemistry	251
Fabric groups	251
Level Vf–e (EB III)	252
Chemistry	253
Fabric groups	253
Level IV (MBA)	253
Chemistry	254
Fabric groups	254
Level III (LBA)	254
Chemistry	256
Fabric groups	257
Level IIa–d	258
Chemistry	259
Fabric groups	259
Level IIe	260
Chemistry	260
Fabric groups	260
Level IIf	261
Chemistry	265
Fabric groups	265
Concluding remarks: the organization of production	267
Level Vj–g	268
Level Vf–e	268
Level IV	269
Level III	269
Level II, phases a–d	270
Level IIe	271

Level IIf	271
Byzantine ceramics	272

Chapter 22 Detailed Fabric Descriptions — **273**

EB II samples (Level Vj–g)	273
Local fabrics	273
Non-local fabrics	279
EB III samples (Level Vf–e)	280
MBA samples (Level IV)	282
LBA samples (Level III)	284
Samples from Level IIa–d	287
Samples from Level IIe	289
Samples from Level IIf	290

Chapter 23 The Early Bronze Age Pottery — **295**

Introduction	295
The fabrics of Levels V and IV	296
Level Vl–k (**193–5**)	296
Early EBA pottery — Level Vj–g	297
Wares	297
*Level Vj (**196–217, 270–73, 280–81**)*	299
*Jugs — Level Vj (**196–203**)*	299
*Cups — Level Vj (**204–9**)*	300
*Bowls — Level Vj (**210–17**)*	301
Level Vi	302
Level Vh	303
Level Vg	303
*Bowls and cups — Level Vi–h (**218–23**)*	303
*Decorated sherds (**224–9**)*	304
*Handles (**230-38**)*	304
*Pottery feet and small bases (**239–44**)*	304
*Bowls — Level Vh–g (**245–63**)*	305
*Jugs and jars — Level Vi–g (**264–9**)*	305
*Coarse ware – Level Vj (**270–72**)*	306
*Coarse ware — Level Vi–g (**273–9**)*	306
*Platters or lids — Level Vj–g (**280–86**)*	306
Level Vf (**287–445**)	306
Introduction	306
*Cooking and storage vessels (**287–94**)*	307
*Bowls (**295–373**)*	307
*Plain bowls (**295–306**)*	308
*Cream-slipped bowls (**307–10**)*	308
*Red- or brown-slipped bowls with S-profiles (**311–23**)*	309
*Red-/brown-slipped bowls with other profiles (**324–32**)*	309
*Partially slipped and red-rim bowls (**333–48**)*	309
*Red cross bowls (**349–59**)*	310
*Handled bowls (**360–67**)*	311
*Miscellaneous bowls (**368–73**)*	311
*Jars and cups (**374–93**)*	311
*Fluted vessels (**387–91**)*	312
*Small red-slipped and red-rim jars/cups (**374–85**)*	312
*Decorated cups and jars (**386–93**)*	312
*Miniature vessels (**394–400**)*	313
*Lids (**401–3**)*	313
*Incised decoration (**404–15**)*	314
Jugs	315
*Decorated jugs and jars (**416–21**)*	316
*Bases (**422–7**)*	316

Handles (428–45)	316
Level Ve *(446–74)*	317
Jugs and jars (446–52)	317
Lid (453)	318
Bowls (454–62)	318
Cups (463–6)	318
Small jars and flasks (467–70)	318
Miscellaneous (471–4)	318

Chapter 24 The Middle Bronze Age Pottery — 319

Level IVa — 319
- *Coarse wares* — 319
- *Medium and fine wares* — 320
- *Jars (475–9)* — 322
- *Bowls (480–89)* — 322
- *Cups (490–94)* — 322
- *Funnel (495)* — 322
- *Handles (498–502)* — 322
- *Decorated sherds (503–5)* — 322
- *Jars (475–9)* — 323
- *Bowls (480–89)* — 323
- *Cups (490–94)* — 323
- *Funnel (495)* — 323
- *Spouts (496–7)* — 323
- *Handles (498–502)* — 323
- *Decorated sherds (503–5)* — 324
- *Cooking and storage pots (506–24)* — 324
- *Combed ware (525–31)* — 324

Level IVb — 325
- *Bowls (532–43)* — 325
- *Jugs and jars (546–58a)* — 325
- *Decorated sherds (561–7)* — 326
- *Bowls (532–43)* — 326
- *Handles (544–5)* — 327
- *Jugs (546–53)* — 327
- *Jars (544–58a)* — 327
- *Lids (559–60)* — 328
- *Decorated sherds (561–7)* — 328

Chapter 25 Pottery from Level III — 329

Introduction — 329
Fabrics — 329
General remarks — 330
Catalogue — 331
- *Plates (568–71)* — 331
- *Deep bowls (572–3)* — 331
- *Open bowls with plain rim (574–9)* — 332
- *Open bowls with external rim (580–87)* — 332
- *Open bowl with incurved rim (588)* — 332
- *Shallow bowls (589–629)* — 333
- *Shallow bowls with flattened rim (589–92)* — 333
- *Shallow bowls with plain thickened rim (593–4)* — 333
- *Large shallow bowls with internal rim (595–602)* — 333
- *Smaller shallow bowls with internal rim (603–24)* — 334
- *Shallow bowls with rim thickened out (625–7)* — 335
- *Large shallow bowls with exterior rim (628–9)* — 335
- *Hole-mouth jars (630–32)* — 335
- *Closed jars with rolled rim (633–7)* — 335
- *Closed jars with vertical plain rim (638–40)* — 336

*Closed jars with vertical band out (**641–3**)*	336
*Closed jars with vertical thickened rim (**644–5**)*	337
*Closed jars with flaring rim (**646–8**)*	337
*Closed jars with everted rims (**649–71**)*	337
*Closed jars with everted plain rims (**649–57**)*	337
*Closed jars with everted rounded rim (**658–61**)*	338
*Closed jars with everted flattened rim (**662–9**)*	338
*Closed jar with everted overhanging rim (**670**)*	338
*Trefoil jug (**671**)*	338
*Lentoid flasks (**672–7**)*	339
*Rhyton (**678**)*	339
*Spindle bottle (**679**)*	340
*'Flower pots' (**680–81**)*	340
*Platter (**682**)*	340
*Painted carinated jar (**683**)*	340
*Libation arms (**684–92**)*	340

Chapter 26   Pottery from Level II — 343

Introduction	343
Local wares	343
Fresh motifs	345
White Painted	346
Black-on-Red	346
Bichrome sherds	347
Pottery from Rm 20 (**693–706**)	347
Pottery from FI96/14 in I19 (**707–35**)	348
Miscellaneous ceramics	353
*Bowls with internal rim (**736–40**)*	353
*Bowls or plates with plain rim (**741–50**)*	353
*Bowls with cross-hatching (**751–7**)*	354
*Bowls with diagonal lines (**758–71**)*	355
*Deep bowls (**772–80**)*	356
*Tray (**781**)*	357
*Lids (**782–3**)*	357
*Jars and jugs with bands (**784–7**)*	357
*Jars with squared rim (**788–800**)*	357
*Jars with cross-hatching (**801–7**)*	359
*Body sherds with cross-hatching (**808–14**)*	360
*Jars with horizontal wavy lines (**815–22**)*	360
*Sherds with bands and lines (**823–36**)*	361
*Black-on-Red sherds (**837–40**)*	362
*Body sherd with concentric circles (**841**)*	362
*Jar sherds with targets (**842–54**)*	362
*Body sherds with pendent semi-circles (**855–9**)*	363
*Miscellaneous jar sherds with decoration (**860–85**)*	364
*Miscellaneous jar rims with decoration (**886–9**)*	365
*Miscellaneous handles (**890–93**)*	366
*Miscellaneous sherds (**894–6**)*	366
*Spindle bottles (**898–903**)*	367
*Small jar (**904**)*	367
*Cooking pots (**905–8**)*	367
*Storage jars (**909–15**)*	367
*Pilgrim flasks (**916–19**)*	368
*Feet from pilgrim flasks (**920–39**)*	368

Chapter 27   Geometric pottery — 371

Chapter 28   The Mycenaean pottery — 373

Chapter 29 **Comparison of the NAA Data for Six Mycenaean-style Samples from Kilise Tepe with Chemical Reference Groups from Mainland Greece, Crete, Cyprus and the Levant**   **377**
    Introduction   377
    Results   377
    Discussion   377

Chapter 30 **Hellenistic Ceramics and Lamps**   **379**
    Summary   379
    Fabrics   379
    Forms   379
        *1. Echinus (**966–7**)*   379
        *2. Large, heavy plate/dish with thick rim (**968–9**)*   380
        *3. Shallow, flat-base saucer (**970–71**)*   380
        *4. Rolled rim dish/saucer (**972–3**)*   380
        *5. Other plate/dish shapes (**974–8**)*   381
        *6. Deep 'skyphos' with vertical handles (**979–80**)*   382
        *7. 'S'-curve kantharos (**981–3**)*   382
        8. Other cup shapes   383
        *9. Jugs and other closed vessels (**984**)*   383
        *10. Krater (**985–9**)*   383
        *11. Unguentarium (**990**)*   383
        *12. Clay lamps (**991–6**)*   384
    Hellenistic or Early Roman ceramics   385

Chapter 31 **Pottery from Level One**   **387**
    Introduction   387
    Summary   387
    Aims and objectives   388
        Preservation of material in the soil   388
        Method and description of the collection of ceramic data   388
    Stratigraphic context of the material   389
    Identification of the material   389
    Analysis of the material in the dighouse/Silifke Museum   390
        Introduction   390
        Method of analysis   390
        Limitations of the analysis   391
        Reliability of interpretations   392
    Summary of Hellenistic and Roman pottery from Level I   392
    Late Roman and Byzantine contexts and assemblages   392
        Pre-courtyard   392
        Courtyard sequence   393
        Level Ic building   393
        Level Id building   393
        I14a–M14b   393
        Less well-stratified material   393
    Glazed wares   394
    Summary   394
        Painted motifs   395
    Conclusion   396
    Character and description of the Late Roman and Byzantine ceramic corpus   396
        Introduction   396
        Late Roman Red Slipped Table Wares   396
        *Late Roman C Ware. Variations of Hayes' Form 3 (**1008–14**)*   396
        *Cypriot Red Slip Ware Form 2. Waagé's Late Roman D Ware (**1015–16**)*   397
        *Spiral burnished ware (**1017**)*   397
        *Other fine wares (**1018–26**)*   397
    Plain and plain painted wares   397

Imported amphorae	402
Level I cooking pot fabric vessels	403
Introduction	403
Cooking pot fabric descriptions	403
Glazed wares	404
Catalogue of pottery from Late Roman and Byzantine deposits	405

Appendix Luminescence Dating of a Single Pottery Sherd from the Byzantine Levels   429

Summary of results	429
Age determination	429
Technical details	429
Sample preparation	429
Palaeodose	429
Dose rate	430

Chapter 20

Introduction to the Pottery

J.N. Postgate

In view of the importance for Kilise Tepe of its relations with the interior and with the Mediterranean, the evidence for local and imported ceramic production is of particular interest. While at different times some or all of the ceramic repertoire may appear closely similar to the material recovered from other regions, the precision afforded by thin-section petrography, supported by chemical analysis, is critical in addressing questions of production. Hence this evidence is presented first, rather than relegated to the usual appendix, followed by reports on the pottery corpus in successive levels.

Recovery and recording

Given that both on the surface of the tepe, and in the excavated deposits, potsherds provided the most abundant and the most chronologically sensitive artefacts, the usual effort went into their recovery and examination. Since we can only present here the merest fraction of what was recovered, it is desirable to describe the process of recording on which the selection is based.

The recovery procedures during the surface clearance have been described above (pp. 48–9). During excavation, potsherds were put in a basket labelled with the unit number of the context being dug, and taken down to the sherd yard, which was on flattish ground in front of the spring at the foot of the north end of the tepe. The sherds were scrubbed by one or two workmen, laid out to dry, and then sorted by the member of the team currently responsible for the on-site pottery work (in 1994 Sara Da Gama Howells; in 1995–8 Connie Hansen).

As part of the sorting process, the sherds were counted (not weighed), and undecorated body sherds discarded on a separate grid (so that the sherds from the unit could be revisited during the season if subsequent study made it desirable; at the close of work each season these sherds were disposed of in a well-defined location off-site).

A form was filled out (on paper in 1994, electronically in later seasons) recording the quantities of this material, including tile fragments. The remaining sherds, principally feature sherds (rims, handles, bases, etc.), but also sherds with various types of decoration, were transferred to the school building at Zeyne, where in due course they were examined by the relevant member of the team (some units from the first season were never systematically re-examined at this stage).

Hand-written notes were kept on the Deep Sounding material. For both the Late Bronze and Iron Age units, recording sheets were introduced in 1996 and used in 1997–98 (see Figs. 362–4). These are the essential record for what was in each unit: they attempt to tabulate for each unit the major recurring types and to sort them by fabric. Notes on other pieces were made below the tabulated section of the forms. In 1997–98 a similar system was devised by Mark Jackson for the Level I pottery (principally Byzantine, but also used for earlier material.

The majority of sherds remained bagged by unit, and at the end of the 1998 season were stored so (within plastic crates) in the Silifke Museum. The exceptions are principally pieces of pottery which for one reason or another were given find numbers of their own: such numbers may have been given by the excavators when the pot was lifted separately from the rest of the sherds in the unit because they were *in situ* whole vessels, or parts of vessels, which required separate numbering to permit their identification on the plan; or they may have been assigned in the house when significant individual pieces were isolated from the rest of the sherds in a unit. These pieces with find numbers, so far as they were kept separate and not discarded, are stored together in crates labelled SFP. Other sherds selected for drawing, but not given a separate finds number were assigned a 'drawing number' (e.g. D1517). These are mostly bagged together with other drawn sherds, and are stored in separate crates, but not consistently, as some were reintegrated with the rest of the kept sherds from their unit. Brief descriptions were written for these drawn sherds, forming the basis for their catalogue entries in this volume.

The drawing numbers and descriptions have been incorporated in the consolidated electronic data

Chapter 20

base, which will be accessible in due course through the Archaeological Data Service in York.

Presentation of the ceramics

Although from the point of view of recovery and initial recording the ceramics from the site all received similar treatment, the material from the different periods varied in character and significance, and the reports which follow vary accordingly. The third-millennium material (Level V), and the two phases of the Middle Bronze Age (Level IVa–b) came exclusively from the Deep Sounding in H19/20. Except for occasional pieces from unstratified contexts, they belong in a single well-defined, if restricted, stratigraphic sequence and were studied as a coherent corpus by Dorit Symington over the five excavation seasons and in a subsequent study season at the Silifke Museum. The total corpus was relatively small, and in some levels there was a fair proportion of whole vessels from primary contexts. Her account of this material is comprehensive, and well informed by familiarity with the Tarsus material in particular. Moreover, as with all our ceramic work, the ware descriptions especially have benefited from joint examination of the material at the site with Carl Knappett.

At the other end of our sequence, the great majority of the Late Roman and Byzantine material was examined either during the excavation or in two study seasons at the museum by Mark Jackson, and was largely incorporated in his doctoral thesis presented to the University of Newcastle in 2001. This section of our pottery report is accordingly a comprehensive survey of our latest ceramics, with due reference to earlier and current work in the Göksu Valley and other sites such as Anamur. Since there were extremely few post-Byzantine sherds in our total surface collection, this corpus did not suffer significantly from later contamination, and in the course of his work Mark Jackson's familiarity with the main bulk of the material from the top level of the site enabled him to isolate certain wares and types which appear to be earlier (see p. 379). He was also able to identify certain contexts excavated in the first two seasons which had yielded virtually uncontaminated Hellenistic assemblages, in addition to those which had already served as the source for the study of the imported Hellenistic wares by Lisa Nevett in 1995 (which therefore does not take into account the material excavated after that season). Nevertheless, the absence of any Hellenistic architecture, except perhaps in I-M14 and on the East Slope, has meant that we have very little satisfactorily provenanced Hellenistic material, and the majority of the pottery described in this section comes from pits.

Sandwiched between the Middle Bronze Age beneath and the patchy Hellenistic presence at the site are Levels II and III which between them account for something over a millennium. This material was processed and described by Connie Hansen, predominantly during the 1995–98 seasons, with the benefit of advice from Dorit Symington. Fabrics were classified and subsequently revised in the light of comments from Carl Knappett. For various reasons these levels have not provided as neat a subject of study as those before and after. In the case of Level III the majority of the material derives from H19/20 and I19/20 at the NW corner. Except for a few large storage vessels it is almost exclusively in the form of sherds, and the same applies to the ceramics from the Late Bronze Age houses in I14. The material from all five stratigraphic phases of Level III in the NW corner was remarkably homogeneous, and as explained below, the decision was taken to treat it as a single corpus, using a few large and safely provenanced units to supply the bulk of the material described. Although we believe the material presented here is a representative sample, we are conscious that our Level III material will repay further study. In particular a review of the fabrics is needed, and in the light of work elsewhere on the chronology of Hittite ceramics of the fifteenth to thirteenth centuries it might well prove useful to re-examine the rather small sample of sherds from phases IIIa–c.

As for Level II, the material included in this report is also very largely from the NW corner. Starting immediately after the end of Level III it runs through (whether continuously or not) to the eighth- to seventh-century IIf kilns and still later pits, which however do not show any traces of ceramics we might date to the sixth–fifth centuries. It seems probable that the earlier phases of Level II (IIa–c) should be contemporary with the end of Tarsus Late Bronze IIa. Level IId belongs in the first half of the twelfth century, in view of the Mycenaean vessels from the IId destruction, studied here in full by Elizabeth French along with the other Mycenaean sherds, and is therefore in Tarsus terms Late Bronze IIb. On the other hand, Level IIf is by any reckoning well into the Iron Age. It might seem logical, therefore, to have treated the Level II material in two halves, the first belonging in conventional terms to the end of the Bronze Age, and the second to the earlier part of the Iron Age, and indeed we considered doing just this.

We have not done so for two main reasons. The first is the nature of the material: the majority of the ceramic evidence for Level II is in sherd form, with the exception of the *in situ* pots in Level IIc (**693–706**) and the contents of a kiln in IIf (**707–35**). In the publication of the ceramics from Tille cogent reasons were given for ignoring the evidence of mere sherds and restricting the account of the ceramics to whole or largely preserved pots in primary contexts (Summers 1993, 3). There is much to recommend this approach: in the case of our NW corner the profusion of Iron Age (and indeed Byzantine) pits has not only removed large swathes of potentially stratified deposits, but also inevitably brought up much earlier sherd material into later levels. The consequences of this are described in more detail below (p. 343).

The second reason is the nature of the contexts: after Level IId most deposits in the NW corner are only marginally associated with architectural phases. There are exceptions (e.g. Room e9), but on the whole most sherds coming from IIe-h are from fill, pits, or courtyard levels. We have tried to attribute the levels in the Western Courtyard to their correct phases, but after IId these are no longer associated with well-defined building phases and the border lines between IIe and IIf, and between IIf and any later deposits remain uncertain.

Unfortunately, the ceramic repertoire of the centuries between about 1200 and 700 BC is the least well known and most controversial. Kilise Tepe itself has demonstrated that we cannot expect the ceramics of this time span to be easily tied in to known repertoires in the same way as the earlier Bronze Age or Byzantine material. As explained below (p. 343), therefore, we have avoided the temptation to assign part of our sequence to the final Bronze Age period, and separate it from a later Iron Age part, precisely because we would be unsure where to place Level IIe in this division of the spoils, and because there must undoubtedly be many sherds fabricated in the earlier, but recovered by us in the later, phases, and we would run the risk of papering over the cracks and prejudging some of the very points at issue.

This is not to say that the sherd material from Levels IIe and IIf is worthless. It is true that it cannot be used by us to pinpoint the date of our levels, nor to provide a stratigraphic sequence which will help with the chronological uncertainties still afflicting the Iron Age in Anatolia and the eastern Mediterranean. Some of the material is previously unknown and evidently of local production, and it is useful to have established its existence; other pieces belong to ceramic types already well attested in Plain Cilicia, Cyprus and elsewhere, and it is valuable to have established their presence further north and west than previously. There is certainly more detailed work to be done here, since there has been neither the time nor the opportunity for the authors to get seriously involved with the complexities and uncertainties of eastern Mediterranean and Levantine wares of the early first millennium. Our catalogue therefore aims to present a typical range of wares without attempting a detailed chronological seriation, which would need a larger corpus of better-stratified material from these phases.

That said, a few suggestions have been made below (pp. 343–6), for possible developments in the local wares, and it is worth noting that at Boğazköy too recent work suggests that there is a progression from the earliest post-Hittite hand-made red-painted wares to the Middle Iron Age tradition associated with Alişar IV. It should be clearly understood, though, that the volume of securely stratified sherds is too small to make this anything more than a first attempt. Whether there is a break in occupation at the site, or we are looking at a continuous occupation between the mid-twelfth century in Level IId and the end of the eighth century in IIf, the ceramic sequence is too thin to be reconstructed with confidence.

Chapter 21

Pottery Fabrics and Technology

Carl Knappett & Vassilis Kilikoglou

Aims of the study

Although this section on pottery technology and composition constitutes a separate section of the publication, the aim from the outset has been to make it fully compatible with the typological sections for each period. It is not our objective to discuss technology and composition as variables somehow independent of style and shape. All aspects of ceramic products are the result of choices being made by pottery producers and consumers at the site. That is to say, the processes of clay selection, paste preparation, vessel construction, surface treatment, decoration and firing are all inputs that are more or less visible in the final output. Shape, style, technology and composition are very much interrelated, and we shall try to remain mindful of this throughout this chapter. An analytical commitment to treating all of these dimensions as part of a coherent totality is part and parcel of the 'chaîne opératoire' approach to ancient technologies, successfully pursued now in both ceramic and lithic studies.

Building from this general perspective, we shall in this chapter attempt to address a number of issues concerning the production and consumption of pottery at the site:
1. Was pottery produced at the site and, if so, what local resources were used? How might production have been organized — is there a single specialized workshop manufacturing all the pottery used at the site, or is each class of pottery made by a different workshop?
2. Was any pottery imported to the site from elsewhere? Can we identify the sources of imported pottery, the quantities involved, and the motivations for such exchange? What sort of regional and long-distance contacts did Kilise Tepe have?
3. The temporal perspective — to what extent can we identify chronological changes in local and imported pottery at the site? What long-term trends in technological innovation and resource exploitation can be identified?
4. The spatial perspective — can production patterns at Kilise Tepe be usefully compared with other sites in or beyond the region? This may prove difficult given the low number of excavated assemblages in Cilicia as a whole.

Methodology

Within these overall aims, the pottery assemblages recovered from each phase of the site were subjected to detailed study of their shapes, wares, decorations, and fabrics. The ceramic fabrics were assessed and described at the macroscopic level before any sort of microscopic analysis was begun. Because of the time and cost involved in microscopic analysis, it is customary to sample only a small percentage of the full ceramic repertoire. However, by conducting extensive study of the entire assemblage at the macroscopic level, there is a very good chance that the samples chosen for further microscopic work are representative of the whole. It is also important to choose samples that are from common shapes and wares, and to select some examples that appear to be of the same fabric but which come from different shapes with different surface treatments. By choosing samples not only on fabric grounds, but also in relation to shape and ware variation, there is a much better chance of piecing together patterns of variation that relate to the choices made by ancient potters throughout their operational sequences.

The main goal at first must be to identify and characterize those fabrics that are most common in each phase. There may be a temptation to sample the odd and exotic fabrics, but such lines of enquiry must be set aside until the predominant local fabrics are determined. Only once the range of variation in the main fabric groups has been established does it make good sense to tackle the minority fabrics. The main fabric groups will tend to be local and the minority fabrics imported, but this is not always the case since some non-local fabrics are imported in such quantities as to constitute major groups at the site (e.g. LBA Red Lustrous Wheel-made ware). In order to define which fabrics are local and which are non-local, it is essential to have some information to hand on the nature of the local geology, a subject to which we now turn.

Local geology and clay resources

Geological information from maps and publications provides some indication of what should be expected petrographically of local resources (Figs. 365 & 366). However, such documentation is not always of sufficient resolution, and clearly has other aims than the identification of clay and sand resources suitable for potting. Thus in order to successfully distinguish local from non-local pottery, and to assess some of the resource choices made by ancient potters, such data as are available must be supplemented by careful sampling of clay and sand resources from the environs of the site. These samples are prepared as clay briquettes, fired in a kiln, and then made into thin sections for petrographic analysis.

Kilise Tepe lies in an area which may be described geographically and geologically as the Mut basin (after the town of Mut, *c.* 25 km up the Göksu from Kilise Tepe), composed predominantly of Lower and Middle Miocene marine sediments (Fig. 366), many of which are calcareous clays suitable for pottery. There are also terrigenous clastics in the form of conglomerates. Much of the surrounding pre-Miocene geology is sedimentary, i.e. limestones and dolomites. On the geological maps there are no metamorphic outcrops documented in the immediate environs of Kilise Tepe (Campbell 1971; Brinkmann 1976), neither have any been observed in the course of the fieldwork and sampling trips. There do exist metamorphic outcrops some distance to the north-east in the Bolkar Mountains (Fig. 365; Demirtaşlı *et al.* 1984). The maps of the area do not appear to show any streams or rivers flowing down from there to the Göksu river valley that might lead to metamorphic rock fragments occurring in river sands of the Kilise Tepe area. This possibility cannot be entirely ruled out though, which means that some metamorphic rock fragments could perhaps find their way into local clay resources. There may also be rocks of metamorphic origin within the varied conglomerate sediments. Yet to encounter a ceramic fabric containing large amounts of metamorphic rock fragments would probably have to mean that the fabric was non-local. It should also be noted that the next nearest metamorphic outcrops occur some distance to the SW in the area of Anamur; the topography of the area, however, means that they could not have eroded into the Mut basin.

Another important feature revealed by the 1:500,000 geological map for the area (Adana sheet) is a very small ribbon of serpentinite outcrops, just 10 km up the Kurtsuyu valley that stretches east from near the site (Fig. 366). These outcrops were visited and sampled in the course of fieldwork, and it was noted that they are located close to and above the Kurtsuyu river. Their exposed position means that they could be eroded into the river and subsequently be transported down-stream towards the confluence with the Göksu river and the site of Kilise Tepe.

In summary, the most relevant features of the local geology for the purposes of the ceramic thin section descriptions are the abundant and varied marine clays, the predominantly sedimentary environment, the serpentinite outcrops up the Kurtsuyu valley, and the occurrence of some metamorphic outcrops in the broader region (Fig. 365). Descriptions of the clay, sand and rock samples taken as part of the project are included below.

Techniques of preparation

Following detailed visual examination of the various ceramic fabrics represented in the pottery assemblage of Kilise Tepe, a number of characteristic fabrics were selected for thin-section analysis. Approximately 200 sherds were chosen as samples from the site, whereupon they were exported to the UK for preparation according to standard thin-section preparation techniques. Ceramic fabrics thus prepared as thin sections can be assessed microscopically for their optical properties, facilitating the process of characterization. Most amenable to such analyses are the minerals and rock fragments that are often included within the fabric, rather than the clay minerals themselves, which are too small to be detected with this technique.

Equipment used
- Nikon Optiphot-Pol polarizing microscope (McDonald Institute, Cambridge);
- Leitz Laborlux 12 polarizing microscope (Fitch Laboratory, British School at Athens);
- Photomicrographs shot with Canon A-1 camera attached to Leitz Laborlux 12.

Descriptive system
A system for the detailed description of ceramic thin sections has recently been devised by Whitbread (1989; 1995). One objective of creating a standardized system for use by ceramic petrographers is to facilitate comparisons between samples studied in different projects. Yet it is not a case of the more detail the better; the endless description of the numerous dimensions of a thin section is not beneficial if those dimensions do not contribute significantly to the characterization and provenancing of the sample,

or to an understanding of the ceramic technology employed. Within Whitbread's system, textural concentration features (Tcfs), amorphous concentration features (Acfs), and crystalline concentration features (Kcfs) are all treated in separate sections. This forms part of a concerted effort to incorporate more elements of soil micromorphology description into the methodology commonly utilized by ceramic petrographers. At present, however, the importance of these features, either in terms of provenancing or technology, does not seem great (although further work may remedy this situation); thus they will not be treated separately and systematically in this study, but will be mentioned as and when they feature. Despite this and other simplifications to Whitbread's system, it is hoped that enough similarities remain for comparisons still to be made with other published descriptions. The format adopted in this study bears strong similarities to, and is partly based on, the system used in Day (1995) and Day & Haskell (1995), which too derives from Whitbread (1989).

The main ceramic fabric groups from each main phase of occupation at Kilise Tepe are classified and described in turn. Although all the samples within each fabric group have of course been fully studied, only representative samples within some groups are published with detailed descriptions. Fabric groups in each phase are assigned higher case letters, i.e. A, B, and C. Within each period there is a division made between local and non-local fabrics at the site, although on many occasions it is impossible to be more specific about the sources of the various non-local fabrics.

Technique of chemical analysis
132 of the ceramic samples were analysed by Instrumental Neutron Activation (NAA) at the Laboratory of Archaeometry, National Centre for Scientific Research (NCSR) Demokritos, Athens (summarized in Table 8). A portion of each specimen was cleaned with a tungsten carbide drill-bit, then removed from it, powdered and kept in glass vials. For the analysis, the powder was left overnight to dry at 120°C and approximately 150 mg from each individual was weighed and heat sealed in polyethylene vials. The same procedure was followed for the reference material used, which was an International Atomic Energy Agency SOIL-7. Individuals and standards were irradiated for 30 min in batches of ten (eight individuals and two standards) at the swimming pool reactor of NCSR 'Demokritos', at a thermal neutron flux of 3×10^{13} n.cm^{-2}.s^{-1}. Seven days after irradiation, the individuals and standards were measured for Sm, Lu, U, Yb, As, Sb, Ca, Na, La and 20 days after irradiation for Ce, Th, Cr, Hf, Zr, Cs, Tb, Sc, Rb, Fe, Ta, Co and Eu.

The samples which were analysed in this project came from many different chronological periods and pottery of diverse style and fabric. For this reason the statistical approach followed treated each period separately and resulting groups were compared with the respective petrographic ones. The standard statistics used was cluster analysis using the majority of the elements determined, in order to get a rough picture of the existing chemical groups within the data. Then the first step for the statistical evaluation of the chemical data was the calculation of the variation matrix (Aitchinson 1990; Buxeda i Garrigós 1999). In this calculation the concentrations of the elements Sb, Tb, Ta and As were excluded for their poor counting statistics and some missing values. The columns of the variation matrix contain the variances resulting from the logratio transformation of each element (in rows) with the element as a devisor shown on the top of the respective column. The sum of the variances in each column is denoted by $\tau_{.i}$, while the sum of all $\tau_{.i}$'s divided by twice the number of elements, gives the total variation (vt), which is a measure of variability within the chemical data set. The absolute value of the total variation is an indication of whether the set of samples considered is monogenic or polygenic (statistically single group or more than one, respectively) (Buxeda i Garrigós & Kilikoglou 2003).

Clay, sand and rock samples

A number of clay, sand and rock samples were taken in the 1997 season from a series of locations in the region around the site of Kilise Tepe. Buff marine clays and marls were selected, as were various sands and silty clays from river and stream margins. Much of the area around Kilise Tepe is composed of buff calcareous clays, which according to the geological map are Neogene marine clays of Lower and Middle Miocene date (Fig. 366). For example, there appear to be a lot of buff clays in the vicinity of Evkafçiftliği, and onwards up to the village of Kurtsuyu. Samples of such clays were taken from:
- halfway between Şarlak and Zeyne (sample 1) going up the hill, in the road cutting;
- a greenish-brown-buff clay (sample 2) from just before crossing to village of Değirmendere, which is halfway down the valley between Kilise Tepe and Silifke;
- Çağlayangedik (sample 3), near Kışla, about 2 km south of Kilise Tepe. Here there are extensive Neogene deposits forming a low hill, exploited by locals for mud brick and plastering of houses;
- silty-clayey sample from beneath bridge at Kurtsuyu village (sample 4). Not a primary marine clay

Table 8. *Kilise Tepe ceramics samples list.*

Level Vj–g (40 samples)					
	Fabric	Chem.	Unit	No.	Description
S1	A	9947	1852		grey burnished ware, rim of open vessel
S2	A	9950	5402		red burnished, exterior only
S3	A	9963	5405		semi-fine crumbly orange
S4	A		5405		closed vessel, red pattern burnish, light brown buff fabric
S5	B	9964	1871		open bowl, red burnish exterior and interior
S6	C		5406		semi-coarse orange scored ware, some black grits
S7	D	9949	1898		black burnished interior and exterior
S8	D		1892		part of tall jar
S9	D		1883		conical bowl
S10	E1	9953	1894	193	globular jar ('earliest pot')
S11	E1		5406		cooking pot
S12	E1	9958	5406		cooking pot
S13	E1	9946	1845		rim sherd, coarse orange brown, roughened exterior
S14	E1		5406		semi-open globular jar, scored, gritty brown fabric
S15	E1	9957	1870		closed vessel with red burnish exterior
S16	E1		1874		closed vessel, red burnished, gritty orange-brown/grey fabric
S17	E2		1851		platter, coarse buff, with organic temper
S18	E2		1851		sandy ware with very thick grey core, red wash
S19	F	9961	1898		cooking pot with roughened exterior
S20	F	9951	1859		brown burnished, 'champagne' cup
S21	G		1847		coarse orange-red ware
S22	G	9965	5402		closed vessel?
S23	G		5402		closed vessel, lumpy interior, faint pink-red slip exterior, brown fabric
S24	H		1872		plain, semi-coarse brown with varied grey grits
S25	I		5406		cooking pot, coarse dark brown with large grey grits
S26	J	9962	1871		cooking pot
S27	J		1871		cooking pot, some wiping, brown and gritty, platy purple grits
S28	K		5429		plain coarse jars (rope cordon at rim), pale buff, low-fired
S29	K	9948	1894		marble-tempered (cooking pot ware?) buff
S30	L	9960	5406		H20/743 very coarse orange-yellow and organics
S31	M	9959	5406		coarse orange, crumbly
S32	N	9944	1851		grey burnished ware, exterior burnish only, dark grey fabric
S33	N	9945	1851		red burnished, exterior only (closed vessel), brown-grey fabric
S34	O	9952	1852		matt painted and red band, semi-fine red
S35	P	9956	1898		plain, thin-walled bowl, dark brown with gritty texture
S36	Q		6305		rim of thin-walled rounded bowl, burnished, gritty red-brown
S37	R	9954	5384	257	rounded bowl, gritty fabric
S38	S		6305		thin-walled closed vessel, red burnish, gritty brown-red
S39	T	9943	1836		clinky metallic ware with grey core
S40	U	9955	6305		closed vessel?, monochrome red exterior, brown-red, grey core
Level V f–e (17 samples)					
	Fabric	Chem.	Unit	No.	Description
S41	A	99102	1825		semi-coarse buff fabric, thick-walled, monochrome exterior
S42	A	99103	1805		orange buff incised ware
S43	A	99104	1813		coarse orange honeycomb ware, plain large jar
S44	A	99105	1823		cream-slipped ware (orange fabric), thick-walled body sherd
S45	A	99106	1807		chocolate speckled buff ware, rim sherd of rounded bowl
S46	A	99108	1829		thin-walled orange honeycomb, rim sherd of rounded bowl
S47	A	99109	1805		dark slip, crossed bowl (cf. **351–8**), buff fabric
S48	A	99112	1826		plain body sherd, coarse pale orange buff, possible organics
S49	A	99114	1826		similar to S48, coarse pale buff, dark wash exterior, thick-walled
S50	A	99115	1826		semi-coarse purplish buff, purple-brown wash interior and exterior

Table 8. *(cont.)*

Level V f–e (17 samples) *(cont.)*					
	Fabric	Chem.	Unit	No.	Description
S52	A	99117	1826		rim sherd, semi-fine to fine wheelmade plain flaring bowl
S53	A	99118			basin, coarse orange fabric
S54	A	99119			basin, coarse orange fabric
S55	A	99110			basin, coarse orange fabric
S56	B	99111	1825		cooking pot ware, handled vessel
S57	C	99113	1805		coarse red with phyllites, plain
Level IV (19 samples)					
	Fabric	Chem.	Unit	No.	Description
S58	A	99130	1258		thick-walled bowl, monochrome red slip, orange buff fabric
S59	A	99126	1258		closed vessel, monochrome red slip exterior, orange buff fabric
S60	A		1258		fine ware with brown/black slip (orange buff?)
S61	A	99127	4267		bowl, all-over red slip, hard orange buff
S62	B	99122	4257		plain buff cup base
S63	B	99123	4254		fine buff, red burnish exterior and interior
S64	B	99124	4257		body from plain fine open vessel (cup?), fine pale buff
S65	B		1258		thick-walled carinated bowl?, red burnish, semi-fine brown grey
S66	B	99129	1258		thick-walled open shape, red burnish, fine grey-brown fabric
S67	B		4254		rounded bowl?, red burnish, dense semi-fine pale buff
S68	B	99132	4255		thick-walled bowl, red burnish, fine pale grey-brown buff
S69	B	99131	4263		open bowl, red burnish all-over, semi-fine buff-grey fabric
S70	B		4271		jug with offset base, red burnish exterior, fine pale buff
S71	C	99125	1227		plain semi-coarse orange fabric
S72	C	99107	1802		grey combed ware
S73	C		1258		combed ware jar, handmade, coarse brown with phyllites
S74	C		1258		combed ware jar, handmade, coarse brown with phyllites
S75	C	99128	4271		plain coarse brown, handmade, pitted interior
S76	D		1258		cooking pot, grooved/twisted handle, very coarse brown
Level III (34 samples)					
	Fabric	Chem.	Unit	No.	Description
S77	A	9997	4211		fine red, lustrous
S78	A		4211		very fine red lustrous, libation arm
S79	A		1428		very fine red lustrous, libation arm?
S80	A	99101	5501		very fine red lustrous
S81	A		5502		very fine red lustrous, rim of open rounded bowl
S82	A	9987	4205		very fine red fabric, lustrous
S83	A	9994	4211		semi-fine version of S84, with red burnish to exterior
S84	A		4211		semi-fine red, from inturned rim bowl
S85	A		4205		semi-fine red
S86	A	9998	4211		semi-fine red
S87	A	9999	4211		semi-fine red, from jar with thickened rim
S88	A		4211		semi-coarse to coarse red
S89	A		4211		semi-coarse to coarse red
S90	A		4211		semi-coarse to coarse red, from large thickened rim jar
S91	A	9988	4205		very coarse red, thick-walled with white grits (calcite?)
S92	A	9995	4211		very thick-walled semi-coarse red fabric with thick grey core
S93	A	99120	1226		coarse orange-red storage vessel fabric
S94	B	9992	4211		fine pale buff thickened rim bowl, plain
S95	B	9981	4205		basin with everted rim, semi-coarse pale buff
S96	B		4205		plain shallow bowl, inturned rim, semi-fine pale buff
S97	B		4205		plain shallow bowl, inturned rim, semi-fine buff
S98	B	9982	4205		plain shallow bowl, inturned rim, semi-fine buff
S99	B		4205		plain shallow bowl, inturned rim, brown buff
S100	B		4211		plain shallow bowl, inturned rim, semi-coarse pale buff
S101	C	9985	4211		semi-fine pale buff (closed vessel body sherd), red slip

Table 8. *(cont.)*

Level III (34 samples) *(cont.)*					
	Fabric	Chem.	Unit	No.	Description
S103	C	9991	4205		fine pale buff thickened rim bowl, dark wash interior and exterior
S104	D	99100	1421		coarse buff, marble/calcite grits (thickened rim jar)
S105	E	9986	4205		coarse brown grey with sparkling grits, plain body sherd
S106	F	9983	4211		very coarse brown fabric, white grits at surface, body sherd
S107	F	9993	4211		very thick-walled coarse pale brown buff
S108	G	9989	4211		closed vessel, coarse orange, platy grits at interior, red slip
S109	H	99121	1226		dark brown cooking pot ware
S110	I	9984	4205		coarse brown, no slip, body sherd
S111	J	9990	4205		coarse brown/grey cooking pot ware, body sherd
Level II a–d (25 samples)					
	Fabric	Chem.	Unit	No.	Description
S112	A	9908	1704	787	banded decoration trefoil amphora
S113	A	9906	1780		square rim basin, cross-hatching
S114	A	9904	2414		square rim basin, diagonal lines
S115	A	9907	2652		rounded bowl, diagonal lines
S116	A	9902	1541	751	rounded bowl, cross-hatching
S117	A		4542		pilgrim flask, grey-brown buff, varied red and grey grits
S118	A		5502		pilgrim flask, semi-coarse sandy orange
S119	A	9912	5502		base of ring-base bowl, half buff and half red (firing)
S120	A	9909	5502		rim of plain bowl, inturned rim, pale silty buff
S121	A		5502		bowl with inturned, grooved rim, fine to semi-fine red
S122	A		5523		inturned rim bowl, washy red slip, gritty buff
S123	A		5523		inturned rim bowl, washy red slip, fine pale green buff
S124	A		5523		inturned rim bowl, red-brown slip, brown buff
S125	A		5523		inturned rim bowl, red-brown slip, brown buff
S126	A		3927		cooking pot, jar on Rm 8 floor
S127	B	9910	5502	790	square rim basin, cross-hatching, semi-fine brown-red fabric
S128	B		2884		square-rim basin, cross-hatching
S129	B		2864		pilgrim flask, semi-fine brown-red with tiny mica grains
S130	B		2880		pilgrim flask, semi-fine red, possibly like LBA red?
S131	B		2877	916	pilgrim flask, semi-fine red
S132	B	9901	2873	917	small pilgrim flask, semi-fine red with white grits
S133	B	9913	4564	693	pilgrim flask (complete), fine red with white silty grits
S134	B	9911	5502		base of ring-base bowl, silty red
S135	C	9903	3927		cooking pot rim, 'marble' temper
S136	D	9905	1387		cooking pot rim, 'marble' temper, orange-red fabric
Mycenaean wares (6 samples)					
	Fabric	Chem.	Unit	No.	Description
S137	E1	9940	3921	957	Mycenaean deep bowl, fine grey buff
S138	E2	9939	1690	955	Mycenaean closed vessel, banded decoration, no rim, fine buff-grey
S139	F	9942	3918	960	Mycenaean deep bowl, orange buff
S140	F	9938	1690	959	Mycenaean deep bowl, fine buff, burnt in places
S141	F	9937	5864	958	Mycenaean deep bowl, fine orange-pink buff, burnt
S142	G	9941	1124	947	Mycenaean stirrup jar, fine salmon pink-orange fabric
Level IIe (7 samples)					
	Fabric	Chem.	Unit	No.	Description
S143	A	9915	1750		lekane, Kindergarten fabric
S144	A	9917	1514		pendent semicircles
S145	A	9916	4353		collar necked jar, Kindergarten fabric
S146	A	9918	2387		large jar? Kindergarten fabric
S147	C		1924		horizontal lines, coarse, pale whitish buff, cf. S176
S148	C		1924		horizontal lines, pale whitish buff with brown grits
S149	C	9919	1924		bichrome jug, semi-fine pale whitish buff, brown grits

Table 8. (cont.)

Level IIf (33 samples)					
	Fabric	Chem.	Unit	No.	Description
S150	A	9914	1783		trefoil jug decorated with target motifs
S151	A		1783		trefoil jug decorated with target motifs
S152	A	9935	1783		trefoil jug decorated with target motifs
S153	A		1783		trefoil jug decorated with target motifs
S154	A		1783		rim of beer jug
S155	A	9924	1783		beer jug, near base
S156	A		1783		juglet
S157	A		1783		juglet
S158	A		1783		pot stand
S159	A	9925	1783		pot stand
S160	A		1783		bevelled-rim bowl
S161	A	9926	1783		bevelled-rim bowl
S162	A		1783		grooved bowl
S163	A		1783		grooved bowl
S164	A		1783		jar
S165	A	9927	1783		jar
S166	A	9928	1627		horiz lines, thin-walled (collared jar?)
S167	A	9930	2201		lines and targets, soft coarse sandy fabric (jar?)
S168	A	9933	1501		lines and targets, greenish buff, relatively coarse
S169	B1	9931	3432		black-on-red bands, red fabric
S170	B1		5941		black-on-red rounded bowl, fine pale red-orange
S171	B1	9923	4500	840	black-on-red rounded bowl, ring base, pale red
S172	B1		6109	845	black-on-red bowl?, target, semi-fine red, varied grits
S173	B2	9920	1571		black-on-red bands, red fabric
S174	B3	9934	3412	847	bichrome targets, semi-fine orange red
S175	B4	9922	1799	846	bichrome jug, targets, semi-fine buff but red core
S176	B5	9932	1704		bichrome targets
S177	B6		5114		bichrome jug?, bands, cream slip, semi-fine orange fabric
S178	B6	9936	1780	828	jug? horizontal lines, orange-red fabric, buff slip
S179	B7		2411	851	trefoil jug, lines and targets, orange buff
S180	B8		2343		bichrome jug, targets, thick cream slip, fine orange-red
S181	C	9921	1799	836	black-on-red closed shape, semi-fine brick-red, varied grits
S182	D	9929	1753		lines and targets, orange-red fabric, buff slip
Byzantine period (4 samples)					
	Fabric	Chem.	Unit	No.	Description
S183		9969	1670		Byzantine painted sherd, with mudstone inclusions
S184		9968	9686		Byzantine painted sherd, with mudstone inclusions
S185		9966	4393	1184	Byzantine painted sherd, with serpentinite
S186		9967	3205	1126	Byzantine spiral-painted sherd, with serpentinite
Clay briquettes (11 samples)					
	Fabric	Chem.	Unit	No.	Description
S187		9970			clay from between Zeyne and Şarlak
S188		9971			clay from Göksu river towards Silifke, on west side
S189		9972			clay from near village of Gedik, close to Kışla
S190		9973			silty clay from river, beneath bridge in Kurtsuyu village
S191		9974			same silty clay as S190, with Göksu river sand from Kışla
S192		9975			silty clay from Tarsus Çay, near motorway
S193		9976			same clay as S192, with serp. sand, river bed NE of Elvanlı
S194		9977			same clay as S192, with limestone sand from Dereköy
S195		9978			brown clay, Kurtsuyu valley, Göbekler village.
S196		9979			light brown clay, cut in river bank of Tarsus Çay, inland
S197		9980			dark brown clay, cut in river bank of Tarsus Çay, inland
Total	197 petrography samples				
	132 chemistry samples				

as such, but derived from one, and redeposited through stream action.

River sands were also sampled from different locations in the Kilise Tepe area:
- from the Göksu river close to Kışla, only 1 or 2 km from the site;
- from Dereköy, in the upper valley of the Kurtsuyu to the east of the Göksu valley.

Finally, rock samples were taken from a location up the Kurtsuyu valley. There is a very distinctive set of low ridges and hillocks that stand out as being quite different from the predominantly sedimentary environment. There are outcrops red and green in colour from which samples were taken, one of which was green and seemingly like a basalt in texture. Another had the soapy feel characteristic of serpentine. Indeed the geological map for the area shows a very narrow ribbon of serpentinite outcrops in this precise area (Fig. 366). When the rock samples were examined petrographically, most proved to be composed of serpentine, whether they were red or green in colour, with a distinctive lattice structure. One of the five samples, however, was a volcanic rock, variolitic in texture, possibly basalt, composed of feldspar laths, epidote, and chlorite, in approximately equal proportions. There is no mention of such volcanic rocks on the geological map.

The geological maps do not suggest the presence of *terra rossas* or any other forms of non-calcareous red clay beds in the areas around the site. Neither did clay prospection lead to the discovery of any such clay deposits in the area of Kilise Tepe. The search for such clay types was extended down the Göksu towards Silifke; along the west side of the valley some limited deposits of red soil were found, but nothing particularly clayey. A more intensive survey of the area may reveal limited pockets of red non-calcareous clays, but it seems clear that there are no significant deposits in the area. It is therefore considered for the purposes of this study that any fabrics that are identified through thin section and chemical analyses as non-calcareous are probably non-local.

Special focus on resources from Tarsus

In the publication of the excavations at Tarsus, samples were taken of pottery from Bronze Age and Iron Age levels and subjected to chemical and petrographic analyses (Norton *et al.*, in Goldman 1963). Although by no means as commonplace today as it might be, this sort of research initiative was rather rare at the time this publication was compiled. Moreover, samples of modern potters' clays from Tarsus were also examined, providing comparanda for the ancient pottery. Indeed when a local clay and an Iron Age sample were compared using X-ray diffraction, they proved to have similar X-ray patterns (Goldman 1963, 403–5). The character of the sampled clays is not described in detail, but they would appear to be calcitic (cf. description of T34 on p. 402).

Against the background of this early pioneering work, and considering the possibility that some pottery may have been imported to Kilise Tepe from Tarsus, it was decided to take new clay samples from the Tarsus area. The exact derivation of the clays studied in Goldman is not clear, but the Tarsus Çay, the river just past Tarsus on the way to Adana, seems a probable source. Clay deposits were therefore selected from two locations along the Tarsus Çay, one beneath a motorway bridge just to the east of Tarsus, another *c.* 2–3 km upstream. Two samples were taken from this source, both from a cutting in the river bank *c.* 2–3 m above river height, one seemingly browner than the other. These samples are described below (samples 6, 10 and 11; see Fig. 528). It is difficult to compare them effectively to the Goldman samples, as the latter were not examined using petrography.

A sand sample was also taken from a location some distance to the west of Tarsus from the bed of the dried-up Karakız river. This river runs southeast down to the coast, emerging roughly halfway along the coast between Erdemli and Mersin, *c.* 2 km to the southeast of the village of Elvanlı. On the geological map the river can be seen to flow just to the east of Elvanlı, and upstream there appear on the map to be significant outcrops of serpentinite. In sample 7 below, the sand can be seen to be composed in large part of serpentine grains derived from these outcrops. One must note that, according to the geological map, these serpentinite outcrops do not stretch as far east as Tarsus, and neither are they present in the clay samples taken from Tarsus.

Clay briquettes in thin section (Fig. 528)
1. S187. Buff Neogene clay from road cutting in between villages of Zeyne and Şarlak. Raw clay only. This is a very fine calcareous pale buff with some microfossils (*globigerina*), and textural concentration features (Tcfs), one or two of which are in the large sand size range. Many of these Tcfs are rather grey-brown in colour with indistinct boundaries, and it is these that make the sample look a little different to sample 3.
2. S188. Buff Neogene clay from half way down the Göksu river towards Silifke, on west side. Raw clay only. Has fired somewhat brown. Really rather fine calcareous clay but calcite and quartz visible in silt-size and subsilt-size fraction. Some Tcfs.
3. S189. Buff Neogene clay from near village of

Çağlayangedik, very close to Kışla. Raw clay only. Extremely fine and pale buff calcareous clay, with some microfossils (*globigerina*). This clay has very strong similarities to some fine buff pottery samples, e.g. MBA Fabric Group B.
4. S190. Silty clay from river edge, beneath bridge in Kurtsuyu village. Raw clay only. A calcareous fabric that is absolutely packed full of all different sorts of microfossils, including *globigerina*, and possibly miliolids, endothyracids, brachiopods, algae, etc.
5. S191. Silty clay from same source and mixed with sand from Göksu river near to Kışla. Unfortunately sand not very prevalent, perhaps not enough mixed into the clay in forming the briquette. Only 1 or 2 grains that are larger than silt-size, and these happen to be red-orange mudstones. Nonetheless, this may be a clue as to the source of the mudstones so prevalent in Level Vf-e Group A.
6. S192. Clay from Tarsus Çay, near motorway. Raw clay only. Silty, mostly quartz and calcite, very few serpentine, Tcfs. Calcareous, but microfossils infrequent if present at all. Surprisingly similar to sample 9. May be a similar sort of marl to sample 9, resulting from riverine redeposition of Neogene marine clays. Both red-brown-grey in colour.
7. S193. Clay from same source, and mixed with sand from dried-up river bed NE of Elvanlı. A great deal of the sand is serpentine, with some of the lattice structure as seen in rock samples 1–4. Presumably it must be at temperatures higher than approx. 700°C that this structure degenerates. Note that on the geological map there are clearly numerous serpentinite outcrops upstream from where this sand was taken. Also some inclusions are calcite/micrite/marble, all mostly sub-rounded to rounded. Quartz and chert also, and some unidentified material.
8. S194. Clay from Tarsus Çay, near motorway, mixed with sand from Dereköy. The sand is almost exclusively limestone, with distinct internal structure, probably microfossiliferous. It is very similar to certain ancient fabrics, e.g Level III Group F.
9. S195. Red-brown-grey clay from a road cutting up the Kurtsuyu valley, just past village of Göbekler. Nowhere near as silty as sample 10, but nonetheless has its fair share of calcite and quartz, much fewer Tcfs, and serpentine. Microfossils are very rare to absent. Similar to sample 6.
10. S. 196. Light brown clay from cut in river bank of Tarsus Çay, inland from motorway. Has fired a good deal less orange than sample 11, also does not have a grey core. Actually this is completely different to sample 11, despite having been taken from adjacent deposits, as it is much siltier. Lots of quartz and calcite, a good deal of it sub-angular and angular. Also Tcfs and serpentine. Seems rather well sorted. Must be calcareous. Some rare plagioclase and muscovite.
11. S197. Dark brown clay from cut in river bank of Tarsus Çay, inland from motorway. Rather fine, nothing like the siltiness of 9, let alone the siltiness of 10. Some microfossils (*globigerina*). Has fired red-orange with a grey core, must have some iron content, and there do appear to be some iron concentrations in silt-size fraction. Very few quartz in silt-size fraction, very rare serpentine.

Level Vj–g (EB II)

One of the most striking aspects of the EB II fabrics is their diversity. Through petrographic examination 21 fabric groups have been identified, of which 15 are local and 6 non-local (Figs. 529–31). The vast majority of all local fabrics in EB II are very calcareous. The finest (Group A) contains nothing but numerous microfossils that are entirely consistent with a local source (judging from the geological maps and similarities with natural clay samples). There is a considerable range from fine through to coarse, with different fabrics containing a variety of inclusion types. Group B, for example, is close to A in being fine and calcareous but contains some plant temper. Group C is another fine calcareous fabric with not only plant temper but also some shell, mudstone, grog and limestone; Group N is yet another, containing both plant temper and serpentine inclusions. Groups D, E1, and F are all very calcareous but rather more silty than Groups A–C, and with a variety of inclusions in the coarse fraction, such as limestone, mudstone, grog, shell, chert and phyllites (see Figs. 529–30). As a whole these fabrics (A–F, N) are employed in the manufacture of a range of vessel and ware types: both red and black burnished closed vessels and bowls, brown burnished 'champagne cups' (e.g. **204–6**), plain fine wares, scored ware, plain coarse wares, and cooking pots.

Groups G, H and I all have a fine calcareous matrix and large inclusions in the coarse fraction. G contains large microfossiliferous limestones, H does too but in combination with mudstones/grog, while I is tempered with micritic mudstones (Fig. 530). These fabrics tend to be associated with coarse closed vessels, probably storage jars (although no complete examples). Fabric Groups J and K seem to be associated largely with cooking pots — J seems to be tempered with the odd combination of brown slate fragments and shell, while K contains angular (crushed?) calcite together with plant temper (an example of a vessel in this fabric is **195**, a jar with rope cordon just below the

Level Vj–g (EB II)

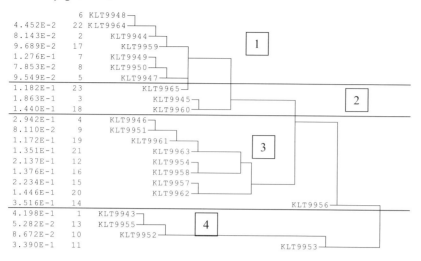

Figure 209. *Dendrogram 1: EB II.*

rim). Fabrics L and M are both from coarse closed vessels, presumably plain storage jars again; the former is plant tempered, the latter grog tempered (Fig. 530).

Thus it can be seen that the nature of the inclusions in the local fabrics gives the impression that resources were selected for their expediency, a sort of 'make do' approach — plant temper, grog, and shell fragments are present in varying quantities and combinations (they barely appear in subsequent periods). Also present are limestones, including some microfossiliferous varieties, mudstones, and limited quantities of slates and phyllites. It seems that calcareous marine clays were the norm, although there is a lot of variation from fine to very silty. Despite the variability in the inclusions, the fact that the underlying clay matrix is basically the same is indicated by the NAA results. The chemistry also provides evidence of just how calcareous these clays are, often between 20 and 25 per cent calcium. Moreover, some of the clay samples taken from near to the site group closely with the EB II calcareous fabrics.

We have already mentioned a number of different wares, and there is indeed almost as much diversity in this dimension as in the fabrics. Some of the many different ware groups are brown burnished, black burnished (e.g. **249**), red burnished (e.g. **248**), red burnished and incised (e.g. **210–12**), red burnished and white painted (e.g. **220**), dark-on-light painted (e.g. **196–9**, **201**), scored, plain, and red slipped, to name but a few. But it seems to be characteristic of the EB II pottery that there are few consistent co-occurrences between ware, shape and fabric. In each ware group there are often three or more different fabrics represented — black burnished ware occurs in at least three different fabrics, as does red burnished ware. Moreover, each fabric group tends to contain a range of wares and shapes. Some shape groups, for example open rounded bowls, have examples made in as many as five different fabrics, also with different surface treatments. Perhaps the only feature common to all of the pottery groups is the construction technology — all pots are hand-made, and there is no sign of the wheel-throwing technique that becomes established in the following period (EB III). Yet the range and diversity of shapes, wares and fabrics is greater than one would expect from any one workshop, or even from any one potting community. It is possible that the Kilise Tepe EB II assemblage represents a non-standardized use of local resources within a household production context.

Non-calcareous fabrics are relatively rare in EB II, represented thus far by only a few samples (Fig. 531). One is a sample of so-called 'metallic ware' (Group T), thought on stylistic grounds to derive from the Konya plain (see typology section), although petrographically there is nothing to tie it definitively to this area. The chemical results (see below) are also suggestive of a non-local source. Another non-calcareous fabric is Group O, represented by a single sample of dark-on-light painted ware. One might note that even though quite a lot of dark-on-light painted ware, such as the jugs **196–9**, is clearly in local calcareous fabrics (for example, sample 316 came from **196**, and forms part of Fabric Group A), this sample seems non-local, judging from both petrographic and chemical information (see below). Its volcanic and granitic inclusions suggest Cyprus or NW Syria as possible sources. Thin-walled rounded bowls were also sampled, and these too seem to be non-calcareous (and micaceous in the fine fraction: Fig. 531), and therefore probably non-local — these are Fabric Groups P, Q and R. Group P (S35) is not unlike Group O in that it contains volcanic and plutonic rock fragments (and associated minerals) which might be indicative of a source in NW Syria or Cyprus. However, it is very different chemically from Group O, and is quite unique among all samples analysed. For its part, Group R, S37 from another burnished rounded bowl (**226**), is somewhat different in having compressed shales dominate the coarse fraction. Such inclusions do not suggest any particular provenance; chemically it actually groups with local samples.

Chemistry
The outstanding characteristic of this EB II group of pottery is the highly calcareous nature of the paste. Some of the ceramics of this period contain Ca, varying from 20 to 28% (9948 (S29), 9964 (S5), 9944 (S32), 9959 (S31), 9949 (S7), 9950 (S2), 9947 (S1), 9965 (S22), 9960 (S30), 9945 (S33)). There is also a group of sherds with 10 to 18% Ca (9946 (S13), 9951 (S20), 9961 (S19), 9963 (S3), 9954 (S37), 9958 (S12), 9957 (S15), 9962 (S26)). The rest of the samples analysed are low calcareous, with Ca values less than 6%. This extreme Ca variability is the main parameter for the classification of those samples in the dendrogram of Figure 209. Although Ca was not included in the elements used for the production of this dendrogram, its variability affected indirectly the concentrations of the rest of the elements determined. The overall variability of this set of samples is reflected in the total variation, which is $vt = 3.29$. This value is relatively high, the highest among the data sets of the chronological periods included and indicates the existence of more than one group in the EB II data set.

The groups formed in the dendrogram are indicated with numbers in Figure 209. Groups 1 and 2 are both very calcareous, but they are discriminated on the basis of Cr, which is lower in group 2. Also 9959 (S31) differs in Cr from the rest of group 1, but it is also different from the members of group 2. Group 3 contains the lower Ca samples. Sample 9956 (S35, Group P) is a loner, while 9957 (S15, Group E 1) and 9962 (S26, Group J) seem to differ from the rest and at the same time between them. The majority of the samples of these three groups probably represent local chemical patterns. All the samples petrographically characterized as local belong to these 3 groups (with the exception of 9956 — S35 'non-local' Group P). Group 4 contains 9943 (S39), 9955 (S40) and 9952 (S34), which have been proposed to be imports on petrographic grounds (Groups T, U and O respectively).

Fabric groups
Local fabrics (Figs. 529–30)
GROUP A (S1–4)
In hand specimen the samples in this group are quite varied in colour, texture and coarseness of fabric. However, thin-section analysis shows them all to have a fine and very calcareous groundmass containing foraminifera. The finest samples have very few inclusions, but the coarser examples tend to contain micritic limestone inclusions and very little else.

GROUP B (S5)
The one sample in this group does relate quite closely to Fabric Group A. However, it is different in containing significant amounts of plant temper, still with plant tissue partially preserved as iron oxide.

GROUP C (S6)
This is another fine calcareous fabric, but containing plant temper, shell, mudstone, grog, and limestone.

GROUP D (S7–9)
A calcareous fabric that is rather more silty than Fabrics A–C, the inclusions are mostly limestone, and very little mudstone. It relates to Fabric A in containing only limestone inclusions, but is much siltier in the fine fraction. Akin to Group E 1 in terms of siltiness, but E 1 members tend to have markedly higher proportions of mudstone, grog, etc.

GROUP E 1 (S10–16)
Similar to Group D in having a silty calcareous groundmass, this fabric nonetheless differs in having a much wider range of inclusion types: not only limestone, but also mudstone, grog, and lesser quantities of chert, schist, and shell.

GROUP E 2 (S17–18)
This fabric is much the same as Group E 1 in its range of inclusions, such as limestone, grog, mudstone, etc. It differs in having a fine (not a silty) calcareous fabric.

GROUP F (S19–20)
Similar to Groups D and E 1 in having a silty calcareous groundmass, this fabric is distinct in containing slate/phyllite inclusions in the coarse fraction.

GROUP G (S21–3)
This is a calcareous fabric, with a relatively fine matrix and a coarse fraction composed almost entirely of large micofossiliferous limestones that must surely have been added as temper.

GROUP H (S24)
Only one sample, with a coarse fraction composed of both microfossiliferous limestones and mudstones/grog. This therefore links quite closely to Group G.

GROUP I (S25)
Coarse fraction dominated by micritic mudstones, which look quite similar to the limestones in the coarse fraction of Groups G and H.

GROUP J (S26–7)
In this group there are two samples with a partially silty calcareous fabric that contains the oddly distinctive combination of brown slate rock fragments, and shell fragments.

GROUP K (S28–9)
The two samples in this group are calcareous, containing notable amounts of both plant temper and calcite.

GROUP L - plant tempered (S30)
The one sample in this group has a fine calcareous fabric with many linear voids that indicate the presence of plant temper before being burnt out in firing.

GROUP M - grog tempered (S31)
The single sample constituting this group is a fine and calcareous fabric with added grog temper.

GROUP N (S32–3)
A fine calcareous fabric containing both plant temper and serpentine.

Non-local fabrics (Fig. 531)
GROUP O (S34)
This is a semi-fine red fabric, micaceous in the fine fraction, with the following inclusions: siltstones, sandstones, limestones, volcanic and granitic rock fragments. These last inclusion types, and the micaceous red fabric, suggest a non-local source, although its precise

Level V f–e (EBIII)

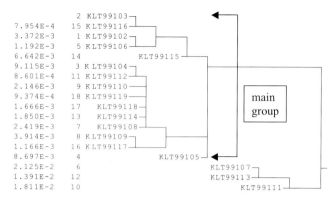

Figure 210. *Dendrogram 2: EB III.*

provenance is unclear. Chemically analysed, and grouping closely with a diverse group of samples from various periods, most having metamorphic inclusions. The group differentiates itself clearly from local calcareous fabrics.

GROUP P (S35)
This is a micaceous (and probably non-calcareous) fabric, with plutonic and volcanic rock fragments, and some associated minerals such as orthopyroxene, plagioclase, and alkali feldspar. The presence of such inclusions makes it almost certainly non-local: indeed this fabric must derive from an igneous environment (Cyprus and NW Syria are possibilities). It has also been analysed chemically — the results show that it is very much a loner, not grouping closely with any other sampled fabric from any period.

GROUP Q (S36)
This is taken from a thin-walled, burnished rounded bowl in a gritty red-brown fabric that looks in hand specimen quite distinct from most fabrics encountered in this period. It is a micaceous and calcareous fabric, with schist/phyllite, and limestone inclusions. Not analysed chemically.

GROUP R (S37)
Rather like the sample constituting Group Q, this comes from a rounded bowl in a rather gritty fabric (**226**). In thin section it shows itself to be both micaceous and calcareous, with compressed shales as the dominant inclusion type in the coarse fraction. Chemically analysed, it falls by itself as a loner, lending support to the idea that this is an imported fabric.

GROUP S (S38)
Like many of the fabrics classified here as non-local, this is a red-firing, non-calcareous fabric; however, it is not micaceous, neither are there metamorphic inclusions. It contains mudstones and micritic limestone, lots of quartz, and sandstone.

GROUP T (S39)
This is so-called 'metallic ware'. Its non-local status is suggested by its micaceous and seemingly non-calcareous fabric: the presence of quartz, micrite, calcite and epidote are not especially diagnostic, but is unlike any other fabric from the site. Chemically analysed, it lies quite close on the dendrogram to Group U.

GROUP U (S40)
Another micaceous and non-calcareous fabric with quartz sandstone, siltstone, and compressed shales. Chemical analysis is not especially conclusive, but it does group relatively closely to Group T.

Level Vf–e (EB III)

The situation represented by the pottery of EB III could hardly be more different from that for EB II. A shift in surface treatment from burnishing to monochrome slipping is matched by an equally major change in fabrics, from highly calcareous to much less calcareous (see chemistry below). The scale and scope of this technological innovation cannot be exaggerated. Not only have potters started using a completely new set of clay resources, but it seems that they have also adapted their firing technology so that the pots are now fired harder. Admittedly, this may be related to the prevalence of burnishing in the previous period and the need to keep temperatures relatively low if the burnish is to survive. Once burnishing is replaced by monochrome slipping, then there is no barrier to the use of higher temperatures. This semi-fine to semi-coarse orange-buff fabric (Group A), as well as being an innovation in EB III, is also much more standardized than any fabric previously. This is not only clear from petrographic examination, but also from the chemistry: all samples analysed clustered together to form a very strong group (see below). Other important technological changes occur, notably with the first evidence for wheel-made pottery at the site. All these strands of evidence taken together provide strong grounds for arguing that production organization changed fundamentally in EB III, perhaps towards a more specialized, full-time scenario.

Fabric Group A (Fig. 532) includes a number of different shapes and wares. Most of the very numerous bowls (**295–373**), many with S-shaped profile, occur in this fabric. Bowls of this type include the red-cross type, as well as plain, red-slipped and brown-coated variants. The fabric is also used for incised ware (e.g. **408–9**), small red-slipped jars/cups (e.g. **374–9**), red-slipped trefoil jugs (**446–7**) and plain storage jars.

The only other two fabric groups in EB III are characterized by the presence of significant quantities of metamorphic rock fragments as inclusions. The absence of any significant metamorphic outcrops in the Kilise Tepe area would tend to imply that these are imported fabrics. However, the possible presence of phyllites in local conglomerates means that a local source cannot be entirely ruled out; this is particularly so when the phyllites occur in conjunction with the types of inclusions to be expected in local fabrics, such as limestones, mudstones, etc. Groups B and C, on the other hand, apart from being non-calcareous, are so dominated by metamorphic inclusions (Fig. 532) that a non-local source seems certain. Moreover, the chemical data suggest a non-local source for both B and C.

It is noteworthy that these two fabrics are associated exclusively with vessels that, judging by their shape and surface treatment, probably functioned as cooking pots. If the only imported classes of pottery in EB III are cooking pots, this marks a distinct change from EB II when the few imports that did exist came in the form of tablewares such as jugs and open rounded bowls.

Chemistry

The picture in EB III pottery is entirely different to that in EB II (as illustrated in the scatterplot Fig. 215, p. 266). Firstly the clay which has been used in this period is much less calcareous than EB II, ranging between 7 and 12%. Secondly, the chemical variability is actually the lowest in comparison to all the other periods. In EB III $vt = 1.07$, which is indicative of the existence of more than one group, but with small chemical differences. Indeed as can be seen in the dendrogram of Figure 210, the majority of the sherds cluster together in the main group. Even the two outliers, 99115 (S50) and 99105 (S44) present small differences from the main group and therefore they could be considered as part of it. The sample 99105 (S44) differs for its high Cs (34.5 ppm) concentration, which is very high in the main group anyway (16–24 ppm). Sample 99115 (S50) differs only in Na, which is higher than the rest of the group. In petrographic terms this group is considered as local, but its chemical difference with the respective local of EB II is significant.

The two metamorphic samples, 99113 (S57) and 99111 (S56), are non-calcareous and very different from the main group. Their petrographic characterization as non-local is compatible with the chemical data.

Fabric groups (Fig. 532)

GROUP A (S41–55)

There are variations in this group between semi-fine and semi-coarse, but there is a remarkable degree of standardization creating links across different wares and types. All have a micaceous, seemingly non-calcareous fabric, or at least much less calcareous than in EB II. It must be noted that foraminifera are almost completely absent, in strong contrast to the fabrics of EB II. In the coarse fraction the EB III Group A fabric samples contain Tcfs/mudstones, and voids created by the loss of $CaCO_3$ (micrite, calcite, or limestone) during firing. Very little else makes its way into the coarse fraction.

GROUP B (S56)

This is a cooking pot fabric containing many metamorphic rock fragments as grits, and shows some similarities to fabrics from later periods, such as S111 from Level III. The combination of a micaceous groundmass with so much schist in the coarse fraction makes it almost certain that this is a non-local fabric. The closest metamorphic environments are some distance to the north, towards the Konya plain, or c. 70 km to the southwest, on the coast near Anamur (see Fig. 365).

GROUP C (S57)

This is a coarse red fabric, probably non-calcareous, containing many phyllites in the coarse fraction, though of rather different character to Group B. But like Group B this must be a non-local cooking pot fabric, with its numerous phyllites: see above for the nearest significant metamorphic outcrops (Fig. 365).

Level IV (MBA)

There is considerable continuity from EB III, albeit with some important developments. MBA Fabric Group A is very similar to EB III Group A, and is still associated with the same sorts of wares, although the shapes have evolved a little. It is a dense orange fabric used for monochrome slipped bowls and closed vessels. The results of chemical analysis also demonstrate the close similarities of this MBA fabric group to EB III Group A.

However, another major fabric in the Middle Bronze Age material — Group B — does not link to any EB III fabrics; in fact it shows more similarities with the highly calcareous fabrics of EB II. Petrography shows that this group includes not only the 'light clay' ware (described in the typology section), but also the 'light brown or beige fabric with multi-coloured grit temper'. It is employed in the manufacture both of plain buff cups (in light clay ware) and of red burnished vessels (often in light brown/beige fabric), notably jugs and open bowls. Although the plain cups are an MBA innovation, red burnished ware was very common in EB II; its reappearance in the Middle Bronze Age in a similar kind of fine calcareous fabric is thus quite striking — does it represent the deliberate resurrection of an older tradition, or is it purely coincidental? It should be noted though that whereas in EB II burnished wares were hand-made, in MBA they are wheel-made. The fabric (Group B) used for this class of pottery is highly calcareous containing many foraminifera (Fig. 533). It also shows very strong links with a clay sampled from an extensive deposit just 1 km from the site of Kilise Tepe itself (Fig. 528). This makes it a very good candidate for being a local product. Chemical analyses also provide strong support for this conclusion.

With this clear differentiation between Fabric Groups A and B, and their association with different wares and even shapes, it is possible to hypothesize as to the nature of production organization. If both Group A and Group B were produced by potters at Kilise Tepe, the co-occurring differences in fabric, ware and shape are not consistent with production in a single workshop. That Kilise Tepe could support two (or more) specialized production traditions may be taken as evidence that Kilise Tepe was something more than just a small hamlet.

Level IV (MBA)

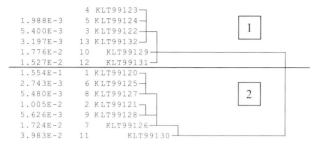

Figure 211. *Dendrogram 3: MBA (with the exception of 99120, which belongs in Level III).*

A semi-coarse brown-orange fabric with brown metamorphic inclusions — Fabric Group C (Fig. 533) — becomes the new standard for most storage and cooking pots in this period, and indeed for the rather common 'combed ware' (see Symington, p. 320 below — where the fabric is described as 'semi-coarse, ... reddish brown or greyish black, with a high proportion of grit temper'). The source of such a fabric with common metamorphic inclusions in the coarse fraction is a puzzle, as there does not appear to be any source of metamorphic rock in the local area. Neither is there any located where it might be transported down rivers towards the Kilise Tepe area. At the same time, it is nonetheless hard to believe that this common fabric could actually be imported from an unknown source outside the immediate area. One possibility is that the deposits of conglomerate that occur frequently in the local area, although sedimentary in nature, might contain some rocks of metamorphic origin.

Chemistry

There is a moderate degree of chemical variability (vt = 1.85), intermediate between that recorded for EB II and LBA. Although only a small number of samples (12) were analysed from this period, they exhibit some clear chemical patterns which can be associated with the two previous periods. The samples cluster in two groups. The first cluster (see Fig. 211) contains samples of a very highly calcareous nature, all belonging to petrographic Group B; they chemically match the first group in the EB II data set. Therefore a local provenance for this group should be suggested. The second cluster of Figure 211 is closely related to the main EB III group, which has a very characteristic chemical pattern. Samples 99126 (S59) and 99130 (S58) create a sub-group in the second cluster; however, the chemical differences of these two samples from the rest of the group are smaller than any other differences within the whole data set.

Fabric groups (Fig. 533)
GROUP A (S58–61)
This fabric is extremely similar to Group A in EB III. It marks a most interesting continuity, being used for the same sorts of wares in the Middle Bronze Age as in EB III. It is micaceous in the fine fraction, non-calcareous, with the coarse fraction predominantly comprised of voids (burnt-out limestone) and Textural concentration features (Tcfs) and/or mudstones.

GROUP B (S62–70)
This is a semi-fine, calcareous fabric with foraminifera, that links in extremely well to the local geology and to clay samples taken from around the site. It is also very interesting that there are no examples of this sort of fabric in EB III, although there are in EB II. The reasons for this discontinuous development are unclear and quite intriguing. After the Middle Bronze Age, such fabrics do seem to continue into Late Bronze, but seemingly not into the Iron Age.

GROUP C (S71–5)
A common semi-coarse to coarse fabric in the Middle Bronze Age levels, orange-brown or sometimes grey in colour, calcareous and with numerous metamorphic rock fragments as well as limestones in the coarse fraction, see Fig. 533 (e.g. S72).

GROUP D (S76)
The single sample constituting this group comes from a cooking pot with a distinctive grooved and twisted handle. It is a very coarse brown with quartz, micritic limestone, compressed shale, quartz sandstone, schist and phyllite inclusions (Fig. 533). The presence of metamorphic inclusions would appear to suggest a non-local source, although some may be present in the conglomerate formations of the area (as discussed for other fabric groups).

Level III (LBA)

Whereas in previous periods there are only minor amounts of imported pottery, in the Late Bronze Age the quantities increase significantly. Fabric Group A is almost certainly imported to the site, although where this pottery is coming from is by no means clear. In its finest variants it is represented by the very distinctive Red Lustrous Wheel-made ware, its most typical shapes being the libation arm, the spindle bottle and the lentoid flask (for these shapes see Eriksson 1993). Also common is a form of shallow bowl with inturned rim more or less identical in shape to those that are locally produced in semi-fine calcareous buff fabrics. The fabric is a very fine, vivid pink-red with practically no inclusions of any size that can be identified petrographically (see Fig. 534). This shape also occurs in a fabric that is the same colour and hardness but containing small white inclusions. Another very similar but coarser fabric is used for storage jars. Macroscopic observation suggested that these fabrics could be seen as fine, semi-fine and coarse variants of a single fabric group (Fig. 534), even though the coarse wares lacked the lustrous surface treatment of the finer specimens. One crucial clue to confirm this suspected continuity comes in the form of a finely-made lentoid flask (**672**), the neck and handle of which are in the very fine pink-red fabric, whilst the main body of the vessel is in the coarser red fabric. In the 16 thin-section samples too a continuity from fine through semi-fine to coarse is quite apparent (see Knappett *et al.* 2005). Moreover, chemical analysis (8 samples) showed that fine and coarse samples of this fabric clustered very closely together to form a single tight group (Fig. 216).

It has already been mentioned above that this is a non-local fabric group, an observation made possible by the combination of petrographic and chemical analysis. Both show that this is far less calcareous than most local fabrics. The coarser variant is typically dominated by white carbonate inclusions, but also contains red textural concentration features (tcfs), probably part of the clay body, and few to common metamorphic rock fragments such as elongate rounded phyllites and schist (Fig. 534). The presence of metamorphic rock fragments is suggestive, although not conclusively, of a non-local source. As for the NAA results, they indicate a tightly clustered group that is clearly very distinct from any local groups (Fig. 212).

Red Lustrous Wheel-made ware has a very wide distribution, being found across Anatolia, on Cyprus, in the Levant, and in Egypt (see map in Eriksson 1991, 85, fig. 10.2). But although the ware is very well known from many consumption contexts, there is as yet no evidence linking it to a production setting. Its source has been something of a puzzle for many years; while Syria and Anatolia have both been raised as serious possibilities, the most recent scholarly synthesis favours Cyprus as the source (Eriksson 1991; 1993). Eriksson presents four main reasons in support of this hypothesis. First, there is more of it found on Cyprus than in the rest of the Near East and Egypt combined. Secondly, it is only on Cyprus that there occurs the full range of shapes and thirdly, it is only on Cyprus that there is a full temporal distribution throughout the Late Bronze Age. The fourth supporting argument is that a number of examples, particularly spindle bottles, bear 'pot-marks', incised before firing, that have similarities with signs in the Cypro-Minoan script. Some of her points do have counter-arguments: for example, the discovery by Jürgen Seeher in 2000–2001 of thousands of sherds of Red Lustrous Wheel-made ware at the Hittite capital Hattusa (Boğazköy) casts a little doubt on the idea that the ware is most abundant on Cyprus (Knappett *et al.* 2005).

That Eriksson's interpretation is not universally accepted is hinted at by Todd, who suggests also that such a conclusion 'sorely needs to be backed up by sci-

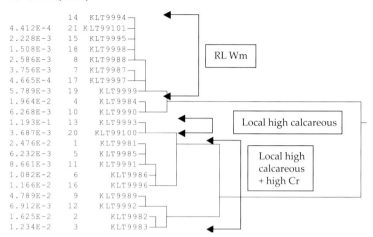

Figure 212. *Dendrogram 4: LBA.*

entific analyses' (Todd 2001, 206). Some Red Lustrous Wheel-made ware was actually analysed by Eriksson, albeit unpublished; she cites some NAA results suggesting that the fabric is similar to the fabrics of other Cypriot products such as Base Ring Ware (Eriksson 1991, 94). However, she goes on to note that these results are ambiguous in that they also show the fabric has an affiliation with samples from clay beds near Boğazköy. This illustrates the limitations of employing solely chemical techniques, rather than using chemistry and petrography together; petrography should be able to differentiate quite clearly between products from Cyprus and from Boğazköy (as indicated by author's recent programme of analysis: Knappett *et al.* 2005). The samples analysed in this study show no petrographic similarities at all with local wares from Boğazköy. But on the other hand, neither do they appear to fit with the geology of Cyprus, much of which is dominated by the igneous rocks of the Troodos mountains. The petrology of the coarser Red Lustrous Wheel-made ware samples from Kilise Tepe points to a geological background of limestone and low-grade metamorphism. Though this is inconsistent with the Troodos, it does seem to fit particularly well with one area of Cyprus — the northern Kyrenia range. Indeed it is here that the site of Kazaphani is located, where especially significant quantities of the ware have been found in tombs (Nicolaou & Nicolaou 1989). Eriksson herself notes, with an appropriate degree of caution, the possibility that the source of Red Lustrous Wheel-made ware may be in the north of the island (Eriksson 1991, 94).

It is important to note that the ware almost certainly does derive from a relatively small area. The visual, petrographic and chemical homogeneity of the fabric, no matter where it is found, points very strongly to a single source. Moreover the standardization in fabric, shape and ware, and the evident skill invested in production, strongly suggest that these are the products of a centralized workshop or set of workshops. It would be most interesting if further analysis could show with more certainty that the single area responsible for the production of this remarkable ware was northern Cyprus, in the region of Kyrenia. As it is, however, we cannot entirely rule out other source areas such as Anatolia or Syria; indeed the present author has noted that the southern coast of Cilicia in the area of Anamur is at least broadly compatible geologically (Knappett *et al.* 2005; see also Symington 2001, 170). Clearly an extensive analytical programme for Red Lustrous Wheel-made ware from all over the eastern Mediterranean and Anatolia is called for; this has been initiated by the author, with samples so far collected and analysed from sites in Turkey (Boğazköy, as well as Kilise Tepe), Cyprus (Kalavassos, Hala Sultan Tekke, Kouklia, Kazaphani) and Egypt (Memphis-Saqqara).

Despite the fact that imports are now more common than ever, local wares still predominate. These are represented principally by the rather standardized, wheel-thrown shallow bowls that are plain and unslipped (burnishing has largely disappeared), occurring in pale semi-fine buff fabrics. One such fabric (Group C) is highly calcareous and hence very similar to that used for plain buff wares and burnished wares in the Middle Bronze Age (Fig. 534; cf. Fig. 212). This similarity is also apparent from the chemical analyses. Another fabric (Group B), though, is a LBA innovation: whilst like most previous buff fabrics it is very calcareous with numerous foraminifera, it is distinct in consistently containing serpentine and chert, along with minor amounts of epidote, amphibole, and igneous rock fragments (Fig. 534). These petrographic features do tally with the local geology, as there is a significant serpentinite and igneous rock outcrop not far to the east of the site (see Fig. 366). The chemistry too suggests a local source, as well as indicating that this fabric group is somewhat distinct from Group B. It is, however, intriguing that fabrics with these kinds of inclusions (i.e. serpentine) only rarely occur in fabrics from earlier periods (e.g. Fabric Group N in EB II). This does suggest that in the Late Bronze Age local potters are beginning to use new resource locations that had previously been underexploited. Whatever the reasons for change, this fabric continues to be produced throughout the Iron Age (e.g. Group B in phases IIa–d, and the kiln group in phase IIf), representing an interesting degree of continuity over time.

Amongst the coarse wares used for storage and cooking, Fabric Group D is very well defined, as it is one of the earliest examples at the site of a calcite-tempered fabric (Fig. 535). Petrographic analysis shows clearly that calcite has been crushed and added as temper to a calcareous fabric containing foraminifera (the presence of which suggests it is a broadly local product). The fact that both samples in this group are from closed jars with rolled rims (e.g. **635**) that served as cooking pots indicates that this is a purposeful functional adaptation. Group E is also a calcite-tempered fabric but is much siltier and much less calcareous. Both these variants of calcite-tempered cooking pots continue into phases IIa–d, after which they disappear.

There is also a coarse fabric used for storage jars that is calcareous with large microfossiliferous limestone inclusions (Group F) that must have been added as temper (Fig. 535). Resource sampling in the area has revealed the occurrence of these sorts of sands in certain streambeds (close to Derekōy, up the Kurtsuyu valley a short distance northeast of Kilise Tepe). This sort of fabric has already been observed in the EB II period. There are four different sorts of coarse metamorphic fabrics, Groups G, H, I and J. Group G is a calcareous fabric that has a range of inclusions, predominantly micritic limestones and phyllite (Fig. 535), and is quite similar to a common Middle Bronze Age fabric (Group C) used for combed ware storage jars. Groups H and I also appear to be calcareous, but contain very large schists as well as phyllites and limestones (Fig. 535). Group J is different again, in being composed of a non-calcareous, micaceous fabric with the coarse fraction completely dominated by very large schist fragments, and no limestones (Fig. 535). This last fabric is almost certainly non-local, whereas Groups G, H and I may actually be local: even though there are no metamorphic rock sources in the vicinity of Kilise Tepe, some fragments may be found in local conglomerate deposits.

Chemistry
The samples that comprise the Level III data set have a high chemical variability ($vt = 2.13$) indicating the existence of several groups. Indeed this is reflected in the structure of the dendrogram of Figure 212, where more than three groups can be identified. The first group is composed solely of the Red Lustrous Wheel-made pottery. This is a very tight and distinct group of calcareous pottery samples, which differs significantly from all the possibly local fabrics. Although calcareous, ranging from 4–10% Ca content, they are far less so than most of the local fabrics. In terms of chemistry

(and indeed petrography) the fabric shares strong similarities with samples of Red Lustrous Wheel-made ware from Memphis-Saqqara and Kalavassos (Egypt and Cyprus respectively) that have been analysed chemically as part of the same project. One should note that chemically the RLWm samples differ from Cypriot imports in phase IIf (Fig. 218).

Next on the dendrogram (Fig. 212) come samples 9984 (S110) and 9990 (S111), Fabrics I and J respectively, both coarse fabrics characterized by significant quantities of metamorphic rock fragments in thin section. Although they do not form a significant chemical cluster as such within the Level III dendrogram, when treated as part of the multi-period data set as a whole they stand out as separate from the local fabric groups.

The remainder of the Level III samples are very similar to the highly calcareous local fabric seen in earlier periods, but with high values of Cr, indicating the presence of serpentinite. This is confirmed in some of the cases by petrography, particularly those belonging to Fabric Group B (i.e. samples 9981 (S95), 9992 (S94), 9982 (S98)). However, some that fall within this high chromium cluster do not contain any visible serpentinite in thin section, such as the three samples of Fabric Group C (9985 (S101), 9991 (S103), 9996 (S102)), and sample 9986, which is calcite tempered (S105, Group E). A sub-group is formed by samples 9993 (S107) and 99100 (S104), Fabric Groups F and D respectively, which contain lesser amounts of Cr (<100 ppm), and which are also local calcareous fabrics.

Fabric groups (Figs. 534–5)

GROUP A (S77–93)
As stated above, this is almost certainly an imported fabric (Red Lustrous Wheel-made ware). It is calcareous, but far less so than most local fabrics, and the coarser examples contain numerous metamorphic rock fragments. There appears to be a continuum of variation from fine through to coarse. The very fine examples are red and micaceous (to varying degrees). Red Tcfs are common in the fine fraction, along with some quartz and micrite (some of which possibly shell). Samples are S77–82.

Next come the semi-fine fabrics (S84, S85, S87), which are very much like the above in terms of groundmass and fine fraction, but there occurs more quartz, Tcfs, and micritic limestone (of which some linear and angular, probably shell) in the coarse fraction. There are very rarely any metamorphic rock fragments.

Samples in the semi-coarse to coarse range (S83, S86, S88–93) are very much like the above fine and semi-fine examples, except for containing more in the coarse fraction including metamorphic rock fragments, i.e. various forms of schist and phyllite. They are commonly 1.0 mm in length, but can be up to 4.0 mm. It should be noted that S92 has a thick dark grey core, and so looks quite different to the other samples (whilst being the same petrographically).

GROUP B (S94–100)
This is a semi-fine calcareous buff fabric in which limestones, serpentine and chert tend to occur in the coarse fraction, also with minor amounts of epidote, amphibole, and igneous rock fragments. This fabric is very similar to a common fabric that is encountered in phases IIa–d, IIe, and IIf. However, it has not been identified in any of the pre-Hittite ceramics from the site. It is almost certainly a local fabric that relates to both the Neogene marine sediments and the serpentinite outcrops in the vicinity of Kilise Tepe.

GROUP C (S101–3)
This too is a semi-fine calcareous buff fabric, but has just micrite and micritic limestones as inclusions (no chert, serpentine, etc.). It is highly likely that this is a local fabric, and is commonly found in earlier periods.

GROUP D (S104)
This is a coarse calcareous fabric with many foraminifera and angular grains of calcite. Judging from its angularity, size and quantity, the calcite quite probably was crushed and added as temper. The single sample in the group is very similar, both in hand specimen and thin section, to a cooking pot fabric from the following period, phases IIa–d.

GROUP E (S105)
The single example in this group has a silty calcareous fabric with abundant angular calcite in fine and coarse fractions. It is different from Group D in being red-brown in colour, silty, and containing far fewer foraminifera. However, it does represent another variant of a common tradition of tempering coarse wares with crushed calcite. Just as there is an analogue to Group D in IIa-d (Group C), so there is an analogue to Group E (IIa–d Group D).

GROUP F (S106–7)
A coarse calcareous fabric, varying in colour from buff to dark brown, containing many large inclusions of microfossiliferous limestone. The numerous and varied foraminifera in a highly calcareous groundmass make a local source very likely. The many large microfossiliferous limestones appear to have been added as temper, and they look very similar to the sand sampled from a stream bed near Dereköy (clay/sand S194), in the Kurtsuyu valley just to the east of the Göksu valley.

GROUP G (S108)
Another calcareous fabric, orange in colour and with a coarse fraction of micritic limestones and dark elongate phyllites. This can be compared with the Level IV fabric group used for combed ware. As with the Level IV group, there is an issue concerning the source of such metamorphic rock fragments, given that there do not appear to be any metamorphic sources in the vicinity of Kilise Tepe. However, in that the local conglomerates may contain a certain amount of metamorphic material, a local origin is not out of the question.

GROUP H (S109)
This is a dark brown cooking pot fabric containing micritic limestones, calcite, quartz, quartz sandstone, and phyllites. Probably a local fabric.

GROUP I (S110)
A coarse brown fabric, this sample is different from many other fabrics in that the fine fraction and groundmass seem to contain significant quantities of both micrite/calcite and mica. The coarse fraction has micritic limestones and phyllites, as does Group G, but also contains a lot of very large schists (not present in Group G). Once again, the issue of local versus non-local is raised by the preponderance of metamorphic rock fragments.

GROUP J (S111)
This has a very micaceous and non-calcareous groundmass and fine fraction. The coarse fraction is composed almost solely of a particular form of schist not seen in previous LBA samples. The

schist inclusions can be very long, up to c. 5.0 mm, some are rounded and some angular. Almost certainly a non-local fabric, given that it is micaceous, and so dominated by a particular form of schist. However, identifying the source of this import is not going to be at all easy in the absence of comparanda from other sites in the broader region.

Level IIa–d

Important changes from the previous period include the decline of Red Lustrous Wheel-made ware, and the appearance of dark-on-light painted pottery. But many shapes go on, even the RLWm lentoid flasks, and fabrics show notable continuities too — the same semi-fine buff fabrics are still used in the manufacture of plain bowls (which have now acquired a ring base), and cooking pots are made with calcite-tempered fabrics.

Fabric A, a semi-fine buff, is the more common fabric and is almost certainly local, given its unique combination of microfossils, carbonates, and serpentine in the coarse fraction, and a very calcareous fine fraction (Fig. 536). This fabric seems to have been first developed in Level III, and continues strongly into Level II. The homogeneity of this fabric is further demonstrated in the NAA results, showing the clustering of Level III, IIa–d and IIf samples close to other local fabric groups. Fabric B is a semi-fine to semi-coarse non-calcareous red fabric, containing frequent quartz grains and many mica laths in the fine fraction (Fig. 536) — it is probably of non-local provenance. Distinct both visually and petrographically from the RLWm ware of the previous period, it is an entirely new fabric, the origin of which is unknown. NAA too shows that it forms its own group, very much separate from local fabrics and close to, though distinct from, the chemistry of Red Lustrous Wheel-made ware (Fig. 213). Whatever the source of this fabric, its producers worked in the same tradition as the local Kilise Tepe potters, creating vessels of the same shapes and with the same surface treatments and decorative patterns. Lentoid flasks, rounded bowls, and square-rim basins are known to occur in each fabric, whilst being more or less identical in all other respects. It should be noted though that pilgrim flasks seem to be particularly common in Fabric B.

Just as in Level III, there is a tradition in IIa–d of tempering cooking pots with angular calcite. Group C is equivalent to Level III Group D, and Group D equivalent to Level III Group E. This is another element of continuity across a transition usually thought to be one of abrupt and disastrous decline into Dark Age social disorder.

Finally, phase IId is characterized by the rather sparse presence of Mycenaean style vessels. Fragments representing nineteen vessels have been recovered —including five stirrup jars, one amphora, and ten deep bowls (see French, Chapter 28; also cf. Postgate 1998b, 134–6, fig. 13.4). French dates the open vessels to LH IIIC (called Myc IIIC 1b in the Near East), i.e. during the twelfth century BC. The closed vessels are earlier, dating between 1350 and 1250 BC.

In terms of provenance it is enormously difficult trying to assign these vessels to a particular source, as the range of possibilities is so vast. Visually the fabrics are well-fired, and fine, with a range of colours from pinkish-buff through to pale grey-brown, differences that are probably attributable to firing. But when these Mycenaean wares are examined in thin section, there is a surprising petrological variety in the fabrics. Three of the deep bowls sampled (**959–61**) occur in a fabric that has fragments of amphibole, as well as serpentine and occasional igneous rock fragments (Group F; Fig. 537). Serpentine does occur locally, but not in conjunction with so much amphibole. Moreover, these fabrics do not appear to be as calcareous as most local fabrics. These features are overall not consistent with a local source, and these vessels are probably imported. From where though is a very difficult question, as Mycenaean-style vessels could have been made in any number of places across the eastern Mediterranean. Two of the remaining samples (**956, 958**, Groups E 1 and E 2) may feasibly be local, judging largely by the presence of calcareous material; French notes some similarities with the fabric from Tarsus (p. 373 on Ware 1). As for the single stirrup jar sample (Group G), it is in yet another fabric,

Level IIa–d

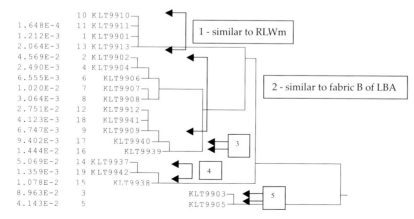

Figure 213. *Dendrogram 5: Level IIa–d.*

but one which is so fine that it is hard to say from thin section whether it is local or not (Fig. 537). The chemical results discussed below are not decisive in establishing a firm provenance for any of these fabric groups, but they do appear to rule out many of the principal exporting areas of Mycenaean pottery, such as the Peloponnese, Boeotia and Crete.

Chemistry
All samples analysed from this period are medium to high calcareous and of quite similar chemistry as the relatively low total variation shows ($vt = 1.21$). The first group (cluster 1) of the dendrogram (Fig. 213) is chemically very tight and has similarities to the RLWm group of Level III. The RLWm group was in itself also tight, which indicates importation from a specific area producing this kind of pottery on a systematic basis. It was noted earlier that this phase IIa–d fabric is used to make forms that were previously popular in RLWm, notably lentoid/pilgrim flasks. The relationship between the two fabrics, suggested by both chemistry and petrography, is thus quite intriguing.

The main group of the highly calcareous sherds forms a cluster (cluster 2 on Fig. 213), practically all the samples of which are from Fabric Group A. This local fabric is more or less identical in thin section to Fabric Group B from Level III, and the chemical composition — highly calcareous with high chromium — is also very similar. However, there are differences in particular elements which indicate a different clay but with the same mineralogical characteristics to that of Level III. The only sample in this chemical cluster that does not belong to this fabric group is 9941 (S142, **947**), a Mycenaean stirrup jar that, being a total one-off in the ceramic assemblage, was previously presumed to be non-local. Although the chemistry alone would not rule out a local source, all other evidence indicates that this is not very probable (see French, p. 373). Cluster 3 on the dendrogram consists of two more Mycenaean samples, 9940 and 9939 (S137, S138), which are related reasonably closely to Cluster 2. The petrography of these two samples (Groups E 1 and E 2) indicate a possible local source in Cilicia, which the chemistry would appear to support. Cluster 4 is also composed of Mycenaean wares (9942, 9938, 9937 - S139–S141), three samples belonging to Fabric F, which in thin section gave strong hints of being non-local. These three samples do form a chemical group that is distinct from the other three Mycenaean samples already mentioned.

Both chemical clusters of Mycenaean samples, the seemingly local (9941 and cluster 3) and the probably non-local (cluster 4), were compared with the main reference groups of Mycenaean pottery that have been formed from the analyses of Perlman and Asaro (Hein *et al.* 2002) as well as the University of Bonn (Hein & Mommsen 1999). These groups represent analyses of ceramics from the major Mycenaean sites of the Peloponnese, Boeotia and Crete. More specifically, the reference groups that the Kilise Tepe Mycenaean sherds were compared against were: Mycenae-Berbati, Tiryns-Asine, Achaia, Aegina, Knossos-Phaistos, Thebes, Locris, and Rhodes. It was found that there were no significant matches with any of the reference groups, suggesting that both chemical groups have a source outside the above-mentioned areas. This would of course make sense for the group that we suspect to be local, and would suggest that the cluster 4/Fabric F samples come from another area; Cyprus is one of the many possibilities that still needs to be investigated.

Lastly, cluster 5 (Fig. 213) consists of two samples of coarse local calcareous wares tempered with calcite. It is this calcite tempering that presumably skews the chemistry so much as to separate them from the local wares to which petrographically they are clearly related.

Fabric groups (Figs. 536–7)
GROUP A (S112–26, except S115)
This is a semi-fine buff fabric that shows clear links to the Level IIf Fabric Group A. It has a calcareous groundmass with foraminifera, and containing inclusions of micritic and sparry limestones, serpentine, chert, and occasional igneous rock fragments. These features are consistent with a local source. There are a number of shapes in this fabric including square-rim basins with cross-hatching, rounded bowls (with diagonal lines or cross-hatching - **751**), inturned rim bowls (both plain and slipped) and pilgrim flasks.

GROUP B (S127–34)
This fabric is unique to phases IIa–d, and the eight samples in this group are all red-orange in colour, non-calcareous, micaceous in the silt-size fraction, containing frequent quartz (*c.* 0.1–0.2 mm), and with varying amounts of micritic limestone. It is felt that this fabric is probably a non-local product, although there is at present little information to connect it with any particular region. It should also be noted that it is different to both of the other main non-calcareous groups in the assemblage, the Red Lustrous Wheel-made ware, and the phase IIf Black-on-Red and Bichrome wares (except for the minor Group D from phase IIf). Most of the pottery in this group consists of pilgrim flasks (**693**, **916**–**17**), although there are some square-rim basins (**790** - S127, and S128).

GROUP C (S135)
There is just one sample in the group, a cooking pot. It has a calcareous buff fabric with foraminifera and angular calcite temper. The foraminifera are seen in many local calcareous fabrics from various periods. The angular calcite, however, is quite rare — it might well have been deliberately crushed up as temper and added to cooking pot fabrics to improve their resistance to thermal shock. This fabric is very similar to one used for cooking pots in Level III (Fabric D).

GROUP D (S136)
Like Group C this comes from a cooking pot, and contains much angular calcite, presumably added as temper. It is not nearly as

calcareous and has no foraminifera, being instead a rather silty red-brown fabric. It corresponds to Fabric Group E from Level III.

GROUP E 1 (S137)
The sample is from a Mycenaean deep bowl (**957**). In being clearly calcareous with a lot of micrite in both groundmass and fine and coarse fractions, this Mycenaean ware is quite unlike the Mycenaean Fabric Groups F and G, which must surely be non-local. Other features include very few serpentine in fine fraction, dark brown Tcfs, very few quartz, rare chert, and very rare altered igneous rock fragments. No foraminifera can be seen, perhaps occasional mica. A local source is a possibility.

GROUP E 2 (S138)
The sample is from a Mycenaean deep bowl (**955**). This is similar to Group E 1 in being calcareous, but is much siltier. It contains more quartz in the small-sand range, and much less serpentine in the fine fraction. There is also very rare plagioclase feldspar, epidote, K-feldspar, amphibole, and sheared quartz. This is therefore different in some ways to S137, and is therefore given a separate sub-group. It is most probably local, although this is by no means a certainty.

GROUP F (S139–41)
The three samples in this group are all from Mycenaean deep bowls (**958–60**). The fabric does not seem particularly calcareous (8.5–11%), but neither is it conspicuously micaceous. The rather rare inclusions in what is a relatively fine fabric are granitic (and occasional volcanic) rock fragments and their associated minerals (plagioclase, quartz, amphibole), as well as serpentine, clinozoisite, and epidote. This must surely be a non-local fabric (judging by the granitic rock fragments and amphibole), but specifying its source area is very difficult. The NAA results are also suggestive of a non-local source, though more precise indications are not possible at present.

GROUP G (S142)
This is a very fine salmon-pink to orange fabric with hardly any inclusions. Its provenance is difficult to establish from thin section as there is very little diagnostic information. It is unlike most local fabrics so one suspects it is non-local, and this is also likely in terms of the type of vessel from which the sample comes — a Mycenaean stirrup jar (**947**). NAA results, while apparently linking the fabric to known local rather than non-local fabrics, are otherwise inconclusive.

Level IIe

Phase IIe of the Iron Age occupation is poorly defined at the site — the excavated units considered to represent the phase have few clear architectural associations. The following pottery groups do tend to come from certain stratigraphic units that can be placed between phase IId and IIf, but they are mostly not linked to a recognizable and coherent building phase or floor. In such circumstances, negative evidence takes on a more important role in linking certain pottery groups to the phase. For example, the highly characteristic pottery that has become known as 'Kindergarten ware' (after its simple and roughly executed 'child-like' painted decoration and crude manufacture) is not found in phases IIa–d or in phase IIf, but must fall somewhere in between the two in stylistic terms. The same sort of argument is used to place in phase IIe the rounded bowls with dark painted decoration of diagonal lines.

The fabric that helps define 'Kindergarten ware' is very distinctive, both visually and in thin section. It appears to be very porous, whilst also being hard and well-fired (indeed, there are many voids seen microscopically, and there is no optical activity in the groundmass). It is very gritty, and thin section shows these grits to be mostly micritic limestone, but also with a fair proportion of serpentine (Fig. 537). This combination of inclusions makes a local source very likely, as it did for the Level IIa–d calcareous buff fabric that had both carbonate and serpentine inclusions. However, the 'Kindergarten ware' fabric is very different in being grittier and seemingly much less calcareous. This fabric has no good parallels in either earlier or later phases.

The shallow rounded bowls (with ring base, grooved rim) are in much the same fabric as they were in the previous phases, i.e. a semi-fine calcareous buff with carbonates, microfossils and serpentine as inclusions. In hand specimen the fabric seems softer than in the previous phases, and it may be that the firing conditions for these vessels were different in phase IIe.

Also worthy of note are three bichrome samples in a semi-fine to semi-coarse, very pale, almost white, buff. All three are from the same unit (1924), which is assigned to phase IIe. Although it does look different in hand specimen, the fabric is very close petrographically to that used for the shallow rounded bowls with grooved rim and diagonal lines or cross-hatching, mentioned above. In phase IIe, the first use of bichrome is only for horizontal bands; in the subsequent phase, when bichrome really comes into its own, concentric target motifs also appear.

Chemistry
As there are only very few samples from this level the chemical results, listed in Table 9, with no separate dendrogram, are necessarily brief. The main feature to comment on is the Kindergarten ware. Of the four samples analysed chemically, three group closely together, characterized in particular by very high concentrations of As (arsenic; between 200 and 400 ppm). The fourth sample, petrographically slightly different, seems to stand apart chemically (e.g. only 56 ppm As). The chemistry does not suggest that this should be considered as anything other than a local ware.

Fabric groups (Fig. 537)
GROUP A (S143–6)
This is the fabric of so-called 'Kindergarten ware'. It is hard to tell in thin section if it is calcareous or non-calcareous. It is not mica-

ceous. In all four samples the coarse fraction is dominated by tightly packed micritic limestone, with Tcfs/mudstones and also significant amounts of serpentine. It is considered to be a local fabric.

GROUP B (S115)

This calcareous fabric with microfossils, and limestone and serpentine inclusions, is much like a fabric (Group A) that is common in Level IIa–d, and which continued little changed in Level IIf. As there are relatively few examples that belong unequivocally to phase IIe, there is only one sample included here as representative of this fabric group, S115, a rounded bowl with diagonal lines from a IIe/f context.

GROUP C (S147–9)

With these samples a bimodal distribution cannot really be identified, as there are many inclusions in the 0.1–0.2 mm range, and so tempering seems much less likely than with samples from phases IIa–d, and phase IIf. But they do all contain the same range of inclusion types, namely limestone, foraminifera, serpentine, chert, mudstones, and much smaller amounts of schist and igneous rock fragments.

Level IIf

Owing to the uncertain stratigraphic and architectural nature of phase IIf, the pottery types securely assigned to this phase are restricted to those that can be identified as 'late' on stylistic grounds. These tend to be decorated tablewares (rather than storage or cooking pot wares), exhibiting features seen in many places throughout the east Mediterranean at this time (c. 750–650 BC).

Thus it follows that most of the samples selected from this phase are from decorated tablewares. These can be divided into two main categories, local and non-local. The local material is extremely well represented in the rich deposits from a very well-preserved kiln, in which more than 3000 sherds were found. What is particularly fascinating about this group of pottery is that stylistically there are extremely close parallels to Cyprus. In the Cypriot terminology the undecorated pieces would be described as 'Plain White IV', and the decorated vessels as 'White Painted IV'. Both these ware groups are usually considered characteristic of the Cypro-Archaic I phase, dated to c. 750–650 BC. The most strikingly 'Cypriote' shape in this Kilise Tepe deposit is the trefoil-lipped jug with concentric targets and bands in dark paint on a light ground. The type is known not only from Cyprus, but is also attested in the excavations at Tarsus (Hanfmann 1963), and at Al Mina, the port for the Amuq plain (Postgate 1998b, 132). Such ceramics were also found at Knossos: some examples appear to be actual imports from Cyprus, whilst others may be local imitations (Coldstream 1984; Coldstream & Catling 1996). At Kilise Tepe one also wonders whether the very strong stylistic links mean that this pottery could possibly be imported, but there are a number of factors that render this unlikely: the sheer quantity of material; the find context — a kiln, suggesting on-site production; and the fact that we are not just dealing with a single type, but a whole range of at least 8 shapes, some plain and some decorated. In addition, petrographic and chemical analysis of the pottery fabrics has provided strong support for a local source.

All the sherds are in exactly the same fabric, a pale semi-fine to semi-coarse buff, and well-fired. The level of paste standardization is so markedly high that all these sherds could be from vessels made in a single production event, from the same large batch of clay. There is some subtle variation in coarseness according to shape and size, which would suggest that the potters tempered their clay variably with respect to the shape and size of the vessel to be produced. The juglets S156–7, and grooved bowl S162–3, are the finest, decorated trefoil-lipped jugs S150–53 are also relatively fine, whilst jug S154 and all other samples are a little coarser, and there is little to distinguish between them. The petrographic analyses confirm the visual impression of an extremely standardized fabric. They also demonstrate that the fabric is local, owing to the presence of serpentine and foraminifera. Furthermore, the chemical analyses confirm both the close similarities between the various samples and the high likelihood of this being a local fabric (see Fig. 217).

This fabric, Group A, is the same fabric as has already been described for the Level III (Group B) and for phases IIa–d (Group A), and therefore marks a significant degree of cultural continuity at the site in ceramic manufacturing traditions.

In addition to these locally produced Plain White and White Painted wares, there are significant quantities of Black-on-Red ware and Bichrome ware. These constitute Fabric Groups B, C, and D, which are all non-calcareous and exhibiting features strongly suggestive of non-local sources. Cyprus must be considered as one of the most likely sources for these imported classes of pottery, on stylistic, petrographic and indeed chemical grounds, but the North Levantine coast is also a distinct possibility. Petrographically the fabrics are quite varied but most seem to be micaceous, and characterized by the presence of rocks and minerals indicative of a predominantly igneous environment, including both volcanic and plutonic rock types (Figs. 538–9). Such features would appear to be consistent with the geology of Cyprus (Jones 1986), but this does not mean that other areas such as the Levant can be ruled out. Although non-calcareous red fabrics do occur in other phases at Kilise Tepe, for example

Table 9. *Chemical data for ceramic samples.*

	Sm	Lu	U	Yb	As	Sb	Ca	Na	La	Ce	Th	Cr	Hf	Cs	Tb	Sc	Rb	Fe	Ta	Co	Eu
KLT99001	7.60	0.38	3.6	3.22	6.0	0.8	90,100	5400	44.2	92.9	14.2	108	5.62	7.17	1.0	15.54	120	45,900	1.3	17.57	1.49
KLT99002	3.63	0.25	3.7	1.73	8.1	1.1	178,500	2500	20.2	42.3	6.5	142	2.38	4.96	0.4	10.44	60	29,300	0.7	16.67	0.76
KLT99003	2.48	0.18	3.3	1.19	8.6	0.8	231,700	1800	13.1	27.7	4.5	99	1.72	3.72	0.3	7.68	40	22,100	0.5	12.25	0.48
KLT99004	3.95	0.23	3.2	1.77	11.5	0.8	175,300	2800	22.3	45.1	7.1	107	2.49	5.72	0.4	10.22	70	28,200	0.7	14.80	0.78
KLT99005	4.18	0.24	1.7	1.94	10.0	0.8	201,900	1400	23.9	51.0	7.1	123	4.53	3.36	0.5	8.10	50	25,600	0.9	12.61	0.90
KLT99006	3.15	0.24	4.4	1.54	8.9	1.0	200,100	2800	16.8	35.4	5.7	193	2.24	5.07	0.5	9.59	60	26,800	0.5	15.79	0.64
KLT99007	4.56	0.29	3.8	2.03	11.6	0.9	184,400	5500	26.6	54.2	8.5	131	2.79	5.90	0.7	11.62	70	32,400	0.8	16.91	0.92
KLT99008	4.13	0.28	4.0	1.87	10.4	0.8	197,500	3900	23.6	48.8	7.4	125	2.64	4.83	0.8	11.25	60	30,900	0.8	16.34	0.87
KLT99009	5.58	0.33	3.6	2.72	13.5	0.9	132,500	8600	32.3	67.1	10.3	145		10.80	0.5	14.41	110	38,800	1.0	19.98	1.13
KLT99010	7.96	0.43	4.0	3.41	7.5	0.8	59,200	4400	46.9	97.3	14.8	95	5.94	6.91	1.2	15.82	130	47,400	1.3	18.46	1.66
KLT99011	7.91	0.42	4.0	3.37	6.9	0.8	52,900	4700	46.4	91.2	15.1	98	5.80	7.02	1.1	15.86	130	46,100	1.2	17.71	1.68
KLT99012	5.07	0.32	3.3	2.20	35.8	1.0	142,300	6900	29.7	61.4	9.2	146	3.21	7.70	0.5	13.52	80	36,000	0.9	18.56	0.94
KLT99013	7.82	0.45	4.1	3.47	12.4	1.0	72,500	3400	44.4	96.5	14.3	101	5.36	7.56	1.1	15.61	130	46,700	1.2	17.79	1.56
KLT99014	3.14	0.22	3.5	1.52	8.1	0.8	195,100	2800	16.6	35.9	5.4	312	2.13	2.93	0.4	9.07	40	26,200	0.5	16.73	0.61
KLT99015	4.43	0.28	6.5	1.62	334.7	2.7	126,900	4700	24.7	62.0	9.3	184	2.68	23.00	0.8	14.80	110	47,600	0.9	19.28	1.03
KLT99016	6.24	0.51	16.8	2.29	397.8	4.2	127,200	5100	28.9	62.6	9.8	276	2.95	25.10	0.5	15.59	110	55,900	0.8	26.40	1.01
KLT99017	5.01	0.34	6.2	2.22	56.4	1.9	129,000	3900	28.2	60.1	9.6	321	3.06	9.90	0.6	14.79	80	41,400	0.9	21.41	0.97
KLT99018	6.07	0.47	12.4	2.37	208.2	3.0	143,000	6500	32.0	69.2	10.0	170	3.05	23.30	0.6	15.82	120	49,300	1.0	21.65	1.07
KLT99019	3.98	0.31	5.7	1.87	23.5	1.0	154,300	2900	21.6	46.2	7.3	274	2.91	9.54	0.5	12.41	70	33,800	0.7	20.59	0.78
KLT99020	3.56	0.29	2.5	2.12	10.3	0.8	85,800	9800	19.0	41.5	6.2	546	3.50	3.39	0.8	20.19	70	52,500	0.7	26.88	0.88
KLT99021	5.85	0.46	3.8	3.57	11.1	1.1		12,500	29.8	107.8	16.6	90	7.48	6.60	0.8	19.31	140	57,800	1.5	24.51	1.19
KLT99022	5.21	0.27	2.7	2.30	9.6	1.1	97,500	7000	28.2	66.8	9.5	800	4.02	5.31	0.6	18.22	80	57,300	1.4	43.63	1.20
KLT99023	3.06	0.26		1.99	7.9	0.8	81,200	13,100	14.5	45.9	3.7	162	2.26	2.67	0.6	25.34	60	54,300	0.5	27.64	0.81
KLT99024	2.96	0.22	3.9	1.49	7.0	0.8	193,500	3100	15.6	32.9	5.7	402	2.35	3.76	0.4	9.39	60	26,500	0.5	16.89	0.60
KLT99024	2.96	0.22	3.9	1.49	7.0	0.8	193,500	3100	15.6	32.9	5.7	402	2.35	3.76	0.4	9.39	60	26,500	0.5	16.89	0.60
KLT99025	2.96	0.2	3.6	1.35	6.4	0.8	199,500	2500	14.8	32.4	5.4	514	2.09	4.58	0.4	8.89	50	25,100	0.5	14.90	0.54
KLT99026	2.82	0.21	4.0	1.37	7.4	0.7	202,900	2900	14.6	32.8	5.7	584	2.00	5.01	0.4	8.66	60	24,500	0.5	14.17	0.56
KLT99027	2.68	0.21	4.1	1.27	6.0	0.6	218,200	2700	13.8	29.7	4.9	388	1.99	3.80	0.5	8.32	50	22,500	0.5	13.76	0.53
KLT99028	6.03	0.39	3.9	2.77	15.6	1.0	137,700	6000	36.0	73.0	11.7	146	3.49	13.40	0.7	17.51	120	46,100	1.1	23.52	1.19
KLT99029	7.93	0.39	2.8	3.42	8.8	0.9	74,600	6700	47.5	98.4	14.4	89	6.16	8.94	1.0	16.21	140	44,700	1.4	19.22	1.69
KLT99030	5.00	0.33	4.6	2.38	19.0	1.2	128,300	4500	28.6	61.2	9.6	202	3.09	12.60	0.5	14.09	100	37,200	0.8	20.43	1.04
KLT99031	3.33	0.27	1.8	2.14	7.5	0.6	80,800	14,400	14.8	29.6	3.3	198	2.53	2.23	0.6	26.75	50	55,400	0.4	26.60	0.89
KLT99032	4.06	0.31	2.9	2.44	7.0	0.8	113,600	7600	18.9	40.3	5.6	237	3.12	3.50	0.7	23.61	70	57,800	0.7	31.33	0.98
KLT99033	5.52	0.37	7.7	2.40	39.4	3.0	138,100	4300	30.4	63.2	10.0	256	3.41	14.80	0.6	15.54	140	42,500	0.9	24.16	1.10
KLT99034	3.94	0.31	2.8	2.33	11.9	0.8	99,200	11,300	18.4	37.0	5.3	318		3.22	0.8	20.62	60	49,700	0.6	27.33	0.99
KLT99035	3.26	0.22	3.2	1.49	8.8	0.7	197,000	3100	17.7	36.7	5.9	241	2.36	4.26	0.4	9.35	50	27,000	0.6	17.35	0.63
KLT99036	3.86	0.28	2.5	2.26	10.3	0.9	120,100	7400	18.9	38.8	5.8	200	2.83	4.30	0.6	22.32	80	55,000	0.7	30.17	1.03
KLT99037	6.16	0.35	3.6	2.84	10.2	1.3	88,500	5500	36.7	78.0	11.2	406	4.04	8.01	0.9	21.00	120	64,200	1.5	47.47	1.32
KLT99038	5.28	0.31	3.0	2.52	11.3	1.2	111,300	7000	29.8	64.5	9.8	678	4.00	5.96	0.8	19.31	80	59,100	1.4	44.38	1.18
KLT99039	4.34	0.31	2.9	2.28	10.4	1.3	115,200	7300	24.1	53.8	9.7	306	4.00	4.66	0.7	13.51	70	37,400	0.8	22.11	0.94
KLT99040	5.83	0.33	4.0	2.60	11.6	1.0	171,500	4400	33.2	71.9	10.5	192	3.87	5.35	0.6	13.82	100	40,800	0.9	23.10	1.20
KLT99041	4.91	0.3	2.9	2.44	6.0	0.9	116,800	5900	26.7	55.9	9.0	156	3.98	6.17	0.6	14.76	110	42,300	1.0	22.35	0.99
KLT99042	5.97	0.36	3.2	2.69	9.1	1.2	85,100	5800	35.7	78.5	11.3	304	4.11	8.16	0.7	20.56	110	63,900	1.6	46.58	1.30
KLT99043	8.83	0.52	4.6	4.11	8.8	1.6	9500	6300	48.3	105.1	19.1	112	6.29	12.30	1.1	19.42	180	45,800	1.5	18.11	1.66
KLT99044	2.34	0.17	3.5	1.16	3.5	0.6	198,600	2800	11.9	24.9	3.7	183	1.59	4.03	0.3	7.26	50	18,800	0.4	11.60	0.48
KLT99045	2.09	0.12	1.6	0.93	4.1	0.5	282,000	1500	11.6	22.7	3.2	92	1.56	0.95	0.2	4.27	20	12,700	0.4	6.93	0.42
KLT99045	2.09	0.12	1.6	0.93	4.1	0.5	282,000	1500	11.6	22.7	3.2	92	1.56	0.95	0.2	4.27	20	12,700	0.4	6.93	0.42
KLT99046	4.32	0.24	2.4	1.85	10.0	1.4	173,900	2100	23.2	51.4	8.8	208	3.52	5.92	0.6	9.58	70	26,700	0.9	12.09	0.83

Table 9. *(cont.)*

	Sm	Lu	U	Yb	As	Sb	Ca	Na	La	Ce	Th	Cr	Hf	Cs	Tb	Sc	Rb	Fe	Ta	Co	Eu
KLT99047	2.20	0.16	2.3	1.07	6.0	0.7	235,700	1900	11.5	24.2	4.0	139	1.83	2.51	0.5	6.30	40	17,700	0.4	8.41	0.44
KLT99048	2.65	0.18	2.5	1.31	4.8	0.6	205,700	2500	14.1	28.4	4.6	148	2.36	3.56	0.4	7.50	40	22,200	0.5	11.66	0.56
KLT99049	2.80	0.16	1.4	1.27	4.2	0.5	239,000	1400	14.8	30.4	4.5	168	2.19	2.61	0.2	5.73	20	16,900	0.4	8.82	0.54
KLT99050	2.77	0.16	1.8	1.25	4.7	0.5	241,900	1600	14.6	32.1	4.6	102	2.13	2.11	0.3	6.01	30	17,900	0.6	8.39	0.56
KLT99051	3.62	0.21	2.1	1.63	5.3	0.7	195,300	2100	19.8	41.9	6.3	197	3.24	4.30	0.5	8.27	50	24,400	0.6	12.95	0.71
KLT99052	7.01	0.42	4.0	3.20	7.4	1.3	30,000	8100	44.5	100.1	15.1	84	5.59	9.73	0.9	16.39	150	50,000	1.5	20.25	1.27
KLT99053	7.53	0.67	20.2	4.00	28.2	1.3	66,500	3000	49.6	103.7	20.4	141	7.11	1.37	0.9	21.41	30	58,900	2.4	21.79	1.21
KLT99053	7.53	0.67	20.2	4.00	28.2	1.3	66,500	3000	49.6	103.7	20.4	141	7.11	1.37	0.9	21.41	30	58,900	2.4	21.79	1.21
KLT99054	6.99	0.37	3.7	2.97	8.2	0.7	88,700	2400	44.2	89.8	13.8	202	4.16	7.07	0.7	16.10	120	46,400	1.2	25.47	1.43
KLT99055	8.27	0.5	4.3	3.93	7.8	1.5	17,300	8500	52.4	114.3	19.3	113	6.94	13.50	0.9	19.86	210	50,300	1.5	21.02	1.37
KLT99056	7.67	0.47	3.4	3.77	5.8	1.1	18,400	11200	43.9	22.7	3.2	79	1.50	3.77	0.3	6.55	50	16,700	0.4	7.90	0.44
KLT99057	5.54	0.4	3.0	3.21	10.0	0.6	150,100	1200	30.2	72.6	12.9	75	7.33	4.77	0.8	11.47	90	32,700	1.2	11.22	1.19
KLT99058	5.58	0.34	3.3	2.58	12.2	1.4	107,900	4000	30.4	64.8	9.1	380	4.06	6.36	0.9	14.37	70	43,300	1.0	25.18	1.20
KLT99059	2.87	0.2	3.2	1.47	4.9	0.7	197,800	2300	16.1	31.9	4.9	94	1.92	5.90	0.3	8.39	50	21,300	0.6	10.36	0.57
KLT99060	2.21	0.17	3.2	1.07	6.5	0.6	218,700	2400	11.6	24.5	4.0	59	1.52	1.80	0.2	6.94	20	18,800	0.4	11.11	0.43
KLT99061	4.54	0.26	2.4	2.18	8.9	0.8	164,900	2900	26.1	57.7	8.7	332	4.35	3.27	0.5	10.01	50	29,900	0.9	15.01	0.98
KLT99062	4.46	0.29	3.7	2.03	10.9	0.7	147,300	1300	24.0	49.3	9.3	65	3.22	7.01	0.4	10.76	100	33,100	0.8	11.13	0.83
KLT99063	4.11	0.27	4.1	1.97	21.5	1.1	154,200	2500	23.0	47.4	7.5	135	2.92	1.99	0.6	10.21	40	29,900	0.8	14.21	0.86
KLT99064	2.84	0.2	3.4	1.35	9.3	1.1	216,200	2100	14.5	31.1	4.8	140	1.81	3.61	0.4	8.42	40	23,500	0.5	12.81	0.58
KLT99065	2.83	0.17	2.5	1.25	6.5	0.6	231,300	1600	15.3	31.9	4.9	61	1.99	3.48	0.4	6.31	40	18,900	0.5	8.36	0.53
KLT99066	5.37	0.33	3.4	2.51	25.9	1.2	134,000	4000	31.4	64.9	9.9	174	3.27	14.80	0.6	14.95	110	41,700	0.9	23.72	1.08
KLT99067	5.01	0.28	2.9	2.29	16.0	0.8	103,100	4200	30.2	66.2	10.8	667	2.86	9.91	0.5	14.69	90	47,100	0.9	42.11	1.05
KLT99068	5.39	0.35	3.7	2.56	27.6	1.2	150,200	4300	30.8	60.8	9.8	94	3.58	15.70	0.9	15.56	120	44,700	0.8	18.80	1.13
KLT99068	5.39	0.35	3.7	2.56	27.6	1.2	150,200	4300	30.8	60.8	9.8	94	3.58	15.70	0.9	15.56	120	44,700	0.8	18.80	1.13
KLT99069	4.35	0.32	4.9	2.13	18.3	1.2	167,500	3800	23.1	47.2	8.0	97	3.10	9.10	0.7	12.68	80	34,300	0.7	17.84	0.85
KLT99070	2.32	0.18	4.6	1.16	7.4	1.0	231,500	2500	11.3	23.6	3.3	62	1.42	4.25	0.3	6.92	40	16,800	0.4	6.93	0.45
KLT99071	4.34	0.27	3.6	2.08	45.1	0.8	186,700	3100	22.6	47.7	7.0	109	2.68	8.42	0.6	11.38	80	29,100	0.8	26.08	0.84
KLT99072	2.18	0.18	3.9	1.00	3.4	0.5	242,600	2300	10.7	95.7	16.4	152	6.46	10.70	1.0	18.92	170	48,900	1.9	20.96	1.41
KLT99073	1.93	0.16	3.6	0.90	10.4	1.1	262,900	1900	9.5	19.5	2.7	102	1.07	2.74	0.3	5.21	30	18,000	0.3	9.55	0.36
KLT99074	1.88	0.16	3.5	0.90	9.7	1.1	251,800	2100	9.2	19.3	2.5	89	1.05	2.50	0.3	4.94	30	16,900	0.2	8.80	0.36
KLT99075	3.71	0.22	2.3	1.77	10.9	0.9	165,300	5400	22.2	46.8	8.1	364	3.34	5.43	0.5	11.28	70	31,900	0.7	19.96	0.79
KLT99076	3.14	0.21	2.1	1.64	8.1	0.7	144,400	5000	16.7	36.5	6.6	800	3.06	3.62	0.4	12.24	50	36,700	0.6	30.13	0.73
KLT99077	3.34	0.21	2.3	1.62	9.9	0.9	196,100	4400	19.5	40.9	7.3	314	2.93	4.62	0.5	9.74	60	27,500	0.6	16.77	0.75
KLT99078	3.69	0.22	2.1	1.87	23.7	0.6	175,000	7000	20.9	43.5	6.7	142	3.23	7.25	0.4	10.02	60	26,500	0.6	12.97	0.82
KLT99079	3.21	0.22	2.1	1.62	10.6	0.7	174,100	5400	17.9	38.0	6.8	450	3.20	4.10	0.4	9.52	50	27,700	0.6	19.53	0.68
KLT99080	4.47	0.27	2.6	2.11	11.9	1.0	139,400	3100	26.9	56.1	10.1	218	3.41	7.73	0.5	14.32	90	39,900	0.9	23.18	0.97
KLT99081	3.14	0.22	4.0	1.46	9.9	0.8	182,900	1900	16.4	34.7	5.4	126	2.03	4.02	0.3	9.65	60	26,500	0.6	17.32	0.63
KLT99082	3.72	0.28	6.0	1.78	17.5	1.0	189,800	3800	18.7	39.0	6.4	230	2.30	4.92	0.5	10.09	60	28,700	0.6	16.12	0.75
KLT99083	3.84	0.23	2.7	1.80	20.5	0.8	201,000	3100	21.5	45.3	7.0	144	2.50	5.61	0.6	9.13	60	30,500	0.6	14.16	0.79
KLT99084	8.09	0.4	3.2	3.26	13.0	1.6	67,200	5600	51.2	110.2	15.5	149	4.95	6.38	0.8	17.26	130	50,200	1.3	19.61	1.59
KLT99085	3.10	0.24	4.1	1.52	14.9	0.9	208,400	2900	16.5	33.7	4.8	213	1.94	4.05	0.6	9.46	50	27,200	0.5	15.39	0.66
KLT99086	2.72	0.2	2.8	1.39	4.7	0.9	216,200	1800	16.2	33.5	7.5	138	1.98	4.85	0.4	8.83	50	24,000	0.5	10.39	0.63
KLT99087	6.75	0.45	4.4	3.27	11.0	1.3	37,700	1800	39.2	88.8	15.4	110	4.90	10.10	1.0	20.10	160	58,200	1.6	22.83	1.33
KLT99088	7.29	0.42	3.9	3.25	29.4	4.7	39,700	2600	44.5	94.8	15.1	100	5.16	11.40	0.8	19.04	170	53,300	1.4	20.89	1.46
KLT99089	5.79	0.32	3.6	2.33	9.5	1.1	110,700	4800	28.6	58.2	10.4	211	3.29	6.26	0.6	14.77	110	37,400	1.0	18.38	1.06
KLT99090	8.70	0.49	3.4	3.93	18.4	1.3	12,900	6100	52.3	116.1	17.0	142	7.49	8.65	1.2	18.51	160	52,400	1.6	27.08	1.73
KLT99091	2.68	0.19	3.4	1.33	9.3	0.8	196,100	2000	13.9	30.3	4.5	193	2.10	2.58	0.5	8.93	40	24,400	0.5	15.00	0.50
KLT99092	4.35	0.3	4.3	2.12	11.7	0.8	162,100	4400	23.4	44.9	7.7	202	3.09	6.47	0.7	12.00	80	29,400	0.8	16.96	0.88

Table 9. (cont.)

	Sm	Lu	U	Yb	As	Sb	Ca	Na	La	Ce	Th	Cr	Hf	Cs	Tb	Sc	Rb	Fe	Ta	Co	Eu
KLT99092	4.35	0.3	4.3	2.12	11.7	0.8	162,100	4400	23.4	44.9	7.7	202	3.09	6.47	0.7	12.00	80	29,400	0.8	16.96	0.88
KLT99093	2.38	0.18	3.3	1.17	6.7	0.7	219,400	2300	12.3	26.6	4.2	97	1.60	2.23	0.5	7.25	40	19,500	0.4	12.08	0.50
KLT99094	6.82	0.42	4.0	3.13	8.8	1.3	86,300	2200	38.2	83.0	13.9	103	5.18	8.28	0.9	17.84	140	52,300	1.5	19.83	1.38
KLT99095	7.19	0.4	3.5	3.15	14.2	2.4	94,800	2700	41.8	91.2	13.5	96	4.71	7.64	1.3	18.35	150	49,700	1.4	18.45	1.48
KLT99096	2.98	0.21	4.2	1.38	12.3	0.8	228,000		15.0	31.0	4.8	163	1.89	3.57	0.4	8.12	40	23,500	0.5	13.19	0.58
KLT99097	7.03	0.46	4.1	3.44	8.2	1.3	44,800	1900	41.0	93.6	16.2	118	4.95	10.60	1.2	20.89	170	59,800	1.6	23.89	1.42
KLT99098	7.20	0.38	3.6	3.15	25.2	3.1	73,400	3100	42.3	91.6	14.6	95	4.34	9.78	1.2	18.76	140	52,900	1.5	21.05	1.38
KLT99099	6.53	0.39	4.2	2.78	10.8	1.1	105,500	2100	36.3	78.8	12.9	85	5.18	7.08	0.7	15.80	110	46,100	1.3	19.74	1.28
KLT99100	2.16	0.14	2.8	1.05	7.9	0.8	223,100	2400	11.1	22.8	3.7	80	1.51	1.88	0.2	6.42	40	18,300	0.2	10.43	0.41
KLT99101	6.58	0.4	4.0	3.05	11.1	1.2	100,400	2100	38.3	82.8	14.1	99	4.61	8.78	1.1	18.82	140	53,800	1.3	20.10	1.26
KLT99102	7.61	0.42	4.6	3.09	40.1	1.5	102,900	7500	48.4	99.5	15.4	123	3.97	19.10	0.9	20.86	160	53,300	1.4	22.83	1.55
KLT99103	8.98	0.45	4.5	3.48	10.2	1.0	72,800	7500	61.2	129.5	18.7	122	4.37	17.80	1.0	22.31	200	49,900	1.6	27.35	1.83
KLT99104	6.94	0.39	4.7	2.79	75.4	2.2	75,700	6000	42.6	91.2	14.0	116	3.75	19.50	1.1	20.71	150	64,000	1.3	26.37	1.43
KLT99105	7.34	0.42	4.7	3.23	45.1	3.4	74,000	5800	46.3	99.4	15.0	131	3.84	34.50	0.6	22.56	200	48,300	1.2	29.73	1.54
KLT99106	7.76	0.41	4.5	3.23	37.0	1.3	124,000	9500	50.3	103.5	15.2	121	3.85	17.00	0.7	19.60	170	48,100	1.3	24.51	1.51
KLT99107	6.68	0.36	3.4	2.79	33.3	1.8	137,600	5400	38.1	78.8	11.5	171	4.30	7.57	1.0	15.40	110	46,600	1.0	19.98	1.37
KLT99107	6.68	0.36	3.4	2.79	33.3	1.8	137,600	5400	38.1	78.8	11.5	171	4.30	7.57	1.0	15.40	110	46,600	1.0	19.98	1.37
KLT99108	6.40	0.4	4.8	2.85	53.6	1.6	83,600	5100	39.1	82.2	13.4	118	4.18	24.00	1.0	20.40	170	51,400	1.2	22.98	1.30
KLT99109	6.64	0.39	3.7	2.90	26.8	1.1	120,100	5400	40.6	84.9	12.6	113	4.01	14.40	0.8	17.69	140	49,300	1.1	23.20	1.44
KLT99110	7.06	0.38	5.3	2.90	98.0	2.4	130,300		44.1	94.9	13.5	111	3.26	18.70	0.6	18.72	150	56,100	1.2	20.91	1.33
KLT99111	7.89	0.44	3.8	3.60	22.6	3.2	6100	4700	53.9	113.3	19.5	122	6.06	7.89	1.3	22.27	190	63,400	1.8	29.19	1.67
KLT99112	7.37	0.4	4.5	3.05	65.1	1.9	96,100	5800	46.2	95.2	14.8	111	4.12	21.70	0.9	20.64	170	59,900	1.3	25.99	1.52
KLT99113	6.92	0.49	6.2	3.39	26.6	5.8	11,000	3000	42.7	87.1	12.3	122	4.97	8.84	0.8	17.13	150	49,400	1.3	16.29	1.36
KLT99114	6.78	0.37	4.7	2.83	63.3	1.8	129,200	6800	40.5	86.5	13.2	115	3.64	19.40	0.7	19.03	130	49,900	1.3	26.45	1.22
KLT99115	8.67	0.45	4.4	3.54	37.9	1.3	78,600	14500	58.7	123.2	18.5	130	4.62	18.50	1.3	22.86	170	51,500	1.5	29.18	1.83
KLT99116	8.70	0.44	4.2	3.52	14.8	1.0	79,800	7100	57.1	119.0	17.5	125	4.48	15.80	0.8	21.26	190	47,300	1.4	24.31	1.71
KLT99117	7.02	0.36	3.9	2.92	7.9	0.8	123,500	6200	44.2	95.4	13.7	133	3.98	13.80	0.8	19.29	140	48,400	1.2	24.43	1.48
KLT99118	6.35	0.41	5.6	2.85	81.7	1.8	50,300	5200	39.5	83.2	13.4	106	4.04	17.80	0.6	19.60	150	51,600	1.1	23.68	1.23
KLT99119	7.07	0.4	4.9	2.95	35.4	1.6	64,600	5900	46.0	96.1	14.6	119	3.56	18.40	0.7	20.26	160	50,700	1.3	24.40	1.34
KLT99120	7.55	0.41	5.5	3.17	11.8	1.6	64,100	3400	45.1	98.9	15.4	98	4.77	10.80	1.1	19.06	140	51,400	1.5	20.94	1.44
KLT99121	6.85	0.37	3.1	3.07	19.8	1.9	78,800	3900	41.8	88.5	13.3	139	5.22	6.88	0.8	15.35	130	47,200	1.3	19.71	1.32
KLT99122	2.43	0.18	3.7	1.21	6.9	0.9	195,700	2200	12.2	25.4	4.2	102	1.65	2.03	0.3	7.24	40	21,100	0.4	13.15	0.49
KLT99123	2.73	0.2	4.3	1.37	7.6	0.9	205,900	2900	13.5	28.7	4.6	115	1.86	3.03	0.3	7.74	40	22,100	0.4	13.96	0.50
KLT99124	2.93	0.21	4.2	1.37	9.0	0.9	207,700	3300	15.0	32.1	5.2	114	1.96	3.28	0.3	8.27	50	24,300	0.5	14.98	0.59
KLT99125	8.00	0.43	5.1	3.20	36.4	2.1	76,600	4000	47.5	100.6	14.1	138	4.58	13.30	0.8	17.69	150	48,900	1.3	22.76	1.52
KLT99126	8.68	0.44	4.3	3.47	32.2	1.2	71,700	6300	59.0	125.7	18.3	128	4.12	18.60	1.0	22.89	200	48,400	1.5	27.09	1.78
KLT99127	7.02	0.4	3.7	3.07	24.7	1.0	98,400	5800	43.3	91.1	13.8	121	4.16	13.60	1.0	18.61	150	53,300	1.3	23.43	1.44
KLT99128	5.85	0.35	3.1	2.87	8.9	1.3	66,300	5600	34.0	77.5	13.1	98	4.37	9.01	0.5	15.97	120	48,100	1.2	21.61	1.19
KLT99129	3.33	0.22	3.4	1.49	11.5	0.8	207,300	3700	18.2	37.5	6.0	234	2.25	3.07	0.5	8.71	40	25,800	0.6	15.23	0.66
KLT99130	8.81	0.47	4.3	3.52	28.6	1.6	91,100		57.3	122.6	17.5	121	4.29	17.90	0.9	22.03	190	52,100	1.5	24.68	1.71
KLT99131	3.68	0.24	3.9	1.65	21.7	0.8	179,500	3000	19.9	42.3	6.4	106	2.25	5.41	0.6	10.20	60	28,500	0.6	17.62	0.73
KLT99132	2.73	0.18	3.7	1.27	10.2	0.7	212,400	2000	14.4	29.6	4.5	109	1.73	2.86	0.3	7.99	50	22,600	0.4	13.69	0.49

the red wares of the Late Bronze Age, no other fabric group is comparable to these phase IIf fabrics in terms of their volcanic and plutonic characteristics.

Chemistry

The total chemical variability amongst the IIf samples is moderate: $vt = 1.91$. All 6 samples forming the first cluster on the dendrogram (Fig. 214) are from the kiln group, and so must clearly be local. The fabric, highly calcareous and with high Cr content (>500 ppm in 2 of the samples), is comparable to Level III Fabric B and IIa–d Fabric A. The next dendrogram cluster is composed entirely of 'Cypriot-style' pottery thought to be non-local on petrographic grounds. Given the plutonic and volcanic inclusions in most of these fabrics, Cyprus itself is a possible source; at present we cannot use the chemistry to either confirm or reject this hypothesis, but what we can say is that chemically the cluster is very different from the main local group (see Fig. 217). It is also distinct from the last small group on the dendrogram, which is something of a mixed bag. Three of the four (9928 (S166), 9933 (S168), 9930 (S167)) are all in Fabric Group A, and so one might have expected them to match chemically with the kiln group. One of the differences seems to lie in the lower quantities of Cr (146–256 ppm), and the samples are perhaps a bit coarser too. Amidst these is sample 9929 (S182), from Fabric Group D, characterized principally by quartz inclusions and comparable in thin section to Group B from Level IIa–d.

Fabric groups (Figs. 538–9)

GROUP A (including kiln group, unit 1783)

This group comprises the 16 samples from the kiln group of unit 1783 (S150–165, described separately below), and a few other phase IIf examples (S166–8). S166 and S168 are slightly different, but only in that they contain more mudstones. It should also be noted that a number of samples from phases IIa–d link in very well to this Middle Iron Age group.

As far as the kiln pottery is concerned, for thin-section analysis 2 samples have been taken from each of the 8 shapes, giving a total of 16 samples. The purpose of taking so many examples of what visually seems to be a single uniform fabric is to assess paste standardization as well as provenance. In terms of provenance the results are very clear, strongly indicative of a local source. The clay matrix is very fine and calcareous, and there are numerous foraminifera. These features are extremely similar to those observed in clay samples taken from very close to Kilise Tepe. Most of the coarse fraction is in the 0.25–0.5 mm range, and the angularity of inclusions is very varied. Serpentine inclusions are also common, with lesser amounts of mudstone, chert and quartz, and very rare epidote and igneous rock fragments.

The presence of common serpentine is very instructive as there are limited serpentine outcrops a short distance to the east of Kilise Tepe, up the Kurtsuyu valley. The presence of very rare igneous rock fragments is also consistent with this source. However, carbonate inclusions (micrite/calcite and microfossils) are the most frequent in the coarse fraction, commonly a feature of local pottery in the

Level IIf

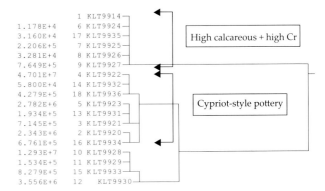

Figure 214. *Dendrogram 6: Level IIf.*

Bronze Age and Iron Age, and entirely consistent with the predominantly sedimentary geology of the area. It is this combination of calcareous clay, carbonate inclusions with distinctive microfossils, and serpentine that testify convincingly to a local origin. It is quite feasible that a fine buff marine clay was selected, and tempered with river sand taken from some point up the Kurtsuyu valley. The fabric is different to most Bronze Age fabrics from the site, but very similar indeed to a limited number of Level III samples, and more commonly to IIa–d fabrics. An interesting further step will be to correlate these broad technological shifts in paste recipes and resource selection with patterns of typological and stylistic change in the ceramic repertoire.

GROUP B (S169–80)

All the samples in this group are from Black-on-Red and Bichrome wares. They tend to be fine to semi-fine, and orange to red in hand specimen. Although there are enough similarities petrographically between them all to place them in this single group, there are nonetheless variations that demand the creation of a number of sub-groups. These fabrics must be non-local: the prevalence of plutonic and volcanic rock fragments and their associated minerals is inconsistent with the local geology. Cyprus is the most likely source. However, it should be noted that the variability shown across the following eight sub-groups indicates that we may be dealing with many different production locales, albeit sharing a comparable background geology.

SUB-GROUP B 1 (S169–72)

This is a red-firing fabric characterized in particular by mica and plagioclase laths in the fine fraction. Also present are quartz, Tcfs, epidote, igneous rock fragments, serpentine, and alkali feldspars. Such inclusions point to an igneous environment (such as the Troodos mountains on Cyprus).

SUB-GROUP B 2 (S173)

This is different to Sub-group B 1 in containing far fewer mica laths, and no plagioclase laths in the fine fraction. The single Black-on-Red sample in this group does show a number of similarities however, not least in that it is non-calcareous. It also has a range of other inclusion types encountered in Sub-group B 1, namely red Tcfs, quartz (large, monocrystalline grains, sa-sr), few to common altered volcanic and plutonic rock fragments, clinozoisite, amphibole, serpentine (relatively rare), few to common micritic limestones, rare chert, and rare alkali feldspars. It has an optically active groundmass, suggesting it was not fired very high. As with all sub-groups of Fabric Group B, an igneous environment such as that on Cyprus constitutes the most likely source.

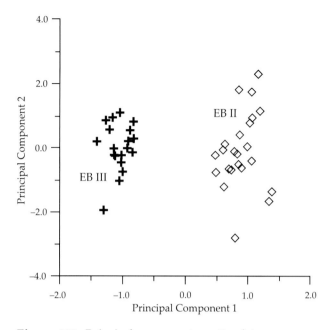

Figure 215. *Principal components scatterplot.*

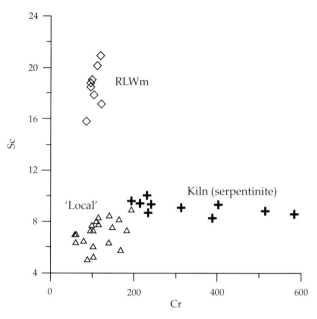

Figure 216. *Sc vs Cr scatterplot.*

SUB-GROUP B 3 (S174)
The sole sample of this group contains substantially more foraminifera and micritic/sparry limestone inclusions than seen in Sub-groups B 1 and B 2. There is little evidence for either mica or plagioclase laths in the fine fraction. Nonetheless, there are Tcfs, quartz, altered volcanic and plutonic rock fragments, serpentine, amphibole, epidote, etc., again pointing to an igneous environment.

SUB-GROUP B 4 (S175)
Once again, this Bichrome sample has many of the same overall features shared by all sub-groups, but contains a lot of both serpentine and amphibole, up to 0.5 mm in size, as well as significant amounts of micrite.

SUB-GROUP B 5 (S176)
The lone Bichrome sample in this sub-group has been highly fired to a pale buff, such that it looks in hand specimen more like a local calcareous semi-fine buff fabric. However, in thin section, micas are still visible in the sub-silt fraction, and there is no identifiable calcareous material. Furthermore, it does contain Tcfs, quartz, amphibole, and plutonic rock fragments composed of alkali feldspar and biotite, once again pointing to a similar source area as other sub-groups (i.e. Cyprus).

SUB-GROUP B 6 (S177–8)
S177 is a mid-body sherd from a closed vessel (jug?), with bichrome bands over a buff-cream slip. The fine to semi-fine orange fabric seems in hand specimen to contain red-brown grits. In thin section it is fine, red-firing, with quartz and tcfs, also granitic rock fragments, chert, metamorphics, volcanics, epidote, clinozoisite. This combination of rocks and minerals is indicative of a varied igneous environment. Also in this group is S178.

SUB-GROUP B 7 (S179)
S179 is from a trefoil jug with white painted bands and targets (**851**). The fabric is a yellow buff that has fired to orange in places — it is fine, but visibly silty in the break. The visual impression that this silt includes quartz is confirmed by thin-section study. Textural concentration features are also prevalent, with plagioclase and granitic rock fragments less common. Amphibole, serpentine, K-feldspar, basalt and chert are rare.

SUB-GROUP B 8 (S180)
This sample comes from a mid-body sherd of a closed vessel (jug?); it has bichrome decoration of targets painted in dark-on-light with a red painted line running through them. The paint adheres to a thick cream slip. The fine orange-red fabric comprises igneous rock fragments, amphibole, serpentine, epidote, micritic inclusions (some foraminifera), and large micritic siltstones. As has been stated with all other sub-groups here discussed, such features indicate Cyprus as the probable source.

GROUP C (S181)
This group, represented by a single Black-on-Red sample **836**, is quite different from all of the above in that it appears to derive from a metamorphic rather than an igneous environment. The coarse fraction is composed of schists, and it has none of the serpentine, amphibole, epidote or igneous rock fragments that are present in all the samples of Group B. Neither is it closely comparable to the Level III red fabrics, although it could feasibly derive from a similar source area (whatever that may be, unknown as it is at present, although the northern coast of Cyprus, around Kyrenia, is geologically compatible).

GROUP D (S182)
White Painted, lines and target motifs. This fabric does not contain any of the serpentine, amphibole, epidote or igneous rock fragments so ubiquitous in Group B, or even any metamorphic rock fragments as in Group C. This is a one-off fabric in phase IIf, although it is rather similar to a common fabric from phases IIa–d, known as Group B. Angular to sub-angular quartz dominates, and it is quite silty — most of the quartz is *c.* 0.1 mm. Also present are some deep red-brown Tcfs, and occasional sandstone. As with Group B from phases IIa–d, a non-local source is suspected, but there is very little material that is petrologically diagnostic.

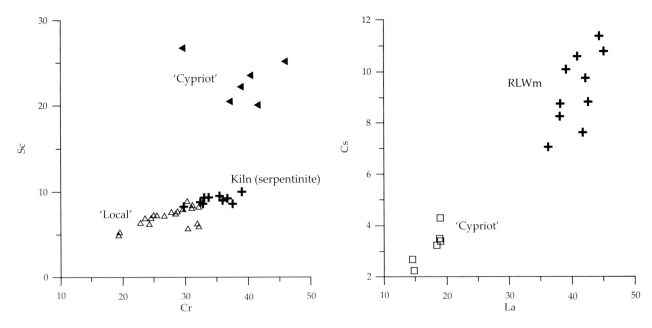

Figure 217. *Sc vs Ce scatterplot.*

Figure 218. *Cs vs La scatterplot.*

Concluding remarks: the organization of production

The principal aim behind the study of the Kilise Tepe ceramics has been to construct a relative sequence of occupation for the site. Through broad ceramic comparisons with other areas, most notably the site of Tarsus (Goldman 1956) on the Adana plain, it has been possible to define the earliest occupation of the site as dating to Early Bronze II, with a more or less continuous sequence thereafter through to the Iron Age. Moreover, the material here published is the only Bronze and Iron Age pottery from the whole Göksu valley to have been stratigraphically excavated. Therefore at present it is the only reliable representative of Göksu valley ceramic traditions over a very broad time span.

An integrated programme of ceramic analysis can contribute still further though, by providing insights into some aspects of economic activity at Kilise Tepe. Studies elsewhere have demonstrated how ceramic data can be effectively used to evaluate how craft production may have been organized at the site level. As well as tackling this issue for each phase in turn, the continuous sequence at Kilise Tepe means that comparisons can be made from phase to phase. This procedure therefore enables a long-term, historical perspective on craft decisions and technological change.

Assessments of production organization are best achieved when comparisons are available at many levels. It has already been noted that pottery from successive phases can be effectively compared, but the Kilise Tepe material is much more limited when it comes to comparisons in the spatial dimension. Firstly, the potential for comparative analyses of pottery recovered from different areas of the site is negligible, as only a small portion of the site has been excavated, especially where the earlier Bronze Age occupation levels are concerned. There are very few deposits from different areas of the site that are at once abundant in material and contemporary with one another. Secondly, moving beyond the site itself, the total lack of other excavated prehistoric sites in the Göksu valley makes it impossible to make any comparisons at the intra-regional level. Other sites are known to exist in the area, but thus far they have not been systematically investigated. Even at the inter-regional level there is little scope, as very few sites have been excavated and even fewer published (Tarsus, Mersin, Beycesultan, Aphrodisias, Karataş, Boğazköy, Troy).

It is thus clear that in this particular context any assessments of production organization have to be made with some caution. Nonetheless, this should not prevent us asking pertinent questions which we may go at least some way towards answering. Was pottery production organized at the household level during the earliest occupation of the site, or was it already a specialized craft? Was all the pottery consumed at the site also produced there, or were certain products manufactured elsewhere? Were there different modes of production for different classes of pottery, i.e. did one set of producers make cooking pots and another set make tablewares? All these questions and many others like them can be asked of the material from each and every phase.

Level Vj–g
Diversity is the watchword of the EB II ceramic assemblage at the site, with many different ware groups, not to mention 15 local and 6 non-local fabrics. Among the calcareous local fabrics the high degree of variability evident both in the petrography and the chemistry gives the impression that resources were selected for their expediency, and that potters were not enormously consistent in their clay paste preparation. It can be argued that the range and diversity of both wares and fabrics is greater than one would expect from any one workshop, or even from any one potting community. It is possible that the Kilise Tepe EB II assemblage represents consumption at the site of products derived from many different workshops or potting communities (within the Göksu valley).

A second conspicuous feature of the EB II pottery is the relative lack of any clear patterns of co-occurrence between ware, shape and fabric. Firstly, in each ware group there are very often three or more different fabrics represented — grey burnished ware occurs in at least three different fabrics, as does red burnished ware, and cooking pot ware. Secondly, each fabric group itself tends to contain a range of wares and shapes. Thirdly, some shape groups, for example open rounded bowls, have examples made in as many as five different fabrics, also with different surface treatments. Finally, perhaps the only feature common to all of the pottery groups is the construction technology — all pots are hand-made, and there is no sign of the wheel-throwing technique that becomes established in the following period (Level Vg–e).

When all of these patterns are assessed alongside the evidence for diversity in the assemblage, the only sensible conclusion that can be reached is that production was non-centralized in its organization. Although taken from a totally different context (Mayan in fact), the following quote is extremely pertinent. Ball (1993, 265) describes:

> ... an industry involving spatially dispersed workshop households, hamlets, or village communities of marginally productive subsistence farmers supplementing their agricultural income by working as part-time potters specializing in the manufacture of workshop-specific ceramic groups.

The question that remains is essentially one of scale. Is the diversity and lack of standardization observed in the assemblage the result of workshop households at Kilise Tepe alone, or attributable to dispersed village communities of which Kilise Tepe was but one? Kilise Tepe would have been no more than a small village site, with only a few households. Such a settlement could probably have been serviced by just one or two full-time pottery specialists; however, considering the diversity and non-standardization of the pottery it would be very difficult to argue for full-time specialists in EB II. If each and every household at the site produced some pottery in a part-time fashion, as suggested by the quote above, then a somewhat diverse and non-standardized assemblage could certainly be the result. Mellink (1986, 141) has suggested that in EB I pottery over much of Anatolia was made at the household level, probably by women. She bases this in part on the parochial nature of pottery traditions at this time, with a high degree of regional variation perhaps due to a lack of intensive contact between regions. In the course of EB II and III, however, this picture changes as regions become more interconnected. Yet in terms of Kilise Tepe I would say that Mellink's general comments on EB I hold true for EB II at the site. Only in EB III at Kilise Tepe are there any truly significant changes in production organization.

The other possibility is that only a few households in the settlement turned their hand to the manufacture of certain types. In this part of the Göksu valley there may well have been a number of other small villages like Kilise Tepe (which archaeologists have yet to identify), each with one or two households choosing to manufacture certain sorts of pottery on a part-time basis. If such settlements were closely connected, as seems likely, then there may well have been frequent exchanges of everyday goods from village to village.

Given that Kilise Tepe is the only prehistoric site in the valley thus far excavated, it is of course very difficult to choose between these two possible scenarios. The excavation of other sites may in the future make feasible the definition of micro-traditions within the region. This might allow archaeologists to assign a particular ware or style to a certain settlement or group of settlements. Further fabric studies of pottery from other sites might also permit the association of specific fabric groups with certain sites or areas. However, the geology of the area is so homogeneous that clay resources cannot be expected to differ very much at all from site to site. Thus further work on neighbouring sites would not necessarily alter the situation currently observed for the EB II fabrics, of local, predominantly calcareous resources showing considerable diversity.

Level Vf–e
Between EB II and EB III there are some dramatic changes in the pottery from Kilise Tepe. There are strong grounds for arguing that production organization underwent a fundamental shift, becoming centralized in EB III. Ceramic diversity decreases, with far fewer ware and fabric groups represented. Indeed, fabrics become immensely standardized, with a single

fabric group dominant (seen in both chemistry and petrography). Other important technological changes occur, notably with the first evidence for wheel-thrown pottery at the site. This is very much consistent with the notion that production was centralized, concentrated in the hands of full-time specialists. Firing technology also appears to have undergone changes in this period, with the use of higher temperatures in oxidizing atmospheres.

Again, the question of scale is important, but difficult to address when faced with material from just one site in the region. Did production become centralized at the community level, or at the regional level? Neither scenario can be ruled out at present. It is possible that much of the pottery consumed at the site was also produced there, perhaps by a handful of specialists working in just one or two workshops. Each of the other settlements presumably located in the wider area may have had a similar arrangement. The alternative scenario is that just one community in the region chose to focus on pottery production, and that this community exchanged its specialized ceramic products with the other communities in the region in return for other sorts of goods.

The other fabric groups in EB III, of which there are only three, are all characterized by the presence of significant quantities of metamorphic rock fragments as inclusions. The absence of any significant metamorphic outcrops in the Kilise Tepe area means that these are probably imported fabrics. It is noteworthy that these fabrics are associated exclusively with vessels that, judging by their shape and surface treatment, probably functioned as cooking pots.

Major changes are postulated for this period (EB III) across broad areas of the east Mediterranean. In Anatolia there are apparent disturbances at many sites from the east (Tarsus) to the west (Troy), with many new ceramic features appearing. Moreover, Anatolian features appear quite strongly in the material culture of sites in the Greek islands and the Greek mainland at this time (cf. Caskey 1986).

Level IV
The pattern of centralized production suggested for Level Vf–e (EB III) seems to carry over into Level IV (the Middle Bronze Age). The principal fabric (Group A) of EB III continues in almost identical fashion, and is still used for the same sorts of wares, although the shapes have evolved a little. There seems little reason to doubt that this represents continuity not only in tradition but also in production organization. Alongside this, though, exists another fabric (Group B), employed in the manufacture both of plain buff tumblers and of red burnished vessels, notably jugs and open bowls. Red burnished ware was very common in Level Vj–g (EB II), but completely absent in Level Vf–e (EB III). Its reappearance in the Middle Bronze Age is thus quite striking — does it represent the deliberate resurrection of an older tradition, or is it purely coincidental? It should also be noted that whereas in EB II burnished wares were hand-made, in MBA they are wheel-thrown. The Fabric Group B used for this class of pottery is very different to Group A — it is highly calcareous containing many foraminifera. It also shows very strong links with clays sampled from an extensive deposit just 1 km from the site of Kilise Tepe itself.

As before, one or two hypothetical scenarios present themselves. Firstly, it may be that both Group A and Group B were produced by potters at Kilise Tepe. If this is the case, the co-occurring differences in fabric, ware and shape are not consistent with production in a single workshop. Instead the patterns suggest quite strongly that one production unit would have been responsible for Group A, and another production unit for Group B. The second scenario is this: Group A represents a class of pottery produced at another site altogether, whilst Group B is produced at Kilise Tepe. Regardless of which of these two hypothesized situations is favoured, one observation holds true: Group A was already in EB III the well established and dominant pottery class for the manufacture of tablewares. But in MBA it appears to come under competition from another class of tableware pottery, the burnished wares of Group B. The question remains as to the scale of this competition — did it operate at the community or at the regional level?

It has been mentioned that both Groups A and B were principally used in the manufacture of tablewares. In the Middle Bronze Age coarse wares (for storage and cooking) tend to occur in a relatively standardized orange-brown fabric (Group C) that contains numerous metamorphic rock fragments as well as limestone fragments in the coarse fraction. The presence of metamorphic inclusions once again raises the provenance question; although this is a common fabric in the assemblage, there is a chance that it is non-local. In this regard it is perhaps not dissimilar to the situation observed for EB III, with the non-local fabrics being the cooking pots.

Level III
The Late Bronze Age sees the continuation at Kilise Tepe of a centralized mode of production. This is represented principally by the rather standardized wheel-thrown bowls that are plain and un-slipped (burnishing has largely disappeared), occurring in pale semi-fine buff fabrics. One such fabric is very similar to

that used for plain buff wares and burnished wares in Level IV (MBA), but another fabric is a Level III (LBA) innovation. Whilst like most previous buff fabrics it is very calcareous with numerous foraminifera, it is distinct in consistently containing serpentine and chert, along with minor amounts of epidote, amphibole, and igneous rock fragments. These petrographic features do tally with the local geology, as there are outcrops of serpentinite and igneous rocks not far to the east of the site. It is, however, intriguing that these inclusions only rarely occur in fabrics from earlier periods (e.g. Fabric Group N in EB II). This does suggest that in LBA local potters are beginning to use new resource locations that had previously been under-exploited. Whatever the reasons for change, which is also clearly apparent in the results of the chemical analyses, this fabric continues to be produced throughout the Iron Age, representing an interesting degree of continuity across the Bronze Age to Iron Age transition.

The other major fabric group of Level III (LBA) is not locally produced, and may well have been imported from some distance. In its finest variants it is represented by the very distinctive Red Lustrous Wheel-made ware, its most typical shapes being the libation arm, the spindle bottle and the lentoid flask (Eriksson 1991; 1993). Also common in this fabric and ware is a form of shallow open bowl with inturned rim more or less identical in shape to those that are locally produced in semi-fine calcareous buff fabrics. Coarser vessel types within this ware group are the same distinctive red but tend not to be lustrous. These coarser variants contain temper of limestone, mudstone, phyllite and schist; the metamorphic rock fragments once again add to the likelihood that such wares are imported to the site and not locally produced. Questions of provenance have been discussed in the section devoted to Level III above — the actual location of manufacture, even in broad regional terms, remains unknown, although northern Cyprus is the most likely candidate (with coastal Cilicia as an alternative: Knappett *et al.* 2005). Even though it is not yet possible to specify the source of this ware, we can characterize the organization of production. The ware is skilfully made and very standardized in fabric, shape and surface treatment, strongly suggesting that it is the product of a centralized workshop or set of workshops.

In the fine wares described above there is a rather neat distinction between plain buff and red lustrous wares. However, when it comes to the coarse wares used for storage and cooking, the picture is much less clear, especially concerning the organization of production. Fabric Group D is of interest in being a local calcareous cooking pot fabric with crushed calcite added as temper. The idea that the addition of calcite is a purposeful functional adaptation receives further support from the fact that Group E is also a calcite-tempered fabric (albeit much siltier and less calcareous) used for cooking pots. Both these variants of calcite-tempered cooking pots continue into Level IIa–d, after which they disappear. As for Fabric Groups F, G, H and I, there is little that can be said about them in terms of production organization.

Level II, phases a–d

The transition from Level III to Level II at the site was for a time thought to mark the end of the Bronze Age and the beginnings of the Iron Age. This was seen as plausible given the major changes in architecture and pottery; in terms of the latter, certain characteristic Red Lustrous Wheel-made ware shapes — libation arms and spindle bottles — totally disappear in Level II, and new forms of pottery emerge with dark-on-light painted decoration. However, the most recent analysis now suggests that the switch from Level III to Level II may actually represent the transition from one Bronze Age phase to another (Hansen & Postgate 1999; Symington 2001). Such an interpretation does at least make sense of the considerable ceramic continuity across this transition. Although spindle bottles and libation arms may disappear, lentoid flasks, another shape associated with RLWm ware, continue into Level II. Moreover, the shallow bowl with inturned rim, a common shape in Level III, carries on into Level II, albeit with some modifications.

Fabrics show notable continuities too — semifine buff fabrics are still used in the manufacture of plain bowls, and cooking pots are made with calcite-tempered fabrics. As for the organization of production, one could certainly argue that the plain bowls mentioned above were created in centralized workshops. They are skilfully made, and just as standardized in shape and fabric as they were in Level III. They even occur in exactly the same fabric in both periods, although in terms of shape the bowl has acquired a ring base by Level II.

A feature of the Level IIa–d pottery is that there are some common types that occur in both fabric types A and B. Lentoid flasks, rounded bowls, and square-rim basins are known to occur in each fabric, whilst being more or less identical in all other respects. This points to a quite different pattern from that seen in, for example, EB II. Fabric B, moreover, is non-calcareous, micaceous, and contains frequent quartz grains (Fig. 536). It is probably of non-local provenance. Distinct petrographically from the Red Lustrous Wheel-made fabric of the previous period, the fabric's origin is unknown. However, it is reasonably close to it chemically, which may with further work provide clues to its provenance. Whatever the source, its producers worked in the same tradition as the local Kilise Tepe potters, creating vessels of the same shapes and with the same surface treatments and decorative patterns.

Just as in the Late Bronze Age, there is a tradition of tempering cooking pots with crushed calcite. Group C is equivalent to Level III Group D, and Group D equivalent to Level III Group E (Fig. 537). As noted above, this is another element of continuity across a transition initially thought to be one of 'dark age' decline, but which may turn out to be from LB I to LB II.

Finally, the phase IId occupation at the site has revealed a small number of Mycenaean-style vessels. Deep bowls are the best represented and date to LH IIIC, i.e. the twelfth century BC. Three of the four deep bowls sampled are almost certainly non-local, but locating their sources is at present difficult, not least because the range of possibilities is so vast, with Mycenaean wares made at a wide range of locations across the eastern Mediterranean. Petrography gives some clues, and the NAA results illuminate the matter further, by indicating that these wares are probably *not* imports from the main areas of the Peloponnese, Boeotia, Crete or Rhodes. Whilst these Mycenaean vessels are extremely useful for dating purposes (Postgate 1998b, 134–5), it is difficult extrapolating much more than this from only a very limited number of examples. However, as with the LH IIIC pottery from Tarsus, we can say that Kilise Tepe was able to participate (albeit in a minor way) in broader networks of exchange despite its position 50 km inland from the main coastal routes used in Mycenaean trade.

Level IIe
The poor definition of this phase and the small quantities of pottery associated with it call for very cautious interpretations. The main class of pottery seeming to belong is the so-called 'Kindergarten ware'. The designs painted on these vessels do sometimes give the impression of a rather unskilled and 'child-like' hand, but it is of course important not to be too affected by these subjective impressions. Petrographic and chemical analysis of these fabrics show that they are evidently standardized, and at least some of these vessels are skilfully wheel-made.

Rounded open bowls with ring bases appear to continue from the previous phases, although with some alterations — they have a grooved rim and dark-on-light painted designs just below the exterior rim (now with diagonal bands, rather than cross-hatching). They are manufactured using the same semi-fine buff fabric as witnessed in phases IIa–d. Another development in phase IIe is the first appearance of bichrome decoration, a feature that becomes more prevalent in phase IIf, on some *oenochoai* for instance.

Level IIf
Most of the samples selected from this phase are from decorated tablewares. These can be divided into two main categories, local and non-local. The local material is extremely well represented in the rich deposits from the kiln assemblages of unit 1783, in which more than 3000 sherds were found. Petrographic (and chemical) analyses show that they are all in an extremely standardized fabric that is clearly identifiable as local due to the presence of serpentine and foraminifera. This is the same fabric as has already been described for the Late Bronze Age and the early Iron Age, and therefore points to cultural continuity in pottery production at the site. All of the ceramic types in this kiln context are very skilfully wheel-made, and the shapes show considerable standardization. Most of the vessels are plain and undecorated but some have dark-on-light painted motifs of bands and concentric targets that are very well executed. The standardization and skill exhibited by these ceramics mean that they must have been made in a centralized workshop in which worked full-time craft specialists.

The close parallels between this kiln pottery and material known from Cyprus are striking. Such pottery is found quite widely in the east Mediterranean, as far west as Rhodes and Crete (e.g. Knossos North Cemetery). To find such abundant evidence for the large-scale local production of these pottery styles and shapes at Kilise Tepe itself tells us that the site was integrated into a phenomenon widespread across the East Mediterranean, in terms of both production and consumption activities.

Whereas the locally produced wares in Cypriot styles are akin to 'Plain White' and 'White Painted', the imports at the site are Black-on-Red and Bichrome wares. The source of these imports is in all likelihood Cyprus, although we cannot entirely discount the north Levantine coast. These imported wares are by no means homogeneous in terms of fabric — Group B consists of eight sub-groups, not to mention Groups C and D. Far from there being a single Cypriot workshop supplying consumers' needs, such variability indicates that imported wares were coming to Kilise Tepe from a variety of locations, quite possibly in different areas of Cyprus.

We are thus seeing a new phenomenon in this phase of the Iron Age, with fine ware ceramics reaching Kilise Tepe in some quantities from areas with which it had not previously been connected. Moreover, even the locally produced ceramics display stylistic traits that betray close links with a tradition of pottery production (and consumption) known to stretch right across the east Mediterranean at this time.

Byzantine ceramics

Samples S183–S186 listed on p. 247 are from the Byzantine period. They will be discussed along with other petrographic samples from Kilise Tepe in connection with Mark Jackson's forthcoming work on contemporary ceramics from both Kilise Tepe and other sites in the Göksu region.

Acknowledgements

CK is extremely grateful to the director of the Kilise Tepe project, Prof. Nicholas Postgate, for making a study of ceramic technology integral to the overall project, and for giving free rein with the material. The project pottery specialists, Dorit Symington and Connie Hansen, have also been incredibly accommodating, and keen to facilitate the fusion of typological and technological information at every stage. The help of other members of the project is also much appreciated, in particular Mark Jackson and Dominique Collon. Many thanks to the authorities in Silifke and Ankara for permission to sample and export the ceramic material from the site.

Much of this research was conducted while CK was a Junior Research Fellow at Christ's College, Cambridge. He is immensely grateful to the College for their continuing support. The McDonald Institute, University of Cambridge, provided the use of microscope facilities. CK thanks also Laurence Smith and Janine Bourriau for free access to their equipment, and for useful discussions of petrographic and other ceramic matters. Much of the petrographic study, and indeed the thin-section photomicrographs, was also conducted in the marvellous facilities of the Fitch Laboratory of the British School at Athens. CK is indebted both to Ian Whitbread, the former Laboratory Director, and to Vangelio Kiriatzi, the present Director. Dr Louise Joyner has also generously shared her expertise in ceramic petrography. Thin sections were expertly prepared by Sean Houlding from the Geology Department of University College, London.

The chemical analysis was carried out in the Laboratory of Archaeometry, National Centre of Scientific Research 'Demokritos', Athens, and supported by a grant from the British Academy.

Chapter 22

Detailed Fabric Descriptions

Carl Knappett

EB II samples (Level Vj–g)

Local fabrics

GROUP A (S1–4)
A fine calcareous fabric with foraminifera.

Sample S1
Grey burnished ware, rim of open vessel.
Microstructure: Rare to very few vughs, no preferred orientation.
Groundmass: Composition fairly homogeneous, except some patches of brown amid the predominantly yellow, and very calcareous groundmass. No optical activity. XP = yellow-brown, PPL = grey-brown.
Inclusions: c:f:v$_{10\,\mu m}$ = 10:85:5 or 5:90:5. Sorting is good.
Fine fraction — mostly sub-silt-size calcite/sparite, and foraminifera of both benthic and planktonic types, such as *globigerina*, which have a thin micritic cell wall and secondary sparite filling the interior. Quartz is present in fine fraction but is rare to very few, *c.* 0.06–0.1 mm.
Coarse fraction — there is very little >0.1 mm, except some planktonic foraminifera, and rare micritic limestone.
Comment: This fine, highly calcareous fabric containing numerous foraminifera is entirely consistent with the dominant local geology of calcareous marine clays dating to the Neogene. Moreover, it shows very close petrographic similarities with a clay sampled from Cağlayangedik, just 1 km from Kilise Tepe. S2 and S5 are quite similar but, as can be seen below, there are some differences observed.

Sample S2
Reddish-brown burnish to exterior only. Fabric is a semi-fine pale grey to yellow buff, with some pale grey inclusions of small-sand-size.
Microstructure: Voids are very rare.
Groundmass: Homogeneous, with no optical activity, and very calcareous and fine. XP = yellow, PPL = slightly brownish yellow.
Inclusions: c:f:v$_{10\,\mu m}$ = 10:87:3. Sorting is moderate.
Fine fraction — very calcareous, with silt-size calcite/sparite and foraminifera, notably planktonic (e.g. *globigerina*) — not as abundant as in sample 22. Quartz is rare, both Tcfs and opaque minerals are rare to very few.
Coarse fraction - some foraminifera are large enough to be classified in coarse fraction (i.e. >0.1 mm). Also some other bioclasts, and bivalves. Micritic limestone is also common, in varying sizes up to 1.0 mm, some seem to be microfossiliferous, showing an internal cellular structure. Rather amorphous and not easy to classify on a-r scale. Chert and quartz are very rare, as are shell fragments. Tcfs are hardly present at all above silt-size range.
Comment: Very similar to S1 in being highly calcareous, although foraminifera are less abundant. A little coarser, with more micritic limestone in the coarse fraction.

Sample S4
Red burnish exterior only. Fabric is semi-fine, pale brown buff, with small sand-size grey inclusions. Looks very similar in hand specimen to S33, which is in Group N.
Microstructure: Voids are rare (vughs), no preferred orientation.
Groundmass: Homogeneous, very calcareous, no optical activity. XP = yellow-brown. PPL = light brown.
Inclusions: c:f:v$_{10\,\mu m}$ = 20:75:5. Sorting is moderate.
Fine fraction is not very silty, but nonetheless some micrite and calcite present (dominant) and quartz very few to few. Tcfs are few, foraminifera are common, also bivalves.
Coarse fraction composed of dominant micritic limestone, up to 1.5 mm, tending to be sr. Some foraminifera and bivalves in coarse fraction, one *globigerina c.* 0.4 mm. Quartz is rare to very few, 0.1–0.2 mm, sa-sr. Chert rare, *c.* 0.2 mm, sr. Tcfs rare, *c.* 0.2 mm. Amphibole very rare, serpentine very rare, 0.3 mm, sa.
Comment: Not quite as fine as most examples in Group A, but can be classed within this group nonetheless. Very calcareous, with foraminifera and bivalves reasonably common though not abundant. Micritic limestones dominant in coarse fraction, little else.

GROUP B (S5)
A fine calcareous fabric with foraminifera and plant temper.

Sample S5
Red burnish interior and exterior, lower body of a bowl. Fabric is semi-fine pale yellow buff with a grey core, grey inclusions and some brown, and some linear voids suggesting plant temper.
Microstructure: Voids are very few to rare, with preferred orientation parallel to vessel walls.
Groundmass: Not very homogeneous, with patches of brown. Yellow-brown in both XP and PPL, with no optical activity.
Inclusions: c:f:v$_{10\,\mu m}$ = 15:80:5.
Fine fraction dominated by calcite/sparite, and foraminifera of both planktonic and benthic varieties. Tcfs are very few, quartz is very rare.
Coarse fraction contains very few Tcfs, *c.* 0.2–0.5 mm, sa-sr. Rare angular calcite, *c.* 0.5 mm. A few rather large benthic foraminifera, and some bivalves too. Micritic limestone is very rare. Very very rare is basalt, with a single rounded grain *c.* 1.0 mm. Central blackened area of section appears to contain relic cell structure of plant tissue, replaced by iron oxide and calcite — points to the use of plant temper.
Comment: Very similar to samples from Group A (especially S2), in being highly calcareous with foraminifera. However, this sample is distinctive in having evidence for plant temper, as well as Tcfs (mudstones, or perhaps even grog?) in the coarse fraction.

GROUP C (S6)
Fine calcareous with plant temper, shell, mudstone, grog, and limestone.

Sample S6
Pale yellowy-orange buff, quite crumbly especially at interior.

Exterior is deeply scored. Fabric is also yellow-buff in colour, with pale grey and brown grits of small sand size.
Microstructure: Very few to few channels and elongate vughs. Some contain secondary growth of well-developed calcite crystals. Some of these voids could be from burnt-out plant temper, with some of the plant tissue replaced by calcite. Note also that looks quite similar to some of the linear shell fragments.
Groundmass: Homogeneous, with a little optical activity. Rather calcareous. XP = yellow-brown to orange-brown, PPL = light brown to orange-brown.
Inclusions: c:f:$v_{10\ \mu m}$ = 15:78:7 to 10:85:5. Sorting is moderate.
Fine fraction is not at all silty, but there is present some micrite/calcite, foraminifera, quartz, shell and Tcfs.
Coarse fraction has burnt-out plant temper, now partially filled in with secondary calcite. Linear shell fragments are angular and common. Micritic and sparry limestones are few to common, with 1 fragment c. 3.0 mm, sr. Mudstones are common, sr, <2.5 mm, dark brown to grey, some of which may be grog. Chert is rare, sa, <1.2 mm.
Comment: This section is quite similar to Group A in terms of fineness of the groundmass, but contains a wide range of inclusions in coarse fraction — plant temper, shell, limestones, mudstones, and possibly grog.

GROUP D (S7–9)
A silty calcareous fabric with limestone inclusions and few mudstones.

Sample S7
Dark grey burnish to interior and exterior. Fabric also is dark grey, with a grey-brown core. Also quite silty, but has small-sand-size grits too, almost all very pale grey-white.
Microstructure: Rare to very few vughs, no preferred orientation as they are equidimensional.
Groundmass: Homogeneous, very calcareous, no optical activity. XP = yellow-brown, PPL = yellow to pale brown/grey.
Inclusions: c:f:$v_{10\ \mu m}$ = 20:75:5 to 25:70:5. Sorting is moderate.
Fine fraction contains dominant calcite/micrite, many rounded micrite grains. Few benthic and planktonic foraminifera, some large enough to be classified within coarse fraction. Few quartz, a-sa, and few dark brown Tcfs/mudstones, sa-sr.
Coarse fraction is composed of dominant to predominant micritic limestone, full range of sizes up to 1.5 mm, varying roundedness. Some have areas of sparite within them, others are microfossiliferous. Very few quartz, mostly sa but also sr, 0.1–0.2 mm. Tcfs larger than 0.1 mm are rare, only up to c. 0.3 mm. Rare foraminifera in coarse fraction, especially benthic types 0.2–0.3 mm, also bivalves. Biotite is very rare, as is chert, 0.1–0.2 mm, sa-sr.

Sample S8
Plain orange interior surface, roughened dark brown exterior. Fabric is pale brown with thick dark grey core. Does not appear too silty, and has medium sand-size grits that are pale grey to white, some look angular.
Microstructure: Very few voids, mostly vughs but some channels too, latter showing preferred orientation parallel to vessel walls.
Groundmass: Not very homogeneous, with patchy areas of brown. Very calcareous, a little optical activity. XP = yellow to brown, PPL = brown to pale brown/yellow.
Inclusions: c:f:$v_{10\ \mu m}$ = 20:70:10 to 25:65:10. Sorting is poor to moderate.
Fine fraction contains dominant calcite/micrite, few to common quartz, also Tcfs. Foraminifera much less common than usual, actually rare. There is however other biogenic material in coarse fraction, such as shell.
Coarse fraction composed of dominant micritic/sparry limestone, some of which microfossiliferous, a-r, up to 2.0 mm. Very few shell fragments, including one with rounded edges c. 1.0 mm, another even larger. Plant tissue burnt out in places, replaced by iron oxide and calcite. Quartz in coarse fraction is rare, 0.1–0.2 mm. Very rare basalt, 1 grain only, c. 0.3 mm, sa. Very rare quartz-mica-schist, r, 0.2 mm.
Comment: Dominated in coarse fraction by limestone inclusions. Also traces of plant temper, probably preserved due to firing conditions of low temperature and reducing atmosphere. Many linear channel voids also can be associated with presence of plant temper (chaff?). Shell is also present. These features are seen in other samples in this group from Vj–g, but not present in later periods.

Sample S9
Thickened rim fragment. Does not seem to be burnished. Very dark surfaces and fabric — medium grey, seems silty, with pale grey to white sand-size grits.
Petrography is extremely similar to S8 — coarse fraction dominated by micritic/sparry limestone. Shell is also present. Little sign of plant tissue. Foraminifera are present in calcareous groundmass. Some quartz in fine fraction but only rare to very few, Tcfs even rarer. Groundmass is a bit darker than in S8, most of core is reduced. No metamorphics, no sandstone. Also note that red slip on surface is quite thick and visible in thin section, hard to tell if it was separately added or not.

GROUP E 1 (S10–16)
Silty calcareous fabric with limestone, mudstone, grog, shell, etc.

Sample S10
Plain grey to brown surfaces, exterior smooth and interior rough, fabric is grey to brown, semi-coarse with dark grey and red grits.
Microstructure: Few channel voids, with some preferred orientation parallel to vessel walls.
Groundmass: Homogeneous, not very calcareous, some optical activity. XP = dark brown/orange brown, PPL = orange brown. Sorting is moderate (to good?)
Fine fraction is not as silty as some in Group B. Not very calcareous, foraminifera seem rare. Micrite/calcite is frequent to dominant, also some Tcfs/mudstones that are very dark brown-red, sr-r, as in coarse fraction. Few quartz.
Coarse fraction contains frequent micritic and sparry limestone, sr-r, up to 2.5 mm. Also common to frequent Tcfs/mudstones, very distinctive dark brown to red colour and fine, mostly r, up to 1.5 mm. Quartz is rare, sa-a, 0.1–0.2 mm. Very rare — 1 large shell fragment c. 1.5 mm. Very rare — 1 grain of phyllite/schist (micaceous), sr, c. 1.0 mm.
Comment: Not as silty as some other members of the group. Coarse fraction looks quite distinctive due to high frequency of red-brown Tcfs/mudstones alongside the ubiquitous limestone fragments. Another example of an EB II cooking pot fabric that falls within a broadly defined fabric group whilst at the same time exhibiting peculiar features that to some extent set it apart (cf. S19 for example). Note that this is the earliest piece examined.

Sample S12
Cooking pot fabric, interior and exterior are plain. Colour is brown to red with grey core. Coarse and crumbly with mostly pale grey grits.
Microstructure: Voids are few to common, with channels and some quite large vughs, no preferred orientation.
Groundmass: Not homogeneous, varying in colour from one side of section to the other, and also in levels of calcite. Also variation in optical activity, with oxidized area seemingly more active. XP = red to yellow-brown, PPL = light brown to reddish brown.
Inclusions: c:f:$v_{10\ \mu m}$ = 25:55:20 to 20:65:15. Sorting is moderate.

Detailed Fabric Descriptions

Micrite and calcite are dominant in fine fraction, and some foraminifera are also present. Quartz is few to common, tending to be sa-a, whilst plagioclase and epidote are both very rare, and chert is rare.

In the coarse fraction, micritic and sparry limestones are dominant, sa-r, <2 mm. Tcfs/mudstones are very few, but some look like grog — very dark and a little silty, with voids. <1.5 mm. Quartz in 0.1–0.3 mm range is few to common, mostly sa-a. Metamorphic rock fragments are very rare to rare, for example phyllite, r, 0.5 mm. Chert is rare, r, <0.5 mm, and shell fragments are very rare.

Sample S11
Looks similar to S25 in hand specimen, i.e. a dark brown cooking pot with irregular interior and slightly smoother exterior. Interior surfaces look very coarse, one or two very large grits protruding. Brown/grey fabric, semi-coarse to coarse, with pale grey grits.
Microstructure: Mostly vughs of various sizes, though some channels too. Overall very few to few.
Groundmass: Homogeneous, very little optical activity, very calcareous. XP = yellow to dark brown, PPL = light brown to dark brown.
Inclusions: $c:f:v_{10\,\mu m}$ = 15:75:10. Sorting is poor to moderate.
In fine fraction dominant micrite/calcite, including some planktonic foraminifera. Quartz is few, Tcfs very few.
Coarse fraction has frequent micritic and sparry limestones, mostly sr-r, all sizes <1.5 mm. Intriguing mudstones/grog are common — dark brown-grey, silty containing micrite and quartz, also voids, and clear boundaries — looks very much like this is grog. Most are quite large, sr-r, <2.5 mm. Note also some linear voids looking very much like burnt-out plant temper, though not as many as in S6. Both quartz and chert are rare in 0.1–0.2 mm range, sa-a.
Comment: Similar to S6 in being a calcareous fabric that falls in between Groups A and B in siltiness. This sample is more silty than S6, and is closer to Group B. No metamorphic rock fragments in either S11 or S6, both have possible grog, both contain some plant temper.

Sample S16
Uneven orange interior surface, red burnish exterior. Fabric is orange at exterior, but grey to interior. Cannot tell if silty, inclusions small to medium-sand size and pale grey to white, or brown in colour.
Petrography: Again very similar to the above, except for obviously greater quantities of Tcfs/mudstones, very dark in colour and homogeneous, mostly in 0.06–0.2 mm range, i.e. silt and small-sand. One larger such fragment, c. 0.6 mm and sa, seems to be alone in having voids and inclusions within it (quartz and calcite of silt-size) — therefore could be grog. Fine fraction dominated by calcite and micrite, with common Tcfs/mudstones and very few quartz. Coarse fraction exhibits similar proportions, although quartz is even less well represented. Micritic and sparry limestone, shell also present but rare. Groundmass is less calcareous than previous samples, and foraminifera fewer.

Sample S14
Smoothed orange surfaces interior and exterior, but exterior is wiped with low grooves. Fabric is yellow buff exterior, but grey interior. Seems to have a lot of linear voids, suggesting plant temper. Semi-coarse, with some light and grey grits, some darker ones too.
Microstructure: Vughs and channels are few, weak preferred orientation parallel to vessel walls.
Groundmass: Not homogeneous — more reduced area of section not only darker in colour but with more voids, especially of channel type. Minimal optical activity in places, quite calcareous. XP = variable, yellow to orange-brown to brown, PPL = light brown to dark brown-grey.

Inclusions: $c:f:v_{10\,\mu m}$ = 20:65:15. Sorting is poor to moderate
Fine fraction is quite silty, with dominant calcite and micrite, <0.1 mm, few quartz (a-sa), few foraminifera and very few Tcfs.
Coarse fraction — dominant micritic limestone, all sizes up to 1.5 mm, sr-r. Rare quartz, sa-a, 0.1–0.2 mm. Dark brown mudstones/Tcfs are common, sr-sa, 0.25–0.75 mm. However, about half of them look rather different — they are silty and c. 0.75–1.0 mm, often containing inclusions of varying types and sizes (e.g. micritic limestones, quartz), up to 0.25 mm. As these grits are also characterized by the presence of voids, and distinct boundaries, it seems they are probably grog.
Comment: A calcareous silty groundmass, with coarse fraction dominated by micritic limestones, also with mudstones and grog.

Sample S13
Cooking pot rim sherd of roughened ware. Brown to pink interior and exterior surfaces, fabric is similar colour but with thick grey core. Semi-coarse with medium-sand size light grey inclusions.
Petrography: Much the same as 3 previous samples in having a silty, calcareous groundmass, and with a coarse fraction dominated by micritic and sparry limestone, some of which microfossiliferous. Mudstones and shell are also represented, as in other samples. However, this sample also contains some metamorphic rock fragments — very few slates/phyllites, r, c. 0.5 mm; and also siltstones and sandstones, rare to very few, up to 2.0 mm in size. These differences probably do not justify the creation of a separate fabric group — rather they should be considered as one pole in the wide spectrum of variation across this rather broad fabric group.

Sample S15
Plain lumpy orange interior, streaky red burnish exterior. Fabric is orange to red-brown. Semi-fine with pale grey grits and fewer brown ones.
Petrography: Not a good quality section — has had broad linear holes dragged through it in preparation. However, it is clearly quite silty and calcareous, but not many foraminifera. A higher than usual amount of quartz in fine fraction, and also in 0.1–0.2 mm size range, sa-a. Micritic limestones again very conspicuous in coarse fraction, as are mudstones, none of which look to be grog. One or two sandstones, not present in previous samples, as well as the occasional micaceous metamorphic rock fragment. As a corollary perhaps, there are rare muscovite laths in the fine fraction. In summary this sample is subtly different to previous ones — seems less calcareous, more quartz, and contains some sandstones and metamorphics. This level of variation is not sufficient to create a separate group; as with S13, this should be attributed to the rather varied Group E 1.

GROUP E 2 (S17–18)

Fine calcareous fabric with limestone inclusions, but also grog, mudstone, etc.

Sample S18
Sandy fabric with very thick grey core, red slip.
Microstructure: Few to very few vughs, most with micrite hypocoatings, and showing weak preferred orientation.
Groundmass: Homogeneous, with no optical activity. Very calcareous, fine groundmass. XP = yellow-brown, PPL = grey-yellow.
Inclusions: $c:f:v_{10\,\mu m}$ = 15:75:10 to 20:70:10
Sorting is poor to moderate.
Fine fraction is very fine and calcareous, surprisingly little in silt-size range. Foraminifera are rare despite the fabric being so calcareous. Dark brown Tcfs are common, quartz is very rare.
Coarse fraction — Tcfs/mudstones are predominant, very dark brown and seemingly overfired, with clear boundaries, and most are 0.5 mm and sa. Few micritic limestone, c. 0.5–1.0 mm, sa-sr. Very rare K-feldspar, 0.5 mm, sa (1 particle only). Very rare calcite, <0.5 mm, a.

Sample S17
Plain surfaces, totally flat, with linear (plant) impressions on one side only. However, there is no plant temper in the fabric proper. Semi-fine to semi-coarse pale buff, slightly yellow, with grey and cream inclusions of medium-sand size.
Microstructure: Few vughs and channels, latter showing preferred orientation parallel to vessel walls.
Groundmass: Not very homogeneous, rather patchy and redder towards sherd edges. Very little optical activity, very fine calcareous groundmass, XP = yellow-brown to orange-brown, PPL = yellow-grey to brown.
Inclusions: c:f:v$_{10\,\mu m}$ = 15:75:10
Fine fraction is very fine and calcareous. Most of the micritic material is sub-silt size, some foraminifera are present but seem to be more benthic than planktonic, and quite large. Quartz more prominent than in some other samples, but still only very few. Dark brown Tcfs common in fine fraction.
Coarse fraction contains common micritic and sparry limestone, up to *c.* 1.5 mm. Very few benthic foraminifera, *c.* 0.3–0.5 mm. Dark brown Tcfs/mudstones very few to few, sa-r, 0.1–0.5 mm. Calcite rare, sa-a, *c.* 0.5 mm, quartz very rare, *c.* 0.2 mm, sa-sr, serpentine very rare, 0.2 mm, r.
Comment: S17 and S18 are very calcareous, relatively fine, and contain foraminifera. These features link them to the samples of Groups A and B, in being fine and calcareous, although the samples of Group E 2 are coarser, with varying amounts of micritic limestones, Tcfs/mudstones, grog, shell, and schist (akin to Group E 1).

GROUP F (S19–20)
A silty calcareous fabric with slate/phyllite inclusions in the coarse fraction.

Sample S20
Brown burnish interior and exterior, quite thin-walled. Fabric also is brown, same 'cognac' colour as the burnish. Fine except rather silty.
Microstructure: Very few vughs, no particular orientation as they are equidimensional. Only some have micrite hypocoatings.
Groundmass: homogeneous, very calcareous, no optical activity. XP = yellow to brown, PPL = pale brown to orange-brown.
Inclusions: c:f:v$_{10\,\mu m}$ = 15:80:5, moderate sorting.
Fine fraction contains dominant to frequent calcite/micrite, few to common benthic and planktonic foraminifera, few quartz, very few to few Tcfs, very rare serpentine and muscovite.
In coarse fraction micrite/calcite is dominant, especially in 0.1–0.5 mm range. Some larger fragments are micritic limestone, including one very large fragment that is microfossiliferous, *c.* 2.5 mm, r. Very few Tcfs. Rare to very few brown slates, very fine-grained, sr-r, 0.5–1.5 mm (not absolutely certain that these are metamorphic, and not shales). Rare quartz, sa-sr, 0.1–0.2 mm.

Sample S19
Interior and exterior pale brown, exterior surface wiped/scored. Fabric also pale brown and semi-coarse with light grey grits but also some distinct brown grits (slates/phyllites).
Microstructure: rare vughs only
Groundmass: Homogeneous, very calcareous, no optical activity. XP = yellow to brown, PPL = brown.
Inclusions: c:f:v$_{10\,\mu m}$ = 25:72:3. Sorting is moderate.
Fine fraction — calcite and micrite are dominant, foraminifera hard to identify, quartz few to common, Tcfs very few.
Coarse fraction — micritic/sparry limestones dominant, some microfossiliferous, tending to be sr-r, all sizes up to 1.0 mm. Quartz sandstone very rare to rare, Tcfs/mudstones rare to very few. Added to this familiar suite are few metamorphic rock fragments, notably some large slates (or fine phyllites?), sr-r, and 0.3–1.5 mm. Also note very rare quartz-mica schist, r, 0.3 mm. Also very rare to rare chert, and occasional bivalves and shell fragments.
Comment: Quite similar to Groups D and E 1, only different in that it contains a relatively high frequency of metamorphic rock fragments, probably slate or phyllite, seemingly added as temper. This does not seem to tally with the local geology, but there may be some metamorphics in local conglomerates.

GROUP G (S21–3)
A calcareous fabric with large microfossiliferous limestones.

Sample S22
Interior very lumpy and plain, exterior is smoothed with orange-pink slip. Fabric is pale brown and semi-coarse, with medium to large sand size grits most of which are pale grey.
Microstructure: Rare to very few small vughs and channels, no preferred orientation, some micrite hypocoatings.
Groundmass: Homogeneous, no optical activity, quite calcareous. XP = brown, PPL = yellow/grey-brown
Inclusions: c:f:v$_{10\,\mu m}$ = 25:68:7. Sorting is poor.
Not very silty in fine fraction, akin to Group A. Mostly micrite/calcite and foraminifera, Tcfs are few, quartz is very few, chert is rare.
Coarse fraction — micritic, sparry, and microfossiliferous limestones are dominant. Mode is *c.* 0.5 mm, but some larger up to 3.0 mm. Most are sr-r, but some sa. Some of limestones are polycrystalline calcite, possibly marble? Also few to very few monocrystalline calcite, a, 0.2–0.5 mm. Microfossils are few to common, benthic and planktonic foraminifera on the whole. Note also very rare bivalve, *c.* 0.5 mm. Very few red-brown Tcfs, sa-r, *c.* 0.2–0.5 mm. Quartz is rare, sa-a, 0.1–0.2 mm, shell fragments also rare.
Comment: Can be characterized as a fine calcareous groundmass containing mostly microfossiliferous limestone inclusions.

Sample S23
This is identical to the above sample, both in hand specimen and in thin section, and so additional description is not needed. S24 is also quite similar, but it is different in containing more mudstones/Tcfs, and a few bits of grog — it will thus be fully described below in a separate grouping, as Fabric H.

Sample S21
Many microfossiliferous limestones.
Seems to be from a large jar. Pink-orange in colour and quite soft, thus different to the above samples. Semi-coarse to coarse, and dominated by pale grey medium to large sand grains, quite angular.
Microstructure: Rare to very few vughs, also rare channels, some of which look like they might be from burnt-out plant temper.
Groundmass: Homogeneous, no optical activity, doesn't seem very calcareous, but may just be oxidation. XP and PPL = dark brown-orange.
Inclusions: c:f:v$_{10\,\mu m}$ = 35:60:5. Sorting is moderate.
In 0.1 mm size range there is much micritic limestone (sr-r) and also foraminifera, benthic and planktonic, as well as other microfossils. Quartz is very rare, and Tcfs are rare.
Coarse fraction — almost entirely comprised of micritic and microfossiliferous limestones, up to 2.5 mm, mode *c.* 0.5 mm but hard to assess as there is such a continuous range from 0.1 to 2.5 mm. Nearly all are sr-r, only a few sa.
Some foraminifera are relatively large, with *globigerina* up to 0.6 mm. Monocrystalline calcite grains are strikingly rare. Micrite is certainly the dominant form.
Comment: Although this does relate broadly to S22 and S23 in terms of the preponderance of microfossiliferous limestones, this sample is different in being coarser, and much rarer in microfossils, as well as having fewer Tcfs than S24.

Group H (S24)

A calcareous fabric with both microfossiliferous limestones and mudstones/grog as inclusions in the coarse fraction.

Sample S24
Very similar visually to S22 and S23, but exterior is plain rather than slipped. Fabric is brown, semi-coarse to coarse, with mostly pale grey-white grits, some angular, and some pale brown grits also visible.
Microstructure: Rare microvughs and very few channels, no preferred orientation, with some micrite hypocoatings.
Groundmass: Homogeneous, no optical activity, fairly calcareous, but less so than S23. XP = orange-brown, PPL = paler orange-brown.
Inclusions: c:f:$v_{10\,\mu m}$ = 30:63:7. Sorting is poor.
Not very silty fine fraction, akin to Group A not B. Micrite/calcite dominant, common to frequent red Tcfs, rare quartz.
Coarse fraction — micritic, sparry, and microfossiliferous limestones dominant. Polycrystalline calcite also present, but does not seem to be marble. Size range is 0.1–5.0 mm, mode *c.* 0.75 mm. Sa-r. Monocrystalline calcite very few, sa-a, 0.2–0.5 mm. Red-brown Tcfs/mudstones are common, from 0.1–1.2 mm, tending to be sr-r. 2 such large fragments appear to be grog rather than Tcfs — they are more grey-brown in colour, they are silty with a range of inclusions such as amphibole, micritic limestone, and voids. They are a-sa, and *c.* 3.0 mm. Clearly different to the very fine red-brown Tcfs/mudstones.
Rare foraminifera, both benthic and planktonic types. Quartz and chert very rare, as are epidote and serpentine. Linear shell fragments are rare, a, <0.75 mm.
Comment: Should this be considered as related to the microfossiliferous limestone Group G, despite the much more common presence of Tcfs (and of grog also)?

Group I (S25)

With micritic mudstones (cf. the limestones of Fabrics G & H).

Sample S25
A very coarse, dark to medium brown cooking pot fabric, quite crumbly with many pale grey and cream-coloured grits. Irregular interior surfaces, smoothed exterior. Quite similar to S21 in being a coarse crumbly cooking pot fabric, but the grits are more cream-coloured, and the petrography also seems different.
Microstructure: Common planar voids, channels, and vughs, but this may in part be due to imperfect section preparation.
Groundmass: Homogeneous, no optical activity. Does not look calcareous, but hard to tell. Little sign of foraminifera. XP and PPL = deep red-brown.
Inclusions: c:f:$v_{10\,\mu m}$ = 30:50:20? Sorting is poor.
In fine fraction quartz is more common than micrite/calcite, and black Tcfs and opaque minerals are also common. No mica.
Coarse fraction — frequent micritic limestone (or micritic mudstone?), sa, <2.5 mm.
Monocrystalline quartz is common, mostly *c.* 0.25 mm, sa-sr. Very few chert, sa-sr, 0.2–0.5 mm. Rare microfossiliferous limestone, very rare globigerina (*c.* 0.2 mm), very rare quartz-mica schist (0.2 mm, sa-sr), and very rare amphibole (0.1 mm, sa).
Comment: If the inclusions are indeed micritic mudstones, then this is a separate group.

Group J (S26–7)

Calcareous with brown slates and shell fragments.

Sample S26
Dark reddish brown, rather coarse, with plain, uneven interior that is rather pitted and lumpy. Brown metamorphic grits very visible, shell less so.
Microstructure: Rare large vughs, no preferred orientation and no hypocoatings.
Groundmass: Homogeneous, fairly fine, and moderate optical activity. XP = orange, PPL = brown-orange.
Inclusions: c:f:$v_{10\,\mu m}$ = 20:77:3. Sorting is poor to moderate.
Fine fraction is not very silty at all, but micrite/calcite dominant. Quartz is rare to very few, red Tcfs with semi-distinct boundaries are common to frequent. These look much more like Tcfs than do those in many previous sections, seems most unlikely that they are grog. Also very rare plagioclase.
In the coarse fraction there are frequent micritic and sparry limestones, sr-r, *c.* 0.2 mm.
Linear shell fragments are common, often angular, and up to 2.0 mm.
Very fine-grained metamorphic rock fragments are few to common. They are mostly brown-red, whilst some are yellow and micaceous. They are probably slates, and are up to 1.5 mm, sr-r. Most are more than 0.5 mm, suggesting that they are part of an added temper (along with the shell).
Dark brown mudstones are very few, sr, 0.25–0.5 mm, with only one fragment much larger at 1.3 mm. Some look rather like grog, whilst others are finer and look not unlike some of the slates but without the birefringence and parallel extinction.
Comment: Seems to be calcareous (with very few foraminifera), though masked somewhat by considerable iron content. Odd combination in coarse fraction of slate, shell, mudstones and perhaps even grog. Hard to think how exactly these components came to be mixed together. Links closely to S27.

Sample S27
Very similar in hand specimen to S26, in colour, coarseness, and pitted interior surface. Shell inclusions are more visible than in S26.
Microstructure: Very few macro- and micro-vughs, rare channels.
Groundmass: Homogeneous, a little optical activity at section edges. XP and PPL = brown-orange
Inclusions: c:f:$v_{10\,\mu m}$ = 25:70:5 to 30:65:5. Sorting is poor to moderate.
Very little to describe in the fine fraction, but red Tcfs are the most frequent, calcite/micrite also common, quartz rare to very few, and foraminifera are rare.
Coarse fraction — brown, fine-grained slates are common, sr-r, and quite large — *c.* 3 mm. Can be difficult to differentiate these from some dark red-brown Tcfs, which show no birefringence.
Micritic/sparry limestones relatively few. Shell is common, tending to be angular and linear, up to *c.* 1.2 mm. No preferred orientation of either the slate or the shell fragments.
Comment: The identification of some of these inclusions as slate is not straightforward — the possibility remains that they are not all metamorphic, which would mean that they could be shales. Samples S26–7 definitely form a small group, as no other EB II samples show this combination of slate/shale and shell fragments. This demonstrates once again the diversity (within certain limits) of EB II ceramic fabrics, especially in the cooking pots.

Group K (S28–9)

Silty calcareous with both plant temper and calcite.

Sample S29
Light grey-brown fabric with grey core, and large calcite grits, with some signs of linear organic temper.
Microstructure: Very few vughs and channels. A closer analysis of the channel voids shows traces of plant tissue, replaced by FeO. This indicates the use of plant temper, perhaps chaff. There are also thin long black FeO inclusions, rather like pencil leads in appearance, that must also be the burnt remains of plant temper (also present in S28). These are common, many are 1.0 mm in length, some are 2–3 mm.

Groundmass: Homogeneous, with no optical activity. XP = yellow-brown, PPL = brown, a little greyish.
Inclusions: c:f:v$_{10\ \mu m}$ = 15:75:10. Sorting is poor to moderate.
Fine fraction is relatively silty, with calcite/micrite dominant. Contains many foraminifera, especially *globigerina*, but also some benthic types. Quartz is very few, as are dark brown Tcfs, and muscovite laths are very rare.
The coarse fraction would have contained plant temper before firing, now just voids and FeO as described above. Angular calcite is frequent, mode probably *c.* 0.5 mm although largest monocrystalline fragment is 3.0 mm. Also 2 very large polycrystalline calcite fragments, angular and *c.* 4.0 mm — lack of clear evidence for triple points means that these are unlikely to be marble, although this possibility cannot be ruled out altogether. Micritic limestone very few, serpentine very rare.
Comment: The groundmass and fine fraction are very calcareous with many foraminifera, and silty like Group B. The presence of both chaff and calcite temper is quite striking, and the angularity and size of the calcite grains do suggest quite strongly that they were added as temper. Compares well to S28.

Sample S28
Buff with grey core, semi-fine to semi-coarse with some calcite grits visible and organic temper too.
Microstructure: Rare vughs, and rare channels with remnants of plant tissue, largely replaced by FeO. Suggests use of plant temper, perhaps chaff, as in S29.
Groundmass: Not very homogeneous, with patches of darker brown, unclear to what these patches relate. Also degree of siltiness varies across section. No optical activity. XP = yellow-brown to dark brown, PPL = brown.
Inclusions: c:f:v$_{10\ \mu m}$ = 15:80:5. Sorting is moderate.
Not very silty in the fine fraction, but micrite/calcite dominate what there is. Also many foraminifera, notably *globigerina*, as well as some benthic types. Quartz is rare, as are Tcfs.
Some of the foraminifera are large enough to be classed in the coarse fraction. The plant temper is very few to few, with size commonly 0.5 mm but also larger. Angular calcite is common to frequent, mostly monocrystalline, but also a few polycrystalline, with mode *c.* 0.25–0.5 mm. One polycrystalline grain is 1.5 mm, a, and has some triple points thus could be marble. Micritic limestone is surprisingly rare, 1 grain is 1.5 mm, sr. Tcfs/mudstones also very rare.
Comment: Definitely links to S29 — a very calcareous groundmass with numerous foraminifera, and tempered with both calcite and chaff.

GROUP L (S30)
Fine calcareous with plant temper.

Sample S30
Coarse orange-yellow fabric with many linear voids from plant (chaff?) temper.
Microstructure: Common to frequent channel voids, varying shapes and sizes but nearly all consistent with the previous presence of plant temper burnt out during firing. Some preferred orientation parallel to vessel walls. Some are thin and some broad, length up to 5 mm. Considerable quantity of calcite crystal growth as hypocoatings, and some of the voids are fully filled in with calcite. Note though the striking lack of FeO replacement seen in some other sections with plant temper.
Groundmass: Homogeneous apart from dense network of linear voids. No optical activity. XP = yellow-brown, PPL = yellow to grey-brown.
Inclusion: c:f:v$_{10\ \mu m}$ = 10:60:30 or 5:60:35. Sorting is poor to moderate.
Fine fraction is very fine, certainly the affinities lie with Group A not B. Very little at all except foraminifera, faint brown Tcfs, and calcite/micrite.
In coarse fraction there is very little at all apart from the voids. Probably foraminifera are dominant, as a number can be classed in c.f. at 0.3–0.4 mm. There are many *globigerina*, especially with serrated edges, but seemingly very few benthic examples. Mudstones are rare, largest is red-brown and *c.* 1.5 mm, r. Serpentine is very rare, 1 grain is *c.* 1.0 mm, r.
Comment: A very fine calcareous clay matrix containing foraminifera, and a lot of added plant temper that could be chaff.

GROUP M (grog tempered - S31)
Fine calcareous with grog temper.

Sample S31
Plain interior and exterior, although affected (by firing, or post-depositionally) at interior and going yellow and crumbly. Fabric is pale yellow buff, semi-fine to semi-coarse, with inclusions almost all brown and rather angular.
Microstructure: Voids are remarkably rare, with just the occasional vugh and channel. Some have secondary calcite infilling.
Groundmass: Homogeneous, some optical activity in places. Extremely calcareous. XP = yellow-brown, PPL = yellow-brown, with a tinge of grey.
Inclusion: c:f:v$_{10\ \mu m}$ = 15:82:3 to 10:87:3. Sorting is moderate.
Very fine in the fine fraction, with very little to describe — micrite/calcite, small foraminifera, Tcfs, rare quartz.
Coarse fraction — dominant angular grog, dark brown to red-brown in colour, up to 2.5 mm. They contain voids and inclusions, and have a void structure around the exterior. Certainly looks like an added temper too, judging by the grog's bimodal distribution, angularity, and size. Also very few to common are large foraminifera, *c.* 0.3–0.4 mm. Micritic limestone is rare, 1 fragment *c.* 2.5 mm and sr. Very rare — a single metamorphic rock fragment, 0.75 mm, sa, composed of quartz grains and biotite — the quartz has undulose extinction and sutured boundaries.
Comment: Like S30, this shows some similarities to Group A, in being very fine and calcareous. This sample differs of course in that the coarse fraction is composed almost entirely of grog added as temper.

GROUP N (S32–3)
A fine calcareous fabric containing plant temper and serpentine.

Sample S32
Black burnish exterior only. Fabric is pale to medium grey, fine to semi-fine, with very few inclusions visible (some very small grey and white).
Microstructure: Very few vughs, no preferred orientation, minimal micrite hypocoatings.
Groundmas: Not homogeneous, with patches of dark brown in places, causes unclear. No optical activity, very calcareous. XP = yellow-brown, PPL = grey to brown.
Inclusions: c:f:v$_{10\ \mu m}$ = 15:75:10. Sorting is moderate to good.
Extremely fine and calcareous, very little in fine fraction. Micrite/calcite dominant, some foraminifera but many are <0.1 mm. Some of the linear fragments of FeO-replaced plant tissue are also <0.1 mm, but most are larger. Few Tcfs, rare quartz, rare serpentine.
Coarse fraction — Common — serpentine, sa-r, <0.7 mm.
Few to common — micritic limestones, sr-r, 0.2–0.5 mm; mono- and polycrystalline calcite, sa-a, 0.2–0.5 mm; chert, sa-r, 0.2–0.5 mm; linear plant remains, FeO replaced, resembling pencil leads. Also one rather large fragment of plant tissue, cellular structure and FeO replaced, *c.* 0.7 mm; foraminifera, both planktonic and benthic types, 0.2–0.5 mm. Note also 1 bivalve, *c.* 2.5 mm.
Few — Tcfs, sr-r, 0.2–0.5 mm.
Rare — quartz, sa-sr, 0.2–0.3 mm.

Detailed Fabric Descriptions

Comment: A one-off fabric, with this unique combination of a highly calcareous groundmass with many small linear plant remains, and serpentine and chert. Well-sorted, largest inclusion is 0.7 mm but most are *c.* 0.25 mm.

Non-local fabrics
GROUP O (S34)

Sample S34
Matt painted, semi-fine red.
Microstructure: Few to common vughs, *c.* 0.1–0.5 mm in size, no preferred orientation.
Groundmass: Composition homogeneous, except colour varies from red along one side to pale brown along the other. No optical activity. Red-firing and quite micaceous (biotite) groundmass means could be non-calcareous. XP = red to pale brown, PPL = red-brown to grey-brown.
Inclusions: c:f:$v_{10 \mu m}$ = 20:65:15. Sorting — moderate.
Fine fraction — most of the biotite is sub-silt size, but there is common quartz, much of which is angular, in the 0.06–0.1 mm range, possibly some K-feldspar too (though hard to identify securely). Many red Tcfs with merging boundaries also in this size range.
Coarse fraction — Few siltstone and meta-siltstone, sr-r, 0.1–2.0 mm. Few quartz, sa-r, 0.1–0.5 mm. Few micritic limestone, sr, 0.3–1.0 mm. Few red Tcfs, 0.1–0.4 mm. Very few sandstone, composed of quartz and a little plagioclase feldspar, sr-r, 0.3–1.2 mm. Rare granitic rock fragments, composed of plagioclase feldspar and biotite, sa, 0.25–0.5 mm. Rare basalt, 0.6 mm, sa. Rare chert, r, 0.25 mm.
Comment: The micaceous, red-firing matrix is unlike all other EB II fabrics, and is suggestive of a non-local source. Whilst the siltstones, sandstones and limestones are not very diagnostic, the presence of both volcanic and granitic rock fragments, although in very limited amounts, is also consistent with a non-local provenance. However, the actual source of this sample cannot be further elucidated at this stage.

GROUP P (S35)

Sample S35
Microstructure: Relatively large vughs (up to 1.5 mm) are common, and very few channel voids. No preferred orientation.
Groundmass: Composition is not homogeneous — there are 'ribbons' of dense red-brown clay minerals, possibly due to incomplete mixing of two clays. A little optical activity. Micaceous, and possibly non-calcareous. XP = brown, slightly orange tinge, PPL = brown, a little grey in places.
Inclusions: c:f:$v_{10 \mu m}$ = 25:60:15. Sorting is poor.
Fine fraction — frequent quartz, a-r, 0.06–0.1 mm, common to frequent muscovite laths, few to common 'clay concentrations', very few plagioclase feldspar.
Coarse fraction — Common to frequent quartz, mostly sa-a, 0.1–0.3 mm. Common dark brown Tcfs, sa-r, 0.1–1.0 mm. Few quartz sandstone, some with mica laths, sa-r, 0.2–3.0 mm. Few muscovite laths, 0.1–0.2 mm. Very few granitic rock fragments, composed of plagioclase, alkali feldspar, and biotite, sa, 0.5 mm. Very few siltstone, r, 0.5–1.0 mm. Rare epidote, a, 0.1–0.2 mm; orthopyroxene, sa, 0.25 mm. V. rare radiolarian chert, r, 0.6 mm; cataclasite, sa, 0.5 mm; basalt, sr, 0.2 mm.
Comment: The very distinctive minerals and rock fragments in this section make it almost certainly non-local. Both plutonic and volcanic rock fragments are present, as are some associated minerals such as orthopyroxene, plagioclase, and alkali feldspar. Although there are numerous rocks of sedimentary origin too, this sample must come from an environment in which a range of igneous rocks outcrop.

GROUP Q (S36)

Sample S36
Relatively micaceous, but also seems much more calcareous than previous two groups. Much schist/phyllite, and carbonates. (The quality of this section is insufficient for a detailed description).

GROUP R (S37)

Sample S37
Brown buff with compressed shales, mica, sparite.
Microstructure: Few vughs, tending to be 0.5 mm in size, no preferred orientation.
Groundmass: Composition is homogeneous, some optical activity. XP = yellow-brown, PPL = pale brown.
Inclusions: c:f:$v_{10 \mu m}$ = 15:75:10. Sorting — moderate to good.
Fine fraction — frequent muscovite laths, although many are sub-silt size, and showing no preferred orientation. Dominant sparite and micrite, but much of this material is also <0.06 mm. very few quartz, *c.* 0.06 mm, a-sa.
Coarse fraction — the above-mentioned minerals very rarely occur above 0.1 mm. Predominant in the coarse fraction are compressed shales, pale brown in colour, containing muscovite laths, up to 1.5 mm, sr-r, and with semi-distinct edges (sometimes hard to distinguish from groundmass). There are also some shales/mudstones present that are not compressed. Practically nothing else in coarse fraction.
Comment: This fabric group has only one sample and thus is something of a one-off. This fact, in combination with the petrography of compressed shales and muscovite, is suggestive of a non-local source, although there is no further evidence available to help pin down its origins.

GROUP S (S38)

Sample S38
Microstructure: Few to common vughs, 0.06–0.5 mm, no preferred orientation.
Groundmass: Composition is homogeneous, a little optical activity. Does not appear to be particularly calcareous, and is not micaceous. XP = red to orange-brown, PPL = brown, slightly orange tinge.
Inclusions: c:f: $_{10 \mu m}$ = 20:65:15. Sorting — moderate.
Fine fraction — frequent quartz, 0.06–0.1 mm, sa-sr. common red tcfs, same size range. Micrite surprisingly rare in fine fraction.
Coarse fraction — common quartz, sa-sr, 0.1–0.2 mm. Few dark brown-red tcfs, 0.1–0.5 mm, sa-r. Fragments of micritic limestone are common, sa, from 0.1 to 1.5 mm. few sandstone, sa-sr, *c.* 0.3–1.0 mm, most consist of dark brown clay matrix with a-sa grains of quartz, and occasionally plagioclase.
Comment: There is very little in this fabric that is not consistent with the local geology, except for the fact that the groundmass appears to be non-calcareous.

GROUP T (S39)

Sample S39
Metallic ware.
Micaceous, quartz in fine fraction, some micrite and calcite, and epidote. (The quality of this section is insufficient for a detailed description).

GROUP U (S40)

Sample S40
Microstructure: Few vughs, 0.1–0.5 mm, and rare channels, no preferred orientation.

Groundmass: Variation in colour with sandwich effect — light grey core, orange-brown either side. Some optical activity. XP = light grey to orange-brown, PPL = grey-green to orange-brown.
Inclusions: c:f:v$_{10\,\mu m}$ = 20:70:10. Sorting is moderate.
Fine fraction — frequent muscovite laths, common quartz, 0.06–0.1 mm, sa, few biotite and few Fe-rich Tcfs.
Coarse fraction — common to frequent quartz sandstone, some with micrite areas and veining, sa, 0.2–2.0 mm. Common grey siltstone, perhaps shale, very low relief so difficult to distinguish from groundmass in either XP or PPL. tending to be sr-r, 0.2–1.2 mm, some also have preferred orientation internally (muscovite laths), probably compressed shales, or meta-siltstones (cf. S37). Few slightly coarser red-brown siltstones, 0.25–1.5 mm, sr, and few micritic limestones, 0.2–2.0 mm, sa.
Comment: Like many of these micaceous (and non-calcareous?) Vj–g fabrics, this is something of a one-off. Very little distinctive amongst the predominantly sedimentary inclusions of this section that is of help in assigning an area of provenance. The compressed shales create a link with Group R, but there are few other similarities.

EB III samples (Level Vf–e)

Group A (S41–55)
Orange-firing, non-calcareous fabric with dominant Tcfs/mudstones, and carbonates.

Sample S48
Thick-walled body sherd, plain interior and exterior. Semi-coarse pale orange buff, with brown and white grits, and voids.
Microstructure: Common (to frequent) vughs, up to 2.5 mm, mode c. 1.0 mm. Many are inclusion-shaped, probably burnt-out limestone. Also note that many of the Tcfs have voids ringing them, suggestive of shrinkage during firing. No preferred orientation.
Groundmass: Homogeneous, moderate optical activity. Non-calcareous, micaceous. XP = reddish-brown, hints of grey-green, PPL = grey-green/brown.
Inclusions: c:f:v$_{10\,\mu m}$ = 20:50:30. Sorting is poor to moderate.
Dominant mica laths, biotite and muscovite, in the fine fraction, many are <0.06 mm. Tcfs common, and flecks of FeO. (Calcite/micrite hardly seem to be present).
Coarse fraction — red-brown Tcfs are dominant, very fine-grained, boundaries are sometimes merging. Mostly sr-r, and ranging 0.1–2.5 mm. Some have overfired to a very dark red-brown. Rare to very few micritic limestones are preserved, up to c. 0.75 mm (not all have burnt out). Siltstone is rare, sr-r, c. 0.1 mm.
Comment: Very little in coarse fraction except for red-brown Tcfs and burnt-out limestone voids. A micaceous groundmass. S49 is almost identical in hand specimen and thin section.

Sample S49
Thick-walled body sherd, plain interior and brown slip exterior. Semi-coarse pale orange buff, brown grits and many voids, something of a honeycomb structure.
Petrography: Much less micaceous in fine fraction than S48. Colour in both XP and PPL is grey-green. Common inclusion-shaped voids as in S48, and some micritic matter is preserved within them, strengthening the hypothesis that they are burnt-out limestones. Otherwise, the coarse fraction is almost entirely comprised of dark red-brown, very fine Tcfs, the darker overfired examples being ringed with voids. Siltstone is rare (as in S48). S48 and S49 have identical structures, and inclusion sizes are the same too.

Sample S43
Thick-walled body sherd, plain interior but creamy slip exterior. Semi-coarse orange buff with honeycomb structure due to burnt-out limestone. Quite light in weight because of this. Hard-fired.
Petrography: Very similar to S48 and S49, and as micaceous as S48 in the silt-size fraction. Inclusion-shaped voids are common to frequent, probably burnt-out limestone. Size up to c. 2.5 mm. Some even have exactly straight sides, perhaps from a calcite grain. Apart from voids, only dark brown, overfired Tcfs occur in the coarse fraction. Siltstone is rare. c:f:v$_{10\,\mu m}$ = 15:55:30, XP = dark brown-red.
To summarize, this is micaceous and non-calcareous, with Tcfs and burnt-out limestones in coarse fraction — thus very similar to S48 and S49. (Note total absence of quartz, serpentine, foraminifera.)

Sample S54
Plain interior and exterior. Semi-coarse orange buff with brown grits and voids, giving it a honeycomb structure. Hard-fired.
Petrography: Again, very similar to previous samples in this group in all respects. Micaceous in silt and sub-silt range, no calcareous material visible. Coarse fraction comprised almost entirely of dark red-brown, fine Tcfs. Common to frequent voids from burnt-out limestone and calcite. Very rare — one metamorphic rock fragment (phyllite or schist), sr-r and 2.0 mm.

Sample S55
Exactly the same as the above in hand specimen.
Petrography: Practically indistinguishable from the above 4 samples. Micaceous in the fine fraction, seemingly non-calcareous, orange-brown, some optical activity. Common limestone voids, with some calcite preserved in places. Otherwise, red-brown, fine Tcfs predominant in coarse fraction, exactly as in S54. Very rare — one metamorphic rock fragment, orange-brown phyllite, 1.5 mm.

Sample S53
Exactly the same as the above two samples in hand specimen.
Petrography: This too is very similar except that more small calcite fragments have survived, some of which appear to be shell. The groundmass is also slightly different — it is very fine and highly optically active, and there are very few micas visible (but still seems non-calcareous). Large inclusion-shaped voids and Tcfs are still predominant in coarse fraction. Very rare — fine-grained metamorphic rock fragments (slate?).

Sample S42
Thick-walled body sherd, plain interior and exterior, but for very finely incised criss-crossing lines. Semi-fine to semi-coarse orange buff, cream and brown grits, and voids (but not honeycomb).
Microstructure: Few to common vughs of all sizes, up to c. 1.2 mm. They are inclusion-shaped, probably from burnt-out limestones. No micrite hypocoatings.
Groundmass: Homogeneous, optically active. Micaceous, non-calcareous. XP = orange-brown to grey, PPL = grey-green/brown.
Inclusions: c:f:v$_{10\,\mu m}$ = 15:65:20 (note more voids than inclusions).
Fine fraction: predominant muscovite and biotite laths in 0.06–0.1 mm range, also appear to be many <0.06 mm. Very few quartz also, but many are <0.06 mm.
Coarse fraction — few quartz-mica schist, with micas showing partial foliation. One fragment is rounded and 2.5 mm, but most are smaller. Also rare to very few silt/sandstones, r, <1.0 mm. Fine red-brown Tcfs (with surrounding voids) are few.
Comment: Also quite similar to the above samples, but fewer Tcfs, and perhaps even more micaceous in the fine fraction, with a little more quartz too. This mica content might be suggestive of a metamorphic source, and indeed tallies with the presence of few metamorphic rock fragments in the coarse fraction. Should the whole group be considered to perhaps relate in some way to a metamorphic source, given that mica laths are quite common in the fine fraction throughout?

Detailed Fabric Descriptions

Sample S50
Medium-walled body sherd, purple-brown slip to interior and exterior. Purplish buff fabric, fine to semi-fine, with few brown grits, few voids.
Petrography: Once again we observe a dark red-brown, micaceous, and non-calcareous groundmass. It is not nearly as micaceous as S42. Mostly inclusion-shaped voids (few to common), though not as large as in some of the coarser examples like S48–49. Some of these voids seem to have vague grey-green rings around them, as if the $CaCO_3$ has leached from them in some way. Apart from these voids there are few to common Tcfs, red-brown and very fine as always in these Vf–e samples, and sr-r, up to 1.0 mm. Fine fraction is very fine, little apart from mostly sub-silt mica laths, and Tcfs. Also note in coarse fraction some micrite preserved, and very rare siltstone. $c:f:v_{10\,\mu m}$ = 10:80:10.

Sample S51
Medium body sherd, red slip interior and exterior. Fine to semi-fine orange buff, small grits, cream and brown.
Petrography: Extremely similar to S50. Dark red to brown micaceous and non-calcareous groundmass. Voids are few rather than common, Tcfs surprisingly rare. Note also very few metamorphic rock fragments, phyllite and schist, sa-sr, up to 1.0 mm. Some micrite preserved, quartz very rare and sub-silt size. $C:f:v_{10\,\mu m}$ = 10:80:10.

Sample S46
Relatively thin-walled rim sherd of a rounded bowl, plain interior and exterior. Semi-fine orange buff, with brown inclusions and some large voids where once limestone grits were.
Petrography: Again very similar, although different to S51 in having common red-brown Tcfs and no metamorphic rock fragments. Groundmass is red-brown (XP), largely inactive optically, micaceous, and non-calcareous. Voids probably burnt-out limestone. The classic combination for this group of mica laths, Tcfs, and limestone voids. It falls towards the finer end of the spectrum (10:80:10), with S48–49 at the coarser end.

Sample S41
Thick-walled body sherd, plain interior with brown slip exterior. Semi-fine pale orange buff, with small, pale orange-brown grits. Not many voids.
Petrography: Section only partially preserved therefore few comments to be made except to say that it seems entirely consistent with the above in colour, mica laths, Tcfs, and voids (some micrite preserved).

Sample S44
Medium to thick-walled body sherd, plain interior and creamy slip exterior. Semi-fine to semi-coarse orange buff, small brown grits and some voids.
Microstructure: Common vughs up to *c.* 2.0 mm, mode *c.* 0.5–1.0 mm. These voids are inclusion-shaped, probably representing burnt-out limestones.
Groundmass: Homogeneous, optically active, non-calcareous. XP = orange-brown, PPL = brown.
Inclusions: $c:f:v_{10\,\mu m}$ = 10:70:20. Sorting is moderate.
Fine fraction consists predominantly of mica laths, and many sub-silt size. Few micrite/calcite, in 0.06–0.1 mm range, also very few quartz, and common Tcfs.
Coarse fraction — mostly voids from burnt-out limestones, but in some instances the micrite has survived, more so than in most samples. Common in 0.1 mm range, very little above this size. Orange-brown Tcfs are common, some with merging boundaries. Full range of sizes exists up to 1.0 mm, and sr-r.

Comment: This sample clearly falls into main Vf–e group — it is micaceous in fine fraction, with Tcfs and voids.

Sample S52
Relatively thin-walled rim sherd of flaring bowl, plain interior and exterior. Pale orange buff (faint orange core) and semi-fine, with very small cream and brown grits.
Microstructure: Few vughs, most only *c.* 0.2 mm. Not obviously due to burnt-out limestone.
Groundmass: Not homogeneous — redder oxidized core at one end of section has less calcareous matter. No optical activity. XP and PPL = red-brown to grey-green-brown.
Inclusions: Mica laths occur in sub-silt range, as well as FeO and Tcfs. Micrite/calcite is also common. In coarse fraction micrite/calcite is few to common, r, <1.0 mm. Siltstone also few to common, sr, <2.0 mm. Very few red-brown Tcfs.
Comment: This sample falls at the finer end of the group.

Sample S47
Medium-walled body sherd, partial dark red slip to interior and exterior (red-cross bowl design). Pale orange buff, semi-fine with small brown and some very small white grits.
Microstructure: Inclusion-shaped vughs are few to common, on average <0.5 mm, but up to 1.0 mm.
Groundmass: Homogeneous, no optical activity. XP = reddish brown, PPL = medium brown.
Inclusions: $c:f:v_{10\,\mu m}$ = 30:55:15. Sorting is moderate.
Fine fraction contains frequent mica laths, though many are <0.06 mm. Common to frequent calcite/micrite, *c.* 0.1 mm, and Tcfs (fine and red-brown). Few quartz.
Coarse fraction — frequent fine red-brown Tcfs, semi-merging boundaries but clear enough to see in PPL, up to *c.* 0.5 mm, mode *c.* 0.1 mm, sr-r. Common micritic limestone, mostly <0.2 mm and sr-r, very little is any larger, up to 0.5 mm. Very few silt/sandstone, sr, *c.* 1.0 mm. Chert is rare to very few, 0.1–0.8 mm, sr-r, and quartz is rare, sr-r, 0.1–0.2 mm.
Comment: Different in having lots more micrite, and more Tcfs than normal too. Still very micaceous, and still part of main Vf–e group.

Sample S45
Rim sherd of rounded bowl, plain interior and exterior. Pale greenish buff, with brown inclusions that have merging boundaries, seeming to spread into clay matrix. 'Chocolate-speckled ware'.
Microstructure: Common to frequent voids, many of which are inclusion-shaped, suggesting previous presence of limestone grits. Some voids very large, up to 4.0 mm.
Groundmass: Not homogeneous, as there are broad bands of calcite speckling at central area of section. No optical activity. Grey green in XP and PPL.
Inclusions: $c:f:v_{10\,\mu m}$ = 10:60:30. Sorting is moderate.
Fine fraction not at all silty, and mica laths less abundant than in most other sections. Calcite/micrite appears disaggregated and scattered across broad areas of section. Quartz is very rare to rare, Tcfs (and/or FeO) few to common.
Coarse fraction — many voids, some burnt-out limestone grits, but others appear to relate to mudstones/Tcfs. Dark brown mudstones/Tcfs are few to common, and some are bloated and overfired. Some so affected by heat that the material has migrated from the inclusion area leaving a void, and FeO is subsequently concentrated around the void, producing a peculiar effect that is visible in hand specimen.
Comment: Odd effect perhaps caused by Tcfs or mudstones breaking down in high firing temperature, with FeO content migrating in immediately surrounding clay body. But in all other respects this falls very well within the main Vf–e group.

GROUP B (S56)
Cooking-pot ware. Non-calcareous, micaceous with schist rock fragments (non-local).

Sample S56
Microstructure: Common vughs and channel voids, no preferred orientation.
Groundmass: Composition is homogeneous, and optically active. Very micaceous, and possibly non-calcareous. XP = orange-brown, PPL = brown.
Inclusions: c:f:v$_{10\,\mu m}$ = 20:45:35. Sorting is poor.
Fine fraction — frequent mica laths, 0.06–0.1 mm, few to common quartz, 0.06–0.1 mm, sa-a.
Coarse fraction — fine-grained schist is totally dominant, in all sizes from 0.1 to 2.0 mm, ranging from a-r, but mostly sa. Where grain sizes are such that minerals can be identified, muscovite laths and quartz feature. Rare micritic limestone, sa, 0.5 mm.
Comment: The combination of a micaceous (non-calcareous?) groundmass with so much schist in the coarse fraction make it almost certain that this is a non-local fabric. As with Group C, a metamorphic area must be sought for its origin, and the closest possibilities are to the north, towards the Konya plain, and to the southwest, on the coast near Anamur.

GROUP C (S57)
Cooking-pot ware. Red-firing, non-calcareous with many phyllites (non-local).

Sample S57
Microstructure: Few to common vughs and channels, no preferred orientation.
Groundmass: Composition is homogeneous, no optical activity. Red-firing and possibly non-calcareous. XP = dark red, slightly pink, PPL = very dark brown.
Inclusions: c:f:v$_{10\,\mu m}$ = 35:50:15. Sorting is poor.
Fine fraction — making the break at 0.06 mm between fine and coarse fractions is important as there is very little *c.* 0.06 mm but quite a lot of material *c.* 0.1 mm. few quartz, sa-a, *c.* 0.06 mm, and very few phyllite in this size range. There is also the problem that the section is cut slightly too thick, making it hard to discern detail in this size range.
Coarse fraction — Metamorphic rock fragments are totally dominant, mostly phyllite but some fine-grained schist too. Size range is 0.1–2.0 mm, mode perhaps 1.0 mm but all sizes well represented. Elongate in shape (but no preferred orientation in the section), ends not fully rounded, indeed angular in many instances. Grain sizes too small to identify minerals securely, but muscovite seems quite common.
Very few quartz, sa-sr, 0.1–0.2 mm, very few dark brown Tcfs, 0.2–0.5 mm.
Comment: The combination of a red-firing, possibly non-calcareous fabric and such enormous quantities of phyllite means this is almost certainly a non-local cooking pot fabric. It is different to Group B in that the groundmass is much less micaceous, and the metamorphic inclusions are finer grained. The question of provenance is hard to resolve at this time, as with Group B, but the nearest significant metamorphic outcrops are some distance to the north of Kilise Tepe, or *c.* 70 km to the southwest, near Anamur.

MBA samples (Level IV)

GROUP A (S58–61)
Non-calcareous, micaceous, with Tcfs/mudstones and voids (once limestone). Cf. Vf–e, Group A.

Sample S58
Monochrome slipped interior and exterior, all fine to semi-fine orange buff.
Microstructure: Few vughs, no preferred orientation.
Groundmass: Homogeneous, optically active. Non-calcareous, and seems micaceous but particles too fine to be sure. XP = orange-brown, PPL = brown.
Inclusions: c:f:v$_{10\,\mu m}$ = 10:80:10. Sorting is good.
Fine fraction is very fine, practically nothing identifiable in 0.06–0.1 mm range. No calcite/micrite, rare quartz. Some mica laths are visible, but most are <0.06 mm. Also Tcfs / FeO.
Coarse fraction — more voids than inclusions, some may have been limestone, but on the whole voids are not inclusion-shaped. Few — very fine brown-red Tcfs, semi-merging boundaries, 1 large grain is 1.2 mm and r, but mode *c.* 0.2 mm. Very few micritic limestone, r, 0.2–0.5 mm. Rare sandstone, sa, 0.5 mm. Siltstone rare to very few, sr, up to 1.0 mm. Rare schist, sa, 0.3 mm.
Comment: This fabric links in very well to the main Vf–e group, in being micaceous and non-calcareous in groundmass, with coarse fraction of Tcfs and limestones. This particular sample is rather fine, so very little at all in the coarse fraction. Also ties into the three samples described below.

Sample S59
Monochrome slipped exterior and plain interior. Fine to semi-fine orange buff.
Microstructure: Few vughs, some preferred orientation parallel to vessel walls. A lot of the voids are 0.1 mm, and most are not inclusion-shaped.
Groundmass: Homogeneous, optically active. Much more clearly micaceous than previous sample.
XP = orange-brown, PPL = brown.
Inclusions: c:f:v$_{10\,\mu m}$ = 10:80:10. Sorting is moderate to good.
Fine fraction contains many muscovite and biotite laths, though many are <0.06 mm. Apart from the frequent micas the fine fraction is very fine, little in 0.06–0.1 mm range. Quartz is very rare, as is calcite, so too are Tcfs.
Coarse fraction — Red-brown, very fine Tcfs are common, sr-r, up to 1.5 mm. Micritic limestones are rare, and most are 0.1–0.2 mm, although one grain is 1.0 mm. Siltstone — rare, r, 0.6 mm.
Comment: Extremely similar to S58 and to members of EB Vf–e Group A.

Sample S60
Monochrome slipped interior and exterior. Fine to semi-fine orange buff fabric.
Microstructure: Common vughs, many of which inclusion-shaped and relating to burnt-out limestone grits. Up to *c.* 1.0 mm in size.
Groundmass: Homogeneous, with some optical activity. Non-calcareous, micaceous. XP = orange/red-brown, PPL = medium brown.
Inclusions: c:f:v$_{10\,\mu m}$ = 10:75:15. Sorting is moderate to good.
Fine fraction is very fine, little in 0.06–0.1 mm range. Muscovite and biotite laths are dominant, some are 0.1 mm but most are smaller. The laths show some preferred orientation parallel to vessel walls. Quartz is also present but in sub-silt range so identification not secure.
Coarse fraction — grey siltstones are few (to common), not very well preserved, sr-r, and some quite large, up to 4.0 mm. Most are *c.* 1.0 mm however. Tcfs are, surprisingly, very rare, and micritic limestones have also only survived in very rare cases.
Comment: Despite differences in proportions of limestone, Tcfs, and siltstones in the coarse fraction, this should certainly be classed in the same group as previous samples.

Sample S61
Monochrome slipped interior and exterior. Fine to semi-fine orange buff fabric.

Microstructure: Few vughs, no preferred orientation.
Groundmass: Homogeneous, a little optical activity. XP = dark brown, PPL = orange-brown.
Inclusions: c:f:$v_{10\,\mu m}$ = 20:70:10 to 25:65:10. Sorting is moderate to good
Fine fraction — frequent muscovite and biotite laths, once again much is <0.06 mm. Calcite/micrite also present, in 0.06–0.1 mm range. Quartz is few. Tcfs, very fine red-brown and with semi-merging boundaries. Serpentine very rare. Fine fraction is more packed with inclusions than was the case with the previous 3 samples.
Coarse fraction — dominated by calcite/micrite (limestone?) and by Tcfs, fine red-brown with semi-merging boundaries. Most inclusions are c. 0.1 mm. There do exist some inclusions > 0.5 mm, but very few indeed. Chert — very few, 0.1–0.5 mm, sa-sr, including 1 fragment of radiolarian chert, r, c. 0.2 mm. Quartz — rare, tending to be sa and 0.1–0.2 mm. Sandstone is very rare, sa, 0.7 mm.
Comment: This sample is coarser than the 3 previous ones, with more varied inclusions in fine and coarse fractions. It links extremely well to some Vf-e samples such as S47. It is certainly part of the MBA Group A, although falling toward the coarser end of the spectrum — it just happens to have a few more Tcfs, and the limestones have been less affected in firing.

GROUP B (S62–70)
Fine calcareous fabric with foraminifera (cf. Vj–g Group A).

Sample S70
Medium to thin-walled, red burnished, and fine pale buff fabric.
Microstructure: Very few vughs, many of which are very small c. 0.1–0.2 mm. No preferred orientation, some micrite hypocoatings.
Groundmass: Homogeneous, no optical activity. XP = yellow-brown, PPL = light brown.
Inclusions: c:f:$v_{10\,\mu m}$ = 10:85:5. Sorting is good.
Fine fraction is very fine. Foraminifera are dominant, especially *globigerina* and perhaps other planktonic types. Quartz is very rare, opaque minerals rare.
Coarse fraction — very similar to fine fraction, just larger foraminifera, both planktonic (*globigerina*) and benthic types. They are dominant to predominant, some are 0.5 mm, but most are c. 0.25 mm, and extremely well preserved. Few are siliceous. Calcite/micrite — few. Bivalves are rare to very few, and dark brown Tcfs are rare, c. 0.2–0.5 mm.
Comment: An incredible range and abundance of foraminifera and other bioclasts, more so than nearly all other samples in the entire assemblage. Clearly very calcareous and links exceptionally well to local clay samples, as well as to a number of other MBA samples, most of which are very similar but perhaps exhibiting a few different features.

Sample S63
Red burnished interior and exterior. Fine pale buff, a little grey silt visible.
Petrography: This sample is utterly similar, and remarkably so, to S70.

Sample S62
Plain interior and exterior, string-cut base of a cup. Fine pale buff fabric.
Petrography: This sample is identical to the above two samples, S70 and S63.

Sample S64
Plain interior and exterior, fine pale buff with some brown grits visible.
Petrography: This too is totally similar, but for the fact that it contains few to common textural concentration features (Tcfs) as inclusions (or perhaps mudstones).

Sample S69
Thick-walled, red burnished, fine to semi-fine pale buff with brown grits.
Microstructure: Voids are rare, mostly micro-vughs, apart from one or two larger, c. 3.0 mm. No preferred orientation.
Groundmass: Homogeneous, no optical activity, very calcareous. XP = yellow-brown, PPL = light to medium brown.
Inclusions: c:f:$v_{10\,\mu m}$ = 20:75:5. Sorting is moderate to good.
Fine fraction — micrite is dominant, as are foraminifera, especially planktonic (*globigerina*). Few to common red-brown Tcfs with semi-merging boundaries. Quartz is rare, muscovite very rare, opaques very few.
Coarse fraction — micrite, calcite and micritic limestones are frequent, many are 0.25 mm. Benthic and planktonic foraminifera are frequent, most 0.1–0.2 mm, some up to 0.5 mm. Common — very fine red-brown Tcfs/mudstones, with distinct boundaries, 0.1–0.2 mm, sr-r (might have been added as temper as tending to cluster in section, not evenly distributed). Quartz and chert are rare, usually 0.1–0.2 mm, sa-sr.
Comment: Very much like most of the above samples within Group B (calcareous, many foraminifera) but for the addition of Tcfs/mudstones. S68 and S65 are very similar.

Sample S68
Thick-walled, red burnished, fine to semi-fine pale buff with brown grits.
Petrography: Very similar to S69, in being very calcareous with many foraminifera. Only different in having fewer Tcfs/mudstones.

Sample S65
Thick-walled, red burnished, fine to semi-fine pale buff with brown grits.
Petrography: Just as many Tcfs/mudstones as S70, but far fewer foraminifera (though still very calcareous of course). Very fine groundmass and fine fraction.

Sample S67
Relatively thin walls, red burnished, fine pale buff fabric.
Microstructure: Few micro-vughs, no preferred orientation.
Groundmass: Homogeneous, no optical activity. XP = yellow-brown, PPL = greyish brown.
Inclusions: c:f:$v_{10\,\mu m}$ = 5:90:5. Well sorted.
Very little in fine fraction, but calcite is dominant, common Tcfs, epidote, quartz and muscovite rare to very rare, serpentine rare, foraminifera very rare.
Coarse fraction — calcite common, 0.1–0.2 mm, sa-sr. Serpentine rare to very few, <0.3 mm, sr. Rare shell fragments, c. 0.2 mm, rare micritic limestones, sr, <0.5 mm, rare Tcfs <0.5 mm, very rare chert and quartz, 0.1–0.2 mm, sa-sr.
Comment: Void structure, homogeneity, fineness, and calcareousness are all very similar to most of the above-mentioned samples in MBA Group B. However, it contains rare to very few serpentine in fine and coarse fraction.

Sample S66
Thick-walled, red burnished, fine to semi-fine pale buff with brown grits.
Microstructure: Few vughs, no preferred orientation.
Groundmass: Homogeneous, no optical activity. XP and PPL = medium brown, faintly orange.
Inclusions: c:f:$v_{10\,\mu m}$ = 10:83:7. Sorting is moderate to good.
Fine fraction contains predominant micrite/calcite, some foraminifera, few to common dark red-brown Tcfs and serpentine, rare quartz, and very rare epidote, amphibole, and muscovite.

Coarse fraction — same suite of minerals as in fine fraction: micrite/calcite dominant to predominant, sa-sr, nearly all 0.1–0.2 mm, rarely 0.5 mm. Serpentine few to common, 0.1–0.3 mm, sr. Few Tcfs, very few chert, sa-sr, 0.1–0.3 mm.
Comment: A quite fine calcareous fabric with mostly micrite and calcite inclusions of small sand size, as well as conspicuous quantities of serpentine. This does not occur in most samples of Group B, but should not in this instance prevent this sample from being included in the same group.

GROUP C (S71–5)
A semi-coarse to coarse orange-brown fabric with schist and limestone inclusions.

Sample S71
Plain surfaces interior and exterior, orange-brown fabric with angular brown grits, also light brown, red and grey grits.
Microstructure: Few vughs and channel voids, no preferred orientation.
Groundmass: Not fully homogeneous as there are patchy differences of colour and only some areas are optically active. Calcareous, but also micaceous. XP = orange-brown to brown, PPL = dark orange-brown to dark brown.
Inclusions: c:f:$v_{10\,\mu m}$ = 25:65:10 to 20:70:10. Sorting is moderate.
Fine fraction — common to frequent micrite and calcite, 0.06–0.1 mm, sa-sr, common quartz, sa-a, common dark brown Tcfs, very few muscovite laths.
Coarse fraction— common metamorphic rock fragments, mostly fine-grained schist, many of which are elongate, r, 0.2–2.5 mm. Common micritic limestone, sa-sr, 0.1–2.5 mm. Few monocrystalline quartz, a-sr, 0.1–0.4 mm. Few quartz sand/siltstone, sa-sr, 0.2–1.2 mm . Few dark brown Tcfs, 0.1–0.5 mm. Rare foraminifera (e.g. planktonic), 0.1–0.3 mm, very rare serpentine, sa, 0.1–0.2 mm.
Comment: In most respects this has most of the features associated with local fabrics, except for the presence of metamorphic inclusions, a combination which makes this a difficult fabric to source. We must remain open to the possibility that a certain amount of metamorphic material may be present in the local environment, perhaps as part of the conglomerate. This is a common MBA fabric amongst the coarse wares, perhaps another reason to suppose that this is a local fabric.

Sample S72
Grey combed ware. Calcareous (+ some muscovite) with micritic limestones and metamorphic rock fragments (local or non-local?).
Microstructure: Very few to few vughs, *c.* 0.25 mm, and rare planar voids. No preferred orientation.
Groundmass: Composition is homogeneous, no optical activity. Groundmass is calcareous. XP and PPL = brown, faintly grey.
Inclusions: c:f:$v_{10\,\mu m}$ = 20:70:10, sorting is moderate.
Fine fraction — frequent micritic inclusions, many of which are sa, 0.06–0.1 mm. In same size range, few quartz, sa-a. Few to common dark brown Tcfs, sr-r. Muscovite laths very few, amphibole very rare, a, 0.06 mm, epidote also very rare.
Coarse fraction — common to frequent micritic limestone, sa-sr, 0.1–2.5 mm. Common to frequent metamorphic rock fragments, mostly fine-grained schist (quartz-mica), sa-r, 0.1–4.0 mm. Very few quartz, a-sa, 0.1–0.5 mm, also in same size range, but very few to rare, is quartzite, with sutured boundaries and undulose extinction clearly showing metamorphic character.
Comment: On the one hand, the calcareous fabric and micritic limestone inclusions are suggestive of a local source. On the other hand, the presence of significant quantities of metamorphic rock fragments, and of some muscovite in the fine fraction, are not, according to present knowledge, consistent with a local source. Thus the provenance of this fabric is rather ambiguous.

Sample S74
Combed ware jar, unslipped surfaces. Fabric very similar to S71, in all respects, a very close match.

Sample S75
Body sherd of a coarse storage or cooking pot ware, plain surfaces. Very similar fabric to S71, except a little coarser. (Some parts of the section are cut rather thin, giving a false impression that the groundmass is different.)

Sample S73
Combed ware jar, seems to be burnished or smoothed at exterior. Fabric is also similar to S72, but differs in being much grittier in the fine fraction, with much more micrite, and many more foraminifera of various sorts. However, it does appear in the coarse fraction to be very close to the above two samples (S74 and S75).

GROUP D (S76)
Cooking pot, very coarse brown, with quartz, compressed shales, limestone, quartz sandstone and schists/phyllites in the coarse fraction.

Sample S76
Microstructure: Common vughs, vesicles, channel voids, and planar voids, the latter infilled with micrite.
Groundmass: Composition is homogeneous, no optical activity. Possibly non-calcareous. XP and PPL = dark brown-red.
Inclusions: c:f:$v_{10\,\mu m}$ = 35:45:20. Sorting is poor.
Fine fraction is quite gritty, and contains common to frequent quartz, sa-a, 0.06–0.1 mm. It appears as if some of the vughs and vesicles in this size range may have been micrite, possibly destroyed in firing. v. rare epidote, a, 0.1 mm.
Coarse fraction — Common to frequent quartz, a-sr, 0.1–2.5 mm. Common grey-brown compressed shale, sr-r, 0.5–5.0 mm. Few micritic limestone, sa-sr, 0.1–2.5 mm. Few quartz sandstone, sa-sr, 0.5–1.0 mm, occasional 2.0 mm. Very few fine-grained schist and phyllite, elongate and r, *c.* 1.0 mm.
Comment: Once again, it is the presence of metamorphic inclusions that renders provenancing problematic. This ought not to be a local fabric, as there should not be any metamorphic rocks in the area, according to the geological maps and the clay samples. If this is non-local, it is difficult to say whence it came. Alternatively, we may have to accept that some metamorphic rocks do find their way into local resources, notably due to the conglomerate formations in the area, and that this may therefore be a local fabric (albeit different to many others described in this study).

LBA samples (Level III)

GROUP A (S77–93)
Red lustrous wheel-made ware

a) Very fine (S77–82)
Sample S82
Microstructure: Rare vughs and vesicles, no preferred orientation.
Groundmass: Composition totally homogeneous, optically active, not very calcareous, micaceous. XP = orange-red, PPL = orange.
Inclusions: c:f:$v_{10\,\mu m}$ = 3:92:5. Sorting is very good.
There is not much sense in discussing separately fine and coarse fractions with a fabric as fine as this. There are only a handful of grains a little larger than 0.1 mm. In the fine fraction there are frequent dark red Tcfs, sr-r, <0.1 mm, few to common quartz, a-sa, and few micritic inclusions. There is also rather a lot of mica, but most is sub-silt size, i.e. <0.06 mm.

Detailed Fabric Descriptions

Comment: The fineness of the fabric indicates that the clay may well have been levigated or thoroughly cleaned and processed. The fact that it is not very calcareous, micaceous, and of such a deep red colour means that this must surely be non-local. There is a clear continuity with the semi-fine and semi-coarse variants, as is seen below.

Sample S81
Very fine salmon-pink to red fabric, well burnished, rim of open rounded bowl.
Microstructure: Very few micro-vughs, no preferred orientation.
Groundmass: Composition is homogeneous, strong optical activity throughout. XP = red-orange-brown, PPL = orange-brown.
Inclusions: c:f:$v_{10 \mu m}$ = 5:90:5 (very fine). Well sorted.
Some particles of micrite/calcite visible in fine fraction, but most are sub-silt size. Same can be said for frequent red-brown Tcfs. Quartz — few to common, but again tending to be <0.06 mm. Some mica also present, but <0.06 mm.
Coarse fraction — hardly anything >0.1 mm. Some micrite *c.* 0.1–0.2 mm, some of which is long and needle-like, so probably shell fragments. Tcfs also common in 0.1–0.2 mm range, and never larger. Quartz >0.1 mm is very rare.

b) Semi-fine (S84–5, 87)
Sample S87
Microstructure: Very few vughs and vesicles, no preferred orientation.
Groundmass: Composition is homogeneous, and some optical activity. XP = orange-red, PPL = orange-brown.
Inclusions: c:f:$v_{10 \mu m}$ = 15:78:7. Sorting is moderate.
Fine fraction - frequent quartz, a-r, 0.06–0.1 mm. Common red Tcfs, sr-r, 0.06–0.1 mm. Few micrite, sa-r, same size range as previous. Micas (muscovite) are barely visible in sub-silt size range.
Coarse fraction — common to frequent quartz, a-r, mostly 0.1–0.25 mm, but up to 0.5 mm. Common micritic limestone, sa-r, 0.1–2.0 mm. Occasionally micritic inclusions are long and curved, suggestive that some may be shell. Few to common red Tcfs (distinct boundaries), sr-r, 0.1–0.25 mm. Rare schist, sr, 0.2 mm, rare chert, sa-sr, 0.1–0.4 mm.
Comment: Very similar to the finer versions but for the presence of some limestone, quartz, and other inclusion in the coarse fraction. It should be noted that there are barely any metamorphic inclusions, in contrast to the semi-coarse variants described below.

c) Semi-coarse (S83, 86, 88–93)
Sample S89
(S86 has quite a lot of metamorphic inclusions, S90 has relatively few. S88 looks a bit odd — optically inactive and lots of voids. S89 is probably a good compromise and most representative of the group).
Microstructure: Very few vughs and vesicles, no preferred orientation.
Groundmass: Composition is homogeneous, optically active. No visible micas, unlike above sections. XP = orange-red, PPL = orange-brown.
Inclusions: c:f:$v_{10 \mu m}$ = 25:65:10. Sorting is poor to moderate.
Fine fraction - common to frequent red-brown Tcfs, sr-r. Common quartz, sa-a, 0.06–0.1 mm. Common micrite, sa-sr.
Coarse fraction — common micritic and sparry limestone, sa-sr, 0.1–2.5 mm, occasional long curved fragments which may be shell. Common schist (some of which quartz-mica), a-r, 0.2–3.0 mm, quite varied in grain size, from fine (almost phyllite) to coarse, and apparently in mineralogy too. Few to common red-brown Tcfs, sr-r, 0.1–0.6 mm. Few quartz, a-sr, 0.1–0.4 mm. V. rare quartz sandstone, sa, 0.7 mm. V. rare chert, sr, 0.25 mm.
Comment: Much as the fine and semi-fine variants but coarser and with many more large inclusions, especially schist.

Sample S93
Microstructure: Common vughs and channel voids, often quite large, up to 2.5 mm. Some at least appear to be where inclusions once were, perhaps having been removed during preparation of the section. There is no preferred orientation.
Groundmass: Composition is homogeneous, and some optical activity. Seems non-calcareous, and quite micaceous. XP = orange-brown, a little red, PPL = orange-brown.
Inclusions: c:f:$v_{10 \mu m}$ = 20:60:20. Sorting is poor to moderate.
Fine fraction — common to frequent Fe-rich red Tcfs, mostly with distinct boundaries, sr-r, 0.06–0.1 mm. Mica and quartz are both common, but a great deal is sub-silt size. Few micrite, 0.06–0.1 mm, rare plagioclase, a, 0.1 mm. Quite striking that there is so much <0.06 m, but rather little in 0.06–0.1 mm range.
Coarse fraction — micritic limestone is common to frequent, sa-sr, 0.1–2.5 mm, but most are *c.* 1.0 mm. Note that many of these inclusions have been damaged, seemingly in section preparation. Common fine-grained schist (some of which quartz-mica), sa-sr, 0.2–2.0 mm. Few to common Fe-rich red Tcfs, sr-r, 0.1–0.3 mm. Few quartz, a-sr, 0.1–0.5 mm, very few quartz sandstone, 0.2–1.0 mm, sa-sr. Rare feldspar, 0.1–0.4 mm. V. rare rock fragment, a, 1.0 mm, composed of well-developed crystals of microcline feldspar, with what may be some biotite veining — rock type unclear though.
Comment: The micaceous (and non-calcareous?) fabric, together with the schist inclusions, suggests a non-local provenance.

GROUP B (S94–100)
Semi-fine calcareous fabric with limestones, serpentine, chert (cf. phase IIa–d Fabric Group A, and phase IIf, Fabric Group A).

Sample S97
Microstructure: Very few vughs, no preferred orientation.
Groundmass: Composition is homogeneous, no optical activity, XP = grey-green to yellow-brown, PPL = grey-green.
Inclusions: c:f:$v_{10 \mu m}$ = 20:75:5. Sorting is poor to moderate.
Fine fraction — very fine but mostly micritic and calcitic inclusions and foraminifera. Also some Tcfs, little more than flecks of red-brown.
Coarse fraction — frequent foraminifera, of numerous types, both benthic and planktonic (e.g. *globigerina*, and many with 'serrated' edges), 0.1–0.5 mm. Common to frequent micritic and sparry limestone (some microfossiliferous), sa-r, 0.1–0.8 mm. Few serpentine (actually ranging from very few to common in different samples), sa-r, 0.1–0.75 mm. Few chert (some radiolarian), sa-sr, 0.1–0.7 mm. Very few monocrystalline quartz, a-sa, 0.1–1.0 mm. Rare to very few calcite, sa-a, 0.1–0.6 mm. Very rare to rare basalt, sr-r, *c.* 0.5 mm, and metamorphic rock fragments (phyllite, schist), sa-sr, *c.* 0.5 mm. Very rare epidote, sa-a, 0.1–0.3 mm, and alkali feldspar, sa, 0.4 mm.
Comment: A local fabric, judging by the predominance of foraminifera and other micritic and calcitic inclusions, and the presence of serpentine. Very similar to one of the main fabric groups from the Iron Age, known as Group A in both phases IIa–d and IIf. Most of the samples in this LBA group come from shallow bowls with inturned rims.

GROUP C (S101–3)
Semi-fine calcareous fabric with foraminifera and micritic limestones.

Sample S102
Microstructure: Very few vughs (most <0.5 mm), no preferred orientation.
Groundmass: Composition is homogeneous, no optical activity,

very calcareous, XP = yellow-brown, PPL = grey-green to greyish pale brown.
Inclusions: c:f:v$_{10\,\mu m}$ = 5:90:5 to 25:70:5, sorting is poor to moderate.
Fine fraction — relatively silty, almost entirely micritic inclusions and foraminifera, with occasional quartz. A few small red-brown flecks, presumably Tcfs.
Coarse fraction — Micritic limestones (some microfossiliferous) and foraminifera are entirely dominant, sa-r, 0.1–1.5 mm. Few large Tcfs, orange-brown and with indistinct boundaries, sr-r, 1.5–2.5 mm. Rare chert, sa, 0.5 mm.
Comment: A typical local calcareous fabric, with limestones and foraminifera as inclusions. This group contains none of the serpentine or other minerals that characterize LBA Group B. There are similarities to certain fabric groups in both the Early Bronze Age and the Middle Bronze Age. Note that S101 does contain rare serpentine, although S102–3 do not.

GROUP D (S104)
Thickened rim jar. Fabric is a coarse pale buff with large glinting grits of calcite. Calcareous with foraminifera and angular calcite temper.

Sample S104
Microstructure: Very few vughs, mostly very small but some are *c.* 0.5 mm. No preferred orientation.
Groundmass: Homogeneous but for one corner that has oxidized and turned red-brown. No optical activity, very calcareous. XP = yellow-brown, PPL = pale brown, slightly yellow.
Inclusions: c:f:v$_{10\,\mu m}$ = 20:75:5. Sorting is poor.
Fine fraction is extremely fine, very little apart from frequent small foraminifera (*globigerina*), and common angular calcite. Few dark brown Tcfs/FeO.
Coarse fraction has predominant angular calcite, mostly monocrystalline, which is up to 2.5 mm, very difficult to identify mode. Polycrystalline calcite also present, no triple points so is not marble (up to 3.0 mm). Few foraminifera, up to *c.* 0.5 mm, some benthic types, but mostly globigerina, some with serrated edges, and also may be silicified rather than calcitic. Quartz is rare, sa, 0.2 mm. Chert very rare, a-sa, 0.4–0.6 mm, very rare shell fragments and bivalves.
Comment: Almost entirely composed of angular calcite in a very calcareous matrix that has many benthic and planktonic foraminifera. These features do tally well with the overwhelmingly sedimentary local geology.

GROUP E (S105)
It is different from the above Group D in being red-brown in colour, silty, and containing far fewer foraminifera. However, it is tempered with abundant angular calcite. It is an analogue to Level IIa–d Group D. Similarity to the above means no thin-section description needed.

GROUP F (S106–7)
Calcareous with foraminifera and microfossiliferous limestones.

Sample S107
Microstructure: Very few to few vughs and channel voids, a degree of preferred orientation parallel to vessel walls.
Groundmass: Composition is homogeneous, no optical activity, very calcareous, XP = yellow-brown, PPL = pale brown.
Inclusions: c:f:v$_{10\,\mu m}$ = 30:60:10 to 35:60:5. Sorting is poor.
Fine fraction — a little silty, with numerous foraminifera (planktonic and benthic), 0.06–0.1 mm. Other micritic inclusions also present, some brown Tcfs, and occasional quartz.
Coarse fraction — dominant microfossiliferous limestones, some very large, *c.* 5.0 mm. Common foraminifera (planktonic and benthic), 0.1–0.5 mm. Very few chert, sa-sr, 0.1–0.5 mm. Rare quartz, sa-sr, 0.1–0.2 mm. Very rare serpentine (one grain), sr, 0.5 mm.
Comment: Note that S106 is very similar in containing many large microfossiliferous limestone inclusions, chert, and a little quartz, but is different in that it is a siltier, red-firing clay (though still apparently calcareous), with more Tcfs, and fewer foraminifera.

GROUP G (S108)
Calcareous with micritic limestones and dark elongate phyllites (cf. MBA Group C).

Sample S108
Microstructure: Very few small vughs (<0.5 mm), no preferred orientation.
Groundmass: Composition is not homogeneous, as there are a few thin streaks of red, perhaps related to clay mixing. No optical activity, XP = orange-brown, PPL = brown.
Inclusions: c:f:v$_{10\,\mu m}$ = 15:80:5 to 20:75:5. Sorting is moderate.
Fine fraction — quite fine, numerous foraminifera and other micritic inclusions, some Tcfs and occasional quartz.
Coarse fraction — common to frequent micritic inclusions and various types of foraminifera, sr-r, on the whole, and mostly 0.1–0.5 mm but occasionally up to 1.0 mm. Common dark brown phyllites, sa-r, 0.1–2.5 mm. Few red-brown Tcfs, sr-r, <1.5 mm. Very few chert, sa-r, 0.1–0.5 mm. Rare quartz, sa-a, 0.1–0.4 mm. Rare calcite, a, one grain 2.0 mm.
Comment: Similar to MBA Group C, and with the same problem of assigning a local/non-local origin. The plentiful foraminifera and calcareous groundmass indicate local, the phyllites would tend to suggest non-local. However, if we accept that the local conglomerates may contain a certain amount of metamorphic material, then overall a local origin seems the most plausible hypothesis.

GROUP H (S109)
Dark brown cooking-pot ware.

Sample S109
Contains odd grains — quartz smashed in the process of thin-section preparation. Calcareous groundmass, coarse fraction has metamorphic (phyllite) and sedimentary.
Microstructure: Relatively large vughs (up to 2.5 mm) are few to common, some may have been created in process of thin-section preparation. No preferred orientation.
Groundmass: Composition appears to be homogeneous, a little optical activity. Calcareous. XP = yellow to orange-brown, PPL = brown to dark brown.
Inclusions: c:f:v$_{10\,\mu m}$ = 35:50:15. Sorting is poor.
Fine fraction — frequent to dominant micrite, sparite, and calcite, few to common quartz, mostly a-sa. Very few muscovite laths.
Coarse fraction — common micritic and sparry limestone, sa-sr, 0.1–2.0 mm, common metamorphic rock fragments, mostly phyllite, sr-r, 0.2–2.0 mm, few to common quartz, badly damaged (in section preparation), sa-sr, 0.1–3.5 mm, few quartz sandstone, sa-r, 0.1–2.5 mm, very few calcite, sa-a, 0.1–0.5 mm, rare foraminifera, 0.1–0.2 mm.
Comment: Presence of metamorphic rock fragments might be taken as evidence for a non-local source. Alternatively, such fragments may derive from local conglomerates, especially when one considers that everything else in the section is consistent with a local source. Moreover, this very coarse sample shows some similarities with certain coarse fabrics in Level Vf–e.

Detailed Fabric Descriptions

GROUP I (S110)
Micrite/calcite and mica, with micritic limestones, phyllites, schist (similar to Group G).

Sample S110
Microstructure: Few vughs, vesicles, and channel voids, no preferred orientation.
Groundmass: Composition is homogeneous, moderate optical activity, XP = orange-brown, PPL = brown.
Inclusions: c:f:v$_{10\,\mu m}$ = 30:60:10. Sorting is poor.
Fine fraction — moderately silty, with common to frequent micritic inclusions and quartz, and common dark brown Tcfs.
Coarse fraction — frequent metamorphic rock fragments, both phyllite and quartz-mica schist, some elongate and others more equidimensional, sr-r, up to 3.0 mm. Common micritic limestone, sa-r, 0.1–2.5 mm. Few quartz, a-r, 0.1–0.7 mm, and very few chert, sa-sr, 0.1–0.7 mm.
Comment: The presence of so much metamorphic material in the coarse fraction raises the question of whether this can be local (possible presence of metamorphic rock fragments in the local conglomerate?). It is similar to Group G but contains much more phyllite and schist.

GROUP J (S111)
Micaceous and non-calcareous with predominant phyllites.

Sample S111
Microstructure: Common vughs and channel voids, some preferred orientation parallel to vessel walls and to elongate inclusions.
Groundmass: Composition is not homogeneous, with broad dark streaks in places, perhaps related to firing. Optically active in places. XP = orange-red to very dark brown, PPL = orange-brown to very dark-brown, almost black.
Inclusions: c:f:v$_{10\,\mu m}$ = 35:50:15, very coarse, sorting is poor.
Fine fraction — quite silty, with common to frequent quartz, common mica laths, few Tcfs, very few to rare micritic inclusions.
Coarse fraction — totally dominated by metamorphic rock fragments, almost all phyllite (and not the same as in Groups G or H), mostly elongate and sr-r, up to 5.00 mm. The fragments fall towards the coarser end of the phyllite range, and individual minerals of quartz, muscovite and biotite can be discerned (i.e. *c.* 0.06 mm). Rare micritic limestone, 0.1–0.5 mm, rare quartz, a-sa, 0.1–0.2 mm.
Comment: The sheer quantities of phyllite in the coarse fraction, coupled with the micaceous nature of the groundmass and fine fraction, as well as the absence of foraminifera, argue for a non-local source. The area of origin though is unclear — perhaps to the southwest, around Anamur, or alternatively at some distance to the north.

Samples from Level IIa–d

GROUP A (S112–26)
Semi-fine calcareous with foraminifera, micritic and sparry limestones, serpentine, chert, and occasional igneous rock fragments. Of the 15 samples in this group, the following are semi-fine: S112 (**787**), S115 (from a IIe/f context), S116 (**751**) and S117. Samples that are a little coarser are S113, S122, S126. Two samples without serpentine are S120 and S123. Four more samples without serpentine, and also a little less calcareous with fewer foraminifera, and somewhat redder in colour, are S119, S121, S124-5. Finally, a single sample (S118 - a pilgrim flask) contains very high amounts of serpentine.

Sample S114 (Fine version of Group A)
Microstructure: Very few vughs, *c.* 0.2–0.5 mm, many with micrite hypocoatings.
Groundmass: Homogeneous, no optical activity, very fine and calcareous. XP = yellow-brown to brown, PPL = medium brown, slightly grey.
Inclusions: c:f:v$_{10\,\mu m}$ = 10:85:5. Sorting is moderate.
A clear bimodal distribution, looks as if must be a tempered fabric, about as fine as S150 (Level IIf), but the inclusions are *c.* 0.5 mm, and thus more like S165 (Level IIf).
Nothing much to describe in fine fraction (very fine). Coarse fraction has frequent sparry limestones, some microfossiliferous, tending to be rounded, mode *c.* 0.5 mm, but some 1.0 mm. Few serpentine, sa-sr, 0.1–0.5 mm, few chert, sa-sr, up to 0.6 mm, very few (altered) igneous rock fragments, including basalt, sa-r, 0.5–1.0 mm. Rare schist, sr, 0.3–1.0 mm, rare foraminifera.
Comment: Very calcareous and fine groundmass with added temper 0.5–1.0 mm in size, including limestone, chert, serpentine, and igneous rock fragments. Links very clearly to the four other Level IIa–d samples listed above, and to samples from the Level IIf kiln group.

Sample S113 (Coarse version of Group A)
Microstructure: Very few vughs, most 0.2–0.5 mm, some as large as 2.5 mm.
Groundmass: Homogeneous, no optical activity, very calcareous. XP = brown-grey-green, PPL = grey-green.
Inclusions: c:f:v$_{10\,\mu m}$ = 25:70:5 (thus a little coarser than S165). Sorting is moderate.
Fine fraction is extremely fine, little to describe. As ever though, calcite/micrite present, many foraminifera, and Tcfs. No mica, practically no quartz.
Coarse fraction — many of the grits are 0.5 mm, and a clear bimodal distribution suggestive of tempering, much like S165.
Frequent — micritic and sparry limestones, some microfossiliferous. Largest is 1.2 mm, but most are 0.5 mm, sr-r, though some sa.
Common — foraminifera, spherical planktonics up to 0.4 mm, some with serrated edges. Benthic types also present, but fewer (one of which is 0.9 mm). Chert is also common, sa-r, up to 0.9 mm but most 0.5 mm. Note also one or two fragments of radiolarian chert.
Few to common — serpentine, sa-sr, 0.2–0.7 mm.
Few — mudstones, sa-r, 0.2–1.0 mm.
Rare — schist, sa-sr, 0.3–0.5 mm. Quartz, sa, 0.1–0.4 mm.
Rare to very rare — igneous rock fragments, including two basalt fragments, sa-r, 0.4–0.5 mm. Epidote is very rare, sa, 0.2 mm, as are small shell fragments, 0.1–0.2 mm.
Comment: The other two samples in this sub-group of Group A also contain mostly limestone inclusions, with significant amounts of chert, serpentine, and foraminifera, and rarer amounts of metamorphic and igneous rock fragments. The combination of serpentine and igneous rock fragments with a sedimentary suite of rocks and minerals is consistent with the local geology, of predominantly Neogene marine sediments, with a very restricted outcropping of serpentine and other volcanic rocks.

GROUP B (S127–34)
Red-firing, non-calcareous and micaceous, with frequent sub-angular quartz, and micritic limestone.

Sample S128
Square rim basin, cross-hatching.
Microstructure: Few to common vughs, mostly small, *c.* 0.1 mm, and very rarely larger *c.* 0.5 mm.

Groundmass: Homogeneous, no optical activity. XP = red to brown, PPL = less red, but red-brown.
Inclusions: c:f:v$_{10\,\mu m}$ = 15:70:15. Sorting is good.
Division between fine and coarse fractions drawn at 0.06 mm because so much material *c.* 0.1 mm.
Coarse fraction — frequent quartz, mostly monocrystalline, much of it sa-a, but also sr-r, and 0.06–0.3 mm. Frequent mica laths, both muscovite and biotite, almost all 0.06–0.1 mm, some smaller but very few larger. Red Tcfs are common, sr-r, also tending to be 0.06–0.1 mm, very rarely >0.1 mm. Very few elongate siltstones, sr, 1.0 mm, very low relief. Some slightly coarser-grained examples have a dark-red brown cement with quartz grains and micas, sa-sr, 1.0 mm, also with low relief. Rare plagioclase feldspar, sa-a, 0.1–0.2 mm. Rare micritic limestone, 1 large grain is 1.0 mm, sa. Others partially preserved are smaller, perhaps burnt-out in firing. Also note what appear to be large clay minerals, *c.* 0.1 mm, and common, only really visible in PPL.
Comment: This combination of mica laths, quartz, and small red Tcfs, with lesser quantities of siltstone and limestone, recurs through all the samples in this group. Also note that particle size and distribution is very similar across all samples. S129, for example, is highly similar — it too contains mica laths, quartz, red Tcfs, large 'clay minerals', voids, limestone, and some siltstones/sandstones. In other samples the ratios of mica, limestone, and siltstone may vary, but they are all much the same nonetheless. This group comes under strong suspicion of being non-local, largely because it is non-calcareous and very micaceous, and no such clay resources seem to be located in the region.

GROUP C (S135)

Sample S135
Buff calcareous cooking pot fabric, with foraminifera and angular calcite temper.
Microstructure: Very few vughs, rare planar voids, no preferred orientation.
Groundmass: Homogeneous, no optical activity, very calcareous and fine. XP and PPL = yellow-brown.
Inclusions: c:f:v$_{10\,\mu m}$ = 20:75:5 to 25:70:5.
Very little in fine fraction, except dominant angular calcite, frequent small foraminifera (*globigerina*), common red Tcfs, very rare quartz.
Coarse fraction — monocrystalline calcite is predominant, all sa-a, sizes from 0.1–2.5 mm. Polycrystalline calcite — few to common, sa-a, 0.5–3.0 mm. Some do have triple points so could be marble. Rare — chert, sa-sr, 0.3–0.5 mm. Very rare — sheared quartz, sr, 0.5 mm. Very few foraminifera in coarse fraction, planktonic and benthic types. Rare Tcfs and mudstones, sr, 0.2–0.5 mm.
Comment: This is a fine calcareous clay containing foraminifera, tempered with crushed calcite, and perhaps some fragments of marble. It is very similar to S105 from Level III. However, it is quite different to the other Level II calcite-tempered fabric, represented by S136.

GROUP D (S136)

Silty red-brown cooking pot fabric with angular calcite temper.

Sample S136
Microstructure: Few vughs, *c.* 0.2–0.4 mm, no preferred orientation.
Groundmass: Homogeneous, no optical activity. Could be calcareous, although very red-brown (oxidation). XP = red-brown, PPL = dark brown.
Inclusions: c:f:v$_{10\,\mu m}$ = 30:65:5 to 35:60:5. Sorting is poor.
So much material in 0.06–0.1 mm range that division between coarse and fine is placed at 0.06 mm for this sample. Dominant — angular (monocrystalline) calcite, 0.06–1.5 mm, mode very hard to estimate, perhaps 0.25 mm (certainly no bimodality). Rare polycrystalline calcite, no clear triple points so not marble. Common — quartz, sa, 0.06–0.2 mm, few micritic limestones, sa-r, 0.2–1.5 mm, very few dark brown Tcfs and opaque minerals, a-r, 0.1 mm. Very rare — chert, shell, bivalves, and foraminifera (*globigerina*).
Comment: This sample has very high quantities of angular calcite, presumably crushed. However, whereas in S135 the calcite was largely in the coarse fraction, in this sample there is much calcite through the full range of sizes, making its identification as temper rather difficult. Either the calcite was crushed very finely before added, or somehow this is a clay with angular calcite occurring naturally within it. Despite the differences between the two samples that constitute Groups C and D respectively, they both represent a tradition of tempering cooking pots with calcite that continues from the Level III, but which is not seen during any other periods at Kilise Tepe.

GROUP E (S137–8)

Mycenaean pottery, phase IId.
There are two samples in this group, representing the possible local production of Mycenaean-style pottery.

Sub-group E 1

Calcareous, with micrite, serpentine, dark brown Tcfs, very few quartz, rare chert (local?).

Sample S137
Mycenaean deep bowl (**957**).
Microstructure: Very few to few small and medium-sized vughs, 0.1–0.5 mm. No preferred orientation.
Groundmass: Composition is homogeneous, appears calcareous, and no optical activity. XP = grey-green-buff, PPL = light grey-brown.
Inclusions: c:f:v$_{10\,\mu m}$ = 5:85:10. Sorting is good.
Not much sense in separating fine from coarse fractions as there are very few inclusions at all, let alone above 0.1 mm. There are numerous micritic aggregations *c.* 0.06–0.1 mm, rarely up to 0.25 mm. Few red-brown Tcfs, never >0.1 mm, and few quartz, <0.25 mm. Clay concentrations, orange in colour, are observed, and are difficult to distinguish from the rare grains of silt-size serpentine also present in the section. Very rare phyllite, elongate and r, 0.3 mm.
Comment: Although by no means conclusively proven, this sample could feasibly be a local product. However, there are none of the foraminifera that are so frequently encountered in the local fine buff fabrics. Chemical data point to a local provenance.

Sub-group E 2

Silty calcareous, quartz, serpentine, very rare plagioclase, epidote, K-feldspar, amphibole, sheared quartz (local/non-local?).

Sample S138
Mycenaean closed shape, rim missing (**956**).
Microstructure: Very few to few small to medium vughs (0.1–0.5 mm), and long channel voids, showing preferred orientation parallel to vessel walls.
Groundmass: Composition is homogeneous, no optical activity, seemingly calcareous. XP = brown, PPL = greyish brown.
Inclusions: c:f:v$_{10\,\mu m}$ = 15:75:10. Sorting is moderate.
Fine fraction — frequent micritic aggregations and common quartz, <0.06 mm, few to common dark brown Tcfs, very few plagioclase, rare to very few orange clay concentrations.

Coarse fraction — frequent micrite, 0.06–1.0 mm (one fragment possible shell, 0.5 mm), common quartz, a-r, 0.06–0.25 mm, very few plagioclase, a-sa, 0.06–0.2 mm, very few amphibole, a-sa, 0.06–0.3 mm, rare alkali feldspar, 0.06–0.4 mm, rare epidote, a-sa, 0.06–0.2 mm, rare mica laths, v. rare foraminifera, poorly preserved.
Comment: A somewhat silty fabric, most of the inclusions <0.2 mm. There is a much broader range of minerals represented than is normally the case with local Kilise Tepe fabrics. Nonetheless, a local provenance seems most likely, and such a conclusion finds support in the chemical results.

GROUP F (S139–41)

Sample S140
Mycenaean deep bowl (**959**).
Common serpentine, up to 0.5 mm but mostly 0.06–0.1 mm. Common amphibole, up to 0.4 mm, but mostly 0.06–0.1 mm. Few quartz, chert, and micritic limestone. Rare volcanic and plutonic rock fragments. Dark brown Tcfs in fine fraction, rare epidote, pyroxenes? and other unidentified mineral. Hard to tell if calcareous or not. It is not micaceous.
Microstructure: Very few small to medium vughs (<1.0 mm), no preferred orientation.
Groundmass: Composition is homogeneous, firing to reddish brown (is it calcareous?), no optical activity. XP = reddish brown, PPL = brown, a tinge of orange.
Inclusions: c:f:v$_{10\,\mu m}$ = 10:83:7. Sorting is moderate to good.
Fine fraction — 0.06–0.1 mm — amphibole, quartz, serpentine, red-brown Tcfs, micrite.
Coarse fraction — common serpentine, sa-r, 0.1–0.5 mm. Common amphibole, sa-sr, 0.1–0.4 mm. Few quartz, sa-sr, 0.1–0.25 mm. Few micritic limestone, sr-r, 0.1–0.8 mm. Rare chert, sr, 0.1–0.8 mm. Rare granitic rock fragments, with amphibole and quartz present, sr, 0.4 mm. Rare clinozoisite and epidote, sa, 0.1–0.4 mm. Very rare (just one grain) basalt, sr, 0.6 mm.
Comment: Almost certainly non-local, the presence of granitic (and occasional volcanic) rock fragments and associated minerals means that this sample probably derives from an igneous environment. Further comparative work and chemical analysis may help pin this down more precisely.

Samples S139 and S141 are less gritty, but are similar enough in most other respects to be grouped with the above sample. A separate description follows.

Sample S139
Mycenaean deep bowl (**960**).
This sample is extremely similar to the above — just as fine, same colour, containing amphibole, some serpentine, also with chert, quartz, occasional feldspar, and odd pyroxene-like minerals, as yet unidentified.
Microstructure: Very few vughs and vesicles, 0.1–0.5 mm, no preferred orientation.
Groundmass: Composition is homogeneous, no optical activity. XP = reddish brown, PPL = brown with a tinge of orange.
Inclusions: c:f:v$_{10\,\mu m}$ = 5:90:5. Sorting is good.
Fine fraction — extremely fine, very little visible except orange clay concentrations, red-brown Tcfs and amphibole.
Coarse fraction — common amphibole, a-sr, 0.1–0.3 mm. Few Tcfs, red-brown, sr-r, 0.1 mm, few quartz, sa-sr, 0.1–0.2 mm, rare orthopyroxene, sa-sr, 0.1–0.4 mm, rare foraminifera, only 2 fragments, both c. 0.4 mm, one rather sponge-like, rare plagioclase, a-sa, 0.1–0.2 mm, very rare granitic rock fragment, sa, 0.1 mm, very rare radiolarian chert (1 grain), sa, 1.1 mm, very rare serpentine, shrunk in firing (with surrounding void), r, 0.6 mm.

Comment: Although a finer fabric than S140, the range of minerals is very similar, meaning that this too must be a non-local fabric from an igneous environment. S141 is incredibly similar to S139, and certainly forms part of the same fabric group. There are some minor differences - it contains a little more serpentine, rare epidote, and some micritic limestone inclusions.

Sample S141
Mycenaean deep bowl (**958**).
Much finer than S140, but similar in some respects, such as the common to few amphibole. But serpentine is very rare, as is quartz, although one can in part attribute this to the fact that it is a finer fabric. Micritic limestone, K-feldspars, epidote, and Tcfs are all present.

GROUP G (S142)
Mycenaean pottery, phase IId.

Sample S142
Small stirrup jar (**947**).
Microstructure: Very few vughs and vesicles, <0.5 mm, most with micritic hypocoatings, and no preferred orientation.
Groundmass: Composition is homogeneous, no optical activity. XP = orange-brown, PPL = brown.
Inclusions: c:f:v$_{10\,\mu m}$ = 2:93:5. Sorting is good.
There is practically nothing in the coarse fraction, just the occasional red-brown Tcf, <0.2 mm. In the fine fraction there is quite a lot of material c. 0.06 mm and smaller, such as micrite, quartz, orange clay concentrations, red-brown Tcfs, and muscovite laths, all in roughly equal proportions. Many of the inclusions are too small for reliable identification.
Comment: Petrographically there is very little diagnostic information to help establish a provenance. It is unlike most local fabrics so one suspects it is non-local, and this is also likely in terms of the type of vessel from which the sample comes — a Mycenaean stirrup jar, which is a rare occurrence at the site. Note, however, that the chemical data do point to the possibility of a broadly local source.

Samples from Level IIe

GROUP A (S143–6)
'Kindergarten ware'. Much micritic limestone, Tcfs/mudstones, and serpentine.

Sample S146
Microstructure: Rare to very few planar voids, and few vughs, some of which are inclusion-shaped, still containing micrite. Varying sizes up to 2.5 mm.
Groundmass: Homogeneous, little optical activity. XP and PPL = red-brown.
Inclusions: c:f:v$_{10\,\mu m}$ = 30:55:15. Sorting is good.
Relatively fine below 0.06 mm, although there is micrite (dominant) in silt-size fraction. Also many Tcfs and FeO. Occasional mica, and quartz.
Coarse fraction — predominant to dominant micritic limestone (few are microfossiliferous), ranging from a-r, mode c. 0.3 mm, but range is 0.06–1.0 mm. Few large planktonic foraminifera, micritized, 0.4 mm. Few — serpentine, 0.2–0.5 mm, surprisingly angular. Common very fine red-brown Tcfs/mudstones, a-r, 0.1–0.2 mm, but some up to 1.0 mm. Chert and quartz both rare, sa, 0.1–0.3 mm.
Comment: It is difficult to tell if groundmass is calcareous or non-calcareous. Not micaceous. In all four samples the coarse fraction is dominated by tightly packed micritic limestone, with Tcfs/mudstones and also significant amounts of serpentine.

Sample S144
This sample is a little different in being finer and apparently calcareous, with more chert, as well as occasional igneous rock fragments, schist, and very rare epidote and amphibole. Although this sample falls very well within the 'Kindergarten ware' fabric group, these minor differences suggest a degree of similarity with the main calcareous group of phases IIa–d and phase IIf. Such links between these two different fabric groups help to support the idea that both are local products, with inclusions at least partially derived from the serpentine and volcanic outcrops a little way up the Kurtsuyu river to the east of Kilise Tepe.

GROUP B (dark-on-light painted bowls)
These are S115 and S116 (**751**) listed in the Level IIa–d section. S115 is from a IIe/f context.

GROUP C (S147–9)
Bichrome decorated wares in a white-buff silty fabric. Calcareous with limestone, foraminifera, serpentine, chert, mudstones etc. (cf. Group A from phases IIa–d).

Sample S149
Bichrome, with 'target' decoration.
Microstructure: Few vughs, tending to be 0.3–0.5 mm, some of which inclusion-shaped and possibly from limestones. Indeed, some are half void/half limestone. Did this carbonate depletion occur in firing?
Groundmass: Homogeneous, no optical activity. Grey-green in both XP and PPL.
Inclusions: c:f:$v_{10\,\mu m}$ = 25:65:10. Sorting is moderate.
Fine fraction is very fine and calcareous (the many micrites in 0.06–0.1 mm range fall into coarse fraction, as division made at 0.06 mm for this sample). Also common Tcfs, very few quartz, rare serpentine, very rare epidote and amphibole.
Coarse fraction can be difficult to discern from fine fraction because so much occurs *c.* 0.1 mm (hence why division has been made at 0.06 mm).
Predominant to dominant — micritic limestone 0.06–1.0 mm.
Common — chert, sa-sr, much is 0.1 mm, up to 0.3 mm (some radiolarian chert).
Common to few — Tcfs/mudstones, sr-r, 0.1–1.0 mm.
Few to common — serpentine, sa-r, 0.1–0.3 mm.
Few — foraminifera, *c.* 0.1–0.3 mm, both planktonic and benthic types.
Very few — quartz, sa-sr, 0.1–0.2 mm.
Very rare — igneous rock fragments (including basalt), sa, 0.3 mm. Schist, sr, 0.1–0.3 mm.
Comment: A very similar range of minerals and rocks as is present in most samples of Group A from phases IIa–d (e.g. S113), and also in many examples from phase IIf.

Samples from Level IIf

GROUP A (S150–68)
Fine calcareous with microfossils, micrite/calcite, serpentine, Tcfs/mudstones, chert, quartz, and very rare igneous rock fragments (cf. IIa–d Group A). Samples S150–65 are all from the kiln group, unit 1783).

Sample S150
White Painted trefoil jug.
Microstructure: Very few to few vughs, tending to be *c.* 0.25 mm.
No preferred orientation.
Groundmass: Homogeneous, no optical activity, very calcareous. XP = medium brown, PPL = brown, slightly grey.
Inclusions: c:f:$v_{10\,\mu m}$ = 10:83:7. Sorting is moderate.
Fine fraction — very fine and calcareous. Micrite/calcite dominant, including some foraminifera (*globigerina*). Quartz rare to very few, muscovite is rare.
Coarse fraction — there seems to be a bimodal distribution, so much of coarse fraction could be temper, inclusions typically 0.25 mm. Frequent — micritic and sparry limestones, some microfossiliferous, sa-sr, none larger than 0.5 mm, most *c.* 0.25 mm. Foraminifera are few, including some large *globigerina*, *c.* 0.5 mm. Chert is few to common, sa-sr, 0.1–0.5 mm, as is serpentine, sr-r, 0.1–0.5 mm. Opaque minerals are few, sa-sr, 0.1 mm. Tcfs/mudstones rare to very few, sr-r, 0.1–0.3 mm, also quartz, sa, 0.1–0.5 mm. Very rare — schist, r, 0.3 mm; phyllite, r, 0.4 mm; amphibole, a, 0.4 mm. Altered igneous rock fragments are very rare, sa-r, 0.1–0.2 mm, including one basalt grain, very rounded, 0.3 mm.
Comment: Largely calcareous in groundmass and temper, but note marked presence of serpentine and rarer amounts of related igneous material that suggest source of temper might be sand from the Kurtsuyu river, close to the Kilise Tepe site.

Sample S165
A little coarser than the above sample S150.
Microstructure: Very few to few vughs mostly 0.25–0.5 mm, but a few are 2.0–3.0 mm. No preferred orientation.
Groundmass: Homogeneous, some optical activity at thinner section edges. Very calcareous. XP = yellow-brown to brown, PPL = brown, slightly grey.
Inclusions: c:f:$v_{10\,\mu m}$ = 20:70:10. Sorting is moderate.
Fine fraction — very calcareous and essentially the same as S150.
Coarse fraction — micritic and sparry limestones, some of which microfossiliferous — frequent, sa-sr, *c.* 0.5 mm. Very consistent size, hardly any >0.5 mm. Common to few foraminifera, benthic and planktonic types, up to *c.* 0.5 mm. Common chert, sa-sr, up to 0.5 mm. Few to very few quartz, sa-sr, up to 0.5 mm. Very few to few serpentine, sa-sr, all <0.5 mm, and Tcfs. Rare — altered igneous rock fragments, sometimes difficult to identify, quite coarse grained. Metamorphic rock fragments (schist/phyllite) rare, r, up to 0.5 mm. Very rare to rare epidote, sa-a, 0.1–0.3 mm, shell fragments also present.
Comment: Very similar range of inclusions, and proportions of inclusion types, as seen in S150, and indeed the whole group. The inclusions are simply a little more frequent, and consistently larger — 0.5 mm, as compared to 0.25 mm in S150. Highly suggestive of the differential use of an added temper, and even the deliberate selection of certain sand sizes, fine sand (0.25 mm) for the finer vessels, medium sand (0.5 mm) for the coarser ones. Could this be achieved through sieving?

GROUP B (S169–80)
Sub-group B 1 (S169–72)
Mica laths and plagioclase laths in the fine fraction are particularly characteristic of this sub-group. They also contain, in varying amounts, quartz, Tcfs, epidote, igneous rock fragments, serpentine, alkali feldspars.

Sample S170 (Black-on-Red)
Lower body sherd of an open shape (a bowl?), decorated with black-on-red horizontal bands at both interior and exterior, and possibly burnished. Very fine pale red-orange, very occasional red grits visible.
Microstructure: Few vughs and vesicles, most <0.5 mm, and rare channel voids. Some of the larger vughs and channels have partial micritic hypocoatings. No preferred orientation.

Groundmass: Composition is not homogeneous, as there are red streaks and patches across the section. These may be due to the imperfect mixing of two clays. There is no optical activity, and the red-firing, micaceous matrix could be non-calcareous. XP = red-brown to yellow-brown, PPL = brown to dark brown.
Inclusions: c:f:$v_{10\,\mu m}$ = 10:80:10. Sorting is moderate to good.
Fine fraction — much silty material <0.1 mm. Muscovite laths and plagioclase laths are both frequent (also equigranular plagioclase present), and there appears to be much biotite, although grains often too small to identify securely — some may just be orange clay concentrations. Quartz, a-sa, is common, fine red-brown Tcfs are few to common. Very few amphibole, rare to very few clinozoisite and epidote, and rare to very few serpentine. Granitic rock fragments (feldspar and biotite) are rare, and there are also rare foraminifera, poorly preserved and hard to make out at all.
Coarse fraction — contains very little. Common Tcfs, sr-r, <0.06 mm, and quartz, sa-sr, 0.1–0.2 mm. Rare grains of epidote and of plagioclase, barely >0.1 mm. Rare altered igneous rock fragments, 0.1–0.3 mm.
Comment: A non-local fabric that must presumably derive from an igneous environment. The petrography is consistent with a Cypriote source, but a source in northwest Syria cannot be ruled out either. S169 and S171 are very similar, although they are of course not identical. S172 also falls into this group.

Sample S171 (Black-on-Red)
Open shape (bowl?) with ring base (**840**). Thick and thin bands at exterior and interior lower body, and well smoothed. Base and mid-body are pale red, with orange sandwich effect in break. Very fine, only occasional grits visible. S171 contains more micritic inclusions, some chert, and what appear to be plutonic rock fragments composed of quartz or plagioclase, with clinozoisite.

Sample S169 (Black-on-Red)
Fine red fabric, with black-on-red bands. It contains most of the features displayed by S171, but also has rare quartz with granophyric texture, and what appear to be rare volcanic rock fragments.

Sample S172 (Black-on-Red)
Lower to mid-body sherd of an open shape (bowl?), with thin black-on-red bands at interior and exterior, and target motif to exterior (**845**). Fabric is quite red and semi-fine, so coarser than most. Various inclusions visible, black, white and red. S172 has fewer plagioclase laths, but many of the other features mentioned above. There are also more rock fragments in the coarse fraction, composed of quartz and epidote/clinozoisite. Although these fragments show no visible schistosity, L. Joyner has identified them as metamorphic. Granophyric textures in quartz are also observed, as in S169.

Sub-group B 2 (S173)
Red-firing, non-calcareous, optically active. Tcfs, quartz, micritic limestones, altered volcanic and plutonic rock fragments, amphibole, serpentine, chert, and alkali feldspar.

Sample S173 (Black-on-Red)
Microstructure: Few to common vughs (<1.5 mm) and vesicles (<0.2 mm), no preferred orientation.
Groundmass: Composition is homogeneous, distinct optical activity, red-firing matrix (could be non-calcareous). XP = red-orange, PPL = orange-brown.
Inclusions: c:f:$v_{10\,\mu m}$ = 15:70:15 to 20:60:20. Sorting is poor to moderate.
Fine fraction — both mica laths and plagioclase laths are absent, notable when compared to their predominance in Sub-group B 1. Common quartz, few to common orange clay concentrations, micritic inclusions, and red Tcfs.

Coarse fraction — common quartz, mono- and polycrystalline, sa-sr, 0.1–0.6 mm (some of the larger grains contain intergrowths of biotite). Few to common micritic inclusions (limestone?), sr-r, 0.1–0.6 mm. Very few amphibole, sa-sr, 0.1–0.3 mm. Very few clinozoisite, a-sr, 0.1–0.3 mm. Very few chert, sr, 0.2–0.3 mm. Rare granitic rock fragments (quartz and biotite), sr, 0.5 mm. Rare metamorphic(?) rock fragments, composed of clinozoisite/epidote, and quartz, no foliation, <0.4 mm. Rare serpentine, <0.3 mm. Rare plagioclase feldspar, sr, 0.25 mm. Rare basalt, r, 0.2 mm. Some possible relic foraminifera.
Comment: Non-local, but the source is not certain. Cyprus or northwest Syria are the two most likely candidates.

Sub-group B 3 (S174)
Red-firing, with foraminifera, micritic/sparry limestone, Tcfs, quartz, altered volcanic and plutonic rock fragments, serpentine, amphibole, epidote, etc.

Sample S174 (Bichrome **847**)
Microstructure: Very few vughs, no preferred orientation. There appear also to be very few channel voids, but these are entirely infilled with sparite/calcite.
Groundmass: Composition is homogeneous. Optically active. XP = orange-red-brown, PPL = orange-brown.
Inclusions: c:f:$v_{10\,\mu m}$ = 15:78:7. Sorting is poor to moderate.
Fine fraction — common quartz, common micritic and calcitic inclusions, few red-brown Tcfs, few amphibole, very few biotite, rare plagioclase.
Coarse fraction — quartz, granitic rock fragments, chert, micritic limestone, amphibole, foraminifera, Tcfs, serpentine, epidote.
Comment: Non-local, but the source is not certain. Cyprus or northwest Syria are the two most likely candidates.

Sub-group B 4 (S175)
Red-firing, with micritic limestone, foraminifera, serpentine, amphibole, quartz, K-feldspar, plagioclase.

Sample S175 (Bichrome **846**)
Microstructure: Few vughs and vesicles, many with micritic hypocoatings, no preferred orientation.
Groundmass: Composition appears homogeneous in XP, but in PPL there are streaks of red that imply imperfect clay mixing. No optical activity. XP = orange-red-brown, PPL = orange-brown to dark brown.
Inclusions: c:f:$v_{10\,\mu m}$ = 15:75:10. Sorting is moderate.
Fine fraction — only moderately silty, with quartz, serpentine, amphibole, and micritic inclusions all common in the 0.06–0.1 mm range.
Coarse fraction — common to frequent micritic limestone, sa-r, 0.1–0.5 mm, amongst which there are few micritized foraminifera (planktonic), 0.1–0.3 mm. Few to common serpentine, sr-r, 0.1–0.7 mm. Few to common amphibole, a-sa, 0.1–0.6 mm. Few quartz, a-sr, 0.1–0.5 mm. Rare alkali feldspar, sr, <0.5 mm. Rare calcite, sa, <0.5 mm. Rare plagioclase feldspar, sa-a, 0.1–0.2 mm. V. rare basalt, sr, 0.2 mm, and v. rare spinel (one grain), a, 0.3 mm (a rare mineral that tends to be associated with basic and ultrabasic igneous rocks). Also what appear to be altered plutonic rock fragments (but could they be metamorphic?), composed of biotite/amphibole, and quartz (rare, sa-sr, <0.5 mm).
Comment: Notable presence of serpentine and amphibole, but no epidote or clinozoisite. Presence of foraminifera and other micritic inclusions also rather distinctive. Also very little if any mica, and feldspars poorly represented. Non-local, but the source is not certain. Cyprus or NW Syria are the two most likely candidates.

Sub-group B 5 (S176)

High-fired pale buff, very fine, with quartz and Tcfs, plagioclase and granitic rock fragments (note lack of amphibole, serpentine or foraminifera).

Sample S176 (Bichrome)
Microstructure: Very few to few vughs and channel voids, showing some preferred orientation parallel to vessel walls.
Groundmass: Composition is homogeneous, no optical activity. XP = grey-green to brown, PPL = pale grey-green. Appears to have been fired to a high temperature.
Inclusions: $c:f:v_{10\,\mu m}$ = 5:90:5. Sorting is good.
Fine fraction — relatively fine with little silty material in 0.06–0.1 mm range — mostly red-brown Tcfs, angular quartz, orange clay concentrations, and perhaps some biotite. Plagioclase feldspar and micritic inclusions also occur, but are rare.
Coarse fraction — very little present, but quartz (a-sa, <0.6 mm) and red-brown Tcfs (one of which c. 2.0 mm) are common. Few plagioclase, a-sa, 0.1–0.2 mm. Very rare epidote, sa, 0.2 mm. Some possible granitic rock fragments (rare, <0.5 mm).
Comment: None of the amphibole and serpentine that are seen in many of these sub-groups of B. Also note lack of micrite/calcite and foraminifera. This is probably a non-local fabric, perhaps derived from a broadly igneous environment (such as Cyprus or northwest Syria).

Sub-group B 6 (S177–8)

Contains granitic rock fragments, quartz, tcfs, chert, metamorphics, volcanics, epidote, clinozoisite.

Sample S177 (Bichrome bands)
Petrography: Very fine groundmass and fine fraction, so quite different to some of the above sub-groups. Sub-silt micas, amphibole, quartz, Tcfs, epidote, chert, altered igneous rock fragments, and plutonic rock fragments composed partly of K-feldspar. Serpentine barely present.
Microstructure: Few vughs and channel voids, some with micritic hypocoatings. Channel voids show distinct preferred orientation parallel to vessel walls.
Groundmass: Composition is homogeneous, some optical activity, XP = orange-brown, PPL = brown.
Inclusions: $c:f:v_{10\,\mu m}$ = 10:80:10. Sorting is poor to moderate.
Fine fraction — very fine indeed, hardly any inclusions present in 0.06–0.1 mm range. Mostly red-brown Tcfs, some micritic inclusions, and only occasional quartz, amphibole, serpentine and mica laths.
Coarse fraction — common quartz, a-sr, 0.1–1.0 mm. Few to common red-brown Tcfs, sr-r, 0.1–0.6 mm. Few granitic rock fragments, composed of plagioclase or alkali feldspar (or quartz) and biotite, sa, 0.2–0.5 mm. Rare chert, sr, 0.2–0.3 mm. Rare metamorphic rock fragments, composed of epidote/clinozoisite and quartz (but with no schistosity), 0.2–0.5 mm. Rare volcanic rock fragments, sa-sr, 0.2–0.5 mm. Rare epidote, sa, 0.1–0.2 mm, very rare clinozoisite, sa, 0.25 mm.
Comment: Another red-firing non-local fabric, probably deriving from an igneous environment such as northwest Syria or Cyprus. Note the very fine groundmass, and the relative absence of amphibole, serpentine, and foraminifera.

Sub-group B 7 (S179)

Mostly quartz and tcfs, also plagioclase, granitic rock fragments, and rare amphibole, serpentine, K-feldspar, basalt, chert, etc.

Sample S179
Trefoil jug with white painted bands and targets (**851**)
Microstructure: Few vughs, no preferred orientation.
Groundmass: Composition is mostly homogeneous save for one area of the section that appears (in PPL) to have a higher concentration of indistinct Tcfs, perhaps due to imperfect clay mixing. No optical activity. XP = red-brown, PPL = dark brown.
Inclusions: $c:f:v_{10\,\mu m}$ = 10:83:7 to 15:75:10. Sorting is moderate.
Fine fraction — does not contain much material — micritic inclusions and red-brown Tcfs mostly, and relatively little quartz, very few mica laths.
Coarse fraction — frequent quartz, a-sa, 0.1–1.5 mm. Common Tcfs. Few plagioclase, very few to rare granitic rock fragments (plagioclase and biotite), Very rare microcline feldspar, sr, 0.25 mm, micritic limestone, foraminifera (v. rare), alkali feldspar, amphibole (rare), serpentine (rare), epidote (v. rare), spinel (v. rare), basalt (rare), chert (rare).
Comment: Again, either Cyprus or northwest Syria would seem to be the most likely source.

Sub-group B 8 (S180)

Sample S180 (Bichrome)
Microstructure: Very few, mostly small vughs and vesicles, many with micritic hypocoatings, no preferred orientation.
Groundmass: Composition is homogeneous, some slight optical activity. XP and PPL = orange-brown.
Inclusions: $c:f:v_{10\,\mu m}$ = 15:80:5. Sorting is moderate.
Fine fraction — common biotite, serpentine, quartz, and micritic inclusions, few red-brown Tcfs, very few plagioclase and amphibole, and rare to very few epidote, and muscovite laths.
Coarse fraction — common to frequent micritic siltstone, sr-r, 0.25–2.5 mm (by far the largest inclusions in this section). Few to common quartz, a-sr, 0.1–0.5 mm. Few micritic limestone, sr-r, 0.1–1.0 mm, some of the smaller ones possible relic foraminifera. Very few serpentine, r, 0.1–0.3 mm. Very few granitic rock fragments, composed of quartz or plagioclase, and biotite or amphibole, a-sa, 0.1–0.4 mm. Rare chert, sr, 0.2–0.4 mm. Rare plagioclase, sr, 0.1 mm. Very rare sheared quartz, sr, 0.5 mm, and very rare basalt, r, 0.2 mm.
Comment: This sample is set apart by the distinctive large micritic siltstones, presumably added as temper. Yet there is the same range of minerals and rock fragments present as in the other samples of this broad group, notably igneous rock fragments, minerals such as amphibole, serpentine and epidote, and micritic inclusions, some of which appear to be foraminifera. Therefore, in line with the rest of the group, a source in northwest Syria or Cyprus seems probable.

GROUP C (S181)

Red-firing, micaceous, non-calcareous, mostly schist, quartz too.

Sample S181
Black-on-Red. Upper body sherd of a closed shape (a jug? **836**) with thickish walls. Burnish to exterior and three black-on-red bands. Interior is plain and untreated. Very red (brick red), semi-fine, with white grits that look like quartz and carbonates, and black grits.
Microstructure: Few vughs and rare channel voids, no preferred orientation.
Groundmass: Composition is homogeneous, with a high level of optical activity, red-firing, micaceous, and perhaps non-calcareous. XP = orange-red, PPL = red-brown.
Inclusions: $c:f:v_{10\,\mu m}$ = 10:80:10, sorting is moderate.
Fine fraction — rather silty, with mica laths and mono- and polycrystalline quartz (a-sa) common to frequent in 0.06–0.1 mm range. Small red Tcfs are few to common.
Coarse fraction — frequent quartz-mica schist, and mica schist, sa-sr (and not elongate like most phyllites in other sections), 0.1–1.25 mm.

Common quartz, mono- and polycrystalline, the latter tending to have sutured boundaries and undulose extinction (indicating metamorphism), a-sr, 0.1–0.5 mm. Few to common red-brown Tcfs, some rather silty, sr-r, 0.1–0.9 mm. Very rare plagioclase, sa-a, 0.1–0.2 mm.

Comment: Totally different to the rest of the Black-on-Red samples in that it must derive from a metamorphic environment. Other than this the actual area of origin is uncertain. Another ware group with much metamorphic material is the Late Bronze Age Red Lustrous Wheel-made ware (LBA Fabric Group A). However, in the LBA group the inclusions are mostly phyllite and not quartz-mica schist, and there are also common limestone inclusions, which do not feature in the current sample.

GROUP D (S182)
Red-firing, non-calcareous, mostly quartz (*c.* 0.1 mm), some Tcfs, occasional sandstone (cf. IIa–d, Group B).

Sample S182
White Painted, lines and target motifs.
Microstructure: Few vughs, varying in size from 0.1–1.0 mm, no preferred orientation.
Groundmass: Composition is not homogeneous — some dark red streaks are suggestive of the imperfect mixing of clays. Moreover, all along one side of the section there is a broad band that is much more micritic than the rest of the section (relating to firing conditions?). No optical activity. XP = dark red to brown, PPL = dark brown, some areas more red.
Inclusions: c:f:$v_{10\,\mu m}$ = 10:80:10 or 15:75:10, difficult to assess due to siltiness. Sorting is moderate to good.
Fine fraction — is very silty with frequent quartz and common mica laths, some micrite (especially at edges of section), and deep red-brown Tcfs.
Coarse fraction — dominant quartz, mostly mono- but also polycrystalline, and some having undulose extinction, a-sr, 0.1–1.0 mm. Very few red-brown Tcfs, sr-r, 0.1–0.8 mm, some contain occasional quartz grains, making them more silty than most Tcfs in other sections. Rare plagioclase, sa, <0.3 mm. Very rare quartz sandstone (1 grain), sr, 0.7 mm.
Comment: Rather similar to a common fabric from the LB/early Iron Age phases IIa–d, known as Group B. Dominated by angular to subangular quartz, and is quite silty — most of the quartz is *c.* 0.1 mm. Also present are some deep red-brown Tcfs, and occasional sandstone. As with Group B from phases IIa–d, a non-local source is suspected, but there is very little material that is petrologically distinctive.

Chapter 23

The Early Bronze Age Pottery

Dorit Symington

Introduction

The EBA pottery presented here comes from a sounding located in quadrants H20c and H20d on the northwestern edge of the mound.

Work began in H20c, an area greatly disturbed by a robber trench, cut into the slope of the tepe at the height of Level IV (MBA). After the removal of the modern fill created by the robber tunnel, well-stratified layers were reached and subsequently excavated down to bedrock at some 13 m from the summit (phases Vf–l). In addition, in Level Ve–Vh, the sounding was extended to the east into H20d — below the MBA levels excavated in the first season — and a 1.50-m-wide strip between the robber cut and the excavated rooms of H20d provided more stratified EBA and MBA pottery (Figs. 367–86).

Although the ceramic material from the Deep Sounding was abundant and varied, it need hardly be stressed that it is unlikely to represent the full spectrum of the sequence given the relatively restricted area excavated and limited sampling. Several of the pottery classes are only known from sherd material and their shapes could not be retrieved.

Furthermore much of the pottery was retrieved from the modern backfill in the robber trench area of the Deep Sounding. This of course makes attribution to a specific occupation phase frequently uncertain, but the redeposited material in question includes some noteworthy ceramics (such as all the lids and fluted jars) and occasional sherds which could be joined with stratified material.

The other major disadvantage in assessing this material lies in the fact that the Göksu valley is still archaeologically *terra incognita*, except for the surveys carried out in this region by Mellaart (1954, 175ff.; 1958a, 311ff.; 1963, 199ff.) and D. French (1965, 179ff.) in the 1950s and 1960s. Therefore correlations rely mainly on sites of neighbouring regions — which may not always be strictly contemporary — such as Tarsus and Mersin in Cilicia and Beycesultan, Kusura, Aphrodisias and Karataş Semayük in southwest Anatolia.

Cultural relations with sites in the Konya plain to the north in the EBA period are still largely unknown since we lack a complete ceramic sequence in that region. EBA levels were reached at Karahöyük Konya but the final publication of the results is still outstanding.

The role of the Göksu valley as an important thoroughfare from the Mediterranean coast to the Anatolian plateau has been frequently stressed and there is some evidence at Kilise Tepe for maritime connections with Cyprus in the Early Bronze Age in the form of an imported Red Polished III vessel (see below).

As already noted in the survey reports, ceramic affinities are probably strongest with Cilicia, although Kilise Tepe — as far as the evidence goes — appears to have missed out on pottery with Syrian affinities in EBA/MBA, prominent at Tarsus and also found as imports at Kültepe (Mellink 1989, 319ff.). As a general observation, contacts with Cilicia are more pronounced in the earlier EBA phases, while pottery of the later EBA period (EB III) seems primarily of West Anatolian inspiration.

The dating of the lowest occupation levels, Level Vl–k, which were sealed by layers of an earthen fill before the construction of Vj, is inconclusive from the ceramic point of view but they may well represent an earlier cultural phase. Above this the EBA deposits in the Deep Sounding fall basically into two major ceramic horizons, clearly distinguishable by different wares and techniques. Phases Vj–g, consisting of six phases and sub-phases, represent the early EBA layers within the sequence for which correlations can be made with pottery types attributed to EB I/II at other sites. The later EBA layers, Level Vf with four sub-phases and Ve divided into three sub-phases, are assigned to EB III and the transition to the Middle Bronze Age.

The following text is by no means an exhaustive study of the Deep Sounding material and does not attempt more than to give a summary account of the EBA ceramic repertoire, leaving ample scope for further analyses and research at a future date.

Chapter 23

The fabrics of Levels V and IV

For the typological study of the pottery the fabrics from Level V (EB) and Level IV (MB) were assigned to groups. These fabric groups, some of which are used in the catalogue entries below, are listed here. Naturally they do not coincide with the petrological classification, which was established later on differing criteria.

Fabric A
Hard orange fabric — grit-tempered with occasionally larger inclusions. In addition most sherds have a small amount of organic temper leaving some voids, particularly on the surface, which are mainly burnt out as circular voids. A variant is a more beige- or buff-coloured fabric with the same temper. Clay is generally well levigated, particularly in the finer pieces.
Firing: medium to medium-high, frequently quite clinky.
This provides the standard fabric for red-slipped ware, brown-coated ware, plain ware, cream-slipped/washed ware and red-cross bowls. It constitutes the most common fabric among the medium and finer wares in the EBA III period (Level Vf–e) and continues to a degree into MBA (Level IVa).

Fabric B
Medium to coarse beige fabric with chocolate-coloured medium size grits (mudstones) and some organic temper which leaves small voids on the surface.
Firing: medium-high.
This fabric features mainly in the brown-coated ware and some medium-sized storage vessels.

Fabric C1
Medium-coarse to coarse hard orange fabric, related to Fabric A but with larger grit inclusions and a small amount of organic temper leaving surface voids. The amount of grit used varies according to vessel size. This fabric occurs occasionally with incised or rilling decoration as well as with a cream wash. Mainly hand-made.
Firing: medium-high.

Fabric C2
Medium-coarse and coarse orange porous fabric with grit and sand temper and a high percentage of organic temper leaving numerous voids, especially on the surface, producing a honeycomb effect. Mainly hand-made.
Firing: medium to medium-high.

Fabric D
The most common fabric for medium and fine wares of EB I/II pottery (Level Vj–g). Generally a soft paste. Colour varies from beige to buff to brown to light grey. Very little temper in finer vessels, dark grits in thicker walled pots. Grey cores are not uncommon in the medium wares. Fabric D is most commonly used in red, black and brown burnished wares. Hand-made.
Firing: low to medium-low.

Fabric E
A relatively fine grit-tempered fabric. Sherds are thin-walled with large grey centre leaving only a thin layer of the original orange fabric on either side. Hand-made.
Firing: very high under very reduced conditions and in many cases overfired, causing distortion of the pottery sherds. Very clean breaks and clinky.
This fabric occurs in 'Metallic Ware', plain or painted. See below on the wares in Vj–g.

Fabric F
Medium to medium-fine red heavily grit-tempered fabric, occasionally with grey cores. Surface mainly left plain, occasionally burnished.
Firing: high.
For this fabric, see under phase Vh on the hemispherical bowl **245**. A coarser version of Fabric F is found in 'scored ware'.

Fabric G
Coarse red/brown/black heavily grit- and stone-tempered fabric, occasionally with added crushed shell(?). Surface generally smoothed, scraped or roughened.
Firing: low.
Fabric G is the standard fabric for cooking pots throughout EBA and a related fabric features in MBA 'combed ware'.

Fabric H
The standard fabric for MBA fine and semi-fine pottery is buff coloured with calcareous inclusions often barely visible, described as 'light clay ware' at Tarsus (see p. 321 on Medium and Fine Wares). The vessels are mainly thin-walled and surfaces are generally left plain except for a red wash around the rim area. This fabric is found mainly in the manufacture of cups and small bowls. Bases are frequently string-cut.
Firing: medium.

Fabric I
Medium-fine buff/light brown dense fabric related to H, tempered with a moderate amount of grits. It occurs in thick-walled fragments of closed vessels (jugs) with a thick red slip and medium burnish.
Firing: medium, evenly fired.

Fabric J
Medium-fine to medium beige fabric with multi-coloured grit (2–5 mm) and some organic temper. Some coarser vessels contain also large white stones (**555**) and chalk(?) inclusions visible on the surface (**549, 559**). Fabric J is mainly found in relatively thin-walled storage jugs and jars of Level IVb.

Level Vl–k (193–5)

The earliest pottery find at Kilise Tepe was a large globular jar (**193**) with flared rim, resting in a shallow pit (P97/30) on bedrock (Level Vl, Fig. 73, p. 89). It was almost complete except for the base part and was made of a semi-coarse fabric, covered in a light brown slip and horizontal burnish. This vessel was accompanied by a few coarse body sherds made of a fabric which contained mica, rarely encountered at Kilise Tepe.

The pottery recovered from Level Vk was sparse and consisted entirely of coarse wares, most of which belonged to cooking pots. A fragment of a hole-mouth jar had a handle attachment and finger-impressed plastic decoration (**195**). Other rim sherds of this ware came from the earthen fill below Vj (5427, 1882–3) which also contained some pottery familiar from Vj, such as red painted wares. Whether phases Vl–k are of EBA date or earlier cannot be resolved by the pottery evidence and the dating of these layers remains open.

193   H20/676   1894
Globular jar with flared rim. Semi-coarse, brown fabric with grit and organic temper. Surface light brown slip. Low horizontal burnishing marks. Reddish wash over rim part. Burnt in places. Hand-made.
Rim di. 11.6; H. (24)
Petrographic sample S10.

194   1892
Cooking pot with flared rim. Fabric G, grey core and chaff faced. Traces of limey wash. Hand-made.
Di. 13; Th. 0.7

195   1892
Rim of cooking pot with plastic decoration. Fabric G, brown. Hand-made.
Di. 18; Th. 0.5

Early EBA pottery — Level Vj–g

Wares[1]

The early EBA phases of Level Vj–g share a number of ceramic links in terms of fabrics and shapes but at the same time reveal a degree of divergence due to development and new introductions. All the pottery recovered from these levels is entirely hand-made.

The most common fabric for medium and fine wares is a soft paste, beige, brown or light grey in colour, and grit-tempered (Fabric D), but the petrographic analysis suggests a much greater variety of fabrics (see Knappett, p. 249). Most characteristic of this ceramic material is a variety of burnished wares. Red burnished pottery appears in all the layers and is overall the dominant type, followed by black burnished wares — particularly prominent in phases Vi–h — while only few examples of the brown burnished category came to light. Slips are thickly applied and burnished to a medium to very high lustre finish. Occasionally a scatter burnish is applied, giving the surface a streaky appearance and a bichrome appearance is created by treating the interior with a darker or lighter shade of red or brown than the exterior. A mottling effect of the burnished surface was also encountered. On the whole this material was very fragmented and apart from a variety of bowls, particularly numerous in phase Vh, few complete shapes could be retrieved.

A number of coarse and medium wares could be traced throughout the early EBA phases indicating that they were in use over a long period, an observation also made in other regions where these pottery types occurred.

Among the coarser wares we noted a pottery type which belongs to the category of 'scored ware' (Fabric F). It occurs at Kilise Tepe deeply scored, or with shallow striation marks going in various directions, and is made in a heavily grit-tempered fabric. Some examples have a red, brown or whitish wash applied after scoring. It was recorded in small quantities in all the early EBA phases but no longer encountered in EB III layers (Fig. 219). The sherd material belongs to fairly large closed vessels but no profiles were obtained.

This type of pottery is described at Troy among the Aegean wares where it was found in Middle and Late Troy I and Troy II a–d (Blegen *et al.* 1950, 53f., figs. 252, 409–10). Scored ware has also a wide distribution on the Konya plain according to Mellaart's survey (Mellaart 1963, 224f., fig. 7) and is known from stratified contexts at Karahöyük Konya in levels XXII–XII — where it occurs in the form of jars — dating it approximately to late EB I and into EB II (Mellink 1965, 136f.; 1967, 161). It was also reported from Tarsus with a similar timespan (Goldman 1956, 97, 109). The chronological aspects of 'scored ware' were discussed in some detail by Yakar (1985, 214ff.).

As suggested by Mellaart, the textured surface finish of scored ware was achieved by brush while the clay was still wet. The shapes that he encountered on the Konya plain survey included not only jars but also large bowls (Mellaart 1963, 224, fig. 13:1–18).

Another pottery class which persisted throughout and is reported from other regions, seems to correspond to the description of so-called 'metallic' ware (Fabric E). The examples found at Kilise Tepe show it to be a relatively fine, white grit-tempered, thin-walled

Figure 219. *Sample 'scored ware' and other sherds with striations.*

Figure 220. *Sample metallic ware sherds.*

Figure 221. *Sample sherds of metallic ware with painted bands.*

and highly fired pottery (Fig. 220). It is clinky with clean breaks. Some of the sherds are severely distorted due to overfiring, and pitting on the surface is evident on some pieces. Apart from the plain 'metallic' ware fragments, it also occurred with irregular wide bands of white matt paint (Fig. 221). This ware was recorded in small quantities in all the early EBA phases, but particularly well represented in phase Vh. None of the material belonging to this pottery group provides information on shapes, except that, once again, most sherds appeared to come from fairly large closed vessels. Metallic ware was not common at Kilise Tepe and is probably not of local manufacture, according to the findings of the petrographic analysis by Knappett (Fabric Group T, sample S39, p. 252).

'Metallic' ware was discussed by Mellaart at some length after finding it on his surveys in considerable quantities on a large number of sites in the Konya plain and Göksu valley (Mellaart 1963, 228f., figs. 6, 14–17). Since then this pottery class has been excavated in stratified contexts at Karahöyük Konya and at Acemhöyük where a date of late EB II and early EB III is indicated (Özten 1989, 409f.). Most characteristic is the red-painted type — of which only one sherd was found at Kilise Tepe, from unit 1836 (Level Vg/h) — in the form of beak-spouted jugs and collar-necked jars also known from Tarsus and Mersin as imports in EB II context (Goldman 1956, fig. 247; Garstang 1953, fig. 122).

The category of 'red gritty ware' from Tarsus of EB I and EB II was taken by Mellaart to represent the same group as 'metallic' ware from the Konya region but D. French in his survey report of the Göksu valley distinguishes between 'Cilician E.B. Metallic or Red gritty ware' and 'Konya Plain E.B. 2 Metallic ware' pointing out the uncertainty that the two wares are completely identical (D. French 1965, 183f.), a view shared by Mellink who refers to it as 'a relative of Tarsus red gritty ware' (Mellink 1989, 322). French also classifies the white-painted 'metallic' ware as 'Cilician' with the comment that it is widely found in the Adana region (D. French 1965, 184). However, matt white-painted specimens were also found by Mellaart in the Konya plain (Mellaart 1963, 228, fig. 16:5, 8–11), leaving the question of the origin of the Kilise Tepe examples open.

Cooking pots and platters also proved rather consistent in the early EBA sequence. They occur in brown or red grit- and stone-tempered fabrics

(Fabric G), occasionally with a wash over the exterior and handles. The most common shapes are jars with handles from rim to shoulder, hole-mouth jars and pots with flared rims. Most characteristic are cooking pots with a roughened outer surface below the rim area, giving the exterior a textured appearance. Some of the pieces were extremely thin-walled. They occurred in the same shapes as mentioned above (**272, 274–5, 277**) but not on pots with flared rims. Cooking pots occasionally have pot-marks (**271–2**), probably noting quantities.

A very common type amongst the cooking wares are 'vegetable impressed' cooking platters which were present in most pottery units. The medium coarse fabric has a grit and stone temper with some organic inclusions and is fired at a low temperature. The top side is covered with a cream coating and burnished, while the underside shows vegetable impressions, possibly from straw matting. Because of its thinness (1.5–2 cm) and low firing this ware is very friable. The size and exact shape of these platters is undetermined but they were either round or oval. Mellaart comments that this 'straw mat impressed' ware was found at nearly every site in the Konya plain (Mellaart 1954, 196), and a very similar ware is also described by Blegen at Troy (Blegen *et al.* 1950, 56) where it was manufactured over a long period.

The other type of thin flat pottery found in Vj–g is a red-burnished or plain platter in a buff or light brown fabric, often with grey cores. The burnished variety is slipped on both sides or the underside only. Rims vary from raised (**282**) to sloping (**283**) to grooved (**284**). Some of the pieces have grain-size excisions on the edge of the rim or depressions (**285–6**) and a decorative example from Vj comes with a scalloped finger-impressed edge and excised lunate pattern (**280**; cf. Goldman 1956, fig. 281:671–5). This group was probably used as serving platters and indeed some of these specimens may also have served as lids, although there are no signs of handle attachments on the surviving fragments.

Level Vj (196–217, 270–73, 280–81)

The pottery repertoire uncovered in Vj proved the most varied and contextually most valuable in the entire EBA sequence of the Deep Sounding and for this reason for the most part is treated jointly here. It also contained pottery types no longer encountered in succeeding layers.

The clutch of whole and restorable pots from the destruction floors of several rooms was rich in ceramic types and shapes and presented a welcome opportunity to study an assemblage of vessels in contemporary use. They belong mainly to the category of kitchen wares but also included some finer pieces. The intense heat of the conflagration which destroyed the building had also affected the consistency and colour of some of the pottery rendering it brittle and a shade of light orange.

Most of the pots were recovered from Rm 82 and Rm 83 and fewer from Rm 81 (Fig. 476). There is no apparent pattern in the distribution of vessel types to suggest that individual rooms fulfilled different functions, although the activities in Rm 82 were probably more varied and specialized. This room contained the base of a large storage vessel (H20/743), in which rested a painted jug (**196**). A cup and another jug were found nearby and three more jugs in Rm 81 to the north. The assemblage also included most of a small oval shaped basin with lug handle(s) and a plug hole at the narrow end (**216**).

An indication of the preparation of red dye or paint is suggested by the remains of a decorated jug (**198**) containing the remains of a red substance (H20/817) for which two red clay artefacts (H20/726) found in the same room, may have been the source. (These have not been analysed. They are described as having two flattened surfaces with rounded sides, with the greatest dimension around 15 cm.) Whether the red pigment(?) was used for dyeing fibres or painting pots (and whether the basin played a role in this activity) remains speculative. The other finds certainly indicate textile production in Rm 82 and neighbouring rooms (see below).

Jugs — Level Vj (196–203)

The most numerous amongst the whole pots were globular jugs with flared rims and handles from neck or rim to shoulder (Figs. 222 & 223). Except for two instances, all were decorated with reddish-brown paint on a light background with diagonally intersecting bands covering most of the vessel or with chevrons painted on the shoulder above a single horizontal band. An example of a more carelessly treated jug is **199** with irregularly painted vertical and horizontal bands. All the examples have an additional band where the neck meets the shoulder. They were made in a semi-coarse grit-tempered fabric and the surface was either smoothed or had received a wash before being painted. The neck is always made separately before being attached to the body. Apart from outcurving rims they also occurred with trefoils and one of the plain jugs (with strap handle) seems to have had a rising spout (**201**).

Figure 222. *Early Bronze Age ceramic assemblage from Level Vj destruction. From left, front row: 217, 204, 199, 207; middle row: 216, 197, 200, 196; back row 198, 201.*

Figure 223. *Selected vessels from Level Vj destruction. Jugs from back left 199, 196; 197; cup 204, hole-mouth jar 217.*

196   H20/725   KLT 89   5406
Hemispherical jug. Light orange with fine white grits. Pinkish wash and red brown paint. Three sets of diagonal bands crossing at apex and single bands around neck, handle and rim. Hand-made.
Rim di. 7; H. 20
Figs. 222 & 223

197   H20/735   KLT 90   5406
Painted juglet. Light orange grit-tempered. Thin walled. Smoothed and painted with diagonal bands on neck and upper body. Hand-made.
Rim di. 6.6; H. 14.5
Figs. 222 & 223

198   H20/816   5406
Painted globular jug with flared rim. Light orange, medium fine with dark grits and white (chalk?) inclusions. Painted with interlaced diagonal red bands on neck and shoulder. Hand-made.
Rim di. 7.5; H. 22.5
Figs. 222 & 223

199   H20/737   KLT 91   5406
Globular jug with flared rim and uneven base. Orange grit temper. Painted with red uneven horizontal and vertical bands running from rim to shoulder. Hand-made.
Rim di. 6.5; H. 16
Fig. 222

200   H20/744   5406
Ovoid jug with uncertain rim shape. Semi-coarse, red brown, grit temper. Covered in creamy wash(?), low burnish in parts. Hand-made.
H. 17
Fig. 222

201   H20/736   5406
Hemispherical jug with strap handle and rising(?) spout. Red very gritty fabric. Remains of burnished areas. Hand-made.
Rim di. c. 5.5; H. 20
Fig. 222

202   H20/614   1871
Piriform painted jug. Semi-coarse, grey with grit and calcareous temper. Striation marks over body. Black painted triple groups of chevrons on shoulder. Hand-made.
Rim di. 4+; H. 18.3+

203   1858
Neck of jug with stopper. Brown fabric, tempered with small black grits. Exterior smoothed, fugitive red paint, including handle. Plug-through handle. Found with foot of a 'champagne' cup placed upside down as a stopper. The latter was found to be a join with 204. Hand-made.
Rim di. 4.6

Cups — Level Vj (204–9)

In the category of fine wares, not as well preserved, we noted foremost a high-stemmed cup (*kylix*) as part of the assemblage in Rms 82–3 in phase Vj. Fragments from this shape were still found in Vi but no longer in Vh. These elegant vessels are made with great skill and care in a fine dense beige fabric, covered in a red, cognac brown or black slip and burnished to a high lustre. Whether these delicate 'champagne' cups served as everyday drinking vessels or were reserved for special liquids can of course not be answered but the only other drinking vessel in this group is a cup with horizontal angular strap handle made in a plain beige fabric (**207**).

Little remained of the burnish on the wine cups from Rm 82 (**204**: Figs. 222 & 223; **206**) which were caught up in the conflagration but a better-preserved example came from Rm 83 (**205**) in which the excavators also unearthed the fragment of a painted jug with an inverted pedestal foot (from a *kylix*) placed inside the neck, functioning here as a form of stopper (**203**).

Although no drinking vessels of the above-described champagne cup type in the EB period are known to us from other sites, there may be a generic connection with the high-stemmed bowls — also referred to as fruit-stands — encountered in NW and Central Anatolia in the Chalcolithic and early EB periods. Burnished pedestalled bowls with low or high stems were particularly frequent and well preserved at Poliochni (Lemnos) in the Blue Phase (EB I) and present close parallels in their proportions, but because of their large shape they are unlikely to be drinking vessels, although they are referred to by the excavator as a *coppa* (Bernabò-Brea 1964, 67, 553f., Tav. IX:a, XXII:a–d). Fruit-stands are also known from Alaca Höyük (Koşay & Akok 1966, pl. 60: j 208, l 112, k 160) and Alişar, attributed to the Chalcolithic period (von der Osten 1937, 67–71, fig. 75). In all the above-quoted examples the vessels were manufactured with hollow stems as opposed to the Kilise Tepe ones which have solid pedestals.

204   H20/734   5406+1858
'Champagne' cup with tan slip and burnish over all. Yellow-brown with dark grits. Cup part has lost most of surface treatment. Pedestal foot retained burnish and was found as stopper in **203**. Hand-made.
Di. 10.5; H. 9.5
Figs. 222 & 223

205   H20/567   1859
Creamy-brown fabric, vegetable tempered, burnt to dark grey/black. Tan slip inside and out. Foot from same unit but no physical join. Hand-made.
Di. 10.5

206   H20/980   5406
'Champagne' cup minus stem. Fine orange with some grits. Both sides red brown slip, partially flaked, low burnish. Hand-made.
Di. 9.9

207   5406
Cup with horizontal strap handle. Light orange fabric. Smoothed, plain. Hand-made.
Di. 7
Fig. 222

208   1871
Small cup with handle attachment. Light brown slip over all, flaked. Hand-made.
Di. c. 7

209   1864
Miniature cup with small pedestal base. Medium, beige, plain. Crudely made, visible finger impressions. Rim uneven.
Di. c. 3

Bowls — Level Vj (210–17)

Part of the same assemblage from the Vj occupation debris is a group of bowls of two basic shapes: hemispherical bowls, some quite thin-walled made in a fine brown fabric, and a fairly deep flat-based type with outward sloping sides. The bowls occurred either plain or burnished but the same shapes were also found with painted or incised decoration. Fragments of at least three bowls of the latter shape were excavated in Rms 81–2 (Fig. 476). They were covered in a red or light brown slip (both sides) and decorated with horizontal and diagonal excised bands (**211–12**) and in one case with inverted intersecting chevrons (**210**), and then filled with a white substance.

The motif of interlaced chevrons recurs in a painted version on a hemispherical bowl with a thick red slip and high burnish. The design is found on both sides of the rim executed in white matt paint (**213**).

Apart from the above bowl from Vj only a few further, intrusive, sherds of this white-painted ware were recorded at Kilise Tepe including two examples from previous surveys (**220**, **224**: Fig. 224; Mellaart 1963, fig. 4: 26; D. French 1965, 185, fig. 8:11). They are all painted on a red background after burnishing

Figure 224. *White painted sherds, including* **224** *(top left) and* **220** *(bottom centre).*

and the paint on most examples adhered well to the body fabric.

There is a long tradition of white-painted pottery, mainly on black background, in Anatolia and neighbouring regions associated with the Late Chalcolithic/EB I/EB II periods (Mellaart 1954, 194ff., 202ff., Map 4). It appeared at Mersin intrusively in Level XIIA with mainly curvilinear patterns, and some unparalleled shapes probably in early EB I context (Garstang 1953, 182ff., fig. 118) and in Kusura in Period B, here decorated with intersecting chevrons (Lamb 1937, 14, fig. 6:12, 13). At Aphrodisias white-painted pottery is characteristic of the Late Chalcolithic period and then reappears in Aphrodisias Bronze Age 2 (Joukowsky 1986, 310), and there is also an EB II white-painted tradition at Karataş Semayük Level V, of jugs decorated with exuberant flowing patterns (Mellink 1966, pl. 58, figs. 11–14).

Seeher has made an exhaustive study of white-painted pottery, also found in some quantities at Demircihüyük (Ware H) mainly in early EBA context, and not intrusive as originally thought (Seeher 1987, 65). This distinctive pottery class is also discussed, and the various descriptions of it from previous publications conveniently summarized, by Thissen in a comparative study of Balkan and Anatolian pottery in the Late Chalcolithic (Thissen 1993, 222ff.).

At Kilise Tepe black white-painted ware was not recorded and our red-painted examples with their criss-cross patterns arranged in pendent triangles and interlaced double chevrons have their closest stylistic parallels with the survey material from the Konya plain, where red burnished examples are common. Mellaart's suggestion that this ware was traded down the Göksu valley (it was also found at Silifke Kale) seems a valid theory. However, his classification of the Konya plain survey material as Late Chalcolithic will need confirmation from a stratified context in that region (Mellaart 1963, 201ff., fig. 4).

210 5406
Decorated bowl fragments. Yellowish fabric, medium with dark grits. Light brown slip and burnish. White-filled incised patterns of horizontal bands and intersecting chevrons. Cf. **211–12**. Hand-made.
Di. 22; Base di. 13

211 H20/738 5406
Bowl with flared sides. Light orange, medium-fine, dark grits. Red slip and burnish, medium lustre. Incised and white-filled decoration. Hand-made.
Di. 22; Base di. 12

212 5406
Flared sided bowl rim sherd. Same as **210–11**. Tan slip. Hand-made.
Di. 22

213 5424
Hemispherical bowl. Fabric D, beige, covered in thick red slip and burnished. Rim area decorated with white matt paint on interior and exterior. Hand-made.
Di. 16

214 5406
Bowl with flat base. Light orange, medium-fine, powdery. Red slip and burnished, partially flaked. Hand-made.
Di. 26

215 1859
Base. Flaky beige fabric with tan slip and burnish over all. Hand-made.
Base di. 5

216 H20/829 5406
Oval basin with plug hole and handle(s). Coarse orange-brown fabric, grit and stone temper. Surface smoothed. Channel leads towards plug hole. Hand-made.
H. 10
Fig. 222

217 H20/720 5406
Small hole-mouth jar. Yellow-brown fabric, grit-tempered. Very low fired. Surface layer crackled, plain. Hand-made.
Base di. 7.5; H. 4.5
Figs. 222 & 223

Level Vi
The archaeological context of the two sub-phases of Vi is poor and only a few rather scrappy architectural features were located.

Noteworthy for the earlier phase is a large pithos (**273**) sunk into the destruction material of Vj, associated with a floor area in the NE corner of H20c (Fig. 477, H20/544). It has an exceptionally elongated base but is overall not dissimilar to examples found at Tarsus and Mersin (Goldman 1956, fig. 352:285, 287; Garstang 1953, fig. 126:12).

An innovation in phase Vi are handles pegged through the body of the vessels in a variety of fabrics, a technique which continues to the end of the early EBA sequence at Kilise Tepe (**233–4**). At Tarsus this technique first appears in EB I and becomes prominent in EB II (Mellink 1989, 320f., pl. 58:3a–b).

Black burnished ware was prominent in Vi, particularly in the later phase, which included a trefoil jug (**264**), a number of handles with incised, punctate (**231**, **238**) or white-filled decoration (**230**: cf. Goldman 1956, fig. 253:249, 252), as well as fragments of a large closed vessel with pattern burnish which could be associated with one of the above handles from the same unit. The steep-sided beaker with a flat base encountered mostly in the succeeding phase Vh is represented here by a black burnished version (**242**).

A single example of a black-topped cup recovered from a floor of the late phase of Vi, and identified for us by Geoff Summers, deserves a mention.

This pottery type has a wide distribution in central and western Anatolia in the mid-third millennium (Brown 1967, 133, figs. 12–13) as well as in Cyprus (Morris 1985, 22, pl. 13c) and this particular surface treatment appears to be another method of creating a bichrome effect on vessels. Our example is a thin-walled hemispherical cup with greyish-brown slip but black in the rim area and with a darker interior with a very glossy burnish (**218**). It can most probably be regarded as an import.

Black-topped cups were reported more recently from Demircihüyük where they are considered typical of the region (Efe 1988, 7, 25, Taf. IX). They occurred in the early and later Early Bronze Age layers, indicating a relatively long time span for this decoration technique in the Demircihüyük and Eskişehir region. (For a detailed discussion on the manufacture of black-topped cups see Seeher 1987, 109.)

Level Vh
The architectural remains of Level Vh were considerably better preserved than in Vi and it too had an early and late phase. Several rooms and their floors were located in H20c and H20d (Figs. 479–80), though disturbed in the latter quadrant by a number of EB III pits.

A few whole vessels were recovered from occupation floors of the early phase: a crudely made, hemispherical bowl (**221**) came from Rm 73 and a plain juglet with rising spout (**268**) accompanied by a clay spit-support (**1627**) was recovered from Rm 70.

The early Vh phase also contained a large repertoire of bowls. They can be grouped into red and black burnished, with only a few examples of brown burnished ones, but no complete profiles could be obtained. The burnished bowls occur mainly with simple or slightly tapered rims and sloping or upright sides, suggesting shallow as well as some very deep bowls. They are consistently made of the same fabric (Fabric D), covered in a thick slip and burnished to a medium or high lustre.

Bowls with horizontal handle(s) (**246**) are an innovation and so are bowls in a red gritty fabric, not previously noted. They appear as thin-walled hemispherical bowls with simple rims. The fabric is red, medium fine with grit and sand, well fired with clean breaks. It is, however, quite distinct from the 'metallic' ware (Fabric E) discussed above. A typical example is **245**, a hemispherical bowl with disproportionately small vertical handle(s) from rim to body which are decorative rather than functional (cf. Goldman 1956, 250: 210). Whether there is a connection between the 'red gritty ware' of Tarsus and the Kilise Tepe material remains to be investigated.

However, a clear link with Tarsus is provided by an almost complete jar of uncommon shape with a rising and pierced tab handle found in the packing below Rm 61 of Level Vg (**265**). Unlike the Tarsus example which is only red slipped (Goldman 1956, fig. 260: 345–8, EB II), the Kilise Tepe vessel is decorated with incised triangles and punctured dots, executed before the slip was applied. Other incised, red burnished pottery with diagonally arranged incised patterns (**226**) decorating jugs are also typical of Tarsus EB II (Goldman 1956, fig. 262: 364, 366).

Level Vg
Level Vg represents the last phase of the early EBA levels at Kilise Tepe and although it revealed several architectural features (Fig. 481), it was not very informative from the ceramic point of view. This is partly because Vg suffered a major conflagration, which destroyed the entire building, baking its walls and floors hard. The absence of objects and scarcity of pottery suggest that the occupants cleared and then abandoned the settlement before the catastrophic event.

All the pottery recovered from Vg was still found to be entirely hand-made, and although limited, it still features some of the standard coarse wares, like scored ware and the cooking pots with the outer roughened surface, as discussed above. Other familiar characteristics are plug-through handles, red and black burnished wares and the thin-walled gritty pottery first recorded in Vh.

The destruction debris of Rm 64 contained a number of bowls with profiles appearing for the first time, among them a pattern-burnished bell-shaped type with tapered rim and rounded bottom (**266**) and a shallow red burnished bowl with interior thickened rim (**258**). Bowls with incised and white-filled decoration applied to the exterior (**259**) and interior (**260**) were found in Rms 62 and 63, respectively. Both examples are thickly slipped and burnished.

*Bowls and cups — Level Vi–h (**218–23**)*

218 1853
Level Vi
Black-topped cup or bowl. Thin-walled, fine fabric, light grey slip, black in the rim area. Highly burnished. Hand-made.
Di. c. 15

219 5405
Level Vh/i
Hemispherical cup or bowl. Beige gritty fabric, plain. Hand-made.
Di. 10

220 1852
Level Vi
Rim sherd. Fabric D, beige. Red burnished with white matt paint. Hand-made.

Di. 26
Fig. 224

221   H20/1058   6307
Level Vh1–2
Small crudely made bowl with rounded base. Coarse beige fabric, much grit temper. Surface lumpy. Hand-made.
Di. 10.5

222   5402
Level Vi
Uneven bowl rim. Medium beige hard-fired fabric. Red band over rim and zigzag pattern on interior. Hand-made.

223   5402
Level Vi
Horned rim with handle attachment. Fabric D, brown slip, high lustre burnish. Reddish over rim area. Hand-made.
Di. *c.* 14

*Decorated sherds (**224–9**)*

224   1838
Level Vg/h
Body sherd. Fabric D, beige. Red slip and burnished both sides. White matt paint on exterior. Hand-made.
Th. 0.6
Fig. 224

225   1847
Level Vg/h
Body sherd from closed shape. Fabric D, beige. Exterior red burnished. Patterns incised and white filled after slipping. Hand-made.
Th. 0.6–1.0

226   1802
Unstratified
Body sherd from closed vessel. Fabric D, beige. Exterior thick red slip, high burnish. Incised decoration. Hand-made.
Th. 0.5–1.0

227   5344
Level Vf?
Body sherd from closed vessel. Fabric D, beige. Exterior thick red slip, high burnish. Incised decoration, herringbone pattern. Hand-made.
Th. 1.2

228   1823
Level Vf3/4
Body sherd. Grey fabric with no visible temper. Exterior cream slip and decorated with barbotine design.
Th. 0.5

229   1826
Level Vf/g
Body sherd from closed shape. Fabric D, beige. Exterior red burnished, incised herringbone pattern. Hand-made.
Th. 1.0

*Handles (**230–38**)*

230   1898
Level Vi
Handle with incised and white-filled decoration. Fabric D, beige. Black slip on top and sides, burnished.

231   1853
Level Vi
Handle fragment. Fabric D, black burnished. Punctate decoration.

232   1853
Level Vi
Handle fragment. Fabric D, brown slip and burnish. Excised decoration.

233   1851
Level Vh/i
Plug-through handle. Black burnished. Mottled appearance.

234   1853
Level Vi
Handle plugged through vessel wall. Semi-coarse, grit and sand tempered. Remains of red slip.

235   1838
Level Vg/h
Plug-through handle. Fabric D, fugitive dark brown slip.

236   1838
Level Vg/h
Handle with grooved decoration. Red gritty fabric, plain.

237   5384
Level Vg
Plug-through handle with longitudinal groove.

238   1856
Unstratified
Decorated handle fragment. Fabric D, black burnished and excised decoration on top side.

*Pottery feet and small bases (**239–44**)*

239   1851
Level Vh/i
Pedestal base of 'champagne cup'. Fabric D, black burnished. Hand-made.
Base di. 2.8

240   1898
Level Vi
Foot of tripod(?) cooking pot. Coarse Fabric G with organic temper. Surface rough.
H. *c.* 7.5

241   1851
Level Vh/i
Base of straight-sided open vessel. Fabric D, black slip, burnished. Hand-made.
Base di. 10

242   1853
Level Vi
Base, same as **241**
Base di. 8

243   1845
Level Vg/h
Cup base, same as **241–2**. Tan slip and burnish.
Base di. 5

244   1838
Level Vg/h
Cup base. Semi-coarse fabric, grey core, plain. Hand-made.
Base di. 6

Bowls — Level Vh–g (245–63)

245   1847
Level Vg/h
Hemispherical bowl. Red gritty fabric, plain. Hand-made.
Di. 16

246   1838
Level Vg/h
Bowl rim with horizontal handle. Red fabric, grit-tempered, grey core. Burnished. Hand-made.
Di. 16

247   1838
Level Vg/h
Bowl rim. Beige with grits, grey core. Painted with red bands both sides. Hand-made.

248   1838
Level Vg/h
Bowl rim. Fabric D, grey core. Red burnished both sides. Hand-made.
Di. 23

249   1838
Level Vg/h
Bowl rim. Fabric D, black burnished. Lighter colour on exterior. Burnished to high lustre. Hand-made.
Di. 14

250   1838
Level Vg/h
Plate rim. Semi-coarse, beige fabric with dark inclusions. Red burnished in interior, brown on exterior, black over rim area. Hand-made.
Di. c. 30

251   1836
Level Vg/h
Rim sherd. Fabric D. Red burnished exterior, brown in interior. Hand-made.
Di. 20

252   1838
Level Vg/h
Small bowl rim. Fine beige fabric. Plain. Hand-made.
Di. 10

253   1836
Level Vg/h
Bowl rim. Fine brown fabric, red-brown slip, low burnish. Hand-made.
Di. 18

254   1836
Level Vg/h
Painted bowl rim. Fabric D, beige slip both sides. Pale orange painted bands. Hand-made.
Di. 18

255   1836
Level Vg/h
Rim sherd. Fabric D, red burnished both sides. Hand-made.
Di. 14

256   1836
Level Vg/h
Fine bowl rim. Fabric D. Black burnished. Hand-made.
Di. 12

257   5384
Level Vg
Hemispherical bowl. Fabric F, brown. Light brown slip overall. Exterior striation marks and blackened in one area. Hand-made.
Di. 16
Petrographic sample S37

258   5384
Level Vg
Rim sherd. Fine orange fabric, grit temper. Thick red slip, medium burnish. Hand-made.

259   1835
Level Vg
Decorated rim sherd. Fabric D, brown. Dark brown slip, burnished both sides. Exterior incised pattern. Hand-made.
Di. 20
Cf. D. French 1965, fig. 5:20

260   5383
Level Vg
Flared rim sherd. Fabric D. Thick red slip both sides. Interior rim area decorated with incised and white-filled cross-hatching. Hand-made.
Di. 33

261   1836
Level Vg/h
Deep bowl rim. Fabric D, black burnished. Lighter colour on exterior. Hand-made.
Di. 20

262   1836
Level Vg/h
Deep bowl rim. Fabric D, black burnished. Hand-made.
Di. 16

263   1831
Level Vg
Deep bowl rim. Soft brown fabric with dark grits, smoothed. Hand-made.
Di. 15

Jugs and jars — Level Vi–g (264–9)

264   6334
Level Vi?
Trefoil neck with handle. Grey-brown, grit-tempered. Exterior black slipped and burnished, severely burnt. Hand-made.
Rim di. 7.6 × 7.0 (outer edge)

265   H20/477   Etütlük 1996   1847
Level Vg/h
Jar with perforated tab handle. Fabric D. Exterior thick red slip. Low to medium burnish. Excised decoration made before slipping. Tab handle incomplete. Hand-made.
Di. c. 5; H. 13+
Cf. Goldman 1956, fig. 260:345–8

266   5384
Level Vg
Deep bowl with rounded base. Fabric D but harder fired. Dark brown slip, medium burnish. Interior pattern burnish. Hand-made.
Di. 15

267   1847
Level Vg/h
Rim sherd. Fabric D, red burnished to high lustre. Hand-made.
Di. 11

268 H20/434 Etütlük 1996 1836
Level Vg/h
Complete juglet. Medium, beige fabric. Plain. Low burnish on shoulder part. Hand-made.
H. 12

269 1838
Level Vg/h
Rim of flask neck or spout(?). Fabric D. Exterior red wash over vertical striations and wavy lines on interior. Hand-made.
Di. 5

Coarse ware — Level Vj (270–72)
270 1859+1874
Rim with vertical handle. Dense light brown fabric, brown wash both sides.
Di. 22; Th. 0.7

271 1858
Horizontal handle with pot mark. Brown fabric, grit-tempered, red wash over handle.
Th. 0.9

272 1899
Hole-mouth cooking jar with handle. Fabric G, pink with roughened outer surface. Three incised lines across rim in handle area. Hand-made.
Di. 15; Th. 1.1

Coarse ware — Level Vi–g (273–9)
273 H20/544 1858
Probably sunk from Vi into Vj level (Fig. 477).
Pithos base and rim fragment. Orange-brown grit-tempered with grits up to 0.7. Exterior smoothed leaving striation marks. Rim wet smoothed. Interior cream coated. Hand-made.
H. (as drawn) 38.5; Di. (max.) 25.

274 5405
Level Vh/i
Cooking pot rim with handle(s). Fabric G, surface roughened below rim. Hand-made.
Di. 14; Th. 0.5

275 1849
Level Vh1
Hole-mouth cooking jar rim. Fabric G, brown. Roughened exterior. Hand-made.
Di. 11

276 1838
Level Vg/h
Hole-mouth cooking pot. Coarse brown fabric, grey core. Hand-made.
Di. 25

277 1838
Level Vg/h
Hole-mouth jar. Coarse fabric, grit and sand temper. Exterior surface roughened below rim. Hand-made.
Di. 24; Th. 0.7

278 1838
Level Vg/h
Rim. Brown, semi-coarse with grits and sand. Grey core. Plastic rope pattern on exterior near rim. Hand-made.
Di. *c*. 35

279 1836
Level Vg/h
Rim with vertical handle. Fabric G, brown gritty fabric, plain. Hand-made.

Platters or lids — Level Vj–g (280–86)
280 5406
Level Vj
Platter or lid with scalloped and finger impressed edge and excised lunate pattern. Fabric D, brown, red wash on both sides. Hand-made.
Th. 0.5–0.7

281 1871
Level Vj
Circular(?) platter with depression. Coarse buff fabric with large chalk inclusions. Cream wash. Hand-made.
Th. 1.5

282 1853
Level Vi
Raised rim of circular(?) platter. Semi-coarse brown fabric, plain.
Di. 18

283 1853
Level Vi
Base of circular(?) platter with depression and grooves. Hand-made.

284 1853
Level Vi
Platter rim. Semi-coarse beige fabric with grits. Grey core. Red slipped, medium burnish. Hand-made.
Di. 22

285 1849
Level Vh1
Rim of oval or round platter. Fabric D, beige, grey core. Light brown slip, burnished on underside. Excised grain pattern near edge. Hand-made.
Di. 19

286 5383
Level Vg
Platter rim with excised grain decoration. Fabric D, traces of red wash.

Level Vf (287–445)

Introduction

The second major ceramic horizon, which can be safely attributed to EB III in Anatolian context, represents a complete departure from the pottery of the lower layers described above. There is a total change in the technology of manufacturing pottery, involving fabrics and surface treatment as well as shapes. The larger percentage of the assemblage is now wheel-made and burnished wares are almost totally absent.

The richest repertoire and greatest volume of pottery came from the layers of Level Vf1–4 and Ve and it is unfortunate that contextually they proved the least satisfactory. The robber trench dug in the H20c quadrant particularly affected these horizons and in

H20d only a few occupation floors could be identified, frequently cut by intrusive pits.

In Level Vf, four architectural sub-phases were identified of which the latest (Vf4) was the best preserved, with a series of rooms that contained a good sampling of pottery and some small finds. The stratigraphic subdivision is, however, generally not reflected in the ceramic repertoire and the overall evidence suggests that fabrics, certain shapes and surface treatments were in use throughout Vf. Therefore no attempt has been made here to present the material by sub-phases. Indeed, the fully developed characteristics of the pottery which followed Vg do raise the question of a possible hiatus in occupation, at least in this particular part of the mound.

The most commonly used fabric for fine and medium wares is a fairly hard orange grit-tempered fabric, not present previously (Fabric A, p. 296). The clay is generally well prepared and the pottery is evenly fired, at times to a high temperature giving it a clinky quality. This provides the standard fabric for red cross bowls and for the plain, the red-slipped, and the brown-coated wares. The fabrics used in the manufacture of coarse vessels (B, C1, C2) are closely related to the above but, as one would expect, with much larger inclusions and added organic temper.

Cooking and storage vessels (287–94)
Storage pots in Vf, in as far as they survived, occurred primarily with flared rims (**290**) or slightly thickened more upright rims (**292**), all with flat bases. The surface treatment consisted of washes, in some cases with incised patterns (**409**).

287 5370
Level Vf2?
Hole-mouth pot rim. Fabric G, reddish brown. Roughened outer surface below rim. Hand-made.
Di. c. 25

288 5356
Level Vf3
Cooking pot with exterior rolled rim. Fabric G, black gritty. Hand-made.
Di. 28

289 5366
Level Vf3?
Large jar rim. Coarse Fabric G, grey core. Purple-red slip both sides. Medium burnish. Hand-made.
Di. 29

290 1829
Level Vf/g
Flared jar rim. Fabric A, light orange. Brown coated, streaky appearance, matt.
Di. 48

291 1823
Level Vf3/4
Flared jar rim. Fabric A, orange, grey brown core. Exterior and rim red-slipped, carried to interior forming band. Matt.
Di. 25

292 5362
Level Vf3?
Storage vessel. Fabric C1, orange. Exterior cream slip, smoothed. Hand-made.
Di. 27

293 1818
Level Vf4
Jar rim. Brown fabric, grit-tempered. Traces of red wash. Hand-made.
Di. 13

294 5354
Level Vf3
Jar neck with flared grooved rim. Medium fabric, brown, grit and sand temper. Exterior self-slipped. Vertical burnishing marks.
Di. 21

Bowls (295–373)
By far the largest percentage of vessels belonged to the category of bowls. They were produced in a variety of shapes with simple, channelled or inverted angular rims but one of the most persistent types is a slightly carinated bowl with an S-shaped profile which occurred throughout Vf. Examples were found as shallow and deeper bowls with an average diameter of 25–30 cm and quite clearly represent mass-produced table ware.

Among the surface-treated pottery — to which most bowls belong — red-slipped and brown-coated wares occur in more or less even quantities and they largely share the same repertoire of shapes. There is, however, a difference in the appearance of the slips; while red wares are evenly covered, the brown examples always have a streaky, smeared look, suggesting a different method of slip application, possibly by brush. Alternatively, as Knappett suggests, both the colour and the streakiness may depend on how thickly the paint was applied. But in all cases slips and paints are consistently left matt, and when covering the whole vessel, the base is included.

The partial application of slips or paint occurs in all phases, but becomes particularly prominent in phase Vf4. Apart from red-rim bowls (**345**), other vessels are only partially slipped or painted, frequently up to the carination which can be on the interior or exterior (**334–5**).

Closely related to the above types are red cross bowls which form a significant group at Kilise Tepe. They make their first appearance in the last phase of Vf and continue into Ve, in which an almost complete example was found, though here they occur also with slightly different profiles. Indeed, red cross bowls were still manufactured in Level IV, now with the cross painted on the exterior (see **564–5**), a method well known from Troy, Kusura and other sites (Easton 2002, 338 & fn. 427). In addition, numerous examples were salvaged from the back fill of the robber trench in H20c, which could frequently be joined with fragments coming from stratified layers. The characteristic shape is a carinated shallow bowl, of the type already discussed above, painted red or brown over a cream slip or wash. The cross is always painted in the interior and surrounded by a wide band of paint in the rim area which reaches the carination, often on both sides. Most of the red cross bowls are rather carelessly painted and the quantity of fragments recovered suggests their mass production, representing, in fact, another version of ordinary table ware. With the exception of one small example (**350**) all our examples were wheel-made.

Red cross bowls have a wide distribution in Anatolia and are known from over thirty sites (Korfmann 1983a, 292). They mark the end of the Early Bronze Age and transition to the Middle Bronze Age at a number of sites, such as Tarsus (Goldman 1956, fig. 273:445, fig. 290:811–12), Beycesultan (Lloyd & Mellaart 1962, 236, fig. P.64:23, 26), Kusura (Lamb 1937, 17 & fig. 6:1a–c.), Troy IV–V (Easton 2002, 324 fn. 200) and indeed Kilise Tepe. But as Korfmann has shown, they occur at Demircihüyük in contexts analogous with Troy I and sporadically at Troy itself from Troy IIc onwards, thus making the time span of their manufacture — at least in NW Anatolia — as wide as their distribution (1983a, 291ff.).

The Kilise Tepe red cross bowls are, however, firmly tied in fabric and shape to the contemporary bowls with red and brown slips which dominate in EB III and continue into the Middle Bronze Age.

Separate bowl categories are plain (**295–306**) or cream-slipped (**307–10**) ones, primarily with simple or slightly thickened rims, and bowls with horizontal loop handle(s) (**360–66**) which belong to the last phase of Level Vf and can be seen to continue into Ve.

*Plain bowls (**295–306**)*

295 1826
Level Vf/g
Bowl rim. Fabric A, self-slipped.
Di. 24

296 1826
Level Vf/g
Bowl rim. Fabric A, with organic inclusions. Smoothed.
Di. 23

297 1812
Level Vf
Bowl rim. Fabric A, plain.
Di. 20

298 1829
Level Vf/g
Shallow bowl rim. Fabric A, but more organic temper, leaving voids on surface.
Di. 26

299 1829
Level Vf/g
Shallow bowl. Fabric A, self-slipped, scraping marks.
Di. 24

300 5368
Level Vf
Bowl rim. Fabric C1, orange, smoothed.
Di. *c*. 20

301 1805
Unstratified
Bowl or jar rim. Fabric A. Smoothed.
Di. 14

302 1805
Unstratified
Shallow bowl. Fabric A, smoothed.
Di. 27

303 1823
Level Vf3/4
Bowl with everted rim. Fabric A, self-slipped. Plain.
Di. 23

304 1805
Unstratified
Bowl rim. Fabric A, plain.
Di. 24

305 5390
Level Vf?
Bowl with corrugated sides and flat base. Fabric A, but larger percentage of grits. Plain.
Di. 28, Base di. 8

306 5366
Level Vf3?
Deep bowl rim. Fabric C1, plain.
Di. *c*. 30

*Cream-slipped bowls (**307–10**)*

307 5370
Level Vf2?
Bowl rim. Fabric A, pink. Cream slip both sides, thicker over rim area.
Di. 26

308 5354
Level Vf3
Small bowl rim. Fabric A, light orange. Thick, light brown slip, matt.
Di. 20

309 1820
Level Vf
Carinated bowl rim. Medium light brown, multi-coloured grits. Exterior and rim cream slip. Horizontal burnishing marks.
Di. 28

The Early Bronze Age Pottery

310   5354
Level Vf3
Bowl with interior thickened rim. Fabric A, orange. Cream slip both sides.
Di. *c.* 24

Red- or brown-slipped bowls with S-profiles (311–23)

311   1829
Level Vf/g
Bowl rim. Fabric A, laminated. Red slip partially flaked off, matt.

312   5376
Level Vf1
Bowl. Fabric A, red slip overall, including base, matt.
Di. 30

313   5368
Level Vf
Bowl rim. Fabric A, red slip both sides, matt.
Di. 28

314   5360
Level Vf3
Bowl rim. Fabric A, orange, dark brown slip, matt.
Di. 28

315   5353
Level Vf
Bowl rim. Fabric A, orange. Interior red slip, exterior brown slip, matt.
Di. 32

316   5350
Level Vf3
Bowl rim. Fabric A, orange. Interior brown slip, exterior red slip, matt.
Di. 27

317   1823
Level Vf3/4
Bowl rim. Fabric A, orange. Both sides dark red slip, matt.
Di. 30

318   1823
Level Vf3/4
Deep bowl rim. Fabric A, little temper. Dark red slip, matt.
Di. 30

319   1825+1826
Level Vf/g
Bowl rim. Fabric A. Brown-coated, streaky appearance. Matt.
Di. 37

320   1826
Level Vf/g
Bowl rim. Fabric A. Brown-coated both sides. Matt.
Di. 29

321   1825
Level Vf/g
Bowl with corrugated exterior. Fabric A, light orange, little temper. Covered in dark brown slip overall, excluding base.
Di. 29

322   1825
Level Vf/g
Bowl rim with corrugated exterior. Fabric A, orange, little temper. Dark red matt slip overall.
Di. 24

323   1823
Level Vf3/4
Bowl with horizontal grooves on exterior. Fabric A, orange. Dark red slip both sides including base. Matt.
Di. 28

Red-/brown-slipped bowls with other profiles (324–32)

324   1826
Level Vf/g
Bowl with angular flattened rim and flat base. Fabric A, orange. Thick dark red slip both sides including base. Matt.
Di. 28

325   1823
Level Vf3/4
Same as **324**.
Di. 24

326   1825
Level Vf/g
Bowl rim. Fabric A, light orange. Dark red slip both sides, low burnish. Uncertain angle and diameter.

327   1829
Level Vf/g
Bowl rim. Fabric A, red slipped both sides, matt.
Di. 28

328   1829
Level Vf/g
Bowl rim. Fabric A. Brown-coated, darker shade on interior, matt.
Di. 27

329   1826
Level Vf/g
Bowl rim. Fabric A, brown-coated both sides, matt.
Di. 29

330   1826
Level Vf/g
Bowl rim. Fabric A, brown-coated both sides, matt.
Di. 28

331   1829
Level Vf/g
Plate rim. Fabric A, light brown slip both sides, matt. Corrugated finish.

332   5368
Level Vf
Bowl rim. Fabric A, orange, brown slip both sides, streaky effect, matt. Hand-made.
Di. 20

Partially slipped and red-rim bowls (333–48)

333   1829
Level Vf/g
Bowl rim. Fabric A. Red slip interior, reddish-brown slip on exterior and over rim forming band in interior.
Di. 26

334   1827
Unstratified
Carinated bowl. Fabric A. Red slip interior over rim to exterior up

Figure 225. *Red cross bowl 352.*

to carination.
Di. 28

335 5347
Level Vf4
Bowl rim with S-shape profile. Fabric A, pale orange. Exterior cream wash. Interior red band up to carination.
Di. 25

336 1813
Level Vf?
Bowl rim. Fabric A, red slip on inside and partially on outside. Wheel marked on exterior.
Di. 16

337 1813
Level Vf?
Red-rim bowl. Fine beige, fugitive red paint over rim.
Di. 19

338 1813
Level Vf?
Bowl rim. Fabric A. Red wash over rim area.
Di. 22

339 5319
Level Ve/f
Shallow red-rim bowl. Fabric A. Red paint carried over rim to interior forming a band. Splashes of paint on exterior. Matt.
Di. 20

340 1813
Level Vf?
Bowl with grooved rim. Fabric A. Red paint over rim and up to carination in interior.
Di. 37

341 1805
Unstratified
Bowl with grooved rim. Fabric A. Red wash in interior.
Di. 35

342 1802
Unstratified
Bowl with broad red band over rim area. Possibly a red cross bowl fragment. Fabric A.
Di. 19

343 1802
Unstratified
Carinated bowl rim. Fabric A, beige slip. On exterior brown wash up to carination. Hand-made.
Di. 26

344 1805
Unstratified
Bowl rim. Fabric A. Red slip interior over rim to exterior.
Di. 25

345 1801
Unstratified
Red rim bowl. Fabric A. Very faint red paint.
Di. 20

346 1805
Unstratified
Red rim bowl. Fine beige fabric, little temper. Faded red paint.
Di. 14

347 1810
Level Ve/f
Bowl with burnt(?) rim. Fine beige fabric, little temper. Exterior brown wash. Burnt in the rim area.
Di. 19

348 5328
Level Vf4
Carinated bowl. Fabric A, with some voids on surface. Interior red wash. Hand-made.
Di. *c.* 16

*Red cross bowls (**349–59**)*

349 5344
Level Vf?
Rim of red cross bowl. Fabric A, medium. Red paint.
Di. 24

350 1812
Level Vf
Small red cross bowl. Fabric A. Orange red paint. Hand-made. Base is **351**.
Di. 11

351 1805
Unstratified
Base of small red cross bowl (join to **350**). Fabric A. Red paint. Hand-made.
Base di. 4.5

352 H20/335 KLT 67 1810
Level Ve/f
Almost complete red cross bowl. Fabric A, orange-brown, medium. Cream slip on exterior, smoothed on interior. Cross painted with broad brown bands in interior. Wide band around rim area reaching carination on exterior.
Di. 20.
Fig. 225

353 1805+1802+1812
Level Vf+unstratified
Rim of red cross bowl. Fabric A, painted brown.
Di. 25

354   1818
Level Vf4
Shallow red cross bowl rim. Fabric A, orange with darker core. Reddish brown paint.
Di. 23

355   1802+1800+1805+1260
Unstratified
Large red cross bowl with flat base. Fabric A, orange red paint.
Di. 24

356   1801
Unstratified
Rim of red cross bowl. Fabric A, dark brown paint. Exterior corrugated.
Di. 22

357   1801
Unstratified
Same as **356**, red-brown paint.
Di. 25

358   1812
Level Vf
Base of red cross bowl. Fabric A, brown paint. Heavily wheel marked on exterior.
Base di. 6

359   1802
Unstratified
Rim of red cross bowl. Fabric A, brown paint.
Di. 23

Handled bowls (360–67)

360   1801+1812
Level Vf+unstratified
Bowl with horizontal high rise handle. Fabric A, light brown wash over rim and interior.
Di. 24

361   1825
Level Vf/g
Carinated bowl rim with handle attachment. Fabric A, pinkish. Red slip on interior, brown slip on exterior.
Di. c. 32

362   5376
Level Vf1
Rim with broken off horizontal handle. Fabric F, red brown slip both sides, low burnish. Hand-made.
Di. 22

363   5362
Level Vf3?
Bowl rim with handle attachment. Fabric C1, orange. Traces of red paint on outer side and over rim forming band on inner side.
Di. c. 30

364   5366
Level Vf3?
Rim with high rise handle. Fabric A, orange, red slip both sides, matt. Hand-made?
Di. 28

365   5328
Level Vf4
Bowl rim with high rise handle and brown wash. Fabric A with many mudstones visible on surface. Hand-made.
Di. 17

366   5328
Level Vf4
Bowl rim with horizontal handle. Fabric A, some voids on surface and traces of reddish wash. Hand-made.
Di. c. 20

367   1805
Unstratified
Bowl rim with vertical tubular handles. Fabric A, fine. Cream slip and traces of brown wash. Exterior horizontally grooved.
Di. 18

Miscellaneous bowls (368–73)

368   5367
Level Vf
Bowl rim. Red gritty fabric, grey core. Thick red slip, medium burnish. Striation marks on exterior. Hand-made.
Di. 28

369   1805
Unstratified
Bowl rim. Soft brown fabric, grit-tempered. Exterior covered in irregular striation marks. Hand-made.
Di. 21

370   1801
Unstratified
Shallow carinated bowl. Fabric A, traces of red wash in interior. Hand-made.
Di. 28

371   1812
Level Vf
Shallow bowl rim. Fabric A, interior red slip, flaked.
Di. c. 20

372   1813
Level Vf?
Horizontal flattened bowl rim. Fabric A with much organic temper. Light brown wash interior and over rim.
Di. 19

373   1805
Unstratified
Bowl rim. Fabric A. Red-slipped exterior, brown on inside, low burnish. Hand-made.
Di. 14(?)

Jars and cups (374–93)

The small vessels with fairly upright sides and everted rim were common throughout the Vf period and the frequency of their appearance would suggest their use as a popular drinking vessel of the period. The larger versions of this shape (**376, 379–80**), however, belong to the category of jars. Their manufacture appears to be standardized including the finish consisting of an exterior slip carried across the rim to form an interior band.

Cups with handles were less frequently encountered but the surviving handles (of the high-rise type) indicate their use (**429**).

Figure 226. *Cup 400, with incised pot mark just visible on left.*

A complete example of a handled cup is **400** (Fig. 226) with an incised pot-mark; a miniature version came from Rm 50 (**398**). They do, however, occur more often in Ve (see below).

In the line of drinking vessels, we noted the absence of any *depas* cups or tankards, both shapes a common EB III feature at most Anatolian sites. The only indication for their possible existence are a few handle fragments (**431–2**) which look remarkably as if they belonged to *depas* cups. Otherwise, no two-handled cups of any shape were recorded at Kilise Tepe.

Fluted vessels (**387–91**)
A small group of vessel fragments with fluted decoration and reddish slip were the only examples found at Kilise Tepe and appear to be of SW Anatolian inspiration. They included globular cups or jars with handles (**387, 389–90**), a vertical grooved strap handle from a closed vessel (**391**). Compare also **367**, a carinated bowl with pierced tubular handles arranged vertically in pairs.

Small red-slipped and red-rim jars/cups (**374–85**)
374 1829
Level Vf/g
Jar with everted and tapered rim. Fabric A, red slip on exterior and over rim to interior forming band.
Di. 7

375 1819
Level Vf4
Same as **374**.
Di. 10

376 1827
Unstratified
Same as **374**.
Di. 8.5

377 1812
Level Vf
Same as **374**.
Di. 8.5

378 1802
Unstratified
Cup rim. Fabric A. Red slip outside and over rim to inside, forming band.
Di. 8

379 H20/1015 5363+5351
Level Vf
Jar with everted tapered rim and slightly curved base. Fabric A, fine, orange. Exterior red slip carried over rim to interior of vessel.
Di. 10

380 1822
Level Ve
Jar rim. Fabric A. Red brown wash exterior and over rim to interior, 3 cm below rim.
Di. 12

381 1822
Level Ve
Cup or jar rim. Fabric A. Red slip outside and partially inside.
Di. 6

382 1810
Level Ve/f
Jar rim. Fabric A. Light brown slip on outside carried over rim to inside.
Di. 11

383 1810
Level Ve/f
Jar rim. Grey fine fabric, few grits. Fugitive yellowish wash.
Di. 10

384 1829
Level Vf/g
Jar neck with flared rim. Fabric A, fine. Brown slip on exterior, rim, and band in interior.
Di. 8.5

385 1801
Unstratified
Jar rim. Fabric A. Red-brown wash exterior and over rim to interior.
Di. 15

Decorated cups and jars (**386–93**)
386 5351
Level Vf
Small globular jar fragment. Fabric C1, plain. Diagonal incised lines.
Th. 0.7

387 5332
Level Vf4
Jar rim with fluted decoration. Fabric A, orange. Outer surface covered in light brown wash. Hand-made?
Di. 14

388   5328
Level Vf4
Jar fragment with pierced lug handle. Fabric A, traces of brown wash.
Th. 0.6

389   1802+1805
Unstratified
Small cup with handle attachment and rounded base. Orange with high grit content. Exterior shallow fluting with traces of brown wash.
Th. 0.8

390   1802
Unstratified
Cup with broken off high rise handle. Fine orange, no visible temper. Red slip on outside surface carried over rim to inside. Shallow fluting. Hand-made.
Di. 7

391   1805
Unstratified
Body sherd with grooved strap handle. Fabric A, reddish brown slip largely flaked off. Hand-made.

392   5333
Level Ve
High rise handle with grooved decoration and red paint. Fabric A.

393   1805
Unstratified
Body sherd with plastic fluted decoration. Orange, hard fired, large percentage of dark grits. Exterior dark red slip. Hand-made.
Th. 1.2

Miniature vessels (394–400)

A small but noteworthy pottery group are miniature pots, mainly in the form of squat, slightly carinated jars with corrugated or incised decoration on the shoulder (**394**, **396**, **399**), and a fine globular almost complete vessel with a collar rim covered in a dark brown slip is also worth a mention (**395**). This group also included a plain, rather crudely made juglet (**397**) which came from the lower fill of a pit.

394   1812
Level Vf
Carinated jar. Dark brown fabric fired to red, gritty. Orange red slip applied over exterior including base and over interior almost down to level of carination.
Di. 6; H. 6.6

395   1823+1825
Level Vf/g+Vf3/4
Miniature globular jar with *omphalos* base. Fine orange fabric (Fabric A). Exterior covered in dark brown slip, worn in parts.
Di. 3; H. 9

396   5344
Level Vf?
Rim and shoulder of small vessel. Fabric A plus sand, orange. Yellowish slip both sides. Exterior low burnish. Decorated on shoulder with incised pattern.
Di. 7

397   H20/920   KLT 123   5362
Level Vf3?
Ovoid juglet, flared rim. Grey fabric, crudely made. Lumpy surface. Hand-made.
Di. 3.1; H. 6

398   H20/359   KLT 63   1813
Level Vf
Miniature cup with high-rise handle. Fabric medium with dark grits. Red wash over exterior, handle, and part of interior. Hand-made.
Di. 2.9; H. 3.5

399   1813
Level Vf?
Cup rim with corrugated decoration on outside. Fine, white grit temper. Red-slipped both sides.
Di. 10

400   H20/292   KLT 64   1801
Unstratified
Cup. Fabric not visible, but surface shows voids and chalk inclusions. Brown wash interior, rim and upper part of exterior and handle. Cross incised in clay while still moist.
Di. 6
Fig. 226

Lids (401–3)

Apart from the group of large EBA/MBA high-sided lids with loop handle which would have fitted over the rim and neck of the vessel (*Stülpdeckel*; Ve: **453**; IV: **531**, **559–60**), there are an additional number of small lids each of a different type known from the ceramic repertoire of other sites. Two of them are representatives of the flat disc type with string holes arranged symmetrically near the edge. **401** is provided with a central knob and **402** has a groove linking the two string holes. Both are hand-made and the former is slipped and burnished. This style of lid was presumably tied on to the vessel.

The type with a central knob is an extremely common shape at Troy and was made over a long period (D14, Blegen *et al.* 1950, I, fig. 232; D15, fig. 405: 36.661). **402** has a close parallel at Tarsus in an EB II context, although here with an additional set of string holes and groove (Goldman 1956, fig. 250: 307). The third example (**403**) represents probably a rather poor attempt at the Troy-type lid with 'ears' covering jars (D11, Blegen 1950, Fig. 231: 33.162). It is plain with two pierced lugs unevenly spaced and is crudely made.

401   H20/574   1860
Unstratified
Lid with two perforation (string) holes. Semi-coarse brown with calcareous and brown stone inclusions. Some mica on surface. Light brown slip both sides, medium burnish.
Di. 9

402   H20/297   1802
Unstratified
Circular clay disc with two perforations (string holes) near the edge

Figure 227. *Incised lid **404**.*

Figure 228. *Cypriot Red polished III juglet **410–11**.*

and on opposite sides connected by a grooved line. Fabric brown grit-tempered. Surfaces smoothed. Both holes are slightly angled on the grooved side. Rather crudely made.
Di. 7.2; Di. Perf.: 0.3–0.4

403   1805
Unstratified
Lid with two pierced 'ear' handles. Fabric A, plain. Poorly made.
Di. 6

Incised decoration (**404–15**)

A small but distinct group belonging to phase Vf4 is in a plain ware with a pale orange fabric and a variety of incised patterns. Most of the pieces were recovered from Rm 53, among them a flask with an irregular chevron design and what appears to be a pot-mark below (**405**). A neighbouring room (Rm 50) produced an attractive lid with incurving sides and an intricate design of herringbone and arc patterns on the top and sides, covered in a red matt slip (**404**: Fig. 227).

A few sherds of black incised and white-filled pottery from miniature or small delicate vessels were also a feature of phase Vf4 (**412–13**: Fig. 229). This type of ware, like other black and grey wares, was rarely encountered at Kilise Tepe, and was most likely not locally made.

Certainly not of local manufacture is a partially preserved vessel with incised and white-filled decoration (**410**: Fig. 228) which was found in Rm 55 (Vf4), associated with a group of loom-weights and several red cross bowl fragments. While the fabric and decoration technique can be matched in Anatolia, the shape with its slightly pointed base cannot, and a Cypriot origin of the vessel seems assured. The original appearance has been partly lost through burning but a light brown slip and burnish, together with the white-filled chevron design survived. The interior does not appear to have been surface treated, indicating a closed shape. It is uncertain whether the neck fragment (**411**, also burnt: Fig. 228) with white-filled grooving, recovered from the same unit (1812), belonged to

Figure 229. *Sherds with incised and white-filled decoration, from miniature vessels.*

the vessel in question, as no traces of a slip remained here, but it is very likely.

The vessel has been classified as a Red Polished III 'gourd' juglet with known counterparts from northern Cyprus, the closest parallel being a jug found at Lapithos (Dikaios & Stewart 1962, fig. XCIV: 7). According to Herscher, these vessels were probably traded for their contents.[2] This find is, therefore, a welcome indication for contacts between the Göksu valley and Cyprus in the latter part of EB III, illustrating once again the strategic importance of Kilise Tepe on a major trade route with links to the Mediterranean coast.

404   5359
Level Vf3/4
Lid with incurving sides. Fabric A, orange, with medium size grits. Interior self-slipped, exterior red slip left matt. Intricate incised design of herringbone, arcs and depressions arranged in four quarters. Herring-bone design on sides.
Di. 13 (top), 12 (bottom)
Fig. 227

405   5328
Level Vf4
Closed vessel fragment with incised decoration. Fabric A, orange, medium with voids on outer surface. Plain. Zigzag incised pattern and pot-marks(?) below.
Th. 0.9

406   5328
Level Vf4
Incised body sherd of closed vessel. Fabric A, orange, medium. Plain. Incised herring-bone pattern.
Th. 0.9

407   5328
Level Vf4
Body sherd with incised decoration. Fabric A, reddish wash on exterior.
Th. 0.7

408   5328
Level Vf4
Body sherd of large vessel with incised decoration. Fabric A, beige, medium. Brown wash.
Th. 1.2

409   1812
Level Vf
Body sherd of storage vessel. Fabric A, light orange, very little temper of grit and some organic. Exterior thin beige slip and incised with linear pattern. Hand-made.
Th. 1.3

410   H20/344   1812
Level Vf
Cypriot Red Polished III 'gourd' juglet. Lower part of vessel with pointed base and incised and white-filled decoration. Fabric greyish-brown, grit-tempered, burnt and friable. Slip and burnish on outer surface, largely disappeared through burning. The colour of the slip is light brown but appears black in certain areas. Decoration: precise multiple incisions forming a zigzag pattern of possibly two bands which are white filled. Hand-made.
Th. 0.4–0.6
Fig. 228

411   H20/1085   1812
Level Vf
Neck fragment, probably belonging to above juglet (**410**). Dark greyish brown fabric, grit-tempered, burnt. Exterior horizontally grooved, remains of white filling.
Fig. 228

412   1822
Level Ve
Body sherd of small closed vessel. Fabric D, grey. Black burnished, incised and white-filled lozenge pattern. Hand-made.
Fig. 229

413   1822
Level Ve
Base of small closed vessel. Black burnished, white-filled incisions. Hand-made.
Di. 3
Fig. 229

414   1801
Unstratified
Body sherd, closed vessel. Semi-coarse, grit-tempered. Incised linear pattern, white-filled. Hand-made.
Th. 0.6

415   5313
Level Ve
Neck of bottle or jug. Grey brown, medium. Black slip, patchy burnishing marks. Irregular rilling and traces of white filling. Hand-made.
Th. 0.7

Jugs

A favoured surface decoration, notably on closed vessels, is rilling and grooving, at times achieving a sort of corrugated effect, clearly in imitation of metal vessels. It is mainly applied to the neck part of jugs or below the rim of jars and bowls, while coarse ware jugs occurred also with a combination of random incisions and combing in the rim area (**420**).

No whole profiles of jugs were recovered but the fragments suggest that apart from flared rims, the most common forms had trefoil rims, whereas beak and cut-away spouts do not appear to have featured.

The remains of a rather splendid jug — of some technical skill — with surface decoration and covered in a bright red slip (**447**) was retrieved, together with a large jar fragment of the same manufacture and style, from a pit thought to have been in use in Level Ve (P97/22). However, the jar (**449**) could be joined with a fragment from a Vf4 occupation floor, indicating that both vessels may belong to the last phase of Vf rather than Ve when the pit was in use. The twisted handles which decorated both pots have several parallels in Level Vf. Other multi-stranded handles excavated occur with plaited rope pattern (**442**) and in one case with a plastic snake decoration (**441**). Identical plaited handles can be seen on jugs found at Tarsus in EB III levels (Goldman 1956, fig. 269:568, fig. 272:560).

*Decorated jugs and jars (**416–21**)*

416 5364
Level Vf
Jug neck and shoulder. Beige, medium, grit-tempered. Dark brown slip, matt. Neck decorated with irregular rilling.
Di. 9

417 1805
Unstratified
Jug neck with flared rim and rilling decoration. Fabric A, red slip applied to exterior over rim to interior.
Di. 7

418 1805
Unstratified
Jar neck with mending hole and horizontal grooves. Fabric A, red slip.
Di. 7

419 1805
Unstratified
Jar rim with horizontal grooves. Fabric A. Exterior red wash over rim to interior.
Di. 16

420 1802
Unstratified
Jug rim. Coarse ware with large inclusions. Exterior scored, striated or combed. Lime wash.

421 1805
Unstratified
Rim sherd. Orange gritty fabric. Rim and exterior red slip. Hand-made.

*Bases (**422–7**)*

422 1823
Level Vf3/4
Base of closed shape. Fabric A, exterior red-brown slip.
Base di. 5

423 1825
Level Vf/g
Small cup(?) base. Fine beige. String cut.
Base di. 2.8

424 1820
Level Vf
Simple base, coil made. Fabric A, exterior traces of red slip.
Base di. 2

425 1801
Unstratified
Base, coil made. Medium, orange. Irregular bands of red paint.
Base di. 2.4

426 1805
Unstratified
Base of closed vessel. Fabric C1. Exterior red wash. Hand-made.
Base di. 13

427 5354
Level Vf3
Base of closed vessel with *omphalos* in interior. Fabric A, beige. Exterior brown coated, excluding base. Smeared effect, matt.
Base di. 6.5

*Handles (**428–45**)*

428 5369
Level Vf1
Push-through handle of cooking pot. Fabric F, red with grey core, plain. Decorated with vertical depression across handle.

429 5378
Level Vf1
High-rise handle. Fabric F, orange, red slip.

430 5353
Level Vf
Vertical handle. Fabric A, red slip.

431 5354
Level Vf3
Vertical handle. Fine pale orange fabric, no visible temper. Light brown slip, low burnish. Belongs most likely to a *depas* cup.

432 5352
Level Vf
Vertical handle. Fine grey with no visible inclusions. Exterior black slip, partly worn and medium burnish. Probably a handle from a *depas amphikypellon*, like **431**.

433 1826
Level Vf/g
Double-stranded handle. Light orange, little temper. Unevenly applied dark red slip.

434 1813
Level Vf?
Long thin double-stranded handle. Red with large percentage of white grits, showing on surface. Partial red wash.

435 1801
Unstratified
Double-stranded handle. Fabric A, light brown slip.

436 1826
Level Vf/g
Twisted handle. Light brown, little temper. Brown slip.

437 1801
Unstratified
Handle. Fabric A, reddish-brown slip. Grooved, giving the appearance of a twisted handle.

438 5362
Level Vf3?
Handle diagonally ridged giving impression of being twisted. Fabric A, pale orange. Plain.

439 5362
Level Vf3?
Body sherd with attached vertical handle of small vessel. Fabric A, pale orange, medium. Smoothed, reddish wash, low burnish. Incised decoration. Handle diagonally ridged.

440   5370
Level Vf2?
Handle with excised zigzag decoration. Pale orange grit and calcareous temper. Red slip, low burnish.

441   5392
Level Vf1/2
Handle with plastic decoration. Fabric A, orange with red slip. Triple-stranded plait of which the central strand has punctured dots, resembling a snake or animal tail.

442   5342
Level Vf?
Multi-stranded plaited handle. Fabric A, red slip.

443   5359
Level Vf3/4
Handle with red splash paint. Fabric A, orange, light orange wash.

444   5350
Level Vf3
Triple-stranded basket handle of multiple vessel(?). Fabric A, brown coated, matt.
Cf. Goldman 1956, fig. 278:623.

445   1805
Unstratified
Handle with two drill holes. Red gritty fabric, grey core.

Level Ve (446–74)

Little can be said about the archaeological context for the pottery of Level Ve, the three sub-phases of which revealed few architectural remains. During this period the excavated area H20d is thought to have served as an outdoor space, a view supported by the numerous pits, which are the source for much of our pottery (Figs. 484–6).

As a general observation, the ceramics of Ve reflect a continuation of EB III traditions, on the one hand, and the appearance of features characteristic of Level IVa (MBA), on the other. Many of the familiar wares of Vf are still to be found in Ve, such as the matt slipped wares in the form of cups or jars with flared rims and carinated bowls (with S-curve profiles). This is also true of the red cross bowl which occurred in all three Ve sub-phases, mainly in the traditional shape, best illustrated by the almost complete example (**352**: Fig. 225) but also with more simple profiles typical of Level IV.

The fragment of a volute foot (**473**) also belongs to the late EB III tradition as seen in the Tarsus red cross bowl on three curled feet (Goldman 1956, fig. 273:445, fig. 355:445) and at Beycesultan (Lloyd & Mellaart 1962, 248, fig. P.70:6).

Although fabrics remain largely unchanged, some new bowl types are introduced, including shallow bowls with simple incurving rims (**455**) and carinated bowls with flat-topped rims (**454**). The bowl with high rise loop handle continues from Vf but new is a small shallow bowl with horizontal handles and exterior grooving (**461**) with counterparts in IVa (**480**–**83**).

Other characteristic Level IV pottery from Level Ve are storage jars with crescentic handles (**452**), some coarse and medium combed ware (**451**, others from 1809, not illustrated), and a large lid with outward curving sides and loop handle (**453**: Fig. 233) which has two parallels in Level IV, although with different decoration (see below).

Cups occurred in two different shapes and fabrics also reflecting the transitional character of Ve. The first type comes with a high-rise handle and *omphalos* base with a partial or overall slip, manufactured in the traditional EB III fabric (Fabric A, **463**, **465**). The second is a simple cup with sloping sides (always with string cut base) of light clay ware (Fabric H), which becomes prominent in Level IV. The latter type comes in a plain or red-rim version (**466**).

While in Vf slips were consistently left matt, in Ve surfaces are frequently given a low or medium burnish, which becomes common practice in the Middle Bronze Age levels.

Jugs and jars (**446–52**)

446   5300
Trefoil neck and shoulder of jug with double-stranded handle. Fabric A, orange-red slip, matt. Decorated on neck with linear grooves and single boss.

447   H20/838   5346
Large trefoil jug with double twisted handle and two bosses on opposite side. Bottom part missing. Dense pale orange fabric, bright red slip left matt. Grooved horizontal lines around neck and shoulder. Neck made separately and attached with prominent finger markings.
H. (42)

448   H20/730   5301
Storage jar with two handles. Red-brown clay with grits and mudstones. Smoothed and burnished in parts. Hand-made.
Rim di. 34; Base di. 11.5; H. 33

449   1299
Large body sherd of closed vessel with twisted horizontal handle and grooved decoration. Fabric A, red slip, matt.
Th. 0.8

450   1289
Rim sherd of cooking jar with plug-through handle. Red cooking fabric (G). Hand-made.
Di. 21; Th. 0.8

451   5306
Rim fragment. Fabric A, red slip, flaked. Decorated on interior with wavy combed lines, incised chevrons on exterior.
Di. 27; Th. 0.5

452   1288
Rim sherd of cooking pot with crescentic handle. Cooking ware (Fabric G) with mudstones. Exterior smoothed. Hand-made.

Lid (453)

453 H20/622 KLT 87 1287
Lid with outward sloping sides and basket handle. Coarse brown fabric, grit temper. Roughly finished, painted with red bands on top, sides and interior. Hand-made.
Di. 19 (rim), 17 (top side)
Fig. 233

Bowls (454–62)

454 5306
Bowl rim. Semi-coarse beige fabric, grit and mudstone temper. Light brown wash on interior over rim. Hand-made?
Di. 19; Th. 0.8

455 1810
Level Ve/f
Shallow bowl with incurving rim. Fabric A, cream slip overall.
Di. 18, Th. 0.5

456 1289
Inverted rim sherd. Coarse fabric, red laminated with dark and white inclusions. Traces of red wash. Hand-made.
Di. 20; Th. 0.8

457 1287
Incurving flat top rim. Semi-coarse beige fabric (B), red slip both sides, matt. Hand-made.
Di. *c.* 25; Th. 1.0

458 1272
Level IVa/Ve?
Tapered incurving rim with flattened top. Fabric A, red. Red-slipped both sides, low burnish. Wheel-made?
Di. 27; Th. 0.6

459 1802
Unstratified
Carinated bowl rim. Fabric A. Red wash both sides.
Di. 24; Th. 0.6

460 5306
Rim with horizontal handle. Fabric A, brown wash interior, over rim and handle.
Di. 30; Th. 0.6

461 1281
Flared bowl rim with handle. Fabric A, red slip overall, matt. Exterior horizontal grooving. Cf. **483**.
Di. 16; Th. 0.4

462 1287
Rim with high-rise handle. Fabric A, traces of red-brown wash. Hand-made.
Di. 18; Th. 0.7

Cups (463–6)

463 5333
Cup with high-rise handle and *omphalos* base. Fabric A, red wash overall.
Di. 7.0

464 5318
Fragment with high-rise handle. Fabric A, red slip on exterior over rim to interior forming band.
Di. 9.0; Th. 0.6

465 5317
Level IVa/Ve - Pit 97/47
Base with *omphalos*. Fabric A, partial red slip, matt.
Di. 2.4 (base)

466 1299
Cup with uneven rim and string-cut base. Fabric H. Light clay ware.
Di. 9.5

Small jars and flasks (467–70)

467 5306
Cylindrical with two handles. Fabric A, plain. Low burnish on shoulder. Grooving below rim.

468 5300
Miniature jar with ring-base. Fabric A, flaked red slip. Hand-made?

469 1289
Small flask with lower part missing. Fine beige fabric burnt to grey-black. Cream wash?
Di. 2.0; Th. 0.4

470 1272
Level IVa/Ve?
Neck of miniature flask. Very fine. Fabric A, light brown slip, matt. Rilling on neck. Hand-made?
Th. 0.3

Miscellaneous (471–4)

471 5318
Sieve fragment. Semi-coarse red, grit-tempered, plain. Hand-made.
Th. *c.* 0.9

472 5302
Sieve fragment from spouted vessel. Semi-coarse grit-tempered, plain. Hand-made.

473 5302
Volute foot from tripod vessel(?). Fabric A, red-brown slip.
Cf. Tarsus (Goldman 1956, 273:445).

474 5344
Level Vf?
Leg of tripod(?) vessel. Fine orange, smoothed, plain. Hand-made.

Notes

1. For the avoidance of doubt, it may be worth stating that we use 'plain' of pottery surfaces to mean without surface treatment (including slip and burnish), or decoration of any kind (German *tongrundig*).
2. We are indebted to Dr Ellen Herscher for identifying the vessel with the help of illustrative material and for her valuable comments and references.

Chapter 24

The Middle Bronze Age Pottery

Dorit Symington

The excavations of the Middle Bronze Age levels extended into the adjoining square H19/a+b to the south of H20/c+d. Two phases could be isolated of which Level IVa represents the earlier layer, followed by IVb as the later one.

After our opening season, these two layers appeared in our preliminary report as phases 'd' (IVa) and 'c' (IVb) respectively and — although we expressed reservations — a possible EBA date for phase 'd' was contemplated (Symington, in Baker *et al.* 1995, 186, fig. 19:2–5, 7), which in subsequent seasons was shown not to be the case. Uncertainty about the dating arose mainly on account of the coarseness of the pottery recovered, best illustrated by the series of unbaked storage vessels (**506–15**; Fig. 230).

There is no perceptible ceramic break between the Early and Middle Bronze Age as demonstrated by the pottery repertoire of the previous Level Ve, summarized above, but a gradual phasing out of EBA fabrics and shapes and the introduction of new ones. To describe the fabrics in Level IV the same classification was used as for Level V (see p. 296 above).

The function of the area investigated in the succeeding period to EBA, continued to be largely domestic although there is a marked emphasis on food storage in the form of large open, unbaked vessels set into benches and groups of jugs for storage of liquids some of which were also set into floors. This accounts for the mainly coarse and medium type of pottery associated with kitchen wares. Finer wares were rare on the occupation floors of rooms and much of the recorded pottery of that category was derived from destruction debris of exterior areas.

Level IVa

Level IVa presented another opportunity (besides Level Vj) to study ceramic material on an occupation floor which had been caught up in a fire, yielding a number of vessels left behind by the occupants. The disadvantage is that their original appearance has often been altered by burning.

The two interconnecting rooms (Rms 41 & 42: Fig. 487) combining storage and cooking activities had numerous *in situ* vessels which provided information on kitchen and storage pottery of the period.

The majority of the pottery was recovered in Rm 41 which had several installations, including a central hearth (Figs. 83, 84 & 86). This room contained the largest group of storage and cooking pots, together with a number of small jars and cups with incised or combed decoration.

Only a small area of Rm 42 survived the digging of the robber trench but from the remaining floor several cooking vessels and some other objects were recovered.

Coarse wares

One of the main features, encountered in Level IVa amongst the coarse wares, were round and irregular-shaped storage pots or bins made of an unbaked vegetable tempered fabric which when first encountered received the name 'Weetabix' (after a breakfast cereal) on account of its friable consistency with many voids.

The crumbly nature of these vessels — frequently set in benches — made their recovery an impossible task, restricting the recording process to their *in situ* position. A major cluster of eight vessels was uncovered in the northern corner of Rm 41 in the form of round and oval containers (**506–8** H19/122, 124, 369: Fig. 230) and more examples were scattered in other parts of the room (**509–11**: Figs. 83, 86 & 487). Weetabix ware in the shape of a shallow oblong dish (**515**) was located in Rm 43 and remains of vessels in the same ware occurred in the east corner of Rm 42 (**512–14**: Fig. 487). There was no indication to determine if these unbaked vessels were used purely for storage or also for the preparation of food.

There were a number of *in situ* cooking pots on the floor of Rms 41 and 42. Typical were cooking pots with single handles rising above a slightly flared rim and occasionally with an added small boss on the opposite side to the handle (**516–17** H20/156, H19/358).

Figure 230. *Unbaked storage vessel* **508** *in situ against north wall of Rm 41.*

Figure 231. *Storage jar* **523** *from Rm 41 (see Fig. 86).*

They are made in a brown or reddish-brown fabric with a large percentage of grit and stone temper and surfaces are roughly smoothed. All the pots are hand-made.

The other characteristic feature of Level IVa amongst the coarse ware, are large vessels with flared rims and crescentic handles. A complete example was recovered from the southern half of Rm 41 in the form of an ovoid jar (**523** H19/359: Fig. 231) nestling next to one of the above described cooking pots (**517** H19/358) set in plaster, which had a smaller vessel sitting inside it (Fig. 86).

Pots with crescentic handles have a wide distribution in Anatolia but the time span in which they occur differs from region to region. Pithoi shaped similarly to **523** were found at Beycesultan in EB III (Lloyd & Mellaart 1962, fig. P.62:1–2, 5) but they are also attested in MBA contexts at Tarsus (Goldman 1956, fig. 299:926) and Mersin (Fitzgerald 1939–40, pl. 69:8). At Kilise Tepe crescentic handles occur also on large vessels with flared rims made from a coarse fabric with added pieces of chalk(?) which also seems to form the basis for the exterior cream coating. Crescentic handles on cooking pots continued into Level IVb.

A characteristic semi-coarse pottery, mainly found in Level IVa, is combed ware, of which a substantial amount was recovered (Fig. 232). Fabrics are reddish-brown or greyish black with a high proportion of grit temper (Petrographic Fabric C, see p. 254). This type of surface decoration is found on all types of vessels, such as jars (**530**), jugs (**529**: Fig. 232) and in one instance on a lid with a basket handle (**531**: Fig. 233). The pattern is usually a combination of undulating bands flanked by straight lines. An *in situ* example of a combed ware vessel was a small jar with one handle (**525** H19/366) in Rm 41 which had been sealed with a clay bung (**1492**: Fig. 87). A very similar jar with combed decoration but with pierced lug handles was recorded at Mersin in an MBA context (Fitzgerald 1939–40, pl. 69:14). The combed decoration is applied horizontally at the widest part of the vessel. On the various pieces found at Kilise Tepe the comb markings occur with 4 and up to 8 strands.

At Tarsus combed ware was first noted in EB II contexts and continued into MBA. It included a lid which is, although rather smaller, a close parallel to the Kilise Tepe one mentioned above (Goldman 1956 fig. 372:922). Combed ware still occurs in early LBA contexts at Tille but here manufactured in a very different fabric, described as friable and vegetable tempered, and the decoration is mostly found on collars of closed vessels which have no parallels at Kilise Tepe (Summers 1993, 43f., figs. 27–31).

Medium and fine wares

There was relatively little finer pottery recorded on the floors of Rms 41 and 42. Two large cups with grooved and incised decoration were exceptions (**490** Fig. 234; **526**). Both vessels have flared rims and high-

The Middle Bronze Age Pottery

rise handles. **490** is a well-known shape and the beige fabric is familiar from Tarsus where it is described as 'light clay ware' which represents the standard fabric for most fine and medium pottery (Goldman 1956, 165).

At Kilise Tepe this fabric (Fabric H) is characterized by a pale cream or buff fabric with calcareous inclusions, wet-smoothed and in some cases covered in a cream wash (Petrographic Fabric B, see pp. 253–4). It represents the standard thin-walled fabric for cups (e.g. **490–92**, **494**), and less frequently for bowls. This ware was first introduced in Level Ve in the form of straight-sided cups and continued throughout the Middle Bronze Age. A related fabric (also included in Petrographic Fabric B) is a fairly thick-walled, hard beige fabric with little visible temper and clean breaks. This fabric type (Fabric I) has only survived as sherd material, all of which came from closed vessels, covered in a thick red slip (**505**).

The greatest variety in terms of wares and shapes came from the destruction material (1258) to the north of Rm 41 with the *in situ* vessels, in an area where no house floors were located and marked as Rm 43 on the plan (Fig. 487). Apart from pottery, this location also yielded a number of small finds, including a large clutch of loomweights (**1702–22**). Although rich in ceramic types, very few whole profiles could be obtained.

The commonest fabrics for open and closed shapes are the 'light clay' ware, and a light brown or beige fabric with multi-coloured grit temper, evenly fired and with clean breaks, both grouped under Petrographic Fabric B. Fast wheel marks are often visible on the interior walls of the vessels.

The standard orange dense fabric of EB III (Petrographic Fabric A; S58-61, see p. 254) is still in use for bowls and closed vessels. Both this and Fabric J are typical for red-slipped wares. An innovative feature of these MBA slipped wares is that they have a low or medium burnish, in contrast to EB III when they were consistently left matt. A small number of black burnished sherds which included some very fine pieces had no other counterparts in Level IV and

Figure 232. *Combed ware jug 529 (on right) and other typical combed ware sherds.*

Figure 233. *Lids: on left 453 with painted decoration; on right 531 with combed decoration.*

Figure 234. *Cup with high-rise handle 490.*

were too fragmentary to retrieve any shapes. Plain finishes were rare. Also noted were fragments of red burnished miniature vessels, some with grooved or corrugated decoration, a technique also used on normal size vessels.

Jars (475–9)

Apart from the cooking ware jars discussed above, examples made in medium and fine fabrics were rare amongst the excavated MBA pottery. Examples of the small jar/cup with everted rim and exterior matt slip, typical of EB III, were still found, but they could be residual (**477–8**).

Two of the vessels in this category have no further parallels at Kilise Tepe: **475** the beige jar with handles emanating from the rim and plugged through the vessel wall and **476**, the pot with a basket handle and slight carination. Closed vessels with basket handles usually belong to the category of 'teapots' being provided with a spout where a handle of this type makes good sense. In the case of the Kilise Tepe fragment we cannot be certain whether the pot was provided with a spout or not, although we note that teapots were known, as demonstrated by the spout fragments recovered (**496–7**). Teapots with basket handles (as opposed to the more common side handle) occur in MBA contexts in — amongst other regions — Cilicia at Mersin (Fitzgerald 1939–40, pl. 69:1), as well as Tarsus. At the latter site, the assemblage also included an example with Syro-Cilician paintwork (Goldman 1956, fig. 297:868–70). Beycesultan recorded two examples (spouts missing) with additional volutes in EB III (Lloyd & Mellaart 1962, fig. P.70:11, 13) and in Level V (MBA) (Lloyd & Mellaart 1965, fig. P.8:5). Basket-handled teapots were also popular in central Anatolia in the Old Assyrian and Old Hittite period as found at Inandık with characteristic trough spouts (T. Özgüç 1988, 80, pl. O:3a & b).

Bowls (480–89)

None of the bowls recovered from Level IVa have yielded a complete profile but fragments reveal the general trends of preferred shapes. The S-profile bowl, typical of EB III and the EB/MB transitional phase, are largely replaced by bowls with gentle carinations, frequently with horizontal handles rising above the rim and mainly of the shallow type. Rims were found to be incurving, everted, or flared but frequently from the carination fairly upright and slightly tapered. The latter type is typical for shallow medium fine bowls (**486**). Red rim bowls, often very fine, and bowls with partial slips were not uncommon (**482, 487**). The carinated bowl is also represented by a miniature version with additional horizontal rilling above the carination (**483**).

Most of the simple bowl bases continue but disc bases are encountered more often (**488–9**).

Cups (490–94)

By far the most popular drinking vessel comes in the shape of a handleless beaker with small base and outward sloping sides (**491–2, 494**). They are made in the above described light clay fabric and are consistently string-cut and at times decorated with a carelessly applied red rim. This type of vessel, which first appears in Level Ve, was encountered in most pottery units and was clearly mass-produced on a grand scale.

Cups with flaring rim and high-rise handle coexist with the above type but in smaller numbers than recorded in Ve (**490, 493**). There are Cilician parallels for this type at Tarsus (Goldman 1956, 294:830) and Mersin (Garstang 1953, fig. 146:5–6; 147:13), sharing the same characteristics and manufacturing method.

Funnel (495)

The fairly coarsely made funnel, recovered from the destruction debris of Rm 43 (to the north of Rm 41), is the only example found at Kilise Tepe. Funnels are a typical item of the MBA ceramic repertoire with rather more refined specimens known from Kültepe where they occur slipped and burnished, also with a handle (Özgüç & Özgüç 1953, 177, pl. 29:173) and Boğazköy in the *karum* level Büyükkale IVd (Bittel *et al.* 1984, 51 fig. 21:196). At Tarsus, funnels formed part of a closed find in the Pottery Storage Room, of largely MBA character, but dated to LB I (Symington 1986, 282).

Handles (498–502)

Popular for jugs and occasionally cups are handles with a longitudinal groove which appears to be a vestige of the double-stranded handle, popular in the Early Bronze Age. While the central groove is still pronounced in Level IVa, it is often barely perceptible in Level IVb.

Another observation is that many handle types increasingly emanate from and rise well above the vessel rim (**493**). There is also evidence for the revival of plug-through handles in both MBA layers, in some cases flattened against the vessel wall but often looking much like their EBA counterparts (**475**).

Decorated sherds (503–5)

Apart from combed ware reserved for fairly coarse kitchen vessels referred to above, decoration of pottery is rare and limited to occasional rilling and excised patterns — executed after slipping — of diagonal, horizontal and wavy lines, mainly found on closed vessel sherds.

Jars (475–9)
475 H19/388 4276
Jar with two handles, lower part of body missing. Plug-through handle(s). Beige medium fine with small grits. Light brown slip carried over rim to interior — matt. Hand-made.
Rim di. 8.2; Th. 0.8

476 H20/272 1263
Jar with basket handle and slight carination. Fragmentary. Pale — orange, fine few grits. Light brown slip, horizontal low burnish.
Rim di. 10; Th. 0.6

477 1242
Jar rim. Buff, no temper. Exterior red wash carried over rim to form band on interior.
Di. 11; Th. 0.4

478 1275
Level IVa/Ve?
Small jar rim. Fabric A. Exterior red slip carried over rim to interior, low burnish.
Di. 8.0

479 1258
Jar rim. Brown with dark grey core, grit-tempered. Slipped.
Di. 11; Th. 0.7

Bowls (480–89)
480 1258
Carinated bowl with handle(s). Creamy-brown with few visible grits. Fugitive red slip. Exterior lightly burnished.
Di. 15; Th. 0.6

481 1258
Carinated bowl with high-rise handle(s). Cream with no visible grits. Fugitive red-brown slip overall.
Di. ?; Th. 0.4

482 1258
Carinated bowl with handle(s). Buff with grit temper. Partially slipped, red.
Di. 13; Th. 0.6

483 1258
Body sherd of miniature carinated bowl with handle(s) and rilling decoration. Black slip, burnished.
Di. ?; Th. 0.3

484 1241
Rim everted. Reddish grit-tempered. Slipped and burnished. Exterior brown, interior red.
Di. 24; Th. 0.6

485 1253
Level IVa/b
Bowl with incurving rim. Orange with grit inclusions. Slipped, low burnish.
Di. 13; Th. 0.5

486 1253
Level IVa/b
Rim of carinated bowl. Beige grit temper. Red wash on exterior.
Di. 22; Th. 0.9

487 1258
Red rim bowl. Fine beige grit-tempered. Orange-red paint over rim area.
Di. 11; Th. 0.3

488 1242
Disc base. Reddish with little temper. Traces of red paint on exterior. Interior red burnished.
Di. 6; Th. 0.3

489 4267
String-cut base. Fine buff fabric. Plain.
Di. 5; Th. 0.5

Cups (490–94)
490 H19/373 Etütlük 1996 4278
Cup with high-rise handle and grooved decoration. Cream, burnt to grey-black in places. Plain.
Di. 7.5; H. 9; Th. 0.5
Fig. 234

491 1272
Level IVa/Ve?
String-cut cup, one third missing. Fine, beige with few inclusions. Red paint over rim area.
Di. 9; H. 5.5; Th. 0.4

492 1258
String-cut base of small cup. Beige, fine with few grits. Plain.
Di. 2.5; Th. 0.6

493 1258
Rim with high-rise handle. Beige with fugitive grey paint overall.
Di. 9

494 1258
String-cut base. Same as **492**.
Di. 3; Th. 0.6

Funnel (495)
495 H20/199 1258
Fairly coarse, grit and stone temper. Surface smoothed. Both rims are rounded. Hand-made.
Di. 4.0–11.4; H. 9.6; Th. 2.1

Spouts (496–7)
496 1258
Beige grit-tempered, red wash on exterior.
Di. 2.2

497 1802
Unstratified
Spouted vessel with handle attachment. Beige soft fabric. Traces of brown wash. Hand-made.
Di. 1.3

Handles (498–502)
498 1243
Coarse reddish horizontal handle with two off-centre ridges.

499 1240
Handle attached to rim. Beige with grits. Exterior partly covered with brown wash.
Di. 1.5

500 1258
Jar handle from rim to body with indentation on base of handle. Brown, coarse very gritty. Smoothed.
8 × 11.2

501 1253
Level IVa/b
Handle with central groove. Coarse cooking ware.
5.6 × 8.8

502 1805
Unstratified
Small handle attached to rim with central groove. Fabric A, Red wash over exterior rim and handle. Hand-made.
W. handle 1.3

Decorated sherds (503–5)
503 1258
Body sherd of carinated closed vessel with bands of triple grooved horizontal lines. Brown with grit inclusions. Burnished.
Th. 1.0

504 1258
Body sherd of closed carinated vessel. Coarse reddish fabric with grits. Grooved decoration of horizontal and diagonal lines.
Th. 1.0

505 1805
Unstratified
Body sherd. Beige, medium fine. Thick red slip on exterior, high burnish. Excised decoration after slipping.

Cooking and storage pots (506–24)
Series of coarse, *in situ* unbaked vessels. Storage bins/containers of irregular shapes, frequently set in benches. Mud-coloured clay with large percentage of vegetation temper. Voids and vegetable impressions seen in breaks. Very friable. Figs. 230 & 487.

[506]	H20/122	1239	Rm 41
[507]	H20/124	1239	Rm 41
[508]	H19/367	4278	Rm 41
[509]	H19/349	4278	Rm 41
[510]	H19/365	4278	Rm 41
[511]	H19/285	4264	Rm 41
[512]	H20/142	1240	Rm 42
[513]	H20/118	1236	Rm 42
[514]	H19/253	4258	Rm 42
[515]	H20/200	1258	Rm 43

516 H20/156 1243
Rm 42, *in situ*
Cooking pot with one handle and one stud. Fabric G, blackish-brown. Complete apart from base and part of one side. Hand-made.
Rim di. 22; H. 6; Th. 1.2

[517] H19/358 4278
Rm 41, *in situ*
Large storage vessel set in plaster with a small pot base resting inside it; located next to **523**. Pot has one handle and a single stud on shoulder of the opposite side. Shape and fabric very similar to **516** above. Reddish-brown grit -and stone-tempered cooking ware. Surface scraped, some burnishing in the shoulder area.
Fig. 86

[518] H20/139 1240
Large storage vessel, base and sides preserved, shoulder and rim missing. Dense beige, crushed stone temper. Smoothed on both sides. Well-fired. Exterior red slip with visible brush strokes. Interior thick coat of red paint. Hand-made.
Base di. 26; Th. 1.0–1.5

519 H20/157 KLT 39 1243
Complete and found *in situ*. Very coarse pot with one handle. Tempered with large grits. Probably originally burnished but burnt black. Hand-made.
Di. 17–18.5; H. *c*. 16; Th. 1.4

520 H20/152 1242
Jar with handle attachment. Coarse orange with white grits and dark stones. Smoothed. Hand-made.
Di. *c*. 25; Th. 1.2

521 H20/123 1239
Storage vessel with straight sides. Fragmentary. Crude, heavily burnt grit-tempered. Possibly crushed out of shape and originally round. Rim missing.

522 1807
Level IVa/Ve
Large coarse bowl with handle(s). Beige grit and stone temper. Traces of red-brown wash both sides. Hand-made.
Di. uncertain; Th. 1.4

523 H19/359 Etütlük 1996 4278
Rm 41, *in situ*
Storage jar with crescentic handles. Very gritty reddish-brown to greyish-brown fabric. Complete, hand-made.
Di. 25; H. 36; Th. 1.2
Figs. 86 & 231

524 1258
Rim sherd of storage jar with crescentic handle. Brown, coarse, very gritty with white chalk-like inclusions. Smoothed. Hand-made.
Di. *c*. 29; Th. 1.1

Combed ware (525–31)
525 H19/366 4278
Rm 41, *in situ* with clay bung **1492**, in place
Small jar or cup with high-rise handle. Reddish-brown, gritty, burnt in parts. Handle broken in antiquity. Combed decoration. Hand-made.
Di. 8.2; H. 9; Th. 0.4
Fig. 87

526 H19/389 4278
Cup with high-rise handle and incised decoration. Brown, medium-fine with white grits. Incised wavy and horizontal decoration.
Di. 8.5; H. *c*. 9.5; Th. 0.3

527 1258
Body sherd of storage vessel with combed decoration. Reddish-brown coarse grit temper. Hand-made.
Th. 1.0

528 4278
Body sherd of closed vessel with combed decoration. Brown, Fabric G. Hand-made.
Th. 0.7

529 1805
Unstratified

Jug fragment with rising spout and combed decoration. Grey coarse fabric with light grits. Hand-made.
Th. 0.7
Fig. 232

530 1240
Rim of closed vessel with combed decoration. Coarse, black, gritty. Exterior greyish wash. Hand-made.
Di. 8

531 H20/593 KLT 86 1272
Level IVa/Ve?
Coarse lid with almost straight sides and broken off loop handle. Orange, medium coarse with large and small inclusions showing also on the surface. Smoothed with traces of red wash on exterior. Decorated with combed straight and wavy lines. Hand-made.
Di. 18
Fig. 233

Level IVb

Later occupational activities in H20d and H19a+b have largely deprived Level IVb (the later MBA phase) of its context. Although occupation floors were located in both squares, yielding a number of *in situ* vessels, there were no associated architectural remains (see Fig. 488). The domestic function of the area, however, is clear from the presence of a hearth and other household paraphernalia and not least by the pottery types recovered. Like its predecessor, Level IVb was burnt.

The pottery industry of Level IVb is overall more refined than in the preceding Level IVa, where coarse wares predominate. Although most of the vessels belonged also to the category of kitchen ware, they were on the whole carefully made with slips applied to the exterior or both sides and in most cases a low lustre burnish was applied.

The cream/buff light clay and related wares common in IVa continue as the chosen fabrics for finer kitchen wares, such as cups and bowls, while the pale orange dense fabric of EB III (Fabric A), still found in IVa, has now disappeared. Combed ware, popular in the previous phase, was rarely found in the IVb, but amongst the cooking ware, crescentic handles are still popular.

Jugs, which were altogether lacking in IVa, were numerous in IVb and well made. The characteristic lid with flared sides and basket handle which fitted over the collar of vessels (*Stülpdeckel*), is still part of the repertoire and represented by a rather crude example (**559**) and by a small specimen with combed decoration (**560**). An unusually elegant vessel in this assemblage is **557** (H20/72), a small jar on tripod feet with a low carination and concave sides. This may have been a *pyxis* but the upper part is broken and hence the final shape of the vessel remains a guess. Nevertheless, the piece is very reminiscent of a *pyxis* found at Tarsus as part of a closed find in the Pottery Storage Room. Although the lid is missing, the flanged rim to accommodate the cover is preserved (Goldman 1956, figs. 308:1056, 383:1056).

Bowls (532–43)

The light clay ware cups or beakers with string-cut base (**491**) continued in Level IVb and were as common as in Level IVa but found in some units with a thick stump base. The same fabric (Petrographic Fabric B, see p. 254) is also used for bowls with upright rims, invariably with a carelessly applied red slip over the rim and string-cut base. Some of the pieces are extremely thin walled, including the only complete bowl recovered in this level (**535**, **540**, **542**; cf. **487**).

As a general observation, characteristic and most numerous are carinated shapes and a preference for shallow bowls, presumably representing the everyday table ware. Most of the carinations are gently sloped and only a few examples are sharply angled. Carinated bowls with horizontal handles rising above the rim were in common use but the fragments cannot tell us if they come from single, double or even quadruple handled bowls (**536–8**) all of which are known from well preserved examples found at Tarsus.

With the exception of the light clay ware, all the bowls are covered with a red slip wash, have a low lustre burnish or — more rarely — are left matt. Decorated examples like **541** with plastic decoration and **539** with painted striped pattern are unusual and have no parallels within the corpus.

Unit 4248 (H19) contained a ceramic mixture of typical Level IV wares and examples of the characteristic shallow bowl with internal thickened rim which becomes the standard table ware in Level III (**603–24**), see p. 109 above.

Jugs and jars (546–58a)

Among the *in situ* vessels, we have a mixture of cooking pots and jugs. Cooking or storage pots occur with a single handle (**556**) but mainly with two handles. They are either oval or rounded in shape and with flared

Figure 235. *Lower part of storage jar 558a with disc base.*

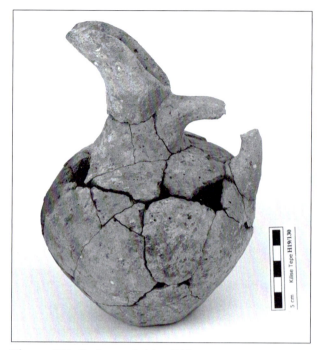

Figure 236. *Beak-spouted jug 549.*

rims (**554-5**). The occasional disc base — as opposed to the usual flat type — makes a rare appearance (**558a**: Fig. 235; see also **488–9**).

Most of the *in situ* vessels belong to the category of jugs (**546–53**) made in cream light brown fabrics and covered in a light brown slip burnished to a low lustre. They are also rather thin walled. The majority have piriform bodies but in most cases neck and rim parts have not survived to determine their final shape. The bases, which are disproportionately small to the body, are at times slightly rounded, indicating the use of pot stands (of which none were found) or their setting into the floor. Jugs with surviving spouts belong to the beak-spouted type, although these are hand-made of a much coarser fabric with large chalk-like inclusions (**549**: Fig. 236) and covered in creamy lime wash (**548**).

Both categories, cooking pots and jugs, share the characteristic of a longitudinal shallow groove on the top of handles, also observed on MBA vessels from Karahöyük Konya in the Konya Museum. This practice can also be seen on 'teapot' and jug handles at Beycesultan in MBA (Lloyd & Mellaart 1965, figs. P17:5, P20:8, 11), but is only rarely found on vessels at Tarsus and Mersin.

Decorated sherds (561–7)

The pottery of Level IVb is predominantly monochrome and decorated wares were extremely rare. Of interest are two brick red sherds with the remains of a 'red cross' painted on the exterior. Red cross bowls were common at Kilise Tepe at the end of EB III and the transitional Level Ve with the cross painted in the interior and manufactured in the traditional pale orange fabric (Fabric A). The exterior cross appears to be a late development which was observed in Troy V (Blegen *et al.* 1951, 250f., fig. 204; Easton 2002, 338 fn. 427) and also at Tarsus (Goldman 1956, figs. 290:811–12, 291:820–22).

The most characteristic Middle Bronze Age ware which Cilicia shared with the Amuq region is the so-called Syro-Cilician painted pottery which was found in large quantities at Tarsus and Mersin and on surveys of the Cilician plain. Neither of the two painted sherds found at Kilise Tepe, illustrated below (**566–7**), can be ascribed with any certainty to this category and it would seem that Kilise Tepe, and probably the whole of the Göksu valley, did not partake in this ceramic tradition. **566** depicts a butterfly motif, well known among the Syro-Cilician repertoire but the fabric is rather denser than the standard light clay ware normally used.

Bowls (532–43)

532 4257
Level IVa/b
Bowl rim. Buff, fine dense fabric some grit temper. Smoothed. Plain.
Di. 15; Th. 0.6

533 4271
Bowl. Plain beige fabric. Self-slipped.
Di. 15; Th. 0.6

534 4275
Carinated bowl. Fine beige, grit-tempered. Red slip overall left matt.
Di. 18; Th. 0.6

535 H19/202 4249
Red rim bowl. Light clay ware, fine. String cut base. Rather burnt. Fugitive red wash over rim (not shown in drawing). Almost complete.
Di. 8; Th. 0.4

536 4257
Level IVa/b
Carinated bowl with horizontal handle. Beige, dense fine fabric, some grits. Red slip both sides.
Di. 20; Th. 0.5

537 4254
Carinated bowl with horizontal handle. Fine beige, grit-tempered. Red slip, medium burnish, mottled effect on exterior.
Di. *c.* 14; Th. 0.5

538 1231
Carinated bowl with horizontal handle. Fine beige, grit-tempered. Red wash overall.
Di. 17; Th. 0.5

539 4235
Level IIIa/IVb
Carinated bowl. Light brown with grit inclusions. Cream slip with

orangey paint of horizontal and vertical stripes.
Di. 19; Th. 0.5

540   4254
Small red rim bowl. Buff fine. Red paint over rim area.
Di. 11; Th. 0.6

541   4248
Level IIIa/IVb
Bowl rim with plastic decoration. Fine orange. Slipped and burnished both sides.
Di. 23; Th. 0.5

542   4268
String-cut bowl base with red slip, matt. Orange medium fabric, many grits.
Di. 4; Th. 0.7

543   4268
Base with pedestal foot. Fine buff, reddish-brown slip overall, matt.
Di. 5; Th. 0.5

Handles (544–5)
544   4251
High-rise handle attached to rim. Beige, medium fine, grit temper. Traces of red wash.

545   4235
Level IIIa/IVb
Jug(?) handle attached to rim with central groove. Coarse, grey with grits, brown slip.

Jugs (546–53)
546   H20/35   KLT 37   1219
Level IVb?
Complete except for top part of neck and rim. Beige grit-tempered. Cream slip, burnt pinkish-red on one side, grey to black on the other, slip flaked in places.
Neck di. 4.3 × 5.0; Th. 0.5; H. 22.5

547   H20/79   1227
Level IIIa/IVb
Complete except for neck and handle. Beige with large grey grits. Cream beige slip in interior and light brown slip on exterior. Emplacement for handle.
H. (22); Th. 0.6

548   H19/205   4249
Top part of beak-spouted jug with horizontal handle and stud. Light-brown, dark grits and small stones. Smoothed. Creamy coating. Hand-made.
Th. 0.6

549   H19/130   Etütlük 1996   4236
Level IIIa/b
Beak-spouted jug. Beige, medium coarse with calcareous and organic temper, and large white inclusions showing on the surface. Surface creamy coating. Burnt on one side. Handle with central ridge.
Base di. 5.5; H. 18; Th. 1.0
Fig. 236

550   H19/193   4249
Jug with rising spout. Most of handle missing. Beige with small grits and grey core. Light-brown slip, low burnish. Burnt on one side.
Th. 0.6

551   H19/191   4249
Piriform jug, neck and handle missing. Slightly curved base. Dense beige with very small grits, some stones. Cream slip on interior and exterior. Burnt in parts.
Base di. 5.0; Th. 0.7

552   H19/192   4249
Base and shoulder of half a piriform jug with handle attachment. Light-brown fired to grey in interior. Calcareous temper, particles showing on surface. Creamy coloured coating. Hand-made(?).
Base di. 5.8; Th. 0.7

553   H19/387   4271+4267
Level IVa+IVb — major part from IVb pit (P96/87), some sherds from IVa fill.
Piriform jug with neck and handle missing. The disc base appears to have undergone some reworking having been perforated in the centre and the outer rim chipped evenly. Dense beige, fine grit temper. Purple-red slip, horizontal. burnishing marks. Mottled effect one side.
H. (21); Th. 0.7

Jars (554–58a)
554   H20/84   1227
Level IIIa/IVb
Rimless vessel broken in half vertically with grooved handle (second handle in drawing restored). Friable, white grit-tempered. Brown burnt to black.
Base di. 8.0; Th. 1.0

555   1231
Large cooking pot with two handles. Coarse reddish-brown, with white stones. Blackened on exterior. Handle with shallow groove. Hand-made.
Rim di. 29; H. 33; Th. 1.0

556   1227
Level IIIa/IVb
Small cooking pot with broken off handle. Coarse light-brown, white grit and stone temper. Barely smoothed.
Rim di. *c.* 10; H. 13; Th. 1.0

557   H20/1091   1220+1226+1227
Level IIIa/IVb
Lower part of jar on tripod feet, one missing. Fine grey-beige some grits. Traces of fugitive red paint below carination. Hand-made(?).
Th. 0.6

558   H20/37   1219
Level IVb?
Base of closed vessel. Semi-coarse, reddish-brown stones and organic temper. Red wash and scatter burnish. Blackened in parts. Hand-made.
Th. 1.4

[558a]   H20/72   1226
Lower part of storage vessel with disc base. Pale orange fabric, medium-fine paste with reddish-brown inclusions and organic temper, judging by voids on the surface. Red wash on exterior, rather worn, with some scatter burnishing.
Th. 0.6
Fig. 235

Lids (559–60)

559   H20/78   KLT 38   1227
Level IIIa/IVb
Lid with sloping sides and loop handle (broken off). Coarse, reddish-brown, white inclusions plus organic temper. Red wash overall, matt.
Di. 20; Th. 1.0

560   4268
Small lid fragment with outward sloping sides. Semi coarse orange, gritty with combed decoration.

Decorated sherds (561–7)

561   4268
Body sherd of closed vessel with combed decoration. Pale orange, gritty. Hand-made.
Th. 0.7

562   4248
Level IIIa/IVb
Body sherd with combed decoration. Same fabric and decoration as **561**.
Th. 1.0

563   4248
Level IIIa/IVb
Body sherd with combed decoration. Same as **561**.
Th. 0.8

564   4248
Level IIIa/IVb
Body sherd with red cross. Medium red, dark grits. Plain, painted with red cross on exterior. Interior traces of coating.
Th. 0.9

565   4248
Level IIIa/IVb
Body sherd with red cross(?) painted on exterior.
Th. 0.9

566   1802
Unstratified
Body sherd, fine beige, cream wash and brown painted butterfly and hatched triangle design. Syro-Cilician(?).

567   4268
Painted body sherd of closed vessel with handle attachment. Beige, semi-coarse, grit-tempered. Burnt on interior. Exterior cream slip and red linear design. Possibly Syro-Cilician.

Chapter 25

Pottery from Level III

Connie Hansen & Nicholas Postgate[1]

Introduction

Although parts of Late Bronze Age houses were excavated in I14 Level 3, deposits of this date were principally found on the NW side of the mound in squares H19, I19/I20, and J20, and the sherds published here mainly come from two prime contexts, the destruction material lying on the IIId floor of the Eastern Courtyard in I20 (especially unit 1428), and well stratified material in H19 (units 4205, IIId, and 4211, IIIc/d). Whole pots in primary contexts are very scarce in Level III. The only *in situ* pots at the NW corner were the two large storage jars, the bases of which were still in place in Room 30 (see p. 115); each had been given a clay coating, perhaps to help keep the contents, very likely water, cool. Two large storage jars were also found *in situ* in the corner of Room 91 in I14 Level 3 (**637a–b**). Apart from this the phase IIId destruction material in the Eastern Courtyard (1428) incorporated some larger fragments of vessels, the size of which entitles us to consider them as secondary material probably contemporary with the context in which they were found; but elsewhere and especially in H19 the ceramic material consists only of sherds small enough to be incorporated in the steady accumulation of occupation deposits, and it is therefore only rarely that we have even a complete profile.

Table 10 gives the occurrence of a selection of rim types, and of libation arms, lentoid flasks and bottles within Level III. This will give an idea of the approximate volume of material in different phases, but it is not intended to provide a basis for statistical study. We found the Level III ceramic material to be extremely consistent throughout the five architectural phases we distinguished, and we have not attempted to find changes through time. This may seem unsatisfactory: given the evidence of continuous occupation and periodic re-building it could correspond to at least two and perhaps three centuries, and some changes must have taken place. However, as the table shows, because the first three phases (IIIa–c) were only reached in H19, the numbers of sherds from them are much lower, and they do not give an adequate basis for identifying changes.

This is particularly the case because very little in the way of change is observable. The same consistency through time is observed at other sites and especially at Boğazköy. Schoop writes of the 'fundamental typological continuity from the beginning of the *karum* period onwards to the very end of the Hittite empire period', and points out that 'if confronted with a Hittite pottery sequence ... lacking a comparative stratigraphy elsewhere, we will not see chronological gaps marked by clear typological breaks' (Schoop 2003, 168). He comments that there is variation in the 'relative numeric portion the distinct types occupy in the assemblage', but in our case it is clear that the sample at our disposal is not large enough, especially for phases IIIa–c, to permit a statistical study of this sort.

Fabrics

The internal consistency of the Level III assemblage and the small repertoire of shapes does not mean that there was not a variety of fabrics in use. On site eleven groups were initially distinguished by the macroscopic physical appearance of the sherds. Later examination of the material by Knappett, backed up in some cases by his petrographical analyses, led us to reduce the number of basic wares by grouping more than one of the original fabrics together. Since the numbers of sherds from each unit were recorded using the original groups, these 'Wares' are listed here, with a note of any corresponding petrographic fabric groups used for Level III (pp. 257–8).

Ware a:
Fine dense brick red with no visible temper. Can be orangey in colour. Red slip. Burnished exterior, interior or both. Burnish is stripy and usually vertical. Both hand-made and wheel-made. Open shapes, lentoid flasks and libation arms.

Ware b
Dense brick red, grit-tempered. Mainly red slipped and burnished. Both hand-made and wheel-made. Both closed and open shapes.

Ware c
Dense brick red with fairly big, mainly white grits. Some with dark red wash. Smoothed but rarely burnished. Both hand-made and wheel-made. Probably all from closed shapes.

Table 10. *Sherd counts for Level III by phase.*

Phase of Level III	a	a–b	b	c	c–d	d	d–e	e
Plate rim					21	18	4	6
Deep bowl rim					3			
Plain rim		14	8	18	19	11	2	5
External rim	7	1		18	13	12		4
Shallow incurred rim	1		1	2	7	4		
Shallow plain flattened rim			1	1	6	2		
Shallow thickened rim				1	2	10		1
Shallow internal large rim				8	10	15	3	8
Shallow internal small rim	3		4	51	85	90	45	27
Shallow internal grooved rim		1				1	1	15
Shallow internal thickened rim				2	1	2	4	3
Shallow external rim				1	1	1		
Hole-mouth rim				1	6	4		1
Rolled rim				5	17	18	2	11
Vertical plain rim	1		2	6	14	5	4	
Vertical band out rim				1	2	3		1
Vertical thickened rim					12	2		
Flaring rim			3	3	16	1	1	3
Everted plain rim		5	4	27	13	27	9	15
Everted rounded rim				2	9	13		3
Everted flattened rim		1		2	8	5		1
Everted overhanging rim					2	1		1
Libation arm				2	28	34		4
Trefoil rim		2		9	4	9	2	1
Pilgrim flask						1		2
Spindle bottle							1	1

These figures are taken from the following units: 1376, 1417, 1421, 1428, 1428, 1436, 4001, 4004, 4010, 4012, 4017–18, 4026–7, 4204, 4211–12, 4214, 4217, 4223–5, 4227–46, 5528–9, 5531–3, 5535–6, 5538–40.

Wares a, b and c all belong to petrographic Fabric Group A, with Ware a in particular corresponding to 'Red Lustrous Wheel-made Ware'.

Ware d
Buff to brownish with soapy surface, grit-tempered. Surface usually yellowish-buff and smoothed. Occasionally reddish and hard-fired. Both hand-made and wheel-made. Mostly closed shapes but also bowls. This ware includes petrographic Fabric Groups B and C.

Ware e
Buff-brownish with large 'oatmeal' grits. External surface wet-smoothed allowing grit temper to show through. Both hand-made and wheel-made. All closed shapes.

Ware f
Buff/yellowish-buff, heavy grit-temper, mostly pebbles. Occasionally dark core. Hand-made. Probably all closed shapes.

Ware g
Very mixed group with reddish wash on exterior (probably also including some residual EBA red burnished sherds). Both hand-made and wheel-made. Open and closed shapes.

Ware h
Yellow-buff/brownish, grit temper. Dull red/purplish-red/brown/blackish monochrome wash on exterior. Sometimes burnished. Hand-made. All closed shapes except for a few bowls.

Ware i
Very varied fabric often dark grey. Lustrous surface often pitted, grit-tempered. Exterior smoothed, sometimes polished. Hand-made. Mostly closed shapes.

Ware j
Hard-fired 'clinky' ware. Mostly fine black or dark grey fabric with very little temper. Some finely burnished. Some possibly EB or MB throw-ups. Both hand-made and wheel-made. Open and closed shapes.

Ware k
Buff-brownish and not very heavy grit-temper. Buff-brown/dull reddish vertical stripy burnishing. Both hand-made and wheel-made. All closed shapes.

General remarks

Despite the small area excavated it is possible to discern some characteristics of the Level III material. The most striking is the presence of the fine red burnished ware both as bowls and libation arms, and occasionally as small jars. In other respects it is a rather homogeneous corpus, with little variety in shapes, the dominant being shallow bowls and jars with everted rims. The homogeneity of the corpus is one of the characteristics of Late Bronze Age assemblages elsewhere in Anatolia (see the quotations from Schoop, p. 329 above). It has long been observed that the standardized wares of the final centuries of Hittite rule are present on any sites which fell under the direct administration of Hattusa. The monotonous repertoire of 'plain pottery with heavy wheel marks of brownish yellow clay' was christened 'drab ware' at Tarsus (Goldman 1935, 534; 1937, 262–3) and more recently it has been recognized by excavators from Gordion in the west to the Altınova in the east, Tarsus and Kinet in the south, and Tille in the southeast on the Euphrates. The homeland of this ware is of course Boğazköy and other cities in the region, and by comparison for instance with Tarsus (Goldman 1956, 205) or with Gordion (Henrickson 2002, 129), a greater variety of types is found there.

The composition of the repertoire of the Upper City at Boğazköy was studied in exemplary detail by Müller-Karpe (1988), and as far as possible we have adapted our terminology to underline the parallels between our material and his. It is clear that our assemblage can correctly be described as 'Hittite', on the basis of the plates and internal rim bowls alone. Nevertheless, there are differences: some shapes are not paralleled in the Upper City corpus (e.g. the pithos rim **637**), and others are scarce (e.g. globular jars like **653–5**). Kilise Tepe seems not to have used much white slipped ware, common at the capital (Müller-Karpe 1988, 20–22, Ware D), but had a distinct preference for the red-slipped wares (see on **603–24**) even though they are apparently not produced in the vicinity (see Knappett, p. 270). Moreover there is a considerable range of wares within each of our prime contexts in Level III, and the repertoire is not by any means rigidly standardized, as is clear from the not infrequent occurrence of hand-made pieces.

One of the notable features of standard LBA Hittite pottery from phases 15–13 at Kinet Höyük, as also at Tarsus (Goldman 1956, 204), was the use of pot-marks (Gates 2001). At Kilise Tepe pot-marks are found occasionally on the base of spindle bottles (**679**; and **897–8** from Level II: see also Symington 2001, 169), as they are on this shape elsewhere (Eriksson 1993; see Knappett, p. 270). In view of their suspected function as containers for valuable liquids one might expect the spindle bottles to have been imported, and the fabric of our pieces supports this. On the other hand, the common and probably locally made plates, a type which had most of the pot-marks both in the Kinet repertoire and at Tarsus, have not yielded any at Kilise Tepe, and it seems as though the function of the marks may have differed between the two sites.

That there were genuine differences from the ceramic repertoire in Plain Cilicia is perhaps suggested by the relative frequency of Red Lustrous Wheel-made wares at Kilise Tepe and other sites along the Göksu compared with both Tarsus and Kinet Höyük. Whether these differences reflect the same conditions that give Kilise Tepe its independent ceramic tradition in the early phases of Level II remains to be researched. One possible explanation which would relate specifically to the Red Lustrous Wheel-made ware is that the Göksu valley was the principal route of import from its centre of manufacture (e.g. northern Cyprus) to the capital at Boğazköy where we know it arrived in great quantities (see Kozal 2003).

Catalogue

In the following catalogue open shapes are listed first, followed by closed shapes (predominantly jars) and special shapes which are readily identified (libation arms, trefoil rims, lentoid flasks and spindle bottles). Where a sherd can be attributed to a specific shape with some confidence this is done, usually with reference to Müller-Karpe (1988), who cites comparisons from other sites. However, not all our forms have clear parallels within that corpus. Further, many rims are insufficient to identify the shape of the entire vessel in the absence of whole pots for comparison, especially with the jars and other closed shapes, and they are grouped according to the rim form.

Plates (568–71)

Plates (sometimes called 'platters') are flat with a plain rim (we have no instances of the string-impressed rims found at Boğazköy). Their fabric is mainly brown or buff and usually they have a slip or wash. **568** is unusually hand-made and of a different fabric. **569–71** are typically wheel-made, and all of about 30 cm diameter. **571** is a little taller than the others and is perhaps more a bowl than a plate. They seem not to be recorded from the earlier phases (see Table 10). Plates are one of the most recognizable and recurrent 'Hittite' types, and very common at other sites such as Porsuk (Dupré 1983, pl. 20–21:128–30 although the rim is a little different), Mersin (Caneva & Sevin 2004, 76), Tarsus (Goldman 1956, pl. 384:1134), and of course Boğazköy (Fischer 1963, Taf. 99:922–7; Taf. 100–101). In the Boğazköy Upper City they constituted 2 to 5 per cent of the production assemblage (Müller-Karpe 1988, 127, Taf. 42–3, Type Te1).

568 1428
Level IIId
Rim to middle body. Hand-made. Orange with yellowish core, grit-tempered. Orangey slip. Rim plain.
Di. 23; Th. 0.6

569 4205
Level IIId
Rim to lower body. Beige, darker core, white grits. Cream slip. Rim plain.
Di. 30; Th. 1.1

570 4211
Level IIIc/d
Rim to lower body. Light brown, grit-tempered. Red wash. Rim plain.
Di. 30; Th. 0.5

571 4205
Level IIId
Rim to middle body. Buff, grit-tempered with big grey grits. Slightly burnished. Rim plain.
Di. 30; Th. 1.5

Deep bowls (572–3)

A few rims from deep bowls were found but in very small fragments. The two illustrated have thickened rims and **572** has dark orange slip and is burnished. Deep bowls or cups have been found at Boğazköy (Fischer 1963, Taf. 52), but they have handles, of which there are no signs on the examples from Kilise Tepe. (For some deeper shapes included under shallow bowls see also **625**, **628** and **629**.)

572   4211
Level IIIc/d
Rim with upper body. Dark orange, very little temper. Dark orange slip, burnished. Rim thickened ext. and int.
Di. 18; Th. 0.5

573   4212
Level IIIc/d
Rim to middle body. Buff-cream, heavily grit-tempered. Smoothed. Rim thickened ext.
Di. 22; Th. 0.9

Open bowls with plain rim (574–9)
A large number of plain rims from bowls were found. They are all made of a fine fabric with very little temper, but a few (e.g. **575** and **579**) are more gritty. The surface treatment is very varied and can be just smoothed (**574**), slipped (**575**), slipped and burnished (**576**) or burnished (**579**). A few have a wash and are burnished (**578**). The diameter also varies from 18 cm (**575**) to 30 cm (**577**). Most of them have thin walls but **579** has walls with a thickness of 2.5 cm. It is also very gritty and has a carinated shape while all the others are rounded. Plain bowls are also a very common shape at other LBA sites as attested in Porsuk (Dupré 1983, pl. 4:2–8, 10), Tarsus (Goldman 1956, pl. 375:960 and 376:953–4, 956–7) and Boğazköy (Fischer 1963, Taf. 83:694, 696–8, 702; 84:706, 711–12).

574   1428
Level IIId
Rim to middle body. Red-brown core with very little temper. Smoothed.
Di. 28; Th. 0.5

575   1428
Level IIId
Rim to middle body. Brown, grit-tempered. Cream slip.
Di. 18; Th. 0.7

576   4211
Level IIIc/d
Rim to lower body. Brown with light brown core, no temper. Brown slip and burnished. Ext. red-brown wash.
Di. 20; Th. 0.3

577   4211
Level IIIc/d
Rim with upper body. Black with very little temper. Brown surfaces with fine lines.
Di. *c.* 30; Th. 0.7

578   4223
Level IIIc
Rim to middle body. Brown, very fine with little temper. Red-brown wash and burnished.
Di. 23; Th. 0.5

579   4223
Level IIIc
Rim to lower body. Brown, heavily grit-tempered. Burnished.
Di. 23; Th. 2.5

Open bowls with external rim (580–87)
A number of bowls with external rim were found. Several are in fine red, orange or brown-yellow fabric, with no temper and burnished, but the fabric can also be brown to grey and gritty to very gritty. The diameter varies from 7 to 24 cm. Both surfaces are either smoothed or burnished and can have wash. One has traces of brown paint on the rim (**583**). They are also attested at Porsuk (Dupré 1983, pls. 14–19) and Boğazköy where, unlike our Kilise Tepe examples, they have handles (Fischer 1963, pl. 103:932–5). Cf. perhaps Müller-Karpe 1988, 115–18, Taf. 38–9, Types S9–11).

580   4211
Level IIIc/d
Rim with upper body. Orangey, no temper. Red slip and smoothed.
Di. 18; Th. 0.5

581   4211
Level IIIc/d
Rim to lower body. Red, heavily grit-tempered. Smoothed.
Di. 21; Th. 0.4

582   4211
Level IIIc/d
Rim to lower body. Brown-yellow, no temper. Brown-yellow slip and smoothed.
Di. 7; Th. 0.6

583   4211
Level IIIc/d
Rim to middle body. Dark grey with lighter grey core, grit-tempered. Smoothed. Traces of brown paint on rim.
Di. 19; Th. 0.6

584   4205
Level IIId
Rim with upper body. Cream, heavily grit-tempered. Smoothed.
Di. 14; Th. 0.5

585   4205
Level IIId
Rim with upper body. Red, no temper. Burnished.
Di. 24; Th. 0.4

586   4211
Level IIIc/d
Rim to middle body. Buff, grit-tempered. Red wash int. and traces ext.
Th. 0.6

587   4205
Level IIId
Rim to middle body. Light brown, grit-tempered. Red wash.
Di. *c.* 20; Th. 0.7

Open bowl with incurved rim (588)
A few sherds with incurved rim were excavated. The fabric is the same as bowls with external rim. Incurved rims do not seem to be very common elsewhere but

some have been found at Maşat Höyük (T. Özgüç 1982, fig. A:16–23). Cf. also Müller-Karpe 1988, 114, Taf. 37, S7.1).

588   4211
Level IIIc/d
Rim to lower body. Dark orange, fine white grits. Ext. smoothed.
Di. 22; Th. 0.7

Shallow bowls (589–629)
Most rims excavated are from shallow bowls and they are listed here under seven different types: plain flattened rims (**589–92**), plain thickened rims (**593–4**), large bowls with internal rims (**595–602**), smaller bowls with internal rims (**603–24**), internal rims thickened out (**625–7**) and external large rims (**628–9**).

Shallow bowls are a common shape at other LBA sites such as Boğazköy (Fischer 1963, Taf. 83–96; Müller-Karpe 1988, 95–123, Taf. 29–37, Type S), Tarsus (Goldman 1956, pl. 384), Maşat Höyük (T. Özgüç 1982, fig. A:37–41, B:1–3) and Porsuk (Dupré 1983, pl. 5–13).

Shallow bowls with flattened rim (589–92)
Several sherds with a flattened rim were found. The fabric is either reddish or brown and all are gritty. The surface is smoothed or slipped and can be burnished. **591** also has red traces of paint/wash on the rim. They are very different in shape although they are all from shallow bowls and have a flattened top. **589** is thickened on its exterior and interior and is diagonally flattened while **590** also is thickened but with a horizontal flat top. **591** is thickened on its exterior, horizontally flat and slightly carinated just below the rim. **592** is plain, horizontally flattened and has a handle attachment on the rim.

589   4205
Level IIId
Rim to middle body. Red-brown with dark grey core, grit-tempered. Dark brown slip and smoothed.
Di. 18; Th. 0.5

590   4211
Level IIIc/d
Rim to middle body. Beige, grit-tempered. Slightly burnished.
Di. 26; Th. 0.5

591   4211
Level IIIc/d
Rim to middle body. Beige with light brown core, grit-tempered. Smoothed. Red wash on ext. and top of rim.
Di. 24; Th. 1.0.

592   4211
Level IIIc/d
Rim to lower body. Light orangey, grit-tempered. Orangey slip and burnished. Rim flattened with handle attachment.
Di. 24; Th. 0.7

Shallow bowls with plain thickened rim (593–4)
A few bowls have a plain thickened rim. They are all in a buff fabric, gritty and with the surface slipped. **593** is red-painted with a band on the rim and uneven diagonal lines on its exterior. In Tarsus LBA I, there are bowls with diagonal lines from the rim (Goldman 1956, pl. 302:993–5; Korbel 1987, Taf. 40–42), but they are very well made compared to this one from Kilise Tepe. This is the only Level III sherd with diagonal lines.

593   4211
Level IIIc/d
Rim to lower body. Buff, grit-tempered. Red paint int. and ext., matt. Band on rim and uneven diagonal lines on ext.
Di. 24; Th. 0.5

594   4205
Level IIId
Rim with upper body. Buff, grit-tempered. Buff slip.
Di. 24; Th. 1.1

Large shallow bowls with internal rim (595–602)
Bowls with an internal rim — the Boğazköy Schwapprand — are a very common shape in Level III. They have been divided in two: internal large and internal small (see next section). The internal large rims come from vessels with a larger diameter between 26–37 cm. They are very varied in fabric and all are gritty; none of the rims are in the fine red fabric (Ware a). The surface is normally smoothed except for **601** which is slightly burnished. **595–7** are slipped. **600** is the only example with painted bands on its exterior, but they can have wash on both surfaces. All are wheel-made with the exception of **596** which is hand-made and also of a coarser fabric.

These are closest to Müller-Karpe 1988, Type S1 (p. 95, Taf. 29–31), which tend to have thicker and steeper sides than his other bowls.

595   1428
Level IIId
Rim with upper body. Yellowish, grit-tempered. Cream slip.
Di. 29; Th. 1.5

596   1428
Level IIId
Rim to middle body. Beige with grey-brown core, grit-tempered and coarse. Hand-made. Cream slip.
Di. 33; Th. 1.2

597   4205
Level IIId
Rim with upper body. Red-brown, heavily grit-tempered. Red-brown slip.
Di. 26; Th. 1.2

598   4211
Level IIIc/d
Rim to middle body. Orange, grit-tempered with big grits.

Smoothed.
Di. 29; Th. 0.9

599   4211
Level IIIc/d
Rim to middle body. Brown, grit-tempered. Int. light brown. Smoothed.
Di. >30; Th. 0.8

600   4217
Level IIIc
Rim to lower body. Reddish, grit-tempered with big grits. Smoothed. Faded red-brown paint or wash, matt.
Di. 35; Th. 1.0

601   4205
Level IIId
Rim to middle body. Buff grit-tempered. Slightly burnished.
Di. 37; Th. 1.1

602   4205
Level IIId
Rim to middle body. Light brown, grit-tempered. Smoothed. Small ridge int.
Di. 32; Th. 1.1

Smaller shallow bowls with internal rim (**603–24**)
By far the most common shape in Level III is the shallow bowl with an internal small rim. It occurs in all fabrics. The surface treatment is either smoothed or burnished and in most cases also slipped. Sometimes paint or wash are added. Commonest are sherds in the fine red fabric with no temper or just a little temper, which have been burnished. They are very uniform in size with diameters usually from 20 to 28 cm; a few have a slightly smaller diameter. At Gordion too smaller (di. ~16 cm) shallow bowls were in fine ware, while the larger range (~25 cm) were in common ware (Henrickson 1994, 105). One rim has a large chip broken off (**617**) perhaps from a handle attachment. Handles on shallow bowls are very rare and this would be the only one from Kilise Tepe.

Müller-Karpe (1988), Type S5 (p. 106, Taf. 34–7); very common (40% of the total of bowls) in level 4 of the Upper City, tailing off to only 15 per cent in level 3.

603   4205
Level IIId
Rim to middle of body. Light brown, grit-tempered. Traces of brown paint.
Di. 22; Th. 0.6

604   4211
Level IIIc/d
Rim to lower part of body. Orange, grit-tempered with big grits. Smoothed.
Di. 24; Th. 0.6

605   1428
Level IIId
Rim with upper part of body. Beige, grit-tempered. Beige slip and smoothed.
Di. 25; Th. 0.7

606   1428
Level IIId
Rim to lower part of body. Orange, heavily grit-tempered. Smoothed.
Di. 22; Th. 0.8

607   1428
Level IIId
Rim to middle of body. Brown, grit-tempered with few big grits. Brown slip and smoothed.
Di. 23; Th. 0.7

608   1428
Level IIId
Rim to middle of body. Orangey, grit-tempered with big grits. Red slip and smoothed.
Di. 20; Th. 0.9

609   1428
Level IIId
Rim with upper part of body. Beige, grit-tempered. Traces of red wash.
Di. 25; Th. 0.5

610   1428
Level IIId
Rim with upper part of body. Yellowish with darker core, grit-tempered with big white grits. Brown wash.
Di. 26; Th. 0.6

611   1428
Level IIId
Rim with upper part of body. Red, grit-tempered. Purple wash.
Di. 20; Th. 0.6

612   1428
Level IIId
Rim with upper part of body. Red, grit-tempered. Slightly burnished.
Di. 28; Th. 0.5

613   1428
Level IIId
Rim to middle of body. Brown with dark grey core, grit-tempered with small grits. Smoothed.
Di. 28; Th. 0.5

614   1428
Level IIId
Rim to lower part of body. Dark brown-red, fine white temper, hard fired. Dark brown slip and burnished.
Di. 28; Th. 0.6

615   1428
Level IIId
Rim to lower part of body. Red with brownish core, fine white temper. Red slip and burnished.
Di. 24; Th. 0.6

616   4211
Level IIIc/d
Rim to lower part of body. Beige, grit-tempered. Smoothed.
Di. 18; Th. 0.7

617 4211
Level IIIc/d
Rim to middle of body. Brown-grey, grit-tempered. Brown-grey slip and smoothed. Traces of red paint, matt. Large chip broken off ext., may be handle attachment.
Di. 22; Th. 0.6

618 4211
Level IIIc/d
Rim with upper part of body. Beige with orange core, grit-tempered. Traces of red paint.
Di. 26; Th. 0.6

619 4211
Level IIIc/d
Rim to lower part of body. Red, no temper. Red slip and burnished.
Di. 24; Th. 0.5

620 4205
Level IIId
Rim to lower part of body. Orange with brown core, grit-tempered. Red wash and smoothed.
Di. 24; Th. 0.5

621 4211
Level IIIc/d
Rim to middle part of body. Brown with fine white grits. Brown slip and burnished.
Di. 18; Th. 0.6

622 4211
Level IIIc/d
Rim to lower part of body. Cream with light brown core, grit-tempered. Cream slip and smoothed.
Di. 24; Th. 0.6

623 4027
Level IIIe/d
Reddish with brown core. Small white grits. Smoothed.
Di. 22

624 4205
Level IIId
Rim to lower part of body. Buff, grit-tempered. Slightly burnished.
Di. 24; Th. 0.7

Shallow bowls with rim thickened out (625–7)
A small group of shallow bowls have an internal rim but are also thickened on the exterior. They are all in reddish to orange fabric with white grits and slipped. The diameter varies from 26 to 28 cm.
  Cf. Müller-Karpe (1988), Type S1g–l (pp. 98–100, Taf. 30–31).

625 1428
Level IIId
Rim to middle body. Orange with fine white grits. Orange slip and smoothed.
Di. 28; Th. 0.9

626 1428
Level IIId
Rim with upper body. Orangey, grit-tempered. Smoothed.
Di. 28; Th. 0.4

627 4217
Level IIIc
Rim to lower body. Reddish with many white grits. Buff slip, smoothed.
Di. 26; Th. 0.9

Large shallow bowls with exterior rim (628–9)
A few bowl sherds have an external rim. The diameter varies from 31 to 39 cm, which is why they have been characterized as large. All have fabrics that correspond with other shallow bowls. Both those illustrated are smoothed. **628** has been burnt and there are traces of brown paint/wash. **629** is very coarse with big voids.
  Cf. Müller-Karpe (1988), Types S10–11 (pp. 115–18, Taf. 38–9).

628 1428
Level IIId
Rim with upper body. Light brown, grit-tempered. Burnt in places ext. Traces of dark brown wash, smoothed.
Di. 31; Th. 0.8

629 4224
Level IIIc
Rim to lower body. Buff-orangey, grit-tempered, coarse with big holes. Smoothed.
Di. 29; Th. 0.9

Hole-mouth jars (630–32)
Sherds from hole-mouth jars were not numerous but some rims were found. Most of them were too fragmentary to measure the rim diameter. They are all slipped and burnished. **632** has traces of brown paint.
  Cf. perhaps Müller-Karpe (1988), Type S7 (p. 114, Taf. 37), but our pieces are probably all smaller.

630 4211
Level IIIc/d
Yellowish with orange core grit-tempered. Ext. brownish slipped and burnished.
Di. 9

631 4211
Level IIIc/d
Rim with upper part of body. Brown, very small grits. Dark red slip, burnished.
3.5 × 3.6; Th. 0.5

632 4211
Level IIIc/d
Rim with upper part of body. Beige with orange core, grit-tempered. Orange slip and burnished. Traces of brown paint.
Th. 0.5

Closed jars with rolled rim (633–7)
A common shape is a jar with a rolled rim. They occur in different fabrics but not in the fine red (Ware a). They are all gritty and some of the fabrics are coarse.

Chapter 25

Figure 237. *Storage jars* in situ *against north wall of Rm 91, looking west. Base of* **637a** *in foreground; mouth of* **637b** *behind.*

It is very difficult to know to which kind of jar these rims belong, especially because only small fragments are preserved. Most of them probably fall within the *Kochtöpfe* category (Müller-Karpe 1988, Type KT, pp. 50–61, Taf. 9–11). Two of those illustrated are of cooking ware (**635–6**). They seem mainly to be wheel-made but **636** is hand-made and has a wide ridge below the rim.

637 is from a pithos with a rim diameter of about 30 cm. At other LBA sites this is also a common shape and they have been found in large quantities at Porsuk (Dupré 1983, pl. 27–31:193–6). Perhaps both the two large storage jars from the NW corner of Rm 91 in Level 3 in I14 (**637a–b**; Figs. 160 & 237) should also belong in this category. A profile reconstructed from **637a** is given as Figure 161 on p. 174.

633 1428
Level IIId
Rim with upper body. Light brown, heavily grit-tempered with grey grits. Light brown slip and smoothed.
Di. 18; Th. 0.7
Cf. Müller-Karpe 1988, Type KT2c–f (pp. 53–4, Taf. 9–10).

634 4211
Level IIIc/d
Rim with upper body. Beige, grit-tempered and coarse with very big grey grits. Smoothed. Below rim a ridge. Cf. **633** for possible parallels.
Th. 1.1

635 4205
Level IIId
Rim with upper body. Brown, grit-tempered, cooking ware. Ext. brown, smoothed.
Di. 17; Th. 0.7
Cf. perhaps Müller-Karpe 1988, Type KT2u (p. 59, Taf. 12).

636 4205
Level IIId
Rim with upper body. Black, grit-tempered, cooking ware. Hand-made. Brown surfaces. Below rim a wide ridge, which should perhaps be compared with **651** and the Boğazköy types cited there.
Di. *c.* 25–30; Th. 0.9

637 4211
Level IIIc/d
Pithos. Rim with upper body. Brown, coarse and grit-tempered with big grits. Hand-made. Smoothed.
Di. *c.* 30; Th. 1.8

[637a] I14/160 3708
Level 3, *in situ* against north wall of Rm 91, to the east of 637b.
Upper part broken, but part of rim present. One handle preserved but probably two originally. Rounded base.
Ext. rim di. 46; Di. (max.) 58; H. 90; Th. of wall (max.) 1.4; Rim th. 5.0
Figs. 161 & 237

[637b] I14/159 3708
Level 3, *in situ*, embedded in floor to a lower level than **637a** to the east (see Fig. 237).
Almost complete; no handles visible (remained *in situ*). Rounded base.
H. 90

Closed jars with vertical plain rim (**638–40**)
A few jars have a plain rim that is almost vertical. The first two pieces are both cooking ware with a rather large diameter. They are both burnished. **640** is a small complete neck of a fine grey fabric with no temper. It is very different from the other two but the rims are the same kind.

638 4211
Level IIIc/d
Rim to middle body. Brown, heavily grit-tempered, cooking ware. Burnished.
Di. 28; Th. 0.8
Cf. Müller-Karpe 1988, Type KT2 (pp. 52–60, Taf. 9–12).

639 4224
Level IIIc
Rim to middle body. Cooking ware with dark green core, heavily grit-tempered. Light brown surfaces, slightly burnished ext.
Di. 29; Th. 0.7

640 4205
Level IIId
Rim with neck. Grey, no temper. Brown slip, burnished.
Di. 5; Th. 0.4

Closed jars with vertical band out (**641–3**)
A number of sherds with a band outside the rim were excavated. They are mainly from small jars; a few rims from larger jars were also found but were too fragmen-

tary to be illustrated or to give a rim diameter. One of those illustrated is a small complete neck of a grey-greenish fabric with no temper (**642**). **641** has very big grits and the surface is smoothed, while **643** has very few grits and is burnished. They are both of reddish fabric. This rim type is seen on bowls from Beycesultan (Mellaart & Murray 1995, pl. 16:9, 14, 16).

641   4211
Level IIIc/d
Rim with upper body. Reddish, grit-tempered with very big grits. Smoothed.
Di. 8; Th. 0.6

642   4231
Level IIIc
Complete neck. Grey-greenish, no temper. Smoothed.
Di. 2; Th. 0.3

643   1376
Level IIId
Rim with upper body. Pinkish-red, few visible grits. Burnished ext.
Di. 6; Th. 0.4

*Closed jars with vertical thickened rim (**644–5**)*
A small group of jar rims are almost vertical and are thickened on both the inner and the outer side. The fabric is brown and gritty and both those illustrated have only been smoothed.

644   1428
Level IIId
Rim with upper body. Brown, grit-tempered. Brown slip and smoothed.
Di. 30; Th. 0.9

645   4211
Level IIIc/d
Rim with upper body. Brown, grit-tempered with big grits. Smoothed.
Di. 24; Th. 0.8

*Closed jar with flaring rim (**646–8**)*
Jars with flaring rim are not very common but a few sherds were found. One of the sherds has a rather large diameter of 26 cm (**647**). It is of fine red fabric, slipped and burnished. The other two are smaller and have a gritty fabric.

646   4211
Level IIIc/d
Rim with upper body. Dark orange, grit-tempered. Dark orange slip and burnished.
Di. 15; Th. 0.5
Cf. Müller-Karpe 1988, Type 15b (p. 87, Taf. 25)?

647   4211
Level IIIc/d
Rim with upper body. Red, no temper. Red slip and burnished.
Di. 26; Th. 0.7
For the shape, but not the ware, cf. Müller-Karpe 1988, Type T12a.3 (p. 83, Taf. 23).

648   4223
Level IIIc
Rim to middle body. Red, grit-tempered with lots of white grits. Smoothed.
Di. 12; Th. 0.5

*Closed jars with everted rims (**649–71**)*
A very large variety of jars with everted rims was found. They have been divided into four different types: everted plain (**649–57**), everted rounded (**658–61**), everted flattened (**662–70**) and everted overhanging (**671**). They can come from many different types of pots.

*Closed jars with everted plain rims (**649–57**)*
Everted plain are the biggest group. All fabrics are represented except for the fine red. They are either smoothed or slipped and can be burnished. A few have traces of wash. **652** has dark brown paint in uneven bands. **651** has a ridge below the rim. The size varies from small jars with a diameter of 10 cm to large jars with diameter up to 48 cm. The everted rim is the most common jar rim shape and is found at all other sites with LBA levels.

649   1428
Level IIId
Rim with upper body. Light orange, grit-tempered. Cream slip.
Di. 30; Th. 1.0
The rounded body and plain everted rims of **649**, **653-655** and also **657** are not typical of the Boğazköy Upper City corpus. The closest parallels for some of them seem to be Müller-Karpe 1988, Type KT3, in cooking pot ware, seen there as an older shape (p. 60, Taf. 12).

650   1428
Level IIId
Rim with upper body. Grey, very little temper. Traces of black wash.
Di. 30; Th. 1.1

651   1428
Level IIId
Rim with upper body. Dark brown, grit-tempered with big grits. Brown slip and smoothed. Traces of dark brown paint. Has a ridge below the rim, which suggests that it should be compared with Müller-Karpe 1988, Type T4 (pp. 71–3, Taf. 18–19), though our ware is different; cf. **636**.
Di. 48; Th. 0.8

652   1428
Level IIId
Rim to middle body. Brown grit-tempered. Brown slip. Dark brown paint ext., matt. Uneven bands.
4.2 × 6.3; Th. 0.6
For the general shape cf. Müller-Karpe 1988, Type T1p (p. 67, Taf. 15).

653   4205
Level IIId
Rim with upper body. Red with white grits. Red slip. Traces of dark

red wash on int. rim. See on **649** for the shape.
Di. 25; Th. 0.5

654   4211
Level IIIc/d
Rim with upper body. Grey, heavily grit-tempered, cooking ware. Smoothed. See on **649** for the shape.
Di. 21; Th. 0.8

655   4205
Level IIId
Rim with upper body. Buff, fine grits. Smoothed. See on **649** for the shape.
Di. 17; Th. 0.8

656   4217
Level IIIc
Rim with upper body. Reddish, grit-tempered with many big white grits. Hand-made. Smoothed.
Di. 10; Th. 0.7

657   1428
Level IIId
Rim to middle body. Beige, grit-tempered. Fired to red or grey in some areas. Brown slip ext. and int. rim. Burnished. See on **649** for the shape.
Di. 23; Th. 0.9
Symington, in Baker *et al.* 1995, fig. 16:6

Closed jars with everted rounded rim (658–61)
Another large group has everted rounded rims. The fabric is mainly buff but it can also occur in the other fabrics, but again not the fine red. Paint or wash is more common on this type. **660** has small incisions below the rim. **661** is a small jar with a rim diameter of 8 cm, while most of the rest have diameters of more than 25 cm.

658   4205
Level IIId
Rim with upper body. Dark orange with darker core, grit-tempered. Hand-made. Smoothed.
Di. 29; Th. 1.5

659   4205
Level IIId
Rim with upper body. Buff with small white grits. Buff slip. Traces of brown paint on top of rim.
Di. 42; Th. 0.7

660   4211
Level IIIc/d
Rim with upper body. Buff, grit-tempered. Buff slip. Small incisions below rim ext. For ridge below rim cf. **636** and **651**, and perhaps Müller-Karpe 1988, Type T4 (p. 71–3, Taf. 18).
Di. 32; Th. 1.2

661   4211
Level IIIc/d
Rim with upper body. Buff with small grits. Red wash.
Di. 8; Th. 0.4

Closed jars with everted flattened rim (662–9)
Quite a number of jars have everted flattened rims. They are either rather large, with a diameter between 27–36 cm, or much smaller (di. 14 cm). The majority are made of a red gritty fabric and a few are hand-made. They are mainly just smoothed but can also be slipped and occasionally have a wash.

662   1428
Level IIId
Rim with upper body. Red, grit-tempered. Smoothed.
Di. 14; Th. 0.5
Cf. Müller-Karpe 1988, Type T19 (p. 89, Taf. 25).

663   1428
Level IIId
Rim with upper body. Beige, grit-tempered with big red grits. Red wash.
Di. 36; Th. 1.0

664   4211
Level IIIc/d
Rim with upper body. Red, grit-tempered. Hand-made. Smoothed.
Di. >30; Th. 1.0

665   4211
Level IIIc/d
Rim with upper body. Beige, grit-tempered. Smoothed.
Th. 0.8

666   4211
Level IIIc/d
Rim with upper body. Orange-brown, grit-tempered. Orange-brown slip and smoothed.
Di. 30; Th. 0.7

667   4205
Level IIId
Rim with upper body. Red, grit-tempered with big red and white grits. Smoothed.
Di. 27; Th. 1.1

668   4205
Level IIId
Rim with upper body. Dark brown, grit-tempered with big grits, coarse. Smoothed.
Th. 1.8
Cf. Müller-Karpe 1988, Type P2 (pp. 94–5, Taf. 28).

669   1428
Level IIId
Rim to middle body. Dark grey, light grey core, grit-tempered. Dark grey slip. Deep groove below rim.
Di. 32; Th. 0.9

Closed jar with everted overhanging rim (670)
A few sherds have an overhanging rim. They all have wash.

670   4224
Level IIIc
Rim with upper body. Brown, heavily grit-tempered. Smoothed. Traces of dark brown paint ext.
Di. 24; Th. 0.8

Trefoil jug (671)
Some trefoil rims were found but most are too fragmentary to be illustrated. The one illustrated has traces of dark brown paint on top of the rim. In Tarsus, sev-

eral pots with trefoil rims were found but it does not seem to be very common at Kilise Tepe in the LBA. The same seems to have been the case at Boğazköy (see Müller-Karpe 1988, Type Kk, pp. 24–7).

671   4205
Level IIId
Rim with upper part of body. Buff, grit-tempered. Buff slip and smoothed. Traces of dark brown paint on rim.
Th. 0.6

Lentoid flasks (672–7)
For this class of vessel see Bilgi 1982. Our examples from Level III all have equal convexity on each side. From Level II we have jars with a profile flatter on one side than the other (see **693–5, 916–19**), for which we have reserved the term 'pilgrim' flask; with individual sherds it is not always possible to distinguish the two forms. In Level III not many sherds from lentoid flasks were found. In the Upper City at Boğazköy they are likewise relatively uncommon, and Müller-Karpe concludes that they were not a regular component of kitchen equipment (1988, 27–8; for whole vessels at Boğazköy see Fischer 1963, Taf. 46–50). **672** (Fig. 238) is from a large example in Red Lustrous Wheel-made Ware, found in pieces lying scattered on the surface of the site; **674**, from the LBA level in I14, is also in a very fine red fabric. **673** has the white slip familiar at Boğazköy; for the concave profile of the base of these two handles see Collon 1995, 168; Müller-Karpe 1988, 141–2 with Taf. 47: Type He 8, three exx. in white slipped ware. **675–6** were found in early Level II contexts but are included here as their fine reddish fabric with small grits seems typical of Level III. **677** is different in having a greyish gritty fabric, with a thick red slip.

Figure 238. *Neck and handle of Red Lustrous Wheel-made ware lentoid flask (**672**).*

672   Q14/1   127, 187, 222
Surface
Neck and handle dense red with no visible temper, surviving part of body (below the white diagonal line in the cross-section on the right half of the drawing) has frequent white grits. Ext. burnished.
Rim di. 10
Fig. 238
Collon 1995, fig. 11:1

673   1428
Level IIId
Part of a handle from a lentoid flask. Fine pinkish-grey with many grits, some quite large, and specks of gold mica. Creamy-white slip, wearing off. Burnished. White slip is not common at Kilise Tepe but more frequent than red at Boğazköy (Fischer 1963, 128, Taf. 47 no. 473; Müller-Karpe 1988, 28, often with mica).
Th. 2.5
Symington, in Baker *et al.* 1995, fig. 16:10

674   3712
Level 3
Handle and part of body from lentoid flask. Fine light red clay with no visible temper, darker red slip on ext. showing burnishing facets.
H. (ext.) 9.3; Handle di. 1.2–1.4

675   1417
Level IIb
Rim, neck and fragment of upper body. Reddish with fine white grits. Smoothed. Handle attachment.
Di. 2.3; Neck di. 2.6

676   1386
Level IIa–b
Handle and part of body. Reddish, grit-tempered. Dark brown wash.
Th. 0.6–0.9; Handle di. 1.4

677   I19/173   5527
Level IIIe
Handle (not joined) and part of body rejoined from several sherds. Greyish, grit-tempered. Very badly burned. Ext. thick red slip.
Th. 0.9–1.2; Handle th. 1.6

Rhyton (678)
678   H19/390   4212
Level IIIc/d
Fragment of zoomorphic spout from rhyton or similar vessel. Bur-

Chapter 25

Figure 239. *Interiors of libation arm fragments from unit 4211, to show manufacturing technique.*

nished dense orange ware with no visible grits. Probably an equid. Part of the neck survives, with diagonal incisions on either side of a crest at the back forming a mane; the ears are broken and there are two diagonal lines across the cheeks. The spout holes from the neck and muzzle join at the back of the head.
Th. 2.5; H. 4

Such pieces are not specially common at contemporary sites (cf. Fischer 1963, 80–84, Taf. 133–9; Parzinger & Sanz 1992, 31, Taf. 74–6).

Spindle bottle (679)

One fragment of a base from a spindle bottle was found in a Level III context. Spindle bottles in red lustrous ware are found all over the Mediterranean area (Eriksson 1993, 185–240). Several more spindle bottles were found in Level II (see below, **898–903**).

679 4211
Level IIIc/d
Base with lower part of body. Orange, no temper. Orange slip, burnished. Ring base. Pot-mark on base.
Di. 5; Th. 0.4

'Flower pots' (680–81)

Two bases from tall vases were excavated. They have ring bases and one had brown wash ext. and on the bottom (**681**). Not a common shape but similar vases have been found at Maşat Höyük (T. Özgüç 1982, pl. 48:2) and Boğazköy (Fischer 1963, Taf. 123:1075; Müller-Karpe 1988, Taf. 46). At Alaca Höyük, a large vase was found (Koşay & Akok 1966, pl. 106:318).

680 1428
Level IIId
Base with most of body. Reddish-brown, grit-tempered. Smoothed.
Base di. 10; Th. 1.2
Symington, in Baker *et al.* 1995, fig. 16:7

681 1426
Level IIIe
Base and lower body. Brown, grit-tempered and coarse. Hand-made. Ext., and under the base, brown wash.
Base di. 10; Th. 1.6

Platter (682)

A single profile from a platter or small tray was found, in cooking ware with a flat base and plain rim. Larger coarse ware examples were found occasionally in the Upper City at Boğazköy (Müller-Karpe 1988, 130, Taf. 43, Type Te2b).

682 4211
Level IIIc/d
Complete profile. Cooking ware with big grits. Rim plain, base flat.
Rim di. (int.) 14; Base di. 16; H. 3.4; Th. 2.8

Painted carinated jar (683)

683 4237
Level IIIa–b
Lower part of closed vessel with carination. Crudely made. Cream soft fabric, grit-tempered. Red painted with cross-hatching above carination. Hand-made.
Base di. 7

Libation arms (684–92)

A relatively large number of libation arm fragments were found both on the surface and in excavated units (Fig. 239). They are mainly body fragments but bases and hands/cups have also been found. They are of fine red ware and a few of a fine dark brown ware. The excavated pieces mostly came from the NW corner but one example in light brown gritty clay was found in Rm 93 in I14 Level 3 (3711). Libation arms have been found in large quantities at Boğazköy (Fischer 1963, Taf. 122:1102, 1124; Taf. 124) and Alaca Höyük (Koşay & Akok 1966, g94, h153, j154) but they have a wide distribution in Anatolia (Eriksson 1993, 258–75). As mentioned above, most are body fragments, some coming from large examples (**686–7**). Another body fragment is from the wrist with a small part of the rim on the cup preserved (**688**). A few ends have been identified. **685** has a ring base which is seen at other sites (Eriksson 1993, 27). Another has a concave base which is also found at other sites (**684**). These two were found in later contexts, but have been included here with the other libation arms as the only examples of these types of base. According to Eriksson, the most common base is the button base but none of these have been found at Kilise Tepe. A number of the hand-shaped cups have, however, been found, although several come from the surface. Three were from good contexts. One is an almost complete miniature cup with carefully made fingers (**692**). Two other fragments also clearly show the fingers (**690–91**).

Pottery from Level III

684   1332
Level IIa
End of arm. Dense brown with no visible temper. Surface orangey. Burnished.
Base di. (3.8); Th. 1.5
Symington, in Baker *et al.* 1995, fig. 17:2

685   1604
Level I
End of arm. Dense red with no visible temper. Burnished. Sign on base ext.
Di. 4.0 (ext. max.); Ring di. 2.2

686   4211
Level IIIc/d
11 cm of arm just before the base. Red, no temper. Burnished.
Di. 9.0 (ext. max.); Th. 1.2

687   1376
Level IIId
Part of arm just before the base. Red, few visible grits. Burnished.
Di. 6.0 (ext. max.); Th. 1.0–1.7

688   I20/94   1428
Level IIId
Part just before cup, part of rim preserved. Brown, no temper. Burnished.
Di. 3.5 (ext. max.); Th. 0.6
Symington, in Baker *et al.* 1995, fig. 17:1

689   4205
Level IIId
Part of arm just before cup. Red, no temper. Burnished.
Th. 0.4–0.9

690   1428
Level IIId
Part of cup. Red, no temper. Slightly burnished ext. Impressions imitating finger nails.
1.9 × 2.2; Di. 3; Th. 0.6

691   1428
Level IIId
Part of cup. Reddish-brown with no visible temper. Hand-made. Impressions to imitate fingers.
2.0 × 2.5; Th. 0.4–0.6
Symington, in Baker *et al.* 1995, fig. 17:3

692   H19/43   4209
Level IIIc/d
Almost complete cup. Red, no temper. Burnished. Impressions to imitate fingers.
2.7 × 2.6; Di. 2.5; Th. 0.4–0.8

Note

1. The catalogue and first draft of the introduction were written by Connie Hansen. The expanded introduction and occasional comments within the catalogue are by Nicholas Postgate.

Chapter 26

Pottery from Level II

Connie Hansen & Nicholas Postgate[1]

Introduction

Pottery of Level II date was found all over the mound but the material published here is mainly from the NW end. Here there was a sequence through from Level III, although the stratigraphy was difficult to disentangle. On the East Slope we did not reach the earliest phases of Level II and in I/J14 there were only two phases present, but some pieces of interest from these areas are included. Table 11 charts the occurrence of the most characteristic features and vessel types through the Level II phases at the NW corner.

As has already been said, the nature of the Level II material and contexts does not lend itself to reconstructing a typological ceramic sequence. These obstacles are further enhanced by the range of wares involved. By contrast with the stability and homogeneity of the preceding Hittite level there is a wide variety of manufacturing techniques, shapes, and decorative schemes represented. Some sherds hark back to Level III, and not all of them are likely to be out of context. Of the new types, some seem to be of purely local origin, others are imports or imitations of east Mediterranean wares, and yet others are local products which seem to incorporate motifs borrowed from elsewhere. The volume of material available is not sufficient to establish a secure succession of types on the basis of their stratigraphic provenance. This may perhaps be seen most clearly in the case of the pilgrim flask feet which were found throughout all phases of Level II (see on **920–39**): their occurrence at other sites gives us no reason to think that this distinctive vessel type was manufactured or used significantly later than the end of the Late Bronze Age. Should we therefore discount the majority of these published examples as stratigraphic strays because they come from phase IIe and later? Or should we look at the clumsy workmanship of some of them and conclude that this type of vessel did continue to be made locally at least into Level IIe and possibly even later?

Because of such uncertainties, all we aim to do in the ensuing discussion is to suggest some possibilities for further consideration. It is partly in order to avoid giving a false impression of certainty that we have refrained from even attempting to divide the Level II material into two or more phases. It is obvious that phases IIa–c could be grouped with IId to yield an 'early' phase, which might accord with LB IIa–b as defined at Tarsus; and that IIf, and the subsequent phases IIg–h which are represented solely by pits, could constitute a 'late' phase. Logically, then, it might seem reasonable to treat IIe as a 'middle' phase, but a glance at the stratigraphic provenances of some classes of sherd in the catalogue which follows will show that there is scarcely anything which is found exclusively in IIe, so that in some respects it seems to belong with what preceded, in others with what followed. Moreover, IIe itself may well correspond to more than one phase, since there is no certainty that the deposits in the Western Courtyard or in Rooms e5–6 are exactly contemporary with Rooms e9 and e10 to the north, or indeed with each other. With this caveat, let us single out some suggestive features of the material.

Local wares

The petrography suggests that there was continuity in the local ceramic production between Level III and Level II, but there are certainly significant changes too. The dominant ware in the early phases of Level II is buff or brown, and one of the clear innovations is a much greater use of paint, usually red. Sherds typical of Level III were indeed found in the earlier Level II phases, such as shallow bowls with internal rim or trefoil jar rims. Although some of these are probably genuinely produced, used and discarded within Level II, it is hard to be certain that any individual piece was not displaced, given the presence of large pits penetrating the Level III strata. We are not convinced, for instance, that any of the pieces of Red Lustrous Wheel-made Ware recovered from Level II were actually in use at that time, since they are mainly fragments of libation arms, which are instantly recognizable and very robust.

Table 11. *Sherd counts for Level II by phase.*

Phase of Level II	a–d	d–e	e	e–f	f–h
Jars					
Square rim with cross-hatching - red or brown paint	19	2		2	1
Square rim with stripes on top	1				1
Square rim with bichrome paint					1
Square rim - plain	15	1		2	7
Other rims with cross-hatching - red or brown paint	14				2
Body sherds with cross-hatching - red or brown paint	19	5	3	3	15
Kindergarten ware	4	>11	3		>12
Wavy lines - red or brown paint	2		1		4
Bands and lines	1	2	7	4	>27
Vertical lines	3		2	1	1
Targets - brown paint		4		1	10
Targets - bichrome paint				1	9
Pendent concentric semi-circles	1			1	5
Black-on-red		3	2		3
Jar with bands	3		3		
Trefoil rims	>66		1	7	>12
Bowls					
Grooved rim with paint	4	1			
Cross-hatching - red or brown paint	2	3			4
Diagonal lines - red or brown paint		2	1	4	5
Bowl with target or semi concentric circles			1		2
Shallow bowl rims - misc.	>83	>16	>11	>11	>20
Shallow bowls rims - grooved	>63	3	2	1	10
Other					
Pilgrim flasks	>23		6		3
Feet from pilgrim flasks	>20	2	5	3	9
Spindle bottles	2				1
Libation arms	12		3		

These figures are taken from the following units: 1117, 1121, 1132, 1332, 1514, 1516, 1527, 1535, 1540–41, 1551, 1555, 1560, 1566, 1568, 1594–5, 1657, 1665, 1667, 1669, 1690–91, 1693, 1766, 1776, 1780–81, 1783, 1787, 1790, 1793, 1911, 1924, 1928, 1930, 1944, 1945, 1982–4, 1994, 2362–3, 2369–70, 2375, 2378, 2381, 2383–4, 2390, 2392, 2399, 2821, 2841, 2846, 2848, 2864, 2871, 2873, 2875, 2877, 2880, 2882, 2884, 2893, 3915, 3925, 3942, 3944, 3960, 4351, 4353, 4363, 4500, 4502, 4513–14, 4521, 4553, 4564, 4573, 4578, 4587, 4594, 4597, 5501–2, 5514, 5523, 5528, 5801, 5812, 5816, 5829, 5837, 5843, 5863, 5894, 5941, 5948, 5954, 5964, 5966–8, 5873, 5975, 5981, 6109, 6113, 6119–21, 6203.

At Tarsus in the LB IIb level, which lay above the major destruction at the end of LB IIa, the excavators reported large quantities of what they came to refer to as 'drab ware', a term which has been borrowed at other sites where the final Late Bronze level is marked by the same ware. Whether we have this precise phenomenon in the early phases of Level II requires further investigation for two main reasons. One is that with the volume of material at our disposal, and the fact that it is all sherds and any individual piece could have been thrown up from below, we are not able to establish the degree of standardization or whether it is comparable to that on other sites. The other is that the Tarsus material itself raises a question of its own to which we do not presume to know the answer: was the 'drab ware' really strictly contemporary with the LH IIIC Mycenaean wares? This was the opinion of the excavators, and it is difficult to contradict in retrospect (Goldman 1956, 205–6, but cf. Ünlü 2005, 145–6); however, if correct, it would imply that at Tarsus a ware now generally associated with the final phase of the centralized Hittite state remained in use some 50 years after the capital at Hattusa was destroyed. This is evidently not inconceivable, but it underlines the caution needed in our intepretation of the ceramics at this date, and it is our hope that future more detailed work on our material will help to clarify what was happening, at Kilise Tepe at least.

New types which make their appearance after Level III include internal rim (Schwapprand) bowls with a 'grooved' outer face, which we did not definitely identify among the Level III material (for examples from Mersin Level VI see Caneva & Sevin 2004, 79, fig. 6). A special version of these had blobs or stripes of paint round the rim (**736–8**), and in some cases red paint inside. Two other bowl sherds with internal (but not grooved) rim are **739–40, 739** also with traces of paint. Painted internal rim bowls are only known from the earliest phases of Level II. Broad red or brown bands round jars and jugs are represented by **784–7**, mostly securely provenanced to Levels IIc–d.

Red or brown paint is also a prime characteristic of the large square-rimmed vessels which make their first appearance in Level II. These we refer to as jars but we have no complete profile, and they are also called basins by Knappett, which reflects their wide open mouths. They often had vertical handles, and sherds with boldly executed cross-hatching, not usually between bands, are commonest. As noted below (on **788–800**), very similar vessels are now known from Mersin in association with the last phase of Hittite ceramics, but the petrography indicates that ours were local products. Our best stratified pieces come from the IIa/b phases of the Western Courtyard. Whether they remained in use in IId and later is hard to say. A later development may be represented by the jar sherds **801** (IIc/d) and **803** from the floor of Rm 21 under the IIc destruction: these lack the squared rim and may both have their cross-hatching confined between bands.

Another very characteristic ware which is seen for the first time is the coarse, badly made ware labelled 'Kindergarten ware'. Petrographic analysis seems to confirm that this forms a distinct group (see p. 260). The fabric is reddish and the vessels are mostly hand-made, but can also be wheel-made especially in the later phases. The paint is usually red, but later bichrome paint occurs (e.g. **870**). The patterns are the same as on the rest of the pottery (though less well executed). The earliest contexts for this ware belong to Level IIe, and this makes sense in that hand-made wares resurface at several Anatolian sites after the disappearance of the Hittite traditions in the twelfth century (see below). The jars do not have the same squared rims, but they do retain cross-hatching or similar designs as their most distinctive decoration. Prime examples of this are **802**, unfortunately poorly stratified, and **811**, which came from a secure context spread across the floor of Rm e9: this context is undoubtedly later than IId, and has been taken to predate IIf largely on the basis of these sherds. Note also the large pieces making up **807** from IIe/f. Kindergarten ware was also used for other large vessels: the very characteristic coarse hand-made bowl **861** is unfortunately not well provenanced, but its cross-hatched triangles, coarse as they are, are a new decorative motif which persists into the later phases of Level II (see on **860–65**).

Bowls with cross-hatching in a band below the rim on the exterior are first attested in Level IIa (**752** from the IIa pit P97/69 visible in Fig. 517, a good provenance though it is only one sherd). Other examples catalogued are from IId to IIf. There is no doubt that in the early courtyard levels these painted bowls are rarer than the cross-hatched jars, but the similarity of the motif suggests that they were at least partly contemporary, while **757** also comes from the layer immediately above Level 3 in I14 and could be relatively early. Similar bowls with groups of diagonal lines in place of cross-hatching occur from IIc (**758**), with at least three examples from IId. The IId examples include very shallow open shapes (**760–61**), but there is also a deeper type of bowl with slightly incurving sides (**758**, **767**, and **771** with handle). They are mostly rim sherds, and only **764** from a pit beneath a IIe surface provides a complete profile with a fairly high ring base. These look as though they are a later version of the cross-hatched bowls, and it would be no surprise if they were still being manufactured in IIe. Functionally, these bowls may replace the Level III internal rim bowls and plates, sherds of which turn up less frequently in the later phases.

All these types with simple geometric designs painted in a single colour, look as though they are local developments. When they turn up in IIf levels it is impossible to be sure if this reflects a longevity of the style, or simply the number of pieces which have been displaced from earlier contexts. These precise painted wares are at present known almost exclusively from Kilise Tepe (except for the cross-hatched jars now known at Mersin). However, other similar red-painted and often hand-made traditions emerge across Anatolia around the end of the Bronze Age. Similar local wares from the early Iron Age have recently been reported on the plateau north of Kilise Tepe at Zoldura (Hatunsaray II), some 40 km SSW of Konya (see Bahar & Koçak 2003). See Hansen & Postgate 1999, 119 for parallels at Boğazköy and its region and at Tille Höyük (and now Blaylock 1999, esp. pp. 266–7 with fig. 1). Note that at Boğazköy these painted hand-made wares are now reassigned to a phase after the major destruction at the site (Genz 2003; 2004). Whether or not these new wares can all be viewed as a reassertion of local craft traditions submerged during the domination of the Hittite state, it has to be borne in mind that at Kilise Tepe the 'red-painted' fashion seems to begin before the end of the thirteenth century, and it is hard to point to any forerunners among our Middle Bronze or earlier ceramics.

Fresh motifs

We have already mentioned the cross-hatched triangles on a Kindergarten ware bowl (**861**). This extremely coarse decoration could of course be an independent development, but from IIf there are numbers of sherds displaying cross-hatched triangles, and it seems likely that **861** borrowed the idea from other vessels. It is found on the square-rimmed jars **798** and **799**, and on jar sherds (for examples and parallels see on **860–85**, with cross-hatched lozenges appearing on **863** and **865**).

Another new motif in IIf is the wavy line, often between bands (see on **815–22**). At Tarsus in the LB I there was a class of Wavy Line ware, but this did not feature in LB II and horizontal wavy lines seem to be uncommon there in the Iron Age decorative repertoire. It is not a common element on Black-on-Red or White Painted wares. Perhaps then this is a rare case of influence from the north and west, since wavy lines are a common element of Phrygian decoration (see Sams 1994, 155–7; also Crespin 1999, 67 from Porsuk).

The open bowl **777** seems to combine a 'local' cross-hatched band with a pendent semi-circle. Such semi-circles are also used below panels with a vertical herring-bone divider and a zigzag line on the large jar **800**, large pieces of which were built into the base of a fire installation of IIe at the earliest, and on the hand-made globular jar **855**. Other pieces with a similar use of the pendent semi-circle are **856, 858–9**. At Tarsus this motif is uncommon outside the Greek wares: there is one piece illustrated from the Early Iron Age (Hanfmann 1963, fig. 55:16). Hanfmann wrote that 'compass drawn half-circles, … seem to be a hall mark of the Greek Protogeometric and of those Western Anatolian styles that depend on it' (1963, 157), but how it reached our Kilise Tepe potters remains unclear.

'Targets', or concentric circles, are found on an open bowl (**773**), but are commoner on jars (see on **842–51**). Our repertoire does not seem to include the rows of small concentric circles typical of some other Iron Age styles (e.g. Bahar & Koçak 2004, Çizim 56–60, Resim 21–2, from Cicek and Şeydişehir II). Concentric circles are of course common on Greek wares from Mycenaean into Geometric, and are a prominent component of White Painted and Black-on-Red wares throughout the eastern Mediterranean (see below).

Jar sherds with panels, or metopal designs, are not uncommon, and these may combine a variety of individual motifs (see on **860–85**). There may be more than one horizontal register, with the panels sometimes divided by nothing more elaborate than a group of vertical lines (**869, 871–3**). In more elaborate designs the dividers may include cross-hatched vertical elements (**866?, 868, 879, 881, 883–4**); herring-bone dividers are found on the large jar **800** (see above), and on a bowl (**776**). The panels may be left blank (**871–2**), or contain cross-hatched triangles (e.g. **869–70, 880**), lozenges (**863, 865**), rectangles (**780, 875**), concentric circles, or other elements. One bowl has a butterfly motif (**774**).

White Painted

For most of the Iron Age much of the ceramic repertoire of Cilicia, as represented by the finds from Tarsus and the surveys of Gjerstad and Seton-Williams (1954, 136–7), has long been acknowledged to belong with the Levant and Cyprus. 'White Painted', 'Black-on-Red' and 'Bichrome' wares are usually present at the same time and place, and often share the same shapes and motifs. Boardman has recently written that 'it begins to look as though the Cypriot style in pottery had become something of a *koine* in this north-eastern recess of the Mediterranean' (1999, 149). Where such materials are found the question always arises as to whether they are locally made or imported from another part of the region. At Tarsus it is reported that unbaked vessels in a kiln included both White Painted and Black-on-Red specimens (Hanfmann 1963, 50), and Hanfmann uses the term 'Cilician painted' to underline the fact that even if such wares are best known from Cypriot contexts, Cilicia was also a leading producer of them.

The material from the IIf kiln at Kilise Tepe therefore extends the range of the ware beyond its previous western limit of Silifke (Hanfmann 1963, 157), but is in other respects no great surprise. It belongs in the White Painted IV bracket, which is presently placed by those working on Cypriot wares around 750–650 BC (see on **707–35**), though without great conviction. **779**, a deep bowl with horizontal handle at rim looks as if it belongs in this tradition and its closest parallel at Tarsus comes from the same period; it may well be an imported piece. A certainly imported piece of typical White Painted IV is **851**, which is of a very different fabric from the material in the kiln (see S179, p. 266). Whether at Kilise Tepe we have any significant earlier White Painted production seems doubtful.

Black-on-Red

This designation is difficult to avoid, when the salient feature of the ware is the use of black painted decoration on a red, usually slipped and polished, surface, but it runs the risk of seeming to claim that the pieces in question belong to the formal category of 'Black-on-Red' as recognized in Cyprus and the Levant. The problem of definition has been addressed by Schreiber, who reserves the formal term for 'the ware described in Gjerstad's typology of 'Black-on-Red' ware in Cyprus' (2002, 3). She comments that both Kinet Höyük and Kilise Tepe 'have produced BoR pottery which resembles the ware from Tarsus …..' and 'is also distinct from the Cypriot wares in quality and decoration' (2002, 278). She assigns these Cilician Black-on-Red pieces to the later Iron Age. This agrees with the Tarsus evidence, which is not contradicted by the IIf and later provenances of our few sherds (**837–40**, also **836**). The petrography of our samples (S169–74, 181) suggests that the Black-on-Red ware at Kilise Tepe would have been imported like the Bichrome pieces, but probably not from a single source and not necessarily all from

Cyprus, since the ware seems to have been made at both Kinet Höyük and Tarsus. Note **877** which although red-slipped with black paint was different from our Black-on-Red pieces.

Bichrome sherds

As observed by Knappett (p. 260), our earliest bichrome pieces (S147–9 which come from unit 1924 in Room e9 in virtually the same context as the rough jar **811**) have purely linear decoration, and target and panel motifs are not found before IIf. Some of these pieces (including **846–7**) resemble 'Bichrome Ware' as defined at Tarsus, and the petrography suggests they are imports (Knappett, S174–7, 180). Other sherds, although painted with more than one colour, seem rather to be local products for which the formal designation would be inappropriate (e.g. **798–9**, square rimmed jars; **831–4**, black and red or dark and light brown; the coarse jar **870**; etc.).

Figure 240. *Lentoid flasks and other storage vessels from Rm 20 Level IIc destruction debris (from back left: **696**, **697**, **694**; front **695**, **698**, **693**).*

Catalogue

The majority of our ceramic material is in the form of sherds, but first we present the two principal assemblages of whole vessels. The first is a group of storage jars from the IIc destruction of Rm 20 in the East Building. With the exception of large storage jars, including **909**, these are virtually the only ceramics which belong *in situ* in Levels IIa–c. (For one pot from the floor see **912**; for pots caught up in the destruction debris see **904** and **913**.) The other assemblage is the varied collection of painted and unpainted shapes from the Level IIf kiln in the Western Courtyard (**707–35**).

Pottery from Rm 20 (693–706)

A varied collection of pottery was recovered from Rm 20 in the destruction layer in the East Building (Fig. 240). It consists of two large pilgrim flasks (**693–4**), one small pilgrim flask (**695**), one piriform jug (**696**), three trefoil jugs (**697–9**), one large jar neck (**700**), a shallow bowl (**701**), three bases of large pithoi (**702–4**), and two storage jars (**705–6**), together with three jar stoppers.

The two large pilgrim flasks (**693–4**) resemble pilgrim flasks found at other places like Tarsus, Maşat Höyük, or Pirot Höyük east of Malatya. The small pilgrim flask (**695**) resembles the two others except for its size. Müller-Karpe plausibly suggests that the smaller examples served as drinking bottles for individual travellers, and larger flasks were used for commercial transport (1988, 28), but this was perhaps not always the case, given that **695** was found here in association with the two large flasks.

The stopper K19/385 was found loose in the destruction fill, but after cleaning fitted perfectly in the trefoil mouth of jug **697**. Its shape is the same as **699** with a vertical handle from the rim. **698** is a little smaller but otherwise of the same type. **700** is from a very large jug but only the neck with the rim and vertical handle is preserved. A single bowl was found (**701**). It is plain with a bevelled rim. Three bases from very large storage jars were excavated. Two (**702, 704**) had the lower walls preserved up to *c.* 25 cm and 33 cm respectively. The third base was found inverted on the floor (**703**). It was heavily burnt and had perhaps been re-used as a fire installation. **706** is a very fragmented storage jar with a flat base. A large number of pithos sherds probably from the same vessel (**705**) were found together. The sherds were in very poor condition and covered with a white layer, which was impossible to get off, so that the vessel could not be reconstructed.

Three jar stoppers were found in Rm 20. That belonging to **697** has been mentioned above. Two others are crudely made and could not confidently be assigned to any of the vessels; these are listed with other stoppers in the clay section of our report (**1498–9**).

693 K19/361 KLT 120 4564
Pilgrim flask, nearly complete. Pinkish, grit-tempered. Red-brown slip. Smoothed. Rounded base, one big grooved vertical handle and two smaller vertical handles. Below handle a horizontal ridge.
Body di. (max.) 47; H. (47); Th. 0.4, Th. of big handle 1.0
Petrographic sample S133.
Fig. 240

694 K19/382 KLT 122 4578
Pilgrim flask, complete. Pale orange, grit-tempered. Smoothed. Rim thickened ext., one vertical handle and two lugs.
Rim di. 10; Body di. (max.) 38; H. 40
Cf. Tarsus (Goldman 1956, pl. 322:1193–4), Maşat and Pirot (Bilgi 1982, Tab. 11 & 16).
Fig. 240

695 K19/387 Etütlük 1998 4578
Pilgrim flask, nearly complete. Joined from several sherds. Beige, grit-tempered. Smoothed and traces of brown slip. Fragment of vertical handle.
Body di. (max.) 23; H. (22); Th. 0.6
Fig. 240

696 K19/386 4578
Jug, nearly complete. Light brown with lots of white grits. Smoothed. Rounded body, rounded base, two vertical handles.
Body di. 18.5; H. (25.5); Th. 0.5

697 K19/383, 385 KLT 121 4578
Trefoil jug. Nearly complete, with clay stopper. Orange-brown, grit-tempered. Smoothed. Trefoil rim, rounded body, flat base, vertical handle.
Rim di. max. 12, Body di. 30, Base di. 7; H. (40); Th. 0.4; Stopper ht 3.9
Fig. 240

698 K19/380 4578
Trefoil jug. Nearly complete. Light orange, grit-tempered. Smoothed. Trefoil rim, rounded body, flat base and vertical rim to body handle.
Rim di. max. 7, Body di. 22, Base di. 4; H. 35; Th. 0.4, Handle th. 2
Fig. 240

699 K19/405 4597
Trefoil jug. Nearly complete, part of rim, neck and handle missing. Light orange, heavily grit-tempered with big grits. Ext. very brittle. Flat base and vertical handle.
Rim di. max. 3.2, Base di. 8, Body di. 21; H. 26; Handle th. 1.6

700 K19/381 4578
Jar. Neck with complete handle. Light brown with many white and black grits. Buff slip ext. Int. is very flakey and fallen off in places. Smoothed.
Rim di. 10; H. (23.5); Handle th. 2.8–4.0

701 K19/391 4564
Bowl. Rim to lower body. Brown, grit-tempered. Smoothed. Rim bevelled.
Di. 21; H. (7.2); Th. 0.7

702 K19/384 4578
Pithos. Base and walls. Dense brown, grit-tempered. Int. cream slip. Ext. smoothed and blackened by fire. Flat base.
Di. 23; H. (25)

703 K19/379 4578
Storage vessel. Base with very little of walls. Grey-brown, grit-tempered. Heavily burnt. Deep ring base.
Di. 17; H. (6)

[704] K19/400 4553
Storage jar. Base and part of walls. Yellow-buff, grit-tempered. Possibly slipped. Smoothed. Base flat, not wheel-finished.
Di. 21; H. (33); Th. 2.0

705 4578
Broken storage jar; only part of rim is illustrated. Light brown, grit-tempered. Smoothed. Most parts covered with a thick white layer. Dark red paint ext., matt. Grid pattern. Plain rim with long neck, two handles and flat base.
Base di. 9; Th. 0.7–1.0

[706] K19/356 4564
Fragmentary storage jar with part of handle, rim and base preserved. Light brown, grit-tempered. Ext. smoothed but very encrusted. Flat base. Above handle stamped decoration (not further described).
Rim di. *c.* 50, Base di. 22; Th. 2.3

Pottery from FI96/14 in I19 (707–35)

From the stone-lined base of the Level IIf kiln FI96/14 more than 3500 sherds were recovered (Fig. 241). They are all of the same fabric except for a few sherds (see Knappett, above p. 261) and were both painted and unpainted. With hundreds of fragments from extremely similar vessels it is certain that we did not succeed in making all possible joins, but the rims, handles and bases must provide a roughly correct indication of the 'minimum number of individuals'. In most cases we were not able to reconstruct entire vessels, despite long searches, and we are forced to conclude that when the pottery was dumped in the kiln it was already in a fragmentary condition. The following descriptions are based on the work of D. Collon.[2]

Painted types:
a. Jugs with one handle from shoulder to rim, a globular body and a low ring base, with decoration of encircling parallel lines and concentric circles (or targets), with a vertical motif of diverging lines. At least nine examples of this type (**707**: Fig. 242a&b).
b. Trumpet-shaped neck with painted stripe and striped handle rising from neck. Two examples, no bodies identified (**708**).
c. Trumpet-shaped neck, with no handle (**709**).
d. Flaring neck with painted stripes and striped basket handle. One example, no body identified (**710**).
e. Small jar with short spout rising from shoulder, globular body and flat base, rim and neck missing. Decoration of band, stripes and small targets. One example (**712**).

Figure 241. *Pottery from fill of Level IIf kiln FI96/14.*

Unpainted types:
f. Small jugs, with trefoil rim and handle, rounded bases. At least twelve examples (**713**).
g. Bowls with everted rims, perhaps flat based. At least four examples (**714**).
h. Cylindrical pot stands, open top and bottom with slight thickening of each rim. H. 14–17 cm, Di. 13–16 cm. At least six examples (**715–17**: Fig. 243).
i. Shallow bowls, with a sharp groove in the top of a wide flat rim, and a flat base with recessed centre. At least four examples (**718**: Fig. 244). A very similar profile with double ring base and grooved rim was recovered from the ditch in I14 which yielded the handful of Geometric sherds (**940–44**), and it is illustrated and catalogued here for comparison (**719**: Fig. 245a&b).
j. Bowl, with bevelled rim and ring base. Numerous examples (**720**: Fig. 246).
k. Miscellaneous plain bowl rims without identified base sherds (**721–7**).
l. Large handled jars; no pouring lip? At least five examples (**728**).
m. Tall jars with cylindrical neck, upper part only surviving with sloping rim and rib encircling body. We have no means of telling whether these were a type of open stand or were closed at the base. At least eight examples (**729–30**).
n. Miscellaneous plain sherds from closed shapes (**731–4**).
o. Large wide-mouthed jugs, with pouring lip and one handle, probably a ring base, though none joined. At least eight examples (**735**).

The painted vessels in this assemblage belong to the tradition known after Gjerstad 1948 as White Painted IV. As well as in Cyprus, similar painted vessels are found at Tarsus (Hanfmann 1963, pl. 64:334, 68:445–6, pl. 74:647–9, 651–9), Al Mina (du Plat Taylor 1959, pls. XXI–XXII), Karatepe (Darga 1986, pl. V), etc. For Knossos (Coldstream & Catling 1996, pl. Tomb 60:22, 229:11), and a wide range of contexts across the eastern Mediterranean, including Crete see Stambolidis & Karetsou 1998.

Although broadly similar in shape and decoration, vessels of this type vary considerably in the details of manufacture and of the design, and it is clear that there was not a single centre of production. At several sites excavators have felt able to distinguish locally made from imported products. Locally produced material was identified at Mersin (Garstang 1953) and Karatepe (Darga 1986), and at the Ialysos necropolis on Rhodes local imitations were excavated alongside presumably imported pieces (Gjerstad *et al.* 1935, 263; for examples see Stambolidis & Karetsou 1998, figs.

Figure 242. *a) Jug **707** (I19/83); b) side view.*

109–10). At the North Cemetery of Knossos a good selection of White Painted *oinochoai* was found, and these were also thought to be a mixture of locally produced and imported items (for examples see Coldstream & Catling 1996, pl. 115, 208 and fig. 146; one piece strikingly similar to the Kilise Tepe assemblage, with the same arrangement of concentric circles and targets and a 'teepee' motif on the front, was found in tomb 229, pl. 208 no. 11).

At Tarsus from their Middle Iron Age levels came several *oinochoai* extremely similar in their decoration to those found at Kilise Tepe (e.g. Hanfmann 1963, pl. 68 nos. 445–6; pl. 74 nos. 647ff.). They are described by Hanfmann under 'Cilician painted wares' (Hanfmann 1963, 120). Unfired pottery which included 'Cilician buff and white-painted' was excavated in the kiln area at Tarsus, and evidently must have been manufactured at the site (Hanfmann 1963, 118). On the other hand, Nos. 648ff. were considered to be imports (Hanfmann 1963, 47).

It is therefore clear that we should not be surprised to find either locally produced or imported wares in the White Painted IV tradition. Thin-section analysis of the sherds from FI96/14 indicates that local clays were used (see p. 261), and suggests that the entire assemblage was made at Kilise Tepe itself or nearby. By contrast, **850** below from R18 is in a very different softer fabric and clearly of different manufacture. It is noticeable that Tarsus provides the closest parallels to the decoration of our jugs, especially in respect of the 'teepee' motif on the front; we would take this as evidence for regional styles within the broad tradition, rather than seeing Tarsus as the sole centre of production for the Cilician area.

Our unpainted vessels, which are shown by the petrography to have been manufactured alongside our painted ware, may belong to Gjerstad's Plain White IV but this needs further research, as publications of pottery with painted decoration rarely include associated plain wares, and only two of our shapes (**713** and **720**) have clear parallels in Cypriot contexts.

At present it is not possible to date this assemblage with great precision. Presumably the excavators had good reason to date the abandonment of the kilns at Tarsus to the same time as the 'Destruction Fill'. However, this was assigned to *c*. 700 BC on the unsafe assumption that it resulted from an Assyrian invasion in 696 BC (see Forsberg 1995). The only real dating criterion can be the associated ceramics, and it has been suggested that the material from the Destruction Fill should in fact be placed some decades later (Boardman 1965). In any case, the Tarsus evidence does not assist us in deriving a date for our White Painted IV material, and developments in Cypriot archaeology in the interim have not yet yielded any safer chronology.[3]

707 I19/82–4+96–7 Etütlük 1996 (I19/83) 1783
The drawing of this number is composed from several different jugs. Parts of at least nine vessels of this type are present in the assemblage, to judge from the number of double handles attached to the backs of trefoil rims. The upper parts of three vessels have been largely reconstructed (I19/83–4, 97) and the base of two other vessels (including I19/82); unfortunately it was not possible to identify the bases belonging to the reconstructed upper parts. The vessels are all wheel-made of fine, friable, beige ware with few visible grits. They are thin-walled and the outer surface is smooth. They are decorated according to a standard scheme in dark brown/black paint. The quality is good except for a fragment of one vessel (I19/96), but different painters seem to have been at work although the pots themselves seem to have been remarkably similar. The standard decorated vessel is as follows:

- A trefoil lip with painted rim from which a double handle, painted on the outside, rises steeply before curving over and descending vertically to join the shoulder of the pot.
- A short neck which flares out towards the bottom. The juncture with the rim is marked by one or, more often, two lines. The juncture with the shoulder is marked by a single line.
- The body of the vessel is globular on a relatively small, low ring base which is unpainted.
- The surface of the vessel is divided into a small upper and a larger lower zone by a band about a third of the way down on the shoulder, consisting of probably no fewer than five and no more than eight multiple parallel lines, carefully executed, probably with the vessel standing on a wheel which was then rotated. The vessel must then have been laid on its side, probably on a stand or cushion, and rotated so that two concentric circles could be painted round each side of the pot. These circles intersect with the multiple band and divide the surface of the vessel vertically into two side zones and a front and a back zone. In only one case the vessel was evidently painted free-hand and the lines are carelessly executed with much correction.
- In the centre of each of these four vertical zones is a large quadruple target (Di. 4.2 cm): those on each side are in the centre of their respective double circles and those in the back and front zones are generally more or less level with them depending on the size of the vessel. Around these large quadruple targets are small triple targets (Di. 1.52–1.57 cm) regularly disposed according to the space available as detailed below. These targets must have been executed with a pair of compasses as there is a central indentation and they are very regular whatever the quality of the vessel's decoration. The outer two circles of the large targets are broader and set close together with a gap between them and the inner circles. The paint on the targets is applied thinner than on the circles or multiple bands and what appear to be concentric brush-strokes are sometimes visible in the broad outer band of the large targets. The decoration is as follows:

Upper zone (above the multiple band):
Sides: Generally three small targets but sometimes fewer or none depending on the space available between the arcs of the double circles and the multiple band.
Back: One or, generally, two small targets one above the other on either side of the base of the handle.
Front: A 'teepee' motif consisting of three divergent vertical lines intersecting just below the neck, at which point there are three short horizontal lines. These perpendicular lines extend into the lower zone. This motif or a variant of it is not uncommon on comparable Tarsus jugs, and is referred to by Hanfmann variously as 'trident pattern', 'three divergent vertical lines crossed below neck', 'bisected triangle' and 'thunderbolts' (1963, 121, 142, 197 and 214). Its significance is not clear to us.

Lower zone (below the multiple band):
The small targets are arranged in a row beneath the multiple band and parallel to it. Their number varies according the size of the vessel and they will run above the large targets if there is the space. A single small target is placed beneath each of the four large targets. In the case of the front, there is room for one or two small targets on either side of the perpendiculars of the 'teepee'; these perpendiculars intersect with the large target where they end in points.

Figure 243. *Cylindrical pot stands 715–17.*

Body di. 17.5, Base di. 7; Th. 0.5–0.8
Figs. 242a&b

708   I19/94   1783
Jar. Rim and handle to base of neck. Creamy-beige with few visible grits. Smoothed. Black paint, matt. Rim flaring and handle from neck to body. Horizontal bands on neck and on rim, int. and ext., stripes on handle.
Rim di. 4.3; Th. 0.4, Handle th. 0.8

709   I19/218   1783
Jar. Rim with neck. Pinkish with few visible grits. Smoothed. Black paint, matt. Bands and target. Rim flaring.
Rim di. 3; Th. 0.3

710   I19/95   1783
Jar. Rim with neck. Beige with few visible grits. Smoothed. Black paint, matt. Bands. Rim slightly flaring and basket handle.
Rim di. 4; Th. 0.4, Handle th. 0.9

711   I19/219   1783
Jar. Body-sherd from upper part of body. Beige, grit-tempered. Smoothed. Black paint, matt. Band and ladder.
1.9 × 2.0; Th. 0.3

712   I19/64   1783
Jug, preserved from shoulder to base, with spout rising from shoulder. Beige, grit-tempered. Fired to creamy beige. Black paint, matt. On shoulder panel band with vertical lines above targets, on middle body horizontal bands and on spout grid pattern. Rounded body, vertical handle and flat base.
Body di. 8.5, Base di. 4; H. (9.4); Th. 0.5

713   I19/65   Etütlük 1996   1783
Complete jug. Beige, grit-tempered. Smoothed. Globular body with trefoil rim, vertical handle and flat base.
Rim di. max. 8.8, Body di. 8.2, Base di. 4; H. 13
Cf. Gjerstad 1948, fig. XLV.15.

714   I19/93   1783
Bowl. Rim to lower body. Orangey-brown with few grits. Smoothed. Rim flattened.
Rim di. 11; Th. 0.5

[715]   I19/90   1783
Pot stand. Complete profile. Beige, grit-tempered. Smoothed.
Rim di. 17; H. 17.5; Th. 1.0
Fig. 243

Figure 244. *Shallow bowl with grooved rim* **718**.

Figure 245. *a) Side view of shallow bowl with grooved rim* **719**; *b) top view.*

Figure 246. *Ring-based bowl with bevelled rim* **720**.

716   I19/91   1783
Pot stand. Complete profile. Beige, grit-tempered. Smoothed.
Di. 14; H. 14.5; Th. 0.7
Fig. 243

717   I19/92   1783
Pot stand. Complete profile. Beige, grit-tempered. Smoothed.
Di. 13; H. 17; Th. 1.0
Fig. 243

718   I19/86   1783
Shallow bowl. Complete profile. Beige, grit-tempered. Smoothed. Flattened rim with fine groove and flat double ring base. At least four examples of this rim type, and one other base (I19/220).
Rim di. 22, Base di. 9.9, Inner ring int. di. *c.* 3.3, ext. di. 6.9; H. 4.7; Th. 0.7
Fig. 244
Similar shallow bowls (or deep plates) with a wide horizontal or nearly horizontal lip are sporadically reported from Tarsus (e.g. Hanfmann 1963, nos. 989, 1145).

719   3465
Level 2k
Shallow bowl. Buff with very little temper. Slightly burnished. 4 grooves on upper surface of rim.
Rim di. 22; Base di. 10.0; H. 4.5
This bowl from the fill of the ditch in I14 is included here for comparison with **718**. The nearest parallel we have noted for a wide lip with multiple grooves is a sherd from Tarsus (Hanfmann 1963, no. 1147 on p. 255 and fig. 137, also with a rim di. of 22 cm).
Fig. 245a&b

720   I19/87   1783
Bowl. Complete profile. Creamy-beige, grit-tempered. Smoothed. Plain rim and ring base.
Rim di. 23, Base di. 7; H. 7; Th. 0.6–0.9
Fig. 246
Cf. Gjerstad 1948, fig. XLIV.2.

721   I19/221   1783
Bowl. Rim to middle body. Cream, grit-tempered. Smoothed. Rim thickened ext.
Rim di. 13; Th. 0.6

722   I19/222   1783
Bowl. Rim to middle body. Creamy-beige, grit-tempered. Smoothed. Rim plain.
Rim di. 7; Th. 0.4

723   I19/223   1783
Jar. Rim with upper body. Beige, grit-tempered. Smoothed. Rim rounded.
Rim di. 12; Th. 0.6

724   I19/224   1783
Jar. Rim to middle body. Beige, grit-tempered. Smoothed. Rim plain, flattened.
Rim di. 15; Th. 0.5

725   I19/225   1783
Bowl. Rim to lower body. Creamy-yellow with few visible grits. Smoothed. Rim plain.
Rim di. 17; Th. 0.5

726   I19/226   1783
Bowl. Rim to middle body. Pale orange, grit-tempered. Smoothed. Rim plain.
Rim di. 18; Th. 0.3

727   I19/227   1783
Bowl. Rim with upper body. Beige with few visible grits. Smoothed. Rim flaring.
Rim di. 12; Th. 0.8

728   I19/89   1783
Two-handled jar. Rim to middle of body with complete handle. Beige, grit-tempered; roughly applied slip with many fine white grits, smoothed. Rim plain, flattened. One vertical handle present, probably originally two.
Rim di. 18; Th. 0.6

729   I19/88a   1783
Jar. Rim with long neck with ridge halfway down. Creamy-beige, grit-tempered. Smoothed. Rim everted and flattened.
Rim di. 10; Th. 0.7–1.0

730   I19/88b   1783
Jar. Rim with long neck with ridge halfway down. Creamy-beige, grit-tempered. Smoothed. Rim everted and flattened.
Rim di. 10; Th. 0.7–1.0

731   I19/228   1783
Jar. Rim with upper body. Creamy-beige, grit-tempered. Smoothed. Rim everted and flattened.
Rim di. 12; Th. 0.6

732   I19/229   1783
Jar. Rim with upper body. Creamy-beige, grit-tempered. Smoothed. Rim everted and flattened.
Rim di. 12; Th. 0.5–0.6

733   I19/230   1783
Jar. Part of base. Creamy-beige. Smoothed. Disc base.
Base di. 7; Th. 0.6

734   I19/231   1783
Jar. Body sherd. Creamy-beige, grit-tempered. Smoothed. Disc base. Knob on ext. surface.
4.9 × 3.9; Th. 0.8

735   I19/85   1783
Big jug. Complete from rim to middle of body. Beige, grit-tempered. Smoothed. Rounded body with pouring lip and vertical handle.
Rim di. max. 10; Th. 0.4

Miscellaneous ceramics

Bowls with internal rim (736–40)
Bowls are very common, and as at other contemporary sites most have an internal rim. Three small fragments with grooved rim and stripes on top (736–8) are from Level IIa–e and seem to continue the tradition of shallow bowls from Level III (see above, p. 334–5). Their diameter varies from 20–31 cm; two have paint all over the inside, while the third is plain. 739–40 have unpainted rims with no groove.

736   5502
Level IIa
Rim to lower body. Buff, grit-tempered. Smoothed. Dark brown paint ext., matt. Stripes on rim. Rim grooved.
Rim di. 20; Th. 0.7
Fig. 247

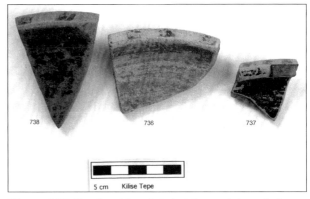

Figure 247. *Bowls with painted strips on internal rim (736–8).*

737   5502
Level IIa
Rim to lower body. Buff, grit-tempered. Smoothed. Dark brown paint. Paint all over inside, stripes on rim and band on exterior. Rim grooved.
4.0 × 3.6; Th. 0.8
Fig. 247

738   5502
Level IIa
Rim to lower body. Buff, grit-tempered. Smoothed. Dark brown paint, matt. Paint all over int., and stripes on rim. Rim grooved.
Rim di. c. 31; Th. 0.7
Fig. 247

739   4012
Level IIa/b
Rim. Brown with light brown core grit-tempered. Slipped. Traces of paint.
Di. 26

740   4004
Level IIb
Rim. Pinkish grit-tempered. Smoothed.
Di. 22

Bowls or plates with plain rim (741–50)
Plain rims were less common; not many complete bowls but several complete profiles were found. All those illustrated are plain bowls with no decoration and plain rims except for **745** and **747–8**. Most have ring bases, which are generally commonest at Kilise Tepe. The fabric varies and they are all smoothed or slipped. Of the two complete bowls found the rim on **747** is not plain but thickened out, and **746** is the only burnished example and is also much bigger than the others (except **743** and **750**) with a diameter of more than 30 cm. **748** has a grooved rim and is blackened on the inside. **750** is a very large plate rim of which we only have a few from Level II.

741   I19/124   2848
Level IIc
Complete profile. Greyish, grit-tempered and few big dark red grits.

Smoothed. Rim plain and base rounded.
Rim di. 16; H. 6.5; Th. 0.6

742 1669
Level IIe/f
Complete profile. Light brown, grit-tempered. Thin walls. Brown wash. Plain rim and flat base.
Rim di. 16, Base di. 6; H. 7; Th. 0.4

743 2390
Level IIf1
Complete profile. Light brown, grit-tempered. Smoothed. Rim plain and ring base.
Rim di. 31, Base di. 11; H. 8; Th. 0.6

744 5523
Level IIa/b
Complete profile. Light brown, grit-tempered. Brown wash. Plain rim and ring base.
Rim di. 18, Base di. 7; H. 6.5; Th. 0.6–1.0

745 6203
Level IIb/c
Complete profile. Reddish, grit-tempered. Red slip int. and 3/4 of ext. Rim grooved and ring base.
Rim di. 12, Base di. 7; H. 4.5; Th. 0.3–0.5

746 6119
Level IIe/f
Complete profile. Reddish-brown, grit-tempered. Reddish-brown slip and burnished. Plain rim but ridged about 3 cm below. Disc base.
Rim di. >30, Base di. 15; H. 11; Th. 1.0

747 K18/227 6113
Level IIf
Complete bowl. Brown, grit-tempered. Smoothed. Rim thickened ext. and flat base.
Rim di. 24, Base di. 10; H. 12; Th. 0.8

748 K20/212 KLT 88 1928
Level I/IIf
Nearly complete bowl. Buff, grit-tempered. Buff slip. Fire blackened inside and on base. Rim slightly thickened and grooved.
Rim di. 19.5, Base di. 9; H. 9.5; Th. 0.5–0.7

749 2378
Level IIf
Complete profile. Buff, grit-tempered. Smoothed. Rim plain. Disc base.
Rim di. 29, Base di. 11; H. 6; Th. 0.6–1.0

750 5502
Level IIa
Complete profile of plate. Joined from two sherds. Brown, grit-tempered. Dark red wash. Rim plain. Flat base.
Rim di. 39, Base di. 9; H. 4; Th. 1.0–1.4

Bowls with cross-hatching (751–7)
These were either smoothed or slipped and with no paint inside, except for a band inside the rim in some instances. They seem to be very uniform in size with a diameter of 17–18 cm. The rim is plain except for **751** which has a thickened rim. Two parallels are found in Porsuk (Dupré 1983, pl. 109:46, 51) but from cups and not a bowl. One bowl (**757**) has cross-hatching in and a handle, with a band out on the lower part of the sherd.

751 1541
Level IId
Rim to lower body. Cream, grit-tempered. Cream slip. Red paint ext., matt. Band on rim and cross-hatching. Rim thickened ext.
Rim di. 17; Th. 0.9
Petrographic sample S116.
Hansen & Postgate 1999, fig. 5; Postgate 1998a, fig. 4
Fig. 248

752 5501
Level IIa
Rim to middle of body. Brown, grit-tempered. Smoothed. Brown paint ext., matt. Cross-hatching. Rim plain.
Rim di. 18; Th. 0.6

753 5812
Level IId/e
Rim to middle body. Reddish, grit-tempered. Smoothed. Red paint ext. and rim, matt. Stripes on rim, cross-hatching on ext. Rim plain, flattened.
Rim di. 18; Th. 1.0

754 4502+4514
Level IId/e and Level I/II
Rim to lower body. Buff, grit-tempered. Smoothed. Brown paint ext., matt. Cross-hatching. Rim thickened ext.
Rim di. 23; Th. 0.8
Fig. 248

755 2362
Level IIf
Rim with upper body. Brown, grit-tempered. Buff slip. Red-brown paint ext., matt. Band int. and cross-hatching. Rim plain.
Rim di. 18; Th. 0.8

756 5801
Level IIf
Rim with upper body. Brown, grit-tempered. Light brown slip. Red paint ext., matt. Cross-

Figure 248. *Bowls with plain rim and cross-hatching on exterior, including 751 (bottom left) and 754 (right).*

hatching. Rim plain.
Rim di. 18; Th. 0.7

757 3489
Level 2/3
Sherd from body of bowl with base of handle. Cream, grit-tempered. Cream slip. Orangey-red paint, matt, cross-hatching exceptionally on int., band and paint on handle ext.
9.1 × 7.0; Th. 0.7

Bowls with diagonal lines (758–71)
At least four rims (**758, 760–62**) are from before Level IIe. Rims are plain or plain flattened. The diagonal lines are on the exterior and the bowls are plain inside except for a band on the internal rim (**760–62**). A complete profile with plain flattened rim and flaring ring base (**764**) was found in a IId/e unit. It is hand-made in contrast to all the other bowls. Two of the bowls are from Level IIf–h (**765–6**) but they do not differ from the earlier phases. Another complete profile is from a very small bowl with a height of 3.5 cm (**765**). It has single diagonal lines from the rim. In all phases the diagonal lines can be very nicely executed (**759–60**) or have more uneven lines (**762, 768**). **758** has a different shape and is not as shallow as the others, but the fabric, rim and decoration are the same. **771**, one of the few provided with a horizontal handle, is like **758** and not as shallow as the rest. The paint is purple and very sloppy.

At Tarsus bowls with parallel diagonal lines are attested from LBA I (Goldman 1956, pl. 302:992–4; Korbel 1987, Taf. 40–42), but at Kilise Tepe they do not appear until Level II. Also they have groups of three or four diagonal lines whereas in LBA Tarsus they seem to be in larger groups. Similar pieces are found at Büyükkaya and Porsuk but from a deeper bowl with a more flaring rim (Seeher 1995, pl. 23:h; Dupré 1983, pl. 41:244).

758 1944
Level IIe
Rim with upper body. Cream with very little temper. Smoothed. Light brown paint ext., matt. Diagonal lines. Rim plain.
Rim di. 20; Th. 0.6
Fig. 249

759 5812
Level IId/e
Shallow bowl. Rim to lower body. Reddish, grit-tempered. Smoothed. Red paint ext., matt. Diagonal lines. Rim plain flattened.
Rim di. 20; Th. 0.8
Fig. 249

760 1132
Level IId
Shallow bowl. Rim to lower body. Orange with big white grits. Orange slip. Purple paint ext., matt. Diagonal lines. Rim plain.
Rim di. 22; Th. 0.8

761 1541
Level IId
Shallow bowl. Rim to lower body. Buff, grit-tempered. Buff slip. Red paint ext., matt. Diagonal lines. Rim plain.
Rim di. 23; Th. 0.8
Postgate 1998a, fig. 4

762 1690
Level IId
Open bowl. Rim with upper body. Brown, grit-tempered. Buff slip. Red paint on rim and ext., matt. Band and diagonal lines. Rim flattened and thickened ext.
Rim di. *c.* 35; Th. 0.8

763 1924
Level IIe
Open bowl. Rim to lower body. Buff, grit-tempered. Smoothed. Red paint ext., matt. Diagonal lines. Rim plain.
Rim di. 24; Th. 1.0
Hansen & Postgate 1999, fig. 7
Fig. 249

764 2399
Level IId/e
Complete profile of open bowl. Orangey, grit-tempered. Hand-made. Buff slip. Red paint. Diagonal lines from rim. Rim plain flattened, ring base flaring.
Rim di. 20, Base di. 10; H. 9.2; Th. 0.8
Hansen & Postgate 1999, fig. 9

765 1799
Level IIf
Complete profile of small bowl. Brown grit-tempered. Coarse and hand-made. Brown slip. Brown paint int. Diagonal lines from rim. Rim plain, base flat and handle attachment.
Rim di. 10, Base di. 4; H. 3.5; Th. 0.7

Figure 249. *Bowls with plain rim and diagonal lines on exterior, including 763 (top centre) and 758 (bottom right).*

766   2370
Level IIf
Open bowl. Rim with upper body. Orangey, grit-tempered. Smoothed. Red-brown paint ext., matt. Diagonal lines from rim. Rim plain.
Rim di. 27; Th. 0.5
Hansen & Postgate 1999, fig. 8

767   4351
Level IId/e
Open bowl. Rim to middle body. Orangey, grit-tempered. Smoothed. Red paint ext., matt. Diagonal lines. Rim plain.
Rim di. *c.* 14; Th. 0.7

768   5863
Level IIe?
Open bowl. Rim with upper body. Brown, grit-tempered. Buff slip. Dark brown paint on ext. and rim. Diagonal lines. Rim plain.
Rim di. 18; Th. 0.5

769   4573
Level IIe
Open bowl. Rim with upper body. Buff, grit-tempered. Buff slip. Red-brown paint ext., matt. Diagonal lines. Rim plain.
Rim di. 20; Th. 0.8

770   1780
Level IIg?
Open bowl. Rim with upper body. Buff, grit-tempered. Buff slip. Red paint ext., matt. Diagonal lines from rim. Rim plain.
Rim di. 18; Th. 0.8

771   4003
Level IIb–e
Open bowl. Rim with upper body. Brown, grit-tempered. Cream slip. Purple paint ext., matt. Diagonal lines. Rim plain and handle attachment.
Di. 15; Th. 0.6
Hansen & Postgate 1999, fig. 10

Deep bowls (772–80)

A number of deep bowls of different types were found. The rim diameters vary from 20 to 30 cm and they occur in different fabrics. The surface is either smoothed or slipped and painted in red or brown. Only one body sherd was from Level IIa–e (**772**). It has cross-hatching above a wide band and is painted in orange-red. Another deep bowl also has cross-hatching out (**775**) but below is a pendent semi-circle. Pendent concentric semi-circles on deep bowls are also seen at Porsuk (Dupré 1983, pl. 50:42). A rather different example with cross-hatching is **778**. The pattern is very uneven and there are stripes on the rim and a band inside. A fine bowl (**773**) has very little temper and painted targets out. The rim is plain whereas most of the others are slightly everted. A similar piece was found at Tarsus (Hanfmann 1963, pl. 69: 480). Another bowl with plain rim is in 'Kindergarten ware' (**776**) and has a very sloppy painted pattern. The painted patterns are very varied, with the previously mentioned cross-hatching, targets, butterfly design (**774**) and vertical lines and triangles with cross-hatching above a band (**780**). The butterfly is also seen in Tarsus (Hanfmann 1963, pl. 73:573). Two sherds had handles. **775** has only the attachment preserved but **779** has a complete horizontal handle on the rim with exterior decoration of thin bands and a single band in. At Tarsus similar deep bowls occur but with the handle attached not to the rim but lower on the body (Hanfmann 1963, pl. 69:482–3).

772   4587
Level IId
Body sherd from upper to lower body. Orangey, grit-tempered. Smoothed. Dark orange-red paint, matt. Bands and cross-hatching. Sharp carination.
6.0 × 8.6; Th. 0.5–0.9

773   2370
Level IIf
Rim with upper body. Brown with a little temper. Smoothed. Dark brown paint ext., matt. Band on rim and targets. Rim plain.
Rim di. 21; Th. 0.6
Hansen & Postgate 1999, fig. 26; cf. Hanfmann 1963, pl. 69:480

774   4353
Level IIe/f
Rim to lower body. Buff, grit-tempered. Smoothed. Red paint ext., matt, bands and butterfly motif. Rim plain.
Rim di. 20; Th. 0.7
Cf. Hanfmann 1963, pl. 73:573

775   6121
Level IIf?
Body sherd from middle body. Light brown, grit-tempered. Buff slip. Dark red paint ext., matt. Panel with paint all over except for small triangle with dot in the middle. Handle attachment.
9.5 × 9.3; Th. 1.2

776   3915
Level IIf
Rim to middle body. Reddish, coarse with heavy grit-temper. Smoothed. Brown paint on ext., matt. Bands and vertical panels with herring-bones and wavy line. Rim plain.
Rim di. 26; Th. 1.0

777   5843
Level IIe/f1
Rim to lower body. Reddish, grit-tempered. Red slip and smoothed. Dark brown paint, matt. Horizontal panel with cross-hatching and pendent semi-circle. Rim plain.
Rim di. 26; Th. 0.9
Cf. Dupré 1983, pl. 50:42

778   2370
Level IIf
Rim to middle of body. Orangey, grit-tempered. Dark brown paint on ext. and rim, matt. Band, cross-hatching; on rim stripes. Rim plain with handle attachment.
Rim di. *c.* 23; Th. 0.4–0.9

779   2370
Level IIf
Rim to lower body. Buff, grit-tempered. Whitish slip. Light brown paint int. and ext.; bands. Rim flattish with round horizontal handle.
Rim di. 30; Th. 0.9

Cf. at Tarsus: Hanfmann 1963, fig. 67:425 ('Cilician buff', from Destruction Level); fig. 69:493 ('Cilician White'); for the 'double-horned' (p. 202) handle on a Black-on-Red bowl see fig. 123:518.

780　　　　　　　　　　　　　　　　　　　　2617
Level I
Rim with upper body. Brown, grit-tempered. Buff slip. Dark brown paint ext., matt. Ext. vertical lines, triangles with cross-hatching. Rim plain.
Rim di. 24; Th. 1.0

Tray (781)
A round tray with handles was found close to the stele in the SE corner of Rm 3 in the destruction debris of the IIc Stele Building (Fig. 108).

781　　　　K19/97　　　　KLT 83　　　　1560
Level IIc
Complete. Cream-grey, grit-tempered. Hand-made. Smoothed. Circular with two raised handles and flat base.
Rim di. 24.5, Base di. 24; H. 2.7, H. with handle 5.5; Th. 1.0–1.3

Lids (782–3)
A complete lid (**782**) was found out of context in L19. It is quite large with a diameter of 40 cm. It is plain with one raised handle and incised lines near the handle. **783** is very strange. It looks like a plate because it has a ring base, but it also had three handles which are probably taller than the base and seem to have been of different sizes, so that it could hardly have stood flat. Perhaps it was made as a plate and then changed to a lid.

782　　　　L19/35　　　　　　　　　　5948
Level I/II
Complete. Light brown with fine grits. Smoothed. Incised lines at one side near handle.
Di. 40; H. 18; Th. 1.0–1.6, Handle th. 2.4

783　　　　J18/395　　　　　　　　　　5894
Level IIc/d
Part of lid or plate. Joined from several sherds. Brown, heavily grit-tempered. Cooking ware. Heavily burnt. Smoothed. Dark red wash ext.
Di. 22; H. without handles (5.5)

Jars and jugs with bands (784–7)
One of the new types in Level IIa–e is jars with horizontal bands. One nearly complete jar and one with base and upper part were found. Both have fairly wide bands in brown paint. A large number of body sherds with bands in red-brown or brown were excavated but some of them could come from jugs as well. Vessels with similar broad bands were not frequent at Tarsus and some were considered imports (Hanfmann 1963, 94 nos. 183–4 (pl. 61:184), with black paint; pl. 93:1351 unstratified, colour of paint not stated).

An almost complete jug with bands in red paint (**786**) was found in P96/121 dug into Rm 4 of the Stele Building. A large shoulder with a vertical handle attached to a possibly trefoil rim has bands in dark red (**787**). Several body sherds with the same paint were found.

784　　　　J19/363　　　　　　　　　　3960
Level IIb/c
Base and upper part, rim missing. Joined from several sherds. Brown, grit-tempered. Smoothed. Red-brown paint, matt. Bands. Rounded body and flat base.
Body di. 18, Base di. 7; H. (19); Th. 0.5

785　　　　K19/117　　　　　　　　　　1568
Level IIc
Almost complete. Joined from several sherds. Reddish with many grits. Buff slip. Light brown paint, matt. Bands. Body rounded, rim everted, base rounded.
Rim di. 10, Body di. 28; H. 28; Th. 0.5

786　　　　K20/211　　　　Etütlük 1996　　　　1994
Level IId
Almost complete, rim missing. Joined from several sherds. Pinky-brown with grey core, grit-tempered. Smoothed. Red paint, matt. Bands. Ring base, part of vertical handle, carinated body.
Body di. 12.5, Base di. 6; H. (15); Th. 0.6
Cf. Hanfmann 1963, pl. 55:25

787　　　　　　　　　　　　　　　　　　　　1704
Level IIe?
Shoulder with handle. Joined from several sherds. Buff, grit-tempered. Smoothed. Dark red paint, matt. Bands. Rim probably trefoil, handle vertical.
20.6 × 15.7; Th. 0.7–0.8, Handle th. 2.2
Petrographic sample S112.

Jars with squared rim (788–800)
A very distinctive feature is the introduction of jars with a squared rim. They can be plain but often they have painted cross-hatching. They are very varied in size, fabric and type. The surface is smoothed or slipped and the jars are painted in red to brown paint. Since we only have sherds it is difficult to say how much of the jar was painted. Some of them have the cross-hatching in a horizontal panel below a band (**792**). They can be large: **789** has a rim diameter of 44 cm, cross-hatching out and stripes on the rim. The rim is squarish and flat on the top, and there is a ridge on the upper part. Another large jar is **788**, which has a complete vertical handle and cross-hatching out and on the flattened top of the rim. The smaller jars have a rim diameter of 22–4 cm (**793, 795–6**) but the decoration is the same. In most cases there are stripes on the rim but it can also be plain (**793**). The cross-hatching can be carefully done or more sloppy (**794–5**). Other patterns occur on the jars and they seem to be more elaborate in the later phases. From Level IIf–h there is a rim with a band and diagonal lines on and below the rim (**797**). Two bichrome painted jars are also from the later phases (**798–9**). They are painted in red and dark brown and have triangles with cross-hatching. **799** is very coarse and not very well made although the

Figure 250. *Jars with squared rim and cross-hatching, including **794** (top left).*

decoration has been carefully applied. **800** is several sherds from a large jar. The decoration is in three horizontal sections. How much of the jar was decorated is impossible to say.

Close parallels for the square-rimmed jars from the end of the Late Bronze Age are now provided by the new excavations at Mersin (Caneva & Sevin 2004, 80 with figs. 7 and 9–10; from the late phase of Level V). One such sherd from there was already published as a 'local ware' by Barnett (1939–40, pl. LII.6). In Early Iron Age Tarsus a few jars with the same kind of rim were published by Hanfmann 1963. They do not have cross-hatching but are painted with bands (pl. 113:20) or no decoration at all (pls. 114:46, 118:225, 119:253). More recently both jars and bowls with painted cross-hatching from the Goldman excavations have been published, and some look much more similar to our early Level II wares (Ünlü 2005, esp. figs. 4–7).

788 I19/112 2848
Level IIc
Rim with upper body and complete handle. Light brown, grit-tempered. Buff slip. Red-brown paint, matt. Cross-hatching below rim. Rim squarish and vertical handle.
Rim di. *c.* 32; Rim W. 3.8; Th. 1.5
Fig. 250

789 2880+2884
Level IIa/b
Rim with upper body, plus joining body sherd with horizontal ridge (drawings pre-date join). Reddish, grit-tempered. Smoothed. Red paint, matt. Stripes on rim, band and cross-hatching below rim. Rim squarish.
Rim di. 44; Th. 1.1–1.4
Hansen & Postgate 1999, figs. 12–13

790 5502
Level IIa
Rim with upper body. Reddish, grit-tempered and coarse, hard-fired. Smoothed. Dark brown paint, matt. Stripes on rim and cross-hatching below rim. Rim squarish.
Rim di. 26; Th. 0.6
Petrographic sample S127.

791 2882
Level IIb
Rim with upper body. Buff, grit-tempered. Smoothed. Brown-red paint, matt. Cross-hatching below rim. Rim squarish.
Rim di. 29; Th. 0.9
Hansen & Postgate 1999, fig. 11

792 2893
Level IIa/b
Rim with upper body. Buff, grit-tempered with many voids. Smoothed. Brown paint, matt. Cross-hatching below rim. Rim rectangular.
Rim di. 28; Th. 1.1

793 5968
Level IId
Rim with upper body. Buff, grit-tempered. Buff slip. Brown paint, matt. Cross-hatching below rim. Rim rectangular, flaring and flattened.
Rim di. 24; Th. 0.8

794 1693
Level IId
Rim with upper body. Buff, grit-tempered. Smoothed. Red paint, matt. Cross-hatching below rim and stripes on rim. Rim squarish and complete horizontal handle.
12.0 × 7.7; Th. 0.6–0.9
Fig. 250

795 3934
Level IIc
Rim with upper body. Greenish, grit-tempered. Smoothed. Brown paint on rim and ext., matt. Stripes on rim and cross-hatching below rim. Rim flattened and squarish.
Rim di. 23; Th. 1.0

796 5966
Level IId/e
Rim with upper body. Buff, grit-tempered. Smoothed. Red paint, matt. Cross-hatching on rim, and possibly ext. Rim rectangular and flaring.
Rim di. 22; Th. 0.5

797 5964
Level IIf
Rim with upper body. Buff, grit-tempered. Buff slip. Dark red paint, matt. Band and diagonal lines below rim and stripes on rim. Rim squarish.
Rim di. 26; Th. 0.8

798 6109
Level IIf?
Rim with upper body. Buff, grit-tempered. Smoothed. Dark brown and red paint, matt. Below rim band, and vertical sections with diagonal lines, zigzags and cross-hatching. Rim squarish.
7.3 × 3.5; Th. 0.7

799 2370
Level IIf
Rim with upper body. Reddish, grit-tempered with many voids. Smoothed. Black and dark red paint, matt. Below rim band, triangle

with cross-hatching and zigzag lines. Rim squarish.
Rim di. 34; Th. 0.6–0.8

800 2821
Level IIf
Rim with shoulder. Joined from several sherds built into base of FI96/11. Reddish, grit-tempered. Buff slip. Red paint, matt. Stripes on rim. Top zigzag lines, middle section with herring-bones and bottom pendent semi-circles. Rim squarish.
Rim di. 25; Th. 0.9–1.3
Hansen & Postgate 1999, fig. 15; Postgate 1998a, fig. 3
Fig. 251

Jars with cross-hatching (801–7)
Several other sherds were found from jars with cross-hatching but not with the rectangular/squarish rim. They seem to be smaller jars with a diameter of up to 22 cm except for **803** which has a diameter of 25 cm. Like the jars with squarish rims it is impossible to say if the entire jar was painted, but **802** seems to have cross-hatching all over. The base is missing. The rim is slightly everted with a complete vertical handle attached. The fabric is very coarse unlike most of the other jars and the paint is crudely applied. It is not 'Kindergarten ware' because it has a softer fabric. **801** and **803** have a slightly everted rim, vertical handle and cross-hatching below the rim. With **801**, it is clear to see the cross-hatching is confined to a band on the upper part of the jar. **807** is made of 'Kindergarten ware' with many voids. The cross-hatching starts on the shoulder and is very badly done. **805–6** differ by having dark brown paint instead of red-brown/red. **805** has diagonal lines inside and **806** has a groove on the interior of the rim and a wide band of paint in. There is not much difference between jars with squared rims and other rims in either fabric or decoration.

801 2841
Level IIc/d
Rim with upper body and complete handle and another sherd with rim to middle body. Light brown, heavily grit-tempered. Smoothed. Red-brown paint, matt. Cross-hatching below rim. Rim everted and vertical handle.
Rim di. 13; Th. 0.5–0.7, Handle th. 1.2
Fig. 252

802 2846
Level IIc-f
Rim to lower body, almost complete profile. Joined from several sherds. Cream, grit-tempered and coarse. Smoothed. Red paint, matt. Cross-hatching below rim. Rounded body, vertical handle.
Rim di. 16, Body di. c. 15; Handle th. 1.0
Fig. 252

803 L19/74 5980
Level IIc
Rim with upper body. Brown, grit-tempered.

Beige slip. Red paint, matt. Cross-hatching. Rim slightly everted and handle grooved.
Rim di. 25; Th. 1.0, Handle th. 1.6
Fig. 252

804 5975
Level IIc
Rim with upper body. Brown, grit-tempered. Smoothed. Dark brown paint, matt. Crude cross-hatching below rim. Rim everted.
Rim di. 34; Th. 1.1

805 2864
Level IIb/c
Rim with small part of upper body. Buff, heavily grit-tempered. Smoothed. Dark brown paint, matt. Int. rim diagonal lines and ext. band and cross-hatching below rim. Rim everted.
Rim di. 19; Th. 0.7
Fig. 252

Figure 251. *Upper part of jar **800** built into base of FI96/11.*

Figure 252. *Miscellaneous jars with cross-hatching: **802** (left), 2 sherds of **801** (top), **805** (bottom right).*

806   5502
Level IIa
Rim with upper body. Reddish, grit-tempered. Smoothed. Brown paint, matt. Band on int. and cross-hatching below. Rim thickened ext. and grooved int.
Rim di. 22; Th. 0.8

807   2375+2392+2399+4353
Level IIe?, IIf, IIf1
Rim, neck and part of shoulder. Reddish, grit-tempered with many voids. Hand-made. Dark red paint, matt. Band with hanging lines on neck and straight herring-bones on shoulder. Rim slightly everted, handle attachment.
Rim di. c. 10; Th. 0.6–1.0

*Body sherds with cross-hatching (**808–14**)*
A large number of body sherds with cross-hatching were found. They are very varied in fabric and decoration but this matches the rim sherds. Unlike most of the other sherds **808** is hand-made, though it looks similar. **810** has very fine cross-hatching above a wide band out. The paint is orange-red whilst the other pieces have red or brown paint. **811** is a large shoulder fragment with cross-hatching below the neck. The decoration is very badly done and the paint is light brown. **813** is from a jar with a probably horizontal handle. The cross-hatching is much thicker than on the others. Furthermore between the cross-hatching are splodges of paint. There are many sherds of 'Kindergarten ware'. For example, **814** is hand-made in a reddish fabric and very coarse. The paint is dark red and not very well executed. The cross-hatching is confined to a band just below the rim.

808   2875
Level IIb
Body sherd from upper body. Buff, grit-tempered. Hand-made. Red paint, matt. Cross-hatching.
4.5 × 4.3; Th. 0.8

809   2873
Level IIb
Body sherd from upper body. Reddish, grit-tempered. Smoothed. Red paint, matt. Cross-hatching.
4.9 × 3.8; Th. 0.9

810   2871
Level IIb
Body sherd from upper and middle body. Reddish, grit-tempered. Pinkish slip. Orange-red paint, matt. Fine cross-hatching above band.
4.4 × 6.6; Th. 0.5–0.8

811   1911
Level IIe
Shoulder to middle body. Joined from several sherds. Buff, grit-tempered. Buff slip. Light brown paint matt. Cross-hatching.
Body di. 26.5; Th. 1.1

812   1799
Level IIf
Body sherd from middle body. Cream, grit-tempered. Buff slip. Red paint, matt. Cross-hatching.
6.2 × 3.8; Th. 0.9

813   3412
Level 1
Body sherd from upper body with root of probably horizontal handle. Pinkish with darker core, fine white grits. Cream slip. Red-brown paint. Lattice with splashes of paint within some of the fields.
13.1 × 10.1; Th. 1.1

814   2401
Unstratified
Complete handle. Red grit-tempered. Coarse and hand-made. Brown paint, matt. Cross-hatching on body and horizontal and vertical lines on handle. Handle attached to wall.
8.6 × 12.2; Th. 0.8

*Jars with horizontal wavy lines (**815–22**)*
From Level IIf–h are body sherds with wavy lines, a motif which is absent in the earlier phases. Wavy lines are attested in Tarsus in LBA I (Goldman 1956, pl. 313), perhaps with MBA antecedents, but none have been found from Level III at Kilise Tepe. The decoration can be very simple with just two or three wavy lines (**817–19**) sometimes framed between two bands (**820–21**). They can also be very elaborate like **816**, part of a shoulder with bichrome decoration. Another bichrome sherd is **822** which is hand-made. One rim sherd (**815**) has decoration also seen at Büyükkaya (Seeher 1995, Abb. 20). The fabric is grey with cream slip and a single wavy line just below the rim. Wavy lines are not unusual elsewhere and are found occasionally on Iron Age sherds from Tarsus but always with other decoration (e.g. Hanfmann 1963, pl. 60:143, 65:344). Of course it not possible to say if the Kilise Tepe sherds with only wavy lines had other decoration. At Porsuk there are a few rim sherds with wavy lines just below the rim (Dupré 1983, pl. 53:60, 62).

815   1595
Level I/II
Rim with upper body. Grey with small white and red grits. Cream slip. Dark brown paint, matt. Bands and wavy line below rim. Rim slightly everted.
Rim di. 14; Th. 0.5
Cf. Seeher 1995, Abb. 20

816   2383
Level IIf
Neck with upper body. Reddish, grit-tempered. Yellowish slip. Light and dark brown paint, matt. Lines on neck, band and wavy line. Neck added separately.
6.3 × 6.0; Th. 0.5

817   1776
Level IIg/h
Body sherd from upper body. Reddish with small black grits. Cream slip. Black paint, matt. Wavy lines.
3.2 × 4.0; Th. 0.7

818   1781
Level IIg
Body sherd from upper body. Brown, grit-tempered. Brown slip. Black paint, matt. Wavy lines.
4.1 × 4.2; Th. 0.8

819   1781
Level IIg
Body sherd from upper body. Buff with very little temper. Buff slip. Red paint, matt. Wavy lines.
6.2 × 4.2; Th. 0.4

820   2370
Level IIf
Body sherd from upper body. Yellowish, grit-tempered. Smoothed. Orange-brown paint, matt. Bands and wavy lines.
6.9 × 5.4; Th. 0.7

821   5829
Level IIf/IIf1
Body sherd from middle body. Brown, grit-tempered. Buff slip. Light and dark brown paint, matt. Lines and wavy line.
5.8 × 4.9; Th. 0.7–1.0

822   5941
Level II
Body sherd from upper body. Buff, grit-tempered. Hand-made. Buff slip. Dark brown and red-brown paint, matt. Band, lines and wavy lines.
4.7 × 5.1; Th. 0.7

Sherds with bands and lines (823–36)
A large number of sherds from jars with bands and lines on the exterior were found. A few are from Level IIa–e but the majority come from Level IIf–h and mark a change in the decoration pattern. Some of the sherds may come from jugs like **707** and **851**. Several of the sherds are a reddish fabric, buff-whitish slip and dark brown paint (**842–3**). They correspond with Cilician White Painted found at Tarsus (Hanfmann 1963, pl. 68:474). There are also bichrome sherds with paint in red and black (**832–3**) or light and dark brown (**831, 834**). One shoulder fragment has a different look (**827**). The fabric and slip are buff but the paint is orange. The paint continues on the neck but as with all the sherds it is impossible to say how much of the rest of the jar was painted. **825** is a neck with different decoration and it probably comes from a different type of jar. The paint is red and the decoration is a band just below the rim with another band just above the shoulder. **826** has a reddish fabric, buff slip and purple paint. The decoration is composed of bands and lines but there seems to be a target on the upper part of the sherd.

823   1781
Level IIg
Rim with small part of neck. Buff, grit-tempered. Buff slip. Black paint, matt. Paint all over rim ext. and horizontal lines. Rim band ext.
Rim di. 6; Th. 0.5

824   1781
Level IIg
Rim with upper body. Buff, grit-tempered. Buff slip. Orange paint, matt. Bands on ext. and band on int. rim. Rim slightly everted, flattened and grooved ext.
Rim di. 9; Th. 0.4

825   2369
Level IIf
Neck. Buff, grit-tempered. Smoothed. Red paint, matt. Bands and two dots above one band.
9.5 × 8.3; Th. 0.8–1.1

826   1332
Level IIa (intrusive?)
Body sherd from middle body. Reddish, grit-tempered. Buff slip. Purple paint, matt. Bands and lines.
12.8 × 8.8; Th. 0.7–1.0

827   1781
Level IIg
Shoulder with upper body. Buff, grit-tempered. Buff slip. Orange paint, matt. Bands and lines.
8.5 × 7.5; Th. 0.4

828   1780
Level IIg?
Body sherd from upper body. Reddish, grit-tempered. Buff-whitish slip. Black paint, matt. Band and lines.
4.9 × 8.1; Th. 0.7
Petrographic sample S178.
Cf. Hanfmann 1963, pl. 68:474

829   1780
Level IIg?
Body sherd from upper body. Reddish, grit-tempered. Buff-whitish slip. Black paint, matt. Bands and lines.
6.0 × 9.4; Th. 0.8
Cf. Hanfmann 1963, pl. 68:474

830   1781
Level IIg
Body sherd from lower body. Brown-reddish, grit-tempered. Buff slip. Red paint, matt. Bands.
4.6 × 7.5; Th. 0.4

831   2384
Level IIf
Body sherd from upper body. Buff, grit-tempered. Smoothed. Light and dark brown paint, matt. Lines.
6.3 × 3.3; Th. 0.6

832   1766
Level IIh
Body sherd from upper body. Reddish with very little temper. Buff slip. Black and red paint, matt. Bands and lines.
4.0 × 4.1; Th. 0.5

833   1790
Level IIf
Body sherd from middle body. Brown-reddish, grit-tempered. Black and red paint, matt. Band and horizontal lines.
6.6 × 4.5; Th. 0.5

834   2370
Level IIf
Body sherd from upper body. Brown, grit-tempered. Buff slip.

Brown and dark brown paint, matt. Lines and bands.
5.3 × 4.8; Th. 0.6

835   2381
Level IIf1?
Body sherd from upper body. Greenish, grit-tempered. Smoothed. Dark green-brown paint, matt. Lines.
4.4 × 5.0; Th. 0.7

836   1799
Level IIf
Body sherd from upper body. Red-brown, grit-tempered. Red-brown slip. Black paint, matt. Bands.
4.4 × 6.2; Th. 0.7
Petrographic sample S181.

Black-on-Red sherds (837–40)
Sherds of orange-reddish fabric, red slip and black decoration first appear in small numbers in Level IIf–h. They match Black-on-Red ware found mainly in Cyprus but distributed all over the East Mediterranean area. One small jar (**838**) has a complete vertical handle and rim; **837** is possibly from the same jar. The exterior decoration consists of horizontal lines. The handle has paint all over. One body sherd (**839**) has a different look. The surface is orange-brown and the paint is dark purple. This may be due to firing. On the upper part is a target. One complete ring base from a bowl was found (**840**). The exterior has bands and lines and the interior just lines. A similar base was found at Tarsus (Hanfmann 1963, pl. 70:502). See also **836** above.

837   2418
Level E5a
Jar rim with upper body. Light orange, grit-tempered. Red slip. Black paint ext. and int. Bands.
Rim di. 7; Th. 0.4

838   2418
Level E5a
Body sherd from upper and middle rounded body of jar with complete vertical handle. Light orange, grit-tempered. Red slip, patches of red on int. Black paint. Horizontal lines, paint all over handle. Same vessel as **837**?
8.3 × 7.0; Th. 0.4
Cf. Hanfmann 1963, pl. 70:502

839   3043
Level 2 upper
Body sherd from upper body of jar. Reddish with little temper, brown core. Ext. burnished. Red and purple paint, matt. Bands.
(8.3 × 6.0); Th. 0.5

840   4500
Level I
Base to middle body of open bowl. Reddish with yellowish core, grit-tempered with big red grits. Red slip. Black paint. Ext. bands and lines, int. lines. Ring base.
Base di. 6; Th. 0.4
Petrographic sample S171.

Body sherd with concentric circles (841)
A large body sherd with a central nipple and concentric circles matches barrel-shaped jugs found at Old Paphos and elsewhere.

841   1117
Level I/II
Body sherd from middle body of barrel-shaped jug. Grey with red core, grit-tempered. Hand-made. Brown slip. Dark brown paint. Concentric circles.
1.7 × 12.3; Th. 0.8
Cf. Karageorghis 1983, pl. XCVI:111; du Plat Taylor 1959, fig. 2:1 (Al Mina); Hrouda 1998, 469 with 478 Abb. 10 (Sirkeli, local product).

Jar sherds with targets (842–54)
In Level IIf–h we see a new pattern well documented in other parts of the Mediterranean area. The decoration consists of concentric circles or targets together with horizontal or vertical lines.

The fabric can vary very much from coarse with many voids ('Kindergarten ware') (**843**), to fine with very little temper (**849**). The fabric is mainly brown and gritty but buff or reddish also occur. A few sherds are hand-made (**842**). This piece also differs from the rest by having several large targets placed vertically.

They mostly seem to come from vessels with rounded body and they may have been decorated all over like **851**. That is the same style as the jugs (**707**) and similar pots from Tarsus (Hanfmann 1963, pl. 68:445) and Al Mina (du Plat Taylor 1959, pl. XXI:9 and XXII, 3b:2–6). The ones from Al-Mina are of a different ware. They are also attested at Karatepe (Darga 1986, pl. V). In Cyprus sherds with targets are found in large quantities at many Iron Age sites.

842–4 and **854** are from different types of jar and it is difficult to say how much of each vessel was painted. **843** comes from a more open jar, coarser and hand-made, with decoration applied very unevenly. **854** is also from a more open shape with rather thick walls and a coarse fabric. It has pinkish slip, purple paint and well executed pattern. Usually the paint is dark brown or black (**844**–**5**) but it may also be bichrome in light and dark brown (**850, 852**) or dark brown and red (**846**–**7**). **849** is a little different in having a fine grey fabric with little temper. The paint is dark brown and black with bands, lines and wavy lines between targets of different size.

842   5941
Level II
Part of neck and shoulder to middle of body. Brown, grit-tempered. Hand-made. Buff slip. Black paint, matt. Bands and large targets. Int. heavily incrusted, neck added to body separately.
12.6 × 11.7; Th. 0.4

843   2646
Level IId/e
Rim with upper body. Brown, grit-tempered. with many voids.

Greenish-grey slip. Dark brown paint, matt. Stripes on rim, lines and targets below rim. Rim flattened and everted.
Rim di. 22; Th. 0.6

844 1766
Level IIh
Body sherd from upper and middle body. Buff, grit-tempered. Smoothed. Dark brown paint, matt. Horizontal and vertical lines and target.
8.9 × 8.8; Th. 0.6–1.1

845 6109
Level IIf?
Body sherd from lower body. Reddish with small black and white grits. Reddish slip. Black paint, matt. Lines and target.
6.1 × 5.9; Th. 0.5–0.8
Petrographic sample S172.

846 1799
Level IIg
Body sherd from upper body. Brown, grit-tempered. Brown slip. Dark brown and red paint, matt. Bands, lines and target.
9.0 × 6.7; Th. 0.5
Petrographic sample S175.

847 3412
Level 1
Body sherd from upper body. Reddish with little temper. Buff slip. Dark red and dark brown paint. Band, lines and target.
5.0 × 4.9; Th. 0.5
Petrographic sample S174.

848 1799
Level IIf
Body sherd from upper body. Brown, grit-tempered. Brown slip. Dark brown paint, matt. Lines and target.
5.1 × 3.4; Th. 0.4

849 2631
Level IIf
Body sherd from upper body. Grey with little temper. Grey-brownish slip. Dark brown and black paint. Lines, bands, wavy line and target. Rounded body.
6.3 × 7.2; Th. 0.5

850 2384
Level IIf
Body sherd from upper body. Buff, grit-tempered. Smoothed. Light and dark brown paint, matt. Bands, one big and several small targets.
8.3 × 7.5; Th. 0.5–0.8
Hansen & Postgate 1999, fig. 28

851 2411
Level E5a
Three-quarters of globular jar. Joined from several sherds. Light brown, grit-tempered. Cream slip. Dark brown paint, matt. Target and intersecting circles. Circular body, ring base.
Body di. 17, Base di. 6.5; H. (16); Th. 0.4
Petrographic sample S179.
Hansen & Postgate 1999, fig. 29; Postgate 1996, fig. 11
Cf. Hanfmann 1963, pl. 68:445

Figure 253. *Jar sherds with pendent semi-circles, including **855** (on left) and **856** (top centre).*

852 2383
Level IIf
Body sherd from upper body with complete handle. Light brown, grit-tempered. Smoothed. Light and dark brown paint, matt. Lines and targets. Oval handle.
8.5 × 8.4; Th. 0.7, Handle th. 1.0
Hansen & Postgate 1999, fig. 27

853 2370
Level IIf
Body sherd with complete handle. Buff, grit-tempered. Light and dark brown paint, matt. Vertical and horizontal lines, target. Vertical handle. Same type as **852**.
5.7 × 7.5; Th. 0.7, Handle th. 1.0

854 3424
Level 2k
Body sherd from upper body. Light brown, grit-tempered with many voids. Pinkish slip. Purple paint, matt. Diagonal stripes, wavy lines and targets.
8.0 × 7.2; Th. 1.2

Body sherds with pendent semi-circles (855–9)
New in Level II are patterns with pendent semi-circles, also attested in Early Iron Age Tarsus (Hanfmann 1963, pl. 55:6). Most of the decoration is not very well made, but one sherd (**857**) has very neat bands and pendent concentric semi-circles. The fabric and paint do not differ from the other sherds. All the sherds are from jars, with a gritty fabric and paint in dark brown or light and dark brown. They also come as 'Kindergarten ware' (**855**). Further pieces from a IId context would have been welcome to support the early provenance of **856**.

855 1516
Level I/II
Large body sherd from upper body of jar with complete vertical handle. Reddish, grit-tempered and very coarse. Hand-made. Cream slip. Brown paint, matt. Vertical and horizontal lines between pendent semi-circle. Stripes on handle.

Hansen & Postgate 1999, fig. 25; Postgate 1998a, fig. 3
Fig. 253

856 1540
Level IId
Body sherd from upper body of jar. Buff, grit-tempered. Smoothed. Brown paint, matt. Vertical lines and pendent semi-circle.
8.0 × 5.4; Th. 1.0–1.4
Hansen & Postgate 1999, fig. 17
Fig. 253

857 6121
Level IIf?
Body sherd from middle body of jar. Buff, grit-tempered. Buff slip. Brown paint, matt. Bands and pendent semi-circles.
11.0 × 8.3; Th. 0.5–0.9

858 2390
Level IIf1
Body sherd from upper body of jar. Brown, grit-tempered. Greyish slip. Dark brown paint, matt. Band and pendent semi-circle.
7.4 × 5.9; Th. 0.9

859 2370
Level IIf
Body sherd from middle body. Orangey, grit-tempered. Smoothed. Light and dark brown paint, matt. Band and pendent semi-circle ext., band on int.
5.9 × 3.8; Th. 0.8

Miscellaneous jar sherds with decoration (860–85)
A large number of body sherds with different kinds of painted patterns were found. The fabric is mainly brown or buff, gritty and slipped. The paint is red, dark brown or light brown. From the earlier phases the patterns seem to be simple cross-hatching, bands and vertical lines, while in the later phases the patterns become more elaborate. Cross-hatching can be in triangles either horizontal (**861, 864–5, 868**) or vertical (**869**) or in vertical panels (**866, 875**). Cross-hatching in triangles is also seen at Tille Höyük (Summers 1993, fig. 37:3, 5), at Xanthos (Metzger 1972, pl. 23:96), at Tarsus (Hanfmann 1963, e.g. pl. 56:37, 60:157) and at Karatepe (Darga 1986, pl. III). **869** has vertical lines together with the cross-hatched triangles, a feature also seen at Xanthos (Metzger 1972, pl. 1:5). A very large sherd of 'Kindergarten ware' with cross-hatching in triangles is **861**. It is very crudely made including the decoration. **862** is a body sherd with a triangular handle. It might come from the same kind of jar as **861** because the fabric is the same. On the handle are stripes and there is a band down each side. **870** looks different. The fabric is very coarse but not quite 'Kindergarten ware'. The bichrome decoration is a triangle with cross-hatching in dark red and dark brown. The decoration can also be thin bands with vertical lines (**873**) or vertical and diagonal lines (**871–2**).

As mentioned, later in Level II the patterns become more elaborate, though the fabric and surface treatment is often the same as in Level IIa–e. Below horizontal lines **876** has triangles with chess boards and groups of dots between. **877** is reddish with red slip and black paint but not the same fabric as Black-on-Red. The pattern is rhombs with cross-hatching within a triangle. A sherd with very elaborate decoration is **863**. In addition to the wavy lines it also has horizontal lines and triangles with cross-hatching. **878** is coarse and has dark red paint. The decoration is diagonal bands with zigzag lines. In between is a cross. **879** has a horizontal panel with diagonal lines and a vertical panel with cross-hatching. The paint on **880** is purple but the pattern is cross-hatched triangles. The fabric and the badly made decoration make it look like 'Kindergarten ware' but it is not so coarse.

860 2401
Unstratified
Body sherd from upper body. Red, grit-tempered, coarse with many voids. Hand-made. Smoothed. Dark brown paint. Cross-hatching and sloppy herring-bones.
6.3 × 7.4; Th. 1.0

861 2407
Unstratified
One third of profile, rim and base missing. Light orangey-brown, grit-tempered with many very fine white grits and some larger dark ones. Hand-made. Red paint. Band and cross-hatching. Applied notched crescentic handle.
19.1 × 16.3; Th. 0.5–0.9, Handle th. 1.0
Postgate 1996, fig. 10

862 1514
Level I
Body sherd from upper body with handle. Reddish, grit-tempered, coarse with many voids. Hand-made. Pinkish slip. Dark red-brown paint. Horizontal stripes. Handle shaped as a triangle.
9.1 × 9.9; Th. 0.9

863 1121
Level IIe?
Body sherd from lower body. Cream, grit-tempered. Light brown slip. Dark brown paint, matt. Wavy lines, bands and triangles with cross-hatching.
8.4 × 8.8; Th. 0.7
An. St. 1995, fig. 14: 10; Barnett 1939–40, pl. XLVI: 7

864 5837
Level IIf1?
Body sherd from middle body. Light brown with very small grits. Buff slip. Dark red paint. Triangles with cross-hatching, band and target.
11.7 × 6.8; Th. 0.4–1.0

865 1667
Level II?
Body sherd from middle body. Reddish, grit-tempered and coarse. Hand-made. Orange-red paint, matt. Triangles with cross-hatching.
9.4 × 7.5; Th. 0.8
Hansen & Postgate 1999, fig. 19

866 2370
Level IIf
Body sherd from middle body. Brown, grit-tempered. Smoothed.

Pottery from Level II

Dark brown paint, matt. Lines and panel with cross-hatching.
4.7 × 5.4; Th. 0.7

867 1781
Level IIg
Body sherd from middle body. Brown, grit-tempered. Brown slip. Black paint, matt. Band, lines, diagonal lines and triangle with cross-hatching.
4.6 × 4.0; Th. 0.9

868 2405
Surface
Body sherd from upper body. Light orange with lots of white grits and many voids. Hand-made. Cream slip. Dark red paint, matt. Band, triangle with cross-hatching, vertical panel with zigzag lines and vertical panel with cross-hatching.
6.0 × 5.4; Th. 0.9

869 2370
Level IIf
Body sherd from upper body. Buff, grit-tempered. Smoothed. Brown paint, matt. Vertical lines and triangle with cross-hatching.
6.2 × 5.0; Th. 0.8
Cf. from Xanthos Metzger 1972, pl. 1:5

870 4500
Level I
Body sherd from upper body. Reddish, grit-tempered with many voids. Hand-made. Pinkish slip. Dark red and dark brown paint, matt. Band and triangle with cross-hatching.
8.8 × 5.7; Th. 0.9

871 6109
Level IIf?
Body sherd from upper body. Buff, grit-tempered. Buff slip. Dark brown paint, matt. Bands, vertical and diagonal lines.
6.9 × 6.4; Th. 0.6

872 2378
Level IIf
Body sherd from upper body. Buff, grit-tempered. Whitish slip. Light brown paint, matt. Vertical and diagonal lines.
8.5 × 6.8; Th. 0.8

873 1766
Level IIh
Body sherd from upper body. Grey, grit-tempered. Beige slip. Light brown paint, matt. Bands and panel with vertical lines.
7.2 × 9.3; Th. 1.0

874 1781
Level IIg
Body sherd from upper body. Brown, grit-tempered. Brown slip. Red paint, matt. Triangle with cross-hatching.
4.6 × 3.0; Th. 0.8

875 1781
Level IIg
Body sherd from middle body. Grey, grit-tempered. Light brown slip. Brown paint, matt. Panel with cross-hatching.
4.0 × 6.7; Th. 0.7

876 2370
Level IIf
Body sherd from upper body. Light brown, grit-tempered. Dark brown paint, matt. Band, lines, triangles with chess board pattern and groups of dots between.
8.1 × 8.2; Th. 0.8–1.0

877 1781
Level IIg
Body sherd from upper body. Reddish, grit-tempered. Reddish slip. Black paint, matt. Lines and triangles with cross-hatching.
8.2 × 5.1; Th. 0.7

878 2369
Level IIf
Body sherd from upper body. Light brown, grit-tempered and coarse. Dark red paint, matt. Diagonal bands with zigzag lines and a cross between.
7.7 × 7.2; Th. 1.0

879 1799
Level IIf
Body sherd from upper body with handle attachment. Brown, grit-tempered. Greyish slip. Dark brown paint, matt. Horizontal panel with diagonal lines, and vertical panel with cross-hatching. Ridge on central part of sherd. Handle attachment.
8.0 × 7.4; Th. 0.6
Hansen & Postgate 1999, fig. 16

880 1780
Level IIg?
Body sherd from upper body. Buff, heavily grit-tempered. Smoothed. Purple paint, matt. Band with diagonal drops and triangles with cross-hatching.
12.1 × 8.0; Th. 1.0

881 1783
Level IIf
Body sherd from upper body. Reddish, grit-tempered and coarse. Hand-made. Buff slip. Red and dark brown paint, matt. Horizontal sections with cross-hatched triangles, wavy lines and diagonal drops.
6.1 × 4.5; Th. 1.0

882 1783
Level IIf
Body sherd from upper body. Buff, grit-tempered. Hand-made. Smoothed. Red and brown paint, matt. Bands and target. Vertical handle.
5.2 × 6.3; Th. 0.5, Handle th. 0.9

883 1945
Level IIc
Body sherd from middle body. Cream, grit-tempered. Cream slip. Brown paint, matt. Vertical panel with zigzag and vertical lines.
5.5 × 7.3; Th. 1.0

884 4358
Level IIe/f
Body sherd from upper body. Brown with very little temper. Red slip. Black paint, matt. Band and panels with cross-hatching and diagonal lines.
2.6 × 4.1; Th. 0.8

885 4594
Level IIe
Body sherd from lower body. Brown, grit-tempered. Smoothed. Dark brown paint, matt. Band, vertical and diagonal lines.
5.8 × 6.6; Th. 0.6

Miscellaneous jar rims with decoration (886–9)
A large number of rim sherds with painted decoration were found. Some of them have been mentioned

under other categories of jars or bowls. They are very varied in fabric and type of decoration. A rim sherd from a jar has on the shoulder a painted wheel above a band (**887**). Another sherd which is not a rim but has a complete handle also has a painted wheel together with vertical lines (**886**). Two rim sherds from the same kind of jars with handles have simple decoration on the shoulder consisting of a panel with zigzag lines (**888-9**). A similar sherd from Porsuk has double zigzag lines (Dupré 1983, pl. 51:50). One of the jars has a horizontal handle while the other handle is vertical.

886   1595
Level I/II
Shoulder to lower body. Brown, grit-tempered with voids. Handmade. Buff slip. Dark brown paint, matt. Bands, vertical lines and circle with cross-hatching (wheel). Rounded body with vertical handle.
11.0 × 9.8; Th. 0.6
Hansen & Postgate 1999, fig. 24

887   4358
Level IIe/f
Rim to middle body. Orangey, grit-tempered with big red grits. Buff slip. Brown paint, matt. Band and wheel. Rim flattened and everted.
Rim di. 20; Th. 0.8–1.0

888   5954
Level IIe/f
Rim to middle body. Reddish, grit-tempered. Pinkish slip. Dark brown paint, matt. Horizontal panel with zigzag lines. Rim slightly everted and complete horizontal handle.
Rim di. 19; Th. 0.4–0.9

889   2378
Level IIf
Rim to lower body. Orange-reddish, grit-tempered. Smoothed. Red paint, matt. Horizontal panel with diagonal lines. Rim slightly everted and complete vertical handle.
Rim di. 11, Body di. 18; Th. 0.6, Handle th. 1.1
Hansen & Postgate 1999, fig. 14

*Miscellaneous handles (**890–93**)*
Many handles were found. They are of the same fabric and decoration as the rest of the pottery but a few should be mentioned. **890** is a small fragment of a vertical handle attached to the rim. The rim is flat and has brown zigzag lines on top. The decoration on the handle is painted herring-bones. **891** is also a small fragment of a vertical handle attached to the rim. The fabric is grey and the decoration consists of stripes in a light brown paint. The stripes continue under the handle. **892** is a shoulder fragment with the rim and a complete vertical handle attached *c.* 4 cm below the rim. The paint is dark brown and the decoration is of bands combined with uneven diagonal lines. On the rim are stripes. The fabric of **893** looks different. It is brown with a brown slip and black paint. The decoration is horizontal bands and stripes.

890   4513
Level IIc
Handle attached to rim. Reddish, grit-tempered. Buff slip. Brown paint, matt. Zigzag lines on rim, herring-bones on handle. Flat handle and rim.
Handle th. 1.9

891   1766
Level IIh
Part of handle. Grey, grit-tempered. Light brown slip. Black paint, matt. Stripes.
Handle th. 1.3, Wall Th. 0.9

892   1780
Level IIg?
Rim with shoulder and handle. Beige with grey core, grit-tempered. Light brown slip. Dark brown paint, matt. Horizontal bands and uneven diagonal lines. Rim slightly everted.
Rim di. 18; Th. 0.8

893   1781
Level IIg
Body sherd from upper body with part of handle. Brown, grit-tempered. Brown slip. Black paint, matt. Horizontal and wavy lines. Vertical handle.
6.7 × 5.6; Th. 0.7, Handle th. 1.7

*Miscellaneous sherds (**894–6**)*
Some sherds come from vessels which are unique at Kilise Tepe. **894** is a fragment of the rim from the middle part of a multiple vessel. Double and multiple vessels are known from several sites in Cyprus (Karageorghis *et al.* 1999, 12–13, no. 32; Morris 1985, 93–5, pl. 167). Too little of the one from Kilise Tepe is preserved to be able establish whether it was a double or a multiple vessel. The rim has cross-hatching in orange-red. Those from Cyprus are plain or incised. **895** is part of a shoulder. The fabric looks a little like the fine red ware from Level III, but is more gritty and not burnished. Attached to the shoulder is an animal head, possibly a dog or a bear. **896** is the neck and part of handle from a composite vessel. Nothing of the lower part was preserved. It looks like a modern coffee-pot but the rim is missing so it is not possible to see if there has been a spout. The execution of the vessel is very bad and the hole is not even in the centre of the neck. The finish of the vessel is very sloppy too.

894   5973
Level IIc/d
One rim and very small part of upper body of a double vessel. Brown, grit-tempered. Smoothed. Red-orange paint, matt. Cross-hatching on flat rim. Four surfaces.
Th. 0.8; Rim W. 1.8

895   1541
Level IId
Jar shoulder. Reddish, grit-tempered. Red slip. Attached to shoulder, animal head.
Th. 0.7–1.1, H. of animal head 3.8

896 1657
Level IId?
Neck and part of handle. Buff, grit-tempered. Red wash ext. Incised diagonal lines on the upper surface of the handle.
Neck di. 5.9–6.8; Handle th. 2.8

897 K19/105 1555
Level IIc
Large jar, fragmentary. Greyish-brown, grit-tempered. Rounded rim; flat base. On the rim sherd part of an incised design, possibly of a ship.
Rim di. c. 40

Spindle bottles (898–903)
A number of sherds from spindle bottles were found throughout Level II, also in I14 and K14. Three of them are of fine red ware with no temper (**898, 900–901**) and one is fine brown with no temper (**903**). Both are a common fabric in Level III, and it is quite possible that all these pieces are throw-ups from that time. Two of the bases have a pot mark underneath (**900, 903**), which is commonly seen on spindle bottles from all over the Mediterranean area. **902** is a different fabric, was painted and has two grooves just above the base. It is also bigger than the others.

898 5514
Level IIa
Base. Fine red with no temper. Burnished.
Di. 3

899 1535
Level IId
Part of neck. Red with fine white grits. Burnished ext. Handle attachment.
Neck di. 2; Th. 0.6

900 1704
Level IIe?
Base. Dense orange with no visible grits. Burnt to brown in places. Traces of vertical burnishing on ext. Pot mark on base.
Di. 3.5; Th. 0.7

901 3424
Level 2k
Long neck with handle attachment. Fine red with no visible temper. Burnished vertical striation.
Di. 2; Th. 0.5

902 3094
Level 2 lower
Base. Reddish, grit-tempered. Int. buff surface. Ext. smoothed. On ext. two grooves and traces of red paint.
Di. 6.5; Th. 0.7

903 2456
Surface
Base. Brown with no visible temper. Hard-fired. Brown slip and burnished ext. Pot mark on base.
Di. 4; Th. 0.5

Small jar (904)
In J18, a small almost complete pot was found. It is plain with no decoration, badly burned and in very bad condition. It is the only one of its kind found.

904 J18/428 5816
Level IIc; Rm 7 destr. debris
Almost complete pot. Joined from several sherds. Brown, grit-tempered. Light brown slip. Rim plain, rounded body and rounded base.
Rim di. 5, Body di. 11.5; H. 13; Th. 0.5–0.7

Cooking pots (905–8)
Sherds from cooking pots were found in all phases all over the mound. Not many complete examples were found but some appear in Level IIa–e. They look very much like cooking pots from other levels. They mostly have rounded bodies, flattened bases and two handles.

905 J19/256 1690
Level IId
Nearly complete pot. Dark brown, heavily grit-tempered. Hand-made. Slightly burnished ext. Flattened rim, rounded body and probably flat base. Two horizontal handles of different sizes.
Rim di. 14–15, Body di. 12.5; H. 22; Th. 1.0

906 K18/134 4363
Level IIe
Nearly complete pot. Dark brown, heavily grit-tempered. Burnt. Hand-made. Smoothed. Rim flattened with raised horizontal handle, base flat.
Rim di. c. 15.5, Body di. 21, Base di. c. 7; H. 12; Th. 0.6–0.8

907 J19/332+333 3942
Level IId
Partially complete pot. Cooking ware. Most of the ext. covered with whitish layer. Rim slightly everted, two vertical handles and rounded body, base missing.
Rim di. 17, Body di. 25; H. (20); Handle th. 1.6

908 K18/238 6120
Level IIf?
Nearly complete pot. Joined from several sherds. Cooking ware, heavily burnt. Rim plain, one vertical handle and the scar of the other; base missing.
Rim di. 15, Body di. 19; H. (13); Handle th. 1.1

Storage jars (909–15)
Different kinds of storage jars have been found at Kilise Tepe including very large jars with a height of up to 120 cm (**909**). In two pits in K20 a large number of heavy sherds were excavated from at least seven very large jars (**910**) and were studied by D. Collon. They had everted flattened rims with diameters from 35–45 cm, rounded bases and two handles centrally on the body. Furthermore they had rope decoration on the upper part of the body and sometimes on the middle. **909** has the same shape but no decoration and two rather small handles placed on the lower part of the body. Another large storage jar (**911**) with a height of 94 cm was found lying on the ground immediately

below the surface but in a IIb/c context. Smaller storage jars include jugs with everted rims and a height of up to 38 cm (**912**, **914–15**). They are plain with flat or rounded base and one vertical handle and look very much like **697**.

909   K19/294   4521
Level IIb/c; SW corner of Rm 4
Complete. Brown, grit-tempered. Smoothed. Rim rounded, body pointed towards base, two small vertical handles on lower part of body.
Rim di. 55, Body di. 72.5, Base di. 17.5; H. 120; Th. 1.0–1.2

910   K20/237   1924+1930
Level IIe
Fragments from a number of similar very large storage jars. One example was reassembled from sherds for drawing. Grey core, grit-tempered, fired cream-brown on surface. Smoothed. Rope decoration below rim and above handle. Rounded pointed base, everted flattened rim and small vertical handles.
Rim di. *c*. 50, estimated Body di. 97; estimated H. 174; Th. 2.0, Handle th. 2.4

Six other vessels were identified from their rims which were all everted and flattened but with slight differences. One rim has rope decoration. Pinky-red, grit-tempered with very fine grits. Creamy-brown slip ext.
Di. 35–45; Th. 1.2–2.0

911   K20/218   1982
Level IIb/c
Complete jar. Joined from several sherds. Buff, grit-tempered. Smoothed. Two vertical handles on lower body.
Rim di. *c*. 50, Base di. 24, Body di. 72; H. 94, Wall th. 1.5–2.0

912   K20/198   1984
Level IIc; on floor of Rm 2
Almost complete jug. Cream-orange, heavily grit-tempered. Buff slip and smoothed. Rim everted, body rounded, flat base and vertical handle.
Rim di. 10, Body di. 25, Base di. 9; H. 38.5; Th. 0.6, Handle th. 1.0

913   K19/115   1566
Level IIc; Rm 4 destr.debris
Complete jug. Grey, grit-tempered. Grey-brown slip. Rounded body, everted rim, flat base and one vertical handle.
Rim di. 8, Body di. 27, Base di. 6; H. 36.5; Th. 0.5, Handle th. 1.0

914   J18/392   5894
Level IIc/d
Nearly complete jug. Brown with small black grits. Burnt and in very poor condition. Pattern burnished ext. Rounded body, vertical handle and possibly trefoil rim.
Base di. 10, Body di. 26; H. 32; Handle th. 1.2

915   J19/320   3925
Level IIe/f
Almost complete jug. Brownish-red, grit-tempered. Smoothed. Trefoil rim, curved base and partly preserved vertical handle.
Body di. 28, Base di. 7; H. 42; Th. 1.0, Handle th. 2.0

*Pilgrim flasks (**916–19**)*
In Level II, apart from those in Rm 20 (**693–5**) we have a few almost complete pilgrim flasks and many sherds. Larger ones (**693**, **916**) had three handles like the lentoid flasks (**672–7**), smaller examples just one from body to rim. Two of those illustrated (**916–17**) are in a gritty red ware that is confined to Levels IIa–d (see Knappett, p. 258 Fabric B). **916** is from a fairly large flask. **918** and **919** which are nearly complete look like similar ones found in Tarsus.

916   2877
Level IIb
Upper part with fragment of one handle. Reddish, grit-tempered. Smoothed.
Neck di. 5; Handle th. 1.6
Petrographic sample S131.

917   2873
Level IIb
Upper part with complete handle. Reddish, grit-tempered with white grits. Brown wash. Plain rim and vertical handle.
Rim di. 2.5; Handle th. 1.1
Petrographic sample S132.

918   K19/100   1555
Level IIc
Nearly complete. Greyish-beige, grit-tempered. Smoothed. Rim missing. One vertical handle.
Body di. (max.) 13.5; H. (17); Th. 0.6
Cf. Goldman 1956, pl. 322:1196.

919   I19/11   KLT 68   1704
Level IIe?
Complete except for chips. Beige, grit-tempered. Smoothed. One vertical handle.
Body di. (max.) 13.2; H. 21

*Feet from pilgrim flasks (**920–39**)*
A total of 87 sherds recognized as feet from pilgrim flasks were found at Kilise Tepe. Furthermore one was found on the surface by James Mellaart during his surveys from 1951–54 (Mellaart 1958, pl. IV:36). This is a surprisingly large number compared to what has been found elsewhere. They are attested in Syria, Cyprus and Tarsus (Eriksson 1993, 26–7). Eriksson states that only eight examples have been found but there are at least two more from Tarsus (Goldman 1956, pl. 328:1226 & pl. 329:1232). Whether this infrequency is really because no more have been found or rather because they have not been recognized as part of vessels is of course difficult to say. At Tarsus, for example, pl. 328:1226 was identified as the leg of a figurine. Unfortunately only fragments of the foot have been identified at Kilise Tepe; obviously sherds from the body must have been present but cannot usually be assigned to this shape. One complete vessel was found at Minet el-Beidha (Schaeffer 1949, fig. 81:8) and another almost complete example at Ras Shamra (Courtois & Courtois 1978, fig. 21:1). In Tarsus they are all from LBA II contexts. The purpose of these feet seems to have been to support a pilgrim flask, probably used for wine or water, in a tilted position. No doubt our ceramic feet imitate wooden or wicker stands separate from the vessels.

At Kilise Tepe they were found all over the mound, but 30 out of 86 were concentrated in K19 on the northwest side of the mound. They mainly come from Level IIa–e but are also found in IIf–h and a few strays came from Level I and the surface. One (**930**) was found in I14 in a Level 3 context, in a fine red fabric, one of the typical wares of Level III. They are very varied in size, from **920** which seems to have supported a very large flask to **934** from a much smaller pot. The fabric is the same as the rest of the pottery. They are all gritty except for **930**. Some are very coarse and look like 'Kindergarten ware' (**927**). The paint is red but can also be brown (**938**). They can broadly be divided into four types:

Figure 254. *A variety of decorated feet from pilgrim flasks, including* **925**, **932**, **936** *and* **938**.

Type 1 – Plain: **920–21** are plain with no decoration. Usually they are slipped and smoothed. Those illustrated are quite big but they appear in all sizes.
Type 2 – Painted: **922–6** are decorated with paint, often as bands along the edges of the foot (**924**). But they can also have painted herring-bones (**925**). **926** has a width of 26 cm, and must have been the support for a very big flask.
Type 3 – Incised: **927–32** have different kinds of incised decoration. Usually it is herring-bones on one face of the foot (**929–30**, **932**) but it can also be diagonal lines (**931**). Another pattern is concentric circles and maybe herring-bones (**928**). The best preserved foot from Kilise Tepe has about 1/3 of the body of the flask preserved (**927**). It is badly made and the actual foot is more a tall ridge with deep grooves on one side.
Type 4 – Painted and Incised: **933–9** have a combination of paint and incised decoration. The paint is still in bands but may also just be spots. The incised herring-bones are also seen here and **934** has concentric circles. One of the pieces from Tarsus looks very much like **938** (Goldman 1956, pl. 329:1234). One foot has an elaborate pattern (**935**). There are splashes of paint and incised cross-hatching with dots in some of the fields. **934** is also different because it has vertical lines. One of the feet from Tarsus has the same pattern but no paint (Goldman 1956, pl. 329:1232). One piece looks very different from the rest (**939**), not in fabric and decoration but in shape. The painted pattern seems to be cross-hatching. It is hollow and may not be a foot from a pilgrim flask.

920 1527
Level IIe
Very big foot. Cream, grit-tempered. Cream slip. Slightly burnished.
H. 11.0

921 1540
Level IId
Very big foot. Orangey, grit-tempered and coarse. Buff slip.
H. 11.9

922 1609
Level I
Greyish-red with many white grits. White slip. Dark reddish-brown paint, matt.
H. 6.1

923 1541
Level IId
Grey, grit-tempered. Buff slip. Red paint on one side and on the bottom, matt.
H. 6.1

924 1551
Level IIc/d
Reddish, grit-tempered. Buff slip. Red paint on one side, matt.
H. 6.0

925 5812
Level IId/e
Reddish, grit-tempered. Light brown slip. Smoothed. Dark red paint on one side, matt. Herring-bones.
H. 7.0
Fig. 254

926 1983+1551
Level IIc/d, IId
Buff, grit-tempered. Buff slip. Dark red paint on one side, matt.
H. 9.6

927 2433
Level E5b
About one third of bowl preserved. Light orange, grit-tempered. Badly made. Central tall ridge decorated with grooves on one side.
H. 3.0

928 3063
Level 2 middle
Very small fragment of foot. Cream, grit-tempered. On surface deep incised concentric circles and vertical lines.
H. 4.1

929 1665
Level II?
Red, grit-tempered and coarse. Smoothed. Incised decoration on one side. Herring-bones.
H. 6.6

930 3712
Level 3
Red with no temper. Red slip. Slightly burnished. Incised herring-bones.
H. 7.1

931 1787
Level IIg
Cream, grit-tempered and coarse. Incised vertical lines on one side.
H. 8.8

932 5975
Level IIc
Brown with very small black grits. Smoothed. Incised on one side. Herring-bones.
H. 7.1
Fig. 254

933 3465
Level 2k
Buff, grit-tempered. Buff slip. Deeply incised on one side. Vertical lines and concentric circles. Faint traces of red paint on the same side as the incised decoration.
H. 7.5

934 1786
Level IIf
Brown, grit-tempered. Light brown slip. Incised lines and traces of red paint on one side of foot.
H. 5.0
Cf. Goldman 1956, pl. 329:1232

935 1527
Level IIe
Greenish, grit-tempered. Buff slip. One side decorated with incised and painted patterns. Red paint, matt. Bands and deep incised cross-hatching with dots.
H. 9.0
Hansen & Postgate 1999, fig. 2

936 1691
Level IId
Buff, grit-tempered and coarse. Smoothed. Incised and red paint on one side, matt. Herring-bones.
H. 9.4
Fig. 254

937 2828
Level IIf
Cream, grit-tempered and coarse. Red paint on both sides of foot, matt. Incised herring-bones on one side.
H. 4.7
Hansen & Postgate 1999, fig. 3

938 5968
Level IId
Reddish-brown, grit-tempered. Dark brown paint on ext., matt. Incised decoration on one side. Herring-bones.
H. 5.2
Cf. Goldman 1956, pl. 329:1234
Fig. 254

939 K20/50 1901
Unstratified
Pinky-buff, grit-tempered. Creamy-buff slip. Orange-red paint, in uneven cross-hatching, matt. Incised herring-bones on one side.
H. 8.2

Notes

1. As for Level III, the catalogue and first draft of the introduction were by Connie Hansen. The introduction in its present form and occasional comments within the catalogue are by Nicholas Postgate.
2. Our thanks also go to Lucy Seffen (née Mutter) for making available to us her undergraduate dissertation (Cambridge 1998). This study of the kiln assemblage has provided important details for our discussion here.
3. Many thanks to Dr Maria Iakovou and Prof. Joanna Smith for their advice and for bibliographical help with the Cypriot dimension. For Prof. Smith's opinion on the date of the kiln material see further Postgate forthcoming.

Chapter 27

Geometric Pottery

J.N. Postgate

A very few pieces at Kilise Tepe are of Greek types from before the Hellenistic period. One piece was identified by Dominique Collon among the surface finds from O9 (**945**). Another (**946**) comes from the later Iron Age levels in the NW corner, but cannot be precisely assigned to a phase. The majority come from the backfill of the ditch in I14, which also yielded a very distinctive shallow bowl profile with grooved rim and double ring base, similar to a type found in the IIf kiln (see above, **718–19**). This might help to sustain a relatively early (seventh-century) date for some of these pieces.

The descriptions and drawings of these few sherds were submitted to Prof. J.N. Coldstream, and his comments on the individual pieces (letter of 30 September 2003) are cited below where relevant. His opinion is that 'as far as I can see, none of your more diagnostic pieces need to be later than the 7th century'. As for the source of some of these pieces, he suggests that this might be the 'colonial workshops in the Rhodian colony of Soloi, ... buried under Roman Soli-Pompeiopolis' (cf. Coldstream 1968, 385–6).

940 3465
Level 2k
Skyphos. Rim with complete handle, brown with very little temper. Thin walls. Cream slip. Brown paint on ext. and int. Ext. vertical and horizontal lines.
Fig. 255 top left
Parallels: for the combination of a rounded open bowl with groups of vertical lines each side of a horizontal handle cf. Coldstream 1968 pl. 17h etc. Prof. Coldstream comments that 'the shape is that of the Corinthian Late Geometric *kotyle* (e.g. Coldstream 1968, pl. 19j) but the clay and cream slip indicate an imitation from elsewhere. I suggest Rhodes, which preserves an old-fashioned habit of a fully coated handle (cf. Coldstream 1968, pl. 18e) but continues to make this type well into a Subgeometric stage in the early seventh century. For Rhodes cf. Coldstream 1968, pl. 62e, and also Gjerstad 1977, pl. VIII 5–6. The apparently empty handle zone may have contained a floating motif, e.g. a row of vertical chevrons — a common Subgeometric type.'

941 3465
Level 2k
Body sherd with handle attachment. Orangey grit-tempered. Ext. burnished and painted in red. Cross-hatched band.
Fig. 255 top right
This seems to be a closed shape and more thick walled. Perhaps a coarse imitation of *oinochoai* with a band of cross-hatched triangles at the level of their handle (e.g. Coldstream, 1968, pl. 18).

942 3465
Level 2k
Skyphos(?) with out-turned rim, no sign of handle on surviving sherd. Grey, grit-tempered. Smoothed and painted in dark brown ext. and int. Ext. band, vertical lines and dot design.
Di. 16
Fig. 255 bottom centre
Coldstream: 'If a *skyphos*, the dotted motif should be a filling ornament near the handle — but the size looks improbably small.'

943 3465
Level 2k
Skyphos(?) body sherd. Cream with very little temper. Smoothed. Painted red-brown int. and ext. Ext. linear design. The thin wall and monochrome painted interior tend to confirm the Greek look of the fragmentary design on this sherd and **944**.
Fig. 255 bottom right
Perhaps a badly executed (or drawn) band of vertical chevrons for which cf. Coldstream 1968, 95f. and pl. 17h, etc.

Figure 255. *'Geometric' sherds from the ditch in I14:* **940–44**.

944   3465
Level 2k
Body sherd. Cream with very little temper. Smoothed. painted red brown int. and ext. It is not clear if the central part of the design at the upper break is a row of dots or the bottom of more vertical lines.
Fig. 255 bottom left.
Coldstream: 'another Subgeometric drinking vessel (*skyphos* or *kotyle*) with a floating motif'.

945   237
O9 surface find
Brown, gritty. Lighter brown slip overall. Brown paint on rim int. and ext. and in brown stripes on top of rim.
Rim di. 12
Coldstream: 'Rim of jug or *hydria*(?). The profile looks Archaic.'
Collon 1995, fig. 9:2. Parallels: Tarsus (Hanfmann 1963, fig. 148 nos. 1570, 1576).

946   1704
Level IIe/f?, Rm e4 packing
Rim. Light greyish-brown grit-tempered. Decoration on top of rim and ext. in dark brown paint with one band in lighter brown (indicated by stippling on the drawing).
Coldstream: 'Not a shape that I know. Perhaps a *pyxis*, or an *amphoriskos*'.

Chapter 28

The Mycenaean Pottery

E.B. French

The sum total of Mycenaean-type pots identified from Kilise Tepe now stands at nineteen. They vary in size from small sherds to an almost complete pot and from good-quality imported sherds to wares clearly manufactured outside the mainstream of production. In fact the most interesting feature of the material as a whole lies in this last group as they are of a ware which is to date totally unparalleled in the eastern Mediterranean. The first group consists of small closed vases for the transport of liquids: five stirrup jars and three other small closed shapes. These typically come from secondary contexts such as pits or packing (**947–9**, **951–3**), in two cases away from the NW corner (**952** in R18 and **953** in K14). All but one of the stirrup jars are of fabrics which can be considered 'mainstream', i.e. of fabrics comparable with those of the mainland though not necessarily produced there. All have the typical lustrous surface. Distinctive are **947** of Petrographic Group G with a true fine buff core (decorated in bright red) and the pale yellow-green fabric of **949** (decorated in black/brown crackling paint).

The small stirrup jar is one of the most popular and profuse export shapes (Leonard 1994). It has generally been assumed that the contents consisted of perfumed oil not least because the manufacture of this is attested in the Linear B texts from Pylos (Shelmerdine 1985). Recent contents analysis of a small stirrup jar from Mycenae (Tzedakis & Martlew 1999, 196 no. 180) has, however, given the unexpected result of wine sealed with olive oil. The profile of **947** can be restored from the fragments as a squat example (FS 178–80). This type is found frequently in the eastern Mediterranean. On the mainland, it is reasonably common in LH IIIA2 (second half of the fourteenth century) but gives way to the globular (FS 171–3) and piriform (FS 166–7), often used in pairs, in LH IIIB1 (first half of the thirteenth century). The red tone of **947–8** probably indicates a late fourteenth-century date, the others are likely to be somewhat later.

Slightly surprising is the presence here of the three sherds of other small closed shapes. Small closed hand-made shapes (FS 126) have only dubiously been identified in the eastern Mediterranean though small wheel-made jugs (FS 114) are known (Leonard 1994). The former are now much better understood on the mainland where they are common in specialist settlement contexts. Mountjoy (1986, 101) is mistaken when she says that they do not occur in LH IIIA2 (E. French 1965, 175, 186). There seems no reason why they should not have formed part of the export repertoire though other closed shapes seem to have been more popular. The chronological range is probably similar to that of the stirrup jars.

The other vessels are a complete contrast. All are of the type that from its dull matt fabric and simple decoration is usually roughly assigned to 'local ware'. Moreover the shape range is quite distinct and, with the preponderance of the deep bowl including an unusual tall thin variant, is clearly later in date. Five of the sherds have been examined petrographically; two belong to Group E and, though not identical one to another, could be of 'local' manufacture; three are assigned to Group F. Under normal examination of the surface and core by a ×30 lens this part of the material can be assigned to three groups:

Ware 1: a buff sandy fabric distinctly softer than wares 2 & 3. This compares well with my own description of the Tarsus material (which I handled in 1973). Petrographic Fabric E 1 (**957**) belongs in this group.

Ware 2: a very fine and very hard, dark buff ware with no sign of a 'gold mica effect'. **958** is the sole example of this ware, and was not examined petrographically.

Ware 3: a very fine and very hard, dark buff ware with a distinct 'gold mica effect', particularly on the surface. Petrographic Fabrics E 2, and F are of this type.

All sherds of wares 2 and 3 came from a burnt context and some have clearly suffered burning so the dark colour *may* result only from this but the fineness and hardness are completely unique.

Mountjoy (1997) has described and illustrated carefully the range of fabrics from Troy and has since compared them with those of other sites from the west coast of Anatolia (pers. comm.). All of these are soft and have actual gold mica. It should be remembered that this effect was also popular as a gold wash to the contemporary plain LBA wares on the west coast (D. French 1969, 72). It is a possibility that fabrics elsewhere, like those from Kilise Tepe, aimed at this effect.

With the exception of **956**, all the pieces from **955–65** effectively come from just two contexts in the Stele Building. Some were *in situ* among the burnt destruction debris on the floor of Rm d10 in Level IId, and sherds from **957–8** and **960** (along with **950** and **954**) came from the removal of the foundations of W764, which, given its position, must originally have been part of the same deposit. That joining pieces came from separate rooms (**962**) may indicate that they had fallen from an upper storey. The remainder came from a pit dug into the destruction debris of the Level IIc Stele Building and filled with black ashy destruction material (P96/102), but these pieces too could well have the same origin, not least because of the joining sherds of **959**.

The combination of a pouring vessel, a large deep bowl or krater and a number of possible drinking vessels in a single context which lacks any other functional identity cannot but suggest that we are dealing with a 'drinking set' (Steel 1997–98).

The most obvious parallels for these pots come from the re-study of the material from neighbouring Tarsus (E. French 1975). Leonard (1994, 119), who calls the type a version of FS 284, lists only four examples from the Levant. Of these the two sherds from the Tell Abu Hawam cannot be definitely assigned to the shape on the drawings available while the restored pots from Sarepta and Byblos are from mixed contexts. In Cyprus the type is well known from Palaeopaphos/Kouklia,[1] and forms half the repertoire at the sites of Tel Miqne-Ekron and Ashdod in Philistia (Dothan & Zuckerman 2004). The identification of an unillustrated example among the deep bowls from the Granary at Mycenae (during re-study in April 2004) leads to the suspicion that others exist among unpublished or unillustrated material both on the mainland and in the Levant.

Dating this group is particularly difficult as none of the parallels have firm contexts but are generally dated in relation to the mainland, which is itself dated by Near Eastern events, a truly circular argument. We now know considerably more about the development of pottery styles on the mainland after destructions around 1200 BC (E. French 1999; forthcoming a,e) and it is clear that there is a long slow build up of the new types which are introduced. It is unlikely that the prototypes which seem to have generated the style found in the East could have been made before 1180 BC (E. French forthcoming d,e).

The presence of stirrup jars dating between 1325 and 1250 BC at Kilise Tepe is not surprising, even in a later context. The shape during this period is found at several quite distant sites, notably Tille Höyük on the Euphrates (Summers 1993, 14; 45 fig. 35.1, pl. 21a) and Tell Brak in North Syria (Oates *et al.* 1997, 79), and of later date Fraktin in the Taurus (T. Özgüç 1948, 267). The pots from Maşat Höyük are of similar date and purpose (T. Özgüç 1978, 66). All indicate the routes by which 'down the line' trading of such low value exotica took place. It may be noted that the river valleys of the West Coast of Anatolia, notably the Gediz and the Küçük Menderes, also formed the routes of penetration to the interior (E. French 1993; forthcoming b).

The recent publication (Yon *et al.* 2000) of a further 500 or so Mycenaean sherds from Ugarit allows an interesting comparison between a major trading station with its sea port where imported items were much used and a small depot further inland on a well known route. At Ugarit the pottery can be divided into:
a) transport and storage vessels which include both large and small examples which are present partly or wholly because of their contents;
b) vessels for everyday or special usage which could not have been used as transport containers, mainly open vessels;
c) cult furnishings. There is an enormous preponderance of peak period Mycenaean wares from the mainland but recently a few pieces of Transitional LH IIIB/C from the very latest levels on the site have been identified.

Until the excavations at Kilise Tepe, there was no new evidence from the Çukurova (Cilicia) either to confirm or amend the assessment by Mee (1978, 150). The Mycenaean- and Aegean-type pottery from Kilise Tepe fits perfectly into the picture already defined (E. French forthcoming c). It is, however, particularly unfortunate that the survey material from this region, both that of Gjerstad (1934)[2] and that of Seton Williams (1954), has not been available for re-study. We need to identify the manufacture sites of the wares which have been assigned to LH IIIC both at Tarsus[3] and at Kilise Tepe. The sherds identified by Seton Williams (presumably, in the early 1950s, on the basis of material such as that from Sinda and Enkomi which she had seen in Cyprus) may have belonged to one of these groups or to yet another. The petrological examination of the Kilise Tepe material does not help as it deals only with the clay base and does not address the methods and standards of manufacture. Wares 2 and 3 from Kilise Tepe are unique for the thin hard wall which has been created. This implies very considerable skill in pottery manufacture unless it is the result of some as yet unidentified component in the clay mix.

In summary, the Kilise Tepe Mycenaean-type material confirms the previously suggested scenario without illuminating, to the benefit of studies on either side of the Aegean, any problems of either manufacture or chronology.

947   K20/34   1124
Level I/II — P94/23+J19 surface find
Stirrup jar. Restored from fragments; top missing though traces of handle and start of neck exist. Wheel-made. Fine orange/pink core with no visible temper; buff slip. Shaded lustrous red-brown paint. Petrological Group G, mainstream fabric. FS 180 squat stirrup jar. Elaborate line groups above and below greatest diameter; band at base.
Body di. 16, Base di. 6; H. (ext.) 8
Petrographic sample S142.
An. St. 1995, fig. 15: 6
Fig. 541

948   4201
Level IIb — H19b packing
Stirrup jar. Body sherd from shoulder with start of neck. Wheel-made. Fine orange core; buff slip. Lustrous red orange paint. Mainstream fabric. FS uncertain. Line group of three thin bands between two broader bands.
2.5 × 1.7; Th. 0.35

949   1405
Level I/II — I20b packing
Stirrup jar. Sherd from shoulder with start of handle. Wheel-made. Fine white to greenish buff core without slip. Black/brown lustrous paint, crackling where thick. Mainstream fabric. Probably FS 180. Line group above greatest diameter.
Di. (at shoulder not max.) 13; 4.5 × 2.8; Th. 0.4

950   3918
Level IIf — J19c W764 removal
Stirrup Jar. Sherd from shoulder with stump of handle; very worn. Wheel-made. Fine pink to dark buff core; buff slip. Black/brown paint probably once lustrous. Mainstream fabric. Probably FS 180. Traces of paint at base of handle on outer side only.
4 × 4; Th. 0.4/0.3

951   1325
Level IIc — Rm 1 floor
Stirrup jar? Sherd with start of handle, very worn and damaged. Abraded to a smooth flat surface at both top and bottom of sherd presumably from secondary usage as a burnisher. Wheel-made. Fine buff core with no slip. Matt brown paint. Not mainstream production (on the basis of matt paint and unusual design). Probably FS 180. Broad band just above greatest diameter; net or net patches in shoulder zone.
Body di. 12; 6.5 × 3.3; Th. 0.5

952   2462
Level E5c — R18c fill
Small closed vessel. Sherd from upper body. Wheel-made. No detailed information on ware though listed as mainstream fabric. FS uncertain. Two thin shaded bands on shoulder.
Th. 0.4/0.6; 2 × 2

953   3090
Level 2 lower — K14 ashy layer
Small closed vessel. Two joining body sherds. Hand-made. Buff core with no slip. Mainstream fabric. Lustrous red stripy paint. FS 126. Irregular band at greatest diameter with thinner band above.
Body di. 9; 3.8 × 3.8; Th. 0.4

954   3918
Level IIf — J19c W764 removal
Small closed vessel. Two joining sherds, very worn, one end heavily burnt. Wheel-made but poorly worked clay. Dark buff core fired pinkish, buff slip. Lustrous red paint. Mainstream fabric. FS uncertain. Two curving vertical bands (from a spiral?) in open field.
Body di. 9; 3.5 × 6; Th. 0.4

955   1690
Level IId — J19b/d P96/102
Amphora/Jug/Hydria. c. 1/3 of pot from base to base of handle. Burnt. Wheel-made. Very thin hard slightly gritty fabric fired to mud colour all through; very very slight traces of surface 'gold mica effect'; no slip. Matt brown paint. Petrological Fabric E2; ware 3. Closed shape with at least one handle. Three broad bands just above greatest diameter; swirl around base of handle.
Body Di. 21, Base di. 7; H. (ext.) 17; Th. 3.5
Petrographic sample S138.
KST 1998, fig. 8
Fig. 540

956   4334+4338
Level IId?, IIe — K18a W421 removal, Rm e6 surface
Krater/Large deep bowl. Two large sherds including handle (combined on paper). Wheel-made. Fine hard gritty buff fabric; no slip. Matt brown paint. Ware 1? Probably large version of FS 285 rather than a krater (because of the angle of the upper body). Int. band at or below rim; ext: band below handle; handle painted on upper surface with tails extending over band; small section of rectilinear design.
Body di. 23?; H. (ext.) 11

957   J19/324   KLT 85   3921
Level IId — Rm d10 occ. deposit
Deep bowl, restored from fragments. Wheel-made. Buff sandy fabric with no slip. Matt black/brown paint. Petrological Fabric E1; ware 1. FS 285. Int. band below rim band, band on lower body; ext: 'Medium' band at rim; thin band below handles.
Di. 14; H. 11
Petrographic sample S137.
KST 1999, Fig. 5
Fig. 256

958   3918+4382+5864
Level IIf, unstratified, IId — J19c W764 removal, K18a, Rm d10 floor
Deep bowl; sherds forming section from base to near rim with one matching sherd. Base cracked probably from burning but no other obvious marks of burning. Wheel-made, pitted with strong wheel marks making grooves on surface. Hard gritty clay, salmon fired ginger with no slip; no 'gold mica effect' apparent on surface. Matt rich brown to red brown paint. Ware 2. FS 285, tall and thin. Int. band on lower body, spiral at centre; ext: two bands on lower body.
Estimated Di. 17, Base di. 4.7; H. (ext.) 10
Petrographic sample S141.
Fig. 541

Figure 256. *Mycenaean deep bowl 957.*

959 1690+5802
Level IId — J19b/d P96/102, Rm d10 destr.
Deep bowl. Two sections of rim and body, burnt? Wheel-made. Fine hard gritty fabric with 'gold mica effect' on surface; fired or burnt to mud colour all through. Matt brown paint. Petrological Fabric F, ware 3. FS 285, tall and thin. Int. band just below rim but no band on lower body; ext: band below rim, two bands on lower body.
Di. 12?; H. (ext.) 10.4; Th. 0.3
Petrographic sample S140.
Fig. 541

960 3918+3921
Level IId, IIf — J19c Rm d10 destr., W764 removal
Deep bowl. Matching sherds of rim (only this section illustrated); body and handles; burnt. Wheel-made. Very hard thin salmon fabric fired mud-coloured; a slight fine 'gold mica effect' on surface. Matt brown paint. Petrological Fabric F; ware 3. FS 285. Int. band on lower body; ext: rim band extends over rim to form narrow line inside, band on lower body.
Estimated Body Di. 17; H. (ext. of rim section) 4.2
Petrographic sample S139.
Fig. 541

961 1690
Level IId — J19b/d P96/102
Deep bowl. Rim sections and several joining body sherds; not apparently burnt. Wheel-made. Gritty buff fabric all through, a little fine 'gold mica effect' apparent on surface. Matt brown shaded paint. Ware 3. FS 285, sinuous. Int. band extending over lip, trace of line (top of band?) on lower body; ext: band below rim; single thin band just below maximum diameter.
Di. 16; H. (ext.) 9.3

962 5802+5864
Level IId — Rm d10 destr. and surface
Deep bowl. Rim and joining body sherds plus two matching sherds (one with start of handle); burnt. Wheel-made. Hard salmon-coloured fabric fired to mud colour with 'gold mica effect' on surface. Matt brown paint. Petrological Fabric F; ware 3. FS 285. Int. bands at and below rim and on lower body; ext: 'Medium' band at rim, two bands on lower body; swirl around base of handle.
Di. 15; H. (ext.) 10
Fig. 541

963 1690
Level IId — J19b/d P96/102
Deep bowl. Single sherd. Wheel-made. Thick sandy pale buff fabric with no slip. Matt brown paint. Ware 1? FS 285. Two thin horizontal lines int. and ext. just below greatest diameter.
4 × 3; Body di. 17; Th. 0.65

964 1690
Level IId — J19b/d P96/102
Deep bowl. Single sherd with trace of handle; very worn inside. Wheel-made. Thick sandy pale buff fabric with no slip. Matt brown paint. Ware 1? FS 285. Two thin bands below handle tail; traces of internal bands, very worn.
4.4 × 3; Th. 0.6

965 1690
Level IId — J19b/d P96/102
Deep bowl. Two sherds which do not appear to join or match any other pot; no profile possible; very worn. Wheel-made. Fine hard fired fabric of mud colour all through, 'gold mica effect' on surface. Matt brown paint. Ware 3. FS 285. Int. thin band; ext: thicker band on either side of greatest diameter.
6 × 3.2

Notes

1. My thanks to Dr Franz Maier who sent me drawings of this material many years ago and who has kindly allowed me to make use of them in comparison with the Kilise Tepe material.

2. This material came to light in the storerooms of the Medelhavsmuseet in Stockholm during the winter of 2001. I thank the authorities and particularly Dr Marie-Louise Winbladh for sending me a set of slides of the Mycenaean wares. More recently the Italian Cilicia Survey (Salmeri & D'Agata 2002) has undertaken the re-study of the Aegean and EIA material in this collection. Unfortunately their preliminary conclusions do not agree with my own assessment of the material nor with the latest work by Dr Mountjoy on the finds from Tarsus, Cyprus and Israel. Full publication and the NAA test results are thus to be awaited with interest.

3. I thank the authorities at Bryn Mawr College and at the Peabody Museum, Harvard, for arranging for me to have photographs illustrating the fabric of the sherds from the Tarsus excavations in their collections for comparative purposes. None of these sherds has been examined petrographically or tested chemically. New work is currently under way at Tarsus and Dr Penelope Mountjoy has restudied the Mycenaean-type material for Dr A. Özyar (Mountjoy 2005).

Chapter 29

Comparison of the NAA Data for Six Mycenaean-style Samples from Kilise Tepe with Chemical Reference Groups from Mainland Greece, Crete, Cyprus and the Levant

Jonathan E. Tomlinson

Introduction

This report presents the results of a comparison of the neutron activation data for six Mycenaean-style samples from Kilise Tepe (S137, S138, S139, S140, S141, S142) (see Knappett, pp. 258–9) against the chemical profiles of a number of reference groups from mainland Greece, Crete, Cyprus and the Levant.

These chemical reference data result from two distinct analysis programmes: 881 sherds analysed at the Lawrence Berkeley Laboratory, University of California in the early 1970s are complemented by a further 1174 sherds analysed at the University of Manchester in the late 1980s and early 1990s. The vast majority of this material is dated to the Late Bronze Age.

The neutron activation analysis procedures used at Berkeley have been well documented (Perlman & Asaro 1969). The procedures used at Manchester are detailed by Taylor and Robinson who also discuss the statistical treatment of the data (Taylor & Robinson 1996).

The data for each of the six samples were tested against the chemical profiles of 113 reference groups (see Table 12) using the Mahalanobis procedures in the MANHATTAN (MAHALA) program, developed at Manchester. Data for all available elements were used in the statistical evaluation.

Results

For the MANHATTAN program, the groups are pre-defined (by cluster analysis in this case) in terms of the mean and standard deviation of each element. For each sample compared against a particular reference group, the Manhattan distance to the centre of that group is defined in units of standard deviation, σ, of each of the elements concerned.

A sample is deemed to 'fit' with a group if its total distance to the group centre is less than the number of elements used in the comparison (i.e. an average of up to 1σ per element). A sample was deemed to have 'possible association' with a group it its average distance from the group centre in question is greater than 1σ, but less than 1.5σ.

Discussion

On the basis of their chemistry, Knappett and Kilikoglou suggest that S137, S138 and S142 are probably local, while S139, S140 and S141 are non-local. However, none of Knappett's non-local samples show a match with any of the 113 chemical reference groups. Indeed, only one sample, S142, shows any 'fits', and these with two groups that are rather

Table 12. *Comparative data.*[1]

Region	Sites/Areas represented	Groups
Attica	Perati	1
Boeotia	Thebes, Gla, Eutresis, Kallithea, Tanagra	3
Argolid-Corinthia	Asine, Berbati, Korakou, Mycenae, Tiryns, Zygouries	33
Peloponnese (other)	Achaea, Ayios Stephanos, Chora Ano Englianos, Menelaion, Nichoria, Olympia-Kolosakos, Palaiokastro, Peristeria, Platanos-Renia	19
Crete	Chania, Kommos, Knossos, Palaikastro, Phaistos	26
Cyprus	Akhera, Arpera, Enkomi, Episkopi Phaneromeni, Hala Sultan Tekke, Kalavassos Ayios Dhimitrios, Kition, Maa, Maroni Zarukas, Pyla Verghi	20
Levant	Lachish, Tell Abu Hawam	11

Table 13. *Similarities found.*

Sample	'Fits' with group (Average d <1.0)	'Possible association' with Group (1.0 < average d <1.5)
S137 – Group E1	-	Cyprus 18 (Mycenaean imports) Chania 2 (west Crete) Mycenaean stirrup jars J B (central Crete)
S138 – Group E2	-	Cyprus 18 (Mycenaean imports) Kommos 4 (central Crete) Mycenaean stirrup jars B (central Crete)
S139 – Group F	-	Mycenaean stirrup jars A2 (west Crete)
S140 – Group F	-	Cyprus 15 (Enkomi) Chania 4 (central Crete) Mycenaean stirrup jars B (central Crete)
S141 – Group F	-	Mycenaean stirrup jars A2 (west Crete)
S142 – Group G	Cyprus 18 (Mycenaean imports) Mycenaean stirrup jars B (central Crete)	Lachish (Argolid) Chania 4 (central Crete)

diffusely defined.[2] These associations, therefore, are unlikely to be meaningful.[3] The same is also true of the 'possible associations' noted.[4]

Notes

1. Attica: Tomlinson 1998; Boeotia: Tomlinson 2000; Argolid-Corinthia: Tomlinson 1995; 1999; forthcoming b; Hoffmann *et al.* forthcoming; Peloponnese (other): Hoffmann *et al.* 1992; Tomlinson 1997; forthcoming a; Crete: Tomlinson 1991; Tomlinson & Robinson in prep.; Cyprus: Bryan *et al.* 1997; Levant: Hoffmann & Robinson 1993; Tomlinson 2004.
2. Cyprus Group 18 (d = 0.84) is a group dominated by Mycenaean imports (Bryan *et al.* 1997), but Hoffmann (pers. comm.) comments 'may not be foreign — one sherd is from Kommos — it is a broad group most probably made up of sherds from different sites and possibly from Palaepaphos...'; Mycenaean stirrup jars Group B (d = 0.90) is of Central Cretan provenance (Tomlinson 1995).
3. Diffuse groups are broadly defined (i.e. with large % standard deviations), thus any sample will have a much greater probability of 'associating' with the group than if the group were more tightly defined.
4. Chania Group 2 is dominated by heavy and coarse wares and is a local west Cretan group (Tomlinson & Robinson in prep.); Kommos Group 4 is a local fineware group. (Tomlinson & Robinson in prep.); Mycenaean Stirrup Jars Group A2 is of west Cretan provenance. (Tomlinson 1995); Cyprus Group 15 is from the Enkomi area (Bryan *et al.* 1997); Chania Group 4 is a group of central Cretan imports, dominated by heavy wares. (Tomlinson & Robinson in prep.); the Lachish Group is of Argolid provenance (Tomlinson 2004).

Chapter 30

Hellenistic Ceramics and Lamps

Lisa Nevett & M.P.C. Jackson

A Hellenistic occupation of the site is attested by the ceramics found both on the surface and within all the main excavation areas. We present first an initial study by Lisa Nevett of the decorated, and probably all imported, material which was recognizably of this date from its similarity to wares well known from contemporary sites (see Figs. 257–8 for a sample of this material). This includes lamps (one of which, **996**, is later). There follows some plain pottery which was excavated in Level I and appears to pre-date the Byzantine wares at the site, selected and described by Mark Jackson.

Summary

The material is domestic in character and is broadly similar to the Hellenistic assemblage published from Tarsus (Goldman 1950), although in contrast with Tarsus there are only a very few pre- and post-Hellenistic pieces. Many of the shapes recovered at Kilise Tepe have close parallels at Tarsus, and the range of fabrics described as local there is also common to this site (see below). Nevertheless, there are also some differences between the assemblages from the two sites. At Kilise Tepe there is a narrower range of 'skyphos' shapes and handle forms, only a very limited amount of stamped pottery and no evidence for Hellenistic mould-made relief bowls ('Megarian bowls'). The assemblage from Kilise Tepe is relatively small compared with that from Tarsus, many pieces coming from a single pit deposit (P94/41 on the East slope; 2106–7) and this small sample size is likely to be part of the reason why a narrower range of forms is represented. In terms of date, the majority of the dish and cup forms which make up the bulk of the assemblage are relatively long-lived, covering the third and much of the second century BC. The presence of a few earlier pieces, the absence of relief bowls and the fact that, for some of the forms, the latest types are not represented, are all indications that material from the earlier end of this period may predominate.

Fabrics

The most common fabrics fall into four main groups, which encompass a similar range to that identified as local at Tarsus (Jones 1950, 153):

Fabric 1
A fine, hard-fired, dark grey-brown-purple fabric with virtually no inclusions.

Fabric 2
A somewhat softer fabric than 1, pink in colour, with a fine texture and few or no inclusions.

Fabric 3
A softer fabric than both 1 and 2, with numerous white grits and other inclusions. A pinkish colour similar to 2.

Fabric 4
A soft pale pinkish, yellowish or whitish chalky fabric with a tendency to de-laminate. Variable numbers of inclusions, which are sometimes large.

Forms

1. Echinus (**966–7**)
This is the shape occurring most frequently at Kilise Tepe and is also noted as forming the bulk of the assemblage at Tarsus (Jones 1950, 156–7, where it is referred to as the 'bowl with incurved rim'). The vessel is paralleled amongst the Hellenistic material from a number of other sites including Tel Anafa (Berlin 1997), Pergamon (Schäfer 1968), and the Athenian Agora (Rotroff 1997). The Kilise Tepe material includes several complete profiles and many base and rim fragments. These are all from the deep form of the vessel, although there is a range of shapes from a rounded profile (**966**) to a relatively straight-walled version, curving in at the top (**967**). The rims vary in the degree to which they are in-turned, and bases vary in size and height.

Fabric: the assemblage includes examples of this shape in all of the fabric groups identified above.
Surface treatment: in most cases there is evidence of a brown, red or black matt wash covering the interior of the vessel and the rim and trickled down the exterior walls of the vessel. In one example there is no trace of any surface coating.

Date: At Tarsus this form occurred in the pre-, early-, middle- and late Hellenistic levels. If Jones is correct in suggesting that the more in-turned rims and smaller, higher bases are later in date (Jones 1950, 157), then the Kilise Tepe material, which provides a similar range of shapes to those found at Tarsus, is likely to include a comparable range of dates, although there is a predominance of more incurving shapes, which in the context of Tarsus are identified as later (Jones 1950, 157 with fig. 180). (Examples from other sites also cover a range of dates: the form occurs in Greece as early as the fifth to fourth centuries, being frequent, for example, at Olynthos, which was destroyed in 348 BC — Robinson 1933, 232, Inv. 879–80. Similarly, at Tel Anafa the vessel is already present by 300 BC and continues through into the Roman period — Berlin 1997, 74).

966   2107
Level E2a
Deep *echinus*. Complete profile. Fabric 1. Grey-brown slip. About 25% of incurved rim preserved, ring base. Faint groove on ext.
Rim di. 12, Base di. 5; H. 4.8; Th. 0.4–0.5
Baker *et al.* 1995, fig. 7:2

967   K14/28   KLT 65   3008
Level 1
Deep *echinus*. Complete bowl apart from chips on rim. Fabric 4. Brown paint int. and partly ext., matt. Rim incurved, ring base.
Rim di. 14, Body Di. 17.2, Base di. 5; H. 6.7; Th. 0.9
Baker *et al.* 1995, fig. 7:1

*2. Large, heavy plate/dish with thick rim (**968–9**)*
A thick-walled, shallow vessel with a thick, grooved rim. The assemblage includes around half a dozen rim fragments but no bases or complete profiles. The published material from Tarsus is also lacking in complete profiles, although Jones suggests that a group of rims comparable to those from Kilise Tepe can be reconstructed as belonging to a form with a simple ring base (Jones 1950, 162). Vessels of this type have been found elsewhere, for example at Ephesos (Moutsopoulos-Leon 1991, 51 Inv. B98 and B99) and in the Athenian Agora (Rotroff 1997, 326, no. 829).

Fabric: this form occurs in Fabrics 1 and 2.
Surface treatment: a dull black or red glaze covers the interior and rim, and either coats the exterior completely or is trickled over the upper part of the vessel wall. In a few instances West Slope decoration runs around the interior of the rim.
Date: the Tarsus rims with this form occurred in Middle and Late Hellenistic units, while a new, drooping form appeared in the top level of the Middle Hellenistic unit. The Kilise Tepe assemblage includes only upward curving rims and lacks the more drooping variety, suggesting that it may cover only the earlier period. This is later than the date of the Athenian vessel, which Rotroff puts at the first quarter of the third century (Rotroff 1997, 326). Nevertheless, it is compatible with the date given to similar vessels at Ephesos, whose context suggests that they belong to the late third or first half of the second century BC (Moutsopoulos-Leon 1991, 51).

968   1517
Level I
Plate. Rim to lower body. Light brown with no visible temper. Black coat int. White paint, matt. Laurel leaf garland running left. Rim rounded and thickened with int. grooves.
Rim di. 23; Th. 0.6

969   194
Surface
Heavy plate or bowl. Rim to lower body. Fabric 1. Grey slip. Rim thickened with deep groove int.
Rim di. *c.* 30; Th. 0.9
Baker *et al.* 1995, fig. 8: 11

*3. Shallow, flat-base saucer (**970–71**)*
A shallow, thin-walled dish with a grooved rim. The assemblage includes a number of rim fragments and one rim and body sherd (**971**). No complete profile is preserved, but a flat base can be reconstructed based on parallels from Tarsus (Jones 1950, 161–2). Similar vessels also occur elsewhere, for example at Paphos (Hayes 1991, 139, Inv. 96).

Fabric: 1 and 2.
Surface treatment: dark grey or black paint or slip on interior, rim and upper part of the exterior. The Tarsus examples are decorated in West Slope style, with a white painted laurel leaf garland running around the interior wall. This is paralleled in one of the Kilise Tepe vessels.
Date: at Tarsus these vessels occur in Middle and Late Hellenistic units (Jones 1950, 162), and the shape may also continue later, since the Paphos example comes from 'a uniform deposit of the late second century BC (*c.* 110–100 BC)' (Hayes 1991, 131).

970   3401
Level 1
Shallow saucer. Rim to lower body. Fabric 2. Black slip int. and part of ext. White paint ext., matt. Laurel leaf garland running right. Rim grooved int.
Rim di. 16–20; Th. 0.4

971   2107
Level E2a
Shallow saucer. Almost complete profile. Fabric 2. Black slip on int. and upper part of ext. Rim grooved int.
Rim di. 20, Base di. 6; Th. 0.4–0.7

*4. Rolled rim dish/saucer (**972–3**)*
No complete profile is preserved, but the vessel is probably to be identified with Jones's 'shallow bowl or saucer with thickened interior rim and low base ring' (Jones 1950, 155–6). There is some variation in the thickness of the rim, which in one case is bevelled. In another example a double groove runs around the interior some 15 mm below the rim. In contrast with Tarsus, where this is the second most common form, at Kilise Tepe the assemblage includes only a handful of rim sherds.

Fabric: 1, also 2 (yellowish-brown with some inclusions).
Surface treatment: the interior and rim are coated in a matt black glaze. In some cases the exterior walls are also covered, while in others, the glaze is trickled down the exterior, in a manner similar to that adopted with the *echinus*. One example has black glaze merging into dark red.
Date: the examples from Kilise Tepe all have the convex wall and incurving rim of the vessels found in the Early Hellenistic unit at Tarsus, while the drooping rim-type which predominates in the middle level of the Middle Hellenistic unit (Jones 1950, 156) is absent here.

972 2106
Level E2a
Rim to lower body. Fabric 1. Black slip on int., rim and upper ext. and paler drips and stripes on lower ext. Rim rolled.
Rim di. 17; Th. 0.5

973 3604
Level 1
Rim to lower body. Grey, very fine. Black slip int. and partly ext., very uneven with reserved band. Rim rolled.
Rim di. 17; Th. 0.5

5. Other plate/dish shapes (974–8)
i) Shallow, flat-base dish with straight sides
A shallow, straight-walled dish with a flat base which is separated from the wall of the vessel by a shallow groove marking the change of angle. The assemblage includes a handful of body sherds, one with a fragment of the base attached (**974**). This form is not noted at Tarsus, nor amongst the Hellenistic assemblages from a variety of other sites, including Pergamon, Samothrace, Corinth or the Athenian Agora.

Fabric: 1.
Surface treatment: a dull black glaze covers the interior and rim and is trickled down exterior. The interior walls feature West Slope decoration.
Date: In the context of Athens, Rotroff dates the myrtle garland West Slope motif to a long period which lasts from the Classical era through to *c.* 275 BC with a few later examples (Rotroff 1997, 48).

ii) Bowl with angular profile and stamped interior
A semi-glazed dish with a ring base, carinated body, thickened rim and stamped interior decoration. The assemblage includes one complete example (**975**) and several base fragments (**976**). The general shape is paralleled at numerous other sites, where it is generally more plentiful (Rotroff 1997, 156). Vessels with a similar profile are also included amongst the material from Tarsus (Jones 1950, 156), although the shape of the rim and the fabric are somewhat different. A closer parallel for the form is a 'bowl with out-curved lip' from Samaria (Kenyon 1957, 221, Inv. Q4898).

Fabric: Group 4 plus one example in a fabric not listed above (**975**).
Surface treatment: the vessel is glazed or semi-glazed with a black or brown slip which varies in density and shine.
Date: at Tarsus this general shape occurs in the Middle Hellenistic and Hellenistic–Roman units and in the Hellenistic levels of the house in Section A (Jones 1950, 213–14; the latter are contemporary with the Late Hellenistic and early part of the Hellenistic–Roman unit: Goldman 1950, 25), and this range of dates corresponds with Kenyon's findings in Samaria (Kenyon 1957, 223). In the context of

Figure 257. *Hellenistic sherds from pit P94/41 in Q19, including **980–81** and **989**.*

Athens Rotroff dates the widely spaced rouletting found on one fragment to the period after 275 BC (Rotroff 1997, 38).

iii) Shallow dish or saucer with horizontal rim
Shallow dish with ring base and horizontal rim. The Kilise Tepe assemblage includes one complete profile (**978**) and a rim fragment. There are no exact parallels for this shallow curving body and broad, flat rim amongst the published material from Tarsus, although a small number of similar vessels have also been found at other sites, for example Samaria (Kenyon 1957, 221, Inv. Q4857) and also (with a somewhat wider base-ring) in the Agora at Athens (Rotroff 1997, 318, Inv. 735).

Fabric: 2 and 3.
Surface treatment: a brown-black wash covers the interior, rim and exterior.
Date: In the absence of close parallels from Tarsus the vessel is difficult to date. Rotroff dates the Athenian example to early in the third century, based on its horizontal rim and shallow body (Rotroff 1997, 150).

974 1501
Level 1
Saucer with straight sides. Body sherd from lower body. Fabric 1. Dull black glaze on int., rim and upper part of ext. White and pinkish paint, matt. West slope decoration featuring incised and painted ivy garland running left, there is also a painted star running up the side from the base.
4.2 × 4.9; Th. 0.4–0.6

975 K14/36 KLT 66 3011+3043
Level 1, 2 upper
Open bowl. Complete except for a few sherds. Buff-pink with very fine grains, similar to Fabric 2. Orange-brown wash int., rim and upper part of ext. Stamped rosette and four palmettes at the bottom of int. Rim bevelled, carination at middle of body, ring base.

Figure 258. *Selected Hellenistic sherds from units 2100 and 2107 (photo: M. Densham).*

Similar to **976**.
Rim di. 12.5, Base di. 5.5; H. 4.2; Th. 0.5

976 H18/178 2602
Level I
Open bowl. Base. Grey-greenish with no temper. Black coat int. and splashed on ext. Stamped rosette and four palmettes at the bottom of the int. Rim bevelled, carination at middle of body, ring base.
Base di. 5; Th. 0.4

977 197
Surface
Open bowl. Part of ring base. Fabric 4. Dull black-brown slip on int. Incised rouletted concentric circles.
Base di. 9; Th. 0.6

978 P20/4 210
Surface
Shallow bowl or saucer. Complete. Fugitive brown-black slip, fired red in places. Rim flattened, ring base. Vessel was warped during firing.
Rim di. 15, Base di. 6.5; H. 3; Th. 0.6
Baker *et al.* 1995, fig. 8:14

*6. Deep 'skyphos' with vertical handles (**979–80**)*
This shape is one of the most common forms at Kilise Tepe and occurs in a variety of sizes. No complete profile is preserved and no bases are identifiable, but the collection includes several handles attached to walls, together with a number of wall fragments, showing that the vessel is usually hemispherical, with the exception of one example, which is conical (**979**). The part most commonly preserved is the handle, which is cylindrical in section, with an applied spur at the top. These handles show a variety of degrees of refinement, from delicate modelling to relatively crude shaping, which it is tempting to interpret as indicating a difference between local and imported vessels. This form was also numerous at Tarsus, where complete profiles show that it had a ring base. The Tarsus handles seem to be more standardized than those from Kilise Tepe.

Fabrics: the assemblage includes this form in a range of all four of the fabrics identified above.
Surface treatment: a red or black wash or slip of varying degrees of lustre generally covers the interior, rim and upper exterior, although one example is unglazed.
Date: The catalogued examples from Tarsus were found in the Middle Hellenistic and Hellenistic-Roman units (Jones 1950, 216–17).

979 2104
Level E2a
Almost complete profile, base missing. Pinkish-grey with no visible grits. Black lustrous coat over int. and most of ext. Rim incurved and handle attachment.
Rim di. 15; Th. 0.5

980 2100
Level E2a
Deep *skyphos*. Complete vertical handle. Creamy-white, no visible temper. Lustrous black slip. Applied spur on top takes the form of a comic mask.
Handle th. 0.6
Cf. Jones 1950, 216–17 (Tarsus 107)

*7. 'S'-curve kantharos (**981–3**)*
A small group of thin-walled sherds, including two rim fragments, appear to be from 'S'-curve *kantharoi*. There are no close parallels amongst the published material from Tarsus, but vessels with similar profiles and decoration have been found at Ephesos (Moutsopoulos-Leon 1991, 33, Inv. B25 and B27), and Pergamon (Schäfer 1968, 61–2, Inv. D52, D63, D64).

Fabric: 1.
Surface treatment: Both interior and exterior are coated in a relatively high quality lustrous black slip. In some instances the exterior wall carries a band of West slope decoration.
Date: At Ephesos vessels of this type are already present in the fourth century BC and continue through to the second century BC (Moutsopoulos-Leon 1991, 33–4). At Pergamon the closest parallels are dated to the third and early second century (Schäfer 1968, 55).

981 2100
Level E2a
Rim with upper body. Lustrous black slip. White-grey paint, matt. Incised ext. and lobed ivy wreath running left with a border of horizontal line and dots. Rim slightly everted.
Rim di. 8; Th. 0.4

982   M14/20   3507
Topsoil
Large *kantharos*. Base with lower body. Light brown with no visible temper, hard-fired. Patchy dark brown slip ext. and base. White paint on base, matt. Incised ext. and lobed ivy wreath border of horizontal line and dots. Elaborate ring base. Body mended with several pairs of small holes.
Base di. 8; Th. 0.6–1.0

983   3011
Level 1
Base with lower body. Brown with no visible temper. Lustrous brownish-grey coat on upper part of ext. Elaborate ring base.
Base di. 8.5; Th. 0.5

8. Other cup shapes

A small number of body and base fragments in Fabric 1 have the moulded foot and waisted profile characteristic of other forms of *kantharos*. The surface is generally black slipped on the exterior but sometimes unglazed on the interior. In addition there are a small number of tapering cylindrical handles in Fabric 1 suggesting the presence of other cup shapes. These have a black or red glaze. Unfortunately, sherds of both shapes are too fragmentary to discuss in detail or to illustrate.

9. Jugs and other closed vessels (**984**)

Numerous out-turned rim fragments of different sizes and one flat grooved handle may belong to jugs of this phase. The fragments occur in Fabrics 1, 2 and 3 and also a coarse, hard whitish fabric. The surface is either left plain or covered or banded with brown or black matt slip or wash. One flat rim fragment may belong to an olla (globular jar), while a neck fragment from a jug or amphora carries an early form of decoration (**984**). Unfortunately, with the exception of the early neck fragment, none of the pieces is well enough preserved to enable its original form to be reconstructed or to merit detailed discussion.

984   2106
Level E2a
Closed jar. Shoulder with part of neck. Cream, grit-temper. Fugitive black-brown wash or slip around the neck. From the neck a droplet or petal pattern.
10.3 × 5.7; Th. 0.7
Cf. Mylonas 1933, 33 Inv. P47.

10. Krater (**985–9**)

The assemblage includes a number of rim, body and base fragments from wide-mouth kraters, including one offering a profile which is complete except for the handles and base (**985**). The form is rare in Hellenistic assemblages (Rotroff 1997, 135–6), although it is paralleled amongst the published material from Tarsus (Jones 1950, 162–3) and a few examples have been found at Athens (Rotroff 1997, 135–6), in Samaria (Kenyon 1957, 225–6) and at Pergamon (Schäfer 1968, 48–9).

Fabric: Vessels are from groups 1, 2 and 3 and comprise a range of fabrics from the relatively coarse and roughly made (**985**), to much finer versions (**986**) (the latter are more common). This range parallels that found amongst the Tarsus material (Jones 1950, 162).
Surface treatment: The exterior is covered in a slip of variable quality which also covers the rim, while the interior may either be glazed or semi-glazed. One body sherd (not illustrated) has vertical ribbing. Some neck and body fragments are decorated with West Slope decoration in a variety of designs, including running ivy, stemless laurel and olive.
Date: The illustrated fragments from Tarsus look similar in form to the Kilise Tepe examples, but are decorated rather differently, with stamped and incised patterns (Jones 1950, 221, Inv. 140–41). The examples from Pergamon and Athens appear to have been finer and more elaborate than those from Kilise Tepe, but a fragment from Samaria (Kenyon 1957, 225, Inv. Q4194) which provides a close parallel in shape and decoration for **985**, is dated to the second century based on the style of the decoration (Kenyon 1957, 226).

985   Q20/23   2103
Level E2a
Column krater. Complete except for foot and handle. Fabric 3. Orange-brown wash on ext. and int. neck and rim. Cream paint, matt. Horizontal bands of dots and laurel leaf. Rim everted with ridge, part of strap handle.
Rim di. 30, max. di. 32; Th. 0.6
Baker *et al.* 1995, fig. 7:4

986   108
Surface
Column krater. Rim to middle body. Fabric 1 or 2. Lustrous black slip. White paint, matt. Olive garland running left with a broad line above and below. Rim everted, flattened.
Rim di. 27; Th. 0.6
Baker *et al.* 1995, fig. 8:1

987   3507
Topsoil
Body sherd from middle of the body. Pale brown, no visible temper, hard-fired. Black lustrous coat. White paint, matt. Relief decoration on middle part of body, above and below laurel leaf garland running right.
20 × 24; Th. 0.5 × 0.8

988   4562
Level IIc — fallen into Level IIc destruction debris near P97/77
Body sherd from middle body. Dark brown, no visible temper. Black lustrous coat. White paint, matt. Relief decoration. Similar to **987**.
4.6 × 4.1; Th. 0.8

989   2100
Level E2b
Body sherd from upper part of body. Cream, no visible temper. Brownish-black coat ext. Deep incised vertical lines ext.
5.6 × 2.7; Th. 0.3–0.5

11. Unguentarium (**990**)

The assemblage includes several rim fragments belonging to the bulbous form of *unguentarium*, which is common amongst the Hellenistic finds from a number of sites including the Athenian Agora (Rotroff 1997, 175–6). Although no bases are preserved, the length of the neck and shape of the upper body (preserved in one example, **990**) suggest that the vessel may have had a ring base. A single example of similar shape, although with a more elongated body and shorter neck, is published from Tarsus (Jones 1950, 231, Inv. 248).

Fabric: all sherds fall into type 1.
Surface treatment: the upper part of the exterior and the rim are covered with matt black slip, which is trickled into the interior of the neck.
Date: the nearest parallel for this form at Tarsus (as above) is dated to the fourth century, on the basis of parallels (Jones 1950, 231) while two similar Athenian vessels are dated to the last quarter of the fourth century and to around 300 BC, respectively (Rotroff 1997, 355, Inv. 1167 & 1169).

990 3012
Topsoil
Rim with neck and upper part of body. Light brown with no visible temper. Dark brown paint, matt. Rim bevelled.
Rim di. 2; Th. 0.3

*12. Clay lamps (**991–6**)*
The assemblage includes a number of lamps and lamp fragments. A later example is also included here (**996**). The most complete examples can be grouped as follows:

i) Lamp with grooved filling-hole and single un-pierced lug (**991**)
The vessel has a flat, raised base, squat body with large filling-hole, a broad, pronounced nozzle with large wick hole, and a single un-pierced lug. The shape has some similarities to Tarsus types I–III (Goldman & Jones 1950, 87–8), although it cannot be identified closely with any one group. It also resembles Howland's Type 34A (Howland 1958, 104–6).

Fabric: 2.
Surface treatment: The exterior surface of the body and nozzle are covered with a matt brown wash or glaze which is trickled onto part of the base. The interior is also partly glazed.
Date: Lamps of types I–III occur in all the Hellenistic levels at Tarsus, down to the Hellenistic–Roman unit. At Athens, Howland's type 34A is dated between the last quarter of the third century and the last quarter of the second century (Howland 1958, 104–5). (Rotroff dates the occurrence of this type at Athens more narrowly between 200 and 140 BC: Rotroff 1997, 502.)

991 L14/9 3601
Topsoil
Complete profile with lug, half of body and most of nozzle. Brown wash or slip, matt.
Body H. 3.4; L. 6.8; W. 6.4

ii) Lamp with raised rim to filling-hole and large nozzle (**992–3**)
The vessel has a flat base and rounded body. The filling-hole has a broad, raised rim. The nozzle is broad, with a large wick hole, although the full length of the nozzle is uncertain since neither example is fully preserved. At the back of the vessel is a tall, thin cylindrical knob.

992 L19/14 Etütlük 1998 5911
Topsoil
Complete body preserved with part of nozzle. Buff, grit-tempered. Brown wash. Raised rim to filling-hole and large nozzle.
Body H. 3.9; L. 9.2; W. 6.7

993 M14/18 3507
Topsoil
Complete except for handle. Buff, grit-tempered. The surface is weathered with sparse traces of brown paint. Flat base, raised rounded rim and broken knob handle.
L. (8.6); H. 2.9; W. 7.0

iii) Lamp with ridge on the shoulder and large nozzle (**994–5**)
Another flat-based vessel with a nozzle and knob similar to the previous type. A raised ridge runs around the shoulder, some 8 mm outside the plain, relatively small, fill-hole.

994 K18/213 Etütlük 1998 4393
Level I
Complete body preserved with base of nozzle. Greenish-cream, grit-tempered. Ridge on shoulder and large nozzle.
Body H. 3.6; L. (8.3); W. 6.5

995 K18/67 4314
Level I
Complete profile with nozzle. Greenish-cream, grit-tempered. Raised ridge around the top. Rim and back broken, flat almost disc base.
L. (8.1); H. 3.3

iv) Mould-made lamp (996)
A vessel resembling the 'leaf-shaped' lamp, with an oval shape in which nozzle and body merge together. In general shape this vessel resembles group XIX from Tarsus (as defined by Goldman & Jones 1950, 97), although it is unusual in that there is no framing ridge or groove outlining the central disc.

The Tarsus examples of this form are dated to mid third to late fifth centuries AD on the basis of parallels from Corinth and Antioch (Goldman & Jones 1950, 97). The Kilise Tepe example seems to fit broadly into Broneer's type XXIX, and its elongated shape is likely to be particularly characteristic of Asia Minor (a number of examples were excavated at Ephesos: for example: Bailey 1988, 389 with previous references).

996 J18/120+147 2343
Level I
Two non-joining fragments, one preserving the profile of the body with handle and part of upper surface, the other preserving the side of the vessel and a section of nozzle. Pale brown with no visible temper, hard-fired. Incised garland inside a border of moulded berries.
H. 3.3; L. 9.0; W. 7.2

Hellenistic or Early Roman ceramics
M.P.C. Jackson

During the course of the analysis of the late Roman and early Byzantine vessels all the material from the Level I units was examined. The majority of this material was plain ware, plain painted ware and cooking ware. Although many of these sherds could be grouped by fabric and form and dated by associated finds and stratigraphy, the Hellenistic units were often not well defined stratigraphically. As a result the Level I pottery report will contain some Hellenistic or Early Roman coarse wares. These may be identifiable by comparison with material from other sites. Although the following vessels belong to Level I units, they appear not to belong to the same groups identified in the Late Roman units, and they derive from units from which Hellenistic fine wares were found. Since these sherds are distinct from material clearly associated with the late Roman/Byzantine ceramics, they are presented here as possible Hellenistic/early Roman period material.

997 was found in packing to the south of W952 in L19c which also contained four Hellenistic fine ware sherds. The fabric is the same as that of **998**. **999** and **1000** were both from the topsoil unit in I14; both had handles atypical of other examples from the site, but **1000** appeared to be made from local clay similar to that of Fabric 1 painted sherds. **1001** was from an apparently well-dated pre-Byzantine unit and was very similar in form and decoration to an over-fired, 'melted' rim fragment also from 2106. This suggests that Kilise Tepe may have been the production site. **1002** has three distinctive grooves on the exterior of the rim but no other decoration. **1003–5** have very similar fabrics and decoration (Fig. 543). **1003–4** have the same form: a large belly and strap handle connected from below the rim to the shoulder. The vessels are painted with a broad horizontal band of red or brown/black paint, which runs from the rims down to the necks and handles.

997   5923
Level I
Rim and handle of closed vessel. Very hard brown fabric, breaks almost concoidally, with white inclusions 0.5 mm and grey inclusions <0.5 mm. Red/brown paint on ext. and int. rim.
Int. rim di. 10, Ext. rim di. 12

998   3001
Level 1
Rim and handle of closed vessel. Orange/brown fabric, fractures concoidally with moderate grey inclusions <0.5 mm and frequent white inclusions <0.5 mm.
Int. rim di. 9, Ext. rim di. 11

999   3400
Topsoil
Rim and handle of closed vessel. Light brown fabric with angular grey/opaque inclusions up to 1.5 mm and light brown sub-angular inclusions up to 1.5 mm. Opaque inclusions very clearly visible on the surface.
Int. rim di.11, Ext. rim di. 12.4

1000   3400
Topsoil
Rim and handle of closed vessel. Orange fabric with frequent grey and red inclusions 0.5 mm and sparse white inclusions 0.5–1 mm.
Int. rim di. 11, Ext. rim di. 14.1

1001   2106
Level E2a
Rim and handle of closed vessel. Green/yellow fabric with sparse white inclusions up to 2 mm and moderate/sparse grey inclusions 0.5 mm, moderate/sparse white inclusions <0.5 mm. Dark brown/brown wash on ext. rim and down handle.
Int. rim di. 10, Ext. rim di. 12
Fig. 542

1002   3322
Level 1
Rim of closed vessel. Orange fabric with grey and white inclusions <0.5 mm.
Int. rim di. 11.4, Ext. rim di. 14

1003   3102
Level 1
Complete rim and strap handle from closed vessel. Pale orange fabric with sparse orange inclusions 0.5 mm and moderate white inclusions less than 0.5 mm.
Int. rim di. 8.5, Ext. rim di. 11
Fig. 543

1004   3001
Level 1
Rim and handle of closed vessel. Cream fabric slightly green, very small sparse black, red and white inclusions, and brown inclusions 0.5 mm. Dark brown/black paint worn on surface
Int. rim di. 7.75, Ext. rim di. 10.5
Fig. 543

1005   3102
Level 1
Handle from closed vessel. Orange fabric with frequent red inclusions up to 1 mm and moderate/sparse white inclusions <0.5 mm. Red paint in horizontal band across vessel and over handle.
Fig. 543 (showing rim omitted from drawing)

1006   Q20/25   2104
Level E2a
Jar found in P94/46 just beneath surface (see Fig. 501); most of rim missing. Rather thin-walled vessel, self-slipped and decorated with red 'splash' paint. Inner surface partially flaked off.
Ext. rim di. *c.* 9, Max. di. *c.* 28, Base di. 11
Fig. 259

1007   Q20/26   2104
Level E2a
Upper part of two-handled cooking-pot, found with **1006**. Heavily burnt grey-black ware with large white grits (<3 mm). Grooving visible on interior.
Ext. rim di. 13, max. di. *c.* 27

Figure 259. *Hellenistic cooking pot* **1007**.

Chapter 31

Pottery from Level One[1]

M.P.C. Jackson

Introduction

The Late Roman/Byzantine levels excavated at Kilise Tepe covered an area of c. 2500 m^2. This section outlines the way in which the Roman and Byzantine ceramic material from the site was recovered during the excavation and the sorting process adopted. A summary interpretation of the material is provided, followed by a catalogue of the material, organized primarily according to fabric and form. The published ceramics from the site are presented by fabric and form and may be examined by provenance also (see Table 14, pp. 424–7).

Summary

The material represents an assemblage of vessels derived from buildings and living areas at a rural settlement. In addition to deposits found within the buildings, stratified deposits were also found associated with refuse disposal pits, courtyards and open areas. Completely closed assemblages e.g. tombs or loaded kilns were not discovered during the course of the excavation.

The fill of certain clay-lined pits, and surfaces in the NW Corner provided the best-stratified deposits in J18 and J19 and material contained within buildings in K18 revealed some useful associated groups of sherds (4395). The significant numbers of sherds from individual broken vessels suggests relatively little post-depositional disturbance of the upper units in K19, despite the proximity to the surface of the mound which had been ploughed.

Hellenistic/Early Roman (see above, Chapter 30) and Late Roman and Byzantine ceramic materials were recovered during the excavations of Level 1. Few deposits or sherds dating to the Roman period were identified during the excavation. The lack of deposits dated stratigraphically to the Roman period and the apparent complete lack of imported Roman material inhibited attribution of coarse wares to this period. It would appear that there was significantly less activity between the Hellenistic/Early Roman period and the Late Roman period, at least in those areas of the site which we excavated. A group of sherds painted with broad areas of red/brown paint was uncovered from beneath the floor at the east end of the Early Byzantine basilica. These were also found in 2343 and may help to provide a date for the construction of the church.

The number of Late Roman fine table wares found was an exceptionally small proportion of the total amount of excavated material, only c. 10 vessels. Parallels for imported sherds found at Kilise Tepe were invariably discovered in the report on the excavations at Anemurium (Williams 1989). Concentrations of sherds from Late Roman 1 amphorae were found in association with these fine ware sherds together with cooking wares and considerable numbers of local painted plain wares.

Large numbers of painted vessels were recovered; these have also been found at Alahan, where they were called 'Monastic Ware' (Williams 1985, 41–7). The clay from which these vessels are made is presumed to be local. The vessels of this tradition most frequently recovered were closed jars which bore dark red/purple painted decoration applied as painted animal, fish, vegetal or loose geometric motifs, or gouged decoration on their shoulders, and ribbing around the bellies. Paint was also splashed and dribbled onto other closed vessels of the same fabric. A wide variety of other forms were also found in this fabric including amphorae, *pithoi* and roof tiles but few open bowls. The fabric was light orange in colour and contained white lime particles and red/brown inclusions. Petrographic analyses (Knappett pers. comm.) showed some variation in the sherds of the fabric group. The white particles are limestone elements and the red/brown inclusions are clay pellets, but not grog. Some samples are micaceous.

The painted vessels were found in association with Late Roman cooking pots with distinctive flat horizontal handles joined to rolled rims. They have a thin, hard cooking fabric. Examples of similar cooking vessels have been reported from kilns on Cyprus and were traded widely in the Mediterranean during the seventh century (especially **1337–48**) and mid to late seventh centuries (notably **1444**). The cooking vessels, Late Roman amphorae, Late Roman fine wares and painted vessels were found in association in K19 in 1500 and 1501 and in K18 in 4395 below 4393. Sizeable concentrations of painted sherds were also found in 2343 and 2350 which represent the earliest stratigraphic deposit containing the material. In 2343 and 2350 a distinctive phalliform amphora toe (**1334**) was recovered together with a fragment of Late Roman 'Spiral Burnished Ware'. These Late Roman pieces provide a *terminus post quem* for the vessels of the painted tradition at Kilise Tepe.

The material from 2343 can be dated stratigraphically by the surface which sealed it, since the sherds must pre-date the surface. The surface contained a worn late fourth-century coin (**2835**) and was cut by pit P95/14 (1604) which contained a mid fifth-century coin (**2837**: see Level 1 stratigraphy conclusion, p. 209). It should be noted that it is not possible to determine the length of time the coins were in circulation before their deposition.

The combination of the evidence from the coins and the imported ceramic material in the assemblage both appear to suggest that the painted pottery may date from the late fifth century. The variety of motifs and styles may be evidence for the continuity of the tradition into later centuries. Since a late Roman *terminus post quem* is suggested by its association with late Roman coins and fine wares in deposits at both Alahan and Kilise Tepe, it is particularly interesting that it is found in such large concentrations in central Isauria along the Calycadnus valley, but not at Anemurium on the coast.

Only a few small fragments of glazed ware were found during the excavations. One was found in a late pit, the rest on the site on the church. A burial to the east of the church has been radiocarbon dated to the twelfth–thirteenth centuries (see p. 186). The later church may date to that period based on its form.

Aims and objectives

The aim of this report will be to illustrate and describe the corpus of Roman and Byzantine pottery recovered from Kilise Tepe, according to form, fabric and archaeological context, presenting a representative sample of the corpus discovered during the excavation. The objective is to present information on the variability and recurrence of types and fabrics and to present interpretations of chronology of types based on consistent associations of deposits.

Preservation of material in the soil
The stratigraphic integrity of the upper units was limited by the intense activity on the site, both in antiquity, and recently by farming on the tepe and the robbing of stones. Material from the surface scrape and up to 0.40 m below the surface of the mound was generally very mixed and fragmented as a result of ploughing. The Level I deposits were rarely more than 1.5 m deep, so this mixed topsoil deposit represented a considerable proportion of the Level I deposit. Squares on the side of the tepe may be expected to have experienced additional post-depositional movement of sherds, and also had comparatively shallow topsoil. In many parts, especially where there were large numbers of walls, the topsoil was less deep and deposits remained somewhat protected within the lines of buildings. However, the walls rarely survived higher than foundation level and were rarely found associated with floors. This may be due largely to levelling between architectural phases or possibly due to the lack of recognizable floor plaster (cf. Postgate above, p. 37). The lack of floors found during excavation of the Byzantine structures means that contexts of Level 1 were rarely securely sealed from above or below.

The quality of the deposits has limited the extent to which clearly stratified Level I pottery assemblages could be produced. However, certain deposits in clay-lined pits, and those representing fill from between the spaces of walls appeared to represent 'good' units with a consistent set of forms and fabrics and a lack of residual material. The relationship between the clay-lined pits and the deposits they cut was considered the most useful starting point for the analysis.

Method and description of the collection of ceramic data
The project's grid and recording system is outlined above (p. 67). The primary information on the pottery labels was the name of the quadrant e.g. J18b, and the unit of excavation e.g. 2343. The majority of the pottery collected during the course of the excavation was recovered when spotted visually by the excavators. Generally soil was not sieved unless from units considered particularly well stratified; most of the Late Roman and Byzantine units were therefore not sieved. It is inevitable that some pottery was lost with the spoil during the excavation process, in particular during the removal of mixed topsoil levels, and some mixed upper layers which were excavated with mattocks and shovels rather than trowels.

All pottery was washed on site, and dried. When dry the content of each unit was divided into groups under specific headings and recorded by Connie Hansen under the following categories: total number of sherds in the whole unit; number of plain body sherds; number of cooking ware sherds; pithos sherds; plain ware; feature; painted/decorated; *tegulae*; and *imbrices*). Excavators marked pottery labels from units containing well-stratified material (WSM); all ceramic material from these units was saved, i.e. all sherds, whether considered diagnostic or not, were washed and kept with the diagnostic material for transportation to the dig-house.

The 'diagnostic' sherds (rims, bases, handles and decorated body sherds) from each unit were put into plastic bags with the original basket labels re-used and stored in polythene bags in plastic crates in the dig-house. Diagnostic material from units within the same 10 m × 10 m square was kept together. All further ceramic analysis took place in the dig-house and subsequently at the Silifke Museum.

Non-diagnostic ceramics, i.e. undecorated body sherds, were laid out in their units for the rest of the season in a 'sherd yard' next to the site, so that material from each unit could be re-examined if necessary. The sherd yard had to be disposed of at the end of each season.

Stratigraphic context of the material

The Roman and Byzantine material occurs within the deposits which were attributed to Level 1, which also contained the Hellenistic material. As has already been mentioned, these Level 1 units were often not ideally stratified: in particular, few floor deposits were identified during the excavation of the Level 1 buildings and many of the building phases cut into the upper levels of earlier deposits. It was equally difficult to attribute some architectural phases to a specific period, rather than a relative one, when they survived only as sub-floor foundation walls dug into earlier layers. This frequently caused units with later Level 1 pottery to contain residual material from earlier phases including Hellenistic and Iron Age material. The poor stratigraphic integrity of many of the units under the broad heading 'Level 1' made close examination of the first occurrence of specific wares necessary.

Identification of the material

In an attempt to provide an overview of Level 1 so that the appearance of the Byzantine material might be studied within its ceramic context, all the material from units labelled 'Level 1', 'Level I', 'Level 1/2' and 'Level I/II' was analysed. However, because of time constraints in the field (a total of 6 weeks) only the Late Roman and Byzantine material was the focus of this study. The vast majority of the assemblage consisted of plain, plain painted and cooking wares, rather than fine wares.

Imported material e.g. Late Roman fine wares, and amphorae clearly stood out both in form and fabric and were generally relatively straight forward to distinguish from local material. They were identified with the help of parallels published from other sites in the Eastern Mediterranean. Particular use was made of reports from: Anemurium (Williams 1977; 1989); Alahan (Williams 1985); Tarsus (Goldman 1950); and sites on Cyprus especially Dhiorios (Catling 1972) and Kornos Cave (Catling & Dikigoropoulos 1970) and the summary paper by Hayes (1980). Bass & van Doornick (1982) and Waagé (1948) also provided comparable examples.

It should be noted that Late Roman fine slipped table wares represented an exceptionally small proportion of the material from the site. This study of the Late Roman and Byzantine pottery therefore has very little to report on these wares which were used, among other things, to provide a *terminus post quem* for units during the processing. They were not, however, always found in Level 1 contexts that were stratigraphically secure.

Analysis of the Hellenistic material from Kilise Tepe had already concentrated on the fine ware but had not considered the coarse and plain wares from the Hellenistic period (see Nevett, Chapter 30). A prime objective in the analysis was the differentiation of the coarse wares from the Late Roman and Byzantine periods from the residual earlier material.

A large repertoire of vessels belonging to a distinctive painted tradition represents the major proportion of the material recovered in the later levels. This group was discovered by Michael Gough at the Byzantine site at Alahan 50 km further north up the Göksu valley where he named it 'Monastic Ware' (Williams 1985, 41). At Alahan this so-called 'Monastic Ware' was dated to the Late Roman/Early Byzantine period (Gough 1985, 28); the site at Alahan had no deposits dating to earlier than the Late Roman period. Occupation at the site may, however, have continued as late as the twelfth century (Gough 1964, 185–90).

Comparison of the fabrics from Kilise Tepe with material from Alahan at Silifke Museum and in the BIAA Reference Collection in 1999 showed a range of fabric and decorational similarities between Alahan and Kilise Tepe but also some differences within the group as a whole. Although variations in the colour, size and proportion of inclusions were apparent to a greater and lesser degree in the fabric of these painted vessels, the Kilise Tepe fabric is generally distinctive and more homogeneous than the fabrics from painted vessels at Alahan. Petrological analysis has confirmed some differences between the mineral composition of the painted vessel fabrics (Knappett pers. comm.). This may be taken to suggest that the ware might have been part of a significant local tradition produced at more than one source.

Analysis of the material in the dighouse/Silifke museum

Introduction
This section summarizes the method by which the diagnostic pottery from each unit was analysed. The major characteristics of the Byzantine material were summarized by Dominique Collon after the initial surface survey in 1994 (Collon, in Baker *et al.* 1995, 157–60). There was unfortunately no time to re-examine the survey material and that from the sub-surface scrape following the study of the excavated sherds. The major conclusions of this preliminary study were, however, borne out by the results of the analysis of the excavated material.

Identification of the Level 1 material continued as part of the pottery sorting process over the next 4 seasons. Certain particularly striking Level 1 sherds were selected and drawn in the seasons they were excavated, but the Roman/Byzantine material was not formally studied until after the excavation had finished at the end of the 1998 season.

Analysis of the later Roman and Byzantine pottery was carried out by the author and took place for two weeks at the dig-house and one week at Silifke in August and September 1998 followed by three weeks of further analysis which took place at Silifke Museum in 1999.

Before the 1998 season, the excavation summaries and notebooks were carefully studied to identify the best-stratified Level 1 units, together with information on the finds and contexts of the units. This enabled the material from the best-stratified units to be selected for examination first. Confirmation of whether there was residual material in the unit was usually apparent when the pottery was laid out. Certain units e.g. (1501) contained a very homogeneous series of forms and fabrics. Some others were much less homogeneous and contained substantial mixture of Late Roman, Hellenistic and Iron Age material. The identification of this material involved invaluable discussions with Connie Hansen and Dorit Symington, the specialists dealing with the pottery from earlier periods at Kilise Tepe, in order to identify many pieces in later contexts which were clearly residual.

At this stage particular note was taken of the presence of dateable imported sherds e.g. amphorae and Late Roman red slip wares and the local types found associated with them.

The completion of this process left remaining the less well stratified units within Level 1, from which the majority of the material came. The units thus contained many types not previously seen in the 'good' Level 1 contexts. Material was considered a candidate for Level 1 pottery if it had not occurred in earlier levels. The difficulty then was determining from which period within Level 1 a group of sherds came. This was not always possible for small groups because of the poor stratigraphic integrity of their provenance. For larger groups, patterns could normally be identified linking the association of the material with certain context groups. Sherds were compared and grouped by fabric and form and cross-referenced by context.

Method of analysis
1. Identification of the best-stratified units from Level 1 in the excavation record. In particular, it remained important to differentiate between sub-phases within Level 1 and to establish the relative relationships between those sub-phases.
2. Following the identification of the potentially most useful units, the saved diagnostic pottery from those bags were found in the store and gathered together in preparation for analysis.
3. The diagnostic sherds from each unit were laid out separately in the dig-house or museum. The characteristic pieces which occurred, especially those typical of the unit whether considered residual or not, were noted to record the character of the unit and the groups were counted. Following this, sherds considered particularly diagnostic either in fabric, form, or decoration, were drawn and marked with the unit number and an individual identification number (the drawing number). At this stage an individual fabric description of the sherd was written on its corresponding drawing.
4. Once marked with unit and drawing numbers, these drawn sherds were then separated from the rest of the unit and placed into groups according to broad categories: cooking ware, plain ware, thick *pithos* type, and fine ware. They were kept in bags according to the square within which they were found, so that they could be found easily.
5. Once the ceramics had been sorted into their various categories (Stage 3), the types within each category were compared and divided into groups according to fabric and shape. At this stage the sherds were grouped into sherds which macroscopically seemed to have the same fabric. By having all the sherds on the same table it was possible to make relatively informed observations and comparisons of fabrics between the sherds.
6. This resulted in an area covered in little piles of pottery, grouped by fabric and form. Each group was given a code name, and all the sherds in the group were then listed. Thus the sherds not only had their own individual fabric description made at the time of drawing but also had been grouped into a fabric group. Fabric details noted for each group were based on those outlined by Peacock: fabric code, colour, hardness, feel, fracture, description of inclusions and general description (Peacock 1977, 23). The individual fabric description recorded on the sherd drawings allowed for individual variation within the group.

This information was recorded on paper and entered later into a computer database (Access 7.0) so that groups of sherds could be cross-referenced with their provenance. The data base contained only information relating to the 800 sherds that had been drawn because their forms, decoration and fabrics were considered to have been the most diagnostic. Information on the material in the rest of a unit was checked manually in the original paper notes on the unit as a whole.

Limitations of the analysis
The major limitation of the analysis is that it has proved difficult to divide the later Roman/Byzantine coarse wares from the Hellenistic/Roman coarse-ware material. The units of excavation could not always be clearly attributed to a phase, and there were frequently residual recognizable fine ware ceramics in later phases, meaning that coarse wares too may have been 'thrown up'. The fact that by the time the study began most of the Level 1 material had already been excavated, and the report on the Hellenistic fine wares completed, in some ways helped; but it also meant that opportunity for re-assessment and dialogue was precluded.

It is regrettable that we are unable to provide more detailed information on the chronology of the local painted vessels, bearing in mind the possible breadth which they might span based on other evidence from the site. For a confirmation of the dating of our most common ware group, we are therefore reliant to a large extent on the results of analysis of material from other sites. Luminescence dating by Durham Luminescence Dating Laboratory of a single sherd (K18/316 from 4395) provided a surprisingly late date of the twelfth century which conflicts with the clear association of the painted sherds found with later Roman sherds in units such as (2343) at Kilise Tepe and with stratified deposits at Alahan. Two eleventh-century coins were noted in the topsoil above the best stratified of the deposits at Alahan but were considered to post-date the context containing painted (Monastic) Ware together with associated late Roman wares and fifth- and sixth-century coins (Harrison 1985, 28). This later date does therefore fit a recurring theme of material associated with later occupation dated to eleventh and twelfth century from both sites, but the strength of the evidence for an early date for the start of the painted vessel tradition is more conclusive at present.

It was unfortunate that analysis of the material could not have taken place during the excavation, rather than afterwards, so that any problems could be addressed. In particular, it would have been helpful if the non-diagnostic material from previous years' sherd yards had been available for consultation. Following excavation at the end of the 1998 season, the discovery of a large number of diagnostic sherds which appeared to derive from two individual vessels in unit (4395) led to the re-examination of the material in the sherd yard. This resulted in the discovery of a considerable number of plain body sherds which were found to join to the diagnostic pieces recovered earlier from the same unit. These in fact facilitated the reconstruction of almost two complete profiles when given to the site conservator Franca Cole. This analysis of the saved 'diagnostic' material in conjunction with 'undiagnostic' material from the sherd yard showed that during the process of selecting diagnostic sherds, certain undiagnostic body sherds which would have connected to diagnostic sherds and added to their profile had been overlooked. The saving of all material from certain WSM units at the time of excavation e.g. 1501 led to the successful reconstruction of **1027** during analysis in the Silifke Museum. This not only tells us about the quality of the unit i.e. that it has not been greatly disturbed by post-depositional processes, but also suggests that others may have been reconstructable. Regrettably the nature of the excavation as a rescue project and the huge quantities of ceramics recovered meant that only diagnostic sherds were saved following sorting and initial counts.

In general, this report contains very few complete profiles. We have a good selection of diagnostic rim, base and handle forms from certain fabrics but rarely complete vessel profiles. Those complete profiles which we do have are heavily biased in favour of pots which were discovered complete, or vessels with a high proportion of diagnostic features to vessel surface area e.g. painted vessels. The report is consequently biased against large storage vessels that have a high proportion of body sherds in relation to 'diagnostic' rim/handle/bases or small amounts of decoration. Fortunately many of the imported storage vessels are more widely traded and therefore not only stand out as non-local fabrics but also have forms and fabric descriptions which may be found within the published literature from other sites.

Although all pottery was washed prior to sorting, and scrubbed using brushes, the processing of some of the late material was hampered by the large amounts of calcareous concretions on the material found in certain units from the upper levels. Removal of such deposits with 1:20 diluted nitric acid, except for a limited number of very heavily encrusted units, was only done to specific diagnostic sherds in order to facilitate reconstruction of joining pieces or photography of painted sherds. However, it should be noted that certain Fabric 1 sherds photographed in the 1994 and 1995 season had completely lost their decoration by 1998, owing to the effects of the acid on the exterior of the fabric. Those sherds treated in the 1998 and 1999 season were soaked for at least an hour in clean water before and for at least two hours in a number of washes after very brief exposure to the acid in an effort to prevent damage to these pieces.

Reliability of interpretations
The major fabric groups were divided up based on macroscopic analysis of the material. Sherds were checked against each other in order to attempt to maintain valid comparisons (rather than relying on purely the objective recording of attributes or memory). Attributes compared during the analysis were based on those outlined by Peacock (1997). It was considered important to compare sherds visually against each other using these attributes as a guide. In order to support the textual fabric descriptions, photographs were taken of fresh breaks of sherds considered diagnostic of the major fabric groups. Samples for petrographic analysis were taken from the fabric groups in order to attempt some comparison between sherds considered macroscopically and based on stratigraphic information to belong to the same group. The main group analysed was the local plain and plain painted material (Fabrics 1a–b). Individual samples were taken of the other wares including cooking vessels and imported amphorae. Samples from the best units were analysed by Knappett and Kilikoglou using Instrumental Neutron Activation analysis (see Knappett, p. 247, 5183–6).

Summary of Hellenistic and Roman pottery from Level 1

The catalogue of material in this section contains certain Hellenistic cooking sherds which were contained within the Level 1 units. It was considered important to present them here since they had not been studied with the Hellenistic fine wares. Their provenance is given in the catalogue. It would appear that the best Hellenistic deposits were from Q10.

It is difficult to argue for a Roman phase following the Hellenistic and preceding the Late Roman at Kilise Tepe. Certainly there is some evidence for fine wares at the site from the period. However, with so little known about the local Roman wares and without coins or a clear phase of architecture attributable to the period, it is difficult to produce much evidence for the local Roman ceramics at the site.

Although it would be unwise to interpret a gap in the Roman fine ware ceramic sequence as a break in the chronology of occupation at the site, it is difficult to attribute any units stratigraphically to the Roman period. The lack of Roman material is confirmed to some extent by the fact that parallels for Roman period cooking vessels from Anemurium were not found at Kilise Tepe (Williams 1989, nos. 360–75).

Terra Sigillata sherds were recovered as part of the pre-excavation surface survey in the S and SW part of the mound (see Thomas, p. 61). This part of the mound remains unexcavated, and so may be the location of Roman deposits.

Following the excavation, a serious attempt was made by the author to identify the stratigraphical relationship between the various archaeological features within Level 1 as well as to study the ceramics from each unit; both of these processes aided interpretations of the phases.

One of the most interesting groups of sherds from early in the Level I phases came from Pit P95/33 (1626) which contained a substantial number of cooking pot fragments and some almost complete cooking vessels. This pit was apparently early in the sequence of Level I pits and possibly pre-dated even the Level Ib walls (see p. 200). It was also cut by the large modern robber pit in J19d. The occurrence of small fragments of both Hellenistic fine ware and painted sherds in (1626) suggests some degree of contamination. But in spite of the possible intrusion of a relatively small number of sherds, the majority of the fill of P95/33 preserved an important collection of data. That the pit remains a very important archaeological feature is confirmed by the fill of (1626) which was sampled also for faunal remains and palaeobotanical evidence which should be considered alongside the ceramic evidence.

Late Roman and Byzantine contexts and assemblages

The analysis of units dated to the Late Roman/Early Byzantine period was facilitated by certain deposits which were considered to be relatively well stratified by the excavators. These appeared to contain few residual sherds from earlier periods. These units were found especially in the NW corner of the mound, in squares: J18, K18, J19, K19 and L19. They were associated with a courtyard area and associated pits, and with Level Ic and Id architecture. Other useful deposits were found in the I14–M14 trench, especially in I14a/b and in L14a/b. Many other areas of the site provided useful examples of individual forms but many of these came from deposits which showed signs of residual material and therefore contamination. The following section will concentrate on material from the best preserved features and deposits. A more detailed discussion of the structural archaeology is to be found in Chapters 14–18.

Pre-courtyard
One of the best-stratified units was 2343 which was excavated in J18b from between two large Level Ib walls W425 and W421. The southern extension of 2343

was 2350, both these units contained significant quantities of painted pottery as well as a spiral burnished ware sherd (**1017**) and the phalliform LR amphora 3 toe (**1334**).

Neighbouring units 2343, 2350 and 2339 probably represent the same archaeological context. The discovery of the Spiral Burnished Ware and amphora sherds in association with the painted sherds appears to confirm the attribution of painted sherds to the Late Roman Period. Williams dates the Spiral Burnished Ware found in significant quantities at Alahan between the fifth–seventh centuries (Williams 1985, 40). The amphora toe, however, has been dated to the Roman period (first–fourth centuries) by Williams at Anemurium (1989, 92).

The packing layers below the ash deposits 2306 and 2308 in J18a contained a variety of plain and cooking vessel sherds, the most notable being the distinctively decorated cooking sherds recovered from 2310 and 2312 (**1404** and **1419**) and a complete vessel from 2316 (**1436**).

Courtyard sequence
In J18a at the bottom of the courtyard sequence, a highly diagnostic cooking pot handle (**1429**) was found in 2308 together with a number of finds including the copper cross (**2294**).

Packing deposit 2336 which sealed pit P97/37 contained a painted sherd (**1211**). It should be noted that these sherds were discovered in the deposits below the ash layers on the courtyard above.

The striated ash layers of the later courtyard generally produced relatively few finds. In J19 ash layers excavated as 1602 contained painted sherds (**1154–7**), as well as the cooking vessel (**1445**). The corresponding ash units in J18b (2337) contained a painted sherd featuring an animal's hind legs and tail (**1174**). The ash layers are relatively late in Level I.

Level Ic building
Significant amounts of Late Roman wares including cooking sherds, imported amphorae and painted sherds were also found in (4393) and (4395) within the Level Ic structure.

Level Id building
The 'lower topsoil' unit (1501) bounded by Level Id walls in K19 contained an almost consistent series of ceramics. The majority of the material in 1501 was painted plain ware, Late Roman amphorae sherds, and Late Roman fine ware.[2] Late Roman cooking pots were also found in this unit. It did however contain at least one residual Hellenistic sherd. Analysis of the material added weight to the excavator's interpretation that the unit may have represented the contents of the phase 1d buildings in K19.

This may be taken to suggest that phase Ic and phase Id were contemporary, in the Late Roman period, although one building may have been constructed earlier than the other.

The phase Id building re-uses a carved stone capital from a monumental building — it is not clear whether it came from the early Kilise Tepe church, but this remains a possibility and thus the contents of the building in K19 could provide a *terminus ante quem* for the destruction of the church.

The discovery of the painted material in both phases Ic, Id and below and in the courtyard phases suggests that the painted tradition was used either for a relatively long period of time, or during a relatively expansive phase of the site. There were more sherds recovered from spiral and dot painted jars than jars with other motifs.

I14a–M14b
In I14a–M14b, the only part of the trench where painted sherds were found in high concentrations was in L14a–b. This was also the only part of the trench in which walls were not excavated. At least three different cooking vessels were discovered in association, and a Late Roman 1 amphora. The rest of the sherds all belonged to closed storage jars made from Fabric 1, many of which featured painted decoration.

Fill below topsoil (3401) in I14a/b revealed both Late Roman 1 amphorae (**1323**) and Fabric 1 sherds with gouged decoration (**1231** and **1233**), as well as a straight-necked cooking vessel (**1354**); the continuation of 3401 was 3402 which produced a cooking sherd (**1434**). A *terminus post quem* for these pieces is provided by the wall collapse (3403) in which lay the spiral-painted sherd (**1133**). In other parts of the I14a–M14b trench, relatively few Late Roman/Early Byzantine sherds were found.

Less well-stratified material
Much of the Late Roman material derived from deposits near the surface of the mound was relatively unstratified. Many of these topsoil units were disturbed but nevertheless they contained sherds significant for the assemblage.

Although not well sealed, topsoil units 3201–2 from N12a for example contained one of the few Late Roman fine rim sherds (**1008**). These units also contained painted sherds and fragments of cooking vessels, but their stratigraphic integrity is too unreliable to attribute their provenance more than limited value.

In the NW Corner, a further Late Roman C Form 3 rim sherd was recovered immediately to the east of 1501 in L19c from the fill below topsoil within the structure formed by phase 1d walls W951 and W950.

Late Roman fine ware sherd **1010** was found in topsoil associated with painted sherds. This material was found above the phase 1c structure located in K18b.

There was a constant association between these Late Roman fine wares and the painted wares, but it should be noted that the numbers of instances when they were sealed together in excellent contexts was rare because of the small total number of fine ware sherds discovered.

Glazed wares

Evidence for later ceramics comes from pit P97/1 (2305) in J18a, which was sealed by late surface 2302. It contained one of the few small glazed sherds recovered from Kilise Tepe. The pit also contained a small fragment of pottery whose painted decoration appeared different in style to other painted sherds (**1148**). In addition, the pit contained the base of a cooking vessel with diagnostic flat strap handle and incised vertical lines (**1420**). A handle similar in both form and fabric (**1421**) was found in another pit P96/16 located nearby in J19a/c. Three other very small sherds of glazed ware found at the site were recovered from topsoil during excavation of the church.

Summary

In general terms the Late Roman assemblage at Kilise Tepe compares well with that from the Late Roman pilgrimage and monastic site at Alahan. No ceramic material, coins or other dateable material was published from Alahan which dates from before the Late Roman period. There a slightly different range of cooking vessels was found. A number of imported vessel types were recovered from both Alahan and Kilise Tepe which included Cypriot-type cooking vessels (Williams 1985, 48–9, esp. no. 53), Kilise Tepe K1 (esp. **1337–51**) (Catling 1972, 47 fig. 29 P433; 49, fig. 30 P210).

Few open bowls were recovered from the later deposits at Kilise Tepe, other than the Late Roman fine wares; a similar observation was made of the material from Alahan. Certain plain painted open bowls were found at Alahan (Williams 1985, 47, nos. 42–3), but similar examples were not discovered at Kilise Tepe. Cooking vessels were closed-shaped round cooking pot type vessels, the open frying pan types found at Anemurium (Williams 1989, 61) were not recovered at Kilise Tepe. This picture may be contrasted with the Hellenistic period for which there are relatively numerous imported open bowls as well as those from the local region.

Only one single sherd of Spiral Burnished ware was recovered from Kilise Tepe, whereas it was the largest single class of fine ware at Alahan, supporting Williams' suggestion that the production centre could have been in central Anatolia rather than closer to the coast (Williams 1985, 39). In addition other imitation Late Roman fine wares including Egyptian 'C' (Williams 1985, 39; Hayes 1972, 399–401) were recovered from Alahan but not Kilise Tepe.

This distribution may be helpful in establishing some understanding of the routes of trade to the sites — which one would assume would have been determined to a large extent by the topography of the area, the major routes being the Calycadnus valley from Seleuceia via either the Sertavul pass or via Dağ Pazarı to get to Lycaonia on the central Anatolian plateau. east–west routes may also have been possible over the mountain to Anemurium via Ermenek.

It is interesting to note the occurrence of almost all the fine ware vessels found at Kilise Tepe and Alahan in the report by Williams on Anemurium, situated on the coast. However, there is relatively little comparability between the cooking wares of the Göksu valley and the coast. Perhaps it is more informative to identify where the differences lie: examination of those fine ware types which were not traded up the Göksu valley provides some evidence for the significance of coastal trade routes. At Kilise Tepe only Cypriot Red Slip ware Form 2 and Late Roman C Form 3, and Spiral Burnished types of imported material were found; at Alahan 26 African Red Slip ware vessels were recovered, only a very few Late Roman C, Cypriot Red Slip and Egyptian C pieces were found (Williams 1985, 36). Williams concludes that they reached Alahan by chance rather than as a result of systematic importation. The discovery of forms dated as early as the early fourth century and certainly not later than the early fifth century (e.g. Williams 1985, nos. 1 & 3) should be considered alongside the numismatic evidence by those attempting to determine the date of the occupation of the site rather than relying merely on the monuments and historical sources. The discovery of a number of sherds datable to the seventh century would also suggest that the site was thriving at least a century after the end of the reign of Zeno.

Perhaps the most interesting difference between the assemblages at Alahan, Kilise Tepe and Anemurium in the Late Roman period is the lack of painted vessels at Anemurium (Williams 1989, 61). Vessels in this fabric represented the greatest proportion of material from both Alahan and Kilise Tepe, yet no vessels of this type were recognized at Anemurium. This may be explained by the fact that the painted vessels found at Kilise Tepe, Alahan and Dağ Pazarı represent a locally produced (i.e. Göksu valley) ware. The evidence from Kilise Tepe seems to suggest a Late Roman date for the initial use of the ware; its continued use in a number of sub-phases of the site is important, but unfortunately those periods of use are not closely dated by other means.

The material archive from excavations at Dağ Pazarı stored in the Silifke museum was catalogued during 1999 and demonstrated that the ceramics from the excavations of the churches were rarely from occupation contexts (hardly surprisingly in view of their provenance). Unstratified grab samples collected by Gough from the surface of the site demonstrated ceramics dating from Hellenistic, Roman, Byzantine and later periods.

The painted vessels from both Alahan[3] and Kilise Tepe were examined in the Silifke Museum and the BIAA library collection in order to facilitate their comparison.[4] There was a good degree of similarity between the fabrics, forms and decoration of many of the vessels which occurred at Kilise Tepe, so similar at times that it was tempting to believe that certain vessels had been made by the same potter. However, in others, the clay fabric was different and the decoration, although within the same tradition, was clearly in a different style to the rest. These differences suggest the possibility of more than a single production site.

The fabric differences tended not to be due to differences in clay inclusions themselves but rather differences may be explained by either clay extraction from a different part of the same clay source or possibly from another extraction site. Styles of decoration and paint colour also varied; some of these variations could be attributed to styles of different producers or to changes through time. Unfortunately the stratigraphy is not clear enough to determine a chronological development. However it should be noted that there was less homogeneity in the fabrics at Alahan than at Kilise Tepe, although the main painted fabric from Kilise Tepe was found at Alahan. The quantity of the material represented at these sites would suggest that it was an important local ceramic tradition; but there is marked similarity between the ware and certain types from North Africa. This may be yet more evidence to suggest that there was trade with communities there — although it is surprising that the material has not been found at Anemurium — or that the local production in Isauria was part of a wider tradition.

It is also interesting to note that this painted pottery has not been found by the Konya Plain Survey where a large number of sites have been identified which date from the Hellenistic through to the Mediaeval period (Baird pers. comm.).

Painted motifs

The significance of the motifs painted on the pottery is very interesting. They appear to be found mostly on closed vessels, which are thought to have been used as water coolers. The discovery of painted decoration on water coolers was noted also on vessels in Lower Egypt at the Monastery of Kellia (Egloff 1977). The motifs fall into a broad category of painted motifs applied to vessels from the Late Roman period in the eastern Mediterranean, often produced in North Africa where they are found on Coptic wares. Vessels bearing these kinds of painted decoration have been discovered in contexts dating into the eighth century at Khirbat al-Karak in Palestine (Delougaz & Haines 1960, 35, pl. 37).

The painted motifs therefore appear to belong, initially at least, to the Early Byzantine period and to be a feature of water cooling vessels. Certain of the motifs belong to a repertoire of images which had religious significance at the time. Crosses were often used for their perceived apotropaic powers and images of birds, animals, and fish represented the various parts of creation: air, sea and land (Maguire 1990).

The significance of the link between water and life, particularly in hot, arid countries, and the symbolic link between water and life in Christianity, may have been one of the reasons why the water cooling jars are found to be decorated with such Christian motifs. It is interesting that when wet the dark painted decoration of these vessels stands out more clearly on the jars than when they are dry: thus the visibility of the motifs depends on the water they contain or when they are wet from dipping.

Thus the vessels were more than functional 'water coolers'; the vessels themselves and the motifs they were decorated with, together with the water they contained served as symbols of their religion for these people. The images are unlikely to have represented apotropaic images as the crosses on doorways may have been (Maguire 1990, 218) since the images are various and the repertoire has more breadth than crosses alone. The combination of motifs on individual vessels suggests a strongly perceived link between water and life and represents a metaphor for Christ as the source of life in Christianity. Maguire has argued that textiles which portray creatures from earth, sea and air represent more than illustrations, and that they were '… magical amulets intended to attract the prosperity that they evoked' (Maguire 1990, 217). The consideration of the motifs in such ways demonstrates something of the significance of the act of drinking from these vessels for their users.

Conclusion

The analysis of the ceramics from the Level 1 deposits at Kilise Tepe revealed that a significant proportion of the material from the assemblage consisted of plain and painted storage vessels and cooking pots. Large *pithoi* and amphorae also made up a significant part of the assemblage. Imported fine wares represented a very small proportion of the total ceramic assemblage, and significantly more Hellenistic than Late Roman fine ware items were recovered. Large numbers of ceramic roof tiles were discovered from the area around the church, as well as in other grid squares suggesting that buildings frequently had tiled roofs in the Late Roman period. These tiles were made of the same local fabric as the majority of the pottery from the site. This pottery bears a characteristic painted decoration found previously only by Gough at Alahan and Dağ Pazarı.

The published ceramics from the site are presented by fabric and form and may be examined by provenance also. Detailed examination of the statistical relationships between groups of sherds and features at the site might be beneficial both to examine the chronological relationship between sherds of different ware groups and the variation of the assemblage between features. However, owing to the large amount of disturbance to upper levels caused by ploughing of the site and the lack of floors identified during the excavation not all units from the site would be suitable for such analysis; time constraints have prevented such analysis in this study.

Relationships between wares were clearly visible in the assemblage. The co-occurrence of Late Roman Cypriot cooking pots, Late Roman 1 amphorae, fine ware bowls and painted vessels in the same contexts was the most apparent. Unlike at Anemurium few frying pans were found and the cooking vessels mostly consisted of rounded pots which would have been placed directly into open fires for the cooking of casserole or stew-type meals. Imported amphorae may have held wine or oil, and large *pithoi* would have been used for the storage of water or seasonal food stuffs. The lack of fine ware bowls provides evidence for not only a lack of trade to Kilise Tepe, but also a difference in everyday domestic life between those at this rural settlement and those living at coastal towns. A similar lack of bowls in the painted 'Monastic Ware' fabric was noted at Alahan (Williams 1985, 42). Epigraphic evidence and excavation at Alahan demonstrates that there was accommodation for guests and living quarters from which amphorae, cooking and fine table wares were excavated. This may be interpreted to suggest that perhaps wooden bowls were used, or that food preparation and eating habits required the use of comparatively few plain ware bowls. Many of the painted vessels had flat bases and single handles; this may be taken to suggest that these vessels were used during meal times. Their motifs provide important evidence for the occurrence of Christian symbolism on everyday objects as well as ecclesiastical vessels. The painted repertoire was applied to a variety of sizes of different closed shapes including those most likely to have been used for a single drink as well as much larger vessels which were probably for water storage.

These various kinds of domestic utensils were recovered from buildings in the NW corner, the I14–M14 strip excavation and from N12a. Certain of these assemblages e.g. 1501, 4393 and 4395 suggested *in situ* deposits had been excavated, whereas other units such as pit P95/33 (1626) represent refuse disposal features. Unfortunately because of the lack of floors identified during the excavation and the fact that no entire buildings were excavated it is difficult to use the ceramics to identify the function of various parts of structures at Kilise Tepe. Nevertheless the ceramic assemblage adds a significant contribution to the narrative of Early Byzantine life at the settlement.

Character and description of the Late Roman and Byzantine ceramic corpus

Introduction

The sherds in the catalogue have been ordered according to the groups discussed in this section, which is organized according to fabric groups and within fabric groups by form and provenance.

Late Roman Red Slipped Table Wares

A very small number of Late Roman Red Slipped Ware vessels were excavated at Kilise Tepe. All excavated examples are listed below. In addition, certain examples were recovered during the 1994 surface survey of the mound and were published by Dominique Collon (1995, 158–60).

Late Roman C Ware. Variations of Hayes' Form 3
(1008–14)

Late Roman C Ware (Phocaean Ware) Form 3 was the most common Late Roman fine ware vessel type found at Kilise Tepe. The pieces have a fine orange fabric and orange/red slip. Certain sherds contain white lime inclusions which caused pitting on the surface of the vessels. The characteristic flanged rim of Form 3 is very common in the eastern Mediterranean during the Late Roman period. It has been noted in deposits from other sites in the region including Alahan (Williams

1985, 38), Anemurium (Williams 1989, figs. 22–3) as well as Antioch (Waagé 1948, 52, pl. XI, esp. nos. 941, 943). This form may be dated to before the middle of the fifth century AD (Williams 1989, 46). She cites the reports from Conimbriga and Corinth and dates it *c.* AD 400–25. This is somewhat earlier than Hayes's attribution of the form to the second half of the fifth and first half of the sixth century; it does not occur before AD 400 (Hayes 1972, 329–38). **1009** was found in unit 6009 above a surface associated with Level Ic in K18d in the narrow trench excavated to examine the relationship between the NW corner and the church.

*Cypriot Red Slip Ware Form 2. Waagé's Late Roman D Ware (**1015–16**)*

It has been suggested that this fine ware may have been produced on Cyprus where it is found in greater quantities than other Late Roman slip wares (Hayes 1972, 385). At Anemurium, it was the most commonly found of the Late Roman fine wares (Williams 1989, 28). The production of CRSW is thought to have started in the fourth century and continued until the eighth century AD. Its distribution primarily by sea has been suggested because of its discovery at a number of coastal towns and cities at and near Cyprus e.g. Anemurium, but in much smaller quantities inland.

At Kilise Tepe relatively few sherds of Cypriot Red Slip were found; these were of the Hayes Form 2 dish. This has been dated to the late fifth/early sixth century (Williams 1989, 30). The rim of this form has grooves and the exterior of the vessel has vertical rouletting on its exterior (Hayes 1972, 373–5). Two examples of this vessel (**1015–16**) were found in (1501) in K19, and a further one in pit P94/13 (1105) in K20 (Fig. 544).

Fabric: A detailed description of the clay fabric is provided by Williams (1989, 29). The fabric is fine grained and occasionally contains very small white lime inclusions. It can vary quite considerably in colour from light red to red-brown; both the clay and slip may have a purplish tinge (Williams 1989, 29).

*Spiral burnished ware (**1017**)*

This ware was first identified at Alahan where many examples were found including an almost complete open bowl with straight sides, flat base and spiral burnishing on the interior. The characteristic decoration may be likened to Hayes ARS Form 109 (Williams 1985, 39–40). A vessel with similar decoration but much poorer-quality clay was found at Anemurium (Williams 1989, 43: nos. 248–9).

The fabric is very fine and dark red in colour with no visible impurities. The exterior is coated in a very fine smooth and shiny slip. The interior is less shiny and decorated with characteristic burnishing. Only one sherd of this ware was found at Kilise Tepe (**1017**: Fig.

545). It is important to note that this sherd was found in 2343 — one of the best stratified Level I units — along with a large amount of painted Fabric 1 sherds.

*Other fine wares (**1018–26**)*

The following fine ware types are not provided; they are probably all of Hellenistic date. **1021–2** may be significant for the dating of 1626, the fill of P95/33. This pit contained many almost complete cooking vessels (including **1437–41**). **1021** has a red slip and may be compared to Anemurium fig. 16:201 (Williams 1989, 201). **1024–6** are sherds of shallow open bowls with orange fabric and forms typical of the Hellenistic period.

The pit may have been contaminated and therefore this material may not be contemporary with the cooking pots. It also contained painted sherds **1159–60**.

Plain and plain painted wares

Fabrics 1a and 1b

Introduction

The largest group of Level 1 sherds was made of a fabric presumed to be local.[5] The group exhibits a range of forms similar to those which were discovered at Alahan and Dağ Pazarı by M. Gough. The group is characterized in particular by a large number of vessels which have painted decoration. Gough named these vessels Monastic Ware (Williams 1985, 41), a somewhat confusing name given that only one of the two sites where it was found is considered to have been a monastery. After preliminary analysis in the 1994 season, similar painted material from Kilise Tepe was reported to be 'non-micaceous' and was contrasted with that from Alahan which was reported to have been micaceous (Baker *et al.* 1995, 157). The analysis of Level 1 material from all five years of excavations at Kilise Tepe confirmed that the fabric of this Kilise Tepe fabric was normally macroscopically non-micaceous. However, certain sherds were micaceous. This was seen as a potentially important differentiation to make, so each sherd, if otherwise considered to be of Fabric 1, was classed Fabric 1a if it was non-micaceous, and Fabric 1b if micaceous. The mica from these sherds was readily distinguishable in good light. The proportion of mica in the sherds was variable, to such an extent that in some the mica was very clear, but in others perhaps only one or two 'glints' were apparent on the whole sherd. A range of these sherds was tested by Carl Knappett (see above, p. 272). The difference between sherds at Kilise Tepe with and without mica may or may not be significant; it was made nevertheless.

The high proportion of sherds from closed painted vessel forms recovered during the preliminary sorting process was due to the fact that some vessels exhibit a large number of features considered to be 'diagnostic', including painted, gouged and ribbed decoration. Rims, handles and bases of other forms including tiles, which are listed in the catalogue demonstrate the range of products received at Kilise Tepe in this fabric (see Fig. 575: 1118, 1134, 1135, 1158, d205).

Fabric: The fabric varied in colour. It was generally a light orange/apricot colour; but could vary towards yellow-orange, yellow-cream and could be slightly green-cream. It was a hard well-fired, smooth fabric, which fractured to produce smooth breaks. Macroscopic analysis of the breaks suggests that it varied slightly between sherds, but usually contained white inclusions less than 0.5 mm and larger dark sub-angular inclusions which were normally red, red/brown or cream. These tended to be up to about 0.5 mm in size, but did occur in some pieces up to 1 mm. When the fabric was fired cream/green these inclusions tended to be very dark brown/black. In certain sherds, particularly those from some large vessels, the red inclusions were much denser and larger; this fabric was called 4A during processing. The fabric — though quite different — may be considered to represent similar clay and inclusions but mixed to produce a much coarser fabric e.g. Fig. 575, d205 (a sherd not in the catalogue, from 3200) which demonstrates the variation in colour of both the fabric and the inclusions depending on firing conditions. The fabric may vary from the orange/apricot colour with red inclusions to a much paler cream/green colour with black inclusions. The only consistent macroscopic difference between the Fabric 1a and Fabric 1b sherds was that mica was visible in those recorded as Fabric 1b.

Forms: As was found at Alahan (Williams 1985), a variety of forms were found in this fabric. The Kilise Tepe material included tiles and *pithoi*, amphorae and smaller closed vessels and cups. Open vessels were unusual; an example is the large basin from P94/13 (1105) — the same pit contained a sherd of Cypriot Red Slip (see above). All vessels were wheel thrown. Handles, where horizontal, were round in cross section (except on *pithoi* where they were grooved — see below), and occurred on the bellies of closed vessels. Where vertical, e.g. on amphorae, they had a characteristic irregular sub-oval profile and were 'pulled' by the potter between thumb and first finger (see **1038**ff.).

Surface treatment: Ribbing or corrugation must have been added by the potter while the vessel was on a wheel and usually consisted of convex ribbing around the belly of closed vessels. This ribbing was mostly rounded, but very occasionally was angular. It was added with some form of tool, rather than with fingers. A tool, probably wooden, was also used to smooth the lower part of the vessel. This burnished the surface slightly but also sometimes caused striations as the inclusions were dragged across the surface (e.g. **1096**).

Decoration: Gouging was applied to the shoulders of certain vessels presumably when they were no more than 'leather hard'. Normally this treatment was given to closed vessels which also had ribbing around their bellies. The gouges tended to have been sharply cut up to 2–4 mm deep and about 5 mm wide and run vertically on the shoulder of the pot, either in straight lines down almost the whole of the length of the shoulder (see **1234–9**: Fig. 563) or in shorter lines extending from a central longer gouge to produce a motif resembling a leaf (see **1231–2**: Fig. 563). Gouging was also used to create cross motifs which were then embellished with further painted decoration (see **1185–6**: Fig. 555).

Painting was the most common form of decoration found on vessels of this fabric. Red/purple paint was applied directly onto the fabric of the pot, normally on the shoulder; but also on the lip of some rims and on certain handles. There was no slip applied to the fabric prior to the addition of the painted decoration. The painted decoration consists of a variety of motifs. Typically these consisted of three separate styles: figurative motifs, loose connected spiral motifs and broad painted lines. The spiral motifs were often associated with dots and wavy lines; the figurative designs included representations of foliage, animals and fish.

Broad painted lines were found on body sherds, most notably from beneath a floor in the church in L16 — (5633–5) — but were also found elsewhere including 2343 and 9658 and 9659. Larger vessels did not have designs and motifs painted on them, but were decorated with both incised lines and brush painted splashes (e.g. **1265–6**: Fig. 565).

Fabric 1 sherds (including painted sherds) were most common in J18b, J19a, J19b, J19d, K18a, K18b, K19 in the NW Corner and in L14a and L14b in the I14a–M14b trench and in N12a. In the NW Corner these sherds are associated with the fill inside the phase Ic building in K18b and phase Id building in K19 and L19. Material was also recovered from the courtyard area in J19, J18 and K18. This included material from packing deposits lying below the ash layers in the courtyard — 2339, 2343, 2350 — but also at least one unit of ash deposit 2337 and a single sherd (**1211**) located in a pit P97/37 (2338) which cut both the ash layers and the packing deposits below. **1211** with its 'wavy' line may therefore be one of the latest pieces of painted pottery from Kilise Tepe. In style it compares well with **1212** from 4308 in K18a.

Parallels: The best parallels are those from Alahan (Williams 1985). Parallels further afield include the 'dark on light' painted wares from Khirbat al-Karak (Delougaz & Haines 1960, pl. 37). Red-brown/purplish-black wares from Carthage were normally applied to closed vessel forms employing naturalistic (birds and foliage) and also geometric motifs. These have been dated to the first half of the sixth century *c*. 500–535 (Fulford & Peacock 1984, 225). At Carthage 'confused patterns' are thought to be later than those where birds, leaves and lattice motifs occur — this would not disagree with the evidence from Kilise Tepe. Jars and basins with red painted motifs including spirals, wavy lines and trees are found in northern Israel, Jordan and Syria in contexts dating eighth and ninth centuries (Sauer & Magness 1997, 476). Painted wares are apparently uncommon in most Late Roman and Byzantine sites except parts of Egypt (Hayes 1997, 474).

Complete vessel — juglet **1027**
(Alahan Form 31, Williams 1985, 45)
This is a closed vessel form, with a disc base, rounded body, sloping shoulders and straight neck (Fig. 546). Surviving rims would suggest that, from a vertical neck, the rim would have sloped outwards at an angle, and would have been sometimes slightly pendulous. A handle was positioned at the bottom of the sloping shoulder, usually rounded and aligned horizontally. Some sherds show that certain vessels had a small raised 'collar', a couple of millimetres high running around the base of the neck.

Decoration: The belly of the vessels was decorated with rounded corrugations/ribbing. These appear to have been made with a tool rather than fingers, but in general they were soft undulating convex corrugations, not angular. Probably the most characteristic feature of the vessel decoration (**1027**) was red/brown paint consisting of horizontal stripes around the rim and neck and raised collar of the vessel with splashes on the shoulder. **1027** has the pale cream/green fabric and black inclusions; it would seem that 'brown' paint seems to occur on fabric fired in this way.

Vessels fired to a pink/orange colour tend to have purple/red colour paint. The form is different from the slightly larger closed vessel form **1094** which has spiral decoration on the shoulder. Unfortunately the small number of complete vessels reconstructed means that a thorough comparison or development of forms is not possible. The diagnostic forms and features of the sherds are thus presented.

Fabric 1: rims, necks and associated handles

The Fabric 1 rims have been grouped into types based on form.

Type 1 (*1027–34*)

This rim form is found on vessels with vertical necks and varying sized rim diameters including **1027**. On the interior, the rim continues the line of the neck vertically, on the exterior the rim slopes outwards, becoming thicker, and is sometimes pendant. Rims of this form are found on closed vessels in varying sizes from small juglets e.g. **1027**, to much larger vessels e.g. **1032**.

Type 1 rim variants (*1035–41*)

Variants of Type 1 are less regular in shape and occur on vessels with a larger internal diameter *c.* 8 cm.

Type 2 rims (*1042–52*)

These rims belong to relatively small vessels. Vessels of this size vary in form and could be subdivided into more types, especially for example **1042–4**. The majority, however, are plain in shape and either vertical or flaring; most have handles, often with knobs connecting to the rim.

Type 3 rims with heavy knobbed handles (*1053–62*)

This group is represented by broken handle fragments originating from storage vessels which had large amphora-like vertical strap handles attached to the top of relatively thin and undecorated rims. A raised knob of clay is often found filling the gap between the handle and the rim; sometimes this is free-standing e.g. **1054** (Fig. 548). In **1060**, a particularly heavy handle, there are two little knobs flanking the main one (Fig. 549). These vessels are often decorated by irregular patches of red wash paint on the handles and exterior.

Type 4 externally thickened rims (*1063–82*)

These rims are found at the top of the necks of closed vessels. They tend to be relatively uncomplicated in form, becoming thicker on the outside near the tops of their rims. These rims tend to be decorated with a thin wash of red or red/brown paint and sometimes with ribbing or painted lines. Where found, handles are placed just below the level of the rim.

Type 5 handles not found attached to rims (*1083–8*)

These handles must have been placed slightly lower on the necks of vessels than those of Type 2, but may be placed no differently from those of Type 4.

Type 6 rarer rims of closed vessels (*1089–93*)

A number of rims were found in Fabric 1 without other parallels from the site. Their occurrence usually in similar units to the better-attested forms, or from units near the surface would support their attribution to the rest of the painted pottery group, but their paucity in numbers and variety in shape casts some doubt on their attribution.

Fabric 1: bases and lower bodies

The majority of bases made in Fabric 1 seem to have been made in different sizes showing little variation in shape in spite of apparent differentiation in the form of the upper parts of the vessels. The material from Alahan complements this picture (Williams 1985).

Disc bases (*1094–106*)

The most common form was the disc base. This was found in a variety of different diameters and thicknesses, but essentially changed little. The flat bases of these vessels suggest that the smaller examples may have been used on flat surfaces e.g. tables.

Ring bases (*1107–8*)

These bases are very similar to the disc bases. It would appear that the vessels would have been turned over and tooled to produce the ring foot. N.B. also **1027**.

Other bases (*1109–11*)

Two unusual forms, **1109**, show clear evidence of the same red painted decoration found on other pieces. **1110** represents an unusual — possibly concave base — form. Four other forms of base, made from Fabric 1, were recognized at Kilise Tepe; most represent variations of ring base.

Fabric 1: body sherds

Body sherds are catalogued here because of the decoration found on them. This is perhaps the most striking part of many of the painted vessels. The styles of decoration and painted motifs are grouped as far as possible into similar types. The decoration itself mostly appears on the shoulders of closed vessels.

It sometimes ran over the top of the corrugations on vessel bellies. The centres of these spirals sometimes contained dots and the 'triangular' space between the tops of the spirals was also often filled with dots, and the space below with wavy lines. A horizontal painted line ran around the base of the neck. Where the vessel had a 'raised collar' the collar was often painted and can be seen at the tops of certain body sherds e.g. **1145–6** (Figs. 552–3).

An attempt has been made to organize the body sherds into squares and within squares into units, so that although the sherds are organized into types, it is also to some extent possible to see their concentrations in certain contexts within the site.

*Painted spirals (**1112–72**)*
Spirals were the most commonly found motif on the painted Fabric 1 vessels (Figs. 554, 562, 573). They are loose running spirals which were painted freehand, and run around the shoulders of closed vessels. Very often dots are painted in the space between the spirals. The paint varies in colour from a red-brown to a red-purple colour and is painted directly onto the vessel biscuit, with no slip applied beforehand. When used to decorate vessels with motifs the paint is relatively thick and the motifs clear.

*Painted birds and fish (**1173–82**, **1199**)*
Fabric 1 vessels were also found painted with representations of birds and fish (Figs. 556–8). These have been found on vessels from Alahan also. Birds were most frequently found.

There was no apparent difference between the fabrics of the vessels painted with these motifs as opposed to the other types. These motifs were also painted on the shoulder area of the vessels usually above a ribbed belly.

*Crosses and painted foliage (**1183–99**)*
A relatively small proportion of the painted motifs are crosses. The most unusual within the group from Kilise Tepe and one of the best-preserved vessel parts is **1183**. This was found in 1501, a unit which had one of the largest concentrations of Fabric 1 material as well as other Late Roman imported material (e.g. **1010–11**, **1017**, **1319**, **1344**). The motifs were painted on the shoulders of the vessels as with other motifs. Although the fabric of **1183** is standard Fabric 1, it is unusual that the vessel has painted circles with motifs inside — no other decoration like this was found at Kilise Tepe. Other sherds decorated with painted crosses were found associated with painted foliage and stars e.g. **1188** (Fig. 559). Painted crosses were found at Alahan (Williams 1985, fig. 6 nos. 44–5).

Gouges forming crosses (**1185–6**) were edged with further incised lines and the interior of the gouged area was painted (Fig. 555).

Various other fragments with painted foliage were recovered, only one example preserves foliage with part of a bird (**1199**: Fig. 557).

Occasionally these sherds were found with lattice decoration e.g. **1198**.

*Linear patterns and dribbled decoration (**1200–204**)*
1200 bears another unusual but distinctive form of decoration found within 1501 (Fig. 561). This vessel is painted with wavy lines which undulate in an apparently haphazard way around its shoulder crossing over each other. They tend to be larger on the right-hand side and thin to points towards the left so that they almost resemble snakes. The strokes of the brush suggest that they were executed by someone with their left hand.

In addition to the quite definite painted lines of **1200**, there is a group of vessels onto which paint seems to have been poured. The paint itself dribbles and runs sometimes down the pot e.g. **1203** but also around the pot e.g. **1202** as if the vessel itself was picked up and paint allowed to run around it.

*Other forms of painted decoration (**1205–12**)*
This group shows a variety of different forms of decoration, painted mostly with a thin brush.

*Broad painted lines (**1213–28**)*
A distinctive group of sherds made of Fabric 1 is characterized by its broad painted lines. The group is not entirely homogeneous as the thickness of paint and the breadth of the painted lines varies. The paint of certain vessels e.g. **1218** and **1220** tends to be thinner than that used to paint the motifs discussed above. The paint used for these lines may be described better as a 'wash'. It varies in thickness, and often bears the marks of bristles.

Little is known about the form of the vessels that bore this decoration as sufficient pieces were not saved in the initial sorting procedure to facilitate reconstruction.

Certain of these sherds come from relatively early deposits. The most important was the group which was found within the matrix and beneath the plaster floor of the church in L16 e.g. **1214–15**, **1217–19**. This floor was laid between the apse and the east wall of the Early Byzantine Church units 5633–4 with which it is thought to be contemporary. These sherds cannot therefore be considered later in date than the floor. Sherds of this type (**1216**, **1218**) were also found in 2343 a deposit containing one of the largest concentrations of painted Fabric 1 material including those with spirals (e.g. **1150**).

The best-preserved vessel with this kind of wash decoration also has handles with a relatively distinctive profile (**1220**: Figs. 564a–b). This particular vessel lay immediately below the topsoil but set against the south exterior wall of the narthex of the Early Byzantine church in 4403. This would suggest that it post-dated the construction of the Early Byzantine church and *may* have been contemporary with its use.

*Gouged, incised and stamped decoration (**1229–46**)*
Various sherds were discovered with gouges cut into them (Fig. 563). Other than those featuring gouged crosses (discussed above) sherds with gouges are not normally found with painted decoration but note **1237–8**, **1240**). Gouges tend to be found on the shoulders of vessels and to be about 3 mm deep. They either run vertically down the shoulder of the vessel e.g. **1235** or at a slight angle e.g. **1230–32** possibly representing a leaf. The only sure gouged representation of a leaf was that of **1245** from a Fabric 1 *pithos*. A single example of a leaf motif made from inscribed lines was found on **1242**. Gouges occur drawn in groups of parallel lines offset at angles to each other forming triangular and diamond-shaped patterns e.g. **1240–41**. Incised, rather than gouged, diamond-shaped decoration is found on **1243**. Also found in K18 was **1244**, a distinctive sherd from a large storage jar which not only has incised combed lines on it, but also small lumps of clay applied onto the surface of the vessel over the joins of the combed lines. **1246** was the only sherd to show evidence of stamped decoration in the form of small square dots stamped in curved lines on a sherd with unusual black wash.

*Fabric 1 handles (**1247–58**)*
Horizontal handles were placed on the upper bellies of the small closed storage vessels with ribbing and painted decoration (Fig. 560). The handles were applied over the ribbing before the vessels were painted. This form of handle occurs on vessels painted with motifs and with 'wash' decoration (**1250–51**).

Small vertical handles, as on **1027**, were also present. These were painted both lengthways as **1254** and with short stripes across the handle, as in **1255**. Horizontal handles with rounded profiles were also found with stripes. All the handles bearing stripes came from L14.

*Large storage jars and pithos rims (**1259–79**)*
The most numerous form for storage vessels was that typified by **1261–6**. The rims of these closed vessels were externally thickened and had an internal diameter of 17–18 cm. The best preserved of them was **1262** from 3002 in K14a (Fig. 566). Although **1265–6** had similar rims, they had distinctive decoration not found on the other vessels (Fig. 565).

1260, **1267–8** were also of similar form and scale (Fig. 567). They may belong to a similar repertoire to each other. **1270–72**, and **1277–9** were all less common forms only occurring once, their dating is uncertain; **1279** was found with the near complete cooking vessels in 1626. **1273–6**, although decorated differently from each other, appear to have some degree of consistency in their internal diameters, rim forms, place of decoration and their provenance (which would appear to be Late Roman/Early Byzantine units).

*Fabric 1 lid (**1280**)*
This example was the only Fabric 1 lid recovered during the excavations. It is not completely preserved but is a typical Late Roman saucer-shaped form e.g. No. 35 from Alahan (Williams 1985, 46, fig. 5) and Anemurium (Williams 1989, figs. 40–41).

*Fabric 1 tiles (**1463–9**)*
Very large quantities of tiles were recovered during the excavation of the Level 1 deposits. These tiles

Figure 260. *Fragments of Byzantine tiles: 1468b, 1468a; 1467, 1467, 1464.*

Figure 261. *Fragments of Byzantine tiles with moulded curve in corners: 1469b, 1466, 1469a; 1469c.*

had two main forms: *tegulae* and *imbrices*. The *tegulae* were rectangular in shape with raised borders around the exterior (Fig. 260). The borders sometimes had a moulded curve in one corner — this may have been decorational (Fig. 261). The *imbrices* were U-shaped tiles which tapered slightly from one end to the other (**1463**). The *imbrices* would have bridged the gap over the *tegulae* thus preventing water from penetrating the roof between *tegulae*. The *tegulae* drawn were found in L14 and are typical of those from Kilise Tepe.

*Fabric 1 large storage jar/pithos handles (**1281–8**)*
Large *pithos* handles were found to have gouges or twisted folds in them (Fig. 566). A *pithos* handle with traces of red paint (L16/16) was used to support the head of the woman buried in a grave to the east of the church (see p. 195). It is not possible to say whether the vessel from which the handle originated would have dated from the same period as the woman (twelfth–thirteenth century) but its context is nevertheless very interesting.

*Fabric 2c (**1289–1307**)*
Diagnostic sherds representing a number of different forms were found in relatively sound Level 1 contexts. This was a hard pale buff fabric, rough to the touch, but with smooth fracture (Fig. 575: **1291**). The fabric has a fine matrix; most sherds were well sorted, with sparse red and grey inclusions and moderate white inclusions all angular and less than 0.5 mm.

Forms included rims and bases of closed vessels not dissimilar to those found in Fabric 1. However, rims of open bowls in this fabric may be considered important as they were not found in Fabric 1.

*Fabric 2h (**1308–17**)*
This was a hard smooth fabric that fractured with a smooth break (Fig. 575: **1311**). It was usually a cream colour but could be brown/cream/green. The clay was very fine and well sorted; tiny white and black inclusions were just visible to the eye.

A variety of different forms were found in this fabric. They tended to be found in similar contexts to the Fabric 1 material, but consisted of different types of forms and decoration. Two open vessels were recovered **1312–13**.

Imported amphorae

A relatively small number of imported amphorae were recovered from the site. The fabrics and forms of these vessels clearly stood out from the local material.

*Fabric 3a: Eastern Mediterranean Type Amphorae (Late Roman 1) (**1318–32**)*
This is the most common form of Late Roman amphora and has been found at a large number of sites in the Mediterranean. Williams lists its occurrence in a number of different amphora typologies including: Anemurium Type B; Thomas's British Series type B(ii), Dressel Type 34, Balance Type 6, Beltran Lloris Form 82, Scorpan (1975) Type B (Williams 1989, 95). LRA 1 are discussed by Van Alfen (1996), Hayes (1980, 379, fig. 15), and Peacock & Williams (1986, 185–7, Class 44); they represent the equivalent of Riley's Late Roman Type 1 from Benghazi.

The fabric has a very characteristic gritty feel owing to the large number of angular inclusions. These tend to be well sorted, measuring *c.* 0.5 mm and occurring in black, brown, red and white colours. Some sherds were micaceous. The fabric reflects the geomorphology of the eastern Mediterranean (Rautman *et al.* 1999, 389) but the form occurs in different fabrics, three of which have been analysed petrographically (Rautman *et al.* 1999, 379).

No complete vessels were recovered but the shape is well known. The rim and handle forms are relatively distinctive: the rims are rounded sometimes with a collar (**1319**) and the handles are characterized by the lines running down their lengths which give them an angular profile. Body sherds have both wide and narrow ridging (Fig. 568). **1331** suggested an internal vessel diameter of *c*. 28 cm. Examples were found at both Alahan and Anemurium (Williams 1985, 51; 1989, 95).

Carthage Late Roman Amphora 3 also known as British Biv (Peacock 1984, 120–21) (**1334**)
Late Roman Amphora 3 spike. The example from Kilise Tepe 1334 has a phalliform toe, which is hollow, with a decorative hole in the tip. It was classed as decorative because the base was sealed behind the hole on the inside. The toe is ribbed on the exterior. The fabric has abundant silt-sized silver mica, as well as white and opaque inclusions and is purplish red/brown in colour. It was sampled for thin sectioning by Knappett (see p. 272). A close parallel was published by Robinson (1959, pl. 41, M373) in a late sixth-century deposit from layer XIII of the Athenian Agora and a second more complete example came from a sixth-century deposit P18:2 (1959, 119; pl. 40, P12861).

Examples of this form have also been published from Ayasoluk (Parman 1989, 284, fig. 7b; Delougaz & Haines 1960, pl. 38, no. 10; pl. 54 no. 18).

Anemurium Amphora Type A (Williams 1989, 91–4)
Mid Roman Amphora 4 (Riley, 1979, 186–7) (**1335–6**)
The amphorae of this type had characteristic handles.

> They are round or oval in cross section and have one deep longitudinal groove in the centre of the upper surface dividing the handle into two distinct rolls. At the point where the handle changes direction it is pinched in on both sides to form a depression for a fingerhold (Williams 1989, 92).

Two such handles were found at Kilise Tepe, **1335–6** (Fig. 569). They were made in fabric also noted at Anemurium (Williams 1989, 91).

This form is common in Rough Cilicia and was found in large quantities at Anemurium where it was dated to the Roman period. It was thought to date from the first to the fourth century AD. The latest dateable deposits are associated with coins of the third and early fourth century (Williams 1989, 92). It is possible that amphora spike 1334 belongs to this type also.

Level 1 cooking pot fabric vessels

Introduction
The catalogue of cooking pots is organized according to form and fabric, but also provides the provenance of each sherd in the form of the unit number. Discussion of individual forms will take place at the beginning of the section on each new form. Specific archaeological features with large concentrations of cooking wares e.g. 1626 pit P95/33 will be discussed below together with a general interpretation of the cooking ware material.

Cooking pot fabric descriptions
Cooking type Fabric K1 (**1337–69**)
Cooking fabric with relatively fine grained inclusions. Surface may be of orange hue with orange core, but normally surface is grey and core orange/red (Fig. 575: **1343**). The fabric is hard, relatively smooth to the touch, and has a hackly fracture. The inclusions are well sorted, less than 0.5 mm and generally contain opaque/white angular inclusions which glint when they catch the sunlight, certain sherds also have angular reddish-brown inclusions less than 0.5 mm. The vessel interiors tend to be red in colour, whereas the exteriors tend to be grey, sometimes purplish grey-brown.

Fabric K1 rims
The majority of K1 fabric sherds were from closed vessels, with everted rolled rims. Relatively thin strap handles were found attached rims. They ran horizontally from the rims before turning vertically down. It is presumed in the reconstruction drawings that the complete vessels would have had two handles — this may or may not have been the case. Two handles, however, would seem a logical necessity in view of the weight of the vessels when full and the stress that would be put on a single handle. No complete vessels of this type were recovered. Rims varied in size mostly *c*. 11–14 cm, but up to 17 cm, diameter. Sherds of this form and fabric were the most numerous of cooking vessels from Level 1 deposits. They were consistently located in the same deposits as painted vessels and with the sherds of imported Late Roman fine ware and amphorae. Parallels can be seen at Alahan (Williams 1985, fig. 9. no. 53) and on Cyprus (Catling 1972, 47 fig. 29 P433; 49, fig. 30 P210). This form was also found in closed well deposit *c*. seventh century at Anemurium (Williams 1977, 179, no. 13) and Carthage (Fulford & Peacock 1984, 186 fig. 70, Form 37).

Sherds considered to be made of K1 fabric but which did not have rolled rims were also recovered. These were of similar relatively fine-grained cooking fabric with thin walls. A variety of characteristic rims were recovered in small numbers. The dating of these is less sure. **1363** was found in the fill of the construction trench of the Early Byzantine church. It can therefore be considered of earlier date.

A number of the cooking pots of this form have a distinctive grey colour on their exteriors, which penetrates less that 0.5 mm into the fabric. The interiors of these vessels remain the same colour as the rest of the fabric core, which suggests that the vessels were stacked during firing and that the kiln may have been 'reduced' at the end of the operation.

A harder, well-fired fine and distinctive cooking vessel, less coarse-grained fabric than K1, was **1444** which was imported from Cyprus (see below) (Williams 1985, 71; Catling 1972, 11, fig. 7, no. P96).

1357 is similar in form to Nile mud of Ptolemaic period (de Paepe & Gratien 1995, 74, no. B172).

1365 is similar to a Hellenistic basin possibly from Rhodes (Salles 1995, 410 fig. 2, no. 442) found at Kition Bamboula, Cyprus.

Cooking type Fabric K2 (**1370–87**)
This fabric varies in colour from orange to very dark brown/black (Fig. 575: **1385**). It is relatively coarse compared to Fabric

K1, containing inclusions up to 1 mm max. These inclusions are angular and red and are visible on the surface of certain pieces. The surfaces are smooth. Sherds tend to be thicker than those made of Fabric K1.

Vessels have flaring or everted rims measuring 10–13 cm in diameter. Certain examples have incised decoration below their rims. Part of only one lid was recovered in this fabric.

Cooking type Fabric K3 (**1387**)
Fabric description: This sherd has a dark red core and grey exterior, with moderate numbers of white and grey inclusions less than 0.5 mm.

This closed vessel has an externally thickened slightly flaring rim.

Cooking type Fabric K4 (**1388–95**)
This distinctive fabric is very coarse, with a large proportion of white/light brown inclusions to dark grey matrix (Fig. 575: **1392**). It is rough on the breaks and relatively brittle and friable.

The cooking vessels in this fabric have wide globular bellies and thickened rims which slope inwards so that they may support a lid. Only one lid was found in this fabric **1395**, it is shaped rather like the base of a plate so that it could fit a variety of rim diameters and has a central domed knob.

Cooking type Fabric K5 (**1396–400**)
Fabric very similar to Fabric K1, but the inclusions much more dense in K5 (Fig. 575: **1397**).

The forms of cooking pot in this fabric are also very similar to those made from K1 — and they may indeed represent merely examples made in a more coarse fabric but part of the same tradition as those of K1. Notable are the rolled rims of **1397–8**. Fabric K5 sherds are found in the same contexts as K1 sherds. The grooved handle of **1400** is particularly distinctive.

Cooking type Fabric K6 (**1401–2**)
Fabric K6 contains very small angular inclusions. The sherds were very blackened, and inclusions measured less than 0.5 mm.

Two cooking rim sherds of the same fabric but very different forms were found. **1401** has a distinctive internally thickened — almost T-shaped rim. **1402** has a slightly everted rim.

Cooking type Fabric K7 (**1403–26**)
Orange/red fabric with large angular red and white inclusions, frequent proportions of inclusions ranging in size up to 1 mm (Fig. 575: **1405**).

Cooking pots made from K7 are relatively thin walled. A variety of rim form is illustrated, the most common being slightly externally thickened or everted (**1405–18**).

1404 has an unusual and very distinctive form comprising slightly everted plain rim with an internal lip. On the exterior, it is decorated with an incised wavy line above a horizontal raised 'collar', and a second wavy line below the collar. A body sherd possibly from the shoulder of the same vessel has horizontal combing (**1405, 1408**).

Examples show handles attached both to the top of the vessels at the rims and also to their shoulders. The handles would appear to be broad and flat strap handles (**1420–21**).

Cooking type Fabric K8 (**1427**)
Fabric: Very small brown/red angular inclusions and very small black inclusions.
Form: Vertical handle attached to vessel below rim.

Cooking type Fabric K11 (**1428**)
Fabric: red/orange fabric with frequent black and white inclusions <0.5 mm and sparse white/opaque 1 mm angular inclusions.
Form: unusual rounded base, possibly domed lid?

Cooking type Fabric K12 (**1429**)
Fabric: brown/grey/green exterior with flakes of mica clearly visible, moderate numbers of white and red inclusions 0.5 mm and red/orange interior (Fig. 575: **1429**).
Form: Flat strap handle attached to the widest part of vessel belly. Only the lower part of the handle survives, this has shallow grooves incised on each side of the outer face of the strap and gouged crescent-shaped 'nicks' in the centre of handle.

Cooking type Fabric K13 (**1430–33**)
Fabric: The fabric is a coarse brown cooking fabric with characteristic frequent angular inclusions up to 1 mm.
Form: Closed cooking vessels with rims from incurving shoulder. Two rims are illustrated, **1430** has a rolled lip with a flat upper surface of the rim. **1431** has lip both interior and exterior thickened, possibly to receive a lid. Base **1432** is slightly rounded, but the fragment from **1433** suggests a flat base.

Cooking type Fabric K20 (**1434–5**)
Distinctive orange/red fabric with frequent white and red inclusions up to 2 mm visible on the interior surfaces of sherds. Figure 575: d1333 shows the cross-section of sherds from d1333, a jar with a vertical handle, which has this fabric.

1434 compares to an example from Alahan (Williams 1985, fig. 7 no. 65).

Cooking type Fabric K21 (**1436–43**)
1436–7 compare to examples found at Carthage dated to the mid sixth century (Fulford & Peacock 1984, 186, fig. 70 Form 31) (Figs. 570–72).

Other cooking fabric sherds (**1444–62**)
1444: A vessel similar to **1444** was found at Anemurium (Williams 1989, fig. 37, no. 407); another at Carthage was found in a context dating from the end of the seventh century (Hayes 1980, 378, fig. 6) — for a distribution map see Hayes (1980, 378, fig. 9.2). Also in Catling & Dikigoropoulos (1970, 45 fig. 3 no. 14, 48–9); Catling reported it from a second half of the seventh-century context (1972, 11, fig. 7 no. P96). A similar vessel was found at Nea Paphos on Cyprus at the castle by A. Megaw associated with eighth-century objects (Hayes 1980, 378, fig. 5).

1445: A vessel with similar rim but different body was found by Catling (1972, 63, fig. 36 no. P07).

1447–9: A vessel similar to Diederichs 1980, 302.

1463–9c: Tiles (see discussion above pp. 401–2).

Glazed wares

Only a very small proportion of sherds recovered during the excavation were glazed (Fig. 574). Four sherds came from topsoil in the area of the church (units 4800, 4801, 5000 and 9600); two from pits (d1378 from 4700, and a sherd from 2305).

Catalogue of pottery from Late Roman and Byzantine deposits[6]

1008 3201
Late Roman C ware (Phocaean Red Slip), Form 3, rim, open vessel; vertical lines on rim, light orange slip on inside; very fine orange fabric.
Int. rim 16, Ext. rim 18
Parallel: Hayes 1972, 329–38

1009 6009
Late Roman C ware (Phocaean Red Slip), Form 3, rim, open vessel; very thin slip on inside. Orange/red fabric with very tiny white inclusions causing pitting in surface of fabric.
Int. rim 17.2, Ext. rim 19

1010 4390
Late Roman C ware (Phocaean Red Slip), Form 3, rim, open vessel. Triple line of fine rouletting on flanged rim; no red slip visible in outside, dull slip on inside; homogeneous dark red fabric with no visible inclusions.
Int. rim 18.8, Ext. rim 20
Parallel: Late Roman C Ware, Form 3, D 13 (Hayes 1972, 332–3); Athens Agora P 27055 (Hayes 1972, 333)

1011 1501
Late Roman C ware (Phocaean Red Slip), Form 3, rim, open vessel.
Int. rim 30, Ext. rim 29
Fig. 544
Parallel: Hayes 1972, 329–38

1012 5904
Late Roman C ware (Phocaean Red Slip), Form 3, rim, open vessel; very fine orange fabric with few inclusions sparse tiny white inclusions.
Int. rim 30, Ext. rim 31.2

1013 1501
Late Roman C ware (Phocaean Red Slip), Form 3, rim, open vessel; orange slip not shiny; worn on int. of rim and ext. of flange; slight raised line below flange; very fine orange fabric, no visible inclusions except pin-prick sized white inclusions.
Int. rim 29, Ext. rim 30

1014 3017
Late Roman C ware (Phocaean Red Slip), Form 3, rim, open vessel.

1015 1501
Cypriot Red Slip Ware, rim; three grooves in rim, rouletting around exterior.
Int. rim 13, Ext. rim 14

1016 1501
Cypriot Red Slip Ware, rim; 2 grooves in rim, rouletting around ext.
Fig. 544

1017 2343
Spiral Burnished Ware, base, open vessel; spiral burnished interior, exterior base very smooth exterior, slip same red colour as core fabric; very fine homogeneous fabric, no visible inclusions.
Base di. 17
Fig. 545
Parallel: Alahan (Williams 1985, 39–40, no. 16)

1018 3606
Rim.
Int. rim 33, Ext. rim 34

1019 3304
Rim.
Int. rim 20, Ext. rim 21

1020 3314
Rim and handle.
Parallel: Cypriot Red Slip; Anemurium No. 202 (Williams 1989, 202)

1021 1626
Rim, open vessel; slip worn on exterior; no slip inside, red slip on outside; hard red fabric.
Int. rim 32.2, Ext. rim 34
Possible parallel: Cypriot Red Slip; Anemurium fig. 16: 201 (Williams 1989, 201)

1022 1626
Rim, open vessel; fine yellow fabric, purple slip inside and outside — worn on interior.
Int. rim 14, Ext. rim 16

1023 3000
Dark red slip on int., purple/brown slip on exterior uneven slip colour, blisters on surface; clay has many inclusions <0.5 mm up to a few sparse 2 mm causing blisters on the surface.
Int. rim 22, Ext. rim 23

1024 3204
Rim, open vessel; red/brown slip ext. rim and int., not shiny; very fine orange fabric with very tiny white inclusions.
Int. rim 18, Ext. rim 15.8

1025 3000
Rim, open vessel; red/slightly purple slip on int., and top of ext. of vessel; orange fabric.
Int. rim 14.4, Ext. rim 16

1026 3200
Rim, open vessel; dark red/black slip almost purple, mottled on ext.; fine orange fabric.
Int. rim 19.8, Ext. rim 22

1027 K19/479 1501+1512
1a; complete profile, closed vessel; ribbing around belly; brown painted horizontal lines on ext. neck and rim, and splashes on shoulder; light green fabric red and white inclusions <0.5 mm.
Int. rim 3.5, Ext. rim 4; Base di. 6; H. 14.5; Body di. 11.3
Fig. 546

1028 2600
1b; rim and handle, closed vessel; red paint splattered around handle; orange fabric with red inclusions 0.5 mm and white/cream inclusions <0.5 mm.
Int. rim 4.5, Ext. rim 6

1029 2343
1a rim, closed vessel; orange fabric with plain white inclusions.
Int. rim 5.6, Ext. rim 7

1030 4309
1a rim, closed vessel; red paint on rim; orange micaceous fabric with frequent tiny white inclusions and sparse grey inclusions.
Int. rim 5, Ext. rim 7.2

1031 3602
1a rim, closed vessel; red painted horizontal lines; orange fabric with brown inclusions <0.5 mm and tiny white inclusions <0.5 mm.
Int. rim 7, Ext. rim 9
Fig. 547

Chapter 31

1032   1501
1a rim, closed vessel; no individual fabric description made.
Int. rim 5, Ext. rim 8

1033   9625
1a rim; white tiny inclusions and 0.5 mm orange inclusions.
Int. rim 7.2, Ext. rim 10

1034   4302
1a rim, closed vessel; red/brown paint on rim; light brown fabric with sparse light brown inclusions 0.5 mm and sparse white inclusions <0.5 mm.
Int. rim 7, Ext. rim 9.8
Fig. 547

1035   1501
1a rim, closed vessel; light brown/orange fabric with moderate angular red inclusions 0.5 mm and tiny sparse white inclusions.
Int. rim 8, Ext. rim 11.4

1036   1605
1a rim, closed vessel; very light brown/cream fabric with moderate sparse grey inclusions 0.5 mm and moderate cream inclusions 0.5 mm.
Int. rim 8, Ext. rim 10.4

1037   4391
1a rim, closed vessel; buff fabric with sparse red inclusions 0.5 mm, white inclusions 1 mm and yellow inclusions 1–2 mm.
Int. rim 8, Ext. rim 10.4

1038   1501
1a rim and handle, closed vessel; splashed, light brown/orange paint; light orange fabric with moderate red angular inclusions 1 mm, moderate white 1 mm inclusions.

1039   9616
1a rim, closed vessel; red wash; orange fabric with tiny white inclusions, large white inclusions 1 mm and orange inclusions <2 mm.
Int. rim 8, Ext. rim 11

1040   4390
1a rim and handle, closed vessel; cream colour fabric with angular red inclusions <2 mm breaking the surface and black and white inclusions <1 mm.
Int. rim 8, Ext. rim 10.4

1041   9650
1a rim, closed vessel; dark orange/red fabric with white inclusions ranging from tiny to 0.5 mm, and red inclusions <0.5 mm.
Int. rim 12, Ext. rim 14

1042   4314
1b rim and handle; paint around rim interior; light orange fabric with frequent very light orange inclusions <1 mm, sparse grey inclusions and white inclusions visible in surface where there is blistering.
Int. rim 4, Ext. rim 5.5

1043   4393
1b rim, closed vessel; splosh red paint neck and handle; orange fabric with sparse white, grey and red inclusions <0.5 mm and sparse tiny mica.
Int. rim 5, Ext. rim 6

1044   3602
1a, rim and handle, closed vessel; dark red painted line around rim; cream colour fabric with red inclusions <0.5 mm.
Int. rim 6, Ext. rim 7.5

1045   3205
1a rim and handle, closed vessel; red/purple paint around neck and on handle, particularly handle; orange fabric with orange inclusions 0.5 mm.
Int. rim 6, Ext. rim 7

1046   3601
1a rim and handle, closed vessel; brown wash on handle and rim; pale orange fabric with light brown inclusions <0.5 mm.
Int. rim 6, Ext. rim 7

1047   3209
1b, rim and handle, closed vessel; orange fabric with moderate orange and red inclusions <0.5 mm.
Int. rim 5.5, Ext. rim 6

1048   4314
1a rim and knobbed handle, closed vessel; purple wash on ext.; coarse light orange fabric with frequent angular large red inclusions 1–2 mm and moderate white inclusions <0.5 mm.
Int. rim 7, Ext. rim 9

1049   3601
1a rim and knobbed handle; orange fabric with moderate orange and white inclusions <0.5 mm.
Int. rim 14, Ext. rim 15.5

1050   4317
1a rim and knobbed handle, closed vessel; pinkish orange fabric with sparse white inclusions <0.5 mm.
Int. rim 7, Ext. rim 8

1051   4392
1a rim, open vessel; dark red painted rim; red inclusions <0.5 mm.
Int. rim 7, Ext. rim 8.4

1052   4393
1a rim and handle; closed vessel; orange fabric with moderate orange inclusions and moderate tiny white/cream inclusions.
Int. rim 7, Ext. rim 7.8

1053   1500
1a, rim and knobbed handle, closed vessel; orange-brown wash over outside, dribble on inside; light orange fabric with moderate white angular 2 mm inclusions, abundant orange/pale red angular inclusions.
Int. rim 6, Ext. rim 6.6
Fig. 548

1054   2305
Rim and knobbed handle, closed vessel; red wash over surface.
Int. rim 6, Ext. rim 8.8
Fig. 548

1055   9671
5b rim and knobbed handle, closed vessel; red wash on exterior; grey core and red exterior, moderate tiny white inclusions and elongated flat black inclusions and cream inclusions <0.5 mm.
Int. rim 7, Ext. rim 8
Fig. 548

1056   4393
1a rim and knobbed handle, closed vessel; abundant white inclu-

sions 1–2 mm and frequent red inclusions.
Fig. 548

1057   1500
1a rim and knobbed handle, closed vessel; orange fabric with red angular inclusions <1 mm and white inclusions <0.5 mm.
Int. rim 7, Ext. rim 7.8

1058   3601
1a rim and handle, closed vessel; purple/brown paint; moderate orange fabric with red/brown inclusions <0.5 mm.
Int. rim 7, Ext. rim 8.2

1059   3100
1a rim and handle, closed vessel; dark brown wash paint on interior rim and ext. below rim and handle top; light green/cream fabric with sparse light orange and grey inclusions <0.5 mm.
Int. rim 10.5, Ext. rim 13

1060   3400
1b rim and triple knobbed handle, closed vessel; handle has triple knob below rim and red paint on handle; orange fabric with frequent red inclusions <0.5 mm and sparse white inclusions <0.5 mm and frequent grey inclusions <0.5 mm.
Int. rim 11, Ext. rim 12
Fig. 549

1061   4391
4a rim and knobbed handle, closed vessel; red paint on top of handle; coarse orange fabric with frequent angular red inclusions 1–2 mm, white inclusions 0.5 mm.
Int. rim 10
Fig. 548

1062   2343
1a rim and knobbed handle, closed vessel; traces of red/brown paint; orange fabric with red up to 3 mm and tiny sparse white/opaque inclusions.
Int. rim 12
Fig. 548

1063   1500
1a rim, open vessel; red wash on outside; light brown fabric with tiny black inclusions, red inclusions <1 mm and linear white inclusions.
Int. rim 10, Ext. rim 12.2

1064   1501
1a rim and handle, closed vessel; orange brown paint on rim and handle; cream colour fabric with moderate white inclusions sparse red inclusions and moderate black inclusions, silver plate-like micaceous particles.
Int. rim 8, Ext. rim 9.4

1065   9616
1a rim, closed vessel; ribbing; horizontal red painted line; orange fabric with tiny white inclusions, large angular orange inclusions up to 2 mm and tiny holes.
Int. rim 8, Ext. rim 10.2

1066   4308
1d rim, closed vessel; ribbing; brown speckled paint on ext.; orange fabric with orange inclusions 1 mm and frequent white inclusions <0.5 mm causing fabric to laminate.
Int. rim 10, Ext. rim 12.8

1067   4320
1a rim, closed vessel; dark red paint on ext.; light orange/cream fabric with frequent white inclusions <1 mm, mostly <0.5 mm.
Int. rim 7.5, Ext. rim 11

1068   4301
1a rim, closed vessel; ribbing below rim; purple paint on ext.; orange fabric with orange inclusions <1 mm and white inclusions <0.5 mm.
Int. rim 9.8, Ext. rim 12
Fig. 547

1069   3602
1a rim, closed vessel; faint raised (not incised) horizontal lines below rim; very light orange fabric with brown-red inclusions <0.5 mm.
Int. rim 11.8, Ext. rim 14
Fig. 547

1070   3423
1a, rim and handle, closed vessel; light brown wash over handle and ext. of rim; very light orange/cream-colour fabric with red inclusions <0.5 mm and sparse light brown/grey inclusions <0.5 mm.
Int. rim 13, Ext. rim 14.6

1071   1567
1a rim, closed vessel; ribbing below rim; worn red paint on ext. rim and over ribbing; orange fabric with red and orange inclusions up to 1 mm, cream inclusions <0.5 mm cream inclusions.
Int. rim 14.2, Ext. rim 17
Fig. 547

1072   1500
1b rim and handle, closed vessel; purple/red wash; orange fabric with large red inclusions <1.5 mm and tiny white inclusions.
Int. rim 12, Ext. rim 14

1073   3602
1a, rim and handle, closed vessel; red/brown wash over handle and rim ext.; very pale brown/orange fabric with moderate sub-rounded brown inclusions <0.5 mm and sparse white inclusions 0.5 mm.
Int. rim 15, Ext. rim 17
Fig. 549

1074   3205
1a rim and handle, closed vessel; orange fabric with moderate orange/red inclusions 1-2 mm and tiny white inclusions 0.5 mm.
Int. rim 17, Ext. rim 20

1075   3202
1a rim, closed vessel; ribbing; purple/red paint.
Int. rim 14.2, Ext. rim 17

1076   1500
1a rim, closed vessel; black/brown wash; light orange fabric with orange angular inclusions <1 mm, and cream-colour inclusions <1 mm.
Int. rim 14, Ext. rim 17

1077   3012
1a rim, closed vessel; light brown paint wash; light orange fabric with moderate orange/red inclusions <0.5 mm and sparse white inclusions <0.5 mm.
Int. rim 15.6, Ext. rim 18
Fig. 547

1078   3000
1a rim, closed vessel; dark brown wash on top of rim; light brown fabric with sparse inclusions: opaque 0.5 mm inclusions, orange/brown 0.5 mm inclusions and white/cream inclusions <0.5 mm.
Int. rim 10.4, Ext. rim 13

1079 3207
1a rim, closed vessel; orange fabric with red and brown inclusions.
Int. rim 13, Ext. rim 14.6

1080 1501
1a rim.
Int. rim 13, Ext. rim 16

1081 1501
1a rim, closed vessel; ribbing; purple paint.
Int. rim 14.2, Ext. rim 17.1

1082 4302
1a rim and handle, closed vessel; ribbing below rim; orange fabric with common orange 0.5 mm inclusions and white inclusions less than 0.5 mm.
Int. rim 17.2, Ext. rim 22

1083 4393
1b knobbed handle; closed vessel; orange fabric with red inclusions 0.5 mm, sparse tiny white inclusions and sparse tiny micaceous particles.
Int. rim 2.75

1084 5900
1a handle, closed vessel; cream fabric with sparse red inclusions 0.5 mm and white inclusions <0.5 mm.
Int. di. 5, Ext. di. 6

1085 4308
1a
Handle, closed vessel, cream fabric, with brown slip varying in thickness from dark to light brown. Moderate brown and sparse white inclusions less than 0.5 mm.

1086 4392
1a handle, closed vessel; fine light orange fabric with sparse white and red inclusions 0.5 mm.
Int. di. 5, Ext. di. 6

1087 3601
1a handle, closed vessel; splashed brown paint on handle ext.; orange fabric with orange and white inclusions.
Int. di. 9

1088 3601
1a, handle, closed vessel; purple/red paint on handle; orange fabric with moderate red inclusions <0.5 mm.
Int. di. 25, Ext. di. 26.2

1089 5922
1a rim, closed vessel; orange fabric with moderate white, orange and sparse grey inclusions all 0.5.
Int. rim 6, Ext. rim 6

1090 1501
1a rim, closed vessel; red-light brown fabric with tiny white inclusions and moderate very tiny silver mica flakes.
Int. rim 11, Ext. rim 12.8

1091 2345
2 m rim, closed vessel; narrow sharp ribbing; very few very small white inclusions, 1 large 1.5 mm red inclusion.
Int. rim 10.8, Ext. rim 13

1092 1501
1a rim, closed vessel; light wash on shoulder; light orange fabric with tiny white inclusions.
Int. rim 15, Ext. rim 19.5

1093 3101
1a rim closed vessel; orange wash on ext.; relatively coarse orange fabric with sub-angular orange inclusions 1–1.5 mm and frequent white inclusions especially visible on interior surface.
Int. rim 14, Ext. rim 17.8

1094 K18/305 4395
1a. Almost complete profile neck and rim not preserved; closed vessel; ribbing on belly; loose painted spiral and dots on shoulder of vessel, horizontal line at base of neck.
Base di. 6.4, Body di. 13.4
Fig. 550

1095 4307
Base, closed vessel; ribbing.
Base di. 6

1096 2343
1a base, closed vessel; slightly burnished, ribbing; relatively soft fabric with 0.5 mm red inclusions.
Base di. 6

1097 1501
1a base; orange fabric with frequent red inclusions <2 mm, 1 mm sparse black inclusions and moderate tiny white inclusions.
Base di. 6

1098 2339
1a base; red/brown inclusions.
Base di. 8

1099 4392
1a base; orange fabric with sparse red inclusions up to 1.5 mm and frequent cream/white inclusions 1 mm.

1100 5631
1a base, red paint; orange fabric with 1.5 mm red inclusions.
Base di. 8

1101 9659
1b base, closed vessel; throwing marks on inside; buff and light brown/orange fabric with tiny white inclusions and red inclusions less than 0.5 mm.
Base di. 3.3

1102 9669
1b base, closed vessel; orange fabric with tiny white inclusions.
Base di. 4

1103 4393
1a base; very light orange fabric with frequent large red inclusions <3 mm, sparse/moderate flat long thin white inclusions.
Base di. 4.3

1104 9659
1b base, closed vessel; throwing marks on inside; light orange fabric with orange/red and brown inclusions less than 0.5 mm.
Base di. 4

1105 4390
1a base; moderate red inclusions up to 2 mm, white inclusions <0.5 mm and sparse grey inclusions 0.5 mm.
Base di. 8

Pottery from Level One

1106   3204
1a base; no individual fabric description made.
Base di. 9

1107   1602
1a? base.
Base di. 7

1108   3316
1a base, open vessel; dark brown painted lines — spiral?; cream fabric with white inclusions <0.5 mm and light brown inclusions <0.5 mm.
Base di. 9

1109   2354
1a base; painted; yellow/cream fabric with very tiny red inclusions.
Base di. 10

1110   3200
1a base?; no individual fabric description made.
Base di. 12

1111   4391
1b base; unusual form possibly residual, but of Fabric 1b, and from a unit with relatively high proportion of other Fabric 1 material; sparse white inclusions 0.5 mm, moderate black inclusions <0.5 mm and sparse red inclusions <0.5 mm and sparse grey plate-like particles 0.5 mm.
Base di. 15

1112   4395
1a. Large reconstructed body sherd with round handle placed horizontally on shoulder; painted shoulder, ribbing, painted horizontal neck line.
Fig. 551

1113   4302
Body sherd, closed vessel; dark brown/red painted spiral and dots; light brown/yellow fabric with moderate light brown inclusions 0.5 mm and sparse white and sparse opaque, and sparse grey inclusions all <0.5 mm.
X 4.3; Y 5

1114   4302
1a body sherd, closed vessel; red painted spiral with three dots in centre; orange fabric with frequent cream inclusions <0.5 mm and white <0.5 mm.
X 5.5; Y 4.3

1115   4302
1a body sherd with handle root, closed vessel; worn; red painted running spiral with three dots in centre; orange fabric with red inclusions 1 mm and white inclusions <0.5 mm.
X 7.3; Y 7.6

1116   4302
1a body sherd, closed vessel; red painted running spiral with dots in centre and between spirals and incised horizontal line; orange fabric with orange inclusions 0.5 mm and white inclusions <0.5 mm.
X 4.5; Y 5.2
Fig. 552

1117   4308
1a body sherd, closed vessel; dark red painted running spiral applied with a thin brush; orange fabric with moderate orange inclusions 0.5 mm and moderate white <0.5 mm.
X 7.2; Y 5.4
Fig. 552

1118   4309
1b body sherd closed vessel; dark red painted spiral with three dots in centre; orange fabric with common tiny white and grey inclusions and possible mica.
X 4.4; Y 5.4
Figs. 573 & 575

1119   4309
Body sherd, closed vessel; dark red painted spiral and horizontal line; micaceous orange fabric with many tiny white inclusions <0.5 mm, sparse grey inclusions.
X 5.3; Y 6.4

1120   4314
Body sherd, closed vessel; light brown painted spiral; frequent fine light brown inclusions and sparse white inclusions all less than 0.5 mm.
X 6; Y 3.8

1121   4390
1a body sherd, closed vessel; worn; brown painted spiral and dot, no collar; light orange fabric with red inclusions <2 mm and very tiny white inclusions.
X 5.2; Y 4

1122   4391
1b body sherd, closed vessel; red painted spiral and dots on shoulder; orange fabric with sparse red and black inclusions <0.5 mm and sparse gold mica flakes.
X 6; Y 6

1123   4391
1b body sherd, closed vessel; red painted spiral; orange fabric with gold mica flakes and flat plate-like white inclusions 2 mm × 0.25 mm, red inclusions 0.5 mm and gold mica.
X 9; Y 6

1124   4391
1a body sherd, closed vessel; red painted spiral on shoulder, painted horizontal neck line; orange fabric with sparse/moderate white inclusions 0.5–1 mm and moderate rounded red inclusions <2 mm.
X 5.4; Y 2.2

1125   4392
1a body sherd, closed vessel; incised horizontal line; red painted spiral thin brush; light orange fabric.
X 4.6; Y 4.4

1126   4393
1a body sherd, closed vessel; ribbing; red painted spiral on shoulder; orange fabric with very rare flecks of gold mica and white and red inclusions <0.5 mm.
X 8.8; Y 7

1127   4395
1b body sherd, closed vessel; painted shoulder, raised collar also painted; very pale orange interior and green exterior, fine fabric with some tiny brown/black moderate inclusions and sparse mica.
X 4.5; Y 3.5

1128   4397
1a body sherd, closed vessel; orange fabric with sparse red inclusions <1 mm and moderate cream/white inclusions <2 mm painted lines thin brush.
X 2.9; Y 5.6

Chapter 31

1129   5625
1a body sherd, closed vessel; painted spiral; cream/slightly orange fabric with red and black inclusions <0.5 mm.
X 2.6; Y 3

1130   5630
1a body sherd, closed vessel; painted; orange fabric with sparse grey and white inclusions.
X 7; Y 3.2

1131   9650
1a body sherd, closed vessel; painted; orange fabric with tiny white and red/orange inclusions.
X 3; Y 2.5

1132   3301
Body sherd, reconstructed; closed vessel; dark red/maroon painted spiral; dark red/maroon paint and very light brown/orange fabric interior, exterior and core with moderate orange/light brown inclusions 0.5 mm and sparse tiny white inclusions much <0.5 mm.
X 11.4; Y 14.7

1133   3403
1a body sherd with handle root, closed vessel; dark red paint.
X 11.6; Y 10.5

1134   3101
1a body sherd, closed vessel; purple paint; orange fabric with moderate red inclusions <0.5–1 mm and white inclusions <0.5 mm.
X 5.3; Y 5.7
Figs. 573 & 575

1135   3000
1a body sherd, closed vessel; red/brown painted spirals; orange fabric with red and white inclusions <0.5 mm.
X 5; Y 5.2
Figs. 573 & 575

1136   3601
1a body sherd, closed vessel.
X 6.4; Y 6.4
Fig. 552

1137   3601
1a body sherd, closed vessel; dark red painted spiral; orange fabric with moderate white and red inclusions <0.5 mm.
X 7.7; Y 3.5

1138   3601
1a body sherd, closed vessel; red painted spiral; orange fabric with moderate pinkish/orange and white inclusions.
X 5; Y 6.3

1139   3603
1a body sherd, closed vessel; orange fabric fired light orange on exterior with moderate red inclusions <0.5–1 mm and sparse white inclusions 0.5 mm.
X 5.2; Y 4.2

1140   3401
1a body sherd, closed vessel.
X 3.3; Y 4.5

1141   3200
1a body sherd, closed vessel; painted spiral, purple.
X 3.7; Y 4.4

1142   3204
1a body sherd, closed vessel; painted spiral motif.
X 6; Y 4.4
Fig. 554

1143   3208
1a body sherd, closed vessel; painted spiral motif.
X 9.7; Y 7
Fig. 554

1144   3208
1a body sherd, closed vessel; painted elaborate motif, spiral and dots.
X 8.1; Y 7.5
Fig. 554

1145   3601
1a body sherd, shoulder and neck with raised collar, closed vessel; worn red paint; light creamy-brown inclusions.
Y 6.6

1146   5902
1a body sherd, closed vessel; thin dark red painted spirals; orange fabric with tiny white sparse inclusions.
X 7.7; Y 6.4
Fig. 552

1147   5904
1a body sherd, closed vessel; red paint; orange fabric with pale cream/white inclusions <0.5 mm.
X 5.6; Y 3.8

1148   2305
1a body sherd, closed vessel; painted.
X 3; Y 2.8

1149   2339
1a body sherd, closed vessel; painted thin spirals on shoulder and narrow neck line painted; white, black and red inclusions well sorted 0.5 mm.
X 4.7; Y 3

1150   2343
1b body sherd, closed vessel; red painted spiral with dots, horizontal painted neckline; orange fabric with very small angular white inclusions, large red inclusions up to 2 mm, rounded cream inclusions 1 mm.
X 9; Y 8

1151   2350
1a body sherd, closed vessel; painted spiral; light orange fabric with 0.5 mm red/brown inclusions, white inclusions <0.5 mm.
X 4.4; Y 3.7

1152   2350
1a body sherd, closed vessel; painted spiral; orange fabric with tiny black inclusions and holes in surface.
X 4; Y 3.7

1153   9650
1a body sherd, closed vessel; painted; yellow/brown fabric with yellow/brown inclusions and very small white sparse paint.
X 2.9; Y 2.7

1154   1602
1a body sherd, closed vessel; painted spiral.
X 9.5; Y 4.5

Pottery from Level One

1155   1602
1b body sherd, closed vessel; painted spiral.
X 5; Y 8
Fig. 554

1156   1602
1a body sherd, closed vessel; painted spirals and dots.
X 2.5; Y 4

1157   1602
1b body sherd, closed vessel; painted dots.
X 2; Y 2.5

1158   1605
1a body sherd, reconstructed; closed vessel; ribbing; painted spiral varies in thickness and colour from dark slightly red brown to lighter brown; micaceous light brown/yellow fabric with relatively coarse matrix and very sparse grey inclusions <0.5 mm, white inclusions 0.5 mm and sparse light brown/yellow inclusions 0.5 mm.
X 12.7; Y 15.2
Figs. 552 & 575

1159   1626
1b body sherd, closed vessel; brown painted spiral and dots; orange/buff fabric with tiny holes in surface, moderate angular red and white inclusions much <0.5 mm.
X 5.7; Y 4.2

1160   1626
1b body sherd, closed vessel; painted spiral and dots.
X 2.6; Y 2.8

1161   1501
1b body sherd, closed vessel; ribbing; painted spiral.
X 9; Y 5.5

1162   1501
1a body sherd, closed vessel; red paint.
X 3.3; Y 3.1

1163   1501
1a body sherd, closed vessel; red paint.
X 5; Y 3.5

1164   1501
1a body sherd.

1165   1501
1a body sherd, closed vessel.

1166   1501
1a body sherd.

1167   1501
1b body sherd, closed vessel; brown painted spiral on shoulder and painted horizontal line round neck; green fabric with angular grey inclusions <0.5 mm, orange and red inclusions <0.5 mm.
Fig. 554

1168   1501
1a body sherd, closed vessel; ribbing; painted.

1169   1501
1a body sherd, closed vessel; brown painted horizontal line around neck with spiral and dots; yellow fabric with moderate white and red inclusions and sparse very small angular grey inclusions.

1170   1501
1a body sherd, closed vessel; ribbing; painted.

1171   1512
1a body sherd, closed vessel; dark red painted spirals; light orange fabric with light orange rounded inclusions 0.5 mm and white 0.5 mm.
X 4.3; Y 2.7

1172   1513
Body sherd, closed vessel; brown painted spirals and stars horizontal line around base of neck; cream-colour fabric with grey/black and light brown inclusions <0.5 mm.
X 4.6; Y 8.5
Fig. 562

1173   1501
1a body sherd, closed vessel; painted bird head.

1174   2337
1a body sherd, closed vessel; ribbing; painted bird motif.
X 10.7; Y 9.7

1175   2343
1a body sherd, closed vessel; brown painted foliage; yellow/cream fabric with large brown inclusions up to 2 mm, sparse white inclusions and a few very small grey inclusions.
X 8; Y 8

1176   2343
1a body sherd, closed vessel; ribbing; painted bird motif; 2 mm light brown inclusions and white inclusions.
X 6; Y 5.5

1177   2355
1a body sherd, closed vessel; painted decoration including fish motif; orange/light brown fabric, very small white inclusions and red inclusions <0.5 mm.
X 10.2; Y 7.7
Fig. 558

1178   4302
1b body sherd, closed vessel; red painted motifs including rear end of fish, and incised lines; orange fabric red paint with white eruptions on surface, red inclusions 0.5 mm and white inclusions <0.5 mm.
X 9.5; Y 8
Fig. 556

1179   4302
Body sherd, closed vessel; red painted bird motif; micaceous orange fabric with moderate cream inclusions 0.5 mm and sparse red inclusions 0.5 mm and sparse white inclusions <0.5 mm.
X 7.1; Y 5
Fig. 559

1180   4307
Body sherd, closed vessel; ribbing; painted bird motif; orange/light brown fabric with orange inclusions <0.5 mm and white inclusions <0.5 mm.
X 4.5; Y 3.8

1181   4320
1a body sherd, closed vessel; painted bird motif; orange fabric with orange inclusions 0.5 mm and white inclusions <0.5 mm.
X 9.7; Y 4.7
Fig. 556

Chapter 31

1182   3601
1a body sherd, closed vessel; painted bird motif.
X 4.5; Y 5
Fig. 556

1183   1501
1a body sherd, closed vessel; painted collar round neck, cross in circle and dot in circle on shoulder of vessel; pale orange fabric with moderate white and red inclusions c. 0.5 mm.

1184   9686
1a body sherd, closed vessel; orange painted leaf motif on shoulder, raised collar unpainted; orange fabric with red inclusion 0.5–1 mm and tiny white inclusions up to 1 mm.
X 5; Y 1.9

1185   4390
1a body sherd, closed vessel; red painted tree motif on shoulder, gouged and incised cross motif; light orange fabric.
X 5.5; Y 7
Fig. 555

1186   4391
1a body sherd, closed vessel; brown/red painted shoulder, gouged, painted and incised cross; cream non-micaceous fabric.
X 3.4; Y 4.8
Fig. 555

1187   4391
1a body sherd, closed vessel; ribbing; red painted shoulder tree motifs, and red painted horizontal line around base of neck; light orange fabric with white inclusions <2 mm.
X 8.8; Y 9.2
Fig. 557

1188   4308
1a body sherd, closed vessel; brown painted cross, stars and foliage; light brown/ light orange fabric with large light orange inclusions up to 2 mm tiny white inclusions <0.5 mm and sparse relatively large white inclusions 1.5 mm.
X 9.4; Y 7.7
Fig. 559

1189   4302
1a body sherd, closed vessel; brown painted foliage motif; yellow/light brown fabric with moderate light brown inclusions 0.5–1 mm and small white inclusions <0.5 mm.
X 4.4; Y 4.4
Fig. 556

1190   2343
1a body sherd, closed vessel; painted leaf motif; 1–2 mm light brown inclusions with occasional black and tiny white inclusions.
X 5; Y 4.5

1191   2339
1a body sherd, closed vessel; painted; cream fabric with 0.5 mm brown inclusions and few tiny black inclusions.
X 8.2; Y 5.1

1192   4393
1a body sherd, closed vessel; red painted motifs; cream fabric with brown inclusions and tiny white inclusions.
X 5.1; Y 5

1193   2343
1b body sherd, closed vessel; tree leaf pattern on shoulder, horizontal painted neck line.
X 6.9; Y 5.2

1194   2343
1b body sherd, closed vessel; tree leaf motif; light brown/cream fabric with 2 mm light brown inclusions, 0.5 mm red and white inclusions <0.5 mm.
X 6.1; Y 6.5

1195   2343
1a body sherd, closed vessel; leaf painted shoulder; cream fabric.
X 3.5; Y 3.1

1196   3204
1a body sherd, closed vessel; painted horizontal neck line and tree? motif.
X 3.5; Y 3.4

1197   3101
1a body sherd, closed vessel; unrecognized dark purple/brown painted design; green/cream fabric with moderate red inclusions <0.5 mm.
X 3.2; Y 3

1198   3101
1a body sherd, closed vessel; dark red/purple painted cross-hatching and other motifs; pale orange fabric with moderate/sparse orange and white inclusions <0.5 mm.
X 5.5; Y 6

1199   3205
Body sherd, closed vessel; painted tree motif and bird; plain buff.
X 7.7; Y 8
Fig. 557

1200   1501
1b body sherd, closed vessel; painted with loose overlapping wavy lines applied with brush; orange fabric with 1 mm angular red inclusions and tiny white inclusions.
Fig. 561

1201   9615
Body sherd, closed vessel; orange/brown splosh painted shoulder and painted raised collar; orange fabric with sparse angular opaque, white and very tiny black inclusions.
X 7; Y 5

1202   4393
1b body sherd, closed vessel; ribbing; black splosh painted; orange fabric with cream and red inclusions <3 mm, and white inclusions 0.5–1 mm and very rare tiny mica particles.
X 7.8; Y 8.7

1203   4393
1a body sherd, closed vessel; splosh black paint and ribbing; cream fabric with cream/red inclusions 1–3 mm and sparse white inclusions 0.5 mm, no visible mica.
X 7.3; Y 5.8

1204   3601
1a body sherd, closed vessel; red paint.
X 6.5; Y 8.5

1205   1501
1a body sherd, closed vessel; herringbone pattern; orange fabric with angular white, and rounded red inclusions up to 1 mm and angular grey/light brown inclusions.
X 5.5; Y 6.5

Pottery from Level One

1206   1501
1a body sherd, closed vessel.
X 3.5; Y 4

1207   1514
1a body sherd, closed vessel; dark red/brown painted decoration; orange fabric with red inclusions <0.5 mm and cream/white inclusions <1 mm.
X 4.8; Y 4.1

1208   4393
1b body sherd, closed vessel; painted horizontal and wavy lines; orange fabric with moderate 1 mm red inclusions and rare white inclusions and very tiny micaceous particles.
X 7.5; Y 5.2

1209   1514
1a body sherd, closed vessel; light brown painted decoration; light brown/orange fabric with moderate/frequent light brown/orange inclusions 0.5 mm and moderate white inclusions <0.5 mm.
X 3.3; Y 4.5

1210   1501
1b body sherd, closed vessel.
X 6.6; Y 5.5

1211   2338
1a body sherd, closed vessel; some paint, painted horizontal neck line; cream colour fabric.
X 4.2; Y 3

1212   4308
1a body sherd, closed vessel; red painted decoration and ribbing; orange fabric with red inclusions up to 2 mm and light brown/yellow inclusions <1.5 mm and very small white inclusions 0.5 mm.
X 3.7; Y 4.2

1213   9659
1a body sherd, closed vessel; painted broad line; orange/buff fabric with red inclusions <0.5 mm and tiny white inclusions.
X 6.3; Y 6.8

1214   5633
1a body sherd, closed vessel; brown broad painted stripe; orange fabric with tiny grey and cream inclusions.
X 4.6; Y 3.2

1215   5634
1a body sherd, closed vessel; red painted stripe; orange fabric with tiny white and 0.5 mm brown inclusions.
X 3.6; Y 4.5

1216   2343
1a body sherd, closed vessel; ribbing; broad painted stripe; orange fabric with brown and white inclusions 0.5 mm.
X 5.5; Y 4.5

1217   5634
1a body sherd, closed vessel; brown broad stripe; orange brown fabric with brown and red 0.5 mm inclusions and tiny black inclusions.
X 4.5; Y 5.3

1218   2343
1a body sherd, closed vessel; broad painted stripe; light orange fabric with orange and white inclusions and tiny black inclusions.
X 7.5; Y 5.3

1219   5634
1a body sherd, closed vessel; white stripe and black wash; orange fabric with red inclusions 0.5 mm and cream inclusions 1 mm and tiny white inclusions.
X 5.6; Y 3.5

1220   4403
1a body profile with handle on shoulder, reconstructed; closed vessel; red paint poured flicked and scrabbled over interior. Thin reddish-brown wash (not as thick as on interior) in broad swathes across exterior. Pale orange with red inclusions.
Fig. 564a–b

1221   4314
1a body sherd, closed vessel; brown/black paint; orange/cream fabric with frequent red inclusions <1.5 mm and sparse red and white inclusions <0.5 mm.
X 6.3; Y 8.2
Fig. 566

1222   4309
1a body sherd, closed vessel; brown wash showing brush marks; cream fabric with light orange/light brown inclusions <1 mm and white inclusions <0.5 mm and grey inclusions <0.5 mm.
X 11.5; Y 9

1223   3501
1a body sherd, closed vessel; red/brown paint showing brush marks; yellow/ light brown fabric with many white inclusions and sparse red inclusions <0.5 mm.
X 9; Y 11.2

1224   4307
1a body sherd, closed vessel; brown/orange wash showing brush marks; light brown/orange with frequent red and white inclusions <0.5 mm.
X 8; Y 6.5

1225   3423
1a body sherd, closed vessel; dark red wash paint; orange fabric with large red inclusions up to 3 mm and small white inclusions.
X 7.8; Y 6.8

1226   3200
1a body sherd, closed vessel; broad purple paint.
X 13.2; Y 13.5

1227   3423
1a body sherd, closed vessel; light brown wash; green/cream colour fabric with sparse grey, and moderate white and orange inclusions all <0.5 mm.
X 4.3; Y 4.2

1228   9658
1a body sherd, closed vessel; ribbing; paint; orange fabric fired yellow near exterior, with red inclusions <0.5 mm and tiny white inclusions.
X 7.7; Y 5.7

1229   1601
1a body sherd, closed vessel; gouged.
X 4; Y 3.5

1230   1600
1a body sherd, closed vessel; gouged.
X 4.5; Y 3

Chapter 31

1231   3401
1a body sherd, closed vessel; paint and gouges.
X 5.2; Y 5
Fig. 563

1232   1501
1a body sherd, closed vessel; wide finger ribbing with gouged decoration on shoulder; gouged shoulder; red inclusions up to 2 mm and white up to 1 mm.
X 10; Y 6.5

1233   3401
1a body sherd, closed vessel; paint and gouges.
X 3.1; Y 5.4
Fig. 563

1234   3204
1a body sherd, closed vessel; paint and gouges.
X 4; Y 5
Fig. 563

1235   3204
1a body sherd with handle root, closed vessel.
X 9; Y 7.5
Fig. 563

1236   3608
1a body sherd, closed vessel; pale orange/white slip applied over gouges; orange fabric with tiny white inclusions and red inclusions <0.5 mm.
X 4.5; Y 4.6
Fig. 563

1237   9657
1a body sherd, closed vessel; vertical gouged, brown paint; orange fabric with tiny white inclusions and red inclusions up to 2 mm.
X 3.6; Y 4.2

1238   4303
1a body sherd, closed vessel; vertical gouges and horizontal red painted line; orange fabric with common orange inclusions 1 mm and sparse white inclusions <0.5 mm.
X 6; Y 3.3

1239   4395
1b body sherd, closed vessel; ribbing; vertical gouges shoulder; orange/light brown fabric with red/brown inclusions 0.5 mm and tiny silver mica inclusions.
X 6.6; Y 8.8

1240   9659
1a body sherd, closed vessel; triangular-shaped areas of parallel gouges and red painted horizontal line.
X 4.4; Y 3.7

1241   4309
1b body sherd, closed vessel; diamond patterned gouges; orange fabric with orange inclusions <1 mm.
X 8.5; Y 7.7
Fig. 563

1242   3601
1a body sherd.
X 4.5; Y 5.5

1243   3404
1a body sherd, closed vessel; incised diagonal lines; very large red inclusions up to 3 mm and sub-angular and white inclusions.
X 11; Y 5.6

1244   4303
1a body sherd, closed vessel; appliqué dots of clay over crossing of incised lines; orange/pink fabric with red 1 mm inclusions and white inclusions <0.5 mm.
X 8; Y 6.3

1245   3200
1a body sherd, closed vessel.
X 9; Y 6.5

1246   4395
1a body sherd, closed vessel; impressed shoulder decoration and black wash; orange fabric with sparse dark red angular inclusions <1–2 mm, sparse angular long thin 3 × 0.5 mm white inclusions and moderate cream inclusions <0.5 mm.
X 4.2; Y 5.5

1247   2339
1a body sherd and handle, closed vessel; ribbing under handle; spirals on shoulder; orange/cream fabric with few holes in surface.
X 8.5; Y 6

1248   1501
Body sherd and handle.
X 7; Y 5.5

1249   1501
1b body sherd and handle, closed vessel; ribbing; splosh painted shoulder; orange fabric with red inclusions up to 1 mm and white inclusions up to 1 mm.
X 8; Y 8

1250   1501
1a body sherd and handle, closed vessel; ribbing; paint on shoulder; light orange fabric with moderate red and white inclusions <1 mm.
X 10; Y 5.5

1251   1501
1a body sherd and handle, closed vessel; brown paint; very light brown/orange fabric with tiny to 0.5 mm to moderate brown inclusions, sparse white 0.5 mm inclusions and sparse silver mica flakes.
X 10.5; Y 6

1252   1501
1a body sherd and handle, closed vessel; light brown wash; cream colour fabric with moderate tiny white inclusions <2 mm, sparse brown inclusions <0.5–1 mm.
X 16.5; Y 14

1253   4390
1a body sherd and round horizontal handle, closed vessel; ribbing on body below handle; orange fabric with tiny white and orange inclusions.
X 6.5; Y 7

1254   3423
1a vertical handle, closed vessel; red paint on ext. side; orange fabric with tiny white inclusions <0.5 mm visible on the surface and 1 mm red inclusions.

1255   3601
1a vertical handle; closed vessel; dark red/purple painted stripes;

414

orange fabric with orange and white inclusions <0.5 mm.
Fig. 560

1256   3602
1a horizontal handle, closed vessel.
Fig. 560

1257   3602
1a horizontal handle, closed vessel; purple/brown stripes on top of handle; green/cream fabric with moderate red inclusions <0.5 mm.
Fig. 560

1258   3600
1a horizontal handle, closed vessel; purple painted tiger stripes on handle; orange fabric with moderate bright red inclusions <0.5 mm.
Fig. 560

1259   4309
1a rim, closed vessel; red/brown paint around rim; coarse orange fabric with frequent large red inclusions <2 mm, sparse white inclusions up to 1 mm.
Int. rim 12, Ext. rim 22.6
Fig. 566

1260   3604
1a rim, closed vessel; scratched wavy line on top of rim and red paint on ext.; coarse orange fabric with frequent angular red and cream inclusions up to 0.5 mm.
Int. rim 17, Ext. rim 21.5

1261   3000
1a rim, closed vessel; red and white inclusions <0.5 mm and sparse larger red inclusions <2 mm and white <1.5 mm.
Int. rim 17, Ext. rim 22

1262   3002
1a rim, closed vessel; green fabric with black inclusions up to 2 mm and light brown/orange inclusions 0.5 mm.
Int. rim 18, Ext. rim 23
Fig. 566

1263   3001
1a rim, closed vessel; green fabric with black inclusions 1 mm and cream/light brown inclusions 1 mm.
Int. rim 18, Ext. rim 23.6

1264   3001
1a rim closed vessel; green fabric with large grey/black inclusions up to <2 mm and frequent cream inclusions <2 mm.
Int. rim 18, Ext. rim 23.4

1265   4600
1a rim, closed vessel. Pithos, externally thickened overhanging rim decorated with both incised lines and brush painted splashes. Decoration divided into registers by horizontal incised lines. The top register beneath the rim is decorated by incised criss-cross lines, the second register by incised wavy lines, the third left blank but decorated with a further wavy line below.
Fig. 565

1266   4600
1a rim, closed vessel. Pithos, probably the same vessel as 1265, with similar decoration, though preserving a second wavy line below the first on the lower wall. Large handle applied to upper body below rim. The hooped horizontal handle has characteristic finger impressions at join with vessel wall.
Fig. 565

1267   3200
6L rim, closed vessel; exterior smooth and interior coarse; splashed with black paint; very coarse cream fabric with frequent angular black and red inclusions up to 2 mm.
Int. rim 14, Ext. rim 18
Fig. 567

1268   5904
6L rim, closed vessel; black/brown paint on ext.; very coarse fabric with red and white inclusions up to 1 mm.
Int. rim 17, Ext. rim 22
Fig. 567

1269   4309
Rim, closed vessel; orange/brown paint splashed on rim top; very light buff/yellow fabric with light brown 0.5–1 mm angular inclusions sparse cream inclusions.
Int. rim 15.4, Ext. rim 22

1270   9659
1a rim, closed vessel; gouges; sparse white tiny inclusions, moderate black inclusions and moderate red inclusions <0.5 mm.
Int. rim 24, Ext. rim 33

1271   1605
1a rim, closed vessel; possible painted decoration; obscured by calcareous deposit on surface coarse orange/yellow fabric with frequent cream/white and red inclusions 0.5 mm and moderate/sparse grey inclusions <0.5 mm.
Int. rim 26, Ext. rim 33

1272   3205
1a rim, closed vessel; incised horizontal bands around belly of vessel; thin red/brown wash with incised wavy lines below rim; orange fabric red inclusions up to 3 mm, 0.5 mm grey/black inclusions and tiny white inclusions.
Int. rim 27, Ext. rim 36.6

1273   1501
5f rim, closed vessel; pie crust ? decoration, light brown wash/paint on rim; light orange, frequent angular black inclusions <0.5 mm and sparse red 0.5 mm angular inclusions and frequent tiny white inclusions.
Int. rim 25, Ext. rim 31.8

1274   4397
1a rim, closed vessel; horizontal incisions below rim and red paint on rim; coarse fabric with moderate red angular inclusions <3.5 mm and sparse white inclusions 0.5 mm.
Int. rim 30, Ext. rim 39.4

1275   4314
1a rim, closed vessel; brown/black paint on ext. and rim top; orange fabric with frequent red inclusions ranging from tiny to 2 mm and sparse cream and white inclusions.
Int. rim 28, Ext. rim 36

1276   2620
1a rim, closed vessel; brown wash on ext. rim; light orange fabric with frequent 1 mm inclusions ranging from red to grey and white inclusions 0.5 mm.
Int. rim 36, Ext. rim 47.4
Fig. 566

1277 4392
1a rim, closed vessel; orange fabric with moderate red inclusions up to 3 mm and sparse tiny white inclusions.
Int. rim 46, Ext. rim 52.6

1278 4302
1a rim, closed vessel; orange fabric with very common large white inclusions up to 3 mm causing blisters on the surface and sparse/common red inclusions <1 mm.
Int. rim 33.6, Ext. rim 42

1279 1626
1a rim; horizontal incised lines.
Int. rim 52.8, Ext. rim 62

1280 3601
Fabric 1a; lid, not completely preserved.

1281 2600
1a handle, closed vessel; red/brown wash paint; very light orange/cream fabric with large red and grey/brown inclusions 0.5–1 mm.
X 4.6; Y 5.9
Fig. 566

1282 1501
1a handle, closed vessel; gouges; light orange fabric with frequent red inclusions up to 2 mm and sparse white inclusions 0.5 mm.

1283 4395
Handle, closed vessel; gouges; green fabric with black rounded inclusions 1 mm and brown 1 mm angular inclusions, red 0.5 mm inclusions.

1284 4309
1a handle, closed vessel; orange fabric with frequent red inclusions ranging form tiny to 2 mm and light brown/cream inclusions <1 mm and white inclusions <0.5 mm.
X 7.9; Y 11
Fig. 566

1285 4314
1a handle, closed vessel; gouges; orange fabric exterior with orange/red inclusions <2 mm and white <0.5 mm, has a dark green/brown core, the inclusions in the core are black.
X 9; Y 9

1286 9643
1a handle, closed vessel; gouges; orange fabric with shiny black, and white inclusions 0.5 mm and red inclusions 1 mm.

1287 3202
1a handle; purple paint.

1288 3205
1a handle, closed vessel.
Fig. 549

1289 9616
2c rim, closed vessel; thin red wash on outside.
Int. rim 9, Ext. rim 12

1290 9615
2c rim, closed vessel; red paint splashed on inside of rim, dribbled down inside and outside.
Int. rim 10, Ext. rim 13.5

1291 2339
2c rim, closed vessel; lightly tooled wavy design.
Int. rim 11.8, Ext. rim 14
Fig. 575

1292 2357
2c rim, open vessel; plain white and grey inclusions, holes in surface.
Int. rim 17.4, Ext. rim 18

1293 9666
2c rim, open vessel; pale buff cream fabric with white inclusions visible on surface and no other visible inclusions.
Int. rim 17.8, Ext. rim 20

1294 2311
2c rim, open vessel; one repair hole.
Int. rim 23.4, Ext. rim 25

1295 2308
2c rim, open vessel; tiny black and white well-sorted inclusions.
Int. rim 27.4, Ext. rim 30

1296 2345
2c rim, open vessel; white and grey inclusions.
Int. rim 27.2, Ext. rim 30

1297 2316
2c rim, open vessel; many very small black inclusions.
Int. rim 29.4, Ext. rim 32

1298 2321
2c rim, open vessel; tiny black, white and red inclusions.
Int. rim 33, Ext. rim 36

1299 2343
2c base; buff fabric and white inclusions 0.5 mm.
Base di. 5.5

1300 2337
2c base; tiny holes in surface no visible inclusions.
Base di. 9

1301 9659
2c body sherd, closed vessel; incised ribbing; black wash/paint; buff colour fabric with moderate tiny white inclusions, and very tiny frequent black inclusions and sparse brown inclusions <0.5 mm.
X 7; Y 7.1

1302 9672
2g rim, closed vessel; pale green fabric with black inclusions up to 1 mm.

1303 1604
2g rim, open vessel.
Int. rim 6.2, Ext. rim 7

1304 9678
2g rim, closed vessel; pale green fabric with sparse cream inclusions 0.5 mm and very tiny moderate black inclusions.
Int. rim 6, Ext. rim 7.6

1305 2350
2g rim, closed vessel; red paint on rim and on shoulder; yellow/green fabric with very small black inclusions.
Int. rim 11, Ext. rim 13

1306 9633
2g rim, closed vessel; medium round ribbing; green/yellow fabric

Pottery from Level One

with brown/black inclusions.
Int. rim 19.2, Ext. rim 22

1307 9649
2g rim; brown/orange paint/wash; yellow/green fabric with large brown inclusions <2 mm.
Int. rim 21, Ext. rim 26

1308 1604
2h rim, open vessel; fine orange fabric.
Int. rim 15.4, Ext. rim 16

1309 4391
2h rim and handle; yellow-colour fabric with moderate tiny black inclusions and tiny white inclusions.
Int. rim 7, Ext. rim 8.4
Fig. 548

1310 4390
2h rim; buff fabric with frequent black inclusions, very tiny white inclusions and tiny silver micaceous flakes.
Int. rim 8, Ext. rim 10.8

1311 4393
2h rim, closed vessel; oval-shaped dents below rim on outside brown paint on outside and rim and wavy incisions; cream fabric with moderate tiny black inclusions and tiny white inclusions.
Int. rim 15, Ext. rim 18.6
Fig. 575

1312 1602
2h rim, open vessel.
Int. rim 24.8, Ext. rim 27

1313 1621
2h rim, open vessel.
Int. rim 27.6, Ext. rim 30

1314 1501
2h handle, closed vessel; very fine light brown fabric with tiny sparse white inclusions.
Int. di. at handle 5, Ext. di. at handle 6

1315 9659
2h handle, closed vessel; relatively fine fabric with brown inclusions <0.5 mm and sparse white inclusions.
Int. rim 10; Ext. rim 11

1316 1501
2h base; cream fabric colour with black angular inclusions from tiny up to 1 mm, light brown inclusions <0.5 mm.
Base di. 6

1317 4393
2h body sherd, closed vessel; vertical gouging and horizontal painted line around neck; cream fabric with sparse red inclusions <0.5 mm, sparse brown inclusions <1.5 mm, sparse tiny white inclusions, and silver mica inclusions.
X 5; Y 5.2

1318 1501
3a (Late Roman Amphora 1) rim, closed vessel; orange fabric, very rough gritty feel, with abundant black/brown angular inclusions less than 0.5 mm, sparse white inclusions and sparse/moderate opaque angular inclusions 0.5–1 mm; also plate-like shiny inclusions-possibly mica.
Int. rim 7, Ext. rim 9
Fig. 568

1319 1501
3a (Late Roman Amphora 1) rim, closed vessel; light orange/cream fabric very gritty feel, abundant tiny black inclusions, sparse 0.5 mm red and white inclusions.
Int. rim 7, Ext. rim 10.2

1320 4393
3a (Late Roman Amphora 1) rim and handle, closed vessel; gritty feel with very frequent tiny black inclusions, sparse/moderate tiny white inclusions and tiny micaceous flakes.
Int. rim 8, Ext. rim 10.2

1321 4393
3a (Late Roman Amphora 1) rim and handle, closed vessel; gritty feel with abundant black/brown inclusions <0.5 mm and occasional white inclusions.

1322 1605
3a (Late Roman Amphora 1) rim and handle, closed vessel; cream slip on exterior; orange fabric with very frequent grey inclusions <0.5 mm and sparse white inclusions <0.5 mm.
Int. rim 8, Ext. rim 11.2

1323 3401
3a (Late Roman Amphora 1) rim and handle, closed vessel; no slip; very gritty fabric with frequent red inclusions <0.5 mm and moderate grey inclusions <0.5 mm and sparse white inclusions 0.5 mm.
Int. rim 10, Ext. rim 12

1324 1501
3a (Late Roman Amphora 1) rim, closed vessel; abundant tiny black inclusions, sparse larger 0.5 mm black inclusions, some shiny particles, sparse white inclusions.
Int. rim 10, Ext. rim 13.4
Fig. 568

1325 4307
3a (Late Roman Amphora 1) body sherd, closed vessel; gritty orange fabric with many tiny grey and white inclusions.

1326 1501
3a (Late Roman Amphora 1) handle, closed vessel; cream slip.

1327 3602
3a (Late Roman Amphora 1) handle, closed vessel; cream slip; pale orangey-red with many small dark grits.

1328 4393
3a (Late Roman Amphora 1) handle, closed vessel; cream colour slip; cream fabric with gritty feel and frequent black and white inclusions <0.5 mm.
Fig. 568

1329 4393
3a (Late Roman Amphora 1) handle, closed vessel; cream colour fabric with gritty feel, and frequent brown and few black inclusions.

1330 1501
3a (Late Roman Amphora 1) body sherd, closed vessel; cream slip on ext. on orange fabric, ribbing; cream colour slip; light orange/buff fabric with abundant black inclusions less than 0.5 mm, sparse large 2–4 mm white inclusions, moderate tiny white inclusions <0.5 mm, sparse tiny red inclusions <0.5 mm and very tiny shiny plate-like inclusions.
X 11; Y 13.4
Fig. 568

1331 4304
3a (Late Roman Amphora 1) body sherd, closed vessel; wide ribbing, cream slip on exterior; many black and grey inclusions and sparse red and white inclusions.
Int. body di. 28; Y 10

1332 9659
3a (Late Roman Amphora 1) body sherd, closed vessel; wide shallow ribbing; coarse fabric with frequent tiny black inclusions, and sparse angular opaque 0.5 mm inclusions and sparse red inclusions <0.5 mm.
X 7.8

1333 5639
5g base, closed vessel; amphora spike; cream wash on amphora exterior; orange/brown fabric with black and white inclusions.

1334 2343
5c (Late Roman Amphora 3), base, closed vessel. Lower wall and base of an amphora which tapers to a hollow point. Bottom sealed inside with decorative hole at tip. Wide smooth ribbing. Fine matrix with micaceous dark red-brown fabric.

1335 1501
Handle, pinched amphora, closed vessel.
Fig. 569

1336 4308
Handle, pinched amphora, closed vessel; very pale cream micaceous slip on ext.; micaceous very fine hard orange fabric with sparse very tiny white inclusions.
Fig. 569

1337 4392
K1 rim, closed vessel; ribbing; evidence of burning; gritty fabric with fine particles.
Int. rim 11, Ext. rim 12.2

1338 4307
K1 rim and handle, closed vessel; ribbing; inclusions very tiny up to 0.5 mm angular opaque.
Int. rim 11, Ext. rim 12.8

1339 4391
K1 rim, closed vessel; red/brown fabric with white inclusions and tiny black inclusions.
Int. rim 11, Ext. rim 13.2

1340 4392
K1 rim, closed vessel; ribbing.
Int. rim 11, Ext. rim 13.2

1341 4308
K1 rim and handle, closed vessel; grey fabric ext. and int. dark brown/ black core with white inclusions much <0.5 mm.
Int. rim 12, Ext. rim 14

1342 4307
K1 rim, closed vessel; narrow ribbing below rim; black/grey vessel ext. dark red int., sparse cream-colour inclusions <0.5 mm and moderate very tiny white, red and opaque inclusions barely large enough to see.
Int. rim 12.4, Ext. rim 14.8

1343 1501
K1 rim, closed vessel; dark red fabric, with moderate tiny white inclusions and moderate dark red angular inclusions <0.5 mm.
Int. rim 11.2, Ext. rim 14
Fig. 575

1344 3309
K1 rim and handle, closed vessel; orange fabric, moderate white inclusions up to 0.5 mm, and red inclusions <0.5 mm and sparse shiny opaque crystals up to 1 mm.
Int. rim 15, Ext. rim 17

1345 4391
K1 rim and handle, closed vessel; red cooking ware fabric with sparse white inclusions and frequent very tiny silver mica.
Int. rim 13, Ext. rim 15

1346 4393
K1 rim, closed vessel; micaceous cooking fabric with white inclusions less than 0.5 mm.
Int. rim 12, Ext. rim 14.4

1347 2339
K1 rim, closed vessel; evidence of burning; dark purple gritty fabric with tiny white inclusions.
Int. rim 16, Ext. rim 19.2

1348 3601
K1 rim and handle, closed vessel; red fabric, sparse white inclusions 0.5 mm.
Int. rim 16, Ext. rim 17.8

1349 2339
K1 rim, closed vessel; narrow ribbing below rim; red/brown purple fabric with white and cream inclusions.
Int. rim 13.2, Ext. rim 16

1350 9659
K1 rim, closed vessel; red/brown fabric with tiny white inclusions and black inclusions both 0.5 mm.
Int. rim 17; Ext. rim 19

1351 4303
K1 rim, closed vessel; red fabric with opaque and white inclusions 0.5 mm.
Int. rim 8, Ext. rim 10

1352 4307
K1 rim, closed vessel; orange fabric with angular opaque crystals.
Int. rim 11, Ext. rim 12.4

1353 9675
K1 rim, closed vessel; evidence of burning; black fabric, inclusions unidentifiable.
Int. rim 11.6, Ext. rim 14

1354 3401
K1 rim, closed vessel; purple/brown colour with sparse grey and white inclusions.
Int. rim 7, Ext. rim 8

1355 4317
K1 rim, closed vessel; white inclusions up to 0.5 mm and dark red inclusions <0.5 mm.
Int. rim 10, Ext. rim 11

1356 9660
K1 rim, closed vessel; relatively fine matrix, no inclusions recognizable.
Int. rim 10.4, Ext. rim 12

Pottery from Level One

1357   4392
K1 rim, closed vessel; micaceous with tiny white inclusions.
Int. rim 12, Ext. rim 12.8

1358   1653
K1 rim, closed vessel; slightly micaceous, tiny white inclusions.
Int. rim 11.6, Ext. rim 13

1359   1501
K1 rim, closed vessel; evidence of burning; grey fabric, tiny sparse white inclusions.
Int. rim 11, Ext. rim 14

1360   3101
K1 rim, closed vessel; red fabric with moderate red inclusions up to 0.5 mm and cream inclusions up to 0.5 mm.
Int. rim 14, Ext. rim 14.4

1361   4303
K1 rim, closed vessel; red/orange fabric with very small white/grey inclusions.
Int. rim 13.8, Ext. rim 15

1362   3200
K1 rim, closed vessel; grey brown core with orange brown ext., sparse opaque/white angular inclusions <0.5 mm, and frequent very tiny white inclusions.
Int. rim 12.8, Ext. rim 15

1363   9666
K1 rim, closed vessel; moderate numbers of tiny white inclusions, round sparse red inclusions 2 mm, and sparse opaque inclusions 0.5 mm, occasional very large white inclusion up to 6 mm long.
Int. rim 19, Ext. rim 20

1364   2350
K1 rim, closed vessel; purple/red brown fabric with white and brown inclusions.
Int. rim 17, Ext. rim 20

1365   3101
K1 rim and handle, closed vessel; red fabric with distinctive moderate cream/white sub-angular inclusions up to 0.5 mm, silt-sized particles reflecting sunlight: mica?
Int. rim 21.2, Ext. rim 22

1366   4391
K1 handle, closed vessel; red fabric with moderate angular red inclusions 1–2 mm and opaque white angular inclusions 1 mm.

1367   1660
K1 handle, closed vessel; gouge (on handle).

1368   1626
K1 rim, closed vessel; black core with large white and opaque angular inclusions and fine white inclusions.
Int. rim 14, Ext. rim 11.6

1369   4391
K1 rim, closed vessel; grey/brown fabric with red core, sparse red inclusions 0.5 mm, opaque/white angular inclusions ranging from tiny up to 1 mm.
Int. rim 9, Ext. rim 10.4

1370   3300
K2 rim and handle, closed vessel; evidence of burning on ext.
Int. rim 12, Ext. rim 13.8

1371   3400
K2 rim, closed vessel; evidence of burning; incised horizontal line on neck below rim; black fabric with grey and white inclusions <0.5 mm.
Int. rim 11.6, Ext. rim 13

1372   3213
K2 rim, closed vessel; brown/red fabric with moderate white, grey, and red inclusions <0.5 mm.
Int. rim 10, Ext. rim 12

1373   3419
K2 rim, closed vessel; evidence of burning; very blackened fabric with frequent angular red inclusions and sparse small yellow angular inclusions.
Int. rim 7.6, Ext. rim 10

1374   3101
K2 rim, closed vessel; light brown/orange fabric with frequent angular opaque inclusions ranging from very tiny to 0.5 mm.
Int. rim 12, Ext. rim 14.6

1375   3212
K2 rim, closed vessel; grey/black fabric with angular black angular inclusions <0.5 mm.
Int. rim 12.2, Ext. rim 14.4

1376   1605
K2 rim, closed vessel; purple brown fabric with red/brown inclusions.
Int. rim 11.6, Ext. rim 14

1377   1626
K2 base; orange fabric with white and brown inclusions.
Base di. 9
Fig. 570

1378   4316
K2 lid, closed vessel; dark brown fabric with many angular shiny crystals <0.5 mm.
Int. rim 12

1379   4393
K2 handle and body sherd, closed vessel; large 2 mm red plate-like inclusions and sparse cream/white inclusions.

1380   4393
K2 rim and handle; red inclusions 1 mm and white inclusions 1 mm and opaque shiny angular inclusions 0.5 mm.

1381   3008
K2 rim, closed vessel; evidence of burning; very black fabric fine with no visible inclusions except mica and very tiny pale inclusions.
Int. rim 8, Ext. rim 9.2

1382   1626
K2 rim, open vessel; few angular white inclusions.
Int. rim 10, Ext. rim 12.4

1383   2336
K2 rim, closed vessel.
Int. rim 9.8, Ext. rim 11

1384   3209
K2 rim, closed vessel; evidence of burning; grey brown fabric, slightly micaceous with sparse angular inclusions up to 3 mm,

mostly <0.5 mm.
Int. rim 14, Ext. rim 12.4

1385   1501
K2 rim and handle, closed vessel; coarse brown/orange fabric with sparse red angular inclusions over 1 mm, and sparse angular black inclusions less than 0.5 mm, sparse white inclusions 0.5 mm.
Ext. rim 14
Fig. 575

1386   1661
K2 rim, closed vessel; 1 mm white inclusions, angular red and opaque inclusions 0.5–1 mm and very small white inclusions.
Int. rim 13, Ext. rim 17

1387   1602
K3 rim, closed vessel; brown/purple fabric with tiny white inclusions.
Int. rim 8.8, Ext. rim 11

1388   2107
K4 rim, closed vessel; burnt exterior; dark/brown/black fabric frequent white/cream inclusions up to 0.5 mm and fine micaceous particles.
Int. rim 11, Ext. rim 13

1389   5636
K4 rim, closed vessel.
Int. rim 13, Ext. rim 14

1390   2321
K4 rim, closed vessel; soft fabric with many white and red angular inclusions.
Int. rim 15, Ext. rim 16.4

1391   1501
K4 rim, closed vessel; many angular red inclusions 0.5 mm and tiny white inclusions.
Int. rim 14, Ext. rim 15.6

1392   3010
K4 rim, closed vessel; burnt on exterior; frequent white inclusions <0.5–1 mm, and dark brown inclusions <0.5–1 mm.
Int. rim 18.8, Ext. rim 20
Fig. 575

1393   3010
K4 rim, closed vessel; grey and angular light brown 0.5 mm angular inclusions.
Int. rim 17, Ext. rim 20

1394   2308
K4 base, closed vessel; burnt on exterior; white and opaque angular and round inclusions less than 1 mm.
Base di. 12

1395   3602
K4 lid, closed vessel.

1396   1501
K5 rim, open vessel; many tiny white inclusions and larger black and red inclusions up to 0.5 mm.
Int. rim 7

1397   4307
K5 rim, closed vessel; ribbing; grey/very dark brown fabric with frequent white inclusions <0.5 mm.
Int. rim 8, Ext. rim 10
Fig. 575

1398   2339
K5 rim, closed vessel; purple/black fabric with many white inclusions less than 0.5 mm.
Int. rim 11, Ext. rim 13

1399   1610
K5 rim, closed vessel; very small white inclusions.
Int. rim 12, Ext. rim 14

1400   2346
K5 handle, closed vessel.

1401   1661
K6 rim, closed vessel; brown inclusions less than 0.5 mm and very small white inclusions.
Int. rim 10.6, Ext. rim 13

1402   1626
K6 rim, closed vessel; no visible inclusions.
Int. rim 14, Ext. rim 16

1403   3400
K7 rim, closed vessel; light brown fabric with common opaque/white inclusions <0.5 mm and sparse grey inclusions <0.5 mm.
Int. rim 9.4, Ext. rim 10

1404   2310
K7 rim, closed vessel; inscribed wavy lines above and below external collar; hard red/brown fabric with black and white inclusions.
Int. rim 10.8, Ext. rim 12

1405   2343
K7 rim, closed vessel; very narrow combing below rim.
Int. rim 10, Ext. rim 12.6
Fig. 575

1406   3203
K7 rim, closed vessel; frequent white and cream inclusions <0.5 mm and sparse red inclusions <0.5 mm.
Int. rim 13, Ext. rim 15.6

1407   4302
K7 rim, closed vessel; light brown/red fabric with red inclusions <0.5 mm and white inclusions <0.5 mm.
Int. rim 11, Ext. rim 13.

1408   4302
K7 rim, closed vessel; ribbing below rim; orange/brown fabric with white and opaque inclusions <0.5 mm.
Int. rim 13, Ext. rim 15

1409   4500
K7 rim, closed vessel; brown/dark red slightly micaceous fabric with browner core and grey inclusions <0.5 mm.
Int. rim 14, Ext. rim 16.2

1410   3106
K7 rim, closed vessel; red fabric with white inclusions <0.5 mm and red inclusions ranging from 0.5–1 mm.
Int. rim 14, Ext. rim 16.4

1411   1732
K7 rim, closed vessel; orange fabric with white inclusions less than 0.5 mm and red inclusions 0.5 mm.
Int. rim 14, Ext. rim 16.6

Pottery from Level One

1412   3102
K7 rim, closed vessel; red brown fabric with frequent opaque angular inclusions <0.5 mm and light brown/orange inclusions <0.5 mm.
Int. rim 14.2, Ext. rim 17

1413   9681
K7 rim, closed vessel; frequent opaque/white angular inclusions less than 0.5 mm.
Int. rim 15.8, Ext. rim 18

1414   3201
K7 rim and handle, closed vessel; orange/brown ext. fabric with opaque white/grey and angular light brown inclusions 0.5 mm.
Int. rim 22, Ext. rim 24.8

1415   4302
K7 rim and handle, closed vessel; red fabric with frequent 1 mm red inclusions, common 1 mm white inclusions and sparse 1 mm opaque inclusions.
Int. rim 16, Ext. rim 18.8

1416   4308
K7 rim and handle, closed vessel; red fabric <0.5 mm.
Int. rim 13, Ext. rim 15

1417   9679
K7 rim, closed vessel.
Int. rim 12, Ext. rim 15

1418   3421
K7 rim and handle, closed vessel; red fabric with frequent white inclusions <0.5 mm and red inclusions <0.5 mm.
Int. rim 13, Ext. rim 16

1419   2312
K7 body sherd, closed vessel; incised horizontal and wavy lines; orange int. and ext. with grey fabric core and white and black inclusions less than 0.5 mm.

1420   2305
K7 handle, closed vessel; many tiny white, grey and angular opaque inclusions.

1421   1652
K7 handle, closed vessel; vertical grooving.

1422   1626
K7 handle, closed vessel; orange/red fabric with very small white and black inclusions.
Int. di. 6, Ext. di. 7

1423   3200
K7 rim, closed vessel; brown/buff fabric with white angular inclusions.
Int. rim 14, Ext. rim 16

1424   3600
K7 rim, closed vessel.
Int. rim 15, Ext. rim 18.8

1425   9674
K7 rim, closed vessel; dark red brown fabric, unable to identify inclusions.
Int. rim 11, Ext. rim 12.2

1426   3205
K7 rim, closed vessel; brown micaceous fabric with frequent angular cream- and brown-coloured inclusions.
Int. rim 21, Ext. rim 20.2

1427   1626
K8 rim, closed vessel; brown/red tiny angular and black inclusions.
Int. rim 8, Ext. rim 8.8

1428   1501
K11 base, closed vessel; red/orange fabric with frequent black and white inclusions <0.5 mm and sparse white/opaque 1 mm angular inclusions.
Base di. 8

1429   2308
K12 handle, closed vessel; shallow grooves along either side of the handle and crescent-shaped gouges up centre of handle; orange interior, brown/grey/green ext. flakes of mica, and moderate white and red inclusions 0.5 mm and red/orange interior.
Fig. 575

1430   4390
K13 rim, closed vessel; dark brown fabric with angular inclusions 1 mm.
Int. rim 11, Ext. rim 13.8

1431   2311
K13 rim, closed vessel; light brown fabric with angular yellow, white and black inclusions less than 0.5 mm.
Int. rim 14, Ext. rim 16.8

1432   1602
K13 base.
Base di. 7

1433   1626
K13 base; frequent angular 1 mm brown inclusions and very small micaceous particles.

1434   3402
K20 rim and handle, closed vessel; bright orange interior with glinting particles visible- mica (?), frequent red inclusions up to 3 mm and moderate white inclusions up to 3 mm visible on pock-marked surface.
Int. rim 11, Ext. rim 13

1435   5912
K20 rim, closed vessel; orange fabric exterior, interior and core, with red inclusions <3 mm, tiny particles glinting on surface.
Int. rim 12, Ext. rim 13

1436   J18/421   2316+2318
K21 complete profile, closed vessel; horizontal lines on shoulder; tiny white inclusions and 0.5 mm grey inclusions.
Int. rim 8.8, Ext. rim 11.3; Base di. 8
Fig. 572

1437   J19/78   1626
K21 complete profile, closed vessel; single horizontal line on shoulder; burnt on opposite side to handle; red/brown fabric and black where burnt, frequent red and white inclusions visible on interior and exterior surfaces: white 0.5 mm up to 2 mm; red/brown up to 2 mm.
Int. rim 10, Ext. rim 12; Base di. 9, Body di. 15.6
Fig. 570

1438 J19/77 1626
K21 base, closed vessel; smooth on exterior; entire base exterior burnt, hole 9 mm diameter off centre of base; orange core and interior surface, inclusions are red and white up to 2 mm clearly visible especially on the interior surface, the white inclusions have blistered especially on the interior.
Base di. 11, Body di. 18.4
Fig. 570

1439 J19/81 1626
K21 base, closed vessel; orange fabric with very light brown central core about 1 mm thick. Fabric has angular red inclusions up to 1.5 mm. The red inclusions are visible on the interior surface; sparse white inclusions <0.5 mm but no evidence for blistering.
Base di. 12, Body di. 23.5
Fig. 570

1440 1626
K21 complete profile, closed vessel; three incised lines on shoulder and three on belly of vessel; burnt on opposite side to handle; orange fabric with white inclusions up to 2 mm and grey inclusions.
Fig. 571

1441 J19/80 1626
K21 base, closed vessel; evidence for burning on exterior; vessel exterior is dull mid brown colour with moderate dark brown angular inclusions up to c. 1 mm.
Base di. 11.6
Fig. 570

1442 3412
K21 rim and handle, closed vessel; angular white/grey/brown inclusions less than 0.5 mm.
Int. rim 14, Ext. rim 15.3

1443 3412
K21 rim, closed vessel; soft orange/pink fabric red and grey inclusions <0.5 mm and sparse white inclusions.
Int. rim 16.8, Ext. rim 19

1444 3204
Rim, S-shaped, closed vessel.
Int. rim 12.4, Ext. rim 13.1

1445 1602
Rim, closed vessel; cooking ware fabric.
Int. rim 15, Ext. rim 19.5

1446 2106
Rim and handle, closed vessel; smooth finish; hard, brittle fabric with smooth finish, relatively fine for cooking ware inclusions very small: unidentifiable.
Int. rim 12.2, Ext. rim 13

1447 3102
Rim, closed vessel; red paint on ext. rim and ext. body; orange fabric with sparse/moderate red inclusions <0.5 mm and a few sparse 1 mm and white inclusions <0.5 mm.
Int. rim 13, Ext. rim 14

1448 3101
Rim, closed vessel; brown fabric with opaque angular inclusions and brown inclusions <0.5 mm.
Int. rim 17, Ext. rim 17.8

1449 3200
Rim, closed vessel; red cooking fabric with moderate angular red 0.5 mm inclusions and moderate angular white inclusions <0.5 mm.
Int. rim 22, Ext. rim 25

1450 3101
Rim, closed vessel; light brown/orange fabric with frequent angular, opaque inclusions ranging from very tiny to 0.5 mm.
Int. rim 21, Ext. rim 22

1451 1514
Rim, closed vessel; grey-brown micaceous fabric with sparse grey inclusions <0.5 mm and sparse light brown/yellow inclusions <0.5 mm.
Int. rim 27, Ext. rim 27.6

1452 3001
Rim and handle, closed vessel; slightly micaceous red fabric with red inclusions 1 mm and grey inclusions 0.5 mm.
Int. rim 13, Ext. rim 14.4

1453 4303
Rim, closed vessel; white angular inclusions.
Int. rim 11, Ext. rim 13

1454 5903
Rim and handle, closed vessel; micaceous, relatively fine matrix for cooking fabric.
Int. rim 16, Ext. rim 13.2

1455 3305
Rim and handle, closed vessel; brown fabric with white/opaque inclusions tiny to 0.5 mm.
Int. rim 17, Ext. rim 18.6

1456 2352
Rim and handle; grey brown ext. and int. slightly red in places with orange core and sparse red inclusions, frequent grey/white inclusions <0.5, and sparse white up to 2 mm.
Int. rim 13, Ext. rim 14

1457 3501
Rim and handle, closed vessel.
Int. rim 12.5, Ext. rim 13

1458 1605
Rim and handle, closed vessel; micaceous fabric with common grey inclusions 0.5 mm, moderate brown inclusions 0.5 mm and sparse white inclusions <0.5 mm.
Int. rim 11.8, Ext. rim 13

1459 3401
Rim, closed vessel; brown fabric with frequent opaque/white inclusions <0.5 mm.
Int. rim 11.2, Ext. rim 12

1460 4500
Rim, closed vessel; raised horizontal line below rim; black/dark grey brown fabric.
Int. rim 12.4, Ext. rim 13

1461 2106
Rim, closed vessel; light brown/orange fabric with 2 mm grey angular inclusions on interior and smooth exterior white and red inclusions <0.5 mm.
Int. rim 11.5, Ext. rim 12

1462 1626
Body sherd, closed vessel; very fine combing: horizontal and wavy

lines; black ext., red/brown outer fabric, brown core with white/clear inclusions up to 0.5 mm.
X 3.6; Y 2

1463　　　　　　　　　　　　　　　　　　　　　　1501
1a imbrex.
Curved imbrex roof tile of fabric 1a. Single large groove running across the upper part of the imbrex from which there are multiple parallel grooves running along the length. Hard light buff/orange fabric with well-sorted red and brown angular inclusions *c*. 2 × 2 mm and poorly sorted white inclusions from very small up to *c*. 1 mm.
L. 9.8+; W. 7.7+; Th. 1.6 (max); Th. Body 1.2; Int. Di. *c*. 8

1464　　　L14/15d　　　　　　　　　　　　　　　　3602
Corner fragment of type 1b. Pale yellow core and upper surface fabric, buff lower surface. Frequent small stones/grog? (same colour as clay) and some red and brown stones. Distinct groove running along inside of ridge and rim.
W. 13.9+; L. 19.5+; Th. rim 4.2; Th. ridge 3.3; Th. body 1.45; Inner edge of ridge to edge 5.6; Outer edge 3.2; W. rim 3.6

1465　　　L14/15b　　　　　　　　　　　　　　　　3602
Corner fragment of type 1b. Pinky-buff core, slightly paler at surface. Medium density of red (grog?) inclusions, and occasional vegetable impressions.
W. 9.9; L. 11.3+; Th. rim 4.05; Th. ridge 3.3; Th. body 2.1; Outer edge of ridge to edge *c*. 1.6; Inner edge 4.5; W. rim 3.45

1466　　　L14/15i　　　　　　　　　　　　　　　　3602
Corner fragment of type 2a. Same fabric as **1469b**.
L. 14.5+; W. 12.7+; Th. rim 4.9; W. rim 4.45; Th. body 2.2; Th. angled ridge 3.5; L. angled ridge 4.8; W. angled ridge 3.7

1467　　　L14/15c　　　　　　　　　　　　　　　　3602
Corner fragment of type 1a. Yellow-buff fabric with red grog?, small stones and fine sand inclusions.
W. 16.2+; L. 12.6+; Th. rim 4.8; Th. ridge 3.4; Th. body 2.6; Outer edge of ridge to tile edge 1.6; Inner edge 3.5; W. rim 3.3

1468a　　　L14/15a　　　　　　　　　　　　　　　3602
Corner fragment of type 1b. Pale greenish-yellow fabric (both core and surface) with frequent sand and small stones. Some finger-impressed grooves on back, which is largely encrusted.
W. 21.8+; L. 13.5+; Th. rim 4.2; Th. ridge. 3.7; Th. body 2.6; Outer edge of ridge to tile edge 1.3; Inner edge of ridge to edge of tile 2.9; W. of rim 3.95

1468b　　　L14/15e　　　　　　　　　　　　　　　3602
Corner fragment of type 1a. Pale yellow fabric, slightly darker at core than surface. Frequent small red stones and sand.
W. 10.4+; L. 12.9+; Th. rim 3.7; Th. Ridge 3.1; Th. body 1.7; Outer edge of ridge to edge 2.1; Inner edge 3.5; W. of rim 3.0.

1469a　　　L14/15f　　　　　　　　　　　　　　　3602
Corner fragment of type 2b. Brick red fabric at core, yellow-buff at surface. Frequent small and medium red stones and occasional white calcareous inclusions.
L. 12.2+; W. 6.3+; Th. rim 4.65; W. rim 3.25; Th. body 2.2; Th. angled ridge 3.6; L. angled ridge 4.9; W. angled ridge 3.8+

1469b　　　L14/15h　　　　　　　　　　　　　　　3602
Corner fragment of type 2a. Pinky-red fabric, slightly paler at surface. Frequent small and medium red stones, occasional large voids, occasional white calcareous inclusions.
L. 12.2+; W. 9.7+; Th. rim 4.4; W. rim 3.6; Th. body 2.4; Th. angled ridge 3.4; L. angled ridge 5.3; W. angled ridge 3.6

1469c　　　L14/15g　　　　　　　　　　　　　　　3602
Corner fragment of type 2a. Yellow-buff fabric with frequent small stones, occasional large white calcareous inclusions, some voids.
L. 12.2+; W. 9.4+; Th. rim 3.75; W. rim 3.7; Th. body 1.7; Th. angled ridge 2.6; L. angled ridge 6.5; W. angled ridge 5.0

Notes

1. For convenience, in this section Level 1 includes Level I, unless Level I is specifically stated — see p. 69 for an explanation of the phasing.
2. Late Roman C form 3 sherds (**1011**, **1013**) and Cypriot Red Slip ware sherds (**1015**, **1016**) were both recovered from the shallow deposits covering the latest (phase 1d) walls in K19.
3. The Alahan material was originally stored at Konya Museum and published, by Caroline Williams (Williams 1985); but this did not represent all the material recovered during the excavations. Much of this is still stored in depots on site (Stephen Hill pers. comm.). In addition, further unpublished photographs, drawings and notes are currently stored within the Gough Archive which is in the care of Dr Stephen Hill, University of Warwick. The Gough archive and the material at Silifke and at the BIAA in Ankara were examined by MPCJ in 1999 (Jackson 1999b).
4. A certain 'lost' sherd was not seen by Williams prior to her publication and was known to her only from photographs and from casts (Williams 1985, 50, no. 72). This sherd was stamped to preserve three oval impressions featuring figures. It was located by MPCJ in 1999 in the British Institute of Archaeology at Ankara reference collection of ceramics from Alahan.
5. The fact that together Fabrics 1a and 1b represent such a large proportion of the Byzantine pottery assemblage including large storage vessels and tiles at Kilise Tepe and that 'Monastic Ware' occurred at both Alahan and Dağ Pazarı would confirm that this is a local fabric.
6. In the catalogue below, the X-measurement represents the maximum distance across the preserved sherd; the Y-measurement represents the maximum length of the sherd along its vertical distance.

Table 14. *Level One pottery provenance, fabric nos. and publication nos.*

Square	Unit	Fabric	Vol. no.	Square	Unit	Fabric	Vol. no.	Square	Unit	Fabric	Vol. no.
H18	2600	1a	1281	J18a	2310	K7	1404	J18b	2354	1a	1109
H18	2600	1b	1088	J18a	2311	2c	1294	J18b	2355	1a	1177
H18d	2620	1a	1276	J18a	2311	K13	1431	J18b	2357	2c	1292
I14a	3402	K20	1434	J18a	2312	K7	1419	J19	1600	1a	1230
I14a	3404	1a	1243	J18a	2316	2c	1297	J19	1660	K1	1367
I14a	3412	K21	1422	J18a	2316	K21	1436	J19a	1653	K1	1358
I14a	3412	K21	1443	J18b	2321	2c	1298	J19a/c	1652	K7	1421
I14a/b	3400	1b	1060	J18b	2321	K4	1390	J19b	1604	2g	1303
I14a/b	3400	K2	1371	J18b	2336	K2	1383	J19b	1604	2h	1308
I14a/b	3400	K7	1403	J18b	2337	1a	1174	J19b/d	1601	1a	1229
I14a/b	3401	1a	1140	J18b	2337	2c	1300	J19b/d	1602	1a	1154
I14a/b	3401	1a	1231	J18b	2338	1a	1211	J19b/d	1602	1a	1156
I14a/b	3401	1a	1233	J18b	2339	1a	1098	J19b/d	1602	1a?	1107
I14a/b	3401	3a	1323	J18b	2339	1a	1149	J19b/d	1602	1b	1155
I14a/b	3401	K1	1354	J18b	2339	1a	1191	J19b/d	1602	1b	1157
I14a/b	3401		1459	J18b	2339	1a	1247	J19b/d	1602	2h	1312
I14a/b	3403	1a	1133	J18b	2339	2c	1291	J19b/d	1602	K1	1445
I14a/b	3403	1a	1467	J18b	2339	K1	1347	J19b/d	1602	K13	1432
I14b	3419	K2	1373	J18b	2339	K1	1349	J19b/d	1602	K3	1387
I14b	3421	K7	1418	J18b	2339	K5	1398	J19b/d	1610	K5	1399
I14b	3423	1a	1070	J18b	2343	1a	1029	J19c	1661	K2	1386
I14b	3423	1a	1225	J18b	2343	1a	1062	J19c	1661	K6	1401
I14b	3423	1a	1227	J18b	2343	1a	1096	J19d	1605	1a	1036
I14b	3423	1a	1254	J18b	2343	1a	1175	J19d	1605	1a	1158
I15	4403	1a	1220	J18b	2343	1a	1176	J19d	1605	1a	1271
I16	4600	1a	1265	J18b	2343	1a	1190	J19d	1605	3a	1322
I16	4600	1a	1266	J18b	2343	1a	1195	J19d	1605	K2	1376
I19d	1732	K7	1411	J18b	2343	1a	1216	J19d	1605		1458
J14a	3309	K1	1344	J18b	2343	1a	1218	J19d	1621	2h	1313
J14a	3314	f	1020	J18b	2343	1b	1150	J19d	1626	1a	1278
J14a	3316	1a	1108	J18b	2343	1b	1193	J19d	1626	1b	1159
J14b	3300	K2	1370	J18b	2343	1b	1194	J19d	1626	1b	1160
J14b	3301	f	1019	J18b	2343	2c	1299	J19d	1626	f	1021
J14b	3301		1132	J18b	2343	5c	1334	J19d	1626	f	1022
J14b	3305		1455	J18b	2343	K7	1405	J19d	1626	K1	1368
J17	5000	fg		J18b	2343	SB	1017	J19d	1626	K13	1433
J18a	2305	1a	1148	J18b	2345	2c	1296	J19d	1626	K2	1377
J18a	2305	fg		J18b	2345	2m	1091	J19d	1626	K2	1382
J18a	2305	K7	1420	J18b	2346	K5	1400	J19d	1626	K21	1437
J18a	2305		1054	J18b	2350	1a	1151	J19d	1626	K21	1438
J18a	2306		1463	J18b	2350	1a	1152	J19d	1626	K21	1439
J18a	2308	2c	1295	J18b	2350	2g	1305	J19d	1626	K21	1440
J18a	2308	K12	1429	J18b	2350	K1	1364	J19d	1626	K21	1441
J18a	2308	K4	1394	J18b	2352		1456	J19d	1626	K6	1402

Table 14. *(cont.)*

Square	Unit	Fabric	Vol. no.	Square	Unit	Fabric	Vol. no.	Square	Unit	Fabric	Vol. no.
J19d	1626	K7	1422	K17d	9660	K1	1356	K18a	4309	1a	1030
J19d	1626	K8	1427	K17d	9666	2c	1293	K18a	4309	1a	1222
J19d	1626		1462	K17d	9666	K1	1363	K18a	4309	1a	1259
K14a	3000	1a	1078	K17d	9669	1b	1102	K18a	4309	1a	1269
K14a	3000	1a	1135	K17d	9671	5b	1055	K18a	4309	1a	1284
K14a	3000	1a	1261	K17d	9674	K7	1425	K18a	4309	1b	1118
K14a	3000	f	1023	K17d	9675	K1	1353	K18a	4309	1b	1241
K14a	3000	f	1025	K17d	9681	K7	1413	K18a	4309		1119
K14a	3001	1a	1263	K18a	4301	1a	1068	K18a	4314	1a	1048
K14a	3001	1a	1264	K18a	4302	1a	1034	K18a	4314	1a	1221
K14a	3001	1a	1464	K18a	4302	1a	1082	K18a	4314	1a	1275
K14a	3001		1452	K18a	4302	1a	1114	K18a	4314	1a	1285
K14a	3002	1a	1262	K18a	4302	1a	1115	K18a	4314	1b	1042
K14a	3008	K2	1381	K18a	4302	1a	1116	K18a	4314		1120
K14a	3010	K4	1392	K18a	4302	1a	1189	K18a	4316	K2	1378
K14a	3010	K4	1393	K18a	4302	1a	1277	K18a	4317	1a	1050
K14b	3012	1a	1077	K18a	4302	1b	1178	K18a	4317	K1	1355
K14b	3017	LRC	1014	K18a	4302	K7	1407	K18a	4320	1a	1067
K17a	9686	1a	1184	K18a	4302	K7	1408	K18a	4320	1a	1181
K17b	9615	2c	1290	K18a	4302	K7	1415	K18b	4390	1a	1040
K17b	9615	K15	1201	K18a	4302		1113	K18b	4390	1a	1105
K17b	9616	1a	1039	K18a	4302		1179	K18b	4390	1a	1121
K17b	9616	1a	1065	K18a	4303	1a	1238	K18b	4390	1a	1185
K17b	9616	2c	1289	K18a	4303	1a	1244	K18b	4390	1a	1253
K17b	9672	2g	1302	K18a	4303	K1	1351	K18b	4390	2h	1310
K17b	9678	2g	1304	K18a	4303	K1	1361	K18b	4390	K13	1430
K17b	9679	K7	1417	K18a	4303		1453	K18b	4390	LRC	1010
K17c	9649	2g	1307	K18a	4304	3a	1331	K18b	4391	1a	1037
K17c	9650	1a	1041	K18a	4307	1a	1224	K18b	4391	1a	1124
K17c	9650	1a	1131	K18a	4307	1a	1466	K18b	4391	1a	1186
K17c	9650	1a	1153	K18a	4307	3a	1325	K18b	4391	1a	1187
K17d	9625	1a	1033	K18a	4307	K1	1338	K18b	4391	1b	1111
K17d	9633	2g	1306	K18a	4307	K1	1342	K18b	4391	1b	1122
K17d	9643	1a	1286	K18a	4307	K1	1352	K18b	4391	1b	1123
K17d	9657	1a	1237	K18a	4307	K5	1397	K18b	4391	2h	1309
K17d	9658	1a	1228	K18a	4307		1095	K18b	4391	4a	1061
K17d	9659	1a	1213	K18a	4307		1180	K18b	4391	K1	1339
K17d	9659	1a	1240	K18a	4308	1a	1085	K18b	4391	K1	1366
K17d	9659	1a	1270	K18a	4308	1a	1117	K18b	4391	K1	1369
K17d	9659	1b	1101	K18a	4308	1a	1188	K18b	4391		1345
K17d	9659	1b	1104	K18a	4308	1a	1212	K18b	4392	1a	1051
K17d	9659	2c	1301	K18a	4308	1d	1066	K18b	4392	1a	1086
K17d	9659	2h	1315	K18a	4308	K1	1341	K18b	4392	1a	1125
K17d	9659	5j	1332	K18a	4308	K7	1416	K18b	4392	1a	1276
K17d	9659	K1	1350	K18a	4308		1336	K18b	4392	1a desc	1099

Table 14. *(cont.)*

Square	Unit	Fabric	Vol. no.
K18b	4392	K1	1337
K18b	4392	K1	1340
K18b	4392	K1	1357
K18b	4393	1a	1052
K18b	4393	1a	1056
K18b	4393	1a	1103
K18b	4393	1a	1126
K18b	4393	1a	1192
K18b	4393	1a desc	1203
K18b	4393	1b	1043
K18b	4393	1b	1083
K18b	4393	1b	1202
K18b	4393	1b	1208
K18b	4393	2h	1311
K18b	4393	2h	1317
K18b	4393	3a	1320
K18b	4393	3a	1321
K18b	4393	3a	1328
K18b	4393	3a	1329
K18b	4393	K1	1346
K18b	4393	K2	1379
K18b	4393	K2	1380
K18b	4395	1a	1094
K18b	4395	1a	1112
K18b	4395	1a	1246
K18b	4395	1b	1127
K18b	4395	1b	1239
K18b	4395		1283
K18b	4397	1a	1128
K18b	4397	1a	1274
K18d	6009	LRC	1009
K19	1500	1a	1053
K19	1500	1a	1057
K19	1500	1a	1063
K19	1500	1a	1080
K19	1500	1a desc	1076
K19	1500	1b	1072
K19	1501	1a	1032
K19	1501	1a	1035
K19	1501	1a	1038
K19	1501	1a	1064
K19	1501	1a	1081
K19	1501	1a	1090
K19	1501	1a	1092
K19	1501	1a	1097
K19	1501	1a	1162
K19	1501	1a	1163
K19	1501	1a	1164
K19	1501	1a	1165
K19	1501	1a	1166
K19	1501	1a	1168
K19	1501	1a	1169
K19	1501	1a	1170
K19	1501	1a	1173
K19	1501	1a	1183
K19	1501	1a	1205
K19	1501	1a	1206
K19	1501	1a	1232
K19	1501	1a	1250
K19	1501	1a	1251
K19	1501	1a	1252
K19	1501	1a	1280
K19	1501	1a	1282
K19	1501	1b	1161
K19	1501	1b	1167
K19	1501	1b	1200
K19	1501	1b	1210
K19	1501	1b	1249
K19	1501	2h	1314
K19	1501	2h	1316
K19	1501	3a	1318
K19	1501	3a	1319
K19	1501	3a	1324
K19	1501	3a	1326
K19	1501	3a	1330
K19	1501	5f	1273
K19	1501	CRS	1015
K19	1501	CRS	1016
K19	1501	K1	1343
K19	1501	K1	1359
K19	1501	K11	1428
K19	1501	K2	1385
K19	1501	K4	1391
K19	1501	K5	1396
K19	1501	LRC	1011
K19	1501	LRC	1013
K19	1501		1248
K19	1501		1335
K19	1512	1a	1027
K19	1512	1a	1171
K19	1513		1172
K19	1514	1a	1207
K19	1514	1a	1209
K19	1514		1451
K19d	1567	1a	1071
K19d	4500	K7	1409
K19d	4500		1460
L14a	3600	1a	1258
L14a	3600	K7	1424
L14a	3602	1a	1031
L14a	3602	1a	1044
L14a	3602	1a	1069
L14a	3602	1a	1073
L14a	3602	1a	1256
L14a	3602	1a	1257
L14a	3602	3a	1327
L14a	3602	K4	1395
L14a	3603	1a	1139
L14a	3606	f	1018
L14b	3601	1a	1046
L14b	3601	1a	1049
L14b	3601	1a	1058
L14b	3601	1a	1087
L14b	3601	1a	1088
L14b	3601	1a	1136
L14b	3601	1a	1137
L14b	3601	1a	1138
L14b	3601	1a	1145
L14b	3601	1a	1182
L14b	3601	1a	1204
L14b	3601	1a	1242
L14b	3601	1a	1255
L14b	3601	1a	1279
L14b	3601	K1	1348
L14b	3604	1a	1260
L14b	3608	1a	1236
L16a	5625	1a	1129
L16a	5630	1a	1130
L16a	5631	1a	1100
L16a	5633	1a	1214
L16a	5634	1a	1215
L16a	5634	1a	1217
L16a	5634	1a	1219
L16a	5636	K4	1389
L16a	5639	5g	1333

Table 14. *(cont.)*

Square	Unit	Fabric	Vol. no.
L19a	5912	K20	1435
L19a/c	5922	1a	1089
L19c	5900	1a	1084
L19c	5902	1a	1146
L19c	5903		1454
L19c	5904	1a	1147
L19c	5904	6L	1268
L19c	5904	LRC	1012
M14a	3501	1a	1223
M14a	3501		1457
N12a	3200	1a	1110
N12a	3200	1a	1141
N12a	3200	1a	1226
N12a	3200	1a	1245
N12a	3200	6L	1267
N12a	3200	f	1026
N12a	3200	K1	1362
N12a	3200	K7	1423
N12a	3200		1449
N12a	3201	K7	1414
N12a	3201	LRC	1008

Square	Unit	Fabric	Vol. no.
N12a	3202	1a	1075
N12a	3202	1a	1287
N12a	3203	K7	1406
N12a	3204	1a	1106
N12a	3204	1a	1142
N12a	3204	1a	1196
N12a	3204	1a	1234
N12a	3204	1a	1235
N12a	3204	f	1024
N12a	3204		1444
N12a	3205	1a	1045
N12a	3205	1a	1074
N12a	3205	1a	1272
N12a	3205	1a	1288
N12a	3205	K7	1426
N12a	3205		1199
N12a	3207	1a	1079
N12a	3208	1a	1143
N12a	3208	1a	1144
N12a	3209	1b	1047
N12a	3209	K2	1384

Square	Unit	Fabric	Vol. no.
N12a	3212	K2	1375
N12a	3213	K2	1372
Q10a	3100	1a	1059
Q10a	3101	1a	1093
Q10a	3101	1a	1134
Q10a	3101	1a	1197
Q10a	3101	1a	1198
Q10a	3101	K1	1360
Q10a	3101	K1	1365
Q10a	3101	K2	1374
Q10a	3101		1448
Q10a	3101		1450
Q10a	3102	1a	1465
Q10a	3102	K7	1412
Q10a	3102		1447
Q10a	3106	K7	1410
Q19c	2106		1446
Q19c	2106		1461
Q19c	2107	K4	1388

Appendix

Luminescence Dating of a Single Pottery Sherd from the Byzantine Levels at Kilise Tepe, Turkey

S.M. Barnett

Summary of results

Table 15. *Summary of luminescence results.*

Lab. ref.	Age (years)	Luminescence date
Dur2000 TL pfg 267-1	840±100±120	AD 1160±100±120

Lab. ref.	Palaeodose (Gy)	Dose rate (mGy/a)	Dose rate components (%)				Water uptake of pottery (%)	Water content of soil (%)
			α	β	γ	cos.		
Dur2000 TL pfg 267-1	4.59±0.52	5.49±0.17	27	55	16	2	5±1	5±1

Age determination

The luminescence age is determined from the Age Equation:

$$\text{Luminescence Age (years)} = \frac{\text{Palaeodose (Gy)}}{\text{Dose rate (Gy/year)}}$$

The luminescence age and date is given with associated errors at the 68% level of confidence. The first error term is the random error and should be used when comparing individual luminescence dates; the second error is the overall error which should be used when comparing luminescence dates with independent dating evidence.

Technical details

Sample preparation
The sherd was cut into four pieces: one each for luminescence, dose-rate and water uptake measurements with the major portion of the sherd retained for reference. Both coarse grain (90–150 μm) quartz inclusions and polymineral fine grain (2–10 μm) sub-samples were extracted from the luminescence portion using standard techniques (Aitken 1985).

Palaeodose
Measurements were made in a Risø TL-DA-12 automated reader, laboratory beta doses were administered by a calibrated ^{90}Sr/^{90}Y beta source mounted on the reader. Thermoluminescence was detected by an EMI photomultiplier with a Kopp 5–60 filter used to isolate the blue luminescence and luminescence due to optical stimulation using green (420–530 nm) light provided by a filtered halogen lamp was detected by an EMI photomultiplier with two Hoya U340 filters to isolate the blue/uv luminescence from the stimulating green light. Alpha doses for the polymineral fine grain fraction were administered by a calibrated ^{241}Am source.

No significant luminescence signal was observed for the quartz inclusions using either thermal or optical stimulation. Measurements therefore concentrated on thermoluminescence from the polymineral fine grain fraction. A multiple aliquot, additive dose procedure was used (Aitken 1985) with a preheat to 220°C held for 600s. The results show a wide plateau in the palaeodose determination over the temperature range 300–420°C; a mean palaeodose was used in the age calculation. Tests of the stability of the luminescence signal after storage for 4 months have not revealed any anomalous fading of the signal.

Dose rate
Laboratory measurements using beta TL dosimetry (Bailiff 1982) and thick source alpha counting were used to calculate the dose rate from both the pottery sample and the burial medium. No sample of the burial medium was submitted with sample 250-6 and the dose rate data for this sample is the mean of the dose rate for the other five samples. Thick source alpha counting of sealed and unsealed samples of the pottery indicates that there is some radon loss which will lead to an overestimate of the burial dose rate and consequently an underestimate of the age. However, for the levels of radon loss detected in this sample, any underestimate will be within the errors quoted.

Part E

The Small Finds

Chapter 32 **The Small Finds: Introduction**	**437**
Levels V (EBA) and IV (MBA)	437
Levels III and II	438
Level I	439
Arrangement in the publication	439
Recovery and recording	440
Chapter 33 **Seals with Hieroglyphic Inscriptions**	**441**
Chapter 34 **Other Glyptic**	**445**
Stamp seals	445
Clay sealings	446
Impressions on potsherds	447
Chapter 35 **Miscellaneous Clay Artefacts**	**449**
Stoppers (**1491–1504**)	449
Figurines (**1505–23**)	450
Wheels and wheel-like objects (**1524–6**)	453
Counters, tokens and gaming pieces (**1527–36**)	453
Pottery discs (**1537–95**)	454
Small discs (2.7–3.8 cm)	455
Medium discs (4.0–5.3 cm)	456
Large discs (from 6.0 cm)	457
Unusual shapes	458
Miscellaneous clay items (**1596–623**)	459
Clay pipe (**1624**)	461
Clay furniture (**1625–33**)	461
Clay crescents (**1634–8**)	463
Clay ovoids from J19 (**1639–78**)	466
Chapter 36 **Loomweights**	**469**
Level Vj (**1679–84**)	470
Level Vg (**1685**)	471
Level Vf (**1686–94**)	471
Level Ve (**1695–701**)	471
Level IVa, unit 1258 (**1702–22**)	472
Miscellaneous Level IV loomweights (**1723–34**)	474
Loomweights from IIe in K20 (**1735–60**)	474
Loomweights from Level IIf in J18 (**1761–82**)	476
Loomweights from Level IIf in K18 (**1783–9**)	477
Predominantly doughnut-shaped loomweights from other locations (**1790–1808**)	477
Loomweights from Q20 (**1809–20**)	478

Rectangular and trapezoidal loomweights (**1821–4**)	479
Possible stone weights (**1825–35**)	479

Chapter 37 Spindle Whorls — 481

- Provenance — 481
- Material — 481
- Shapes — 481
- Perforations — 481
- Weight — 482
- Decoration — 483
- Parallels — 483
- Levels V and IV — 483
  - *Level Vj–g* — 483
  - *Level Vf* — 484
  - *Level Ve* — 486
  - *Level IVa–b* — 488
- Levels III to I — 490
  - *Bi-conoids (**1909–28**)* — 490
  - *Spheroids (**1929–62**)* — 492
  - *Ovoids (**1963–74**)* — 494
  - *'Spinning tops' (**1975–83**)* — 495
  - *Hemispheroids (**1984–2000**)* — 495

Chapter 38 Beads — 499

- Clay, stone, copper and shell — 499
  - *Bi-conoid* — 499
  - *Cylindrical* — 499
  - *Miscellaneous shapes* — 499
- Glass, frit or faience — 500
  - *Spheroid (ratio of height to diameter not less than 2:3)* — 500
  - *Round tabular* — 501
  - *Lobed spheroid* — 501
  - *Ovoid (ratio of height to diameter about 1:2 or less)* — 501
  - *Double conoid* — 501
  - *Annular (diameter greater than height; mostly straight-sided)* — 502
  - *Cylindrical (diameter less than height)* — 502
  - *Grooved cylinder* — 502
  - *Barrel-shaped* — 503
  - *Miscellaneous shapes* — 503
  - *Unidentifiable fragments* — 503

Chapter 39 Glass — 505

- Level II — 505
- Later glass — 505
  - *Vessels* — 505
  - *Colour* — 505
  - *Rims* — 506
  - *Body fragments* — 506
  - *Handles* — 506
  - *Bases* — 507
  - *Bangles* — 508
  - *Ring* — 510
  - *Rod* — 510
  - *Glass distribution by square and unit* — 510

Chapter 40 Mosaic Tesserae — 511

- Description — 511

    Distribution of mosaic tesserae   511

Chapter 41   Metalwork   515
   Copper or bronze (**2213–96**)   515
      Adze   515
      Blade   515
      Bracelets   515
      Celt   516
      Haft and tang   516
      Hooks   516
      Nails   516
      Needles   516
      Needle or pin shafts   517
      Pins   517
      Projectile points   518
      Rings and chain links   519
      Shields   521
      Spatula   521
      Tweezers   521
      Wick-holders   521
      Wires, strips and rods   522
      Miscellaneous   522
   Fragments of copper/bronze   523
   Lead and silver (**2297–307**)   523
      Lead strips   523
      Wire   524
      Miscellaneous   524
   Iron (**2308–420**)   525
      Blades   525
      Buckle   526
      Fork   526
      Hafts, tangs and sockets   526
      Nails   526
      Pins   528
      Projectile points   528
      Rings and chain links   528
      Rods and strips   529
      Spatula   529
      Miscellaneous   529
      Fragments of iron   529
      Fragments of unspecified metal or slag   529

Chapter 42   Bone, Horn and Ivory   531
   Astragali (**2421–52**)   531
   Awls and points (**2453–4**)   535
   Pins or needles (**2464–8**)   536
   Notched pins (**2469–70**)   536
   Bone tubes (**2471–8**)   537
   Spatulas (**2479–80**)   538
   Miscellaneous (**2481–92**)   538
   Unworked bone (**2493–9**)   539

Chapter 43   Fossils   541
   Shells: bivalves (**2500–507**)   541
   Shells: spiraliform univalves (**2508–15**)   541
   Dentalium(?) (**2516**)   542
   Sponge(?) (**2517**)   542

Coral(?) (**2518–23**)	542
Shark's tooth (**2524**)	543
Vegetal(?) (**2525–8**)	543
Unidentified (**2529–32**)	543

Chapter 44 **Lithics** — 545
  Introduction — 545
  Methodology — 545
  Results — 545
  Typology — 546
    Arrowhead — 546
    Sickles — 546
    Borer — 547
    Microliths — 547
    Scrapers — 547
    Blades — 547
    Knives — 548
    Denticulates — 548
    Hammerstone — 548
  Technology — 549
    Cores — 549
    Flaked lumps — 550
    Blanks — 550
    Edge conditions — 551
    Raw materials — 552
    Chronology — 553
    The larger samples — 554
  Conclusions — 554

Chapter 45 **Smaller Stone Artefacts** — 559
  Axes or celts (**2597–601**) — 559
  Bobbin(?) (**2602**) — 559
  Decorated stone objects (**2603–11**) — 559
  Incense burner(?) (**2611**) — 561
  Gaming-pieces or counters(?) (**2612–13**) — 561
  Maceheads (**2614–15**) — 561
  Mould for metal (**2616**) — 562
  Mould for jewellery (**2617**) — 562
  Palettes (**2618–23**) — 563
  Sling-shots (**2624–6**) — 563
  Stone tools (**2627–37**) — 563
  Stone vessels (**2638–46**) — 564
  Weights (**2647–8**) — 565
  Whetstones (**2649–64**) — 565
  Worked stones of uncertain use (**2665–70**) — 566

Chapter 46 **Larger Stone Artefacts** — 567
  Mortars — 567
    Mortars from H19 and H20 — 567
      *Early Bronze Age (**2671–5**)* — 567
      *Middle Bronze Age (**2676–7**)* — 567
      *Late Bronze Age (**2678–83**)* — 568
      *Level II and above (**2684–99**)* — 568
  Querns and grinders — 569
    *Early Bronze Age (**2700–12**)* — 569
    *Middle Bronze Age (**2713–19**)* — 570

Late Bronze Age (2720–34)	570
Level II and later (2735–78)	571
Unclassified (2779–80)	573
Pounders, hammerstones and rubbers	573
Pounders and hammerstones (2781–808)	573
Rubbers (2810–20)	575
Doorsockets and related objects (2821–8)	575
Stelae (2829–30)	576

Chapter 47 Coins 577

Chapter 32

The Small Finds: Introduction

J.N. Postgate

The heading 'Small Finds' has an old-fashioned ring to it, but has been chosen because, with the architectural elements already treated above, it most accurately reflects the contents of this section of our report (if we exclude the stele or stelae listed under **2829–30**). The purpose of this Part is to give a comprehensive account of the full range of items recovered from all levels. Given the time range and the variety of contexts involved, the collected material is naturally very heterogeneous, and most items lack the kind of primary context which can give meaning to the humblest artefact. The material is presented here by the categories in which it was studied by the various authors. In their jointly authored sections Symington has contributed the account of finds from Levels IV and V, Collon of the later material from Levels III, II and I. With the exception of the loomweights and perhaps the spindle whorls, individual classes of object are not represented in sufficient quantity or from sufficiently well-provenanced contexts to merit a study in their own right, or to serve as the basis for a general review of their class across contemporary Anatolia. It may nevertheless be helpful to review how human activity at the site at different times is reflected in the range of materials recovered.

Levels V (EBA) and IV (MBA)

Taken as a whole, the Early and Middle Bronze Age repertoire from Levels V and IV comprises the imperishable components of everyday life, whether these are stone or bone tools, lithic blades, the occasional copper tool, or various baked or unbaked clay items. In so far as these are culturally specific, they tend to reinforce the links with the Early and Middle Bronze Age repertoire of Tarsus and other Anatolian sites which are suggested by the ceramics: see the commentaries on the clay 'ball' **1596**, with parallels at Alişar and further west, the kitchen furniture (**1625–33**), and the typically MBA clay crescents (**1634–8**).

Positioned as it is on a potential major trade route between the Mediterranean littoral and the interior, Kilise Tepe seems likely to have been a minor player in the commercial world of Bronze Age Anatolia. Level IV was at least in part contemporary with the lively trading scene attested in the Kültepe archives. Evidence for commercial activities was present, although scarce. One fragmentary sealing came from Level IVa (**1483**), and couple of others bear impressions made by seals of the early second millennium, even though found in later contexts (**1480–81**). Three jar rims impressed with stamp seals were also from later levels, but may belong to the same period (**1484–6**). Imported items are very scarce. The single probable Cypriot ceramic import (**410–11**) is matched by the decorated stone lid(?) **2603**. We have no reason to think that the Göksu valley fell within the geographical range of the Assyrian traders, and are therefore not surprised to find no sign of inscribed documents.

Most finds reflect the domestic activities concerned with the preparation, storage and consumption of food. Containers, both baked and unbaked, are already described under pottery, but there are several pieces of kitchen equipment in clay (**1625–33**), the best-provenanced pieces from the destroyed rooms in Vj (**1625–6**). Some storage jars would have been closed with clay stoppers, but by contrast with Level II only two were found in these earlier periods: one (**1491**) came from Level Vj and and another was still in place on a jar found *in situ* in Level IVa (**1492**; see Fig. 87). Flint and other chipped stone tools were distinctly commoner in the EBA and MBA levels than later, but except for sickle blades (**2534–45**) it is difficult to attribute any very specific functions to them (see p. 545). The same applies to various bone artefacts such as points (**2453–6**, **2464–5**), tubes (**2471–3**) and the miscellaneous items **2481–4**. Antler tines were found in the ashes of a hearth in Level IVb (**2493**), suggesting they were used as a poker. Domestic ground stone tools for pounding, grinding or polishing were also present as expected (**2627–33**; **2782–9**; **2810**). Some of these will have been used in combination with mortars (**2671–7**) or flat grindstones (**2700–719**), none of which regrettably were found *in situ*. The function of the stone palettes, two of which (**2618–19**) came from these levels, must remain uncertain, though one may note the possible pigment found in Level Vj (see Symington, p. 300).

No doubt the great majority of this equipment served for food preparation. Most of the evidence for other activities revolves round textile production. The spindle whorls and especially the loomweights from Levels IVa and Ve, Vf and Vj, indicate that in Level IV and Level V the buildings or courtyards regularly accommodated household textile production. The broken mould for two different metal objects (**2616** from Level IVa or Ve) suggests that somewhere in the vicinity copper was being worked in the late EBA or early MBA. This is also suggested by a fragment of jewellery mould of Bronze Age type (**2617**) from a much later context, but we did not identify any fire installations which from their appearance or contents could be called remotely industrial. Nor were there any discoveries of raw materials or waste products, whether in pottery, clay, stone, lithics or metal which suggested production on site (except perhaps the red pigment, mentioned above). It is possible though that some of the bone artefacts, especially antler, were worked on the premises (see **2488**; **2493**).

Despite the presence of the mould, only small copper items were recovered from Level IV and V: these included **2221**, a possible fish-hook from Level Vf, and the tweezers **2276**. Other pieces are mostly fragments of pins or needles (**2226–7, 2236–9**). One at least of the metal shapes formed by **2616** could have served as a weapon, but there is little else to hint at either hunting or war. The pressure-flaked obsidian arrowhead **2533**, from an EB III context, is notable for its uniqueness at the site. The two stone maceheads **2614–15**, one black and one white, are not out of place in the Bronze Age, and may have been more ceremonial than utilitarian. The occasional beads from scattered contexts in these levels were of clay, stone or shell (**2001–16**).

Levels III and II

The same absence of evidence for craft activity other than textile production applies also to Levels III and II. In Level III indeed, there was virtually no evidence for textile work either, with only the very occasional spindle whorl; this may reflect the nature of the single building which accounts for most of our exposure in Level III, and which we suspect was not a purely domestic house but may have been a predecessor of the Stele Building in some respects. In Level II the loomweights in phases IIe and IIf attest to continued textile production at the site. Possibly also connected with textile work is the group of more than 40 similar bone tools (**2469**) from a pit in the IIc Stele Building; unfortunately their function at present remains unknown although it was obviously very specific. Whether or not they had any significant connection with the pit in which they were found must remain in doubt, if only because the function of the pit itself remains uncertain.

Another find from the IIc Stele Building which undoubtedly relates to its function is the collection of nearly 100 astragali found sealed under the floor of Room 7 (**2421**). These had been deliberately placed here, perhaps in a container now perished. Similar collections of animal astragali have been found in cultic buildings across the Near East. Their presence here tends to reinforce our assumption that the miscellaneous group of items recovered from in and behind the suspected altar in Room 3, which includes more astragali, in addition to shells and clay whorls (see Fig. 105, p. 125), were not there by accident. The non-utilitarian function of the stele **2829** from Level IIc and its relationship to the building are self-evident; it is to our knowledge unique, although there is a possibility that the fragment **2830** belonged to a similar object from a later phase.

A few copper or bronze items came from Level III, principally two needles (**2228–9**), a pin (**2240**) and a solid ring (**2255**) with unknown purpose. A single fragment of metal slag from the Late Bronze Age level in I14 is the sole hint of any metalworking at this date (I14/157 under **2420**). From Level II came the majority of the projectile points found at the site (**2246–53**), some surely of military purpose since there is no evidence in the faunal remains for hunting as a significant component of the economy. They mostly came from unhelpful contexts, with just one (**2247**) caught up in the Level IIc destruction of the Stele Building. The only substantial copper implement, the adze **2213**, likewise came from destruction debris in Room 3 of the IIc Stele Building, but at this date seems more likely to be a tool than a weapon. As one might expect, iron is first attested in Level II, and only rarely as early as Level IIc or IId (a nail, J20/176 (in **2388**); a link(?) **2399**). The most striking piece is the three-pronged fork **2322** which was lying over the remains of a hearth of IId/e date. Later, iron is predominantly used for nails, though there are a few blades (**2308–11**), projectile points (**2392–3**), and fragments of tools (**2323–5**) in later Level II contexts. From Levels II and III there is an absence of any definite agricultural implements. Most metal slag or similar material came from Level II or Level I (**2420**), and analysis of some of these pieces might shed light on metal production at these dates.

There is a singular dearth of decorative items. Apart from the spindle whorls, the majority of which still have a pattern, no doubt in part to distinguish one from another, the principal ornamental items are the beads. A few stone and shell examples came from Level II and the equivalent level on the East Slope (**2010–15**), but the majority are in a composite material, whether frit/faience or glass (see **2017**ff.). Most of these are simple shapes, but a few are more elaborate, like the lobed spheroid **2026** from IIe, the leaf-shaped **2074**, or the lozenge-shaped pair of blue glass beads (**2070**) from a IIa/b context. Most are also of a single colour, with **2025**, **2069**, **2079** the main exceptions. Most beads turned up in random contexts, no doubt accidentally mislaid, but a small group (**2018**, **2035** and **2043**) was found within the calcined destruction debris of Room 20, together with two pins (**2241**, copper, and **2307**, silver) and the silver figurine of a divine triad (**2306**).

Other items which are more than strictly functional include the slender bone strut from a delicate but unidentifiable object (**2486**), and the tiny fragment of a carved stone bowl (**2641**) with the figure of a lion in relief. Apart from the beads, no glass was recovered from Level II, although a single multi-coloured sherd from the surface (**2080**) is assigned to the sixth–fourth centuries BC.

Other than a variety of imported pottery at different dates — most notably the Red Lustrous Wheel-Made Ware in Level III, the Mycenaean pieces from Level IId, and occasional east Mediterranean pieces, e.g. Black-on-Red wares, later in Level II — there are few items which can confidently be identified as trade goods. Unsealed clay jar stoppers (**1493–1504**) attest to the possibility of the transport of wet or dry commodities in pottery vessels; they were commonest in Level II and noticeably absent from later levels. The only inscribed material from Level II is the four bifacial stamp seals (**1470–73**); these may derive more from the practices of government administration than from trade as such.

Level I

Very few finds in the top layers of the site had a respectable context. The numerous mosaic tesserae from the church area (**2160–212**) were presumably distributed more or less where they fell. Other architectural fragments which must almost all derive from the church in one of its phases are listed at the end of the excavation section above (**1–192**), or in the case of the roof-tiles as items **1463–9**. The group of loomweights from the eastern edge of the site in Q20 (**1809–20**) must obviously have belonged in the vicinity to have survived as a group, but no good architectural context remained.

On purely stratigraphic grounds it is usually difficult to determine if objects belong broadly to our Hellenistic or Byzantine time-span, and one always has to allow for material displaced from the upper phases of Level II. Therefore attribution to one period or another usually derives from the internal evidence of the item itself.

In addition to the coins (**2832–9**), some items from the topmost level are plainly of Late Roman or Byzantine date. These include the flat bronze cross **2294**, and the wick-holders **2278–80**, both perhaps connected with activities in the church, though only one of the wick-holders came from there, the remainder being recovered by us from the NW corner of the site.

Probably the most surprising finds are the fragments of Greek hoplite shields (**2272–4**), which came from two different parts of the site, though in no very meaningful context. These appear to fall in the time between our latest Iron Age and the beginning of the Hellenistic, which is not attested in the ceramics; obviously the presence of fragments of shield does not have to reflect any permanent settlement at the site. In addition to the imported Hellenistic ceramics, a few stray items must be remnants of a late first millennium BC occupation. These include a bronze bracelet terminal (**2215**) and two terracotta figurines (**1511** and **1519**). To judge from its stratigraphic association, the miniature metal column **2293** would also have been of Hellenistic date. One intriguing possibility is that the tightly rolled lead strip **2297** was inscribed, but we were not able to resolve this.

Glass ware from Level I was no doubt imported, although not necessarily from a great distance (cf. Tobin 2004, 83 for glass production as close as Corycus and Seleucia in the Late Roman/Byzantine period).

Although there is no reason to suppose the mound was occupied after the twelfth century AD, a few finds may be of recent origin. These include miscellaneous metal items (e.g. **2295**, **2313**, **2415** and **2418**), and of course the Ottoman clay pipe (**1624**).

Arrangement in the publication

The individual catalogue entries should be self-explanatory. Within categories they are generally arranged with those from earlier provenances first, though for various reasons this principle is not rigidly applied. It should perhaps be stressed that the indication of level for each item refers to its stratigraphic provenance and does not constitute an opinion as to its date of manufacture. The division of the artefacts into categories is broadly on the basis of their material and/or function, and calls for little explanation. Uncertainties mainly concern the many objects recovered from the Bronze and Iron Age levels which may or may not have derived from textile production. Principal among these are the spindle whorls and loomweights. Perforated discs cut from sherds and other objects of this type could have been used as spindle whorls but do not conform to a well-defined category. Their perforations are not properly centred and this would make them unsuitable for spinning (Crewe 1998, 9). They have been classified with unperforated sherd discs under the general category of clay objects (as **1537**–**95**).

It is notoriously difficult to make the distinction between a small spindle whorl and a large bead and for this reason several publications have presented this material jointly (Goldman 1956, 328). To base the distinction purely on size ('no bead is larger than 2 cm in diameter': Barber 1991, 51) seems unduly arbitrary. Here, clay beads are treated in a separate section (Chapter 38), but the Early and Middle Bronze Age spindle whorl corpus may well include examples which originally had the function of beads, as indicated in the catalogue. This is less of an issue in the later corpus, where beads are mostly of glass and are typologically different.

Recovery and recording

Artefacts, bones, shells, and other items retained were numbered, bagged and sent to the house for cleaning and registration, and, where appropriate, conservation. (For the 'object numbers' used to identify them see above, p. xxiii). The basic details of each item were entered on a hand-written card and at the same time into a computerized data base (using FileMaker Pro). This data base will be made available through the internet by the good offices of the Archaeology Data Service at York (http://ads.ahds.ac.uk/). The catalogue entries here have usually, but not always, been revised by the authors in the light of further study.

The majority of the finds were transferred to the depot in the Silifke Museum at the end of the 1998 season. They are stored in numbered crates and the location of each item will be found on the electronic data base and on lists deposited with the Museum. Relatively few items were selected each season for formal incorporation in the Museum's holdings, and therefore stored in the main Museum storeroom. These received a Museum Number of the type KLT 67 which is also listed in the catalogues. In 1997–98 some finds were placed in the museum category of Etütlük; although not given KLT numbers these are also stored in the central museum storeroom.

In August 2000 with the very obliging help of the museum Director, İlhame Öztürk, we were able to install a display of finds from Kilise Tepe in one of the museum vitrines (see Fig. 1, p. 4). This includes some of the museum-registered objects with KLT numbers, and other finds from the depot, and their inclusion in the display is noted on the electronic data base.

Chapter 33

Seals with Hieroglyphic Inscriptions

Dorit Symington

Four classic Hittite seals with hieroglyphic inscriptions were recovered at Kilise Tepe. They belong to the category of biconvex, also referred to as lentoid seals, which became the preferred seal type in the thirteenth century BC (among the non-royal seals). They are known from several Hittite centres in central Anatolia and elsewhere. Biconvex seals are usually inscribed on both sides and typical too for that period are husband and wife seals with the male name written on one side and the female one on the other.

The Kilise Tepe seals were not a closed find but were recovered from different locations in and around the Stele Building. All may be associated with Level IIb. The best stratified seals are **1473**, found beneath the IIc floor in Rm 3, and **1470** which was recovered from a layer of fill in the Western Courtyard just outside the Stele Building. **1472** came from a context in J20 near the base of a wall, not known to be contaminated but close to the surface, while **1471** was found in the fill of a pit in the Western Courtyard which is probably of Level II date but cannot be dated more precisely. The archaeological context of the Kilise Tepe seals would thus suggest an association with the function of the Stele Building (see p. 137).

Two shapes of biconvex seals are represented in the Kilise Tepe assemblage; **1471–3** have a smooth flat edge with a slight curvature when seen in profile, while **1470** is more convex and has a double grooved edge. All the seals are perforated at the widest diameter, in most cases at random in relation to the inscription. They would have been suspended on a string or provided with a metal mount (on which they could pivot) and hence act as a type of stamp seal (Gorny 1993, 166f., fig. 1). The most recent find of this kind is reported from Büyükkaya at Boğazköy consisting of a bronze biconvex seal with an iron ring. It was recovered in an Iron Age context but is thought to have had its origin in the Lower City, together with other objects of Hittite Empire date which had been re-deposited in antiquity (Seeher 1998, 231–5).

The Kilise Tepe seals were cut with precision and the glyptic and epigraphic content is well spaced and in most cases encircled by a single groove on each face. All the names of the seal owners, inscribed on both sides, are clearly legible. Apart from **1473** which has a crack on one side, the remaining seals are in relatively good condition.

In recent years there have been a number of important publications and studies on biconvex seals with hieroglyphic inscriptions: Güterbock presented the Boğazköy examples from Temple I and other parts of the city (Boehmer & Güterbock 1987), to which we can now add well-stratified seals/seal impressions of more recent excavations from the Nişantepe archive where 58 per cent of the bullae are said to come from biconvex or hemispheroid seals (Herbordt 1998, 310; Herbordt 2005). A considerable amount of additional material recovered from the Upper City was reported by Neve (1985, 338; 1987, 390; 1993, 30, Abb. 80) and this seal corpus is presently in preparation by A. & B. Dinçol.

Biconvex seals are also discussed by Mora in her study of the glyptic on Hittite seals with hieroglyphic inscriptions, in which she dates lentoid seals of her Group VI (b) to the thirteenth century with the exception of the Alişar and Hama seals which are considered later (second half of thirteenth to first half of twelfth century) on account of their sketchy and at times illegible inscriptions (Mora 1987, 164ff., table 169f.).

By far the most extensive review of biconvex seals from Anatolia and Syria was made by Gorny (1993, 163–91) in the context of the Alişar seals, formerly dated to the Iron Age by the excavators, in which he argued for an Empire date for this seal category and considers them as a chronological indicator for LB II (Gorny 1993, 176). More difficult to follow is Gorny's theory (Gorny 1993, 190) for the origin of the biconvex seal in southeast Anatolia and its arrival on the plateau on account of the transfer of the capital from Tarhuntassa back to Hattusa (at the time of Mursilis III) which in his view explains why the biconvex seals enjoyed their greatest popularity in LBIIb (1280–1175 BC).

Crucial in the discussion for dating of the biconvex seals is the archaeological context in which they were recovered, although they are often not well stratified. Furthermore, many examples of this seal category now in museum collections have no provenance at all (Dinçol 1983, 213ff.; Dinçol & Dinçol 1985, 33ff.). However, there is now sufficient archaeological evidence from Boğazköy tying the majority of biconvex seals to the last building phase of the Empire Period in the Temple I area, the Nişantepe archive building and in the Upper City (O.St. 4). Güterbock described the biconvex seal as the most abundant type of hieroglyphically inscribed seals at Boğazköy in the Late Empire Period and dated them to the second half of the thirteenth century (Boehmer & Güterbock 1987, 61). A late Empire date is also suggested by the biconvex seals found at Maşat in Hittite Level I, the last Hittite level which ended in a conflagration. It belongs to a male with an uncertain title and depicts a striding male on one side, as seen on our **1470** (Özgüç 1982, 118, pl. 58:5a–c).

The other aspect to be considered in the dating of the Kilise Tepe seals is their orthography and glyptic content. As remarked above, the individual signs are precisely cut and the repertoire of sign forms found on the seals is entirely consistent with those of the Empire Period and does not include late forms. Equally, the iconographic content, which can only be studied on **1470**, suggests an Empire date. Hence a post-Hittite or Neo-Hittite date for their manufacture can be excluded.

Biconvex seals with sketchy and carelessly executed script are to be dated later, according to Güterbock (Boehmer & Güterbock 1987, 65). The subject of post-Hittite and Neo-Hittite seals was addressed by Mora (1990, 443–59, figs. 1–6) who notes some survivals of biconvex seals into the twelfth century which generally display a more cursive script than those of the Empire Period (Mora 1990, 445f., see figs. 3.1–2).

The seals recovered at Kilise Tepe presumably belonged to resident officials and their activities are most likely to be connected with the function of the Stele Building.

1470   I19/126   KLT 93   2882
Level IIb
Biconvex seal manufactured in a dense black stone, most probably serpentine. The seal is drilled diagonally to the inscriptions and has double rilling on the edge.
Side A: In the centre a striding figure wearing a short kilt and horned skull cap and carrying a bow over his left shoulder. Above his outstretched right hand is the Weather God sign forming part of his name, which reads TONITRUS-*pi-ya* (Tarhunta-piya), and behind the figure his title AURIGA (L. 289) 'charioteer'.
Side B: Largely filled with the depiction of a lion with raised tail and open mouth. Facing the animal is a repeat of the owner's name TONITRUS-*pi-ya*. Presumably for reasons of space, the title is not repeated in Side B. The remaining symbols above the lion appear to be fillers.

Di. 2.5; Th. 1.45; Di. perf. 0.35
Also illustrated in Jackson & Postgate 1999, 554, fig. 4

Striding male figures (most likely depicting a deity) are not uncommon in Hittite iconography, and probably a reflection of similar images on Hittite rock reliefs, most of which were created in the thirteenth century BC. These figures can also appear with conical head-dresses, carrying an axe or *lituus* instead of a bow, and occasionally in addition holding a staff in the other outstretched hand. Examples for this type of seal are to be found in Mora's Groups VI (a) and XI (1987, Tav. 31–3; Tav. 72–6).

The shape of **1470** and the neat style of seal cutting, as well as its glyptic content, have parallels at Boğazköy in a number of examples: Nos. 184, 185, 186, 194, 197. These are mainly from the Temple I area and other locations of the Lower City, and they may have originated in contemporary workshops. These seals belong to charioteers, temple officials and scribes (Boehmer & Güterbock 1987, 66ff.; Taf. XX–XXIV; see Fig. 431).

The name Tarhunta-piya is attested on a number of other Hittite seals or seal impressions, mainly from Boğazköy, written in the same manner as found on **1470** or with an added phonetic complement: TONITRUS-tà-piya (Güterbock 1942, SBo II nos. 23, 141–5). The name is, however, rarely attested in cuneiform texts. A Tarhuntapiya (^{md}U-SUM) appears in the witness list of the treaty with Ulmi-Tesub of Tarhuntassa (Güterbock 1942, KBo IV 10 Rs. 31) with the title 'prince' and could conceivably be the seal owner of SBo II Nr. 23 (see above) which reads TONITRUS-*piya* FILIUS.REX.

The title of 'charioteer' is not infrequently found on Hittite seals. Among the Nişantepe seal impressions over 100 examples belong to the military, among them chariot drivers (AURIGA) and chief charioteers (MAGNUS.AURIGA) (Herbordt 1998, 311, fig. 2). The hieroglyphic sign for 'charioteer' (L. 289 which represents the reins with an object above) was identified by Laroche as 'charioteer' with the help of documents from Ras Shamra bearing Syro-Hittite seal impressions and he demonstrated the correspondence of L. 289 with cuneiform *KARTAPPU*. (Laroche 1956, 29f.). The records of Boğazköy and Ugarit contain numerous references to the *KARTAPPU* and indicate that he was a high-ranking official (Beal 1992a, 155–62). Indeed, royal chariot drivers are seen to be trusted individuals and being mobile were sent on missions, thus acting as envoys. A text from Ugarit relates that the chariot driver of the king of Carchemish supervises a legal case between the merchants of Ura and the state of Ugarit (Beal 1992a, 159–60).
Figs. 262 & 431

1471   I20/43   KLT 40   4001
Level IIb–e
Biconvex seal of dark red stone, each face slightly convex, with a smooth edge. The perforation is bored horizontally to the inscription and slightly damaged at both ends on Side A. The hieroglyphic inscription is identical on both sides but only on Side A is it encircled by a groove. The signs making up the name fill most of the seal surface and read *mi - nú - wa/i - za/i* (Minuwa(n)za) flanked on either side by BONUS$_2$.VIR$_2$. There are two additional fillers on either side of the *zi/a* sign. This name does not appear to be attested elsewhere.
Di. 1.8; Th. 0.9; Di. perf. 0.4
Figs. 262 & 431

1472   J20/33   KLT 1   1317
Level IIb
Biconvex seal in a dark grey stone varying to light grey, probably chlorite. Seal faces only slightly convex, the edge is smooth. Perforated slightly off central axis.

The name of the seal owner is written on both sides and reads *sà - tu - wa/i - li* BONUS$_2$.VIR$_2$ X. The gazelle head *sà* (L. 104) has the serrated horns as seen in the seal impressions of Sahuranuwa (Beyer 1982, 73, fig. 11 a–c). The sign facing L. 104 on Side B, and

Figure 262. *Hieroglyphic seals (**1470**, **1471**, **1472**, **1473**).*

on the opposite Side of A, represents most likely the title of the seal owner. This sign — which at present cannot be identified — is basically an oval with vertical lines emerging from the top on Side B, while on Side A it almost resembles a triton.
Di. 1.6; Th. 0.7; Di. perf. 0.3
Figs. 262 & 431

1473　　　　K19/342　　　　KLT 92　　　　4551
Level IIb
Biconvex seal of yellow, rather soft limestone(?). The edge of the seal is not ridged but smooth. One side has a crack. The hieroglyphic legend is encircled by a single groove on both faces. The PN written in the centre consists of three signs *ta - ti - ya* which is flanked on either side by BONUS$_2$.VIR$_2$. The remaining signs are fillers. The first sign I take to be L.100 '*ta*' (head of a donkey) which is normally written with the head pointing downwards but there are variants as can be seen on a biconvex seal illustrated by Mora which writes the same name on Side A with the head pointing downwards and on Side B with the head upright (Mora 1987, Tav. 39: 1.23; 153).
The name Tatiya is attested in cuneiform records where he appears as a priest and in another text as a scribe (Laroche 1966, 181).
Di. 2.2; Th. 1.1; Di. perf. 0.3
Figs. 262 & 431

Acknowledgements

I am indebted to Professor J.D. Hawkins for discussing the hieroglyphic content of the Kilise Tepe seals with me on a number of occasions.

Chapter 34

Other Glyptic

Dominique Collon

Other evidence for the use of seals at Kilise Tepe is varied but difficult to quantify. The material consists almost entirely of stamp seals and stamp seal impressions, but all are of clay with the exception of the one prehistoric seal, **1489**. On stylistic grounds these seals and impressions can tentatively be divided into the following broad chronological groups:

    Prehistoric seal: **1479**
    EB: **1483**
    MB and Assyrian Colony Periods:
        cylinder seal impressions (**1480**, **1482**)
        stamp seal (**1478**)
        stamp seal impressions (**1481**, **1484–6**)
    LB: **1487**
    First millennium BC–AD: **1475**, **1489–90**

Parallels for **1476** come from all periods and it was found in topsoil.

Stamp seals

1475–8 are asymmetrical truncated cones of clay, with their design on the roughly circular base (except for **1477** which is blank). The parallels for **1478** would suggest a date in the Assyrian Colony period (eighteenth century BC), but the horse rider on **1475** points to a late second-millennium date at the earliest and it is probably much later. The asymmetrical cone shape would seem to be a feature of clay seals and probably has functional rather than chronological implications.

1474   L19/33   KLT 125   5949
Level IIf
A crudely made, small, cylindrical clay object, with an uneven surface, possibly chipped at one end and with traces of burning. Around each end there is a line border crudely incised in the damp clay in separate, non-joining sections. Between the line borders are diagonal slashes leaning towards the right, but they slant at different angles.
L. 2.2; Di. 1.6

This object could be thought to be a crude cylinder seal but it is unperforated. It could, however, be the base of a clay stamp-cylinder of a type known from Boğazköy around 1700 BC (Boehmer & Güterbock 1987, nos. 279 - stone, and 280 - clay, 93, pl. XXXV, and cf. 94, Abb. 72b from Alişar), but these both have designs on the base, and the Kilise Tepe example would therefore be unfinished, perhaps because the handle broke off during manufacture. It is, however, much cruder than the other examples.

1475   I14/13   KLT 41   3402
Level 1
Asymmetrical truncated cone of creamy-brown clay with occasional medium-sized calcareous inclusions and some coarse ones, with the handle flattened and pierced, flaring to a roughly circular base which bears the impression of a circular seal (Di. *c*. 3.2). The seal which made this impression bore the design of man on a horse, facing left, surrounded by a line border from the left side of which extend four points (i.e. in front of the rider and horse). The man's torso is depicted frontally and he holds the horse's mane or bridle with his right hand and raises his left hand to touch the line border on the right, but no details of features or dress are visible. The cone is perforated as if this were a seal but this stamp's impression would have been in *intaglio*. Hence this could be some type of bulla rather than a seal.
H. 2.9; Di. 3.0-3.2; W. at top 1.0–1.6

The closest parallel is a Sasanian pottery stamp from Samarra (Sarre 1925, 11. Abb. 23–4, Tafel III top).

1476   J19/94   KLT 78   1641
Topsoil
Asymmetrical truncated cone of greyish-pink grit-tempered clay with the handle flattened and pierced, flaring to a roughly circular base; the handle is broken, probably along the line of the perforation. The design on the base consists of a leaf or herring-bone pattern surrounded by a circular groove, forming a line border, which is punctuated by four small circular holes at the top and bottom of the leaf's stem (which forms the diameter of the circle) and on either side.
H. (2.3); Di. *c*. 1.5–2.9 (top-base)

For similar designs from Boğazköy, see Seidl 1972, 36–49, Abb. 11–17; A 121–82 = twigs or branches; A 183–203 = grapes; see also pl. 4. These are elongated impressions applied to the bases of handles of Hittite pottery from all levels at Boğazköy. Seidl discusses them and believes they could have indicated the contents of the vessels (Seidl 1972, 73–5). The round Kilise Tepe stamp may have fulfilled the same function, probably at a later date.

1477   K19/17   1501
Level 1
Asymmetrical truncated cone of creamy-beige clay with few visible grits. The top is broken level with the perforation, and the base, which is blank, is chipped.
H. (3.3); Di. *c*. 2.3 (top), *c*. 3.7 (base)

1478   R18/112   KLT 42   2406
Level E5a
Asymmetrical truncated cone-shaped stamp seal of greyish-pink, grit-tempered clay, with coarse calcareous inclusions. The flattened perforated handle flares to the flat circular base. The design consists of a hollow made in the damp clay at the centre of the base with a pointed stick, and ten roughly radiating lines impressed between this hole and the edge of the base.
H. 2.6; Di. 2.7; W. of handle 0.8–1.7

Boehmer has pointed out that radiating designs with a central depression are typical of stamp seals of the Assyrian Colony period at Boğazköy (first half of the eighteenth century BC), although the shapes are more complex (Boehmer & Güterbock 1987, 19 and pl. 1, especially no. 9). A clay seal of this shape and type of design (judging from the photograph, although the description indicates that the design was more complex) was found in Level Ib at Karum Kanesh (Özgüç 1968, 73, no. 3, pl. XXXVII:3).

1479   J9/7   KLT 43   313
Surface
Stamp seal of soft black-and-white banded stone, originally probably square, but one side is broken; pointed perforated loop on the back. The white banding of the stone forms a diagonal across the base, and up to four diagonal lines have been filed from each edge of the seal, all leaning towards the left.
H. 0.85; L. 1.9; W. (1.75)

This type of seal is well-attested from Neolithic times onwards (von Wickede 1990). The stone has been selected for its patterning and has been carefully shaped to incorporate the white band in the design on the base. The incised lines were simple to produce, either by running a piece of wet string dipped in abrasive, or a flint, backwards and forwards from a notch in the edge. However, this type of design is more common on round seals, whereas square seals tend to have grids. The shape is also well attested.

Clay sealings

Sealings from all types of containers were found in large numbers at Kültepe and Acemhöyük and formed an important part of the trade mechanism in the Middle Bronze Age. To gain access to the merchandise the sealings had to be broken but they have largely survived and were found scattered in rooms or special repositories (Özgüç 1989, 377f.). Bullae from sealed merchandise or other items also came to light at Karahöyük Konya, most examples showing impressions of string, others of textiles or wood (Alp 1968, 70ff., pls. 139:427 & 140:432).

Karahöyük is also noted for the presence of enigmatic curved and stamped objects, probably tokens of some sort, but often called loomweights, and it should be noted that several objects of this type were found at Kilise Tepe (see **1634–8**; Fig. 440), but they bore very faint impressions of small stamps, either simple rosettes or unfortunately unidentifiable.

1480   H19/44   4209
Level IIIc/d
Small strip of pale brown clay, broken at one end and on both sides, with the smooth impression of the neck (Di. 3.2) of a small vessel on its reverse. On the side is the double impression of the upper edge of a Classic Syrian cylinder seal of the eighteenth–seventeenth century BC (1.0 × 1.6 max.). All that survives of the design is part of a line border, part of the first sign of a cuneiform inscription which ran from top to bottom of the seal, and the left end of a horizontal guilloche or plait, perhaps with a horizontal line beneath it.
L. (2.4); W. (1.1)

For plaits on a seal from Mari and, with an inscription, on an impression from Ugarit, see Otto 2000, nos. 106, 315. Inscribed seals of this period have been shown to belong to kings or high officials who formed an elite (Otto 2000, 173–8). Unfortunately, owing to the double impression of the cuneiform sign, it is very difficult to reconstruct. Seals with inscriptions and guilloches or, more rarely, plaits in close proximity are particularly popular on cylinder seals belonging to servants of Shamshi-Adad I of Assyria and Hammurabi of Babylon in eastern Syria and northern Iraq in the first half of the eighteenth century BC (Otto 2000, nos. 140, 314–15, 317, 363, 368, 415, 418, 460–61, 463). None, however, shows the guilloche at the top of the seal alongside the inscription, as on the Kilise Tepe fragment, although uninscribed elite seals do show guilloches or plaits framing parts of a design (Otto 2000, nos. 325, 335, 350).

1481   I20/67   4017
Level IIIe
Small piece of pinky-brown, unbaked clay with one shapeless rough side and one side broken along the line of two string impressions. Fragmentary stamp seal impression (original Di. c. 2.5) of which less than a quarter survives, with part of the edge and curved line-border framing a ladder-pattern of six 'rungs', and four further lines parallel to one of the 'uprights'.
L. (1.5); W. (1.0); Th. 1.5

A fragmentary clay seal of the Assyrian Colony period (nineteenth to mid-eighteenth centuries BC), bearing a similar design, was found at Boğazköy (Boehmer & Güterbock 1987, 19, 21, no. 4, pl. 1:4). Stamp seals with similar designs in Adana Museum are, unfortunately, unprovenanced (Dinçol et al. 1998, nos. 7 & 9).

1482   J19/280   1690
Level IId; found through wet-sieving
Very small piece of brown clay with rough, broken back, flat base and two indented, grooved impressions. These could have been made by the metal caps of a cylinder seal. Many of the cylinder seal impressions from Alalakh indicate that the seals had grooved metal caps, possibly made of gold (Collon 1975, 162).
H. 1.8; L. (2.4); Th. 1.1

1483   H20/252   1258
Level IVa, destruction debris of Rm 43; found together with a large clutch of loomweights (**1702–22**).
Fragment of bulla of buff-coloured, fine, unbaked clay. Some of the outer part has broken off, leaving a very clear string impression around the rest of the circumference. On the outer faces are traces of a fine faint seal(?) impression, but these are too indistinct to interpret.
H. 1.7; L. (1.9); W. (1.7)

Impressions on potsherds

Four large jar-rims with a stamp seal impressed in the clay before firing can be dated to MB or LB on stylistic grounds despite their varied provenances.

1484 J20/126 KLT 82 1376
Level IIId
Rim sherd of brick-red clay, with a temper of red, white and black grits. The flaring rim belonged to a jar (outer Rim di. 29.0; inner Rim di. 21.0), and a circular stamp seal (Di. c. 2.15) was impressed on the flat sloping upper surface of the rim, near its inner edge. The design consists of a circular line-border surrounding three interlocking hollow-sided equilateral triangles made up of triple strands; these enclose an irregular eight-pointed star within a nine-sided, hollow-based shape echoing the shape formed by the interlocking triangles. See **1485** for a similar stamped rim from Level IIa/b.
H. (8.4); L. (18.0); W of rim 5

A seal impression on a bulla from Acemhöyük has a meander pattern surrounding a similar motif, but with two interlocking triangles rather than three (Özgüç 1983, 420, no. 10 & pl. 83); the central motif is a sun-burst rather than a star. The motif with two interlocking triangles enclosing a star is also found on a sealing and, in a simpler version, on a seal, from Proto-Palatial Phaestos on Crete (Levi 1976, pls. 224k, 229q). Two interlocking hollow-sided squares are found on jar-sealings and bullae from Karahöyük (Konya), but the central motif is no longer visible (Alp 1968, 235–6, no. 260, Abb. 211, and e.g. pl. 32 alongside an Old Babylonian cylinder seal impression). All these examples can probably be dated to the second half of the eighteenth century BC.

1485 J20/169 1395
Level IIa/b
Stamped rim sherd from pithos of smoothed, reddish, grit-tempered clay (many white grits) with, on its upper surface, a stamp impression (Di. 1.9) with a 12-petalled rosette. Note that the rim is of a similar type and fabric to **1484** from Level III, though slightly larger.
H. (7.1); L. (10.4); Rim w.: 5.4; Rim di. c. 40

1486 X14/2 1000
Unstratified
Stamped rim sherd. Pale orange fabric with medium density of small, red stones and occasional white, calcareous inclusions; the surface is yellow-buff and smooth. The stamp was applied to the top of a ledge-rim from a wide-diameter vessel; the inner upper edge of the rim formed an overhanging ledge which is broken so that only about half the impression survives; beneath this broken ledge there are several indentations which probably indicate that the clay was folded over several times to form the rim. The design of the stamp is difficult to interpret: it could be a floral motif or the frontal head of a demon such as a bull-man or, more probably, Humbaba. There are a variety of Humbaba heads on Classic Syrian cylinder seals belonging to servants of Shamshi-Adad I of Assyria and Hammurabi of Babylon in northeast Syria and northern Iraq, during the first half of the eighteenth century BC (Otto 2000, nos. 439, 462–3, 471). However, the segmented design is not paralleled on these examples.
L. (8.7); Rim w. 2.6; Rim di. c. 30

1487 P7/4 KLT 44 246
Surface
Rim sherd of pinky-red grit-tempered ware (some large brown and white grits <0.5); fired to beige on exterior. The exact angle of the rim is difficult to establish; near the edge is the incomplete impression of a circular stamp seal (Di. c. 2.0). The actual seal had a recessed rim; the design consists of a circle from which radiate six long petals alternating with six short petals forming a star with six points linked by fringe-filled arcs.
H. (7.5); L. 10.6

I have found no close parallels, but arcs filled with fringed circles occur on the back of a dome-shaped stamp-seal from Boğazköy, dated to the thirteenth century BC, and the base of a similar seal has an eight-petalled rosette with hatching between the petals (Boehmer & Güterbock 1987, no. 219, pl. XXVI and no. 231, pl. XXVIII).

Three jar handles with a stamp seal impressed next to the junction with the rim are unfortunately all surface finds (**1488–90**). The only close parallel for this we have noted is at Tarsus, where a very similar handle with a stamp seal impressed in the same position is said to be 'unequivocally dated in a sixth century B.C. level' (Goldman 1963, 354 no. 22). That seal shows a lion, but like **1489–90** has an exergue. Glyptic parallels from Cyprus and Syria suggest that these handles belong in the early first millennium BC, but quite likely earlier than the sixth century.

1488 P12/1 202
Surface
Jar handle fragment of pale-grey grit-tempered clay with occasional calcareous inclusions, fired to orange-buff on the surface, with the impression of a rectangular stamp with rounded corners (1.5 × 1.7) on the upper side. The stamp is impressed twice, once very shallowly so that the design is not visible, and once deeply and partly overlapping the first impression. The design may be a herringbone pattern or, if view turned through 90 degrees, it may be a tree on the right. The left side is damaged but there are traces of lines that do not seem to be part of a herringbone design. Moorey (pers. comm.) suggests they may come from the back end of a quadruped.
L. (7.5); W. 9.2 (body), 5.9 (handle).

For the distinctive frame of the seal, Moorey (pers. comm.) compares Buchanan & Moorey 1984 no. 197, suggesting it may have had a 'stud-shaped' back or similar shape current in LB to IA. A similar design appears on a stamp seal from Proto-Palatial Phaestos on Crete (late eighteenth century BC: Levi 1976, pl. 229c & cf. 229a). See also stamp seal impressions on pottery from Boğazköy (Seidl 1972, Abb. 15:A170, Abb. 16:A182, both lacking the border; for a similar shape with border see Abb. 18:A204. These are respectively attributed to Unterstadt 1, unprovenanced and Büyükkale IIIa – Phrygian and Old Hittite).

1489 Q10/45 230
Surface
Large jar handle of grey-brown to buff, grit-tempered clay with large calcareous inclusions and some vegetable temper, fired to buff on the surface, with half of a large, circular stamped impression extant (Di. c. 5.6) at the top, impressed upside-down (the handle is shown in the drawing the right way up for the impression but not for the handle). The design consists of a central gazelle(?) eating a tree to its left. To its right is a man stretching out his arm towards the horn of the animal. To the bottom right, at the man's feet, are two large, outlined petals which may be part of half a rosette which would have occupied the remaining half of the seal.
L. (7.0); W. (7.8)

The gazelle is somewhat similar to that on **1490** but that seal is much smaller. Designs like this, showing an animal passant with some object in the upper field within a circular frame, are known from the early Iron Age in the northern Levant (Buchanan's so-called 'horse group': see Buchanan & Moorey 1984, pl. V; for the design cf. also Riis & Buhl 1990, 89–91 fig. 44 from Hama, but this is a bifacial lentoid and probably earlier).

1490   Q12/5   220
Surface
Fragment of handle of beige clay, with frequent red and white calcareous inclusions, fired to orangey-red on the exterior, with a circular stamp (Di. *c.* 2.3) on the upper part of the handle near to the junction with the body. The design consists of a line border within which is a gazelle(?) standing on a base-line, with a star in the space above its tail and behind its backward-curving horn; there may be some hatching beneath the base-line.
L. 4.8; W. 5.3; Th. 1.7

The gazelle is somewhat similar to that on **1489** but that seal is much larger.

Chapter 35

Miscellaneous Clay Artefacts

Dominique Collon & Dorit Symington

This chapter covers the wide variety of items made of clay, baked and unbaked, which are not listed in other sections. Thus it does not include sealings (Chapter 34), loomweights (Chapter 36), spindle whorls (Chapter 37) or beads (Chapter 38). The main headings are as follows:

1491–1504 Stoppers
1505–1523 Figurines
1524–1526 Wheels and wheel-like objects
1527–1536 Counters, tokens and gaming pieces
1537–1595 Sherd discs, etc.
1596–1623 Miscellaneous clay items
1624   Clay pipe
1625–1633 Clay furniture
1634–1638 Clay crescents
1639–1678 Clay ovoids

Stoppers (1491–1504)

Some of the following objects were found with or close to a jar, into the mouth of which they plainly fitted, and the similarity of other pieces indicates that they too were jar stoppers. Several examples were found in the IIc destruction level of the East Building (**1495–1501**; also K19/385, catalogued with the trefoil jar to which it belonged, **697**), underlining the presence of whole storage vessels in these rooms. Similarly, the two earliest vessel stoppers were found with jars: **1491** was found on the floor in Rm 82 of Level Vj (EB II) and most probably sealed the contents of **197**, a small painted jug. The dome-shaped clay bung **1492** was found still sealing the mouth of a small combed ware jar (**525** H19/366: Figs. 87 & 487) on the floor of Rm 41 in Level IVa.

1526, catalogued below as a possible wheel, may also, in fact, have been a stopper.

1491   H20/770   5406
Level Vj
Mushroom-shaped stopper of unbaked clay with almost circular head and tapering end. The edge of the round top, where it would have met the vessel which it sealed, is sharply defined. Fabric semi-coarse with some grits and organic temper. Barely smoothed, rather lumpy in parts.
H. 6.3; Di. 5.7

[1492]   H19/371   4278
Level IVa
Clay bung, domed top. Fitted into the mouth of vessel **525** to seal contents.
Di. 9.0
Fig. 87, p. 104

[1493]   J19/385   3977
Level IIb
Light brown, gritty clay; upper surface smoothed; traces of burning.
L. 7.0; W. 5.5

[1494]   K20/167   1971
Level IIb
Unbaked clay with a flattened underside and convex top in which are two pairs of small holes, but these do not go through to the other side and could not have been used to tie on the stopper; bears the faint impression of the grooved rim of a vessel (Ext di. 8.0, Int. di. c. 6.0).
H. 12.1; W. 10.2; Th. 4.0

[1495]   K19/102   1561
Level IIc
Circular stopper made out of dark brown, coarse clay; slight rim around it; the surface is curved and smooth.
W. c. 9.0

[1496]   K19/130   1572
Level IIc
Similar to **1498**, but very friable; no measurements possible.

[1497]   K19/403   4596
Level IIc
Large fragment of a crudely-made jar stopper; brown, gritty, very porous clay; smoothed with traces of burning on upper surface and the impression of the neck of a vessel on the underside. Similar to **1498**.
W. 9.5

1498   K19/409   4597
Level IIc
Complete. Brown clay with black grits. Crudely made, surface smoothed with black spots. Lower part plainly shows impression of a large trefoil rim. Domed top rises c. 4 cm above line of rim.
H. 8.5–9.1; Di. 9.7

[1499]   K19/406   4597
Level IIc
One edge broken away. Brown, grit-tempered clay, crudely made but surface smoothed. Flattish top, rounded beneath. Had been pushed into vessel with slightly flaring lip (Rim di. 7.4).
H. 4.4; Di. 7.9 max.

1500 L19/65 5975
Level IIc
Greyish-green, gritty clay; flaky surface, traces of burning on top. Probably a stopper.
H. 5.0; W. 6.0

[**1501**] K19/436 6202
Level IIc/d
Brown, gritty, smoothed clay. Probably a jar stopper similar to **1497–8**.
H. 3.9; Di. 7.4 max.

1502 K18/111 4353
Level IIe/f
Flaring cylinder of beige, vegetable-tempered, unbaked clay; bottom missing.
Di. 5.4 (top)–4.3; L. (7.0)

[**1503**] I19/68 1781
Level IIg
A fragment of dark grey, coarse clay with a rounded edge, possibly a rim. The fragment widens at the 'base' to its max. thickness. There are rough (W. 1.0) grooves on the inside of the piece. Uneven and irregular. Slightly curved.
Th. 3.3

[**1504**] K20/210 1990
Level II
Several crumbling fragments of light grey, unbaked clay with a smooth, curved surface on the upper part of the largest fragment; coarse fabric with some blackened patches; impression of the neck of a jar (Int. di. *c.* 10.0) on the underside.

Figurines (1505–23)

It is unfortunate that almost all the figurines from Kilise Tepe are surface finds. The few examples from Level II are unsophisticated and crude, and their fragmentary state means that they are often difficult to interpret. Only the Hellenistic examples are sufficiently distinctive to have significant parallels elsewhere. The zoomorphic spout from a vessel (**678**) and the arm-shaped libation vessels (**684–92**) have been presented in the pottery report.

1505 L19/53 Etütlük 1998 5973
Level IIc/d
Bovid figurine made out of baked, grit-tempered, beige clay. The ears, left front leg and the whole of the back half are missing. The animal has a pronounced dewlap below its triangular muzzle and a small hump; its eyes are not indicated, nor its hooves. A line of orangey-red paint runs from its muzzle, over its head and along its back to the break. Transverse lines run under its chin, over its hump and across its back and there is also paint on the left side of the dewlap and front of the broken leg.
H. 6.5; L. (7.2); W. (5.3)
Fig. 263

1506 K19/402 Etütlük 1998 4594
Level IIe
Part of a bird(?), similar to **1514**, made out of pale brown, grit-tempered clay, fired to grey with the remains of a cream slip. The beak, left side of the head, legs and back of the body were broken off. The bird's long neck is set at an angle to the body, with the smooth,

Figure 263. *Bovid figurine* **1505.**

round head at right angles to the neck. The eyes are indicated by roughly incised circles.
H. (5.7); L. (5.8); W. (2.7)

[**1507**] K19/62 1535
Level IId
Grey leg-like object with a flat 'base' (the diameter is widest at the base edge, which is slightly wider than the main body) and narrowing towards the opposite end. Perhaps a tripod leg or stand, see **1520**.
H. 4.3; W. 4.5; Di. 5.3

1508 J18/288 5827
Level IIe?
Perhaps a crudely-formed quadruped, made out of cream, probably unfired, clay. Depending on which way up it is viewed, it either has large ears or horns, a long muzzle, a long neck and no body, or it has large ears or horns, but no head, one foreleg, a tail but no hindlegs; or its front is missing, it has a tail and two stumpy hindlegs; alternatively, it could be a piece of twisted clay discarded by a potter. Cf. **1607**, found in the vicinity, which may be another such piece.
L. (3.5); W. (1.8); H. (2.3)

[**1509**] J18/230 2396
Level IIf1
Animal(?) horn or head-dress(?) made out of cream, grit-tempered, baked clay. It is oval in section where broken and has two grooves on one broad side, tapering to a curved tip.
L. 4.2; W. 2.4; Th. 3.0

1510 L14/10 KLT 58 3602
Level 1
Statuette base consisting of a flat disc with two feet attached at the centre. The clay is buff-coloured with fine, sand temper and occasional small, red grits and white, calcareous inclusions. The underside has distinct marks indicating that it was cut by means of a string from the surface on which it was shaped. The edge of the base is slightly bevelled and its top is concave. On the upper side there is a painted band around the edge, and within that, a series of overlapping, crude semi-circles, all in yellow-brown paint. The toes and sides of the feet are painted with solid colour, while the upper parts of the feet are decorated with sandals(?) of criss-cross design with dots in between. One foot has only a small part of the upper surface preserved, while the figure's left foot is broken off slightly further up. We have not identified parallels to this piece.

Figure 264. *Base of statuette* **1510**.

Figure 265. *Hellenistic plaque* **1511**, *showing comic actor*.

Figure 266. *Human figurine* **1512**.

H. (3.2); Base th. 1.3 max.; Di. 13.7–13.9
Fig. 264

1511 N12/22 KLT 4 3205
Level 1
Hellenistic, mould-made human figurine of yellowish-buff clay with some sand and occasional white, calcareous inclusions; the surface is largely coated in a dirty brown wash with traces of red paint. The back of the mould is slightly concave and the edges are very thin. Seated male with legs crossed at the ankles, chin resting on his left hand, and his left elbow supported by his right arm which is folded across the middle. He has the wide open mouth of a comic actor. There are traces of red paint especially on his left shoulder and side, his chest, below his right arm and behind his right leg.
H. 6.7; W. 3.1; Th. 2.0
Fig. 265

Figurines in the round of this character are widely attested in the Hellenistic world (e.g. Webster *et al.* 1995, vol. I pl. 3 IA T16), and examples are known from Tarsus (Goldman 1950, nos. 259–64, p. 345, fig. 234, and nos. 471–2, fig. 246 with crossed legs). Plaques may be less common.[1]

1512 N12/39 3208
Level 1
Human figurine of creamy yellow, baked clay with fine grit temper. The figure is a hollow cone, the top of which is broken off so that it is headless, while the lower part forms a flaring skirt. Its short arms are extended laterally and bent forwards (one arm is broken at the shoulder and the other above the elbow). The skirt, which is decorated with two narrow, horizontal bands of blackish-brown paint, is broken around the hem, although part of the hem, tilted upwards towards the front, may survive, and there are traces of two small holes poked through it at the back on the line of the break.
H. 7.4; W. (4.9) at the arms; Base th. 0.7, Base di. 3.9–4.3
Fig. 266

Hollow-based free-standing figures from Tarsus were dated to the Early Iron Age and Assyrian Period (Goldman 1963, figs. 153:1–2, both with broken arms).

1513 G13/2 304
Surface
Cream, grit-tempered, fired clay that appears to have been carved when leather-hard. From a convex knob *c.* 4.0 in diameter with edges 1.1 high, rises an inverted cone with shaved sides, the top of which is broken diagonally. There are four grooves on the best-preserved side in which pinky-brown paint survives. Traces indicate that the knob was also painted and perhaps the whole piece was coloured. The object resembles the metal door-knockers known as 'Hands of Fat(i)ma' found throughout the Near East and North Africa. They are shaped in the form of a hand holding a ball (the knocker) with a hinge at the wrist, but this could not have been the purpose of this piece and it is difficult to suggest what it may have been.
L. 7.4; W. 3.9; Th. 5.3; Di. 4.0 (knob)

1514 I20/2 1400
Surface
Head of a bird(?) made out of greyish-brown, fired clay with fine grits; the surface has a cream, burnished slip. The tip of the beak and the body are missing; the neck is fairly long, the head (at right angles to the neck) is smooth and round. Two hollows indicate the eyes which were formed by pellets, one of which survives. There are indications of a groove along the top of the beak. The bird looks like a somewhat startled seal; see also **1508**.
W. (2.7); Th. (2.2); H. (4.8)

For a figure with a similar bird head with pellet eyes, but described as bearded and tilted back, see Goldman 1963, 338, fig. 153:6 (and cf. fig. 157:38, p. 342) from Tarsus, dated to the early first millennium BC. The 'arms' are broken and the cylindrical body is broken at the bottom. There are traces of paint. The parallel from Alişar, quoted by Goldman, is closer to the Tarsus figure than to the ones discussed here.

451

Chapter 35

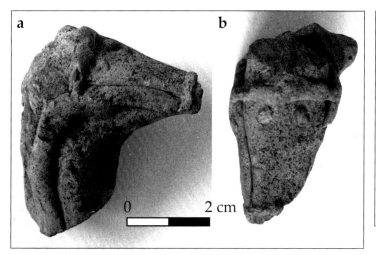

Figure 267. *Head of horse head figurine **1515**: a) side view; b) front view.*

Figure 268. *Head of animal figurine **1516**, side view.*

1515 J20/123 KLT 81 1346
Topsoil
Small, pale brown to grey clay horse's head with bridle and pellet eyes; broken at ears, nose and neck.
H. (4.8); L. (4.8); W. 4.8 at top; Di. 2.3 at neck
Fig. 267
Goldman 1963, fig. 158:46–9 and p. 343.

1516 K7/3 320
Surface
Animal's head of baked clay, with fine grit temper and a pink core, fired to beige on the exterior. It is broken at the neck, its ears or horns are broken off and it has a roughly triangular head into which a stick has been poked to create eyes and the cleft lower lip, while nostrils have been made with a smaller stick, with creases below them, and an impressed line forms the mouth. Diagonal lines on the right cheek and left side of the neck might perhaps indicate an incomplete harness. The species of animal cannot be determined.
H. 4.6; Th. (3.4); W. 3.8
Fig. 268

Similar examples with grooved mouths are recorded from Tarsus (Goldman 1956, 377, fig. 452:14, with wide spreading horns, from an LB I level; Goldman 1963, figs. 156:28, 30, 31, 33; 157:43, from early first-millennium levels).

1517 K8/5 315
Surface
Pair of animals made out of brown clay with many grits (some of them up to 4 mm), fired to creamy beige and shaped as one body with two heads (both broken off) and four legs which are also missing. There are two further breaks, one on each side of the rump, possibly the emplacement of their tails, one of which may lie along the body. The clay at the back of the necks is pinched into a crest, possibly indicating a mane, and traces of orangey-red paint extend from these 'manes' and meet in a V-shape within a rectangle on the back while a further painted line runs horizontally all around the body and intersects with lines running down the necks and up the front legs. These painted lines may represent a harness.
L. (4.7); W. (5.0); H. (4.7)

1518 M7/1 323
Surface
Front of a horse's head? This fragment of fine, dense, orangey-red, fired clay, with no visible temper, resembles the front of the headless body of a buxom, naked lady with small, stumpy arms. It is more likely, however, to be the top of a horse's head with the nose broken off at an angle (the 'arms' being the horse's ears and the 'neck' being its forelock). It has blinkers, and curved lines indicate the harness.
H. 4.9; L. 3.2; W. 1.9; Th. 1.8

1519 O20/6 185
Surface
The head of a Hellenistic female figurine, hollow and mould-made in two halves out of fine, light brown, grit-tempered, fired clay. The head is broken beneath the chin and down the left side, and most of the back is missing. The features are hard to distinguish, but the nose and chin are prominent, the eyes are just visible as slight swellings and the ears are absent. The woman wears a veil which forms a double arch over her hair which is indicated by two rows of vertical ridges rising from her forehead.
H. (4.3); W. (3.5); Th. 2.0
Fig. 269

1520 P15/5 101
Surface
Leg of an animal(?), made of pink clay with large grits and a beige slip on the exterior. There is a clean break at the top. The leg is set at an angle and widens towards the front at the bottom, rather like that of an elephant, but there is no indication of a hoof or toes, etc. This could be a tripod foot (cf. **1507**).
H. (5.8); L. 3.7 (foot); W. 3.5

1521 R13/1 200
Surface
Torso of a female figurine made out of creamy brown, grit-tempered, fired clay. The head and arms are missing and the figure is broken just below the narrow waist (3.0), where the swelling buttocks and hips begin. Judging from the angles of the breaks, the figure held her right arm up and her left arm down. Two lines of purplish brown paint run from the base of the neck along the broad shoulders, and there are two little splashes of paint on her flat front, between the small applied pellets that mark her breasts. Two diagonal lines of brown paint intersect across her curved back.
H. (5.1); W. 6.5; Th. 2.3

See Goldman 1963, figs. 153:1–2 and 160:76 for similar painted lines on the backs of figurines of the early first millennium BC.

Figure 269. *Head of Hellenistic female figurine* **1519**.

Figure 270. *Head of horse figurine* **1523**.

1522 R13/2 200
Surface
Perhaps an arm intended for inlay, made out of soft, cream clay, with a flat back left rough, and front carefully shaped into a rounded, V-shape resembling the bent elbow of a figure. The line running around the piece some 0.3 cm above the base may indicate its use as an inlay; alternatively, it could be part of the decoration of a relief vase (cf. Boehmer 1983).
H. (3.4); W. 3.7; Th. 1.1

1523 T11/1 275
Surface
Horse's head of hard-fired, pinky-brown clay, broken at the bottom of the neck. The ears are broken off, the mane is shown by incised, inverted V-shapes down the ridge at the back of the neck, the eyes are indicated by crudely-drawn circles and there are applied blinkers. Brown painted lines on either side of the neck, down across the blinkers, down the front of the head and across beneath the eyes, from the mouth down the underside of the head and neck probably indicate a harness.
H. (5.5); L. (7.8); W. 3.5
Fig. 270

Wheels and wheel-like objects (1524–6)

Clay wheels resembling **1524** have been found at other sites, connected with large animal or chariot figurines to which they would have been linked by a wooden axle (e.g. Woolley 1934, 591, pl. 188, U.14461, an animal-shaped pot on wheels, found loose in the soil of the lower grave stratum in the Royal Cemetery at Ur). These were presumably used as toys and they are sometimes included in burials. Whether **1526** was a wheel is debatable; it may, as also suggested above, have been a stopper.

1524 K20/209 1988
Level IId
Wheel; hand-made, crumbly, grit-tempered, layered clay; the rim of the wheel is missing, there is a conical hub on each side (one damaged), pierced for an axle (diameter of perforation 0.6). Orange-brown paint has been roughly applied around the hubs, with four radial lines indicating spokes. The presence of four spokes would favour a date in the second millennium BC when spokes first appear on Near Eastern vehicles; in the first millennium, spokes become more numerous (see Littauer & Crouwel 1979, figs. 24–5, 28–35, 39–40, 42–3).
Di. (5.6); Th. 4.3

1525 R18/32 KLT 3 2018
Level E5b
Centrally pierced disc with a raised knob on one side — probably a wheel. Chipped around the edge. The flatter side is slightly thickened around the hole. The clay is orange with occasional white, calcareous inclusions; the surface is orange-buff. The flatter side is roughly finished but the other side has been wheel-finished.
Di. 10.0; H. 2.8

1526 K19/13 1501
Level I
Hand-made, wheel-shaped object made out of grit-tempered, grey-brown clay, narrowing on either side to two badly damaged 'hubs' (where one of the hubs has broken, there is a large pebble, 0.6 wide, in the clay). In view of the fact that there is no perforation for an axle, it is possible that this piece was used as a stopper and there is, indeed, a circular groove on one side of the 'wheel' which could have been impressed in the damp clay by the rim of a vessel.
Di. 4.9; W. (3.5); H. (3.4)

Counters, tokens and gaming pieces (1527–36)

1527 H19/320 4267
Level IVa
Small circular clay disc with a shallow depression on each face and roughly rounded edges. Fine buff fabric with small dark grits.

Rather crude. See **1528** for comments.
Th. 0.8; Di. 1.8

1528   H19/208   4249
Level IVb
Small circular clay ball flattened at each end, with roughly rounded edges. Fine buff fabric with small dark grits. Rather crude.
Di. 3.4; H. 2.7
Plain clay discs with slightly concave faces like this and **1527** were numerous at Alişar in Stratum II, where they are referred to as 'clay cakes'. They were found in association with clay crescents and miniature wheels, which also fits the MBA Kilise Tepe context but unlike our examples, the Alişar specimens are frequently decorated (von der Osten & Schmidt 1932, 120, fig. 146).

1529   J19/427   KLT 126   6414
Level IIb
Disc of fine, soft clay with a groove around both faces (edges chipped), and a raised, round central section; side decorated with impressed, unevenly-spaced, centre-dot circles in four pairs with one single one: 1.3 × 2.3.
Di. 2.3; H. 2.2; H. of rim 0.95; Di. of raised part 1.4; Di. perf. 0.4
Fig. 271

Similar objects, but made of stone and described as 'whorls or large beads', were found at Tille Höyük on the Euphrates in the Atatürk Dam area in contexts dated between 1300 and 1200 BC (Summers 1993, fig. 63:1–3, pp. 137, 150). At Malatya, stone, bone and clay examples, some of them undecorated, were found in contexts which range from Neo-Hittite to late first millennium BC or Early Byzantine (Pecorella 1975, figs. 2:1–3, 11:1–6). The examples from Alişar, described as 'whorls', are usually of serpentine and are dated to the 'Post Hittite-Phrygian' period (von der Osten 1937, 427, 430, fig. 485:d.289, d.1105, d.1266, d.1939, d.217). At Boğazköy, all the examples are unstratified and made of stone (Boehmer 1972, nos. 2400–403; only no. 2402 is decorated, also with centre-dot circles). For an undecorated example, see **1532**, and for one made of bone see **2487**. Both the Kilise Tepe examples date to Level II; the decorated piece was found in a IIb context and the undecorated example in IId–e.

[**1530**]   J19/410   6400
Level IIc
Disc of grey unbaked clay with one concave face; uneven.
Di. 1.8; Th. 1.0

[**1531**]   K19/90   1554
Level IIc
Ball of cream, unbaked clay, perhaps used as a marble.
Di. *c.* 1.8

1532   K20/121   1938
Level IId/e
Disc of greyish-brown clay with a deep groove running around both faces; pierced.
Di. 3.2; Di. perf. 0.65; H. 1.1
Fig. 272
See **1529**, for a decorated version of this type of object, and for parallels quoted there.

[**1533**]   L19/34   5950
Level IIf
Tapering cylinder of unbaked, pale grey clay with concave (chipped) ends.
Di. 1.1; L. 2.8

[**1534**]   K20/188   1985
Level II
Concave-sided, slightly tapering cylinder of unbaked, pale grey clay with concave ends; one side is broken.
Di. 2.3 max., 1.7 (at centre); H. 2.6

1535   K19/53   1527
Level IIe
Concave-sided disc made out of pale grey clay. See **1536**.
Di. 2.9 (ends), 2.4 (middle); H. 2.2

1536   L18/27   99
Surface
Concave-sided disc of unbaked, pale grey clay. See **1535**.
Di. 3.1 (ends), 2.9 (middle); H. 1.8

Pottery discs (1537–95)

Potsherds roughly turned into discs or other secondary shapes were found at all levels. They are generally relatively flat sherds from the walls or bases of pots — the larger ones from large, thick-walled pots and the smaller ones generally from thinner-walled vessels. In

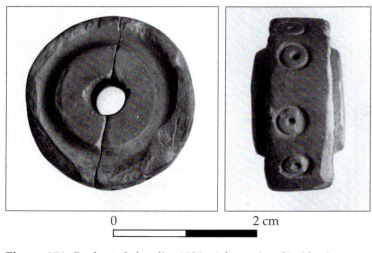

Figure 271. *Perforated clay disc* **1529**: *a) front view; b) side view.*

Figure 272. *Perforated clay disc* **1532**.

the examples from Levels III–V the thicknesses vary from 0.5–1.1 cm, and it is clear that they were fashioned from discarded pottery in fabrics well known at the periods concerned. These range from *pithos* wares to finer fabrics such as the classic dense pale orange fabric of EB III/MBA (Fabric A; see pp. 252–3). They were taken from both open and closed vessels, occasionally with red slips (**1537**, **1549**).

Unless otherwise stated, they are roughly circular in shape with approximately vertical edges which have clearly been intentionally chipped into shape. Except in the case of some of the smaller discs, there is not usually any attempt to smooth the edges. They come in three, clearly distinguishable, sizes: small (12 examples, from 2.7–3.8 cm), medium (25 examples, from 4.0–5.3 cm) and large (13 examples, from 6.0–7.3 cm). These variations do not seem to have any chronological significance, but whether they have functional implications remains to be established.

The crude nature of the material and small sizes of the objects mean that it is not generally possible to be certain whether a piece was wheel-made or hand-made, and that the measurements are approximate. Int. and ext. refer to the interior and exterior of the pot from which the discs were cut and are equivalent respectively to the bottom and top of the discs, assuming the smoother, sometimes slightly convex side to be the top.

Some of the discs are perforated, usually through the centre. None of those from Level IV or earlier is pierced, though two have signs of an attempted central perforation on the interior side (**1550**, **1574**). Where discs are pierced, this is indicated in **bold** in the following entries.

Such re-worked pottery sherds used as artefacts are extremely common throughout western Anatolia and the Aegean (Joukowsky 1986, 381), and their distribution in time and place has been explored at great length by Obladen-Kauder (1996, 214–24). Examples have also been recorded in northern Iraq, in Neo-Assyrian and surface levels at Khirbet Khatuniyeh (Curtis & Green 1997, 19, nos. 73–4, 110).

Unlike at Kilise Tepe where the edges are almost always rough, sherds with ground and smoothed edges are reported at other sites. A mixture of perforated and unperforated discs, and examples with attempted perforation is commonly observed but the ratio varies from site to site. At Demircihüyük, perforated far outnumbered unperforated ones. At Aphrodisias out of 525 examples from the Late Neolithic to the IA (reaching their peak in EB IV to MBA levels) 59 per cent were unperforated (Joukowsky 1986, 381). They were of similar sizes, ranging from about 3.5–7.0 cm in diameter. At Kinet Höyük, the chronological distribution extends into the medieval period. Many have probably gone unrecognized and unrecorded, as suggested by Joukowsky with reference to Troy, where Blegen apparently found only 19 examples in the first five levels whereas Schliemann records finding 'many hundreds', drawing parallels with Hungarian and German examples (Schliemann 1880, 422).

For their use numerous explanations have been put forward, such as lids (at Aphrodisias), spindle whorls and labels for the perforated type. Some of the pierced examples may have been intended for use as spindle whorls, but Crewe (1998, 9) argues that only objects with properly centred perforations would have been suitable for spinning (see below, p. 481; for a possible stone example which is perforated, see **2613**). An association with the textile industry, but with a different purpose, is attested at Lisht in Egypt, where X-rays of two balls of linen yarn revealed that roughly chipped clay discs were used as a base for winding thread into a ball; in one case two overlying unperforated discs were used, the other ball had only one (Cartland 1918, 139, pl. 22).

Another possibility is that the discs were tokens or counters of some kind, with the few which are pierced perhaps being worn on a thong around the neck. There are iconographical parallels for discs being worn in this way, from Susa in the fourth millennium BC (Amiet 1980, nos. 118, 122), and from Sar-i Pul-i Zohab at the end of the third millennium (Börker-Klähn 1982, no. 33).

1586–95 are a variety of shapes including roughly triangular and rectangular pieces and unusual types of disc. For re-used potsherds in square, oval and triangular shapes from other sites see Obladen-Kauder 1996, 215 Abb. 142.

Small discs (2.7–3.8 cm)
[**1537**]   H20/1013   5363
Level Vf2/3
Small pottery disc with chipped outer edges. Fabric fine orange with red slip on both sides.
Di. 2.8; Th. 0.6

[**1538**]   H20/1014   5363
Level Vf2/3
Small pottery disc chipped around the edges. Fabric fine orange-red, plain.
Di. 2.7; Th. 0.5

1539   H20/29   1215
Level IIIa–c
Body sherd roughly worked into a circular disc. Fabric red, grit-tempered with some calcareous inclusions. Ext. smoothed and treated with a low burnish; int. covered in a lime deposit.
Di. 3.6; Th. 0.7

Chapter 35

Figure 273. *Assorted clay discs, drawn examples: 1540, 1546, 1570, 1575, 1582 and 1595.*

1540   J19/317   3927
Level IIc
Fine, reddish-brown, grit-tempered; very carefully finished.
Di. 3.2; Th. 0.5
Fig. 273

[1541]   K20/200   1992
Level IId
Dense, grit-tempered with dark red core; orange slip on the int. and ext. and a smoothed ext.; unusually thick.
Di. 3.3-4.0; Th. 1.7

[1542]   H18/142   2640
Level IId/e
Wheel-made, creamy-grey, grit-tempered; orange to brown slip on the ext.; irregular shape.
Di. 3.2–3.4; Th. 1.0

[1543]   H18/161   2659
Level IId/e
Hand-made, coarse, vegetable-tempered; heavily burnt to pale grey on the worn int. and to black on the ext.; flaring hole in the centre, **pierced** from both sides; neatly finished but one edge damaged.
Di. 1.7-3.6; Th. 1.7

1544   H18/61   2619
Level IIf
Brick red, grit-tempered, with surface carefully removed; **pierced** neatly; carefully finished.
Di. 2.7–3.0; Th. 0.9

[1545]   I19/78   1781
Level IIg
Creamy orange-brown, grit-tempered; traces of orange slip on the int., reddish-orange slip on the ext.
Di. 3.6; Th. 0.7

1546   J14/85   3354
Level 1/2
Cream, tempered with very fine, black grits; dark grey slip on the ext.; carefully smoothed edges.
Di. 2.8; Th. 0.8
Fig. 273

[1547]   K14/53   3016
Level 1
Dense, pinky brown, concreted; neatly cut.
Di. 2.7; Th. 0.8

[1548]   I16/16   4601
Topsoil
Hand-made, reddish-brown, grit-tempered, with pattern burnish just visible on the ext.
Di. 3.6–4.0; Th. 1.2

Medium discs (4.0–5.3 cm)
[1549]   H20/1075   5392
Level Vf1–2
Irregular-shaped pottery disc with chipped edges. Red slipped on both sides. Comes from EB III type vessel of dense orange fabric (Fabric A).
Di. 4.4; Th. 1.1

[1550]   H20/983   5370
Level Vf2?
A roughly circular pottery disc, chipped on the edges. Attempted perforation on int. Dense orange red fabric with orange wash both sides.
Di. 4.3; Th. 0.9

[1551]   H19/329   4270
Level IVb
Sherd reworked into a roughly round disc-shaped object. Medium coarse, orange fabric, grit- and mudstone-tempered with traces of a wash on ext.
Di. 4.4–4.6; Th. 1.0

1552   H20/34   1217
Level IIIa–c
Body sherd reworked to a roughly circular disc. Pale orange medium fabric with grit and mudstone temper. Ext. smoothed, plain.
Di. 4.1; Th. 1.2

[1553]   I19/106   2832
Level IIe
Brick red, grit-tempered; burnished int. and ext. (worn); one face is more carefully finished than the other.
Di. 4.0; Th. 0.7

[1554]   I19/199   5536
Level IIId/e
Grit-tempered, greyish-brown; traces of burnish on the ext. and smoothing on the int.
Di. 4.8; Th. 1.0

[1555] I14/188 3717
Level 3
Hand-made, pinky-brown, grit- and vegetable-tempered; smoothed ext.
Di. 4.0–4.5; Th. 1.3

[1556] I14/175 3489
Level 2/3
Cream; many small, black grits, with a brown wash on the ext.; straight break on one side.
Di. 3.8–4.2; Th. 0.9

[1557] J19/394 3981
Level IIb
Pinky-brown; tempered with fine grits; almost rectangular, with rounded corners and a rounded end.
Di. 4.5–5.1; Th. 1.2

[1558] J20/188 1393
Level IIb
Wheel-made, creamy grey-brown.
Di. 3.9–4.1; Th. 0.8

[1559] K19/82 1550
Level IId
Grit-tempered; pale orange-brown on the int. and grey-brown on the ext.
Di. 5.2; Th. 1.0

[1560] J19/257 1690
Level IId
Coarse, hand-made, grit- and vegetable-tempered; orange on the int. and burnt black on the ext.
Di. 5.0; Th. 0.5–1.1

[1561] H18/156 2649
Level IIe/f
Dense, orange, grit-tempered; smoothed on the ext.; roughly oval.
Di. 3.8–4.3; Th. 1.1

[1562] K14/155 3090
Level 2 lower
Grit-tempered, very worn; pale grey on the int. and smoothed grey-brown on the ext.; roughly oval.
Di. 4.0–4.7; Th. 1.2

[1563] R18/171 2435
Level E5a/b
Hand-made, heavily concreted; dense orangey-brown; smoothed on the ext.; hole **pierced** in the centre, chipped from both sides; rather a jagged circle.
Di. 4.8; Th. 1.2

[1564] R18/188 2446
Level E5b
Dense, grey, grit-tempered; fired to orange on the int. and pale brown on the ext. which is smoothed.
Di. 4.7; Th. 1.5

[1565] K19/140 1575
Level I/II
Dense, orange, grit-tempered (some large grits).
Di. 4.6; Th. 1.5

[1566] J14/89 3356
Level 1/2
Hand-made, pale orangey-brown, coarse, grit- and vegetable-tempered (some large grits); smoothed ext.
Di. 4.8; Th. 1.0

1567 K18/1 4300
Topsoil
Hand-made cooking ware, dark red, grit-tempered; made from the centre of a slightly concave base; ext. burnt, with impressed(?) cross.
Di. 5.0–5.3; Th. 0.6

[1568] K8/8 315
Surface
Crumbly, hand-made, grit-tempered (with large white grits); orange on the int. and grey-brown on the ext. with a lighter brown, streaky burnish.
Di. 5.3; Th. 0.9

[1569] P6/2 328
Surface
Wheel-made, orangey-brown, dense, grit-tempered; slightly oval.
Di. 4.2–4.8; Th. 0.7

1570 R14/1 189
Surface
Hand-made, very coarse; many large grits; reddish-brown to grey on int. and reddish-brown on the ext.; the hole in the centre was **pierced** from both sides; very irregular in shape.
Di. 4.3–4.7; Th. 1.2
Fig. 273

[1571] J14/104 3367
Level 2k
Dense, pinky-red, grit-tempered; many red grits (some large); smoothed ext.
Di. 4.1; Th. 1.2

[1572] I19/111 2846
Level IIc–f
Cream, grit-tempered; burnt black on the ext. with traces of burning on the sides (i.e. after the disc was made); made from the centre of the flat base of a vessel.
Di. 4.8–5.1; Th. 1.0

Large discs (from 6.0 cm)
[1573] H20/665 5300
Level Ve
A disc-shaped potsherd, re-worked presumably from a broken vessel. Medium coarse (Fabric C1) pink fabric with grit and some dark stone temper. Ext. covered in thick cream slip, left matt.
W. 6.0

[1574] H20/261 1260
Unstratified
Roughly circular disc from a re-worked pot sherd. The int. shows the beginning of a drill hole. Medium coarse, orange fabric, grit and sand temper fired under reduced conditions which has rendered most of the fabric grey. Int. orange wash.
Di. 6.0–6.1; Th. 1.2–1.4

1575 I20/60 4010
Level IIb
Hand-made, reddish-brown, coarse, grit-tempered (some large grits); cut from a *pithos*, with two rows of string impressions across the ext.; one edge is damaged.
Di. 6.5; Th. 1.4
Fig. 273

[1576]   J18/159   2338
Level I
Pinky-brown, grit-tempered; pinky-orange with red wash on the ext. and pink on the int.
Di. 6.1; Th. 1.1

[1577]   K14/156   3097
Level 2 lower
Hand-made, grey, coarse, grit-tempered with many large grits; fired to creamy-brown on the int. and greyish-cream on the ext. which is burnt; roughly oval.
Di. 6.2–7.2; Th. 0.9

[1578]   K20/106   1928
Level I/IIf
Hand-made, cream, grit-tempered, burnt; the int. face is missing and rough, the ext. smoothed; roughly sliced from the bottom of a round-based pot and therefore rounded on the ext.; the edges are sharp.
Di. 6.6; Th. 1.1 (at centre)

[1579]   L19/24   5930
Level I/II
Pinky-cream, grit-tempered (with red grits).
Di. 7.3; Th. 2.0

[1580]   I14/65   3430
Level 1/2k
Pinky-brown, grit-tempered; the underside is uneven; perhaps originally part of a sieve as it was **pierced** by a small funnel-shaped hole which has been re-used (the diameter is uncertain as the piece is broken here); irregular in shape with three straight edges preserved.
Di. 5.5–6.5; Th. 1.5

[1581]   J14/74   3348
Level 1/2
Wheel-made, grey, grit-tempered; fired to light greyish-brown; ext. smoothed; probably cut from the bottom of a vessel which had a ring-base, as it is slightly thicker in the centre.
Di. 7.2; Th. 0.9–1.3

1582   Q19/80   2127
Level E4b
Pinky-cream, grit-tempered with red grits; smoothed ext.; a hollow was chipped in the centre from both sides (carefully on the ext. and roughly on the int.) but not pierced through; just over half remains.
Di. 7.2; Th. 1.2
Fig. 273

[1583]   J14/27   3314
Level 1
Possibly hand-made, pinky-orange, grit-tempered (some large grits).
Di. 7.0; Th. 0.8

[1584]   L14/27   3608
Level 1
Pitted, orangey-brown, grit- and vegetable-tempered; from a *pithos* with string impression (preserved across one end); worn edges.
Di. 7.0–7.3; Th. 1.7

[1585]   I8/3   317
Surface
Wheel-made, grey, grit-tempered (some large); fired to grey-brown; reddish-brown slip on the ext.; roughly oval.
Di. 6.7–7.0; Th. 1.1

Unusual shapes

1586   H20/424   1829
Level Vf/g
Clay scraper(?). Thin-walled clay object with three smoothed and rounded sides. The lower end and part of one side have fresh breaks. This object may have started its life as a rim sherd and was either re-worked for a different purpose or smoothed by water action. Medium-fine fabric, pale orange, grit-tempered.
H. 4.0; W. 6.0; Th. 0.4

[1587]   H19/21   4205
Level IIId
Triangular sherd with well rounded corners and smoothed edges. Edges are very well-worn; one corner is broken off. Medium fine fabric, pale buff, grit- and some sand-temper. Ext. self-slipped, smooth.
L. 4.2; W. 4.0; Th. 0.9

[1588]   J20/117   1376
Level IIId
Fine, soft, pale brown with very small grits and fine wheel marks on the int.; carefully shaped like a rectangle, tapering slightly towards a rounded end, with the sides smoothed and rounded.
L. 3.2; W. 2.6; Th. 0.5

1589   I19/192   KLT 135   5536
Level IIId/e
Undecorated domed disc; creamy-grey with black grits; **pierced**.
Di. 2.8; Th. 1.5; H. (dome) 0.6; Di. perf. 0.5

[1590]   K20/122   1938
Level IId/e
Unusually large pot disc formed out of the convex base of a large vessel; dense, sand and small white calcareous inclusions; light orange-red core; orange-buff ext. smoothed rather haphazardly, buff int. with pronounced spiral markings from manufacture; round the edge are distinct diagonal notches where the disc has been cut down and shaped.
Di. *c.* 23.5; Th. 2.3; H. *c.* 6.1

[1591]   K18/92   4337
Level IIe/f?
Abraded, brick red, grit-tempered; square with a shallow depression on the inner face.
L. 6.2; W. 6.5; Th. 1.9; Di. of depression 2.8 × 0.6 deep

[1592]   J19/217   1667
Level II?
Dense, orangey-red with many white grits (some large); carefully shaped into a roughly triangular shape with two rounded corners and a curved apex, with smoothed sides.
L. 5.2; W. 4.9; Th. 1.0

1593   K19/111   1564
Level I
Disc of pale brown clay resembling a button, with a concave ext. and convex int. and a rounded rim; **pierced** through the middle.
Di. 3.1; Th. 0.4; Max. H. 0.7

[1594   number not used]

1595   S18/23   174
Surface
Wheel-made, dense ware with many very small grits; grey fired to creamy-brown, brown burnished slip on the ext.; roughly diamond-shaped with a flattened top, with five holes, one drilled at each corner with one of the top ones too near the edge so that it broke.

L. 6.7; W. 5.5; Th. 1.9; Di. 6.8
Fig. 273

Miscellaneous clay items (1596–623)

Many of these objects, especially those coming from J18, are rough balls, lumps or twists of clay and could be the by-products of the making of clay objects or pottery.

1596 H20/666 KLT 104 5302
Level Ve
Decorated clay ball made of grey fabric with incised, approximately parallel lines running all around its surface with small holes interspaced (like a golf ball!).
Di. 2.7
Fig. 274

This decorated clay ball is the only example of its kind from the site. It is an object of no obvious practical use but must have enjoyed great popularity judging by the wide distribution of these clay 'marbles'. At Alişar, they are most common in Stratum I–III with a variety of incised, punctured and pricked designs covering the whole surface (von der Osten & Schmidt 1932, 109, fig. 89; 1937, fig. 204). In western Anatolia, clay balls are known from Kusura (Lamb 1937, fig. 12:9) and in Troy, with two close parallels to the Kilise Tepe pattern found in Troy III (Blegen *et al.* 1951, fig. 56: 34–54, 34–287).

1597 H20/655 5300
Level Ve
Perforated clay object. The two faces are flattened and edges are round. Perforated near the narrow edge with an additional drill hole not pierced through on the longer side. Fabric is a friable, grey beige with much organic temper leaving many voids visible in the break. Some signs of burning on one side.
L. (4.2); W. 4.0; Th. 1.05

1598 H20/823 5340
Level Vf4
Incomplete, perforated clay object. Extant portion is slightly trapezoidal in plan and 2.5 cm (max.) high. One face has four perforations at one end, and a fifth which pierces the centre of the object. The face opposing the perforations has a part of a complete raised edge that rises 0.76 cm from the solid portion. One end has a perforation *c.* 2 cm in length that intersects the central perforation but does not continue through. The other end has the remains of a raised edge that is curved, indicating the possibility that this end had a hole or dip in it at least 0.86 cm wide. Medium fine beige fabric with little temper. Smoothed. Probably unfired.
L.3.5; W. 2.0; Th. 1.8

[1599] H20/76 1226
Level IIIa/IVb
Unbaked, sand-coloured ceramic disc. Not included with sherd discs as recorded as unbaked; no dimensions available.

1600 H19/167 4247
Level IIIa
Wheel-shaped object with a circular indent and a central ridge (and perforation) on one side; reverse flat; edges broken and there are traces of holes pierced through the object at the edge; the thickness was measured at the outside edge. Fabric grit-tempered, varying from pale orange to buff, with grey core. No evidence of surface treatment.
Di. 5.5; Th. 2.0 max.

Figure 274. *Decorated clay ball* **1596**.

Cf. a small, vertical-sided sieve from Karahöyük (Colony Period) in Konya Museum which is grooved in a similar way. This would be the central part of such a vessel. A similar ring base from a jar, pierced approximately through the centre and reused, was found at Demircihüyük, unfortunately not well stratified (Kull 1988, Taf. 49:6).

[1600a] J20/143 1388
Level IIIe
Fragment from centre of a large flat ceramic tile, medium fine baked clay with small inclusions. One face is in plain, orange, clay; the other is painted red, with one reserved strip.
L. (28); W. (22.5); Th. 2.28

[1601] I14/161 3708
Level 3
Wheel-shaped clay object; mid-brown, with a groove running around inside the edge and a raised, central area; coarse, friable fabric with stone inclusions.
Di. *c.* 6.3

[1602] I14/151 3489
Level 2/3
Small lump of unbaked clay with one end flattened and pierced diagonally.
L. 2.0; W. 1.9; Th. 1.4

[1603] I14/164 3703
Level 2/3
Oddly-shaped, yellowy-brown object; coarse fabric; the surface is rounded into a blunt point, smooth, although uneven; broken across the widest area.
L. *c.* 7.0; H. *c.* 6.5

[1604] K19/451 6209
Level IIc?
Three fragments of a roughly cylindrical lump of beige, grit-tempered (large grits) unbaked clay, two of them joining; very rough; cf. **1610** for a similar (but better made) type of object.
Di. *c.* 3.0; L. (16.0 + 3.6)

[1605] K19/66 1541
Level IId
Concave-sided, cylindrical, unbaked, coarse, grey-white clay object; one end flattened and the other broken, but not much missing.
Di. 3.3; L. 6.2

[1606] H18/155 2650
Level IId/e
Coarse, unbaked beige-grey clay object with one face curved and smoothed.
H. 6.0; L. 6.0; Th. (3.0)

[1607] J18/327 5850
Level IIe
Twist of unbaked clay, horn-shaped but probably a by-product of potting.
L. 2.8; Th. 0.9

[1608] I19/61 2812
Level IIe
Brown, cylindrical object with bluntly rounded ends and a smooth, even surface along the length. One end has broken off but was included in the dimensions.
L. 7.5; Th. 3.3

[1609] J18/299 5843
Level IIe/f1
Fragment; holes could have held pebbles to weight it. Beige clay.
H. 3.3; Di. 5.1; Wt (30.0)

1610 K18/113 4353
Level IIe/f
Very roughly cylindrical piece of grey, grit- and vegetable-tempered clay which looks (and feels) as though it has been shaped in the fist (fingers fit well into the shape); the ends do not look broken.
Di. *c.* 3.3; L. 5.4

1611 J18/309 5849
Level IIe
Object resembling a lop-sided finger-ring of unbaked, grit-tempered, white, very weathered, powdery clay. The 'bezel' is cartouche-shaped and set at an angle and there is no trace of any surviving design on it; the 'hoop' (int. di. 1.65) is not quite complete.
(H. 3.7); W. 3.2; Th. 1.9

It has been suggested that this could have been a loomweight. However, this could have been a crude, even playful, imitation of the turquoise faience finger-rings which were popular in Egypt in the second half of the second millennium BC (Hayes 1959, 396–7, figs. 249–50), but no trace of any colour survives.

[1612] J18/210 2391
Level IIf1
Roughly shaped ball of unbaked, creamy-grey clay, with a semi-circular groove (W. 1.8) running across one side.
Di. *c.* 4.5

[1613] J18/343 5867
Level IIe?
Six fragments of an unbaked, rounded, clay object, burnt on exterior.
L. (4.0); W. (3.5); H. 2.2; Wt (28.9)

[1614] I14/60 3424
Level 2k
Roughly shaped ball of unbaked clay with three small stones sticking out of it. Perhaps a weighted slingshot.
Di. 3.0

[1615] I14/107 3466
Level 2
Oval-ended, light brown, asymmetrical clay object.
13.0 × 11.0 (at base); 8.0 × 5.0 (at top)

[1616] I14/125 3477
Level 2
Burnt(?), unbaked, dark grey object with a flat 'base' and curved edges, narrowing towards a (broken) 'top' surface; a shell is lodged in the broken end. A stand or a stopper? Cf. **1618**.
Di. 7.0

[1617] I14/127 3478
Level 2
Roughly circular object with one end wider than the other; coarse fabric.
Di. 9.0

[1618] K19/52 1527
Level IIe
Similar to **1616**, but creamy, without the shell inclusion; top and side broken.
Di. 8.2; H. (6.4)

[1619] K19/56 1537
Level I/II
Dark grey, unbaked clay object; curving widely, including one 'rim' piece; very coarse fabric with small stone and vegetable temper; uneven outer and inner surfaces. Possibly a pot stand.
W. *c.* 3.0 max.

1620 J18/41 2303
Level I
Small fragment or lump of clay with a grey core, fired to reddish-brown on the ext.; two small, irregular strips of clay have been applied on one side; red wash overall. Perhaps part of a handle or of a figurine.
L. 2.5; W. 1.9; Th. 0.9

[1621] I14/5 3400
Topsoil
Corner of a large, tile-like object. A hole in the corner and another 6.3 from one edge and 4.9 from the other have been pierced from both sides; they are *c.* 0.7 in diameter and flare out at the ends to *c.* 1.5.
L. (12.3); W. (11.1); Th. 3.1

1622 K15/7 100
Surface
Curved piece of clay, hand-made, grit-tempered, grey, fired to brown with reddish-brown wash on the ext., with a grooved outer edge (ext. di. 8.0; int. di. irregular; outer th. *c.* 1.0) and one face smoothly finished while the other is rough. Perhaps part of a pot-stand, or (less likely because of the one rough side) the horn of a large figurine.
L. 5.6; W. 2.6; Th. 1.9

[1623] M17/2 118
Surface
Flat sherd of grey grit-tempered ware, fired to brownish-pink; re-used. On one side (probably originally the int.) a line has been incised and dots have been gouged on either side of it. Cf. the stone incense-burner **2611**.

Clay pipe (1624)

1624   Q19/17   2100
Level E2b
Ottoman pipe bowl, broken diagonally and missing most of the stem. Dense red fabric with no visible temper, tan exterior surface with traces of burning on the bowl interior. Rounded bowl decorated with a row of notch-rouletting around the bottom, followed by a horizontal stamped leaf pattern, a row of vertically impressed 'eye' motifs with irregularly spaced and separately impressed, upper and lower, curved 'lashes', and two further rows of notch-rouletting at the base of a tall (H. 1.6), flaring lip. The lip is decorated by two fine horizontal grooves and, below the rim, a row of stamped ornamented stepped U-shaped (*ogee*) motifs and a further band of notch-rouletting at the top. The bowl-stem junction is marked by a large V-shape of notch-rouletting and double-incised lines on the bottom of the bowl and by a row of notch-rouletting on the upper part of the stem itself. On the right side of the stem, close to the bowl-stem junction, is a small oval pipe-maker's stamp impression containing up to three lines of a highly stylized inscription. Although the stamping of the decoration has been done somewhat carelessly, the overall effect is elegant.
Di. *c.* 4.0 (bowl rim), 3.3 (bowl), 1.8 (stem); L. (4.0); H. 4.0
Fig. 276

We are indebted to Dr St John Simpson of the British Museum for the following comments:

> This single fragmentary Late Ottoman clay pipe bowl was recovered from the surface in 1994. It probably dates to the nineteenth century and is likely to be of Turkish manufacture.
>
> The best-documented centre of pipe manufacture within Turkey is Istanbul itself where the main focus of production was between Tophane and Galata. During the nineteenth century burnished red-slipped pipes were the most popular type to be produced here but small numbers of black or caramel-coloured pipes were also made; the same range of colours was mirrored in contemporary pipe-makers' ceramic sidelines, such as coffee cups, bowls and ewers (Bakla 1993). During the eighteenth and nineteenth centuries most, if not all, other Turkish towns and cities probably also had pipe-making industries in order to cope with the huge demand from smokers. Avanos, Lüleburgaz, Diyarbakır, Edirne, Iznik, Kayseri, Mardin, Siirt and Sivas are among those cities that are documented by contemporary European authors or through analysis of pipe-makers' stamps.
>
> The publication of further groups of Ottoman pipes should allow the identification of specific workshop traditions. Until then, the place of manufacture of this Kilise Tepe pipe remains uncertain; the pipe-maker's mark is unfortunately illegible. The overall scheme of the decoration is not found on published Ottoman pipes but this is hardly surprising as very few pipes have yet been published from within Anatolia itself. The V-shaped decoration on the base of the bowl is not diagnostic and is a feature occurring on eighteenth–nineteenth century Ottoman pipes found from Greece to Palestine. Likewise, the stepped U-shaped stamped decoration on the bowl also recurs on the upper bowls of nineteenth-century pipes found at Corinth (Robinson 1985, 185–6, 190, pls. 55, 58 C87–8, C118) and Bursa (pers. observ. 1993).

Figure 275. *Re-used sherd with incised design* **1623**.

Figure 276. *Ottoman pipe bowl* **1624**.

Clay furniture (1625–33)

A most intriguing and substantial item of domestic paraphernalia is a two-horned clay artefact with a triangular base and handle mounted at right angles to the horns (**1625**). It was found on an EB II domestic floor in Rm 82 of Level Vj. A second object of this type (**1626**), although rather fragmentary, came from the same room, and the two items may well have acted as a pair. The handle, preserved in both examples, suggests that the objects were portable, although the opening (perforation) of the handle is quite small (c. 1.2).

Significant is the context in which they were found which suggests some specialized activity involving red dye preparation which, together with a number of loomweights, may hint at some form of textile production at Kilise Tepe (see p. 300 on Level Vj).

Horned objects of this kind — although frequently without handles — are not unique to Kilise Tepe and occur at various Anatolian and some Near Eastern sites (for a study of various classes of horned objects in Anatolia and the Near East see Diamant & Rutter 1969). The closest parallels can be found at Mersin where a series of horned artefacts of this type came to light in Middle and Late Chalcolithic Levels, indicating their use over a lengthy period. The earliest from Rm 166 in Level XVI was found in association with a domed oven and three others came from later levels (XIV–XII) but their context is not discussed. Garstang called them 'andirons' and suggested their use as supports for cooking pots with the idea that the space between the horns would 'permit the flame of the fire to circulate freely' (Garstang 1953, 166, fig. 90, 106). It is not stated whether the horned objects showed signs of burning.

At Tarsus there is one 'horned' example, but with a domed top and no handle, which is described as a 'loom support' on the basis of a find from Nuzi with the idea that the loom bar would have rested between the horns with a cord passed through the hole positioned in front (Goldman 1956, 319f., fig. 442:15). Horned 'supports' are also reported from the Konya plain at Karahöyük in Level XXV (EB I): 'one side has a pair of horns, the other has a handle for lifting' (Mellink 1967, 161), and at Alişar (von der Osten 1937 II, fig. 278).

Returning to the Kilise Tepe examples, we should stress that no burning marks were noted to connect them to hearth activities, while the context in which they were excavated would favour a role in textile production rather than food preparation. The small perforation through the handle may have served the same purpose as the one in the base of the Tarsus specimen (see above).

1625   H20/742   5406
Level Vj
A horned clay object with a handle and triangular flat base. Opposite the two horns, which are tapered towards the top, is a handle running at right angles to the horns. The fabric is medium coarse, beige, with a moderate amount of grit and organic temper. Surface smoothed and covered with a cream lime coating.
H. 14.5; L. 14.0; W. 17.0
Fig. 277

Figure 277. *Horned clay support* **1625**.

Found with a similar clay object **1626** in the same unit and the two may have acted as a pair.

[1626]   H20/755   5406
Level Vj
Similar object to **1625**, but fragmentary. Two joining fragments provide the handle part and one of the horned parts of which most has broken off. Beige coarse fabric with grit and stone temper. Fired.
W. 15.0

Items of note connected with cooking are so-called spit supports and a hearth guard fragment. **1627** came from the destruction fill of Level Vh (EB II) located next to a small jug. The rectangular shape with outward curving top and bottom is provided with three grooves on the top and two holes on opposite sides, making it suitable for spits resting in the grooves as well as inserted into the sides. Presumably these artefacts could only have worked as a pair with the fire arranged between them.

The majority of spit supports encountered at other Anatolian sites are pyramidal in shape and were recorded at Kusura (Lamb 1937, 34, fig. 16:4–6), Demircihüyük (Obladen-Kauder 1996, 245f., Abb. 175) and other sites. They occur either plain, with added holes, or more rarely transversely perforated. The Kilise Tepe 'spit support' has a close parallel at Alaca Hüyük (Koşay & Akok 1973, 79 Taf. 37 Al.t.19), also grooved on the top, a feature also seen at Tarsus (Goldman 1956, 320, fig. 442:16–22).

Of related function are horned or crenellated portable hearth-guards, in our case (**1631**) of the straight variety from an MBA/LBA context with counterparts at Tarsus of LB I date and Aphrodisias. They may have had a double function of containing the fire as well as supporting spits laid across them, again functioning as a pair (Goldman 1956, 320, fig. 443:28–9; Joukowsky 1986, fig. 423:22).

A cylindrical clay stand (**1632**) was excavated on a domestic house floor in Rm 42 of Level IVa (MBA) among a collection of cooking pots and other vessels (Fig. 487), indicating here a domestic use of a kind. Contemporary parallels of similar dimensions can be found at Kusura (Lamb 1937, 37, fig. 16:1, 3) from Period C (from a shrine) and Period B, and at Tarsus where three specimens were found of similar date (Goldman 1956, 320, fig. 442:23–4). They could have served as a stand or support for a variety of things including, in the Kilise Tepe context, for some of the pots found in close proximity.

1627   H20/435   KLT 84   1836
Level Vg/h
Clay 'spit support'. The shape is roughly rectangular, flared at the top and bottom and contracted in the centre. The top part has 3 grooves which are smoothed and slightly blackened. The object is pierced transversely at the centre. Presumably spits could be placed in the grooves or inserted into the holes. Very crumbly fabric with little temper, probably unbaked. Surface smoothed, some areas are blackened.
H. 7.9; W. 5.9
Fig. 278
Cf. Goldman 1956, 320, fig. 442:18.

1628   H20/561   1859
Level Vj
One fragment from the corner of a spit support. The preserved faces are well smoothed. The fragment has one entire groove and part of a second preserved. Similar to, but smaller than, the one recovered from Level Vg/h (**1627**). Orange-brown, medium fine fabric with multi-coloured grit temper. Unfired.
H. (3.0); L. (5.0); Th. (3.0)

[1629]   H20/1082   5391
Level Vg
Clay object in the shape of a foot or — when tilted 90° — a horn-shaped object as seen in the so-called horned loom supports. The object tapers at one end and is broken diagonally at the other. Apart from a small chip, the pointed end is intact. The fabric is similar to that used in loomweights. Coarse with dark grits and some stones as well as a large percentage of vegetation temper. Traces of red paint at the 'foot' end. Unbaked.
H. 11.5; W. 7.8 max.

1630   H20/836   5427
Level Vj/k
One end of a curved piece of pottery. Fabric orange/yellow with large grit inclusions. It has an obvious base and stands up on this, making a low circular enclosure with a rounded top and an opening. Perhaps a hearth guard similar to one at Tarsus (cf. Goldman 1956, fig. 443:30).
H. 6.0; W. 2.4; Th. 2.0

1631   H20/68   1223
Level IIIa–IVb
Fragment of a horned hearth guard, cf. Goldman 1956 fig. 443:28–9, of the straight rather than curved type. Flat base preserved on one side and damaged on the opposite side, tapering upwards to the horned or crenellated ridge. Only two of the crenellations are preserved as it is broken at both ends. Mid-brown coarse fabric with small stone and little organic temper. Surface is barely smoothed and slightly lighter in colour.
H. 11.4; L. (12.5)

Figure 278. *Clay spit support 1627.*

1632   H20/155   1243
Level IVa
Clay support. Large object of unbaked clay, like a cylinder but narrowing at the centre. The edges are rounded and one end is slightly concave, though the surface is largely missing. The other side (bottom?) is slightly blackened. The beige fabric is coarse with grit, stones and large amounts of organic matter, leaving voids.
H. 14.5; W. 5.9; Di. 9.5
Cf. Goldman 1956, fig. 442, nos. 23-4.

1633   K20/227   1131
Level IIc
Half of a stand(?) with two horns, one broken away. Coarse fired clay, vegetable temper. On one face there is a perforation 3.4 cm above the base extending into the interior of the object to a depth of 3.7 cm. The diameter of the perforation is 1.85 cm at the exterior and tapers to 1.0 cm.

Clay crescents (1634–8)

At Kilise Tepe a small number of clay crescents were recovered during the opening season in 1994 (Baker *et al.* 1995, 186f.). No further examples were encountered in the following campaigns.

Most of the crescents came from destruction debris on an occupation floor in the proximity of a hearth (FI94/3) and a number of complete or partly preserved vessels (Fig. 488); one was at the very base of the Level III packing, and it is uncertain whether it had been incorporated in the packing material or belonged to the IVb layer below. There was no further contextual information to provide clues to the nature of their use which remains controversial (see below).

The five, or possibly six, clay crescents are not very well preserved. With the exception of **1634**, which was neatly made with a smooth surface and pale red slip, they were fragmentary, unbaked and frequently friable. Their shapes differ only marginally, showing

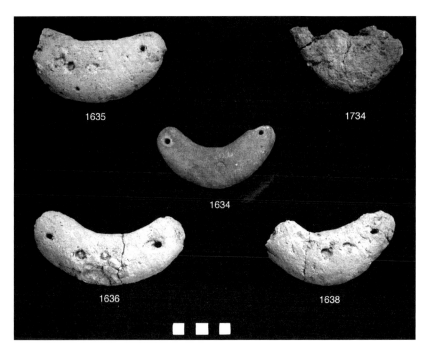

Figure 279. *Clay crescents: top) **1635**, **1734**; centre) **1634**; bottom) **1636**, **1638**.*

similar curvature but with varying width, and all are perforated at both ends, when preserved (Fig. 279).

Most of our examples are stamped in the central area of one side. The impressions are often indistinct, but **1634** has a single rosette and **1636** bears two impressions of which one is in the form of a type of cross, motifs which can be paralleled on crescents from Karahöyük Konya (Alp 1968, pls. 170:521 & 171:524) and Beycesultan (Mellaart & Murray 1995, 165, fig. O.15.170).

Clay crescents are not uncommon at Anatolian sites. Closest to Kilise Tepe in Cilicia are Tarsus with 26 crescents attributed to the level of LB I (Goldman 1956, 319, fig. 441:11), and Mersin from where two examples were reported (Garstang 1953, 217, fig. 137). The richest find in terms of numbers and variety of decoration is still Karahöyük Konya, excavated in the 1960s, where over 300 clay crescents with a vast repertoire of stamp impressions and incised markings came to light (Alp 1968, 73ff.).

Crescents are primarily associated with the MBA, although they already feature in the EBA (see below). The most recent major find in MBA contexts occurred at Demircihüyük with 74 specimens, of which 23 were decorated. Six different shape variants were isolated and wear marks near the perforations were consistent, clearly indicating that the crescents had been suspended (Kull 1988, 200ff., fig. 190, 195). The author made a case for their use as loomweights in her discussion and reconstruction drawings. This was firmly rejected by Vogelsang-Eastwood (1990, 97ff.) on technical grounds and lack of context to suggest such a function. The context appears to have been provided more recently, however, with the publication of the EB I examples from the same site where clay crescents feature as part of an *in situ* loomweight group and it would appear that in this particular context the crescents must have had some function associated with textile production (Obladen-Kauder 1996, 238f., pl. 1; photograph of crescents and other weights *in situ* in Korfmann 1983b, 33–4 Abb. 45). Some of these crescents were also found to have been augmented with additional clay as observed on other loomweights (see p. 470).

At Aphrodisias, clay crescents also make their debut in EB I, followed by a long gap after which they reappear in EB IV to MBA and then continue into the Iron Age (Joukowsky 1986, 379f.).

As the evidence stands at present, there appears to be a considerable time gap between the introduction of clay crescents in EB I and their re-appearance in the MBA, during which the specific use of them may have undergone some transformation. The elaborate markings, created by stamping and incising, of clay crescents, especially at Karahöyük Konya, must have a significance beyond mere decorative purposes, as already argued by Alp who suggested that stamped crescents, in the absence of currency, represent 'receipts' for goods, presented by the buyer to the seller as a form of guarantee (Alp 1968, 75). Whatever their role, one would like to think that stamped clay crescents in general were associated with the textile industry, not least because they were found associated with loomweights at Troy (Blegen *et al.* 1950, 338, Abb. 369), Demircihüyük, Kusura (Lamb 1938, 256) and Tarsus. Thus, if not used as loomweights, they may possibly have identified workshops, or types of textiles or fibres, while the crescents with horizontal and vertical incised markings could have had numerical value as proposed by Alp (1968, 75).[2]

However, if one rejects their use as loomweights, there is still a role to be found for the crescents that were fired but otherwise left plain which are the majority at Demircihüyük and Aphrodisias and, indeed, for the two MBA examples manufactured in stone found in Level V at Beycesultan (Mellaart & Murray 1995, 177, fig. O.27: 239–41). Worth mentioning too is the comment by the excavators of Alişar regarding clay crescents who reported that 'Heavy wooden weights similarly shaped are now used as loomweights in certain districts of Central Anatolia' (von der Osten & Schmidt 1932, 106).

We are most grateful to J.P. Wild (Manchester) for his comments on the question of crescentic weights, and in particular for referring us to the survey of Iron Age loomweights from SE Spain by Castro Curel (1985). Here too half-moon or crescent-shaped weights with holes at the two upper corners are found alongside more normal shapes, and there are also numerous examples of small impressed designs on weights of various shapes, some of the designs strikingly similar to those on Anatolian crescents a thousand years earlier.

While it may well be that Vogelsang-Eastwood's objections on the technical detail of how they were used are still valid, these Iberian parallels do indicate that neither the dual perforations nor the impressed designs can be taken as clear proof that the crescents were not somehow used in association with warp-weighted looms. Earlier sources for European crescents, including EBA Tiryns, (also found in conjunction with loomweights), are listed by Kull (1988, 205, fn. 860), and their function has been recently discussed by Feldtkeller 2003. Nevertheless, to acknowledge the uncertainties, we have catalogued the crescents here rather than under loomweights.

Figure 280. *Stamped clay crescent* **1634**.

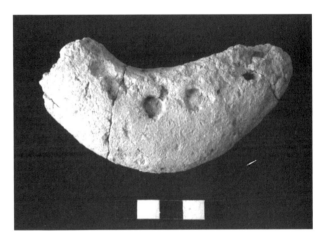

Figure 281. *Stamped clay crescent* **1638**.

1634　　　H20/27　　　KLT 8　　　1215
Level IIIa–c
Crescentic clay object pierced at both ends. Stamped with a rosette in the centre of one side. Very fine yellow-buff sandy fabric, with remains of an orange-red slip on surface, worn through in places. Both ends have a slight groove along their outer edges where the slip is well preserved. Baked. This one baked example from Kilise Tepe is not only significantly lighter than the other complete examples, but also lighter than any of those found at Demircihüyük (which range from 110–328 g).
L. 10.0; W. 3.4; Th. 2.4; Wt 97.5
Figs. 279–80

[1635]　　　H20/47　　　KLT 9　　　1220
Level IVb
Clay crescent, unbaked. One end broken off; a piece of it is extant but does not include the perforation. One surface has one clear circular stamp impression and traces of two more. No motif visible. The fabric is buff-coloured with dense coarse vegetable temper and occasional white calcareous stones.
L. 12.2; W. 5.0; Th. 3.3; Wt 217.9
Fig. 279

1636　　　H20/53a　　　KLT 10　　　1220
Level IVb
Crescent of unbaked clay, pierced at both ends and stamped twice in the centre of one side, one appears to represent a cross, the other is indeterminable. The clay is yellow-buff with vegetable temper (coarse) and pebbles up to 1.5 cm visible at surface.
L. 12.4; W. 3.8; Th. 3.7; Wt 221.1
Fig. 279

[1637]　　　H20/53b　　　　　　1220
Level IVb
Three fragments of a clay crescent, unbaked. Two join to form an end with perforation. Clay buff with organic temper and calcareous stones.
Central piece: L. (7.4); W. (3.8); Th. (7.4)

[1638]　　　H20/54　　　KLT 11　　　1220
Level IVb
Crescent fragment of unbaked clay, friable. One perforated end is extant, the other broken off. A first attempt at perforation failed owing to the presence of a stone in the fabric, so that there is a partial hole on one side, near the successful perforation. The crescent is stamped three times in the centre on one side; the circular impressions are indistinct.
L. 11.0; W. 4.2; Th. 3.2; Wt 182.2
Fig. 279, 281

Clay ovoids from J19 (1639–78)

A group of some 40 strange objects was found in the lower fill of Pit 96/56 in J19a (probably of Level IIe or IIf date). Owing to their uniformity, we have not described each one individually. The quantitative data for all the objects are presented in Table 16 and Figure 282. Those specifically mentioned in the text or illustrated in Figure 440 (**1639–41**) are, however, described below. Similar descriptions of the remainder will be found on the electronic data base.

Unless otherwise specified, they are sausage-like objects and have blunt or roughly shaped ends, but some have carefully rounded ends and a few have pointed ends and are fusiform. They are made of vegetable-tempered unbaked clay, occasionally with the addition of fairly large, isolated grits, either white or grey and plaster-like ('white', 'grey') or light brown and more clayey ('brown'). They are either carefully shaped and smoothed (defined as 'smooth') or are roughly squashed into shape (defined as 'rough').

They are unperforated, but most have a hole in the middle of the fabric which has weakened it and caused the pieces to break or crumble ('hole' or 'no hole'; otherwise the piece is not intact and there is no evidence for a hole available). This hole could have been caused by the weathering of a large wooden inclusion; however, in some cases there are hollows on the exterior which must also have contained an inclusion, and in the case of **1669** and **1671**, the hole is actually still filled with a more crumbly version of, respectively, the same brown or plastery clay, and it may be that the clay was not homogeneous and that areas of the core were not as well sun-dried. These holes are rounded and differ from the irregularly shaped holes found in the K20 loomweights. In a few cases, root, and perhaps animal, action are probably responsible. A few examples are particularly homogeneous, denser, feel heavier, are better finished and harder (**1647**, **1672**, **1675–6**).

When found, these objects were tentatively called 'loomweight blanks' since like loomweights they are unbaked. However, their shape differs from that of other loomweights and it would have been difficult to keep a string tied round the middle of them without a notch to stop it slipping; there is no evidence for such a notch. None bears traces of burning. The weights of complete examples range from 129 to 333 g, with **1642** as an outlier weighing 423 g. No very obvious pattern emerges, but there is a tendency for weights to cluster (e.g. **1646** and **1666** at 333 and 332 g respectively, or a group of five weighing between 269.5–277 g. This could indicate that there was some value in having examples of matching weight. However, the pit from

Table 16. *Clay ovoid data.*

Vol. no.	J19 no.	Length	Diameter	Weight	Complete?
1639	J19/190	14	4.8	247.8	y
1640	J19/195	12.2	2.2	276	y
1641	J19/196	13	5	270	y
1642	J19/149	16.2	5.5	423	y
1643	J19/150	5.7	4.6	92	n
1644	J19/151	9.5	5.1	178	n
1645	J19/167a	6	3.5	178	n
1646	J19/172	13.2	5.35	333	y
1647	J19/173	11.7	4.9	269.5	y
1648	J19/174	7.8	4	129	y
1649	J19/175	12	5.2	251	y
1650	J19/176	13.4	4.6	215.5	n
1651	J19/177	8.9	4.45	133.5	n
1652	J19/178			150.5	n
1653	J19/179	8.6	4.9	110	n
1654	J19/180a	6.85	3.7	105.5	n
1655	J19/180b	3.6	4		n
1656	J19/181	8.6	4.4	159.5	n
1657	J19/182			110.8	n
1658	J19/183	6.5	4.75	137.7	n
1659	J19/184			122	n
1660	J19/185	11.3	4.7	175	y
1661	J19/186			171.5	n
1662	J19/187	9.8	4.65	139.8	y
1663	J19/188	12.5	4.8	186.5	y
1664	J19/189	8.7	4.7	159.2	n
1665	J19/191	10.8	4.8	190	y
1666	J19/192	12.3	4.65	332	y
1667	J19/193	10.5	5	210.7	y
1668	J19/194	11.3	4.8	138	y
1669	J19/197	8.5	4.2	148.3	y
1670	J19/198	10.7	5.3	233	n
1671	J19/199	11.9	4.7	238	y
1672	J19/200	11.35	5	277	y
1673	J19/205	11.8	5.2	274.5	y
1674	J19/206			173	n
1675	J19/207	12.5	5.1	320	y
1676	J19/208	12.5	5	300.6	y
1677	J19/209	9.6	4.7	216.5	n
1678	J19/210	9.8	5.1	217	y

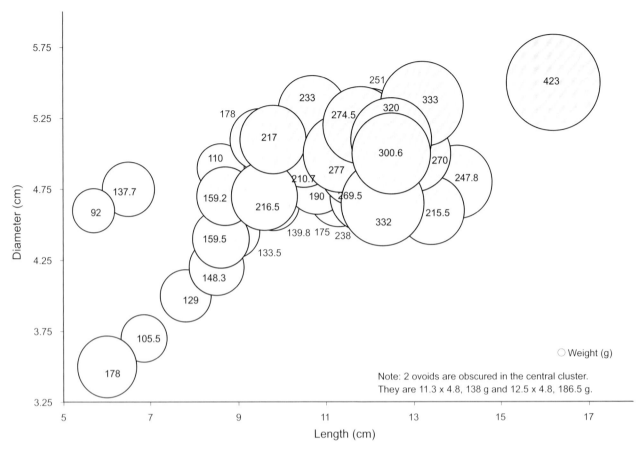

Figure 282. *Dimensions of clay ovoids (**1639–78**)*.

which the ovoids were recovered lay directly beneath the remains of a pebble-based hearth (FI96/12), and they probably therefore acted as a lower layer performing a function similar to that of the pebbles.

We have not identified any convincing parallels for these ovoids from other Anatolian sites, but they are sufficiently unglamorous to have been ignored and so may have existed elsewhere.

1639 J19/190 1669
White; fairly smooth with pointed ends (one chipped); no hole; c. 14 × 4.8 cm.
L. c. 14.0; Di. 4.8; Wt 247.8

1640 J19/195 1669
White; smooth, with rounded ends; one fairly shallow but wide hole near centre.
L. 12.2; Di. 2.2; Wt 276.0

1641 J19/196 1669
White; smooth with rounded ends; two large holes near ends.
L. 13.0; Di. 5.0; Wt 270.0

[1642] J19/149 1669
White; fairly smooth, but weathered with slightly squashed profile and rounded ends; holes and diagonal groove on ext.; unusually large.
L. 16.2; Di. 4.8–5.5; Wt 423.0

[1646] J19/172 1669
White; very smooth; rounded ends; one very small hole at centre.
L. 13.2; Di. 5.35; Wt 333.0

[1647] J19/173 1669
White; very smooth with well-rounded ends and hard finish; no hole.
L. 11.7; Di. 4.9; Wt 269.5

[1666] J19/192 1669
White; weathered with tapering ends.
L. 12.3; Di. 4.65; Wt 332.0

[1669] J19/197 1669
Brown; fairly smooth but weathered, with rounded ends.
L. 8.5; Di. 4.2; Wt. 148.3

[1671] J19/199 1669
White; fairly smooth with roughly rounded ends (one chipped); hole filled with crumbly white clay (see above).
L. c. 11.9; Di. 4.7; Wt 238.0

[1672] J19/200 1669
White, smooth with tapering rounded ends; part of the surface weathered; several small (root?) holes.
L. 11.35; Di. 5.0; Wt 277.0

[1675] J19/207 1669
White; smooth with rounded ends, one slightly tapering; two tiny, shallow holes — one at the centre and one at one end (di. 0.2 cm) with a narrow exterior groove, and four other holes, all equally

small, filled with crumbly material, also at the end.
L. 12.5; Di. 5.1; Wt 320.0

[1676]　　　J19/208　　　　　　　　　　1669
White; smooth with rounded ends and hard finish.
L. 12.5; Di. 5.0; Wt 300.6

Notes

1. Our thanks to Lucilla Burn and Eric Handley for the identification and references.
2. For a comparative study of sealing practices at Karahöyük Konya and Minoan Crete (Phaistos) see Weingarten 1990, 63ff.

Chapter 36

Loomweights

Dominique Collon & Dorit Symington

Although it is unsafe to call every large perforated clay artefact a loomweight, the majority of finds in this section can confidently be identified as such, either because they were found in a group or because they closely resemble pieces which were. Clay crescents, which have been described as, and may indeed have been, loomweights, and a group of unidentified objects we have called 'clay ovoids', are listed and discussed in the preceding section (**1634–78**).

From our earliest levels (V–IV) in H19 and H20 some 58 loomweights and loomweight fragments were excavated. The majority belong to the early phase of the MBA, Level IVa (32 examples), with smaller groups of late EB III date (Levels Vf and e) and from Level Vj of the early EBA. After the MBA, the vast majority of the loomweights come from the later Iron Age (Level IIe–f). Indeed, none was found in the building in Level III or in phases IIa–d of the Stele Building (except **1828** from IIa/b and **1829** from IIc, which are both stone). Apart from a group found immediately below the surface on the eastern edge of the mound in Q20 (**1809–20**), only stray examples come from Level I.

Throughout our sequence there is a strong tendency for the loomweights to be found in groups, either lying *in situ* on a floor beneath a burnt destruction layer (Level IVa, Level Vj, Level IIe in K20, and Level I in Q20) or distributed through a single layer in a way which suggests they were originally a group (Level Vf Rm 55, and Level IIf in J18 and K18).

The discovery of groups of perforated clay weights, often showing traces of suspension, is generally, and no doubt correctly, taken to betray the use of a vertical loom in which several warp threads were tied to a loomweight at the bottom, holding the warp taut (Broudy 1979, 23ff.). Collective finds of this kind are not unusual and are reported from several Anatolian sites (Barber 1991, 387–90). These include Tarsus (Goldman 1956, 319), Kusura (Lamb 1938, 256), and Troy IIg (Barber 1991, 93, fig. 3.14). At Kuruçay in the Late Chalcolithic 100 weights were excavated in one area (Duru 1983, 44, pl. 18.2), and in EBA levels at Demircihüyük Phase E (EB I) there were 28 *in situ* loomweights (Obladen-Kauder 1996, 239 Taf. 1). They are also found in Middle Minoan Crete (Sheffer 1981, 82).[1]

The great majority of our loomweights were made of clay. Most were unbaked, with the exception of the Middle Bronze Age examples, 70 per cent of which were baked or even fired (as noted in the catalogue). A few pierced stones are included in our loomweight section, either because of their similarity to, or because they were found in association with, clay examples (see **1716**, **1825–7**; **1828–35**).

The general shape of the weights varies from period to period but is usually fairly standard within a single group. Oval or ovoid loomweights[2] are much the commonest in the MBA and EBA Levels IV and V (except Vj); other shapes represented in these levels are pyramidal, tear-drop and conoid. In these levels (IV and V) all the weights have a single perforation (usually quite regular, as though formed round a cylindrical stick) positioned near the upper edge, the diameter of which varies from 0.5–2.1 cm but on average lies around 1.5 cm. We also noted traces of suspension wear on the upper part of the perforation in some instances (**1691**, **1709**, **1711**, **1726**), in the form of lines or polished grooves caused by the warp thread. Such wear marks are less evident in Levels I and II (but see **1773** and **1797**). Although particular shapes or sizes are not generally characteristic of a specific period, an exception is the flattened loomweight type of the MBA of Level IVa and in particular the fired fine fabric examples from the collective find (unit 1258) which have no counterparts at Kilise Tepe.

Elsewhere in the Near East there is clearly a break in tradition after the MBA, and the Demircihüyük and MBA Taannek loomweights are quite different from the Iron Age doughnuts found at Taannek and Kilise Tepe (Obladen-Kauder 1996, 237–45, esp. fig. 165, pls. 96–8, I–II; Friend 1998, 13–35, figs. 5–8). This break is also reflected in the Kilise Tepe material. After the MBA there are no weights from Level III, and in Level II doughnut-shaped[3] weights form the largest

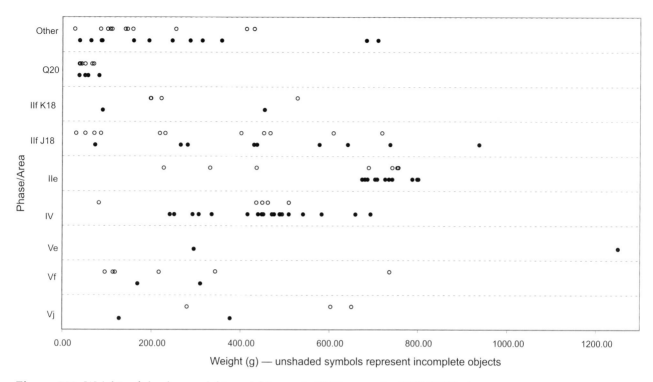

Figure 283. *Weights of clay loomweights weighing up to 1250 g; see also* **1760** *(3800 g).*

category. These are generally flattened spheres of whitish-yellow, friable unbaked clay, with a central perforation and little visible temper. The ratio of height to diameter varies from group to group and some doughnuts are almost spherical. They are most common in the Iron Age throughout the Near East and have been discussed by Sheffer (1981), who deals predominantly with the material from Israel, and by Curtis & Green (1997, 18) in connection with the material from Khirbet Khatuniyeh in northern Iraq.

Seen overall, the weight of loomweights, when complete, varied from 80 g for the smallest (**1725**) to 1250 g for the largest specimen (**1695**). Heavier weights are used for heavier textiles (Friend 1998, 7, 9). As shown in Figure 283, the weights in the two main collective finds (IIe and IVa) cluster respectively between 673–800 g and 416–540 g.

Two of the loomweights from the Vf group (**1688**, **1690**) have an additional amount of clay added to the lower half (cf. also **1682** from Vj). This was also noted on two examples from Level IVa (**1711**, **1726**). The added lumps are often of a different coloured clay. The best example of this technique is **1726**, a large ovoid from Level IVa, which had an added piece of clay stuck to it to increase its weight to a total of 582.4 g. The augmentation with lumps of clay, in order to increase the weight of a particular loomweight appears to have been common practice and is mentioned in the Tarsus report (Goldman 1956, 319), at Troy (Blegen *et al*. 1951, 350, fig. 369) and Demircihüyük (Obladen-Kauder 1996, 238), though there is no evidence of its use with the later Kilise Tepe weights.

It seems clear that in general the upper limit lies around 800 g, but there are a few exceptional 'giant' weights. A complete ovoid specimen was found in Level Ve (**1695**), but **1679–80** came from Level Vj or even earlier. Two large loomweights of similar weight (1200–1300 g) were also uncovered at Demircihüyük as part of the MBA group deposit, though sub-circular in shape, and with two perforations (Type VII). It is suggested there that they were mounted at either side of the loom with the front warp tied to one hole and the back warp to the other (Obladen-Kauder 1996, p. 237 Abb. 164, p. 238f. figs. 168, 173). Whether this could also be achieved with a single perforation of a giant loomweight must remain speculative, but at any rate positioning an extra heavy weight at either side of the loom may also have served to stabilize the loom itself. Occasionally weights much heavier than the average turn up in later levels also (see, of clay, **1760** 3800 g and **1761** 936 g, and the stones **1829**, **1832** and **1834**).

Level Vj (1679–84)

The recovery of loomweights from the house floors of the earliest architectural phase of the EBA Level Vj suggests that textiles were produced at the site from the beginning. Other textile production items — so-called loom supports and spindle whorls — were found in close proximity and these are discussed above (**1626–7**) and below (**1836–7**), respectively.

1679   H20/794   5427
Level Vj/k
Upper part of a giant loomweight(?), fabric beige with grey core. Sides flattened, edges rounded, perforated.
H. (11.5); W. (6.4); Th. (6.4); Di. perf. 1.2; Wt (603)

[1680]   H20/545   1858
Level Vj
Top half of a giant loomweight.
H. (11.5); W. (9.6); Di. perf. 1.0; Wt (650)

1681   H20/551   1858
Level Vj
Conoid with flattened sides and bottom. Surface partly smoothed, lumpy. Beige, grit and stone temper. Fairly hard fired. Perforation at right angles. Traces of red paint near apex.
H. 8.8; W. 8.1; Th. 5.5; Di. perf. 1.1; Wt 376.5

1682   H20/623   1875
Level Vj
Pyramidal with an added piece of clay on one side, flattened on the other. Underside flat, rounded edges. Grit and vegetable temper. Smoothed. Damaged.
H. 8.3; W. (7.65); Th. 4.7; Di. perf. 1.1; Wt (280)

1683   H20/741   5406
Level Vj
Small tear-drop shaped, medium coarse brown clay. Rounded edges, bottom flattened. Diagonally running perforation. Slightly chipped.
H. 6.95; W. 4.9; Th. 4.0; Di. perf. 0.5; Wt 127.2

[1684]   H20/740   5406
Level Vj
Very small fragment of loomweight. Remains of perforation. Vegetable tempered unbaked clay.

Level Vg (1685)

[1685]   H20/987   5388
Two fragments of loomweight. Remains of perforation visible. Baked clay with burning marks.

Level Vf (1686–94)

The loomweights of unit 1812 from Rm 55 of Level Vf date to the latter part of EB III and are the earliest to be recovered as a group, consisting of nine complete or fragmentary loomweights. They are consistently oval or ovoid shaped and much smaller than those encountered in the MBA. A creamy-yellow medium coarse fabric persists and the surfaces are barely smoothed. There is also little attempt at flattening the sides when seen in profile and **1689** is almost globular. Weights vary from 117–737 g, but the weight of most lies around 200–300 g. **1688** and **1690** have an additional lump of clay stuck on to one side (see above on this practice).

[1686]   H20/347   1812
Oval with flattened front and back. Yellow-buff clay with organic and calcareous stone temper. Surface damaged.
H. 9.6; W. 9.6; Th. 7.2; Di. perf. 1.3; Wt (216.6)

[1687]   H20/350   1812
Two small non-joining fragments, clay as above. Remains of perforation in one fragment, the other comes from rounded lower part.
a. H. (7.6); W. (5.3); Th. (3.9)
b. H. (6.9); W. (5.5); Th. (4.9)

[1688]   H20/352   1812
Ovoid with rounded sides, bottom slightly flattened. Perforation near apex. Fabric cream, few grits. Surface smoothed. Lower part has additional lump of clay added to increase weight.
H. 10.0; W. 7.2; Di. perf. 1.3; Wt 309.9

[1689]   H20/351   1812
Oval with perforation at one end, also oval in profile. Fabric cream, very coarse with stones (up to 1.2 cm) and organic temper. Surface lumpy. Chipped, about 90 per cent of original remaining.
H. 11.0; W. 6.0; Di. perf. 1.1; Wt (342.85)

[1690]   H20/354   1812
Small oval with perforation at slightly narrower end. Buff, grit and organic tempered fabric. Surface smoothed. An additional lump of clay is added to increase weight.
H. 9.9; W. 6.5; Di. perf. 0.6; Wt 168.25

[1691]   H20/355   1812
Partially restored ovoid, badly chipped. Buff clay grit and organic temper. Smoothed. Linear marks of wear on perforation.
H. 11.0(?); Wt (735.6)

[1692]   H20/345   1812
Small ovoid made of greenish-yellow clay with grit, stone and organic temper. Surface flaked but smooth where preserved.
H. 9.1; W. 4.0; Di. perf. 1.2; Wt (112.6) — fragments estimated as 65 per cent of original

[1693]   H20/349   1812
Small ovoid of greenish-yellow clay, organic temper. Surface barely smoothed.
H. 8.3; W. 5.6; Di. perf. 0.9; Wt (117.6) — fragments estimated as 75 per cent of original

[1694]   H20/348   1812
Approximately half of ovoid(?) of greenish-yellow clay with dark and white inclusions. Surface damaged.
Wt (94.6)

Level Ve (1695–701)

1695   H20/654   5300
Giant oval loomweight — much larger than normal. Coarse vegetable tempered fabric. Almost complete.
H. 17.0; W. 14.2; Th. 6.0; Di. perf. 1.6; Wt 1250

[1696]   H20/713   5318
Fragment of loomweight, top half, flattened sides, rounded edges. Probably top half of **1697**, same fabric.
W. (5.05); Th. (2.5)

[1697]   H20/660   5301
Bottom fragment of a pyramidal loomweight. Buff medium coarse, calcareous and organic temper. Surface smoothed. Lower half of **1696**?
H. (5.6); W. 7.8; Th. 3.2

Figure 284. *Group of 14 loomweights from Middle Bronze unit 1258 (Level IVa; from top left: 1712, 1705, 1704, 1713, 1706; 1717, 1716, 1714, 1711; 1707, 1708, 1710, 1709, 1702).*

[1698]   H20/712   5318
A pale grey, unbaked clay object which may be a loomweight fragment. Smooth surfaces.
W. 7.3; Th. 2.9

[1699]   H20/678   1288
Fragment of lower half. Coarse beige fabric. Surface flaked.
H. (5.6); Th. (4.6)

1700   H20/619   1283
Almost circular with perforation at tapered end. Flattened front and back faces. Cream dense fabric, grit and organic temper. Smoothed, chipped on one side.
H. 9.8; W. 8.73; Th. 3.6; Di. perf. 2.1; Wt 295

[1701]   H20/637   1289
Fragment of top part. Coarse brown clay with organic temper. Part of perforation preserved.
H. (7.5); W. (3.4)

Level IVa, unit 1258 (1702–22)

The 21 loomweights and loomweight fragments found as a group in the destruction debris of Level IVa (see Figs. 91 & 284) offer a considerable variety in fabric shape and size. Most of the members of this group were baked. One was a naturally perforated stone (**1716**).

Generally speaking the Kilise Tepe MBA loomweights, including those found outside this deposit (**1723–34**), are flattened on the front and back, a feature also remarked on in the Tarsus report where they are described as 'flat oval pats' (Goldman 1956, 319).

The most striking group, consisting of five specimens (**1702, 1704–7**) of almost identical shape and weight (450–500 g), are made of a fine light-orange fabric with small white grits resembling the EB III and early MBA pottery fabrics. The surfaces are carefully smoothed and all of them are well fired, in total contrast to the majority of loomweights encountered at Kilise Tepe. All are oval shaped, flattened on their sides and have rounded edges, including the bottom. In profile they widen only marginally towards the bottom. These weights are also characterized by a relatively large perforation in relation to their size — measuring around 1.5–1.6 cm and at a consistent distance from the apex of 1.5–2.0 cm. This is an unusually consistent group, indicating that it was understood that ideally loomweights should be of similar size and weight to create even tension on the warp threads for a smoother weave.

A curious pair are **1712–13**, two pyramidal loomweights provided with an additional circular hollow in the lower right-hand corner of one side. Both have flattened faces and a large perforation at the apex (1.9 cm). In profile they taper only marginally towards the top. Both are well finished and fired. Presumably they acted as a pair, although in what manner is not clear at present; perhaps the depressions held the heddle or shed rod which separated the front from the back warp.

The remaining loomweights from 1258 are made of a coarser fabric with grits and stones (up to 1 cm) and large amounts of organic temper. Some are quite rounded in profile and widen more noticeably towards the bottom. There is also evidence for additional lumps of clay being added to increase their weight (**1711** and **1726**).

The majority are ovoid which also goes for the MBA loomweights found outside this group. In addition the following shapes are also represented: teardrop (**1708–9**), sub-circular (**1710**), and a miniature tear-drop-shaped weight of fine dense fabric with tiny perforation, found in the vicinity but not as part of the group (**1725**).

1702 H20/190 1258
Oval, flattened front and back. Fabric medium, grit and organic temper. Smoothed, fired.
H. 11.6; W. 9.1; Th. 4.2; Di. perf. 1.7–1.9; Wt 439.2
Fig. 284

1703 H20/191 1258
Flattened pyramidal with rounded corners, uneven base. Brown coarse clay, grit, stone and organic temper. Smoothed but flaked on one face. Other side has diagonal cut and percussion mark. Burnt. Tapering towards top when seen in profile.
H. 11.6; W. 9.3; Th. 5.1; Di. perf. 1.4; Wt 508.1

1704 H20/194 1258
Oval of lightly baked clay, flattened on one face. Pale brown coarse, large amount of organic temper, voids. Smoothed, cream wash.
H. 12.4; W. 9.1; Th. 4.6; Di. perf. 1.1–1.7; Wt (461.3)
Fig. 284

1705 H20/222 1258
Oval of medium coarse, beige/pale orange, grit-tempered fabric. Fired. Patches of cream slip. Front and back flattened, rounded edges. Surface rough, chipped.
H. 12.8; W. 8.9; Th. 4.7; Di. perf. 1.1; Wt 416.1
Fig. 284

1706 H20/208 1258
Oval of fired clay, flattened front and back with large perforation at narrower end. Well smoothed, blackened on one side. Fabric medium beige, grit, organic temper.
H. 11.35; W. 9.29; Th. 4.0; Di. perf. 1.8; Wt 487.2
Fig. 284

1707 H20/207 1258
Flattened oval shape made of fired clay. Angled perforation. Fabric pale-orange, some grits and voids. Slightly blackened on one side.
H. 11.28; W. 8.94; Th. 4.03; Di. perf. 1.8; Wt (508.2)
Fig. 284

1708 H20/206 1258
Tear-drop of baked clay with tapered apex and flattened faces. Wear marks on perforation. Very coarse fabric, stone (1.2 cm) and vegetable temper, leaving voids.
H. 12.2; W. 8.96; Th. 4.8; Di. perf. 1.4; Wt (448.8)
Fig. 284

1709 H20/205 1258
Tear-drop shape tapering towards apex. Clay buff, grit and vegetable temper leaving voids. Traces of wear near perforation, both sides, caused by suspension.
H. 11.4; W. 9.4; Th. 3.9; Di. perf. 0.6–0.8; Wt (435.4)
Fig. 284

1710 H20/192 1258
Almost circular, lightly baked coarse light brown/dark grey fabric. Flattened front and back, tapering towards perforation (seen in profile), slightly flat bottom. Rough surface.
H. 9.5; W. 9.4; Th. 4.3; Di. perf. 1.5–1.9; Wt. 334.9
Fig. 284

1711 H20/198 1258
Baked ovoid with one flattened side and remains of added lump of clay on the other. Four grooves (string marks) at top of perforation. Fabric buff, grit and vegetable temper, cream wash.
H. 10.6; W. 8.5; Th. 5.4; Di. perf. 1.2–1.3; Wt 447.6
Fig. 284

1712 H20/193 1258
Flattened pyramidal loomweight with rounded corners, flat bottom and large perforation. One side has a depression (di. 1.3) in bottom right-hand corner. Fabric buff with multiple grit and organic temper. Baked. For companion piece see **1713** below.
H. 11.4; W. 10.8; Th. 3.8; Di. perf. 2.1; Wt 540.5
Fig. 284

1713 H20/197 1258
Companion piece to **1712** above. Slightly better preserved, otherwise identical.
H. 11.7; W. 9.8; Th. 3.6; Di. perf. 1.8–1.9; Wt 450.9
Fig. 284

[**1714**] H20/221 1258
Flattened ovoid, fire blackened on one side. Dense medium orange fabric, surface smoothed, flaked in places.
H. 11.1; W. 9.2; Th. 4.5; Di. perf. 1.6; Wt 493.2
Fig. 284

1715 H20/195 1258
Fragmentary ovoid of lightly baked clay. Very coarse beige fabric, smoothed but surface mostly lost. Damaged near perforation and edges.
H. (10.4); W. (9.1); Th. 5.1; Di. perf. 1.6; Wt 292.3

[**1716**] H20/226 1258
Irregular-shaped stone with two holes, most probably natural and chosen to serve as loomweight. Encrusted with lime and clay.
H. 9.5; W. 10.5; Th. 7.5; Wt 692.5
Fig. 284

[**1717**] H20/237 1258
Ovoid of unbaked(?) buff clay, grit and organic temper, surface smoothed. Top and bottom end chipped.
H. 9.9; W. 8.8; Th. 3.9; Di. perf. 1.7; Wt 250.9
Fig. 284

[**1718**] H20/220 1258
Ovoid with small perforation at tapered end and flattened faces. Thickness is uniform. Fabric dense pale-orange, surface smoothed and lime encrusted.
H. 13.6; W. 10.0; Th. 4.5; Di. perf. 0.5; Wt 658.5

[**1719**] H20/210 1258
Conoid loomweight with rounded corners and sides. Very coarse fabric with heavy inclusions. Surface lumpy and flaked, lower half chipped.
H. 10.1; W. 8.0; Th. 5.6; Di. perf. 0.7–1.2; Wt 474.9

[**1720**] H20/224 1258
Loomweight fragment, lower half. Most of perforation lost. Coarse buff fabric.
H. (8.6.); W. 10.1; Th. 4.6

[**1721**] H20/250 1258
Small fragment, soft beige clay. Part of perforation preserved.
H. (3.0); W. (2.2); Th. (1.9); Di. perf. (0.4)

[**1722**] H20/196 1258
Two loomweight fragments. Fabric grey/brown. No measurements possible.

Miscellaneous Level IV loomweights (1723–34)

[**1723**]   H20/274   1263
Level IVa
Baked ovoid with large perforation, flattened on both faces and tapered towards apex in section. Dense pale orange fabric, surface smoothed. Top half burnt.
H. 11.5; W. 9.5; Th. 4.0; Di. perf. 1.6; Wt 488.2

[**1724**]   H20/275   1263
Level IVa
Ovoid with flattened faces. Coarse pale orange fabric with large inclusions, friable. Surface damaged and chipped on edges. Baked.
H. 13.5; W. 10.0; Th. 4.8; Di. perf. 1.7–1.8; Wt 470.0

1725   H20/276   1263
Level IVa
Small tear-drop shape. Fabric medium-fine, small grits. Smoothed, traces of cream slip. Chipped on one side. Baked.
H. 6.6; W. 5.0; Th. 2.9; Di. perf. 0.3; Wt (80.8)

1726   H20/316   1806
Level IVa
Flattened ovoid with additional lump of clay on one side — medium-coarse fabric. String wear marks on upper part of perforation.
H. 12.5; W. 9.1; Th. 4.4 (6.1 inc. applied lump); Di. perf. 1.7–1.9; Wt 582.4

[**1727**]   H20/591   1272
Level IVa/Ve
Ovoid with upper part missing, part of perforation visible. Flattened on both faces, bottom rounded. Fabric buff, medium-coarse, smoothed in parts.
H. (9.0); W. 6.8; Th. 2.9; Di. perf. 0.5

1728   H20/147   1241
Level IVa
Ovoid rather damaged with flattened faces. Most of perforation lost. Dense pale orange fabric. Well fired.
H. 11.0; W. 6.7; Th. 4.0

1729   H20/576   1269
Level IVa
Pyramidal with flattened front and back. Part of lower half broken off. Yellowish medium-coarse clay, smoothed surface. Baked.
H. 11.5; W. 8.0; Th. 4.5; Di. perf. 1.8–2.0

1730   H20/577   1269
Level IVa
Small ovoid with slightly flattened bottom and faces. Dense cream fabric, smoothed, flaked in parts.
H. 9.0; W. 7.0; Th. 4.0; Di. perf. 1.0; Wt 240.7

[**1731**]   H20/113   1233
Level IVa/b
Tear-drop-shaped loomweight. Grey-brown coarse fabric, baked. Burning marks on one face. Broken at the top.
H. 11.5; W. 8.5; Th. 4.0; Di. perf. 1.5

[**1732**]   H19/301   4264
Level IVa
Tear-drop shape, flattened on both faces. Coarse beige fabric, surface smoothed and vegetable impressions. Patches of burning.
H. 11.1; W. 9.2; Th. 3.5; Di. perf. 0.8; Wt 305.8

[**1733**]   H19/283   4264
Level IVa
Loomweight fragment (lower part?) blackened by fire. Semi-coarse fabric.

[**1734**]   H20/89   1227
Level IIIa–IVb
Fragment of ovoid(?) loomweight of coarse brown fabric. Surface mostly flaked.
H. (6.6.); W. (6.2); Th. (2.9)

Loomweights from IIe in K20 (1735–60)

Some 25 'doughnut' loomweights, in this case roughly spherical, were found in the NE corner of Rm e9 (unit 1911). **1735–7** were found close to W712 but the others were found closely grouped in rows (see p. 157, Fig. 498). **1738–41**, **1742–5** and **1752–4** formed three rows orientated roughly north–south with **1759** close by, and **1746–51** and **1757** forming a row roughly east–west. **1755** and **1758** lay about 1 m away to the southeast and west respectively. They may have belonged to one or more vertical looms standing by the wall. They are all doughnut-shaped, of unbaked, vegetable-tempered clay, sometimes with the addition of large grits or small pebbles. They often have large holes, as a result of which they are very crumbly and many are fragmentary. The holes do not seem to be due to animal action or to the disappearance of some constituent (wood?). Possibly they were intended to reduce weight while retaining a standard diameter. Where they are well preserved, the perforations are often oval, probably intentionally rather than through wear. Some of these loomweights are unusually large, with heights ranging between 5.2–7.8 cm (but mostly between 6.6–7.0), and diameters between 8.2–14.0 cm (but mostly between 11.0–11.9). The weights, despite the holes, range between 680–800 g. A selection is illustrated on Figure 285. Found separately in 1924, but from the same general stratigraphic context was an exceptionally large weight **1760**. Two fragmentary 'doughnut'-shaped weights found in K19 and listed below as **1799** and **1800** were dissimilar and probably did not derive from the same group.

[**1735**]   K20/64   1911
Several fragments; the largest piece is hemispherical. Light grey.
H. 5.7; Di. 8.3; Di. perf. 2.2; Wt (227.1)
Fig. 285

[**1736**]   K20/65   1911
Roughly spherical; fragments, two joining to make up *c.* 75% of the object; a further two fragments do not join; smoothed, but uneven surface. Buff-coloured, coarse, friable clay with some stone inclusions.
H. 6.2; Di. 8.2; Di. perf. *c.* 2.4
Fig. 285

[1737]   K20/66   1911
Five fragments. Yellow-buff.

[1738]   K20/67   1911
Roughly spherical; the surface on the lower side is badly damaged, but there are a couple of seemingly deliberate grooves, possibly made by a finger. A hole, again possibly deliberate, runs from the side through to the central perforation. Coarse, pale buff clay with dense vegetable temper and occasional stones.
H. 6.6; Di. 12.2; Di. perf. 2.6; Wt 679.5

1739   K20/68   1911
Roughly spherical; some surface damage, otherwise it is smoothed, but uneven, with coarse vegetable impressions visible. On one side there are two extra holes, and on the other side, a single extra hole; all three reach though to the lower side. Buff, coarse, friable clay.
H. 6.9; Di. 11.4; Di. perf. 2.3; Wt 685.0

1740   K20/69   1911
Roughly spherical; the surface is smoothed, but uneven, with vegetable impressions visible. On one side, a hole near the perforation curves through the body of the object to join the central perforation about halfway along its length. Another, angled hole lies opposite this one but is not finished and ends within the body of the object. On the underside is a curving finger-impressed(?) groove c. 5.5 cm long. Buff, coarse, friable clay.
H. 6.9; Di. 11.5; Di. perf. 2.2; Wt 733.7

[1741]   K20/70   1911
Roughly spherical; some surface damage, otherwise it is smoothed, but uneven, with vegetable impressions visible. Two additional holes on the upper surface, one of which runs through to the lower side, as does one which begins in the side of the other hole. On the opposite side to the two extraneous holes, a groove runs from the central hole to the edge. Buff, coarse, friable clay.
H. 6.0; Di. 11.1; Di. perf. 2.2; Wt 673.1

[1742]   K20/71   1911
Roughly spherical. Apart from the central perforation, there are three other holes in the upper side, none of which goes all the way through. There is also a hole, possibly deliberate, on the upper side which joins up with the central perforation. Buff, coarse, friable clay.
H. 7.3; Di. 11.1; Di. perf. 2.7; Wt 797.6

[1743]   K20/72   1911
Roughly spherical; complete; one side is badly pitted, otherwise the surface is smoothed, but uneven, with many vegetable impressions. Buff, coarse, friable clay with dense vegetable temper and some stone inclusions.
H. 6.3; Di. 11.7; Di. perf. 2.3; Wt (687.9)

[1744]   K20/73   1911
Roughly spherical; some surface damage, otherwise it is smoothed, but uneven, with vegetable impressions. An extra hole next to the central perforation curves and comes out on the lower side. This side has indentations as if it has been laid on something organic when

Figure 285. Selected loomweights from floor of Rm e9 (**1735–59**), showing examples with single and multiple perforations. At back, large trapezoidal weight from unit 1924 (**1760**); in vertical rows, from top left: **1742**, **1751**, **1740**; **1739**, **1741**; **1745**, **1744**, **1753**; **1748**, **1747**, **1756**; **1750**, **1757**, **1754**; **1743**, **1738**, **1752**.

wet. Buff, coarse, friable clay with occasional stone inclusions.
H. 6.2; Di. 11.2; Di. perf. 2.1; Wt 707.3

1745   K20/74   1911
Roughly spherical; much surface damage (c. 30 per cent), otherwise it is smoothed, but uneven, with vegetable impressions. Apart from the central perforation, there are two other holes on one side, both of which exit on the lower face. Buff, coarse, friable clay with dense vegetable temper.
H. 7.7; Di. 11.9; Di. perf. 2.6; Wt (753.0)

[1746]   K20/76   1911
Large; one large, fragile piece and several smaller fragments, one of which joins. Buff, coarse, friable clay with vegetable impressions and some stone inclusions.

[1747]   K20/77   1911
Roughly spherical; some surface damage, otherwise it is smoothed, but uneven, with vegetable impressions. Buff, coarse, friable clay with occasional white stone inclusions.
H. 7.3; Di. 10.5; Di. perf. 1.9; Wt 741.2

[1748]   K20/78   1911
Roughly spherical; some surface damage, otherwise it is smoothed, but uneven, with vegetable impressions. On one side it is not quite rounded, but has a slight carination. Buff, coarse, friable clay with frequent vegetable temper.
H. 7.8; Di. 11.0; Di. perf. 2.1; Wt 706.5

[1749]   K20/79   1911
Large, fragmentary.
H. 6.7; Di. 11.1; Di. perf. 2.2

[1750]   K20/80   1911
Roughly spherical; some surface damage, otherwise it is smoothed, but uneven, with vegetable impressions. Buff, coarse, friable clay

with frequent vegetable temper.
H. 6.8; Di. 9.9; Di. perf. 2.2; Wt 702.3

[1751]   K20/81   1911
Roughly spherical; much surface damage, otherwise it is smoothed, but uneven. Buff, coarse, friable clay with some stone inclusions.
H. 6.9; Di. 14.0; Di. perf. 2.6; Wt (752.5)

[1752]   K20/82   1911
Roughly spherical; lower part has entirely broken off, but even without that, its dimensions are somewhat smaller than all the other loomweights from this cache; the surface, where preserved, is smoothed and uneven, with vegetable impressions. Near to the central perforation is a small hole which runs through to the other side. Buff, coarse, friable clay with some calcareous pebbles.
H. 5.2; Di. 9.5; Di. perf. 2.1; Wt (331.2)

[1753]   K20/83   1911
Roughly spherical; the surface is smoothed, but uneven, with vegetable impressions, and is well preserved except for a couple of missing chunks on one side, and a deliberate(?) hole which doesn't run very deep. Buff, coarse, friable clay with much vegetable temper and occasional stone inclusions.
H. 6.7; Di. 11.1; Di. perf. 2.2; Wt (741.5)

[1754]   K20/84   1911
Roughly spherical; some surface damage, otherwise it is smoothed, but uneven, with some vegetable impressions. On the underside is an organic (possibly coarse textile?) impression. Buff, coarse, friable clay with much vegetable temper and occasional calcareous inclusions.
H. 7.6; Di. 11.0; Di. perf. 2.2; Wt 725.1

[1755]   K20/85   1911
Roughly spherical; broken vertically along the central perforation so that *c*. 50% remains: one main piece with several small, non-joining fragments; surface smoothed, but uneven and much cracked, with vegetable impressions visible. Buff, coarse, friable clay with occasional calcareous inclusions.
H. 6.8; Di. 10.5; Di. perf. 2.3; Wt (436.1)

1756   K20/86   1911
Roughly spherical; some surface damage, otherwise it is smoothed, but uneven, with some vegetable impressions. Buff, coarse, friable clay with dense vegetable temper and occasional calcareous inclusions.
H. 6.9; Di. 11.5; Di. perf. 2.5; Wt 786.5

1757   K20/87   1911
Roughly spherical; surface quite damaged on lower face, and cracked, otherwise it is smoothed but uneven, with vegetable impressions. Buff, coarse, friable clay with occasional calcareous inclusions.
H. 7.0; Di. 11.0; Di. perf. 2.9; Wt 800.1

[1758]   K20/88   1911
Fragments of a large, roughly spherical, loomweight; dimensions cannot be determined, but the form is the same as all the others from the K20 (1911) cache. Buff clay, very friable, with much vegetable temper and occasional calcareous inclusions.

[1759]   K20/98   1923
Roughly spherical; fragments. Buff with dense vegetable temper and some stone inclusions.

1760   K20/104   1924
Large trapezoidal weight; oval, almost rectangular base. Crumbly creamy-grey clay with grit and vegetable temper.
H. 14.8; 16.8 x 22.0; Di. perf. 4.1; Wt 3800.0

Loomweights from Level IIf in J18 (1761–82)

Most of these loomweights were found in quadrant J18a, Level IIf, but of the few from quadrant J18b three are from pits assigned to IIe (**1779**) or IId (**1777**, **1782**). Some of these loomweights, which we have described as 'doughnuts', are almost spherical (**1762**, **1764–6**, **1768**, **1779**). They are made of very crumbly unbaked clay although they look very solid. Heights range from 3.5 to 7.9 cm and diameters from 4.6 to 13.0 cm. Their weights vary considerably, depending on the density of the clay; complete examples range between 72.5 and 936.0 g. Loomweights **1763–5** were found in unit 2378 together with an undecorated, ovoid spindle-whorl (**1967**). **1766** and **1768** are too large to be spindle-whorls, but too small and light to be loomweights and it is unclear to which category they should belong, although they are included here. Also included here is **1777**, a concave-sided cylinder which may also have been a loomweight.

1761   J18/177   2376
Doughnut. Brownish grey.
H. 7.0; Di. 12.2; Di. perf. 2.2; Wt 936.0

[1762]   J18/183   2378
Several fragments of coarse clay which fit together to form a round loomweight perhaps similar to **1764**.
H. 7.9; Di. 10.2; Di. perf. 2.0; Wt 641.0

[1763]   J18/184   2378
Large but in fragments; one fragment may have a perforation at its edge. Vegetable temper and a pottery sherd inclusion.
Wt (608.5)

1764   J18/185   2378
Almost spherical; now fragmentary. Light grey.
H. 7.5; Di. *c*. 9.6; Di. perf. *c*. 2.2; Wt 736.6

1765   J18/188   2378
Almost spherical; sliced across on one side, probably in antiquity. Light brown.
H. 5.2; Di. 7.1; Di. perf. 2.0; Wt (218.0)

[1766]   J18/203   2391
Level IIf1
Almost spherical; roughly made. Cream.
H. 3.85; Di. 4.6; Di. perf. 1.4–1.7; Wt 72.5

[1767]   J18/204   2391
Almost spherical; half remaining. Soft clay.
H. 3.2; Di. 4.8; Di. perf. 1.3; Wt (50.6)

[1768]   J18/208   2391
Almost spherical; broken but almost complete; smooth outer surface. Soft, cream-coloured clay.
H. 3.7; Di. 4.6; Di. perf. 1.4; Wt (70.3)

[1769]   J18/209   2391
Doughnut; chipped on one side; one loose fragment. Soft light brown clay.
H. 4.2; Di. 8.0–8.7; Di. perf. 1.8; Wt 265.0

[1770]   J18/212   2392
Level IIf1
Almost spherical; almost complete, in three large fragments which appear to fit together. Soft clay.
H. 4.7; Di. 7.4; Wt (230.5)

[1771]   J18/213   2392
Level IIf1
Doughnut, with a large central perforation. Very soft greyish-cream clay.
H. 4.7; Di. 8.3; Di. perf. 1.8; Wt 280.8

[1772]   J18/218   2393
Level IIe
Fragmentary. Soft, cream clay.
H. (7.6); Di. 13.0; Di. perf. c. 2.0; Wt (400.9)

[1773]   J18/227   2396
Level IIf1
Almost spherical; string groove; damaged surface opposite groove, probably where the weight was dropped on the floor in antiquity. Soft cream clay.
H. 6.1; Di. 9.7; Di. perf. 1.9; Wt (466.3)

[1774]   J18/229   2396
Level IIf1
Basically spherical but small and irregularly shaped; half missing. Soft light grey clay; one large grit is visible in the break.
H. 3.5; Di. 5.8; Di. perf. 1.5; Wt (85.1)

1775   J18/232   2399
Level IId/e
Almost spherical; perforation at one end is small and irregular (1.4–2.0), but at the other end it flares funnel-like. Soft cream clay.
H. 6.8; Di. 9.5; Di. perf. 2.0–3.5; Wt 577.0

[1776]   J18/233   2399
Level IId/e
Almost spherical; roughly made; broken into three fragments. Soft brown-grey clay.
H. 5.9; Di. 9.5; Di. perf. 2.1; Wt 430.3

1777   J18/258   5814
Level IIc/d
Concave-sided cylinder with convex ends; unperforated; carefully smoothed. Cream-yellow clay with large, gritty inclusions.
H. 11.3; Di. 6.3 (middle)–7.3 (ends); Wt (718.0)
For the shape cf. Barber 1991, 98 fig. 3.19 from Bulgaria.

[1778   number not used]

1779   J18/306   5847
Level IIe/f1
Spheroid; buff-coloured with grit and vegetable temper. Unevenly made.
H. 6.9; Di. 7.5; Di. perf. 2.4; Wt 436.7

[1780   number not used]

[1781   number not used]

[1782]   J18/353   5874
Level IId?
Large, almost spherical; half remains; crudely made, uneven surface with pebble inclusions.
H. 7.4; Di. 11.1; Di. perf. 2.0; Wt (452.0)

Loomweights from Level IIf in K18 (1783–9)

The only disc-shaped loomweights were found, together with the more common doughnut-shaped loomweights, in a pit sealed by W438 in K18b (P98/70), and must date to phase IIf. A possible stone loomweight was also found in the same pit (**1831**). Also from pits in K18 came one rather ovoid weight **1788** (P96/68, probably IIf) and one further doughnut-shaped weight **1789** (P97/48, not sealed but possibly also IIf). Some may have been lightly fired or baked.

1783   K18/241   6121
Disc; nearly complete (seven joining pieces). Baked(?) clay with grit and vegetable temper.
H. 3.5; Di. 12.5; Di. perf. 1.8; Wt (527.0)

1784   K18/242   6121
Doughnut. Grey clay with inclusions, but with material missing from the inclusions.
H. 4.2; Di. 8.6; Di. perf. 2.0; Wt (221.3)

[1785]   K18/243   6121
Fragments.
Wt (198.0)

[1786]   K18/245a-d   6121
Four fragments found with a possible loomweight of stone (**1831**):
a) Disc: H. 3.9; Di. 11.2; Di. perf. 2.3
b) Disc fragment: H. 3.4
c) Fragment of a thicker loomweight; very crumbly clay with large holes (see the loomweights from K20 for similar fabric).
d) Doughnut: H. 3.4; Di. c. 8.5

[1787]   K18/249   6121
Disc; baked grey clay with vegetable temper, a fragment of shell and a small piece of stone.
H. 4.0; Di. 6.0; Di. perf. 1.6; Wt (199.6)

1788   K18/234   6118
Doughnut.
H. 4.9; Di. 10.0; Di. perf. 2.2; Wt 453.7

1789   K18/99   4319
Level I/II
Roughly hemispheroid with rounded edges. Fine grit-tempered creamy-grey clay; lightly fired?
H. 3.4; Di. 5.4; Di. perf. 0.95–0.8; Wt 89.0

Predominantly doughnut-shaped loomweights from other locations (1790–1808)

[1790]   J19/243   1691
Level IId
Doughnut. White, coarse, crumbling clay.
H. 4.9; Di. 8.9; Di. perf. 2.2; Wt 313.0

[1791]   J19/244   1691
Level IId
Doughnut. Very soft cream clay with a number of air pockets in it.
H. 5.0; Di. 9.5; Di. perf. 2.3; Wt 356.5

[1792]   J19/53   1615
Level IId/e
Drum-shaped. Greyish-cream clay.
H. 6.6; Di. 10.4; Di. perf. 1.7; Wt 708.0

1793   J19/55   1615
Level IId/e
Cylinder or drum shape with rounded angles; fragmentary. Light grey clay.
H. 6.7; Di. 10.3; Di. perf. 1.7; Wt (412.5)

[1794]   J19/255   1698
Level IIe?
Roughly spherical; large and fragmentary.
H. *c.* 7.0; Di. *c.* 9.0; Di. perf. *c.* 2.5; Wt (430.0)

[1795]   J19/260   1698
Level IIe?
Doughnut; fragmentary. Light grey clay.
H. 5.4; Di. 11.0; Di. perf. 1.5; Wt (253.7)

[1796]   I19/8   1704
Level IIe?
Roughly spherical; roughly shaped. Buff, coarse clay with some vegetable temper.
H. 3.7; Di. 5.6; Di. perf. 1.7; Wt 87.6

[1797]   I19/9   1704
Level IIe?
Irregularly shaped. A slight groove on one side, next to the perforation, possibly worn by the string. Pale buff, chalky-textured clay with some stone inclusions.
H. 4.2; Di. 7.4; Di. perf. 1.7; Wt 193.0

[1798]   I19/73   1783
Level IIf
Roughly spherical. Greyish-cream clay.
H. 4.6; Di. 6.5; Di. perf. 1.8; Wt 158.4

[1799]   K19/37   1522
Level I
Doughnut; half remains. Pale grey, coarse, vegetable-tempered clay.
H. 4.0; Di. 7.0; Di. perf. 1.8; Wt (106.0)

[1800]   K19/45   1516
Level I/II
Doughnut; about a third remains. White clay.
H. (6.0); Di. *c.* 9.0; Di. perf. *c.* 1.4; Wt (140.0)

[1801]   H18/102   2632
Level IIe/f
Doughnut; about 25% remains; no trace of perforation survives; broken in antiquity. Grey-brown, unbaked clay.
H. (5.0); Di. 8.0; Wt (110.0)

[1802]   H18/107   2633
Level IIe/f
Doughnut; about half remains.
H. 4.7; Di. 7.0; Di. perf. *c.* 2.0; Wt (100.0)

[1803]   H18/71   2622
Level I/II
Doughnut; about a third remains. Traces of perforation. Grey-brown, vegetable-tempered, unbaked clay.
H. 5.0; Di. *c.* 12.0; Wt (84.0)

[1804]   K14/19   3005
Level 1
Doughnut; small; half remains.
H. 2.7; Di. 5.0; Di. perf. *c.* 0.9; Wt (26.5)

[1805]   K14/38   KLT 36   3011
Level 1
Doughnut; one side broken. Very friable, pale green-buff, sandy clay.
Di. 4.6; Di. perf. 1.6; Wt 37.8

[1806]   K14/58   3016
Level 1
Doughnut; fragmentary; perforation off-centre. Powdery cream clay.
H. 4.5; Di. *c.* 6.0; Wt (157.0)

1807   K14/167   KLT 20   3001
Level 1
Almost spherical; extended round one end of the perforation. Dense orange-brown clay with fine grit temper.
H. 4.5; Di. 5.7; Di. perf. 1.1; Wt 144.5

1808   Q19/38   KLT 19   2107
Level E2a
Bi-conical; no central perforation, but two small perforations on one side which are oval at one end; carefully shaped. Creamy-grey clay.
H. 4.0; Di. 5.0; Di. perf. 0.6–1.2; 0.8–1.0; Wt 62.9

Loomweights from Q20 (1809–20)

The objects catalogued here were found on the surface or in the topsoil in Q20, together with a stone spindle whorl (**2000**). Although not securely stratified, they are probably of Hellenistic or Byzantine date. As noted below (**1821–4**), pyramidal examples are known from Tarsus, but apparently none of the 'doughnut'-shaped ones found here in association with pyramidal ones. Note that these loomweights are much smaller and lighter than those catalogued above. They are of unbaked clay unless otherwise specified.

[1809]   Q20/3   184
Fragmentary circular loomweight with a carination; centrally-perforated; surface smoothed, but largely encrusted. Soft grey-brown clay with some vegetable temper and a large stone.
H. 2.9; Di. 5.2; Di. perf. l.0; Wt (37.0)

[1810]   Q20/4   KLT 16   184
Doughnut; surface uneven, with chip broken off one side. Light brown, sandy fabric with occasional small, red grits.
H. 2.3; Di. 4.2-4.7; Di. perf. 1.3; Wt. (42.5)
Baker *et al.* 1995, pl. XXVI(a)

[1811]   Q20/5   KLT 15   184
Doughnut; small, fragmentary. Soft, grey, grit-tempered clay; burnt.
H. *c.* 2.45; Di. 5.4; Di. perf. 1.1; Wt (39.0)
Baker *et al.* 1995, pl. XXVI(a)

1812 Q20/6 KLT 17 184
Doughnut. Grey clay.
H. 2.2; Di. 4.7-5.3; Di. perf. 0.6–1.4; Wt 56.0
Baker et al. 1995, pl. XXVI(a)

1813 Q20/7 KLT 18 184
Doughnut. A small diagonal hole goes through one side from top to bottom (Di. 0.3). Grey clay.
H. 2.55; Di. 4.55–4.9; Di. perf. 1.25; Wt 49.4
Baker et al. 1995, pl. XXVI(a)

1814 Q20/8 184
Four-sided, pyramidal loomweight with flat top and bottom; horizontal perforation near the top; surface smoothed. Clay is grey at core, yellow/buff at surface, with frequent coarse vegetable impressions.
H. 6.7; W. (3.4); Th. (2.6); Wt (68.9)
Baker et al. 1995, pl. XXVI(a) ['184/7']

1815 Q20/9 KLT 12 184
Elongated, pyramidal; four-sided, with flat base and top; horizontally-perforated near the top. Grey-brown clay.
H. 7.0; W. 2.0–3.5; Th. 1.7–3.3; Di. perf. 0.55; Wt 80.7
Baker et al. 1995, pl. XXVI(a)

1816 Q20/10 KLT 13 184
Four-sided pyramidal; fragments. Crumbly grey clay with lots of vegetable temper; burnt rather than baked.
H. 6.0; W. 2.9–3.8; Th. 1.6–2.2; Wt (50.0)
Baker et al. 1995, pl. XXVI(a)

[1817] Q20/11 184
Rectangular; two fragments; the surface is smoothed, but largely encrusted; chipped; perforation at one end, slightly off-centre through wide face.
H. 7.0; Th. 2.7; W. 3.1 at top

1818 Q20/12 184
Fragments of a four-sided pyramidal loomweight with flat top and bottom; surface smoothed, but one face is missing. The top end is broken at the horizontal perforation. The junction between bottom and sides is rounded. The clay is grey-brown at the core, yellow-buff at the surface, with heavy vegetable temper and occasional stone inclusions.
H. (6.2); W. 3.4–3.6; Th. 2.4–2.7; Di. perf. 0.9; Wt (65.4)
Baker et al. 1995, pl. XXVI(a) ['184/11']

[1819] Q20/19 184
Doughnut fragment. Grey, vegetable-tempered clay.
H. (2.9)

1820 Q20/21 KLT 21 2151
Doughnut; grey, unbaked clay. Coarse fabric, with vegetable temper. Surface chipped or damaged in places.
H. 2.5 ; Di. 4.1; Di. perf. 4.1; Wt 36.5

Rectangular and trapezoidal loomweights (1821–4)

Loomweights of this type have been found in Hellenistic or later levels in Tarsus (Goldman 1950, 394, fig. 267), but some were found in Median levels at Tepe Nush-i Jan (Curtis 1984, 39–40). For further examples, see **1814–18** above.

1821 I14/134 3474
Level 2
Rounded weight on oval base; complete apart from chipped base; perforation near top. Burnt blackish-brown; vegetable temper and small stone inclusions.
H. 8.5; Base 6.0 × 6.8; Di. perf. 1.3; Wt 286.0

1822 I14/31 3410
Level 1
Rectangular; perforation off-centre near one end of the wide sides. Three of the long sides are finished off; part of the fourth side projected further, but has been cut off flush with the rest of the original surface. One end is also finished off, but the end near the perforation is broken. Baked creamy-yellow clay with frequent red stones, calcareous and vegetable inclusions, resembling the fabric of some Byzantine tiles.
H. 9.9; W. 4.7; Th. 4.4; Di. perf. 0.95; Wt 245.5

[1823] J7/3 319
Surface
Trapezoidal slab; flat ends, rounded corners and angles; perforated. Cream clay, grit- and vegetable-tempered, originally with pale orange surface, now worn and encrusted.
H. 14.7; Top 4.75 × 4.25; Base 4.74 × 6.0; Di. perf. 1.3; Wt 682.3

1824 P20/6 KLT 14 210
Surface
Four-sided, rectangular; horizontally pierced near the top; surface smoothed. There is a slight facet at one side at the bottom, and the front is slightly narrower than the back. One corner is chipped at the bottom. Clay is yellow-buff, with coarse vegetable temper and occasional white calcareous inclusions.
H. 7.0; W. 3.4–4.0; Th. 2.55–2.6; Di. perf. 0.7; Wt 85.5
Baker et al. 1995, pl. XXVI(a)

Possible stone weights (1825–35)

Small stones with perforations, some perhaps fishing weights, have been catalogued below with the stones (**2647–8, 2665**). The following are either very large or at least approximate the clay loomweights in size or shape.

1825 H20/154 1243
Level IVa
Stone of sub-rectangular shape with hole close to one side, probably natural but was shaped and smoothed. Surface polished. Loomweight?
H. 7.6; W. 6.8; Th. 4.1; Di. perf. 1.2; Wt 293.5

1826 H20/58 1220
Level IVb
Perforated stone of white chert, chipped around edges, probably roughly shaped. Loomweight?
H. 7.6; W. 7.6; Th. 3.6; Di. perf. 1.5; Wt 303.1

[1827] H19/182 4248
Level IIIa/IVb
Yellow limestone with oval perforation, which may have served as a loomweight.
H. (14.0); W. 8.2; Th. 5.9

[1828] J20/168 1395
Level IIa/b
Roughly rectangular grey stone with hole drilled through it.
H. 7.8; W. 6.0; Th. 3.0; Wt 196.5

[1829] L19/64 5976
Level IIc
Large, rounded stone with large, loop-like hole through the centre of the thinnest angle; certainly partly, if not entirely, natural.
H. 10.8; Di. perf. *c.* 3.0; Wt 2988.0

[1830] K18/117 4356
Level IIe
Small drum with rounded edges and inward-tapering sides; bottom broken; carefully shaped from cream limestone. A drill-hole (di. 0.95, 0.55 cm deep) was started at the top and never completed; a second, very thin drill-hole was started laterally 0.5 cm below the top, where there is a chip in the stone, and aimed towards the centre, but it too was never completed (di. 0.36, 0.95 cm deep).
Di. 2.8 × 4.9 (top)–3.8 (at break); Wt (89.7)

[1831] K18/245e 6121
Level IIf?
Fragment of pitted stone; part of a loomweight or possibly a rubber.

[1832] I14/56 3424
Level 2k
Very irregular, eroded piece of sandstone with a hole in the middle which is wider on one side than the other. Perhaps natural, but could have been used as a loomweight.
H. 7.2; Di. perf. 5.2; Wt 2014.5

[1833] J18/85 2321
Level IIf
Half a natural, pale brown stone, concreted on one face, with a hole, probably natural, through it; broken at hole. Note that even though natural, this stone may have served as a loomweight since artefacts connected with weaving activities were so prominent in J18 (see **1761–82**).
H. 4.55; W. 4.4; Th. 3.1; Wt (77.8)

[1834] L19/11 5907
Level I
Roughly dressed, approx. rectangular, cream stone with large, almost central hole.
H. 9.8; Di. 14.9 max.; Di. perf. 3.6; Wt 2132.0

1835 I16/3 4601
Topsoil
Ovoid; pale grey stone, heavily concreted with large chip. Small hole drilled through from one side.
H. 3.36; Di. 5.4; Di. perf. 0.75; Wt (81.0)

Notes

1. There are claims of Neolithic occurrences in central Europe and Switzerland, but it should be remembered that the Neolithic there continues into the second half of the fourth millennium BC (Barber 1991, 94, fig. 3.16 is unconvincing as the weights are bunched together; p. 96 fig. 3.18 belongs to a context dated to the first half of the third millennium BC).
2. 'Oval' is used here for weights whose outline is genuinely and regularly oval, 'ovoid' for those whose outline is more tapered towards the top and wider at the base.
3. This term, used by Sheffer (1981), Curtis & Green 1997, 18–19, Barber (1991) and Friend (1998), refers to more or less flattened circular weights with a central hole through the lesser dimension; however, at Kilise Tepe there is a good number of roughly spherical examples which seem to cluster as a group.

Chapter 37

Spindle Whorls

Dorit Symington & Dominique Collon

'Besides pottery no class of object is as common at Anatolian sites as baked clay spindle whorls' (Lloyd & Mellaart 1962, 277), and in this respect Kilise Tepe, where some 160 examples were recovered, is no exception, indicating the importance of textile production at the site.

As an object, spindle whorls are easily re-deposited and much of the material is contextually uncertain. Nevertheless, there were numerous examples with a secure context and, viewed as a whole, a clear pattern of typological development in shape and decoration can be observed.

Provenance

74 spindle whorls were recovered from EBA/MBA levels in H20 and H19, of which 50 were complete, or only slightly damaged. In Level II and later they are also frequent, but like the loomweights, spindle whorls are strikingly absent from Level III, with the exception of **1986**.

Material

The spindle whorls are almost all made of clay. Of the 74 whorls from Levels IV and V only one was carved in stone (**1867**). In the higher levels the rare exceptions are hemispheroids, including a fossilized sea-urchin which has been perforated (**1998**). Most clay whorls appear to have been unfired but many show traces of burning and were perhaps placed among the ashes of a domestic fire to bake them. The fabrics, in Levels IV and V at least, reflect to a degree the particular clays or fabrics used for pottery in these levels. Slipped and burnished examples are also represented.

Shapes

In our catalogue within each period the spindle whorls have been arranged according to shape. The top of the spindle whorl is here taken to be the decorated surface (see below); in some categories this means that the base is narrower than the top and undecorated examples have been classified with this in mind.

Typologically, the shapes of the spindle whorls fall into several distinct categories. Typologies are almost as numerous as the discussions of spindle whorls. Crewe (1998, 22), for instance, has no ovoid whorls; Joukowsky (1986, 373f. Tab. 127), on the other hand, has an 'irregular squat' and a 'flat' category to reflect what may be an Anatolian preference. Here the categories have been simplified and are those which best reflect the Kilise Tepe repertory of shapes. In the catalogue whorls from Levels IV and V are listed first, arranged according to level, beginning with the earliest. Unstratified examples from H19 and H20 are included in this section when they seem likely typologically to belong here (**1842**, **1859–61**, **1866**, **1884**). Other unstratified examples are listed with the spindle whorls from Levels I to III, which are arranged typologically by shape, and in stratigraphic order within each category.

There has been much discussion as to which way up spindle whorls were used and should be described and illustrated. There are ethnographic comparisons and technical reasons for considering the 'flat' end, which often has a concave depression, to have been uppermost when the spindle was in use. This flat end would have served as a resting area for the accumulating fibre bundle (Kull 1988, 197–8, fig. 187). These considerations are supported in our Kilise Tepe corpus by the fact that whorls decorated on only one end have their decoration on the 'flat' end. We have consistently illustrated the whorls with the flat side uppermost, but this is not necessarily correct in all cases. For the possible high- and low-whorl positions on the spindle, which are culturally determined, see Barber (1991, 53), and Crewe (1998, 6–8).

Perforations

All our whorls are perforated vertically and centrally, as required for efficient spinning (Barber 1991, 52). The ends of the perforation are usually smoothed.

Chapter 37

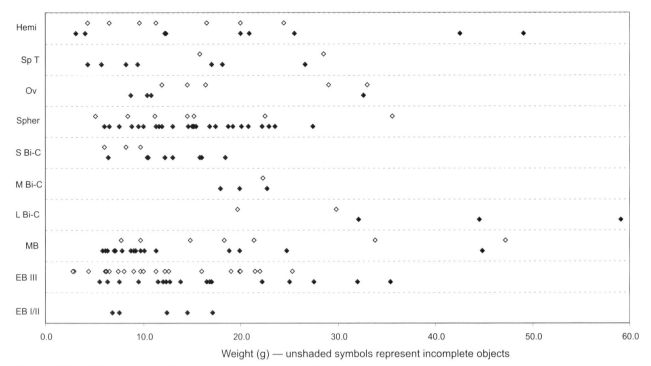

Figure 286. *Weights of spindle whorls, grouped by period or type.*

In Levels IV and V the diameters range between 0.3 and 0.8 cm, and average 0.5 to 0.6 cm. From Level III onward the perforations almost all fall between 0.4 and 0.9 cm. The perforations are generally straight and were probably made by pushing a smooth stick through the damp clay and perhaps twisting it (cf. Crewe 1998, 23).

The hole is sometimes wider at one end than at the other. In Levels IV and V for about half the whorls a difference in the diameter of the perforation was recorded, ranging from 0.1 to 0.3 cm. A varying diameter was found more rarely in symmetrical whorls (spherical, bi-conoid, ovoid) — where the top and bottom cannot be determined — but frequently in the asymmetrical group which includes conical, hemispherical, and the 'spinning top' whorls. Here the flat upper and decorated side was found to have the smaller diameter, and the lower conical end the larger one. An exception is **1881**, where the larger perforation is at the decorated end. In the catalogue the diameter of the smaller perforation is given first throughout. Where only one diameter is noted the whorl was fragmentary.

Tapering perforations were also noted among the Early and Middle Cypriote whorls where 73 per cent had a different hole diameter, varying from 1–3 mm (Crewe 1998, 12). Similar observations were made on the MBA whorls at Demircihüyük, where the greater diameter of the pointed end was attributed to use wear caused by the spindle (Kull 1988, 197, 199 Katalog and Abb. 187). Crewe (1998, 7) suggested that this feature has relevance in differentiating the top from the bottom of the spindle whorl because the tapered spindle would be wider at the top. It might also indicate from which end the stick was being twisted. Only further detailed study would resolve some of these uncertainties in our corpus.

Weight

Within a period or a type of whorl the weight can vary widely. For instance, in Levels IV–V the 'spinning top' weights varied from 6.0–44.8 g. Figure 286 gives an idea of the variation of weights from different levels and, for the later periods, by category of shape. Hollow diamonds indicate fragmentary whorls: it may be thought these should have been excluded, but in a few cases even the incomplete weight is heavier than some complete examples and its inclusion therefore has some value. No very striking patterns emerge, but it is noticeable that in the later types the small and medium bi-conical and spherical share a similar range between about 6 and 23 g, with the occasional heavier outlier.

The weights are given to one-tenth of a gramme, but should only be taken as accurate to a gramme. In our records we noted discrepancies between weights recorded in the field and taken in the Museum. Testing the results achieved by two different members of the team indicated that the reading often varied by

0.1 g, and in a few cases by 0.2 g. A second test indicated that a larger variation might be caused by the dryness of the whorl. This showed that if a whorl had been weighed shortly after washing it might appear up to 10 per cent heavier.

Decoration

The two categories where 'top' and 'bottom' are differentiated ('spinning tops' and hemispheroids) are also the categories which are most often decorated, but all shapes can be decorated with designs incised in the damp clay. Dots are impressed with the end of a sharp stick or pin. EBA and MBA spindle whorls are more frequently and more finely decorated, and the designs are occasionally white-filled. Only 15 from Levels IV and V were left plain. The decoration, which is geometric and abstract, covers the whole or part of the whorl. Slipped and burnished examples are also represented, particularly in the early levels. Plastic decoration, popular at other sites, was not encountered.

Figure 287. *Spindle whorls from Level V: a) view from above (from left) 1841 (Vg), 1836 (Vj), 1839 (Vg); b) view from side (from left) 1841, 1836, 1839.*

Parallels

Viewing the collection as a whole, the Kilise Tepe spindle whorls belong very much to the Anatolian tradition of spindle whorl production with parallels in shape and decoration at other sites, in particular at Tarsus, Beycesultan and Troy II–V.

Levels V and IV

The main shapes in the EBA and MBA corpus include spheroids, hemispheroids, conoids, bi-conoids, spinning tops and ovoids, although the latter are not always strictly of a 1:2 ratio, i.e. height to diameter. Rare are so-called 'turnips', conical, and disc-shaped whorls.

Level Vj–g
The early EBA phases have yielded only a small number of whorls, with two recorded from Vj and four examples in Vg (Fig. 287). The predominant shape for both levels is spherical and in all cases the whorls are left undecorated.

1836–7 from Vj are fairly coarse and unbaked while the Vg examples have a denser fabric and appear to be baked. **1841** (Vg) is a small bi-conoid orange whorl with a simple radial design with numerous parallels at several sites and **1840** also

of phase Vg could be a bead but was classified as a spindle whorl.

No spindle whorls were found in Level Vi or Vh.

1836 H20/563 1859
Level Vj
Spherical but slightly lop-sided. Orange-brown with small inclusions, unbaked. Surface lumpy, undecorated.
H. 2.5; Di. 2.5; Di. perf. 0.5, 0.5; Wt 12.4
Fig. 287

1837 H20/566 1859
Level Vj
Spherical, brown medium-coarse, partly burnt. Surface uneven, undecorated, unbaked(?).
H. 2.5; Di. 2.7; Di. perf. 0.4, 0.4; Wt 17.1

1838 H20/474 1845
Level Vg/h
Spherical, fine buff fabric, well smoothed. Undecorated.
H. 2.3; Di. 2.8; Di. perf. 0.5, 0.5; Wt 17.1

1839 H20/1011 5388
Level Vg
Spherical. Pale-orange fabric, grit and sand tempered, smoothed. Undecorated.
H. 2.1; Di. 2.8; Di. perf. 0.4, 0.5; Wt 14.5
Fig. 287

1840 H20/1004 KLT 138 5388
Level Vg
Small spherical. Fabric as **1839**, smoothed. Undecorated.
H. 1.7; Di. 2.1; Di. perf. 0.5, 0.6; Wt 6.8

1841　　　H20/1005　　　　　　　　　　5388
Level Vg
Bi-conical whorl or bead. Fine pale orange fabric. Surface smoothed, low burnish. Incised with diagonally running lines from perforation to carination, both sides.
H. 2.2; Di. 2.1; Di. perf. 0.3, 0.3; Wt 7.5
Fig. 287

Level Vf

At Kilise Tepe the EB III phases proved to be the most prolific and the most accomplished period for spindle whorl production. A very marked increase of whorls was also noted at other Anatolian sites. Aphrodisias reported a three-fold increase from Bronze Age 3 to Bronze Age 4 (Joukowsky 1986, 373) and at Tarsus too the greatest number occurred in EB III (Goldman 1956, 328). At Kilise Tepe this period yielded the largest group with 27 examples from Level Vf1–4 and 15 from the transitional Level Ve.

The predominant shapes of spindle whorls in the EB III period are bi-conoid (**1844**, **1852–3**) or ovoid (**1848**, **1854**, **1858**), but hemispherical examples were also found (**1850**, **1861–2**). Undecorated whorls, favoured in the early EBA levels, still occur but they are now manufactured in medium or fine fabrics and are well fired (**1843**, **1845**, **1855**, **1868**). Some of these are covered in a black slip and burnished but otherwise left plain (**1847**). The majority, however, are decorated with incised patterns and in several cases the incisions are white-filled.

The fabric used for all decorated whorls is notably fine, dense grey or beige in colour and they are often slipped and burnished before the decoration is applied. The favoured designs are triple chevrons (**1850**, **1852**) and triple arcs (**1851**, **1863**).

A noteworthy group was excavated in Rm 53 (Level Vf4) of late EB III date. Characteristic for this level are ovoid spindle whorls and the dominant decorative patterns are concentric ovals in sets of four, the so-called 'eye' motif (**1854**, **1856–7**; cf. Goldman 1956, fig. 449:67) and interlocking triple arcs, some encasing dots and slashes (**1858–60**) — the incisions are frequently white-filled — thus dating these particular designs towards the end of EB III. This is a type also encountered at Karataş Semayük in late EBA context (Periods IV and V; Warner 1994, pls. 183:i & 185:h).

Unusual examples from H19 and H20 are **1853**, a bi-conoid with sharp carination, decorated on both sides with a series of vertical lines and punctured dots (white-filled), and **1848** made in an uncharacteristic red, gritty fabric with a four-pointed star motif on each side.

1842　　　H20/301　　　　　　　　　　1804
Unstratified
Small bi-conoid, fragment of whorl or bead. Fabric mid-brown with sand and vegetable temper. Surface smoothed, high burnish.
H. 2.15; Di. 2.5; Di. perf. 0.4, 0.4; Wt 5.5

1843　　　H20/900　　　　　　　　　　5361
Level Vf3?
Bi-conoid with one slightly flattened side. Medium pale-orange fabric, grit tempered. Traces of red slip. Undecorated.
H. 2.6; Di. 3.3; Di. perf. 0.5, 06; Wt 22.2

1844　　　H20/1023　　　KLT 127　　　5397
Level Vf/g
Bi-conoid, dense orange fabric, grit tempered. Slipped, low burnish. Damaged around perforation both ends. Decorated both sides with lines radiating from perforation to carination.
H. 2.6; Di. 3.7; Di. perf. 0.6, 06; Wt 27.5

1845　　　H20/893　　　　　　　　　　5359
Level Vf3/4
Half a spheroid. Fabric brown, medium-fine with grit inclusions. Undecorated. Blackened by fire on one side.
H. 2.5; Di. 3.6; Di. perf. 0.8, 0.8; Wt (21.5)

[1846]　　　H20/346　　　　　　　　　　1812
Level Vf
Half of a spheroid. Dense greyish-brown, fine vegetable and calcareous inclusions, grey core. Surface colour buff to black. Smoothed and well burnished.
H. 2.1; Di. 3.3; Di. perf. 0.6, 0.7; Wt (12.2)

[1847]　　　H20/924　　　　　　　　　　5363
Level Vf2/3
Small fragment of spheroid(?). Grey fabric with fine grits. Surface black slip and burnish.
H. 2.7; Wt (6.5)

1848　　　H20/855　　　　　　　　　　5350
Level Vf3
Ovoid. Red medium-fine fabric with small white grits. Decorated both sides with a four-pointed star filled with short strokes.
H. 1.6; Di. 2.8; Di. perf. 0.5, 06; Wt 12.7
Fig. 288

1849　　　H20/607　　　　　　　　　　1863
Level Vi/j (intrusive)
Fragment of a hemispheroid. Fine, grey fabric, grit-tempered. Surface dark grey slip, well burnished. Decorated on flat top with connected arcs meeting at the outer edge and series of white-filled dots.
H. 1.75; Di. (3.35); Di. perf. 0.6; Wt (8.0)

1850　　　H20/904　　　　　　　　　　5362
Level Vf3?
Half a hemispheroid. Brown grit-tempered fabric. Surface smoothed, burnished, partly worn. Sets of triple chevrons with apex towards perforation, filled with white-filled dots. Decorated on under and upper side.
H. 1.8; Di. 3.9; Di. perf. 0.7, 0.8; Wt (11.3)

1851　　　H20/380　　　　　　　　　　1820
Level Vf
Half a hemispheroid. Orange-red fabric with calcareous and stone inclusions (0.2 cm). Decorated on top and sides with three sets of roughly incised triple arcs. Surface varies from red to yellow.
H. 2.6; Di. 4.2; Di. perf. 0.5, 0.8; Wt (22)
Fig. 290

1852   H20/1009   5397
Level Vf/g
Squat bi-conoid with sharp carination. More than half preserved. Fine, grey grit-tempered fabric. Surface black slip and high burnish. Pattern: sets of pendent chevrons from central perforation both sides, meeting at carination.
H. 1.8; Di. 3.2; Di. perf. (0.5); Wt (6.5)
Fig. 288

1853   H20/1010   5397
Level Vf
'Turnip'-shaped bi-conoid. Fine beige/brown fabric. Surface slipped(?), medium burnish. Identical decoration both sides, four sets of triple lines, two with enclosed punctured dots. White-filled.
H. 1.9; Di. 3.0; Di. perf. 0.5, 0.6; Wt 12.0
Fig. 288

1854   H20/813   5334
Level Vf4
Half of an ovoid. Fine beige fabric, grit-tempered. Traces of black slip and burnish. Decoration 'eye' motif, four sets (when complete) of three ovals on the side and double circle around perforation. White-filled(?). Cf. **1856**.
H. 2.4; Di. 3.8; Di.perf. 0.7, 0.7; Wt (16.0)
Fig. 288

[1855]   H20/774   5332
Level Vf4
Fragment of 'turnip'-shaped spindle whorl. Gritty beige fabric. Surface light-brown slip, burnish, traces of burning. Undecorated.
H. (3.0); Di. 4.8; Di. perf. (0.5); Wt (25.3)
Fig. 288

1856   H20/750   5327
Level Vf4
Ovoid. Slight depression around perforation. Grey fabric, dark grits, black slip and burnish, worn. Four sets of triple ovals on sides, 'eye' motif.
H. 1.72; Di. 2.78; Di. perf. 0.6, 0.6; Wt 11.5
Fig. 289

1857   H20/757   5328
Level Vf4
Half of ovoid. Fine, grit-tempered, blackened through burning. Decoration: 'eye' motif, for this design see also **1854** and **1856**.
H. 1.95; Di. 3.0; Di. perf. 0.5; Wt (9.0)
Fig. 289

1858   H20/805   5328
Level Vf4
Half an ovoid, made from unfired clay with fine grits. Exterior blackened through fire. Decoration: sets of triple arcs top and bottom, interlocking, offset by lines and dots.
H. 1.9; Di. 3.2; Di. perf. 0.7, 0.7; Wt (9.7)
Fig. 289

Figure 288. *Spindle whorls from Level Vf, views from above and side. From top left:* **1852, 1848, 1854, 1853, 1855**.

Figure 289. *Spindle whorls from Level Vf: a) view from above; b) view from side. From top left:* **1858, 1857, 1868, 1856, 1863, 1864**.

1859   H20/296   KLT 50   1802
Unstratified
Ovoid. Fine beige fabric with grit inclusions. Burnt on one side. Four sets of triple arcs top and bottom, interlocking, and four sets of vertical double lines with punctured dots.
H. 1.8; Di. 2.9; Di. perf. 0.6, 0.6; Wt 13.8
Cf. Goldman 1956, fig. 449:63.

1860   H20/309   1805
Unstratified
Half an ovoid. Grey-brown dense clay with sand and vegetable temper. Surface high burnish, chipped in one place. Interlocking triple arcs with dots, similar to **1858–9**.
H. 2.5; Di. 4.1; Di. perf. 0.7, 0.7; Wt (19.0)

1861 H20/423 1828
Unstratified
Half of a small hemispherical whorl. Fine orange fabric with calcareous inclusions. Red slip, all-over decoration of strokes, arcs and outer circles.
H. 1.1; Di. 2.2; Di. perf. 0.5, 0.5; Wt (2.9)

[1862] H20/826 5328
Level Vf4
Fragments (2) of hemispheroid. Grey with grit inclusions. Surface smooth, exterior blackened through burning. Decorated on upper surface and base with triple lines forming herringbone pattern.
Wt (3.6)

1863 H20/753 5327
Level Vf4
Half of conoid. Orange/pink fabric, small inclusions. Decorated on flat surface with triple arcs arranged radially.
H. 1.7; Di. 3.33; Di. perf. 0.5, 0.6; Wt (6.1)
Fig. 289

1864 H20/392 1823
Level Vf3/4
Fragment of bi-conical spindle whorl or bead with sharp carination. Orange fabric, grey core, darker orange slip. Set of three radial incisions on one surface, two on the other.
H. 1.9; Di. 2.4; Di. perf. 0.4, 0.4; Wt (2.8)
Fig. 289

1865 H20/394 1823
Level Vf3/4
Squat bi-conoid, burnt, very friable. Chipped. Orange fabric, large white inclusions. Irregular strokes around perforation, both sides. Groove round carination (cf. **1916**, **1974**, **1976**).
H. 1.7; Di. 3.0; Di. perf. 0.5, 0.5; Wt (12.6)

1866 H20/306 1805
Unstratified
Small ovoid whorl or bead. Fine buff fabric, well smoothed, undecorated.
H. 1.4; Di. 2.6; Di. perf. 0.7, 0.7; Wt 9.5

1867 H20/752 5327
Level Vf4
Small ovoid made in light brown stone. Fine incised concentric circles around perforation and edge both sides. Chipped.
H. 1.2; Di. 2.47; Di. perf. 0.5, 0.6; Wt (7.4)

1868 H20/756 5327
Level Vf4
Fragment of bi-conoid, slightly asymmetrical. Orange fabric with dark and white grits, smoothed. Exterior cream slip(?), undecorated.
H. 3.5; Di. 3.5; Di. perf. 0.6; Wt (21.5)
Fig. 289

Level Ve

The spindle whorls from Level Ve form the most varied group, particularly in design, and contain some examples with close parallels from other sites.

This phase also sees the introduction of the 'spinning top' type, i.e. an asymmetrical bi-conical shaped whorl with a deep depressed centre, leaving a bevelled edge which is always decorated (**1876–80**). This type is generally regarded as the classic shape of the MBA in Anatolia and is the favoured type over a long period, particularly at Troy where it is most prominent in Troy III–V (Blegen *et al.* 1951, figs. 152–3, 237; see quantitative distribution chart of Troy spindle whorl shapes in Levels I–VII by Kull 1988, fig. 189) but has almost totally disappeared in Troy VI (LBA), similarly at Tarsus. However, although typical of MBA, the 'spinning top' spindle whorl makes an appearance already in EB III as seen at Troy, where, in fact, it is first encountered in Troy II, and also at Beycesultan (Lloyd & Mellaart 1962, 277f.) and at Aphrodisias (Joukowsky 1986, 374). Therefore, the Kilise Tepe evidence fits in well with the findings from other sites.

The remaining shapes which occur in Level Ve are ovoid and hemispheroid/conoid, decorated overall, or more often on the 'flat' or concave (top) face only (**1872**, **1877–8**). One example of the ovoid black burnished type with the 'eye' motif survived into Ve, but the remainder display a different repertoire of designs, mainly of arcs arranged in a variety of ways, forming various shapes and covering the whole or part of the whorl.

Fabrics vary greatly from dense grey or brown, and well fired to coarser grit-tempered in bright orange and buff, possibly not all of local manufacture.

Possible imports could be **1879**, a 'spinning top' decorated with a star motif and hatched background which has an identical counterpart at Tarsus (Goldman 1956, fig. 446:46), and **1870**, an ovoid whorl with an unusual pattern of diagonal double lines filled with slashes forming a triangle, that again has an exact parallel at Tarsus (Goldman 1956, fig. 448:26). Another example of an unusual decoration at Kilise Tepe, with no parallel, is **1881** with four deep drill holes and stroke-filled arcs arranged on the edge.

1869 H20/719 5319
Level Ve/f
Ovoid. Grey medium-fine clay, grit and vegetable temper. Black slip, medium burnish. Decorated with 'eye' motif (see **1854–5**), white-filled.
H. 2.5; Di. 4.3; Di. perf. 0.7, 0.8; Wt 35.4

1870 H20/792 5333
Level Ve
Ovoid. Medium-fine grit-tempered fabric. Well fired. Surface smoothed and decorated with three sets of parallel lines forming a triangle and encasing a series of slashes.
H. 1.9; Di. 3.5; Di. perf. 0.7, 0.7; Wt 25.0
Fig. 290
Cf. Blegen *et al.* 1951, fig. 237, 35–457.

[1871] H20/784 5333
Level Ve
Fragments of ovoid(?) made from unfired beige clay with fine grit temper. Traces of black slip and burnish. Set of three diagonal lines encasing small dots.
Wt (4.4)

1872　　　H20/674　　　5304
Level Ve
Flattened hemispheroid with slightly concave top. Orange fabric with grit and sand temper, smoothed. Decoration on flat side only, six sets of triple interlacing arcs giving the impression of a guilloche pattern, enclosed by a single circle.
H. 1.6; Di. 3.7; Di. perf. 0.5, 0.6; Wt 16.8
Fig. 290

1873　　　H20/336　　　KLT 52　　　1810
Level Ve/f
Flattened hemispheroid with slightly concave flat side. Medium-fine clay, very gritty, orange with grey core. Domed surface decorated with four sets of quadruple arcs, similar pattern on the flat side, five sets of more pointed arcs forming a star. Chipped.
H. 1.5; Di. 3.7; Di. perf. 0.8, 0.8; Wt (19.9)

1874　　　H20/672　　　5304
Level Ve
Conoid. Brown semi-coarse clay with grit and small stones. Smoothed, flat side burnished with four sets of triple arcs (one missing due to damage). Four sets of triple pendent arcs on dome part and two circles around perforation. Chipped both sides.
H. 2.0; Di. 3.6; Di. perf. 0.6, 0.7; Wt (20.0)
Fig. 290

1875　　　H20/656　　　KLT 102　　　5301
Level Ve
Small hemispheroid. Fine orange-pink fabric, cream slip. Both surfaces decorated with four sets of irregularly spaced double arcs resting on a line running around the edge.
H. 1.5; Di. 2.85; Di. perf. 0.6, 0.7; Wt 7.5
Fig. 294

1876　　　H20/695　　　KLT 100　　　5313
Level Ve
'Spinning top' type. Fine pale-orange fabric, white grits. Surface red-brown slip. Decoration: on flat top, arcs resting on a grooved line running round the edge and forming a seven-pointed star. On domed face, five sets of double arcs pendent from the grooved line. Chipped.
H. 1.7; Di. 3.1; Di. perf. 0.6, 0.6; Wt (10.0)
Fig. 294
Cf. Goldman 1956, fig. 450:77.

1877　　　H20/670　　　5302
Level Ve
'Spinning top', yellowish fine clay with grits. Surface smooth. Bevelled edge of upper side decorated with three groups of triple arcs and one with a double arc, compensating for poor spacing.
H. 2.0; Di. 3.2; Di. perf. 0.6, 0.7; Wt 12.3
Fig. 290

1878　　　H20/636　　　1289
Level Ve
Small 'spinning top'. Fine beige clay with little grit temper. Surface brown slipped, matt. Bevelled edge decorated with four groups of triple arcs interrupted by radiating lines of dots.
H. 1.0; Di. 2.6; Di. perf. 0.5, 0.5; Wt 6.3
Fig. 290

1879　　　H20/639　　　1290
Level Ve
'Spinning top'. Dark-brown fabric with white and dark grits,

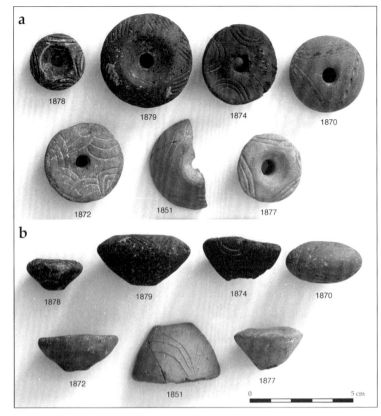

Figure 290. *Spindle whorls from Level Ve (except* **1851** *from Vf): a) view from above; b) view from side. From top left:* **1878**, **1879**, **1874**, **1870**; **1872**, **1851**, **1877**.

dark grey slip, some burnishing marks. Worn in carination area. Bevelled edge of top decorated with six-pointed star and hatched background.
H. 2.2; Di. 4.25; Di. perf. 0.5, 0.6; Wt 32.0
Fig. 290
Cf. Goldman 1956, fig. 446:46.

1880　　　H20/643　　　1289
Level Ve
Fragment of a 'spinning top', medium-fine dense grey-brown fabric, small grits. Surface slipped(?) and burnished. Bevelled rim and depression decorated with arcs and punctured dots around inner rim and inside depression.
H. 3.0; Di. (4.6); Di. perf. 0.7

1881　　　H20/699　　　5315
Level IVa/Ve
Hemispheroid with slightly convex top, made from fine orange clay with some grits, smoothed. The flattish side is slightly convex and is decorated with four arcs filled with vertical strokes forming a rhomboid shape containing four large punctured dots of 0.5 cm depth. The larger perforation is on the decorated side.
H. 1.65; Di. 3.5; Di. perf. 0.9, 0.5; Wt 17.0

1882　　　H20/722　　　5321
Level Ve
Fragment of small hemispheroid. Fabric orange with small inclusions. Surface red slip, incised with triple diagonal lines on flat surface only.
H. 1.85; Di. (2.88); Di. perf. 0.6; Wt (6.2)

1883   H20/689   5310
Level Vf4
Spheroid, chipped on one side. Fabric almost white with few inclusions, unbaked, lumpy surface, undecorated. Intrusive?
H. 2.5; Di. 2.8; Di. perf. 0.5, 0.5; Wt 16.5

Level IVa–b
The spindle whorls of Level IVa are a more mixed group and on the whole less well made than seen in the EB III phases. The fabrics are often coarser and vary in colour from beige or orange to grey. The 'spinning top' is still the most common form, some with a larger concave centre than in the previous level, but more importantly the decoration is now always confined to the bevelled edge of the top adjoining the depression (**1884**, **1886**, **1898**), and is not found below the carination. Triple arcs and radiating strokes are the favoured designs, and they are often applied to one side only on other whorl shapes, apart from the 'spinning tops'.

Other types include conoids (**1889**), some of which now appear with a slightly convex 'upper' side (**1890**). Without parallel among the EB/MB corpus are the disc-shaped whorls **1894** and **1907** (from IVb).

In Level IVb there is a slight decline in spindle whorl tradition — they are less well finished and also on the whole much smaller in size, indicating the spinning of finer fibres. The clays vary from medium to fine in colours of beige, grey and orange.

The 'spinning top' shape still continues but the concave part on some examples has become rather shallow, as in **1900** and **1901**.

The favoured incised decoration is still triple arcs and strokes. There are also two examples harking back to EB III tradition with familiar motifs and white filling (**1903–4**), but these examples may well be intrusive.

1884   H20/572   1268
Unstratified
Large 'spinning top' with deep depression on top leaving bevelled rim divided by four sets of shallow arcs irregularly spaced. Fabric greyish-brown with burnished surface.
H. 2.8; Di. 4.85; Di. perf. 0.6, 0.7; Wt 44.8
Fig. 292

1885   H20/588   1272
Level IVa/Ve?
'Spinning top' with large depression leaving narrow bevelled rim incised with sets of arcs, similar to previous example **1884**. Coarse orange fabric, medium grits, barely smoothed, traces of brown slip. Chipped.
H. 2.2; Di. 4.7; Di. perf. 0.5, 0.7; Wt (33.8)

1886   H19/282   4264
Level IVa
'Spinning top' made of brown grit-tempered medium fabric, smoothed. Traces of white (lime?) coating, blackened in parts. Depression has additional circular groove. Bevelled part incised with four sets of triple arcs and three arrow-shaped incisions pointing towards perforation. Chipped.
H. 1.9; Di. 3.6; Di. perf. 0.6; Wt (18.3)
Fig. 291

[**1887**]   H19/316   4271
Level IVb
Small fragment of conical shape with slight depression on top. Fabric coarse, beige with dark stone inclusions, exterior cream. Three vertical incisions on top edge.
H. 1.9; Di. perf. 0.5

1888   H20/589   1272
Level IVa/Ve?
Small 'spinning top' with shallow depression, brown fabric, small white grits. Slip and burnish, worn in parts. Undecorated.
H. 1.2; Di. 2.45; Di. perf. 0.4, 0.5; Wt 7.0
Fig. 291

1889   H20/647   1298
Level IVa
Conoid. Orange fabric with medium size grits, smoothed. Flat top decorated with single grooved circle around perforation and five sets of double arcs arranged near the outer edge.
H. 1.9; Di. 3.8; Di. perf. 0.6, 0.7; Wt 18.8
Fig. 291

1890   H20/145   KLT 29   1241
Level IVa
Small conoid with a slightly convex top, decorated with a single circle around the perforation and a five-pointed star. The lower surface has two concentric circles and four sets of irregularly spaced triple arcs. Yellowish dense clay with tiny black inclusions, smoothed, light burnish.
H. 1.4; Di. 2.45; Di. perf. 0.4, 0.4; Wt 7.1

[**1891**]   H20/146   KLT 30   1241
Level IVa
Bi-conical, chipped on one side. Light-brown medium fabric, multi-coloured grits. Orange-brown slip, flaked. Partly burnt. Undecorated.
H. 3.5; Di. 4.2; Di. perf. 0.6, 0.6; Wt (47.2)

1892   H20/703   KLT 101   5317
Level IVa/Ve
Hemispheroid, pale orange fabric, fine grit temper. Flat face decorated with concentric circles around perforation and edge and seven groups of triple radiating strokes — rather crudely executed.
H. 1.3; Di. 3.01; Di. perf. 0.5, 0.6; Wt. 8.7
Fig. 294

1893   H20/586   KLT 99   1272
Level IVa/Ve?
Small hemispheroid of fine pale orange fabric with small inclusions and cream slip. Decorated on upper and lower surfaces with sets of swirling triple arcs radiating from the perforation.
H. 1.8; Di. 2.9; Di. perf. 0.3, 0.4; Wt 9.0
Fig. 294

1894   H20/151   KLT 31   1242
Level IVa
Disc-shaped with off-centre perforation — possibly a bead. Fabric beige, medium, calcareous inclusions. Brown slip, burnished, worn. Sides decorated with two rows of irregular diagonal slashes.
H. 1.15; Di. 2.5; Di. perf. 0.5, 0.5; Wt 9.2

Spindle Whorls

1895   H20/280   1263
Level IVa
Squat bi-conoid. Coarse grey-brown clay with stone and calcareous inclusions, friable. Surface brown to orange, burnished(?), partly chipped. One face crudely incised with radial grooves.
H. 1.8; Di. 3.7; Di. perf. 0.4, 0.4; Wt 19.9
Fig. 291

1896   H20/234   1258
Level IVa
Squat bi-conoid of orange baked clay with some small stone inclusions. Radial grooves on one surface. Friable.
H. 1.4; Di. 2.7; Di. perf. 0.5, 0.5; Wt 9.7

1897   H19/235   4254
Level IVb
Small fragment of hemispheroid(?). Grey fabric with black stone inclusions. Pattern of sketchy triple arcs.
H. 1.9; Di. 3.2; Wt (7.7)

1898   H19/239   4255
Level IVa/b
'Spinning top'. Pale orange fabric, calcareous inclusions, orange slip, worn. Bevelled edge of top incised with five groups of triple arcs.
H. 1.9; Di. 3.1; Di. perf. 0.5, 0.6; Wt 11.3
Fig. 292

1899   H20/178   1253
Level IVa/b
'Spinning top' of yellow buff clay, dark grits and calcareous inclusions. Upper surface with bevelled edge and depression decorated with four sets of quadruple arcs and lower part with four bands of radial grooves. Chipped.
H. 1.6; Di. 3.1; Di. perf. 0.5, 0.6; Wt (9.7)
Fig. 293

1900   H20/268   1262
Level IVb
'Spinning top'. Light brown clay, small grits and calcareous inclusions. Rim area incised with crude slashes, chipped near perforation at bottom end.
H. 1.8; Di. 3.35; Di. perf. 0.7, 0.7; Wt (14.8)
Fig. 293

1901   H19/247   4257
Level IVa/b
Small 'spinning top' with shallow depression. Dark brown clay with small white particles. Black slip, light burnish. Upper face decorated with concentric groove near depression and four sets of triple arcs. Incisions white-filled.
H. 1.3; Di. 3.5; Di. perf. 0.5, 0.5; Wt 7.8
Fig. 292

1902   H19/211   4249
Level IVb
'Spinning top' with deep concave depression. Beige fabric, fine inclusions. Traces of burnishing, partially blackened. Bevelled edge has four groups of triple radiating lines. Chipped in one place.
H. 1.8; Di. 3.9; Di. perf. 0.5, 0.6; Wt (21.4)
Fig. 292

Figure 291. *Spindle whorls from Level IVa (except **1975** from IIIc): a) view from above; b) view from side. From top left: **1975**, **1889**, **1895**, **1886**, **1888**.*

1903   H20/30   KLT 27   1216
Level IIIa–c
Truncated spheroid made of fine brown clay with small grits. Circular groove around perforation on both faces enclosing four adjoining ovals made up of two lines encasing a series of dashes. White-filled. Type of 'eye' motif.
H. 1.7; Di. 2.6; Di. perf. 0.7, 0.7; Wt 24.7

1904   H19/194   4249
Level IVb
Bi-conoid with slight depression on top and bottom. Fabric grey, medium inclusions. Sides are incised with three pairs of concentric ovals. Type of 'eye' motif.
H. 1.5; Di. 2.9; Di. perf. 0.5, 0.6; Wt 10.1
Fig. 292

1905   H19/309   KLT 79   4271
Level IVb
'Turnip' shape, slightly concave one side and drawn out on the opposite side. Fine dense orange fabric, grits. Upper area decorated with three groups of triple or quadruple arcs which alternate with a series of dashes, the latter white-filled.
H. 1.6; Di. 2.2; Di. perf. 0.4, 0.4; Wt 6.1

1906   H20/90   1227
Level IIIa/IVb
Fragment of truncated spheroid. Grey dense fabric with few inclusions, smoothed. Undecorated.
H. 1.7; Di. (2.7); Di. perf. 0.6

Chapter 37

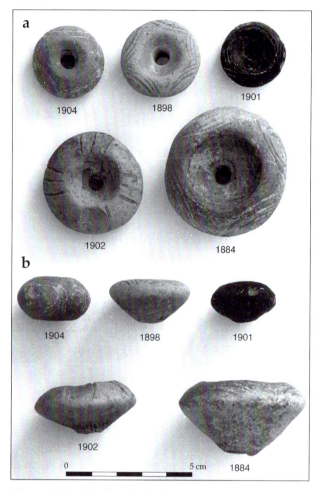

Figure 292. *Spindle whorls from Level IV: a) view from above; b) view from side. From top left:* **1904**, **1898**, **1901**, **1902**, **1884** *[unstratified].*

Figure 293. *Spindle whorls from Level IV: a) view from above; b) view from side. From left:* **1900**, **1899**.

distinct categories, with probable functional and chronological implications. Many come from Squares J19, J20, K19 and K20.

a) Large undecorated bi-conoids (**1909–13**)
These are fired and are often made of clay with a high proportion of quite sizeable stone grits, probably with the aim of making them heavier. The surface is carefully smoothed and is often reddish, sometimes with traces of burnish surviving. They are undecorated. The height varies from 2.8 to 3.8 cm, the diameter from 3.2 to 3.8 cm and the weight from around 30 to 45 g. One unstratified bi-conoid from H20 is catalogued with EBA stratified examples above (**1842**).

1907 H19/134 4237
Level IIIa–b
Disc shaped, slightly concave on both faces and ridge running around perforation. Pale orange clay, medium-fine, dark brown inclusions.
H. 1.1; Di. 2.2; Di. perf. 0.6, 0.8; Wt 5.8

1908 H20/59 KLT 28 1221
Level IIIa/IVb
Very small 'spinning top' with ridge running around the perforation on the concave top. Fine light brown fabric, few grits, traces of red slip, smoothed. Undecorated.
H. 1.1; Di. 2.4; Di. perf. 0.3, 0.4; Wt 6.3

Levels III to I

*Bi-conoids (**1909–28**)*
These spindle whorls are regular bi-conoids with the height less than the maximum diameter (an average of 4:5) and a marked carination. The ends around the perforation are slightly flattened. They fall into three

1909 H20/310 1805
Unstratified
Bi-conoid. Orange to buff fabric, with calcareous and micaceous inclusions. Surface smoothed, traces of burnish, worn at ends. Undecorated.
H. 3.8; Di. 4.3; Di. perf. 0.6, 0.7; Wt 59.1

1910 J19/56 1615
Level IId/e
Bi-conoid, large, with rounded carination and one end slightly broken and the other flattened. Coarse, grey clay with frequent grits and some calcareous inclusions. The surface is orange and quite smooth.
H. (2.8); Di. 3.4; Di. perf. 0.55; ?; Wt (29.8)

1911 K20/58 1905
Level I/II
Bi-conoid, large; half remains. Dense brown clay with few visible inclusions, fired to grey. Surface smooth.
H. 3.3; Di. 3.8; Di. perf. 0.5, 0.5; Wt (19.7)

1912   K9/5   314
Surface
Bi-conoid, large. Grey-brown clay with white grits.
H. 2.8; Di. 3.2; Di. perf. 0.65, 0.65; Wt 32.1

1913   M6/2   325
Surface
Bi-conoid, large, with ends rounded. Greyish-brown clay, with many grey grits and white, calcareous inclusions. Surface smooth.
H. 3.3; Di. 3.8; Di. perf. 0.68, 0.69; Wt 44.5

b) Medium decorated bi-conoids (**1914–17**)
All these bi-conoids are 2.5 cm high and 3.2 cm in diameter, with weights varying between 17.5 and 22.7 g. They thus fall between categories a) and c) as regards size and weight and are the only bi-conoids which are decorated (apart from those from earlier levels). All are from Level II.

[**1914**]   J19/374   3963
Level IIb
Bi-conoid, medium, decorated, with one end chipped. Fired clay with medium grit inclusions. Surface smoothed and blackened, showing evidence of burning. Decorated by a row of small vertical lines around the carination.
H. 2.5; Di. 3.2; Di. perf. 0.5; ?; Wt (22.3)

1915   K19/343   4563
Level IIc
Bi-conoid, medium, decorated, with uneven carination. Burnt grit-tempered clay. Surface smoothed but cracked. Decorated with impressed dots arranged unevenly across the whole surface.
H. 2.5; Di. 3.2; Di. perf. 0.55, 0.55; Wt 22.7

1916   K19/317   4546
Level IIc/d
Bi-conoid, medium, decorated, with sharp carination. Fired clay with large grit inclusions. Surface with orange patches and traces of burnish. Decoration consists of an incised line around the carination and four sets of double lines radiating from the perforation at each end; between these sets of lines are four sets of two dots arranged radially.
H. 2.5; Di. 3.2; Di. perf. 0.63, 0.63; Wt 19.9

1917   K19/437   KLT 131   6204
Level II?
Bi-conoid, medium, with flattened ends, decorated. Brown clay, very worn around the carination, with impressed circles (di. 0.5) in a row above and below the carination.
H. 2.5; Di. (3.2); Di. perf. 0.55, 0.55; Wt 17.9

c) Small undecorated bi-conoids (**1918–28**)
These are generally unfired clay but many show traces of burning. They are normally grey or brown in colour. They range in size from 1.5 to 2.6 cm high, and 2.1 to 3.0 cm in diameter, and weigh around 6 to 18 g. They are predominantly found in Level II.

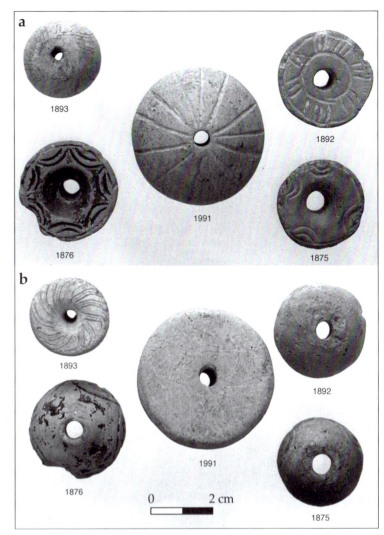

Figure 294. *Spindle whorls from various levels: a) view from above; b) view from below. From top left:* **1893** *[IVa/Ve],* **1991** *[I/II],* **1892** *[IVa/Ve];* **1876, 1875** *[both Ve].*

[**1918**]   J20/55   KLT 32   1328
Level IIa/b
Bi-conoid, small, with pronounced carination and flattened ends; half remains. Black grit-tempered clay with white, calcareous and occasional micaceous inclusions. Surface mid-grey and well smoothed.
H. 2.5; Di. c. 2.9; Di. perf. 0.45, 0.6; Wt (9.7)

[**1919**]   K19/163   1592
Level IId
Bi-conoid(?), small; two pieces joining but the original shape is not clear. Creamy-brown clay. Surface smooth and polished.
H. c. 2.0; Di. c. 1.75; Di. perf. 0.6; ?; Wt (8.2)

1920   K20/203   1994
Level IId
Bi-conoid, small, with sharp carination and flattened ends; two halves, joining. Burnt vegetable-tempered clay.
H. 2.0; Di. 2.8; Di. perf. 0.52, 0.54; Wt 10.4

[1921]   K20/207   KLT 80   1994
Level IId
Bi-conoid, small, with rounded carination and flattened ends. Reddish-brown clay.
H. 1.5; Di. 2.1; Di. perf. 0.4, 0.4; Wt 6.4

1922   K18/120   4356
Level IIe
Bi-conoid, small, with rounded carination. Clay with large grit inclusions fired to orange.
H. 1.2; Di. 3.0; Di. perf. 0.6; Wt 16.0

1923   I19/7   1704
Level IIe?
Bi-conoid, small, with flattened ends. Hard-fired light brown clay. Surface smooth and highly burnished.
H. 2.1; Di. 2.3; Di. perf. 0.4, 0.4; Wt 10.5

1924   J18/374   KLT 129   5822
Unstratified
Bi-conoid, small, with flattened ends. Greyish-black clay.
H. 2.6; Di. 2.8; Di. perf. 0.9, 0.9; Wt 18.4

1925   I14/120   3473
Level 2
Biconoid, small, with fairly sharp carination. Burnt greyish-brown clay with fine white and black grits and one large grit (<6 mm).
H. 2.0; Di. 2.5; Di. perf. 0.45, 0.45; Wt 13.0

1926   I14/133   3474
Level 2
Bi-conoid, small, with flattened ends and pronounced carination. Brown clay.
H. 2.0; Di. 3.0; Di. perf. 0.56, 0.56; Wt 15.8

1927   R18/80   2047
Level E5a
Bi-conoid, small, with rounded carination; one third remains. Brown and black clay with medium vegetable temper. Surface well burnished.
H. 1.9; Di. 2.8; Di. perf. 0.65, ?; Wt (6.0)

1928   K19/26   1514
Level I
Bi-conoid, small, flatter at one end than the other. Burnt grey clay.
H. 1.9; Di. 2.6; Di. perf. 0.4, 0.5; Wt 12.2

Spheroids (**1929–62**)
Spheroids are generally slightly flattened spheres but are quite distinct from the ovoids in that the relation of height to diameter is closer (*c.* 2:3). Some have a slight carination but this is more rounded than is the case with the bi-conoids. Over a quarter are decorated, and the type of decoration, with slashes, 'eye' motifs and interlocking arcs, is related to that of the ovoids. Almost all are made of unfired clay, but most show signs of burning and were probably placed among the ashes of a domestic fire to bake them; as a result, several are brittle and crumbly and most are grey, while some are black. They generally have a fine grit temper. The height ranges between 1.4 and 2.5 cm but is generally around 2.0 cm; the diameter ranges between 2.3 and 3.8 cm but is generally around 3.0 cm; the weights range between around 11 to 23 g. Four examples do not fall within this range. **1945** is exceptionally small and light, whereas **1946**, **1951** and **1961**, are exceptionally large and heavy for this category of spindle whorl, although within the range for spindle whorls generally.

A few spheroids and one ovoid are somewhat turnip-shaped, drawn out into an extension terminating in a ring or rim round the perforation at one end, here taken to be the base: a decorated example was found in Level IV and is discussed above (**1890**), as is one undecorated example from Level Vf (**1846**). One undecorated example came from Level III (**1963**); all the other examples, **1935**, **1939–41** and **1956**, were found in Level IIc and only **1956** bears any form of decoration.

a) Undecorated spheroids (**1929–54**)
[1929]   I14/182   3714
Level 3
Possible fragment of a spheroid spindle whorl found with two other fragments probably belonging to some other object.

1930   I19/151   5518
Level IIa/IIIe
Spheroid, flattened on one face to form a dome. Burnt, gritty dark grey clay.
H. 2.0; Di. 2.0; Di. perf. 0.7, 0.7; Wt 10.0

1931   I14/147   3495
Level 2/3
Spheroid; almost carinated on one side. Clay burnt black.
H. 1.8; Di. 2.6; Di. perf. 0.52, 0.52; Wt 11.6

1932   I14/150   3489
Level 2/3
Spheroid; half survives. Pale grey, slightly powdery, unfired clay. Surface smoothed.
H. 2.1; Di. 3.8; Di. perf. *c.* 0.4, ?; Wt (8.4)

1933   I19/153   5517
Level IIa
Spheroid, slightly drum-shaped. Grey clay. Roughly made.
H. 1.7; Di. 2.6; Di. perf. 0.7, 0.7; Wt 15.0

1934   J20/56   KLT 33   1331
Level IIb
Spheroid, almost an ovoid. Fine brown clay with few visible inclusions. Surface smooth grey-brown.
H. 1.6; Di. 2.7; Di. perf. 0.6, 0.6; Wt 13.0

1935   K20/153   1962
Level IIb/c
Turnip-shaped spheroid with rim round the lower, oval end of the perforation. Grey clay. Small nicks around the round upper end of the perforation.
H. 2.0; Di. 2.9; Di. perf. 0.7, 0.65–0.7; Wt 15.2

1936   K19/450   KLT 132   6209
Level IIc
Spheroid, drum-shaped with flattened sides; perforation at an angle and off-centre. Pale grey clay.
H. 2.2; Di. 2.8; Di. perf. 0.6; Wt 11.3

1937 K19/453 KLT 133 6209
Level IIc
Spheroid, slightly drum-shaped. Grey-brown, baked clay with pitted surface where inclusions are missing. Perforation is off-centre.
H. 2.1; Di. 2.7; Di. perf. 0.61, 0.6; Wt 19.2

[1938] K19/454 6209
Level IIc
Spheroid, crudely-made; broken. Crumbly, creamy grey, vegetable-tempered clay.
H. 2.1; Di. 3.1; Wt (11.2)

1939 K20/145 1945
Level IIc
Turnip-shaped spheroid with thick ring round the lower end of the perforation. Fine beige clay burnt black, with very sparse burnt calcareous inclusions.
H. 2.0; Di. 2.3; Di. perf. 0.4, 0.4; Wt 8.8

1940 L19/61 KLT 134 5976
Level IIc
Turnip-shaped spheroid with rim round the bottom of the perforation. Grey-brown clay.
H. 1.8; Di. 3.2; Di. perf. 0.7, 0.7; Wt 17.4

1941 J20/50 1325
Level IIc
Turnip-shaped spheroid with ridge of clay round the lower perforation. Fine, dense grey clay burnt to dark grey. Surface smooth with some traces of light burnish.
H. 1.8; Di. 3.3; Di. perf. 0.6; Wt 17.4

1942 J18/380 5889
Level IIc/d
Spheroid, crudely made; encrusted. Grey-brown burnt clay.
H. 1.8; Di. 3.0; Di. perf. 0.4; Wt 16.8

1943 K20/219 1942
Level IIc/d, found with decorated spheroid **1956** and with two further small fragments of spheroids (not recorded).
Spheroid. Grey clay. Small wedge-shaped indentation round perforation at one end; little nicks round ends of perforation.
H. 1.9; Di. 2.8; Di. perf. 0.5, 0.5; Wt 14.6

[1944] K18/143 4367
Level IId
Spheroid with the middle slightly flattened. Light brown clay with fine grit temper. Surface smoothed.
H. 1.7; Di. 2.9; Di. perf. 0.5, 0.55; Wt 15.1

1945 K20/205 1994
Level IId
Spheroid, very small. Creamy clay. Surface rough.
H. 1.4; Di. 2.3; Di. perf. 0.45, 0.45; Wt 6.0

1946 I19/40 1776
Level IIg/h
Spheroid; worn. Crumbly grey clay with many large, multi-coloured inclusions.
H. 2.7; Di. 4.2; Di. perf. c. 0.6; Wt (35.6)

1947 I14/85 3455
Level 2
Spheroid with slight, rounded carination; cracked and slightly split. Creamy-grey clay with some white grits. Perforation at an angle.
H. 2.3; Di. 3.4; Di. perf. 0.5, 0.5; Wt 18.7

1948 I14/116 3474
Level 2
Spheroid with slight, rounded carination. Burnt blackish-brown clay with fine white grits.
H. 2.5; Di. 3.3; Di. perf. 0.64, 0.7; Wt 27.4

1949 J19/164 1672
Level II?
Spheroid; about a quarter remains. Light greyish-brown clay with fairly large grey stone inclusions (<5 mm).
H. 1.9; Di. 3.0?; Di. perf. 0.4?; Wt (5.1)

1950 R18/29 2016
Level E5b
Spheroid; half remains. Buff clay with sparse calcareous inclusions.
H. 2.1; Di. 3.2; Di. perf. 0.68, 0.7; Wt 9.5

1951 R18/51 2030
Level E5a
Spheroid, flattened around the middle; about half remains. Burnt grey-brown clay with sandy temper and occasional small, white, calcareous inclusions.
H. 2.7; Di. c. 3.8; Di. perf. 0.7; Wt (22.5)

1952 K20/25 KLT 26 1116
Level I/II
Spheroid; slightly irregular shape. Surface smoothed brownish-red clay. Perforation at a slight angle.
H. 2.2; Di. 3.2; Di. perf. 0.6, 0.6; Wt 23.5

[1953] K19/301 4536
Level I
Spheroid, uneven, almost carinated. Powdery cream clay.
H. 2.5; Di. 3.3; Di. perf. 0.5, 0.5; Wt 20.1

1954 K19/369 4571
Surface
Spheroid; small hole on one side where inclusion is missing. Lightly fired beige clay with fine grit temper.
H. 2.3; Di. 2.7; Di. perf. 0.6, 0.6; Wt (14.5)

b) Decorated spheroids (**1955–62**)
The decoration is distinguished by the fact that it is generally applied so as to be visible from the sides as well as on the top and bottom. It is much simpler than that found on the earlier spheroids (see above), consisting of incised lines and impressed dots somewhat randomly arranged. Decorated spheroids are found both in Level II and in Byzantine contexts.

1955 I14/153 3704
Level 2/3
Spheroid, decorated. Beige clay. The perforation narrows in the middle. Three rows of small incised strokes: one row radiating round the perforation on both faces and one row vertically around the widest part, making the edge look deckled. Cf. Ovoid **1972** from Level IIc for an untidier version of this design.
H. 1.9; Di. 2.6; Di. perf. 0.54, 0.55; Wt 11.9

1956 K20/125 1942
Level IIc/d; found with undecorated spheroid **1943** and with two further small fragments of spheroids (not recorded).
Turnip-shaped spheroid, with rim round lower end of the perforation,

decorated. Burnt grey clay. On the upper surface, which is burnt dark grey, there is a circle of impressed dots around perforation.
H. 2.2; Di. 3.4; Di. perf. 0.54, 0.54; Wt 22.2

1957　　　　K19/165　　　　　　　　1592
Level IId
Spheroid, decorated. Greyish-brown clay with grit inclusions. Indented wedges and lines, apparently at random, on one face.
H. 1.5; Di. 2.4; Di. perf. 0.5, 0.5; Wt 6.5

1958　　　　K20/102　　　　　　　　1924
Level IIe
Spheroid, decorated. Grey clay with sparse fine sand and calcareous inclusions. A row of small vertical strokes around the widest part, probably finger-nail impressions.
H. 2.5; Di. 3.1; Di. perf. 0.6, 0.6; Wt 22.9

1959　　　　K20/24　　　　KLT 25　　　1116
Level I/II
Spheroid, decorated. Dark greyish-brown clay. Traces of burnish. A spiral on one face and an incomplete circle and random radiating strokes on the other face.
H. 2.1; Di. 2.9; Di. perf. 0.7, 0.7; Wt 15.4

1960　　　　K19/31　　　　　　　　1514
Level I
Spheroid, decorated. Crumbly grey clay with grits. Four pairs of small almost vertical strokes on either side of a faint groove around the widest part.
H. 2.4; Di. 2.7; Di. perf. 0.73, 0.75; Wt 20.8

1961　　　　J20/5　　　　　　　　　1301
Surface
Spheroid with slight carination, decorated; half remains. Dark grey clay burnt to reddish-brown at the surface, with fine sandy temper. Impressed dots and grooves on one face, and deep, vertical grooves at the widest part extending onto the other face.
H. 2.7; Di. 3.7; Di. perf. 0.56, 0.56; Wt (15.2)
Baker *et al.* 1995, 189, fig. 20

1962　　　　N8/2　　　　　　　　　331
Surface
Spheroid, drum-shaped with ring round one end of the perforation decorated. Creamy-grey, grit-tempered, burnt clay. Concave at one end around perforation. Sides decorated with four pairs of vertical thumb-nail impressions.
H. 1.4; Di. 2.1; Di. perf. 0.47, 0.47; Wt 7.5

*Ovoids (**1963-74**)*
As stated above, these may be related to the spheroids because of the similarity in decoration, but the proportions of height to diameter are closer to 1:2 and even 1:3. Like the spheroids, they are made of unfired clay and most show signs of burning; they too were probably placed among the ashes of a domestic fire to bake them. As a result, several are brittle and crumbly, but although some are partly grey, most show traces of brown, buff, orange or red. They generally have a fine grit temper. The heights range between 1.0–2.7 cm, the diameters between 2.8–5.9 cm and the weights between around 10–33 g. These ovoids were found in early and late phases of Level II as well as Level I.

a) Undecorated ovoids (**1963–71**)
1963　　　　H19/18　　　　　　　　4205
Level IIId
Turnip-shaped ovoid, with ring around one end of the perforation. Undecorated. Buff clay.
H. 1.3; Di. 3.1; Di. perf. 0.65; Wt 8.7

[**1964**　　　　number not used]

[**1965**　　　　number not used]

1966　　　　I20/44　　　　　　　　4001
Level IIb-e
Ovoid; in two halves with sliver missing. Burnt grey clay, originally beige with fine grit temper. Perforation (now cracked) made by pushing a stick backwards and forwards so that ends are rough and uneven.
H. 1.8; Di. 3.1; Di. perf. 0.35, 0.6; Wt (16.4)

1967　　　　J18/187　　　　　　　　2378
Level IIf
Ovoid, slightly carinated, chipped. Hard-fired, greyish-brown, grit-tempered clay with largish stone inclusions.
H. 2.2; Di. 4.2; Di. perf. 0.8; ?; Wt (33.0)

1968　　　　K19/93　　　　　　　　1554
Level IIc
Spheroid, slightly irregular. Beige, probably grit-tempered, lightly-baked clay.
H. 1.6; Di. 2.8; Di. perf. 0.6, 0.57–0.65; Wt 10.4

[**1969**　　　　number not used]

1970　　　　K14/164　　　　　　　　3001
Level 1
Ovoid, disc-shaped; half remains. Reddish-brown clay.
H. 1.7; Di. (5.4); Di. perf. 0.9, 0.9; Wt (29.0)

1971　　　　T11/2　　　　　　　　　275
Surface
Ovoid, fragment. Hard, light brown, grit-tempered clay.
H. 1.4; Di. 3.2; Di. perf. 0.88, 0.95; Wt (11.9)

b) Decorated ovoids (**1972–2000**)
The decoration is simple, like that of the decorated spheroids.

1972　　　　K19/458　　　　　　　　6210
Level IIc
Ovoid, decorated; half missing. Creamy-brown clay with black inclusions (<2 mm). Random nail impressions all over and along the carination. Cf. Decorated spheroid **1955** from Level 2/3 where the grooves are more tidily arranged, longer and more apparent as a deckled edge around the carination.
H. 1.7; Di. 2.7; Di. perf. 0.6, 0.6; Wt (14.5)

1973　　　　J19/52　　　　KLT 51　　　1615
Level IId/e
Ovoid, decorated. Greyish-brown, grit-tempered clay. Decorated on each face with four groups of arcs which form eye-shapes when seen from the side.
H. 1.1; Di. 3.0; Di. perf. 0.7, 0.7; Wt 10.8

1974   H19/3   KLT 53   4200
Topsoil
Sand-tempered clay; buff-coloured at surface, wearing through to dark grey in places. Horizontal groove around widest part. Decorated on both faces with a design of four groups of arcs which interlock when viewed from the side. Traces of a circular groove around the perforation survive at both ends. Design very similar to **1859** (note both unstratified).
H. 2.3; Di. 4.0; Di. perf. 0.9, 0.9; Wt 32.6

'Spinning tops' (1975–83)

These are basically bi-conoids, but differ from that category in that the upper part is considerably shallower than the lower and bears a concave depression in the middle. The carination is generally sharply marked. Almost all are decorated. The base is often slightly elongated around the end of the perforation — hence the resemblance to 'spinning tops'. They seem to have been made of unfired clay but most are burnt and may have been baked in the ashes of a domestic fire. All are between 1.1 and 1.9 cm in height and 2.2 and 3.9 cm in diameter, with weights varying from 4.3 to 28.3 g.

All are decorated except **1977**. With the exception of **1976**, the decoration is restricted to the upper slope or bevel surrounding the central depression above the carination, and the sides below the carination are undecorated. The decoration is simple with groups of lines forming Vs or arcs, carefully executed but often unevenly spaced.

This shape is found in the latest EBA level, throughout the MBA and into the earliest LBA levels (see above). The sporadic later occurrences are catalogued here. The decorative scheme, with groups of arcs creating star-shapes, and groups of Vs, is similar to that of the earlier examples, although it differs in not having the groups of three lines and arcs characteristic of the earlier levels. It seems, therefore, that these later examples are revivals rather than survivals.

The recessed top seems to be particularly popular at Kilise Tepe. The equivalent shape is described as 'truncated bi-conoid' by Crewe (1998, 22), but this is flat-topped and higher in relation to the diameter, and she illustrates few Cypriote examples with recessed tops. This is also the case as regards the Aphrodisias examples, which are described as 'conical' and 'conical with flattened top and bottom' (Joukowsky 1986, 373). At Tarsus, however, the recessed top has the same chronological distribution as at Kilise Tepe and is described as occurring 'chiefly in Middle Bronze and in Late Bronze I when it is the characteristic shape' (Goldman 1956, 328-34, nos. 42, 44–8 and 76–7, 80). The same pattern is repeated at Troy (Blegen *et al.* 1951, fig. 56, no. 33.289, p. 39) and at Alişar (von der Osten 1937 I, figs. 199–203, pp. 198–207, fig. 276, p. 270).

1975   H19/155   4244
Level IIIc
'Spinning top', decorated. Burnt grey clay with traces of paint(?) now brown. Eight groups of three lines rotating from centre.
H. 1.3; Di. 3.9; Di. perf. 0.6; Wt 9.4
Fig. 291

1976   J19/351   3960
Level IIb/c
'Spinning top', decorated. Unfired, burnt clay. Groove around the carination, groups of two lines forming six Vs on the bevel, five pendent double arcs below the carination, and a partial groove around the lower end of the perforation.
H. 1.7; Di. 3.5; Di. perf. 0.7; Wt 18.1

1977   J18/219   2393
Level IIe
'Spinning top'. Brown, fired clay with large grit inclusions and evidence of slight burnishing.
H. 1.9; Di. 4.1; Di. perf. 0.75; Wt 26.6

1978   K19/27   1514
Level I
'Spinning top', decorated; part missing. Burnt black clay with very small white inclusions. Six groups of triple, unevenly-spaced arcs.
H. 1.5; Di. 3.5; Di. perf. 0.65, 0.57; Wt (15.8)

1979   H19/6   KLT 49   4200
Topsoil
'Spinning top', decorated. Fine, dense, orange/brown fabric with few visible inclusions, very fine, white. Sets of diagonal grooves in opposing directions, separated by radial grooves. Smooth and burnished.
H. 1.2; Di. 2.6; Di. perf. 0.4, 0.4; Wt 8.2

1980   I10/1   KLT 54   310
Surface
'Spinning top', decorated. Fine, grey clay without visible inclusions. Four groups of four lines forming radiating Vs.
H. 1.1; Di. 2.2; Di. perf. 0.6, 0.6; Wt 4.3

1981   K17/10   9603
Surface
'Spinning top', decorated; crude and uneven. Creamy greenish-yellow grit-tempered fired clay. Surface smoothed. Bevel with a single groove around its inner edge and adjacent intersecting arcs.
H. 1.9; Di. 3.6; Di. perf. 0.6; Wt 17.0

1982   K19/368   KLT 130   4571
Surface
'Spinning top', flat top with shallow indentation, decorated; worn. Grey clay. Double inverted Vs on the top.
H. 1.1; Di. 2.4; Di. perf. 0.6; Wt 5.7

1983   R18/256   KLT 23   181
Surface
'Spinning top', decorated; very worn. Greyish-brown grit-tempered clay. Spaced groups of triple arcs around the bevel; two groups survive, but there were probably originally five.
H. 1.9; Di. 3.9; Di. perf. 0.8, 0.8; Wt (28.5)

Hemispheroids (1984–2000)

There are few undecorated hemispheroids and most are decorated on the top (i.e. flat) surface and on the sides, so that if they are turned over, the domed base also appears to be decorated. One example (**1987**) is not absolutely flat on top and should perhaps be considered as an ovoid; however, it resembles neither category in that its design of arcs is restricted to the top, and it is unusually large.

In contrast to the earlier hemispheroids (see pp. 483 ff.) which range from white through pinky-cream and pinky-red to bright orangey-red and brownish-red, these later hemispheroids are mostly grey and brown and some may have been burnt. The heights range from 1.1 to 2.4 cm, the diameters vary from 2.1 to 4.6 cm and the weights range from 20.0 to *c*. 49.05 g.

The decoration, with groups of arcs forming stars, is related to that of the 'spinning tops', the other category where the top and bottom are clearly differentiated, but the V-shaped decoration is missing. The domed base of the hemispheroids is, however, more frequently decorated than the bottom of the 'spinning tops'.

The hemispheroid spindle whorls in the undecorated category a) were both found in Byzantine levels. The decorated hemispheroids in category b) should probably be dated to the Late Bronze and Iron Ages. The only spindle whorls from Kilise Tepe made of materials other than clay are hemispheroids and they are discussed separately in category c) below.

a) Undecorated hemispheroids (**1984–5**)
1984　　　　　I19/31　　　　　　　　　　1753
Level I
Grey, grit-tempered clay.
H. 1.9; Di. 3.7; Di. perf. 1.05, 0.85; Wt 25.5

1985　　　　　K20/59　　　　　　　　　　1906
Level I
Upper part curving in slightly; half remains. Grey-black burnt clay with very fine inclusions. Surface smoothed.
H. 2.3; Di. 3.9; Di. perf. 0.75, 0.6; Wt (16.5)

b) Decorated hemispheroids (**1986–92**)
1986　　　　　H19/152　　　　　　　　　4243
Level IIIa
Pinky-cream clay with small red grits; chipped. Base is flat. Widest diameter is 0.8 from base. Three (originally four) groups of four incised arcs on top.
H. 2.6; Di. 3.5; Di. perf. 0.7; Wt (24.4)

1987　　　　　I20/38　　　　KLT 34　　　1436
Level II/IIIe
Slightly ovoid, decorated; top worn, bottom chipped. Brownish-red, grit-tempered clay with largish red and white grits (<5 mm). Surface pinkish-beige. Three spaced groups of four or five incised arcs on the top.
H. 2.4; Di. 4.6; Di. perf. 0.8, 0.5; Wt 49.05

1988　　　　　I14/156　　　　　　　　　3704
Level 2/3
Flat-based, lobed; chipped. Light greyish-brown clay. Some small incisions on the top, and deeply-incised lines on the sides, from top to bottom defining lobes and extending onto the base up to the perforation.
H. 1.5; Di. 2.1; Di. perf. 0.67, 0.69; Wt (4.3)

1989　　　　　K20/135　　　　　　　　　1943
Level IIc/d
Concave top; very worn. Dark greyish-brown clay, grit-tempered with some calcareous inclusions. Surface black. Top originally decorated with five(?) double arcs of which traces of four remain.
H. 1.8; Di. 3.6; Di. perf. 0.8, 0.75; Wt (20.0)

1990　　　　　J18/317　　　　　　　　　5846
Level IIf1
Irregular top; less than half remains. Brown clay. Pairs of arcs set around a groove on the flat top, and groups of three parallel lines on the domed base.
H. 1.9; Di. *c*. 3.0; Di. perf. 0.7; ?; Wt (6.5)

1991　　　　　K19/162　　　　KLT 103　　1591
Level I/II
Light creamy-grey hard-fired clay with fine inclusions. Top undecorated. Single straight incised lines radiate up the sides from the lower end of the perforation. Cf. **1988** which has similar decoration cut much more deeply to produce a very different lobed effect.
H. 2.1; Di. 4.4; Di. perf. 0.5, 0.55; Wt 42.5
Fig. 294

1992　　　　　99/12　　　　KLT 22　　　99
Unstratified
Creamy-white, slightly powdery clay. Top decorated with two incised lines round the edge and six adjacent arcs enclosing a star-shape. There is a single line just below the top edge from which hang four groups of triple arcs.
H. 1.3; Di. 3.3; Di. perf. 0.5, 0.4; Wt 12.2

c) Hemispheroids in materials other than clay (**1993–2000**)
These stone and bone examples all come from late levels and are probably Iron Age and later, but have no distinguishing characteristics with the exception of **1996–7**, which bear decoration. Both these were found in the same Byzantine level and both are carefully worked in bone and possibly turned on a lathe. The dating of **1997** is, however, problematic. It is a geographically widespread type with several excavated in Late Sasanian levels at Merv in Turkmenistan (Simpson *et al.* forthcoming), and one example from a Mediaeval level at Tille Höyük in eastern Turkey (Moore 1993, fig. 76:158 & p. 134). However there are also Late Bronze Age examples from Tarsus (Goldman 1956, fig. 439:104 & p. 317), Megiddo (Loud 1948, pls. 171:15, 17 from Stratum X, and 172:22 from Stratum IX), and one example from Perati in Attica. The Perati spindle whorl is described as imported (Barber 1991, 64, fig. 2.30). It is mounted near the bottom of its decorated ivory spindle and, from the photograph, it is clear that it has a deep groove around the perforation at its flat end, which Barber believes to have been the top. The context would indicate that **1997** probably

belongs to the later group and this would be confirmed if it was indeed turned on a lathe.

1993   H19/111   4231
Level IIIc
Bone. Shallow conical. Undecorated.
H. 0.9; Di. 2.8; Di. perf. 0.4; Wt 3.1

1994   J18/362   5881
Level IId
Chipped. Bone, probably from a large mammal, perhaps a femur head. Perforation damaged and off-centre.
H. 1.4; Di. 4.0; Di. perf. 0.7; Wt (9.6)

1995   J18/282   KLT 128   5829
Level IIf/f1
Black stone, probably haematite. Surface smooth.
H. 1.5; Di. 2.5; Di. perf. 0.98, 0.98; Wt 12.3

1996   J19/83   1626
Level I
Bone. The top is flat and rather uneven with circular marks from turning or polishing. The rounded base is polished apart from the slight depression round the end of the perforation. Decorated with single grooves just below the upper edge and around the bottom.
H. 0.7; Di. 2.4; Di. perf. 0.55, 0.55; Wt 4.05

1997   J19/79   KLT 48   1626
Level I
Bone or ivory. Round the centre there is a row of six unevenly-spaced double circles round a pierced central dot, with two opposite each other damaged. One groove above and three below. Uneven pink staining over the base.
H. 1.84; Di. 2.4; Di. perf. 0.92, 0.87; Wt 9.8

1998   J19/125   1653
Level I
Fossilized sea urchin which has been drilled through from both ends and reused as a spindle whorl.
H. 1.7; Di. 3.0; Di. perf. 0.8, 0.7–0.75; Wt 20.0

1999   N12/8   KLT 35   3200
Surface
Shallow. Hard stone which is black at the surface but dark brown where chipped, and has minute 'gold' inclusions visible on the rougher under side.
H. 1.2; Di. 3.3; Di. perf. 0.8, 0.8; Wt 20.9

2000   Q20/17   KLT 24   184
Surface
Shallow; chipped. Dark greenish-black stone (chlorite?). Perforation slightly off-centre at bottom. Well polished, slightly chipped around edge and upper surface.
H. 1.2; Di. 2.7; Di. perf. 0.5, 0.4; Wt (11.3)

Chapter 38

Beads

Dominique Collon & Dorit Symington

In the absence of graves almost all our beads are not surprisingly stray finds, found singly. Exceptions are the four beads found with the silver figurine in Rm 20 destruction debris (two beads, **2018**; bead fragment **2035**; **2043**), the two lozenge-shaped beads **2070**, a pair of small annular beads **2054**, and three beads found in a flotation sample from beneath the IIc floor of Rm 3 (**2033** and **2051**). Some of the smallest beads and fragments were recovered (and could only have been recovered) through flotation and sieving. This is mentioned in each relevant entry.

The majority of the beads from Kilise Tepe come from Levels I and II and are almost all made of glass or some other composition material (**2017–79**). Beads in other materials come predominantly from the earlier levels, and are listed first.

Clay, stone, copper and shell

In the earlier levels the beads are made in a variety of materials of which stone and clay are the most frequent, followed by shell, and a single copper bead.

The clay beads (**2001–3**) are all decorated with incised patterns known from the spindle whorl repertoire and, indeed, the distinction between the two categories is not always easily made (see p. 440). They are all bi-conoid, the classic shape for whorls and beads at Anatolian sites during the Early Bronze Age, particularly in the earlier part.

Cylindrical beads are made in a variety of materials, such as stone and shell. The only hemispherical example is made in shell (**2008**) and is contextually one of our earliest beads, dated to EB II.

Bi-conoid
2001   H20/931   KLT 136   5369
Level Vf base
Black clay bead of bi-conoid shape with pronounced carination and central perforation. Fine fabric, dark brown. Surface slipped and slightly burnished. Blackened on one side, possibly through baking. Decorated on both sides with a series of impressed circles which have traces of white filling.
H. 1.4; Di. 1.6; Di. perf. 0.2

2002   H20/825   5328
Level Vf4, from flotation
Small clay biconoid bead fragment, cream-coloured. Fired. Central perforation. Decorated with sets of triple ovals — 'eye' motif on its side.
H. 1.97; Di. (1.8); Di. perf. 0.3–0.4
Fig. 295

[2003]   H20/1086   1260
Unstratified
Bead of orange clay of medium density with calcareous inclusions. Bi-conoid shape with sharp carination. Decorated with four incised concentric circles arranged on one side and three on the other.
H. 1.7; Di. 1.9; Di. perf. 0.3

Cylindrical
[2004]   H20/1000 Etkülük 1998   5394
Level Vf
Very small cylindrical black stone bead with central perforation. Undecorated. Chipped at one end.
L. 0.95; Di. 0.6; Di. perf. 0.1

[2005]   H20/337   1810
Level Ve/f
Small cylindrical bead of white stone(?) with a small hole drilled off-centre.
L. 0.4; Di. 0.41; Di. perf. 0.11

[2006]   H20/241   1258
Level IVa
Bead of tubular white shell; intact at narrower end, broken at other. Polished.
L. 1.6; Di. 0.24–0.33; Di. perf. 0.2

2007   H19/293   4261
Level IVa/b
Small copper bead. Oval piece of metal folded to form a bead. Heavily corroded.
L. 0.6

Miscellaneous shapes
2008   H20/969   KLT 137   5384
Level Vg
Truncated hemispherical bead made from a thin shell, with rather large perforation. The underside shows fine circular toolmarks.
H. 0.5; Di. 1.7; Di. perf. 0.4

[2009]   H19/254   4257
Level IVa/b
Fragment of a spherical(?) black stone or clay bead, broken in half horizontally with a central perforation. Surface matt.
Th. (0.8); Di. 1.7; Di. perf. 0.3

Chapter 38

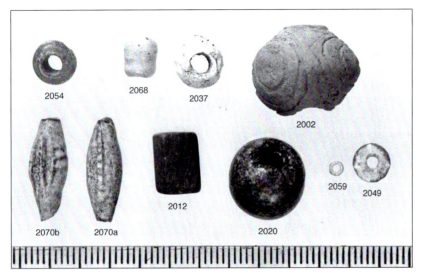

Figure 295. *Assorted beads from Level II (except **2002** from Vf). From top left: **2054**, **2068**, **2037**, **2002**; **2070** x 2, **2012**, **2020**, **2059**, **2049**.*

[2010] I19/186 5526
Level II/III
Orange, stone(?), approximately square and very irregular.
H. 0.15; 0.35 × 0.4

[2011] K20/173 1971
Level IIb, from flotation
Grey, streaked stone(?), possibly imitating, or fossilized, dentalian.
H. 0.2; Di. 0.5

2012 K19/146 KLT 94 1572
Level IIc
Small, orange-brown, veined stone with polished surface and perforation drilled from both ends slightly off-centre. Rectangular with two of the sides sloping slightly in the same direction.
H. 0.95; W. 0.65; Th. 0.45
Fig. 295

[2013] K20/130 1942
Level IIc/d
Fragment of a bead(?), made of light brown stone with a polished surface. The shape is rounded but not of even thickness. It is too small to determine the original form.

[2014] R18/215 2464
Level E5b
Elongated and vertically-ridged tubular shell fragment which could have been used as a bead. Small end smooth; other end broken.
L. 1.56; Di. 0.55–0.65

[2015] R18/258 2463
Level E5c
Dentalian.
H. 0.35; Di. 0.35

[2016] K20/1 1100
Topsoil
Fragment; buff-coloured stone or shell tube, dentalian(?). Broken at both ends.
L. (0.95); Di. 0.62

Glass, frit or faience

From the first phase of Level II onwards the earlier materials are almost completely replaced by glass, or sometimes perhaps frit or faience (see Moorey 1994, 168 for the problems surrounding the terminology of frit and similar materials. None of our pieces has been subjected to laboratory analysis and with very small white beads it is sometimes difficult to tell with the naked eye, if they are unbroken, whether they are faience, frit or glass). Very few such beads are recorded from Level III or earlier. With items so small it is difficult to be certain that they are securely stratified, but there is no particular reason to doubt the provenance of **2027–8**, **2057** from Level IIIc in H19, **2066** from Level 3 in I14, or **2044** from Vf.

The glass is opaque and may have been so in antiquity since the glass bangles (**2116–57**) are still mostly translucent. The smaller glass beads are often of very irregular height, culminating in a point where the bead was pulled away from the molten glass (e.g. **2038**). All are perforated. However, as demonstrated by Küçükerman (1988), the process of glass bead manufacture in Turkey has remained virtually unchanged until the present, so that dating according to technological development is inappropriate.

Spheroid (ratio of height to diameter not less than 2:3)
[2017] I20/46 4001
Level IIb–e
Yellowish-pink.
Di. 0.4

[2018] K19/350 4553
Level IIc
Two complete but burnt beads of similar size, now white but one with traces of yellow.
H. 0.6, 0.6; Di. 0.75, 0.8

[2019] K20/131 1942
Level IIc/d
White.
H. 1.05; Di. 1.3

2020 J18/178 KLT 95 2377
Level IIf?
Small, spherical bead. The surface is the silvery to dark grey colour of discoloured glass.
H. 1.15; Di. 1.25
Fig. 295

[2021]   K14/153   3087
Level 2 lower
White.
H. 0.3; Di. 0.45

[2022]   H18/90   2625
Level I/II
Turquoise, now black, with yellow blotches.
H. 0.8; Di. c. 1.1

[2023]   J19/62   1621
Level I
White; plus some tiny fragments.
Di. 0.66

2024   J14/29   3314
Level 1
Complete, concretions on the surface.
H. 1.29; Di. 1.41

Round tabular
2025   K20/163   1965
Level IIb
Almost circular; white with black lines across. Perforated from top to bottom.
H. 1.02; W. 1.22; Th. 0.45; Di. perf. 0.2

Lobed spheroid
2026   K20/94   1918
Level IIe
Opaque, black. Longitudinal grooves producing a five-lobed rosette in cross-section; somewhat uneven in shape.
H. 1.0; Di. 1.15

Ovoid (ratio of height to diameter about 1:2 or less)
Similar beads are still made near Idlib in Syria and in Lebanon (Simpson 1999).

[2027]   H19/41   4209
Level IIIc/d
Fragments; complete; mottled bluish-grey.
H. 0.2–0.3; Di. 0.6

[2028]   H19/45   4209
Level IIIc/d
Complete; white.
H. 0.2–0.3; Di. 0.5

[2029]   I19/174   5519
Level IIIe
Complete; white.
H. 0.15–0.2; Di. 0.5

[2030]   I19/158   5501
Level IIa, from flotation
Complete, but broken; cream.
H. 0.15; Di. 0.39

[2031]   I19/145   2883
Level IIb
Complete; white with a large perforation (c. 0.23).
H. 0.12–0.21; Di. 0.45

[2032]   J19/372   3963
Level IIb
Complete but broken; cream.
H. 0.3; Di. 0.6

2033a-b   K19/345a   4551
Level IIb, from flotation
Two ovoids; complete; creamy yellow. Found with an annular bead (2051).
a) H. 0.11–0.23; Di. 0.4
b) H. 0.09–0.13; Di. 0.35

[2034]   K20/168   1971
Level IIb
Complete; orangey-pink.
H. 0.33; Di. 0.66

[2035]   K19/351   4553
Level IIc
Heavily burnt and mis-shaped.
Di. 0.9

[2036]   I19/100   2814
Level IIf
Complete; purplish-black.
H. 0.2–0.5; Di. 0.42

[2037]   J18/214   2392
Level IIf1
Complete; white with an excrescence on one side, possibly due to weathering.
H. 0.47; Di. 0.8
Fig. 295

2038   J18/236   2370
Level IIf
Complete; white.
H. 0.24–0.9; Di. 0.41

[2039]   I14/191   3446
Level 2
Cream glass(?), with a groove around the perforation at one end.
H. 0.3–0.34; Di. 0.58

[2040]   K14/152   3083
Level 2 middle
Complete; grey.
H. 0.21; Di. 0.5

[2041]   R18/175   2436
Level E5b
Turquoise glass.
H. 0.2; Di. 0.6

2042   I14/11   3401
Level 1
Complete; black with median, undulating, white band, ending in an eye-shape on one side.
H. 1.0; Di. 0.53

Double conoid
2043   K19/349   4553
Level IIc
Complete, but irregular in shape with slanted perforation. Probably

originally turquoise but burnt black, yellow and green.
H. 1.2; Di. 1.6

Annular (diameter greater than height; mostly straight-sided)
[2044] H20/807 5310
Level Vf4
Circular frit bead with central perforation.
Di. 0.4; Di. perf. 0.15

[2045] I19/169 5526
Level II/III
Turquoise.
H. 0.09; Di. 0.6

[2046   number not used]

[2047] K20/189 1986
Level IIa?
Very pale turquoise, almost white.
H. 0.15; Di. 0.44

[2048] J20/103a 1370
Level IIa/b
Complete; pale blue.
H. 0.15; Di. 0.62; Di. perf. 0.33

[2049] J20/135 1365
Level IIb
Turquoise.
H. 0.08; Di. 0.6
Fig. 295

[2050] J19/393 Etütlük 1998 3981
Level IIb
Small annular bead of blue faience.
H. 0.2; Di. 0.4

[2051] K19/345b 4551
Level IIb, from flotation
Complete; white. Found with two ovoids (2033).
H. 0.1; Di. 0.5

2052 K20/116 1935
Level IIb
Complete; pale blue.
H. 0.1; Di. 0.55; Di. perf. 0.24

[2053] K20/44 1135
Level IIc?
Two annular; complete; pale turquoise.
H. 0.2, 0.2; Di. 0.5, 0.7; Di. perf. 0.2, 0.2

2054 J18/224 KLT 96 2394
Level IIe
Small, circular, thin bead. Light green, fairly translucent glass. There are two small projections, one at each end of the bead, due to the process of manufacture.
H. 0.3; Di. 0.7
Fig. 295

[2055] K14/177 3067
Level 2 upper, from flotation
Complete; turquoise-blue.
H. 0.17; Di. 0.3

[2056] I14/195 3446
Level 2, from flotation
Small annular bead in a white material.
Di. 0.6; Di. perf. 0.2

Cylindrical (diameter less than height)
2057 H19/100 4229
Level IIIc
Acid green.
H. 1.93; Di. 0.73

[2058] I14/168 3705
Level 3
Complete; turquoise.
H. 0.2; Di. 0.36

[2059] J20/160 1395
Level IIa/b
Complete; turquoise.
H. 0.14; Di. 0.24
Fig. 295

[2060] K19/322 4535
Level IIb/c
Brick-red material, possibly not glass, with very small perforation; surface and ends missing.
H. (0.45); Di. 0.32

[2061] I19/114 2848
Level IIc
Complete; grey.
H. 0.8; Di. 0.43

[2062] J18/321 5854
Level IIe
Two joining pieces. Dark brown (where broken) glass with concretions, tapering with the wider end rounded and a tiny hole for the perforation at that end.
H. 1.34; Di. 0.42–0.49

[2063] I19/211 2806
Level IIe–h
Complete; turquoise.
H. 0.25; Di. 0.38

[2064] K14/132 3078
Level 2 middle
Black with white streaks.
Di. 0.45

[2065] K20/5 1101
Topsoil
Complete; powdery turquoise, perhaps faience, squashed into a roughly triangular shape.
H. 1.29; Di. 0.9

Grooved cylinder
2066 I14/186 3708
Level 3
Complete, very pale turquoise or white; divided into two equal halves by a median groove. Perhaps intended as two separate beads which fused together or did not separate.
H. 0.45; Di. 0.35

2067 J20/127 1363
Level IIb–d
Complete; white with a spiral groove running around it about seven times, the result of twisting the glass tube upon itself.
H. 1.3; Di. 0.6

2068 K19/208 KLT 98 4509
Level IIc
Small, white bead, cylindrical with shallow groove round it. Made of similar material to bead **2067**.
H. 0.6; Di. 0.5
Fig. 295

Barrel-shaped
2069 R18/210 2462
Level E5c
Complete; white with a band of black wrapped spirally around three times.
H. 1.33; Di. 0.9

Miscellaneous shapes
2070 J20/161a, b KLT 97 1395
Level IIa/b
Two dark blue glass beads. Long, tubular and lozenge-shaped, with rounded sides and two slightly flattened faces. Central, longitudinal perforation. J20/161a is decorated with a groove running along the centre of each flattened face. On one side the groove is segmented by further parallel grooves within it, at 90 degrees to it forming a ladder pattern. The other bead, J20/161b, has two grooves running down one of its faces, one of which has dots in it. Around the sides of this bead are several parallel, perpendicular grooves. These stop on the other face which has a short groove to one side and a longer one with diagonal lines across it.
J20/161a: L. 1.68; Di. of ends 0.25; W. 0.6 max.; Th. 0.45 max.
J20/161b: L. 1.65; Di. of ends 0.3; W. 0.63 max.; Th. 0.48 max.
Fig. 295

[**2071**] J20/103b 1370
Level IIa/b
Complete; white, made from an asymmetrical dollop of glass, with sloping perforation. From one angle, it (probably unintentionally) resembles a jug with a handle.
H. 0.66; Di. 0.85–1.05

[**2072**] K20/147 1945
Level IIc
Irregularly-shaped bead probably made of white glass.
H. 0.9; L. 1.1; Di. perf. 0.25

2073 J20/69 KLT 47 1342
Level IId–f
Small glass bead in the shape of a pendent pointed leaf with a horizontal perforation at the other end. The perforated part is blue, and the leaf itself is yellow at the centre and light green around the edges. The back is flat, with a projecting lump at the tip. The front is impressed with a leaf pattern: a central groove from which extend diagonal grooved veins angled towards the point.
L. 1.6; W. 0.45 max.; Th. 0.15–0-2

2074 I19/18 1712
Level IIc/d
Complete; bluish-grey glass, one face convex with deckled edges, the other flat.
Di. 1.23–1.34; Di. of perf. 0.24

Unidentifiable fragments
[**2075**] I20/54 4004
Level IIb
Small spheroid bead or barrel; white.

[**2076**] J19/298 3927
Level IIc
Turquoise; originally quite large.

[**2077**] J19/326 3927
Level IIc, from flotation
Very small; black.
Di. 0.5

[**2078**] K20/140 1944
Level IIc
White glass(?).
Di. 0.4

2079 K14/135 3087
Level 2 lower
Two fragments of large spheroid(?), not joined; perhaps originally green or blue (now black), with a yellow line, probably around the middle, bordered by white arcs.
H. (1.6)

Chapter 39

Glass

Dominique Collon

Level II

Other than beads, only one fragment of glass (**2080**) was definitely of Iron Age date. This surface find is a sherd which stands out from the others due to its brilliant royal blue colour with a band of yellow and two wavy strands of pale blue across it. It is probably from a vessel of the sixth to fourth centuries BC when this combination of colours and type of decoration was particularly common. Such vessels were probably made in Phoenician workshops and were exported throughout the Mediterranean. Unfortunately, without evidence for the shape, a closer dating is impossible. For parallels, see Barag 1985, nos. 80–89, pls. 10–11.

2080   O20/7   185
2.4 × 2.7; Th. 0.35

Later glass

All the remaining pieces of glass came from the surface, topsoil, or Level I. Only a small selection of characteristic pieces is listed here: a full list of the distribution by square and unit will be found at the end of this section. Sherds of glass were usually grouped together under a single find number by the excavators, and for the purposes of the publication individual sherds have been given supplementary letters (e.g. K18/195a) although these have not been marked on the pieces themselves. See also Chapters 38 (Beads), and 40 (Mosaic Tesserae, which are predominantly made of glass).

Vessels
The glass from Kilise Tepe is in the form of small fragments; no complete profile of a glass vessel can be reconstructed, or anything approaching it. This poor state of preservation is probably due to the fact that the glass belongs to the latest level of the site and was damaged throughout the centuries by successive robbing or ploughing operations. Glass was frequently melted down and recycled and a wreck of the Islamic period (eleventh century AD) carrying glass for such a purpose has been recovered (Bass 1984). There is, furthermore, evidence that glass vessels were being cut up to provide cubes for mosaics for one of the Byzantine churches (see p. 511). It seems probable, therefore, that the glass belongs to the early Byzantine occupation of the site, but as only one possible waster was found, in K18/191, it is unlikely that it was manufactured on the site.

The assemblage from unit 4393 (K18/191) is typical of those found — 37 fragments: 4 rims made of discoloured, clear glass; 3 decorated fragments (2 from the same object), green glass with ridge decoration; 1 rim with ridge decoration; 28 discoloured, clear glass fragments; 1 clear green glass fragment.

The indented cups and cups with ribs discussed by Stern (1989) as probably or possibly being products of Roman Cilicia do not seem to be represented at Kilise Tepe.

Colour
The dominant colours are pale blue (over 120 fragments) and three shades of green (45 pale green; 30 olive green, 25 mid green — these numbers are approximate). There are also almost 200 fragments of 'clear glass'; all are very badly weathered, with dark blotches, so that the clarity of the glass can only be seen by holding the fragment to the light. However, in view of the way most of these fragments reflect green (or occasionally blue) light, it may be that their present 'colourless' state has been produced by weathering. This could explain the discrepancy between the predominance of clear body and rim fragments, most of them very thin, and the virtually absent bases of colourless glass, where the glass is thicker and better preserved. Two fragments, one yellow (**2092**) and one brown (**2082**), are anomalous; neither, however, looks recent, and the yellow fragment in **2092** bears a small fragment of decoration in blue. A small, olive green fragment, one of four sherds in **2081**, has what looks like a pointed leaf of dark blue glass applied to it but this could be accidental.

For a discussion of glass from sites in Cilicia, and the relevance of colour, see Tobin 2004, 82–3.

[2081] K18/195 4393
Sherd of olive green glass with an irregularly-shaped ridge of dark blue glaze applied to it.

[2082] K14/56a 3016
Rim sherd of brown transparent glass. **2086** was found with it.
H. (1.9); W. (3.4); Th. at rim 0.1

Rims
These are only slightly thickened. In contrast to what so frequently occurs elsewhere, for example in the atrium church of probable fifth- to sixth-century date at Apamea-on-the-Orontes (Napoleone-Lemaire & Balty 1969, e.g. figs. 18: 1–3, 8–13, 19:1–4, 8–10), there are but three cases where a rim is formed by folding the glass over, **2083–4** which are both very fragmentary, and **2199** (reused as a mosaic tessera with gilding added). Often only the very tops of the rims survive but it seems that they belonged to thin-walled, straight-sided (**2085**) or only slightly-flaring vessels, with diameters (when these can be measured) between 6 and 13 cm but clustering around 8 cm. One rim of green glass flares out more sharply near the top (**2086**).

[2083] H18/6 2601
Clear, green.

[2084] K16/35 4812
Green.
Di. 16

2085 J18/114a 2343
Pale blue.

2086 K14/56b 3016
Green. **2082** was found with it.
Di. 7.0

Body fragments
There is very little evidence for the shapes of the vessels. Six fragments belong to fairly straight-sided vessels and then swell out (without any thickening of the glass), but here they are broken and no rims are preserved. Four fragments of thicker glass are flat and curved over to form a letter C (**2087–90**); interestingly, they all come from square K18 but without knowing more about the shape it is impossible to ascertain whether this is significant in any way. There is a parallel from Apamea-on-the-Orontes, also broken (Napoleone-Lemaire & Balty 1969, fig. 27:14). There are flat-based bottles from Sardis (von Saldern 1980, pls. 6: 13, 8:155), but one is eggshell glass and has a ring base, while the other has a concave base (**2107–8** inverted), and both lack the thickened curve of the

Kilise Tepe and Apamea fragments; furthermore, the Sardis pieces come from first- to second-century deposits which are probably not present at Kilise Tepe. Three fragments are S-shaped and must have belonged to globular bottles (**2093**). Several fragments survive of the neck of a bottle of pale blue glass with a very thin line of white trailed decoration around it (**2091**). Other fragments are shaped but are too small for any comment to be possible.

2087 K18/12 4302
Pale blue.

2088 K18/29 4309
Pale green.

2089 K18/48 4316
Olive green.

2090 K18/59 4320
Pale blue.

2091 K19/434a 1501
Pale blue with a very thin line of white trailed glass decoration wound around.
Di. 2.3

2092 L8/2 318
Yellow with small fragment of blue decoration.

2093 L14/28 3608
Pale blue; three fragments from the same vessel.

Handles
Only ten small handles have been preserved and even these are mostly broken; they were attached to thin-walled vessels, of which the profiles cannot be reconstructed. They were made by applying thick molten glass to the side of the vessel, drawing it into shape, applying the lower end to the vessel and twisting it off (**2094–5, 2097–101, 2103**). One piece of green glass with relief decoration has a smoothed edge and may be part of an applied handle (**2102**). One anomalous handle of pale olive glass is flat and straight but its ends are missing (**2096**). Another strap handle of clear glass is curved (**2099**).

2094 H20/180 1253
Level IVa/b
Clear.
W. 0.5
Fig. 296

2095 I16/17 4601
Olive green.
L. 3.0; W. 0.5

2096 K8/10 315
Green.
L. (4.0); W. 1.5 max.
Fig. 296

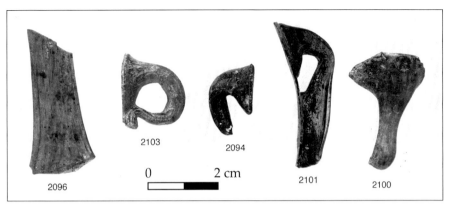

Figure 296. *Glass handles. From left: 2096, 2103, 2094, 2101, 2100.*

2097   K17/79   9659
Pale green.
L. 2.6

2098   K18/60   4320
Pale green.

[2099]   K18/182   4391
Clear glass.

2100   K19/434b   1501
Pale blue.
H. 3.3; W. 2.2, W. of handle 0.6; Th. 0.9, Th. of handle 0.4.
Fig. 296

2101   K19/430   1501
Pale green.
L. 5.0
Fig. 296

2102   L14/1   3600
Green.
L. (1.5); W. (2.0)

2103   99/19   99
Pale blue.
W. 2.0
Fig. 296

Bases

These are thicker than the rims but scarcely better preserved. Some 23 consist of a hollow circle with a diameter between 3.5 and 9.0 cm but clustering around 5.0 cm (**2110** and **2113**); 5 other bases are variants. From this circle, the foot rises towards a stem which is preserved in only five cases (**2104, 2106, 2110** and **2113–14**). The poor preservation of these stems is surprising since they are generally tubes of thicker glass and should survive well even if their ends are frequently broken off, but only one broken piece was identified. One of the variant bases belonged to a flat-edged foot or to a lid, with a diameter of 17.0 cm. There are also two ring-bases, one small and low (di. 5.0) and one high (**2112**), two heavy-ridged bases (**2109** and **2111**), a small fragment of a foot with relief decoration in the form of a leaf (**2105**) and two shallow pointed bases (**2107–8**).

2104   I14/9   3401
Green; part of base and stem.
H. (2.6); W. (2.9); Th. 0.3

2105   I18/6   2701
Green; fragment of base with incised lines decorating the upper surface.
Di. 8.0; W. 2.4

2106   J16/8   4600
Green; stem.
L. (4.4); W. (2.9)

2107   J18/114b   2343
Clear; shallow pointed base fragment.

2108   J18/132a   2350
Level IIf
Clear; shallow pointed base.

2109   K10/7   226
Green; horizontally ribbed base.
Di. 11.0

2110   K14/46   3013
Pale blue; part of a foot and stem.

2111   K17/72   9657
Olive green; fragment of horizontally ridged base.
Di. 8.5

2112   K19/8c   1501
Green; part of a ring base.
Di. 10.0

2113   L19/12   5907
Pale blue; base and part of stem.
Di. 4.0; H. 2.8; Th. of edge 0.43

2114   S18/5   177
Clear; part of stem and base.
H. (1.9); W. (2.3); Th. 0.3

[2115]   K19/431   1501
Base and lower part of an egg-shaped vessel; probably not ancient.

Bangles

Not surprisingly, only one complete bangle has been recovered and of the others only fragments remain. The bangles seem to have been round rather than oval, and the internal diameter of the bangle has been given wherever the fragment is large enough, together with the measurements of the width and thickness of the bangle. Most are flat on the inner face and rounded on the outer face into an elongated D-shape when seen in section, but sometimes the D resembles a triangle set on its side, and some bangles are round, oval or square in section. Unless otherwise stated, the bangles should be taken as being of the elongated D-shape. Most are in a royal blue glass or a slightly paler version of this; more rarely the glass is ultramarine or bright green. These colours are not attested for glass vessels. This could reflect a chronological difference but since glasses and bangles were often recovered from the same units, it is more likely to reflect fashion and the working-practices of different workshops. Some of the bangles are decorated but as the decoration is restricted to the very surface of the glass it was probably painted on subsequent to manufacture. Drawings have been made of all the decorated bangle fragments, except where only traces of the decoration are visible. The small diameters of many of these bangles would indicate that they belonged to children. The majority have been found in J19, either in the topsoil, in Byzantine levels or in Byzantine pits. The five from pits might have come from discarded material from disturbed burials but corroborative evidence is lacking since these pits contained only unidentifiable bone fragments recovered from sieving. Several bangles were also found in J18, an adjacent square.

Bangles are a feature of Late Roman and Byzantine sites from the third century AD onwards. There are two main types: the seamless ones are streaked vertically on the interior and often have rust spots on them, probably from the metal tool used to make them; the seamed bangles are made by bending and closing a glass cane. There is no evidence for seamless bangles at Kilise Tepe, and the only complete bangle (**2157**) is clearly of the seamed type. The bangles of Palestine have received the most attention recently, but the glass is predominantly black, possibly in imitation of jet, and the decoration is twisted, trailed and fused; neither the Pre-Islamic (Spaer 1988), nor the Islamic examples (Spaer 1992) provide close parallels for the distinctive translucent royal-blue glass and type of 'painted' decoration. Only two bangle fragments were recorded from Early Byzantine levels at Sardis, and one of these was of blue glass, but it had a bi-conical section unparalleled at Kilise Tepe (von Saldern 1980,

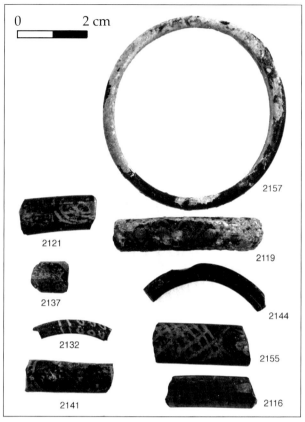

Figure 297. *Glass bangles. Left, from top:* **2121**, **2137**, **2132**, **2141**; *Right, from top:* **2157**, **2119**, **2144**, **2155**, **2116**.

no. 679, p. 91 & pl. 16). Among the more than forty Middle Byzantine bangles of the tenth–fourteenth centuries AD from Sardis, there are only four of blue glass: three of them are plain and the last has 'painted' decoration which sounds similar but had not been seen by von Saldern (1980, 98–101, esp. nos. 776–9). The bangles from medieval Harran are also different (Rice 1952, 72–3, nos. 26–35). There are two blue glass bangles from Boğazköy, apparently from a Phrygian level and therefore presumably not of translucent glass (Boehmer 1972, nos. 1852–3).

[**2116**]   I14/4   3400
Blue.
Di. 5; W. 0.85; Th. 0.35
Fig. 297

[**2117**]   I14/54   3424
Level 2k
Royal blue.
Di. 8; W. 1.8; Th. 0.32

[**2118**]   I19/23   1732
Blue, minute fragment; oval in section.
W. 0.6; Th. 0.4

Glass

2119   J16/3   4600
Ultramarine; pale blue decoration of adjacent diamond shapes with dots in their centre, and a band along either side.
Di. 7; W. 0.89; Th. 0.56
Fig. 297

[2120]   J16/33   4700
Blue, now iridescent, two fragments; oval in section.
Di. 5; W. 0.44; Th. 0.38

2121   J18/27   2307
Emerald green; elongated oval in section; white decoration.
Di. 5; W. 0.99; Th. 0.43
Fig. 297

[2122]   J18/36   2308
Blue, very small fragment; oval in section; pale yellowish linear decoration.
W. (0.8); Th. 0.7

[2123]   J18/46   2310
Blue, weathered; kidney-shaped in section due to groove on int.; faint traces of white decoration (perhaps transverse lines) framing red zigzag.
Di. 6; W. 0.63; Th. 0.56

[2124]   J18/53   2311
Ultramarine; twisted glass; round in section with a diameter of 0.7.
Di. 6

[2125]   J18/121a   2344
Level I/II?
Now weathered to grey; approximately round in section with a diameter of 0.53.
Di. 5

[2126]   J18/121b   2344
Level I/II?
Now weathered to grey; approximately round in section with a diameter of 0.7.
Di. 8

[2127]   J18/132b   2350
Blue; elongated oval (broken) in section; white lines. [Some doubt as to correct provenance — originally recorded as from unit 2356.]
W. 0.69

[2128]   J19/12   1601
Dark green glass, now very weathered; oval in section; traces of arcs of white paint on the edge but design not clear because of incrustation.
Di. 8; W. 0.85; Th. 0.6

[2129]   J19/19   1602
Royal blue, now iridescent; elongated kidney-shape in section.
Di. 8; W. 1.1; Th. 0.32

[2130]   J19/33   1605
Blue glass, now iridescent, two fragments from same bangle; one diameter 4, the other of irregular shape, oval in section.
W. 0.44; Th. 0.35

[2131]   J19/38   1609
Now black with grey streaks.
Di. 4; W. 0.74; Th. 0.3

2132   J19/43b   1609
Blue glass, square in section with sides 0.35; three outer sides decorated with yellow lines and circles.
Di. 5
Fig. 297

[2133]   J19/48   1610
Probably pale blue, now dark and very iridescent; traces of white scalloped lines along one side.
Di. 7; W. 0.91; Th. 0.72

[2134]   J19/68   1622
Probably blue, now black.
Di. 6.5; W. 1.1; Th. 0.41

[2135]   J19/71a   1626
Pale blue; round in section with a diameter of 0.84.

[2136]   J19/71b   1626
Blue; elongated oval in section with irregular ridge on ext.; traces of the central part of an elongated figure-of-eight decoration in pale blue paint with traces of pale blue paint in one part and red paint in the other.
Di. 5; W. 1.1; Th. 0.36

[2137]   J19/85a   1626
Green, very small fragment; traces of green decoration (a flake — perhaps from this bracelet — bears an eye motif with dots instead of lashes).
Fig. 297

[2138]   J19/85b, c, d   1626
Blue, three very small fragments.

2139   J19/85e   1626
Blue, very small fragment; round in section with a diameter of 0.87; decorated with a red and pale blue design.

[2140]   J19/99   1641
Blue glass, now iridescent; almost round in section.
Di. 7; W. 0.66; Th. 0.58

2141   J19/104   1650
Blue; decorated with red and pale blue design.
Di. 13; W. 0.87; Th. 6.9
Fig. 297

[2142]   J19/105   1650
Discoloured; oval in section.
Di. 6; W. 0.84; Th. 0.71

[2143]   J19/140a   1653
Green; rounded triangular section.
W. 1.0; Th. 0.57

[2144]   J19/142   1661
Royal blue; ridged triangular D-section.
Di. 3; W. 0.85; Th. 0.53
Fig. 297

[2145]   J19/145   1662
Level IIf
Royal blue; oval in section.
W. 0.84; Th. 0.56

[2146]   K16/17   4804
Now dark grey; oval in section.
Di. 8; W. 0.62; Th. 0.5

[2147]   K16/24   4805
Blue, now iridescent; round in section with a diameter of 0.7.
Di. 6

[2148]   K17/44   9624
Discoloured; round in section with a diameter of 0.35; groove twisting round it.
Di. 5

[2149]   K17/58   9643
Blue; with swelling at one end to 0.7; elongated oval in section.
Di. 5; W. 0.62

[2150]   K18/31   4308
Royal blue, three minute fragments, probably from a bangle.

[2151]   K19/8d   1501
Green; almost round in section.
Di. 5; W. 0.5; Th. 0.45

[2152]   K19/107a   1564
Blue.
W. 1.5; Th. 0.4

[2153]   K19/107b   1564
Green and yellow (possibly the result of weathering) divided lengthways; triangular D-shaped section.
W. 0.7; Th. 0.4

[2154]   Q19/2   173
Royal blue.
W. 0.96

2155   Q19/8   178
Royal blue; decorated in pale blue.
Di. 6; W. 1.06; Th. 0.53
Fig. 297

[2156]   Q20/16   184
Royal blue, exceptionally transparent.
Di. 7; W. 0.39

2157   S18/4   2500
Blue glass, the only complete example; slightly thicker in one place where the two ends were joined; kidney-shaped in section; traces of a red design on a yellow ground, much flaked.
Di. 4–4.5
Fig. 297

Ring
2158   Q10/7   3100
Twisted, iridescent but perhaps originally with two strands of gold glass alternating with two of silver glass.
Di. of int. 1.3, Di. of section 0.39

Rod
[2159]   I14/43   3415
A short length of rod with both ends broken; emerald green glass, now partly iridescent.
Di. 0.35; (L.) 2.6

Glass distribution by square and unit
H18: 1805, 1812, 2600, 2601, 2606
H20: 1253
I14: 3400, 3401, 3403, 3409, 3481, 3708
I15: 4400
I16: 4600, 4601
I17: 4901
I18: 2701, 2704
I20: 1400
J14: 3319, 3326
J16: 4600, 4700
J17: 5000
J18: 2315, 2318, 2337, 2353, 2354, 2369, 2392, 5823, 5824
J19: 1600, 1602, 1604, 1605, 1609, 1610, 1622, 1626, 1627, 1641, 1644, 1650, 1653, 1656, 1661, 1696
J20: 1304, 1307, 1353, 1356
K8: 315
K14: 3000, 3001, 3002, 3003, 3004, 3012, 3014, 3015, 3016, 3078
K15: 100
K16: 4800, 4801, 4812
K17: 9603, 9643, 9656, 9657, 9659, 9666, 9671
K18: 4212, 4301, 4302, 4303, 4304, 4314, 4316, 4317, 4390, 4391, 4392, 4393, 4395, 6003, 6102
K19: 1500, 1501, 1514, 1567
K20: 1101, 1105, 1115, 1905, 1909
L8: 318
L14: 3600, 3603, 3608
L16: 5601, 5629, 5632, 5634
L17: 119, 5108
L19: 5902, 5903, 5904, 5906, 5907
M14: 191, 3501, 3504, 3506, 3507
M20: 231
N8: 331
N12: 3205, 3209
O8: 243
Q10: 3100, 3101, 3102
Q12: 220
Q18: 2201
Q19: 2102, 2103
Q20: 184, 185
R18: 2432
S18: 174, 177, 2508
T7: 255
Misc.: 99

Chapter 40

Mosaic Tesserae

Dominique Collon

Description

The distribution of the mosaic tesserae indicates that the cubes are found predominantly in the area of the church, especially at the east end of the north aisle where a group of 767 tesserae (**2199**) was recovered (see p. 190). A further 25 had previously been found in K17 units. Fewer than 60 tesserae, however, were found in all the other units put together, so it is unlikely that the church was richly decorated with mosaics.

Distribution of mosaic tesserae
H19: **2160** (162)
I14: **2161** (3455)
I16: **2165–6** (4600); **2162–4** (4601)
I18: **2167** (2703)
J16: **2168–9** (4700);
J18: **2170** (2308); **2171–3** (2311), **2174** (2337)
J19: **2175** (1602); **2176–7**, **2210** (1604); **2178** (1609); **2179** (1626), **2180–82** (1653)
K15: **2183** (100)
K16: **2184** (4812)
K17: **2185–8**, **2211** (9603); **2186** (9600); **2190** (9614); **2191–2** (9615); **2193** (9623); **2194** (9625); **2195** (9628); **2196** (9642); **2197–8**, **2212** (9643); **2199** (9682)
K18: **2200** (4300), **2201** (4393)
K20: **2202** (1909); **2203** (1942)
L16: **2204** (5601); **2205**, **2208** (5626); **2206–7** (5623)
L17: **2209** (5104)

The cubes are small, between 0.8 and 1.0 cm. They are rarely completely square, although most are fairly flat on top; thicknesses vary considerably. Some are irregularly shaped; the five small, beige or cream limestone cubes are slightly smaller than the average, however. Most tesserae are made of glass; the glass is well preserved with iridescence obscuring the original colour in many cases. The material into which the tesserae were set has not adhered to them; any discolouration is generally caused by dirt on their rougher surfaces or by the cloudiness of the glass. The following colours are represented and unless otherwise specified all these tesserae are made of glass and probably were originally transparent or translucent; the number of tesserae is indicated in brackets:

- now iridescent or dark, original colour unidentifiable (408);
- gold (189);
- blue (5);
- turquoise opaque (47);
- green transparent (24);
- green opaque (81);
- blood red opaque (17);
- black (4);
- white stone (39);
- pink stone (24);
- small beige stone (5);
- orange ceramic cut from sherds (8);
- brown clay (1).

The gold tesserae consist of a very thin coat of gold paint(?) applied to a glass base which may have been clear originally but is now generally black (or at any rate very dark). There are also thin, square slivers of dark glass with gold colouring, but whether these have broken off tesserae is not clear, since the glass of the complete tesserae appears homogeneous and not layered. The opaque, green glass tesserae range in colour from an intense shade of apple green to emerald; they are particularly irregular in shape, some of them being wedges, and may not all have been tesserae, but they differ from material used for glass vessels. The transparent, pale or olive green glass cubes, however, were made from recycled glass vessels. The only white stone cubes were recovered from **2199** but others scattered elsewhere on the site may not have been recognized.

Small fragments of glass were recovered along with the cubes from **2199** — they were probably discarded when vessels were being cut up for reuse. One square-cut piece of rim sherd of thick folded glass had been gilded while another had mortar adhering to it. As there was also a flake of pink stone, this suggests that some of the cubes were made on site.

The tesserae were recovered from very powdery, white plaster. It is unlikely that they came from a floor mosaic because the church seems to have been paved and no *terrazzo* layer has been identified. They could have adorned a cupola or an item of church furniture. One piece of flat, iridescent glass, originally square or rectangular (2.2 × 1.5+ × 0.1 cm), had part of a circle (di. 2 cm) carefully cut out of it; a piece of transparent, pale green glass (2.2 × 1.7+ × 0.4 cm) was also originally square or rectangular and a dark red layer on the back (now black where it adheres to the glass) may have been intended to be seen through it. Some 24 very small pieces of pinky-red, painted plaster were also recovered.

[2160]   H19/404   162
Turquoise-coloured glass tessera.
L. 0.9+; W.0.7+

[2161]   I14/92   3455
Level 2
Light blue glass tessera.

[2162]   I16/4   4601
Green tessera.
L. <1.0

[2163]   I16/9   4601
Discoloured glass tessera.
L. <1.0

[2164]   I16/14   4601
Small, wedge-shaped, opaque, green stone tessera with mortar attached to it.
L. <1.0

[2165]   I16/28   4600
Two small tesserae:
a) dark green glass with gold leaf on one surface. 0.9 × 0.8 × 0.4.
b) red, opaque glass, irregular in shape. 1.0 × 0.8 × 0.5.

[2166]   I16/36   4600
One fragment of plain, discoloured glass mosaic tessera. Perhaps complete.
L. 0.8

[2167]   I18/16   2703
Faience fragment. Squared tessera, turquoise in colour.
L. 0.9; W. 0.8

[2168]   J16/16   4700
One tessera of dark blue-green, weathered glass.
L. 1.0; W. 0.8

[2169]   J16/34   4700
Seven glass tesserae fragments: mixed yellow and opaque in colour.

[2170]   J18/42   2308
Small, dark red, square object, perhaps a tessera.
L. 0.9; W. 0.8

[2171]   J18/56   2311
Small fragment of clear glass tessera. Very discoloured.
L. <1.0

[2172]   J18/57   2311
A small, turquoise-coloured tessera; roughly square.
L. <1.0

[2173]   J18/62   2311
Two green tesserae.
L. <1.0

[2174]   J18/111   2337
Blue, square(ish) mosaic tessera(?).
L. <1.0

[2175]   J19/20   1602
Five small fragments, including one tessera of turquoise-coloured glass.

[2176]   J19/25   1604
Ten mosaic tesserae fragments of various types of glass. Colours include turquoise and green; plain and opaque pieces. Collected during dry sieving.
L. <1.5; W. <1.5

[2177]   J19/31   1604
Five small fragments of glass, including one lime-green tessera (0.7 × 0.8 × 0.4) and a small, very pale blue, rounded rim.

[2178]   J19/43a   2308
Three tiny tesserae fragments.

[2179]   J19/71   1626
Eleven fragments of glass tesserae, of various colours including one turquoise handle piece(?) patterned in yellow. Also one opaque, red mosaic square (incomplete).

[2180]   J19/115   1653
Square, turquoise mosaic tessera piece.
L. 0.6

[2181]   J19/124   1653
Mosaic tessera.
L. 0.5; W. 0.8

[2182]   J19/140b   1653
Tessera fragment(?).

[2183]   K15/4   100
Two irregular tesserae:
a) pink marble-like stone.
b) black glass.
L. 1.1, 0.8; W. 0.8, 0.8

[2184]   K16/34   4812
A very small fragment of greeny glass tessera.

[2185]   K17/12   9603
A squarish, opaque, black glass tessera.
L. <1.0

[2186]   K17/13   9603
Thick and opaque, very discoloured tessera.
L. 1.0

[2187]   K17/19   9603
A small, bright green tessera of a glassy type material. Perhaps a mosaic piece.
L. *c.* 1.0

[2188]   K17/20   9603
Squarish tessera of pink stone.
L. 0.8; W. 0.8

Mosaic Tesserae

[2189] K17/29 9600
Tessera.

[2190] K17/30 9614
Seven tesserae, some with gold colouring.
L. <1.0

[2191] K17/31 9615
Very thin mosaic tesserae fragments.

[2192] K17/32 9615
Tessera with evidence of green paint.
L. <1.0

[2193] K17/40 9623
Tessera with evidence of gold colouring.
L. <1.0

[2194] K17/43 9625
Tessera with gold colouring.
L. <1.0

[2195] K17/48 9628
Two very small tesserae with gold colouring.
L. <1.0

[2196] K17/57 9642
Two tesserae with evidence of gold colouring.
L. <1.0

[2197] K17/62 9643
Very small, dark coloured tessera.
L. 1.0

[2198] K17/64 9643
Four tesserae. Irregularly shaped. One blue piece, the rest of indeterminate colour.
L. <1.0

[2199] K17/94 9682
767 assorted mosaic tesserae, made of glass and stone. Colours include: cream, pink, red, green, blue, clear, gold, black. The pink and cream fragments are mostly cube shaped, the others are irregularly shaped. Pieces of plaster with pink colouring were also collected.

[2200] K18/2 4300
Rectangular, pale orange piece of tessera.
L. 1.5

[2201] K18/196 4393
Blue tessera.
L. <1.0

[2202] K20/63 1909
Level I/II
Red-coloured glass tessera.

[2203] K20/228 1942
Level IIc/d
Tiny, turquoise tesserae (<2 mm).

[2204] L16/1 5601
Two possible tesserae of same width; one turquoise blue, the other darker.
L. <1.0

[2205] L16/5 5626
Two tesserae with evidence of gold colouring.
L. <1.0

[2206] L16/13 5623
Pink stone tessera.
L. <1.0

[2207] L16/14 5623
Mosaic tessera with black and silver colouring. Also various tiny fragments of similar colour.
L. <1.0

[2208] L16/17 5626
Two tesserae with little discernible colour.
L. <1.0

[2209] L17/2 5104
Square mosaic tessera with gold colouring.
L. <1.0

The following three pieces were not studied at the same time as the others:

[2210] J19/33b 1605
Tessera of green, transparent glass with red coating on one surface; $0.9 \times 0.7 \times 0.6$

[2211] K17/21 9603
A turquoise square tessera, broken in two pieces.
L. <1.0

[2212] K17/60 9643
Irregularly-shaped tessera with glass on upper surface.
L. 1.3

Chapter 41

Metalwork

Dominique Collon & Dorit Symington

In Levels V, IV and III the only metals represented in our finds are of copper or copper alloy. No analyses have been carried out to determine the composition of the metals, and 'copper' should therefore always be understood to mean 'copper or a copper alloy'.

A surprisingly small number of metal artefacts were noted for the early periods (EBA/MBA, Levels V and IV) at Kilise Tepe. Indeed, the early layers of the EBA Level Vj–g did not produce any metal artefacts at all. This is not unusual in non-funerary third-millennium contexts, and no doubt in part reflects the fact that metal was a valuable substance which in normal circumstances could easily be recycled, and in times of crisis would be removed by the occupants. Here, as indeed throughout all periods except the later part of Level II, there is a dearth of weapons.

Probably the earliest metal artefact recovered at Kilise Tepe, from the lower layers of EB III, is a pair of copper alloy tweezers (**2276**), still in remarkably good condition and looking much like a modern counterpart. The only other noteworthy early finds are pins (**2236–8**) and needles (**2226–7**), and a metal hook (**2221**). The latter came from the same context as a number of spindle whorls (**1858, 1863**) in Rm 53 of Level Vf. The two long, round-headed pins are both neatly made and in good condition; **2237** came from an EBA/MBA transitional context, while **2238** is of MBA date. The only other copper piece from the EBA/MBA levels is **2239**.

In the later levels the metalwork was predominantly of iron, some of which was probably of fairly recent manufacture.

Copper or bronze (2213–96)

Adze
2213   J19/270   3906
Level IIc
Well-preserved adze made from a T-shaped piece of metal with the rounded arms of the T rolled so that they touch to form the socket (5.2 × 3.7 × 3.2); the blade (7.5) tapers slightly from 3.3 × 0.8 at the socket to 2.6 × 0.2 at the rounded end which was sharp.
L. 12.7; W. 3.7; Th. 0.2–0.8
Fig. 298

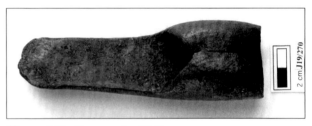

Figure 298. *Copper adze 2213.*

Similar tools are widely distributed in the Near East in the later second millennium BC (Deshayes 1960, II, pp. 62–3 and pl. XVI (esp. nos. 1207 and 1211 from Ugarit). From Boğazköy: Boehmer 1972, 134 no. 1223 with Taf. XLII, and (shape less similar) 1979, 31–2 no. 3404 with Taf. XIX.

Blade
No complete copper/bronze blade was found and only two possible blade fragments. One, however, K18/138 from Level II, is a shapeless strip and has been listed under Miscellaneous (**2296**) below.

2214   H19/181   4248
Level IIIa/IVb
Perhaps a blade or the edge of a disc-shaped object; the metal is smooth and sharp on one of the long edges.
L. 4.8; W. 0.9; Th. 0.4

Bracelets
Only one certain metal bracelet was found, although there are several coils of thick or thin wire which could have been used as bracelets (see **2255–7** and **2270** below, under Rings).

2215   K18/24   4307
Level I
Bracelet fragment with a terminal shaped like a dragon's head (1.7 × 0.9 × 0.5) with open mouth, elongated wrinkled snout, two small hollows for eyes, an inverted V incised on its head and two small lateral Vs for its ears. The juncture with the bracelet consists of a diagonally-hatched band, a plain band and three grooves; a piece of the bracelet survives (0.3 × 0.8 × 0.1), made of thin metal with the edges bent over towards the inside to make them thicker.
L. (3.6); W. (max.) 0.5; Wt (5.6)
Fig. 299

There are two close parallels from the cemetery at Deve Hüyük in northern Syria, dated to between 480 and 380 BC (Moorey 1980, 75, Fig. 11, nos. 272–3).

Figure 299. *Copper bracelet terminal* **2215**.

Celt

2216 I14/78 3446
Level 2
Flat celt, widening but getting progressively thinner from haft end to curved, sharpened blade end.
L. 7.1; W. 1.1–2.5; Th. 0.5

Haft and tang
These are fragments and the tool or weapon of which they were part is missing.

2217 J19/370 KLT 115 3969
Level IIc
Long thin tool with a square-sectioned tang, becoming cylindrical and then flattened at the other end, the tip of which is probably missing. Central part corroded.
L. (10.7); Wt (8.1)
Fig. 301

2218 I14/79 3446
Level 2
Fragment with broken square haft [(2.9) × 0.4 × 0.4], widening to a square section [0.6 × 0.6] with the tip broken.
L. (7.6); W. 0.4–0.6; Th. 0.4–0.6

2219 Q19/62 2118
Level E4a
Flat tang, thin at the complete, narrow end and widening and thickening to the broken end.
L. (3.5); W. 1.2–1.6; Th. 0.5 max.

2220 J19/82 KLT 57 1626
Level I
Small tanged tool with both tang [L. (1.5)] and point broken.
L. (5.2); W. 0.25–0.55; Th. 0.3

Hooks

[2221] H20/808 5328
Level Vf4
A small metal hook broken into two pieces. The top of the hook is bulbous. The hook curves round to a sharp point.
W. of hook 1.2; Di. of wire (0.18); Wt 0.5
Purpose unknown. Fish-hooks are occasionally referred to in the literature but there is always the uncertainty whether they were actually used as such (Goldman 1956, fig. 429:122–3; at Thermi, Lamb 1936, pl. XLVII:32.59).

2222 J19/158 1667
Level II?
Probably a copper pin reused as a fish-hook.
L. 3.1; W. 1.3; Th. 0.2 max.

Nails
Almost all the nails recovered were made of iron (see below). **2223** was the only copper nail with its head preserved.

2223 K19/178 4500
Level I
Head rounded and flattened.
L. *c.* 10; Di. of head 1.4; H. of head 0.5; Wt 11.7

2224 K19/196 4507
Level IIc
Roughly square in cross-section, tapering to a point, with tang tapering to a chisel-like end (W. 0.25).
L. *c.* 9.3; Di. 0.6 max.; Th. 0.4 × 0.4 at top of blade

2225 Four other fragments possibly belonging to copper nails:
a: Level IIb: I20/26 (1421)
b: Level IIc: K18/286 (6145)
c: Level IId?: J18/350 (5874)
Nail without its head. Incomplete, broken and corroded.
L. 3.7; Th. 0.8 max.; Wt 5.9
d: Level II?: J19/159 (1667)

Needles
All the identifiable surviving needles are made of copper or bronze and they come predominantly from Level II with a few earlier instances. There are no iron examples, but the technology for making such fine iron objects would have been slow to develop and they would probably not have survived.

Where the method of construction of a needle's eye can be identified, this is specified. The small number of needles (**2226–7**) among the earlier metal finds all have an integrated eye, as opposed to the very common type where the end part of the metal rod is flattened and then bent over itself to form the eye, a style which was popular throughout the Bronze Age (Boehmer 1972, 83 fig. 33:m), and is found at Kilise Tepe in Levels II and III.

Only those needles which can be securely identified as such are catalogued here; fragments of shafts are listed below. The shafts are all round and taper towards the point.

2226 H20/902 5362
Level Vf3?
Fragment of a needle damaged at the tip and eye.
L. (4.0); Di. 0.3.

2227 H20/775 5333
Level Ve
The shaft is thickened between 1.0–2.0 cm from top end to accommodate the eye. At the lower end the needle tapers to a point.
L. 7.0; L. of eye 0.45; W. at eye 0.35; W. of eye 0.12; Di. of shaft below eye 0.2; Wt 1.2
Fig. 301

[2228] H19/63 4212
Level IIIc/d
Rather contorted, very tip broken but top with needle eye intact.

Figure 300. *Detail of needle 2233 head to show folded eye.*

Round in section.
L. *c*. (7.5); Di. of shaft 0.16; L. of eye 0.25; W. of eye 0.05

[2229]   I19/172   5527
Level IIIe
Bent over at one end to form the eye (now opened).
L. *c*. 6.3; W. 0.2; Wt 1.4

[2230]   I19/150   5514
Level IIa
Needle with eye.
L. *c*. 7.6; Di. of shaft 0.15; W. of shaft at eye 0.25; L. of eye 0.25; W. of eye 0.09

2231   J19/424   Etütlük 1998   6411
Level IIb/c
Needle with shaft in two pieces and point probably missing; the round shaft is flattened at the end and folded over to form the eye.
L. (12.7); Di. 0.2

[2232]   J20/158   1396
Level IIc
Heavily corroded needle broken into four fragments with tip missing; shaft flattened and folded over to form the eye (0.6).
L. (6.9); Di. 0.3; W. at eye 0.3; L. of eye 0.15; W. of eye 0.1

2233   J19/310   3930
Level IId/f
Needle; eye probably formed by cutting the shaft obliquely, bending the narrower piece of metal over and tucking the end into a hole made for the purpose.
L. 10.9; W. at head 0.34; Di. of shaft 0.2; L. of eye 0.25; W. of eye 0.1
Fig. 300
There are numerous parallels from Boğazköy (Boehmer 1979, nos. 337–8, 352–3, 372, 430, 432–4 from Büyükkale Level IV and 501–4, 506–8, 510–11 from Büyükkale Level III), and see especially Maşat Höyük (T. Özgüç 1982, fig. 17).

2234   K18/192   KLT 139   4393
Level I
Needle, complete but bent; flattened at the end (2.2 × 1.1), where the leaf-shaped eye (L. 0.5) has been pierced.
L. 6.8; Th. 0.2

Needle or pin shafts
Fragments of copper or bronze pin or needle shafts are differentiated from nail fragments not only by their material, but by their smaller size and the fact that they are round in section rather than square.

They were found in the following squares and units, again, as with the needles, predominantly in Level II, suggesting a possible concentration of sewing activity in the area of square J19.

[2235]
Level IIIc: **H19**/375 (4227)
Level IIId: **J20**/162 (1390)
Level IIIe: **J20**/164 (1388)
Level IIb: **I19**/144 (2883)
Level IIc: **I19**/115 (2843); **J18**/389 (5893); **J19**/116 (1642); **J20**/90 (1353); **K19**/203 (4507), /282 (4518)
Level IIc/d: **J19**/234, 278 (1690), /296 (3928), /321 (3935)
Level IId: **I19**/105 (2842); **J19**/328 (3942)
Level IId–f: **J20**/68 (1342)
Level I: **J19**/26 (1604), /76c (1626)

Level E5d: **R18**/227 (2476)
Level 2: **I14**/166 (3491)

Pins
Although there are some iron pins (see below), pins were generally made of copper or bronze, as were the needles, and are complete unless otherwise specified. The dimensions are overall length × diameter of shaft, followed by details of the head. Again, as with the needles, most came from Level II. In view of the frequency of spindle-whorls at the site, it is perhaps worth noting that two items described as blunt-ended copper 'pins' from mid-third millennium Abu Salabikh (Postgate & Moon 1982, 134 with pl. Vc) have been identified as spindle shafts by Barber (1991, 57).

[2236]   H20/642   1289
Level Ve
Pin(?) fragments.
L.(5.8); Di. 0.23

2237   H20/834   KLT 117   5301
Level Ve
Pin with round domed head, tapering to a fine point. Pin is bent about halfway along its shaft where it is corroded. Otherwise in good condition.
L. 11.8; Di. of head 0.7
Fig. 301
Pins like this one and **2238** have a wide distribution in terms of place and time. A detailed discussion and classification of pins by Boehmer can be found in the Boğazköy small finds volume with further literature for parallel examples (Boehmer 1972, 79–101, fig. 33, pl. XVII–XXIV).

[2237a]   H19/304   4269
Level IVa
Complete, but bent and slightly corroded.
L. (when straight) *c*. 5.5

2238   H19/338   4272
Level IVb
Long thin pin, slightly bent. The head is rounded and has two horizontal grooves below it.
L. 10.5–11.0; Di. of head 0.8; Di. of shaft 0.26; H. of head from upper groove 0.65
See on **2237**.

[2239]   H19/355   4278
Level IVa
Small object of uncertain type (pin?), complete but bent back on itself.
L. (original unfolded) *c*. 2.8; Di. of head 0.4

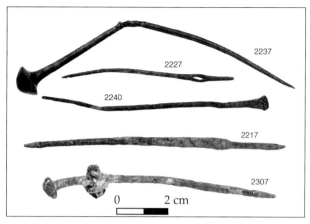

Figure 301. *Copper pins and needles from Levels II, III and V. From top:* **2240** *(IIIe),* **2227** *(Ve),* **2237** *(Ve),* **2217** *(IIc),* **2307** *(IIc)*

2240 I19/179 KLT 116 5527
Level IIIe
Long, thin pin, with a square, flat-topped head with bevelled edges.
L. 9.2; Th. 0.2; Di. of head 0.7
Fig. 301

[2241] K19/348 4553
Level IIc; found with **2306**
Pin of which the shaft has exploded and is broken; head (H. 0.1 × Di. 0.5) is well preserved and rounded.
L. (1.9); Di. of shaft 0.3

[2242] K19/168 1592
Level IId
Pin with its tip missing. Round head flaring from the shaft.
L. (4.1); Di. 0.3; H. of head 0.7; Di. of head 0.7

2243 I14/88 KLT 73 3455
Level 2 upper
Pin with round shaft, now bent; melon-shaped head divided into six uneven segments, with a circular moulding beneath it.
L. 10.4; Di. of shaft 0.35; Di. of head 1.15

2244 K14/78 3037
Level 2 upper
Pin with the head formed by rolling the end of the shaft.
L. 7.3; Di. of shaft 0.3; L. of head 0.5

2245 J19/218 1682
Topsoil
Pin with crook-shaped head and swelling at the top of the round shaft.
L. 6.6; Di. 0.4–0.7

Projectile points
In view of the difficulty in ascertaining whether fragmentary objects in this category are large arrowheads or small spearheads, they have been grouped together. Virtually all the arrowheads come from pits, but **2247** was found embedded in the destruction debris of Level IIc Rm 4; **2246** is of a very similar type, but the other arrowheads are remarkable for their dissimilarity.

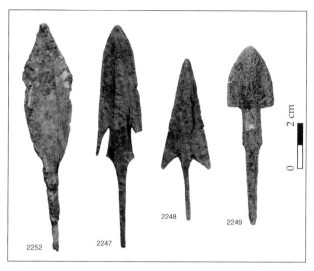

Figure 302. *Projectile points from Level II. From left:* **2252**, **2247**, **2248**, **2249**.

2246 I20/52 KLT 69 4004
Level IIb
Broad arrowhead with long barbs and a flat midrib with a square section extending into the tang.
L. 9.4; L. of tang 4.9; W. 2.0; Th. 0.6; Di. of shaft 0.5; Wt 9.05.

Similar barbed arrow-heads of the period of the Hittite Empire were found at Ortaköy (Süel 1998, 59, fig. 21), at Tarsus (Goldman 1956, fig. 427:70–80, 82–3) and Boğazköy (Boehmer 1972, no. 833). There are Neo-Hittite/Early Iron Age barbed arrowheads from Malatya (Pecorella 1975, fig. 13:1–11, Level III, and fig. 21:2 Level IV), from Tarsus (Goldman 1963, 372, fig. 172–3) and from Delos (Gallet de Santerre & Tréheux 1947–48, no. 82, pp. 233–4, fig. 27 in a deposit dated to the second half of the eighth century but containing objects ranging in date from Mycenaean to Geometric). **2247** is very similar, though with a more sharply angled swelling above the tang. These two are surely arrowheads, and their weight is comparable to that of copper/bronze arrowheads from third-millennium Mesopotamia (see Martin 1985, 15 on examples from Abu Salabikh, ranging from 6.7–10.1 g, and for the idea that such relatively heavy points were used for fighting at close range).

2247 K19/150 KLT 109 1572
Level IIc
Projectile point with thin barbs and a flat midrib, widening and then cut away sharply to merge with the square-sectioned tang.
L. 9.8; W. 2.0; Th. 0.3; Wt 10.4
Fig. 302

No good parallels for this very distinctive barbed type have been found (but cf. Boehmer 1972, no. 822 from Boğazköy, Level IVb). **2246** is similar but lacks the sharply-angled swelling above the tang, as do all the examples quoted in that entry.

2248 K18/121 KLT 108 4359
Level IIe
Narrow triangular arrowhead with two barbs. After conservation, it was possible to see a small engraved X on one side (visible in Fig. 303), but this is no longer clear on the object owing to its poor state of preservation.
L. 7.2; W. 2.2; Th. 0.2; Wt. 5.1
Figs. 302–3

Metalwork

Figure 303. *Detail of blade 2248 to show X mark.*

Similar arrowheads were excavated at the Hittite sites of Maşat Höyük (T. Özgüç 1982, pl. 55:6) and Boğazköy (Boehmer 1972, no. 820, Level IVb). See also Buchholz & Karageorghis 1973, nos. 600–604 and 606 from Mycenaean tombs at Ialysos on Rhodes; Gallet de Santerre & Tréheux 1947–48, no. 82, pp. 233–4, fig. 27 from Delos (see **2246** for the date).

2249   J18/237   KLT 110   2399
Level IId/e
Arrowhead with a small spade-shaped head and a flat midrib extending into the tang, which has a square section and tapers to a point.
L. 7.9, L. of head 2.9, L. of tang 5.0; W. of head 2.2; Wt 12.6
Fig. 302

No exact parallels, but cf. perhaps Gallet de Santerre & Tréheux 1947–48, no. 82, pp. 235, fig. 28 (on left) from Delos (see **2246** for the date); and Catling 1964, 132 type (d) with Fig. 16:7–8 (from Cyprus). References courtesy A.M. Snodgrass.

2250   I19/60   2806
Level IIe–h
Projectile point with edges broken and a wide central midrib with rectangular section. Cf. **2254** and **2251** which it may have resembled.
L. c. 14.6, L. of head 9.3; tang 5.3 × 0.7 tapering to 0.5 × 0.4; W. (1.5); midrib 0.8 × 0.5

2251   J19/162   KLT 70   1667
Level II? Found associated with iron slag fragments **2420**.
Spearhead with very faintly defined midrib, sloping shoulders and rectangular-sectioned tang (end broken).
L. (14.0); W. 1.8; Th. 0.35; Wt 28.5
Gallet de Santerre & Tréheux 1947–48, no. 82, pp. 233–5, fig. 28 (bottom) from Delos (see **2246** for date).

2252   K19/173   KLT 111   1598
Level I/II
Leaf-shaped projectile point with a narrow square tang and faint midrib.
L. 10.0; W. 2.3 (max); Th. 0.3; Wt 16.0
Fig. 302
There are Bronze Age parallels from Tarsus (Goldman 1950, fig. 427: 85). See also Gallet de Santerre & Tréheux 1947–48, no. 82, pp. 233–5, fig. 28 from Delos (see **2246** for date).

2253   K19/180   1577
Level I
Flat leaf-shaped arrowhead with the remains of a tang

[(0.3) × 0.5 × 0.2].
L. 3.0; W. 1.2; Th. 0.2

[2254]   99/24   99
Surface
Spearhead; badly preserved with tip, tang, and edges broken. Cf. **2250** and see **2251** which it may have resembled.
L. (7.2); W. (1.9); Th. 0.4 (at midrib)–0.2 (at sides); tang (0.8) × 1.1 × 0.6

Rings and chain links

Catalogued here are finger-rings (**2259**, **2266**?, **2269**?, **2271**), coils of wire, links from chains, and objects which may fall into these categories.

Figure 304. *Copper ring 2259, side view to show herring-bone design.*

2255   I19/178   KLT 112   5527
Level IIIe
Open ring, probably hammered from a thick strip of metal, with its sides folded towards the middle. One end was drawn out, hammered into a flat oval and pierced, but it is broken so that it now looks like a fish-tail; the other end was roughly clipped off. Could be part of a bracelet.
Di. 5.7 (ext.), 4.5 (int.); Th. 1.7 max.

[2256]   K20/229   Etütlük 1998   2904
Level IIb
Complete; rod with slightly tapering squared-off ends, bent to form a roughly oval bangle or chain link (int. dimensions 5.3–7.0) with a c. 1.9 cm overlap of the ends.
L. c. 23.5; Di. 0.6–0.5

2257   K19/457   Etütlük 1998   6210
Level IIc
Complete; rod with one tapering end (di. 0.4 tapering to 0.35) rolled on itself to form a bangle or chain link (int. di. 3.9) with c. 6.5 overlap of the ends.
L. c. 23.0

[2258]   K19/337   4557
Level IIc
Fragments of wire coil.
Di. of wire 0.2 × 0.3.

2259   J20/45   1324
Level IId
Finger-ring with tapering ends touching, decorated with incised herring-bone design. Cf. **2260**.
Di. 2.6 (ext.), 2.15 (int.); W. 1.0; Th. 0.3
Fig. 304

2260   J20/46   1324
Level IId
Wire ring.
Di. 3.1; Di. of wire 0.2–0.3.

[2261]   K20/202   1994
Level IId
Two wire coils corroded together; one broken, one complete and circular.
L. c. 2.1; W. 0.9; Di. of wire 0.2.

519

Figure 305. *Copper chain links* 2268.

Figure 306. *Copper ring* 2271: *a) one face; b) other face; c) side view.*

Figure 307. *Section from copper rim of hoplite shield* 2272.

[2262] K18/255 6127
Level IIe
Fragmentary ring made from a piece of wire, folded round with the ends overlapping.
Di. *c.* 1.8 (ext.); Di. of wire 0.2

[2263] I19/156 2882
Level IIb
Wire coil. Di. originally *c.* 1.8 but crushed out of shape.
Di. of wire *c.* 0.3

[2264] K19/123 1567
Level I/II
Fragments of wire coil.
Di. 1.0; Di. of wire 0.3

2265 J14/8 3302
Level 1
Ring with overlapping ends.
Di. 2.6; Di. of wire *c.* 0.3

2266 J18/40 2308
Level I
Curved tapering segment, decorated with incised, elongated guilloche. Perhaps part of a finger-ring. Cf. **2269** for fragments of what was probably a similar ring.
L. (2.0); W. 0.6–1.0; Th. 0.2

[2267 number not used]

2268 J19/409 1626
Level I
Four strips bent to form figure-of-eight chain links (one flattened). Cf. **2267** from same unit.
L. 0.9–1.0; W. of strip 0.2; Th. 0.1
Fig. 305

These small figure-of-eight links may have been parts of chains used for suspending a polycandilion (Balty 1981, 103, no. 107, from Apamea on the Orontes): a disc of bronze with holes in it into which glasses of oil were inserted to provide lighting. The wick-holders listed below would have been inserted into such glasses.

2269 J19/445 1604
Level I
Seven small flat fragments with deeply-incised linear decoration consisting of a line border and pairs of diagonal lines. A rather different eighth fragment (2.0 × 2.3) consisting of two of the pieces riveted together has relief decoration and is curved over at one end. Perhaps a finger-ring? Cf. **2266**.
Largest fragment: 1.7 × 2.0; Th. *c.* 0.1

[2270] L19/19 5929
Level I
Thin wire with one thicker round end (Th. 0.4), curved into a ring-shape (or bracelet?). Four other small fragments of thick corroded wire (Di. 0.4) with slight curve.
L. *c.* 15.5; Th. 0.3; Di. (int.) 4.3–5.2

2271 J19/3 KLT 55 1600
Surface
Finger-ring with circular hoop with double lines at the end of the hoop; sides bevelled at the top and decorated with centre-dot circles to form an eight-sided setting for an oval stone (now missing).
Di. (int.) 1.83; Th. 0.12–0.2
Fig. 306a–c

520

Metalwork

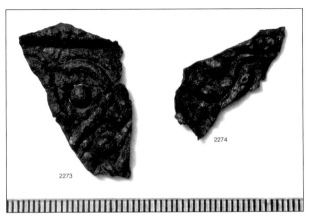

Figure 308. *Copper fragments from rim of hoplite shield(s) 2273–4.*

A close parallel for the type of ring was found in the Roman-Byzantine village at Malatya (Equini Schneider 1970, 44, pl. XXX:5).

Shields

2272 K19/313 KLT 114 4539
Level I
Nineteen fragments of sheet metal with *repoussé* decoration on most of them. They fit together to form a flat slightly-curved strip from the edge of a shield, with the outer edge folded over for added strength. Between an outer concentric ridge and two inner ones is a panel decorated with an elaborate three-stranded quadruple plait winding in and out of three rows of raised dots (36 preserved).
L. (16.5); W. (6.8); Th. 0.1
Fig. 307

The identification of this object is due to Prof. A.M. Snodgrass. Exactly similar designs form the edges of votive shields from Olympia (Bol 1989, 6–15 and Taf. 4–16). This type of decoration on shields is dated from the late seventh century to the mid-fifth century BC.

2273 J14/24 3314
Level 1
Possibly from the same shield as **2274**.
2.7 × 2.5; Th. 0.1
Fig. 308

2274 J14/33 3316
Level 1
Possibly from the same shield as **2273**.
2.55 × 1.2; Th. 0.1
Fig. 308

Two small fragments with *repoussé* decoration similar to that of **2272**, but the plait, though probably also quadruple, is single-stranded instead of triple, and the raised dots are smaller (Di. 0.4).

Spatula

2275 J16/4 KLT 74 4600
Surface
Copper, well preserved. Flaring spatula with straight edge at the end of a long pin with a square section and slightly swelling rounded extremity. Immediately above the spatula head are three narrow double mouldings separated by broader ball-like mouldings.
L. 15.1, L. of splayed end 2.7; W. 0.75; Th. 0.3; Wt 9.25

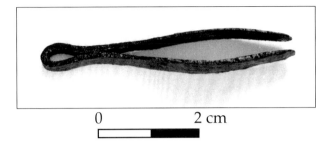

Figure 309. *Tweezers 2276 from Level Vf.*

Tweezers

2276 H20/921 KLT 140 5367
Level Vf
Pair of tweezers made from a strip of metal with rounded ends and narrowing towards the centre at which point it is folded over and pinched together forming a loop at the top. The ends are slightly bent inwards for a better grip. Object still usable. Complete but slightly corroded.
L. 5.1; W. and Th. vary from 0.35 × 0.03 at the ends to 0.2 × 0.13 in the centre increasing to 0.5 × 0.5–0.8 at the loop end.
Fig. 309

Tweezers are not a common item in the metal repertoire at other sites but in Troy II (EBA) another example manufactured by the same method (and with similar dimensions) was recorded, made in silver. According to Blegen tweezers are also known from Early Cycladic and Early Minoan contexts (Blegen *et al.* 1950, 281, fig. 359:36–369). An impressive number of tweezers (11 in all) were noted for the later periods at Boğazköy, with the earliest example from Level IVd (*karum* period), followed by some from Hittite Empire and Phrygian levels. They were usually made in bronze, except for two specimens which were manufactured in iron, and occur in a variety of styles (Boehmer 1972, 118, 155, pl. XXXIV 1006–13A; pl. LIV 1625–27).

2277 K20/57 1905
Level I/II
Tapering strip which has been folded in two to form a loop at one end. Could have been tweezers (now bent) or a hold-fast.
L. *c.* 11.9; W. 0.3; Th. 0.05–0.1.

Wick-holders

Wick- or taper-holders are found in Byzantine churches (e.g. at Apamea and Antioch on the Orontes: see Kondoleon 2000, 83–4 & fig. 5). They are made of a strip of copper or bronze which is split along most of its length while the un-slit part is rolled into a tube to hold a wick; the long extensions or 'legs' are pushed apart to form a spring so that they will hold the wick upright when inserted into a glass of oil. The dimensions given below are the original length, width and thickness of the strip before cutting; the length of the uncut part which held the wick is given in brackets.

[2278] J19/34 1605
Level I/II
Long flat strip, rolled over at one end and tapering at the other. Probably part of a wick-holder.
L. 5.1; W. 0.5; Th. 0.1

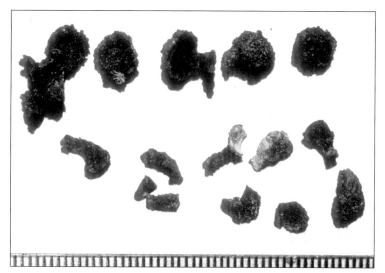

Figure 310. *Copper studs **2290**, found with astragali **2421**. Scale in mm.*

2279   K18/203   Etütlük 1998   4393
Level I
Broken wick-holder, with a short section of one 'leg' missing.
L. *c.* 12.0 (3.2); W. 1.3; Th. 0.7

2280   L14/13   3602
Level 1
Complete wick-holder; the 'legs' have irregular edges.
L. *c.* 7.5 (3.5); W. 1.2; Th. 0.01

Wires, strips and rods
Various miscellaneous fragments have been grouped in this category; other fragments of rod or wire may have been listed above as fragmentary nails or pins.

2281   K19/410   4597
Level IIc
Piece of twisted wire.
L. *c.* 6.0; Di. 0.4

2282   K19/411   4596
Level IIc
Twisted fragments of rod, the longest with one rounded end.
L. *c.* 12.0 (longest); Di. 0.6

2283   J18/387   Etütlük 1998   5894
Level IIc/d
Piece of wire with a square section, twisted upon itself to form a loop (W. 1.0) and two prongs (1.5 apart), one of which tapers.
L. *c.* 7.5; W. 0.1–0.2; Th. 0.3

2284   J18/354   5873
Level IId
Flat arc, perhaps part of a rim, broken on its inner edge and at both ends.
L. (6.3); W. (1.2); Th. 0.1 (outer edge)–0.3 (inner edge); Di. 11.0 (8.5 inner).

2285   J18/285   5832
Level I/II
Twisted fragment of wire of uneven thickness.
L. 2.4; W. 1.3; Th. 0.5 max.

[2286]   K19/159   1593
Level I/II
Short length of wire with one end twisted and rolled around to form a double loop, and the other ending in a point.
L. 2.8; W. 1.0; Th. 0.3

[2287]   J16/166   4706
Level 1
Irregularly-shaped sheet with pieces cut from its edges; after conservation appears to have had a split-pin rivet.
L. *c.* 8.0; W. 1.5 max.; Th. 0.2

2288   J19/76a   1626
Level I
Trapezoidal sheet, broken along sloping edges where it has been bent.
L. (1.8)–(2.4); W. 2.2; Th. 0.1

2289   K18/207   Etütlük 1998   4393
Level I
Complete length of tapering wire with a rectangular section (tapers to W. 0.2 × Th. 0.1).
L. 15.0; W. 0.3; Th. 0.2

Miscellaneous
2290   J18/346   5870
Level IIc
About 12 small hollow dome-shaped studs; the better preserved have a hollow strap-like appendage, possibly the remains of a hoop. Some contain the remains of a brown fibrous material, possibly a textile or leather.
Di. *c.* 0.7; H. of domes 0.4; L. of 'straps' *c.* 0.55
Fig. 310
As they were found in a pit with a hoard of astragali (**2421**), they may have been the studs decorating a bag in which the astragali were once held.

[2291]   K19/277   4515
Level IIc?
Small, corroded fragment, almost triangular in shape, like a flattened cone; possibly part of a larger object.
L. 1.6; W. 0.9; Th. 0.6

[2292]   J14/3   3301
Level 1
Roughly triangular flat fragment with shaved ends (one of which has been hammered flat) and sides.
L. 3.8; W. 0.9–1.6; Th. 0.5

2293   I14/45   KLT 72   3419
Level 1, Hellenistic context
Miniature Ionic column round a central iron peg. Traces visible before cleaning seemed to indicate that the object might have been covered with silver but what survives seems to be copper or bronze. The end of the peg is visible at the top and has caused the base to explode. The entablature (2.1 × 1.65) rests on an Ionic capital and double moulding, all probably separate pieces, and the column and base were also separate pieces. The column (Di. 0.9 top, 1.0 bottom) is fluted (× 15); the very bottom is slightly wider due to cracks caused by the expanding iron peg. The peg and another metal element extended below the base, presumably fixing the column to the object it decorated. Before cleaning, a piece of wood was noted, adhering to one side of the capital. N.B. all but the top drawing show the column as it would have been; the photograph shows its present condition after cleaning.

Figure 311. *Metal column* **2293**.

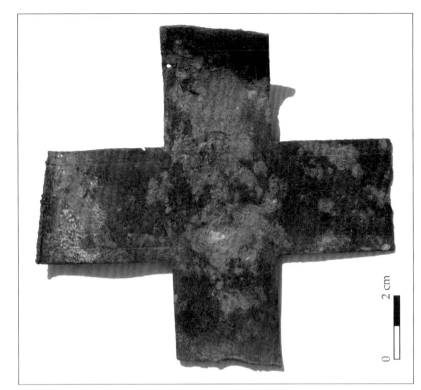

Figure 312. *Copper cross* **2294**.

H. 7.1; W. 2.5 (at base); Wt 51
Fig. 311
The column could have decorated a wooden box or similar item. It was carefully made and was evidently part of a valuable and high-quality object, particularly if it was covered with silver. This is not a provincial piece.

2294   J18/34   KLT 113   2308
Level I
Symmetrical cross, cut from a sheet of metal. The arms of the cross have been bent and pieces have been broken off them. In the case of two of the arms these breaks occur along the edge of an excised curved cut, but there is no trace of similar cuts on the other two arms, although one of them had an incised circle, about a third of which remains, with double border and two small punched centre-dot circles on its periphery, possibly with remains of some motif in the centre. There is an incised circle at the point of intersection of the arms of the cross, which may also have contained an incised motif now obscured by corrosion. There is an incised line around the cross, on the outer side of which is a row of roughly aligned small centre-dot circles, probably executed with a punch and sometimes overlapping. Up the centre of each arm is a row of similar but more spaced centre-dot circles linked by incised curved lines to form a rough guilloche motif. On the back of the cross are two incised lines on both sides of two of the arms, and on one side of the other two arms. There is a small neatly-punched hole (Di. 0.1) on the edge of two of the arms, presumably so that the cross could be fixed by small nails to a backing, for they seem too small to have held a chain enabling the cross to be suspended.
L. (11.9); W. (10.9); Th. 0.15
Fig. 312
Though now cruciform, this object was not necessarily originally just a cross, as all the arms are now broken. It could have been applied decoration to a processional cross or chest, or part of a furniture fitting, but more fixing holes would be expected.

2295   P15/2   101
Surface
Curved shield-shape with small rectangular hole at the centre. Substance uncertain, probably a modern alloy.
L. 2.5; W. 2.1; Th. 0.5

Fragments of copper/bronze

Unidentifiable fragments were also found in the following squares and units:
[2296]
Level IIc/d: **J19**/274 (1690), **K19**/78 (1543)
Level IIe: **K18**/138 (4364)
Level 2 upper: **K14**/129 (3067)
Level 2 lower: **K14**/141 (3095)
Level I: **K16**/9 (4801)

Lead and silver (2297–307)

Lead and silver are difficult to distinguish without laboratory analysis. The objects in these materials are therefore grouped together, but where an identification seems reasonably certain, one or other is specified.

Lead strips
2297   I14/152   3489
Level 2/3
Lead strip tightly rolled at least 4 times (L. therefore c. 15–20 cm;

the drawing does not clearly indicate the rolling); also one small fragment. This could have been an inscribed strip, but there is no sign of an inscription on the visible portion and we did not attempt to unroll it.
W. 1.9; Di. 1.8
For lead and silver strips, some inscribed, from Antioch see Kondoleon 2000, 164–5.

[2298]   J14/63   3340
Level 1/2
Lead; strip folded in two lengthways.
L. 3.4; W. *c.* 2.3; Th. 0.3

[2299]   K14/7   3003
Level 1
Lead; twisted fragment of sheet. Possibly two parallel diagonal incisions at one broken edge.
L. (3.2); W. (2.6); Th. 0.2

[2300]   Q20/22   2151
Level E2a
A lead rectangle folded lengthwise.
L. 4.7; W. *c.* 3.0; Th. 0.35

[2301]   I16/21   4600
Surface
Silver(?) or lead; strip, tapering to a complete end; bent in two and the other end (broken) rolled up.
L. *c.* (10.0); W. 1.6; Th. 0.1

Wire
[2302]   H19/331   4272
Level IVb
One small lead rod bent into a rough horseshoe shape.
H. 1.5; W. 1.5; Di. 0.3

[2303]   H19/23   4205
Level IIId
Lead; four small fragments of wire, two of them bent.
Di. 0.2

[2304]   M14/14   3506
Level 1
Silver; small curved fragments of wire.
Di. of wire 0.3

[2305]   J19/291   3923
Topsoil
Silver or lead(?); small, elongated ring or earring fragment, made out of wire of uneven thickness.
L. 2.2; W. 1.5; Di. of wire 0.3–0.5

Miscellaneous
2306   K19/327   KLT 119   4553
Level IIc
Silver; group of three figures standing on a base plate (3.6 × 1.5). They are linked by a round-ended strip (*c.* 3.7 × *c.* 1.5) behind their heads and extending above the group and beyond it at each end. The end at the right is damaged with one piece missing and the remainder bent round like a blinker with four small circular depressions at the edge. The end on the left is thicker and a copper-coloured lump (corrosion from some other object) adheres to it at the back. The silver is reasonably well preserved, but the figures have been pushed sideways on their base so that they lean towards the left. They have also been pushed closer together than they would have been originally. There are traces of copper corrosion on the figure on the left extending onto the head of the central figure.

Figure 313. *Silver figurine of divine triad* **2306**: *a) before conservation, concreted to silver pin* **2307**; *b) after conservation — front view; c) after conservation — back view.*

The central and right-hand figures have long robes, and mantles hanging open over them; they also wear necklace counterweights or long plaits hanging down their backs. The central figure is a woman holding a baby in the crook of her left arm and her right arm is folded. The baby's features are well preserved and its head touches its mother's cheek. Her headdress is not clear and it may be that her hair is swept back and up. The right-hand figure, probably also a woman, wears a small, rounded, triangular headdress, has one arm bent and her right arm extended: its end is broken so that any object she may have held is missing. The figure on the left wears a tall headdress which may have vertical decoration. This figure wears a straight robe and has no necklace counterweight or plait and may be male. In both hands he holds an object formed by a concertinaed strip of metal 1.35 cm wide as if he were unfurling it.
H. 3.8 ; W. 4.05; Th. 2.15
Fig. 313

A close parallel is provided by a silver triad on a base-plate from Ugarit on the north Syrian coast (Schaeffer 1956, 94ff., figs. 113–14); it was the same size as the Kilise Tepe triad and a loop on the back indicates that it was a pendant. The two outer figures wear tall conical headdresses and hold curved sticks; that in the centre is either animal-headed or wears a mask. It has been suggested that they could be priests. A small triad of similar figures, but in ivory, was found in Temple 20 at Boğazköy (Neve 1998, 29–30, 33, Abb. 81; size not given but also about the same size). Boehmer (1979, 30–31, pl. XLII, No. 3394A–C) suggests that three bronze legs, found in a house in Boğazköy, may also have belonged to a triad but this would have been a much larger object built in sections. Single-figure pendants on base-plates have also been found at Boğazköy and both have been interpreted as deities: a seated goddess 2 cm high in gold is a surface find (Kulaçoglu 1992, no. 138), and a bronze standing god with arms folded was excavated in Temple 4 (Neve 1992, 81, Abb. 228 — size not given). The Kilise Tepe triad consists of a different set of figures from the other triads; they are more likely to be deities. That on the left could be a god of writing, the central figure could be a mother goddess or divine consort, but the identity of the figure on the right is not clear.

2307   K19/346   KLT 118   4553
Level IIc
Silver; pin recovered from the concreted material around figurine **2306**. It has a round domed head, and tapers to a point at the other end.
L. 9.4; Th. 0.35; Di. of head 0.9
Figs. 301 & 313a

Iron (2308–420)

A note of caution is needed here since some of the iron objects, by definition found in the upper levels, may be of recent manufacture.

Blades
These end in a tip unless otherwise stated. The term blade is used for the whole object and, more specifically, for the cutting edge (as opposed to the back). With the exception of **2214** all the identifiable blades are made of iron.

[2308]   K18/116   4356
Level IIe
Very corroded with straight sides, round tip and taper towards handle end.
L. 13.6; W. 2.8 (max.)–1.6; Th. 0.8

2309   K18/247   6120
Level IIf?
Chopper with slightly concave back, possibly also used for cutting, and very convex blade which is still quite sharp; tip broken; narrows at handle end for hafting with break at possible rivet hole (corroded).
L. (12.4); W. 2.0–3.8 max.; Th. 0.2–1.0

2310   I19/45   1792
Level IIg
Straight back and curved blade with tang. Width tapers to a point.
L. 14.9; W. 2.0 max.; Th. 0.7 max.

2311   I19/57   2806
Level IIe–h
Concave back and convex blade; handle end cut at an angle with a hole through it. Thickness tapers to the tip.
L. 7.9; W. 2.0 max.; Th. 0.75 max.

2312   J18/35   2308
Level I
Sickle-blade with tip and part of tang missing; width constant throughout, as is the thickness for most of the length; see also below, **2315**.
L. (24.0); W. 3.1; Th. 1.2; tang (1.9) × 2.0 × 0.9

[2313]   J18/39   2308
Level I
Perhaps several iron blades fused together or one object that has exploded and laminated, or a penknife(?); the end is missing.
L. (9.0); W. 1.8–0.7; Th. 0.6–1.1

[2314]   K18/204   4393
Level I
Broken at handle end; slightly convex back and straight blade; width tapers to the tip; thickness tapers to the cutting edge.
L. (9.8); W. 1.6; Th. 0.5

2315   K20/54   1903
Level I
Very corroded; part of a sickle-shaped blade, tapering to a point; cf. **2312**.
L. 14.0; W. 4.0; Th. 1.0

[2316]   L14/8   3602
Level I
Both ends missing; straight back and straight, sloping blade; thickness tapers to blade.
L. (7.2); W. 0.8–1.5; Th. 0.3 max.

2317   I17/4   4901
Topsoil
Iron, with variations in thickness due to corrosion; long, flat, blade-like object with parallel sides and one rounded end; at the other end is a rounded tang which has been bent upwards.
L. 21.7; W. c. 3.7; Th. 0.5–0.9; L. of tang 2.5, Di. 0.9

[2318]   K17/105   120
Surface
Rounded tip of a large blade with a straight back and convex cutting edge.
L. 4.8; W. 2.8; Th. 0.7

2319   S18/21   177
Surface
Small convex blade with straight back, and slightly upward-curving

tip; handle end broken.
L. (6.3); W. 0.8–1.3 max.

[2320]
Iron blade (or possible blade) fragments were also found in the following squares and units:
Level IIc/d: **J18**/249 (5811)
Level IId: **K18**/146 (4367)
Level IId/e: **J18**/231 (2399)
Level IIe: **K18**/144 (4364)
Level IIf: **H18**/112 (2631); **J18**/164 (2366)
Level II: **K18**/70 (4321); **K20**/193 (1985)
Level I/II: **K20**/92 (1915)
Level 1: **I14**/34 (3412); **I18**/14 (2704); **J16**/113 (4700); **J18**/6 (2301); **K14**/67 (3031)
Surface/unstratified: **J19**/219 (1682); **M8**/3 (322); **R12**/5 (221)

Buckle
2321   K18/205   Etütlük 1998   4393
Level I
Complete but corroded; small, oval buckle with slightly pointed ends; tine (2.2 × 0.6 × 0.3) preserved.
L. 3.2; W. 1.7; Th. 0.4

Fork
2322   H18/146   2643
Level IId/e
Nine iron fragments which, when put together, form a long-handled, three-pronged fork. Five of these fragments definitely join. The ends of the prongs bend in towards each other, possibly due to damage to the object before or during burial. Three-pronged forks are generally more elaborate, for instance examples from Boğazköy (Boehmer 1982, no. 1268, and no. 1270 which is socketed, both of bronze).
L. *c.* 42.0; W. at prongs 5.0; Di. of prongs *c.* 1.0; L. of central prong *c.* 7.0

Hafts, tangs and sockets
These are fragments; the tool or weapon of which they were part is missing.

[2323]   K20/100   1924
Level IIe
Rectangular tang (2.3 × 0.4 × 0.8) but the shape of the rest of the tool is not clear due to corrosion (circular or rectangular in section?) nor is it clear whether the length is complete (6.7 × 1.1 × 1.2).
Overall L. 9.0

[2324]   I19/51   1799
Level IIf
Flat, tapering tang with two rivets preserved; best-preserved rivet 0.3–0.4 and bent on the other side.
L. (4.1); W. 1.2–1.5; Th. 0.3

[2325]   K19/57   1537
Level I/II
Square haft (2.0 × 0.5 × 0.6) but the shape of the rest of the tool is not clear due to corrosion (circular or square in section?), nor is it clear whether the length is complete (4.7 × 0.9 tapering to 0.5).
Overall L. 6.7

[2326]   I14/131   3471
Level 2
Flattened at one end (broken) and rolled up to form a wedge.
Di. 1.0–1.1 tapering to 0.5–0.9; L. (4.5); W. 1.5; Th. 0.4

[2327]   K18/188   4393
Level I
Square haft (4.1 × 0.1 × 0.1) but the shape of the piece of which it is part is not clear owing to corrosion, although at the broken end it seems to be a circular tube (Di. 1.5).
L. (6.5)

[2328]   K18/201   4393
Level I
Circular socket, tapering at broken end.
L. (4.3); W. 1.3–1.8
There is a good parallel from Tarsus (Goldman 1963, fig. 172: 111, p. 367).

[2329]   Q12/1   220
Surface
Fragment with square section [(0.4) × 0.8 × 1.0 at one end and 0.8 × 0.8 at the other].

Nails
The nails are heavily corroded so dimensions are approximate. Almost all have square shafts, tapering to a point, and circular heads. Exceptions are listed separately below. The dimensions for representative nails are listed as follows: overall length, width, thickness of shaft; diameter and thickness of head (some have three dimensions for the head e.g. **2383**, **2386–7**). Owing to the corrosion, it is not always possible to tell whether the point is missing, and the nail is judged to be complete unless it is either clear that it is broken or the break is recent. For others, only the length is given. Most are surface, topsoil and Level I finds.

Level IIb
[2330] I20/53 (4004) — probably modern!

Level I/II
[2331] K19/119 (1567) — (3.0) (+ fragments) × 0.8 × 0.9; 2.6 × 0.5 Fig. 314
[2332] K19/44 (1516) — (6.4)

Level I/II?
[2333] K20/13 (1104) — 3.7 × 0.5 × 0.5; 1.4 × 0.4

Level I
[2334] J18/134 (2350) — 7.5 × 0.9 × 0.9; 1.8 × 0.7
[2335] J18/274 (5824) — (11.0)
[2336] K18/63 (4314) — (9.2) and (11.5) Fig. 314
[2337] I18/12 (2708) — (4.8) × 1.0; 1.9 × 1.8
[2338] J18/4 (2300) — complete with shaft hammered flat at the point; 2.8 × 0.9 × 0.6; 1.8 × 0.4
[2339] J18/23 (2306) — (7.7) Fig. 314
[2340] J18/32 (2308) — (7.8)
[2341] J18/37 (2308) — complete, bent; 10.3 × 1.2 × 1.2; 2.8 × 0.6 Fig. 314
[2342] J18/38 (2308) — (8.6) × 1.1 × 1.15; 2.5 × 1.0
[2343] J18/119 (2343) — two pieces of one or two nails; very corroded and laminated; square shaft; 1.0 × 1.3; 1.9 × 0.7 Fig. 314
[2344] J19/18 (1602) — complete; 5.2 × 0.6 × 0.6; 1.5 × 0.4
[2345] K18/209 (4393) — four nails; L. 12.9, 11.8, 10.5, (9.2); square shafts and round heads.

Level 1
[2346] J16/152 (4706) — complete, bent; 10.7 × 1.0 × 1.0; 2.7 × 0.5
[2347] J16/165 (4706) — (8.5) and *c.* (11.4) fragment

[2348] K17/52 (9636) — (5.3)
[2349] L17/7 (5103) — (9.1)
[2350] I14/18 (3403) — complete with tip bent; 5.4 × 0.9 × 0.8; 0.9 × 0.6
[2351] I14/197 (3403) — (4.6) × 1.4 × 1.2; 2.2 × 0.6
[2352] I14/198 (3403) — complete with curled head(?); 8.3 × 0.9 × 0.9; head is an extension of pin. H. 1.5 × Th. 1.0
[2353] N12/16 (3204) — (10.8) × 0.9 × 0.8
[2354] N12/17 (3204) — complete; 8.1 × 1.0 × 0.9; 0.7 × 0.3
[2355] N12/20 (3205) — (c. 8.6)

Surface or topsoil
[2356] J18/86 (2320) — complete with flattened tip; 3.7 × 0.6 × 0.5; 0.6 × 0.4
[2357] H15/1 (159) — 4.5
[2358] I16/31 (4600) — complete; 9.7 × 0.9 × 0.8; 2.1 × 0.4
[2359] I16/20 (4600) — complete; 8.4 × 0.4 × 0.5; 1.8 × 0.5
[2360] I16/22 (4600) — complete; 7.5 × 0.8 × 0.7; 1.3 tapering to shaft
[2361] I16/32 (4600) — complete; 3.3 × 0.4 × 0.4; 1.8 × 0.45
[2362] I17/8 (4903) — (9.4)
[2363] J16/11 (4700) — almost complete except for tip; (7.4) × 0.7 × 0.8; rectangular head 1.2 × 2.4 × Th. 0.7
[2364] J16/28 (4700) — complete apart from chipped head, bent; c. 7.0 × 1.8 × 0.2
[2365] J16/29 (4700) — complete; 7.6 × 0.9 × 0.8; 0.9 × 0.5
[2366] J16/30 (4700) — 4.3
[2367] J17/12 (5000) — complete apart from chipped head; 9.4 × 0.9 × 0.7; 2.2 × 0.5
[2368] K17/1 (9600) — 13.7
[2369] K17/2 (9600) — (6.6) × 1.0 × 0.8; 1.9 × 0.6
[2370] K17/8 (9602) — complete; 3.3 × 0.8 × 0.5; 1.9 × 0.5 Fig. 314
[2371 number not used]
[2372] K17/22 (9603) — complete, bent; 9.5 × 0.9 × 0.8; 2.0 × 0.5 Fig. 314
[2373] K18/5a (4301) — (3.1) × 0.5 × 0.4; 1.3 × 0.3
[2374] K18/5b (4301) — (3.5) × 0.6 × 2.0 × 1.7
[2375] K20/3 (1101) — (2.8)
[2376] N12/11 (3200) — 12.0

Some iron nails had rounded convex-concave heads like umbrellas. There were probably more examples than those listed, but corrosion has obscured the details:

[2377] I14/29 (3409) Level 1/2 — (1.4) × 0.5 × ?; 1.1 × 0.5
[2378] J19/448 (1602) Level I — complete with bent shaft; 3.3 × 0.8 × 0.8; 2.3 × 0.6
[2379] Q19/25 (2102) E2b — (2.9) × 0.6 × 0.5; 2.2 × 0.8

Some nails had heads formed by flattening the end of the shaft into a rounded tongue and bending it over at right angles. Dimensions given are diameter × width × height. All the examples are from the topsoil, except **2383**:

[2380] H20/3 (1200) — (2.0) × 0.5 (top)–0.2 × 0.4; sides of head broken off, 2.1 × (0.7)
[2381] I16/29 (4600) Level I — tip bent; c. 5.7 × 0.5 × 0.4; 1.3 × 1.1 × 0.2

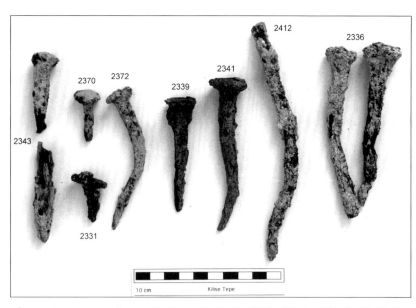

Figure 314. *Iron nails etc.* **2343**, **2370**, **2331**, **2370**, **2331**, **2372**, **2339**, **2341**, **2412**, **2336**.

[2382] J16/25 (4700) — c. 9.4 (bent) × 0.9 × 0.8; 1.7 × 1.4 × 0.7
[2383] J18/52 (2311) — complete, bent; 10.5 × 1.3 × 1.2; 1.8 × 1.6 × 0.7
[2384] L17/5 (5112) — complete; 9.5 × 0.9 × 0.7; 1.9 × 2.0 × 0.4; it is possible that the head was forged separately.
[2385] Q19/11 (178) — complete; 6.3 × 0.4 × 0.4; 0.9 × 0.8 × 0.2

Another type of nail had its head formed by hammering the end of the shaft into a fan shape:

[2386] I14/22 (3405) Level 1/2k — (4.5) × 1.0 × 0.9; 1.5 × 2.0 × 1.1

One nail had a flat, semi-circular head and a short shaft like a tack:

2387 L17/1 (5101) Topsoil — 3.0 × 0.5 × 0.4; 1.6 × 0.8 × 0.6

[2388] The following fragments may have belonged to iron nails, generally large:
Level IIc/d: **J20**/176 (1397); **K19**/194 (4506)
Level IIf/IIf1: **J18**/291 (5829)
Level IIf?: **J18**/427 (2365); **K18**/273 (6120)
Level II: **L19**/20 (5941)
Level I/II: **K18**/38 (4310)
Level I: **H18**/7 (2600); **J16**/167 (4722); **J18**/29 (2310), /54 (2311), /66 (2310); **J19**/111 (1653); **K17**/84 (9670); **K18**/44 (4314); **K19**/14 (1501); **L19**/4 (5903); **Q10**/43 (3118)
Topsoil: **H20**/11 (1205); **I16**/7 (4601), /33 (4600); **K16**/16 (4802)

Level E5a: **R18**/68 (2043)

Level 2: **I14**/193 (3446)
Level 1/2: **I14**/53 (3422); **J14**/90 (3357)
Level 1/2k: **I14**/63 (3430)
Level I: **I14**/34 (3412); **J14**/7 (3302), /16 (3306); **M14**/9 (3501)
Topsoil: **I14**/3 (3400) ; **M14**/3 (191)

Pins
See p. 517 above, for discussion.

[**2389**]　　　J19/139　　　　　　1653
Level I
Round head and very short piece of shaft.
L. (1.3); Di. 0.4; Head h. 0.8 × Di. 0.9

[**2390**]　　　K18/206　　　　　　4393
Level I
Tip missing, flattened triangular(?) head.
L. (4.2); Di. 0.3; head 0.5 × 0.6 × 0.4

Fragments of iron pin, needle or small nail shafts were found as follows:

[**2391**]
Level I: **J19**/40, 86 (1626); **L16**/15 (5626)
Level E5a: **R18**/68 (2043)
Level 1: **I14**/8 (3401) (possibly square)

Projectile points
See p. 518 above on **2246–54**, for discussion.

2392　　　J18/296　　　Etütlük 1998　　5840
Level IIf1
Corroded; complete (broken and repaired) leaf-shaped projectile point with swelling at the base (6.1 × 0.6–1.1) and long, square-sectioned tang (7.8 × 0.7) narrowing to 0.5 and ending in a point.
L. 14.0; Th. 2.0

[**2393**]　　　J18/308　　　　　　5849
Level IIe
Two leaf-shaped spearheads fused together with broken tangs; dimensions of each approximately the same, narrowing to 0.6 (Di. of tang).
L. (12.9); W. 2.1 max.; L. of head: *c.* 8.0; combined Wt 52.0

2394　　　J14/34　　　　　　3316
Level 1
Spearhead, well-preserved, socketed, leaf-shaped with pronounced midrib (H. 0.2 × W. 0.5) with rectangular section; only the very tip missing and a chip on the side.
L. (21.3); W. 4.4 max.; Th. 0.5; Socket L. 8.8, Di. 1.8 widening to 2.0; Wt 156.5 (but includes some earth in socket)
Similar spearheads, though in bronze, were found at Tarsus (Goldman 1956, fig. 427:97), Ugarit (Schaeffer 1939, pl. XXIII) and Tepe Sialk (Ghirshman 1939, 45, pl. XCII:24).

[**2395**]　　　J18/47　　　　　　2310
Level I
Corroded; complete (broken and repaired) leaf-shaped arrowhead, with tip bent and a bent, round-sectioned tang (4.1 × 0.6).
L. 6.0; W. 1.5; Th. 0.5; Wt 18 (but some of this is dirt)

2396　　　N12/25　　　　　　3207
Level 1
Corroded; spearhead shaped like an elongated triangle (L. 11.2) with inward-sloping shoulders; broken tang (2.0) tapering from 1.1 to 0.6 × 0.5 at break.
L. (13.2); W. 2.2; Wt 33.9

[**2396a**]　　　Q19/37　　　　　　2107
Level E2a
Two badly corroded objects described as iron spearheads were recorded from P94/41 but for some reason were not seen during the preparation of the publication.
L. 6.5 and 7.2

[**2397**]　　　I15/8　　　　　　4400
Topsoil
Flat, leaf-shaped arrowhead with tang broken off.
L. (4.8); W. 1.4 max.; Th. 0.3; Wt 4.9

[**2398**]　　　K14/41　　　　　　3012
Topsoil
Leaf-shaped arrowhead, possibly with a midrib (corroded), with tang broken off.
L. 3.5; W.1.2; Th. 0.8; Wt 4.0

Rings and chain links
[**2399**]　　　K19/338　　　　　　4561
Level IIc/d
Fragment of elongated chain link(?).
Di. of rod: 0.6

[**2400**]　　　J18/142　　　　　　2338
Level I
Half preserved.
L. 3.5; W. 2.1; Th. 0.5

[**2401**]　　　I18/22　　　　　　2709
Level I
Link fragment.
L. 2.1; Di. of rod: 0.5

[**2402**]　　　K18/208　　　　　　4393
Level I
Chain link, elongated and pinched in towards the middle, one end broken. Made from a rod, roughly round in section, of uneven diameter.
L. (6.1); W. 1.9; W. at middle 1.2; Di. as preserved *c.* 0.5?.

[**2403**]　　　L19/13　　　　　　5907
Level I
Elongated chain link or part of buckle.
L. 5.5; W. 3.5; Di. of rod 0.5

[**2404**]　　　N12/18　　　　　　3205
Level 1
Two fragments of chain links with part of the next link corroded on.
Di. 3.2; Di. of rod 0.6

2405　　　J16/5　　　　　　4600
Topsoil
Heavy; perhaps a link of a chain with a fragment of corrosion where the next link touched it(?).
Di. 6.5; Di. of section 1.0.

[**2406**]　　　J16/31　　　　　　4700
Topsoil
Chain link, elongated and pinched in towards the middle; made from a rod with a rectangular section (0.6 × 0.7).
L. 6.3; Di. 2.3 (max.)–1.7 (at middle)

[**2407**]　　　J17/11　　　　　　5000
Topsoil
Band forming a ring with overlapping ends, one tapering.
Di. 2.8 × 0.6 × 0.5.

[**2408**]　　　K19/4　　　　　　1500
Surface
Unclosed ring of round wire.
Di. 2.7; Di. of wire 0.4

Rods and strips

[2409] K19/181 1577
Level I
Narrow strip.
L. 3.1; W. 0.6; Th. 0.3

[2410] J18/24 2305
Level I
Narrow strip with one rounded end.
L. (3.8); W. 0.8; Th. 0.3

2411 K14/21 3005
Level 1
Two joining fragments, forming a strip with rounded ends.
10.3 × 3.1 × 0.3; 6.6 × 2.9 × 0.4

[2412] I17/9 4903
Topsoil
Rod with square section; slightly bent.
L. 15.5; W. 1.0; Th. 0.8
Fig. 314

[2413] J16/12 4700
Topsoil
Strip of uneven width and thickness now bent into a hook-shape with one flattened end.
L. c. 12.0; W. 0.3–0.7; Th. 0.2–0.6

[2414] J17/9 5000
Topsoil
Strip.
L. c. 6.2; W. 0.5; Th. 0.4

[2415] O12/1 203
Surface
Fitting consisting of a T-shaped piece of metal [4.1 × 1.4 – (c. 4.0) × 0.4] with arms of the T (one broken) folded round three sides of a square or rectangular upright with a row of four small holes for attachment in front; there is a bent extension on one side (2.4 × 1.2 × 0.4).
H. 5.1

Spatula

2416 I14/196 3403
Level 1
Complete, with a pointed end and a round shaft hammered flat at the other end to form a spatula (2.7 × 1.2 × 0.2) with the blade cut at an angle.
L. 11.2; Di. of shaft 0.5

Miscellaneous

[2417] J18/19 2365
Level IIf?
Well-preserved piece of iron with square section tapering to a point at both ends.
L. 4.0; W. 0.4; Th. 0.4

[2418] K18/39 4308
Level I
Arc-shaped handle of chest-of-drawers or similar object; probably modern.
L. 2.0; W. 3.0; Th. 0.6

Fragments of iron

Unidentifiable fragments of iron have been found in the following units and squares:

[2419]
Level IIf: **H18**/97 (2631), /120, 168 (2636); **I19**/77 (2802)
Level IIf?: **J18**/95 (2331)
Level IId: **K19**/61 (1535)
Level II: **L19**/21 (5941)
Level I: **J18**/55 (2311)

Fragments of unspecified metal or slag

The concentration of slag and other pieces of metal in certain squares may indicate that metal-working took place in these areas.

[2420]
Level IIId: **H19**/411 (4214)
Level IIc: **K19**/407 (4597)
Level IId/e: **K19**/300 (4533)
Level IIe: **K20**/221 (1929)
Level IIf: **J18**/164 (2366), /281 (5829)
Level II?: **L19**/22 (5927)
Level I: **I18**/7 (2702); **J16**/160 (4706); **J18**/50, 59 (2311); **J19**/16 (1602), /30 (1604), /126 (1653), /138 (1661), /403 (1602), /439 (1626); **K17**/78 (9659); **K18**/26 (4307), /202 (4393); **K19**/177 (4500)

Level 3: **I14**/157 (3702)
Level 2: **I14**/128 (3478), /193 (3446); **K14**/76 (3036), /133 (3078), /150 (3800)
Level 2k: **I14**/104 (3465); **J14**/106 (3368)
Level 1: **J14**/12 (3305); **L16**/8 (5626), /25 (5632), /32 (5638)

Chapter 42

Bone, Horn and Ivory

Polydora Baker & Dominique Collon

This chapter is primarily concerned with worked bone artefacts. The catalogue entries and descriptions of Dominique Collon have been combined with the osteological expertise of Polydora Baker. At all periods the repertoire of bone artefacts is poor, and many fragments do not permit proper classification. Evidence of use or working is usually indicated by polished or smoothed surfaces and cut marks.

The great bulk of unworked animal bone from Kilise Tepe has been the object of a separate study by Baker, which is to be published later, with full statistical details. Here she only describes pieces whose location *in situ* was noted during excavation, and other individual finds of particular interest. These include a number of unworked astragali and fragments of antler, which require description alongside visibly worked or used examples from similar contexts.

Astragali (2421–52)

Sheep and/or goat unless specified. Two groups are described first. **2421** is a hoard of knuckle-bones deliberately buried beneath the floor of the IIc Stele Building. This obliges us to consider the concentration of some 20 astragali in and behind the altar in Room 3 (**2422**) as significant, and for comparison with these two groups, to give attention to the nature and context of other worked and even unworked astragali. After **2422** the entries are arranged by level.

For caches of astragali in Near Eastern buildings see Gilmour 1997, mentioning instances from Alishar, Gordion and Tarsus. We may add to the list of Anatolian examples Hacilar (Mellaart 1970, [12] Level VI) and Beycesultan (a group of 77 in Level II Room 13, a secular Late Bronze Age context: Lloyd 1972, 12 with pl. VIa). Further east, but closer in time, 19 sheep/goat astragali were found on the floor in Room 11 of the Mitanni Palace at Tell Brak, Syria, while a total of 93 pierced sheep/goat astragali were in and between the two 'vestry' rooms of the nearby Mitanni Temple (Oates *et al.* 1997, 26, 29, 31, 32).

2421   J18/345   5870
Level IIc, Stele Building Rm 7
This deposit of 99 astragali, mainly from sheep and goat, was found in a small pit contrived beneath the floor plaster near the south wall of the room. It includes worked and/or cut astragali, as well as unworked ones. Although worked caprine astragali are ubiquitous in all areas and periods at Kilise Tepe, this is by far the largest deposit. Most other finds consist of single or a few associated specimens.

The methods of study are described below, followed by a description of the finds. The data are presented in Tables 17–18, with further details to be included in the digital data base.
Fig. 315

Methods: The astragali were identified to species where possible. The criteria of Boessneck (1969) were followed for distinguishing between sheep and goat, and for determining sex. It was not always possible to arrive at a secure identification. Where the identification is probable, this is indicated by cf., and where a less secure (possible) identification was recorded, this is indicated by cf. cf. The criteria of Lister (1996) were followed for distinguishing between fallow and red deer. Measurements were taken following von den Driesch (1976). In the case of the burnt specimens, the data will not be included in the wider osteometric study, as burning is known to cause bone to shrink (Gilchrist & Mytum 1986; Shipman *et al.* 1984). The presence of working or butchery marks was recorded. Most of the evidence for working consists of bone facets that are worked flat; in some cases this is very

Table 17. *Deposit 5870: distribution of astragali by species, sex and body side. Numbers in brackets are not included in totals, as they are included in main species group.*

Species	Side						Total
	Female?		Male?		Indeterminate		
	left	right	left	right	left	right	
Goat, *Capra hircus*			1		21	25	47
(cf. *Capra hircus*)					3	5	8)
(cf. cf. *Capra hircus*)						4	4)
Sheep, *Ovis aries*	3		6	7	8	10	34
(cf. *Ovis aries*)	1			2	2	3	8)
(cf. cf. *Ovis aries*)			1	1	3	5	10)
Sheep/goat					7	9	16
Fallow deer, cf. *Dama dama*						2	2
Total	3	0	7	7	38	44	99

Table 18. *2421: deposit under floor of Rm 7 (unit 5870). Distribution of modifications by species and side.*

Species	Total		Worked		Cutmarks		Charred		Battered		Rodent		Semi-digestion		Modern breakage	
	left	right	left	right	left	right	left	right	left	right	left	right	left	right	left	right
Goat, *Capra hircus*	22	25	2(+3)	11	8	13	19	14(+2)								1
Sheep, *Ovis aries*	17	17	2(+1)	6(+1)	5	6	4(+3)	13	1			1				
Sheep/goat	7	9	3	6	4	2	5	7(+1)						1	1	1
Fallow deer, cf. *Dama dama*	2		2				2									
Total	48	51	9(+4)	23(+1)	17	21	30(+3)	34(+3)	1			1		1	1	2

Goat includes cf. Goat and cf. cf. Goat; Sheep includes cf. Sheep and cf. cf. Sheep. Additional numbers (+n) refer to specimens in which evidence of modification is uncertain.

marked. Polished surfaces were occasionally observed. The worked finds are described in detail and those with more severe or unusual modification are illustrated. Many of the bones also show cut-marks. The type and number of marks, as well as the location (proximal, mid, distal) and facet (anterior, posterior, medial, lateral) on which the marks were observed was recorded, in order to understand better the purpose and procedure of cutting. So, an astragalus with cutmarks on the 'distal anterior-lateral facet' is cut on the anterior surface near the lateral side/edge, at the distal end of the bone. Most of the bones are charred and the degree of burning was recorded. Other modifications, including weathering, root etching and gnawing by carnivores or rodents, were recorded where present.

Taxonomic distribution: The deposit includes 97 astragali of sheep or goat and two of large cervid, probably fallow deer (Table 17). The caprine bones include 47 goat, 34 sheep, and a further 16 indeterminate sheep/goat elements. The relative frequency of sheep and goat reflects that recorded in the wider animal bone assemblage from Kilise Tepe, in which approximately 60 per cent goat and 40 per cent sheep may be observed (Baker 2005). The bones are distributed evenly between the right and left sides (Table 17). Sex distinction was successful in only a few cases, and mainly for sheep; the results show a majority of male elements (see Table 17).

Sheep/goat
Worked bones: A total of 32 astragali show clear evidence of working and a further five elements may be worked. A higher proportion of right astragali (23) are modified than left astragali (9), and the ratio (c. 2.5:1) changes little if the possibly worked specimens are included: 24 right versus 13 left (c. 2:1). The ratio does not reflect the fairly even distribution of right and left elements in the deposit, but the reason for the discrepancy is not known.

The evidence for working consists mainly of flattening on various facets of the bones. In some cases only one facet is worked flat, but on most bones two or more sides are worked. The degree of modification varies widely from very slight abrasion of the more prominent ridges, to complete wearing away of all surface features. In addition to the presence of worked facets, a few specimens are partly or completely pierced. One right goat astragalus has a hole in the anterior side, just above the centre of the bone; a right sheep/goat astragalus has a hole in the centre of the anterior side; a left sheep/goat astragalus has a hole pierced through the middle of the lateral-anterior edge.

Butchery marks: A total of 38 specimens show cut-marks. Cut marks were observed primarily on the distal and less commonly on the mid anterior surface, near the medial and lateral edges. Cut marks are much less common on the posterior side, or on the lateral and medial facets. The location of the marks suggests that these result from disarticulation of the feet. They may also have resulted during the skinning process. Modern procedures of skinning and butchery were observed in 1995 in South Central Turkey. To facilitate removal of the skins, an incision is made at the location of the ankle joint, into which the butcher blows air; this releases the skin from the muscle. Unfortunately, the bones from this activity were not collected so it is uncertain if this procedure resulted in marks in the same location as observed on the archaeological bones.

Burning: A total of 64 specimens, including all but seven of the worked/possibly worked specimens, are burnt and an additional six may also be burnt (see Table 18). The burning ranges from light (brown colour) to complete charring (blackening). None of the bones are calcined, which indicates that they were not exposed to a very high heat; this results instead in a grey to white colour and may even lead to twisting and cracking of the bones. Most of the burnt specimens appear to be completely charred

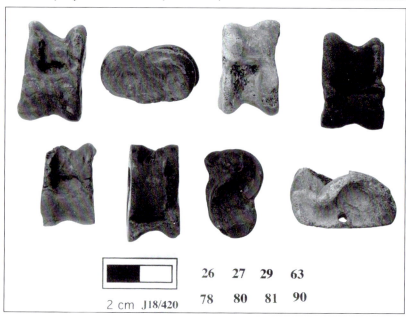

Figure 315. *Selected astragali from hoard* **2421** *in Level IIc, Rm 7.*

but five bones show partial charring. The differential charring may result from the position of the bones, with those placed at the centre of the deposit being least affected. This cannot be verified, as the exact location of each astragalus was not recorded during excavation.

Other modifications: One astragalus shows possible rodent gnawing, one specimen is battered, and three show modern breakage. The surface of one astragalus appears very irregular, as if corroded, and it may be semi-digested. The presence of a semi-digested specimen as well as the possibly gnawed bone suggests that astragali that were at one point discarded as rubbish, were collected for inclusion in the deposit. A semi-digested bone also occurs in the smaller group of astragali from unit 6209 (**2422**).

Fallow deer, cf. *Dama dama*
Two left astragali of probable fallow deer are included in the deposit. Identification is based on the presence of criteria 1 and 2 after Lister (1996) (shape of curvature of proximal end). The identification of one of the finds (no. 99) is supported by the metric data. The length (GL1 42.5 mm) and breadth (Bd 25.7) measurements compare closely to a large group of fallow deer astragali from the Neolithic site of Khirokitia, Cyprus (Davis 1994). The specimen is worked flat on the lateral, anterior and medial sides, and shows many cuts or scratch marks at the distal end of the lateral and medial sides. The second astragalus (no. 98) is worn almost completely flat on the anterior and posterior facets, reducing it to a rectangular disk (see Figs. 316 & 469). Wear on the medial and lateral sides is less pronounced. Both specimens are charred.

[2422]   Collections of astragali in K19   6209
Groups of astragali were found in association with the Level IIb/c altar in Rm 3 of the Stele Building. Some were behind it but others were actually incorporated into the plaster on its face.
K19/448: This group consists of twenty-one astragali and three fragments (see Table 19). Only one sheep left astragalus is worked — the anterior and medial facets are worked flat — and a few show cut-marks (possibly associated with disarticulation). A few astragali are partly or completely charred or calcined. The relatively infrequent occurrence of charring indicates that the bones were not burnt as a single unit, but rather that a few burnt bones were collected prior to deposition. The partly charred specimens may indicate that some carcasses were roasted. The natural modifications observed on the bones also suggest that the astragali were obtained from different sources. A number of specimens show abrasion, rodent gnawing and possibly semi-digestion, suggesting that they had been exposed for a period of time prior to burial or incorporation into the altar

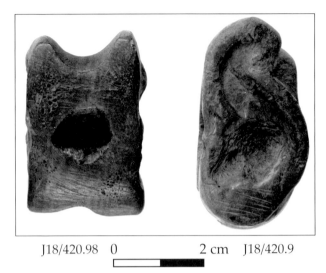

Figure 316. *Two deer astragali from 2421.*

structure. It also indicates that these bones, even if waste, were collected. An abraded and charred fragment of a probable sheep/goat tarsal (centrotarsale) is included in the deposit.
K19/460: goat right astragalus, not worked or butchered/cut.
K19/461: a sheep/goat left astragalus (medial side only), not worked or butchered/cut.
K19/472: from plaster face of altar. Two unworked astragali: one goat, left, not worked or butchered/cut, one sheep, right, not worked or butchered/cut.
K19/473: from plaster face of altar. One sheep/goat left astragalus, worked flat on lateral and anterior sides.
K19/474: from behind altar. Three astragali: one goat left astragalus, cut-marks on anterior distal medial and lateral sides; one possible goat left astragalus, not worked or butchered/cut; one possible goat right astragalus, with rodent gnawing on medial and lateral sides of proximal end and anterior-lateral side at distal end.

2423   H20/1032   5362
Level Vf3?
a. Possible sheep left astragalus, worked flat on lateral and medial sides. Hole present in proximal anterior side but not pierced through.
b. Probable goat left astragalus, worked flat on lateral and medial sides.
c. Possible fallow deer left astragalus, worked flat on lateral and medial sides; possible polish on distal anterior surface and proxi-

Table 19. *2422: astragali from altar area in Rm 3 (unit 6209). Distribution of species, body side and modifications.*

Species	Total left	Total right	Worked left	Worked right	Cutmarks left	Cutmarks right	Charred left	Charred right	Calcined left	Calcined right	Abrasion left	Abrasion right	Erosion left	Erosion right	Rodent left	Rodent right	Semi-digestion left	Semi-digestion right
Goat, *Capra hircus*	2	5			1	1	3							1		1		
cf. Goat	2												2					
cf. cf. Goat	1	2				2	1				1			1	1			
Sheep, *Ovis aries*	2	1	1								1					1		
cf. Sheep	2	1											1					
Sheep/goat		1										1						1
cf. Sheep/goat	1					1					1		1					
Medium artiodactyla	1						1						1					
Total	11	10	1	0	1	3	3	3	0	1	3	1	3	3	1	2	0	1

Figure 317. *Three worked astragali **2423** from 5362 (Level Vf).*

mal surface. This specimen was originally identified as possible deer (species not indicated), but was not verified subsequently. The shape of the proximal end (criteria 1 and 2 in Lister 1996) and the measurements, which place it within, albeit at the low end of, the range of Fallow deer measurements from Cyprus (Davis 1994), suggest that it is from Fallow deer.
Fig. 317

2424   H20/1031   5347
Level Vf4
Sheep/goat left astragalus, worked flat on medial and lateral sides; worked on proximal-anterior facets; possible polish on posterior proximal-medial corner; two cut-marks on anterior distal-lateral surface. Two small holes pierced into the astragalus but not pierced through.

[2425]   H20/916a   5363
Level Vf2/3
Four unworked astragali. one sheep/goat right (with one cut-mark in the proximal-mid area on posterior-lateral surface); two sheep, left; one probable sheep, right.

[2426]   H20/1076   5372
Level Vf
Sheep/goat right astragalus; worked flat on medial, lateral, anterior and posterior sides.

[2427]   H19/327   4272
Level IVb
Fifteeen astragali: 7 sheep, 4 goat, 4 sheep/goat; 3 sheep and 1 goat were worked.

[2428]   H19/318   4268
Level IVb
Eighteen astragali: 6 sheep, 7 goat, and 5 sheep/goat; 4 sheep, 2 goat and 2 unattributed were worked.

[2429]   H19/49   4211
Level IIIc/d
Goat right astragalus, worked flat on anterior side.

[2430]   I20/51a   4004
Level IIb
Two astragali:
a. Goat left astragalus, possibly worked and polished, cut down posterior lateral surface, polished
b. Probable goat right astragalus, worked flat on anterior, medial and lateral sides (lateral side completely flat).

[2431]   K20/240   1975
Level IIb
Sheep left astragalus, worked completely flat on lateral side and on medial side at proximal end. Cut-marks on mid-distal anterior-medial side, distal lateral side, middle of medial side.

[2432]   K19/464   6203
Level IIb/c
Possible sheep left astragalus, worked flat on lateral side.

[2433]   K20/239   1962
Level IIb/c
Sheep/goat left astragalus, worked flat on lateral side, polished at distal anterior end.

[2434]   J18/412   5893
Level IIc
Probable goat right astragalus, worked flat on lateral and medial sides (associated with unworked goat left astragalus, fine cut marks on distal anterior-medial surface).

[2435]   K19/475   4507
Level IIc
Three astragali:
a. Deer left astragalus, charred; hole pierced through lateral proximal corner, hole incompletely pierced through lateral anterior edge above centre of bone; small area of bone shaved off mid anterior-lateral facet, many fine cut-marks along anterior medial and lateral facets. This specimen was originally identified as red deer following Lister's (1996) criteria (1, 2, 4 and 5). However, criterion 3 is more like Fallow deer, and the measurements suggest that it is from this species (GLl 43.3 mm, Bd 27.0 mm, Dl 23.8 mm after von den Driesch 1976).
b. Possible sheep right astragalus, charred, worked flat on lateral and medial sides; cut-marks at the middle of medial side and on distal anterior-lateral facet.
c. Unworked charred possible sheep left astragalus.

[2436]   K19/341   4562
Level IIc
Sheep/goat right astragalus, hole pierced through centre, slight polish on anterior side, abrasion on lateral and anterior sides but uncertain if this is cultural or natural; worked on lateral and medial anterior side.

[2437]   J19/225a   1690
Level IId
Six astragali:
a. Goat left astragalus, worked flat on anterior side, one cut-mark on medial-anterior distal edge.
b. Sheep right astragalus, worked flat on anterior side, one longitudinal cut-mark on mid-posterior side, slight polish on medial-proximal corner.
c. Possible goat right astragalus, generalized polish on corners and surface, two longitudinal cut-marks on distal posterior surface.
d. Sheep right astragalus, hole pierced through centre, not worked flat on sides but heavy rubbing or polishing has rounded edges.
e–f. Two unworked, one sheep left, one goat right.

[2438]   K19/465   6200
Level IIc/d
Probable sheep left astragalus, worked flat on lateral, medial and anterior sides.

[2439] K19/435 6202
Level IIc/d
Probable sheep left astragalus, with cut-marks on anterior distal medial and lateral surface. Not worked.

[2440] J18/410 5880
Level IId
Goat left astragalus, worked flat on lateral and medial sides; fine cuts on distal anterior-medial side.

[2441] J18/429 5808
Level IId/e
Goat right astragalus, worked flat on lateral side; fine cut-mark on distal anterior-medial side, possible cut-marks on mid anterior medial and lateral side.

[2442] J18/413 5822
Unstratified
Goat right astragalus, hole pierced through the middle of the proximal end.

[2443] K18/226 6111
Level IIf
Sheep/goat right astragalus, possibly worked flat on medial side (heavy erosion impedes secure determination), worked flat on lateral side.

[2444] K18/304 6111
Level IIf
Sheep/goat right astragalus, worked flat on lateral side; possibly worked flat or eroded on medial side.

2445 I19/205 1781
Level IIg
Sheep/goat right, worked flat on lateral, anterior and medial sides.

2446 I14/86 3455
Level 2
Probable sheep/goat, right astragalus; heavily calcined; hole at proximal end with a small copper/bronze wire through it, folded round to form a ring.
Also from the same pit were two sheep/goat astragali, three or more pieces of tusk (**2490**), a metal pin (**2243**) and some fragments of blue glass tessera (**2161**).

[2447] I14/114 3474
Level 2
Sheep/goat left astragalus, hole pierced through middle.

[2448] K14/157 3091
Level 2 lower
Goat right astragalus, worked flat on lateral side and proximal posterior lateral surface; slight polish on proximal and distal anterior-lateral surface.

[2449] K14/159 3097
Level 2 lower
Possible sheep right astragalus, worked flat on medial, lateral, anterior and posterior sides; fine cut marks on mid and distal anterior lateral surface.

[2450] K19/116 1567
Level I/II
Sheep/goat left astragalus, worked flat on anterior and posterior sides.

[2451] R18/147 2428
Level E5a
Probable goat left astragalus, worked flat on lateral and medial sides; wear on distal lateral end is very heavy and on slight diagonal.

[2452 number not used]

Awls and points (2453–4)

These are the tips of antler tines, unless otherwise specified. As with astragali, the examples from H20 are Early Bronze Age, and all the other examples come from Level II. The working and use of the various parts of an antler in archaeological context is discussed by Kull, together with a summary of antler products from other Anatolian sites (Kull 1988, 188f., fig. 182; cf. also Choyke 2000).

[2453] H20/569 1859
Level Vj
Black polished point — grey core — part of a burnishing tool? Found with 'champagne cup' **205**. Possibly not bone but polished clay.
L. (1.6); W. 0.8; Th. 0.5

[2454] H20/799 1852
Level Vi
Tip of a pointed and well-polished bone object.
L. 1.3; Th. 0.2

2455 H20/692 5313
Level Ve
Awl? Fragment of antler or large mammal bone, showing some cortical and cancellous bone; tip missing; widens and, at the other end, is also broken; it is tapered forming a collar with faint horizontal cuts.
L. (5.6); W. 0.8; Th. 0.7; Di. 0.7 max.

[2456] H20/698 5313
Level Ve
Bone or antler tine(?); sharp intact tip, polished. Broken at other end.
L. 3.1

[2457] I19/157 2880
Level IIa/b
Probable sheep metatarsal used at its distal end as an awl; there are cuts across the proximal end on the anterior side.
L. 10.4

[2458] I19/208 5537
Level IIb
Worked bone splinter, from large mammal bone, rounded and smoothed at one end. Dark colour at tip may indicate charring.
L. 6.9

[2459] J19/228 1690
Level IId
Three smoothed, rounded tips; burnt. The smallest piece has transverse cut marks; the largest (measured) may be from a red deer.
L. 8.9; W. 3.9; Th. 3.1

2460 J20/131 1364
Level IIb–d
Smoothed and rounded at the point, with the other end squared

(perhaps a handle or for attachment to something else).
L. 8.7; Th. 0.7

[2461] J20/186 1363
Level IIb–d
Antler or large mammal bone, showing some cortical and cancellous bone; both ends broken. Rounded into a cylinder and smoothed. At one end a groove runs across the top surface.
L. 2.9

[2462] K18/263 6126
Level IIc
Small fish(?) bone — 'nail' shaped(?).
L. 1.8

2463 K20/134 1943
Level IIc/d
Large mammal bone, probably not antler, worked to a point at both ends. Surface badly preserved, otherwise complete.
L. 14.9; Di. 1.0 max.

Pins or needles (2464–8)

[2464] H20/786 5333
Level Ve
Tip of a pin or needle; broken off piece of bone, fashioned into a long, thin cylinder, oval in cross-section with two flattened sides. It tapers almost to a point at one end. The other end is missing.
L. 4.6; W. 0.3; Th. 0.15

[2465] H20/886 5347
Level Vf4
Fragment of a bone needle(?), very slender. Broken at both ends.
L. 5.5; Th. 0.2

[2466] I20/51b 4004
Level IIb
Pin? Polished sliver of bone.
L. *c.* 2.3; W. 0.4–0.5; Th. 0.2–0.25

[2467 number not used]

[2468] J18/133 2347
Level I/II?
Smoothed, rounded and cut transversally.
L. 5.8

Notched pins (2469–70)

These objects numbered **2469** were all found together in the lower fill of a pit in the NW corner of Rm 7 in the IIc Stele Building (see above p. 134 for the problem of the pit's exact date). They were all burnt and very liable to break. Each one tapers to a rounded point, often polished as though from use, but is flattened towards the head, with one side more or less flat (or even slightly concave) and the other gently convex (or occasionally sliced flat). The head is either straight across or gabled with two joining sloping surfaces, which often look as though they are freshly broken along one or two cut lines. Invariably on the right edge of the flatter side two notches have been cut diago-

Table 20. *2469: dimensions of notched bone implements, giving overall length, and distance between top (A), notches (B and C), and bottom (D). Photos of the examples marked P are shown in Figure 318. Incomplete dimensions in round brackets.*

	Condition	Length	A–B	B–C	C–D	Photo
1	Complete	7.4	0.45	0.7	6.2	P
2	Complete	7.2	0.6	0.7	5.9	
3	Complete	6.6	0.5	0.7	5.4	
4	Lacks upper end	6.6	–	0.6	5.3	P
5	Complete	6.5	0.45	0.7	5.4	
6	Complete	7.0	0.6	0.7	5.7	
7	Lacks very tip	7.1	0.6	0.7	~6.0	
8	Complete	7.3	0.3	0.6	6.3	
9	Complete	7.7	0.5	0.6	6.6	
10	Complete	6.7	0.5	0.6	5.6	P
11	Lacks very tip	(6.5)	0.55	0.65	(5.3)	P
12	Lacks tip	(6.4)	0.5	0.6	(5.2)	
13	Lacks tip	(5.2)	0.4	0.8	(3.9)	
14	Lacks lower part	(4.5)	0.5	0.7	(3.3)	
15	Lacks lower part	(5.2)	0.3	0.5	(4.4)	
16	Lacks tip	(5.9)	0.5	0.7	(4.7)	
17	Lacks upper end	7.0	(0.4)	0.8	5.7	
18	Complete	6.7	0.6	0.6	5.5	
19	Complete	7.0	0.5	0.7	5.7	
20	Complete	6.65	0.6	0.7	5.3	
21	Complete	6.8	0.5	0.7	5.6	
22	Complete	6.9	0.5	0.7	5.7	
23	Complete	6.6	0.45	0.8	5.3	
24	Complete	6.7	0.7	0.75	5.2	
25	Lacks tip	(4.8)	(0.45)	0.45	(3.7)	
26	Lacks tip	(5.5)	0.5	0.8	(4.2)	
27	Complete	5.5	0.55	0.75	4.25	
28	Lacks tip	(4.8)	0.45	0.6	(3.8)	
29	End damaged?	(6.1)	(0.3)	0.65	5.2	
30	Complete	7.25	0.5	0.85	5.9	
31	Complete	6.7	0.55	0.7	5.25	
32	Lacks tip	(6.2)	0.45	0.7	(5.0)	
33	Complete	6.3	0.4	0.8	6.3	
34	Complete	7.2	0.4	0.8	7.2	
35	Complete	7.3	0.65	0.7	7.3	

nally, mostly at a distance of 7 mm apart, but sometimes as close as 4.5 mm or as far as 8.5 mm apart. 35 complete or nearly complete examples were rejoined, and there were at least 11 others, making a minimum total of 46. The normal length is about 7 cm, but they vary; one complete example was only 5.5 cm long, and another as much as 8.5 cm. In a few cases (Nos.

4, 11, 24, 36) there are one or more cuts transversely across the rounded back; these may be the accidental result of manufacture or in some cases aborted cuts along an intended break line. Instead of the usual diagonal notches, No. 8 has rough squarish, and No. 15 semi-circular notches, but in other respects these tools are remarkably uniform. It is pointless to describe each instance individually, but because the precise dimensions may assist in identifying the technical purpose of these very specific tools, Table 20 gives the dimensions of the 35 reconstructed ones.

The closest parallels to these tools appear to come from Mound A at Alişar, in Level 3. Schmidt writes that 'The most common type of bone point has a head marked off by a notch', and the examples illustrated appear like ours to be flattened, with a side notch (Schmidt 1933, 79–80 fig. 124, in particular a1145, 1475 and a801); none however has the two notches which are so characteristic of our group. As to their purpose, we remain in the dark. The pointed end and the notches might be taken to support a use with a thread or string of some kind, such as netting or crotcheting. There is also a distinct resemblance to flattened implements from Gordion identified as weaving shuttles (some on display in the site museum), with one pointed end and notches in the side of the other end. These are referred to in Burke 1998, 202, on the basis of descriptions in Sheftel 1974 (not seen); however our examples seem smaller and surprisingly light if they fulfilled this function.

Figure 318. *Notched bone implements 2469 (nos. 1, 4, 10 and 11).*

2469   J19/322/1–35   3935
Level IIc/d
In P97/49, dug into the NW corner of Level IIc Rm 7 of the Stele Building. More than 35 bone implements; for dimensions see Table 20.
Fig. 318

2470   R18/195   2453
Level E5b
Antler tine(?). One side is flattened; notch at top of rounded side and another at right-angles to it; the notches are cut straight across at the top and at an angle at the bottom.
L. 5.9; Th. 0.6

Bone tubes (2471–8)

The bone tubes appear in levels from the Early Bronze Age onwards. They may have fulfilled a number of functions, but most were probably handles for knives or tools.

2471   H20/404   1826
Level Vf/g
Outer surface is highly polished. Both ends have a number of grooves incised on the inner edge. Cut from lower tibia shaft of a medium-sized mammal.
L. 7.25; Th. 1.3; W. 1.5

2472   H20/769   5313
Level Ve
Medium artiodactyl tibia, right mid-shaft hollowed out; natural erosion on outside; cut transversally at distal end and probably at proximal end.
L. 9.0; W. 1.4

[2473]   H19/376   4248
Level IIIa/IVb
Probable artiodactyl left tibia distal shaft. Probably cut at both ends; edges not well-defined due to erosion.
L. (3.0)

2474   J19/378   3970
Level IIc
Slightly flattened cylinder, broken at both ends and cut back at one end. Core hollowed out and, apparently, finished off with a drill.
L. 2.0; Di. perf. 0.2

[2475]   H18/128   2636
Level IIf
Possible hare-sized to medium mammal-sized bone, cut transversally at both ends.
L. 2.3

[2476]   J18/192   2381
Level IIf1?
Medium mammal long-bone or antler? Cut across section and hollowed out. The surface and ends are polished.
L. 1.9

[2477]   J19/210   1744
Level I/IIh?
Bone tube made from distal half of a sheep/goat metatarsal (identification based on slight groove on anterior facet of bone); cut at both ends. A very similar piece was recorded from unit 1781.
L. 3.5

2478 R18/173 2436
Level E5b
Medium mammal long-bone; cut transversely at both ends with a short transverse cut near one end.
L. 3.4; Th. 0.2

Spatulas (2479–80)

The spatulas were both found near the surface. They could have been used for weaving (Friend 1998, 10, 61–6 & pl. 3, suggests pattern-weaving for which such tools are still used), burnishing, or for other functions (Obladen-Kauder 1996, 301–4, pls. 143–4, who gives a list of published Neolithic to Early Bronze Age occurrences). They are ubiquitous at all periods and probably well beyond the Near East. Their use in Mesopotamia is discussed by Moorey (1994, 113).

2479 H18/86 2626
Level IIf
Long-bone, probably of a large mammal, with the inside of the bone structure visible on one side and the other highly polished. One end has been carefully rounded and the edges have been smoothed.
L. (5.3); Th. 0.2

[2480] J18/415 2317
Level IIg/h?
Slightly curved rib with weathered, rounded end; other end broken. Shaved lengthways; one side pitted from use(?).
L. (7.8); Th. 0.6

Miscellaneous (2481–92)

[2481] H20/550 1857
Level Vh/i
Three broken but joining fragments of antler(?) that have been polished smooth. It is cut and rounded at the wide end. The very tip is missing.
Di. 1.6

[2482] H20/570 1859
Level Vj
Fragments of highly polished bone — both on main surface and edges. Black. Possibly used as a burnishing tool for pottery.

2483 H20/581 1270
Level IVa
Two fragments, probably from the antler of a large deer, using its natural curvature, to form a hollow tube or a semi-circular shape (less than 180° survives). There are perforations through the wall, and one rounded end which is slightly thickened (perhaps the beginning of the burr); the other end is broken away.
Di. c. 3.5–4.0
(a) L. (3.5); W. (3.6); ten holes bored through it (one of Di. 0.5; nine of Di. 0.3).
(b) L. (5.1); W. 2.4; six holes bored through it (one of Di. 0.5; five of Di. 0.3).
Fig. 319
Hollowed and perforated antler objects are known from Beycesultan, and identified as cheek pieces for a horse bridle (Mellaart & Murray 1995, 125, 186 fig. 0.36:311–12; Late Bronze Age). Here and at Boğazköy they were found in pairs (Boehmer 1972, 201f., pl. LXXV: 2114–15). The Kilise Tepe fragments are by no means identical but if semi-circular rather than cylindrical conceivably served the same purpose.

[2484] H19/175 4248
Level IIIa/IVb
Worked bone. Hollowed medium mammal long bone cut transversely and polished. Notches incised on surfaces. Bone bead?
L.1.2

[2485] H19/146 4240
Level IIIb
Worked bone. Two metatarsal fragments, possibly cattle or deer. Worn on one broken edge and polished on outer surfaces. Burnt black.
L. 3.5

2486 I20/70 4018
Level IIIe
Two long, probably joining, squared pieces of bone each with a round dowel at one end; carefully cut from cortical bone of a large mammal long-bone.
(a) L. (10.1) × 0.8 × 0.6 (dowel - L. 0.7 × Di. 0.3).
(b) (6.3) × 0.7 tapering to 0.8 × 0.5 (dowel - L. 0.4; Di. 0.3).
Fig. 320

2487 K19/303 4521
Level IIb/c
Dark brown disc of bone or antler with central perforation; one side flat, the other with a raised rim and the centre rising in two steps. There is a groove and row of small dots around the edge. For a similar disc in clay and references to parallels see **1530**.
Di. 2.4; Di. perf. 0.3; Th. 0.4 (edge), 0.5 (middle).
Fig. 460

Figure 319. *Perforated tube of antler* **2483**.

[2488] K20/191 1989
Level IIc
Worked burr and stem of large deer antler, entirely calcined (it was in destruction debris). Burr and stem with three step-like cut surfaces: 2 edges around antler, 1 through stem. Perhaps an unfinished object.

2489 J18/411 5800
Level IIf1
Ivory cylinder, broken lengthways; drilled through half way along its length (Di. 0.4), with a round dowel-hole below the drill-hole (Di. 0.6; 1.0 deep). The top is decorated with a deeply incised cross with drill-holes between the arms, and the bottom had eight radiating lines. This could have been used as a toggle.
L. 2.8

2490 I14/87 3455
Level 2
Curved fragment of some kind of ivory with lines incised transversely across the interior surface. Burnt black, as are other items from this pit (see **2446**).
L. (5.0); W. (at break) 0.8

2491 I20/9 KLT 7 1404
Level I/II
Carefully made from the bone of a large mammal. The inside of the bone structure is visible on one side. The other side is now rough. This could be part of a stylized figurine but is more likely to have had a utilitarian function such as a bobbin.
L. (8.5); W. 2.0; Th. 0.6 max.
Fig. 321

2492 K17/36 9618
Level 1
Squared piece of bone with blunt ends; possibly worked.
L. 3.4; Th. 0.5

Unworked bone (2493–9)

[2493] Antler
In addition to the pieces listed above, fragments of antler were frequent among the routine collections of bone from each unit. Some of these may have served as tools without showing any signs of working. They included the following pieces: **H18**/57 (2618); **H20**/97–8 (1230), /916b (5363); **I20**/76 (4024); **J14**/105 (3368); **J18**/25 (2307); **J19**/100 (1650), /225b, /229, /232, /236 (1690); **K18**/61 (4314), /96 (4348) Fig. 322, /98 (4349); **K19**/68 (1542), /156 (1591), /182 (4502), /275 (4514); **K20**/158–9 (1968), /162 (1965); **Q19**/98 (2138); **R18**/99, 101 (2402).

[2494] J18/393 5894
Level IIc/d
Horn core of a male goat, in good condition and almost complete. Completely charred, ranging in colour from grey to black.

[2495] J18/323 5855
Level IIe
Third phalanx of a bear's claw. Greatest length 49.0 mm. Proximal breadth 13.4 mm.

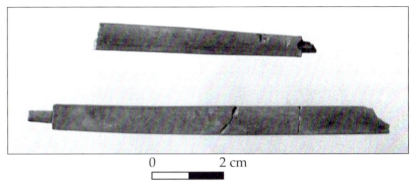

Figure 320. *Bone bar* **2486** *with dowels each end.*

Figure 321. *Carved bone artefact* **2491**.

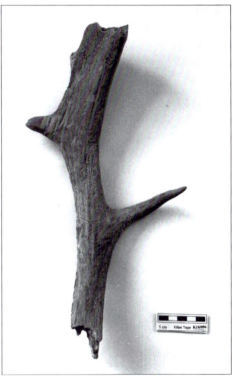

Figure 322. *Antler* 2493 *(K18/96).*

[2496] J19/443 1006
Level 1
This is a partial skeleton of a kid (based on the morphology of the lower deciduous third and fourth premolars, after Payne 1985). It includes the left mandible, in which the dP4 shows very light wear. The deciduous incisors are present, except for one di3. The forelimb elements and unfused epiphyses are present (scapulae, humeri, radii, ulnae, metacarpals). The bones are small and none of the epiphyses are fused, indicating a juvenile animal under 6–8 months (after Silver 1969). The third and fourth metacarpals are incompletely fused together at the distal ends. Some of the carpals have been lost. Four first and second phalanges and epiphyses, and four third phalanges are present; presumably these are associated

with the forelimbs. The unfused greater trochanter of the left femur is present also. A few other bone fragments, not associated with the skeleton are present.

[2497] K19/179 4500-1
Level I
Complete skeleton of an adult dog. All the major limb bones, metapodia, cranium, mandibles, vertebrae, manubrium and many fragmented ribs are present. Approximately half of the phalanges and carpals/tarsals are missing which is probably due to recovery bias. The absence of the baculum (*os penis*), which is much longer than the small bones is probably not due to recovery bias however, so the animal is probably a female. The cranium, mandible, atlas, axis, forelimb elements and some phalanges, carpals and tarsals are recorded from 4501 and the hindlimb elements, phalanges, and most carpals and tarsals are recorded from 4500. All the epiphyses are fused and the adult teeth are erupted, so the animal was at least 18 months at death. Three of the ribs show evidence of fractures or trauma. One rib has a partially healed fracture, with extra bony growth forming at both ends of the fracture and partially bridging the break. A second rib has a partially healed fracture, and is swollen with remodelled bone; the fracture is still visible. A third rib is swollen at about mid shaft, possibly a reaction to the trauma which caused the fractures in the above ribs. The skeleton is very well preserved.

[2498] K19/297 (4533), K19/291 & K19/295 (4528), K19/288 (4524)
Level IId/e
Partial skeleton of a juvenile dog, including the main limb bones and metapodia of the right side (except humerus, radio-ulna and innominate), miscellaneous left and right metacarpi, first, second and third phalanges, the right and left mandibles (4524 and 4528). The epiphyses of the main limb bones, metapodia and phalanges are unfused. In the right mandible (4524), P_2 and P_3 are almost fully erupted, P_4 is half erupted, and M_1 and M_2 are fully erupted. In the left mandible (4528; K19/295), P_1 and P_2 are not fully erupted, P_3 is almost fully erupted, M_1 and M_2 are fully erupted and M_3 is erupting. P_4 is not yet erupted and the alveoli of dP_4 are still visible. In the left maxilla (also from 4528), the dP^2 is present, P^3 is erupting and P^4, M^1 and M^2 are erupted. In the right maxilla, P^3, P^4, M^1 and M^2 are fully erupted. P^2 may have been lost during excavation. P^3 is pathological, with extra enamel which had formed on the occlusal surface. The roots of P^4 are slightly closer together at the aboral end, than in the left maxilla, possibly due to crowding caused by P^3. In the axis (4528) the epiphysis is unfused. The fusion and tooth eruption data indicate that the animal was less than 6–7 months at death (after Silver 1969). Four vertebrae, 21 cranial fragments and a possible ear ossicle were recovered also.

2499 K19/135 1577
Level I
Right cranial fragments, left mandible and right forelimb elements (scapula, humerus, ulna, radius) of a very juvenile, possibly foetal or neonatal, dog. All elements are very small and incompletely ossified. All of the epiphyses were unfused and the dP4 is unerupted or just beginning to erupt through the bone, indicating an age of less than 5–8 weeks (after Silver 1969).

2499a K18/79 4331
Level IIe/f
Almost complete skeleton of a juvenile dog, including all the major limb bones, cranium (broken), mandibles, axis and atlas, some metacarpals, metatarsals, carpals, tarsals and phalanges, and many rib and vertebral fragments. The epiphyses of the limb bones, metapodials and phalanges are unfused. The main bones of the pelvis are not fused together but the permanent teeth are erupted, so the animal was probably just under or *c.* 6–7 months (after Silver 1969).

Chapter 43

Fossils

Dominique Collon

Fossils were found at all levels. Most are marine fossils. These are to be expected in limestone terrain and many would have been unintentional constituents of mud brick. However, there is some evidence for an interest in fossils. The larger shells, sponge and coral fragments could hardly have been accidental inclusions; indeed a large coral fossil, **2519** (*c.* 28.0 × 14.0 cm), was recovered in Rm 5 of the (Level IIc) Stele Building where it had been built into the inner face of a wall with the adjacent brick cut away to accommodate it. Equally significantly, perhaps, the sea-urchin fossil, **1998**, was drilled through and used as a spindle whorl. The following descriptions are written by a non-specialist and are for reference only. The photographs will provide a better indication for the specialist of the types of fossils present.

Figure 323. *Fossil bi-valve shells from different levels: **2503**, **2505**, **2500**, **2504**.*

Shells: bivalves (2500–507)

The bivalve shells are all of the scallop variety and range in size from a maximum diameter of 0.9–7.0 cm. The best-preserved have markings on both sides.

[2500] H20/789 5333
Level Ve
L. 5.2; W. 4.9
Fig. 323

[2501] H19/246 4257
Level IVa/b
Small.

[2502] H19/50 4211
Level IIIc/d
Large.

[2503] H19/117 4232
Level IIIc/d
W. 2.2
Fig. 323

[2504] K19/395 4586
Level IId
Large.
Fig. 323

[2505] J18/123 2343
Level I
Fig. 323

[2506] J18/190 2373
Level I
W. <1.0

[2507] Q19/5 178
Surface
Small, orange-coloured, in a buff stone matrix.
L. 1.3; W. 1.9

Shells: spiraliform univalves (2508–15)

The spiraliform shells are of various types: two resemble snail shells (max. W. 3.6 and 10.5 cm) but the others are upright varieties, all incomplete, and ranging in height from 2.8–5.1 cm.

[2508] H20/852 5349
Level Vf3
Fig. 324

[2509] H20/286 1267
Level Ve
L. 4.0; W. 2.0
Fig. 324

Chapter 43

Figure 324. *Fossilized univalve shells: 2510a, 2509, 2510, 2508, 2511, 2512, 2514, 2513.*

Figure 325. *Fossils: 2517, 2521.*

Figure 326. *Fossilized coral (?) 2518.*

[2510] K19/113 1566
Level IIc
Fig. 324

[2510a] I19/22 1732
Level I
White stone with fossil of a large univalve shell on one side.
L. 10.5; W. 8.5
Fig. 324

[2511] L14/16 3602
Level 1
L. 5.1; W. 2.2
Fig. 324

[2512] R18/104 2403
Level E5b
L. (2.7); W. 2.1
Fig. 324

[2513] N12/2 3200
Topsoil
L. 3.8; W. 3.3
Fig. 324

[2514] J9/3 313
Surface
L. (4.2)
Fig. 324

[2515] Q20/2 183
Surface
Broken, elongated, encased in calcareous material.

Dentalium(?) (2516)

[2516] I20/91 1631
Level IId/e
Small cylinder, which is broken at one end. It has a knob on top where the perforation would normally be.
L. 1.1

Sponge(?) (2517)

[2517] S15/2 168
Surface
Coral, or possibly a loofah.
L. (4.3); W. (3.4)
Fig. 325

Coral(?) (2518–23)

See also **2517**, which could be a loofah rather than a coral.

[2518] H19/78 4217
Level IIIc
Cream-coloured with many round holes, like a bees' nest.
L. 13.2; W. 7.4; Th. 6.0
Fig. 326

[2519]   K19/466   4589
Level IIc; built into inner face of the E wall of Rm 5 of the Stele Building.
H. 14.0; Di. *c.* 28.0

[2520]   K18/303   6161
Level IIc

[2521]   K14/79   3037
Level 2 upper
Grey.
Fig. 325

[2522]   R18/17   2010
Unstratified
L. (6.5)

[2523]   P20/2   210
Surface

Shark's tooth (2524)

[2524]   K19/152   1587
Level IId/e
A light brown, smooth outer surface and dark inside. Very sharp pointed end which may be natural or worked.

Vegetal(?) (2525–8)

[2525]   H20/408   1829
Level Vf/g
Three pieces of fossil wood, all approximately the same length.
L. 2.0

[2526]   H20/236   1258
Level IVa
Fossil root cast.

[2527]   H19/250   4257
Level IVa/b
Three fragments that fit together to form a long, tube-like shape. There is a hole in the centre.
L. 4.5 (combined)

[2528]   K19/127   1567
Level I/II
Half a leaf impression(?) with both sides preserved; alternatively, this could be part of the spine of a fish.
L. <6.0

Unidentified (2529–32)

[2529]   J19/417   6403
Level IIc
Long, thin, bent cylinder, perhaps a worm-cast or the stalk of a plant.
L. 4.9

[2530]   K19/191   4506
Level IIc/d
Small fragment of stalk — a flaring, central portion with ribs on either side; coral(?).
L. 1.9

[2531]   J18/113   2344
Level I/II?
Small disc showing, on one side, a very fine, closely-hatched coil — perhaps a small centipede-like creature rolled up on itself four times, or the end of a plant or a seed.
L. 0.23; Di. 0.6

[2532]   L16/6   5626
Level 1
Sickle-shaped, with a rough surface.
L. 7.3; W. 5.4; Th. 6.6

Chapter 44

Lithics

Tim Reynolds

Introduction

A study has been undertaken of the chipped stone assemblage excavated at Kilise Tepe. A total of 480 units (contexts) have been examined; of these 435 proved to have chipped stone artefacts. All the contexts yielded only a small collection each, the largest single collection being 19 pieces from 5333 (H20/780). A total of 817 artefacts comprise the entire assemblage. The site has been occupied since the Early Bronze Age and there is a high degree of residuality of pieces. The total assemblage is rather nondescript comprising a random collection of discarded pieces and its potential to inform on prehistoric activities at the site is limited (see Conclusions, below pp. 554 ff.). The collection also lacks significant typological indicators; a borer, an obsidian arrowhead and a collection of sickle blades would be wholly consistent with an EBA date but could not be used to rule out earlier occupation. A variety of raw materials was used, most of it local, either derived from a pebble conglomerate in the Göksu river valley or from the surrounding limestone hills. Exploitation of material sources does not seem to have been intensive, nor is any material singled out for special technological or typological treatment. The reduction sequence employed generated flakes and blades with the former predominating. Blades and blade segments were selected for use as sickles. There is an amount of burnt material but this does not show any marked patterning. Certainly the manufacture of temper for pottery is unlikely given the frequencies of burnt material and its size.

In summary, the assemblage collected is small and difficult to characterize. It would seem most appropriate to assign an EB date but elements within it could be earlier. Activities identifiable from the collection include cereal harvesting, stone tool manufacture, cutting both soft and more durable substances, and scraping.

There are single examples of a borer and an arrowhead.

Methodology

All materials were examined in natural light, using a hand lens of ×5 when appropriate. The following variables were recorded:

1. Raw material. See below; all pieces are of chert unless otherwise specified.
2. Blank type (to include identification of primary, secondary and tertiary blanks and whether a piece was whole or fragmentary).
3. Striking platform type (categories used are plain, cortical, crushed, prepared and dihedral).
4. Edge damage (the presence of gloss, microflaking, lateral and transverse snaps, and half-moon snaps).
5. Retouch (its presence, location and form).
6. Maximum dimensions (Length, Width and Thickness measured in cm; Weight (g) was generally not recorded but was not necessary because there is a direct relationship between the volume and weight of a piece).
7. Presence of formal tool types.
8. Blank form (flake, blade, bladelet or chip).
9. Miscellaneous technological components (presence/absence of Janus flakes, Siret flakes, double-bulbs, plunged pieces, hinges and burning).
10. A cursory attempt was made at refitting within each sample. Refits were found where single pieces had been broken recently or burnt lumps had fragmented but no prehistoric refits were found.
11. All tools were drawn and a selection of utilized pieces and cores were also drawn.

Results

A total of 480 contexts were examined, of which 435 contained artefacts. All pieces were analysed for the variables noted above and a total of 62 drawings made from a total collection of tools, utilized pieces and cores of 79 pieces (i.e. 78 per cent were drawn).

It should be stressed that the majority of contexts were small and even the richest (5333 H20/780)

Table 21. *Total numbers of tools.*

Arrowhead	1	2533
Sickles	16	2534–49
Borer	1	2550
Microliths	2	2551–2
Scrapers	3	2553–5
Endscrapers	3	2556–8
Nosed scraper	1	2559
Backed blades	4	2560–63
Retouched blade	1	2564
Inversely retouched blade	1	2565
Truncated blade	1	2566
Serrated blade	1	2567
Knives	4	2568–71
Denticulates	2	2572–3
Hammerstone	1	2574

contains only 19 pieces. It is clear that the behavioural and other information potentially held in these collections is limited. Given these limitations this report will be structured to draw out as much data as possible without having to list the entire collection. There are a total of thirteen contexts with ten or more pieces and seventeen with between five and ten pieces (see Tables 29 & 30). The remaining 405 contexts have fewer than five pieces each.

Typology

A total of 41 chipped stone tools plus a single hammerstone were identified amongst the contexts studied. A tool list is presented in Table 21.

There are no specific chronological indicators within this collection with the exception of the arrowhead which is Late Neolithic/EBA in date.

Arrowhead
2533   H20/629   KLT 105   1289
Level Ve
Elongated bifacial pressure-flaked foliate point, with serrated edges. Black obsidian.
L. 5.4; W. 1.36; Th. 0.4; Wt 3

Sickles
The presence of sickle blades, including two with retouched crescentic backs (**2538** and **2542**) could argue for either a PPNA or EBA date but variations in sickle blade morphology are a poor indicator of chronology.

2534   H20/379   1820
Level Vf
Sickle on naturally-backed blade fragment; has gloss.
L. 3.5; W. 2.2; Th. 0.7

2535   H20/754   5323
Level Vf
Sickle on tertiary medial blade element; glossed.
L. 3.6; W. 2.3; Th. 0.6

2536   H20/657a   5301
Level Ve
Sickle on burnt tertiary blade fragment; gloss on both edges.
L. 4.8; W. 1.9; Th. 0.4

2537   H20/657b   5301
Level Ve
Sickle on plain platformed tertiary backed blade; glossed.
L. 4.8; W. 1.7; Th. 0.5

2538   H20/673   5302
Level Ve
Plain platformed secondary flake with edge damage.
L. 3.4; W. 3.4; Th. 1.0

2539   H20/684   5302
Level Ve
Sickle on tertiary medial blade element; glossed on both edges and sides.
L. 4.4; W 1.8; Th. 0.5

2540   H20/937   5368
Level Vf
Sickle on blade tertiary fragment.
L. 2.3; W. 2.1; Th. 0.6

2541   H20/966   5379
Level Vg
Sickle on an inversely truncated medial tertiary blade element; glossed.
L. 3.8; W. 3.4; Th. 0.8

2542   H20/992   5392
Level Vf1–2
Sickle on backed secondary blade crescent; glossed.
L. 3.7; W. 1.4; Th. 0.7

2543   H20/1062   6320
Level Vh/i
Sickle on cortical platformed secondary bladelet; glossed.
L. 3.1; W. 1.3; Th. 0.4

2544   H20/242   1258
Level IVa
Sickle on plain platformed, tertiary chert blade; gloss on both edges and sides.
L. 3.7; W. 1.3; Th. 0.4

2545   H19/277   4264
Level IVa
Sickle on truncated tertiary medial blade element; glossed; flint.
L. 3.9; W. 1.8; Th. 0.6

2546   H19/138   4238
Level IIIc/d
Sickle on a burnt tertiary distal flake fragment; has gloss on both sides.
L. 1.8; W. 1.3; Th. 0.3

2547   J19/161   1667
Level II?
Sickle on a tertiary obsidian blade fragment, identified by use damage.
L. 2.4; W. 1.2; Th. 0.5

Lithics

2548 K18/294 6147
Level IId
Sickle on plain platformed tertiary proximal blade fragment; black flint; glossed.
L. 3.2; W. 1.8; Th. 0.4

2549 Q19/6 178
Surface
Sickle on distal tertiary blade fragment; glossed.
L. 1.7; W. 1.3; Th. 0.3

Borer

There is a single flake-blade based borer, but it is not of a typical form; the long 'bit' of the borer seen in more typical forms is missing and its form reflects the shape of the original blank more than any template of a specific tool form.

2550 S7/1 252
Surface
Borer on a cortical platformed secondary flake/blade; flint.
L. 5.5; W. 2.3; Th. 1.3

Microliths

The two microliths recovered are both truncation forms of bladelets with rounded rather than oblique edges. These pieces could date from the Epi-Palaeolithic onwards although their informal morphology makes them difficult to place within the chronological sequence.

2551 H19/266 4261
Level IVa/b
Microlith on a secondary distal bladelet fragment; translucent honey-colour flint.
L. 1.9; W. 0.7; Th. 0.2

2552 K8/6 315
Surface
Microlith on medial tertiary bladelet; flint.
L. 1.4; W. 1.0; Th. 0.4

Scrapers

The scrapers as a general grouping are again informal, made on a mixture of both flake and blade blanks, and the endscrapers (**2556–8**) also follow this pattern. The nosed scraper (**2559**) has a steep, carinated working edge which could equally serve as a bladelet core but lacks the damage forms usually associated with core edge maintenance.

[**2553**] H20/913 5364
Level Vf
Sickle on tertiary medial blade fragment, sickle by use damage.
L. 5.2; W. 1.5; Th. 0.3

2554 H20/461 1838
Level Vg/h
Scraper on a secondary distal flake/blade fragment, milk quartz.
L. 4.3; W. 2.7; Th. 1.3

2555 K19/15 1501
Level I
Inversely retouched scraper on tertiary distal flake fragment; chert.
L. 2.9; W. 4.8; Th. 0.8

2556 H20/343 1812
Level Vf
Carinate endscraper on plain platformed tertiary flake, flint.
L. 5.8; W. 3.7; Th. 2.1

2557 K18/106 4352
Level IIe
Endscraper on distal tertiary flake fragment.
L. 2.3; W. 2.9; Th. 1.0

2558 H20/258 1260
Unstratified
Endscraper on tertiary obsidian blade (platform lost) and use on edges.
L. 3.2; W. 1.4; Th. 0.4

2559 99/21 99
Surface.
Nosed scraper on a plain platformed tertiary flake, brown flint. Palaeolithic?
L. 4.4; W. 4.7; Th. 1.7

Blades

The backed blades are of typical form, steeply retouched blades worked on one edge facing a sharp even cutting edge on the opposite side. In terms of chronology such pieces could be dated as early as the Upper Palaeolithic but a mid-Holocene date would probably be more reasonable given the contexts from which the pieces derive.

2560 H20/578 1269
Level IVa
Backed blade, tertiary, on limestone.
L. 4.0; W. 1.6; Th. 0.7

2561 H19/337 4272
Level IVb
Inversely backed blade, tertiary fragment; chert, burnt.
L. 3.6; W. 1.4; Th. 0.6

2562 H20/230 1258
Level IVa
Backed and utilized tertiary blade; flint.
L. 6.0; W. 1.9; Th. 0.6

2563 H20/315 1806
Level IVa
Backed blade on a secondary blade element, utilized as sickle.
L. 5.3; W. 1.8; Th. 0.4

Variously retouched blades such as the truncated blade (**2564**), retouched blade (**2565**) and the inversely retouched blade (**2566**) are all *ad hoc* classes which do not have culture-chronological significance on their own. However, relative frequencies of these pieces can be used in conjunction with other type fossils to order assemblages. Unfortunately, there are only single examples of each and they come from different contexts and so cannot be used in this way for Kilise Tepe.

2564   N19/2   153
Surface
Retouched distal tertiary obsidian bladelet fragment.
L. 2.2; W. 1.4; Th. 0.3

2565   J19/475   1002
Modern robber pit
Inversely retouched medial tertiary blade fragment.
L. 3.6; W. 1.4; Th. 0.4

2566   H20/812   5334
Level Vf4
Truncated and retouched medial tertiary blade element; utilized.
L. 1.7; W. 1.2; Th. 0.6

The serrated blade (**2567**) is most commonly associated with Natufian and PPNA and B cultures but does continue as part of the general cereal harvesting component of assemblages up into the EB. Once again with large sample sizes, relative frequency of such pieces can be a useful chronological indicator but the presence of a single such piece can be no more than remarked upon.

[**2567**]   H20/887   5344
Level Vf?
Serrated blade on a cortical platformed secondary blade.
L. 2.7; W. 1.4; Th. 0.4

Knives
There is a particularly fine well-made knife on a flake (**2568**). It lacks any damage to use for assigning anything other than a broad functional category. Other knives are less formal, including an inversely retouched piece on a large flake blade (**2569**). All are on relatively large blanks and would have probably been hand held.

2568   H20/652   5300
Level Ve
Retouched knife on naturally backed blade.
L. 6.7; W. 3.0; Th. 1.8

2569   H20/892   5359
Level Vf3/4
Retouched knife on a plain platformed secondary proximal blade fragment.
L. 3.0; W. 1.6; Th. 0.7

2570   I19/35   1770
Level IIg/h
Knife on a plain platformed secondary chert flake.
L. 6.6; W. 4.3; Th. 0.4

2571   P8/1b   245
Surface
Knife on a tertiary distal blade fragment, obsidian.
L. 3.5; W. 22.0; Th. 0.4

Denticulates
The denticulates are an informal grouping of mostly flakes or flake fragments which have been retouched to create a toothed edge, although none are regular, even or thin enough to have served as saws. Once again their presence could be significant in culture-chronological terms when measured against the frequencies of other tool groupings but sample sizes do not permit useful comparisons.

2572   H20/375   1819
Level Vf4
Denticulate on cortical platformed tertiary flake; flint.
L. 3.5; W. 3.1; Th. 0.8

2573   O8/4   243
Surface
Denticulate, inversely retouched onto a plain platformed secondary flake, white flint.
L. 4.7; W. 3.5; Th. 1.0

Hammerstone
The single hammerstone from among the chipped stone collection is a rounded natural pebble, unmodified for use but damaged by it. A small area of battering and flake removal indicates where the piece has been used. Other such pieces are described amongst the grinding stones elsewhere.

[**2574**]   Y13/1   290
Surface
Possible hammerstone.
L. 6.4; W. 5.0; Th. 5.4

In summary, the Kilise Tepe collection contains a limited number of formal tool types which comprise 5 per cent of the whole collection. This frequency of tools to debris is not unusual from excavated assemblages but the information value of these tools is further reduced because of the low sample sizes for each unit. Additionally, the contexts excavated are a series of pit fills, packing layers and disturbed units with high residuality and so the associations between artefacts within a sample may be due to discard and mixing rather than activity-linked behaviour.

It is apparent that blade blanks were preferred for supporting tools — of the 41 tools recorded 26 were made on blades or bladelets. This is in marked contrast to the availability of blanks where flakes predominate (see below).

The forms of retouch for shaping tools are limited to simple direct flaking and backing. There is little use of 'nibbling' or invasive retouch while stepped and scaly retouch forms are absent. The absence of the latter two forms might suggest that refreshing tool edges was not a significant factor in the use of materials.

The glossing on the edges of some sickles demonstrates that they were used on one side then turned around in their haft and used again.

Technology

This report concentrates upon the chipped stone component and the main variables for this discussion are the blank form, type, striking platform, retouch character, dimensions and the different core types and forms.

Cores
There are a total of 24 cores and a further 12 flaked lumps. The majority of cores are single platform and direction cores for the production of chips (15), flakes (5) and bladelets (4). 19 cores were single platform and flaking direction (79 per cent of all cores).

There were four double platform and flaking direction cores and a single three platform and flaking direction core. The latter was informal and the double platform and flaking direction cores were also informal. There was no opposed platform working. Three of the single platform and flaking direction cores could be termed prismatic, the rest reflected the shape of the original nodule/pebble. Most of the cores were made on pebbles or fragments derived from pebbles. It is significant that the average core size is smaller than that of the average blank size and therefore, the frequency of cores for chips (flakes less than 1.5 cm in maximum dimension) is unsurprising. This small size of cores could be used to suggest pressure on stone resources (maximizing the returns from each piece) but equally it may reflect time constraint (using up one pebble before having to go and get another). It also reflects the small size of pebbles being used. The latter two suggestions might be supported by the fact that the pebbles used seem in plentiful supply around the site. No true blade cores were recovered, nor were there any levallois cores. The platform edges of all cores show little sign of systematic control of the edges although there is some abrasion and microflaking. No core shows signs of core edge rejuvenation or core tablets having been removed. Examination of the cores suggests that simple direct percussion with a hard hammer was the main means of reduction.

Single platform and flaking direction
2575 H20/479 1847
Level Vg/h
Core for chips. Single platform and direction for flakes on chert pebble.
L. 3.9; W. 4.4; Th. 1.7

2576 I19/3 1700
Topsoil
Core for chips. Single platform and direction flake core on small pebble.
L. 1.6; W. 3.0; Th. 3.3

2577 H20/321 1807
Level IVa/Ve
Core for chips. Single platform and direction flake core, secondary, flint.
L. 2.3; W. 4.4; Th. 4.1

2578 O8/1 243
Surface
Core for bladelets. Single platform and flaking direction bladelet core, tertiary, quartz.
3.9 × 1.5 × 2.0

2579 P8/1a 245
Surface
Core for bladelets. Carinate scraper on crushed platform, secondary flake.
4.6 × 2.6 × 1.8

2580 H20/751 5327
Level Vf4
Core for chips. Single platform and direction flake core, secondary.
L. 2.4; W. 2.8; Th. 3.3

2581 H20/759 5328
Level Vf4
Core for chips. Single platform and direction flake core; obsidian.
L. 1.5; W. 1.8; Th. 1.7

2582 J18/250 5811
Level IIc/d
Core for bladelets. Single platform and direction bladelet core on quartz pebble.
L. 2.4; W. 2.1; Th. 1.7

2583 H20/797 5334
Level Vf4
Core for bladelets. Single platform and direction bladelet core, secondary.
L. 3.3; W. 1.7; Th. 2.5

2584 H20/780a 5333
Level Ve
Core for chips. Single platform and direction flake core on chalky flint pebble.
L. 6.3; W. 4.5; Th. 3.8

2585 J18/366 5878
Level IIe
Core for chips. Single platform and direction flake core, tertiary; obsidian.
L. 2.7; W. 2.4; Th. 2.0

[2586]	H20/305	1805	chips
	K18/32	4308	chips
	H20/704	5317	chips
	H20/780	5333	chips
	R12/2	221	chips
	Q18/1	127	flakes
	H20/1063	6323	chips

Double platform and flaking direction
2587 H19/31 4206
Level IIId
Core for chips. Two direction and platform flake tertiary core; chert.
L. 2.3; W. 4.4; Th. 3.6

[2588]   H20/933   5372   flakes
         O19/2   154   flakes
         K20/208   1994   obsidian, chips

Treble platform and flaking direction
[2589]   T7/2   255   flake

Flaked lumps
The flaked lumps are an informal category of struck pebbles where flake removal appears to be the intention (as opposed to hammerstones where accidental flaking can occur). The size of flakes removed is generally larger than for formal cores and it may be that it is only once a pebble has been worked down to a certain size that it becomes necessary to use a formal platform to control the flaking angle. Flaked lumps may then simply be an earlier stage in reduction than the more obviously reduced cores. Once again direct percussion with a hard hammer is the reduction method.

[2590]
H20/265 (1261), /333 (1810), /780 (5333) limestone, /780 (5333), /797 (5334), /827 (5340), /1003 (5396); **J18**/20 (2306); **O15**/1 (105); **R11**/2 (222); **W10**/1a (271), /1b (271) quartz.

The core tablet H20/641 (1290) removes the face of flaking and platform edge which rejuvenates the working face of the core. This is the only example of this and so no systematic rejuvenation is taking place.

Despite the use of pebbles there is no sign of systematic reduction using either 'salami-slice' or 'orange segment' methods, neither were larger pebbles quartered prior to further reduction.

Blanks
A total of 676 blanks have been examined; of this group, 450 had platforms that could be categorized. A total of 320 (71 per cent) had plain platforms, 67 (15 per cent) had crushed platforms, 62 (14 per cent) had cortical platforms, one had a prepared platform (0.22 per cent) and there were no dihedral platforms. It is clear from this that no significant effort was being made to control the platform edge formally by preparation. Equally, the frequency of large plain platforms and crushed platforms could directly reflect the use of hard hammer percussion. There were no lipped platforms and none of the blanks showed signs of the reverse 's' twist found in the dorsal *arete* patterns of pressure flaked pieces. It is possible that softer hammers were used for the removal of some blanks (despite the lack of lipped platforms) but there is no evidence for the use of punches. Removals were made precisely, with little evidence of mis-hits. A small number of pieces had double bulbs (4 out of 320 — 1.25 per cent) but this figure is not significant. Equally, there are a small number of Siret pieces (five — 1.5 per cent) and plunged pieces (four — 1.25 per cent). There is a moderate number of hinged pieces (32) for this size of collection but yet again this shows that overall reduction was controlled and confident. There was a single Janus flake present so reclaiming material from blanks was not an urgent need.

Table 22 shows that flake production dominates the reduction sequence overall, with blades as a minor component to reduction but important when the production of tools is concerned (see above). The lack of the smaller element is probably due to a mixture of sampling (the smaller pieces are fragile and do not preserve well and are also prone to being lost during excavation) and the lack of *in situ* knapping or discard directly from a knapping area. It is important to note that sediment samples were floated but still very few chips were recovered. Micro-debitage analysis is

Table 22. *Blank form distribution.*

		Whole	Fragmentary	Total	
Flakes	Primary	8	2	10	
	Secondary	135	55	190	Total flakes 451 (66.7%)
	Tertiary	174	77	251	
Chips	Primary	0	0	0	
	Secondary	4	3	7	Total chips 47 (6.9%)
	Tertiary	21	19	40	
Bladelets	Primary	0	0	0	
	Secondary	8	3	11	Total bladelets 49 (7.2%)
	Tertiary	13	25	38	
Blades	Primary	0	1	1	
	Secondary	12	8	20	Total blades 78 (11.5%)
	Tertiary	17	40	57	
Flake-blades	Primary	1	0	1	
	Secondary	18	5	23	Total flake-blades 51 (7.5%)
	Tertiary	14	13	27	
Total		425	251	676	

Total Primary blanks   12   (1.8%)
Total Secondary blanks 251   (37%)
Total Tertiary blanks   413   (61%)

therefore not likely to be particularly informative on this part of the site.

The lack of *in situ* knapping is confirmed by the paucity of primary blanks, the pieces that would normally be removed first in the knapping sequence. These are very rare, just 1.8 per cent of the total and so clearly decortication and any roughing out were not occurring within the excavated area. The proportion of secondary flakes is within the range to be expected when compared with that of tertiary flakes if pebble cores are being used (in working with nodules there is proportionately more non-cortical material available for exploitation and so the ratio between secondary and tertiary flakes is usually higher). It is surprising, however, that secondary and primary flake production is not higher given the pebble materials used. This may be due to differential discard, the cortex[1] covered pieces being produced in one area (not sampled) and later working in another area which is represented in the deposits excavated.

It is worth noting that although blades and bladelets and blade segments are present there is no evidence for crested blade technique nor for microburin technique for dividing up blades. Division of blades and bladelets was simply by snapping.

There were no traces of mastic on any of the pieces examined. The backing retouch observed on blades and blade segments regularizes their edges and could permit hafting. Given the presence of use wear and gloss on the opposite edges of such pieces, this is probably how they were hafted. Certain pieces were taken out of their hafts, turned around and the backed edge used. This is attested by the presence of use wear on both edges. No haft wear, abrasion polished spots, striations or similar were noted in the middle of pieces so they must have been hafted along the edge not centrally. None of the other tools exhibited signs of haft wear.

Edge conditions
The edge conditions of pieces can provide information on the use and depositional environment of those pieces. There were fourteen pieces that had wear on an edge that suggested they had been utilized. This use wear took three main forms: localized microflaking, smoothing of an area and striations. Most of the utilized pieces listed below showed some or combinations of these. The main use for the utilized blades was cutting and apart from the generation of gloss on the edges, the wear pattern was the same as that for sickle blades. It is not possible to identify any other functions from use wear on the listed pieces.

The frequency of blades in the utilized category reinforces the suggestion that they are the preferred blank form for use. Of the 14 utilized pieces 12 are blades or bladelets (85 per cent) whilst only 2 (14 per cent) are on flakes. Although sample size is low, this does resemble the situation for formal tools where blade-based tools predominate.

2591 H20/634 1288
Level Ve
Backed plain platformed secondary flake/blade, utilized.
L. 3.8; W. 1.7; Th. 0.4

2592 H20/765 5331
Level Vf4
Backed blade (bladelet?) on plain platformed secondary blade, utilized.
L. 5.5; W. 1.1; Th. 0.4

2593 H18/3 2600
Topsoil
Utilized tertiary medial blade element; honey-coloured flint.
L. 2.3; W. 1.7; Th. 0.4

2594 H20/657c 5301
Level Ve
Utilized tertiary medial blade fragment; obsidian.
L. 2.2; W. 1.2; Th. 0.2

2595 J20/1 1300
Topsoil
Utilized tertiary blade medial element; obsidian.
L. 2.7; W. 1.4; Th. 0.3

[2596]

H19/222	4243	blade
H20/305	1805	blade
H20/683	1860	blade
H20/914	5362	flake
H20/915	5364	blade
H20/999	5394	blade
H20/1007	5397	blade
Q10/19	3103	obsidian, bladelet
R18/62	2040	bladelet

Amongst other edge condition variables, rolled pieces (pieces that have been subject to heavy mechanical erosion such as movement by rivers) are absent and only three pieces were part-patinated. The rest were generally fresh.

A total of 107 pieces (15.8 per cent of the total number of blanks) showed edge damage; of these, 43 (6.3 per cent) had either lateral or transverse snaps, 41 (6 per cent) had micro-flaking and 23 (3.4 per cent) had half-moon snaps. These figures are low for any area where trampling by stock or people has taken place and does not suggest high energy depositional contexts.

A specialized form of damage to projectile points — impact damage — was looked for but no evidence for it was found.

Also indicative of depositional environments is the degree to which an assemblage is burnt. Material can be burnt deliberately to make temper for pottery and to heat water or accidentally when hearths are placed over a lithic scatter or when pieces are thrown into fire. Generally, uncontrolled burning of flint can be hazardous as it tends to crack violently and send fragments flying. Seventy-seven (9 per cent of total number of pieces) burnt pieces were recorded. This figure includes burnt tools such as the borer noted above and unworked flint fragments. There does not, on the basis of this figure, or indeed of the amount of burnt material from any single context, seem to be any evidence of deliberate burning of flint and the burnt component may best be attributed to the random inclusion of flint amongst burning materials, especially during the phases of building destruction by fire.

There were 104 pieces of shatter amongst the collection. This figure represents 12.7 per cent of the whole collection and is within the expected ranges from extensive knapping of derived raw material sources (as opposed to mined sources).

Raw materials

A total of nine raw materials were noted (see Table 23). Five of these were variations of chert, locally available from the surrounding limestone hills and present as pebbles in the conglomerate and river valley. These five cherts have been lumped together for the purposes of analysis. The next most common material is obsidian from the Konya basin. Two forms were observed, black and a single piece of red and black mottled obsidian. In terms of numbers of pieces, obsidian makes up 10 per cent of the collection.

The successively less frequent raw materials are limestone (3.9 per cent) and quartz (2.7 per cent). Once again both are available locally, the limestone both as pebbles and blocks whilst the quartz occurs as pebbles in the river valley and the conglomerate. There was a single pebble of greenstone.

The differential treatment of raw materials may be seen from a comparison on Tables 24–8. In terms of use for tools, obsidian is not preferentially selected but it does seem to be better represented in the utilized class. It must be stressed, however, that sample sizes are very small. No patterns of special treatment or selection can be discerned from the exploitation of cores or bashed lumps.

Table 23. *Raw materials in the collection.*

General chert	631	(77.3%)
Translucent chert	19	(2.3%)
Fossiliferous chert	10	(1.2%)
Red/white/black chert	16	(2.0%)
Variegated chert	2	(-)
Obsidian	83	(10.0%)
Quartz	22	(2.7%)
Limestone	32	(3.9%)
Greenstone	1	(-)
n = 816		

Table 24. *Raw material usage.*

Tool type	Raw material	Number	
Sickles	Obsidian	1	
Sickles	Chert	15	
Scrapers	Chert	4	
Endscrapers	Obsidian	1	
Endscrapers	Chert	2	
Knives	Chert	4	
Backed blades	Obsidian	1	
Backed blades	Chert	4	
Truncated blades	Obsidian	1	
Microliths	Chert	2	
Denticulate	Chert	3	
Serrated blade	Chert	1	
Borer	Chert	1	
Arrowhead	Obsidian	1	
Totals	Obsidian	4	(13.3%)
	Chert	36	(86.6%)
Utilized blades	Obsidian	2	
Utilized blades	Chert	7	
Utilized bladelets	Obsidian	1	
Utilized bladelets	Chert	2	
Utilized flakes	Chert	2	
Totals	Obsidian	3	(21.4%)
	Chert	11	(78.6%)
Cores:			
Bladelets	Chert	2	
Bladelets	Quartz	2	
Flakes	Chert	4	
Flake	Quartz	1	
Chips	Obsidian	3	
Chips	Chert	12	
Totals	Obsidian	3	(12.5%)
	Chert	18	(75.0%)
	Quartz	3	(12.5%)
Flaked lumps	Chert	9	
Flaked lumps	Quartz	1	
Flaked lumps	Limestone	1	
Flaked lumps	Greenstone	1	

Total 12 1.3% of total collection of 815 pieces
Cores are 2.9% of entire collection
Shatter is 12.7% of entire collection

In terms of edge damage, obsidian shows higher frequencies of all categories when compared with other raw materials, this is probably because obsidian is both softer and more brittle than the other materials

Table 25. *Chert blank composition.*

Blank type		Whole		Fragments	
Flakes:	Primary	8	(1.4%)	2	(0.4%)
	Secondary	216	(38.7%)	47	(6.9%)
	Tertiary	140	(25.1%)	64	(11.5%)
Chips:	Primary	0		0	
	Secondary	4	(0.7%)	2	(0.4%)
	Tertiary	9	(1.6%)	9	(1.6%)
Bladelets:	Primary	0		0	
	Secondary	8	(1.4%)	3	(0.5%)
	Tertiary	10	(1.8%)	16	(2.9%)
Blades:	Primary	0		1	(0.2%)
	Secondary	12	(2.2%)	7	(1.3%)
	Tertiary	14	(2.5%)	32	(5.7%)
Flakes/blades:	Primary	1	(0.2%)	0	
	Secondary	17	(3.0%)	4	(0.7%)
	Tertiary	11	(2.0%)	11	(2.0%)
Blanks total		558	(82.3%)		
Shatter		93	(13.7%)		
Flaked lumps		9	(1.3%)		
Cores		18	(2.7%)		
Total chert		678	(100.0%)		
Technological aspects:					
	Microflaking	14	(2.5%)		
	Snaps	34	(6.0%)		
	Half-moon snaps	17	(3.0%)		
	Hinges	29	(5.1%)		
	Siret	5	(0.9%)		
	Plunged	4	(0.7%)		
	Double-bulbed	3	(0.5%)		
	Janus	1	(0.2%)		
Platforms:					
	Plain	281	(73.4%)		
	Crushed	46	(12.0%)		
	Cortical	55	(14.4%)		
	Prepared	1	(0.2%)		
	Dihedral	0			
	Total	383	(100.0%)		

Table 26. *Obsidian blank composition.*

Blank type		Whole		Fragments	
Flakes:	Primary	0		0	
	Secondary	3	(3.8%)	6	(7.7%)
	Tertiary	13	(16.8%)	10	(12.0%)
Chips:	Primary	0		0	
	Secondary	0		0	
	Tertiary	12	(15.5%)	10	(21.9%)
Bladelets:	Primary	0		0	
	Secondary	0		0	
	Tertiary	2	(2.5%)	9	(11.7%)
Blades:	Primary	0		0	
	Secondary	0		0	
	Tertiary	1	(1.2%)	7	(9.0%)
Flakes/blades:	Primary	0		0	
	Secondary	0		0	
	Tertiary	2	(2.5%)	2	(2.5%)
Blanks total		77	(92.8%)		
Cores		3	(3.6%)		
Shatter		3	(3.6%)		
Flaked lumps		0			
Total obsidian		83	(100%)		
Technological aspects:					
	Microflaking	26	(33.8%)		
	Snaps	7	(9%)		
	Half-moon snaps	5	(6.5%)		
	Hinges	2	(2.3%)		
Platforms:					
	Plain	19	(55.9%)		
	Crushed	15	(44.1%)		
	Cortical	0			
	Dihedral	0			
	Prepared	0			

and so will become damaged more easily. Equally, the proportion of striking platforms crushed is higher for obsidian pieces, for the same reasons. Cortical pieces are rare for obsidian, this may be because obsidian is being imported as rough-out blocks with decortication having already taken place elsewhere.

Chronology

There is no single sample which provides clear dating evidence for the context from which it comes. There are no chronologically distinctive type fossils present in the collection and on the basis of type pieces the collection is best characterized as 'mid-Holocene'. However, given the nature of the site, there is also nothing present in the assemblage that would rule out an EBA date.

Chronology for the site can be more effectively derived from the study of other materials.

Table 27. *Quartz blank composition.*

	Blank type	Whole		Fragments	
Flakes:	Primary	0		0	
	Secondary	2	(12%)	0	
	Tertiary	11	(65.0%)	0	
Chips:	Primary	0		0	
	Secondary	0		0	
	Tertiary	0		0	
Bladelets:	Primary	0		0	
	Secondary	0		0	
	Tertiary	1	(5.8%)	0	
Blades:	Primary	0		0	
	Secondary	0		1	(5.8%)
	Tertiary	1	(5.8%)	0	
Flakes/blades:	Primary	0		0	
	Secondary	0		1	(5.8%)
	Tertiary	0		0	
Blanks total		17	(81.0%)		
Shatter		1	(4.7%)		
Cores		3	(14.3%)		
Total		**22**	**(100.0%)**		
Technological aspects:					
	Microflaking	1	(5.9%)		
	Snaps	1	(5.9%)		
	Hinges	1	(5.9%)		
Platforms:					
	Plain	11	(73.3%)		
	Crushed	3	(20.0%)		
	Cortical	1	(6.7%)		
	Prepared	0			
	Dihedral	0			

Table 28. *Limestone blank composition.*

	Blank type	Whole		Fragments	
Flakes:	Primary	0		0	
	Secondary	4	(16.6%)	2	(8.3%)
	Tertiary	10	(41.7%)	3	(12.5%)
Chips:	Primary	0		0	
	Secondary	0		1	(4.1%)
	Tertiary	0		0	
Bladelets:	Primary	0		0	
	Secondary	0		0	
	Tertiary	0		0	
Blades:	Primary	0		0	
	Secondary	0		0	
	Tertiary	1	(4.1%)	1	(4.1%)
Flakes/blades:	Primary	0		0	
	Secondary	1	(4.1%)	0	
	Tertiary	1	(4.1%)	0	
Blanks total		24	(74%)		
Shatter		7	(22%)		
Flaked lumps		1	(3.1%)		
Total		**32**	**(100%)**		
Technological aspects:					
	Snaps	1	(4.1%)		
	Half-moon snaps	1	(4.1%)		
	Double-bulbed	1	(4.1%)		
Platforms:					
	Plain	9	(52.9%)		
	Crushed	2	(11.8%)		
	Cortical	6	(35.3%)		

The larger samples

These are arranged approximately in stratigraphic sequence, earliest first. All measurements are given in cm and refer to length, width and thickness respectively (Tables 29 & 30).

Conclusions

Study of the chipped stone collection has not been able to add any great insights into specific contexts or their dating but some general observations are possible.

The first point to comment on is the general lack of material. Kilise Tepe is a settlement occupied over many years. Domestic rubbish would be expected to accumulate rapidly but there is little evidence of flint work. Any single knapping event will produce hundreds of chips, flakes and a core at the least, so why is there not more material?

It is likely that chert was a regular but occasional component of the everyday life of the site. The majority of tools and utilized pieces were for cutting purposes suggesting that metal knives had yet to make an impact in this range of behaviour. It is possible that much of the everyday tasks involving cutting took place outside and so would not lead to discard of pieces amongst the rooms of buildings. Equally, flint working is dusty and creates noise and many hazardous sharp chips — it is not an activity for family rooms. Once again this would argue for activity areas away from residential areas. It is clear that this might explain the general lack of material; what has

Table 29. *Data for units yielding ten or more pieces.*

6321	H20/1070
Level Vh/i. A destruction layer.	
A cortical platformed tertiary limestone flake	5.2, 3.1, 1.5
A naturally backed secondary single arete medial chert blade fragment	2.1, 1.2, 0.4
A cortical platformed tertiary chert flake	2.2, 1.6, 0.4
A plain platformed primary chert flake	1.4, 2.9, 1.1
A plain platformed proximal tertiary chert flake fragment	1.7, 1.8, 0.5
A distal secondary chert flake fragment	1.3, 1.7, 0.3
A crushed platformed tertiary chert flake	1.5, 1.1, 0.4
A burnt medial tertiary chert flake-blade fragment	1.7, 1.0, 0.2
A chert shatter fragment	3.1, 2.6, 1.6
A chert shatter fragment	2.5, 2.3, 2.0
A distal tertiary flake fragment	1.8, 3.4, 1.5
A burnt medial secondary chert flake fragment	1.8, 2.2, 0.8
A burnt tertiary chert fragment	1.5, 2.3, 0.5
Also an obsidian flake (H20/1074).	

6304	H20/1030
Level Vg. Destruction rubble overlying floor 5389.	
A plain platformed triple arete secondary chert blade	5.6, 3.4, 0.9
A plain platformed secondary chert flake	4.3, 5.1, 1.4
A cortical platformed tertiary chert flake	3.4, 4.6, 1.5
A plain platformed secondary chert flake	4.9, 4.0, 2.0
A burnt secondary chert fragment	3.8, 2.2, 1.3
A cortical platformed burnt tertiary chert flake	3.4, 3.7, 1.7
A cortical platformed secondary chert flake	2.9, 2.4, 0.8
A burnt chert lump	2.6, 2.3, 1.2
A crushed platformed secondary chert flake-blade	4.2, 1.9, 0.9
A medial single arete tertiary chert bladelet fragment	1.8, 1.1, 0.2
A chert shatter fragment	2.4, 2.3, 0.7
A distal chert flake? fragment	1.1, 1.9, 0.3
A burnt chert fragment	0.8, 1.1, 0.6
A crushed platformed, hinged tertiary chert flake	1.3, 2.1, 1.2

5397	H20/1007
Level Vf/g. A packing layer, i.e. dumped material linked to Phase Vf.	
A plain platformed single arete secondary chert blade	6.3, 3.0, 0.7
A cortical platformed secondary chert flake-blade with half-moon snaps	3.6, 2.0, 0.5
A crushed platformed tertiary chert flake with an edge notch	2.6, 4.3, 0.8
A plain platformed secondary chert flake	2.7, 2.5, 0.3
A crushed platformed single arete tertiary chert blade	4.0, 1.8, 1.2
A medial double arete tertiary utilized obsidian blade fragment	3.1, 1.7, 0.5
A plain platformed tertiary chert flake	1.2, 1.2, 0.3
A distal secondary chert flake fragment	1.2, 2.1, 0.6
A cortical platformed hinged tertiary chert flake	1.9, 2.2, 0.4
A plain platformed secondary chert flake	2.6, 2.0, 0.8

A crushed platformed secondary chert flake	1.2, 1.9, 0.5
A plain platformed hinged tertiary chert flake	1.8, 1.8, 0.4
A chert shatter fragment	1.7, 1.0, 0.8
A chert shatter fragment, refits the above piece	1.3, 1.2, 0.7
A plain platformed tertiary chert flake	1.4, 1.9, 0.4
A medial secondary chert flake fragment	2.6, 1.2, 0.8

5392	H20/992
Level Vf1–2. Pit fill, grey fairly compact material	
A chert pebble fragment	2.7, 2.4, 5.1
A plain platformed secondary chert blade	5.2, 2.7, 0.8
A large plain platformed tertiary chert flake	2.4, 5.2, 0.8
A plain platformed double arete proximal chert blade fragment	3.7, 2.0, 0.8
A chert shatter fragment	3.2, 3.4, 1.0
A plain platformed secondary chert blade	4.3, 1.6, 1.4
A backed secondary double arete chert cresentic blade sickle with gloss	3.7, 1.4, 0.7
A distal secondary chert flake fragment with half-moon snaps	2.6, 1.9, 0.8
A cortical platformed secondary chert flake	2.0, 2.2, 0.5
A cortical platformed tertiary chert flake	1.6, 2.7, 0.9
A cortical platformed tertiary chert flake	2.0, 2.2, 0.3
A secondary chert shatter fragment	2.3, 1.4, 1.1
A crushed platformed secondary chert flake	1.6, 2.1, 0.5
A burnt chert tertiary fragment	2.0, 1.1, 0.7
A plain platformed secondary chert flake	2.4, 2.8, 0.9
A tertiary chert shatter fragment	2.2, 1.1, 0.9
A burnt tertiary flake? Fragment	1.4, 0.4, 0.4

5363	H20/905
Level Vf2/3. A packing layer, compact mid brown/grey material underlying Phase f surface.	
A plain platformed secondary chert flake	3.4, 3.2, 0.9
A cortical platformed secondary chert flake	4.7, 3.3, 1.5
A plain platformed secondary chert flake	2.8, 4.0, 1.0
A tertiary chert shatter fragment	3.1, 1.7, 0.9
A crushed platformed secondary chert bladelet	2.9, 1.2, 0.4
A burnt tertiary chert fragment	1.8, 1.4, 0.3
A burnt distal tertiary chert flake fragment	0.9, 1.1, 0.3
A burnt secondary flaked chert lump	3.6, 3.6, 4.2
A distal tertiary limestone flake fragment	1.1, 3.4, 0.8
A plain platformed single arete tertiary chert bladelet	2.9, 1.1, 0.4
Also 2 obsidian flakes (H20/907).	

5362	H20/914
Level Vf3? Pit fill. Loose fine-grained silty with a few inclusions.	
A crushed platformed hinged utilized secondary chert flake	4.7, 4.6, 1.7
A plain platformed tertiary chert flake	4.3, 4.5, 1.0
A chert shatter fragment	2.2, 2.1, 1.5
A crushed platformed tertiary chert flake with half-moon snaps	3.8, 5.4, 0.3

Table 29. *(cont.)*

A plain platformed tertiary quartz flake	2.3, 2.6, 1.0
A plain platformed tertiary chert flake	1.9, 3.8, 0.7
A limestone shatter fragment	1.5, 1.6, 1.4
A flaked chert shatter fragment	1.3, 2.7, 1.8
A burnt chert lump	1.6, 0.9, 2.3
A secondary limestone chip	1.2, 1.8, 0.3
A secondary chert pebble fragment	3.7, 2.8, 1.5
Also an obsidian flake (H20/911).	

1823	**H20/389**
Level Vf3/4. A hard grey brown fill, a compact layer with an ash dump.	
A tertiary chert shatter fragment	4.7, 3.1, 1.4
A plain platformed secondary chert flake fragment	3.4, 2.9, 0.8
A distal secondary chert flake fragment	2.7, 2.5, 0.8
A distal tertiary chert flake fragment with many lateral snaps	3.4, 1.9, 0.2
A plain platformed tertiary chert flake fragment, refits the above piece	3.8, 3.2, 0.3
A burnt secondary chert flake with lost platform	1.9, 2.1, 0.8
A plain platformed secondary chert flake	2.5, 3.6, 1.0
A distal tertiary chert flake fragment	1.7, 2.8, 0.7
A plain platformed hinged secondary chert flake	1.5, 1.7, 0.4
A distal secondary chert flake fragment	2.7, 1.8, 0.9
A distal secondary chert chip	0.8, 1.1, 0.3

5340	**H20/827**
Level Vf4. Pit fill, mid-brown deposit	
A plain platformed proximal single arete tertiary chert blade fragment	4.9, 2.4, 0.6
A tertiary chert shatter fragment	2.2, 3.8, 1.6
A flaked chert lump	5.2, 4.8, 3.8
A distal tertiary chert flake fragment with edge snaps	2.2, 3.6, 0.5
A plain platformed tertiary chert flake	2.6, 3.0, 1.0
A plain platformed secondary chert flake	3.9, 3.6, 0.5
A plain platformed secondary chert flake-blade	3.8, 1.6, 0.7
A plain platformed tertiary chert flake	2.8, 2.0, 0.8
A distal tertiary chert flake fragment	2.2, 2.2, 0.3
A cortical platformed hinged secondary chert flake	1.8, 3.1, 0.5
A plain platformed secondary Siret chert flake	2.9, 1.6, 0.8
A plain platformed double arete tertiary chert blade	4.5, 1.8, 0.3
A medial single arete tertiary chert blade fragment	1.2, 1.9, 0.3
A plain platformed secondary chert flake	5.0, 2.7, 0.8
A distal secondary chert flake with edge snaps	5.5, 3.6, 0.3

5328	**H20/758**
Level Vf4. A consolidation layer, a light brown compact fill.	
A plain platformed hinged single arete tertiary chert blade	3.9, 2.0, 0.7
A plain platformed tertiary chert flake	2.7, 3.5, 1.2

A distal tertiary chert flake fragment	3.0, 3.2, 0.7
A plain platformed secondary chert flake	1.9, 2.1, 1.0
A plain platformed proximal tertiary chert flake fragment	2.2, 3.7, 1.0
A plain platformed secondary chert flake	1.7, 4.2, 1.0
A plain platformed proximal tertiary chert flake-blade fragment	1.9, 2.0, 0.5
A plain platformed denticulate on a single arete proximal tertiary chert blade fragment	3.5, 2.6, 0.7
A crushed platformed hinged secondary chert flake	2.5, 2.8, 1.2
A plain platformed secondary chert flake	2.0, 1.8, 1.3
A chert shatter fragment	3.0, 1.8, 0.7
A chert shatter fragment	1.5, 1.2, 0.6
A tertiary chert chip fragment	0.9, 1.1, 0.2
A burnt chert tertiary fragment	1.0, 1.0, 0.9
Also 2 obsidian flakes (H20/759)	

1819	**H20/375**
Level Vf4. A burnt soil forming fill under walls.	
A burnt tertiary chert flaked fragment	2.8, 3.3, 1.6
A plain platformed secondary chert flake	4.3, 2.3, 1.3
A plain platformed tertiary chert bladelet	3.5, 1.2, 0.5
A plain platformed tertiary chert flake	1.9, 1.7, 0.3
A cortical platformed tertiary chert flake denticulate	3.5, 3.1, 0.8
A plain platformed tertiary chert flake	2.6, 2.2, 1.0
A plain platformed tertiary chert flake	2.4, 3.1, 0.8
A tabular primary chert fragment with snaps	1.7, 1.3, 0.4
A plain platformed tertiary chert flake	2.3, 1.8, 0.8
A tabular primary chert fragment with snaps	1.5, 1.3, 0.5
A tertiary chert shatter fragment	2.5, 1.2, 0.6
A tertiary chert shatter fragment	1.9, 0.9, 0.4
A distal double arete tertiary chert blade fragment	2.5, 1.5, 0.4
A plain platformed tertiary chert flake	2.5, 2.7, 0.8
Also an obsidian flake (H20/376)	

1810	**H20/333**
Level Ve/f. A clay packing layer below IVa.	
A flaked secondary chert lump	4.7, 2.8, 1.7
A burnt plain platformed tertiary chert Siret flake	2.9, 2.0, 1.1
A plain platformed end-snapped tertiary chert flake	3.1, 3.2, 0.7
A plain platformed microflaked tertiary chert flake	3.5, 2.5, 0.5
A large plain platformed secondary chert flake on a small pebble	1.8, 2.8, 0.9
A corticated platformed tertiary chert flake	1.6, 1.2, 0.4
A distal tertiary chert bladelet fragment	2.1, 1.0, 0.2
A crushed platformed tertiary chert flake	2.7, 1.3, 0.3
A plain platformed burnt proximal tertiary chert flake fragment	0.7, 1.4, 0.3
A distal tertiary chert flake fragment	1.3, 2.1, 0.3
A tertiary chert shatter fragment	1.6, 1.2, 0.5
Also an obsidian flake (H20/338)	

Table 29. *(cont.)*

5333	H20/780
Level Ve. Pit fill	
A single platform and direction of flaking core on a chert pebble	6.3, 4.5, 3.8
A flaked secondary chert lump	4.8, 4.2, 2.7
A distal microflaked secondary chert flake fragment	4.5, 4.7, 1.7
A plain platformed secondary chert flake	5.7, 2.8, 1.2
A large plain platformed secondary chert flake	4.2, 4.7, 1.7
A flaked chert lump	5.3, 3.8, 2.4
A flaked limestone lump	4.7, 4.2, 2.2
A plain platformed secondary chert flake	4.3, 2.5, 1.7
A single platformed and flaking direction chip chert core	1.7, 3.6, 3.8
A cortex platformed secondary limestone flake	3.2, 4.4, 1.5
A crushed platformed, double arete secondary chert flake-blade	5.3, 2.9, 1.2
A distal secondary chert flake fragment	2.1, 2.8, 0.3
A plain platformed tertiary chert flake with edge snaps	3.3, 2.6, 0.7
A distal tertiary chert flake fragment	1.7, 2.5, 1.0
A plain platformed secondary chert flake	3.2, 2.0, 0.8
A plain platformed secondary chert flake	1.8, 1.4, 0.4
A chert shatter fragment	0.6, 1.5, 0.3
A distal tertiary chert flake fragment	0.8, 1.2, 0.2
A plain platformed double arete tertiary chert blade with many edge snaps	6.9, 2.1, 0.4
Also 3 obsidian flakes (H20/702)	

Table 30. *List of units yielding between five and nine pieces.*

9	1838	H20/467 w/s (includes micro-debitage)
8	1814	H20/363
7	5384	H20/968
	5362	H20/901
	5394	H20/999
6	1820	H20/379
	1826	H20/402
	5332	H20/773
5	4249	H19/189 (all refit into a single burnt lump)
	2406	R18/110
	1272	H20/585
	1289	H20/630
	5300	H20/652
	5334	H20/797
	178	Q19/6
	5344	H20/887
	6323	H20/1063
	5370	H20/934 (4 of these refit to a burnt lump)

been recovered is likely to be casual losses, occasional discard and material imported from rubbish accumulations elsewhere to make up ground for building. At present there is no evidence for lithic production on an industrial scale.

The main purpose of the lithics collected would be blade and bladelet production for tool manufacture and then tool use. Although flakes dominate the blank production, it is usually necessary to produce a quantity of flakes in preparing blades, particularly where cresting technique is absent. It is interesting that true blade cores are absent so perhaps a production area for blades did exist and has not been sampled in the present excavations. Certainly, blades dominate both the tools and utilized categories.

The significance of the lithic component to living can be assessed in terms of investment made in the materials. In these terms very little effort is being put into the chipped stone industry. Exploitation is dominated by locally available materials, regardless of quality, with occasional use of obsidian. The latter, whilst attractive and versatile as a material, is not singled out for any special treatment or uses. Obsidian is reduced in the same way as all the other materials. It is likely that the proportions of the different raw materials used is determined by their local availability in the conglomerate and river valley. Obsidian from the Konya basin may be an exception to this. The materials used are also of variable quality; whilst durable, reliable cherts are widely available, poorly consolidated and fossiliferous pieces are also used. Limestone, of very variable quality, is also used. It would seem that there was very little investment of time into lithic artefact production.

On a more detailed level there is no evidence for the bringing back of hunted game from the presence of utilized or broken arrowheads. Once again this may be a problem of sampling and the role of hunted game is best analysed through the faunal assemblage. There is also no evidence of single knapping events taking place and then being discarded as a unit into the rubbish pits recorded. Chipped stone debris has a nuisance value and would be likely to be discarded away from living areas and busy route ways. The knapping areas must lie outside the sampled area. This knapping elsewhere would include not just the basic roughing out, but tool manufacture, retouching and a significant amount of tool maintenance.

The small number of scrapers is interesting for a domestic site as these often form the largest single component of stone tool assemblages. Once again this could be a sampling problem but it could also be a sign of the role of textiles — hide working is one of the most common functions for scrapers.

The tools recovered comprise a mixture of hand-held and hafted pieces but no trace of the haft material now survives.

Finally, there is no evidence for pieces which were chipped to rough-out and then polished.

Sample sizes have been a major limiting factor in this analysis. The low numbers of pieces are, however, in themselves, an indicator of the nature of the site. It must have been structured and organized with lithic production centred away from the occupied area. The excavation has only sampled a very small area of EBA occupation and significant spatial variation in stone artefact distribution is likely. In the EBA, chipped stone tool use was in decline and so if there is no earlier occupation than this on the site, low frequencies of stone artefacts could be expected.

Notes

1. In this report 'cortex' is taken to be unmodified external surfaces of the material in its natural state.

Chapter 45

Smaller Stone Artefacts

Dominique Collon & Dorit Symington

The stone industry at Kilise Tepe for the early periods is mainly represented by objects recovered from the Middle Bronze Age levels (IVa/IVb). The exception are grinding stones which are as common in the Early Bronze Age levels (from Level Vi onwards) as in the succeeding periods (see next section).

Axes or celts (2597–601)

From the Middle Bronze Age period we recorded three small, well-made greenstone axes in perfect state of preservation. They are well polished with sharp cutting edges and worked symmetrically when seen in profile. Their find spots give no contextual information as they were retrieved from an EBA/MBA pit (**2597**) and packing material of Level IVb (**2598–9**). Two examples from higher levels, one of them also in greenstone, are not from a good context either.

Greenstone would not have been available locally and the stone — or possibly even the finished product — would have been imported. There are three close counterparts from Mersin in Level XI, also from Middle Bronze Age layers (Garstang 1953, fig. 150:9–11). For stone axes, adzes and axe-shaped chisels from Ugarit (the distinction is not evident), see Elliott 1991, 61–3 and figs. 17–18. Elliott believes that these small stone axes are of Neolithic and Chalcolithic date and are reused, either as tools or as amulets, when they occur in later contexts. However greenstone axes seem to have enjoyed great popularity throughout the Bronze Age in Anatolia. Considering their small size, these axes would have been designed for delicate work on wood or other softer materials. It is likely that they continued to be made and used long after alternative metal tools were available, and that their aesthetic value was as important as their use.

2597 H20/721 KLT 107 5321
Level Ve
A complete greenstone hand axe with a very sharp working edge. Symmetrical profile. The upper end is slightly rounded. All surfaces are very smooth. Complete.
L. 2.46; W. 3.03; Th. 1.25

2598 H19/314 KLT 75 4268
Level IVb
Smooth, polished greenstone axe head, slightly asymmetrical in profile, with a slanting cutting edge and sharply angled on one side. The top is rounded. Upper part less well polished. Complete.
L. 3.5; W. 3.1; Th. 1.4; Wt 26.5

2599 H19/330 KLT 76 4272
Level IVb
Greenstone axe head; green and orangey mottled in colour with highly polished surfaces. The working edge is very sharp and perfectly even and the sides are symmetrical. The top end is rounded into a blunt point with some concretion. Complete, good condition.
H. 4.2; W. 3.4; Th. 1.5; Wt 32.8

2600 K19/336 KLT 106 4555
Level IIc?
Greenstone. Small, symmetrical, with a sharp, curved edge, a rounded butt and very smooth surfaces. Complete.
L. 5.1; W. 3.3 max.; Th. 1.8 max.

2601 K19/175 1598
Level I/II
Dark, slate-like stone. Small, slightly asymmetrical, smooth on one face with some chips down one side but the other face is more weathered with a slight depression; the slightly curved cutting edge is barely chipped, but worn, indicating that the soft stone was re-ground after use.
L. 5.5; W. 4.0; Th. 1.1; Wt 45.3

Elsewhere asymmetry in axe heads is common and represents the left- or right-handedness of the tool which was hafted — hence the slight depression on the upper surface.

Bobbin(?) (2602)

2602 I19/10 KLT 46 1704
Level IIe?
Deep red-coloured stone. Perforated slightly off-centre, with a flat top and bottom. The edge has two deeply-worn grooves, and traces of several shallower ones. On one flat surface there are roughly-incised, radial grooves and other haphazard, but deliberate scratches. Perhaps a bobbin for winding thread onto.
Di. 2.9; H. 1.3; Di. perf. 0.6

Decorated stone objects (2603–11)

2603 H20/837 5335
Level Vf4; recovered in the wet-sieving of a sample from the fill of Rm 51 (Level Vf4), but of course subject to the same uncertainties

Figure 327. *Fragment of decorated disc* **2603**.

Figure 328. *Segment of carved disc* **2605**.

Figure 329. *Carved stone* **2610**.

that apply to the stratigraphic context of any small item.
Incised disc — a small segment from a disc, possibly but not certainly of stone, which seems to have fine micaceous inclusions. The reverse is smooth and greyish, perhaps discoloured by heat. There is a thick creamy white layer on the obverse into which a decorative pattern has been cut. This consists of a narrow circular band of opposed excised triangles leaving diamonds, and inside this parts of four Y-shaped incised lines hanging from a single circular line and radiating from a central perforation. The piece has no curvature and is derived from a flat object (tapering very slightly towards the outer edge), such as a lid. The perforation from which the design radiates may indicate the location of a central knob or pivot.
H. (3.3); W. (2.2); Th. 0.93 at centre, 0.91 at outer edge; Di. perf. *c.* 0.5
Fig. 327

The decorative motifs of this small fragment suggest that it originated from an object of Egyptian inspiration, even if not of Egyptian workmanship. The influence of Egyptian artistic elements in the Levant, Syria and Cyprus is well documented. The lid could have belonged to a cosmetic box, as frequently seen amongst Egyptian cosmetic paraphernalia often made of wood with a swivel lid (Vandier d'Abbadie 1972, no. 125 on p. 46 — bowl with attached lid, XVIIIth Dyn.). For a wooden lid to a balance-pan case with central perforation for the lid to pivot on a nail, see Petrie 1927, pl. XL no. 73. Compare also Freed 1982, 61 no. 32 case for balance pans and arm, rosette decoration on circular part, and the kohl pots on pp. 218–20 nos. 264 and 268.
  For smaller (di. 3–5.5 cm) cylindrical bone boxes with lids in Anatolia cf. von der Osten 1937, 248 with fig. 274 (boxes d186, d370, and lids with central perforation c151, c763), a stone lid p. 431 fig. 486 d2006; floral motifs p. 434 fig. 489 (e350, e2511). For the ivory lid of a cosmetic box with incised rosette decoration and central depression from Emar see Margueron 1982, 123f., fig. 1.

[**2604** number not used]

2605   I14/67   3431
Level 1/2k
Corner of a soft, cream stone (or stucco) disc with a convex underside, partly discoloured by burning, and flat, upper face, neatly divided by thin, incised lines into a grid of squares some 2 cm across. Each of these squares is divided diagonally by a St Andrew's cross, formed by the excision of four triangles. The shape and design resemble those of wooden bread-stamps.

L. (5.7); W. (5.4); H. 1.7 at edge; Di. 12.0
Fig. 328

For Byzantine parallels to this design cf. Woolley & Lawrence 1936, fig. 50, p. 130 from Raheiba; pl. XXXVIII, figs. 19–20 from Esbeila.

2606   J18/67   2313
Level IIg/h?
Small fragment; pale grey, turned slightly pink and dark grey in patches from the effects of fire. It may originally have been part of a stele or architectural fragment with a curved and rounded top(?). There are faint traces of an edge with a pendant circle and part of an oval in high relief (0.8). Alternatively, this could be an '*objet trouvé*'.
W. (4.9); H. 7.2; Th. 6.2

2607   K20/17   1105
Level I
Flat, roughly square pebble; greyish pink, heavily encrusted on one face. The other face is bisected by a deeply incised groove. There is a second groove below it at an angle; two pairs of lines run into the upper groove at an angle and two of these lines extend below it, running into each other and intersecting with the lower groove.
L. 3.5; W. 3.2; H. 1.2

This object resembles some of the Neolithic seal-amulets of the Near East (e.g. Wickede 1990, nos. 25, 78–9, 83, 173) but may be merely a crude doodle.

[**2608**]   J18/69   2315
Level IIg/h?
Flat, shaped like a scaraboid; black with grey mottling; broken at the tip and down one side. The back is slightly convex, the base is smooth with one diagonal fault, and there is a band of discoloration 1.3 cm wide running around the lower edge of the piece, perhaps indicating the presence of a setting. Possibly a natural pebble.
L. 6.2; W. (3.7); Th. 2.9

2609   99/11   99
Surface
Flat, grey with roughly parallel edges; broken at an angle at both ends. A straight, median, rounded V-shaped groove runs along each face leaving a thickness of 0.5 of stone between. It is not clear what purpose this object may have served.
L. (5.3); W. 3.3; H. 0.8 (0.5 at groove)

Smaller Stone Artefacts

Figure 330. *Fragment of stone incense burner(?) 2611.*

Figure 331. *Stone maceheads from Level IVa: 2614 & 2615.*

2610   I12/2   306
Surface
Part of a fine-grained cylinder or rounded corner. Broken along the lines of five radiating holes which have been drilled into it from the approximate centre of the top (the drilling is at the end of a groove), at approximately 90 degrees from two sides (the point of one drilling is marked on the exterior by the juncture of three short, radiating lines) and by two further diagonal drillings. The broken surface thus shows a star-pattern of drillings, two of which run into each other while the others touch. Two of the drillings have a diameter of 0.8 and three of 0.6. They are straight and smooth, but one of the narrow drillings shows distinctive 'collars' indicative of wear on a copper drill-bit (see Gorelick & Gwinnett 1989) and this drilling flares at the outer end. This flaring was presumably caused when the craftsman was trying to free his drill, possibly resulting in the fracture of the stone. The purpose the drilled piece served is unclear: it may have been merely practice drilling on a discarded piece of stone.
W. (4.1); H. (3.6); Di. *c.* 6.0
Fig. 329

Incense burner(?) (2611)

2611   J17/8   5000
Topsoil
Fragment of a rough cube of cream to pale brown limestone, with one side and the bottom broken off. Its top is undecorated, with a circular recess (Di. 3.0; depth 2.0). Front: decoration is roughly incised with a rough-tipped tool; it consisted originally of a vertical panel divided into triangles by a vertical line and two diagonals, with a haphazard pattern of small, gouged dots (five each in the almost complete top triangle and five in the incomplete right triangle), within a border of small, gouged dots (five preserved on the left side and two along the top). Left side: a partially preserved pattern of thin, incised lines — part of a diagonal grid with one central vertical. Back: chiselled flat.
W. (9.7); H. 7.4; Di. 3.0 × 2.0 deep
Fig. 330

The decoration is strongly reminiscent of that of a widespread class of incense-burner found in second-millennium Emar (Margueron 1982, 95–7, esp. fig. 1, found in fill below occupation levels), but far more prevalent in the sixth–fifth centuries BC, corresponding to a period when the spice trade flourished (Ziegler 1942; Stern 1982, 182–5 & 191). Normally the incense burners are completely hol- lowed-out and it may be that this is an unfinished piece that broke during manufacture. This could imply that the object was locally produced and was not an import.

Gaming-pieces or counters(?) (2612–13)

[2612]   K14/151   3096
Level 2 middle
White, very powdery gypsum burnt to plaster. Conoid object with a wide, flat base, tapering to an end about 1.0 cm across. Similar to a stamp seal shape, but with no visible design.
H. 2.0; Di. 3.2
A similar object is recorded from Kamid el Loz in Lebanon.

2613   S18/1   2500
Surface
Greyish-brown disc with smooth, rounded edges and a central hole pierced from both sides. About 50 per cent is preserved. Both faces are roughly flat, although somewhat irregular. Perhaps the stone equivalent of sherd discs (see **1537–95** above) or a counter.
Th. 0.7; Di. 3.3

Maceheads (2614–15)

Two maceheads of very different appearance came from Level IVa. **2615** is almost spherical, made of carefully polished grey-black igneous stone. In contrast, **2614** is biconoid and manufactured from a soft white stone which appears to have undergone some chemical process rendering it to a powdery consistency. Whatever the original property of the stone, it could hardly have served the same purpose as its counterpart **2615**, being far too soft.

Maceheads are not everyday objects and are often classified as weapons, but there is also the ceremonial type as represented by the tomb gifts at Alaca Hüyük (Koşay 1951, pl. 182:1–2). Particularly close counterparts to the Kilise Tepe ones can be found at Kusura of Period B and C (Lamb 1937, 47, fig. 22; 1938, 263ff., fig. 25:2–4).

2614   H20/592   1272
Level IVa/Ve?
White macehead, biconoid with central perforation, resembling a giant spindle whorl. Made from talc-like stone which has disintegrated to a white powdery consistency.
H. 4.65; Di. 6.5; Di. perf. 1.4; Wt 255
Fig. 331

2615   H20/583   1270
Level IVa
Complete spherical macehead of grey-black igneous stone with carefully polished surface. Clearly visible drilling marks show that the large central perforation was drilled from both sides with an imperfect join at the centre. Slightly flattened top and bottom. Some discoloration on outside surface possibly due to chemical action.
H. 5.0; Di. 5.6; Di. perf. 1.9; Wt 206
Fig. 331

Mould for metal (2616)

2616   H20/323   KLT 60   1807
Level IVa/Ve
Open mould of red-brown sandstone. The preserved part tapers to one narrow end. The upper surface has two straight-sided channels with rounded ends. Both are discoloured from use. The sides are roughly worked, as is the underside, while the upper face is smooth.
L. (12.3); H. 5.3; W. (10.0)
Fig. 332

This mould for the production of metal artefacts was found in the packing material below an early MBA occupation floor in Rm 42 and may have been broken and discarded in antiquity. One of the two matrices is slightly more tapered than the other. In the mould's incomplete state, we can only speculate on the complete shape of the negatives and hence of the particular items that were cast in it.

Moulds of the 'open' kind — as opposed to piece-moulds — are the easiest form of casting metal. In Anatolia they are first attested towards the end of the fourth millennium, but are most frequent during the third and second millennia (Müller-Karpe 1994, 134f.). Almost 100 examples are recorded, coming from most major sites (Müller-Karpe 1994, 131, fig. 89). Many of the known examples are multi-sided, i.e. more than one side has been worked to create several negatives, often with a combination of differing implements incorporated in the same mould (Müller-Karpe 1994, pls. 22–34). The most commonly encountered mould negatives belong to the category of bar-shaped ingots, also referred to as slab ingots, followed by flat and lugged axes. The slab ingots, of which 120 matrices are known, are narrow elongated bars with rounded corners. This type may be represented on the Kilise Tepe mould by the example shown on the left side of the drawing (Fig. 464), while the remains of the right negative possibly suggest an axe. The combination on the same mould of ingot negatives with those for other artefacts, particularly flat axes, is not uncommon (Müller-Karpe 1994, 143).

It is not clear whether slab ingots were trade items or raw material for cold metal working. There is, however, clear evidence later for the standardization of ingots from the Cape Gelidonya shipwreck where 19 slab ingots were found, all weighing c. 1.0 kg (equivalent to 2 Babylonian minas), prompting the suggestion that they may have been used as a form of currency (Bass 1967, 81f., fig. 96; Müller-Karpe 1994, 136ff., 181, pls. 15, 19, 21–3).

Mould for jewellery (2617)

2617   K20/9   KLT 2   1102
Level I?
Broken end of a jewellery mould; hard, smooth, black stone with white specks with a patchy brown corner. The piece has been carefully finished and polished. Along the sloping broken edge, the stone has been roughly abraded, leaving clear striations. On the upper face is an excised design consisting of a horizontal groove, damaged by a chip at one end, decorated with two vertical slashes, and surmounted by a crescent embracing a small indentation in the centre. Along the line of the break are a couple of slightly diagonal grooves running from edge to edge; one groove is a continuation of the other, but slightly off-set and slightly deeper. On one edge is a hole drilled near to the adjacent edge to a depth of c. 0.8, which may have been used to clamp the mould to its other half although one would have expected it on the upper face. On the lower face is a horizontal groove which widens at one end into a deeper, oval-shaped depression that runs into the break.
L. 3.3; W. (2.6); H. 1.9
Fig. 333

A number of similar moulds have been found in Late Bronze Age contexts at Ugarit and other Levantine sites (Elliott 1991, 49–51, figs. 14:23 & 22:6–10, esp. nos. 7 & 9). The moulds are generally referred to in the literature as being made of steatite. However, the Ugarit

Figure 332. *Sandstone mould for metalwork* **2616**.

Figure 333. *Stone jewellery mould* **2617**.

moulds have been analysed and are all of chlorite, which is more resistant to heat than steatite; limestone is too coarse for jewellery moulds. The moulds are almost invariably found broken and may have been kept for re-use. However, the main documented period for the use of such moulds in Anatolia is in the Late Early Bronze Age and Middle Bronze Age, particularly at Kültepe where many complete examples have been found (Emre 1971, esp. pl. I:2–3, II:2, III:1). Some of these moulds are very elaborate but parts of others, particularly in the Middle Bronze Age, are similar to that from Kilise Tepe, and the fragment may be a survival from that period.

Palettes (2618–23)

These are flat, rectangular stones with rounded edges and slightly concave sides. The material is dense and fine-grained. They have been found in most levels. They are small enough to have been held in the palm of the hand and may have been used for grinding small quantities of spices or pigments. Most are broken, but one from Level IV (**2619**) and a thicker example from the surface (**2622**) are complete.

2618   H20/1008   5397
Level Vf/g
Rectangular fragment of a palette of reddish-brown sandstone with rounded edges. Smooth on both sides.
L. 6.5; W. 7.6; Th. 1.3

2619   H20/109   1232
Level IVa/b
Tabular palette of light brown sandstone of rectangular shape. The upper surface is grey and slightly concave.
L. 8.9; W. 6.1; Th.1.0

2619a   I19/107   2848
Level IIc
Large, tear-shaped; grey with lighter veining and darker discoloration from burning. Probably originally a pebble, ground flat on both faces.
L. 7.1; W. 4.0; H. 1.0
Fig. 334

2620   K19/190   4506
Level IIc/d
Corner of a large example of a dark grey stone palette. Judging by the concavity of the two partly-preserved sides, it is likely that relatively little is missing. Smooth surfaces and right-angled corners at one end.
L. 9.1; W. 13.8; Th. 1.5

2621   K14/70   3031
Level I
Rounded end of a slightly chalky, spatula-shaped, cream, object (other end broken), concave on one face and convex on the other, with rounded edges. Probably another type of palette.
L. (7.2); W. 4.8; Th. 1.4

[**2622**]   M6/1c   325
Surface
Complete grey quartz-like stone palette. Worn on one face; the other face is encrusted.
L. 11.0; W. 7.0; Th. 2.5

2623   O20/5   185

Figure 334. *Stone palette 2619a.*

Surface
Orangey-brown stone (or perhaps hard clay) end of a palette.
L. (4.3); W. 5.5; Th. 1.1

Sling-shots (2624–6)

Possible sling-shots; pebbles selected for their near-spherical shape; although smooth, they are somewhat abrasive on the surface.

[**2624**]   K18/136   4364
Level IIe
Grey; one side is covered with a hard, cream coating, possibly clay, and patches of the same material can also be seen on the other side.
Di. 3.3–4.0; Wt 60.8

[**2625**]   J18/117   2343
Level I
Asymmetrical, roundish, reddish-brown; slightly flatter on one surface. Possibly natural.
Di. 2.8–3.6; Wt 36.9

[**2626**]   K18/177   6002
Topsoil
Small, roundish, beige; a small dent on one side.
Di. 2.5–3.0; Wt 28.2

Stone tools (2627–37)

This category includes a variety of stones showing use-wear; some are no doubt hammer stones, others pestles, and some irregularly shaped stones with worked surfaces probably acted as rubbers or polishing tools, such as **2627**, found in association with other polishing implements made from bone (**2465, 2471**) in Rm 83 of Level Vj. The majority of rough stone tools are listed below with the larger stone objects (**2781** ff.).

[**2627**]   H20/562   1859
Level Vj
Purple oval-shaped stone with two flat surfaces. The side edges are smooth and curved. Polisher?
L. 11.8; W. 9.0; Th. 3.0

Chapter 45

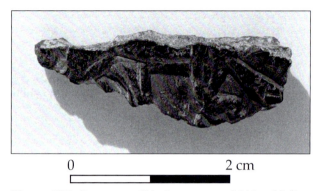

Figure 335. *Fragment of black stone vase **2641**, with lion in relief.*

[2628]   H20/617   1863
Level Vi/j
Hammerstone or pestle, limestone. Cylindrical, well-rounded and slighly wider at the working end. Some percussion marks visible; chipped on two sides. Smooth.
L. (8.6); Di. 4.1; Wt 224.2

[2629]   H20/707   5402
Level Vi
Hammerstone. A smooth yellow stone with chips taken off it. This may be a core although there is no cortical surface. Rounded triangular shape.
7.3 × 6.5 × 4.3; Wt 314

2630   H20/1037   KLT 124   6305
Level Vg
Cylindrical black stone pounder tapering slightly towards the top. Surfaces smooth. Chipped on lower edges.
H. 9.7; Di. 6.5 max.

[2631]   H20/659b   5301
Level Ve
Ovoid pebble that has been worked as a rubber or polishing tool. Brown-grey overall appearance but on flattened polished side it is light brown.
3.5 × 4.9

2632   H20/729   5322
Level IVa/Ve
A large, heavy rounded stone. The shape appears largely natural, with some chips taken off it to make it spherical. Perhaps a hammer or pounder.
Di. 10.2; Wt 1430.2

[2633]   H19/210   4249
Level IVb
Grey hammerstone, complete, with percussion marks on narrower end which led the tip to flake off eventually.
L. (7.2); W. 3.5; H. 2.7; Wt 100.5

2634   I20/82   KLT 59   4028
Level IIId/e
Grey and white, crystalline stone. Rounded, very well-worn head on a short stem which flares out slightly to a rounded butt, like a champagne cork.
Di. 6.5 (head), 4.9 (stem, max.)

[2635]   J19/422   6411
Level IIb/c
Plano-convex with rounded ends; smoothed. Probably natural but could have been used as a rubber.
L. 9.2; W. 4.7; Th. 1.9

2636   J19/309   1711?
Provenance possibly P95/2 (Level IIg–h)
Complete, mottled, black and green cylinder, tapering at one end. The ends are flattened and carefully polished overall. Larger than the whetstones; the polished surface bears no marks of having been used for sharpening a blade; there are, however, several hairline fractures running from the wider end which could have been caused by this implement having been used as the pestle it resembles.
L. 5.7; Di. 2.4; Wt 62.5

2637   K14/102   3060
Level 1
End of a transversely broken pick or wedge of cream, smooth-surfaced stone; damage (flaking) at the tip, indicating that it was used for striking blows and the tool probably snapped at the haft where jarring was being absorbed.
L. (12.8); W. 5.7 tapering to 2.9 at the tip; Th. 3.5

[2638   number not used]

Stone vessels (2639–46)

Apart from mortars and similar large vessels (see below) only fragments of stone vessels survive. The manufacture or acquisition of stone vessels was clearly not a priority at Kilise Tepe.

2639   I19/123   2840
Level IIc
Rough, grey, basalt-like stone with black and brown inclusions carved into a bowl of which only a section of the plain rounded rim survives. The rim widens at one point to 2.3 cm; a swelling at the point of breakage about 4.5 cm below the rim may indicate the presence of a foot (Th. 3.8), so that this may have been a tripod vessel similar in shape to a mortar (see **2671** ff.), but not as thick.
L. (12.0); Th. 1.1–2.5; H. (9.0); Di. 28.0

2640   J18/251   5811
Level IIc/d
Beige; fine-grained with some darker veining forming what seems to be the base of a small handle with an oval section (1.6 × 2.0). None of the surfaces, however, is finished in any way. Possibly a natural stone formation.
H. (4.5); W. (4.3)

2641   I19/39   KLT 77   1776
Level IIg/h
Black stone resembling steatite; small fragment carved in relief with the lower part of a lion pacing towards the right with its tail tucked between its legs. The thickness of the wall of the vessel varies considerably.
L. (3.2); H. (0.8); Th. 0.3–1.2; Di. unmeasurable
Fig. 335

Similar 'steatite' vessels of the early first millennium BC have been found at Carchemish (Woolley 1921, pl. 28:3 & 4) and some North Syrian ivory pyxides are also related (Barnett 1957, pls. XVI–XXVII many of which depict pacing animals).

2642   K18/35   4310
Level I/II
Beige; formed into a tubular spout (of which less than half survives)

with a ridge-edged rim. The walls are thin and irregular but widen towards the juncture with the vessel (missing) and the spout develops a slight ridge on what is probably its underside.
L. (3.3); Th. 0.4; Di. 2.0

2643   Q19/43   2108
Level E2b/c
Off-white calcareous stone, with many cracks; possibly from a vessel; the curvature of the fragment is regular but the actual external and internal surfaces are somewhat rough. The wall of the vessel becomes increasingly thinner from bottom to top (if that is the right way up).
L. (6.0); W. 1.2

2644   L14/22   3604
Level 1
White, crystalline stone, carved into a bowl of which only part of the rim survives. Plain, rounded rim, slightly thickened in relation to the walls of the vessel. Well-finished surfaces, but concretions on exterior.
L. (5.0); H. (6.7); Th. 0.65; Di. 22.0

2645   Q19/13   178
Surface
Dense; creamy-white, burnt to grey on one side, carved into a shallow platter(?) of which only part of the plain rim survives. The underside has been left rough and the surface is irregular.
L. (4.2); W. (4.1); Th. 1.8–2.2; Di. 12.0

2646   H19/2   4200
Surface
Lid fragment? Veined dark brown stone; smooth; roughly circular with a ridge rising towards the centre which could have formed a handle. This could be a natural stone which was 'improved'.
L. (7.0); W. (4.2); H. (2.5)

Weights (2647–8)

It is not suggested that the objects listed here belonged to any weight system but they were probably used as fishing weights or to weigh down objects, perhaps connected with weaving. For other perforated stones see under the loomweights (above, **1825–35**).

2647   J18/312   5849
Level IIe
Orangey-pink chert fragment with an irregular hole through it. Probably natural.
L. (3.7); W. 3.0; H. 1.7; Wt 17.7

[2648]   R18/38   2023
Topsoil
Smooth, roughly circular, grey-brown, chert pebble with white markings and a curious lustre. It has been bored through in one corner from both sides; the hole is irregular and much wider at the surfaces than at the middle. Recently chipped in the lower part.
L. 3.8; W. 3.0; H. 1.7; Di. 0.5; Wt 25.7

Whetstones (2649–64)

Whetstones used for sharpening blades and tools vary from carefully shaped, elongated stones to larger, smooth but uncut stones which bear marks of having been similarly used. Among the former are cylindrical, rectangular-sectioned and flat examples, which were pierced for suspension and may have been carried on a belt. In many of the male burials of *c.* 2600 BC in the Royal Cemetery of Ur in southern Iraq, the owner was buried with a seal, dagger, toilet set and whetstone suspended from his belt (Woolley 1934, 156). Where the perforation is preserved, it has generally been bored from both sides. A surprising number of whetstones come from the surface of the mound and some may, therefore be recent, whereas others may have been ancient ones re-used.

For whetstones found in Late Bronze Age contexts at Ugarit see Elliott 1991, 23–5 and fig. 6:3–7, with a discussion of types, distribution and use, predominantly in Cyprus and the Levant. For Iron Age examples from Tarsus, see Goldman 1963, 388, pl. 180 Nos. 4–7, and for Boğazköy, see Boehmer 1972, 229ff. Taf. XCVII–XCVIII, and most recently Boehmer 1979, 63, nos. 3852–67.

2649   H20/580   1272
Level IVa/Ve?
Long, narrow stone object with perforation hole at one end and tapered at the other. One face is flat the other rounded, making it D-shaped in section. Surface very smooth. Possibly a whetstone. Complete.
L. 6.2; W. 1.2; Di. perf. 0.42

2650   H19/169   4248
Level IIIa/IVb
Rectangular whetstone of grey sandstone with well executed perforation hole at one end which was drilled from both sides, leaving a bevelled edge. Broken at the lower end.
L. (3.5); W. 2.0; Th. 1.0; Di. perf. 0.9

2651   J20/110   KLT 45   1372
Level IIIe
Hard, black; very smooth and rounded, with a triangular cross-section, perforated from both sides. Tapering at the perforated end; the other end has a pronounced groove around it, giving the whetstone a phallic appearance; next to the groove, on one side, is a neat, circular hole with traces of white inlay. On all three sides, but especially on the flattest, there are striations from use.
L. 8.8; W. 1.8 max.; Di. perf. 0.3

2652   J19/226   1690
Level IId
Dense, dark grey; cylindrical with one broken end and one rounded. No trace of a perforation. Heavily used on one side, which is worn into a hollow.
L. (6.5); Di. 1.4

[2653]   J19/350   3959
Level II
Dense, purplish-red, fine-grained; cylindrical, but worn down in places from much use. Perforated from both sides and broken at the perforation, with a tapering break at the other end which has been bored through from one side at an angle with a small replacement hole.
L. (6.0); Di. *c.* 1.3

2654 H12/3 307
Surface
Blackish-grey; flat, slightly tapering rectangle, with rounded edges and a perforation at the wider end; chisel-shaped at the other end. The hole, perforated from both sides, is slightly off-centre. Diagonal scoring on one side and polishing marks on the other.
L. 4.5; W. 1.5–1.8; Th. 0.5

[2655] I14/179 3715
Unstratified
Dense, dark grey with very fine, darker mottling and lighter veining. Cylindrical, perforated from both sides, and tapering at the perforated end; broken at the perforation and a clean break at the other end. Very faint, transverse cut marks and longitudinal, orangey-brown streaks on two sides.
L. (4.3); Di. 1.6 tapering to 1.2

2656 I14/180 3715
Unstratified
Dense, purplish-red; rectangular in section, perforated from both sides, tapering towards the perforation. Broken at the perforation and at the other end. Heavy transverse cuts on one side below the perforation.
L. (4.3); W. 1.2; Th. 1.3

[2657] K18/7 4301
Surface
Dense, dark grey; cylindrical with an oval section. One end is flat, with rounded edges, the other broken. There is no trace of a perforation. Heavily used on one side.
L. (2.7); Di. 1.2–1.4

2658 L8/5 318
Surface
Dense, pale greyish-brown; trapezoidal section, with one narrow side rounded and the other squared; slightly tapering at the smoothed end and broken at the other; no trace of a perforation survives. Diagonal cuts on the narrow, rounded side and longitudinal marks and striations on the narrow, flat side.
L. (4.8); W. 1.3–1.7; Th. 1.3

2659 Q9/2 235
Surface
Fine, dense, grey; cylindrical but broken longitudinally; flat end with a perforation drilled from one side; other end broken. Heavy scoring on sides, at right angles to the perforation.
L. (4.3); Di. 1.2

[2660] R6/1 330
Surface
Dark brownish-grey, grainy; weathered to grey on unbroken areas; flat on one face and rounded on the other, wedge-shaped in section with edges carefully rounded, broken at both ends, with no trace of a perforation surviving. Faint traces of use on the rounded face.
L. (4.2); W. 2.8; Th. 1.5

The following are examples of less portable whetstones (or possible whetstones):

[2661] I19/109 2851
Level IIc
Long pebble with rounded ends; dark grey with white streaks and veining; approximately flat on one side. Heavily used in the middle of the rounded side which has worn down, with traces of transverse cuts.
L. 9.0; W. 2.8 max.; Th. 1.9 max.

[2662] K19/365 4569
Level IIe
Greyish-yellow, very abrasive sandstone; rectangular, with one side broken. One surface seems smoothed.
L. 7.8; W. (3.8); Th. 3.0

[2663] K18/13 4302
Level I
Slate-like; flat, irregularly-shaped rhomboid, with one side (c. 4.0) possibly smoothed (concretions) but the others rough. Diagonal scored lines on one face.
L. c. 5.0; W. 4.2; Th. 0.6

[2664] K18/6 4301
Surface
Dense, black limestone; shaped as a tapering, irregular rectangle, flat, but not smoothed on one face and at one end. Used on all the smoothed sides with particularly heavy use on the sloping edge.
L. 5.1–5.7; W. 2.3–3.4 and 2.8–3.3; Th. 1.8–2.2

Worked stones of uncertain use (2665–70)

2665 H20/830 5326
Level Vf4
Half of circular ground stone with large central perforation which widens considerably towards the two faces, leaving a ridge in the centre. Sides well rounded and polished.
H. 6.1; Di. 13.4; Di. perf. 2.6

[2666] H20/57 1220
Level IVb
Worked stone shaped into very smooth rounded shell form, hollowed on one side.
L. 2.7; W. 1.7; Th. 1.2

2667 H20/929 5368
Level Vf
Finger-shaped brown sandstone object with outer layer of white encrustation. Snapped off at one end. One surface is polished. Could be natural.
L.(5.5); W. (2.2); Th. 1.5

[2668] H19/249 4257
Level IVa/b
Unevenly-shaped pebble of a light brown colour with a perforation through its narrow end. No traces of being worked and the hole could be natural.
L. 4.0; W. 3.0

[2669] H19/236 4254
Level IVb
Pierced calcareous white stone, uneven and asymmetrical with a perforation running through — slightly off centre.
L. (10.0); W. 9.2; Di. perf. (max.) 2.1

2670 I16/19 4601
Surface
Cylindrical stone, with a broad V-shaped circular depression in the rounded top, widening to a sloping ledge and a flattened rounded base.
L. 5.05; Di. 1.27

This is too small to be a door socket. It may be the socket for a bearing for a potter's wheel such as have been found at Lachish (Tufnell 1958, 90–91, pl. 21:1 and cf. pl. 49:12–13 for bearings).

Chapter 46

Larger Stone Artefacts

Dominique Collon

The study of querns, grinders, mortars and other large stone objects has, over the years, become a specialist subject, with its own parameters and terminology (see for example Procopiou & Treuil 2002; Baysal & Wright 2002 with further references). Unfortunately, the present material has not benefited from such specialist treatment and has been catalogued by a non-specialist. However, the material was examined as a whole and every attempt has been made to be consistent both in the classification of the objects and in the stone identifications. The latter are tentative and should be taken as a means of differentiating the different types rather than an accurate geological determination (see especially below under 'Querns and Grinders'). Dimensions are given as length × width × height with incomplete dimensions enclosed in brackets ( ); given the nature of the material, the dimensions are often approximate.

Mortars

In contrast to the querns (see below) these are made of fine-grained stone and have a hollow area or bowl for pounding or mixing ingredients. Two Late Bronze Age examples (**2679** and **2681**) were extremely large and were evidently fixtures, although they were found reused in or beside the foundations of W740. Some have a pecked surface rather than a smooth surface and as this pecking extends over the whole of the bowl's interior it seems to have been intentional rather than the result of extensive use; this pecking is distinct from the pitting due to weathering noted in some cases below. Here the well-stratified sequence of mortars from H19 and H20 will be dealt with first and other examples will be grouped separately at the end.

For mortars found in Late Bronze Age contexts at Ugarit see Elliott 1991, 28–33 and figs. 7:3–9:5, with a discussion of types and distribution, predominantly in Cyprus and the Levant. For Boğazköy, see most recently Boehmer 1979, 53–4, nos. 3704–26.

Mortars from H19 and H20
Early Bronze Age (2671–5)
The EB II examples are carefully-shaped, small, circular, round-bottomed bowls which, in cross-section, are flattened spheres with the bowl scooped out at the top. The exterior is rougher than the interior but both surfaces were carefully finished although both are now affected by pitting due to weathering. They look like chunky ashtrays.

2671 H20/534 1853
Level Vi
Beige.
Ext. di. 13 × H. 6.5; Int. di. 8 × 3.5 deep

[2672] H20/450 1838
Level Vg/h
Greyish-brown.
Ext. di. 20 × H. 7.25; Int. di. 8 × 4 deep

A single example was found in EB III and is of a different type.

[2673] H20/427 1836
Level Vg/h
Cream limestone; carefully-shaped rim fragment with the outer edge broken. The top of the rim is flat and polished (max. preserved smoothed area 8 cm) with a stepped area 1.5 cm higher, L. (7) × W. (8). The interior is almost vertical (Top di. 16; Bottom di. 12).
(22.5) × (10.5) × (9.5)

[2674] H20/973 5370
Level Vf2?
Light brown limestone; fragment with smoothed curved section with near vertical side (Di. 20 × H. (6.5)).
(22) × (15) × (6.5)

[2675] H20/988 5349
Level Vf3
Grey sandstone (white inclusions); roughly oval, flat-bottomed piece, with shallow depression 7–8.5 × 1 cm deep.
11 × 9 × 2.8

Middle Bronze Age (2676–7)
Both the preserved examples come from the latter part of this period.

[2676]   H19/315   4268
Level IVb
Roughly-shaped lump of cream stone which no longer sits square, heavily pitted due to weathering. The upper part is worn around the edges; the bowl is smoothed (Di. *c.* 16 × (6) deep).
(22) × (17) × (17)

[2677]   H19/324   4268
Level IVb
Beige limestone; probably with straight sides and curved ends but only one end is preserved and the edges are broken. The smoothed depression is oval (16 × *c.* 20 × *c.* 2.5 deep).
(17) × *c.* 26 × 7

Late Bronze Age (2678–83)

[2678]   H19/164   4247
Level IIIa
Grey stone with white inclusions; roughly triangular fragment with rounded apex (sides (29) and (28) × W. 26), and curve of a deeply sloping bowl (round? oval? max. W. 18 × 8 deep); carefully chipped into shape.

2679   H19/108   4241
Level IIIc
Cream stone; large, carefully-shaped, boat-like with a longitudinal groove along the interior, with one end and side broken; depth of grinding area 11.5.
L. probably originally 45 (now 43) × 24 × 17

[2680]   H19/109   4241
Level IIIc
Grey limestone; end of roughly rectangular mortar with flat base (natural line of cleavage), upper edges broken but most of width probably preserved. The smoothed depression was probably oval and deepens at the break (now 8 cm deep but deeper originally when the edges were preserved).
(19.5) × (16) × 12

[2681]   H19/76   4217
Level IIIc
Beige weathered to grey limestone; large, shapeless block, with shallow, smoothed depression (Di. *c.* 18 × 3.5 deep).
33 × 35 × 13

[2682]   H19/66   4212
Level IIIc/d
Fine-grained limestone; end of a rectangular mortar with rounded corners and smoothed exterior. The shallow bowl seems to have had a pecked interior, (15) × 16 × 4.5 deep.
(17) × 19 × 11.5

[2683]   H20/14   1209
Level IIId
Creamy-grey flaky limestone; fragment of large bowl with ext. damaged by fractures, edges missing and flat base on line of cleavage (Th. *c.* 4 cm). The curved area is smooth (5.5 deep).
(16) × (13) × 10

Level II and above (2684–99)

[2684]   J18/379   5887
Level IIc
Beige; large roughly-shaped stone with flat base and roughly-squared end with rounded corners (or roughly-rounded end); smoothed bowl (Di. 22 × 7 cm deep).
(17) × 27 × 10

2685   K20/40   1131
Level IIc
Fragment of a (three?)-footed mortar of dark grey sandstone (black inclusions), burnt, with pitted surfaces due to weathering. Complete profile but less than a quarter of the diameter survives; rounded rim (Int. di. 19, Ext. di. 20.5) thickening to 2.3 cm at the centre of bowl. The surviving vertical foot tapers from just below the rim (W. 7–3.6) and is roughly semicircular at the bottom, with the flat side outermost.
H. of bowl 9.0, H. with foot 12.5

[2686]   K20/101   1924
Level IIe
Perhaps similar to **2671–2** (see above) and therefore possibly EB II. Pinky-grey fossiliferous limestone; fragmentary with edges missing and base flattened (Th. 5.0).
(20) × (14); W. of bowl (14.5) × (3.4) deep

[2687]   K18/282   6142
Level IId/e?
Grey limestone; rim fragment, too small for diameter to be established; thin and rounded at the top, flaring to Th. 5.
L. 6; H. 8.5

[2688]   K14/124   3080
Level 2 middle
Cream; pitted due to weathering; rounded rim (*c.* 15 cm preserved; Di. *c.* 28). Th. at base of fragment 6.25.

[2689]   I14/136   3465
Level 2k
Cream with very worn and weathered surfaces; fragment with flat base. Bowl Di. *c.* 14? × 2.5 deep.
(18) × (12) × 8

[2690]   I19/28   1751
Level I/IIh
Similar to **2671–2** (see above) and therefore probably EB II. Beige and pitted due to weathering; its rim is less well preserved.
Ext. di. 16.5 × H. 7.5; Int. di. 11 × 3.7 deep

[2691]   I18/9   2701
Topsoil
Pale grey, fine-grain limestone. Curved fragment 18 × 20 × 4.5 with large Di., *c.* 30–40.

[2692]   K19/30   1518
Level I
Pale brown limestone; approximately a quarter preserved of a large bowl; ext. chip-smoothed with part flattened, perhaps so that it can be rested on its side to enable its contents to be decanted; base flattened along natural cleavage. The interior of the bowl (Di. *c.* 26) is smoothed.
(16) × max. H. 13 × base Th. 7.5

[2693]   R18/208   2461
Level E5a
Grey limestone; fragment of large mortar. Curved surface with no edge preserved.
(12.5) × (7.5) × H. of base 3.7–6.6

[2694]   K17/26   9607
Level 1
Pale brown stone; flattish surfaces and an edge at 90 degrees; fragmentary.

[2695]   J16/13   4700
Topsoil
Cream; fragment of rim, from large, steep-sided bowl (Int. di. 34) with a flat rim (Th. 4) which steps outwards for 7 cm (Th. 6) and forms a wedge along the bowl 12 cm high.
(19) × (16); Th. at bottom 7

[2696]   I12/7   306
Surface
Part of a large, smoothed boulder of fossiliferous limestone, carved out for use as a mortar of which about half remains (Di. *c.* 20 at the top and 7.3 at the bottom × 11 deep). The surface of the hole is smooth but its base was small and thin and finally fell away, taking part of the smoothed surface of the bottom of the boulder with it.
(36) × (20) × 12

[2697]   Y19/1   301
Surface
Fragment of grey vesicular basalt with small part of mid-section of bowl. The bottom of a large ear-lug survives, with outer face like an inverted triangle, H. (5) × max. surviving W. at top 3.5 (outer face)–4.7 (where attached to the vessel).
Max. surviving W. 9.5; Int. di. 15; Th. 2.5–3.0

Other mortar fragments found on the surface are as follows:

[2698]
Shallow depressions in large stones (cf. **2679**): H12/4 (307); K8/4 (315); L6/1b (324).

[2699]
Bowl-shaped fragments: I13/1 (302); K9/1 (314); K15/6 (100) medium, /9 (100); M7/4 (323) large; U10/2 (269); O7/2 (244) small.

Querns and grinders

These have been grouped together, as many are fragmentary and it is not easy to differentiate between them except on the basis of size; where a reasonable presumption can be made, this is stated. Here, the quern is defined as the nether millstone, whilst the 'grinder' is the upper stone.

The stones fall into clear groups but the terms used here are to enable differentiation of the main types used and are not necessarily geologically accurate:

a) *Sandstone*: this has many small gritty inclusions of which the colour is specified in brackets.
b) *Conglomerate*: differs from sandstone in having many larger inclusions 1 cm or more across; their colour and that of the matrix are specified in brackets. Not attested in H19 and H20 before the Late Bronze Age.
c) *Schist*: hard, dark with white inclusions and layered; this is rare.
d) *Volcanic*: black, crumbly with lots of holes (vesicular), some large. Where the holes are smaller and the stone is closer to pumice (but still not so fine) this is specified as 'Fine volcanic'. Only small pieces have survived but it seems likely that these are from small grinders and never querns.

Unless otherwise stated, these objects are curved lengthwise and widthwise on the underside with relatively sharp edges (often broken or chipped) and are flat on top with rounded ends and straight sides (for grinders the top would strictly speaking be the bottom but is still referred to here as top for convenience). Unless otherwise specified, they are broken, with one end preserved unless they are described as fragments.

What strikes the non-specialist is the remarkable consistency of these objects through time and space. They appear in the earliest sedentary contexts, which given their weight is scarcely surprising (e.g. Mellaart 1975, 43, fig. 13:o from Mureybet, eighth millennium BC, and p. 81 fig. 35 from Jarmo, *c.* 6000 BC; de Contenson 1993 from Ramad, *c.* 6300-6000 BC), and it seems that once the shapes best suited for the purposes of grinding had been developed, they remained virtually unaltered for millennia. This would seem to make dating by typology impossible (at least to the non-specialist), and given the consistency of shape, even stratified finds may well be reused objects. Since the stones from which these heavy objects are made do not necessarily occur locally, their reuse would make considerable economic sense.

A rare example of a room full of querns and grinders preserved *in situ* occurs at Ebla in northwest Syria in a palace dated between 1800 and 1600 BC (Matthiae *et al.* 1995, 173 and cf. p. 349 no. 149 found in Palace G dated 2400–2300 BC). For querns and grinders found in Late Bronze Age contexts at Ugarit see Elliott 1991, 25–7 and fig. 6:8–14, with a discussion of types and distribution, predominantly in Cyprus and the Levant. For Tarsus, see Goldman 1956, 275, and for Boğazköy, see most recently Boehmer 1979, 56–7, nos. 3757–67 and 3770.

Early Bronze Age (**2700–12**)
[2700]   H20/506   1852
Level Vi
Grinder, almost complete; grey sandstone (white).
(25) × 14 × 5

[2701]   H20/509   1851
Level Vh/i
Quern; grey sandstone (white and white streaks); flat bottom; very slight concavity of the width.
(14) × 20 × 6

[2702]   H20/512   1851
Level Vh/i
Quern; grey sandstone (white); large with concave width (up to 4 cm deep) and slightly concave length.
(19) × (25) × (15)

[2703] H20/1049 6330
Level Vh1–2
Schist; fragment.
Max. th. 3.4

[2704] H20/888 5374
Level Vg
Grey sandstone; fragment.

[2705] H20/1020 5398
Level Vg
Volcanic; fragment.

[2706] H20/1052 6315
Level Vg
Volcanic; fragments.

[2707] H20/1061 6316
Level Vg
Quern or mortar?; dark grey schist; fragment with a flat base, part of a rounded edge, and a round depression (max. surviving width 15 × c. 4 deep).
(18) × (16) × 6.5

[2708] H20/957 5363
Level Vf2/3
Volcanic; fragment.
Max. th. 3

[2709] H20/897 5360
Level Vf3
Volcanic; fragment.

[2710] H20/930 5370
Level Vf2?
Quern; black sandstone (grey, black); fragment probably with part of edge.
(21) × (18) × (4.3)

[2711   number not used]

[2712] H20/659a 5301
Level Ve
Cream limestone.
(18) × 14 × 4.5

*Middle Bronze Age (**2713–19**)*

[2713] H20/587 1272
Level IVa/Ve?
Grinder; grey sandstone.
(13) × 13 × 4

[2714] H20/166 1245
Level IVa
Grinder, complete; grey sandstone (black and white).
28 × 16.5 × 6.5

[2715] H19/186 4249
Level IVb
Grinder; mottled grey and beige sandstone.
(23) × 18 × 4

[2716] H19/200 4249
Level IVb
Grinder; mottled grey and beige sandstone.
(22) × 14 × 4.5

[2717] H19/207 4249
Level IVb
Grinder; dark grey sandstone.
(24) × (17–probably c. 24) × 3.5

2718 H19/226 4251
Level IVb
Quern, probably almost complete; beige to dark grey sandstone (grey, black); square ends, length concave (2.5 deep at centre).
(41) × (19) × 3; 5.5 above horizontal at ends

2719 H19/227 4251
Level IVb
Complete grinder; light grey sandstone (red, white, grey).
28.5 × 15 × 4

*Late Bronze Age (**2720–34**)*

[2720] H19/161 4247
Level IIIa
Grinder; square end with rounded corners and concave edges, and ridge along back (triangular section).
(18) × 18 (end)–14 (middle) × 5 (end)–4 (middle)

[2721] H19/165 4247
Level IIIa
Schist.
(14) × (20) × (4)

[2722] H19/172 4248
Level IIIa/IVb
Quern; dark grey mottled igneous rock.
(19) × 20 × 6

[2723] H19/173 4248
Level IIIa/IVb
Grinder; triangular with rounded end.
(19) × (18) × 5.5

[2724] H19/174 4248
Level IIIa/IVb
Grinder; grey sandstone.
(26) × (15) × 4.5

[2725] H19/176 4248
Level IIIa/IVb
Grey sandstone; fragment.
(6) × (8)

[2726] H19/179 4248
Level IIIa/IVb
Grinder; schist.
21 × (18–probably originally 24) × 5.5

[2727] H19/160 4245
Level IIIb
Quern; greyish-brown sandstone (white, pink); intentionally pecked surface.
(12.5) × 17 × (10)

[2728] H19/106 4241
Level IIIc
Grinder; almost complete but upper surface missing; grey sandstone (white).
(18) × 19 × (6)

[2729] H19/107 4241
Level IIIc
Quern; conglomerate (black, green, dark red, orange in grey matrix).
(18) × 19 × 6

[2730] H20/20 1210
Level IIIc
Schist; lentoid fragment.
Di. c. 38 × H. 5.5

[2731] H20/846 5344
Level Vf?
Quern fragment and grinder; volcanic but greyer, with smaller holes and less friable than usual; both pieces are very flat on one face, with the quern uneven on the other face and the grinder convex on the other face.
Quern: (24) × (20) × 2.5-4
Grinder: probably complete, 21 × 16 × max. 3

[2732] H20/70 1224
Unstratified
Fragment of a low, plano-convex grinding stone made out of grey and black, mottled, quartz-like stone. Almost the entire cross-section has been preserved, (7.6) × (15.2) × 4.1.

[2733] I14/183 3714
Level 3
Quern; creamy-grey sandstone; flat surfaces above and below; thick, probably rounded end.
(21) × (26) × 12

[2734] I19/165 5506
Level IIIe
Grey sandstone with brown streaks; fragment.
(23.5) × (19) × 5

Level II and later (2735–78)
[2735] I19/163 5523
Level IIa/b
Hand-grinder, almost complete with damage on one side; conglomerate (multi-coloured in grey matrix); flat circular surface (Di. 8.3) and asymmetrical, domed back, probably with one vertical side, which fits into the hand.
H. 5.5

[2736] K20/157 Etütlük 1996 1967
Level IIb
Quern or mortar; cream sandstone with concretions; huge fragment with convex base and shallow concavity (i.e. like a shallow bowl); triangular 'handle' at one end, perhaps one of four, and fairly straight rounded edge leading to next 'handle' (missing).
(46) × (41) × 13.5 (to top of 'handle') × 7 (Th. of base)

[2737] K20/178 1976
Level IIb
Grinder; conglomerate (pinky-orange in pinky-orange matrix).
(18) × 14 × 6

[2738] K20/156 1962
Level IIb/c
Greyish-cream sandstone (multi-coloured); fragment.
(23) × 19 × 4.5

[2739] K18/277 6139
Level IIc
Grey sandstone.
(10) × (17.5) × 4

[2740] J19/349 3951
Level IIc?
Grinder, almost complete; cream sandstone (very small grey and brown); one end slightly triangular and the other probably more rounded.
(28) × 15 × 3

2741 I19/118 2861
Level IIc/d
Quern, almost complete but edges and ends chipped; grey sandstone (white); length concave (3.5 deep at centre).
56 × 22 × 7; 10 cm above horizontal at each end

[2742] J18/391 5894
Level IIc/d
Quern; conglomerate, heavily burnt and now friable (black and red); flat base; top sloping, perhaps originally concave lengthwise.
(16) × (16) × 8 at one end and 3 at the other

[2743] J19/375 3968
Level IIc
Dark grey sandstone (white); end shaped like a triangle with a flattened apex.
(13) × 15 × 5.5

[2744] I19/206 1726
Level IIc; in foundation of W733
Quern; pinkish with darker pink and yellow/brown inclusions, also larger flint-like nodules. Upper surface very gently concave, smoothed. Irregular shape.
41.5 × 39.8 × Th. 8.2

[2745] J18/364 5882
Level IId
Grey sandstone (white, black); fragment across concave width with much of underside broken.
(15.5) × (26) × 5

[2746] J18/371 5888
Level IId
Quern; grey sandstone; thick rounded end and irregular underside.
(24) × (23) × 7.5

[2747] K19/279 4517
Level IId
Reddish-grey burnt to rusty red sandstone (red); rectangular cross-section with rounded lower corners.
(12) × 13.5 × 3.5

[2748] H18/167 2661
Level IId/e
Quern; grey sandstone; thick rounded end.
(14) × 16.5 × 7.5

[2749] K18/101 4350
Level IIe
Dark grey sandstone (grey); fragment with part of one edge.
(12.5) × (18) × 3.5

[2750] K19/366 4570
Level IIe
Quern; grey sandstone (grey, black); round edge at end; part of edge preserved.
(23) × (23.5) × 10

Chapter 46

[**2751**]   K19/404   4593
Level IIe
Quern; cream conglomerate (white, grey, black, pink, red, fossils); fragment with rounded sides.
(9) × (20) (probably almost complete) × 9

[**2752**]   L19/36   5954
Level IIe/f
Grey sandstone (white); perhaps a roughly-squared end, or broken and smoothed.
(27) × 22 × 6.5

[**2753**]   L19/37   5954
Level IIe/f
Quern; grey sandstone; irregular lozenge-shape but large enough to be usable so it may be complete or nearly so; sits crooked.
44.5 × 24 × 7 (on one side) and 12 (on the other)

[**2754**]   J18/138   2351
Level IIf
Conglomerate (red), heavily incrusted; fragment.
(7.5) × 8 × (2.5)

[**2755**]   I19/207
Level II; no further details of provenance.
Quern; greenish. Dimensions not recorded, but L. *c.* 58.

[**2756**]   I14/99   3458
Level 2
Quern; grey sandstone (black, white, brown); end shaped like a triangle with a rounded apex.
(26) × (24–probably originally 29 at widest surviving point) × 4

[**2757**]   I14/24   3406
Level 1/2k
Grinder; volcanic; roughly squared end and very uneven thickness.
(21) × 13.5 × *c.* 5.5

[**2758**]   R18/212   2463
Level E5c
Very dense conglomerate (green, brown, red in white matrix).
(12) × 18 × 5.5

[**2759**]   Q19/63   2118
Level E4a
Cream sandstone, pitted due to weathering; carefully rounded end and back; very slightly convex upper face.
(14) × 20 × 6

[**2760**]   J18/79   2320
Level I?
Conglomerate; fragment.
(18) × (15) × 4

[**2761**]   K18/219   6105
Level I
Grinder; cream sandstone (grey, red, black).
(13) × 13 × 4.5

[**2762**]   K18/244   6121
Level IIf?
Schist; fragments.
(10) ×18 × 4.5

[**2763**]   K19/10   1501
Level I
Quern; dark red sandstone (red); concave fragment.
(21) × (17) × 10

[**2764**]   K19/84   1520
Level I
Cream sandstone; carefully rounded end and back; very slightly convex upper face.
(18) × 20 × 7

[**2765**]   K19/469   1520
Level I
Probably quern fragment.
(20.5) × (16) × 7

[**2766**]   I14/20   3403
Level 1
Grinder; fine volcanic; thicker ends than usual, probably to avoid breakage of this friable material.
(9) × 15 × 4

[**2767**]   S18/19   2506
Level E1
Conglomerate (red, yellow in white matrix); fragment.
(11) × (19.5) × 6.5

[**2768**]   S18/20   2506
Level E1
Grey limestone with upper layer resembling a gritty sandstone (green, grey, red); underside rough; flat, pointed end with round concavity of which about half remains (Di. 15 × 1.5 deep).
14+ × 12+ × 5.5

The following fragments found on the surface were probably all quern fragments:

[**2769**]
H12/2a (307); **I16**/45 (156); **J11**/9 (213); **J12**/1+8 (212); **K12**/3 (207); **L6**/1a (324); **L7**/1c–d (321); **L8**/1a (318); **M6**/1a–b (325); **M15**/5 (103); **O6**/2b, f (327); **P15**/3 (101); **R8**/2b (249); **T6**/1b (254); **T12**/1e (278); **T17**/3 (171); **U7**/258b (258); **V7**/1 (261); **V8**/1b–c (260); **V12**/1d (288); **V14**/1 (292).

The following fragments, most of which were surface finds, were too small and non-descript to merit measuring but show how grinders were used until they broke; they also illustrate the distribution of the fragments and of the various materials.

a) Sandstone (also described in the data base as granular quartz)
[**2770**] **Excavated**
H20/779 (5333; Level Ve), black, white and grey, with orange, red and purple staining; **J19**/262 (1691; Level IId), rounded edge; **J18**/254 (5813; Level IId/e), grey; **K18**/102 (4350; Level IIe); **H18**/166 (2664; Level IIe/f), grey, pitted with large grits (green, grey) but smoother than conglomerate; **K18**/276 (6138; Level IIe/f?); **J19**/336 (3944; Level II); **I14**/141 (3493; Level 2), grey and black (multicoloured); **I18**/25 (2710; Level I), thick end; **J18**/13 (2303; Level I), light sandstone?; **K18**/41 (4312; Level I); **R18**/229 (2476; Level E5d), dark grey; /81 (2048; Level E5a), cream (red, black); /83 (2048; Level E5a), grey, white and black with red stains; /119 (2407; unstratified), dark grey and white.

[**2771**] **Surface finds**
G13/1a dark grey, 1b grey, 1d grey and white, 1e dark and light grey (304); **H11**/1b grey (308); **H12**/2c grey (pink and white), 2d light grey (307); **H13**/2 red (grey and white) (303); **I8**/1b grey (white), 1c red

and grey (317); **I11**/1b white (309); **I12**/1a, b, c, d grey (306); **I20**/93 (163), black (white, transparent); **J7**/1b grey (white), 1c grey (green and white) (319); **J8**/1a, b grey (white) (316); **K8**/1a red, grey white, 1b dark grey (315); **K9**/3a grey, 3c red and grey (314); **L7**/1a, 1b dark grey (321); **L7**/2 dark grey (321); **L8**/1e grey and white (318); **M12**/1 beige (crystals etc.) (205); **N6**/1b grey (326); **N7**/1 red (orange, some large) (242); **N11**/2 grey, black and white (217); **O6**/2a black and white (327); **O7**/1 (244); **O19**/5 black (white, translucent, some red) (154); **P6**/1 dark grey (white and translucent) (328); **P7**/2 grey (white) (246); **P15**/6 pink and pale grey (101); **Q6**/1 dark grey and red (329); **Q11**/1 dark grey (223); **Q18**/3a black (white), 3c and 3d grey, 3e grey and white (red) (128); **S6**/1 grey (253); **S9**/2b red and brown (bands of white quartz) (266); **S11**/1b mid-grey (276); **S19**/1 dark grey and white (299); **T7**/1 grey (255); **T9**/1 dark grey (265); **T12**/1b reddish, 1c grey, 1d grey (278); **T14**/2a, 2b, 2c grey (284); **T15**/5 mottled grey and black (169); **T15**/8 (169) grey; **T16**/2 black (white) (170); **U6**/1 grey (257); **U7**/1a grey (258); **U11**/1 (274); **U12**/1 grey (279); **U13**/1 (282); **U14**/1 grey (white and transparent) (283); **U15**/1 grey (286); **V11**/2 grey (273); **V12**/1a–1c grey (288); **V13**/2a grey and red, 2b dark grey (290); **V15**/1a, 1b grey (294); **V16**/1b (296); **W11**/1 (272); **W12**/1b grey and white, 1c, 1d (289); **W13**/1b grey (beige) (291); **W14**/2b and 2c grey, 2d white (293); **W17**/1a dark grey and white, 1b light grey and white (298).

b) Conglomerate

[2772] Excavated

I14/174 (3489; Level 2/3), reddish; **I20**/23 (1417; Level IIb), brown (black, brown, some red and white); **J19**/224 (1686; Level IIc); **K19**/325 (4552; Level IIc); **K18**/87 (4338; Level IIe); /88 (4338; Level IIe); /159 (4377; Level IIe); **J18**/101 (2335; Level IIf); **K18**/53 (4315; Level I/II); **R18**/16 (2010; before Level E5b), white, cream, grey, red in grey matrix; /144 (2424; Level E5a/b).

[2773] Surface finds

G13/1 red (305); **H11**/1a red (308); **H12**/2e red (red and orange) (307); **J8**/1c red (red and orange) (316); **J10**/3 white (red and yellow) (311); **J17**/17 beige (145); **K9**/3b red (314); **L15**/6a grey (102); **M8**/2e red (327); **O8**/2 red and orange (red and orange) (243); **R8**/2a (red, orange, green) (249); **R15**/2b red (133); **S10**/2 (267), red (orange) (170); **T15**/1 light brown (red and yellow) (169); **T16**/4 black, white and red (170); **T19**/1 green (green) (299); **V8**/1a grey (red and yellow) (260); **V11**/1 banded red grey and white (red) (273); **W12**/1a red (white and grey), 1f off-white (289); **W13**/1a red (white) (291); **W16**/1 pink and yellow (297).

c) Schist

[2774] Excavated

R18/165 (2434; Level E5a); **J20**/24 (1310; Level I/II).

d) Volcanic (vesicular basalt, black unless otherwise specified)

[2775] Excavated

H20/367a–c, with a–b joining (1817; Level Vf4); /824 (5340; Level Vf4), dark grey; /778 (5333; Level Ve); **K19**/92 (1554; Level IIc); **H18**/170 (1611; Level IIe/f); **K18**/36 (4310; Level I/II); **L19**/6 (5903; Level I); /17 (5907; Level I); **I14**/105 (3465; Level 2k); **J14**/26 (3314; Level 1); /97a–b (3362; Level 1/2); **M14**/10 (3501; Level 1); **J16**/17 (4700; Topsoil), fine, flat slab; **J20**/7 (1301; Topsoil), fine; **R18**/130 (2412; Level E5a); **Q19**/60 (2118; Level E4a); /71 (2122; Level E2b), × 7.

[2776] Surface finds

(square not known), × 2, one fine (99); **H12**/2b fine (307); **I8**/1a (317); **I11**/1a (309); **J7**/1a (319); **J11**/4 (213); **J12**/5 (212); **L8**/1b–c (318); **M8**/2a (322); **M10**/7 (224); **M18**/1 (123); **N14**/2, fine (190); **N16**/5 (109); **O16**/1 (110); **P11**/1a, 1b (219); **Q14**/4 (187); **Q18**/3b (128); **R18**/253 (179); **S11**/1a, fine (276); **T12**/1a (265); **T17**/1 (171); **U11**/2 (274); **W14**/2a (293).

e) Limestone (with shell inclusions)

[2777] Excavated

K18/11 (4302; Level I), without shell; **K19**/9 (1501; Level II); **R18**/169 (2435; Level E5a/b); /82 (2048; Level E5a).

[2778] Surface finds

G13/1c (304); **H15**/2 (159); **I12**/1e, 1g (306); **J9**/1a (313); **J16**/104 (144); **L7**/1d (321); **L8**/1f with black 'crystals' as well as shell (318); **L13**/1 (194); **N6**/1a (326); **N16**/8 (109); **O18**/1 (125); **O19**/1 (154); **P11**/5 (219); **S18**/2 (2500); **U9**/1 (264); **V16**/1a, 1c (296); **W12**/1e (289).

Unclassified (2779–80)

[2779] Excavated

H20/528 (1856; unstratified), grey; /732 (5323; Level Vf), black; **K18**/28 (4309; Level I), grey; **K19**/476 (1501; Level I).

[2780] Surface finds

T15/6 (169); **U10**/1 (269).

Pounders, hammerstones and rubbers

These are stones which were chosen for their shape and suitability for pounding, grinding or polishing. Some, at least, were certainly not local (e.g. the pounders of volcanic stone) and were obviously specially imported. A pounder is taken to be a large, rounded stone that fits well in the hand and can be used for pounding. See also **2636** for a pestle which is, in contrast, a carefully-worked object. When a diameter is given, this implies that the stone is approximately round. Rubbers are oval or elongated stones that have been selected for their flat face and abrasive qualities.

For examples found in Late Bronze Age contexts at Ugarit see Elliott 1991, 17–25 and figs. 4–5, with a discussion of types and distribution, predominantly in Cyprus and the Levant. At Tarsus, pounders and polishers are only listed in Neolithic to Bronze Age levels: Goldman, 1956, 264–5, 270–71, figs. 414–15; for Boğazköy, see most recently Boehmer 1979, 56–8, nos. 3753A–56, 3769, 3771–86.

Pounders and hammerstones (2781–808)

[2781]   H20/715   5403
Level Vi
Cream with pitted surface; flattened sphere.
Di. 10 × H. 6.3

[2782]   H20/498   1851
Level Vh/i
Dark greyish-brown with pink veining; large, smooth, elongated stone, perhaps an anvil fragment, broken diagonally, with one rounded end, a flat surface which could be used as a rubber, and a rounded upper part which could be held; pitting on one surface.
(14) × 7.5 × 5.3

[2783]   H20/460a   1838
Level Vg/h
Greyish-pink fossiliferous stone with the inclusions weathered away to leave it resembling a sponge, particularly on one face, while much of the other surface is smooth.
8.1 × 6.25 × 3.6

[2784] H20/460b 1838
Level Vg/h
Pinky-brown on one face and reddish-brown on the other; hammerstone shaped like a smooth triangle with rounded angles and edges, with areas of polish on surfaces and a large dent in the paler face which shows how it was hafted; the edges were used for hammering or pounding and one 'angle' is chipped.
6.3 × 6.9 × 3

[2785] H20/964 5380
Level Vg
Yellowish-grey soapstone; very smooth, elongated pebble with signs of wear on one side.
6.6 × 2.9

[2786] H20/1040 5393
Level Vg
Beige.
Di. 7 × 6.3

[2787 number not used]

[2788] H20/849 5349
Level Vf3
Grey limestone, traces of burning; rounded fragment with flattish base along line of natural cleavage; pitting over top and at one blunted end indicating use as an anvil and hammer.
(9) × 12.4 × 6.65

[2789] H20/848 5347
Level Vf4
Badly burnt and fractured; three smooth surfaces, one flat and two rounded, surviving.
6.7+ × (5) × 5

[2790 number not used]

[2791] J19/373 3963
Level IIb
Grey with large white inclusions; smooth and spherical.
Di. 7.5

[2792] I19/110 2851
Level IIc
Dark brown, very smooth with battering on one end. Perhaps a hammer.
4.45 × 5.85

2793 J19/319 3927
Level IIc
Large rounded stone, burnt and fractured, with flaked surface burnt to plaster and heavily incrusted.
10.8 × 9.1 × 7.65

[2794] K19/314 4537
Level IIc
Grey, burnt; slightly flattened sphere with pitting on both faces and an indentation on one face probably caused by use as a hammer.
Di. 8 × 5.6–6.3

[2795] K20/195 1989
Level IIc
Flint 'cobble'; smoothed with chipping in one place possibly due to use; flattened sphere.
Di. 6.7–7.4; H. 5.0

[2796] K20/196 1989
Level IIc
Pale grey-brown stone; flattened sphere with periphery battered through use.
Di. 7.7; H. 4.9

[2797] J19/294 3926
Level IId
Dark grey; spherical.
Di. 6.0

[2798] K18/97 4348
Level IIe
Beige with pitted surface.
Di. 6.5–7.2

[2799] K18/104 4346
Level IIe
Grey-brown to pinky-grey; irregular flattened sphere; localized patch of battering indicating use as a hammer/pounder.
Di. 8.6–9.0; H. 7.0

[2800] K19/373 4574
Level IIe
Dark brown volcanic stone with black obsidian inclusions; roughly hemispheroid with pitted domed surface and fractured flat surface.
Di. 6.7–7.1; H. 3.6

[2801] J18/186a 2380
Level IIf
Flint 'cobble'; broken, rounded edge preserved; traces of use on both faces.
(4.6) × (4.2) × 3.9

[2802] J18/186b 2380
Level IIf
Grey sandstone; fragment with part of curved, pitted surface preserved.
(9.8) × (6.65) × (3.6)

[2803] J18/186c 2380
Level IIf
Grey limestone; fragment with part of rounded edge and slightly concave face with traces of use.
(6.3) × (7.5) × (7)

[2804] J18/28 2307
Unstratified
Grey; large, elongated stone hammer, with rounded ends, both slightly battered, a flat surface (now weathered), and a rounded upper part which could be held.
18 × 8.35 max. × 4.7

[2805] J18/45 2310
Level I
Grey; polyhedral hammer/pounder.
Di. 6.7–7.75

[2806] H20/294 1802
Unstratified
Brown volcanic stone with obsidian inclusions; spheroid with two flattened and shiny surfaces.
Di. 5.8–6.4

[2807] J17/7 5000
Topsoil
Pumice?; wedge with two flattish surfaces and end, and rounded

edges.
13.75 × 12 × 7 max.

[2808]   K17/7   9601
Topsoil
Dark grey volcanic stone; flattened sphere.
Di. 7.3; H. 6.0

[2809   number not used]

Rubbers (2810–20)
See also **2782** which has been classified as a pounder but could also have been used as a rubber.

[2810]   H20/179   1253
Level IVa/b
Pinky-grey; roughly rectangular with one flat and one rounded face, and one flat and one rounded end; could have been used as a pounder, hammerstone or rubber and chipping at the ends and along one edge of the flat face could have resulted from use as a hammer.
10.7 × 6.6 × 4.0

[2811   number not used]

[2812]   K20/194   1989
Level IIc
Pale brown; rectangular stone with rounded corners, with the two largest faces flat and the four smaller ones slightly convex; one of the large faces is pitted, with recoil damage on the other side, indicating use as an anvil.
6.9 × 5.3 × 4.45

[2813]   J18/365   5882
Level IId
Pale grey; large, egg-shaped with a rounded back and a slightly concave face and some chipping of the ends; possibly natural but could have been used as a rubber or even pounder, though the user would have had large hands.
15 × 11 × 5

[2814]   K18/161   4379
Level IIe
Creamy-grey limestone with pitted surface; broken, with rounded surviving end and two flat surfaces showing battering through use as a hammer.
(8) × 9.6 × 4.2

[2815]   K18/260   6129
Level IIe
Grey stone; broken with surviving end rounded, and two flat surfaces.
(7) × (4.3) × 2.8

[2816]   K18/246   6121
Level IIf?
Grey stone; broken with one flattened surface which bears traces of work — striations and wear.
(8) × (11) × 4.3

[2817]   J19/29   1751
Level I/IIh
Creamy-grey, pitted; elongated and rounded, with one side thinner than the other.
11.2 × 4.5 × 3

[2818]   K18/239   6107
Level IIf?
Creamy-grey; large natural stone, egg-shaped with rounded back, and fairly flat but very incrusted face, which could have been used as a rubber or grinder, but the stone is probably too large and heavy to have been used as a pounder or hammer; some wear on the back could have been caused by weathering but could indicate use as a whetstone although no striations or cuts are visible.
27 × 13 × 7.5

2819   L19/18   5913
Topsoil
Black volcanic with large and small holes; irregular cone with rounded point at the top and pear-shaped base.
6.7 × 5.8 × 7.3

[2820]
The following fragments of what may have been rubbers have been recorded, unstratified or from the surface: **L17**/12 (119); **M6**/1c (325); **O18**/5 (125); **P15**/7 (101); **R11**/5 (222); **T13**/1 (281); **T16**/9 (170); **U9**/2 (2640).

Doorsockets and related objects (2821–8)

[2821]   K19/109   1565
Level IIc/d
Light-coloured stone, flattened sides with reddish lines along one side which could be natural. Shallow depression (Di. 6.0) on one side.
L. (16.0)

[2822]   K18/261   6123
Level IIf
Cream limestone, flaky; irregularly shaped but with flattish top and base along lines of natural cleavage (Th. 8) and five approximately straight sides (15, 31, 23, 22 cm). Socket off-centre (Di. 10 × 1.3 deep); within it and to one side is a deeper hole (Di. 5 × 0.9 deeper); this may have been the original hole and the pivot may have slipped and worn a larger, shallower hole.

[2823]   K19/20   Etütlük 1996   1518
Level I
Grey limestone; large irregular stone, roughly trapezoidal with one corner missing (sides 39, 29, 20, 22, 47, H. 18–20 cm). Centrally-placed cylindrical depression (Di. 18 × 3.5 deep) with rough sides and bottom.

[2824]   K17/6   9601
Topsoil
Cream limestone; rectangular with one end and part of base broken. Socket centrally placed (Di. 5 × 2 deep).
(17) × 12 × 10

[2825]   J9/1   312
Surface
Grey, incrusted limestone; irregularly shaped but with flattish top and base along lines of natural cleavage and one approximately straight side. Centrally-placed socket (Di. 5 × 1.5 deep); concentric lines indicate use.
20 × 14.5 × 5.5

[2826]   J12/5   306
Surface
Beige limestone; squared end with other end broken or unshaped, upper surface pecked and base formed by line of natural cleavage. A small, funnel-shaped hole is centrally placed (Di. 2.5 at top × 2.3 deep, ending in a point).
(10) × 9.6 × 5.5

[2827]   O13/1   197
Surface
Beige limestone, weathered; roughly triangular (sides 11.3, 11.6, 12.7) with base formed by line of natural cleavage (Th. 5.5). Shallow depression (very weathered) placed centrally (Di. 5.8 × 1.5 deep).

[2828]
Beige limestone; irregularly shaped with flat base along natural line of cleavage, two straight sides at right-angles to each other, separated by a rounded corner (25 × 9) with the other two sides irregularly shaped (29 × 16); top sloping (H. 8.5–13). At the higher squared end is a shallow depression (Di. 6 × 1.5 deep approximately).

Stelae (2829–30)
2829   K19/104   Etütlük 1996   1554
Level IIc; in destruction debris, lying face down in SE corner of Rm 3 of the Stele Building (see Fig. 108).
Single piece of sandstone, perhaps originally reddish but discoloured red and black by the fire which had fragmented it into over 70 pieces, a few of which from the 'reverse' were not recovered. It looks as though this was a natural boulder, with uneven sides and ends. The 'obverse' was almost flat and perhaps deliberately smoothed, and a very faint design, in narrow lines of red paint is discernible: a thicker inverted L-shape runs parallel to the top and left edges at about 3 to 7 cm in from the edge, and is matched by a thinner line another 9.7–11.0 cm further in. There is also a very fine line of paint surviving on the lower right hand part of the obverse. Without any comparable examples, it is impossible to suggest whether this is a purely abstract design, or representational. On the 'reverse', which is less flat and rougher, there are minute traces of red paint, insufficient to be drawn.
H. 77; W. 49; Th. 16–17.5
Fig. 336

Figure 336. *Stele* **2829** *obverse with red-painted design, after cleaning and re-assembling (see Fig. 469).*

[2830]   K18/283   6131
Level IId
Large block of limestone; only a tiny section of the original surface survives at the top of one edge. Flattened base along line of natural cleavage. Smoothed upper surface divided into panels by roughly incised approximately vertical lines (panel width 4.5 (left side missing), 6, 8,5, 9 (tapering to 7 towards the bottom). At the end where the edge is preserved, two roughly parallel slightly diagonal lines close off these panels.
(33) × (34) × 15.5

[2831   number not used]

Chapter 47

Coins

Koray Konuk

Editors' note: Eight coins were recovered by us from Kilise Tepe, all naturally from the surface or Level I. We are very grateful to Koray Konuk for preparing the following catalogue on the basis of casts and/or photographs; and to Adrian Popescu for some additional comments on **2833–5**. One piece of copper (R18/224) was initially identified as a coin but shows no clear details and is probably not one. Weights are not accurate to less than 0.1 g.

Figure 338. *Coin of Arcadius (2nd period — AD 402–408) (2936): a) obverse; b) reverse.*

Figure 337. *Coin of Gordian III, obverse (2832).*

2832 Q10/6 Etütlük 1998 3100
AE 36 mm, Gordian III (AD 238–244), provincial issue from Tarsos. *Obv.* AVT K ANT ΓΟΡΔΙΑΝΟC CEB ΠΠ; radiate bust of Gordian right. *Rev.* ΤΑΡΣΟΥ ΜΗΤΡΟΠΟΛΕΩΣ ΑΜΚ ΓΒ; Tyche Panthea standing left, winged and wearing kalathos, holding rudder and cornucopia. Wt after cleaning not known.
Fig. 337
SNG France 2, 1648; SNG Levante, 1136.

2833 99/25 KLT 56 99
AE, very worn and corroded. Constans? (AD 333–350). *Obv.* Head of the emperor to right. *Rev.* [...]-AVGG; Victory advancing l.; in exergue [S]MALΔ.
Wt 1.7
RIC VIII, 31.

2834 K9/2 Etütlük 1998 314
AE, 16 mm, Valentinian I (AD 364–375) or Valens (AD 364–378), Constantinople AD 367–375, chipped and legend off-flan. *Obv.* DN[...]; diademed bust of emperor right. *Rev.* [...]PVBLICAE; Victory advancing left; in exergue, CONSA or Λ.
Wt 1.9

2835 J18/58 2311
AE, 19 mm, very worn and corroded. Arcadius (AD 383–408) or Honorius (AD 393–423). Eastern mint, AD 395–401. *Obv.* [...] Bust of emperor. *Rev.* [...] Victory to left crowning emperor.
Wt 1.7

2836 I17/12 4900
AE, 14 mm, Arcadius (AD 383–408), Western Empire, Rome (AD 404–408). *Obv.* DNARCAD IVSPFAUG; diademed bust of Arcadius right. *Rev.* VRBS RO-MA FELIX; Roma standing facing, looking right, holding trophy on spear and globe surmounted by Victory; in field, OF and officina letter P.
Wt 1.9
Fig. 338
RIC X, 1271 or 1277.

2837 J19/27 1604
AE, 10 mm, Leo I (AD 457–474), Constantinople. *Obv.* DN L-EO; diademed bust of Leo right. *Rev.* No legend; Leo standing facing, head left, holding long cross and placing left hand on head of kneeling captive.
Wt 1.6
Fig. 339
RIC X, pl. 36, 708.

2838 K19/185 KLT 141 4502
Level I/II
AE, 29 mm, follis, anonymous type, Class A2 (*c.* AD 980–1025), Constantinople. *Obv.* +EMMA NOVHA; bust of bearded Christ facing,

Figure 339. *Coin of Leo I (2837): a) obverse; b) reverse.*

Figure 340. *Anonymous follis, c. AD 980–1025 (2838): a) obverse; b) reverse.*

Figure 341. *Follis of Michael VII Ducas (2839): a) obverse; b) reverse.*

holding book with his left hand and raising his right hand before breast in blessing; in field, IC - XC. *Rev.* Four-line legend: +IhSYS XRISTYS BASILEY' BASILE'.
Wt 12.6.
Fig. 340
DOC A2.47.11.

2839   K19/28   KLT 71   1514
AE, 25 mm, follis, Michael VII Ducas (AD 1071–1078), Constantinople, overstruck, undertype unclear. *Obv.* No legend. Bust of bearded Christ facing (Type Ve), holding book with his left hand and raising his right hand before breast in blessing; in field, IC - XC above lateral arms of cross, six-pointed stars beneath. *Rev.* +MIX AHΛ RACIOΔ. Bust of Michael VII facing.
Wt 3.1
Fig. 341
DOC, p. 818, 14.

Part F

Environmental Studies

Chapter 48	Environmental Studies: Introduction	**581**
Chapter 49	The Archaeobotanical Assemblages	**583**
	Introduction	583
	Aims	583
	Methods	583
	On-site sampling strategy	583
	Processing	583
	Identification and quantification	584
	Analysis of data	584
	The overall composition of samples	585
	Potential crop species	585
	Data preparation for statistical analyses	585
	Wild species and crop processing	586
	On-site patterning: external influences on the composition of samples	587
	Results	587
	Overall composition of samples	587
	Presence of potential crop types by phase	587
	Crop-processing stages	588
	On-site patterning: external influences on the composition of samples	590
	Discussion	590
	Possible sources for the archaeobotanical assemblages	590
	Implications for activities carried out on-site	590
	Internal variation of sub-sampled units	591
	Evidence for the storage of crops	591
	Potential crops recovered from non-storage contexts	593
	Kilise Tepe and its surroundings	594
	Conclusion	594
Chapter 50	Processing, Storing, Eating and Disposing: the Phytolith Evidence from Iron Age Kilise Tepe	**597**
	Phytoliths — the stones from plants	597
	The samples	597
	Phytolith assemblage formation and taphonomy	598
	Methodology	598
	Results	599
	Interpreting the phytolith assemblages	600
	Coprolite	600
	Residues from pots	602
	House floor	602
	Courtyards	602
	Pits	602
	White layer on floor	604
	Agricultural practice in Kilise Tepe	604
	Conclusions	605

Chapter 51 **Fish Remains from Bronze Age to Byzantine Levels**   **607**
    Introduction   607
    Description of the material   607
    Discussion and conclusions   609

Chapter 52 **Human Remains**   **613**
    Introduction   613
    Ageing and sexing   613
    Palaeopathology   613
    Byzantine remains   613
    Bronze Age remains   615
    Catalogue of scattered human bone   616

Chapter 53 **Dating**   **619**
    Dendrochronology   619
    Radiocarbon dating   622
        Excavator's comment   622

Chapter 48

Environmental Studies: Introduction

J.N. Postgate

The majority of the environmental work undertaken at Kilise Tepe fell within the project entitled *Contextual analysis of the use of space at two Near Eastern Bronze Age sites*, which was funded by a Leverhulme Trust research grant and jointly directed by Roger Matthews (for Tell Brak) and Nicholas Postgate (for Kilise Tepe). The results of this project are available electronically on http://ads.ahds.ac.uk/catalogue/projArch/TellBrak/index.cfm. Most of the data there comprise quantitative information about the frequency and distribution of plant and animal remains in the archaeological deposits, together with analysis of micromorphological thin sections by Wendy Matthews.

The recovery programme at both sites was managed by Sue Colledge, who also directed, analysed and wrote up the archaeobotanical evidence. In this she was assisted at Kilise Tepe in particular by Joanna Bending, whose report on the individual finds of botanical material from outside the controlled recovery programme comprises Chapter 49 below.

Decayed plant material frequently formed a white layer at the base of, or within the fill of, pits. Samples were often taken from this, with a view to identifying the phytolith component. A selection of these samples was studied by Marco Madella in Cambridge, and they provide valuable evidence for the usage of these pits (see Chapter 50).

The other major body of evidence in the Leverhulme programme is the animal bones. The full analysis of results from the contexts used in the Leverhulme programme is presented in the electronic archive (see above). However, animal remains were recovered from most excavated contexts, and although these were not usually samples controlled by sieving, the material was mostly examined by Polydora Baker both during and after her work on the comparative project. Her report on this material would be too long for inclusion within the present report, and will appear shortly either in printed or electronic format.

In Chapter 42 we have listed the majority of worked bone items, most of which have also been examined by Baker.

Baker also identified and separated out fish bones from the main body of material. These, with the kind consent of the Turkish authorities, were sent for study to Wim Van Neer, and his report appears here as Chapter 51.

Shells, both fresh water and marine, were frequent in the cultural deposits at the site. The entire collection was examined by Sarah Blakeney in 1999, and a total of 39 types distinguished. It is hoped that a specialist report on this collection by Sofie Debrayne will also be forthcoming shortly.

Human remains at the site were extremely scarce. Intramural burial was certainly not the norm during any period, and at least one pre-Christian burial ground was present to the east of the modern main road (see p. 33). Of the burials identified as such during excavation three belonged to the Early Bronze Age levels, another was behind the apse at the east of the late Byzantine church and a second, probably Byzantine burial was encountered near the surface in K14. These individuals and a variety of scattered human bones from various levels and contexts are described by Jessica Pearson in Chapter 52.

Despite a number of destructions by fire at the site, pieces of carbonized wood large enough for dendrochronological analysis were infrequent. Samples were taken from two contexts — an oven in Level IIId and wall-foundations in Room 7 of the IIc Stele Building — and sent to the Malcolm and Carolyn Wiener laboratory in Cornell for examination by Peter Ian Kuniholm and his team. To them, and to Bernd Kromer at Heidelberg who carried out C14 determinations on some of the same samples, we are very grateful for their results, given below in Chapter 53, and their collaboration.

While the precision afforded by a successful dendrochronological determination cannot be matched by C14 analyses, the chronology of the Anatolian Bronze Age is not yet so precisely fixed that they are without interest, and we selected a sequence of five charcoal samples from Levels III to V in the NW corner. These were submitted to Roy Switsur at Anglia University in Cambridge for analysis. His results in Chapter 53, for which we are very grateful, agree broadly with our expectations but suggest that analyses of more suitable and well-stratified samples would be no bad thing.

Chapter 49

The Archaeobotanical Assemblages

Joanna Bending & Sue Colledge[1]

1.0. Introduction

This chapter concerns the 61 archaeobotanical samples from Kilise Tepe not analysed in the Leverhulme Trust funded project (whose aims and conclusions are outlined in Colledge 2001). The majority of these samples were originally analysed as MSc dissertations at the Department of Archaeology and Prehistory, University of Sheffield, by Dione Miller (1998) and Joanna Bending (1999). All samples remaining after the completion of the above research programmes were analysed by Joanna Bending in Sheffield, in accordance with the methods of the MSc dissertations.

The samples represent all phases of occupation from Late Bronze/Iron Age (IIb) to Byzantine (I), as well as selected samples from the underlying deposits (Late Bronze Age IIIe, and Middle Bronze Age IVa and IVb — these deposits were subject to less extensive excavation as they were only exposed in the deep sounding (trench H20) or on the edges of the mound). Trenches H18, H19, I14, I19, I20, J18, J19, J20, K18, K19 and K20 are all represented by at least one sample. Some trenches and phases are represented more frequently than others. The IIc storage rooms, for example, were excavated in trenches J19 and K19, and were extensively sampled due to the visible concentration of charred botanical remains.[2]

2.0. Aims

The aims of this report are to:
- Investigate the range of plant species recovered from Kilise Tepe: What were they? Which species were economically significant? Was there any change in the suites of plants represented over time? How were they processed and stored?
- Establish how the botanical material recovered from Kilise Tepe may have come to the site: are they likely to be the products/by-products of the processing of crops, or result from other activities e.g. burning of dung cakes as fuel. This will give an indication of some activities relating to plant material carried out on site.
- Discuss in broad terms whether there is any botanical evidence for change in the environment of Kilise Tepe between the time of occupation and the modern day.

3.0. Methods

3.1. On-site sampling strategy

The main sampling strategy for archaeobotanical samples was defined by the research brief of the Leverhulme Trust funded project. The aim of this project was to

> ... recover a statistical characterisation of context type, including household rooms of varying function, streets and open areas, so as to provide a new tool for understanding the anatomy of different settlements (Postgate & Matthews 1995).

This required a rigorous sampling of a specific range of contexts, focusing on those related to the use of space (e.g. occupation deposits, occupation sequences, structural fills, external fills). Samples had to be at least 60 litres in volume.

Samples were also taken at the discretion of the excavators, particularly from visibly rich deposits and potentially interesting features (e.g. the fill of complete pots). The following samples were taken in this fashion: 6–7, 12, 16, 26, 37, 39–41, 43–4, 47, 49–50, 52 and 55. Some units were sub-sampled, particularly when they exhibited a visible degree of variation in the distribution of plant remains. The burnt destruction levels were sampled extensively.

3.2. Processing

The majority of the samples analysed were processed in the field by the authors. To fulfil the remit of the Leverhulme Trust funded project, it was necessary to recover all 'environmental' materials (bone, shell, pottery etc.). The charred plant remains were recovered by the water separation method using a flotation machine. Floating plant remains were collected on a 250 μm mesh. The heavy residue resulting from the first 10 litres of material processed was wet sieved on a 1 mm mesh, the remainder on 3.5 mm.[3] Samples 7,

Table 31. *Context details of archaeobotanical samples analysed in this report.*

Sample no.	Trench	Unit no.	Sample no.	Trench	Unit no.
1	H18/20	2607	32	J19/252	1696
2	H18/98	2629	33	J19/297	3927
3	H18/116	2640	34	J19/308	3927
4	H18/116	2640	35	J19/323	3927
5	H18/117	2636	36	J19/334	3943
6	H18/131	4263	37	J19/341	3927
7	H19/224	4251	38	J19/356	3963
8	I14/101	3459	39	J19/396	6423
9	I14/98	3458	40	J20/147	1388
10	I19/26	1743	41	J20/153	1389
11	I19/44	1781	42	K18/173	4344
12	I19/50	2802	43	K18/256	6125
13	I19/52	2802	44	K18/279	6141
14	I19/70	2818	45	K19/72	1540
15	I19/71	2817	46	K19/96	1560
16	I19/72	2818	47	K19/99	1561
17	I19/80	2823	48	K19/99	1561
18	I19/81	2825	49	K19/99	1561
19	I20/47	4003	50	K19/199	4507
20	J18/265	2370	51	K19/204	4510
21	J18/266	2391	52	K19/206	4510
22	J19/74	1626	53	K19/210	4510
23	J19/74	1626	54	K19/211	4511
24	J19/98	1644	55	K19/287	4822
25	J19/110	1653	56	K19/354	1566
26	J19/129	1653	57	K20/154	1965
27	J19/204	1656	58	K20/166	1971
28	J19/204	1656	59	K20/171	1976
29	J19/222	1686	60	K20/183	1988
30	J19/233	1690	61	K20/204	1994
31	J19/249	1688			

12, 37, 43, 44, 49, 50 and 52 were bucket floated at the Department of Archaeology, University of Sheffield. The same mesh sizes as in the field were used to collect each fraction respectively.

Owing to time constraints, very large or rich flots were split into fractions using a riffle box. At least 50 ml of the coarse flot and 25 ml of the fine flot of each sample was sorted. Ideally, the whole of the heavy residue was processed, but this did not occur for very large or very rich samples due to time limitations. In these cases, flots were fractioned to produce a volume which could be sorted within the time available.

3.3. *Identification and quantification*

All identifications were supervised closely by Mike Charles and Amy Bogaard, following the criteria and methodology used by Glynis Jones (after Hillman unpublished). Extensive use was made of the modern and archaeological reference collections housed in the Bioarchaeology Laboratory, Department of Archaeology, University of Sheffield. All material was identified using a binocular microscope (magnification ×7 to ×45).

A considerable amount of reworking of the data sets produced during the MSc research was carried out to ensure that the identifications were equivalent. It was assumed that the categorization of crop types by each analyst was internally consistent, although much of the material was checked in the course of further analysis. Comparisons of these categories were made, and it was found that few changes were necessary. All fruit, nut, wild and unidentified items were reanalysed and quantified accordingly.

Identifiable plant items were quantified in the following ways:
- Cereal grain, legumes and grasses: whole items and embryo end fragments counted as 1.
- Cereal chaff: glume bases were considered the basic unit, spikelet forks counted as 2.
- Grape: each fossette counted as half. Other fragments not quantified.
- Olive: weight of fragments measured.
- Wood charcoal and dung fragments: volume of fragments >1 mm.
- Non-quantifiable items (legume pods etc.): presence or absence.

These results are presented as Appendix 1.7 (pp. 633–9).

4.0. Analysis of data

By far the majority of the archaeobotanical material recovered from Kilise Tepe, and all the material recovered during the analysis of the 61 samples discussed in this report, was preserved due to charring. Human behaviour will have affected the composition of the plant material brought to Kilise Tepe — consciously (choice of building materials, animal fodder, crops and their stage of processing etc.) as well as unconsciously (weeds brought in with crops or attached to clothing, plants allowed to grow wild in the settlement). Activities would also have affected the plant material likely to come into contact with fire, and thus be preserved — differential food processing and cooking techniques would make some crop species far more likely to be burned accidentally than others, and refuse would have a greater chance of being purposefully burned than foodstuffs. The conditions during burning (temperature, proximity to flames etc.) would have meant that some items of the plant assemblage would be more likely to burn to ash than char. The most fragile elements would also be less likely to endure post-depositional attrition. Human behaviour and taphonomic processes, as well as mixing of material from various sources at the time of deposition or afterwards, result in assemblages that may bear little relation to the original, thus making interpretation of past human behaviour difficult to untangle. This should be borne in mind when considering the techniques of analysis appropriate to the Kilise Tepe archaeobotanical assemblages.

4.1. The overall composition of samples

In order to assess variations in composition between samples the relative proportions of taxa, rather than absolute numbers, were compared. Differences in the morphology of the cereal plants represented in the samples meant that an estimation of the overall content of each sample could not simply be calculated as percentages based on the original counts. The spikelets of einkorn, emmer and spelt, free-threshing wheats and barley tend to have different ratios of grain: quantifiable chaff elements, and this must be allowed for in any comparison of counts for each species.[4] It should also be noted that glume wheats (einkorn, emmer and spelt) tend to be processed rather differently to free-threshing wheats and barley, again due to their morphological characteristics (see Hillman 1984 and Jones 1990). In an attempt to establish the broad composition of the 61 samples, four sets of summary data were produced:

- the percentages of cereal grain, legumes and wild seeds;
- the overall percentages of glume wheat grain (einkorn+emmer+spelt), free-threshing grain (free-threshing wheats + barley) and wild seeds;[5]
- the percentage of grain of each cereal species and wild seeds;
- the percentage of grain to chaff, taking into account the ratios expected for each species.

These figures enabled an assessment of the major crop component(s), and the proportion of wild seeds and chaff, in a manner that is not misleading for the species present in each sample. This summary data will simplify interpretation of each assemblage, providing a broad picture of the relative proportion of the major components.

The summary percentages are presented as Appendix 1.1.

4.2. Potential crop species

The preservation of archaeobotanical material by charring means that readily interpretable assemblages, such as the Late Bronze/Iron Age storerooms from phase IIc at Kilise Tepe, are rare. Not only does an unusual event need to take place (i.e. the catastrophic burning of stored goods), but the conditions of burning need to be right for the material to become charred (rather than, say, burning to ash). In most situations, prior assumptions must be made about the economic significance of certain species. Most of the archaeobotanical material from Kilise Tepe is likely to represent material charred incidentally during every-day activities, for example in ovens and hearths, and is therefore more ambiguous. The distinction between 'wild' and 'domesticated' species in the past might not have been as it is outlined in modern botany. Many of the 'wild' types identified from Kilise Tepe could have been useful, collected in the wild or managed in semi-wild conditions – the seeds from various types of *Crucifer* can be processed into oil, and *Malva sylvestris* is often used as a fodder crop. The intention here is to discuss the taxa perceived as the major domesticated/managed/regularly collected types.

The presence and absence of potential crop species for each phase was noted in the hope that, at a very general level, this material may be used to say something about the plant species present at Kilise Tepe, and assess temporal change in the crop-related activities. The results are presented in section 5.2 below.

4.3. Data preparation for statistical analyses

Various forms of statistical analysis can be applied to archaeobotanical data. These tools enable more elaborate interpretation of the assemblages than the production of a straightforward species list and general observations based on context. Two widely used techniques in archaeobotany are discriminant analysis (to assess the degree of similarity between groups of modern samples of known provenance and archaeobotanical assemblages) and multivariant correspondence analysis (a useful 'pattern searching' tool, which allows categorization of samples by external factors such as phase).

In order to prepare the data for these statistical analyses, it was necessary to amalgamate some of the identification categories, and give each amalgamation a code (summarized in Table 32). This allows the overall composition of samples to be considered, dissociating it to some extent from other aspects of the material which may have an effect on a more detailed level of categorization e.g. the effects of preservation on the ability to identify items. Identifications to the species and genus level, and probable identifications to the genus level, were amalgamated. This was not done on occasions when types tended to occur independently

Table 32. *Summary of codes used in statistical analyses and the identification categories they represent.*

Code	Amalgamated identification category	Code	Amalgamated identification category	Code	Amalgamated identification category
EINEMGR[6]	*T. monococcum* and *T. dicoccum* grain	OLIVE	*Olea* (Olive)	GRAM<	Graminae <2 mm
EINEMGL	*T. monococcum* and *T. dicoccum* glume	VITIS	*Vitis* (Grape)	HRDWILD	Wild *Hordeum*
SPGR	*T. spelta* grain	FICUS	*Ficus* (Fig)	LEGUM	Leguminosae
GLWHGR	Glume wheat indet. grains	POME	*Punica* (Pomegranate)	LOL	*Lolium*
FTWGR	*T. aestivum/durum*	STONE	Fruit stone/nut shell	MALV	Malvaceae
FTWRAC	Free-threshing wheat rachis	ADON	*Adonis*	MEDI	*Medicago*
WHGR	Wheat grains identified to general level	ASTTRIG	*Astragalus/Trigonella*	NESLIA	*Neslia*
BARGR[7]	*Hordeum distichum/vulgare* grain	AVEN	*Avena*	PAPAV	*Papaver*
BARRAC	*Hordeum* rachis	BRO	*Bromus*	PHAL	*Phalaris*
CERGR	*Triticum/Hordeum* and Cereal indet.	BUPL	*Bupleurum*	PIMP	*Pimpinella*
CULM	Culm nodes and bases	CHENO	*Chenopodium*	RUBI	Rubiaceae
VIER	*Vicia ervilia* (Bitter vetch)	COMP	Compositae	RUME	*Rumex*
LASA	*Lathyrus sativus* (Grass pea)	CORO	*Coronilla*	SCIR	*Scirpus*
PISUM	*Pisum* (Common pea)	CRUC	Cruciferae	SMGRA	Small Graminae (<0.5 mm)
LENS	*Lens* (Lentil)	CRUCSQ	Square Cruciferae type	TRIMEL	*Trifolium/Melilotis*
LAAST	Large *Astragalus* type	CYPER	Cyperaceae	UMBEL	Umbelliferae
LALEG	Large legumes	GALI	*Galium*	VACC	*Vaccaria*
MILL	*Panicum* (Millet)	GRAM>	Graminae >2 mm	WILD	Wild species indet.

of each other. When types could not be assigned to an amalgamated category, or occurred in less than 10 per cent of the samples, they were amalgamated at the broadest level. (N.B. Amalgamated categories occurring in less than 6 of the samples (10 per cent of the total number) and identification categories not easily converted into M.N.I. equivalents (e.g. pomegranate flesh) were eliminated at this stage.)

4.4. Wild species and crop processing
The processing of seed crops for consumption generally comprises various stages. These selectively remove impurities such as chaff and the seeds of wild (weed) species which have been harvested with the crop. Some of these techniques can be identified in archaeobotanical samples as they systematically affect the content of the assemblage by the removal of items with certain physical features. For example, winnowing will remove the lighter chaff and seeds, coarse sieving the large-headed weeds and fine sieving the small seeds. Seeds which bear morphological similarity to the crop will remain with it, and will often be removed by hand picking directly before use. If wild seeds from archaeological samples can be categorized in terms of the physical features that will determine their behaviour during these stages of crop processing (i.e. size, headedness and aerodynamic features), it may be possible to interpret assemblages in terms of their stage of crop processing (after Jones 1984). This information can then be used to further our understanding of the plant-related activities taking place at Kilise Tepe, as well as the taphonomic processes affecting the composition of samples (e.g. mixing of waste by-products).

In order to investigate the possibility of the contents of the Kilise Tepe samples originating from crop processing, discriminant analysis was used to see if the composition of wild plant seeds was similar to an existing ethnographic data from Kolofana, on the Greek island of Amorgos.[8] These data represent the physical features of the wild species found in various products and by-products of crop processing, providing control groups with which to compare the archaeological data from Kilise Tepe. The stages represented by the ethnographic data are those which result in a significant change in the composition of the assemblage, and which were considered by Hillman (1984) to be the most likely to come into contact with fire, and thus be preserved archaeologically. It should be noted that the ethnographic data is based on free-threshing cereals only, and that its comparability to glume wheats should be considered in a broad sense (see Hillman (1984) for comparison of generalized processing stages for free-threshing and glume wheats). The ethnographic comparison does however appear to be applicable to pulses (Jones 1984).

Classifications for the Kilise Tepe wild types were taken, where possible, from previously determined categories resulting from research at the Department of Archaeology, University of Sheffield. If a category had not been previously decided, material from the reference collection was used to develop one in consultation with Dr Charles (* in Table 33). The characteristics of the weeds present in the Kilise Tepe assemblages were borne in mind whilst carrying out this task — for example, the Bupleurum present in the Kilise Tepe samples were all of a similar size (c. 1 mm in length) and the predicted behaviour of the extremely small-seeded species known to occur in modern times did not need to be taken into consideration.

Wild seeds were categorized as:
- Small or Big: greater or less than 2 mm;
- Free or Headed: dispersed at threshing, or still contained in 'heads', spikes or clusters, or with appendages;
- Light or Heavy: aerodynamic features, or lack of.

They were then coded by all three features to take account of the behaviour of particular combinations during crop processing (Table 33).

Only the 35 samples containing more than 10 wild seeds which could be categorized were analysed to ensure the results were based on a valid data set. Samples containing high proportions of species which would not be associated with the processing of cereal or legume crops (fruit seeds and olive pips, for example) were included in the analysis, as it was considered that the wild species present in the sample may have originated from crop processing and become associated with other categories of charred material at a later date.

The analysis was run twice:
- Kilise Tepe samples as ungrouped data — each sample having to group with one of the four ethnographic categories;
- Kilise Tepe samples as grouped data — samples can group with ethnographically known categories, or other Kilise Tepe samples (i.e. derived from a recognizable crop-processing stage or more similar to other archaeological samples).

The diagrams are discussed in section 5.3, and the sample-by-sample classifications presented in Appendix 1.5.

Table 33. *Categorization of wild seed characteristics expected to influence behaviour in crop processing.* * *indicates category developed especially for the assemblages at Kilise Tepe.*

Genus	Category	Genus	Category	Genus	Category
Adonis	BFH	Galium	BFH	Neslia	BFH
Astragalus/Trigonella	SFH	Gramineae >2 mm	BFH	Papaver	SHL
Avena	BFH	Hordeum	BFH	Phalaris	SFH
Bromus	SFL	Lolium	BFH	Scirpus	SFH
Bupleurum*	BFH	Malvaceae	SHH	Trifolium/Melilotis	SFH
Chenopodiaceae	SFH	Medicago	BHH	Vaccaria	SFH
Coronilla	SHH				

4.5. On-site patterning: external influences on the composition of samples

In order to establish whether the composition of samples appears to relate to external factors, the data was explored using multivariant correspondence analysis. This displays samples without external reference i.e. located on axes in terms of their degree of similarity to other samples entered into the program. As a consideration of the results produced in sections 4.2 and 4.4 above would be expected to result in the categorization of many of the samples, multivariant correspondence analysis was used as a tool to investigate patterning at a broader level, helping to distinguish categories of sample. Samples were coded by phase, context type and unit number in order to establish whether potentially meaningful patterning relating to time or functional location became apparent, as well as to assess the internal consistency of sub-sampled units. Amalgamated categories (see Table 32) present in less than 10 per cent of the total number of samples (i.e. 6) were ignored to prevent skewing of data by background 'noise' (Jones 1984). The results are presented in section 5.4.

5.0. Results

5.1. Overall composition of samples

From the summary percentages, the following aspects of each sample were established:
- whether the sample is dominated by wild seeds, legumes (Appendix 1.1), or a category of cereal grain that is likely to have been processed together (Appendix 1.2);
- where dominated by a cereal-processing category, whether this consists largely of one particular species (Appendix 1.3);
- the percentage of grain and rachis occurring for each species present (Appendix 1.4).

5.2. Presence of potential crop types by phase

From Table 34 it can be seen that einkorn and emmer, free-threshing wheats, barley and lentil, were recovered consistently from all phases sampled. Spelt, bitter

Table 34. *Presence of potential crop types by phase. Presence is indicated by the percentage of the samples from each phase containing the crop type. One sample was taken from phase IVa, but contained no recognizable crop species. 8 samples were left out due to uncertain phasing.*

	Byzantine	Iron Age			Late Bronze/Iron Age				Late Bronze Age	Middle Bronze Age
	I	IIg	IIf	IIe	IId/e	IId	IIc	IIb	IIIe	IVb
Einkorn + Emmer	38	100	86	100	40	50	72	50		
Spelt	50				40	50	17	33		
Free-threshing wheat	63	100	29		40	50	6			
Barley	100	100	100	100	80	100	72	83		100
Common vetch					20					
Bitter vetch	13		29		60		6			
Grass pea	13				40	50	11			
Common pea	38		14			75	17	33		
Lentil	50	100	14	100	60	75	28	33		
Millet	50	100	71		40	50				
Flax	25	100			25					
Olive	50		57	100	60	50	44	83		
Grape	38		86	100	80	75	50	100		
Fig	13	100	57		40	75	17		100	
Pomegranate	25		57							100
Tuber	13				25					
No. of samples	8	1	7	1	5	4	18	6	2	1

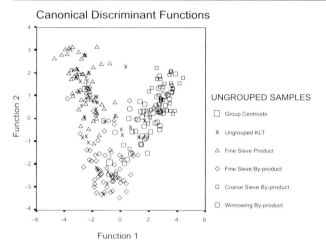

Figure 342. *Results of discriminant analysis comparing ungrouped Kilise Tepe wild type assemblages to ethnographic data.*

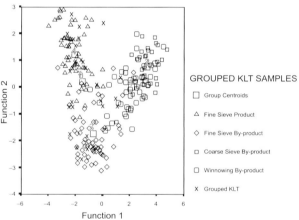

Figure 343. *Results of discriminant analysis comparing grouped Kilise Tepe wild type assemblages to ethnographic data.*

vetch, grass pea, common pea, olive, grape and fig were present in the majority of phases. Millet and flax occur from phase IId (twelfth century BC) onwards. Pomegranate and tuber occur intermittently throughout.

Under-representation of phases due to the number of samples available/nature of the archaeology may be responsible for a lot of the variation — many taxa are absent from Level IIb (a sequence of floors with generally low concentrations of charred plant material) and IIg (one sample). It should be noted that the single samples from phases IIe and IVb contained low item counts, and that both samples from IIIe were grab samples of whole figs.

5.3. Crop-processing stages

The patterning produced by the discriminant analysis of ungrouped weed assemblages in terms of their predicted behaviour during crop processing (Fig. 342) indicated that all the Kilise Tepe weed assemblages fell within the general scatter of ethnographic samples. Of the four possible categories, the majority of samples were most similar to fine sieve by-products (29 per cent) or fine sieve products (63 per cent).

When the Kilise Tepe samples were entered as a separate group (Fig. 343) 63 per cent of the samples analysed grouped independently of the ethnographic samples. It should be noted that the centroid of the

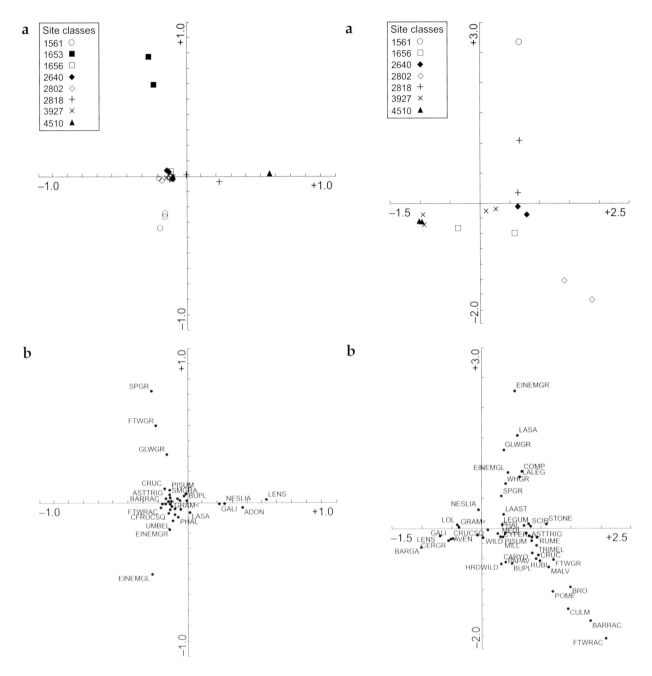

Figure 344. *Results of multivariant correspondence analysis showing: a) grouping of all samples taken from sub-sampled units, b) equivalent plot of amalgamated identification categories. See Table 32 for explanation of codes. N.B. BARGR lies on x-axis at –0.9.*

Figure 345. *The seven outlying samples in Figure 344 have been excluded from multivariant correspondence analysis to focus on the cluster present around the origin. Results showing: a) grouping of samples taken from sub-sampled units; b) equivalent plot of amalgamated identification categories. See Table 32 for explanation of codes.*

Kilise Tepe group lies between the scatters representing fine sieve by-products and clean products, indicating that these samples exhibit characteristics intermediate between the two groups i.e. they are likely to be a mixture of material from recognizable crop-processing stages, rather than from another source.

These categorizations are presented in Appendix 1.5.

Table 35. *Categorization of samples based on their overall composition and the results of crop-processing analysis. The full list of categories is presented in Appendix 1.6.*

Category	No. of samples
Cleaned product grain/legumes (<5% wild seeds)	7
Figs (whole)	2
Fine sieve products (cereal)	4
Fine sieve products (legume)	1
Coarse sieve products (cereal)	9
Coarse sieve products (legume)	1
Fine sieve by-products (cereal)	4
Late crop-processing stage(s) by-product	8
Mixed crop and late crop-processing stage(s) by-product	10
Wild seed dominated (>75% wild seeds)	4
Mixed crop and wild	2
Low counts (<25 items)	11

5.4. On-site patterning: external influences on the composition of samples

Of the plots produced, only the categorization by unit number (Figs. 344 & 345) showed any significant patterning. It indicates that, although sub-samples taken from the same unit do tend to group together, there is still a notable amount of variation in archaeobotanical remains within the excavated units. From Figure 344 it can be seen that samples taken from units 1653 (lying near SPGR), 1561 (between EINEMGR and EINEMGL) and 2818 (LASA) show a good degree of consistency. The content of samples from 2640 and 2802 lie within the cluster of taxa located between the origin and –0.20 on the x-axis, implying their contents may be more mixed. Two of the four samples from 3927 lie near BARGR, whilst the others locate near the origin. The samples from unit 4510 appear to show a degree of consistency, but this is related to the fact that LENS and BARGR are located close to each other in the third quadrant of Figure 345.

Little distinction between the samples of different phases or context types on the basis of overall composition of assemblages was apparent. The patterning which did occur was largely explicable by reference to Figures 344–5, i.e. sub-samples from the same unit tended to group together, and were taken from the same phase and context type. These plots are, therefore, not presented here.

6.0. Discussion

The most abundant cereal species from the Kilise Tepe assemblages were hulled barley (*Hordeum distichum/vulgare*) and glume wheats (einkorn and emmer — *Triticum monococcum* and *T. dicoccum*). Cereal grain was generally more abundant than chaff. The most widespread legumes were lentil (*Lens culinaris*) and grass pea (*Lathyrus sativus*). Spelt (*Triticum spelta*), free-threshing wheats and millet (*Panicum/Setaria* spp.) were also present, as were olive (*Olea* sp.), fig (*Ficus* sp.) and grape (*Vitis* sp.).

6.1. Possible sources for the archaeobotanical assemblages

As the analysis of the samples in terms of crop processing is only based on the physical characteristics of wild seed types that can be categorized (sections 4.4 & 5.3), the overall composition of each sample (sections 4.1 & 5.1, and Appendix 1.7) must also be considered if a meaningful interpretation is to be attempted. A level of <5 per cent contamination by species processed in a different way (and therefore not expected to come from the same source) was deemed acceptable due to the presence of background levels of material and mixing between archaeological contexts. Wild-seed dominated samples were considered to contain over 75 per cent wild seeds. Less than 25 quantifiable items was too low for any comment on the source of the material to be valid. A consideration of these aspects of the samples, as well as the counts for culm nodes, allowed samples to be categorized into broad groups (see Table 35).

6.2. Implications for activities carried out on-site

The Kilise Tepe assemblages analysed predominantly contain material appearing to represent the products and by-products of the later stages of crop processing. It would appear that the earlier stages of processing were carried out off-site, or in an area not excavated or represented in these samples. The evidence would suggest that crops were brought on to site as coarse-sieved products, fine sieved and stored. Any remaining wild seeds would probably be removed by hand picking before use.

The presence of culm nodes in at least 17 per cent of samples at low levels indicates that straw was being used on site but probably not becoming charred very often. Culm seems to occur at a general level, similar to fruit pips and olives, possibly representative of the background rubbish present across the site.

The exceptions to this are the samples taken from unit 1653, the contents of a Byzantine clay-lined pit, and sample 13 (unit 2802), from a Late Iron Age kiln. The basal few centimetres of the pit fill contained a concentration of semi-clean spelt (samples 25 and 26) associated with a high concentration of culm nodes (1881:1677 grain:culm for context overall). It could be tentatively suggested that straw was being used as tinder to clean the pit by burning its contents, the light straw burning to ash whilst the culm, grain and

Table 36. *Summary of content of sub-samples taken from the same archaeological units.*

Unit no.	Sample nos.	Category	Degree of consistency
1561	47 48 49	Clean and semi-clean einkorn	High
1653	25 26	Semi-clean spelt	High
2640	3 4	Fine sieve by-products	High
2802	12 13	Mixed wild species	High
2818	14 16	Clean and semi-clean grass pea	High
3927	33 34	Semi-clean barley	See discussion in 6.3
	37	Low counts	
	35	Late crop-processing stage by-product	
4510	51	Clean lentil	See discussion in 6.3
	52 53	Clean and coarse sieve product barley	

wild seeds were subject to charring. Sample 13 was predominantly made up of the chaff of free-threshing crops — rachis internodes of barley and free-threshing wheats — 78 grain: 648 chaff: 159 wild seeds. If the deposit was *in situ*, this may represent the burning of chaff as fuel in the kiln. The majority of evidence for fuels at Kilise Tepe comes from wood charcoal. The results of discriminant analysis presented in Figure 343 indicate that there is little reason to believe that external sources — such as dung fuel — contributed a large amount of material to the assemblages, and fragments of charred dung were recovered from only one sample. It is, however, likely that chaff would have been used as a fuel source on particular occasions — perhaps as tinder, or for particular heating regimes.

6.3. Internal variation of sub-sampled units
The data presented in Table 36 indicates that most sub-sampled units show a good degree of internal consistency. This can be related to the categories produced in section 6.1 to explain the variations that are apparent.

The variation within unit 3927, the IIc destruction of Room 8, may represent samples taken from the *in situ* burning of crop in the lower fill (33 and 34) or collapse of rubble into a jar (37) and forming an upper layer of the fill. The contents of the jar may have had different heating conditions and not charred (e.g. burned to ash) or may have been a product unlikely to char (e.g. oil or another liquid).

The two sub-samples taken from unit 4510, IIc destruction in Room 5, were purposefully selected by the excavator to represent visible differences in the type of charred botanical remains within the same archaeological unit.

6.4. Evidence for the storage of crops
Of the samples containing clean and semi-clean crops listed in Table 35 the majority were taken from the IIc destruction of the Stele Building (13 of 22 samples). The IIb sample may also be associated with this, although it may be intrusive. Three samples were taken from phase I, two from phases IId/e and two from IIIe.

6.4.1. Level I: Byzantine storage pits
Two of the Byzantine contexts sampled were the burned clean/semi-clean crops recovered from the basal fill of large clay-lined storage pits (barley from 1656, spelt from 1653). It was stated above (section 6.2) that this may represent the cleaning of the inside of the pits by burning, although it is just as likely that it represents the contents of the pit — either as packing, or a product in its own right. It is also possible that it represents burned debris deposited once the pits had gone out of use. Although no culm was recovered from 1656, concentrations of charred plant remains were so low that the burning conditions may have not been right to result in charring, or the pit may have been 'clean' of plant material in the first place.

6.4.2. Level IIc: Late Bronze/Iron Age storerooms
The rooms mentioned in Table 37 are part of the complex known as the Stele Building, which focuses on Room 3 where a fragmented sandstone slab with fine red-painted lines was uncovered in the destruction debris of a severe conflagration. Other rooms appear to have been used for storage. The destruction probably took place not much later than 1100 BC. The samples taken from this level are generally focused on concentrations of charred crops within larger units of destruction debris. All deposits were associated with sherds of, or emplacements for, storage jars.

From Table 37 it is apparent that cleaned or semi-clean products were being stored in this complex of rooms. Legumes appear to be stored as clean products, whilst the glume wheat and barley were stored awaiting the later stages of processing. Glume wheats do not appear to have been stored as spikelets. Einkorn spikelets (the dominant glume wheat in the storerooms) usually comprise one grain enclosed by two glume bases. A higher percentage of glumes would be expected in the figures presented in Appendix 1.4 if storage as spikelets were to be suggested.

The variety of crops recovered from the IIc destruction level represents some of the most commonly occurring taxa at Kilise Tepe, and could be considered the dietary staples of the period (cereals, legumes etc.). Their storage as cleaned or semi-clean products, as well as the general absence of early-stage crop process-

Table 37. *Summary of samples from Level IIc. A concentration of olive stones was also recovered during excavation in Room 8, near east wall.*

Room	Unit	Sample no.(s)	Category	Description	Trench	Charred plant density cm³/l
3 'stele room'	1560	46	Barley - coarse-sieve product	Destruction debris - southeast corner of room, near stele	K19a	4.5
	1686	29	Grass pea - clean	Destruction debris	J19b	8.6
	1690	30	Mixed crop and late crop-processing stage by2-product	Pit P96/102	J19b/d	6.1
4 'storeroom'	1561	47	Einkorn - coarse-sieve product	Small area of floor cut by pits	K19b	N/A
		48	Einkorn - coarse-sieve product	Small area of floor cut by pits	K19b	N/A
	1566	56	Low counts of charred plant material	Destruction fill containing complete jar	K19a/b	N/A
5 'storeroom'	4510	51	Lentil - clean	Concentration within destruction debris	K19c	27.13
		52	Barley - coarse-sieve product	Concentration within destruction debris	K19c	285.0
		53	Barley - fine-sieve product	Concentration within destruction debris	K19c	17.4
6 'open space'	4511	54	Einkorn - semi-clean	Other side of plastered wall from 4510	K19c	3.5
7 and 8 'storeroom'	3927	33	Barley - fine-sieve product	Main level destruction debris directly on floor of plastered room	J19c	2.94
		34	Barley - fine-sieve product	Main level destruction debris directly on floor of plastered room	J19c	6.94
		35	Late crop-processing stage by-product	Main level destruction debris directly on floor of plastered room	J19c	1.2
		37	Low counts	Fill of whole pot in debris	J19c	0.83

ing products and by-products at Kilise Tepe, indicates that tasks associated with the bulk separation of grain from chaff, such as threshing, winnowing and coarse sieving, were probably carried out away from the area of habitation. These tasks tend to be more efficiently carried out when crops are processed in large quantities, and create a lot of waste material (although this is a desirable product in its own right — as animal fodder, construction material etc.). Once the bulk of chaff has been removed, the crop can be further processed, or stored in a semi-clean state — fine sieving and hand picking being performed as the final stages in preparation for consumption.

As not all the samples taken from the Stele Building were analysed as part of this report, any attempt to look at the spatial patterning of the material must be kept to a basic level. The presence of both lentil and barley in Room 5 indicates that each room was probably not reserved for a particular crop. The location of clean products with those not fully cleaned in Rooms 3 and 5 indicates that their level of processing was not an important criterion either. The storage of cleaned grass pea (often considered a fodder crop) with food crops may indicate its status as a human food during the period, although ethnographic work by Jones (1998) indicates that it may not be possible to distinguish food from fodder by storage facility. The categorization of samples analysed as part of the Leverhulme-funded project by crop-processing stage would obviously shed more light on this.

6.4.3. Level IId/e: Late Bronze/Iron Age destruction debris

The samples containing semi-clean grass pea were taken from a layer of destruction debris cut by two pits, and little can be said about their conditions of storage.

6.4.4. Level IIIe: preparation of fruit for drying in the Late Bronze Age

The most remarkable archaeobotanical find from Kilise Tepe was recovered during the 1997 digging season — a concentration of figs from a burnt occupation layer (sample 40, 1388) and the packing below (sample 41, 1389) in the Eastern Courtyard (trench J20). The majority of the figs were flattened and had holes through their centres, much like the fresh figs strung up to dry in the open air in modern times (see Fig. 95, p. 118). Figs which had not been prepared in this way were also present in the same contexts, and could be interpreted in a number of ways. Perhaps these fruit were selected for a different method of preparation, or for discard if they were of an unsatisfactory quality for drying. It is also possible 'work in progress' was interrupted by the fire, and they represent fruit yet to be prepared for drying.[9]

6.5. Potential crops recovered from non-storage contexts

Crops recovered from contexts where they appear to have been stored are only part of the story of the plant economy at Kilise Tepe. The presence of potential crops at low concentrations may give a broader view of the species used in every-day life on the site, taking into account material recovered from contexts other than storage.

Glume wheats are present in all phases from IIb onwards (Late Bronze/Early Iron Age), although their cultivation becomes more limited in the Anatolian archaeobotanical record during the Early Bronze Age (Nesbitt 1995). They are present until much later at Kilise Tepe, and appear as clean and semi-clean crops in the Late Bronze/Early Iron Age (einkorn, phase IIc) and the Byzantine period (spelt, phase I). The almost consistent presence of emmer at low levels does not indicate whether the material is rubbish from its processing/storage/consumption on site, or implies its presence at low levels as a weed of other crops. Free-threshing wheats are present from phase IId onwards, indicating their possible use alongside glume wheats. Hulled barley, the most common cereal in archaeobotanical deposits (Nesbitt 1995), is also consistently present. There were not enough samples analysed from the Early and Middle Bronze Age (phase IV) to fully compare the material analysed here with the general trend in crop species change noted in the report for the Leverhulme-funded project. It was noted that

> The earlier periods (Bronze Age, with the exception of one of the phases) comprise samples in which there are greater proportions of barley grains than wheat grains, in the later periods the proportions are reversed. Free threshing wheat grains increase in abundance in the samples from the latest periods at the site (Colledge 2001).

Figure 346 presents a very rough summary of the cereal grain content of samples with definite phase associations and containing more than 50 cereal grains. Free threshing wheats are present from phase IId (Late Bronze/Early Iron Age) onwards, and wheat occurs in greater frequency than barley, fitting with these trends. It should be noted that 12 of the 18 samples are from phase IIc storerooms, and may not be representative of the range of crop species in use across the site during this phase.

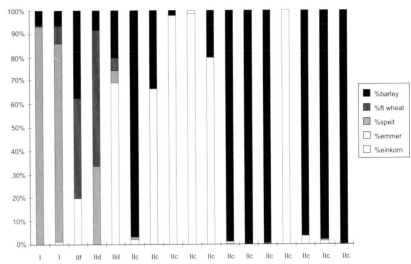

Figure 346. *Percentage bars showing cereal grain composition for samples containing 50 grains or more and from definite phases (18 samples). Bars presented in order of phase. 'Ft wheat' refers to free-threshing wheat.*

Lentil is the most consistently present legume from phase IIc onwards. Bitter vetch, grass pea and common pea are also present in the majority of phases represented by more than one sample. These are all commonly found in archaeobotanical assemblages from other sites in Anatolia (Nesbitt 1995). Chickpeas are also generally common, although absent from Kilise Tepe. Common vetch is not documented from other sites until the early modern period. It could easily have been present at Kilise Tepe as a weed due to its infrequent appearance.

The presence of flax, albeit at low levels, from phase IId (twelfth century BC) onwards is very important. It is a widespread crop used for oil and fibre, and is commonly present in Anatolian archaeobotanical assemblages from the Bronze Age onwards (Zohary & Hopf 2000). The high oil content (over 40 per cent) means that it is likely to combust, rather than become charred. Its presence at low levels is likely to under-represent its importance in the economy of Kilise Tepe.

The occurrence of low numbers of millet grain from phase IId (twelfth century BC) onwards, roughly fits with the general pattern of uptake as a crop. It is not until the Early Bronze Age that millets appear in the archaeobotanical record of the Near East, and only then in small quantities, probably as a minor weed. Its establishment as a crop is not apparent until the first half of the second millennium in northwest Iran, and only in the seventh and sixth centuries BC does it become widely established (Nesbitt & Summers 1988). The evidence from Kilise Tepe is too scant to suggest much more than the presence of this crop at the site — its role as a weed or crop is unclear.

The relatively consistent presence of olive, grape and fig fits well with their increasing importance in the archaeobotanical record from the Early Bronze Age. They may well be local produce, as the geography and climate in the region around Kilise Tepe was probably more in keeping with the Mediterranean zone than the mountainous regions or central plains. Pomegranate has been recovered from Bronze Age sites outside Anatolia. These occur outside the geographical distribution of wild *Punica* types, and strongly suggest well-established cultivation in the Early Bronze Age (Zohary & Hopf 2000).

The infrequent presence of tubers may be related to the techniques often employed in their preparation (they may be less likely to become charred if boiled and/or pulverized), or problems with identification (fragments of tuber are often very similar in appearance to charcoal, and may be overlooked during sorting. Analysis of the charcoal from Kilise Tepe may provide more evidence of the use of tubers at the site). Unidentifiable types of fruit, including skin and flesh, and fragments of fruit stone or nutshell were also recovered from Kilise Tepe. They were present in a low number of samples (13 per cent or less), so their economic status is open to question.

The taxa identified at Kilise Tepe show a considerable diversity in the species of crop potentially exploited. There is a notable temporal consistency from the Hittite Late Bronze Age through to the Byzantine period, especially considering the hiatus between Level IIg and the Byzantine occupation. The main trends, suggested by the analysis of a greater number of samples for the Leverhulme-funded project, are supported by the samples analysed here — the increasing importance of free-threshing wheats and decreasing importance of barley in the later phases of occupation. Considerable comparability with the pattern of crops known from archaeobotanical assemblages in Anatolia and the wider region was exhibited.

6.6. Kilise Tepe and its surroundings

No systematic survey of the flora or conditions in the area surrounding Kilise Tepe has been carried out, and the identification of the wild seeds recovered from Kilise Tepe was somewhat limited. Even though preservation was on the whole good, modern Turkey has perhaps the richest flora known. This made it extremely difficult to narrow down the list of possible species for each wild type, as a species could not be discounted unless seeds from the reference collection had been compared to the archaeological material. The identifications cannot, therefore, be reliably related to modern growing conditions. This means that any discussion of past environmental conditions must be kept to a very general level.

6.6.1. The area in modern times

The climate of the area is hot and dry during the summer, with temperatures over 40°C not unusual in July and August. The annual precipitation is low, less than 500 mm, and less than 5 mm of rain per month is typical for July, August and September (Baker *et al.* 1995). Small springs scattered across the landscape (including one at the foot of Kilise Tepe, with now unused steps cut into the rock to assure access from the mound itself) provide water, but main supplies are taken from the Kurtsuyu and the large spring at Pinarbasi. Both unirrigated and irrigated crops (olives and cereals; vegetables, tree fruit, vines, poplar etc.) are grown successfully. Away from areas of cultivation the landscape is sparsely vegetated, and prone to erosion, with steep scarps. Livestock in the area is predominantly goat, with some sheep and dairy cows. (Postgate 1998).[10]

6.6.2. Conditions at the time of occupation

A brief summary of the modern habitats of the wild types recovered from the archaeobotanical samples, based on Davis (1965–88), suggests that environmental niches existing in the area surrounding Kilise Tepe at the time of occupation were similar to those that can be observed today. The majority of the types for which a habitat was indicated tended to be found in crop or fallow fields, open areas and hillsides, all of which are visible in the immediate environs of the mound. Irrigation may well have been essential to encourage yields in general, especially for fruit crops.

7.0. Conclusion

The 61 archaeobotanical assemblages analysed from Kilise Tepe are of major importance to our understanding of the plant economy of the site. The assemblages suggest that, throughout its occupation, the range of crops being exploited was relatively consistent, focusing on cereals (einkorn and hulled barley), pulses (lentils and grass pea), and fruits/tree products (olive, grape and fig). The main changes in the suite of crops exploited are the more frequent presence of free threshing wheats and the decrease in the importance of barley in the later phases of occupation (phase IId onwards), and the appearance of millet and flax at very low levels from the twelfth century onwards. Spelt, common and bitter vetches, common pea and pomegranate were also recovered, as were low numbers of unidentifiable fruit and nut items. This indicates that the inhabitants of the site participated in a stable, broad-based plant economy.

Although the archaeobotanical assemblages may not in themselves indicate the sites participation in wider relations (in terms of large-scale storage for trade or evidence of traded crops), the apparently local nature of production and consumption of plant foodstuffs (in contrast to its interaction in other spheres) is just as important. The material present in the samples appears to be most likely to have arrived on the site in association with semi-clean (coarse-sieved) cereal or legume products, or as crop in its own right (e.g. fruit). The later stages of crop processing (sieving) appear to have been carried out on-site, and products stored in their cleaned or semi-clean form. The Late Bronze/Iron Age burnt storerooms, with settings for jars and scatters of charred clean and semi-clean einkorn, hulled barley and lentil, provide a spectacular insight into how this was done — and a more clear indication of a selection of crops which were economically important at the time. The preparation of figs for drying, evident from Late Bronze Age levels, provides a unique link between past and present crop preparation techniques. Thus, the archaeobotanical assemblages appear to owe more to the various stages of crop processing (products, by-products and mixed by-products) than variations over time or space, or between context types. There is little reason to believe that external sources, such as dung fuel, contributed a large amount of material to the assemblages.

The importance of Kilise Tepe in terms of the scarcity of excavated sites, both for the region and the periods, is clear. The quality of preservation and variety of material recovered (in terms of associated environmental materials, as well as archaeobotanical remains), plus the systematic sampling of a range of contexts, makes them potentially important for understanding agricultural economies in the area.

Notes

1. The text is essentially the work of Joanna Bending, while Sue Colledge directed the archaeobotanical work on site and provided expertise and encouragement at all stages. This paper benefited greatly throughout from the help and advice given by Dr Mike Charles and Dr Amy Bogaard. Many thanks to Dr Anaya Sarpaki for her invaluable comments on the final draft.

2. Samples were taken from various context types. The majority came from pit fills (23% of samples analysed), destruction debris (23%) or construction materials (20%). Occupation sequences (13%), occupation surfaces (8%), fire installations (3%), a kiln (2%), an occupation deposit (2%), packing fill (2%), an in situ ash patch (2%), a burnt surface (2%) and the sounding below a floor (2%) were also sampled.

3. The mesh sizes and volumes for heavy residues were suggested by the archaeozoologist in order to provide maximum recovery of faunal remains.

4. Einkorn tends to have 1 grain per 2 glume bases, emmer and spelt 1 grain per 1 glume base and free-threshing wheat c. 3 grains per 1 rachis internode. 2-row barley has one grain per internode, and 6-row 3 per internode (obviously there are exceptions to this — these figures are intended to aid in establishing general patterns only). Due to the frequency of barley grains distorted by lateral splitting, it was impossible to reliably establish the number of asymmetric grains present in the samples, an indicator of 6-row barley. The ratios for 2-row were, therefore, utilized in the calculations, and it should be noted that the percentage of rachis would be lower if the barley is indeed 6-row.

5. The sub-division of wheat means that items identified to an intermediate category (i.e. *Triticum aestivum/durum/spelta*) could not be counted. Wheat will, therefore, be underrepresented in these calculations compared to barley, which did not need to be sub-divided.

6. Einkorn (*Triticum monococcum*) appears to be the major crop, with emmer (*T. dicoccum*) occurring less frequently, perhaps growing as a 'weed' in the same field. This mixture of edible grains may have been tolerated, or seen as undesirable.

7. Almost all barley grains appear to be hulled — there were no definite identifications of naked types.

8. Available from the Department of Archaeology, University of Sheffield.

9. Inspection of the material under low magnification indicated that these samples did not contain hazel nuts or any other type of soft fruit, as was originally thought and stated in publication.

10. A survey of the agricultural regions of Turkey (Erinç & Tunçdilek 1952) was carried out during the period when major public works (such as irrigation systems) were beginning to have an effect on the Turkish agricultural system (agriculture had been bypassed by the reforms implemented by the Atatürk regime of the 1930s — it was not until later that 'modernization' of the system took place). The survey placed Kilise Tepe in the Mediterranean region, and its location in a valley bottom in the foothills of the Taurus Mountains seems to imply a similar range of crops as seen today.

Chapter 50

Processing, Storing, Eating and Disposing: the Phytolith Evidence from Iron Age Kilise Tepe

Marco Madella

Phytoliths — the stones from plants

Phytoliths — literally stones from plants — are microscopic bodies of opal silica (the same substance that makes up glass) that are formed within and between the cells of plants. The production of phytoliths encompasses the entire Plant Kingdom but certain families of plants accumulate opal silica more than others. The plants of the grass family (Gramineae or Poaceae) have one of the highest silica deposition rates and opal silica can account for up to 6 per cent of their dry weight (Carnelli *et al.* 2001). However, other Monocotyledons, like the palms, or woody plants, such as the Gymnosperms or the fig-tree family (Moraceae), also produce an abundance of phytoliths (Albert & Weiner 2001; Carnelli *et al.* 2001; Piperno 1988).

Vegetal cells can be almost completely filled during the life of the plant by the opal silica deposit and phytoliths are almost perfect casts of the original cell. This is probably their most important attribute, as they maintain the anatomical — and therefore often taxonomical — characteristics of the original cells, allowing for the identification of the tissue and plant where they have formed (Piperno 1988; Madella 2003). A further important characteristic of phytoliths is their durability in the sediments. Once the phytoliths have been deposited by decay or burning of the organic matter, they tend to be preserved in most depositional environments. Opal silica does admittedly become unstable and is likely to go into solution at high temperatures in moist environments. However, as the preservation of phytoliths also seems to be influenced by the presence of organic matter, humic acid and other soil variables, they have in fact been recovered from disparate deposits and climatic conditions (e.g. Blinnikov *et al.* 2001; Bowdery 2001; Runge 2001).

When the silicification of the plant epidermis (the outermost layer of cells covering the plant) is particularly severe owing to high evapo-transpiration, most of the epidermal cells are filled with opal silica and the epidermal sheets that result can remain in articulation, keeping the tissue's anatomical characteristics. In such cases, the preserved taxonomical information is very detailed, further helping the identification of the original taxon. These silicified epidermal sheets are called silica skeletons and have been recovered from many geological and archaeological sites (e.g. Rosen 1992; Madella 2003).

The samples

Several bulk samples for phytolith analysis were collected during the excavations at Kilise Tepe (Table 38). Some of the samples are from general architectural fill contexts while others were identified in the field as 'white ashy layers' and therefore sampled, having been recognized as rich in phytoliths. Further samples are from very specific contexts that were considered important for gathering detailed information on diet, such as a coprolite or the residue in a pot.

A particular set of samples was collected as being part of the contents of some of the many Iron Age pits excavated at the site. Indeed, one substantial interpretative problem at Kilise Tepe, which was left unanswered by the archaeological evidence, was understanding the original structure and function of the numerous pits scattered all over the settlement. It was difficult to interpret the original purpose of these pits because of their partial preservation and their apparently random distribution across the site. Bones, pottery and botanical charred remains were commonly found in the pits, with charcoal showing the highest density in these contexts (Colledge 2001). However, the charred remains from pits normally pertain to a secondary use of the feature, as rubbish bins, after their primary use had ceased. Nonetheless, in many of the pits, a 'white ashy layer' was found at the bottom, sometimes partially rising up the sides. These layers were interpreted, during the excavation, as concentrated deposits of phytoliths and were carefully sampled.

Table 38. *List of contexts sampled for the analysis of phytoliths with level and unit of provenance and the field description.*

Sample no.	Level	Unit no.	Unit location	Description
L19/75	IIc	5981	Rm 22	floor
K19/99	IIc	1561	Rm 4	residue from pot
I19/142	IIe/f	2859	P97/12	thick phytolith layer at base
J19/166	IId	1318	W121	coprolite
J20/173	IIId	5705	FI97/10	ashy courtyard deposit by oven FI97/10
J20/181	IIId	5705	FI97/10	ashy courtyard deposit by oven FI97/10
I19/184	II/III	5526	West Courtyard	pinky-white occupation deposit in courtyard
K19/480	IIc/d	1551	Rm 4	residue from pot 918 K19/100
H20/635	5e	1288	P97/7	phytoliths from pit fill
R18/146	E5a	2426	P95/46 upper	white layer of phytoliths(?)
R18/154	E5a	2430	P95/46 base	white layer of phytoliths(?)
R18/167	E5a	2434	P95/53	white layer of phytoliths(?)
R18/193	E5b	2451	P95/60	white layer of phytoliths(?)
I14/41	1	3414	P95/27	compact, silty-loam soil
I14/138	2	3478	P96/29	white layer of phytoliths(?)
I19/236	IIf	2819	P96/93	white layer of phytoliths(?)
I19/98	IIe/f	2804	P96/70	white layer of phytoliths(?)
I14/145	2	3493	P96/59	compact, silty-loam soil
I14/102a	2	3459	Rm 97 burnt occ. deposit	white thin layer of phytoliths(?) on floor
I14/102b	2	3459	Rm 97 burnt occ. deposit	white thin layer of phytoliths(?) on floor

Phytolith assemblage formation and taphonomy

It is important to note here that, unlike other plant remains that have been preserved in Kilise Tepe (basically charred seeds and wood), phytoliths recovered from the site had survived because of their mineral composition — the plant material did not need to have come into contact with fire to enhance preservation. This is an important difference from the macro-remains that has to be taken into consideration when interpreting the phytolith assemblages. The overall composition of an archaeological phytolith assemblage is related to four major processes of accumulation:
1. the plant assemblages of anthropic origin, deliberately brought into the site (e.g. plants for food, building material, fodder, fuel, etc.);
2. the plants coming into the site accidentally (e.g. crop weeds);
3. the phytoliths already present in the sediments;
4. the taphonomic processes.

While the anthropic and accidental inputs can be incredibly varied, the phytoliths already present in the sediments can be considered as background noise and constant in the site, and therefore ignored. Taphonomic processes can be important in affecting the preservation of the phytoliths but heavy dissolution and/or breakage can easily be detected and accounted for. The overall composition of an archaeological phytolith assemblage should therefore be considered as related to source formation and to identifiable secondary formation processes (taphonomy).

Another important point needs to be stressed. Not all plants produce phytoliths (the deposition of opal silica in plants is both environmentally and genetically controlled). Therefore, some plants are not recorded in the phytolith evidence, and sometimes phytolith typologies can be redundant, as they are produced in different taxa. Grasses are one of the major producers of phytoliths in the Plant Kingdom but many of the plants of economic interest, in both the Old and New Worlds, have characteristic typologies that can be positively used to identify ancient crops, crop processing and the ancient use of vegetal material (Piperno 1998). Also, one of the major points of phytolith analysis, vital for the understanding of ancient agricultural economies, is the possibility to identify the non-dietary use of plants — what part of a plant was exploited in a particular context and in which proportions.

Methodology

Five grams of sediment were sub-sampled from the 20 samples collected for phytolith analysis at Kilise Tepe (Table 38). They were processed according to the extraction method of Madella *et al.* (1998). A phytolith count in three slide fields (a field is a passage from side to side of the cover slip) and for at least 200 phytoliths, both single-celled and articulated, was carried out for each sample (Table 39). Exceptions were samples L19/75 and J19/166, where the full count of the slide's fields yielded only 20 and 121 phytoliths respectively.

The processing of the data from the phytolith assemblages was performed at two different mo-

Phytolith Evidence

ments in time and correspondence analysis was only carried out on the pit samples, with the addition of samples I14/102a and I14/102b (both from unit 3459) as controls (Tables 38 & 39; Madella 2001). Statistical analysis was carried out on the pit samples to highlight possible relationships between these features.

Results

The results of the breakdown of the data set from Kilise Tepe into individual morphologies and silica skeletons, given as absolute numbers and proportional frequencies (%), are shown in Table 39. The composition of silica skeletons expressed as proportional frequencies is also shown in Figures 347–9.

The phytolith assemblages from Kilise Tepe are characterized by fresh-looking phytoliths. However, some silica bodies show a low degree of chemical dissolution with rugose or pitted surfaces. Ornamentation (e.g. spines) and weak morphologies (e.g. dumbbells), on the other hand, are always well preserved underlining the fact that physical weathering can be considered absent. Besides this, some of the samples were constituted of almost pure phytoliths, in the form of characteristic white layers where the soil fraction is almost non-existent. These white layers should represent the primary deposition of phytoliths owing to *in situ* decay of the plant organic matter.

Despite the varied nature of the assemblages, grass phytoliths are always dominant. In most of the samples, long cell phytoliths from grasses — both as single cells and silica skeletons — show a predominance of spiny and dendritic forms from the inflorescence parts (glumes, paleas and lemmas: Table 39, Figs. 347–9 & 576). However, the input of silica bodies from the culm[1] and the leaves, represented by long smooth cells (Fig. 577) and bulliform cells (Fig. 578), is also important. Articulated phytoliths from the pits attest to the presence of not insignificant amounts of the culm/leaves (Figs. 349 & 577), with the characteristic epidermis made by long smooth cells.

The correspondence analysis of the pit samples (Table 40 & Fig. 350) displays a total inertia of almost 50 per cent, pointing to a good significance expressed on the first two axes of the correspondence analysis graph. The graph shows that there is some variability in the phytolith suites' composition. It is notable, however, that the samples from the control contexts (the white layer on a floor — samples I14/102a and I14/102b) lay clearly separate in the graph on the basis of their different phytolith composition.

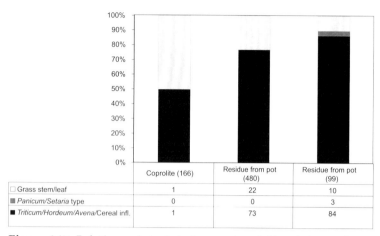

Figure 347. *Relative and absolute frequencies of silica skeletons from the coprolite and the residues from pots.*

Interpreting the phytolith assemblages

Phytolith samples from Kilise Tepe represent several different depositional contexts — a coprolite, house floors, courtyards and pits. Each of these categories will be discussed separately below.

Coprolite

The ingestion of phytoliths in humans should be considered as accidental with phytoliths entering with the vegetable food or during some stages of crop processing (e.g. winnowing) and wild plant processing (e.g. chewing grass stems to soften them). Phytoliths from glumes, lemmas and paleas (husks) are commonly found even in the most clean grains and there is an intake of phytoliths when food produced from cereals and/or other grasses is eaten. Grains may also form silica bodies in their epidermal tissues (Kaplan *et al.* 1992). Variability in the frequency of phytolith typologies from coprolites should therefore be dependent on:

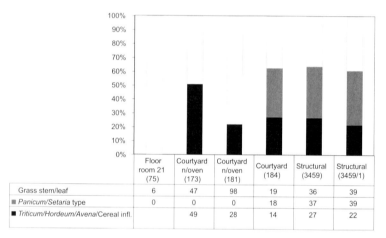

Figure 348. *Relative and absolute frequencies of silica skeletons from the floor, the courtyards and the structural fill samples.*

Ingestion with food:
- phytoliths produced in the grass grain epidermis;
- phytoliths produced in the tissues of leafy vegetables;
- phytoliths from impurities related to inaccurate cleaning of the grains.

Ingestion during plant processing:
- cereals crop processing;
- processing of plant parts using teeth.

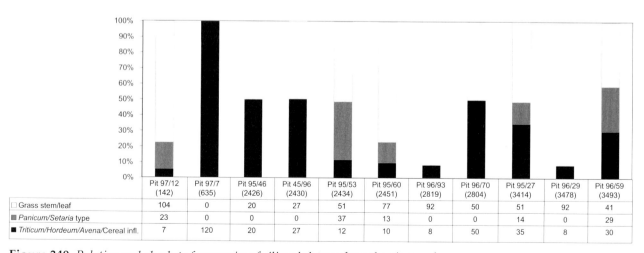

Figure 349. *Relative and absolute frequencies of silica skeletons from the pit samples.*

It is interesting to note that about half of the grass phytoliths in sample J19/166 originated from inflorescence (spiny and dendritic long cells) and intake was probably mainly related to impurities in the food.

The coprolite assemblage also presents a particular and rare type of phytolith — perforated blocks. This particular phytolith was also observed in the pot-residue sample K19/480 (Table 39, Fig. 579) and it does not appear in any other sample from Kilise Tepe. The presence of the perforated blocks only in contexts directly related to food seems to suggest that this phytolith type is produced in a dietary plant. The characteristics of the phytolith rule out the possibility of it coming from grasses (e.g. cereals), and show that the plant was a Dicotyledon and that it might have been used for its leaves. It is not possible to exclude *a priori* that a fruit might have been the source of this phytolith type. If the phytolith came from a dicot plant or fruit, this might also explain the scarceness of the type in Kilise Tepe samples, as dicots have a much lower level of silicification than grasses (Albert & Weiner 2001; Carnelli *et al.* 2001). The presence and noticeable quantity of these phytoliths in the coprolite and pot residue might indicate that the plant/fruit had undergone some kind of preparation and/or cooking that was responsible for the phytoliths' concentration. As an example of this process of 'concentration', think of the loss of volume of spinach leaves that occurs during cooking and the consequential concentration of the calcium oxalate crystals normally present in the leaves of this plant. As for which plant it was, it is currently not possible to identify the taxon.

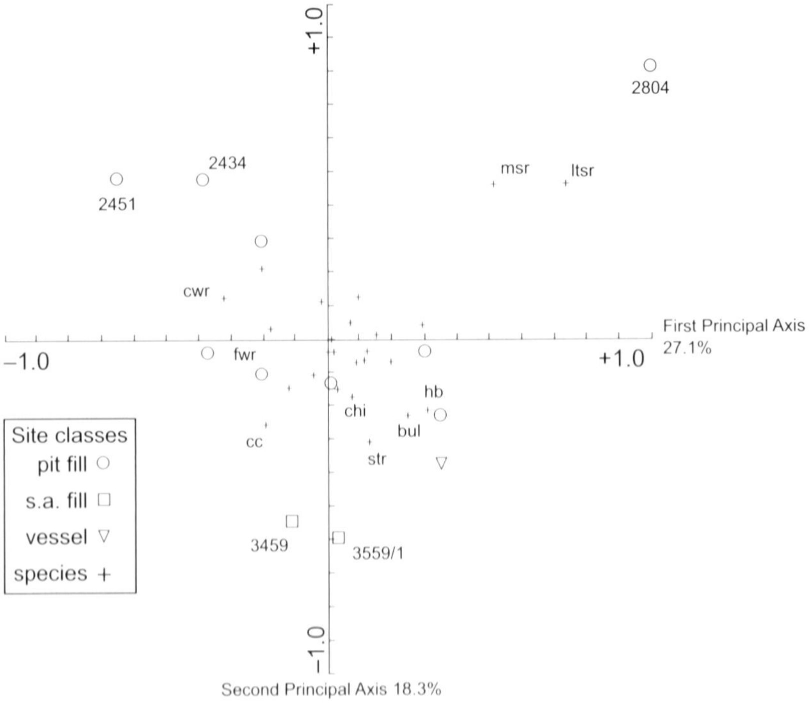

Figure 350. *Correspondence analysis plot of the pit samples and two controls (3459 = 114/102a and 3459/1 = 114/102b). Almost 50 per cent of the inertia represented on the two principal axes.*

Table 40. *Results of the correspondence analysis of Kilise Tepe samples with the identified clusters and the characterizing phytolith types. (Abbreviations = ltsr: long cells, smooth or wavy; chi: short cells; den: long cells, dendritic; tri: trichomes; cc: cork cells; fsr: long cells, spiny; irr-s: irregular spiny)*

	sub-clusters	samples	morphotypes
cluster A		2804	ltsr
cluster B		the average composition of the samples is similar but they can be divided into two sub-clusters:	
	B1	3493 2819	chi
	B2	3478 1561	den
cluster C		3459 3459/1	tri
cluster D		2430 3414	cc
cluster E		2451 2434	fsr
outlier		2426	fsr & irr-s

Residues from pots
Two samples of residues associated with pots were analysed. The phytolith composition of the residue from sample K19/99 (Table 39) indicates that the food cooked in the pot was from cereal grains. At least some of this grain was wheat, and the grains were not particularly clean (see Bending, p. 589 Samples 47–8). The phytoliths recovered are typical of the floral structures surrounding the cereal grain (glumes, paleas and lemmas, collectively referred to as husks) that are normally removed during winnowing and sieving (Hillman 1981). However, if no great care is taken during cleaning, some of these parts are stored with the grains and eventually end up in the food when the grains are processed and cooked. Phytoliths from the stems and leaves of grasses (probably cereals) were also found in the residue, which once more underlines the fact that the grains were not particularly clean.

The same seems to be true for sample K19/480, from pot **918** (Table 39). It is difficult to offer generalizations on how carefully the grains were cleaned before cooking and to what extent impurities entered the food chain on the basis of only two pots from a settlement the size of Kilise Tepe. The results from the coprolite sample, however, seem to support further the impression that grains were not cleaned thoroughly before cooking. Nevertheless, more samples — both coprolites and residues from pots — need to be investigated before such a hypothesis can be confirmed.

The residue from sample K19/480 contains the same perforated blocks observed in the coprolite sample (J19/166). The phytoliths have a high frequency (about 8 per cent of the total assemblage: Table 39), which, as already discussed, indicates that some sort of concentration of the phytoliths happened due to processing and/or cooking.

House floor
The sample from the floor of Rm 22 (sample L19/75) is very poor in phytoliths, with a total count of only 20 (Table 39). Rm 22 seems to lack completely the characteristics of a domestic floor where activities related to food storage, food preparation and cooking were regularly carried on. The paucity of phytoliths and the types recovered (from stem/leaf as might be expected when the input is related to bedding or grass scattering) may point to the use of this structure for purposes other than merely domestic. The low quantities of phytoliths also suggest that the floor was kept rather clean during its lifespan (ethnoarchaeological studies note the regular sweeping of domestic spaces and periodic sweeping of animal pens, to gather dung and straw as fuel: e.g. Kramer 1982, 106, 109) and/or that vegetal material was not greatly used in this particular structure. There is no reason to think of less good preservation of the phytoliths in this context, as those recovered have a fresh look and are well preserved.

Courtyards
The samples from the courtyards (J20/173, J20/181, I19/184: Table 39) have a good frequency of phytoliths, which seems to represent the input from several activities that were carried out in the courtyards. These activities seem to have been crop processing (phytoliths from the inflorescence), hay storage (phytoliths from stem and leaves) and probably animal penning. In this respect, the presence of scalloped spherical and plates phytoliths (Fig. 580) indicate input from the leaves of dicot plants that could have been used as fodder. Ethnoarchaeology in the Indus valley has shown that animals are often kept in the courtyard of compound houses and hay and fodder are stored alongside (Madella, unpublished data). Ethnoarchaeological studies in Turkey record that part of the ground floor of houses is often used for stabling animals, and for the storage of fuel, while the rear is used to store fodder (Yakar 2000, 153). Similarly, a 'wrecked building' on a threshing floor near a village in Iran was used to pen animals and piled with harvested fodder prior to threshing (Kramer 1982, 86). Thus, in both the courtyards sampled at Kilise Tepe, it is possible to hypothesize the storage of hay (samples J20/173 and J20/181 from the Eastern Courtyard: Fig. 491; and I19/184 from the Western Courtyard: Fig. 495) and fodder (samples J20/181 and I19/184).

Pits
The correspondence analysis of the pits and the control samples shows that there are differences within contexts (the pits) and between contexts (the pits versus the floor sediments: Table 40, Fig. 350). One might expect pit sediments to exhibit some variation in the frequency of the typologies or in assemblage composition due to variation in pre- and post-depositional taphonomic processes. However, phytoliths are well preserved and post-depositional taphonomic processes seem to have played a negligible role in all the samples. Samples R18/146 (2426), R18/154 (2430), R18/167 (2434), and I14/41 (3414) (Table 39) have high frequencies of spiny long cells that suggest an important input of plant material from inflorescence, while samples I19/98 (2804) and I14/145 (3493) have substantial frequencies of smooth long cells from culm epidermal tissues. Sample I14/138 (3478) (Table 39) has a not insignificant presence of bulliforms and stomata, which suggests an input from leaves. This variability is also represented in the silica skeletons (Fig. 349)

and it indicates input of different classes of vegetal material, possibly related to both the pit structure and the stored goods.

According to the archaeological record, the sampled pits can be divided into two main groups, on the basis of the presence or absence of a white, ashy layer at the interface between the fill and the bottom of the pit. However, for both the suites and correspondence analyses of the data set, there is no evidence of dissimilarities in the phytolith assemblages depending on whether the original sediment was from the 'white layers' or the compact silty loam (see Table 39, Fig. 349). This homogeneity of the assemblages may suggest that the plant material signal is more related to the original function of the features than to the secondary deposit (the filling of the pits after the end of their use as storage installations) and that both the phytoliths from the white layer and those from the silty loam deposit originate from a similar source. Further evidence supporting this hypothesis comes from the fact that there is no sign of burning on the walls of the pits, suggesting that the phytoliths from the white lined pits, and probably the ones incorporated in the wall sediments, are the result of *in situ* decay of the plant material pertaining to the original structure of the pits and not the residues from rubbish burning at the end of their use life. The different proportions of inflorescence and culm/leaves material may be due to a variable presence of husk in the stored grains or to a differential incorporation of this part in the sediments.

Straw lining of storage pits was a common storage practice in prehistoric and historic times (Panagiotakopulu *et al.* 1995). It improved the preservation of the grains by preventing germination and the development of food pests, by reducing the oxygen content of the pit. Several Classical sources provide evidence of this practice and advice in the preparation of the feature. Storage pits with the base and/or sides covered by straw were described by Varro (RRI, Cvii2) and Pliny (NH XVIII, 306) in Cappadocia and Thrace. The exclusion of air from the pits is claimed by Pliny to achieve successful preservation of wheat (for up to 50 years) and millet (for up to a century: Pliny, NH XVIII). The results of phytolith analysis in association with the archaeological evidence from the white lined pits seem to corroborate the hypothesis of this storage practice in Kilise Tepe. A possible reconstruction of the storage pits in Kilise Tepe is given in Figure 581. The fact that there is no great variation of phytolith suites between the two types of pits (with and without the white layer) may suggest that the pits were constructed similarly but they might have had a slightly different fate at the end of their life. For the pits lacking an apparent white layer of concentrated phytoliths, the original structure may have altered quite substantially after abandonment. However, the phytolith signature related to the original structure seems to persist in the phytolith assemblages.

A further important question that can be asked about the pits at Kilise Tepe is what sort of cereal grains were kept in these features. Charred remains present in the pit fills cannot lead to a secure interpretation of what grains were stored in these structures because of the secondary provenance of this material. The pattern that arises from the analysis of the charred material, bones and pottery in the pits seems to indicate clearance from 'living spaces' (Bending & Colledge this volume). An answer, however, may come from the analysis of the articulated phytoliths (silica skeletons). The silica bodies deposited along the walls of the pits should primarily be the result of the straw lining but they may also carry some information about the stored goods. Spiny and dendritic long cells identified during the scanning of the microscopy slides have already underlined the substantial contribution from inflorescence anatomical parts to the constitution of the assemblages. Furthermore, silica skeletons identified as originating from inflorescence have been examined for their anatomical characteristics: pattern of the joints (Rosen 1992), and size and number of pits in the papillae (Hodson & Sangster 1988; Sangster & Hodson 1997; Ball *et al.* 2001). The preliminary results from the silica skeleton seem to point to the presence of three different crops: wheat, barley and *Panicum/Setaria* type (millets: Table 40). Wheat and barley articulated phytoliths have the typical spiny/dendritic long cells (Fig. 582). Fragments are of variable dimension, formed by from 2 to several tens of long cells (ranging from about 30 μm to 3000 μm of maximum dimension). Silica skeletons with long cells showing coarse wavy and somewhat erratic sides were also identified (Fig. 583). These silica skeletons have smaller dimensions (between about 40–165 μm of maximum dimension) in respect to the wheat and barley silica skeletons. After comparison of the silica skeletons with material from reference collections, it was possible to highlight anatomical similarities with inflorescence epidermis from *Setaria* sp. and *Panicum* sp. (millets). The presence of these cereals in the settlement is supported by the results of the charred seed analysis that reveal the presence of grains, glumes and forks from *Hordeum sativum*, *Triticum monococcum* and *T. dicoccum*, *Avena* sp. and *Panicum/Setaria* spp. (Bending & Colledge Chapter 49).

In some pits the presence of both cereal and millet inflorescence phytoliths might suggest that the features were used for different types of crops during their lifetime.

White layer on floor
Finally, the two samples (I14/102a–b — 3459, 3459/1), used as a control, need to be mentioned (Table 39). The deposit was described during excavation as 'a thin layer (between 5–7 cm) of white phytoliths(?) lying upon a floor'. No pottery or bones were associated with this deposit but animal dung was observed and einkorn grains were recovered by wet sieving. The phytolith composition of this context is quite different from the pit samples, confirming the sensitivity of phytoliths in differentiating distinct vegetal inputs. The two samples have similar average composition and they have, in respect to the pits, a higher presence of short cells. In the light of the phytolith assemblages composition, context of deposition and the observation made during excavation, these two samples may be interpreted as the remains of straw scatter upon a floor in an animal shed. The thin white layer may represent the *in situ* decay of the plant material originating from the accumulation of organic matter from dung and from several episodes of straw scattering, probably compacted by the action of animal trampling.

Agricultural practice in Kilise Tepe

Some of the silica skeletons recovered from Kilise Tepe show smooth, straight or stepped cuts, perpendicular to the cell length (Figs. 584–5). These do not follow the natural lines of weakness between phytoliths (the joins); instead, they break the long cell in the middle like a breakage made by the action of a blade. Ethnoarchaeological experiments have shown that these cuts are produced when a threshing sledge (*tribulum*) is used (Anderson-Gerfaud 1992). The *tribulum* was an implement made of wooden planks or straight, robust branches securely tied together with leather strings. A series of flint blades were inserted in slots in the lower part of the sledge and fixed with bitumen; sometimes the entire lower surface was covered in bitumen. The *tribulum* was pulled, using a traction animal, over the cereal crop scattered on an earth or stone threshing floor and a person would have normally stood or sat on it to add weight. In this way, the grains were separated from the husk as well as the straw chopped (Young 1956; Gjerstad 1980). The threshing sledge is probably one of the most efficient traditional methods of threshing, others being lashing, the flail, the feet of animals or metal rollers (Cheetham 1982). Threshing is an important part of the crop processing as it separates the grain from the chaff. For certain cereals, such as hulled barley, the *tribulum* separates the spikelets of the spike and eliminates the long awns. This is an indispensable step for both human and animal use of the grains. Threshing with the sledge also produces finely chopped straw, a raw material with multiple uses in the prehistoric economy, important in the production of earthen floors and mud bricks, for plastering, animal feed and, mixed with dung, as fuel.

The threshing sledge must have been a common implement throughout the Mediterranean and Black Sea basins and survived till recently (Anderson & Inizan 1994; Garstang 1953, pl. XIII; Kardulias & Yerkes 1996; Yakar 2000, 170–72). However, the presence and use of the threshing sledge has not always been clearly identified in the archaeological record, as the sledge flints can be mistaken for sickle blades, bifaces or other chipped stone tools. The earliest written references to the threshing sledge are to be found in the 'Farmer's Almanac', a Sumerian text that possibly dates to shortly after 2000 BC (Civil 1994). Later, several Classical Roman authors cite or discuss the *tribulum* in their writing: Columella (*De Re Rustica* I.vi.24; first century AD), Varro (*Res Rusticae* I.lii.1; last part of first century BC), Vergil (*Georgics* I.164), Pliny (XVIII.298) and Cato (CXXXV.1). It is possible to identify the use of the *tribulum* from the archaeological record on the basis of typology and microwear of flints (Anderson-Gerfaud 1992; Kardulias & Yerkes 1996). Archaeological evidence (in the form of threshing flints) for the use of the threshing sledge comes from as early as the Pre-Pottery Neolithic B (*c.* 6000–7000 BC) in Syria (Anderson-Gerfaud 1992) and from the Eneolithic in Bulgaria and the Ukraine (*c.* 3500 BC: Skakun 1993). There is also evidence of the use of *tribulum* from the lithic assemblages of the fourth or fifth millennium BC at Ali Kosh in Iran (Anderson-Gerfaud 1992) and the lithic assemblages of the beginning of the third millennium BC at Kutan (Ninevite V) in Iraq (Anderson & Inizan 1994).

Further archaeological evidence for the use of the *tribulum* can come from the study of the articulated phytoliths (silica skeletons). Once the organic matter decays, silica skeletons would naturally tend to disarticulate following the weak lines of intersections between single phytoliths. However, when the plants are threshed with a *tribulum* the flint blades will cut the plant tissues made up by the dry organic matter and the phytoliths. The organic matter, in this case, efficiently keeps together the phytoliths and the blades will cut both through the phytoliths and between the phytoliths creating the typical straight or stepped cuts (Anderson 1998; see Figs. 584–5).

In Kilise Tepe there is an interesting pattern in the presence/absence of silica skeletons with *tribulum* cuts in the different contexts. The pits never have silica skeletons with breakage attributable to the *tribulum* while clearly threshed silica skeletons make up almost 40 per cent of the skeletons from the courtyard samples (J20/173, J20/181, I19/184) and about 25 per cent of the skeletons from the pot residues (sample K19/480 and K19/99). This seems to highlight differential treatment for the straw, depending on the use for which it was intended. When straw is used as fodder, it is often finely chopped and sometimes mixed with fresh leaves from trees or bushes and this practice can produce the phytolith input observed in the courtyard samples (with cuts pertaining both to threshing and chopping). On the other hand, if straw has to be used as a liner, it would probably be kept as whole stems. This is the possible scenario for the pits, where the straw lining would have been made up of long straw as is shown by the absence of silica skeletons with threshing cuts.

Conclusions

Notwithstanding the small data set and heterogeneous contexts sampled at Iron Age Kilise Tepe, phytolith analysis has shown the great potential of these microfossils for interpreting agricultural practices and economy, archaeological structures and ancient diet. Phytolith assemblages are sensitive to pre-depositional material selection and when taphonomic processes are under control, they can be an important indicator of the source of vegetal material and the processes this material underwent at the site. Moreover, silica skeletons can positively identify ancient crops and wild plant exploitation when macro-remains are less informative.

Notes

1. Culm is the correct botanical name for the stem of grasses.

Chapter 51

Fish Remains from Bronze Age to Byzantine Levels

Wim Van Neer & Marc Waelkens[1]

Introduction

The fish remains described in this contribution were excavated at Kilise Tepe during the 1995–97 seasons and date between the Early Bronze Age II and Byzantine period. For Turkey, a similar long sequence with fish bones is thus far only available from Troy (Van Neer & Uerpmann 1998). For that site only hand-picked remains have been described, but a small amount of sieved material is available as well (Uerpmann & Van Neer 2000). The material from Kilise Tepe comprises few hand-collected specimens and a larger number of bones retrieved during water sieving of large volumes of sediment on a 3.5-mm mesh. The depositional contexts from which the fish bones were collected were mainly pit fills and constructional materials ('packing', 'fill'). In these type of deposits, rapid burial of bone occurs which allows good preservation of tiny fish remains.

Kilise Tepe is located close to the junction of the Göksu river and the Kurtsuyu tributary, and is at less than 40 km from the Mediterranean. Hence, both freshwater and marine fish may be expected to occur on the site.

Description of the material

The material comprises 190 remains and was identified by comparison with the reference collection housed at the Royal Belgian Institute of Natural Sciences in Brussels. This comparative material was collected, amongst others, during three field campaigns in Turkey (Van Neer *et al.* 2000a,b; in press) and one in northern Syria. The skeletal elements of each taxon present at Kilise Tepe were noted and, when the specimens were sufficiently preserved, a size reconstruction was carried out. This was done by direct comparison with modern skeletons of known length. Reconstructed sizes are given in 5 or 10 cm length classes and expressed as standard length (SL), i.e. the length of the fish measured from the tip of the snout to the base of the tail.

Table 41 gives an overview of the taxa represented in the different chronological units. The species have not been arranged in systematical order but rather in terms of the environment from which they are derived.

The eel (*Anguilla anguilla*) is exclusively represented by vertebrae and occurs throughout most of the sequence. The reconstructed sizes indicate that the fish were mainly between 40 and 50 cm SL, with only one specimen of 30–40 cm SL. All the other Anatolian freshwater species found at Kilise Tepe belong to the family of the minnows (Cyprinidae). In terms of number of fragments, this taxon is the most common at the site with 77 per cent of the identified material. The number of specimens identified beyond family level is rather low, as is usually the case with Cyprinidae. The Göksu basin does not have many cyprinid taxa that are valuable as food fishes, but in the small collection studied here, three out of four species that can attain large sizes are represented. The barbel *Barbus capito* is attested by a dentary of a fish that measured 30–40 cm SL, and by two precaudal vertebrae I and one vertebra II+III of smaller fish. The reconstructed lengths for the vertebrae were 10–15 cm (two specimens) and 15–20 cm SL (one specimen). *Capoeta capoeta* is represented by a cleithrum, an opercular and an epihyal, all of fish measuring between 30 and 40 cm SL, whereas the presence of *Chondrostoma regium* is only indicated by a basioccipital of an individual that measured 15–20 cm SL. The chub (*Leuciscus cephalus*) which is also expected to occur in the Göksu (Geldiay & Balık 1996; Bogutskaya 1997) was not found among the Kilise Tepe remains, despite the fact that it can attain sizes of more than 60 cm SL. Since it is unlikely that this species would have been disliked by the inhabitants of Kilise Tepe its absence is probably due to small sample size and the difficulty of identifying cyprinids to species. In addition to the aforementioned species, another cyprinid has been identified which has never been reported from the Göksu in the ichthyological literature. The gudgeon (*Gobio gobio*) is represented at Kilise Tepe in a Late Bronze Age context by a highly diagnostic pharyngeal plate of an individual that measured 10–15 cm SL. The presence

Table 41. *The fish remains in the various levels of Kilise Tepe.*

	Sieved material												Hand-collected material									
	Byzantine	Later Iron Age	Middle Iron Age	Early Iron Age	Later or Middle Iron Age	Iron Age	total Iron Age	Late Bronze Age	Middle Bronze Age	Early Bronze III	Early Bronze II	*total sieved*	no provenance	Byzantine	Later Iron Age	Middle Iron Age	Late Bronze Age	Middle Bronze Age	Early Bronze III	Early Bronze II	*total hand*	grand total
Anatolian freshwater species																						
eel (*Anguilla anguilla*)	-	-	1	2	-	1	4	1	-	3	-	*8*	-	-	-	-	-	-	-	-	*-*	8
barbel (*Barbus capito*)	-	2	-	-	-	-	2	-	-	2	-	*4*	-	-	-	-	-	-	-	-	*-*	4
Capoeta capoeta	-	-	-	1	-	-	1	-	-	-	-	*1*	1	-	-	-	-	1	-	-	*2*	3
nase (*Chondrostoma* sp.)	-	-	-	-	-	-	-	1	-	-	-	*1*	-	-	-	-	-	-	-	-	*-*	1
gudgeon (*Gobio gobio*)	-	-	-	-	-	-	-	1	-	-	-	*1*	-	-	-	-	-	-	-	-	*-*	1
Cyprinidae indet.	22	6	3	34	8	6	57	5	2	2	2	*90*	-	1	-	1	-	-	-	-	*2*	92
Marine species																						
shark (*Carcharhinus* sp.)	-	-	-	-	-	-	-	1	-	-	-	*1*	-	-	-	-	-	1	-	-	*1*	2
twaite shad (*Alosa fallax*)	1	-	-	-	-	-	-	1	-	-	-	*2*	-	-	-	-	1	-	-	-	*1*	3
Clupeidae indet.	-	-	-	1	-	-	1	-	-	-	-	*1*	-	-	-	-	-	-	-	-	*-*	1
skipjack tuna (*Katsuwonus pelamis*)	-	-	-	1	-	-	1	-	-	-	-	*1*	-	-	-	-	-	-	-	-	*-*	1
seabreams (Sparidae indet.)	1	-	-	-	-	-	-	-	-	-	-	*1*	1	-	-	-	-	-	-	1	*2*	3
corb (*Umbrina cirrosa*)	-	-	-	-	-	-	-	-	-	-	-	*-*	-	-	-	-	-	-	1	-	*1*	1
mullets (Mugilidae indet.)	-	1	-	-	-	-	1	-	-	-	-	*1*	-	-	-	-	-	-	-	-	*-*	1
Perciformes indet.	-	2	-	-	-	-	2	1	-	-	-	*3*	-	-	-	-	-	-	-	-	*-*	3
Exotic freshwater species																						
walking catfish (Clariidae indet.)	2	1	-	-	-	-	1	-	-	-	-	*3*	-	1	1	-	-	-	-	-	*2*	5
Nile perch (*Lates niloticus*)	-	-	-	-	-	-	-	-	-	-	-	*-*	-	-	1	1	-	-	-	-	*2*	2
total identified fish	26	12	4	39	8	7	70	10	3	7	2	*118*	2	2	2	2	1	2	1	1	*13*	131
unidentified fish	13	10	4	9	3	-	26	2	4	9	2	*56*	-	-	2	-	-	-	1	-	*3*	59
grand total	39	22	8	48	11	7	96	12	7	16	4	*174*	2	2	4	2	1	2	2	1	*16*	190

Table 42. *Skeletal element representation of the unidentified cyprinids.*

neurocranium fragments	3
articular	1
branchiostegal	1
hyomandibular	1
interopercular	1
pharyngeal plate	1
pharyngeal tooth	1
cleithrum	2
precaudal vertebrae	22
caudal vertebrae	35
ribs	20
pterygiophores	4
Total	92

of two rows of pharyngeal teeth and the typical shape of the pharyngeal bone exclude an identification as one of the other cyprinid species occurring in Anatolia. It is unlikely that the species has become extinct since the Late Bronze Age and its apparent absence from the Göksu river today is probably due to insufficient exploration of the present-day ichthyofauna. A similar poor knowledge of the modern freshwater fish fauna was encountered during the interpretation of the fish remains from Sagalassos (Burdur Province) and prompted us to a series of field campaigns in order to establish the modern distribution of fishes in the region (Van Neer *et al.* 2000a; in press). The majority of the fish remains from Kilise Tepe were classified as 'Cyprinidae indet.'. The skeletal elements of these unidentified cyprinids are listed in Table 42 and the size reconstructions are given in Figure 351.

Marine fish are numerically less represented than the Anatolian freshwater fish, but their diversity is higher. Two specimens indicate the presence of cartilagenous fish. An upper and a lower tooth of Carcharhinidae were found in Middle Bronze Age contexts. The specimens can be assigned to the genus *Carcharhinus* but a more precise identification cannot be given due to the incompleteness of the reference material for this group. Two species of *Carcharhinus* have been reported off the Turkish coast (Branstetter 1989): the spinner shark (*Carcharhinus brevipinna*) and the sandbar shark (*C. plumbeus*), whereas the blacktip shark (*C. limbatus*) occurs from Tunisia to Israel. The smooth cusp of the lower tooth found at Kilise Tepe excludes an identification as sandbar or blacktip shark which have serrated teeth. The specimen is therefore tentatively identified as *Carcharhinus brevipinna*. All three species have serrate upper teeth, hence the upper tooth from Kilise Tepe cannot be identified beyond genus level. Although these sharks sometimes occur in coastal waters, it is likely that their presence at Kilise Tepe is related to the fishing in an open marine environment.

The Clupeidae, which is the family of herring-like fishes, are represented by two species at Kilise Tepe. The twaite shad (*Alosa fallax*) is attested by a urohyal (20–30 cm SL), a precaudal and a caudal vertebra (both 30–40 cm SL). Another clupeid vertebra is poorly preserved and comes from a specimen that is about 20 cm SL. Owing to its poor state of preservation it is impossible to decide whether it is derived from a pilchard (*Sardina pilchardus*) or a round sardinella (*Sardinella aurita*). All the aforementioned clupeids occur in coastal waters and the twaite shad enters Turkish estuaries in May–June to spawn in freshwater near the tidal limit (Geldiay & Balık 1996). It is likely that the shad remains found at Kilise Tepe are from specimens captured in the Göksu estuary during the spawning season when they are more accessible and vulnerable to fishing. The juveniles of pilchard are also known to enter river mouths but the large size of the specimen from Kilise indicates that the fish was rather captured in coastal marine waters. The skipjack tuna (*Katsuwonus pelamis*) probably indicates fishing in open marine environments since it only rarely occurs inshore. This species is represented in an Early Iron Age level by a typical caudal vertebra of an individual measuring 30–40 cm SL. Three remains of sea breams (Sparidae) were found but none of them could be identified more precisely. The recovered bones are an articular (30–40 cm SL), a caudal vertebra (50–60 cm SL) and a ceratohyal fragment (20–30 cm SL). Sea breams are important commercial species living mainly inshore. Certain species such as the gilthead (*Sparus aurata*) support brackish waters and enter estuaries. The corb (*Umbrina cirrosa*) is attested at Kilise Tepe by a well-preserved cleithrum of an individual of 30–40 cm. This drum species lives inshore although juveniles enter estuaries. The reconstructed size indicates again coastal fishing.

A Later Iron Age context yielded a basipterygium of a mullet (Mugilidae) of small size (10–15 cm). Five species of these very common inshore and estuarine fishes are listed for the Mediterranean (Miller & Loates 1997) but no attempt was made to identify the bone beyond family level. Three bones have been classified as 'Perciformes indet.' (perch-like fishes) and were retained as marine taxa since the freshwater fauna from

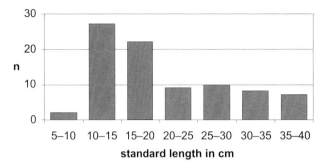

Figure 351. *Size distribution of all the cyprinids.*

the Göksu does not comprise any such species. These include a dorsal spine that corresponds well to that of a mullet, and which was found in the same sieved sample as the mullet basipterygium. The two other bones are a fragment of a dorsal or anal fin spine and a dorsal or anal pterygiophore.

Two fish taxa found at Kilise Tepe are believed to be allochthonous and are considered as imports through long-distance trade. There is some controversy about the former distribution of the Nile perch and there are also new data on the modern distribution of the catfish *Clarias* which complicate the interpretation. The arguments for considering the Nile perch and the catfish as imports will be elaborated in the discussion. Catfish of the Clariidae family are represented by a Weberian apparatus (30–40 cm SL), a branchiostegal (40–50 cm SL), a coracoid (30–40 cm SL), a precaudal vertebra (90–100 cm SL) and a caudal vertebra (30–40 cm SL). The catfish remains occur exclusively in the Late Iron Age and Byzantine levels. The Nile perch (*Lates niloticus*) is attested by a cleithrum of a specimen of 80–90 cm SL and by a ventral spine of an individual that measured 70–80 cm SL. These specimens come from a Late and a Middle Iron Age context.

Discussion and conclusions

All the fish remains found at Kilise Tepe are considered as food refuse, including the shark teeth. The lower tooth from *Carcharhinus* cf. *brevipinna* is small and was probably unattractive as an ornament. Moreover, its root does not show any sign of perforation or wear resulting from use as a pendant. The upper tooth of *Carcharhinus* sp. is rather large but the root is lacking. Although shark teeth can be used as ornaments and may have been exchanged over long distances, it is supposed here that they are from sharks that were brought in from the Mediterranean for human consumption. The fact that no other skeletal elements of sharks are found is not necessarily an indication of the contrary since teeth and calcified vertebral centra

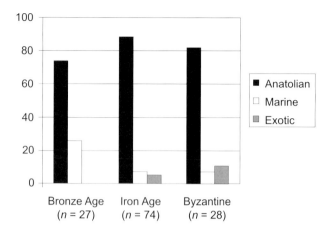

Figure 352. *Percentage contribution of Anatolian freshwater fish, marine species and exotic freshwater fish through time. The sample size is indicated in brackets.*

of cartilagenous fish are the only hard parts that have reasonable preservation chances.

It is obvious from Table 41 and from Figure 352 that local freshwater species were the most commonly consumed fish throughout the attested periods of occupation. The Göksu, as most of the other Anatolian rivers draining into the Mediterranean, has an ichthyofauna that consists mainly of cyprinids. This family is the richest in terms of number of species and also as far as biomass is concerned. Three out of four cyprinid species, known from the Göksu and attractive as food fish because of the size they can attain, are attested at Kilise Tepe, but it is not excluded that the missing species — *Leuciscus cephalus* — is represented among the unidentified cyprinid remains. The only other large food fish of which no trace has been found thus far is the brown trout (*Salmo trutta*). This species has, however, rather poor chances of preservation owing to the high fat content and the porosity of its bones. The cyprinids and the eel are the only species which may have been captured locally, although they may have been partly brought in from other areas along the Göksu basin. However, the large number of cyprinids of small size (Fig. 351) could rather point to local fishing. It is possible that the twait shad (*Alosa fallax*) was captured in the river mouth of the Göksu during its yearly spawning season. Other marine species that may have been taken from the estuary are the mullets and, possibly, some of the seabreams. Coastal water species consumed at Kilise Tepe include the unidentified clupeid (pilchard or round sardinella) and the corb (*Umbrina cirrosa*). The two shark species and the skipjack tuna, finally, are considered as fish that were taken from the open sea. All these marine species, including the ones taken from the Göksu estuary, were transported to the site over land, a journey that must have taken at least a day or two. It is unclear if the Mediterranean fish were cured for the purpose of transport. In summer, small clupeids like the pilchard or sardinella would need treatment to prevent spoilage during transport. All the other species, could in principle arrive in a rather fresh state when transport was efficient.

Two other fish species occurring exclusively in Byzantine and Iron Age levels must have been brought to Kilise Tepe in a cured form because of the large distances over which they were transported. The Nile perch presently lives in many large rivers and lakes of Africa and it is supposed here that the specimens found in a Late and Middle Iron Age context from Kilise Tepe were imported from the Nile. It has been argued by Lernau (1986/87) that the species may have been part of the autochthonous ichthyofauna of the southern Levant in the past, but this hypothesis is not accepted here. The Nile perch occurs in various sites in Israel, Lebanon and Jordan from the Bronze Age onwards but it was never found in archaeological sites predating the period that trade with Egypt existed (Rose 1994; Van Neer *et al.* 2004). Catfish of the Clariidae family, on the other hand, occur today in Africa and in the Near East. The Egyptian Nile hosts the genera *Clarias* and *Heterobranchus*, both with two species, whereas in the Levant only *Clarias gariepinus* is found. The specimens from Kilise Tepe could not be identified beyond family level due to the lack of the very diagnostic pectoral spines. The present-day distribution of *Clarias gariepinus* was traditionally believed to reach as far as the Ceyhan (Kosswig 1969; Skelton & Teugels 1992), but fieldwork recently carried out has shown that the species occurs much farther west as well (Van Neer *et al.* 2000b). Its presence was attested in the Seyhan river, the Tarsus river and near Akgöl, which is part of the Göksu basin, and even in the Aksu basin near Antalya. It remains unclear thus far whether this wider distribution was due to insufficient exploration in the past of the rivers flowing into the Mediterranean or if it was a result of recent artificial introductions. The absence of Clariidae from the Bronze Age levels of Kilise Tepe seems to indicate that these fish are not indigenous to the Göksu basin. Clariidae are easy to catch during their yearly spawning season when they are found in very shallow waters. During the Bronze Age, Mediterranean fish were brought to the site indicating that commercial contacts existed already with the coastal region. If *Clarias gariepinus* was already present in the lower Göksu it would be strange that it was not imported as well. A similar problem was encountered at the Roman–early Byzantine town of Sagalassos. The site yielded remains of exotic freshwater fish from the Nile (Nile perch and bagrid catfish *Bagrus* sp.) and of two taxa that occur both in the Nile and the Levant (tilapia and *Clarias* sp). During exploration of the freshwater fish fauna, *Clarias gariepinus* was found to be present in the Aksu and Acısu basin as well (Van Neer *et al.* 2000a,b; in press). If the original distribution of the clariid would indeed have included these basins south of Sagalassos, an import from that area would be more logical. Mitochondrial DNA analysis was carried out on modern tissue samples from *Clarias gariepinus* from rivers in Turkey, Syria, Israel and Egypt and indicated several variable regions containing point mutations that distinguish the haplotypes from each other (Van Neer *et al.* 2000b). Primer sets were designed to amplify very small fragments (between 100 and 150 nucleotides) containing these informative regions. Ancient DNA extracted from six catfish bones from Sagalassos matched the DNA from the modern Egyptian samples and excluded a Turkish or Syrian origin for the catfish (Arndt *et al.* 2003).

The diachronic changes in the fish fauna presented in Figure 352 are based on a small number of specimens, especially for the Byzantine and Bronze Age levels. The major trends are that local freshwater fish are the most frequently consumed species in all periods and that the highest proportion of marine fish was consumed in Bronze Age times. Bronze Age levels lack imported fish from Egypt which is present in higher proportions in Byzantine levels than in those from the Iron Age.

The dietary importance of fish versus that of other animal food resources at Kilise Tepe is difficult to quantify. Fish probably contributed very little, even when the poor chances of preservation, with respect to other vertebrates, are taken into account. Because of the low yield of the Göksu river, it is likely that fishing in freshwater was only an occasional activity, as it is the case today in the Anatolian rivers running towards the Mediterranean. Professional fishing was probably practised along the coast and possibly in the estuary, whereby the surplus of the catch was exported inland. Dried freshwater fish from Egypt have probably been a rather common trade item in the eastern Mediterranean since the Bronze Age. Nile perch remains have been found, for instance, in Late Bronze Age to Roman sites in Cyprus (Rose 1994), in Hellenistic levels at Miletus (von den Driesch pers. comm.), at Roman Sagalassos (Van Neer *et al.* 2000b), and in a second-century AD context at Ostia, the antique port of Rome (Van Neer unpublished). *Clarias* is attested, amongst others, at Kommos (Crete, c. 375 BC–AD 200: Rose 1994), at Salamis (Cyprus, c. 700 BC: Greenwood & Howes 1973), at Sagalassos (first–seventh centuries AD: Van Neer *et al.* 1997) and as far as Vallerano, 10 km south of Rome in a context dated to the first–second centuries AD (de Grossi Mazzorin 2000). Finds in the southern Levant, which are closer to the source area, are even more common (e.g. Lernau 1986/1987; 1996; Rose 1994; Van Neer *et al.* 2004).

Apart from a possible Egyptian item from a Middle Bronze Age context (**2603**), no Egyptian artefacts have been found at Kilise Tepe. However, the fish bones indicate that some kind of contacts, perhaps nothing more than simple 'down-the-line' conveyance of Egyptian goods, persisted during the Middle Iron Age (eighth–seventh centuries BC), the Late Iron Age (probably around the sixth century) and Byzantine times (fifth–sixth/seventh centuries AD).

As we have seen (Chapter 3), occupation continued at Kilise Tepe after the collapse of the Late Bronze Age palace cultures, and from at least the eighth century BC onwards, in Level IIf, its inhabitants certainly had cultural links with Cyprus. As during this period Nile perch and *Clarias* were also reaching Cyprus (see above), it should come as no surprise that Cypriot traders or other traders dealing with Cyprus also handed 'down-the-line' through the Göksu valley Egyptian fish reaching the island. The emergence of new states such as Tabal, a bit later also Phrygia, and eventually Lydia, must have stimulated the movement of goods in this area during the Middle to Late Iron Ages, including Egyptian fish which may have been a luxury item. Only the excavation of the capital of Tabal, and that of some cities of Hilakku and Pirindu, might fully document the real nature of international trade at that moment.

Only in Hellenistic times may direct contacts with Egypt have been established. In fact, the Ptolemies very quickly became interested in both Rough Cilicia and Cyprus. A first attempt in 311 BC by Ptolemy I to free the Greek cities in Rough Cilicia from the rule of Antigonos Monophthalmos, motivated by its favourable location opposite Cyprus, which fell partially under Ptolemaic control already in 311/310 BC and definitively in 295/4 BC, foundered (Hölbl 2001, 19, 23). Cilicia only fell into the hands of Ptolemy II during the so-called 'Syrian War of Succession' in 280–279 BC, as it is included in Theocritus's list of Ptolemaic possessions in the 270s. But large parts of the Cilician territories may have been lost again to Antiochos II and his Seleucid kingdom around the middle of the century (Hölbl 2001, 38, 44). However, the fortress of Meydancıkkale briefly served as a Ptolemaic administrative centre (Davesne 1991, 349–53; Mitchell 1999, 189). Much later, Mark Antony, who appointed his son Ptolemaios Philadelphos as its ruler (Hölbl 2001, 244) was to give Cilicia back to Egypt. So in Hellenistic times there must have been many links connecting Rough Cilicia with Cyprus and Egypt. This strengthening of the ties between these areas might explain why even in early Byzantine times Egyptian fish still reached Kilise Tepe. As shown by the examples from Sagalassos, and from other locations in Anatolia, Cyprus, the Aegean and even Italy, such a trade in Nilotic fish was far from exceptional. One can only expect more coastal and inland sites located along major trade routes to produce additional evidence for this in future.

Notes

1. This text presents research results of the Belgian Programme on Interuniversity Poles of Attraction initiated by the Belgian State, Prime Minister's Office, Science Policy Programming.

Chapter 52

Human Remains

J.A. Pearson[1]

Introduction

Human remains recovered at Kilise Tepe from 1995 to 1998 include a minimum of six distinct individuals from the Bronze Age and the Byzantine period. In addition, a number of isolated, scattered human bones were found in a variety of units across the extent of the excavation. The human remains described here were documented entirely in summer 1999 at the Silifke Museum. The majority of skeletal elements had been exposed to taphonomic factors resulting in their deterioration. Many of the individual bones were highly friable and much of the cortical bone had been exposed, probably due to disturbance, and soil could often be found inside the bone cavity. Preserving chemicals (B72 in toluene administered by F. Cole) were restricted to pelvic elements allowing sex identification to be optimal, and to prevent compromising bones which may in the future be required for radiocarbon dating or other analyses.

Demographic interpretations were not attempted owing to the small number of individuals recovered. However, the morphological identification of genetic traits suggests that if a larger population were available some interesting data could be obtained. The inventory of scattered remains could not be assigned to any of the burials nor to each other, although this should not be considered as conclusive evidence given the inherent difficulties of such a task (Kilgore & Jurmain 1988).

Ageing and sexing

The five key publications used include: Mays 1998; Acsádi & Nemeskéri 1970; Brothwell 1981; Bass 1995 and Workshop of European Anthropologists 1980. Sex was assigned primarily by pelvic morphology observations, age was identified for the subadults by a combination of epiphyseal union/obliteration and dental development. The adults were more tentatively aged according to a larger combination of observations including: cranial suture union and obliteration; pubic symphysis erosion; osteophytosis of the vertebrae and osteoarthritis of the appendicular skeleton (Bass 1998; Workshop of European Anthropologists 1980). However, owing to the small number of adults recovered it was not possible to establish a seriation of these changes which would have made the identifications more secure.

Palaeopathology

Although it is often not possible to ascertain the cause of death from osteology alone, the identification of pathology in ancient populations can provide information regarding overall health and nutritional status. The dental hygiene of the Byzantine population at Kilise Tepe was poor in comparison to the Bronze Age individuals. The adult Byzantine individual (**2840** L16/31) showed signs of caries, severe grades of attrition (Brothwell 1981), and the beginnings of periodontal disease. Although little intra-site comparison can be made, the dental pathology of the Byzantine population of Kilise Tepe shows no analogy with that of Domuztepe on the Kahramanmaraş plain, east Turkey (author's own unpublished data). Degenerative modifications were observed on the axial skeleton of the adult Byzantine individual (**2840**). No traumatic lesions or inflammatory reactions were observed in either population. Two cases of the metabolic disorder *Cribra orbitalia*, an osteological modification caused by increased blood supply to the orbits, brought on by iron deficiency and anaemia, were identified, one from the Bronze Age juvenile (**2842**) and the other in the juvenile skeleton recovered from the topsoil (**2841**).

Byzantine remains

A single primary inhumation (**2840**) was recovered during the 1998 season of excavation from beneath church foundations subsequently built on top of this burial (see Jackson above, p. 195; Fig. 177). This burial appears not to have been disturbed, as was deduced by the presence of terminal phalanges, patellae and

Figure 353. *Cranium 2840, from grave at east end of Church: a) left side; b) back.*

hyoid. The remains of a juvenile skeleton (**2841**) were recovered from the topsoil and may also represent an individual from this period.

The burial (**2840**) contained the complete and well preserved skeleton of a mature female. The sex was identified from the sciatic notch and pubic symphysis (Bass 1995; Mays 1998; Acsádi & Nemeskéri 1970; Workshop of European Anthropologists 1980). Although the skeletal gracility complemented this deduction, the supraorbital ridges (frontal brow ridges) were markedly large for a female (Bass 1995). The cranium (Fig. 353a–b) seemed very round and less angular than the Byzantine remains from Domuztepe (author's own unpublished data) and Çatalhöyük (author's own unpublished data). This phenomenon is unlikely to represent a deliberate modification. Examination of the cranium also revealed the presence of two 'Inca' bones at the Lambda landmark of the cranium (Fig. 353a–b). Such extra bones in the cranium are generally accepted as inherited (Finnegan 1978). The future recovery of human remains from the Byzantine period could provide information on kinship.

Skeletal age was approximated to 40 years based upon full dental eruption (Brothwell 1981) and epiphyseal fusion to obliteration. Some clues to age were also given by slight degeneration at some points of the axial skeleton: osteophytes were present on all vertebral groups. Although the skeletal elements seemed porotic, this may also be attributed to diagenetic factors in the burial environment. However, osteo-arthritis was observed on the terminal phalanges of both hands. The fact that this individual has not been classified as an 'old' adult was due to the failure of the outer cranial suture lines to obliterate. *Cribra orbitalia* was found to be absent as were any other skeletal pathologies.

A metric comparison was made between this individual and a suite of Byzantine skeletons recovered from the site of Domuztepe (author's own unpublished data). The females of a younger adolescent/adult age group at Domuztepe were generally smaller and shorter. But when this individual is compared to the females of similar age from Domuztepe we find that the Kilise Tepe individual is markedly smaller and shorter. In one femur comparison, the maximum length measurements differed by as much as 5 cm, a phenomenon which cannot be resolved purely by observer error. On other elements less indicative of stature, very few measurements can be confidently identified as larger or smaller. This metric skeletal difference could be explained as geographical/environmental differences or else a chronological difference. Since neither Domuztepe nor Kilise Tepe have radiocarbon dates for these skeletons as yet, the latter explanation cannot yet be discussed. If these Byzantine remains prove to be a few hundred years different to one another, this could be the result of a new influence in the already diverse population.

The dental health of this individual is interesting. Almost every tooth has a large occlusal or distal caries, which on many occasions has resulted in collapse of the tooth crown, leaving only the roots. Where the crown of the tooth does survive, it is always heavily worn. The caries development seems not to have been counteracted by the attritional processes, although no calculus is observed suggesting that some attrition has occurred. This is the result of frequent intake of carbohydrate-rich foods. The absence of hypoplasias, an interruption in the development of tooth enamel usually triggered by nutritional deficit or infection, has also been noted. The dentition also revealed agenesis of the third maxillary molar on both left and right sides.

A juvenile aged 4–5 years (**2841**) was recovered from the topsoil and assigned to the Byzantine Period. This individual was very fragmented. Much of the cranium was recovered — examination of the orbits revealed a medium degree of *Cribra orbitalia*. The teeth from the maxilla and mandible had been lost post-mortem and were recovered in excavation. The development of the dentition allowed age to be estimated. Very little of the post-crania was preserved and no osteological measurements could be taken.

[**2840**]   L16/31   5626
Mature adult female (*c.* 30–40 years). Complete except: right femur (taken for C14); a few tarsals, metatarsals and phalanges were also missing. Most osteological measurements were possible owing to good preservation.
2 Inca bones at Lambda.
Agenesis of the third maxillary molars.
Large quantity of caries, high grade of dental attrition and moderate hypoplasia present on the incisors.
Fig. 353a–b

[**2841**]   K14/40   3012
Juvenile skull with some postcrania. Orbits on the skull show medium degree of *Cribra orbitalia*. Majority of cranial areas are represented. Complete maxillary and mandibular dentition, mandible is slightly better preserved. Individual teeth were separate from the mandible and maxilla. Development of the maxillary canine crowns and maxillary central incisor development indicate an age of 4–5 years.
A selection of ribs.
A fragment of long bone (humerus?).
Right clavicle.

Bronze Age remains

The remains from this period were better preserved: three near-complete individuals were recovered. They comprised the lower half of an adult skeleton (**2845**) found in the fill of a pit from phase Vi (late), and the complete skeleton of a juvenile aged 8–10 years (**2842**), deposited in the destruction of phase Vj (see Fig. 75). This population was easily distinguishable from the Byzantine population. The patellae, for example, were as much as 1.5 cm narrower compared with the much later Byzantine population.

The sex of the adult from this period (**2845**) could not be ascertained owing to absence of all skeletal elements bearing secondary sex characteristics. The skeleton was only complete from the below the pelvis. A full range of metric measurements were taken of the legs and feet. No squatting facets were observed between the articulations for the tibiae and tali, though the tibial distal articulations were badly preserved. The first metatarsals provided evidence for kneeling with the toes curled under (Molleson 1994) and were photographed in articulation (Fig. 354a–b).

Figure 354. *Metatarsal* **2845** *to show kneeling facets: a) top; b) side.*

The complete juvenile skeleton (**2843**) recovered was aged at 8–10 years according to dental development (Brothwell 1981) and epiphyseal fusion. Few metric measurements were possible owing to fragmentation of all diagnostic bones. Examination of cranial bones suggested severe *Cribra orbitalia*. Examination of the dentition revealed marked attrition for a young individual. Heavy calculus was found together with slight hypoplasias on the mandibular central incisors and maxillary central and lateral incisors. It seems unusual that the heavy attrition was insufficient to disturb calculus deposition on the teeth.

The infants (**2843–4**) were entirely retrieved from the faunal remains indicating that they were not afforded disposal or burial such as could be identified by the excavators, providing an insight into the regard in which the newly born and infantile were held in Bronze Age Anatolia. A comparison with the Neolithic infants and neonates from Çatalhöyük may provide details pertaining to the *in utero* or *ex utero* status of these infants. The only indicator of age was the calcification of the second deciduous molar, where the cusps of the crown had recently united. All diagnostic bones were fragmented though a few metric measurements were estimated and some mid-shaft diameters were possible.

Level Vj
[**2842**]   H20/785   5407
Juvenile 8–10 years
Skeleton is complete (except for left calcaneus and a number of epiphyses) but friable.
Fragmentation prevented most osteological measurements.
Heavy *Cribra orbitalia* observed in orbits.

High attrition grade on dentition.
Marked calculus.
Fig. 75

[2843]   H20/879   1859
Infant
6 rib fragments.
4 metacarpals.
1 humerus fragment.
1 fibula fragment.
1 ulna fragment.
1 right proximal femur, broken (estimated total length: 75 mm).
Indicates <1 years.
1 maxillary lateral incisor.

Level Vi/j
[2844]   H20/863   1863
Infant/neonate skeleton
Left and right ilia (estimated height 33 mm).
Deciduous second molar crown.
Left femur with epiphyses.
Midshaft AP: 6 mm.
Left and right tibiae with epiphyses.
Fibula: estimated length: 68 mm.
Two vertebrae fragments.
Two rib fragments.
Left and right pubis.
Right ischium.
Skull fragments, cranial with some facial.

Level Vi
[2845]   H20/615   1872
The lower torso of an adult.
Sex could not be assigned.
Poor preservation.
Left and right femora present, but proximal ends are missing.
Left and right patellae.
Left and right tibiae, fragmented.
Left and right fibulae, fragmented.
Both feet intact except for second right cuneiform; a few phalanges are also missing. Kneeling facets were found on 1st metatarsals and articulating proximal phalanges.
Fig. 354a–b

Catalogue of scattered human bone

In addition to the individuals described above, human bone was recovered in small quantities from most areas and strata of the site, usually only recognized later among the faunal collection. A list of these follows, arranged chronologically.

Level Vj
[2846]   H20/872   1899
Adult axis, dark orange in colour, heated?

Level Vi
[2847]   H20/554   1852
Very thick adult cranial bone, interior is carbonized and beginning to become calcined (human?).

[2848]   H20/798   5403
Adult atlas vertebra (bridged).

[2849]   H20/875   1898
Adult thoracic vertebra.
Adult lower lateral incisor with anomalous deposit on root.

Level Vg
[2850]   H20/1033   5384
Juvenile/adult 1st metacarpal, proximal head fusing, distal epiphysis unfused.

Level Vf/g
[2851]   H20/877   1824
Lower left permanent lateral incisor (32: FDI system).

[2852]   H20/878   1829
1 adult fused distal metacarpal end, broken.

Level Vf?
[2853]   H20/839   5344
Three adult metacarpal phalanges.
Two adult carpals.

Level Ve/f
[2854]   H20/869   5319
Three adult tarsal fragments.
2 juvenile ischia.
Juvenile distal femur condyle epiphysis.
1 juvenile femoral head epiphysis.

Level Ve
[2855]   H20/861   5318
1 adult fibula fragment.
1 adult ulna fragment.

[2856]   H20/862   5304
1 left adult talus, robust; maximum length: 53.6 mm; articulation: 35.7 mm.
1 adult molar 37 (FDI system), enamel wear only.

[2857]   H20/864   5318
Right juvenile tibia, distal and proximal articulations are broken, proximal tuberosity is also broken (same individual as **2862**?).
Estimated length: 200 mm.
Juvenile fibula fragment.

[2858]   H20/866   5321
Adult left distal humerus, condyle broken.
Juvenile fibula distal epiphysis missing.
Juvenile distal femur condyle epiphysis.

[2859]   H20/870   5300
Adult permanent lateral incisor.

[2860]   H20/871   5313
1 adult left maxillary molar 26 or 27 (FDI system) anomalous shaped.

[2861]   H20/873   1287
Adult cervical vertebra, left transverse foramen is bipartite.

[2862]   H20/876   5313
Juvenile left fragment of a mandible, only 74 and 75 (FDI system) remain, age estimated to 4–6 years.
1 juvenile premolar unassociated with mandible, estimated age 8–10 years.

Human Remains

Level IVa/Ve
[2863] H20/865 5317
Juvenile left tibia; Length: 205 mm.
Nutrient foramen AP: 19.2 mm.
Nutrient foramen ML: 15.1 mm.
Juvenile right ilium; breadth: 95 mm; length: broken.
Juvenile left pubis.

Level IVa/Ve?
[2864] H20/874 1272
Adult permanent left lower canine (33: FDI system).

Level IVa
[2865] H19/383 4258
Human bone retrieved from H19/252 (animal bones). 1 adult angular long bone midshaft, 70 mm long (fibula?).

[2866] H19/385 4258
Adult proximal left ulna, appears dark brown in places suggesting heating.

Level IVa/b
[2867] H19/382 4257
1 adult cranial fragment, sutures closing (parietal?).
1 permanent premolar.
1 long bone shaft, unfused, compact bone seems thick for human.

[2868] H19/384 4261
Juvenile mandible, front apex only. Alveolae preserved for 85, 84, 83, 82, 82, 71, 72 (FDI system); only 84 is still in socket and unworn suggesting recent eruption, indicative of age 3–5 years.

Level IIIa/IVb
[2869] H19/125 4235
Adult metacarpal proximal phalanx (not worked).

[2870] H19/386 4235
Young adult metacarpal, epiphyseal lines have not yet obliterated.

Level IIIa–b
[2871] H19/380 4237
Juvenile/Adult (mid/late teens) metacarpal phalanx, distal epiphysis not yet fused.
1 carpal.

[2872] H19/379 4236
1 adult phalanx.
1 adult permanent molar 47 (FDI system) enamel wear only.

Level IIIc
[2873] H19/378 4234
Two juvenile/adult metacarpals, proximal heads are unfused.
Three juvenile/adult phalanges, distal epiphyses are fusing.
Right young adult clavicle, sternal epiphysis unfused, broken distal metaphysis and splintered midshaft; age estimated 16–25 years (Webb & Suchey 1985). Estimated length: 130 mm.

Level IIIc/d
[2874] H19/381 4238
1 adult metacarpal phalanx.

Level 2/3
[2875] I14/190 3703
Juvenile deciduous incisor root has not been reabsorbed.

Level IIb
[2876] K20/238 1971
Juvenile deciduous second molar, total root has reabsorbed.

Level IIc
[2877] I19/187 2848
Adult permanent premolar.

Level IIc/d
[2878] L19/51 5973
Adult right tibia, two shaft fragments, proximal and distal heads are missing.
Adult left scapula fragment.
Adult proximal radius fragment, epiphysis nearly obliterated.
Adult ulna fragment.

Level IId
[2879] L19/71 5968
Adult left distal radius fragment.
Adult fibula shaft fragment.
Adult ulna shaft fragment.
Two metatarsals (4th and 5th) missing proximal heads.
Three adult clavicles (all from different individuals).

Level IIe
[2880] K18/264 4352
Adult right, 1st metatarsal (MT1), anterior kneeling articulation; maximum length: 60.3 mm.
Midshaft minimum AP: 11.6 mm.
Midshaft minimum ML: 11.1 mm.

Level E5a
[2881] R18/263 2414
Deciduous canine, tooth has been almost totally reabsorbed.

Level E5b
[2882] R18/264 2453
Adult right humerus, midshaft fragment:
Midshaft AP: 16.5 mm.
Midshaft ML: 16.6 mm.

Level IIg?
[2883] I19/209 1780
Adult left acetabulum and ilium fragment.

Level 2 lower
[2884] K14/158 3097
Adult right distal humerus fragment, distal condyle is missing.

Level I
[2885] K18/265 4312
Juvenile recently erupted lateral incisor.

[2886] J18/414 2308
Three adult cranial fragments, irregular colouring: deep brown/black, heating?

Level 1
[2887] K16/31 4812
Approximately 50 adult cranial fragments, all areas of the skull are represented although maxilla and mandible are absent.

[2888]   K16/38   4812
Five fragments mature adult crania (parietal?) sutures are closed inside but still fusing outside.

[2889]   K16/36   4813
Juvenile crania, left temporal maxilla, orbit fragment.

Unstratified
[2890]   J19/449   3923
Adult distal ulna.
Adult distal radius.
Adult proximal 1st metacarpal.

Notes

1. This research was funded by a grant from the British Institute of Archaeology at Ankara.

Chapter 53

Dating

Peter Ian Kuniholm, Maryanne W. Newton, Roy Switsur & Nicholas Postgate

Dendrochronology
by PETER IAN KUNIHOLM & MARYANNE W. NEWTON

Over the years of the Kilise Tepe excavations, 1994–198, Professor Postgate kindly furnished the Aegean Dendrochronology Project with twenty sets of charcoal. One lot was *Cedrus* sp., one *Salix* sp., one *Populus* sp., and seventeen were *Pinus* sp. The most common variety of pine in the region today is *P. brutia*. In its carbonized state with no bark or needles or cones preserved, a distinction between the subspecies of pine cannot be made.

One pine sequence from a single tree, a combination of three charcoal samples, KLT-3 (J20/172), KLT-6 (J20/180), and KLT-7 (also J20/180), forms a ring-sequence 194 years long. The sample is from Unit 5703, in the excavator's phase IIId. Some years ago we reported to Professor Postgate that the combined ring-sequence looked good against the Bronze Age/Iron Age tree-ring chronology at 1381 BC +4/–7[1] (t-score 4.61, overlap 194 years, r-correlation .32, trend coefficient 59.1%, D-score 41.7), but since then (1996) additional work on the radiocarbon basis upon which the absolute dates were based required the shifting up of all dates connected to that floating dendrochronology, i.e. everything is now older by 22 years. Because this floating chronology is not yet connected to the living trees of the Anatolian plateau, largely because of a major gap in the Roman period, we have been using radiocarbon wiggle-matching[2] to approximate absolute dates for the Bronze Age/Iron Age tree-ring chronology until such time as it can stand on its own.

The argumentation for the first placement was set out by Kuniholm *et al.* in *Nature* in 1996 (and see also the comment by Renfrew in the same volume, 733–4) and then, with more than triple the number of radiocarbon determinations for the wiggle-match of Gordion timbers, in *Science* in 2001 (Manning *et al.* 2001; Kromer *et al.* 2001, and see also comment by Reimer in the same volume, 2494–5). The revised date for the whole dendrochronological sequence (up 22 years) plus additional radiocarbon dates obtained since 2001, support the placement for KLT-3&6 at 1403 BC ± 3.[3]

Since this dendrochronological fit for KLT-3&6 was less robust than we might have wished,[4] we submitted samples to Bernd Kromer at the Institut für Umweltphysik radiocarbon facility in Heidelberg to try to confirm it by radiocarbon wiggle-matching. The 1403 BC tree-ring date is now reinforced by two near-decadal radiocarbon dates from the Heidelberg laboratory (see Fig. 356b). Because of the shape of the calibration

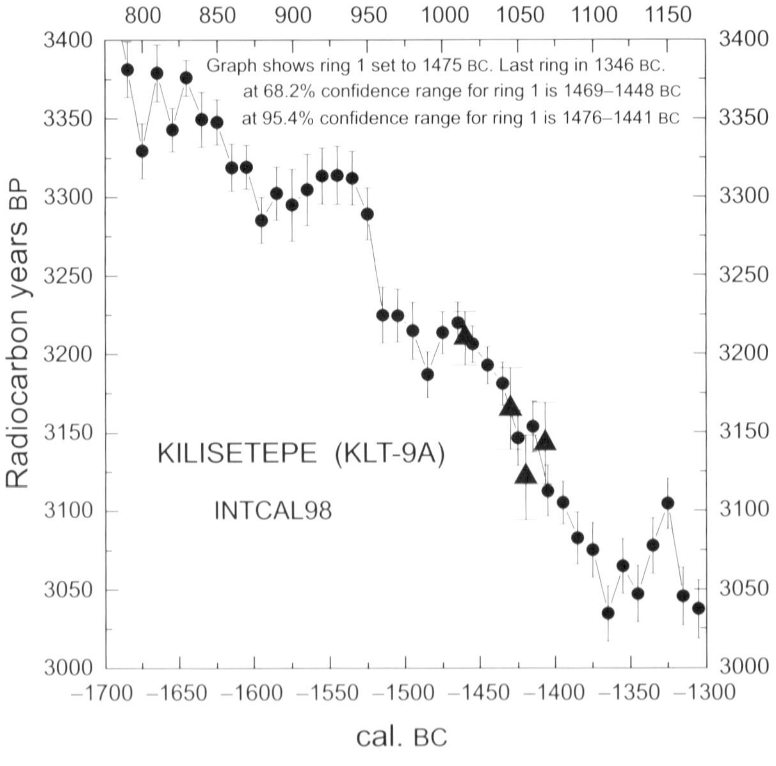

Figure 355. *Dendrochronology chart.*

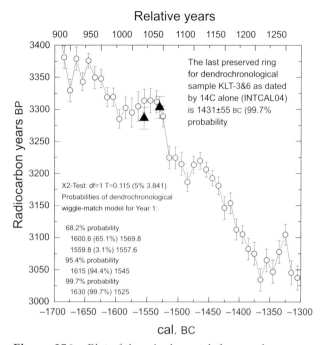

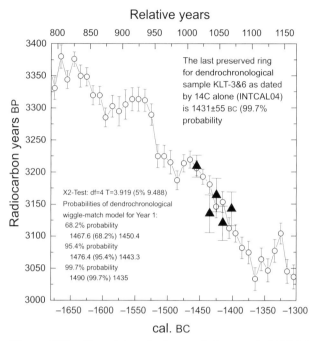

Figure 356a. *Plot of the wiggle-match for sample J20/172 against the INTCAL04 calibration data set (Reimer et al. 2004). The last preserved ring of the dendrochronological sample KLT-3&6 is 134 years after the midpoint of the last dated decade, i.e. 1431±55 BC. The dendrochronological date is 1403±3 BC.*

Figure 357a. *Plot of the wiggle-match for sample J18/398 against the INTCAL04 calibration data set (Reimer et al. 2004). The last preserved ring of the dendrochronological sample KLT-9A&15 is 59.5 years after the midpoint of the last dated decade, i.e. 1345.5±30 BC.*

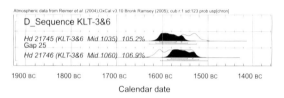

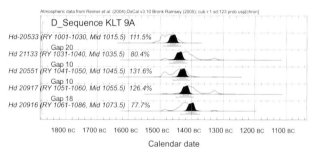

Figure 356b. *Composite probability plot of the radiocarbon dated decades calculated for the Kilise Tepe sample J20/172 wiggle-match model using the program OxCal v3.10 (Bronk Ramsey 1995; 2001) and the INTCAL04 calibration data set (Reimer et al. 2004). The last preserved ring of the dendrochronological sample KLT-3&6 is 134 years after the midpoint of the last dated decade, i.e. 1431±55 @ 3σ BC. The unshaded (hollow) background histograms show the total dating probability for each sample in isolation, while the black (solid) histograms show the same, but for each decade as a part of the wiggle-match.*

curve in the sixteenth century BC (i.e., relatively flat) and the low sample number (only two dates, and those for years earlier in the tree's life[5]) for the wiggle-match model, the match is not conclusive; it does, however, support an end date for the tree ring sequence in the last half of the fifteenth century BC.[6]

Figure 357b. *Composite probability plot of the radiocarbon dated decades calculated for the Kilise Tepe sample J18/398 wiggle-match model using the program OxCal v3.10 (Bronk Ramsey 1995; 2001) and the INTCAL04 calibration data set (Reimer et al. 2004). The last preserved ring of the dendrochronological sample KLT-9A&15 is 59.5 years after the midpoint of the last dated decade, i.e. 1345.5 ± 30 BC. The unshaded (hollow) background histograms show the total dating probability for each sample in isolation, while the black (solid) histograms show the same, but for each decade as a part of the wiggle-match.*

A second pine sequence from a single tree, a combination of KLT-9 and KLT-15 (J18/398 from 6504 in the excavator's phase IIc: see Fig. 122), has 134 years preserved, but with no bark present. We first reported

Table 43. *Radiocarbon data. The date ranges for the samples that comprise dendrochronological radiocarbon wiggle-matches are the same for each sample that is part of the wiggle-match; in each case the samples are ten-year segments of carbonized wood, and the date ranges reflect the date of the last preserved ring of the wiggle-match.*

Sample code	Unit	Level	^{14}C lab ID	^{14}C yrs BP	Relative years (for DWM)	Calibrated date range cal. BC at 1σ (68.2% probability)	Calibrated date range cal. BC at 2σ (95.4 % probability)	Calibrated date range cal. BC at 3σ (99.7% probability)
H20/456 wood charcoal	1838	Vg/h	Q	4290±75		3080–3070 (1.2%) 3030–2860 (59.0%) 2810–2760 (8.0%)	3300–3200 (1.0%) 3150–2600 (94.4%)	3350–2550
H19/357 wood charcoal	4278	IVa	Q	3610±60		2120–2100 (2.8%) 2040–1880 (65.4%)	2140–1860 (87.8%) 1850–1770 (7.6%)	2300–1650
H19/197 wood charcoal	4249	IVb	Q	3585±45		2020–1990 (9.9%) 1980–1880 (58.3%)	2120–2090 (2.1%) 2040–1860 (82.8%) 1850–1770 (10.5%)	2140–1740
H19/157 wood charcoal	4245	IIIb	Q	3450±55		1880–1840 (15.8%) 1830–1680 (52.4%)	1920–1610	1980–1520
J20/172 Architectural timber /dendro sequence	5703	IIId	Hd 21745	3286±17	KLT-3 RY 1030–1040 (mid 1035)	1448–1411 (65.1%) 1401–1399 (3.1%)	1456–1396	1471–1366
J20/172 Architectural timber /dendro sequence	5703	IIId	Hd 21746	3303±17	KLT-3 RY 1050–1070 (mid 1060)	1448–1411 (65.1%) 1401–1399 (3.1%)	1456–1396	1471–1366
J20/125 burned figs	1372	IIIe	Q	3070±45		1410–1290	1440–1210	1460–1120
J18/398 Architectural timber/ dendro sequence	6504	IIc	Hd 20553	3210±17	KLT-9 RY 1001–1030 (mid 1015.5)	1353.6–1336.4	1362.4–1329.3	1379–1319
J18/398 Architectural timber/ dendro sequence	6504	IIc	Hd 21133	3136±17	KLT-9 RY 1031–1040 (mid 1035.5)	1353.6–1336.4	1362.4–1329.3	1379–1319
J18/398 Architectural timber/ dendro sequence	6504	IIc	Hd 20551	3165±26	KLT-9 RY 1041–1050 (mid 1045.5)	1353.6–1336.4	1362.4–1329.3	1379–1319
J18/398 Architectural timber/ dendro sequence	6504	IIc	Hd 20917	3121±27	KLT-9 RY 1051–1060 (mid 1055.5)	1353.6–1336.4	1362.4–1329.3	1379–1319
J18/398 Architectural timber/ dendro sequence	6504	IIc	Hd 20916	3143±26	KLT-9 RY 1061–1086 (mid 1073.5)	1353.6–1336.4	1362.4–1329.3	1379–1319

to Professor Postgate what we thought was a good crossdate against the Bronze Age/Iron Age Master Tree-Ring Chronology at 1350 BC (using the dating scheme published in *Nature* in 1996), but re-analysis of samples KLT-9 & KLT-15, prompted by results of a second radiocarbon wiggle-match (Fig. 357a), produced a revision of the series. What had previously been measured as an annual ring proved to be a false ring, thereby ruining the 'fit' we had reported. We also found four additional rings on another radius at the exterior. Now nothing at all in the second millennium looks good dendrochronologically.

Because the 1350 BC date for KLT-9&15 that we had first reported was from a single tree (and not a very long-lived one at that), we selected five decadal or near-decadal samples and sent them to Kromer at Heidelberg for a second exercise in radiocarbon wiggle-matching. Fig. 357a shows where Kromer thinks the five Kilise Tepe samples (shown as triangles) fit on the 2004 radiocarbon calibration curve. The best visual fit is at 1346 BC plus or minus not very much at all.[7] The Oxford Calibration program adds calculations of the probabilities for the fits at 1σ [68.2% probability], 2σ [95.4% probability], and 3σ [99.7% probability]), respectively, so that the last preserved ring is dated to 1345±9 (1σ), 1346±17 (2σ), and 1349±30 (3σ) BC. There is no longer any dendrochronological fit with which this determination can be matched, so any scientific dating for KLT-9&15 will have to be based on the radiocarbon alone.

A third piece of pine, KLT-11 (K19/467 from 6212, also phase IIc), although it has 128 rings preserved, does not crossdate with either our Bronze Age/Iron Age master tree-ring chronology or with KLT-9 & 15.

Experience has shown us that we can usually get cross-dating in Anatolian conifers when we have a century and a quarter's worth of rings preserved, but KLT-11 is one of the exceptions.[8]

While the dendrochronological results are less than we had hoped to provide, we can at least incorporate them into a model that takes advantage of both the radiocarbon results, and the archaeologists' recording of the stratigraphy.[9]

Radiocarbon dating
by Roy Switsur

Five samples were submitted to the Environmental Sciences Research Centre Radiocarbon Dating Research Laboratory at Anglia University in Cambridge. With the exception of the carbonized figs (J20/125), the samples consisted of carbonized wood.

The results are shown in Table 43. The 'conventional radiocarbon ages' are based on the Libby half-life of 5568 years for the radiocarbon isotope and the base year AD 1950, using the BP notation. The numbers have been rounded to the nearest 5 years. The uncertainty is based on the one standard deviation of the counting statistics of the sample and the standards.

The radiocarbon ages and uncertainty have been calibrated with INTCAL04 to give date ranges on the Christian calendar. These ranges have the notation cal. BC. Because of the properties of the calibration curve, it is not correct to take the mid point of the date range and allocate an uncertainty as is possible with the radiocarbon age. The calibrated date ranges are given at 1σ (68.2%), 2σ (95.4%) and 3σ (99.7%) probability levels (Table 43), and were calculated with the program OxCal v3.10 (Bronk Ramsey 1995; 2001) using the INTCAL04 calibration data set (Reimer *et al.* 2004).

Excavator's comment
by J.N. Postgate

The dates seem generally quite plausible, not least because their chronological sequence agrees with their stratigraphic sequence. In several cases they come out earlier than we would have predicted. The likeliest reasons for this would be the re-use of timbers or mistaken assumptions about the position of our Levels in the historical and cultural sequence. At present the number of determinations is not adequate to enable us to opt for one or another explanation. These comments begin with the most recent samples.

J18/398 These dendrochronological samples (KLT-9 and KLT-15) were taken from timbers in the foundation of Rm 7 in the IIc Stele Building. If the trees were felled around 1350 BC, the implication would be that about two centuries elapsed between the construction of the IIc building and the burning of the IId phase (if we accept a broad date of 1150 BC for the Mycenaean ceramics caught up in that destruction). This is rather longer than might have been predicted on stratigraphic grounds, and puts the new ceramics of Level IIa–c further back in time than we expected. The date for this timber also falls towards the earlier end of the date range for the burnt figs from phase IIIe, given to us by J20/125. These considerations mean, I think, that we may have to allow for the timber in the foundations being recycled from an earlier building.

J20/125 This date from carbonized figs belongs in our latest Level III phase. A date between 1410 and 1290 would be quite acceptable in the context of our expected historical dates, and the earlier part of this range falls before the dendrochronological/radiocarbon date of about 1350 for J18/398.

J20/172, 180 These dendrochronological samples (KLT-3, -6, -7) come from a relatively small unshaped branch in the remains of a large hearth of phase IIId. With the agreement between the revised dendrochronological date of 1403±3 and the Heidelberg radiocarbon range pointing to the second half of the fifteenth century BC, it seems increasingly possible that the transition from Level III to Level II falls earlier than we guessed.

H19/157 This is close to the beginning of the dense sequence of occupation layers constituting our Level III, and in conventional terms belonging to 'Late Bronze Age I'. Given the dendrochronologically determined dates of about 1770 and about 1830 for the construction of the major Middle Bronze Age palaces at Acem Höyük and Kültepe respectively (Manning *et al.* 2001, 2534), a calendar date of between 1880–1680 seems surprisingly early, although the fact that 1830–1680 is the most likely helps a little. These pieces were not found in a primary context (e.g. in a destruction level) and one cannot therefore exclude the possibility that they are recycled material from an earlier phase.

H19/197 These pieces were, by contrast, found among burnt debris on an occupation surface. This phase (IVb) is the later of our two 'Middle Bronze Age' strata. We expect it to be close in time to H19/157 above, and H19/357 below. Its highest and lowest ranges do in fact overlap with them, but the likeliest range (1980–1880) seems very acceptable (especially since before 1500 BC, our conventional historical dates still have at least a century of leeway).

H19/357 This sample also came from primary debris on a well-preserved floor. It is the occupation phase immediately preceding Level IVb and a date in the range 2040–1880 would therefore fit well.

H20/456 The context (packing below phase Vg floors) means that this material should be contemporary with phase Vh, which is separated from Level IVa by three distinct building levels, each with a number of phases. It should therefore be separated from the other samples by a considerable length of time. In conventional terms, on the basis of the ceramics, this should be the later part of Early Bronze Age I, and I think we would have expected a date later, but perhaps not much later, than 2700. It follows that the likeliest range of 3030–2860 is earlier than we would have predicted, but here again, as with H19/157, the sample was contained within packing material, and we have to admit the possibility that it is recycled material from an earlier time.[10]

Notes

1. Hansen & Postgate 1999, 111.
2. In this report 'wiggle-matching' means the matching of radiocarbon determinations from sets of selected tree-rings, say rings 1–10 and rings 50–60 from a single tree-ring sequence (i.e. with mid-points precisely 50 years apart) against the master radiocarbon curve. It is therefore different from 'archaeological' wiggle-matching as discussed by Manning & Weninger 1992, where the difference between the samples from one stratum to another is on the basis of best-estimates by the excavator.
3. The placement of KLT-3&6 versus the master chronology is the same as it was when we made our first report. The only difference is that the master chronology itself (and therefore KLT-3&6) had to be moved back in time. For the low calculated error estimate, see Manning *et al.* 2003.
4. The ring series is long, but it is, after all, from only a single tree. It is perhaps because the mean sensitivity of this tree-ring sequence, at .331, is comparable to those from the Anatolian *Juniperus* spp. trees that make up most of the samples in the Bronze Age–Iron Age master dendrochronology, that the crossdate was identified at all.
5. The average ring size for the entire series is .28 mm, but .47 for the first 70 years of the tree's life (from which we retrieved the samples), and only .18 mm for the last 124 years). Because the rings are so small, we have been unable to cut charcoal of sufficient weight for sampling the whole of the series at the Heidelberg Laboratory.
6. Note that in Figure 5:2a the two triangles have been set at the lowest possible fit (in accord with the dendrochronological fit). If there were nothing else to confirm this late placement, it would be equally easy to slide the triangles to the left, i.e. back in time, by some thirty years.
7. As sloppy as Figure 357a appears to be, with an outlier to the left and another to the right of the radiocarbon curve, there is nowhere else for KLT-9&15 to go. The last ring remains in the middle of the fourteenth century.
8. The reader is reminded that we are talking about a total of three potentially datable trees with ring-sequences of 128 years to 194 years. Additional charcoal collection at sites in the Mut basin might very well show us where these trees fit. Compare the situation at Kilise Tepe with Urartian Ayanis where we have almost 500 samples from many trees, several dozen of which have the bark preserved. We are able to make a number of informed estimates about Ayanis where we can do nothing of the sort at Kilise Tepe.
9. Of course, rings missing from the exterior of any of these pieces, either from shaping by the carpenter or by the action of the fire which destroyed the building, could bring down the date. The excavator must also consider whether the building was long-lived, and whether the timber could have been re-used. Lacking additional dateable samples from these levels, there is nothing more we can say other than to remind the reader of the various possibilities posed when one has only single trees representing a building, or archaeological phase, to analyze.
10. Our thanks go to John Meadows for his advice on radiocarbon matters, and for modelling some of our determinations with OxCal 3.10. The samples cannot be pin-pointed sufficiently accurately to single events to call for the publication of these 'modelled' results, but they do add further weight to the arguments that H19/357 pre-dates 1880 BC and H19/197 post-dates 2030 BC.